The Seed Search

Second Edition

Devised, compiled and edited by
Karen Platt

Published by Karen Platt

KP

This second edition of the Seed Search is dedicated to Bel Amri Mokhtar Ben Hmida, to Joshua and to my Mother.

British Library Cataloguing in publication Data.
A Catalogue record of this book is available from the British Library.

ISBN   0 9528810 1 2
ISSN   1365-9863

Second Edition: December 1997

Compiled, Edited, Typeset and Published by:
Karen Platt
35 Longfield Rd
Crookes
Sheffield
S10 1QW
www.seedsearch.demon.co.uk

Front Cover:
Scabiosa Black

Cover Design:
Alan Coventry Design
Sheffield
Tel: 0114 234 6708
www.ac-design.demon.co.uk

Abbreviations

coll	collection
coll.ref	collector's references
c.s.	coated seed
cv(s)	cultivar(s)
cw	collected wild
dbl	double
d.m.p.	dried mycelium preparation
dw	dwarf
f	forma (botanical form)
fl	flower(ed)
fl.pl.	flore pleno
g	germinated
Gr	group
h.	hort
h-p	hand pollinated
hyb(s)	hybrid(s)
imp	improved
(o)	organic
o-p	open pollinated
poll	pollenless
p.s	pelleted seed
pr.s	primed seed
r-v	revegetation
sel	selected
s-c	separate colours
sp	species
sp.s	sprinter seed
ssp	subspecies
st	stratified
(u-g)	unknown genus
v(ars)	varietas (botanical variety)
(V)	variegated plant
w.a.	widely available
x witt	x wittrochiana (Pansy)

TABLE OF CONTENTS

Preface - Second Edition

IMPORTANT NOTE TO USERS

This is the second edition of The Seed Search I have compiled and published. It is a unique directory of seed catalogues to enable the gardener to access the vast array of seeds available from sources around the world.

The suppliers in The Seed Search offer a wide range of seeds from the common to the rare, from open-pollinated to F1's. There are limitations put on our choice of vegetables by the existence of the National List. Thanks to the HDRA, vegetables not on the National List were listed in the first edition as well as many sources of organic seeds. In this edition, I am pleased to have included many sources of more unusual and heritage heirloom vegetables. So, you can make the choice - hand-pollinated F1 seed or organically grown and open-pollinated types. F1 seed is usually far more expensive and seed which is saved from F1's will not breed true.
Similarly, I believe we should all be aware of CITES (Convention on International Trade in Endangered Species of Wild Fauna and Flora) which regulates trade in wild plants and forbids the import and export of those species which are listed as endangered as well as restricting trade in those which are at risk.

There exists a wider choice of seeds than many people would imagine and I hope the book will entice you to contact the suppliers and get growing. I aim to include as many small suppliers as possible together with their specialities in the world of seed.

Sad to lose Chris Chadwell who is taking time off this year and asked to be deleted so as to avoid the influx of requests, Chris listed 190 seeds, for 42 of which he was the sole supplier, and also Hillview Hardy Plants who have ceased to sell seed.

This second Edition lists over 33,000 seeds of flowers shrubs, trees etc., and almost 6,000 vegetables plus herbs and green manures from over 150 suppliers. Growing from seed is one of the most satisfying pleasures and I hope The Seed Search will make it easier for you to find the seeds you have been searching for and have not been able to find in the past.
Karen Platt
November 1997

Acknowledgements

I am eternally grateful to Ralph Wheatley for his help and expertise with the database without which I would never have managed to complete the first edition and therefore subsequent editions.
My thanks also go to Ray Brown of Plant World, and to Dirk Van Der Werff of Plants for their continued support. Also to those seed suppliers who, by sending in their catalogues and information make the possibility of the book a reality.
I would also like to acknowledge Chris Philip for the invaluable work he undertook in producing The Plant Finder, which formed the inspiration for The Seed Search. I am also extremely grateful for the welcome support of the advertisers.

To avoid disappointment, please

Check the information for each supplier you wish to contact and whether wholesale or retail. Most retail suppliers are mail order only.for retail outlets, those welcoming callers - see details of opening times - Code-Supplier index.

If a request is made for stamps or payment for their catalogue please honour their request.
Early orders i.e. Jan/Feb will avoid disappointment where stocks are low.

N.B. Do please bear in mind I rely upon the information given to me to be accurate i.e. lists to be what is available for the current year. In some cases supplies will be short, in others a crop failure may prevent fulfilment of the order. Please check with suppliers , before ordering and sending money that the seed you require is still available.

THE SEED SEARCH exists to put you, the grower, in touch with suppliers. It does not offer value judgments on those included nor intend any reflection on those not included in this edition. In some cases, lists come too late, in many others it is possible I simply did not know of the existence of the supplier, although I have made every effort to make the SEED SEARCH as comprehensive as possible.

I have made many cross-references to the only correct and valid name, and I will continue to do this in future years. It is clearly the responsibility of suppliers to check what they are selling and ensure seeds are accurately named in their catalogues.

Disclaimer

As the compiler and Editor of THE SEED SEARCH I have taken every care, in the time available, to check all the information supplied to me by the seed suppliers. Nevertheless, in a work of this nature, containing many thousands of records, errors and omissions are likely to occur. The compiler and editor of THE SEED SEARCH cannot be held responsibile for any consequences arising from any such errors.
Please let me know if you do find any errors, so that I may correct them for the next edition.

HOW TO USE THE DIRECTORY

Code-Supplier Index
Suppliers each ahve their own code. This code is given for each seed supplied, except where the number of suppliers exceeds 30, where you will find the words widely available (w.a.).
In the Code-supplier index on page 333, you will find codes listed for each supplier in alphabetical order, together with detailed information on each supplier.

Supplier-Code Index
For ease of use, a reverse supplier-code index is included on page 343, giving the names of seed suppliers in alphabetical order of their name followed by their code.

Societies- Please note
Societies and other horticultural groups which offer seed exchanges have been included here on the understanding that seed exchanges are only offered to members.

Searching for Seeds
If you cannot immediately find the seeds you want, look through the complete listing of that genera and note where reference has been made to name changes. If you still cannot find what you want I am happy to answer any requests provided you send an sae.

Cross references
There are cross-references to enable you to find seeds that are sadly still listed by synonyms in seed catalogues. The list of synonyms and common names will also be of use.
Vegetables, herbs and green manures have their own sections ,please also refer to the main list for suppliers who do not list these seeds separately.

Suppliers' Details
The details given for each supplier are compiled from a questionnaire sent to each supplier. I make no personal comment on this. If information is not included it is because it was not given by the supplier. Minimum order is given where appropriate. Opening times, where stated will mostly refer to telephone lines for mail order. Please bear in mind, the different time zones throughout the world. A charge for catalogues is given where appropriate and the time of year you can expect a new catalogue to be issued. If postage is charged on orders this is also shown. Seed count on the seed packet, or in catalogues, is indicated along with whether you can expect information on growing from seed. Specialities, seed collections and other information the supplier wished to be included is noted. Days of the week have been abbreviated. So too, have the credit card organisations' names.

Catalogues
Please assume the latest catalogue is entered. It costs nothing for companies to be listed, but I only list those who complete the questionnaire and send their catalogue. For societies a selection of seeds are entered, those that crop up on a regular basis.

Import and Export
The Plant Health Order 1993 rules over import and export of plant material. Check with seed suppliers for any necessary photosanitary certificates.

Plant Breeders' Rights
If you are raising from seed and come across something different, and are intersted in Plant Breedes' Rights, for further information contact:
Mrs. M. Vaughan at the Plant Variety Rights Office, White House Lane, Huntingdon Rd, Cambridge. CB3 0LF. Telephone (01223) 342350. Fax (01223) 342386.

New Entries
If you are a supplier wishing to be included in THE SEED SEARCH 1999, please send sae for details to:
Karen Platt. 35 Longfield Rd. Crookes. Sheffield. S10 1QW.
Closing date for new entries 10 September 1998.

Collector's References
Where possible, I have indicated seeds collected with the reference. This has not been possible in every case. Please refer to individual catalogues for full references.

Nomenclature
I have followed the Rules of Nomenclature set out in the International Code of Botanical Nomenclature 1994 (ICBN) and the International Code of Nomenclature for Cultivated Plants 1995 (ICNCP), perhaps with the exception of Chrysanthemum.
The use of botanical names avoids confusion. There is only one valid name, although many seeds are listed under synonyms in catalogues. Other catalogues use common names, and these can lead to confusion as the common name may refer to more than one plant.
It is essential for suppliers to keep their catalogues and nomenclature up-to-date and I know the recent name changes have made this difficult.

Karen Platt
November 1997

SEED - CULTURAL NOTES

GROWING FROM SEED

Seed is a sexual method of propagation and the commonest way of reproduction found in nature. Resulting seedlings can be variable owing to the variety of genetic combinations. Such variation allows for the breeding and selection of cultivars with combinations of the most desirable characteristics of each parent plant.

Collecting and storing seed

Seed should be collected as soon as it is ripe and stored in a dry, dark, airy place at 1-5°C (34-41°F) until it is used. Some seeds have special requirements.

Viability - Those which are only viable for short periods need to be sown as soon as possible.

Fleshy Fruits - Soften fleshy fruits by soaking them in water, remove the seed and air dry at 10-20°C (50-68°F). Harvest fruits that split to release their seed, if not quite mature, dry in clean paper bags before separating out the seeds.

Wind Disribution - Seeds distributed by the wind can be collected by covering the seed heads.

Storing - The length of time for which seed is viable varies greatly. and depends on the species and the storage conditions. Oily seeds do not store well and should be sown soon after collection. Parsnip seed also needs to be used quickly. The viability of seed may be prolonged if stored at 3-5°C (37-41°F) in sealed containers.

Dormancy

Scarification is used to break down the hardened seed coat to enable water to penetrate and therefore speed up the process of germination. Carefully nick the hard-coated seed with a sharp knife. Alternatively, rub the seed between two sheets of abrasive paper.

Warm stratification is used for hard-coated seeds of many woody species. Place the seed in a plastic bag in equal amounts of sand and leaf mould, or peat substitute and sand. Store for 4-12 weeks at 20-25°C (68-77°F). This method is normally followed by a period of cold stratification.

Cold stratification is used following warm stratification and for many alpines. Put the seeds in a plastic bag in a mixture of 50/50 peat or peat substitute and sand, place in the fridge, not the freezer, for 4-12 weeks until germination starts. You will need to check the seeds regularly for germination and sow as soon as germination has occurred. Alternatively, plunge the seeds outdoors in a pot, covering to keep out mice, and check regularly for signs of germination. Sow seeds immediately this occurs.

Germination

The necessary requirements for germination are water, air, warmth and for some species - light.

Use a fine compost, lightly firmed but not compressed. Check the temperature as low temperatures will inhibit the germination of some seeds and high temperatures will inhibit others. Heated propagators will maintain an even temperature, however seeds can also be successfully raised on a windowsill. A small pot or seed try covered with a plastic bag to conserve the right atmosphere, shaded from strong sunlight.

There is no way of distinguishing which seeds need dark and which need light to germinate. If the requirement is unknown, sow the seed in the dark, if germination does not occur after a number of weeks, place it in the light. Some seeds germinate erratically, prick out germinated seedlings, whilst trying not to disturb those which have not germinated. Be prepared to keep pots for up to two years before discarding the contents.

Pelleted or coated seed is available to enable sowing of very tiny seed such as Begonia or Lobelia.

Aftercare

After sowing do not allow compost to dry out or become waterlogged. Cover the seeds to maintain the appropriate environment. When the seedlings are large enough to handle, prick out to avoid weak growth. Gradually harden off by placing in cooler conditions.

Pollination

Open pollination occurs naturally in nature and is the transfer of pollen from the anthers to the stigma.

Cross pollination is the transfer of pollen from the anther of a flower on one plant to the stigma of a flower on another plant.

Self pollination is the transfer of pollen from the anthers to the stigma of the same flower, or to another flower on the same plant.

Open-pollinated varieties are often better adapted to the home garden and small farm. They deliver the performance, flower and nutrition that is lacking in many selected hybrids.

Hybrids

When hybridising it is important to prevent self-pollination. Petals, sepals and stamens are removed from the proposed female parent and the denuded flower is protected by a plastic or paper bag until the stigmas are sticky and receptive. Pollen is then transferred to the stigmas and the flowers protected again until fertilisation has occurred. The seed can then be collected when ripe.

The attraction of hybrids lies in their vigour and uniformity which I feel is not always a necessity to the home gardener.

True From Seed

A listing in the directory is not a guarantee that seeds will come true. Some cultivars will come true from seed, many will not. Suppliers should be able to advise upon this.

Some genera are not normally propagated from seed, coming much better from vegetative propagation, and therefore you may find that seed is not available.

F1 Hybrids will not breed true from seed collected from them.

SEED DIRECTORY

Abelia biflora	B,C		VE
Abelia chinensis	B	Abies procera Glauca Group	B,FW
Abelia floribunda	B	Abies recurvata	B,EL,FW
Abelia mosanensis	B	Abies recurvata v ernestii	B
Abelia x grandiflora	B	Abies religiosa	B,FW
Abeliophyllum distichum	B	Abies sachalinensis	B,FW,LN,SA
Abelmoschus esculentus 'Star of David'	DD	Abies sibirica	B,FW,LN,SA
Abelmoschus ficulneus	B	Abies sibirica 'Argentea'	B,FW
Abelmoschus manihot	C,G,HU,JE,SA	Abies sp mix	C
Abelmoschus manihot 'Cream Cup'	B,BS,DE,T	Abies veitchii	B,FW,SA,SG,VE
Abelmoschus manihot oriental red	DD,HU,PK	Abroma augusta	B
Abelmoschus manihot pink	PK	Abroma fastuosa	B,EL
Abelmoschus manihot 'Sunset Grandifl'	B	Abronia calyptrata	DD
Abelmoschus moschatus	B,EL,HP,JE,PI,SA	Abronia fragrans v fragrans	B,SW
Abelmoschus moschatus 'Pacific' mix	BS,C,CA,DE	Abronia latifolia	AB,B
Abelmoschus moschatus ssp palustris	B	Abronia maritima	B
Aberia caffra	B	Abronia villosa	AV,B,SW
Abies alba	B,EL,FW,LN,SA,T,VE	Abronia villosa 'Milka'	B
Abies amabilis	A,AB,B,FW,LN,SA	Abrus precatorius	B,DD,DV,EL,FW,HA,NI,
Abies balsamea	A,B,C,FW,LN,SA,VE		SA,SI
Abies balsamea 'Cook's Blue Imp'	B,FW	Abrus precatorius, white seeded	B
Abies borisii regis	B,FW,LN,SA	Abutilon amplum	B,NI,SA
Abies bornmulleriana	FW,SA,VE	Abutilon arboreum	B,EL
Abies bracteata	B,SA	Abutilon 'Ashford Red'	HP
Abies cephalonica	B,CA,CG,FW,LN,SA,VE	Abutilon auritum	B
Abies chinensis	B,FW	Abutilon 'Benary's Giant'	B,BS,C,MO,PK
Abies cilicica	B,FW,LN,SA	Abutilon 'Canary Bird'	B,HP
Abies cilicica ssp cilicica	VO	Abutilon 'Feuerglocke'	CG
Abies concolor	B,C,CA,CG,EL,FW,LN,N,	Abutilon geranioides	B,NI
	NO,SA,SG,VE	Abutilon grandiflorum	B,DD
Abies concolor f atroviolacea	SG	Abutilon indicum	B
Abies concolor ssp lowiana	B,FW,LN,SA,VE	Abutilon 'Maximum' mix	BS,BY,CL,DE,SA,V
Abies concolor 'Swift's Silver'	B	Abutilon megapotamicum	B
Abies delavayi	B,EL,FW,LN,SA,SG	Abutilon mix	D,F,HP,J,L,O,T
Abies delavayi v smithii	B	Abutilon mix pink	E
Abies densa	B	Abutilon muticum	B,NI,SA
Abies equitrojani	FW,LN,SA	Abutilon 'Nabob'	B
Abies ernestii	EL,SA	Abutilon otocarpum	AU,B,HU,NI,RS
Abies fabri	B,C,FW,SA	Abutilon oxycarpum	B
Abies fargesii	B,EL,FW,LN,SA	Abutilon palmeri	SZ
Abies firma	B,C,FW,LN,SA	Abutilon sonneratianum	B,SI
Abies forrestii see A.delavayi v smithii		Abutilon striatum x suntense	JD
Abies fraseri	B,FW,LN,SA,SG	Abutilon theophrasti	AP,B,CG,G
Abies grandis	A,AB,B,C,CA,DD,EL,FW,	Abutilon vitifolium	AP,B,C,HP,HU,JD,JE,LG,
	G,LN,NO,SA,VE		PL,RH,SA,SC,T
Abies holophylla	B,EL,FW,LN,SA	Abutilon vitifolium 'Ralph Gould'	C
Abies homolepis	B,C,CG,FW,G,LN,	Abutilon vitifolium 'Tennant's White'	HP
	N,SA,VE	Abutilon vitifolium Treseder form	X
Abies kawakamii	B	Abutilon vitifolium v album	C,HP,LG,SC,X
Abies koreana	AP,B,C,CG,FW,LN,N,SA,	Abutilon vitifolium 'Veronica Tennant'	C,HP
	SC,SG,T,VE,X	Abutilon white flowers	N
Abies lasiocarpa	B,C,CA,DD,FW,LN,NO,	Abutilon x hybridum	EL,G,HU
	SA	Abutilon x suntense	AP,B,HP,RH,SC
Abies lasiocarpa ssp arizonica	B,CA,FW,LN,N,SA	Abutilon x suntense 'Violetta'	HP
Abies magnifica	B,CA,FW,LN,SA	Acacia abyssinica	B,SI
Abies magnifica v shastensis	B,FW,LN,SA	Acacia acanthoclada	B,NI
Abies mayriana	SA	Acacia acinacea	B,EL,HA,NI,O,SA
Abies nephrolepis	B,EL,FW,LN,SA,SG	Acacia acradenia	AU,B,NI,O
Abies nordmanniana	B,CG,EL,FW,LN,N,T,VE	Acacia acuminata	AU,B,EL,HA,NI,O
Abies nordmanniana 'Ambrolauri'	B,FW,SA	Acacia acuminata inland form	B
Abies nordmanniana ssp equitrojani	LN	Acacia acutaetissima	CG,HA
Abies numidica	LN	Acacia adsurgens	B,EL,HA,NI,O
Abies pindrow	B,C,EL,FW,G,HA,LN,SA	Acacia adunca	B,EL,HA,NI,O
Abies pinsapo	B,FW,LN,N,SA,VE	Acacia aestivalis	B,NI
Abies pinsapo 'Glauca'	B,C,CA,FW,SA	Acacia alata	B,CG,NI
Abies procera	AB,B,C,CA,FW,G,LN,SA,	Acacia albida	SA

ACACIA

Acacia amoena	B,HA,NI,O
Acacia ampliceps	B,NI,O
Acacia anaticeps	B,NI
Acacia anceps	AU,B,NI
Acacia anceps v angustifolia	B,NI
Acacia ancistrocarpa	B,NI,O
Acacia andrewsii	B,NI
Acacia aneura	B,CA,DD,EL,HA,HU,NI,O
Acacia angusta	B,NI
Acacia angustissima	B,HU,RE
Acacia anthochaea	B,NI
Acacia aphylla	B,NI
Acacia arabica	FW,SA,VE
Acacia arenaria	B,SI
Acacia argyrophylla	AU,B,NI
Acacia arida	B,NI
Acacia arrecta	B,NI
Acacia ashbyae	B,NI
Acacia aspera	B,NI
Acacia assimilis	B,NI
Acacia ataxacantha	B,SI
Acacia atkinsiana	B,NI
Acacia aulacocarpa	B,EL,HA,NI,O
Acacia aulacophylla	B,NI
Acacia auriculiformis	B,CA,EL,HA,HU,NI,O,SA
Acacia ausfeldii	B,HA,NI
Acacia baileyana	AU,B,C,CA,EL,HA,HU, NI,O,RE,SA,SH,VE,WA
Acacia baileyana 'Purpurea'	B,C,CA,EL,HA,HU,NI, O,SA,SH,VE
Acacia bancroftii	AU,B,HA,NI,O
Acacia barattensis	B,NI
Acacia baxteri	AU,B,NI
Acacia beauverdiana aff	B,NI
Acacia beckleri	AU,B,NI
Acacia berlandieri	B,CA
Acacia betchei	AU,B,HA,NI
Acacia bidwillii	B,NI
Acacia biflora	B,NI
Acacia binata	B,NI
Acacia binervata	B,EL,HA,NI
Acacia binervia	B,EL,HA,NI,O,SA,SH
Acacia bivenosa	AU,B,NI
Acacia blakei	B,HA,NI
Acacia blakelyi	B,NI
Acacia boormanii	AU,B,EL,HA,HP,HU, NI,O,SA
Acacia botrycephala	AU,B,HA,LN,NI,O,SA
Acacia brachybotrya	AU,B,DD,HA,HU,NI
Acacia brachystachya	B,NI
Acacia brassii	O
Acacia browniana v browniana	B,NI
Acacia browniana v endlicheri	B
Acacia browniana v intermedia	B,NI
Acacia brownii	EL,HA
Acacia brunioides	AU,B,NI
Acacia burkei	B,SI,WA
Acacia burkittii	AU,B,HU,NI
Acacia burrowii	B,NI,O
Acacia buxifolia	B,EL,HA,NI,O,SH
Acacia buxifolia ssp pubiflora	B,HA
Acacia caerulescens	AU,NI
Acacia caesia	B
Acacia caesiella	B,HA,NI
Acacia caffra	B,HU,KB,SA,SI,WA

Acacia calamifolia	AU,B,HA,NI
Acacia cambagei	B,O
Acacia cardiophylla	AU,B,C,EL,HA,NI,SA
Acacia caroleae	B,NI
Acacia catechu	B,SA
Acacia celastrifolia	B,NI
Acacia cheelii	AU,B,NI
Acacia chinchillensis	AU,B,NI
Acacia chisholmii	B,NI
Acacia chrysella	B,NI
Acacia chrysocephala	AU,B,NI
Acacia cibaria	B
Acacia cincinnata	B,NI,O
Acacia citrinoviridis	B,NI
Acacia cochlearis	AU,B,NI
Acacia cognata	B,EL,HA,NI,O
Acacia colei	B,NI
Acacia colletioides	B,NI
Acacia complanata	B,HA,HU,NI,O
Acacia concinna	B
Acacia concurrens	B,EL,HA,NI
Acacia conferta	B,EL,HA,NI,SA
Acacia confusa	B,HU
Acacia constricta	B,CA
Acacia continua	AU,B,NI
Acacia convenyi	HA
Acacia coolgardiensis	B,NI
Acacia coriacea	B,EL,HA,NI,O
Acacia cowleana	B,DD,EL,HA,NI,O
Acacia craspedocarpa	B,NI
Acacia crassa	B,NI
Acacia crassicarpa	B,NI,O
Acacia cultriformis	AU,B,CA,EL,HA,NI,SA, VE,WA
Acacia cunninghamii	B,NI,SA
Acacia cupularis	AU,B,NI
Acacia curranii	B
Acacia curvata	AU,B,NI
Acacia curvinervia	B,NI
Acacia cuthbertsonii	B,EL,HA,NI,O
Acacia cyanophylla see A.saligna	
Acacia cyclops	AU,B,CA,EL,HA,LN,NI, O,SA,VE
Acacia cyperophylla	B,NI
Acacia davyi	B
Acacia dawsonii	B,EL,HA,NI,SH
Acacia dealbata	AU,B,BS,C,CA,DE,EL, HA,HP,HU,LN,N,NI,O, SA,SH,T,V,VE,X
Acacia deanei	AU,B,EL,HA,NI,O
Acacia declinata	B,NI
Acacia decora	B,C,EL,HA,NI,O,SA,VE
Acacia decurrens	B,CA,EL,FW,HA,NI,O,SA
Acacia decurrens dealbata	FW
Acacia decurrens mollis	FW
Acacia delphina	B,NI
Acacia dempsteri	B,NI
Acacia denticulosa	B,NI,O
Acacia dentifera	B,CG,NI
Acacia dictyoneura	B,NI
Acacia dictyophleba	B,EL,NI
Acacia dielsii	B,NI
Acacia dietrichiana	B,NI
Acacia difficilis	B,NI,O
Acacia difformis	B,EL,NI
Acacia discolor	C,HA

8

ACACIA

Acacia divergens	B,NI
Acacia dodonaeifolia	B,NI
Acacia donaldsonii	B,NI
Acacia dorotoxylon	AU,B,EL,HS,NI
Acacia drepanocarpa	B,NI
Acacia drepanolobium	B
Acacia drummondii	AU,B,C,HA,SA
Acacia drummondii 'Grossus'	B,NI
Acacia drummondii ssp affinis	B,NI,O
Acacia drummondii ssp candolleana	B,NI,O
Acacia drummondii ssp drummondii	NI,O
Acacia drummondii ssp elegans	B,HU,NI,O
Acacia dunnii	B,C,EL,HA,NI,O
Acacia dystyla	B,EL
Acacia elata	AU,B,EL,HA,HU,NI,O, WA
Acacia elongata	AU,B,CA,EL,HA,NI,SA
Acacia empelioclada	B,NI
Acacia eremaea	B,NI
Acacia eremophila	B,NI
Acacia ericifolia	B
Acacia ericifolia aff	AU,B,NI
Acacia erinacea	AU,B,NI
Acacia erioloba	B,LN,SI,WA
Acacia erioloba giraffae	SA
Acacia eriopoda	B,NI
Acacia erubescens	B
Acacia estrophiolata	AU,B,NI,O
Acacia euthycarpa	AU,B,NI
Acacia everestii	B,NI
Acacia excelsa	B
Acacia exilis	B,NI
Acacia exocarpoides	B,NI
Acacia extensa	AU,B,NI
Acacia falcata	B,EL,HA,NI,SA
Acacia falciformis	B,EL,HA,NI,O
Acacia farnesiana	B,CA,DD,EL,HA,HU,LN, NI,O,SA,SH,VE
Acacia farnesiana v smallii	CA
Acacia fasciculifera	B,NI
Acacia fauntleroyi	AU,B,CG,NI,O
Acacia ferruginea	B
Acacia filicifolia	AU,B,HA,NI
Acacia filifolia	AU,B,NI
Acacia fimbriata	B,C,EL,HA,HP,NI,O,SA
Acacia fimbriata v perangusta	HA
Acacia flagelliformis	B,NI
Acacia flavescens	B,EL,NI
Acacia fleckii	B,SI
Acacia flexifolia	B,HA,NI
Acacia floribunda	AU,B,CA,EL,HA,HU,NI, O,SA,SH,VE
Acacia frigescens	B,HA,NI
Acacia galpinii	B,LN,SA,SI,WA
Acacia genistifolia	AU,B,NI
Acacia georginae	B,NI,O
Acacia gerrardii	B,SI
Acacia gilbertii	B,NI
Acacia gillii	AU,B,NI
Acacia giraffae	C,HU,LN
Acacia gittinsii	B,NI
Acacia gladiiformis	B,EL,HA,NI
Acacia glaucescens see A.binervia	
Acacia glaucissima	B,NI
Acacia glaucocarpa	B,EL,NI,O
Acacia glaucoptera	B,C,HU,NI,O
Acacia gnidium	B,NI
Acacia gnidium v latifolia	HA
Acacia gonoclada	B,NI
Acacia gonophylla	B,NI
Acacia gracilifolia	AU,B,NI
Acacia grandicornuta	B,SI
Acacia granitica	AU,B,HA,HU,NI
Acacia grasbyi	B,NI
Acacia greggii	B,CA
Acacia gregorii	AU,B,NI
Acacia guinetii	AU,B,NI
Acacia gunnii	HA
Acacia hadrophylla	B,NI
Acacia haematoxylon	B
Acacia hakeoides	B,HA,NI
Acacia halliana	B,NI
Acacia hamersleyensis	B,NI
Acacia hamiltoniana	HA
Acacia harpophylla	B,EL,HA,NI,O
Acacia harveyi	B,NI
Acacia hastulata	B,NI
Acacia havilandii	AU,B,NI
Acacia hebeclada ssp chobiensis	B,SI
Acacia hemignosta	B,NI
Acacia hemiteles	AU,B,NI
Acacia hemsleyi	B,NI
Acacia heteroclita	AU,B,NI
Acacia heteroneura	B,NI
Acacia heterophylla	B
Acacia hilliana	B,NI
Acacia hockii	B
Acacia holosericea	B,EL,HA,NI,O
Acacia homalophylla	HA
Acacia horridula	B,NI
Acacia howittii	AP,AU,B,CG,EL,HA,NI,O
Acacia hubbardiana	B,NI
Acacia idiomorpha	B,NI
Acacia imbricata	AU,B,NI
Acacia implexa	AU,B,EL,HA,NI,O
Acacia inaequilatera	B,NI
Acacia inaequiloba	B,NI
Acacia incurva	B,NI
Acacia irrorata	EL,HA
Acacia irrorata ssp irrorata	B,NI
Acacia iteaphylla	AU,B,EL,HA,NI,O,SH
Acacia ixiophylla	B,HA,NI,O
Acacia ixodes	B,NI
Acacia jamesiana	B,NI
Acacia jennerae	B,NI,O
Acacia jensenii	B,NI
Acacia jibberdingensis	B,NI
Acacia jonesii	AU,B,NI
Acacia julibrissin see Albizia	
Acacia julifera	AU,B,NI
Acacia julifera ssp julifera	O
Acacia juncifolia	B,HA,NI
Acacia juncunda	HA
Acacia juniperina	HA
Acacia karroo	B,C,SA,SI,WA
Acacia kempeana	B,NI
Acacia kirkii	B,SI
Acacia koa	B
Acacia kybeanensis	AU,B,CA,EL,HA,NI,O, SA,SH
Acacia laccata	B,NI
Acacia lanigera	AU,B,HA,NI

9

ACACIA

Acacia lasiocalyx	B,NI	Acacia myrtifolia	AU,B,EL,HA,NI,O,SA
Acacia lasiocarpa	AU,B,NI,SA	Acacia myrtifolia v angustifolia	B,NI
Acacia lasiocarpa v sedifolia	AU,B,NI	Acacia nematophylla	B,NI
Acacia latericicola	B,NI	Acacia neriifolia	B,C,CG,EL,HA,NI,O
Acacia latescens	B,NI	Acacia nervosa	B,NI
Acacia latisepala	B,NI	Acacia neurophylla	B,NI
Acacia leichhardtii	B,NI	Acacia nigrescens	B,LN,SA,SI,WA
Acacia leiocalyx	B,EL,HA,NI	Acacia nigricans	AU,B,NI
Acacia leiocladia ssp argentifolia	HA	Acacia nilotica	B,SA
Acacia leioderma	B,NI	Acacia nilotica ssp adansonii	B
Acacia leiophylla	AU,B,HA,NI	Acacia nilotica ssp indica	B
Acacia leptocarpa	B,EL,HA,NI	Acacia nilotica ssp kraussiana	B,SI
Acacia leptoneura	AU,B,NI	Acacia nilotica ssp tomentosa	B
Acacia leucoclada	B,HA,NI	Acacia nodiflora v ferox	B,NI
Acacia leucophloea	B	Acacia notabilis	AU,B,DD,HA,NI,O
Acacia ligulata	AU,B,DD,EL,HA,NI,O	Acacia nyssophylla	B,NI
Acacia ligustrina	B,NI	Acacia obliquinerva	AU,B,NI
Acacia linearifolia	AU,B,NI,SA	Acacia obovata	B,NI
Acacia lineata	AU,B,HA,HU,NI	Acacia obtecta	B,NI
Acacia linifolia	AU,B,EL,HA,NI,VE	Acacia obtusata	B,HA
Acacia linophylla	B,NI	Acacia obtusifolia	B,HA,HU,NI,O
Acacia littorea	B,NI	Acacia oldfieldii	B,NI
Acacia loderi	B,NI	Acacia olsenii	B,HA,NI
Acacia longifolia	B,C,CA,DD,EL,HA,HU, NI,O,SA,SC,VE	Acacia omalophylla	B
		Acacia oncinocarpa	B,NI
Acacia longiphyllodinea	B,NI	Acacia oraria	B,NI,O
Acacia longispicata	B,NI	Acacia orthocarpa	B,NI
Acacia longissima	B,EL,HA,HU,NI,O	Acacia oswaldii	B,DD,HA,NI,O
Acacia luteola	B,NI	Acacia oxycedrus	AU,B,NI
Acacia lysiphloia	B,NI	Acacia oxyclada	B,NI
Acacia mabellae	B,EL,NI,O	Acacia pachycarpa	B,NI
Acacia macdonelliensis	B,NI	Acacia palustris	B,NI
Acacia macradenia	B,EL,HA,HU,N,NI,O	Acacia papyrocarpa	AU,B,NI,O
Acacia macrothyrsa	B,SI	Acacia paradoxa	B,HA,NI,SA,VE
Acacia maidenii	B,EL,HA,O	Acacia paraneura	B,NI
Acacia maitlandii	B,NI	Acacia parramattensis	AU,B,EL,HA,NI
Acacia mangium	B,CA,EL,HA,NI,O	Acacia parvipinnula	AU,B,HA,NI
Acacia maslinii	B,NI	Acacia patagiata	B,NI
Acacia 'Maxwellii'	B	Acacia pellita	B,NI
Acacia mearnsii	AU,B,CG,DD,EL,HA,LN, NI,O,SA,VE	Acacia pendula	B,C,CA,EL,HA,HU,NI,O, SA,VE,WA
Acacia meisneri	AU,B,NI	Acacia pennatula	B
Acacia melanoxylon	AU,B,C,CA,EL,FW,HA, HU,LN,NI,O,SA,SG,VE, WA	Acacia penninervis	B,EL,HA,HU,NI,O,VE
		Acacia pentadenia	B,NI
		Acacia perangusta	B,HA,NI
Acacia melleodora	B,NI	Acacia phlebopetala	B,NI
Acacia mellifera	B,SI	Acacia pilligaensis	B,NI
Acacia menzelii	AU,B,NI	Acacia pinguifolia	B,NI
Acacia merinthophora	B,NI,O	Acacia platycarpa	B,NI
Acacia merrallii	AU,B,NI	Acacia podalyriifolia	AU,B,C,CA,EL,HA,NI,O, SA,SC,SH,VE,WA
Acacia microbotrya	AU,B,NI		
Acacia microcarpa	B,NI	Acacia polyacantha	B,SI
Acacia mimula	B,NI	Acacia polybotrya	AU,B,EL,HA,NI,O
Acacia mitchellii	B	Acacia polystachya	B,NI
Acacia mix blue foliage	C,EL	Acacia prainii	B,NI
Acacia modesta	B,SA	Acacia pravissima	B,CA,EL,HA,HP,HU,N, NI,O,SA,SH
Acacia moirii ssp dasycarpa	AU,B,NI		
Acacia mollifolia	AU,B,NI	Acacia prominens	B,EL,HA,NI,O
Acacia mollisima see A.mearnsii		Acacia pruinocarpa	B,NI,O
Acacia montana	B,HA,NI	Acacia pruinosa	B,HA,NI,O
Acacia monticola	B,NI	Acacia pubescens	HA
Acacia montis-usti	B,SI	Acacia pubicosta	B,NI
Acacia mucronata	AU,B,EL,HU,NI,O,SA	Acacia pubifolia	B,NI
Acacia muellerana	B,HA,NI	Acacia pulchella	B,DD,SA
Acacia multispicata	AU,B,NI	Acacia pulchella v glaberrima	AU,B,NI
Acacia murrayana	B,EL,HA,NI	Acacia pulchella v goadbyi	B,NI

ACACIA

Acacia pustula	B,NI
Acacia pycnantha	AU,B,EL,HA,NI,O,SA
Acacia pyrifolia	B,NI
Acacia quadrimarginea	B,NI
Acacia quadrisulcata	B,NI
Acacia raddiana	B
Acacia ramulosa	AU,B,NI
Acacia redolens	B,CA,EL,NI,O
Acacia redolens compacta	CA
Acacia redolens 'Prostrata'	B
Acacia reficiens	B,SI
Acacia rehmanniana	B,SI
Acacia retinodes	AP,AU,B,C,CG,EL,HA, NI,O,SA,VE
Acacia retinodes blue leaf	B,NI
Acacia retivenia	B,NI
Acacia rhigiophylla	AU,B,NI
Acacia rhodophloia	B,NI
Acacia riceana	AU,B,C,N,NI,O,SA,SG
Acacia rivalis	B,NI
Acacia robusta	B,SI,WA
Acacia rossei	AU,B,NI
Acacia rostellifera	AU,B,NI
Acacia rotundifolia	B,NI
Acacia rubida	B,CA,DV,EL,HA,NI,O,SH
Acacia rupicola	B,NI
Acacia saliciformis	B,NI
Acacia salicina	B,CA,EL,HA,NI,O
Acacia saligna	AU,B,C,CA,CG,EL,FW, HA,NI,O,SA,VE
Acacia saligna desert form	B
Acacia scirpifolia	B,NI
Acacia sclerophylla	B,C,NI
Acacia sclerophylla v lissophylla	B,NI
Acacia sclerosperma	AU,B,NI
Acacia semilunata	B,EL,HA,NI,O
Acacia semirigida	B,NI
Acacia senegal	B,SA
Acacia senegal v rostrata	B,SI
Acacia sessilis	B,NI
Acacia sessilispica	B,NI
Acacia shirleyi	B,NI
Acacia sibina	B,NI
Acacia siculiformis	AU,B,HA,NI
Acacia sieberana	B
Acacia sieberana v woodii	B,LN,SI,WA
Acacia signata	AU,B,NI
Acacia silvestris	AU,B,EL,NI
Acacia simsii	B,NI,O
Acacia sophorae	AU,B,DD,EL,HA,HU, NI,O
Acacia sp dwarf mix	C,EL
Acacia sp mix	C
Acacia spathulifolia	B,NI
Acacia spectabilis	B,EL,HA,NI,O,SA,SH
Acacia spondylophylla	B,NI,O
Acacia steedmanii	B,NI
Acacia stenophylla	B,CA,EL,HA,NI,O
Acacia stenoptera	B,NI
Acacia stereophylla	B,DD,NI
Acacia stipuligera	B,NI
Acacia stricta	B,EL,HA,NI
Acacia stuhlmanii	B,SI
Acacia suaveolens	B,EL,HA,HU,NI,O,SA
Acacia subcaerulea	B,NI
Acacia subflexuosa	B,NI

Acacia subglauca	B,NI
Acacia subporosa	CA
Acacia subulata	AU,B,NI
Acacia sulcata	AU,B,NI
Acacia sulcata v platyphylla	AU,B,NI
Acacia suma	SA
Acacia sylvestris	HA
Acacia tanumbirinensis	B,NI
Acacia tenuissima	B,NI
Acacia teretifolia	AU,B,NI
Acacia terminalis see A.botrycephala	
Acacia tetragonocarpa	B,NI
Acacia tetragonophylla	AU,B,NI
Acacia torta	B
Acacia tortilis	B,SA,SI,VE,WA
Acacia torulosa	B,NI
Acacia trachycarpa	B,NI
Acacia trachyphloia	B,EL,HA,NI
Acacia translucens	B,HU,NI
Acacia trigonophylla	B,NI
Acacia trineura	AU,B,NI
Acacia triptera	B,HU,NI
Acacia triptycha	B,NI
Acacia triquetra	B,NI
Acacia truncata	AU,B,NI
Acacia tumida	B,NI
Acacia tysonii	B,NI
Acacia ulicifolia	AU,B,HA,HP,NI
Acacia ulicifolia v brownei	AU,B,NI,O
Acacia ulicina	B,NI
Acacia umbellata	B,NI
Acacia uncinata	AU,B,EL,HA,HU,NI
Acacia uncinella	B,NI
Acacia urophylla	B,NI
Acacia validinervia	B,NI
Acacia venulosa	B,HA,NI
Acacia verniciflua	AU,B,C,EL,HA,NI,SA
Acacia verticillata	AU,B,C,CA,CG,HA,NI,SA
Acacia vestita	AU,B,EL,HA,LN,NI,O, SA,SH
Acacia victoriae	AU,B,DD,EL,HA,LN,NI, O,SA
Acacia viscidula	B,HA,NI
Acacia visite	B,WA
Acacia wanyu	B,NI
Acacia wattsiana	B,NI
Acacia wilhelmiana	AU,B
Acacia willdenowiana	B,NI
Acacia williamsonii	AU,B,HA,NI
Acacia xanthina	B,NI
Acacia xanthocarpa	B,NI
Acacia xanthophloea	B,SI,WA
Acacia xiphophylla	B,NI
Acaena anserinifolia	B,HP,JE,SC,SS
Acaena argentea	G
Acaena 'Blue Haze'	C,HP,I,SC
Acaena buchananii	AP,B,C,JE
Acaena caesiglauca	AU,B,HP,JE,SA,SC,SG, SS
Acaena fissistipula	AP,B,CG
Acaena glabra	B,KL,SC,SS
Acaena glauca	C
Acaena inermis	B,C,HP,JE,SC,SG,SS
Acaena magellanica	AR,B,JE,SA
Acaena magellanica ssp laevigata	E
Acaena microphylla	AP,AU,B,C,G,HP,KI,SA,

	SC,SG
Acaena microphylla 'Copper Carpet'	E,JE,SC,ST
Acaena microphylla 'Green & Purple Carpet' see 'Copper Carpet'	
Acaena minor	B,SC
Acaena myriophylla	B,BS,C,P
Acaena novae-zelandiae	AP,B,C,G,I,JE,RH,SA,SC
Acaena ovalifolia	AP,B,C,KL,SC
Acaena pinnatifida	AP,RH
Acaena saccaticupula	AP,AU,HP,SC,SG
Acaena sericea	AP,B,CG,P,SC
Acaena viridior see A. anserinifolia Druce	
Acalypha hispida	B,CA
Acalypha indica	B
Acalypha peduncularis	B,C,SI
Acanthocaclycium violaceum see Echinopsis sniniflora	
Acanthocalycium aurantiacum see Echinopsis thionantha	
Acanthocalycium brevispinum	DV
Acanthocalycium catamarcense	B
Acanthocalycium chionanthum	DV
Acanthocalycium glaucum	B,DV,Y
Acanthocalycium klimpelianum	B,BC,DV
Acanthocalycium peitscherianum	B,DV,Y
Acanthocalycium sp	C,Y
Acanthocalycium spiniflorum	B,DV,Y
Acanthocalycium thionanthum	BC,DV
Acanthocalycium variifolium	BC,DV
Acanthocalycium violaceum see Echinopsis spiniflora	
Acanthocarpus preissii	B,NI
Acantholimon acerosum	AP,B,RM,VO
Acantholimon acerosum v acerosum	KL
Acantholimon albanicum	SC
Acantholimon armenum	VO
Acantholimon armenum v armenum	KL
Acantholimon bracteatum	VO
Acantholimon caryophyllaceum	AP,KL,SC
Acantholimon caryophyllum ssp parvifl.	KL
Acantholimon confertifolium	KL
Acantholimon glumaceum	AP,B,RM,SG
Acantholimon glumaceum blue leaf	RM
Acantholimon hohenackeri	B,I,RM
Acantholimon litvinovii	AP
Acantholimon olivieri	G
Acantholimon puberulum	AP
Acantholimon sp	AP,JE
Acantholimon tenuifolium	B,RM
Acantholimon ulicinum	PM,VO
Acantholimon ulicinum ssp ulicinum	KL
Acantholimon ulicinum v purpurascens	KL
Acantholimon venustum	B,RM,SC
Acanthopanax see Eleutherococcus	
Acanthophoenix crinita	O
Acanthophoenix rubra	B,O
Acanthosicyos naudinianus	B,SI
Acanthospermum hispidum	B
Acanthostachys strobilacea	B,SG
Acanthus balcanicus see A.hungaricus	
Acanthus caroli-alexandri	HP
Acanthus hungaricus	AP,B,G,HP,JE,SA,SC,SG,T
Acanthus longifolius see A.hungaricus	
Acanthus mollis	B,BD,BS,BY,C,CA,CL,CN,DE,DT,F,FW,G,HP,JE,L,O,MO,SA,SU,T,TH,VE
Acanthus mollis Latifolius Group	U
Acanthus peringii	JE
Acanthus spinosus	AP,G,HP,SA,SC
Acanthus syriacus	JE
Acca sellowiana	B,C,CA,CG,FW,HU,SA,T,VE
Acca sellowiana 'Magnifica'	B
Aceitillo amarillo	B
Aceitillo blanco	B
Acer aconitifolium	X
Acer acuminatum	B
Acer argutum	B,N
Acer barbatum	SA
Acer barbinerve	B,FW,LN,SA,SG
Acer buergeranum	B,C,CA,CG,EL,G,HA,LN,N,SA,VE,WA
Acer caesium	B,FW,LN,SA
Acer cambelii ssp wilsonii	N
Acer campestre	A,B,C,CG,EL,FW,LN,N,SA,SG,VE
Acer capillipes	CG,LN,N,SA,SG,X
Acer cappadocicum	B,CG,FW,SA,X
Acer cappadocicum 'Aureum'	B,N,SA
Acer carpinifolium	B,LN,SA
Acer caudatifolium	N
Acer cinnamomifolium see A. coriaceifolium	
Acer circinatum	AB,B,C,CG,FW,HP,KL,LN,N,NO,SA,X
Acer cissifolium	B
Acer cissifolium ssp henryii	B
Acer coriaceifolium	B,EI,FW,SA
Acer crataegifolium	CG,N
Acer davidii	B,C,CA,EL,FW,LN,N,SA,VE
Acer davidii AC1471	X
Acer davidii 'George Forrest'	NG
Acer davidii ssp grosseri	AP,B,C,FW,LN,N,SA,X
Acer diabolicum	B,CG,SA
Acer divergens	G,SG
Acer drummondii	SA
Acer elegantulum	B,EL,FW,LN,SA
Acer erianthum	N
Acer fabri	B,C,FW,SA
Acer glabrum	B,C,FW,NO,SA,SG
Acer glabrum v douglasii	B,LN
Acer granatense	SG
Acer griseum	AP,B,C,CA,EL,FW,G,HP,LN,N,NG,SA,VE
Acer heldreichii	B,N,SA
Acer heldreichii ssp trautvetteri	B,LN
Acer henryi	C,LN,SA
Acer hybrids autumn col	DT
Acer hyrcanum	B,FW,LN,SA
Acer japonicum	B,C,LN,MN,SA,SG
Acer japonicum 'Aconitifolium'	B,CG,LN,N
Acer japonicum 'Aureum' see A. shirasawanum 'Aureum'	
Acer kawakamii see A.caudatifolium	
Acer komarovii	FW,SA
Acer laxiflorum	C
Acer lobelii	SA
Acer longipes	B,C,FW,SA
Acer macranthum	CG
Acer macrophyllum	A,AB,B,CA,FW,LN,NO,SA
Acer mandschuricum	B,C,EL,FW,G,LN,SA
Acer maximowiczianum	B,CG,N,SA
Acer metcalfii	N,SA
Acer micranthum	AP,B,N

ACER

Acer mix bonsai — C
Acer mix snake bark — C,N
Acer miyabei — SA
Acer mono — B,C,EL,LN,SA,SG
Acer monspessulanum — B,CG,EL,HA,LN,SA,SG, VE
Acer negundo — A,B,C,CA,CG,EL,FW,HA, LN,SA,SG,VE,WA
Acer negundo v interius — SG
Acer negundo v pseudocalifornicum — SG
Acer negundo 'Variegatum' — B,VE
Acer nigrum — LN,SA
Acer oblongum — B,EL,FW,LN,SA
Acer obtusatum — FW,SA
Acer oliverianum — B,EL,FW,LN,N,SA
Acer opalus — B,CG,LN,SA,VE
Acer opalus ssp obtusatum — B
Acer palmatum — B,C,CA,CG,EL,FW,G,HA, HP,KL,LN,N,SA,SG,T,VE
Acer palmatum Dissectum Atrop.p. Group — B,C,CA,HP,N,SA
Acer palmatum Dissectum Viride Group — B,N
Acer palmatum f atropurpureum — B,C,CA,CG,EL,FW,HA, KL,LN,N,SA,V,VE
Acer palmatum Heptalobum Gr. — KL
Acer palmatum 'Hessei' — N
Acer palmatum 'Kagiri-nishiki' — CG
Acer palmatum 'Linearilobum' — N
Acer palmatum 'Matsumurae' — B,C
Acer palmatum 'Osakazuki' — HP,N,SA,SC,X
Acer palmatum 'Roseomarginatum' see A. palmatum 'Kagiri-nishiki'
Acer palmatum 'Sango-kaku' — N
Acer palmatum 'Sanguineum' — N
Acer palmatum 'Sazanami' — N
Acer palmatum 'Senkaki' see A. palmatum 'Sango-kaku'
Acer palmatum 'Shigitatsu sawa' — N
Acer palmatum sp mix — N
Acer palmatum ssp palmatum — N
Acer palmatum st — CA
Acer palmatum 'Tsukomo' — N
Acer palmatum v dissectum — B,C,FW,HP,SA,SC
Acer palmatum v heptalobum 'Lutescens' — B,N
Acer palmatum v koreanum — N
Acer pectatum ssp laxiflorum — SA
Acer pensylvanicum — B,FW,N,SA,SG,VE
Acer platanoides — A,B,C,CA.CG,EL,FW, LN,SA,VE
Acer platanoides 'Columnare' — B
Acer platanoides 'Crimson King' — LN,N
Acer platanoides 'Laciniatum' — CG
Acer platanoides 'Schwedleri' — B,FW,LN,VE
Acer pseudo-sieboldianum — B,FW,N
Acer pseudo-sieboldianum v macrocarp. — SG
Acer pseudoplatanus — A,B,CA,CG,EL,FW,LN, SA,VE
Acer pseudoplatanus 'Atropurpureum' — B,FW,HA,RS,SA,VE
Acer pseudoplatanus f variegatum — RS
Acer pseudosieboldianum — AP,EL,LN,SA,SC
Acer robustum — C,LN,SA
Acer rubrum — A,B,C,CA,EL,FW,G,SA, VE
Acer rufinerve — B,C,CG,FW,G,N,SA
Acer saccharinum — B,CA,FW,LN,N,SA,VE
Acer saccharum — A,AB,B,C,CA,CG,EL,FW, LN,SA,VE
Acer saccharum ssp grandidentatum — B,NO,SA
Acer saccharum ssp nigrum — B

Acer schwedleri — SA
Acer semenovii — CG
Acer shirasawanum 'Aureum' — AP,B,HP,SC
Acer shirasawanum 'Junihitoe' — N
Acer shirasawanum 'Microphyllum' — N
Acer shirasawanum 'Palmatifolium' — N
Acer sieboldianum — B,N
Acer sikkimense ssp metcalfii see A.metcalfii
Acer sinense — B,EL,FW
Acer sp collection — N
Acer sp mix — C
Acer spicatum — B,FW,LN,N,SA,SG
Acer sterculiaeceum franchettii — SA
Acer tataricum — B,C,CG,FW,G,LN,RS, SA,SG
Acer tataricum ssp ginnala — A,AP,B,C,CA,CG,EL,FW, HP,KL,LN,N,SA,SG,VE
Acer tataricum ssp ginnala 'Flame' — LN,SA
Acer tataricum ssp semenovii — N
Acer tegmentosum — AP,B,C,EL,FW,LN,SA,SG
Acer trautvetteri — C,N,RH,SA
Acer triffidum — CG
Acer triflorum — B,C,EL,FW,LN,SA
Acer truncatum — B,C,CA,EL,FW,LN,N,SA
Acer truncatum v mono — CA,FW
Acer tschonoski — B,N
Acer tschonoski v koreanum — N
Acer turkestanicum — CG
Acer ukurunduense — B,C,EL,FW,LN,SA
Acer velutinum — B,LN,SA
Acetosa alpestris — CG
Acetosella tenuifolia — SG
Achillea abrotanoides — G
Achillea acuminata — SG
Achillea ageratum — BH,G,KL
Achillea ageratum 'Golden Princess' — B
Achillea ageratum 'Moonwalker' — B,BS,C,CN,JE,MO,SA
Achillea 'Appleblossom' — HP
Achillea asiatica — SG
Achillea atrata — B,SA
Achillea cartilaginea — HP,MA
Achillea cartilaginea 'Silver Spray' — B,C
Achillea chrysocoma — SG
Achillea clavennae — AP,B,C,G,JE,KL,SC,T
Achillea clypeolata — B,BS,JE
Achillea coarctaca — B,T
Achillea erba-rotta ssp moschata — B,JE
Achillea 'Fanal' — HP
Achillea filipendulina — B,CN,CP,G,PI,SG
Achillea filipendulina 'Cloth Of Gold' — B,BS,CL,CO,D,DE,F,FR, J,KS,KI,MO,SE,SK,ST, SU,T,V
Achillea filipendulina 'Gold Plate' — HP
Achillea filipendulina 'Parker's Variety' — C,HU,JE,JO,PK,SA,SG
Achillea fraasii — B,JE,SA
Achillea glaberrima 'Gold Spray' — B
Achillea grandifolia — B,HP,P
Achillea holosericea — AP,B,KL,SC,SG
Achillea impatiens — SG
Achillea lanulosa — SG
Achillea macrophylla — B,G,HU,SC,SG
Achillea millefolium — AB,B,C,CA,CN,CP,DD,G, HU,HW,JE,LA,NO,NT,PI, SA,SD,SG,TH,Z
Achillea millefolium 'Colorado' — B,C,JE,JO
Achillea millefolium 'Debutante' — GO,PK

13

ACHILLEA

Achillea millefolium F2 'Summer Pastels'	BD,BS,C,CL,CN,D,DE, DT,F,G,HP,J,L,MO,PK,S, SA,SE,SK,T,U,V,VY
Achillea millefolium 'Red Beauty'	B
Achillea millefolium 'Reine Cerise'	B,BH,BS,C,CL,CN,DE, HU,JE,JO,L,KS,MO,PI, PK,SA,SK,SU,T
Achillea millefolium 'Rosea'	B,FR
Achillea millefolium 'Rosy Red'	JE
Achillea millefolium 'Rubra'	CA
Achillea millefolium 'Silver Queen'	B
Achillea nana	B,C
Achillea nobilis	B,G,JE,SA
Achillea nobilis ssp neilreichii	B
Achillea ptarmica	B,CN,JE,SG,TH
Achillea ptarmica 'Ballerina'	B,BS,CO,JE,KI,SA
Achillea ptarmica 'Mother of Pearl'	D
Achillea ptarmica 'The Pearl'	B,BS,BY,C,CL,CN,DE, HP,J,JE,KS,L,MO,O,SA, SE,SK,T,VY
Achillea ptarmica 'The Pearl Superior'	B,C,JE,PK
Achillea ptarmica white	B,FR
Achillea pyrenaica	B,G
Achillea setacea	SG
Achillea sibirica	AP,B,G,JE,SC,SG,T
Achillea 'Tickled Pink'	BS,KI
Achillea tomentosa	BH,G
Achillea tomentosa 'Aurea'	B,BS,BY,C,CL,CN,JE, L,MO,SA
Achillea umbellata	AP,G,SG
Achimenes f1 'Carmencita'	B,BS,C,MO
Achimenes f1 Cupid's Bower mix	V
Achimenes f1 'Palette' mix	BS,C,CL,D,DE,L,MO, N,SK,T
Achimenes f1 'Prima Donna'	B,BS,C,MO
Achyrachaena mollis	CG
Achyranthes aspera	B
Achyranthes bidentata	CP
Achyrophorus maculatus	SG
Acianthus caudatus	B
Acidanthera see Gladiolus	
Acinos alpinus	AP,B,KL,SC,SG
Acinos arvensis	B,SG
Aciphylla aurea	B,C,CG,SA,SC,SS
Aciphylla colensoi	B,SA
Aciphylla crenulata	B,SS
Aciphylla dieffenbachii	B,SS
Aciphylla dissecta	B
Aciphylla dobsonii	SC
Aciphylla hookeri	B,SS
Aciphylla horrida	B,C
Aciphylla monroi	B,SC,SS
Aciphylla montana	B,SS
Aciphylla pinnatifida	B,SA,SC
Aciphylla polita	B
Aciphylla scott-thomsonii	B,SS
Aciphylla similis	B,SS
Aciphylla squarrosa	B,KL,SS
Aciphylla subflabellata	CG,SC
Ackama rosaefolia	B
Acmadenia alternifolia	B
Acmella oleracea	B
Acmella oppositifolia	B
Acmena brachyandra	B
Acmena hemilampra	B
Acmena smithii	B,EL,HA,O,SA,SH
Acmena smithii purple	B,EL,SH
Acnatherum see Stipa	
Acnistus australis see Dunalia	
Acoelorraphe wrightii	B,CA,EL,HA,O,SA
Acokanthera oblongifolia	B,CG,SA
Acokanthera oppositifolia	B,SI
Aconitum altaicum	SG
Aconitum anglicum see A.napellus ssp n. Anglicum Group	
Aconitum anthora	AP,B,C,G,HP,JE,SA
Aconitum anthoroideum	SG
Aconitum arcuatum	G
Aconitum arendsii	SA
Aconitum barbatum	KL,SG
Aconitum carmichaelii	AP,C,DE,HP,P,SC,T
Aconitum carmichaelii 'Arendsii'	B,C,G,JE
Aconitum carmichaelii wilsonii	AP,G,HP,JE,SA
Aconitum carneum	C
Aconitum columbianum	C,NO,SG
Aconitum cvs mix	HP
Aconitum czekanovskyi	CG,G,SG
Aconitum delphinifolium delphinifolium	SG
Aconitum ferrox	AP,HP
Aconitum firmum	CG,SG
Aconitum forrestii	SG
Aconitum gmelinii	HP
Aconitum hemsleyanum	HP
Aconitum heterophyllum	AP,G,SC
Aconitum 'Ivorine'	AP,B,C,JE,P,SC
Aconitum komarovii	SG
Aconitum krylovii	SG
Aconitum lasiostomum	CG,G
Aconitum loczyanum	SG
Aconitum lycoctonum	AP,B,C,G,HP,JE,KL,SA, SG,T
Aconitum lycoctonum ssp	B,G
Aconitum lycoctonum ssp lycoctonum	C,HP,JE,SG
Aconitum lycoctonum ssp neapolitanum	HP,JE,SC
Aconitum lycoctonum ssp vulparia	AP,C,G,HP,PO,SC
Aconitum moldavicum	SG
Aconitum napellus	AP,B,BS,C,CN,DE,FR,G, HP,HU,JE,KI,KL,RH,SA, SC,SG,ST,SU,T,TH,V, VO,W
Aconitum napellus 'Albiflorus' see A.n. ssp vulgare 'Albidum'	
Aconitum napellus 'Carneum' see A.n. ssp vulgare 'Carneum'	
Aconitum napellus 'Newry Blue'	B,BS,C,CL,JE,L,MO,PK
Aconitum napellus ssp napellus	B,HP
Aconitum napellus ssp n. Anglicum Gr.	AP,C,HP,I,SC
Aconitum napellus ssp vulgare 'Albidum'	AP,B,G,HP,JE
Aconitum napellus ssp vulgare 'Carneum'	B,G,HP
Aconitum napellus v bicolor	C
Aconitum noveboracensis	G
Aconitum orientale	VO
Aconitum pubiceps	SG
Aconitum sachalinense v compactum	SG
Aconitum septentrionale see A.lycoctonum ssp lycoctonum	
Aconitum soongaricum	SG
Aconitum tauricum	KL
Aconitum variegatum	B,G,JE,SG
Aconitum volubile	B,C,NG,SC,SG,T
Aconitum vulparia/orientalis see A. lyconitum	
Aconitum wardii	SG
Acorus calamus	B,JE,PR,SG
Acorus calamus 'Variegatus'	B
Acorus gramineus	B
Acorus gramineus 'Variegatus'	B

ACOSMIUM

Acosmium panamensis	B
Acridocarpus natalitius	B,C,SI
Acrocarpus fraxinifolius	B,EL,SA,WA
Acrocomia aculeata	B,CA,EL
Acrocomia chunta	B
Acrocomia totai	B
Acrodon subulatus	B,DV
Acrostichum aureum	B
Actaea acuminata	SG
Actaea alba	AP,B,C,G,HP,JE,KL,NG,
	P,PO,RS,SA,SC,SG,T
Actaea arguta	SG
Actaea asiatica	AP,HP
Actaea erythrocarpa Fisher	B,HP,JE,SA,SG
Actaea pachypoda see A.alba	
Actaea rubra	AP,B,C,CG,G,JE,NG,NO,
	SC,SG
Actaea rubra f neglecta	AP,B,HP,NG,SC
Actaea rubra ssp arguta	B,HP
Actaea spicata	B,C,G,HP,JE,KL,NG,PO,
	RH,RS,SA,SC,SG
Actaea spicata v rubra see A. erythrocarpa Fisher	
Actinidia arguta	A,B,C,CG,FW,LN,RS,SA
Actinidia arguta 'Issai'	B
Actinidia callosa	CG
Actinidia chinensis h. see A. deliciosa	
Actinidia deliciosa	B,C,CA,G,DV,EL,FW,
	LN,SA,SG,T,V
Actinidia deliciosa 'Bruno'	B
Actinidia deliciosa 'Hayward'	B
Actinidia kolomikta	A,B,C,CA,DD,FW,HU,
	LN,SA,SG
Actinidia melanandra	B
Actinidia polygama	B,C,LN,RS,SA
Actinidia purpurea	B,LN
Actiniopteris radiata	B
Actinomeris alternifolia see Verbesina	
Actinorhytis calapparia	O
Actinostrobus acuminatus	B,NI,O
Actinostrobus arenarius	B,NI,O,SA
Actinostrobus pyramidalis	B,NI,O,SA
Actinotus helianthi	AP,AU,B,C,DI,EL,HA,
	NI,O,SA,SH
Actinotus leucocephalus	B,C,NI,O
Actinotus minor	HA
Adansonia digitata	B,C,DD,DV,EL,SA,SI,T,
	WA
Adansonia fony	DV,SI
Adansonia grandidieri	DV,SI
Adansonia gregorii	B,EL,HU,NI,O,SA
Adansonia madagascariensis	B
Adenandra brachyphylla	B,SI
Adenandra marginata	B
Adenandra uniflora	B,C
Adenanthera pavonina	DD,EL,HA,NI,O,SA
Adenia digitata	B,SI
Adenia glauca	B,DV,SI,Y
Adenia hastata	B,SI
Adenia keramanthus	B
Adenia spinosa	DV
Adenium obesum	B,C,CA,CH,DV,EL,SA,Y
Adenium obesum 'Multiflorum'	B
Adenium obesum ssp swazicum	B
Adenocarpus decorticans	SA
Adenolobus gariepensis	B
Adenolobus pechuellii	B

Adenophora aurita	AP,HP,W
Adenophora aurita stricta	SA
Adenophora bulleyana	AP,B,C,G,HP,PM,SG,T,W
Adenophora confusa	HP,SG
Adenophora forrestii	AP,MA
Adenophora himalayana	AP,G,HP
Adenophora khasiana	B,P
Adenophora kirilense	DD
Adenophora koreana	AP,HP,PM,SC
Adenophora liliifolia	AP,B,C,CG,G,HP,HU,JE,
	SA,SC,T
Adenophora nikoensis	AP,B,G,HP,KL,SC
Adenophora nikoensis v stenophylla	HP
Adenophora pereskiifolia	B,G,HP,RS,SC,SG
Adenophora polyantha	AP,B,HP,P,SG
Adenophora potaninii	B,C,HP
Adenophora stricta	SG
Adenophora takedae	B,C,JE,SA
Adenophora takedae alba	JE
Adenophora tashiroi	AP,CG,HP
Adenophora triphylla	AP,C,SC
Adenophora triphylla v hakusanensis	AP,B,HP
Adenophora triphylla v japonica	G,SG
Adenophora x confusa?	T
Adenopodia spicata	B,SI
Adenostoma fasciculatum	B
Adenostoma sparsifolium	B
Adenostyles alliariae	AP,CG,SG
Adenostyles alpina see Cacalia glabra	
Adiantum aethiopicum	B,C,EL,HA,SA
Adiantum ancens	SG
Adiantum capillus fimbriatum	SG
Adiantum capillus veneris	B,SG
Adiantum caudatum	B,SG
Adiantum cuneatum see A.raddianum	
Adiantum edgeworthii	B
Adiantum formosum	B,EL,SG
Adiantum fulvum	B,SG
Adiantum grossum	SG
Adiantum 'Harlequin'	B
Adiantum hispidulum	B,EL,HA,SA
Adiantum imbricata	B
Adiantum macrophyllum	SG
Adiantum peruvianum	B,SA
Adiantum pubescens	B
Adiantum raddianum	B,SA,SG
Adiantum raddianum cvs	B,C,SA
Adiantum raddianum v majus	B
Adiantum tenerum	SG
Adiantum tenerum 'Bessoniae'	B
Adiantum tenerum 'Fergusonii'	B
Adiantum tenerum 'Scutum Roseum'	B,SA
Adiantum tenerum 'Sleeping Beauty'	B
Adiantum trapeziforme	B,SG
Adiantum trapeziforme 'Kuranda'	B
Adlumia fungosa	AP,C,HP,KL,P,SC
Adonis aestivalis	AP,B,C,DE,FR,G,HP,HU,
	KS,SC,SG,SU,T,V
Adonis altaicus	B
Adonis amurensis	AP,B
Adonis annua	AP,B,CN,CO,TH
Adonis brevistyla	HP
Adonis davurica	SG
Adonis flammea	SG
Adonis vernalis	AP,B,C,CG,G,JE,KL,PO,
	SA,SC,SG,T

ADOXA

Adoxa moschatellina	B
Adriana quadripartita	B
Adriana tomentosa	B
Aechmea aquilegia	B,CG
Aechmea bromeliifolia	B,CG
Aechmea coelestis	B,SG
Aechmea melinonii	SG
Aechmea mertensa	B,CG
Aechmea miniata	DV
Aechmea recurvata	DV
Aechmea sp	B
Aechmea tillandsioidea	B,CG
Aegilops geniculata	CG,G
Aegilops neglecta	SG
Aegilops ovata	B
Aegilops ventricosa	G
Aeginetia indica	C,SG
Aegle marmelos	B,EL,HA,SA
Aegopodium podagraria	B
Aeluropus lagopodoides	B
Aeolanthus parvifolius	B
Aeollanthus buchnerianus	B,KB
Aeollanthus parvifolius	KB
Aeollanthus suaveolens	B,KB
Aeonium arboreum v holochrysum	B
Aeonium canariense	C
Aeonium canariense v subplanum	DV
Aeonium glutinosum	B
Aeonium haworthii	B,KL
Aeonium nobile	C
Aeonium simsii	DV
Aeonium sp mix	C
Aeonium spathulatum	HP
Aeonium subplanum see A.canariense v subplanum	
Aeranthes grandiflora	B
Aerva lanata	B
Aeschynanthus longicaulis	C
Aesculus californica	B,LN,N,SA
Aesculus chinensis	B
Aesculus flava	B,FW,LN,N,SA
Aesculus glabra	B,LN
Aesculus glabra v arguta	B
Aesculus hippocastanum	B,LN,SA,VE
Aesculus indica	B,SA
Aesculus parviflora	G,SA
Aesculus pavia	B,FW,LN,N,SA
Aesculus sylvatica	B
Aesculus turbinata	B,LN
Aesculus wilsonii	B,LN,SA
Aesculus x carnea	B,SA,VE
Aesculus x carnea 'Briotti'	B
Aesculus x hybrida	N
Aesculus x woerlitzensis	B,LN
Aetheopappus pulcherrimus	VO
Aethionema anittaurus	SG
Aethionema arabicum	B,SG
Aethionema armenum	AP,B,SC,SG
Aethionema armenum 'Warley Rose'	AP,B,G,HP,JD
Aethionema cappadocium	CG
Aethionema coridifolium	B,BS,C,JE,PK,SA,SC,SG
Aethionema creticum	CG
Aethionema glaucescens	B,RM
Aethionema grandiflorum	AP,B,C,CG,G,I,JE,KL, PM,SC,SG
Aethionema iberideum	B,RM
Aethionema kotschyi	JE

Aethionema oppositifolium	AP,B,SG
Aethionema Pulchellum Group	AP,HP
Aethionema saxatile	AP,B,G,KL,SC,SG,VO
Aethionema schistosum	AP,JE,SC,SG
Aethionema x warleyense	KL
Aethiopappus pulcherrimum	T
Aethusa cynapium	B,SG
Aethyrium spicatum	B
Afrocarpus falcatus v elongatus	B
Afrocarpus gracilior	B
Afrocarpus usambarensis	B
Afromomum thonneri	B
Afzelia quanzensis	B,SA,SI,WA
Agalinis besseyana	B
Agalinis purpurea	B,PR
Agalinis tenuifolia	B
Agapanthus africanus	B,C,CA,G,HP,I,JE,SA, SI,T
Agapanthus africanus 'Albus'	B,CA,HU,JE,SA
Agapanthus africanus 'Albus Nanus'	B,CA,HA
Agapanthus africanus blue	HU
Agapanthus africanus 'Getty White'	B,HA
Agapanthus angustifolius	CG
Agapanthus campanulatus	BY,C,G,HP,RU
Agapanthus campanulatus 'Isis'	PM
Agapanthus campanulatus ssp camp.	B,KB,SI
Agapanthus campanulatus ssp patens	B,SI
Agapanthus campanulatus white form	T
Agapanthus caulescens ssp angustifolius	B,KB,SI
Agapanthus caulescens ssp caulescens	B,KB,SI
Agapanthus coddii	B,SI
Agapanthus comptonii	CG
Agapanthus comptonii ssp comptonii	B,SI
Agapanthus comptonii ssp longitubus	B,KB,SI
Agapanthus dw blue	C
Agapanthus Headbourne hybrids	AP,BS,C,G,HP,JE,L,MO, N,PL,SA,SC,T,V
Agapanthus Headbourne white	PL
Agapanthus hybrid	B,EL
Agapanthus hybrid miniature	N
Agapanthus hybrids new	T
Agapanthus hybrids white	C
Agapanthus inapertus	RU
Agapanthus inapertus ssp ho. 'Lydenburg'	B,SI
Agapanthus inapertus ssp inapertus	B,SI
Agapanthus inapertus ssp intermedius	B,KB
Agapanthus inapertus ssp pendulus	G
Agapanthus 'Kingston Blue'	HP
Agapanthus 'Lilliput'	AP,G,HP,PM
Agapanthus 'Midnight Blue'	HP
Agapanthus minor alba	C
Agapanthus Mooreanus minor hybrids	C
Agapanthus nutans	B,KB,SI
Agapanthus 'Peter Pan'	B,CA,EL,HA,JE,SA
Agapanthus praecox	AP,CG,DV,G,HP,RU,SG, SI
Agapanthus praecox 'Blue Baby'	B,HA,T
Agapanthus praecox 'Dwarf White'	B,KB
Agapanthus praecox 'Grey Pearl'	B
Agapanthus praecox 'Medium White'	B,KB,SI
Agapanthus praecox ssp minimus	B,C,CG,RU,SI
Agapanthus praecox ssp min. 'Adelaide'	B,KB,SI
Agapanthus praec. ssp m. 'Storms River'	B,KB,SI
Agapanthus praecox ssp orientalis	B,CG,CN,LG,SI
Agapanthus praecox ssp orientalis blue	B,DE,EL,HA,KB,O,RU, SA,SH

AGAPANTHUS

Agapanthus praecox ssp o. 'Mt.Thomas'	B,G,KB
Agapanthus praecox ssp o. 'Weaver'	B,KB,SI
Agapanthus praecox ssp orientalis white	EL,HA,KB,N,O,RU,SA, SH
Agapanthus praecox ssp praecox	B,KB,RU,SI
Agapanthus praecox ssp praecox 'Azure'	B,CG,G,KB,SI
Agapanthus praecox ssp pr. 'Floribunda'	B,CG,KB,SI
Agapanthus praecox tall white	B,SI
Agapanthus praecox v floribundus	RU
Agapanthus 'Purple Cloud'	C
Agapanthus 'Queen Anne'	B,CA,EL,HA
Agapanthus sp mix	AP,C,SI
Agapanthus umbellatus	BS,JE,VE
Agapanthus umbellatus 'Albus'	BS,DE,JE,VE
Agapanthus 'Wavy Navy'	B
Agapetes serpens	B
Agaricus campestris d.m.p.	B
Agastache anisata see A. foeniculum	
Agastache barberi	B,SW
Agastache 'Camphor Hyssop'	B
Agastache cana	B,RM,SW,T
Agastache cana 'Heather Queen'	PK
Agastache foeniculum	AP,B,C,CN,CP,DD,DT,F, G,HP,HU,JE,KL,KS,P, PR,RH,SC,SG,T
Agastache foeniculum 'Alabaster'	E
Agastache foeniculum 'Album'	B,C,CN,HP,SC
Agastache 'Fragrant'	D,J,SE,T,V
Agastache hyb	SZ
Agastache 'Liquorice Blue'	B,BD,BS,C,HP,JO,KI,L, MO,SK
Agastache 'Liquorice White'	B,BD,BS,C,JO,L,MO,SK
Agastache mexicana	B,C,DD,G,HP,SZ
Agastache mexicana 'Carille Carmine'	B
Agastache mexicana 'Champagne'	B,T,KS
Agastache mexicana 'Rosea' see A.cana	
Agastache micrantha	B,SW
Agastache 'Neapolitan Mix'	F
Agastache nepetoides	B,C,CG,CP,G,HP,HU,PR
Agastache pallidiflora ssp neomexicana	B,SW
Agastache pallidiflora ssp pallidiflora	B,SW
Agastache pink large	SZ
Agastache pringlei	B,HP,SW
Agastache rugosa	AP,B,C,CN,CP,G,HP,JE, SA,SG
Agastache rugosa alba	BH,JE,SA
Agastache rugosa B&SWJ 735	E
Agastache rupestris	B,HP,RM,SW
Agastache scrophulariifolia	B,DD,G,PR
Agastache sp	AP,C,CP,G
Agastache 'Tangerine Dreams'	SZ
Agastache urticifolia	B,C,HP,NO,SW
Agastache wrightii	B,HP,SW
Agastachys odorata	B,O
Agathis australis	B,SA
Agathis robusta	B,HA,O,SA
Agathosma betulina	B,SI
Agathosma cerefolium	B,KB
Agathosma ciliaris	B,SI
Agathosma ciliata	SI
Agathosma crenulata	B,EL,SA,SI
Agathosma ovata	B,BH,KB,SI
Agathosma sp	SI
Agave americana	B,DV,EL,HA,SA
Agave angustifolia	B,EL,SA
Agave angustifolia 'Marginata'	B,EL,HU,SA
Agave attenuata	B,CA,EL,SA
Agave celsii v albicans	B,DV
Agave celsius	SA
Agave chrysantha	B,DV
Agave desertii	B,DV,SW,Y
Agave ferdinandi-regis	DV,Y
Agave filifera	B,DV,EL,Y
Agave gheisbreghtii	DV
Agave goldmanniana	DV
Agave havardiana	B
Agave kerchovei	DV
Agave lechuguilla	B
Agave mckelveyana	B,DV
Agave neomexicana	B
Agave palmeri	B,DD,DV
Agave parryi	B,C,DV,SA,SW,Y
Agave parryi v cousei	B,DV,SW
Agave parryi v huachucensis	B,HU,SW
Agave parryi v parryi	B,SW
Agave parryi v truncata	B,DV
Agave patrense	Y
Agave potatorum	B,Y
Agave schavii	CH
Agave schidigera	B,SW
Agave schottii	B,DV,SG
Agave sisalana	B
Agave sp mix	EL,HA,T
Agave striata	B,DV
Agave stricta	B,DV,GC,Y
Agave tourneyana	B,CH,DV
Agave univittata	DV
Agave utahensis	B,DV,SA,SW
Agave utahensis v eborispina	B,DV
Agave utahensis v kaibabensis	B,DV,G
Agave utahensis v nevadensis	B,DV
Agave victoriae-reginae	B,C,CG,DV,EL,HU,N, SA,SG
Agave vilmoriniana	B
Ageratum 'Atlantic Plus'	BS
Ageratum 'Blue Blanket'	BS
Ageratum 'Blue Cap'	BS
Ageratum blue dw	FR,SK
Ageratum conyzoides	B
Ageratum f1 'Hawaii' blue p.s.	SK
Ageratum f1 'Hawaii' royal p.s.	SK
Ageratum f1 'Hawaii' white p.s.	SK
Ageratum houstonianum	SG,TH
Ageratum houstonianum 'Bavaria'	B,BS,C,DT,J,O,SK,U
Ageratum houstonianum 'Blue Ball'	B,BS,CO,KI,ST
Ageratum houstonianum 'Blue Bouquet'	C,J,V
Ageratum houstonianum blue imp	PK
Ageratum houstonianum 'Blue Mink'	B,BD,BS,BY,C,CL,CN,D, DT,F,J,L,M,MO,O,PI,R,S, SE,SG,SK,SU,T,TU,U,V, VH,VY,YA
Ageratum houstonianum 'Capri'	F,PK
Ageratum houstonianum 'Dondoblue'	B
Ageratum houstonianum 'Dondowhite'	B
Ageratum houstonianum f1 'Adriatic'	B,BD,BS,C,D,DT,KI,L, MO,O,PK,S,SK,T,YA
Ageratum houstonianum f1 'Blue Blazer'	B,BS,BU,BY,CA,CN,J, KI,MO,ST,TU
Ageratum houst. f1 'Blue Danube' p.s	B,BD,BS,CA,CL,D,DT, F,M,MO,S,SE,T,U,YA
Ageratum houstonianum f1 'Blue Horizon'	B,BS,C,CL,D,JO,MO,PI, PK,SK

17

AGERATUM

Ageratum houstonianum f1 'Blue Lagoon'	BS,MO,PK,SK
Ageratum houstonianum f1 'Blue Swords'	S
Ageratum houst. f1 'Champion' s-c	CL
Ageratum houst. f1 'Champion' s-c p.s	CL
Ageratum houstonianum f1 'Hawaii Blue'	B,BD,L,MO,SK,VY
Ageratum houstonianum f1 'Hawaii Mix'	DT
Ageratum houstonianum f1 'Hawaii Royal'	B,BD,BS,L,MO,PK,SK
Ageratum houstonianum f1 'Hawaii White'	B,BD,BS,DE,DT,KI,L, MO,O,S,SK,YA
Ageratum houstonianum f1 'Madison'	BS,FR
Ageratum houstonianum f1 'Mauritius'	BS,KI
Ageratum houst. f1 'Neptune Blue'	CL
Ageratum houst. f1 'Neptune Blue' p.s	CL
Ageratum houstonianum f1 'North Sea'	BS,D,J
Ageratum houstonianum f1 'Pacific'	BS,CL,J,L
Ageratum houstonianum f1 'Pacific Plus'	MO
Ageratum houstonianum f1 'Snowball'	F
Ageratum houst. f1 'Summer Snow'	T,VH
Ageratum houstonianum f1 'Summit'	BS,DT,F,S,T
Ageratum houstonianum f1 'Swing'	BS,F,KI,T
Ageratum houstonianum f1 'White Raven'	B
Ageratum houstonianum 'Florists Blue'	B,BS
Ageratum houstonianum 'Pink Beauty'	J,V
Ageratum houst. 'Pink Powder Puffs'	BS,CA,F,KI,SE
Ageratum houstonianum 'Pinky Imp'	T
Ageratum houstonianum 'Snowdrop'	KI
Ageratum houstonianum 'Southern Cross'	SE,T
Ageratum houstonianum 'White Bouquet'	JO
Ageratum houstonianum white imp	PK
Ageratum 'Wedgewood'	BS
Aglaia roxburghiana v courtallensis	B
Aglaomorpha meyeriana	SG
Aglaonema commutatum	B,CA
Aglaonema commutatum 'Tricolor'	B
Aglaonema commutatum v maculatum	B
Aglaonema commutatum 'White Rajah'	B
Aglaonema crispum	B
Aglaonema modestum	B
Aglaonema 'Purple Stem'	B
Agonis flexuosa	B,CA,EL,HA,HU,NI,O, SA,VE
Agonis floribunda	B,NI
Agonis hypericifolia	B,NI
Agonis juniperina	B,NI,O,SA
Agonis linearifolia	B,NI,O
Agonis marginata	B,NI
Agonis obtusissima	B,NI
Agonis parviceps	B,NI,O,SA
Agonis spathulata	B,NI
Agoseris cuspidita	PR
Agoseris grandiflora	B,DD,HU
Agrimonia eupatoria	AP,B,C,CN,DD,HU,JE, KL,LA,SA,SG,TH
Agrimonia eupatoria 'Topaz'	B
Agrimonia pilosa	AP,B,SG
Agrimonia procera	B,G,SG
Agrimonia sp	SG
Agropyron cristatum	B,SG
Agropyron magellanicum see Elymus	
Agropyron pectinatum	B,SG
Agropyron pubiflorum see Elymus magellanicus	
Agropyron repens	B
Agropyron smithii	B
Agropyron spicatum	NO
Agropyron trachycaulum	PR
Agropyron trichophorum	B

Agrostemma 'Atrosanguinea'	BS,V
Agrostemma githago	AB,AP,B,C,CN,CO,G,HP, KL,LA,LG,SD,SG,SU, TH,TU,V
Agrostemma githago coeli rosea	KS
Agrostemma githago 'Milas'	B,BS,BY,C,D,DI,HU,J, KS,L,SG,T
Agrostemma githago 'Purple Queen'	B,C,DE,SP
Agrostemma githago 'Rose Queen'	B
Agrostemma gracilis	B,SG
Agrostemma linicola	B
Agrostemma 'Ocean Pearl'	T
Agrostemma 'Rose of Heaven'	KI
Agrostis alpina	G
Agrostis canina	SG
Agrostis canina 'Silver Needles'	B
Agrostis canina ssp canina	B
Agrostis castellana	B
Agrostis delicatula	SG
Agrostis geminata	SG
Agrostis gigantea	SG
Agrostis nebulosa	B,BS,C,DE,KI,MO,SU
Agrostis rupestris	SG
Agrostis sp	SG
Agrostis stolonifera	B,FR
Agrostis stolonifera 'Cobra'	B
Agrostis tenuis	B,FR
Agrostocrinum scabrum	B,C,HU,NI
Aichryson laxum	B,DV
Aichryson palmense	DV
Aichryson punctatum	DV
Ailanthus altissima	A,C,CA,EL,FW,LN,N,SA, VE,WA
Ailanthus altissima umbracifera	FW
Ailanthus excelsa	B,EL,SA
Ailanthus giraldii	CG
Ainsliaea acerifolia	B
Ainsworthia trachycarpa	B
Aiphanes caryotifolia	B,O,SA
Aiphanes erosa	B,EL
Aizoon paniculatum	B,SI
Ajuga chamaepitys	AP,SC
Ajuga chamaepitys ssp chia	RM
Ajuga chamaepitys v glareosa	B
Ajuga genevensis	B,JE,SA
Ajuga reptans	B,BS,C,CN,DE,G,HP,JE, L,MO,RH,SA,SC,SU,TH
Ajuga reptans 'Atropurpurea'	B,JE,SA
Akebia quinata	A,C,EL,G,LN,SA
Akebia trifoliata	A,C,G,LN,SA
Alangium chinensis	B,SA
Alangium plantanifolium	B,G,LN,SA,SG
Alangium salviifolium	B
Alaskan wild flower sp	B
Alberta magna	B,BH,EL,KB,LN,SA,SI, WA
Albizia adianthifolia	B,BH,C,SA,SI,WA
Albizia amara	B,SI,WA
Albizia anthelmintica	B,SI
Albizia bermudiana	B
Albizia caribaea	B
Albizia chinensis	B,EL,LN,WA
Albizia falcataria	B
Albizia forbesii	B,WA
Albizia guachepele	B,RE,TT
Albizia gummifera	B

ALBIZIA

Albizia harveyi	B,SI	Alcea rosea 'Chater's Dble,scarlet'	B,JE
Albizia julibrissin	C,CA,CG,DD,EL,G,HA,	Alcea rosea 'Chater's Dble,white'	B,JE
	HU,LN,O,SA,SC,T,VE,	Alcea rosea 'Chater's Dble,Yellow'	B,JE
	WA	Alcea rosea 'Chater's Dble,yellow,soft'	B,JE
Albizia julibrissin 'E H Wilson'	B	Alcea rosea 'Chater's' mix	BU,JE,S
Albizia julibrissin f rosea	B,C,FW,N,SA,VE	Alcea rosea dbl dark red	PL,SP,TH
Albizia kalkora	B,FW	Alcea rosea East Coast hybrids	PL,SE
Albizia lebbeck	B,CA,EL,HA,LN,O,SA,	Alcea rosea 'Indian Spring' white/ pink	B,DE,HU
	VE,WA	Alcea rosea 'Lemon Light'	B,P
Albizia lophantha see Paraserianthes		Alcea rosea 'Majorette'	BS,C,KS,MO,PI,T,U
Albizia lucida	B,EL	Alcea rosea 'Nigra'	AP,B,BS,C,CN,CO,G,HP,
Albizia moluccana	VE		HU,JE,KI,KS,PG,PK,SA,
Albizia occidentalis	DD		SD,SE,SG,SU,T,TH,V
Albizia procera	B	Alcea rosea nigra dbl	PL
Albizia richardiana	B,EL	Alcea rosea old fashioned mix	PG,U
Albizia saman	B	Alcea rosea 'Powder Puffs'	C,T
Albizia schimperana	B,SI	Alcea rosea s-c	G,HU,PG
Albizia sinensis	SA	Alcea rosea 'Simplex'	C,JE,V
Albizia stipulata	B,EL	Alcea rosea 'Summer Carnival'	BD,BS,BY,C,CL,D,DE,
Albizia tanganyicensis	B		DT,FR,J,KS,L,M,MO,PI,
Albizia viris	DV		S,SE,SK,T,V,VY
Albuca acuminata	B,RU	Alcea rosea v nigra plena 'Negrita'	B,JE
Albuca africana	DV	Alcea rosea 'Watchman'	JO,L,SE
Albuca altissima	B,C,DV,RU,SI	Alcea roseus country garden mix	PK
Albuca angolensis	B,G,RU	Alcea rugosa	AP,B,C,HP,JD,JE,PG,SA
Albuca canadensis	AP,B,LG,RU,SC,SI	Alcea 'Salmon Queen' dbl	PL
Albuca gloriae clanwilliamiae	B,SI	Alcea 'Sawyer's' single mix	CN
Albuca humilis	AP,HP,LG,PM,SC	Alchemilla alpina	B,C,I,JE,SA,SG
Albuca juncifolia	HP,MN	Alchemilla anisiaca	SG
Albuca maxima	B,SI	Alchemilla arvensis see Aphanes	
Albuca nelsonii	B,C,KB,SC,SI	Alchemilla caucasica	SG
Albuca setosa	B,SI,T	Alchemilla conjuncta	B,HP,SG
Albuca shawii	AP,B,G,HP,LG,SC,SG,SI	Alchemilla epipsila	B,G,JE,SG
Albuca sp	AP,BH,RU,SC,SI	Alchemilla erythropoda	B,C,JE,T
Albuca spiralis	B,C,CF,RU,SI	Alchemilla fulgens	B
Alcea 'Black Beauty'	P	Alchemilla glaucescens	SG
Alcea 'Blackcurrant Whirl'	PL	Alchemilla gracilis	SG
Alcea cetosa	B	Alchemilla hoppeana h. see A. plicatula	
Alcea ficifolia	HP,HU,PG	Alchemilla mollis	AP,BD,BS,C,CL,CN,DE,
Alcea ficifolia butter yellow	HU		F,G,HP,JE,KI,L,MO,RH,
Alcea ficifolia 'Cottage Mix'	P		SC,ST,SU,T,V
Alcea ficifolia 'Golden Eye'	B,P	Alchemilla mollis 'Auslese'	BH,C,JE
Alcea ficifolia hybrids mix	AP,C,DT,JE,PG,SA	Alchemilla mollis 'Robustica'	C,F
Alcea froloviana	SG	Alchemilla mollis 'Select'	B,JE,T
Alcea 'Icicle' dbl	PL	Alchemilla mollis 'Thriller'	B,BH,JO,KS,PK,T
Alcea 'Lavender Lady'	PL	Alchemilla monticola	B,JE,SA
Alcea 'Loganberry Fizz'	PL	Alchemilla plicatula	JE
Alcea pallida	B,JE,NG,SG	Alchemilla saxatilis	B,BH,C,JE,SG
Alcea 'Peaches n Dreams' TM	T	Alchemilla sericea	B
Alcea reds & pinks	P	Alchemilla vulgaris h. see A. xanthochlora	
Alcea rosea	B,DD,DI,HP,I,SG,SP,TH,	Alchemilla xanthochlora	CN,JE,SG,TH
	V	Alchryson dichotomum	SG
Alcea rosea annual Dble mix	F,J,ST	Alciope tabularis	B
Alcea rosea annual Single mix	AB,BS,BY,C,F,HU,J,JO,	Alectra sessiliflora	B,SI
	KI,KS,MO,ST,SU,T	Alectra sp	SI
Alcea rosea 'Apricot'	P	Alectris farinosa	DD
Alcea rosea 'Chater's Dble,apricot'	B,DT,PL,SE,T,V	Alectryon excelsus	B,SI
Alcea rosea 'Chater's Dble,chestnut'	B,JE	Alepidea thodei	B,SI
Alcea rosea 'Chater's Dble' mix	BD,BS,BY,C,CL,CN,CO,	Alepidia amatymbica	B,SI
	D,DE,DT,JE,KI,L,MO,R,	Alepidia natalensis	B,SI
	SA,SK,TU,U,YA	Aletris farinosa	B
Alcea rosea 'Chater's Dble,pink,bright'	B,F,JE,SE	Aleurites fordii	B,CA,EL,HA,LN,S
Alcea rosea 'Chater's Dble,purple'	B,JE	Aleurites moluccana	B,EL,HA,NI,O,SA
Alcea rosea 'Chater's Dble' s-c	B,C,DT,F,JE,PL,SA,SE,	Alfedia cernus	SG
	T,V	Alisma gramineum	SG
Alcea rosea 'Chater's Dble,salmon-pink'	B,F,JE	Alisma lanceolatum	B,HP,JE,SA,SG

ALISMA

Alisma parviflora	C,JE,SA
Alisma plantago-aquatica	C,G,HP,JE,KL,RH,SA, SC,SG
Alisma plantago-aquatica v parviflorum	B
Alisma subcordatum	PR
Alkanna graeca	HP
Alkanna orientalis	CG
Allamanda blanchetii	B
Allamanda cathartica	B
Allamanda neriifolia see A. schottii	
Allamanda schottii	B,EL,SA,SG
Allanblackia stuhlmanii	B
Allardia tridactylites	VO
Alliaria officinalis	DD
Alliaria petiolata	B,C,G,LA,SG,Th
Allionia incarnata	B
Allium acuminatum	AP,B,C,JE,KL
Allium acuminatum v album	B,JE
Allium aflatunense see A. hollandicum	
Allium akaka	KL,SG
Allium albidum see A.denudatum	
Allium altaicum	B,G,SG
Allium altissimum	AP,G
Allium amabile see A. mairei v a.	
Allium amethystinum	B,JE,LG,NG
Allium ampeloprasum	B,DD
Allium ampeloprasum v babingtonii	SG
Allium angulosum	AP,B,SC,SG
Allium atropurpureum	AP,B,G,JE,KL,LG,NG
Allium babingtonii	NS
Allium basticum	SG
Allium beesianum see A.cyaneum	
Allium bodeanum	AP,SG,SC
Allium bucharicum	B
Allium buriatum	G
Allium caeruleum	AP,B,G,JE,SC
Allium callimischon	B,SC,SG
Allium callimishon ssp haemostrictum	NG
Allium campanulatum	AP,B,SC,SW
Allium canadense	AP,C,G,PR
Allium canum	SG
Allium carinatum	AP,B,G,I
Allium carinatum ssp pulchellum	AP,B,C,G,I,JE,KL,LG, MN,NG,PA,RS,SC,SG,T
Allium carinatum ssp pulchellum 'Album'	AP,B,G,HP,PM
Allium carinatum ssp pulchellum pink	C
Allium cepa Proliferum Group	HP
Allium cernuum	AB,AP,B,BS,C,G,JE,KL, LG,MN,NO,PA,PM,PR, RM,SC,SA,SG,SW,T
Allium chamaemoly v littoralis	B
Allium chamaemoly v littoralis A.B.S4387	MN
Allium chrysonemum	B
Allium chrysonemum HMS379	MN
Allium cristophii	AP,B,C,DE,G,I,JD,JE,KL, LG,RH,SA,SC,SG,T
Allium cyaneum	B,KL,SG,SC
Allium cyathophorum	AP,SC
Allium cyathophorum v farreri	AP,B,C,G,JE,KL,LG,SC, SG
Allium cyrillii	G
Allium decipens	SG
Allium denudatum	AP,B,VO
Allium dichlamydeum	AP,B,MN,NG,SC
Allium dregeanum	B,SI
Allium elatum see A. macleanii	
Allium elegans	KL
Allium ellisii	B
Allium ellisii PF2571 Iran	MN
Allium ericetorum	B
Allium falcifolium	AP,G,SZ
Allium fistulosum	NG,TH
Allium flavum	AP,B,C,G,I,JD,JE,KL,LG, MN,NG,SC,SG
Allium flavum 'Blue leaf'	AP,PM,SC
Allium flavum ssp tauricum	KL
Allium flavum v minus	AP,B,G,KL,MN,SC
Allium flavum v nanum	KL
Allium fuscovoilaceum	KL
Allium geyeri	AP,B,SC,SW
Allium giganteum	AP,B,BD,G,JE,KL,SA,SC
Allium globosum	G,SG
Allium haematochiton	B
Allium hierochuntinum	B,MN
Allium hollandicum	AP,B,C,G,I,JE,KL,LG, RS,SA,SC
Allium hollandicum 'Purple Sensation'	AP,B,KL,LG,SC,T
Allium hymenorrhizum	CG
Allium insubricum	AP,B,C,JE,KL,SC
Allium jesdianum	B,CG,G,JE,KL
Allium karataviense	AP,B,C,E,G,I,JE,KL,PM, RM,RS,SA,SC,SG
Allium komarovianum	KL,SG
Allium ledebourianum	SG
Allium libani	G,RS,SG
Allium longicuspis	SG
Allium macleanii	B,G,KL
Allium macropetalum	B,SW
Allium mairei v amabile	I,KL
Allium mix rock garden	C
Allium moly	AP,B,C,G,JE,SA,SC,SG
Allium montanum	JE,SG
Allium narcissiflorum h. see A.insubricum	
Allium neapolitanum	AP,B,C,G,JE,KL,SC,SG
Allium neapolitanum v cowanii	AP,B,KL,SC
Allium nigrum	B,JE,KL,SA
Allium nutans	AP,B,G,LG,SC,SG
Allium obliquum	AP,B,C,NG,RS,SC
Allium ochroleucum	B
Allium odorum see A. ramosum	
Allium oleraceum	AP
Allium oliganthum	SG
Allium olympicum	AP,NG
Allium oreophilum	AP,B,C,G,JE,KL,LG,SC, SG
Allium oreophilum 'Zwanenberg'	PM
Allium oreoprasum	SG
Allium ostrowskianum see A. oreophilum	
Allium paniculatum	KL,NG
Allium paradoxum	AP,B
Allium paradoxum PF5085 Iran	MN
Allium peninsulare	AP,B,SC,SW
Allium pskemense	KL
Allium pyrenaicum	CG
Allium ramosum	B,BD,CN,G,JE,RS,SA, SC,SG
Allium rosenbachianum	B,G,JE,PM
Allium rosenbachianum 'Album'	B,JE
Allium roseum	AP,B,G,KL,SC
Allium rotundum	B
Allium rubrovittatum	B
Allium rubrovittatum C.Barclay	MN

ALLIUM

Allium sativum	G
Allium sativum v ophioscorodon	B,CP
Allium scabriscapum	B,MN
Allium schoenoprasum	AP,B,CP,G,JE,KS,RH,SC, SG,TH
Allium schoenoprasum f1 'Hylau Cut'	B,CN
Allium schoenoprasum v sibericum	SG
Allium schubertii	B,C,G,LG,NG,SC,SG
Allium scorodoprasum	B,G,SG
Allium senescens	AP,B,G,JE,KL,LG,SC
Allium senescens ssp montanum	AP,B,I,JE,RH
Allium sibthorpianum see A. paniculatum	
Allium sikkimense	AP,B,G,KL,NG,RS,SC, SG
Allium sp	KI
Allium sp mix	C,G,SC
Allium sp orange	RS,SG
Allium sphaerocephalum	AP,B,C,CN,G,JE,RM,RS, SA,SC,TH
Allium splendens	AP,SC
Allium stellatum	B,JE,PR,SG
Allium stipitatum	AP,B,C,G,JE,SC,SG
Allium stipitatum 'Album'	G
Allium strictum	B,SG
Allium subtilissimum	G,SG
Allium tanguticum	AP,B
Allium telavivense	B
Allium textile	AP,B,SG,SW
Allium tricoccum	B,PR,SC
Allium trifolium	B
Allium trifolium L/Cu 124/1 Cyprus	MN
Allium trifolium S.L53 Jordan	MN
Allium triquetrum	KL,SG
Allium tuberosum	AP,CN,CP,G,HU,KL,KS, SG,TH
Allium turkestanicum	B
Allium unifolium	AP,B,C,G,KL,LG,MN,P, SC,SG,SZ
Allium ursinum	A,AP,B,C,G,JE,KL,SC,TH
Allium victorialis	AP,B,C,G,JE,SG
Allium vineale	AP,B,KL,SC
Allium vineale v compactum	G
Allium violaceum see A.carinatum	
Allium wallichii	B,SC,SG
Allium winklerianum	KL,LG
Allium zebdanense	AP,B,G,SG
Allium zebrina	B
Allmania nodiflora	B
Allocasuarina campestris	NI,O
Allocasuarina decaisneana	NI,O
Allocasuarina distyla	AU,EL,HA,NI,O
Allocasuarina huegeliana	NI,O
Allocasuarina littoralis	B,C,EL,HA,NI,SA
Allocasuarina muellerana	AU,HA,NI
Allocasuarina nana	EL,HA,NI
Allocasuarina paludosa	EL,HA,NI
Allocasuarina pusilla	HA,NI
Allocasuarina sp	AU
Allocasuarina stricta	EL,HA,NI,O
Allocasuarina torulosa	EL,HA,N,NI,O
Allocasuarina verticillata	B,CA,SA
Allophylus africanus	B,SI
Allophylus dregeanus	B,SI
Allophylus natalensis	B,C,KB,SI
Allophylus serratus	B
Alloplectus dodsonii	B

Alloteropsis cimicina	B
Alluadia procera	DV
Alnus acuminata	B
Alnus acuminata ssp arguta	SG
Alnus acuminata ssp glabrata	SG
Alnus cordata	A,B,C,CA,EL,FW,LN,SA, SG,VE
Alnus cremastogyne	B,EL,FW,LN
Alnus crispa see A.viridis ssp c.	
Alnus firma	LN,SG
Alnus formosana	SA
Alnus glutinosa	A,B,C,EL,FW,LN,RH,SA, VE
Alnus hirsuta	B,EL,FW,LN,SA,SG
Alnus incana	A,B,C,CA,CG,EL,FW,LN, NO,RH,SA,VE
Alnus incana f aurea	SG
Alnus japonica	B,LN,RH,SA
Alnus jorullensis	B,EL
Alnus maximowiczii	B,SG
Alnus nepalensis	B,CA,FW,LN,SA,SG
Alnus nepalensis AC1862	X
Alnus nepalensis CNW778	X
Alnus nitida	B,FW,SA
Alnus pendula	SG
Alnus rhombifolia	B,CA,FW,LN,NO,RH,SA
Alnus rubra	A,AB,B,C,CA,EL,FW,LN, NO,RH,SA,SG,VE
Alnus rugosa	B,LN
Alnus serrulata	B,CG,FW,LN,NO
Alnus sieboldiana	SG
Alnus sinuata	A,B,C,FW,LN,NO,RH,SG
Alnus tenuifolia	B,FW,LN,RH,SA,SG
Alnus viridis	A,B,CG,LN,RH,SA,SG
Alnus viridis ssp crispa	B,FW,LN,RH,SG
Alnus x mayrii	RH
Alocasia macrorrhiza	B,EL,HA,O
Alocasia sanderana	B
Aloe abyssinica JBG12358	BC
Aloe aculeata	B,DV,SI
Aloe affinis	B,DV
Aloe africana	B,SA,SI
Aloe albiflora	B,SI
Aloe alferdii	SI
Aloe ammophila	B,DV
Aloe arborea	BH
Aloe arborescens	B,C,DV,SA,SI,Y
Aloe aristata	B
Aloe asperifolia	B,SI
Aloe bainesii	B,SI
Aloe bakeri	SI
Aloe bellatula	B
Aloe bowiea	B,SI
Aloe boylei	SI
Aloe bracteata	B,Y
Aloe branddraaiensis	B,DV,SI
Aloe brevifolia	B,SI
Aloe broomii	B,DV,KB,SI
Aloe buhrii	B,DV,SI
Aloe burgersfortensis	B,DV,SI
Aloe camperi	DV,SI
Aloe camperi 'Maculata'	B
Aloe capitata	B,DV,SI
Aloe capitata v cipolinicola	B,SI
Aloe capitata v quartziticola	DV
Aloe castanea	B,DV,SI,Y

ALOE

Aloe chabaudii	B,DV,SI
Aloe claviflora	B,DV,KB,SI,Y
Aloe comosa	B,DV,SI,Y
Aloe compressa v schistophylla	B
Aloe comptonii	B,SI
Aloe conifera	B,SI
Aloe cooperi	B,C,SI
Aloe cryptopoda	DV,SI
Aloe davyana	B,DV,Y
Aloe davyana v subulifera	B,Y
Aloe dichotoma	B,CH,DV,KB,SA,SI,Y
Aloe distans	B
Aloe dolomitica	B
Aloe dominella	B,SA,SI
Aloe ecklonis	B,SI
Aloe erinacea	B,SA,SI
Aloe excelsa	DV
Aloe falcata	B,DV
Aloe ferox	B,BH,DV,KB,SA,SI,Y
Aloe fosteri	B,Y
Aloe gariepensis	B,DV,KB,SI,Y
Aloe glauca	B,SI
Aloe globuligemma	B,DV,SI
Aloe graciliflora	B,BC
Aloe graminicola	B
Aloe grandidentata	B,DV,SI
Aloe greatheadii	B,DV
Aloe greatheadii ssp davyana	B,SI
Aloe greenii	B,DV
Aloe greenwayi	B,DV
Aloe haemanthifolia	B,SI
Aloe harlana	B
Aloe haworthoides	B
Aloe hereroensis	B,DV,KB,SI,Y
Aloe howmanii	B,SI
Aloe humilis	B,DV,SI
Aloe immaculata	B,DV
Aloe inyangensis	B,SI
Aloe jacksonii	B,SI,Y
Aloe karasbergensis see A.striata ssp k.	
Aloe kedongensis	DV
Aloe khamiesensis	B,SI
Aloe krapohliana	B,DV,SI
Aloe kraussii	SI
Aloe lineata	B,SI
Aloe lineata v muirii	B,SI
Aloe littoralis	B,DV,SI,Y
Aloe littoralis v rubro-lutea	B,Y
Aloe longibracteata	B
Aloe lutescens	B,DV,Y
Aloe maculata	B,SI
Aloe madecassa	B,DV,SI
Aloe marlothii	B,DV,SA,SI,Y
Aloe melanacantha	B,DV,SI
Aloe microstigma	B,DV,SI,Y
Aloe miebuhriana	DV
Aloe mieburgiana	DV
Aloe minima	SI
Aloe mitis	B
Aloe mitriformis	B,SI
Aloe modesta	SI
Aloe mudenensis	DV
Aloe munchii	DV
Aloe mutabilis	B,DV,Y
Aloe mutans	DV
Aloe pachygasta	BC,DV

Aloe parvibracteata	B,DV,SI,Y
Aloe peglerae	B,DV,SI
Aloe petricola	B,DV
Aloe pictifolia	B,SI
Aloe pirottae	B
Aloe plicatilis	B,DV,SI
Aloe pluridens	B,SI
Aloe pratensis	B,DV,SA,SI
Aloe pretoriensis	B,SI
Aloe prinslooi	B
Aloe ramosissima	B,SI
Aloe rauhii	B
Aloe reitzii	B,DV
Aloe reynoldsii	DV
Aloe rupestris	B,DV,SI,Y
Aloe saponaria	B,DV
Aloe sinkatana	B,DV,SI
Aloe sp	C,CA,DE,DV,EL,SI
Aloe speciosa	B,DV,SI
Aloe spectabilis	B,DV
Aloe spicata	SI
Aloe spinossisima	DV
Aloe squarrosa	SI
Aloe striata	B,BC,DV,SA,SI,Y
Aloe striata ssp karasbergensis	B,KB,SI
Aloe striatula	B,SI
Aloe succotrina	B,SI
Aloe suprafoliata	B,SI
Aloe suzannae	DV
Aloe thraskii	B,CH,DV,SI
Aloe tidmarshii	B
Aloe tomentosa	B,DV
Aloe transvaalensis	B,SI
Aloe trichosantha	DV
Aloe vacillans	B
Aloe vahombe	DV
Aloe variegata	B,C,CF,CH,DV,SA,SI
Aloe vera	SA,SI
Aloe viridiflora	B,DV,KB
Aloe vogtsii	DV
Aloe wickensii	DV
Aloe zebrina	B,DV,SI
Aloinopsis hilmarii	B
Aloinopsis jamesii	B
Aloinopsis luckhoffii	B,DV,GC,SI,Y
Aloinopsis malherbei	B,DV,SI,Y
Aloinopsis mix	Y
Aloinopsis orpenii	B,SI
Aloinopsis peersii	B,SI
Aloinopsis rosulata	B,DV,SI,Y
Aloinopsis rubrolineata	B,DV,SI
Aloinopsis schooneesii	B,DV,GC,Y
Aloinopsis setifera	B,DV,Y
Aloinopsis spathulata	B,DV
Aloinopsis thudichumi	B
Aloinopsis villetii	B,DV,SI,Y
Alonsoa acutifolia	HP
Alonsoa albiflora	P
Alonsoa albiflora 'Snowflake'	C
Alonsoa hyb new mix	J
Alonsoa linearis	AP,B,C
Alonsoa meridionalis	B,C,G,HP,JE,SA,V
Alonsoa meridionalis 'Firestone Jewels'	F,T
Alonsoa meridionalis mix	JE
Alonsoa meridionalis 'Pink Beauty'	B,I,P
Alonsoa meridionalis 'Salmon Beauty'	T

ALONSOA

Alonsoa meridionalis shell pink	JE
Alonsoa warscewiczii	AP,B,BS,C,DT,HP,HU,SG,T
Alonsoa warscewiczii 'Sutton's Scarlet'	B,PI
Alopecurus arundinaceus	SG
Alopecurus geniculatus	B
Alopecurus myosuroides	B
Alopecurus pratensis	B,SG
Alopecurus pratensis 'Aureovariegatus'	B
Aloysia triphylla	B
Alphitonia excelsa	B,HA,NI,O,SA
Alphitonia petriei	B,NI,O
Alphitonia philippinensis	B
Alpine compositae B&SWJ 1659 (u-g)	E
Alpinia caerulea	B,EL,SA
Alpinia calcarata	B
Alpinia galanga	B
Alpinia purpurata red	B
Alpinia zerumbet	B,BS,O,SA
Alpinia zerumbet 'Variegata'	B
Alstonia macrophylla	B
Alstonia scholaris	B,HA,SA
Alstroemeria aff exserens	AR,B
Alstroemeria aff garaventae	AR,B
Alstroemeria aff zoellneri	AR
Alstroemeria angustifolia	AP,B,SC
Alstroemeria aurantiaca see A.aurea	
Alstroemeria aurea	AP,B,C,G,HP,JE,P,SA,SC,SG
Alstroemeria aurea 'Cally Fire'	C
Alstroemeria aurea 'Dover Orange'	HP
Alstroemeria aurea 'Moorheim Orange'	C,T
Alstroemeria aurea 'Orange King'	AP,B,HP
Alstroemeria brasiliensis	RS,SC,SG
Alstroemeria diluta	B
Alstroemeria hookeri	AP,AR,B,SC
Alstroemeria ligtu hybrids	AP,BD,BS,BY,C,CL,D,DT,F,G,HP,JE,KI,LG,MO,N,PL,S,SA,SC,SE,SG,SU,SY,T
Alstroemeria ligtu ssp incarnata	AR,B
Alstroemeria ligtu ssp simsii	AR,B
Alstroemeria ligtu x Dr Salter's hybrids	B,HP,J,L,PK,T,V
Alstroemeria magenta	B
Alstroemeria magnifica	B,HP,P
Alstroemeria magnifica ssp maxima	AR,B
Alstroemeria 'Mona Lisa' (Stablaco)	B,JE
Alstroemeria mutabilis	B
Alstroemeria pallida	AP,AR,B,SC
Alstroemeria patagonica	AP,AR,HP
Alstroemeria paupercula	B
Alstroemeria pelegrina	AP,B,MN,SC,SG
Alstroemeria polyphylla	B
Alstroemeria presliana ssp australis	AR,B
Alstroemeria pseudospathulata	B,P
Alstroemeria psittacina	AP,B,CG,EL,HP,PL,SC
Alstroemeria pulchra	B,P
Alstroemeria pygmea	AP,NG
Alstroemeria revoluta	B
Alstroemeria schizanthoides	B
Alstroemeria sp S.American	PL
Alstroemeria umbellata	AP,B,SC
Alstroemeria versicolor	AP,B
Alternanthera denticulata	B,NI
Alternanthera ficoidea v amoena 'Sessilis'	B
Alternanthera sessilis	B

Althaea armeniaca	B,JE,NG
Althaea cannabina	B,C,HP,JE,P
Althaea hispida	B,NS
Althaea officinalis	B,C,CG,CO,CN,CP,DD,HP,HU,JE,KS,SA,SG,T,TH,Z
Althaea officinalis alba	AP,B,HP,P,PG
Althaea sp white	AB
Althaea zebrina	DD,HP
Alvaradoa amorphoides	B
Alyogyne cuneiformis	AU
Alyogyne hakeifolia	AU,B,HU,NI,O,SA
Alyogyne huegelii	AP,B,C,HP,NI,O,SA
Alysicarpus monilifer	B
Alysicarpus rugosus	B,NI
Alyssoides utriculata	AP,B,C,CO,G,HP,JE,KI,KL,NG,SC,SG
Alyssoides utriculata 'Lost April'	B
Alyssoides utriculata 'Tinkerbells'	B,KS
Alyssoides utriculata v graeca	AP,SC
Alyssum alpestre	AP,B,C,GG,VO
Alyssum alpestre ssp serpyllifolium	B
Alyssum argenteum h. see A. murale	
Alyssum armenum	B
Alyssum bornmuelleri	KL
Alyssum borzeanum	KL,SG
Alyssum caespitosum	B
Alyssum corymbosum see Aurinia corymbosa	
Alyssum cuneifolium	B,JE,KL
Alyssum desertorum	B
Alyssum lesbicum	B,RM
Alyssum maritimum see Lobularia maritima	
Alyssum moellendorfianum	SG
Alyssum montanum	AP,B,BS,BY,C,DE,G,HP,KL,SA,SC,SG,T
Alyssum montanum 'Berggold'	BD,BS,CL,CN,D,F,JE,L,MO,PK,R,VY
Alyssum montanum 'Mountain Gold' see 'Berggold'	
Alyssum montanum v serpentini	KL
Alyssum murale	AP,B,C,CG,G,JE,RH,SA,SC,SG
Alyssum obtusifolium	KL
Alyssum poderi v poderi	B
Alyssum pulvinare	B,KL,P
Alyssum repens	B,JE,KL
Alyssum saxatile see Aurinia saxatilis	
Alyssum serpyllifolium	C,JE,SC
Alyssum sp	KL
Alyssum spinosum	B,C,G,JD,JE,KL,VO
Alyssum spinosum 'Roseum'	KL,T
Alyssum wulfenianum	AP,B,G,KL,SC,SG
Alyxia buxifolia	B,NI
Alyxia ruscifolia	B
Amaranthus acutilobus	CG
Amaranthus albus	B
Amaranthus biltoides	SG
Amaranthus caudatus	AB,B,BS,BY,C,CG,CO,DE,DI,DT,F,FR,G,HU,J,JO,MO,O,PI,S,SD,SG,SK,SU,T,TE,TH,TU,V,YA
Amaranthus caudatus 'Albiflorus'	CG
Amaranthus caudatus 'Crimson'	D,F
Amaranthus caudatus 'Flavus'	SG
Amaranthus caudatus 'Grunschwanz'	V
Amaranthus caudatus 'Kiwicha'	B
Amaranthus caudatus red	BD,KS,ST,V

AMARANTHUS

Amaranthus caudatus 'Red/Green Tassels'	U
Amaranthus caudatus 'Viridis'	B,BS,BY,C,HU,JO,KI, KS,ST,SU,T
Amaranthus chlorostachys	B,SG
Amaranthus cruentus	C,CG,DD,RH
Amaranthus cruentus 'Alegria'	B
Amaranthus cruentus 'Bronze Standard'	B
Amaranthus cruentus 'Chihuahuan Orn.'	B
Amaranthus cruentus ecuador	B
Amaranthus cruentus 'Foxtail'	B,BS,CL,MO
Amaranthus cruentus 'Golden Giant'	B
Amaranthus cruentus 'Mayo Red'	B
Amaranthus cruentus 'Mexican Grain'	B,C
Amaranthus cruentus 'Multicolor'	B
Amaranthus cruentus 'Oeschberg'	B,KS,V
Amaranthus cruentus 'Popping'	B
Amaranthus cruentus red	BS,J,SE
Amaranthus cruentus 'Red Cathedral'	B,C
Amaranthus cruentus 'Red Cathedral Sup.'	B
Amaranthus cruentus 'Rodale Multiflora'	B
Amaranthus cr. x 'Hopi Red Dye Amar.'	B,C,DD
Amaranthus cruentus x powellii	CP
Amaranthus 'Green Thumb'	B,BD,BS,BY,C,CN,JO, KS,MO,PI,T,VY
Amaranthus hybridus	SG
Amaranthus hypochondriacus	B,C,CP,SG
Amaranthus hypochondriacus 'Burgundy'	B,DD
Amaranthus hypochondriacus 'Dreadicus'	B,DD
Amaranthus hypochond. 'Golden Giant'	B,DD,T
Amaranthus hypochondr.s 'Guarijio Grain'	B
Amaranthus hypochondriacus 'Nepalese'	B,DD
Amaranthus hypochond. 'Pigmy Torch'	B,BS,C,CN,HU,JO,KS, MO,PI,T,VY
Amaranthus hypochond. 'Prima Nepal'	B,DD
Amaranthus hypochond. 'Rio S. Lorenzo'	B
Amaranthus 'Intense Pink'	T
Amaranthus lividus	B,SG
Amaranthus mangostanus	DD
Amaranthus orientalis	B
Amaranthus paniculatus	PL,SG
Amaranthus paniculatus 'Split Personality'	F,JO
Amaranthus powellii	CG
Amaranthus 'Quintonil'	B,HU
Amaranthus 'Red Fox'	BS,KI
Amaranthus retroflexus	B
Amaranthus sp mix	BH,SK
Amaranthus spinosus	B,SG
Amaranthus tricolor	BD,SE,SK,T,TH,V
Amaranthus tricolor 'Amar Kiran'	B
Amaranthus tricolor 'Amar Peet'	B
Amaranthus tricolor 'Aurora'	B,BS,T
Amaranthus tricolor 'Blood Red'	B
Amaranthus tricolor 'Early Splendour'	B,BS,C,HU,J,MO,PI,SK
Amaranthus tricolor 'Elephant's Head'	B,DD,SD
Amaranthus tricolor 'Flaming Fountain'	B,DE
Amaranthus tricolor 'Hartman's Giant'	B,DD
Amaranthus tricolor 'Illumination'	B,BS,KI,MO,PK,U
Amaranthus tricolor 'Lotus Purple'	B
Amaranthus tricolor 'Merah'	B
Amaranthus tricolor mix special	PK
Amaranthus tricolor 'Molten Fire'	B,BY,DD,KI
Amaranthus tricolor 'Perfecta'	B,FR,PK
Amaranthus tricolor 'Pinang'	B
Amaranthus tricolor 'Puteh'	B
Amaranthus tricolor 'Splendens'	B,BS,L,MO
Amaranthus tricolor 'Splendens Perfecta'	C
Amaryllis belladonna	B,C,RU
Amaryllis belladonna v purpurea major	B,C
Amberboa moschata Crown mix	CO
Amberboa moschata 'Dairy Maid'	T
Amberboa moschata 'Imperialis' mix	BS,C,D,PK,V
Amberboa moschata 'Imperialis' s-c	B
Amberboa moschata mix	BY,DE,DT,F,HU,J,KS,PI, SK,SP,SU,T,TH,TU
Amberboa moschata ssp suaveolens	B,DE
Amberboa moschata ssp suav. 'Magnus'	B
Amberboa moschata 'The Bride'	PL,T
Ambrometiella brevifolius	B
Ambrosia artemisiifolia	CO,CG,SG
Ambrosia chamissonis	B
Ambrosia dumosa	B
Ambrosia maritima	B
Amelanchier alnifolia	A,AB,AP,B,C,DD,FW,LN, NO,SA,SC,SG
Amelanchier alnifolia v semi-integrifolia	SG
Amelanchier arborea	B,LN,N
Amelanchier bartramiana	SG
Amelanchier canadensis	B,C,FW,LN,N,SA,VE
Amelanchier florida see A.alnifolia v semi-integrifolia	
Amelanchier humilis	SG
Amelanchier laevis	B,FW,LN,SA,SC
Amelanchier lamarckii	A,B,FW,LN,SA
Amelanchier oblongifolia	SG
Amelanchier ovalis	LN,SA,SG,VE
Amelanchier pumila	AP,B,G,SC,SG
Amelanchier sanguinea	CG
Amelanchier spicata	B,SG
Amelanchier utahensis	B,LN
Amellus asteroides	B,SI
Amethystea caerulea	C
Amethystea caerulea 'Turquoise'	B,HU
Ammannia baccifera	B
Ammi majus	B,BH,BS,C,CN,CP,DE,DI, HP,HU,JO,KS,MO,PI,PK, V
Ammi visagna 'Green Mist'	PK
Ammi visnaga	AB,B,CG,CN,CP,DD,KS
Ammobium alatum	B,BD,BS,C,CO,DE,HP, HU,J,KI,L,MO,O,TU,V, VY
Ammobium alatum 'Bikini'	B,BS,C,CA,CL,JO,MO,O, PK
Ammobium alatum 'Grandiflorum'	B,CN,KS,PI,T,SU
Ammodendon conollyi	B
Ammophila arenaria	B,EL,JE,SA
Ammophila littoralis	B
Amoreuxia palmatifida	B,SW
Amorpha californica	B
Amorpha canescens	B,C,G,JE,NO,PR,SA
Amorpha cyanostachys	B
Amorpha fruticosa	A,AP,C,CA,CG,LN,PR, SA,VE
Amorpha fruticosa pods	B,FW
Amorpha nana	B,PR
Amorpha paniculata	B
Amorphophallus bulifer	SG
Amorphophallus konjac	B
Ampelocissus elephantina	DV
Ampelodesmos mauritanicus	B,C,JE,SA
Ampelopsis arborea	B
Ampelopsis brevipedunculata see A.glandulosa v b.	
Ampelopsis glandulosa v b.	B,SA

24

AMPELOPSIS

Ampelopsis megalophylla	AP,SA
Amsonia ciliata	B,G,JE
Amsonia elliptica	B
Amsonia hubrichtii	B,JE
Amsonia illustris	B,SG
Amsonia orientalis	HP,NG
Amsonia tabernaemontana	AP,B,C,CG,G,HP,JE,NG, T
Amsonia tabernaemontana v salicifolia	B,SA
Amsonia tomentosa	B,SW
Anacampseros affinis	DV
Anacampseros albidiflora	B,DV
Anacampseros albissima	B,C,DV
Anacampseros alstonii	B,BC
Anacampseros angustifolia	DV
Anacampseros arachnoides	B,C,Y
Anacampseros australiana	B,DV
Anacampseros avasmontana	DV
Anacampseros baeseckii	B,DV
Anacampseros buderiana	B,DV
Anacampseros comptonii	B,Y
Anacampseros crinita	DV
Anacampseros filamentosa	B,DV
Anacampseros gracilis	DV
Anacampseros lanceolata	B,DV,SI
Anacampseros lanigera	DV
Anacampseros meyeri	B
Anacampseros namaquensis	B,SI
Anacampseros papyraceae	B,DV
Anacampseros parviflorus	DV
Anacampseros recurvata	B
Anacampseros retusa	B,SI,Y
Anacampseros rufescens	AP,B,SI,Y
Anacampseros sp	DV,SI
Anacampseros subnuda	DV
Anacampseros telephiastrum	B,DV,SI
Anacampseros tomentosa	B,Y
Anacampseros ustulata	B,DV,Y
Anacamptis pyramidalis	B
Anacardium excelsum	B,SS
Anacardium occidentale	B,EL,HA,RE,WA
Anacistrocactus scheeri	BC
Anacyclus maroccanus	B,JE
Anacyclus officinarum	SG
Anacyclus pyrethrum	B,CG,KL,PO,SG
Anacyclus pyrethrum v depressus	AP,B,BS,CG,CL,CN,G, HP,HU,KL,L,SA,SC,SG,T
Anacyclus pyrethrum v d. 'Garden Gnome'	BS,C,D,JE,KI,MO
Anacyclus pyrethrum v d. 'Silberkissen'	B,JE
Anadenanthera colubrina	B
Anadenanthera peregrina	B
Anagallis arvensis	B,C,CN,HU,SG,SU,TH,V
Anagallis arvensis v caerulea	B,C,NG
Anagallis blue	C,S,U
Anagallis 'Blue Light'	C,KS
Anagallis linifolia see A.monellii ssp l.	
Anagallis monellii	AP,B,CL,CN,MO,SE,SG, T
Anagallis monellii 'Gentian Blue'	J,KS,T,V
Anagallis monellii ssp linifolia	B,HU,SE
Anagyris foetidus	SA
Ananas comosus	B
Anapalina caffra	BH
Anapalina nervosa	SI
Anaphalis alpicola	AP,B,SG
Anaphalis margaritacea	AB,AP,B,BS,CN,HP,KS,

	NO,PK,SA,SC,SG,SU, T,U
Anaphalis 'Neuschnee' (New Snow)	B,BS,C,CL,DE,HU,JE, JO,KI,MO
Anarcardium occidentalis	SA
Anarrhinum bellidifolium	B,HP
Anastrabe integerrima	B,KB
Anchusa americanus	PR
Anchusa arvensis	B
Anchusa azurea	B,C,HP,JE,SA,SP
Anchusa azurea 'Blue Angel'	B,BS,CL,CO,D,J,KI,KS, MO,S,SK,SU,T,TU,U,V
Anchusa azurea 'Dropmore'	B,BS,BY,C,DE,HP,KI,SU, T,V
Anchusa azurea 'Feltham Pride'	CL,HP
Anchusa azurea 'Royal Blue'	HP
Anchusa capensis	B,BH,G,KB,SI
Anchusa capensis 'Blue Bird'	BS,C,T
Anchusa capensis mix dw	KS
Anchusa 'Dawn'	D,J,S
Anchusa leptophylla	KL
Anchusa leptophylla ssp incana	AP,HP
Anchusa officinalis	B,C,CN,CP,JE,SA,SG
Anchusa undulata	AP,B,SC
Ancistrocactus megarhizus see Sclerocactus scheeri	
Ancistrocactus see Sclerocactus	
Andersonia involucrata	B,NI,SA
Andersonia lehmanniana	B,NI
Andira inermis	B
Androcymbium capense	B,RU,SI
Androcymbium ciliolatum	B,RU,SI
Androcymbium dregei	B,RU
Androcymbium europaeum	B
Androcymbium europaeum MS510 Spain	MN
Androcymbium gramineum	B
Androcymbium gramineum S.F13 Mor.	MN
Androcymbium longipes	B,SI
Androcymbium melanthioides f striatum	AP,B,SC,SI
Androcymbium pulchrum	B,RU,SI
Androcymbium sp	SI
Andrographis paniculata	B
Andromeda polifolia	C,CG,KL
Andromischus umbraticola	SI
Andropogon gerardii	B,C,DE,HU,JE,NO,SA
Andropogon gerardii 'Roundtree'	B
Andropogon glomeratus	NT
Andropogon hallii	NO,PR
Andropogon ischaemum see Botriochloa i.	
Andropogon scoparius see Schizachyrium scoparium	
Andropogon virginicus	JE
Androsace albana	AP,B,G,KL,SC,SG
Androsace alpina	AP,B,C,CG,G,JE,SA,SC
Androsace arachnoides	SG
Androsace armenaica v macrantha	HP
Androsace barbulata	VO
Androsace caduca	B
Androsace carnea	AP,B,C,CG,JE,KL,SC,SG
Androsace carnea 'Alba'	KL
Androsace carnea ssp brigantiaca	AP,B,CG,G,JE,KL,SC,SG
Androsace carnea ssp laggeri	AP,CG,SC,VO
Androsace carnea ssp rosea	AP,G,KL,SG
Androsace carnea x pyrenaica	AP,PM,SC
Androsace chaixii	AP,CG,G,KL,SC,SG
Androsace chamaejasme	B,C,JE,SW,VO
Androsace ciliata	AP,SC,SG,VO
Androsace cylindrica	AP,KL,SG,SC

ANDROSACE

Androsace fedtschenkoi	SG
Androsace foliosa	B
Androsace hausmannii	KL
Androsace hediseantha	PM
Androsace hedraeantha	AP,KL,SG,SC
Androsace helvetica	B,C,CG
Androsace hirtella	AP,G,KL,SC,VO
Androsace hybrids	KL
Androsace lactea	AP,B,G,JE,KL,SC
Androsace lactiflora	AP,CG,HP,JE,KL,SA
Androsace lanuginosa	B
Androsace mathildae	AP,G,KL,SC,SG
Androsace maxima	CG
Androsace mix	JE
Androsace montana	B,SW
Androsace muscoidea	SG
Androsace obtusifolia	AP,B,C,G,JE,KL,SC
Androsace primuloides	B
Androsace pubescens	AP,CG,KL,SC
Androsace pyrenaica	AP,B,CG,G,SC
Androsace rotundifolia	AP,B,C,RM,SC
Androsace sarmentosa	AP,B,SG
Androsace sarmentosa v chumbyi	SG
Androsace sempervivoides	AP,B,SC,SG
Androsace septentrionalis	AP,B,CG,DV,G,RM,SC, SG
Androsace septentrionalis 'Stardust'	B,BS,JE,MO
Androsace sericea	VO
Androsace strigillosa	AP,B,SC
Androsace vandellii	AP,B,CG,KL,SC,SG,VO
Androsace villosa	B,C,CG,G,JE,KL,SA,SC, VO
Androsace villosa ssp palandoekenensis	VO
Androsace villosa v arachnoidea	KL
Androsace villosa v congesta	B
Andryala aghardii	AP,G,KL,SC,SG,T
Andryala integrifolia	SG
Anemarrhena asphodeloides	B,HP
Anemathele lessoniana	B
Anemocarpa podolepidium	B,NI,O
Anemone altaica	AP,C,G,JE,KL,LG,SC
Anemone apennina	B,SC
Anemone baldensis	AP,B,C,CG,G,HP,JE,KL, SA,SC
Anemone biarmiensis see A.narcissiflora spp b.	
Anemone blanda	AR,KL
Anemone blanda hybrids new mix	C
Anemone blanda 'White Splendour'	B
Anemone canadensis	AP,B,CG,G,HP,JE,P,PR, SG
Anemone caroliniana	AP,C,CG,G,HP,KL,PM, SC
Anemone coronaria De Caen Group	AP,C,D,G,J,S,V
Anemone coronaria 'De Caen Hollandia'	B
Anemone coronaria 'De Caen Sylphide'	B,BD,BS,C,CL,DT,L, MO,T
Anemone coronaria 'De Caen The Bride'	B,C
Anemone coronaria f1 'Cleopatra'	BS,C,DE,PK
Anemone coronaria f1 'Mona Lisa' see Sylphide	
Anemone coronaria f1 St Brigid Group	BD,BS,C,J,KI,PK,V
Anemone coronaria 'Gloria Mix'	F
Anemone coronaria 'St B. Lord Lieutenant'	B
Anemone coronaria 'St B. Mount Everest'	B
Anemone coronaria 'St B. The Governor'	B,C
Anemone coronaria white, ex Turkey	G
Anemone crinita	AP,HP,SC,SG

Anemone cylindrica	AP,B,G,HP,JE,KL,NO, PR,SC,SG
Anemone daurica	SA
Anemone debilis	VO
Anemone dichotoma	SG
Anemone drummondii	AP,B,HP,KL,P,SC
Anemone elongata	B,SC
Anemone fannini	B,SI
Anemone fasciculata see A.narcissiflora	
Anemone fistulosa	KL
Anemone hortensis	AR,B,C,JE,NG
Anemone hupehensis	B,G,JE,SA,SG
Anemone hupehensis v japonica	AP,B,BH,BS,C,HP,KL, PK,SG,TH,V
Anemone leveillei	AP,B,BS,C,CG,F,G,JE,P, SC,SG,T
Anemone lyallii	HP,KL
Anemone magellanica see A.multifida	
Anemone multifida	AP,B,C,CG,G,HP,JE,KL, P,RH,SC,SG
Anemone multifida 'Major'	AP,B,G,HP,JE,SC
Anemone multifida red form	AP,B,F,HP,SC
Anemone multifida 'Rubra'	G,JE
Anemone narcissiflora	AP,B,BS,C,CG,G,HP,I, JE,KL,SA,SC,V,VO
Anemone narcissiflora spp biarmiensis	B,SC
Anemone narcissiflora v nipponica	B
Anemone nemorosa	B,C,G,JE,PM,RH,SA,SU, T
Anemone nemorosa 'Alba Plena'	B
Anemone obtusiloba	KL
Anemone obtusiloba 'Alba'	KL
Anemone palmata	AP,B,CG,G,JE,PM,SC
Anemone palmata v lutea	KL
Anemone parviflora	AP,HP,KL
Anemone patens see Pulsatilla patens	
Anemone pavonina	AP,AR,B,G,MN
Anemone pavonina S.L165/3 Greece	MN
Anemone polyanthes	AP,B,JE,SC
Anemone pulsatilla see Pulsatilla vulgaris	
Anemone quinquefolia	SW
Anemone racemosa	RS
Anemone ranunculoides	B,C,G,JE,SC,SG
Anemone reflexa	SG
Anemone riparia	AP,HP
Anemone rivularis	AP,B,C,G,HP,JE,NG,P, PM,RH,SC,SG,T,V
Anemone rivularis v flore-minoris	KL
Anemone rotundifolia	KL
Anemone rupicola	AP,B,SC
Anemone sp China	SG
Anemone speciosa	KL,VO
Anemone stellata MS938 France	MN
Anemone sulphurea see Pulsatilla alpina ssp apiifolia	
Anemone sylvestris	B,C,CG,CL,CN,DE,G,HP, JE,KL,MO,RM,SA,SG,T, TH,Z
Anemone sylvestris 'Grandiflora'	KL
Anemone tenuifolia	B,SI
Anemone tomentosa	B,C,JE
Anemone trullifolia	AR,KL
Anemone tschernjaewii	KL
Anemone tuberosa	B,SW
Anemone vernalis see Pulsatilla vernalis	
Anemone virginiana	AP,B,C,G,HP,JE,NT,SG,T
Anemone vitifolia	AP,B,C,HP,SG

ANEMONE

Anemone x fulgens	B,G,SC	Annona atemoya	B,EL,SA
Anemone x lesseri	B,C,G,HP,KL,LG,PL,SG,	Annona aurantiaca	B
	T,V	Annona cherimola	B,C,G,SA
Anemopsis californica	B	Annona diversifolia	B
Anemopsis macrophylla	AP,G,HP,JE,KL,SC	Annona glabra	B
Angelica archangelica	B,CN,HP,JE,KS,RH,SA,	Annona montana	B
	SC,SG	Annona muricata	B,C,RE
Angelica arguta	B,DD	Annona reticulata	B
Angelica atropurpurea	B,DD,HP,JE,PR,T	Annona senegalensis	B
Angelica dahurica	B,SA	Annona squamosa	B,C,EL,LN,SA
Angelica decurrens	SG	Annonidium mannii	B
Angelica gigas	B,C,HP,JE,KL,NG,PK,	Anoda cristata	G
	SA,SC,SZ	Anoda cristata 'Opal Cup'	B,BS,C,HP,HU,J,KS,MO,
Angelica grayi	B,RM		PK
Angelica maximowizii	BH	Anoda cristata 'Silver Cup'	C
Angelica officinalis	KL	Anoda cristata 'Snow Cup'	B
Angelica pachycarpa	AP,B,HP,KS	Anoda cristata v violacea	B
Angelica paniculata	B	Anoda wrightii 'Butter Cup'	B,C
Angelica pinnata	B,DD	Anomatheca cruenta see A.laxa	
Angelica sylvestris	B,C,CG,LA,SA,SG	Anomatheca fistulosa	B,RU,SI
Angelica sylvestris 'Naini's Wood'	B	Anomatheca grandiflora	AP,B,SC,SI
Angelica ursina	B,DD	Anomatheca laxa	AP,B,C,G,HP,HU,KL,LG,
Angianthus cunninghamii	B,NI		MN,NG,PM,RH,RU,SC,
Angianthus milnei	B,NI		SG,SI
Angianthus tomentosus	B,C,NI,SA	Anomatheca laxa 'Joan Evans'	AP,HP,PM
Angophora bakeri	B,CA,EL,HA,O,SA	Anomatheca laxa mix forms	C
Angophora cordifolia	CA	Anomatheca laxa v alba	AP,B,G,HP,PM,MN,RU,
Angophora costata	B,CA,EL,HA,O		SC
Angophora floribunda	B,EL,HA,NI,O,SA	Anomatheca laxa viridis	MN
Angophora hispida	B,HA,NI,O	Anomatheca viridis	AP,B,C,RU,SC,SI
Angophora melanoxylon	HA	Anomyrtus luma	SA
Anigozanthos bicolor	B,C,EL,NI,O,SA,SH	Anopterus glandulosus	B,C,SA
Anigozanthos flavidus	AP,AU,C,EL,HA,HU,NI,	Anredera cordifolia	B,DD
	O,SA,SC,SH	Antegibbaeum fissoides	B
Anigozanthos flavidus orange & red	B,SH	Antennaria alpina	SG
Anigozanthos flavidus red	B,EL,HA,O,SA	Antennaria aprica see A. parvifolia	
Anigozanthos gabrielae	B,NI,O	Antennaria carpatica	B,CG,JE
Anigozanthos humilis	B,C,EL,NI,O,SH	Antennaria compacta	KL
Anigozanthos manglesii	AU,B,EL,HA,HU,NI,O,	Antennaria dioica	AP,B,C,CL,CN,DE,G,HP,
	SA,SG,SH,V		JE,KL,MO,SA,SC,SG,T
Anigozanthos onycis	O	Antennaria dioica red	I
Anigozanthos preissii	B,C,EL,NI,O,SH	Antennaria dioica 'Roy Davidson'	KL
Anigozanthos pulcherrimus	B,O	Antennaria dioica 'Rubra'	JE
Anigozanthos rufus	B,EL,NI,O,SH	Antennaria dioica ssp borealis	CG
Anigozanthos sp mix	C	Antennaria dioica v rosea see A.microphylla	
Anigozanthos viridis	B,C,EL,NI,O,SA,SH	Antennaria howellii	AP,B,JE,SC
Anisacanthus wrightii	SA	Antennaria hybrids new mix	B,C,JE
Anisacanthus thurberi	SW	Antennaria hybrids red mix	JE
Anisochilis carnosus	B	Antennaria magellanica	B,C,JE
Anisodontea anomala	B,SI	Antennaria microphylla	AP,B,BS,JE,KL,NO,SA,
Anisodontea biflora	B,SA,SI	Antennaria neglecta	AP,B,JE
Anisodontea capensis	AP,B,HP,SI	Antennaria oelandica	KL
Anisodontea elegans	B,SI	Antennaria parvifolia	AP,B,KL,SG
Anisodontea julii	B,KB,P,SA,SI	Antennaria plantaginifolia	AP,B
Anisodontea malvastroides	HP	Antennaria rosea	SG
Anisodontea scabrosa	B,HP,SC,SI	Antennaria sp	AP,KL,RM
Anisodontea sp	SI	Anthemis arabica 'Criss Cross'	B,BD,BS,KI,MO,T
Anisodontea triloba	B	Anthemis arvensis	B,CN
Anisomeles indica	B	Anthemis austriaca	G
Anisomeles malabarica	B	Anthemis carpatica	HP
Anisotome aromatica	B,SC,SS	Anthemis carpatica 'Karpatenschnee'	B,JE
Anisotome filifolia	B,SS	Anthemis cotula	B
Anisotome flexuosa	B,SS	Anthemis cretica ssp argaea	VO
Anisotome haastii	B,SA,SC,SS	Anthemis cretica ssp cretica	SC
Anisotome intermedia	B	Anthemis leucanthemifolia	B
Anisotome pilifera	B,SC,SS	Anthemis maritima	B,JE

ANTHEMIS

Anthemis marschalliana	KL,VO
Anthemis nobilis see Chamaemelum nobile	
Anthemis palaestinus	B
Anthemis pseudocotula	B
Anthemis punctata	SG
Anthemis punctata ssp cupaniana	AP,HP
Anthemis sachokiana	KL,VO
Anthemis sancti-johannis	B,C,CN,DE,G,HP,HU, JE,SA,T
Anthemis sosnovskyana	SG
Anthemis sp Turkey	I
Anthemis tinctoria	AP,B,C,CG,CN,CP,F,G, HP,JE,SC,SG,TH,V
Anthemis tinctoria alba	HP
Anthemis tinctoria 'E.C.Buxton'	HP
Anthemis tinctoria 'Grallach Gold'	HP
Anthemis tinctoria 'Kelwayii'	B,BS,C,CL,DE,DT,HP,JE, O,SA,SK,T
Anthemis tinctoria 'Pride of Grallach'	HP
Anthemis tinctoria 'Sauce Hollandaise'	AP,HP
Anthemis triumfetii	CG
Anthemis tuberculata	I
Anthericum angulicaule	B,SI
Anthericum baeticum	AP,LG,SC
Anthericum floribundum	SG
Anthericum liliago	AP,B,C,G,HP,I,JE,KL,LG, MN,RH,SA,SC
Anthericum liliago v major	AP,HP,NG
Anthericum ramosum	AP,B,C,G,HP,JE,KL,LG, MN,NG,RH,SC,SG
Anthericum saundersiae	B,SI
Anthocephalus chinensis	B
Anthocercis littorea	AP,B,C,DD,NI,SA
Anthocleista grandiflora	B,LN,WA
Anthocleista zambesiaca	C
Anthotium humile	B,NI
Anthoxanthum alpinum	SG
Anthoxanthum odoratum	B,C,DE,JE,PO,SA,SC
Anthriscus cerefolium	CN,DD,HP,HU,TH
Anthriscus sylvestris	B,C,HU,JE,KS,LA,NS,P, SA,SG,V
Anthriscus sylvestris 'Ravenswing'	AP,B,C,HP,NG,P
Anthropodium candidum	SG
Anthropodium cirrhatum	SG
Anthurium coriaceum	B,EL,SA
Anthurium gracile	B
Anthurium hookeri	B
Anthurium hybrids new	CA
Anthurium imperiale	B
Anthurium pallidiflorum	B
Anthurium scandens	B
Anthurium scherzeranum	B
Anthurium schlechtendalii	B
Anthurium wildenovii	SG
Anthyllis aurea	VO
Anthyllis cretica cretica	HP
Anthyllis cytisoides	SA
Anthyllis dillenii	B
Anthyllis montana	B,BS,KL,SA,SC,VO
Anthyllis montana 'Carminea'	B,C
Anthyllis montana 'Rubra'	AP,B,HP,JE,SC,SG
Anthyllis polyphylla	B
Anthyllis vulneraria	AP,B,BS,C,HP,I,JE,KL, LA,SA,SC,SG,SU
Anthyllis vulneraria orange	KL
Anthyllis vulneraria ssp vulneraria	T

Anthyllis vulneraria v alpestris	B,CG
Anthyllis vulneraria v coccinea	AP,B,G,HP,JD,JE,P,PL, RS,SC,SG
Anthyllis vulneraria v ibirica	AP,HP
Anthyllis vulneraria v rosea	KL
Anthyllis vulneraria v rubra	AP,SC
Antidesma bunius	B,EL
Antidesma dallachyanum	B
Antidesma venosum	B
Antigonon leptopus	B,C,CA,DD,EL,G,HA, HU,O,SA
Antigonon leptopus 'Album'	B,SA
Antigonon leptopus v alba 'White Bride'	C
Antimima 'Nelii'	B
Antimima pulchella	B,SI
Antimima sp	SI
Antirrhinum 'Appleblossom'	B,C
Antirrhinum 'Apricot Mist'	PL
Antirrhinum asarina see Asarina procumbens	
Antirrhinum Azalea fl. s-c	PL
Antirrhinum barrelieri	HP
Antirrhinum 'Bizarre'	J,V
Antirrhinum braun-blanquetii	AP,B,C,G,HP,HU,JE,P,SC
Antirrhinum 'Brighton Rock'	F,PI
Antirrhinum 'Candyman' mix	S
Antirrhinum 'Carioca'	BS
Antirrhinum Crown mix	BS,CO
Antirrhinum Cut Fl mix	BS
Antirrhinum f1 'Bells' mix	BS,D,DT,J,MO,PK,SK
Antirrhinum f1 'Bells' s-c	CL
Antirrhinum f1 'Blue Bird'	JE
Antirrhinum f1 'Blue Jay'	JE
Antirrhinum f1 'Bright Butterflies'	B,BS,BY,J,KI,MO,SK
Antirrhinum f1 'Bunting'	JE
Antirrhinum f1 'Caerulea Heterosis Musik'	JE
Antirrhinum f1 'Caerulea Het. Olympia'	JE
Antirrhinum f1 'Cardinal'	JE
Antirrhinum f1 'Chimes' mix	BS,J,MO,SK
Antirrhinum f1 'Chimes' s-c	CL
Antirrhinum f1 'Coronette' bronze	B,BS,MO
Antirrhinum f1 'Coronette' cherry	B,BS,MO
Antirrhinum f1 'Coronette' crimson	B,BS,MO
Antirrhinum f1 'Coronette' mix	CL,DT,J,KI,MO,S,SE
Antirrhinum f1 'Coronette' orchid	B,BS,MO
Antirrhinum f1 'Coronette' pink	B,BS,MO
Antirrhinum f1 'Coronette' rose	B,BS,MO
Antirrhinum f1 'Coronette' scarlet	B,BS,MO
Antirrhinum f1 'Coronette' white	B,BS,MO
Antirrhinum f1 'Coronette' yellow	B,BS,MO
Antirrhinum f1 'Dove'	JE
Antirrhinum f1 'Floral Carpet'	BS,BY,C,CA,CL,L,MO
Antirrhinum f1 'Floral Showers' apricot	PL
Antirrhinum f1 'Floral Showers' copper	SK
Antirrhinum f1 'Floral Showers' crimson	B,BS,MO,SK
Antirrhinum f1 'Floral Showers' dp bronze	B,BS,MO
Antirrhinum f1 'Floral Showers' fuchsia	B,MO
Antirrhinum f1 'Floral Showers' lavender	B,BS,MO,SK
Antirrhinum f1 'Floral Showers' lilac	B,BS,MO,SK
Antirrhinum f1 'Floral Showers' mix	BD,CA,DT,KI,MO,PL,SE, SK,ST,YA
Antirrhinum f1 'Floral Showers' purple	B,BS,MO,SK
Antirrhinum f1 'Floral Showers' rose	B,BS,MO,SK
Antirrhinum f1 'Floral Showers' rose pink	B,BS,MO
Antirrhinum f1 'Floral Showers' scarlet	B,BS,MO
Antirrhinum f1 'Floral Showers' white	B,BS,MO,SK
Antirrhinum f1 'Floral Showers' yellow	B,BS,MO,SK

ANTIRRHINUM

Antirrhinum f1 'Forerunner'	BS,C,T
Antirrhinum f1 'Goldfinch'	JE
Antirrhinum f1 'Jewel' blue	JE
Antirrhinum f1 'Jewel' pink	JE
Antirrhinum f1 'Jewel' purple	JE
Antirrhinum f1 'Jewel' white	JE
Antirrhinum f1 'Liberty' Series mix	CA,F,T
Antirrhinum f1 'Liberty' Series s-c	BS,CL,M
Antirrhinum f1 'Madame Butterfly'	B,BD,BS,CL,CN,D,DT,F,J,M,MO,O,S,SE,SK,T,U,
Antirrhinum f1 mix florist	CL
Antirrhinum f1 mix supreme dble giant	C,DE
Antirrhinum f1 'Pixie'	BS,CA,CL,D,L,MO,YA
Antirrhinum f1 'Princess'	BS,CL,KI,L,U
Antirrhinum f1 'Robin'	JE
Antirrhinum f1 'Rocket' s-c	SK
Antirrhinum f1 'Royal Carpet' mix	BS,S,T
Antirrhinum f1 'Royal Carpet' s-c	BS
Antirrhinum f1 'Sonnet Bronze'	B,BS,CN,MO,SK,YA
Antirrhinum f1 'Sonnet Burgundy'	B,BS,CN,MO,SK,YA
Antirrhinum f1 'Sonnet Carmine'	B,BS,CN,MO,SK,YA
Antirrhinum f1 'Sonnet Crimson'	B,BS,CN,MO,SK,YA
Antirrhinum f1 'Sonnet' mix	BD,BS,CN,D,DT,KI,L,MO,PK,SK,YA
Antirrhinum f1 'Sonnet Orange-scarlet'	B,BS,CN,MO,SK,YA
Antirrhinum f1 'Sonnet Pink'	B,BS,CN,MO,SK,YA
Antirrhinum f1 'Sonnet Rose'	B,BS,CN,MO,SK,YA
Antirrhinum f1 'Sonnet White'	B,BS,CN,MO,SK,YA
Antirrhinum f1 'Sonnet Yellow'	B,BS,CN,MO,SK,YA
Antirrhinum f1 'Sweetheart' mix	BS,D,DT,F,L,M,S,SK,T
Antirrhinum f1 'Tahiti' mix	BS,F,MO,PK,S,SK
Antirrhinum f1 'Tahiti' s-c, mix	SK
Antirrhinum f1 'Tetra Ruffled Giants'	C,HU,VY
Antirrhinum f2 'Cheerio'	BD,BS,BY,C,DT,L,MO
Antirrhinum f2 'Corona' mix	BS,CL,MO,S
Antirrhinum f2 mix outdoor finest	SK
Antirrhinum f2 'Popette'	T,V
Antirrhinum f2 'Vanity Fayre' mix	BS,D,J
Antirrhinum 'Glamour Shades'	BS,VH
Antirrhinum hispanicum	AP,HP
Antirrhinum 'Kelvedon Pride'	BS,KI,SU
Antirrhinum 'Kimosy'	B,F
Antirrhinum lavender bicolour	T
Antirrhinum 'Lipstick Gold'	F,T,V
Antirrhinum 'Lipstick' mix	J
Antirrhinum 'Lipstick Silver'	F,PK,S,V
Antirrhinum 'Little Darling' mix	BS,CA,CL,SK,VY
Antirrhinum 'Lollipop'	SE
Antirrhinum 'Madonna' dw	BS
Antirrhinum 'Magic Carpet'	BD,BS,BY,C,CN,D,DE,DN,F,J,MO,PI,S,SK,TU,V
Antirrhinum majus	AP,B,DD,G,SG,TH
Antirrhinum majus f1 'Rocket'	JO,PK,SD,SK
Antirrhinum majus 'Maximum' mix	AB,T
Antirrhinum majus 'Maximum' old gold	B
Antirrhinum majus 'Rosovyi'	SG
Antirrhinum majus sempervirens	SG
Antirrhinum majus ssp linkianum	RS
Antirrhinum maximum	V
Antirrhinum mix choice	DT
Antirrhinum mix col	S
Antirrhinum mix dwarf bedding	FR,T
Antirrhinum mix dwarf lg fl	J
Antirrhinum mix giant fl. bedding	D,M
Antirrhinum mix tall	BS,FR,KI,PI,SE

Antirrhinum mix tetraploid	DE
Antirrhinum molle	AP,HP,KL,PM,RS,SC
Antirrhinum 'Monarch' mix	BS,C,DT,F,PL,T
Antirrhinum 'Monarch' s-c	BS,L,T
Antirrhinum multiflorum	B
Antirrhinum nanum	V
Antirrhinum nanum 'Black Prince'	F,L,PI,SE,T
Antirrhinum nanum 'Rust Resistant'	BS,L,MO
Antirrhinum 'Night & Day'	C,F,V
Antirrhinum orontium	C,DD,HU
Antirrhinum 'Panorama' mix	BU,DE
Antirrhinum 'Peaches & Cream'	B,BS,D,DT,J,MO,SE,T
Antirrhinum pendula 'Chinese Lanterns'	T
Antirrhinum pendula 'Lampion'	DT,PL,R
Antirrhinum 'Picturatum'	BS,DT
Antirrhinum 'Powys Pride'	B,HP,P,PL
Antirrhinum pulverulentum	RS
Antirrhinum pumila 'Tom Thumb'	BS,CO,D,DE,DT,F,J,KI,L,M,O,ST,V,VH
Antirrhinum 'Purity'	L
Antirrhinum 'Purple King'	T
Antirrhinum 'Rainbow'	BS,R,TE
Antirrhinum 'Rembrandt'	BS,F
Antirrhinum 'Rust Resistant' tall mix	BU
Antirrhinum 'Sawyer's Old-Fash.Snapdr.'	C,CN,SU
Antirrhinum 'Scarlet Giant'	C
Antirrhinum sempervirens	AP,B,G,HP,SC
Antirrhinum siculum	B,P
Antirrhinum 'Snap Happy'	KI,ST
Antirrhinum 'Snowflake'	B,DE
Antirrhinum sp	RS
Antirrhinum 'Spring Giants' mix	CA
Antirrhinum 'St. Clements'	U
Antirrhinum 'Tiara' s-c,mix	BS
Antirrhinum 'Torbay Rock'	B,P
Antirrhinum 'Trumpet Serenade' mix	B,BS,D,F,J,S,T,VH
Antirrhinum villosum	KL
Antirrhinum 'Welcome'	B,BS
Antirrhinum white dw	BS
Antirrhinum 'White Wonder'	B,C,T
Antisdesma venosum	SI
Aotus 'Diffusa'	B,NI,SA
Aotus ericoides	AU,B,HA,NI,SA
Aotus lanigera	B,NI
Aotus preissii	B
Apatesia helianthoides	B,SI
Apeiba aspera	B,RE,SA
Apera spica-venti	B
Aphanes arvensis	B
Aphloia theiformis	B
Aphyllanthes monspeliensis	B,C,SC
Apios americana	B,DD
Apium graveolens	B,C,CN,DD
Apluda mutica	B
Apocynum androsaemifolium	B
Apocynum cannabinum	B,CP,HU
Apodytes dimidiata	C,SI,WA
Apodytes dimidiata ssp dimidiata	B,KB
Apollonias barbujana	B
Aponogeton distachyos	B
Apophyllum anomalum	HA
Aporocactus sp mix	C
Aptenia cordifolia	B,C,CG,DV,SG
Aptenia lancifolia	B
Aptosimum indivisum	B,SI
Aptosimum procumbens	B,SI

APTOSIMUM

Aptosimum sp — SI
Aptosimum spinescens — B,SI
Aquilefia clematiflora see A. vulgaris v stellata
Aquilegia ageratifolia — KL
Aquilegia akitensis h. see A. flabellata v pumila
Aquilegia 'Aline Fairweather' — B
Aquilegia alpina — AP,B,BS,C,CG,CN,CO, F,G,HP,HU,JD,JE,KL,KS, MO,P,PI,SA,SC,SG,SU,V
Aquilegia alpina 'Alba' — AP,B,C,P,SC
Aquilegia alpina 'Carl Ziepke' — B,JD
Aquilegia alpina German Form — B,JD
Aquilegia atrata — AP,B,C,CG,G,HP,JD,JE, KL,PL,SA,SC,SG
Aquilegia atrata v nigra — HU
Aquilegia atropurpurea — SG
Aquilegia aurea — AP,HP
Aquilegia baicalensis see A. vulgaris Baicalensis Group
Aquilegia 'Ballerina' — B,P
Aquilegia barnebyi — AP,B,P
Aquilegia 'Beidermeier' — BS,CG,DE,HP,HU,JE,KS, MO,PI,SA,SG,SK
Aquilegia bernardii — CG,SA
Aquilegia bertolonii — AP,B,C,G,HP,KL,PM,SC, SG
Aquilegia borodinii — SG
Aquilegia brevicalcarata — B,P
Aquilegia brevistyla — SG
Aquilegia buergeriana — AP,B,CT,HP,JE,KL,RS,
Aquilegia buergeriana v oxysepala — HP,P
Aquilegia buergeriana x flavescens — B,JD
Aquilegia caerulea — AB,AP,B,C,G,HP,JE,NO, PK,RM,SC,SW
Aquilegia caerulea 'Harmony' — SG
Aquilegia caerulea 'Koralle' — B,JD,JE,SA
Aquilegia caerulea 'Snow Queen' — B,SA,T
Aquilegia caerulea v ochroleuca — AP,B,JD
Aquilegia caerulea v pinetorum — B,SW
Aquilegia californica — SA
Aquilegia canadensis — AB,AP,B,BS,C,F,G,HP, HU,HW,JD,JE,KL,KS, NO,NT,P,PK,PL,PR,SA, SC,SE,T,TH
Aquilegia canadensis 'Corbett' — AP,B,JE
Aquilegia canadensis 'Nana' — AP,B,G,HP,P,SC
Aquilegia 'Celestial Queen' — B
Aquilegia chrysantha — AP,B,C,CG,G,HP,KS,SA, SC,SW
Aquilegia chrysantha (wild form) — JE
Aquilegia chrysantha 'Yellow Queen' — B,DE,F,JE,SA
Aquilegia clematiflora see A.vulgaris v stellata
Aquilegia 'Cream Dainty' — V
Aquilegia 'Crystal Star' — B,HU
Aquilegia cvs mix — HP
Aquilegia desertorum — AP,B,HP,SC,SW
Aquilegia discolor — AP,C,G,HP,KL,P,SC,SG
Aquilegia 'Dorothy' — CT
Aquilegia double blue — C,HU
Aquilegia 'Double Pleat' — B,BS,PL,SE,T
Aquilegia 'Double Quilled Purple' — B,P
Aquilegia 'Double Rubies' — B,P
Aquilegia double s-c — HU,PL
Aquilegia 'Dragonfly Hybrids' — BS,C,CL,CN,DN,DT,F, JE,L,MO,R,SA,SC,YA
Aquilegia einseleana — B,C,G,SA,SG
Aquilegia 'Elegantissima' — B,P

Aquilegia elegantula — AP,KL,RS,SC,SW
Aquilegia f1 'Music Harmony' — BS,C,D,J,MO,PK,U
Aquilegia f1 'Music Series' mix — CA,CL
Aquilegia f1 'Olympia' — C
Aquilegia f1 'Olympia' mix — C
Aquilegia f1 'Olympia' red, gold — C
Aquilegia f1 'Songbird' s-c — BS,CL,JE,MO,SE
Aquilegia 'Fairyland' mix, dw — T
Aquilegia 'Fantasy Series' s-c, dw — T
Aquilegia flabellata — AP,C,CG,G,HP,KL,RM, SC,SG,T,V
Aquilegia flabellata 'Blue Angel' — B,JE,SA
Aquilegia flabellata 'Cameo' s-c,mix — B,BS,PL
Aquilegia flabellata f alba — AP,HP,KL
Aquilegia flabellata 'Mini-Star' — AP,B,BS,C,CL,G,JE,KL, MO,SC
Aquilegia flabellata nana — AP,SC
Aquilegia flabellata nana alba fl pl see A.flabellata v pumila f alba
Aquilegia flabellata pink — B,P
Aquilegia flabellata v pumila — AP,B,C,CG,G,I,KL,RS,SC
Aquilegia flabellata v pumila f alba — B,G,HP,JE,KL,SC
Aquilegia flabellata v pumila f alba fl.pl — AP,B,C,PL
Aquilegia flabellata v pumila f kurilensis — JE
Aquilegia flabellata v pumila 'Rosea' — AP,B,SC
Aquilegia flabellata v pumila 'Rubra' — KL
Aquilegia flabellata v pumila selection — JE
Aquilegia flab. v p 'Shimmering Breeze' — SE
Aquilegia flabellata v pumila 'Silver Edge' — B,P
Aquilegia flabellata 'White Angel' — SA
Aquilegia flavescens — B,NO,SA,SG,SW
Aquilegia formosa — AB,AP,AV,B,C,CG,DD,G, HP,JD,JE,KL,NO,SC,SG
Aquilegia formosa v truncata — AP,B,HP,SC,SW
Aquilegia fragrans — AP,B,C,HP,JD,P,SC,T
Aquilegia 'Frilly-Dilly' see dble s-c
Aquilegia glandulosa — AP,B,KL,P,SC,SG
Aquilegia glandulosa v jucunda — SG
Aquilegia glandulosa v transsilvanica — B
Aquilegia grata — AP,P,SC,T
Aquilegia 'Hensoll Harebell' — B,JD
Aquilegia hyb tall — I
Aquilegia 'Iceberg' — B,P
Aquilegia 'Irish Elegance' — B,P,PK,SE
Aquilegia 'Isabel Allen' — B
Aquilegia 'Jewel Dwarf' — AP,PM
Aquilegia jonesii — AP,HP,KL
Aquilegia jonesii saximontana — AP,HP,KL
Aquilegia karelinii — HP
Aquilegia kitaibelii — AP,CG
Aquilegia 'Kristall' — B,C,JE
Aquilegia laramiensis — AP,B,KL,RM,SC
Aquilegia litardieri — HP
Aquilegia Long Spurred Hybrids — D,S,SE,U
Aquilegia longisiliqua — KL
Aquilegia longissima — AP,B,CG,CT,HP,JD,KL,P, SA,SC
Aquilegia 'Magpie' see William Guiness
Aquilegia Mckana Group — AP,BD,BS,BU,BY,C,CG, CN,CO,DN,DT,F,FR,G, HP,HU,J,JD,JE,JO,KS,L, M,MO,PI,PK,SA,SC,SK, ST,T,TU,V,VH,VY
Aquilegia 'Mellow Yellow' — AP,B,P,S
Aquilegia 'Melton Rapids'
Aquilegia micrantha — C,SW
Aquilegia mix cottage garden — P

AQUILEGIA

Aquilegia mix singles & doubles — HU
Aquilegia moorcroftiana — B,JD,KL
Aquilegia Mrs Scott-Elliott Hybrids — B,BS,C,CL,HU,MO
Aquilegia nevadensis see A. vulgaris ssp n.
Aquilegia 'Nosegay' — C
Aquilegia olympica — AP,B,C,G,HP,JE,KL,P, SA,SG,VO
Aquilegia oxysepala — B,CG,SA,SG,T
Aquilegia parviflora — SG
Aquilegia 'Petticoats' — U
Aquilegia 'Pink Bonnets' — T
Aquilegia pink tall — I
Aquilegia Plena mix — SK
Aquilegia pyrenaica — AP,B,CG,G,JD,KL,SC,SG
Aquilegia 'Red Hobbit' — B,C,JE
Aquilegia rockii ex KGB176 — I
Aquilegia 'Roman Bronze' — B,P
Aquilegia 'Royal Purple' — P
Aquilegia 'Ruby Port' — T
Aquilegia saximontana — AP,B,G,HP,RM,SC,SG
Aquilegia 'Schneekonigen' — T
Aquilegia schokleyi — AP,G,KL,SG
Aquilegia scopularium — AP,B,KL,RS,SC,SG,SW
Aquilegia scopularium perplexans — SG
Aquilegia secundiflora — C,RS
Aquilegia sibirica — AP,B,CG,SG
Aquilegia single dk blue — HU
Aquilegia skinneri — AP,B,BS,CT,F,HP,JD,KL, P,PL,SA,SE,SW,T
Aquilegia 'Snow Queen' see Schneekonogen
Aquilegia 'Snowflakes' — P
Aquilegia 'Snowlight White' — T
Aquilegia sp — AP,HP,KL,RS,SC,SW
Aquilegia sp mix, cultivars & forms — BL,C
Aquilegia sp white dbl — PM
Aquilegia 'Star' blue — B,BS,DE,JE,KS,MO,SA
Aquilegia 'Star' crimson — B,BS,C,DE,HU,JE,MO, SA
Aquilegia 'Star' gold — B
Aquilegia 'Star' mix — BS,F,KI,PK
Aquilegia 'Star' red — AP,BS,KS,MO,SC
Aquilegia 'Star' white — B,BS,KS,MO
Aquilegia 'Star' yellow — SE,T
Aquilegia 'Strawberry Ice-cream' — B,P
Aquilegia 'Sunburst Ruby' — P
Aquilegia 'Sweet Lemon Drops' — B,P
Aquilegia 'Sweet Surprise' — B,P
Aquilegia thalictrifolia — AP,B,CG,G,HP,SC,SG
Aquilegia triternata — AP,B,HP,P,SC,SW
Aquilegia vernardii — SA
Aquilegia Vervaeneana group (V) — AP,B,BS,C,CG,CT,DT, F,HP,I,J,JD,JE,KS,LG, P,PL,PM,SC,SE,V
Aquilegia viridiflora — AP,B,C,F,G,HP,KS,LG, PL,SC,SE,SG,T,V
Aquilegia viridiflora 'Chocolate Soldier' see viridiflora
Aquilegia vulgaris — AB,AP,B,BS,C,DE,G,HP, HW,JD,JE,LG,PO,RS, SA,SC,SG,TH,V
Aquilegia vulgaris 'Adelaide Addison' — AP,B,JD,SC
Aquilegia vulgaris 'Altrosa' — B,JE
Aquilegia vulgaris 'Anemonaeflora' — B,HU,JE,SA
Aquilegia vulgaris Baicalensis Group — AP,SC,SG
Aquilegia vulgaris 'Bicolour Barlow' — PL
Aquilegia vulgaris 'Black Barlow' — B,C,HU,JO,PI,PL,SA
Aquilegia vulgaris 'Blue Barlow' — B,C,JO,PL,SA

Aquilegia vulgaris 'Brno' — B
Aquilegia vulgaris 'Burgundy' — B,JD
Aquilegia vulgaris 'Christa Barlow' — B,C,JO,SA
Aquilegia vulgaris clematiflora see A.vulgaris v stellata
Aquilegia vulgaris Dk purple — E,JD
Aquilegia vulgaris 'Gisela Powell' — B,JD
Aquilegia vulgaris 'Grandmother's Garden' — JE,T
Aquilegia vulgaris 'Heidi' — B,BS,JE,KI
Aquilegia vulgaris inverso — B,JD
Aquilegia vulgaris 'Jane Hollow' — B,P
Aquilegia vulgaris light pink — E
Aquilegia vulgaris 'Michael Strominger' — B,T
Aquilegia vulgaris 'Mrs Fincham' — B,JD
Aquilegia vulgaris 'Munstead White' see A.vulgaris 'Nivea'
Aquilegia vulgaris 'Nivea' — AP,B,C,CT,JD,MA,P
Aquilegia vulgaris 'Nora Barlow' — w.a
Aquilegia vulgaris 'Nora Barlow' mix — BS,CN,DT,F,J,KS,MO, PL,SE
Aquilegia vulgaris 'Nora B's Relatives' mix — C
Aquilegia v. Old-fash Granny's Bonnets — C
Aquilegia vulgaris pale mauve/blue bic. — C
Aquilegia vulgaris 'Patricia Zavros' — B,JD
Aquilegia vulgaris 'Pom-poms' mix — C,P
Aquilegia vulgaris 'Pom-poms' s-c — B,JD,P
Aquilegia vulgaris 'Rize' — JD
Aquilegia vulgaris 'Rose Barlow' — B,C,PL,SA
Aquilegia vulgaris 'Ruby Port' — AP,C,JE,T
Aquilegia vulgaris ssp nevadensis — JE
Aquilegia vulgaris Tall Blue Form — B,JD
Aquilegia vulgaris v alba — AP,F,HP,JE,SA,SC
Aquilegia vulgaris v fl.pl — C,HP,SC,TH
Aquilegia vulgaris v stellata — AP,C,HP,P,SC
Aquilegia vulgaris v stellata 'Alba' — AP,B,C,JD,MA,P
Aquilegia vulgaris v stellata 'Firewheel' — P
Aquilegia vulgaris v stellata fl.pl. s-c — B,P
Aquilegia vulgaris v stellata 'Green Apples' — P
Aquilegia vulgaris v stellata hybrids — B,JE
Aquilegia vulgaris v stellata pink — AP,HU,JD
Aquilegia vulgaris v stellata red — JD
Aquilegia vulgaris v stellata s-c — P,SA
Aquilegia vulgaris v stellata 'The Bride' — P
Aquilegia vulgaris 'Warwick' — JD
Aquilegia vulgaris 'White Barlow' — B,JO,PL,SA
Aquilegia vulgaris 'William Guiness' — BD,BS,C,CN,CT,D,DT, F,I,KS,L,LG,MO,P,PL, PM,SA,SC,SE,T,V
Aquilegia 'Westfaeld' — C
Aquilegia 'Winkie' — B,T
Aquilegia x cultorum blue shades — JE
Aquilegia x cultorum 'Heavenly Blue' — JE
Aquilegia x cultorum 'Maxi' — JE
Aquilegia x cultorum 'Spezialrasse' — JE
Aquilegia x helenae — SG
Aquilegia x hybrida — KL,SG
Aquilegia yabeana — AP,B,G,SA
Arabidopsis thaliana — B,BS
Arabis alpina — AP,B,BS,JE,KI,KL,SA, SC,SG
Arabis alpina 'Pink Pearl' — J,S,T,V
Arabis alpina pure white — BS,BY,J,S,V,YA
Arabis alpina 'Snowdrop' — CL
Arabis alpina ssp caucasica — AP,B,KL,SG,T
Arabis alpina ssp caucasica 'Schneehaube' — B,BD,BS,C,D,DE,JE, L,MO,SK
Arabis alpina v rosea — BD,BS,BY,C,CL,DV,SU
Arabis androsacea — AP,B,G,HP,KL,SC

ARABIS

Arabis aubrietoides	AP,B,G,SC
Arabis blepharophylla	AP,C,G,HP,KS,SA,SC,SG
Arabis blepharophylla 'Frulingszauber'	AP,B,BS,C,CL,CN,D, JE,L,MO,SK
Arabis blepharophylla 'Rote Sensation'	B,JE,R,S,SE,V
Arabis blepharophylla 'Spring Charm' see 'Fruhlingszauber'	
Arabis breweri	KL
Arabis bryoides	AP,B,KL,SC
Arabis caerulea	KL
Arabis caucasica see alpina ssp caucasica	
Arabis collina	KL
Arabis cypria	SG
Arabis flaviflora	VO
Arabis hirsuta	B,G,SG
Arabis lyallii	C,JE,SG
Arabis muralis see A. collina	
Arabis procurrens	B,KL
Arabis procurrens 'Glacier'	B,JE
Arabis pumila	AP,B,G,KL,SC
Arabis scabra	B,NS,SG
Arabis scopoliana	B,JE
Arabis serrata v japonica	SG
Arabis 'Snow Cap' see alpina ssp c. 'Schneehaube'	
Arabis 'Snowball'	B,CN,JE,SA
Arabis soyerii	AP,G,KL,SG
Arabis soyerii ssp coriacea	B
Arabis sp	KL
Arabis stelleri	B,JE
Arabis stelleri v japonica	AP,HP,KL,SG
Arabis stricta see A.scabra	
Arabis turrita	B,G,SG
Arabis vochinensis	SG
Arabis x arendsii 'Compinkie'	B,BS,C,CN,CO,D,JE, KI,MO,SK,ST,YA
Arabis x arendsii 'La Fraicheur'	B,JE
Arabis x arendsii 'Rosabella'	SG
Arabis x arendsii 'Rosea'	B,CN,HU,L,MO,SA
Arachis hypogaea	B,C,SA,SE,V
Arachis hypogaea 'Tennessee Red'	B
Arachis pintoi	B
Arachnoides adiantiformis	B
Arachnoides standishii	G
Aralia californica	B,DD,G,JE,SA
Aralia cashmeriana	B,JE,SA
Aralia chinensis see A.elata	
Aralia continentalis	B
Aralia cordata	B,JE,SA,SG
Aralia elata	A,C,DD,FW,LN,N,SA
Aralia elata v palmata	B
Aralia elegantissima	CA
Aralia nudicaulis	SG
Aralia racemosa	B,C,JE,PR,SG
Aralia spinosa	B,C,DV,EL,FW
Araucaria angustifolia	B,FW,LN,WA
Araucaria araucana	B,C,CA,CG,HA,LN,N, SA,VE
Araucaria bidwillii	B,C,CA,CG,EL,HA,O, SA,WA
Araucaria columnaris	B,O,WA
Araucaria cunninghamii	B,EL,HA,LN,O,SA,WA
Araucaria excelsa see A.heterophylla	
Araucaria heterophylla	B,CA,EL,FW,HA,LN,N, O,SA,SH,VE,WA
Araujia hortorum	C
Araujia sericifera	AP,B,C,CG,DD,HP,SC,T
Arbutus andrachne	B,SA

Arbutus arizonica	B,SW
Arbutus menziesii	AB,B,C,CA,LN,SA
Arbutus menziesii 'Madrona'	N
Arbutus unedo	A,B,C,CA,CG,EL,HA,LN, O,SA,T,VE
Arbutus xalapensis	B,SA
Archontophoenix alexandrae	B,C,CA,EL,HA,O,SA
Archontophoenix alexandrae v beatricea	B,EL
Archontophoenix cunninghamiana	B,C,CA,EL,HA,N,O,SA
Archontophoenix cunning. 'Illawarra'	B,EL
Archontophoenix 'Mount Lewis'	EL,O
Arctanthemum arcticum	B,G,JE
Arctium lappa	C,CP,DD,HU,JE,SG
Arctium minus	B,SG
Arctogeron gramineum	SG
Arctopus echinatus	B,SI
Arctostaphylos alpina	B,C,KL
Arctostaphylos columbiana	AB
Arctostaphylos glauca	CG,SA
Arctostaphylos manzanita	A,B,SA
Arctostaphylos nevadensis	B,C,NO
Arctostaphylos patula	B,C,FW,LN,NO,SA
Arctostaphylos pungens	B
Arctostaphylos uva-ursi	A,AB,B,C,CG,DD,FH,FW, JE,LN,NO,PO,SA,VE
Arctostaphylos viscida	B,FW,LN
Arctotheca calendula	B,SG,SI
Arctotis acaulis	AP,B,C,KB,SA,SI,V
Arctotis acaulis Harlequin New Hybrids	BS,BY,C,D,DE,J,KI,MO
Arctotis acaulis new hybrids	B,DT,FR,T
Arctotis aspera	B,SI
Arctotis auriculata	B,C,KB,SI
Arctotis auriculata yellow	B,KB
Arctotis diffusa	B,SI
Arctotis fastuosa	B,BD,BS,C,DE,F,KB,SI, T,VY
Arctotis fastuosa v alba 'Zulu Prince'	B,BS,DT,KS,PL,SD,SE, SK,T,V
Arctotis gumbletonii	B,SI
Arctotis hirsuta	AP,B,C,KB,T
Arctotis hirsuta orange	B,KB
Arctotis laevis	B,KB,SI
Arctotis mix special	S
Arctotis revoluta	B,SI
Arctotis scullyi	B,SI
Arctotis semipapposa	B,SI
Arctotis sp	SI
Arctotis stoechadifolia see A.venusta	
Arctotis venusta	AB,B,C,DD,G,HU,KB,PI, PK,PL,SA,SE,SG,SI
Arctotis venusta v grandis	SG
Ardisia crenata	B,G,SA,SG
Ardisia crenata 'Porcelain'	B
Ardisia crispa	B,BS,C,CA,EL,HA,O,SA
Ardisia crispa 'Alba'	EL,SA
Ardisia escallonoides	CG
Ardisia humilis	B,BS,CA,EL,HA,O
Ardisia humilis 'Aurea'	B
Ardisia littoralis	B
Ardisia macrocarpa	B,EL
Ardisia polycephala	B,BS
Ardisiandra wettsteinii	CG
Areca catechu	B,CA,O,SA
Areca ipot	O
Areca lutescens	CA
Areca triandra	B,CA,O

32

ARECA

Areca vestiaria	B
Arecastrum see Syagrus	
Aregelia corolinae see Neoregelia	
Arenaria aggregata	B
Arenaria armerina	KL
Arenaria balearica	AP,C,I,KL,SC,SG
Arenaria blepharophylla v parviflora	B
Arenaria congesta v liphophila	SG
Arenaria erinacea	C
Arenaria glomerata	B
Arenaria gottica	KL
Arenaria gracilis	B,JE,SG
Arenaria graminea	B
Arenaria grandiflora	AP,B,KL,SC,SG
Arenaria hookeri	B,RM
Arenaria kingii	G,SG
Arenaria longifolia	SG
Arenaria lychnidea	B,VO
Arenaria montana	AP,B,BD,BS,BY,C,CN, CO,DE,J,JE,MO,S,SA, SC,SK,V
Arenaria norvegica	AP,SC,SG
Arenaria obtusiloba see Minuartia	
Arenaria procera ssp glabra	B,CG,JE,KL,SG
Arenaria purparescens	AP,B,C,JE,SC,SG,VO
Arenaria recurva ssp oreina see Minuartia	
Arenaria rigida	KL
Arenaria serpyllifolia	SG
Arenaria serpyllifolia ssp leptocladus	CG
Arenaria stricta	B,PR
Arenaria tmolea	AP,B,SC
Arenaria tweedyi	KL
Arenga ambong	O
Arenga caudata	B,EL,O,SA
Arenga engleri	B,CA,EL,O,SA
Arenga pinnata	B,O,SA
Arenga tremula	B,O,SA
Arenga undulatifolia	O
Arequipa erectocylindrica	B,DV
Arequipa weingartiana	B
Argemone glauca	B
Argemone grandiflora	AP,B,DI,HP,PL
Argemone hispida	B,HU
Argemone mexicana	AP,B,C,G,KL,NG,SG
Argemone mexicana 'Chicalote'	HU
Argemone mexicana 'White Lustre'	B,C
Argemone mexicana 'Yellow Lustre'	B,C,SG,T
Argemone munita	B,HP
Argemone platyceras	B,G,SG
Argemone platyceras 'Silver Charm'	B
Argemone pleiacantha	B,DD
Argemone polyanthemos	AP,B,T,V
Argemone squarrosa ssp glabrata	T
Argyranthemum frutescens	B,FR
Argyranthemum frutescens 'Whity'	B
Argyranthemum 'Jamaica Primrose'	HP
Argyreia nervosa	B,C,CP,SA
Argyroderma congregatum	B,KB,SI
Argyroderma crateriforme	B,SI
Argyroderma delaetii	B,DV,GC,KB,SI,Y
Argyroderma delaetii f delaettii	SI
Argyroderma delaetii v aureum	B,DV,Y
Argyroderma delaetii v roseum	B,DV,SI,Y
Argyroderma fissum	B,DV,KB,SI,Y
Argyroderma fissum 'Brevipes'	B
Argyroderma fissum 'Littorale'	B

Argyroderma framesii	B,SI
Argyroderma framesii 'Hallii'	B,DV,SI
Argyroderma framesii 'Minus'	B,BC
Argyroderma patens	B,DV,SI,Y
Argyroderma pearsonii	B,DV,GC,KB,Y
Argyroderma pearsonii v luckhoffii	B,DV,SI
Argyroderma ringens	B,DV,KB,SI,Y
Argyroderma sp mix	C
Argyroderma subalbum	B,DV,SI,Y
Argyroderma subalbum 'Villetii'	B,BC
Argyroderma testiculare	B,SI
Argyrolobium pilosum	B
Ariocarpus agavoides	B
Ariocarpus fissuratus	B,BC,CH,DV,GC,Y
Ariocarpus fissuratus v hintonii	B,BC
Ariocarpus fissuratus v intermedius	B
Ariocarpus fissuratus v lloydii	B
Ariocarpus furfuraceus	CH,DV,Y
Ariocarpus furfuraceus v rostratus	Y
Ariocarpus kotschoubeyanus	B,CH,DV
Ariocarpus kotschoubeyanus v albiflorus	B,Y
Ariocarpus kotschoub. v macdowelli	B,BC
Ariocarpus lloydii	CH
Ariocarpus retusus	B,DV,Y
Ariocarpus retusus v elongatus	B,DV,GC
Ariocarpus sp mix	C
Ariocarpus trigonus	B,CH,DV,Y
Ariocarpus trigonus v elongatus	B,DV,GC
Ariocarpus trigonus v minor	DV
Arisaema amurense	AP,B,C,G,KL,LG,PM,SA, SC,SG
Arisaema anatolicum	B,MN
Arisaema candidissimum	KL
Arisaema ciliatum	G,N,SC
Arisaema concinnum	G,B
Arisaema consanguineum	AP,SA
Arisaema elephas	AR
Arisaema flavum	AP,B,C,G,I,KL,LG,MN, SC
Arisaema griffithii	B,G
Arisaema jacquemontii	B,G,HP,SC
Arisaema kishidai	B
Arisaema nepenthoides	C
Arisaema ostiolatum	KL
Arisaema propinquum	B
Arisaema ringens h. see A.robustum	
Arisaema robustum	AP,B,G,KL,SC,SG
Arisaema serratum	AP,B,CG,G,KL
Arisaema sikokianum	B,PK
Arisaema sp	AP,KL,SC,SG
Arisaema speciosum	C,PM
Arisaema tortuosum	AP,B,C,NG
Arisaema tortuosum v helleborifolium	C
Arisaema triphyllum	AP,B,G,HU,JE,SA,SC
Arisaema triphyllum 'Zebrinum'	KL
Arisaema yamatense	B
Arisarum proboscideum	B
Arisarum vulgare	B
Aristea africana	B,SA,SI
Aristea angolensis	B,SI
Aristea biflora	SI
Aristea cognata	SI
Aristea confusa	B,BH,SI
Aristea ecklonii	B,C,CA,EL,G,HP,HU,SC, SG,SI
Aristea ensifolia	SI

ARISTEA

Aristea juncifolia	B,SI
Aristea lugens	B,SI
Aristea macrocarpa	B,SI
Aristea major	B,BH,C,DV,KB,RU,SI
Aristea monticola	B,SI
Aristea sp	SI
Aristea spiralis	B,SA,SI
Aristea woodii	B,SG,SI
Aristida hystrix	B
Aristida purpurea	B
Aristida setacea	B
Aristolochia argentina	CG
Aristolochia baetica	B
Aristolochia bodemae	CG
Aristolochia bracteolata	B
Aristolochia californica	C
Aristolochia clematitis	AP,B,C,CG,G,JE,SG
Aristolochia elegans see A.littoralis	
Aristolochia fimbriata	B,CG
Aristolochia gibbosa	CG
Aristolochia grandiflora	B,CG
Aristolochia imbriata	CG
Aristolochia indica	B,EL
Aristolochia kaempferi	B
Aristolochia labiata	B,CG
Aristolochia littoralis	AB,B,C,CG,HA,HP,HU, PK,SA,SG
Aristolochia longa ssp paucinervis	AR
Aristolochia macrophylla	B,CG,SA
Aristolochia maxima	B
Aristolochia peucinervis	CG
Aristolochia pistolochia	B
Aristolochia ringens	B,EL
Aristolochia rotunda	B
Aristolochia sempervirens	B,CG
Aristolochia tomentosa	B
Aristolochia trilobata	B
Aristolochia watsonii	B
Aristotelia fruticosa	B,SS
Aristotelia peduncularis	B
Aristotelia serrata	B
Armatocereus arboreus	B,DV
Armatocereus laetus	B,DV,HU
Armatocereus matucanensis	B,DV
Armeniaca sibirica	SG
Armeria alliacea	AP,B,G,HP,JE,PK,SA, SC,SG
Armeria alliacea v leucantha	B,G,JE,SA,SG
Armeria alpina	AP,B,HP,KL
Armeria caespitosa see A. juniperifolia	
Armeria filicaulis	KL,SG
Armeria formosa hybrids	AP,BS,C,DE,HP,L,SA, SK,T
Armeria formosa 'Joystick'	B,BS,MO
Armeria girardii	PM
Armeria hybrida 'Ornament'	AP,BS,C,CL,G,J,JE,KI, MO,PK,U
Armeria juniperifolia	AP,B,G,HP,KL
Armeria juniperifolia 'Alba'	KL
Armeria juniperifolia 'Bevan's Variety'	AP,PM,SC,SG
Armeria juniperifolia x maritima	I
Armeria latifolia mix special lg fl	HU,JO
Armeria macloviana	AR
Armeria maritima	AB,AP,B,C,CN,CO,D,DD, HP,KL,PI,R,SC,SG,TH
Armeria maritima 'Alba'	AP,B,BD,BS,CL,CN,D,

	G,HP,JE,MO,PM,RS,SA, SC,SG,SK
Armeria maritima alpina	SG
Armeria maritima 'Bloodstone'	KL
Armeria maritima 'Carlux Rose'	B
Armeria maritima 'Carlux White'	B
Armeria maritima 'Corsica'	KL
Armeria maritima 'Pink Lusitanica'	B,JE
Armeria maritima 'Sea Spray'	U
Armeria maritima 'Snowball'	HP
Armeria maritima 'Splendens'	B,BD,BS,CL,CN,HU,JE, L,MO,SA,SK,SU,VO
Armeria maritima ssp sibirica	SG
Armeria maritima v laucheana	AP,C
Armeria mix dwarf	S
Armeria morisii	SG
Armeria pseudarmeria	AP,G,HP,JE,SC,V
Armeria pseudarmeria Bee's Hybrids	B,C,SC,SE,T
Armeria pseudarmeria hybs	B,BS,KI
Armeria pungens	AP,G,SC,SG
Armeria setacea	SG
Armeria sp ex Patagonia	AP,PM
Armeria tweedyi	AP,P,PM,SC
Armeria welwitschii	AP,HP
Armillaria mellea d.m.p	B
Arnebia pulchra	KL,VO
Arnica alpina	B,G,I
Arnica amplexicaulis	BH
Arnica chamissonis	AP,BS,CG,CN,DD,G,HP, JE,KL,SC
Arnica cordifolia	B,DD,NO,RS
Arnica foliosa	SG
Arnica fulgens	AP,B,HP
Arnica latifolia	AP,B,NO,SC
Arnica lessingii	AP,SC
Arnica mollis	CG,SG
Arnica montana	AP,B,BS,BY,C,CG,CN,G, HP,JE,KI,KL,SA,SC,SG,T
Arnica nevadensis	AP,B,HP,SC
Arnica parryi	B,DD
Arnica sp mix	BH
Aronia arbutifolia	RH,SA
Aronia melanocarpa	A,B,FW,LN,RH,SA,SG
Aronia x prunifolia	B,FW,RH,SA
Arrhenatherum elatius	B
Arrhenatherum elatius ssp bulb. 'V'	B
Arrojadoa albiflora	B,DV
Arrojadoa albispina	DV
Arrojadoa reflexa	BC,DV
Arrojadoa rhodantha	B,CH,DV,Y
Artabotrys hexapetalus	B,CG,EL
Artemisia abrotanum	B,KL
Artemisia absinthium	B,C,CN,DE,HU,JE,KS, SA,SG,TH
Artemisia afra	B,BH,C,KB,SI
Artemisia annua	C,CN,CP,DD,DE,GO,HU, JO,KS,PI,PK,T
Artemisia arborescens	B
Artemisia arborescens 'Powis Castle'	B
Artemisia assoana see caucasica	
Artemisia californica	B,CA,LN
Artemisia campestris	G
Artemisia campestris ssp borealis	B
Artemisia campestris ssp campestris	B
Artemisia campestris ssp maritima	B
Artemisia cana see Seriphidium canum	

ARTEMISIA

Artemisia canariensis see A.thuscula	
Artemisia caucasica	B,I,SG
Artemisia chamaemelifolia	B,BH,CG,G,JE,SA
Artemisia douglasiana	B
Artemisia dracunculus	B,CN,JE,KS,SG,TH
Artemisia filifolia	B
Artemisia frigida	B,LN,NO,SG
Artemisia genipi	B,CG,JE
Artemisia glacialis	C,CG,SC
Artemisia glauca	SG
Artemisia gmelinii	B
Artemisia gmelinii 'Viridis'	B
Artemisia herba-alba	B
Artemisia lactiflora green	PA
Artemisia lactiflora Guizhou Group	G,P
Artemisia ludoviciana	B,C,JE,NO,PR
Artemisia ludoviciana v latiloba	HP
Artemisia ludoviciana 'Valerie Finnis'	AP,HP
Artemisia monosperma	B
Artemisia mutellina see A.umbelliformis	
Artemisia nova	B
Artemisia pontica	B
Artemisia pycnocephala	B
Artemisia rupestris	SG
Artemisia sosnowskyi	SG
Artemisia sp mix	BH
Artemisia stelleriana	B,JE
Artemisia thuscula	B,CG
Artemisia umbelliformis	B,C,CG,G,JE
Artemisia valesiaca	C
Artemisia viridis	B
Artemisia vulgaris	CN,CP,HU,JE,SG,TH
Arthropodium candidum	AP,AU,B,G,HP,PM,SC, SG,SS
Arthropodium candidum maculatum	AP,HP
Arthropodium candidum purpureum	AP,HP,NG
Arthropodium capillipes	NI,SA
Arthropodium cirratum	AP,AU,B,C,G,HP,KL,SA, SC,SG,SS
Arthropodium milleflorum	AP,AU,HA,HP,KL,NI,SC
Arthropodium sp	AU
Artocarpus altilis	B
Artocarpus heterophyllus	B
Artocarpus hyb	B
Artocarpus lakoocha	B
Artocarpus odoratissimus	B
Arum albispathum	KL
Arum concinnatum	B,C,G,MN,SC
Arum concinnatum NL1234 Iran	MN
Arum creticum	AP,B,C,G,JE,SA,SC
Arum dioscoridis	B,JE
Arum dioscoridis S.L570/1 Turkey	MN
Arum hygrophilum	B
Arum italicum	AP,B,G,JE,KL,SA,SC, SG,VO
Arum italicum 'Marmoratum'	AP,G,I,KL,N,NG,P,SC
Arum italicum 'Pictum' see A.i. ssp i. 'Marmoratum'	
Arum italicum S.F336 Morocco	MN
Arum italicum ssp italicum	AP,B,PM
Arum maculatum	AP,B,C,CG,JE,KL,PO,SA, SC,SG
Arum orientale	G
Arum orientale orientale	SG
Arum pictum	B,C,P,MN,SC,SG
Arum purpureospathum	AP,B,SC
Arum purpureospathum PB49 Crete	MN

Arum rupicola v rupicola	B
Arum sp	KL
Aruncus aethusifolius	AP,B,BS,C,G,HP,I,JE,KL, RH,SA,SC,SG
Aruncus asiaticus	SG
Aruncus chinensis	SA
Aruncus dioicus	AB,B,BS,C,DD,DE,G,HP, JE,KI,KL,PK,SA,SC,SG, T,V
Aruncus dioicus 'Kneiffii'	AP,HP,KL,SG
Aruncus sinensis	B,JE
Aruncus sinensis 'Zweiweltenkind'	B,JE
Aruncus sylvester see A. dioicus	
Aruncus vulgaris	SG
Arundo donax	B
Arytera divaricata	B,NI,O
Asarina antirrhiniflora see Maurandella a.	
Asarina barclayana see Maurandya b.	
Asarina procumbens	AP,B,C,HU,I,JE,KL,P, PM,RH,SA,SC,SG
Asarina procumbens 'Iberian Trail'	C,HU
Asarina procumbens 'Sierra Nevada'	B
Asarina scandens see Maurandya s.	
Asarina sp	F,SG
Asarina 'Victoria Falls'	B,BD,C,DT,MO,T
Asarum canadense	B,JE
Asarum caudatum	B,JE,SG
Asarum europaeum	B,C,EL,G,JE
Asarum lemmonii	SG
Asarum shuttleworthii	B,JE
Asclepia sp	SI
Asclepias amplexicaulis	B
Asclepias asperula	B
Asclepias brevipes	B,SI
Asclepias burchellii	B,DD
Asclepias cancellata	B,SI
Asclepias 'Cinderella'	U,V
Asclepias crispa	SI
Asclepias curassavica	B,BS,C,CP,DD,EL,G,HP, HU,J,JE,KI,KS,SA,SG,V
Asclepias curassavica aff 'Rejalgar Rojo'	B,HU
Asclepias curassavica Gay Butterflies Gr.	B,C,JE,JO,PI,PL,SA,T
Asclepias curassavica 'Serenade'	B
Asclepias curassavica 'Silky Gold'	B,JO
Asclepias eriocarpa	B
Asclepias hirtella	B,PR
Asclepias incarnata	B,BS,DD,G,HP,HU,JE, NT,PK,PR,SA,SC
Asclepias incarnata 'Ice Ballet'	C,HP,JE,PK
Asclepias incarnata 'Ice Follies'	JO
Asclepias incarnata 'Soulmate'	B,C,JO
Asclepias incarnata white	B
Asclepias physocarpa see Gomphocarpus fruticosus	
Asclepias purpurascens	B,C,G
Asclepias speciosa	B,HP,SZ
Asclepias sullivantii	B,PR
Asclepias syriaca	AB,B,C,CG,CP,G,HP,HU, JE,PR,SA,SG
Asclepias tuberosa	AB,B,BS,C,CA,CN,CP, DD,DE,HP,HU,HW,JE, KL,NO,PK,PR,SA,SC, SK,SW
Asclepias tuberosa 'Hello Yellow'	B,JE
Asclepias verticillata	B,JE,PR
Asclepias viridiflora	B
Asimina triloba	A,B,C,CA,G,LN,N,SA,VE

ASIMINA

Asimina triloba Improved	B,FW
Asimina parviflora	SA
Askidiosperma chartaceum	B,SI
Askidiosperma esterhuyseniae	B,SI
Askidiosperma paniculatum	B,SI
Aspalanthus linearis	B,SI
Aspalathus elliptica	B,SA,SI
Aspalathus nivea	B
Aspalathus sp	SI
Asparagus cooperi	CA,EL,SA
Asparagus davuricuus	SG
Asparagus deflexus scandens	B,CA,EL,SA
Asparagus densiflorus	B
Asparagus densiflorus 'Flagstaff'	B,KB
Asparagus densiflorus 'Meyeri'	B,BS,C,CA,CL,DE,EL, HA,KB,PK,SA,V
Asparagus densiflorus 'Sprengeri'	B,BD,BS,C,CA,CL,DE, EL,FW,HA,KB,L,MO,PK, SA,SK,V,VE
Asparagus dens. 'Sprengeri Compacta'	B,CA,EL,SA
Asparagus dens. 'Sprengeri Variegatus'	B,BS,EL,L
Asparagus falcatus	B,CA,SA
Asparagus hybridus	B
Asparagus laricinus	B
Asparagus maritimus	SG
Asparagus medeloides	EL,HA
Asparagus mix ferns	T
Asparagus myriocladus	CA,EL,SA
Asparagus officinalis	CG,SG
Asparagus officinalis 'Spitzenschleier'	C,JE
Asparagus officinalis v pseudoscaber	PK
Asparagus plumosus see A.setaceus	
Asparagus pseudoscaber	B
Asparagus racemosus	B,EL,LN,SA
Asparagus retrofractus	B
Asparagus scandens	C,KB
Asparagus scoparius	C
Asparagus setaceus	B,CA,DD
Asparagus setaceus 'Nanus'	B,BD,BS,BY,C,CL,DE, EL,FW,KI,L,MO,SA,SK, ST,V,VE
Asparagus setaceus 'Pyramidalis'	B,CA,EL,SA
Asparagus setaceus 'Robustus'	B
Asparagus sp	SI
Asparagus umbellatus	B,EL
Asparagus verticillatus	B,C,G,JE,SA
Asparagus virgatus	B,CA,EL,KB,SA
Asperula orientalis	AP,B,BS,C,CN,HU,J,KI, KS,S,SG,SP,T,TH,V
Asperula orientalis 'Blue Mist'	U
Asperula taurina	B
Asperula tinctoria	B,G
Asphodeline liburnica	AP,B,C,G,HP,JE,LG,SA
Asphodeline lutea	AP,B,BS,C,CH,CL,G,HP, HU,JE,KI,KL,MN,MO, PA,PM,SA,SC,SG,TH
Asphodeline taurica	B,JE
Asphodelus acaulis	AP,B
Asphodelus acaulis S.F. 156 Morocco	MN
Asphodelus aestivus	AP,B,G,HP,JE,SC,SG
Asphodelus albus	AP,B,C,CG,G,HP,JD,JE, KL,LG,NG,SA,SC,SG,T
Asphodelus cerasiferus see A.ramosus	
Asphodelus fistulosus see A.tenuifolius	
Asphodelus microcarpus see A.aestivus	
Asphodelus ramosus	AP,B,C,CG,G,HP,JE,SG

Asphodelus sp	KL
Asphodelus tenuifolius	AP,C,HP,SG
Asplenium australasicum	B,EL,HA
Asplenium bulbiferum	B,SG
Asplenium dimorphum	SG
Asplenium nidus	B,C,SA
Asplenium scolopendrium	B,CG
Asplenium scolopendrium f marginatum	SG
Asplenium septentrionale	CG,G
Asplenium trichomanes	B,CG,G
Asplenium viride	B,G
Asrtophytum capricornis	B,CH,Y
Astartea ambigua	B,NI
Astartea fascicularis	AU,B,NI,O,SA
Astelia banksii	AR
Astelia fragrans	B,C,SA
Astelia graminea	B,SS
Astelia linearis	B,SS
Astelia nervosa	B,SS
Astelia nervosa v chathamica	B,SA
Astelia nivicola	B,SS
Aster 'All Change'	T
Aster Allsorts	F
Aster alpine fairy mix	U
Aster alpinus	AP,B,BS,C,CG,CL,CN, ,FR,G,HP,I,JE,KL,L,RI, RM,SA,SG,ST,T,V,VO
Aster alpinus 'Abendschein' fl.pl.	KL
Aster alpinus 'Albus'	AP,B,G,JE,KL,SC,SG
Aster alpinus 'Dunkle Schone'	AP,C,JE
Aster alpinus fl.pl 'Marchenland'	AP,C,JE,PL
Aster alpinus 'Goliath'	B,DE,JE,SA
Aster alpinus 'Happy End'	AP,C,G,JE
Aster alpinus mix	BD,JE,KI,MO,PK,SK
Aster alpinus 'Rose'	AP,B,KL,SA
Aster alpinus 'Trimix'	BS,C,CL,D,J,JE,MO,R,T
Aster alpinus v dolomiticus	KL
Aster alpinus v speciosus	SG
Aster alpinus white	SA
Aster alpinus 'White Beauty'	C,HP
Aster altaicus	SG
Aster amellus	AP,B,C,CG,CO,G,HP,JE, KL,SA,SG
Aster amellus hyb mix	BS,JE,KI,T
Aster amellus 'Rosa Erfullung'	HP
Aster amellus 'Rudolph Goethe'	B,C,JE
Aster andersonii	KL
Aster 'Apricot Giant'	F,S
Aster 'Asteroid' mix	B,BS
Aster azureus	G,JE,PR,SA
Aster bakerianus	B,SI
Aster bellidiastrum	B,CG
Aster bigelovii	JE
Aster bigelovii 'Happiness'	T
Aster 'Blue Magic'	U
Aster 'Burpeeana'	BS
Aster 'Candy Stripe' mix	BS
Aster 'Carousel' mix	BS,KI
Aster 'Carpet Ball' mix	T,VH
Aster chinensis see Callistephus	
Aster Chrysanthemum Fl mix	S
Aster ciliolatus	SG
Aster coloradoensis	B,RM
Aster 'Colour Star'	L
Aster conspicuus	NO
Aster Contraster mix	SK

ASTER

Aster cordifolius	B,CG,G,PR	Aster oolentangiensis	B
Aster cordifolius ssp sagittifolius	B	Aster 'Operetta' mix	T
Aster 'Crego Giants'	BU,PI,SK	Aster 'Opus'	SE
Aster 'Crimson Sunset'	T	Aster paeony fl	FR,L,SK
Aster cut flower mix	D,DT,M,PK,T	Aster patens	G,NT
Aster 'Devon Riviera' mix	S	Aster pattersonii	RM
Aster divaricatus	B,CG,G,HP,JE,KL,NT	Aster 'Petite Bedders' mix	FR,YA
Aster drummondii	B,PR	Aster petite mix	S
Aster dubius v glabratus	B	Aster pilosus	B,PR
Aster dumosus	B,KL	Aster pilosus v demotus	B
Aster dumosus s-c	KL,SG	Aster 'Pink Magic'	U
Aster dw bedding s-c	D	Aster pinnatisectus	SG
Aster 'Dwarf Queen'	BS,CA,CO,KI,M,MO,SK, ST,U	Aster pot 'n' patio	SE,SK
		Aster prenanthoides	B,PR
Aster 'Early Charm'	BS	Aster 'Prinette' mix	S
Aster ericoides	B,G,I,JE,PR	Aster 'Pruhonicer' dw	T
Aster falcatus	SG	Aster ptarmicoides	B,C,JE,KS,PR
Aster farreri	AP,B,CG,JE,SC	Aster puniceus	B,G,JE,PR,SG
Aster flaccidus	AP,B,HP,SC	Aster pyrenaeus	B,JE,SC,SG
Aster 'Florette Champagne'	T	Aster 'Queen of the Market'	BS,L
Aster foliaceus	AP,B,RM	Aster radula	HP
Aster 'Germannia'	D	Aster 'Red Ribbon'	T
Aster giant single	BS,J,KI,ST,SU,TU,U,V, VH	Aster 'Ribbon' mix	BS,KI
		Aster 'Riviera'	F
Aster 'Giants of California'	BS,BY,CO,F,KI,MO,SK, ST,TU	Aster 'Roundabout' mix	CL
		Aster scaber	HP
Aster grandiflorus	B	Aster sedifolius	B,HP
Aster 'Gusford Supreme'	PL	Aster 'Serene' light blue	C
Aster 'Harz' mix	BS	Aster 'Serene' rose	C
Aster hesperius	SG	Aster sericeus	B,HP,PR
Aster himalaicus	AP,CG,HP,SC,SG	Aster sibiricus	AP,B,G,JE,KL,SG
Aster himalaicus luteus	KL	Aster sinensis mix	BY,S
Aster ibericus	KL,VO	Aster sinensis super mix	S
Aster 'Koningin der Hallen'	V	Aster Spider dw s-c	SK
Aster laevis	B,G,JE,PR,SG	Aster squamatus	CG
Aster lanceolatus ssp simplex	B	Aster 'Starburst'	U
Aster lateriflorus	AP,B,CG,G,PR	Aster 'Starlet' mix	BS,CO,KI,U
Aster linariifolius	AP,B	Aster 'Starwort'	J
Aster linosyris	B,C,G,HP,JE,SG	Aster Stripes	SE
Aster 'Love Me'	BS,U	Aster subcaeruleus	SG
Aster 'Lutins' mix	BD,BS,MO	Aster subcaeruleus 'Lavender Star'	C
Aster macrophyllus	B,G,HP,JE,NG,NT,SC	Aster subspicatus	AB,NO,SC,SG
Aster 'Madeleine' mix	BS,CL,MO	Aster tanacetifolius	NO
Aster Massagno mix	SK	Aster tataricus	B,SG
Aster 'Matador' mix	BS,CL,CO,KI,MO,SK, SU,YA	Aster 'Teisa Stars'	F,J,S
		Aster thomsonii	G,SG
Aster 'Meteor'	BS,U	Aster tibeticus	KL,SG
Aster 'Mini Lady'	SK	Aster tibeticus v albus	SG
Aster mix lg Fl Imp	BS	Aster 'Tiger Paw' mix	BD,BS,D,MO,SE,SK
Aster mix pastel	T	Aster tongolensis	AP,B,G,PK,SA,SC,SG
Aster modestus	B,DD,SG	Aster tongolensis 'Dunkelviolett'	C
Aster 'Moraketa'	SE,T	Aster tradescantii	HP
Aster natalensis see Felicia rosulata		Aster tripolium	AP,B
Aster nepalensis	AP	Aster tripolium ssp polonius	B
Aster novae-angliae	AB,B,BD,BY,G,HU,HW, J,JE,JO,NO,PR,V	Aster 'Truffaunt's Paeony Mix'	DT
		Aster turbellinus h	C
Aster novae-angliae Autumn fl	CL,M	Aster uliginosus	SG
Aster novae-angliae 'Benary's Comp.'	B,BS,C,CN,F,J,JE,MO, PK	Aster umbellatus	B,C,G,HP,JE,PR
		Aster undulatus	NT
Aster novae-angliae 'Composition Mix'	DT,T,U	Aster vahlii	AU,AP,SC
Aster novae-angliae 'Dr Eckener'	B	Aster 'Wartburgstern'	B,BS,G,JE,KI,SK
Aster novae-angliae lg fl	S	Aster x frikartii	AV,B,G,HP,SC
Aster novae-angliae 'Lucida'	B	Asteridea athrixioides	B,NI
Aster novae-angliae 'Septemberrubin'	B,JE	Asteridea chaetopoda	B,NI
Aster novi-belgii	DE,G,JE,KS,SG,SU	Asteridea pulverulenta	B,NI
Aster oblongifolius	NT	Asteriscus graveolens	B

ASTERISCUS

Asteriscus maritimus	AP,PM,SC
Asterogyne martiana	B
Asteromyrtus magnifica	B
Astilbe biternata	B,JE
Astilbe chinensis	B,CG,JE,KL,RH,SG
Astilbe chinensis japonica hyb	JE
Astilbe chinensis v davidii	B,G,JE,SG
Astilbe chinensis v pumila	B,BS,C,CO,G,JE,KI,PK, SG,SU,T
Astilbe chinensis v taquettii hyb	C,CG,JE,RH
Astilbe chinensis v taquettii 'Superba'	AP,B,C,P
Astilbe glaberrima	KL
Astilbe grandis	SG
Astilbe koreana	SG
Astilbe microphylla	SG
Astilbe myriantha	B,JE,SG
Astilbe simplicifolia mix	DE,JE
Astilbe sp	KL
Astilbe sp China	SG
Astilbe sp Coll Ref	X
Astilbe thunbergii hybrid	JE
Astilbe thunbergii v congesta	B,CG,SG
Astilbe x arendsii 'Bunter Zauber'	JE
Astilbe x arendsii 'Garden Delight'	J,SE,T,V
Astilbe x arendsii mix	BD,BS,C,CL,L,MO,PK, SK
Astilbe x arendsii mix hyb	B,CN,D,S
Astilbe x arendsii pink	B,JE
Astilbe x arendsii red	B,JE
Astilbe x arendsii 'Roman Dancers'	F
Astilbe x arendsii 'Showstar'	B,C,CL,DT,JE,MO,YA
Astilboides tabularis	B,BS,C,G,JE,SA,SC
Astragalus aboriginum	SG
Astragalus allochrous	B
Astragalus alopecuroides	C,G,SG
Astragalus alpinus	AP,B,C
Astragalus angustifolius	KL
Astragalus antisellii	B,CG
Astragalus arnottianus	AP,RS,SC
Astragalus atropurpureus	KL
Astragalus australis	B
Astragalus austrosibiricus	KL
Astragalus callichrous	B
Astragalus canadensis	B,G,KL,PR,SG
Astragalus centralpinus	B,KL,SG
Astragalus ceratoides	SG
Astragalus cicer	AP,B,DD,RH,SG
Astragalus crassicarpus	B,PR
Astragalus danicus	SG
Astragalus fruticosusus	SG
Astragalus glycyphyllos	A,AP,B,C,DD,G,HP,JE, LA,NS,SA,SC,SG
Astragalus kentrophyta ssp implexus	B,RM,SG
Astragalus lentiginosus	B,DD
Astragalus macrocarpus	B
Astragalus melilotoides	SG
Astragalus membranaceus	AB,HU,JO,SD
Astragalus monspessulanus	AP,B,KL,SC
Astragalus onobrychis	B,SG
Astragalus penduliflorus	B,SG
Astragalus plattensis	B,PR
Astragalus polaris	B
Astragalus ponoensis	CG
Astragalus purpureus	B,C
Astragalus purshii	B
Astragalus schelichowii	B,SG

Astragalus simplicifolius	B
Astragalus sp	KL
Astragalus sulcatus	SG
Astragalus tephroides	B
Astragalus thurberi	B
Astragalus uliginosus	SG
Astragalus utahensis	AP,B,SC,SW
Astragalus vesicarius ssp albidus	B
Astragalus wootonii	B
Astrantia bavarica	HP,SG
Astrantia carniolica	AP,G,HP,RH,SC
Astrantia carniolica major see A.major	
Astrantia carniolica v rubra	AP,B,HP,JE,SC,SG
Astrantia major	AP,B,BS,C,CG,CN,G,HP, I,JE,KI,KL,PA,RH,SA, SC,SG,ST,T,TH,V
Astrantia major 'Alba'	B,C,G,HP,JE,SA
Astrantia major bieberstanii	SG
Astrantia major f rubra	AP,C,HP,PL,SG
Astrantia major 'Hadspen Blood'	NG
Astrantia major 'Moira Reid'	C,NG
Astrantia major 'Primadonna'	B,BS,C,CL,HP,HU,JE, MO,PK
Astrantia major 'Rosea'	B,HP,JE,SA
Astrantia major 'Rosensinfonie'	B,C,HP,JE,SA
Astrantia major 'Ruby Cloud'	B,JE
Astrantia major 'Ruby Wedding Series'	AP,HP,LG,P
Astrantia major ssp involucrata 'Margery Fish' see 'Shaggy'	
Astrantia major ssp involucrata 'Shaggy'	AP,B,C,HP,NG,P
Astrantia major ssp major	SG
Astrantia major 'Sunningdale' (V)	AP,G,HP,I,PL,SG
Astrantia maxima	AP,B,C,G,HP,JE,NG,SA, SC,SG
Astrantia maxima extra lg fl	T
Astrantia minor	B,C,HP,SC
Astrantia 'Rainbow'	B,JE
Astrebla lappacea	B,HA,NI
Astrebla pectinata	B,NI
Astridia alba	B
Astridia citrina aff	B
Astridia dinteri	B
Astridia hallii	B
Astrocaryum alatum	B
Astrocaryum standleyanum	B
Astroloba spiralis	B
Astroloma ciliatum	B,NI
Astroloma epacridis	B,NI
Astroloma foliosum	B,NI
Astroloma glaucescens	B,NI
Astroloma pallidum	B,NI
Astronium graveolens	B
Astrophytum asterias	B,CH,DV,GC,Y
Astrophytum capricornis	DV,Y
Astrophytum capricornis f aureum	B,Y
Astrophytum capricornis v crassispinoides	B,Y
Astrophytum capricornis v major	Y
Astrophytum capricornis v minor	B,Y
Astrophytum capricornis v niveum	B,Y
Astrophytum capricornis v senile	Y
Astrophytum capricornis x asterias	B
Astrophytum coahuilense	B,DV,Y
Astrophytum mix	DV,Y
Astrophytum myriostigma	B,CH,DV,Y
Astrophytum myriostigma v columnare	B,BC,Y
Astrophytum myriostigma v jamauvense	B
Astrophytum myriostigma v nudum	B,Y

ASTROPHYTUM

Astrophytum myriostigma v potosinum	B,Y	Atriplex 'Pintharuka'	B,NI
Astrophytum myr. v quadricostatum	B,GC	Atriplex polycarpa	B
Astrophytum my. v strongylogonum	B,DV	Atriplex prostrata	B
Astrophytum myriostigma v tulense	B,BC,Y	Atriplex semibaccata	B,CA,EL,LN,NI,O
Astrophytum ornatum	B,CH,DV,Y	Atriplex semilunaris	B,NI
Astrophytum ornatum v glabrescens	B,Y	Atriplex undulata	B,O
Astrophytum ornatum v mirbellii	DV	Atriplex vesicaria	B,DD,EL,HA,NI,O
Astrophytum senile	DV	Atriplex vesicaria v sphaerocarpa	B,NI
Astrophytum sp/hyb	Y	Atropa belladonna	AP,B,C,CP,HU,NG,PO,
Asyneuma canescens	AP,B,C,HP,JE,P,SG		SG
Asyneuma limonifolium ssp pestalozae	T	Atropa belladonna lutea	B,C,CP,NG
Atalantia monophylla	B	Atropanthe sinensis	B
Atalaya hemiglauca	B,EL,HA,NI,O,SA	Atylosia scarabaeoides	B
Atalaya variifolia	B,NI	Aubrieta Bengal Hybrids	BD,BS,C,JE,MO
Athamanta cretensis	B,JE,SA	Aubrieta 'Campbellii'	B,DT,JE,SA
Athamanta turbith	HP	Aubrieta canescens	VO
Athanasia crithmifolia	B,KB,SI	Aubrieta 'Carnival' s-c & mix	BS
Athanasia parviflora	C	Aubrieta 'Cascade Blue'	B,JE,SA
Athanasia trifurcata	B,SA,SI	Aubrieta 'Cascade Lilac'	BS
Atherosperma moschatum	B,SA	Aubrieta 'Cascade' mix	BD,BS,CL,CN,MO
Athrixia fontana	B,SI	Aubrieta 'Cascade Purple'	B,BD,BY,JE,R,SA,ST,T,U
Athrixia phylicoides	SI	Aubrieta 'Cascade Red'	B,BD,JE,R,SA,ST,U
Athrotaxis cupressoides	B	Aubrieta 'Cascade Rose'	B,BD
Athrotaxis selaginoides	B,C	Aubrieta dbl & semi-dbl	YA
Athrotaxis x laxifolia	B,SA	Aubrieta deltoidea red	KL
Athyrium filix-femina	AP,G	Aubrieta 'Double Manon'	U,V
Atractylis phaeolepis	B	Aubrieta f1 'Novalis Blue'	BS,C,JE,MO,PK,SK
Atragene see Clematis		Aubrieta 'Fruhlingszauber'	D
Atriplex amnicola	B,DD,NI,O	Aubrieta 'Galaxy' lg fl	YA
Atriplex amnicola 'Rivermor'	B,NI	Aubrieta 'Graeca'	B,BS,MO
Atriplex angulata	B,NI	Aubrieta 'Grandiflora'	B,DE,HU,JE
Atriplex bunburyana	B,NI,O	Aubrieta 'Hendersonii'	B,BS,HU,JE,L,SA
Atriplex canescens	A,C,CA,DD,EL,LN,NO,	Aubrieta hybrids mix	BS,BY,C,CO,F,FR,J,L,M,
	O,SA		S,SE,SK,T,TU,U,V,VH
Atriplex cinerea	B,NI	Aubrieta 'King Blue'	J,V
Atriplex codonocarpa	B,NI	Aubrieta 'King Red'	J,V
Atriplex confertifolia	B,LN,NO	Aubrieta 'Leichtlinii'	B,BS,BY,DE,HU,JE,L,KI,
Atriplex gardneri	NO		SA
Atriplex glauca	B,CA,O	Aubrieta 'Light Series' s-c	YA
Atriplex halimus	A,B,C,EL,SA,VE	Aubrieta 'Monarch'	BS,C,DT
Atriplex holocarpa	B,NI	Aubrieta purpurea	BS,KI,TH
Atriplex hortensis	AP,B,KS,SG,V	Aubrieta 'Rich Rose'	F,S
Atriplex hortensis cupreata	T	Aubrieta 'Royal Blue'	B,BS,CL,CN,JE,MO,SA
Atriplex hortensis 'Plume Crimson'	B	Aubrieta 'Royal' mix	BS
Atriplex hortensis 'Plume Gold'	B,CN,G	Aubrieta 'Royal Red'	B,BS,C,CL,CN,JE,MO,
Atriplex hortensis 'Plume Green'	B,BS,CN,DD,DE,HU,MO		SA
Atriplex hortensis 'Plume Red'	B,BS,BY,CN,DD,DE,G,	Aubrieta 'Royal Violet'	B,BS,CL,CN,JE,KI,MO,
	HU,MO,SG		SA
Atriplex hortensis 'Plumes' mix	C	Aubrieta semi-dbl	D
Atriplex hortensis 'Rubra'	AP,RH	Aubrieta sp ex Mt Olympus	HP
Atriplex hortensis v purpurea	C	Aubrieta 'Spring Falls'	KI,ST
Atriplex hortensis white/yellow	HU	Aubrieta 'Whitewell Gem'	B,BS,CG,CN,DE,HU,JE,
Atriplex hymenelytra	B		L,SA
Atriplex isatidea	B,NI,O	Aubrieta x cultorum	AP,B,CG,SA,SC,SU
Atriplex lentiformis	B,CA,DD,LN,O	Aucuba japonica	B,C,CA,G,LN,SA,VE
Atriplex lentiformis ssp breweri	B	Aucuba japonica 'Variegata'	B,SA,VE
Atriplex leucoclada	B	Augea capensis	B,SI
Atriplex lindleyi	B,NI	Aulacospermum anomalum	SG
Atriplex muelleri	B,NI	Aulax cancellata	B,O,SI
Atriplex nummularia	B,C,EL,HA,HU,LN,NI,	Aulax pallasii	B,SI
	O,SA,WA	Aulax umbellata	B,KB,O,SI
Atriplex nummularia 'De Kock'	B,NI	Aureolaria flava	B,HU
Atriplex nummularia ssp spathulata	B,NI	Aureolaria grandiflora	B
Atriplex nuttallii	B,EL,LN,NO,SA	Aureolaria virginica	B,HU
Atriplex paludosa	B,NI,O	Aurinia corymbosa	B,P
Atriplex patula	B	Aurinia saxatilis	AP,B,BS,BY,CA,HP,KL

AURINIA

Aurinia saxatilis 'Alpinum'	CG
Aurinia saxatilis 'Basket of Gold'	AB,PK
Aurinia saxatilis 'Citrina'	AP,CG
Aurinia saxatilis 'Compacta'	AP,B,BD,BS,CG,CN,CO, HP,J,JE,KI,RH,SA,SG, ST,V
Aurinia saxatilis 'Coupe D'or'	B
Aurinia saxatilis 'Gold Ball' see 'Goldkugel'	
Aurinia saxatilis 'Gold Dust'	AP,B,BS,C,F,FR,PI,R,SK
Aurinia saxatilis 'Gold' mix p.s.	U
Aurinia saxatilis 'Golden Queen'	DT,S,T
Aurinia saxatilis 'Goldkugel'	B,CL,DE,JE,L,MO
Aurinia saxatilis 'Sulphureum'	B,JE,SA
Austrocedrus chilensis	B,C,SA
Austrocephalocereus dolichospermaticus	B,DV
Austrocephalocereus dybowski	B,DV,Y
Austrocephalocereus estevesii	B,DV,Y
Austrocephalocereus purpureus	B,DV,Y
Austrocylindropuntia haematacantha	B,DV
Austrocylindropuntia humahuacana	DV
Austrocylindropuntia inarmata	B,DV
Austrocylindropuntia miquelii	DV
Austrocylindropuntia vestita	DV
Austrocylindropuntia weingartiana	DV
Austromyrtus dulcis	B,NI
Avena abyssinica	SG
Avena fatua	CG,G
Avena nuda	SG
Avena persica	SG
Avena pubescens	SG
Avena sativa	B,T
Avena sativa 'French Black'	B,JO
Avena sterilis	B,MO
Avena strigosa	B
Avenula see Helictotrichon	
Averia javanica	B
Averrhoa bilimbi	B,SA
Averrhoa carambola	B,RE,SA
Avicennia germinans	B
Axonopus affinis	B,EL
Axyris amaranthoides	B,SG
Aylostera albiareolata	DV
Aylostera albipilosa	Y
Aylostera aureispina	DV
Aylostera cajasensis	Y
Aylostera carminifilamentosa	Y
Aylostera cintiensis	Y
Aylostera fiebrigii	DV,Y
Aylostera flavistyla	Y
Aylostera fulviseta	DV,Y
Aylostera fusca	Y
Aylostera horstii	DV
Aylostera keisligiana	DV
Aylostera kupperiana	DV,Y
Aylostera muscula	SO,Y
Aylostera narvaecensis	Y
Aylostera pulvinosa	Y
Aylostera robustispina	Y
Aylostera rubiginosa LAU 402	Y
Aylostera sanguinea	DV
Aylostera sp	DV
Aylostera tamboensis	Y
Aylostera tuberosa	Y
Azadirachta indica	B,EL,HA,SA
Azanza garckeana	B
Azara integrifolia	B,SA

Azara microphylla	B,C,SA
Azara serrata	B,HP,SA
Azima tetracantha	B,KB
Azolla filiculoides	B
Azorella filamentosa	AU
Azorella trifurcata	KL
Azorina vidalii	AP,G,HP,JE,KS,SC,SG
Azorina vidalii 'Rosea'	AP,B,JE,PL,T,V
Aztekium hintonii	DV,Y
Aztekium ritteri	B,CH,DV,GC,Y
Azureocereus hertlingianus see Browningia hertlingiana	
Babiana ambigua	B,RU
Babiana angustifolia	B,G,RU,SI
Babiana attenuata	B,RU
Babiana blanda	B
Babiana cedarbergensis	B,SI
Babiana crispa	B,SI
Babiana curviscapa	B,RU,SI
Babiana dregei	AP,B,G,RU,SC,SI
Babiana ecklonii	B,RU
Babiana fimbriata	B,SI
Babiana hyb	SZ
Babiana klaverensis	B,SI
Babiana leipoldtii	B,RU
Babiana nana	AP,B,CG,RU,SI
Babiana odorata	B,RU,SI
Babiana patersoniae	B,CG,RU,SI
Babiana plicata	B,RU,SI
Babiana purpurea	B,RU
Babiana pygmaea	B,MN,RU
Babiana 'Queen Fabiola'	PM
Babiana ringens	B,SI
Babiana rubrocyanea	AP,B,C,CG,RU,SI
Babiana salteri	B
Babiana sambucina	B
Babiana scabrifolia	B
Babiana scariosa	B,RU
Babiana secunda	B,RU
Babiana sinuata	B,SI
Babiana sp mix	C,SC,SI
Babiana spathacea	B,SI
Babiana stricta	AP,B,KB,RU,SI
Babiana thunbergii	B,SI
Babiana truncata	B,RU,SI
Babiana tubiflora	KL
Babiana tubulosa	AP,G,SC,SI
Babiana tubulosa v tubiflora	AP,B,RU
Babiana vanzyliae	B,RU,SI
Babiana villosa blue	B,RU,SA,SI
Babiana villosa red	SA,SI
Babiana villosa v grandis	B,RU
Babiana villosula	B,RU,SI
Baccharis emoryi	B
Baccharis halimifolia	B,JE,S,SA,SG
Baccharis magellanica	AR
Baccharis microphylla	B
Baccharis pilularis	B,CA
Baccharis pilularis ssp pilularis	B
Baccharis pilularis v consanguinea	B
Baccharis salicifolia	B
Baccharis sarothroides	B,SA
Backhousia anisata	HA
Backhousia citriodora	HA,O
Backhousia myrtifolia	B,HA
Bactris cubensis	B
Bactris gasipaes	B,CA,O,SA

BAECKEA

Baeckea camphorosmae	B,C,NI,O
Baeckea corynophylla	B,NI
Baeckea crispiflora	B,NI
Baeckea densifolia	B,HA
Baeckea floribunda	B
Baeckea linifolia	B,EL,NI
Baeckea preissiana	B,NI
Baeckea thryptomenoides	B,NI
Baeckea virgata	B,EL,HA,HU,NI,O,SA,SH
Baeometra uniflora	AP,B,RU,SC,SI
Baikiaea plurijuga	B,SI
Baileya multiradiata	B,C,CA,KS,NO,SA,SW
Baileya pleniradiata	B
Balanites aegyptiaca	B,SA
Balanites maughamii	B,SI
Balaustion pulcherrimum	B,NI,O,SA
Baldellia ranunculoides	B,JE,SA
Ballota africana	B,BH,SI
Ballota hirsuta	SA
Ballota nigra	B,CN,LA,SG,TH
Ballota nigra 'Archer's Variegated' (V)	B,P
Ballota rupestris	SG
Ballota saxatilis	SG
Balsamorhiza hookeri	NO
Balsamorhiza sagittata	AV,B,C,DD,,JE,NO,SA
Bambusa arundinacea	B,C,SA
Bambusa nutans	DV,SA
Banisteriopsis caapi	B
Banksia aculeata	B,NI,O
Banksia aemula	B,NI,O
Banksia ashbyi	B,EL,NI,O,SA
Banksia aspenifolia	EL,HA,SA,SH
Banksia attenuata	B,EL,NI,O
Banksia attenuata dw	B,NI,O
Banksia audax	B,EL,NI,O
Banksia baueri	B,C,EL,NI,O
Banksia baxteri	B,EL,NI,O
Banksia benthamiana	B,EL,NI,O
Banksia blechnifolia	B,NI,O
Banksia brownii	B,EL,NI,O
Banksia burdettii	B,NI,O
Banksia caleyi	B,C,EL,NI,O,SA
Banksia candolleana	B,NI,O
Banksia canei	AU,B,C,NI,O
Banksia coccinea	B,NI,O,SA
Banksia collection	C
Banksia collina	C,EL,SA,SH
Banksia conferta ssp penicillata	AU
Banksia conferta v conferta	B,NI,O
Banksia cunninghamii	B
Banksia dentata	B,NI,O
Banksia dryandroides	B,NI,O
Banksia elderana	B,NI,O
Banksia 'Ellisonii'	B,EL,SH
Banksia ericifolia	DV,EL,HA,N,NI,SA,SH
Banksia ericifolia ericifolia	B,O
Banksia ericifolia v macrantha	B,NI,O
Banksia gardneri v gardneri	B,NI,O
Banksia gardneri v hiemalis	B
Banksia grandis	B,EL,NI,O,SA
Banksia grossa	B,NI,O
Banksia hookerana	B,EL,NI,O,SA,T
Banksia ilicifolia	B,NI,O
Banksia incana	B,NI,O
Banksia integrifolia	AP,B,EL,HA,NI,O,SA,SH
Banksia laevigata v fuscoluta	B,NI,O

Banksia laevigata v laevigata	B,NI,O
Banksia lanata	B,NI,O
Banksia laricina	B,NI,O
Banksia lemanniana	B,NI,O
Banksia leptophylla	B,NI,O
Banksia lindleyana	B,NI,O
Banksia littoralis	B,NI,O
Banksia lullfitzii	B,NI,O
Banksia marginata	AU,B,EL,HA,NI,O,SA,SH
Banksia media	B,EL,NI,O,SA
Banksia meisneri	B,NI,O
Banksia menziesii	B,EL,NI,O
Banksia menziesii dw	B,NI,O
Banksia nutans v cernuella	B,NI,O
Banksia nutans v nutans	B,NI,O
Banksia oblongifolia	B,NI,O
Banksia occidentalis	B,EL,NI,O,SA
Banksia oreophila	B,NI,O
Banksia ornata	B,C,EL,HA,NI,O,SA
Banksia paludosa	B,EL,HA,NI,O,SA,SH
Banksia petiolaris	B,NI,O
Banksia pilostylis	B,NI,O
Banksia praemorsa	B,EL,NI,O,SA
Banksia prionotes	B,EL,NI,O,SA
Banksia pulchella	B,NI,O
Banksia quercifolia	B,NI,O
Banksia repens	B,NI,O
Banksia robur	B,C,EL,HA,NI,O,SA
Banksia saxicola	B,O
Banksia scabrella	B,NI,O
Banksia sceptrum	B,NI,O
Banksia seminuda	B,NI,O
Banksia serrata	B,C,EL,N,NI,O,SA,SH
Banksia serratifolia	C,EL,HA
Banksia solandri	B,NI,O
Banksia sp	AU,CA
Banksia speciosa	B,C,EL,NI,O
Banksia sphaerocarpa v caesia	B,NI,O
Banksia sphaerocarpa v sphaerocarpa	B,NI,O
Banksia spinulosa	EL,SA,SH
Banksia spinulosa v collina	B,HA,NI,O
Banksia spinulosa v neoanglica	O
Banksia spinulosa v spinulosa	B,HA,NI,O
Banksia telmatiaea	B,NI,O
Banksia tricuspis	B,NI,O
Banksia verticillata	B,NI,O
Banksia victoriae	B,EL,NI,O
Banksia violaceae	B,EL,NI,O,SA
Baphia massaiensis	B,SA,SI
Baptisia australis	AB,AP,B,BS,C,CG,DD, DE,G,HP,HU,JE,NG,LG, PK,PL,PR,SA,SC,SE,T
Baptisia australis 'Exaltata'	HP
Baptisia bracteata	B,JE
Baptisia lactea	AP,B,JE,PR,SA,SG
Baptisia leucantha see B.lactea	
Baptisia leucophaea see B.bracteata	
Baptisia pendula	B,JE,NT,SA
Baptisia sphaerocarpa	B,PK
Baptisia tinctoria	B
Barbarea intermedia	B
Barbarea orthoceras variegata	SG
Barbarea sp	KL
Barbarea stricta	SG
Barbarea verna	B,DD,KS
Barbarea vulgaris	B,G

BARBAREA

Barbarea vulgaris 'Variegata'	AP,C,HP,I,P
Barklya syringifolia	AU,B,EL,HU,O
Barleria buxifolia	B
Barleria cristata	B
Barleria longiflora	B
Barleria obtusa	B,C,KB,SC,SI
Barleria prionitis	B
Barleria saxatilis	B,KB
Barleria sp	BH,SI
Barnardiella spiralis	SI
Barringtonia aculatangula	B,HA
Bartlettina sordida see Eupatorium	
Bartschella schumannii	B,BC,DV,Y
Bartschella schumannii v globosa	BC,DV
Bartsia alpina	B,C
Basella alba	B,FW
Basella alba 'Rubra'	B
Bassia scoparia 'Evergreen'	AP,B,BS,SK,T
Bassia scoparia f trichophylla	AP,BD,BS,BY,C,CL,D,F,
	FR,J,KI,KS,L,MO,PI,
	PK,S,SK,ST,T,TU,V,YA
Bauhinia acuminata	B,SA
Bauhinia alba	EL,HA,O,RE,SA,TT
Bauhinia carronii	HA
Bauhinia galpinii	B,C,CA,EL,HA,HU,RS,
	O,SA,SI,WA
Bauhinia hookeri	EL,HA,SA
Bauhinia monandra	B,CA,DD,EL
Bauhinia natalensis	B,KB,O,SI
Bauhinia petersiana	B,SI
Bauhinia petersiana ssp serpae	B,WA
Bauhinia purpurea	B,CA,DV,EL,HU,FW,
	LN,SA,TT,VE
Bauhinia purpurea variegata	DV,HA,O,VE
Bauhinia racemosa	B,EL,HA,HU,SA
Bauhinia retusa	B,EL,HA,SA
Bauhinia rufescens	B
Bauhinia scandens	B,EL
Bauhinia sp	RE,T,V
Bauhinia tomentosa	B,EL,KB,O,SI
Bauhinia vahlii	B
Bauhinia variegata	B,DD,EL,FW,HA,LN,
	SA,WA
Bauhinia variegata 'Candida'	B,C,CA,EL,LN,SA,WA
Bauhinia x blakeana	B
Bauhinia yunnanensis	T
Beaucarnea see Nolina	
Beaufortia elegans	B,NI
Beaufortia heterophylla	B,NI
Beaufortia incana	B,EL,NI,O,SA
Beaufortia macrostemon	B,NI
Beaufortia micrantha	B,NI,O
Beaufortia micrantha v empetrifolia	B,NI,O
Beaufortia orbifolia	B,NI,O
Beaufortia purpurea	B
Beaufortia schaueri	B,NI,O
Beaufortia sparsa	B,C,EL,NI,O,SA
Beaufortia squarrosa	B,NI,O
Beaumontia grandiflora	B,C,CA,SA
Beccariophoenix madagascariensis	B,EL
Becium grandiflorum v obovatum	B,SI
Beckmannia eruciformis	B,CG,HP
Beckmannia syzigachne	B,SG
Begonia conchaefolia	CG
Begonia Container/Hanging Basket Mix	T
Begonia crassicaulis	DV

Begonia dregei	SG
Begonia elatior f1 'Charisma' s-c	CL,MO,YA
Begonia f1 'All Round Series' s-c	BS,MO,SK,YA
Begonia f1 fib 'Ascot' br.leaf s-c,mix	BS
Begonia f1 fib 'Ascot Complete' mix	BS
Begonia f1 fib 'Ascot' s-c,mix	BS
Begonia f1 fib 'Expresso' mix p.s	MO
Begonia f1 fib 'Focus' s-c,mix	BS
Begonia f1 fib 'Hi-fi' Series	BS,MO
Begonia f1 fib 'Hi-fi' Series p.s	MO
Begonia f1 fib 'Lotto' Series p.s	MO
Begonia f1 fib 'Olympia' mix p.s	MO
Begonia f1 fib 'President' mix p.s	MO
Begonia f1 fib 'Rio' mix	BS
Begonia f1 fib 'Royale'	MO
Begonia f1 fib 'Senator' mix p.s	MO,SK
Begonia f1 fib 'Vision' Series p.s	MO
Begonia f1 hyb 'Marshall's Fantasy'	M
Begonia f1 'Illumination Apricot'	BS,C,CL,MO,SE,SK,YA
Begonia f1 'Illumination' mix	C,DE,L
Begonia f1 'Illumination Orange'	BS,C,CL,KI,MO,SE,SK,
	V,YA
Begonia f1 'Illumination Pink'	BS,C,CL,KI,MO,PK,SE,
	SK,YA
Begonia f1 'Inferno Series' mix	BS,DT
Begonia f1 'Inferno Series' s-c	DT,YA
Begonia f1 tub 'Bl. & Lang. basket mix	MO
Begonia f1 tub 'Bl. & Langdon's dbl mix	MO
Begonia f1 tub 'Lorraine Love-Me'	BS,CL,MO
Begonia fib f1 'Devil' mix	CL
Begonia fib f1 'Devil Series' s-c	CL
Begonia fib mix o-p	S
Begonia fib 'Scarlanda'	CA
Begonia fib 'Scarletta'	SK
Begonia fib 'Sunshine Carpet'	CO,KI,ST
Begonia fib 'Tausendschoen' Series s-c	SK
Begonia fib 'Total Victory' mix	CA,DT
Begonia fib 'Varsity' s-c	SK
Begonia foliosa v miniata 'Rosea'	B
Begonia grandis ssp evansiana	B,C,HU,I,SC
Begonia grandis ssp evansiana v alba	B,C,I
Begonia hirtella	DV
Begonia incana	CG
Begonia leptotricha	CG,SG
Begonia limmingheiana see B.radicans	
Begonia lindleyana	CG
Begonia masoniana	B,C
Begonia metallica	HP
Begonia nelumbiifolia	SG
Begonia partita 'Bonsai'	C,DV
Begonia peltata	DV
Begonia pendula f1 'Finale' mix	CL
Begonia pendula f1 'Musical' mix	BD,CL,YA
Begonia pendula 'Happy End'	BD,BS,C,DT,MO,R,V
Begonia pendula mix h-p	BL
Begonia pendula 'Picotee' mix h-p	BL
Begonia pendula 'Pink Avalanche'	SK
Begonia pendula 'Show Angels' p.s	SK
Begonia pendula 'Show Angels' s-c	SK
Begonia petisitifolia	CG
Begonia radicans	DV
Begonia rex	B,DT,F,V
Begonia rex f1 'Colorvision'	BD,BS,C,DE,L,MO,PK,
	SK
Begonia rex 'Imperial'	CL
Begonia sanguinea	CG

BEGONIA

Begonia schmidtia	CG
Begonia semp 'Atlanta' s-c p.s	U
Begonia semp Crown mix	BS
Begonia semp dw mix	D
Begonia semp f1 'Alpha Series' s-c, mix	BS,MO,YA
Begonia semp f1 'Ambassador' mix	BS,D,MO,SK
Begonia semp f1 'Ambassador' mix p.s	D,MO,SK
Begonia semp f1 'Ambassador Series' s-c	BS,MO,SK,YA
Begonia semp f1 'Ambra Mix'	BS,YA
Begonia semp f1 'Ambra Mix' s-c	BS
Begonia semp f1 'Bella Vista'	J,TU
Begonia semp f1 'Bellavista Mix'	BS,YA
Begonia semp f1 'Bellavista' s-c	BS
Begonia semp f1 'Cocktail' c.s	BS,MO,S,SK
Begonia semp f1 'Cocktail' s-c/mix	CA,CN,MO,PK,SK
Begonia semp f1 'Coco Mix'	T
Begonia semp f1 'Devon Gems' c.s	S
Begonia semp f1 'Excel' mix	F,J,T
Begonia semp f1 'Expresso' s-c, mix	BS,MO,YA
Begonia semp f1 'Kalinka'	CL
Begonia semp f1 'Lotto' mix	BS
Begonia semp f1 'Lotto' s-c	BS,MO,PK,SK
Begonia semp f1 'New Generation' mix	D
Begonia semp f1 'Olympia' mix	CL,J,KI,L,MO,SE,SK
Begonia semp f1 'Olympia' red	CN,MO,SK
Begonia semp f1 'Olympia' s-c	CL,D,FR,L,MO,SK
Begonia semp f1 'Olympia' s-c c.s	CL,MO,S
Begonia semp f1 'Olympia' white	CL,CN,D,MO,SK,U
Begonia semp f1 'Options'	T
Begonia semp f1 'Organdy' mix	BD,BS,BY,CA,CL,CN,D, DT,F,J,L,MO,R,SE,SK,V
Begonia semp f1 'Organdy' p.s	BD,CL,MO
Begonia semp f1 'Party' Series s-c	CA,MO
Begonia semp f1 'Partyfun' mix	BS,C,J
Begonia semp f1 'Partyfun' mix p.s	MO
Begonia semp f1 'Pizzazz'	PK
Begonia semp f1 'President Mix'	BS,MO,T,YA
Begonia semp f1 'Royale' p.s	CL
Begonia semp f1 'Senator Series' s-c	BS,MO,YA
Begonia semp f1 'Symphony Mix'	YA
Begonia semp f1 'Total Victory Series' p.s	CL
Begonia semp f1 'Total Victory Series' s-c	CL
Begonia semp f1 'Treasure Trove'	S
Begonia semp f1 triploid 'Rusher Red'	C
Begonia semp f1 'Victory Series' s-c, gr lf	BS,CL,DT,PI
Begonia semp f1 'Vision' s-c, mix	BS,MO
Begonia semp f1 'Viva'	CA,SK
Begonia semp f1 'Wings'	BS,KI
Begonia semp 'Festival Dw'	BS
Begonia semp 'Happy Choice'	BS
Begonia semp 'Indian Maid'	BS,MO
Begonia semp 'Mardi Gras'	U
Begonia semp mix	BY,C,DT,VH
Begonia semp mix o-p	DT,SU
Begonia semp 'Paint Splash' (V)	DT,T
Begonia semp 'Pink Sundae'	F
Begonia semp 'Roselyn'	U
Begonia semp 'Scarlet Bedder'	D
Begonia semp 'Summer Rainbow'	F
Begonia semp 'Supernova Mix'	CL
Begonia sempeflorens o-p	BD,FR,MO
Begonia semperflorens alba	DV
Begonia semperflorens 'Feuermer'	DV
Begonia semperflorens 'Flamingo'	DV
Begonia semperflorens 'Papillon Rouge'	DV
Begonia semperflorens 'Rote Perle'	DV

Begonia semperflorens 'Trophee Rose'	DV
Begonia semps f1 'Cocktail'	BS,C,D,F,J,KI,L,SE,V
Begonia semps f1 'Colorita Mix'	YA
Begonia semps f1 'Danica Scarlet'	T
Begonia semps f1 'Kalinka' s-c	YA
Begonia semps f1 'Royale' mix	BS,CL
Begonia semps f1 'Stara'	S,U
Begonia semps f1 'Thousand Wonders'	KI
Begonia semps f1 'Victory' s-c, br. leaf	BS,CL,DT
Begonia sp	HU,SI
Begonia sp mix Malaysian	C
Begonia sutherlandii	C,I,P,SI
Begonia tub choice prize dbl	L
Begonia tub, f1 'Clips' mix	BS,CL,L,MO,PK,T
Begonia tub, f1 'Fortune Series' s-c	T,YA
Begonia tub, f1 'Galaxy'	BS,MO,YA
Begonia tub f1 giant hyb mix	C
Begonia tub f1 'Memory'	BS,CL,MO
Begonia tub f1 'Midnight Beauty'	PK
Begonia tub f1 'Musical'	BS,L,MO
Begonia tub, f1 'Nonstop' mix	BS,C,CA,CL,CN,D,DT,J, KI,L,MO,R,SE,SK,T,V,YA
Begonia tub, f1 'Nonstop' mix p.s	BD,CL,MO,S,SK
Begonia tub, f1 'Nonstop Orn.' mix	BS,CL,DT,F,MO,SK
Begonia tub, f1 'Nonstop Orn.' mix p.s	CL,D,L
Begonia tub, f1 'Nonstop Ornament' s-c	BS,CL,SK
Begonia tub, f1 'Nonstop' s-c	BS,C,L,MO,SE,SK,T
Begonia tub f1 'Panorama' p.s	CL
Begonia tub f1 'Panorama' s-c/mix	BS,CL,MO
Begonia tub f1 'Pin-Up'	BS,C,CL,KI,L,MO,O,PK, SK,V
Begonia tub f1 'Pin-Up' c.s	S,SK
Begonia tub f1 'Royal Harlequin'	BS,L,MO,SE
Begonia tub f1 'Royal Picotee'	BS,DT,L,MO,T
Begonia tub, f1 'Show Angels' mix	BD,BS,DT,MO,PK,SE, SK,T
Begonia tub 'Fortune' s-c,mix	SK
Begonia tub 'Fortunes' p.s	SK
Begonia tub tub mix	CA
Begonia un-named sp ex-Sabah	C
Begonia venosa	CG,DV,SG
Begonia vitifolia	CG
Behria tenuiflora	B,SW
Beilschmiedia tawa	B
Belamcanda chinensis	AP,C,CG,DE,E,EL,G,JE, KL,LG,KS,NT,PO,SA,SC
Belamcanda mix	T
Bellardia trixago	B
Bellendena montana	B,O,SA
Bellevalia dalmatica	B
Bellevalia dubia	AP,AR,B,LG,MN
Bellevalia forniculata	AR
Bellevalia hackelii	AP,B
Bellevalia hackelii MS439 Portugal	MN
Bellevalia kurdistanica	AR
Bellevalia longipes	AR
Bellevalia longistyla	AR
Bellevalia paradoxa	AP,KL,NG,PM,SC
Bellevalia pycnantha	AR,KL
Bellevalia pycnantha h. see B.paradoxa	
Bellevalia rixii	AR
Bellevalia romana	AP,AR,B,G,KL,NG,SG
Bellevalia romana JCA523	MN
Bellevalia sarmatica	SG
Bellevalia sp	KL
Bellevalia sp Jordan	MN

BELLEVALIA

Bellevalia webbiana	AR
Bellida graminea	B,NI,O
Bellidiastrum mitchelli	SG,VO
Bellis annua 'White Stars'	B
Bellis caerulescens 'Lilac Pixie'	B
Bellis perennis	AB,B,BY,C,DI,FR,JE, SU,V
Bellis perennis 'Buttons Box' s-c	YA
Bellis perennis 'Buttons' mix	BS,BY,CO,DT
Bellis perennis 'Carpet Bright'	C,T
Bellis perennis 'Carpet' dbl mix	BS,CL,KI,MO,S,SU
Bellis perennis 'Carpet' s-c	B,BS,C,CL,MO
Bellis perennis 'Clutch of Pearls'	U
Bellis perennis 'Crown Double Mix'	KI
Bellis perennis 'Galaxy' p.s.	YA
Bellis perennis 'Galaxy' Series s-c/mix	B,BS,MO
Bellis perennis giant mix	D,U
Bellis perennis 'Goliath'	F,S,T
Bellis perennis 'Grandiflora dbl' s-c, mix	SK
Bellis perennis 'Habanera' mix	CL,D,DT,KI,L,MO
Bellis perennis 'Habanera' s-c	B,BS,CL,J,MO,PL,S, SE,SK
Bellis perennis 'Kito Cherry Pink'	B,T
Bellis perennis 'Medici Button'	BS,F,TU
Bellis perennis 'Medicis Red'	BS,KI
Bellis perennis 'Medicis' s-c	BS,YA
Bellis perennis 'Miniature Buttons' s-c	L,SK
Bellis perennis 'Monstrosa Double' mix	BS,CL,DE,J,TU,V,VY
Bellis perennis 'Monstrosa' s-c	BS,BY,CL
Bellis perennis 'Pomponette' mix	BD,BS,C,CL,J,JE,MO, T,V
Bellis perennis 'Pomponette Pink Buttons'	D
Bellis perennis 'Pomponette' s-c	B,BS,CL,CN,JE,MO
Bellis perennis 'Radar' mix	BD,BS,MO
Bellis perennis 'Radar' s-c	B,BS,MO
Bellis perennis 'Robella'	B,BS,MO,O
Bellis perennis 'Rosina'	SE
Bellis perennis 'Spring Star'	S
Bellis perennis 'Super Enorma Salmon'	B,C
Bellis perennis 'Super Enorma' mix	BS,DT,L,PK,R
Bellis perennis 'Super Enorma' s-c	B,BS
Bellis perennis Super Giant Fl	M
Bellis perennis 'Swift'	BS
Bellis perennis 'Tasso' mix	B,BS,CL,MO
Bellis perennis 'Tasso' s-c	B,BS,CL,MO
Bellis perennis wild type	HU
Bellis sylvestris	SG
Bellium bellidioides	B,KL
Bellium minutum 'Fairy Princess'	B
Benincasa hispida v chieh-que	B
Benkara malabarica	B
Bensoniella oregana	AP,G,SC,SG
Bentinckia nicobarica	B
Berardia subacaulis	B,C,JE
Berberidopsis corallina	B,SA
Berberis aetnensis	CG
Berberis aggregata	A,B,C,SA,SG
Berberis amurensis	B,CG,SG
Berberis angulosa	SG
Berberis aquifolium see Mahonia	
Berberis arido-calida	RH
Berberis aristata	A,RH,SA
Berberis asiatica	A,SA
Berberis beanianii	CG,SG
Berberis bergmanniae	SA
Berberis brachypoda	B,CG,SG

Berberis bretschneideri	SG
Berberis buchananii tawangensis	SG
Berberis buxifolia	AU,SA
Berberis centiflora	SG
Berberis chinensis	B,CG
Berberis chitra	SG
Berberis congestiflora	SA
Berberis consimilis	SG
Berberis coxii	SA
Berberis crataegina	SG
Berberis darwinii	A,B,C,RH,SA
Berberis dasystachya	SG
Berberis dictiophylla	B,RH
Berberis dictiophylla v epruinesa	SG
Berberis dielsiana	B,SG
Berberis dolichobotrys	B
Berberis edgeworthiana	SG
Berberis faxoniana	SG
Berberis francisci-ferdinande	B
Berberis fremontii	B,SW
Berberis fremontii x haematocarpa	B,SW
Berberis gagnepainii v lanceifolia	B,C,CG,SA,SG,VE
Berberis georgei	SG
Berberis gilgiana	CG
Berberis globosa	SG
Berberis hakodate	CG
Berberis henryana	SG
Berberis heteropoda	SG
Berberis honanensis	SG
Berberis hookeri	CG,SG
Berberis hypokerina	SG
Berberis integerrima	SG
Berberis jaeschkeana v jaeschkeana	SG
Berberis jaeschkeana v usteriana	SG
Berberis jamesiana	CG,RH,SA,SG
Berberis julianae	B,C,CG,G,SA,VE
Berberis julianae 'Nana'	B,FW
Berberis kewensis	CG
Berberis koreana	B,CG,SG
Berberis lepidifolia	SG
Berberis linearifolium	SA
Berberis lycium	A,SA
Berberis mitifolia	CG
Berberis montana	SA
Berberis nervosa	AB,NO
Berberis oblonga	SG
Berberis phanera	SG
Berberis prattii	B
Berberis pruinosa	SG
Berberis regeliana	SG
Berberis repens	NO,SW
Berberis sherriffii	CG,RH,SG
Berberis sibirica	SG
Berberis ssp	SG
Berberis stiebritziana	SG
Berberis talliensis	SG
Berberis thunbergii	B,BS,FW,KL,LN,SA,SG, VE
Berberis thunbergii f atropurpurea	B,C,CA,CG,FW,KL,LN,N, SA,SG,T,VE
Berberis valdiviana	SA
Berberis veitchii	CG
Berberis vernus	B,CG
Berberis vulgaris	A,B,C,SA,SG,VE
Berberis vulgaris 'Atropurpurea'	B,SA
Berberis wilcoxii	B,SW

44

BERBERIS

Berberis wilsoniae	A,B,HP,RH,SA,SG	Betula fontinalis	B,FW,LN,NO,RH,SA,SG
Berberis wilsonii v subcaulialata	B	Betula fruticosa see B.humilis	
Berberis wisonii v stapfiana	SG	Betula glandulifera v glandulifera	SG
Berberis x mistabilis	SG	Betula glandulosa	B,FW,LN,RM,SG
Berberis x ottawnsis	SG	Betula globispica	SG
Berchemia discolor	B,SI	Betula grossa	SG
Berchemia zeyheri	B,WA	Betula humilis	RH,SG
Bergenia ciliata	B	Betula insignis	B,EL,N,SG
Bergenia cordifolia	B,BS,C,CL,CN,DE,JE,L,	Betula japonica	CA
	MO,PK,PL,SA,SK	Betula lenta	B,FW,LN,RH,SA,SG
Bergenia cordifolia new hybrids	JE	Betula litwinowii	B,FW,SA,SG
Bergenia cordifolia new winter Fl	B,D,JE,T,V	Betula maximowicziana	B,C,FW,LN,SA
Bergenia cordifolia 'Redstart'	B,T,V	Betula medwediewii	AP,RH,SG
Bergenia 'Glockenturm'	SG	Betula megrelica	SG
Bergenia purpurascens	B,C,JE,SA	Betula microphylla	SG
Bergenia purpurascens 'Rotblum'	JE	Betula mix Bonsai	C
Bergenia 'Silberlicht'	HP	Betula nana	AP,C,CG,KL,LN,SC,SG
Bergenia x crassifolia see B. x schmidtii		Betula neoalaskana	B,FW,LN
Bergenia x schmidtii	AP,B,SG	Betula nigra	B,C,CA,FW,LN,N,RH,SA,
Bergeranthus artus	B,DV		VE
Bergeranthus longisepalus	B,SI	Betula obscura	B,G,SG
Bergeranthus multiceps	B,DV	Betula occidentalis see B.fontinalis	
Bergeranthus scapiger	DV	Betula ovalifolia	SG
Bergerocactus emoryi	B	Betula papyrifera	A,AB,B,BH,C,CA,CG,EL,
Berkheya cuneata	B,SI		FW,LN,N,NO,RH,SA,SG,
Berkheya latifolia	B,SI		T,VE
Berkheya macrocephala	B,SI	Betula pendula	A,B,C,CA,CG,EL,FW,HA,
Berkheya maritima	B,C,SI		LN,SA,SG,T,V,VE,WA
Berkheya mutijuga	B,SI	Betula pendula 'Dalecarlica' hort see B.p. 'Laciniata'	
Berkheya purpurea	B,SI	Betula pendula 'Laciniata'	B
Berkheya setifera	B,SI	Betula pendula 'Purpurea'	B,BH,SA
Berkheya speciosa	B,SI	Betula pendula v pendula dissectum	FW
Berlandiera lyrata	B,JE,NO,SA,SW	Betula pendula 'Youngii'	B
Berrya cordifolia	B	Betula platyphylla	B,EL,FW,SG
Berrya javanica	B,EL	Betula platyphylla kamtschatica	B,LN,N,SA
Berula erecta	B	Betula platyphylla v japonica	B,C,FW,LN,SA,SG
Berzelia abrotanoides	B,KB,O,SI	Betula platyphyllum AC1731	X
Berzelia commutata	B,SI	Betula populifolia	B,FW,LN,RH,SA,SG
Berzelia galpinii	B,KB,SC,SI	Betula potaninii	SG
Berzelia intermedia	B,SI	Betula procurva	SG
Berzelia lanuginosa	B,KB,O,SA,SI	Betula pubescens	A,B,LN,SA,SG
Beschorneria calcicola	DV	Betula pubescens ssp carpatica v munthii	B,RH
Bessera elegans	B,SW	Betula raddeana	B,FW,SG
Bessera tuitensis	B	Betula rotundifolia	SG
Besseya alpina	B,RM,SW	Betula szechuanica	B,SG
Besseya bullii	B	Betula tatewakiana see B.ovalifolia	
Besseya wyomingensis	B,RM	Betula tianshanica	B,EL,FW,LN,N,SA
Beta 'McGregor's Favourite'	BS,C,TH	Betula tuskesanica	CG
Beta trigyna	AP,CG,HP	Betula uber	B
Beta vulgaris ssp cicla 'Bull's Blood'	B,BS,HP	Betula utilis	B,C,CG,FW,LN,N,SA,SG
Beta vulgaris ssp maritima	B	Betula utilis AC1824	X
Beta vulgaris strap leaved	BS	Betula utilis v jacquemontii	B,FW,LN,N,SA,SC
Betonica see Stachys		Betula x aschersoniana	SG
Betula alba see B.pendula		Biarum arundanum	AR
Betula albosinensis	B,C,EL,FW,LN,N,SA,SG	Biarum bovei	B
Betula alleghaniensis	B,C,FW,LN,RH,SG,VE	Biarum bovei S.B.L199 Morocco	MN
Betula alnoides	B,FW,LN	Biarum carratracense	AP,B
Betula apoiensis	SG	Biarum carratracense S.B.L217 Morocco	MN
Betula attractive bark sp	C	Biarum carratracense S.F226 Spain	MN
Betula chichibuensis	SG	Biarum carratracense S.F236 Spain	MN
Betula chinensis	B,FW,SA	Biarum dispar	B
Betula costata	AP,CA	Biarum dispar A.B.S4455 Morocco	MN
Betula davurica	B,EL,FW,LN,SA,SG	Biarum dispar A.B.S4613 Morocco	MN
Betula divaricataa	SG	Biarum dispar S.F265 Morocco	MN
Betula ermanii	B,C,CA,EL,FW,LN,SA	Biarum dispar S.L261 Tunisia	MN
Betula ermanii 'Grayswood Hill'	B,FW,N,SA	Biarum dispar S.L282 Tunisia	MN

BIARUM

Biarum dispar S.L290/2 Tunisia	MN	Blackstonia serotina	B
Biarum dispar S.L294 Tunisia	MN	Blaeria ericoides	B,SI
Biarum dispar v hispanica	B	Blancoa canescens	B,O
Biarum dispar v hispanica B.S465 Spain	MN	Blandfordia grandiflora	B,C,DD,EL,HA,O,SA
Biarum dispar v hispanica S.F226 Spain	MN	Blandfordia nobilis	O
Biarum dispar v hispanica S.F235 Spain	MN	Blandfordia punicea	AR,AU,B,C,NI,O,SA
Biarum frassianum	B	Blechnum brasiliense	B,EL
Biarum frassianum PB64 Greece	MN	Blechnum capense	B,G
Biarum idomenaeum	B	Blechnum cartilagineum	B,EL,SA
Biarum idomenaeum MS698 Crete	MN	Blechnum gibbum	B,SA
Biarum idomenaeum MS758 Crete	MN	Blechnum moorei	B
Biarum pyrami	B	Blechnum nudum	HA
Biarum pyrami PB238 Turkey	MN	Blechnum occidentale	B
Biarum pyrami PB253 Turkey	MN	Blechnum orientale	B
Biarum sp S.L185 Greece	MN	Blechnum patersonii	B,SA
Biarum tenuifolium	AP,B,SC	Blechnum spicant	B,KL
Biarum tenuifolium PB154 Greece	MN	Blechnum tabulare	C
Biarum tenuifolium S.B.L228 Morocco	MN	Blepharis maderaspatensis	B
Biarum zeleborei	B	Blepharocarya involucrigera	O
Biarum zeleborei Coll ref	MN	Blephilia ciliata	B,PR
Bidens aurea 'Bit Of Sunshine'	B,BS,MO,S	Blephilia hirsuta	B,PR
Bidens cernua	B,DD,PR	Bletilla striata	AP,HP,SG
Bidens connata	B,PR	Bletilla striata alba see B.s. f gebina	
Bidens coronata	B,PR	Bletilla striata f gebina	B
Bidens ferulifolia	HP,SG	Blighia sapida	B
Bidens ferulifolia 'Golden Goddess'	AP,B,BS,C,DT,F,HP,J,	Bloomeria crocea	AP,B,C,SC,SW
	MO,PK,T,U,V	Blossfeldia albida	DV
Bidens frondosa	SG	Blossfeldia campaniflora	DV
Bidens 'Golden Eye'	BS	Blossfeldia fechseri	B,DV,Y
Bidens humilis see B.triplinervia v macrantha		Blossfeldia flocculosa	Y
Bidens parviflore	SG	Blossfeldia grandiflora	BC,DV
Bidens pilosa	CG	Blossfeldia liliputana	B,CH,DV,GC,Y
Bidens sp	HU	Blossfeldia liliputana alba	BC,DV
Bidens tripartita	B,CG,SG	Blossfeldia minima	Y
Bidens triplinervia v macrantha	SZ	Blossfeldia pedicellata	DV,Y
Bidens vulgata	DD	Blossfeldia sp	C,DV
Bignonia capreolata	B	Blossfeldia subterranea	DV,Y
Bignonia tweediana	CA,EL,HA	Blossfeldia sucrensis	DV
Bijlia cana	B,DV,KB,SI,Y	Blossfeldia tarabucensis	DV
Bijlia tugwelliae	B	Blossfeldia tominense	DV
Billardiera bicolor	B,C,NI,O,SA	Blumea obliqua	B
Billardiera candida	B,NI	Blumenbachia insignis	B
Billardiera coeruleo-punctata	B,NI	Blumenbachia laterita	SG
Billardiera coriacea	B,NI	Blysmus compressus	SG
Billardiera cymosa	B,NI	Bobartia indica	B,SI
Billardiera drummondiana	B,NI	Bobartia longicyma v longicyma	B,SI
Billardiera erubescens	B,C,NI,SA	Bobartia robusta	B,SI
Billardiera floribunda	B,NI,O,SA	Bobartia sp	SI
Billardiera granulata	B,NI	Bochloe dactyloides	DE
Billardiera lehmanniana	B,NI	Boehmeria nivea	B
Billardiera longiflora	AU,B,DV,HP,NG,NI,O,	Boehmeria penduliflora	B
	P,SA,SC,SG	Boerhavia diffusa	B
Billardiera ringens	O	Boerhavia erecta	B
Billardiera sp prostrate	NI,SA	Boisduvalia densiflora	CG
Billardiera variifolia	B	Bolax glebaria see Azorella trifurcata	
Billardiera variifolia blue	NI,SA	Bolboschoenus maritimus	SG
Billbergia magnifica v escuticephala	SG	Bolivicereus samaipatanus	B,Y
Billbergia sp,cvs,&vars	B	Boltonia asteroides	B,G,PR,SA
Billtanthus beuckeri	B	Boltonia asteroides v laisquama	B,G,JE
Bischofia javanica	B,CA,EL,HA,SA	Boltonia asteroides v latisquama 'Nana'	C,JE
Bischofia polycarpa	SA	Boltonia decurrens	B,PR
Biscutella coronopifolia	B,SC	Bolusafra bituminosa	B,SI
Biscutella laevigata	AP,B,G,JE,KL,SC	Bolusanthus speciosus	B,BH,C,EL,HU,O,SA,SI,
Bismarckia nobilis	B,CA,EL,HA,O		WA
Bixa orellana	B,BS,C,EL,HA,HU,O,RE,	Bomarea caldasii	B,C,HP,PL
	SA,TT,WA	Bomarea edulis	SG

46

BOMAREA

Bomarea hirtella	PL
Bomarea lobbiana	B,C
Bomarea salsilla	AP,B,P,PL,SG
Bomarea 'Senorita'	B
Bombacopsis glabra	B
Bombacopsis quinata	B,RE
Bombax ceiba	B,DV,EL,HA,HU,O,SA
Bombax ellipticum	CA,DV
Bombax malabaricum see B.ceiba	
Bombax palmeri	DV
Bombax rhodhognaphalon	B,SA
Bonafousia longituba	B
Boophane haemanthoides	RU
Boophone disticha	C,CF
Boophone guttata	B,RU
Borago officinalis	B,CG,CN,CP,HU,KS,SD,
	SG,SU,TH
Borago officinalis 'Alba'	B,CN,NG,PL
Borago officinalis 'Bill Archer' (V)	B,NS
Borago pygmaea	AP,B,G,HP,SG,T
Borassus flabellifer	B
Borojoa patinoi	B
Boronia caerulescens	B
Boronia crenulata	AU,B,NI,O,SA
Boronia crenulata v gracilis	B,NI,O
Boronia cymosa	AU,B,NI,O
Boronia denticulata	B,NI,O,SA
Boronia dichotoma	B,NI
Boronia falcifolia	B,NI,O
Boronia fastigiata	AU,B,NI
Boronia glabra	B
Boronia heterophylla	B,C,NI,O,SA
Boronia inornata	B,NI,O
Boronia ledifolia	B,EL,O,SH
Boronia ledifolia v glabra	HA
Boronia megastigma	AU,B,C,EL,O,SA
Boronia microphylla	HA
Boronia molloyae	B,NI
Boronia ovata	B,NI
Boronia pinnata	B,EL,HA,NI,O,SH
Boronia ramosa	B,EL,NI,O,SA
Boronia rosmarinifolia	B,NI,O,SA
Boronia spathulata	B,NI,O
Boronia stricta	B,NI,O
Boronia ternata v elongata	B,NI,O
Boronia viminea	B,NI,O
Borrichia frutescens	B
Boscia albitrunca	B,C,SA,SI,WA
Boscia foetida	B,SI
Boscia mossambicensis	B,SA,SI
Bossiaea aquifolium	B,NI,SA
Bossiaea dentata	B,NI,SA
Bossiaea ensata	B,HA,NI
Bossiaea eriocarpa	B,NI
Bossiaea foliosa	B,HA,NI
Bossiaea heterophylla	B,HA,NI
Bossiaea laidlawiana	B,NI
Bossiaea linophylla	B,C,NI,SA
Bossiaea obcordata	HA
Bossiaea ornata	B,NI,SA
Bossiaea preissii	B,NI
Bossiaea pulchella	B,NI,SA
Bossiaea rhombifolia	B,HA,NI
Bossiaea scolopendria	B,HA,NI
Bossiaea walkeri	B,NI
Bossiaea webbii	B,NI

Bothrichloa decipiens	HA
Bothrichloa ischaemum	B,C
Bothrichloa macra	HA
Bothrichloa petusa	B,EL
Bothriochloa insculpta	B
Bothriochloa pertusa	B
Botryostege bracteata see Elliottia	
Bouea macrophylla	B
Bouteloua aristidoides	B
Bouteloua curtipendula	B,C,CA,JE,PR,SA
Bouteloua gracilis	B,C,CA,DE,JE,NO,PR,
	SA
Bouteloua hirsuta	B,PR
Bouvardia glaberrima	B,SW
Bowenia serrulata	B,C,EL,HA,O
Bowenia spectabilis	EL,O
Bowenia 'Tinaroo'	O
Bowiea volubilis	B,DV,G,SG,SI,Y
Bowkeria citrina	B,SI
Bowkeria verticillata	B,SI
Boykinia aconitifolia	AP,B,DV,G,HP,P,SC,SG
Boykinia jamesii	B,JE,KL,SC
Boykinia rotundifolia	AP,B,CG,DV,HP,SC
Brabejum stellatifolium	B,SI
Brachiaria decumbens	B
Brachiaria humidicola	B
Brachiaria miliiformis	B,NI
Brachiaria mutica	B
Brachycarpaea juncea	B
Brachycereus nesiocactus	B
Brachychiton acerifolius	B,C,CA,EL,HA,LN,NI,O,
	SA,VE,WA
Brachychiton acuminatus	NI,O
Brachychiton australis	B,EL,O,SA
Brachychiton bidwillii	B,EL,O
Brachychiton discolor	B,C,CA,DV,EL,HA,LN,NI,
	O,SA,WA
Brachychiton diversifolius	B,DV,NI,O
Brachychiton gregorii	B,DV,NI,O,SA
Brachychiton paradoxum	O
Brachychiton populneus	B,CA,DV,EL,HA,LN,SA,
	VE,WA
Brachychiton rupestris	B,C,DV,EL,HA,NI,O,SA
Brachyglottis bellidioides	AU,B,SS
Brachyglottis bidwillii	B,SS
Brachyglottis cassinioides	B,SS
Brachyglottis greyii	B,SC,SS
Brachyglottis haasti	B,SS
Brachyglottis kirkii	B,SA
Brachyglottis lagopus	B,SS
Brachyglottis 'Moira Reid' (Dunedin Gr.)	HP
Brachyglottis monroi	AU,B,HP,SS
Brachyglottis repanda	B
Brachylaena discolor	SA,WA
Brachylaena discolor v discolor	B,SI
Brachylaena elliptica	B,BH
Brachylaena neriifolia	B,SI
Brachylaena rotundata	B,SI
Brachyloma daphnoides	HA
Brachypodium pinnatum	B,SG
Brachypodium sylvaticum	B,JE,SA,SG
Brachyscome ciliaris ssp ciliaris	B,NI,O
Brachyscome iberidifolia	BD,BS,BY,C,CO,D,DE,
	DI,DT,HU,KI,L,MO,NI,
	,SA,SG,ST,SU,T,TH,TU
Brachyscome iberidifolia 'Blue Star'	B,BD,BS,CL,D,F,HA,KS,

BRACHYSCOME

	M,MO,PK,S,T,U
Brachyscome iberidifolia 'Brachy Blue' dw	B,BS,C,HA,KI,MO,ST, VY,YA
Brachyscome iberidifolia 'Bravo' mix	BS,D,DT,F,PL,T,VH
Brachyscome iberidifolia 'Bravo' s-c	B,BS
Brachyscome iberidifolia 'Gleam Blue'	C
Brachyscome iberidifolia 'Splendour Blue'	B,BS,HA,JO,PK
Brachyscome iberidifolia 'Splendour mix'	BS,J,KS,V
Brachyscome iberidifolia 'Splend.r Purple'	B,BS,C,DT,F,HA,J,T,V,VH
Brachyscome iberidifolia 'Splendour Violet'	B,BS,C,SK
Brachyscome iberidifolia 'Splend.r White'	B,BD,BS,CL,D,DT,F, HA,MO,PK,SK,T
Brachyscome iberidifolia 'Starshine' mix	HA
Brachyscome iberidifolia 'Summer Skies'	F
Brachyscome latisquamata	B,C,NI,O
Brachyscome rigidula	AP,B,SC,SG
Brachyscome sinclairii	B,SS
Brachysema latifolium	B,NI,SA
Brachystegia glaucescens	B,SI
Brachystegia spiciformis	B,SA,SI
Brachystelma caffrum	DV
Brachystelma circinatum	B,SI
Brachystelma meyerianum	B,SI
Brachystelma pygmaeum ssp pygmaeum	B,SI
Bracteantha bracteata	AB,AP,AU,B,BU,CG,DI, HA,O,R,SD,SG
Bracteantha bracteata alba	B,SG
Bracteantha bracteata 'Bikini Bright'	BS,BY,C,CL,CO,D,DT, HA,KI,MO,PK,S,T,VY,YA
Bracteantha bracteata 'Bikini Crimson'	C
Bracteantha bracteata 'Bikini Golden'	C
Bracteantha bracteata 'Bikini Hot'	C,S,T,VY
Bracteantha bracteata 'Bikini' mix	JO,KS
Bracteantha bracteata 'Bikini' s-c	B,C
Bracteantha bracteata 'Chico' mix	BS,MO
Bracteantha bracteata 'Chico' s-c	BS
Bracteantha bracteata 'Coco'	AP,HP
Bracteantha bract. 'Dargan Hill Monarch'	T
Bracteantha bracteata dbl	BS,CA,CO,DT,FR,HA, J,ST,TU
Bracteantha bracteata 'Drakkar Pastel'	BS,DT,F,M
Bracteantha b. 'Frost. Sulphur/ Silv. Rose'	F,JO,SK,T,V
Bracteantha bracteata 'Golden Sun'	BS,BY
Bracteantha bracteata 'Icicle Mix'	SE
Bracteantha bracteata 'King Size' mix	BD,BS,CN,HA,KS,MO, NI,O
Bracteantha bracteata 'King Size New' s-c	B,BS,C,MO
Bracteantha bracteata 'King Size' s-c	B,BS,C,KS,MO
Bracteantha b. 'King Size Tall Choice mix'	BS,C,F,S
Bracteantha b. 'M.'s Dbl Swiss Giant Mix'	M
Bracteantha bracteata mix dbl	BS
Bracteantha bracteata mix Dutch	DE
Bracteantha bracteata mix dw	BS,BU,F,NI,PI
Bracteantha bracteata mix tall	DN,PI
Bracteantha bracteata 'Monstr. Dbl' Mix	B,D,MO,YA
Bracteantha bracteata 'Monstrosum Mix'	BS,L,T
Bracteantha bracteata 'Monstrosum' s-c	BS,BY,KI,L,PK,SU,VY
Bracteantha b. 'Monstr. Tetra. Dbl Mix' s-c	T
Bracteantha bracteata 'New Select' s-c	BS
Bracteantha bracteata 'Pastel'	BS,D,KS,MO,PK,S,T
Bracteantha bracteata 'Pastel Sombrero'	U
Bracteantha bracteata 'Rosa'	V
Bracteantha bracteata 'Spangle' mix dw	BS
Bracteantha bracteata special	JO,SK
Bracteantha b. 'Standard Series' s-c	B
Bracteantha bracteata 'Sultane' s-c	BS,MO
Bracteantha bracteata 'Swiss Giants'	BS,U
Bracteantha bracteata v albidum	B
Bracteantha bracteata v macranthum	B
Bracteantha bracteata v viscosum	B
Bracteantha bracteatam 'Paper Daisy'	BS,KI
Bracteantha subundulata	AP,AU
Brahea armata	B,CA,EL,O
Brahea brandegeei	CA
Brahea dulcis	CG
Brahea edulis	B,CA,EL,O
Brasilicactus graesneri	DV,Y
Brasilicactus graesneri v aureiflorus	DV
Brasilicactus haselbergii	B,DV,Y
Brasilicactus haselbergii v albolanatus	DV
Brasilicactus haselbergii v haseltonianus	DV
Brasilicactus haselb. v pseudograesneri	Y
Brasilicactus haselbergii v stellatus	DV,Y
Brassica nigra	HU
Brassica oleracea	TH
Brassica ol. f1 'Orn.Cabb.Bright Lights'	B
Brassica ol. f1 'Orn. Cabb. Cherry Sundae'	T
Brassica ol. f1 'Orn. Cabb. Osaka mix'	BS,CA,F,J,PI,SK
Brassica oleracea f1 'Orn. Cabbage Tokyo'	BD,BS,CL,DE,F,KI,MO, YA
Brassica ol. f1 'Orn. K. Chidora' s-c	BS,PI,SK
Brassica oleracea f1 'Orn. Kale Kamone'	BS,CL
Brassica oleracea f1 'Orn. Kale' mix	BY,FR,L,M,S,ST,VY
Brassica oleracea f1 'Orn. K. Nagoya' mix	BS,C,CA,CL,MO,PK,SK, YA
Brassica ol. f1 'Orn. K. North. Lights' mix	TU
Brassica ol. f1 'Orn. K. North. Lights' s-c	CL,T
Brassica oleracea f1 'Orn. Kale Peacock' mix	BD,PK,T,U,V,VH
Brassica ol. f1 'Orn. Kale Peacock Red'	BS,CA,CL,KS,L,MO,PI, PK,SK
Brassica ol. f1 'Orn. Kale Peacock White'	BS,CA,CL,KS,L,MO,PI, PK,SK
Brassica ol. f1 'Orn. Kale Pidgeon' mix	BD,BS,MO,U
Brassica ol. f1 'Orn. Kale Pidgeon pink'	BS,MO
Brassica ol. f1 'Orn. Kale Pidgeon Red'	BS,MO
Brassica ol. f1 'Orn. Kale Sparrow' mix	BD
Brassica ol. f1 'Orn. Kale Sparrow Red'	BS,MO,SK
Brassica ol. f1 'Orn K. Sparrow White'	BS,MO,SK
Brassica oleracea f1 'Orn. Kale Sunrise'	KS
Brassica oleracea f1 'Orn. Kale Sunset'	KS
Brassica ol. Orn. Cabb. 'Color-Up' s-c, mix	PK
Brassica oleracea 'Orn. Cabb. Delight mix'	BS
Brassica oleracea 'Orn. Cabbage, mix'	B,BY,C,CO,D,KI,R,ST, SU,T,VH,VY
Brassica oleracea 'Orn Cabb.,white/green'	B
Brassica oleracea, orn f1 'Chidori' s-c	BS
Brassica oleracea 'Orn. K.Dec. Fringe Mix'	CO,BS
Brassica oleracea 'Orn. K. Feather Series'	CL,DN,PI
Brassica oleracea, orn. Kale 'Pigeon' white	PI
Brassica oleracea 'Orn. Kale,Tassels'	KI,SU
Brassica oleracea 'Orn. K. Winter Beauty'	DT
Brassica oleracea 'Orn. Nagoya' red	SK
Brassica oleracea 'Orn. Nagoya' rose	SK
Brassica oleracea 'Orn. Nagoya' white	SK
Brassica oleracea 'Orn. Osaka' pink	SK
Brassica oleracea 'Orn. Osaka' red	SK
Brassica oleracea 'Orn. Osaka' white	Sk
Brassica ol. f1 Or..K.Illumination' s-c,mix	BS
Brassica ol.orn.l Kale, 'Pidgeon white'	MO
Braunsia apiculata	B,SI
Breonadia salicina	B,KB
Breynia retusa	B

BREYNIA

Breynia vitis-idaea	B
Bridelia micrantha	B,SI,WA
Bridelia mollis	B,SI
Bridelia retusa	B
Briggsia muscicola	AP,C,SC
Brimeura amethystina	AP,AR,B,G,KL,NG,MN, PM,SC,SG
Brimeura amethystina alba	AP,NG,SC,SG
Brimeura fastigiata	AR
Brionia dioica	B
Briza maxima	AP,B,BY,C,CA,DE,G,HU, I,JO,KI,KS,L,MO,PI,PK, PM,SC,SK,SU,T,V,VY
Briza media	B,C,G,HP,LA,JE,SA, SC,SG,SU
Briza minor	B,C,CA,DD,HU,KS,L, MO,SG
Briza triloba	SG
Brodiaea albus roseus	MN
Brodiaea amoenas USA	MN
Brodiaea clavatus v avius	MN
Brodiaea coronaria	AP,B,JE,SG,SW
Brodiaea douglasii	C,JE,NO
Brodiaea elegans	B,LG,MN
Brodiaea minor violet	B
Brodiaea sp	AP,NG
Bromelia antiacantha	B
Bromelia balansae	B
Bromelia karatas	B
Bromelia pinguin	B
Bromopsis bebekenii	SG
Bromopsis inermis	SG
Bromopsis pumpelliana	SG
Bromus benekenii	SG
Bromus breviaristatus	B
Bromus briziformis	SG
Bromus canadensis	B
Bromus carinatus	B,DD
Bromus catharticus see B.unioloides	
Bromus ciliatus	PR
Bromus commutatis	SG
Bromus erectus	B,SA,SG
Bromus inermis	B
Bromus interruptus	SG
Bromus kalmii	B,PR
Bromus lanceolatus	B,C,CA,L,MO,SG,V
Bromus macrostachys see B.lanceolatus	
Bromus madritensis	B
Bromus marginata	B
Bromus mollis	B,CA
Bromus monocladus	SG
Bromus purgans	B,PR,SG
Bromus ramosus	B,C
Bromus rubens	B
Bromus secalinus	B
Bromus secalinus v velutinus	B
Bromus squarrosus	AP,B
Bromus sterilis	B,SG
Bromus unioloides	B,DE,SA
Brosimum alicastrum	B
Brosimum utile	B
Broussonetia papyrifera	B,C,EL,FW,HA,HU,VE
Browallia americana	G
Browallia americana 'Skyblue'	B
Browallia americana 'Snowwhite'	B
Browallia 'Bluetta'	YA

Browallia speciosa	SG
Browallia speciosa 'Amethyst'	B,C
Browallia speciosa 'Blue Bells'	BY,C,DE,HU
Browallia speciosa 'Blue Bells' imp	PK
Browallia speciosa 'Blue Troll'	B,BS,CA,CL,D,L,MO,PK, S,T,V
Browallia speciosa 'Daniella'	CL
Browallia speciosa 'Heavenly Bells'	B,BS,MO
Browallia speciosa 'Jingle Bells'	PK,S
Browallia speciosa 'Powder Blue'	PK
Browallia speciosa 'Silver Bells'	PK
Browallia speciosa 'Violetta'	CL
Browallia speciosa 'White Troll'	B,BS,C,CA,CL,DE,MO, PK,S
Browallia viscosa	SG
Browallia viscosa 'Sapphire'	B,D,J
Browallia viscosa 'Sapphire Reselected'	B
Browallia viscosa 'Starlight' mix	BS,SK
Browallia viscosa 'Starlight' s-c	BS,CO,KI,SK
Browningia candelaris	B,DV
Browningia hertlingianus	B,C,HU,Y
Brucea macrophylla	B
Bruckenthalia spiculifolia	AP,B,C,JE,KL,SC,SG
Bruckenthalia spiculifolia 'Alba'	KL
Brugmansia arborea	B,C,SA,V
Brugmansia aurea	C
Brugmansia candida x aurea	PL
Brugmansia Hairy Yellow Tree Datura	B
Brugmansia sanguinea	B,C,PL,T
Brugmansia suaveolens	AP,C,F,HP,JE,SC,T
Brugmansia versicolor	B
Brugmansia x candida pink	B,C
Brugmansia x candida white	B,C,CA,SA
Brugmansia x insignis pink	B
Brunfelsia americana	B
Brunfelsia australis	B
Brunfelsia floribunda	CA
Brunfelsia grandiflora ssp schultesii	B
Brunfelsia jamaicensis	B
Brunfelsia lactea	B
Brunfelsia latifolia	B,C,EL,HA
Brunfelsia pauciflora	B,SA
Brunfelsia pauciflora 'Floribunda'	B,C
Brunfelsia sp	SG
Brunfelsia undulata	B
Brunia albiflora	B,KB,SA,SI
Brunia alopecuroides	B,SI
Brunia laevis	B,SI
Brunia nodiflora	B,SI
Brunia stokoei	B,SI
Brunnera macrophylla	B,HP
Brunnichia cirrosa	B
Brunonia australis	B,C,NI,O,SA
Brunsvigia appendiculata	B,RU
Brunsvigia bosmanii	B,RU
Brunsvigia comptonii	B
Brunsvigia gregaria	CF
Brunsvigia litoralis	RU
Brunsvigia minor	B,RU
Brunsvigia orientalis	B,CF,RU
Bryonia alba	G,SG
Bryonia dioica	B,G,HU
Buchaniana axillaris	B
Buchaniana obovata	B,NI
Buchloe dactyloides	AV,B,CA,DI,JE,NO,PR
Bucida buceras	B,SA

BUCKINGHAMIA

Buckinghamia celsissima	B,EL,HA,NI,O,SA
Buddleja albiflora	B,G
Buddleja alternifolia	LN,SA
Buddleja asiatica	B
Buddleja australis	SG
Buddleja 'Butterfly'	B,BD,BS,L,MO,PL
Buddleja colvilei	B
Buddleja davidii	B,C,CA,CN,F,FW,HU,J,
	LN,PK,RH,SA,SU,T,V,VE
Buddleja davidii 'Black Knight'	HP
Buddleja davidii 'Royal Red'	HP
Buddleja davidii v nanhoensis alba	HP
Buddleja davidii violet	PK,SK
Buddleja fallowiana	B
Buddleja fallowiana AC1483	X
Buddleja forrestii AC1339	X
Buddleja globosa	B,C,SA,SG
Buddleja glomerata	B
Buddleja lindleyana	B,CG,SA
Buddleja longiflora	SA
Buddleja loricata	B,SI
Buddleja saligna	B,SI
Buddleja salviifolia	B
Buddleja sp AC1200	X
Buglossoides purpureocaeruleum	B,JE,SA
Buiningia aurea	B,DV,Y
Buiningia brevicylindrica	B,Y
Buiningia brevicylindrica v longispina	Y
Buiningia purpurea	Y
Bulbine abyssinica	B,DV,SI
Bulbine annua	B,DV
Bulbine bulbosa	AP,B,NI,SC
Bulbine caulescens see B.frutescens	
Bulbine frutescens	AP,B,BH,C,DV,HP,P,SI
Bulbine glauca	B
Bulbine haworthioides	B
Bulbine lagopus	B,SI
Bulbine latifolia	B,C,DV,KB,SI,Y
Bulbine margarethae	B,CH,DV,Y
Bulbine narcissifolia	B,SI
Bulbine praemorsa	B,RU
Bulbine sedifolia	B,SI
Bulbine semibarbata	CG,G,HP,KL,SC
Bulbine semibarbata 'Stargazer'	C
Bulbine sp	BH,SI
Bulbine torta	SI
Bulbine wiesei	B,RU
Bulbinella aloides	DV,SI
Bulbinella angustifolia	AP,B,CG,SA,SC,SS
Bulbinella cauda-felis	AP,B,KB,RU,SI
Bulbinella eburnifolia	B,SI
Bulbinella elata	B,SI
Bulbinella floribunda	B,BH,SZ
Bulbinella gibbsii	B,SS
Bulbinella graminifolia	B,RU
Bulbinella hookeri	AP,B,C,CG,G,JE,P,PM,
	SA,SC
Bulbinella latifolia	RU,SA
Bulbinella latifolia ssp doleritica	B,RU,SI
Bulbinella latifolia ssp latifolia	B,RU,SI
Bulbinella nutans	B,C,SA,SI
Bulbinella nutans v turfosicola	B,SI
Bulbinella punctulata	B,SI
Bulbinella sp	RU,SI
Bulbinella triquetra	B,SI
Bulbocodium vernum	AP,B,G,KL

Bulbophyllum bracteatum	B
Bulbophyllum elisae	B
Bumelia celastrina	B
Bumelia lycioides	CG
Bumelia tenax	B
Bunchosia argentea	B,EL
Bunias orientalis	B,CG,DD,G,JD,SG
Bunium bulbocastanum	B,C,DD,G
Buphthalmum salicifolium	B,CG,HP,JE,KL,SG,V
Buphthalmum salicifolium 'Alpengold'	B,JE
Buphthalmum salicifolium 'Sunwheel'	B,CA,SA
Bupleurum angulosum	AP,HP,KL
Bupleurum aureum	B,RM
Bupleurum falcatum	AP,G,HP,JE,SC,SG
Bupleurum fruticosum	B,C,HP,SA,VE
Bupleurum gibraltaricum	SA
Bupleurum longifolium	AP,G,HP,SC,SG
Bupleurum longifolium ssp aureum	JE,SA
Bupleurum multinerve	C,SG
Bupleurum petraeum	AP,B
Bupleurum ranunculoides	B,C,HP,JE,SA
Bupleurum rotundifolium	AP,C,CN,G,LG,SG,TH,V
Bupleurum rotundifolium 'Garibaldi'	B
Bupleurum rotundifolium 'Green Gold'	B,F,JO,KS,PK,T
Bupleurum rotundifolium 'Griffithii'	B,BS,DD,MO
Bupleurum rotundifolium 'Griffithii Decor'	C,DE,HU
Bupleurum stellatum	B
Bupleurum sylvatica	NG
Bupthalmnum salicifolium	T
Burbidgea schizocheila	B
Burchardia multiflora	B,NI
Burchellia bubalina	B,C,EL,KB,SA,SI,WA
Burkea africana	B,SA,SI,WA
Bursaria spinosa	AU,B,C,EL,HA,NI,SA
Bursaria spinosa r-v	EL,HA
Bursera aptera	DV
Bursera arborea	DV
Bursera arencis	DV
Bursera arida	DV
Bursera bolivari	DV
Bursera copalifera	DV
Bursera cuneata	DV
Bursera excelsis	DV
Bursera fagaroides	B,BC,DV,GC,Y
Bursera filicifolia	DD
Bursera galeotiana	DV
Bursera glabrifolia	DV
Bursera grandifolia	CH,DV
Bursera lancifolia	DV
Bursera longipes	DV
Bursera microphylla	B,SW
Bursera morelensis	DV
Bursera schlectendalii	DV
Bursera submoniliformis	DV
Bursera suntui	DV
Burtonia hendersonii	SA
Burtonia scabra	SA
Butea frondosa see B.monosperma	
Butea monosperma	B,EL,HA,SA
Butia capitata	B,C,CA,EL,FW,HA,LN,O,
	SA,VE
Butia eriospatha	CG
Butia yatay	B,C,EL,HA,SA
Butomis umbellatus	SG
Buxus microphylla v koreana see B.sinica v insularis	
Buxus sempervirens	B,C,CA,FW,G,LN,SA,VE

BUXUS

Buxus sempervirens 'Elegantissima'	B
Buxus sempervirens 'Suffruticosa'	B
Buxus sinica	SA
Buxus sinica v insularis	B,FW,SA
Byblis gigantea	B
Byblis liniflora	B,DV
Byblis liniflora ssp liniflora	B
Byblis liniflora ssp occidentalis	B,DV
Byrsonima crassifolia	B,RE
Byrsonima spicata	B
Cacalia glabra	AP,C,CG,HU,JE,SC
Cacalia sonchifolia	DI
Caccinia macranthera v crassifolia	SG
Caccinia strigosa	B
Cactus Chilean mix	CH
Cactus columnar	C
Cactus Crown mix	BS
Cactus mix	BD,C,CA,DE,DT,FR,FW, L,MO,PK,S,SK,SO,T,Y
Cactus Old Man mix	C
Cactus sp	V
Cactus Superfine mix	BS,J,U
Cadaba aphylla	B,SI
Cadaba fruticosa	B
Cadia purpurea	B
Caesalpinia bonduc	DD
Caesalpinia cacalaco	B,CA,HU
Caesalpinia californica	DD
Caesalpinia decapetala	DD
Caesalpinia ferrea	B,EL,HA,O,SA,WA
Caesalpinia gilliesii	B,C,CA,CG,DD,DV,EL, FW,JE,KL,O,SA,SW,T,VE
Caesalpinia mexicana yellow	CA,HU
Caesalpinia pulcherrima	B,BS,C,CA,DD,EL,HA, HU,O,RE,SA,SW,TT
Caesalpinia pulcherrima pink	C,CA
Caesalpinia regia	HA,VE
Cajanus cajan	B,DD,WA
Cajanus cinereus	B,NI
Cajophora acuminata 'Orange Supreme'	T
Cajophora coronata	KL,RS
Cajophora laterita	HP,HU
Cajophora laterita 'Frothy'	V
Cakile maritima	B
Caladenia sp	B
Calamagrostis arundinacea	B,SG
Calamagrostis brachytricha	B
Calamagrostis canadensis	B,PR
Calamagrostis epigioides	B
Calamagrostis rubescens	NO
Calamagrostis sp Canada	SG
Calamagrostis varia	SG
Calamagrostis villosa	SG
Calamagrostis x acutiflora	HP
Calamintha cretica	G,SC,SG
Calamintha grandiflora	AP,B,C,G,HP,JE,P,SA, SC,SG,T
Calamintha grandiflora 'Variegata'	B,HP,P
Calamintha nepeta	AP,B,CN,CP,G,JE,SA, SC,T,TH,V
Calamintha nepeta ssp glandulosa	B
Calamintha officinalis	CP
Calamintha sp	C
Calamintha sylvatica	B,C,DD,G,JE,NS
Calamus australis	B
Calamus caryatoides	O
Calamus discolor	O
Calamus moti	O
Calamus radicales	O
Calamus rotang	B
Calamus tenuis	B,SA
Calandrinia ciliata	B,I
Calandrinia compressa	B,SC
Calandrinia grandiflora	AP,B,C,HP,P,SC,SG,T
Calandrinia grandiflora 'Rosemarie'	D
Calandrinia 'Neon'	U
Calandrinia sericea alba	AP,P
Calandrinia umbellata	AP,B,BS,CL,EL,G,HU,J, JE,KI,KL,MO,S,SC,SG,V
Calandrinia umbellata amarantha	AP,C,SC,T
Calandrinia umbellata 'Ruby Tuesday'	B,HU,PK
Calathea crotalifera	B
Calathea inocephala	B
Calathea lancefolia	B,RE
Calathea lutea	B
Calceolaria alba	B,P
Calceolaria biflora	AP,B,C,G,HP,SC,SG
Calceolaria biflora 'Goldcap'	B,JE
Calceolaria biflora 'Goldcrest'	AP,HP,KL,MO
Calceolaria biflora 'Goldcrest Amber'	CN,SC,T,V
Calceolaria chelidonioides	C,I
Calceolaria crenatiflora	DD
Calceolaria crenatiflora 'Goldcut'	B
Calceolaria cymbiflora	B,P
Calceolaria darwinii	C,SG
Calceolaria ericoides	RS
Calceolaria f1 'Anytime'	BD,BS,C,CL,D,DT,F,J, MO,PK,S,SK,T,V
Calceolaria f1 'Bright Bikini'	C
Calceolaria f1 'Dainty'	CL,KI,T,YA
Calceolaria f1 'Melody'	CL
Calceolaria f1 'Memory'	L
Calceolaria falklandica	C,HP,JE,KL,SC
Calceolaria fiebrigiana	CG,JE
Calceolaria filicaulis	PM
Calceolaria fothergillii	AP,AU,C,RS,SC,SG
Calceolaria 'Gold Fever'	SK
Calceolaria gracilis	AP,PM
Calceolaria 'Grandiflora'	BS,BY,KI
Calceolaria helianthemoides	RS
Calceolaria hyssopifolia	RS
Calceolaria integrifolia	B,HP
Calceolaria integrifolia f1 'Cinderella'	BS,MO
Calceolaria integrifolia f1 'Dainty Mix'	BS,MO
Calceolaria integrifolia f1 'Goldari'	BS,MO,V
Calceolaria integrifolia f1 'Goldari' p.s	B,J
Calceolaria integrifolia f1 'Golden Bunch'	B,BS,CL,MO
Calceolaria integrifolia f1 'Sunset'	BS,CL,D,DT,EL,J,L,MO, PM,S,V,YA
Calceolaria integrifolia f1 'Sunshine'	B,BS,CL,DT,L,MO,S,YA
Calceolaria integrifolia f1 'Sunshine' p.s	CL
Calceolaria integrifolia 'Little Sweeties'	J,T
Calceolaria 'Jewel Cluster'	S
Calceolaria lagunae-blancae	RS
Calceolaria lanceolata	HP
Calceolaria lanigera	B,P,RS
Calceolaria mendocina	RS
Calceolaria mexicana	AP,B,NG,RS,SC
Calceolaria nivalis	RS
Calceolaria picta	B
Calceolaria purpurea	B,RS
Calceolaria sp	AP,RS,SC

CALCEOLARIA

Calceolaria tenella — B,I,PM,RS,SC
Calceolaria 'Tigered' dw mix — C,DE,FR,SK
Calceolaria tripartita — CG,RS,SC
Calceolaria volckmannii — RS
Calceolaria x banksii — HP
Calceolaris scabiosifolia — SG
Calea zacatachichi — B
Calendula arvensis — C,G,SG
Calendula 'Cheddar Dw' mix — PI
Calendula 'Golden Beauty' — SK
Calendula mix — C,FR
Calendula officinalis — A,AB,B,CA,CG,CN,CO,F, G,JE,RH,SD,SG,T,TH,V
Calendula officinalis 'Apricot Pygmy' — SE
Calendula officinalis 'Art Shades' — BD,BS,C,CO,DE,DT,F,J, KI,KS,L,MO,ST,T,V
Calendula officinalis 'Balls Apricot' — B
Calendula officinalis 'Balls Imp Orange' — B,BD,BS,MO
Calendula officinalis 'Balls Lemon' — B
Calendula officinalis 'Balls Long Orange' — B
Calendula officinalis 'Beauty Apricot' — C
Calendula officinalis 'Beauty Lemon' — C,SK
Calendula officinalis 'Beauty Pacific' — C,D,F,GO,HU,JO,SD,U, VY
Calendula officinalis 'Black Eyes' — F
Calendula officinalis 'Bon Bon' — CA,PK,SE,SK,VY
Calendula officinalis 'Bon Bon' s-c — SK
Calendula officinalis 'Campfire' — DT
Calendula officinalis 'Coffee Cream' — PL
Calendula off. 'Erfurter Orangefarbige' — JO
Calendula officinalis 'Fiesta Gitana' — B,BD,BS,C,CL,CN,CO,D, DN,DT,J,L,M,MO,S,SK, T,U,V,VY,YA
Calendula officinalis 'Geisha Girl' — F
Calendula officinalis 'Gitana Yellow' — S
Calendula officinalis 'Greenheart Gold' — B
Calendula officinalis 'Greenheart Orange' — B,DI,F,PI,T
Calendula officinalis 'Gypsy Festival' — BS,KI,TU
Calendula officinalis 'Hen & Chickens' — B,C,HU,KS,PI
Calendula officinalis 'Kablouna Golden' — B,KS
Calendula officinalis 'Kablouna Lemon' — T
Calendula officinalis 'Kablouna' mix — AB,BS,DE,DT,J,SD,T
Calendula officinalis 'Kablouna Orange' — B,DD,KS
Calendula officinalis 'King Golden' — BS
Calendula officinalis 'King Orange' — B,BS,BY,CO,J,KI,R,S,ST, V
Calendula officinalis mix dbl — BS,MO
Calendula officinalis mix dw — KS
Calendula officinalis 'Pacific Apricot' — B,S,SK,T
Calendula officinalis 'Pacific' mix — AB,BU,PI,SK,T,TE
Calendula officinalis 'Pink Surprise' — D
Calendula officinalis 'Prince Golden' — B,SK
Calendula officinalis 'Prince Indian' — B,D,HU,SK
Calendula officinalis 'Prince' mix — JO,PK
Calendula officinalis 'Prince Orange' — B,HU,SK
Calendula officinalis 'Princess Golden' — C,HU
Calendula officinalis 'Princess' mix — C,S
Calendula officinalis 'Prolifera' — B,C,P
Calendula officinalis 'Pygmy' mix — F
Calendula officinalis 'Queen Lemon' — S
Calendula officinalis 'Radio' — B,BS,BY,C,DE,KS,SE
Calendula officinalis 'Red Splash' — SD
Calendula officinalis 'Resina' — JO
Calendula officinalis single — KS
Calendula officinalis 'Tangerine Pink' — PL
Calendula officinalis 'Touch Of' s-c — DT,F,KS,PI,SE,SK,T

Calibanus hookeri — B,C,DV
Calla palustris — B,I,JE,KL
Calliandra anomala — B,HU
Calliandra calothyrsus — B,EL,HU,RE,SA,TT
Calliandra emarginata — B,EL
Calliandra eriophylla — B,C,CA,HU,SW
Calliandra haematocephala — B,EL
Calliandra hyb 'Rosea' — B,EL
Calliandra surinamensis — B,EL
Callianthemum anemonoides — KL
Callicarpa americana — B,EL,HU,FW,LN,SA
Callicarpa americana 'Lactea' — B,HU
Callicarpa bodinieri 'Profusion' — KL
Callicarpa dichotoma — B,FW,SA
Callicarpa japonica — B
Callicarpa japonica 'Leucocarpa' — B
Callicarpa mollis — B
Callicarpa pedunculata — B,EL
Callicoma serratifolia — B,C,HA,NI
Calligonum comosum — B
Callilepis laureola — B
Callirhoe involucrata — AP,B,G,HP,JE,RM,SC,T
Callirhoe involucrata v tenuissima — SZ
Callirhoe triangulata — B,PR
Callistachys lanceolata — B,NI
Callistemon brachyandrus — B,CA,EL,HA,O,SA,SC
Callistemon 'Buranda Station' — B
Callistemon 'Burgundy Supreme' — B
Callistemon citrinus — B,C,CA,DV,EL,HA,HP, LN,NI,O,RH,SA,SG,SH, V,VE
Callistemon citrinus 'Splendens' — AU,B,LN
Callistemon coccineus — DV
Callistemon comboynensis — B
Callistemon flavovirens — B,NI
Callistemon formosus — B,HA,O
Callistemon glaucus see C.speciosus
Callistemon 'Injune Pink' — B
Callistemon 'Jeffersii' — B
Callistemon lanceolatum see C.citrinum
Callistemon linearifolius — B,CA,DV,NI,O
Callistemon linearis — AU,B,C,EL,HA,N,NI,RH, SA,SG
Callistemon macropunctatus — DV,EL,HA
Callistemon montanus — B,DV,HA,O
Callistemon pachyphyllus — AU,B,EL,HA,NI,O
Callistemon pachyphyllus green — B,NI
Callistemon pallidus — AU,B,EL,HA,HP,NI,O,SA
Callistemon phoeniceus — AU,B,DV,EL,HA,NI,O, SA,SH
Callistemon pinifolius green — AU,CA,HA,NI
Callistemon pinifolius red — AU,B,EL,NI,SA
Callistemon pityoides — AU,B,NI,SG
Callistemon polandii — AU,B,EL,HA,NI,O,SH
Callistemon pungens 'Gilesii' — B
Callistemon 'Pygmy Pink' — B
Callistemon rigidus — B,CA,CG,EL,HA,HP,NI, RH,SA,VE,WA
Callistemon rugulosus — AU,B,NI
Callistemon salignus — B,C,CA,DV,EL,HA,NI,O, SA,SH,VE
Callistemon salignus 'Rubra' — B,EL,SA,SH
Callistemon sieberi — B,C,EL,HA,NI,O
Callistemon sieberi pink — B
Callistemon sp mix — C,EL,SG
Callistemon speciosus — AU,B,CA,EL,HA,LN,NI,

CALLISTEMON

	O,VE
Callistemon subulatus	AU,B,C,EL,HA,HP,SG,T
Callistemon teretifolius	AU,B,HA,NI
Callistemon viminalis	AU,B,C,CA,EL,HA,LN, NI,O,SA,SH,VE,WA
Callistemon viminalis 'Captain Cook'	B,EL,HA,N,SH
Callistemon viminalis 'Dawson River'	B
Callistemon viminalis nanus	SA
Callistemon violaceus	AU,B,CA,EL,NI,O
Callistemon viridiflorus	AP,AU,B,HA,O,P
Callistephus 'Bouquet'	B,BY
Callistephus chinensis	AB,B,BS,DD,DT,F,G, NO,SG,SP,TH,VY
Callistephus 'Colour Carpet'	BS,BY,DT,F,J,L,MO
Callistephus 'Comet' dw mix	BS,D,F,J,L,MO,PK,SE, SK,T
Callistephus 'Comet' dw s-c	B,BS,BY,CL,MO,SK
Callistephus 'Compliment' mix	BS,MO
Callistephus 'Compliment' s-c	B,BS,MO
Callistephus Cut Fl mix	BS
Callistephus 'Doe's'	BY
Callistephus 'Duchess' mix	BD,BO,BS,BY,CL,D,DT, FR,J,KI,M,MC,MO,R, S,T,TU,U,YA
Callistephus 'Dw Thousand Wonders' mix	C
Callistephus 'Early Dawn'	PI
Callistephus 'Fan' s-c,mix	BS
Callistephus 'Giant Comet'	BS,KI
Callistephus 'Giant Princess' mix	BS,BY,C,MO,SD,SK
Callistephus 'Ivica'	C
Callistephus 'Kamo' s-c	B
Callistephus 'Lilliput'	BS,CO,KI,MO,S,ST
Callistephus 'Lilliput' s-c	B
Callistephus 'Matsumoto' mix	B,BD,BS,C,J,JO,L,MO, PI,S,SK,TE,YA
Callistephus 'Matsumoto' s-c	B,C,SK
Callistephus 'Matsumoto' White	B,C,DT,PI,SK
Callistephus 'Milady' mix	BD,BS,D,DT,J,KI,L,M, MO,S,SE,SU,T,TU,U,YA
Callistephus 'Milady' s-c	CL
Callistephus 'Nova'	D
Callistephus 'Olga'	C
Callistephus 'Ostrich Plume' mix	BD,BO,BS,BY,CL,CN, CO,D,DT,F,J,KI,L,M,R,S, ST,T,TU,U,VH,YA
Callistephus 'Ostrich Plume' s-c	B,C
Callistephus 'Perfection' mix	CA
Callistephus 'Pinocchio'	BS,CN,D,DT,F,FR,J,KI, L,S,SE,SK,V,VH
Callistephus 'Pommax' mix	SK
Callistephus 'Pompom' s-c	C
Callistephus 'Pompon' mix	BS,D,DT,F,FR,J,MO,SK, T,TU,U
Callistephus 'Powderpuffs' mix	BS,BU,CA,JO,L,MO,PI, SK,YA
Callistephus 'Princess' mix	BS,FR,KI,ST,T,U,V
Callistephus 'Quadrille' mix	C
Callistephus 'Rainbow'	DN,PI
Callistephus 'Starlight' mix	BS,M
Callistephus 'Starlight Rose'	O
Callistephus 'Starlight' s-c	BS
Callistephus 'Starlight Scarlet'	BS,M
Callistephus 'Turandot'	C
Callistephus Waldersee 'Starlet'	C
Callistephus 'Wheelies'	PK
Callitris canescens	B,NI,O

Callitris columellaris	B,EL,HA,NI,O
Callitris drummondii	B,NI,O
Callitris endlicheri	B,EL,HA,NI,O,SA,WA
Callitris glaucophylla	B,NI,O
Callitris hugelii	B
Callitris intratropica	B,NI,O
Callitris macleayana	B
Callitris monticola	B,C,NI,O,SA
Callitris muelleri	O
Callitris oblonga	B,C,O
Callitris preissii	B,DD,EL,HA,NI,O,SA
Callitris preissii ssp murrayensis	B,NI,O
Callitris preissii ssp preissii	O
Callitris preissii ssp verrucosa	B,DD,NI,O
Callitris rhomboidea	AU,B,C,EL,HA,HU,NI,O
Callitris roei	B,NI,O
Calluna vulgaris	A,B,C,FW,HU,JE,LN,PK, SA,V
Calmagrostis varia	SA
Calocedrus decurrens	AB,B,C,CA,FW,LN,SA, VE
Calocedrus formosana	SA
Calochilis holtzei	B
Calochortus albus	AP,B,NG,SC,SW
Calochortus albus v rubellus	AP,B
Calochortus ambiguus	B,RS,SW
Calochortus amoenus	AP,B,HP
Calochortus apiculatus	B,RS
Calochortus aureus	B,SW
Calochortus barbatus	AP,B,G,PM,SW
Calochortus catalinae	AP,B,SW
Calochortus clavatus	AP,CG,PM,SC
Calochortus clavatus v avius	B
Calochortus concolor	B,SW
Calochortus davidsonianus	PM
Calochortus eurycarpus see C.nitidus	
Calochortus exilis	B,RS,SW
Calochortus flexuosus	B,SW
Calochortus gunnisonii	AP,B,SW
Calochortus invenustus	AP,B,SW
Calochortus kennedyi	B,SW
Calochortus kennedyi munzii	SW
Calochortus kennedyi v aurea	B
Calochortus luteus	AP,B,SC
Calochortus macrocarpus	B,NO
Calochortus nitidus	B,C,NO,RS
Calochortus nuttallii	B,NO,SW
Calochortus purpureus	B,RS,SW
Calochortus splendens	AP,B,PM,SC
Calochortus uniflorus	AP,PM,SC
Calochortus venustulus	B,SW
Calochortus venustus	AP,B,G
Calochortus weedii	AP,B,SW
Calodendrum capense	B,BH,CA,EL,HA,KB,SA, SI,WA
Calomeria amaranthoides	AU,B,NI,SG
Calophyllum brasiliense	B
Calophyllum inophyllum	B,EL,NI
Caloscordum neriniflorum	AP,HP
Calothamnus aridus	B,NI
Calothamnus asper	B,HA,NI
Calothamnus blepharospermus	AU,B,NI
Calothamnus chrysantherus	B,HA,O,SA
Calothamnus gilesii	B,C,HA,NI,O
Calothamnus gracilis	B,NI
Calothamnus graniticus	B,NI

CALOTHAMNUS

Calothamnus hirsutus	B,NI
Calothamnus homalophyllus	AU,B,NI,O
Calothamnus lehmannii	B,NI
Calothamnus pinifolius	B,NI,O,SA
Calothamnus planifolius	B,NI
Calothamnus quadrifidus	AU,B,EL,HA,NI,O,SA
Calothamnus rupestris	AU,B,EL,NI,SA
Calothamnus sanguineus	AU,B,HA,NI
Calothamnus tuberosus	B,NI
Calothamnus validus	B,C,NI,O,SA
Calothamnus villosus	B,EL,HA,HU,NI,O,SA
Calotis cuneifolia	B,DD,NI
Calotis erinacea	B,NI
Calotis lappulacea	B,NI
Calotis multicaulis	B,NI
Calotropis gigantea	B
Calotropis procera	B
Calpurnia aurea	SA
Calpurnia aurea ssp aurea	B,KB,SI
Calpurnia sericea	B,SI
Caltha leptosepala	B,C,HP,RM,SC,SW
Caltha obtusa	B,SS
Caltha palustris	AP,B,BS,C,CG,CN,CO,G, HP,JE,KI,KL,PR,SA,SG, SU,T,TH
Caltha palustris fl.pl.	B
Caltha palustris v alba	AP,B,C,G,HP,JE,SC
Caltha palustris v palustris	B,G,HP,JE
Caltha sagittata	AR,AU
Calycanthus chinensis	SA
Calycanthus floridus	A,AP,B,C,CA,CG,EL,FW, G,HU,LN,SA,VE
Calycanthus occidentalis	AP,B,C,CG,HA,LN,RH, SA
Calycanthus praecox	VE
Calycotome spinosa	SA
Calycotome villosa	B
Calyptridium umbellatum see Spraguea	
Calyptrogyne dulcis	B
Calyptrogyne sarapiquensis	B
Calystegia sepium	B
Calytrix acutifolia	B,NI
Calytrix angulata	B,NI
Calytrix aurea	B,NI
Calytrix ericoides	C,NI
Calytrix exstipula	B,NI,SA
Calytrix flavescens	B,NI
Calytrix fraseri	B,NI
Calytrix glutinosa	AU,B,NI
Calytrix leschenaultii	B,NI
Calytrix tenuifolia	B
Calytrix tetragona	B,EL,HA,NI,SA
Camassia cusickii	AB,AP,B,CG,G,KL,NO, RH,SC
Camassia leichtlinii	AB,AP,B,C,DD,G,JE,KL, LN,RH,SA,SC,SG
Camassia leichtlinii 'Alba' see C.l.ssp leichtlinii	
Camassia leichtlinii ssp leichtlinii	AP,B,C,G,KL,LG,SC
Camassia quamash	AB,AP,B,C,HUJE,NO,SA, SC,SG
Camassia quamash v utahensis	B
Camassia scilloides	B,PR
Camassia sucksdorfii	SG
Camassia viridiflora	AP
Camelina sativa	B,SG
Camellia japonica	B,BS,BY,C,CA,CG,EL, FW,LN,SA,VE
Camellia japonica cvs	B
Camellia oleifera	B,EL,LN,SA
Camellia saluenensis	B
Camellia sasanqua	B,CG,EL,FW,SA
Camellia sinensis	B,CA,FW,LN,V,VE
Camellia x williamsii 'Wilber Foss'	B
Camissonia bistorta	B,KS
Camissonia bistorta 'Sunflakes'	PK,S
Camissonia californica	B,BS,L,MO,SE
Camissonia cheiranthifolia	B,T
Camissonia claviformis	B
Campanula acaulis	B
Campanula alaskana see C.rotundifolia v alaskana	
Campanula alliariifolia	AP,B,C,CG,DV,F,G,HP,JE, KL,P,PK,SA,SC,SG,VO
Campanula allionii see C.alpestris	
Campanula alpestris	AP,B,C,CG,JE,KL,SC,VO
Campanula alpina	AP,B,C,CG,KL,SC,VO
Campanula alsinoides	SG
Campanula americana	B,HP,PR
Campanula angustifolia	SG
Campanula ardonensis	VO
Campanula arguensis	VO
Campanula argyrotricha	KL
Campanula aucheri	AP,B,C,JE,KL,SC,SG,VO
Campanula autraniana	CG,VO
Campanula barbata	AP,B,C,CG,DV,F,G,HP, HU,JE,KL,RS,SA,SC,SG
Campanula barbata 'Alba'	AP,B,G,SC
Campanula bellidifolia	B,G,JE,KL,SC,SG
Campanula bellidifolia 'Alba'	KL
Campanula besenginica	VO
Campanula betulifolia	AP,G,I,P,SC
Campanula 'Blue Basket'	S
Campanula bononiensis	AP,B,CG,DV,G,HP,SC
Campanula 'Burghaltii'	HP
Campanula caespitosa	B
Campanula calaminthifolia	AP,KL,SC
Campanula carnica	B
Campanula carpatica	AP,B,BD,BS,C,CG,CO, DV,G,HP,JE,KL,L,MA, MO,RI,SC,SG
Campanula carpatica blue	BS,F,J,KI,MO,PI,SA,ST,V
Campanula carpatica 'Blue Gem'	S
Campanula carpatica 'Clips Blue'	B,BS,C,CA,CL,DE,DT,G, JE,MO,PK,SA,SK
Campanula carpatica 'Clips Deep Blue'	B,BS,CL,JE,MO
Campanula carpatica 'Clips Light Blue'	B,BS,CL,JE,MO,PK,SK
Campanula carpatica 'Clips' mix	BS
Campanula carpatica 'Clips White'	AP,B,BS,C,CA,CL,DT,G, HP,JE,MO,PK,SA,SK
Campanula carpatica Dwarf Hybrids	D
Campanula carpatica f alba	AP,B,BS,HP,HU,JE,KL, MA,MO,ST
Campanula carpatica f1 'Bellissimo' mix	SE
Campanula carpatica f1 'Uniform Blue'	B,JE
Campanula carpatica f1 'Uniform White'	B,JE
Campanula carpatica 'Isobel'	CG,G,SG
Campanula carpatica 'Jingle Bells'	T
Campanula carpatica New Hybrids	B
Campanula carpatica 'Silberschale'	B,JE
Campanula carpatica 'Star Blue'	YA
Campanula carpatica 'Star White'	YA
Campanula carpatica v turbinata	AP,C,CG,JE,SC
Campanula carpatica v t.. 'Wheatley Violet'	B,SG

CAMPANULA

Campanula carpatica white   CN,F,J,KI,V
Campanula cashmeriana   AP,G,HP,I,KL,PK,SG,T
Campanula cenisia   B,C,JE,VO
Campanula cephallenica see C.garganica ssp cephallenica
Campanula cervicaria   AP,DV,G,HP,KL,SG
Campanula chamissonis   KL
Campanula chamissonis 'Superba'   KL
Campanula 'Champion Blue'   U
Campanula choruhensis   VO
Campanula ciliata   VO
Campanula cochlearifolia 'Pixie'   S,T
Campanula cochleariifolia   AB,AP,B,C,CG,CL,CN,
    EL,G,HU,I,JE,L,MO,RM,
    SA,SC,U
Campanula cochleariifolia 'Alba'   AP,B,I,JE,SA,T
Campanula cochleariifolia 'Baby Series' s-c B,F
Campanula cochleariifolia 'Bavaria Blue'   B,JE
Campanula cochleariifolia 'Bavaria White'   B,JE
Campanula collina   AP,B,BS,C,CG,G,JE,KL,
    SA,SC,SG
Campanula cordifolia   B
Campanula coriacea   KL
Campanula dzaaku   VO
Campanula elatines v elatinoides   B,C,SC
Campanula elatines v fenestrellata   B,F
Campanula 'Elizabeth'   PM
Campanula erinus   CG,DV
Campanula excisa   B,C,SC
Campanula excisa 'Alba'   B
Campanula f1 'Champion' s-c, p.s.   YA
Campanula fenestrellata   CG,JE
Campanula formanekiana   AP,B,C,CG,SG
Campanula fragilis   B,BS,BY,CN,L,MO,SC
Campanula fragilis 'Jewel'   C
Campanula garganica   AP,B,BS,C,CL,CN,D,DV,
    G,JE,L,MO,SA,SC,T
Campanula glomerata   AP,B,C,CG,CN,DV,G,
    HP,LA,SA,SG,SU,T,V
Campanula glomerata 'Alba'   AP,B,C,G,JE,JO,KL,SA
Campanula glomerata 'Alba Nana'   KL
Campanula glomerata ssp elliptica   SG
Campanula glomerata 'Superba'   B,DV,HP,HU,JO,L,P,SA,T
Campanula glomerata v acaulis   AP,B,BS,C,CL,HP,JE,
    MO,PM,SC
Campanula glomerata v dahurica   BS,C,F,G,JE,PK
Campanula grossekii   B,G,HP,RS,SC
Campanula grossheimii   DV,G,SG
Campanula hawkinsiana   T
Campanula herzegovina   G,I
Campanula hierosolymitana   B
Campanula hohenackeri   CG
Campanula hondoensis   KL,SG
Campanula incurva   AP,B,C,CG,G,HP,P,RM
Campanula isophylla 'Alba'   B
Campanula isophylla 'Caerulea'   B
Campanula isophylla f1 'Top Star'   YA
Campanula isophylla imp, s-c   B
Campanula isophylla 'Stella Blue'   C,CL,DE,DT,L,PK
Campanula isophylla 'Stella mix'   C
Campanula isophylla 'Stella White'   C,CL,DE,DT,L,PK
Campanula justiniana   B,CG
Campanula kemulariae   B,G,JE
Campanula kolenatiana   B,C,SC
Campanula kryophila   VO
Campanula lactiflora   A,AP,B,CG,F,G,HP,JE,
    MA,PK,RS,SA,SC,SG,T

Campanula lactiflora 'Loddon Anna'   HP
Campanula lactiflora New Hybrids   B,C,JE
Campanula lactiflora 'Pouffe'   HP
Campanula lactiflora 'Pritchards Variety'   HP
Campanula lactiflora s-c   PK
Campanula lanata   B,CG,G,P,SG
Campanula lasiocarpa   AP,G,JE,KL,SC,VO
Campanula latifolia   A,AP,B,C,CG,CN,DV,G,
    HP,JE,KL,LA,PA,PM,SA,
    SC,SG,VO
Campanula latifolia 'Alba'   AP,B,C,JE,KL,SC,SG
Campanula latifolia 'Amethyst'   T
Campanula latifolia 'Brantwood'   HP,T
Campanula latifolia 'Gloaming'   HP
Campanula latifolia v macrantha   AP,B,C,CG,DV,G,HP,HU,
    JE,SA,SC,SG
Campanula latifolia v macrantha 'Alba'   B,G,JE,SA,SC,T
Campanula latifolia v mac. 'Blue Master'   B
Campanula latifolia v mac. 'Snow Master'   B
Campanula latiloba   HP,W
Campanula latiloba 'Alba'   HP,MA
Campanula latiloba 'Hidcote Amethyst'   HP
Campanula lingulata   B,CG
Campanula linifolia see C.carnica
Campanula lusitanica   CG
Campanula macrorhiza   KL
Campanula macrostachya   B
Campanula malacitana   I
Campanula medium   AP,B,C,CA,CG,DI,FR,G,
    KS,PI,PK,R,SG,SK,ST,
    TH,VH
Campanula medium 'Bella Series' s-c   F
Campanula medium 'Bells of Holland'   BD,BS,C,MO,S
Campanula medium 'Calycanthema'   AB,B,BS,CL,CN,D,DD,
    F,HU,KI,L,MO,SE,SU,
    T,U,YA
Campanula medium 'Calyc. Ringing Bells'   C
Campanula medium 'Cantebury Pink'   U
Campanula medium 'Champion' s-c   PL
Campanula medium 'Chelsea Pink'   B,BS,C,CL,DT,F,MO,
    SE,U,V
Campanula med. 'Cup & Saucer' special   BY,CO,DE,J,S,V,VY
Campanula medium 'Dean's Hybrids'   L
Campanula medium dw bedding   D
Campanula medium 'Dw Bell Tower'   U
Campanula medium fl.pl. finest mix   C,TH
Campanula medium fl.pl. violet-blue   B
Campanula medium fl.pl. white   B
Campanula medium mix dbl   BS,BY,L,TU
Campanula medium 'Rosea'   D
Campanula medium 'Russian Pink'   T
Campanula medium 'Single Blue'   B,C,JE
Campanula medium 'Single Lilac'   B
Campanula medium 'Single' Mix   BS,HU,KI,L,ST,TU
Campanula medium 'Single Rose'   B,C,JE
Campanula medium 'Single White'   B,JE
Campanula mirabilis   HP
Campanula mix border sp   FR,T
Campanula mix erect border   C,FR
Campanula moesiaca   AP,B,C,P
Campanula moravica   CG
Campanula ochroleuca   AP,B,G,HP,JE,T,VO
Campanula olympica h. see C.rotundifolia 'Olympica'
Campanula orphanidea   AP,CG
Campanula pallida   HP
Campanula patula   AP,B,C,DV,G,JE,SC,V

CAMPANULA

Campanula persicifolia	A,AB,AP,B,BY,CG,CL, CN,DV,G,HP,HU,I,KI, RM,SA,SG,SU,TH,V,W
Campanula persicifolia 'Alba'	AP,B,F,G,HP,HU,I,MO, RM,SA,SC,SG
Campanula persicifolia 'Blue Bell'	C,KS,MO,PK,SK
Campanula persicifolia 'Caerulea'	SA
Campanula persicifolia 'Chettle Charm'	C
Campanula persicifolia 'Coronata'	HP
Campanula persicifolia grandiflora	B,JE
Campanula persicifolia grandiflora 'Alba'	B,JE
Campanula persicifolia grand. 'Caerulea'	G,JE
Campanula persicifolia new giant hyb	T
Campanula persicifolia s-c	BS
Campanula persicifolia 'Telham Beauty'	AP,B,BS,BY,C,F,HP,HU, MO,SA
Campanula persicifolia v planiflora	AP,B,KL
Campanula persicifolia v planiflora f alba	HP,KL
Campanula persicifolia 'White Bell'	C,KS,PK,SK
Campanula persicifolia 'White Queen'	HP,S
Campanula petraea	CG,DV
Campanula pilosa see C. chamissonis	
Campanula polymorpha	CG
Campanula portenschlagiana	AP,B,C,F,JE,SA,SC
Campanula poscharskyana	B,BS,C,CG,CL,CN,DV, I,JE,MO,SA,U
Campanula prenanthoides	C
Campanula primulifolia	AP,B,CG,G,HP,P,SA,,SZ
Campanula pulla	B,G,HP,SC
Campanula pulla alba	KL
Campanula punctata	AP,B,C,CN,F,G,HP,JE, KL,PA,SA,SC,SG
Campanula punctata f albiflora	AP,B,HP,JE
Campanula punctata 'Nana Alba'	B,P,SC
Campanula punctata 'Rubriflora'	AP,B,C,F,HP,KL,P,SA
Campanula punctata v hondoensis	AP,B,DV,HP,P
Campanula puntata 'Rosea'	KL
Campanula pusilla see C.cochleariifolia	
Campanula pyramidalis	AP,B,C,F,G,HP,HU,JE, KI,S,SA,U,V
Campanula pyramidalis 'Alba'	B,BS,C,CG,HP,HU,JE,SA
Campanula pyramidalis f caerulea	CG
Campanula pyramidalis mix	AB,BS,C,DT,JE,L,MO
Campanula raddeana	B,JE
Campanula raineri	AP,B,C,CG,JE,KL,SA,VO
Campanula rapunculoides	A,AP,B,C,CG,CN,DV,HP, HU,JE,SA,SG
Campanula rapunculoides 'Alba'	HP
Campanula rapunculus	B,C,DV,G,JE,SG
Campanula reiseri	C
Campanula retrorsa	B
Campanula rhomboidalis	AP,B,C,SC,SG
Campanula rigidipila	KL
Campanula rock garden mix	C,JE,P,T
Campanula rotundifolia	AB,AP,B,BD,BS,C,CG, CN,CO,D,DV,F,G,HP,HU, JE,KI,KL,LA,NO,PR,SA, SC,SE,SG,SU,TH,V,Z
Campanula rotundifolia 'Olympica'	B,C,MO,SG
Campanula rotundifolia v alaskana	CG
Campanula rotundifolia v marchsettii	B,T,W
Campanula rupestris	AP,SC,W
Campanula rupestris anchusifolia	PM
Campanula ruprechtii	VO
Campanula sarmatica	AP,B,C,CG,G,HP,KL,P, SC,SG,VO
Campanula sartorii	AP,SC,SG,T,W
Campanula saxifraga	B,KL,RM,SC,SG,VO
Campanula scheuchzeri	AP,CG,DV,JE
Campanula sibirica	AP,B,C,JE
Campanula speciosa	AP,B,C,CG,G,JE,SC,T,VO
Campanula spicata	AP,B,G,SC
Campanula sporadum	RM
Campanula stellaris	B
Campanula stricta	KL
Campanula strigosa	B
Campanula suanetica	VO
Campanula sulphurea	B
Campanula takesimana	AP,B,F,G,HP,JE,P,PM,T
Campanula takesimana 'Alba'	B,P
Campanula tatrae	B,CG,DV,SG
Campanula thessala	AP,B,RS,SC
Campanula thyrsoides	AP,B,C,CG,F,G,HP,HU, JE,KL,NG,SA,SC,SG,VO
Campanula thyrsoides ssp carniolica	AP,CG,G,KL,SC,SG,W
Campanula tommasiniana	AP,B,I,G,JE,KL,SC,SG
Campanula tommasiniana hyb	I
Campanula trachelium	AP,B,C,CG,CN,DV,G,HP, LA,JE,KL,PM,SA,SC, SG,SU,TH,TU
Campanula trachelium 'Alba'	AP,C,HP,SA,SC,SG
Campanula trachelium 'Bernice'	B,P
Campanula trachelium 'Faichem Lilac'	B,C,P
Campanula trachelium v urticifolia	SG
Campanula tridens	KL
Campanula tridentata	C,G,JE,KL,SC,SG,VO
Campanula versicolor	AP,B,C,G,HP,JE
Campanula waldsteiniana	B,C,CG,JE
Campanula woronowii	VO
Campanula x pseudoraineri	G
Campanula x pulloides	G
Campanula xylocarpa	B
Campomanesia lineatifolia	B
Campsis grandiflora	B,EL,FW,G,HP,SA
Campsis radicans	AP,B,C,CA,CP,DV,EL,FW, G,HU,LN,NO,O,SA,T,VE
Campsis x tagliabuana 'Mdm Galen'	B,RS
Camptotheca acuminata	B,CG,FW,LN,SA
Cananga odorata	B,SA
Canarium madagascariensis	B
Canarium schweinfurthii	B
Canavalia cathartica	B,DD
Canavalia ensiformis	B
Canavalia kawaiensis	DD
Canavalia maritima	HA,NI,SA
Canavalia rosea	AU,B
Canavalia virosa	B,SI
Canistrum sp	B
Canna altensteinii	G
Canna americana	B
Canna coccinea	CG
Canna Colour Carnival	EL,O
Canna Crozy's New Hybrids	B,BS
Canna edulis see C.indica	
Canna flaccida	B,G
Canna glauca	CG
Canna hortensis	DD
Canna indica	B,BS,C,CG,DD,EL,HA, HU,LG,O,RE,SA,SG,TT
Canna indica hyb	T
Canna indica 'Tropical Rose'	B,DE,MO,SK,T,V
Canna lutea	SG

CANNA

Canna mix lg fl	F	Carduncellus monspeliensis	B,C
Canna mix new hybrids	BS,BY,MO	Carduncellus rhaponticoides	AP,PM
Canna polymorpha	SG	Carduus acaulis	B
Canna 'Seven Dwarfs Cherry' s-c	B	Carduus benedictus see Cnicus	
Canna warscewiczii	SG	Carduus carlinoides ssp carlinoides	CG
Canna x generalis	AB,HU	Carduus crispus	SG
Cananga odorata	RE	Carduus dahuricus	SG
Canthium dicoccum	B	Carduus nutans	B,C
Canthium inerme	B	Carduus tenuiflorus	B
Canthium mundianum	B,SI	Cardwellia sublimis	B,O
Canthium odoratum	B	Carex acuta	B,JE
Canthium oleifolium	HA	Carex acutiformis	AP,B,JE
Canthium parviflorum	B	Carex alba	B,JE,SG
Capparis brevispina	B	Carex alopecoidea	B,PR
Capparis mitchellii	B,NI	Carex annectens xanthocarpa	B,PR
Capparis spinosa	B,C,FW,HP,SA,VE	Carex appressa	B
Capparis spinosa v inermis	B,SA,VE	Carex aqualilis	NO
Capparis spinosa v inermis select	B	Carex arenaria	B,JE,SA,SG
Capparis spinosa v nummularia	B,NI	Carex atrata ssp aterrima	SG
Capparis tomentosa	B,SI	Carex baccans	SG
Capparis zeylanica	B	Carex baldensis	KL
Capsella bursa-pastoris	AB,DD,SG	Carex bergrenii	AP,AU,B,JE,PM,SG
Capsicum annuum conoides	TT	Carex bicknelii	B
Capsicum annuum Ornamental	BS,CA,KI,MO,SK	Carex boottiana	HP
Capsicum annuum Ornamental (V) mix	HU	Carex buchananii	AP,B,CA,G,HP,JE,KL,SA
Caragana arborescens	A,AB,AP,B,C,FW,G,HP,	Carex buchananii 'Viridis'	B,JE
	HU,LN,NO,SA,SG,VE	Carex caespitosa	SG
Caragana arborescens v crasseaculeata	B	Carex capillaris	SG
Caragana aurantiaca	B,LN,SA,SG	Carex comans	AP,B,C,G,HP,SA,SC,SG
Caragana boisii	SA,SG	Carex comans bronze	AP,B,HP
Caragana frutex	B,LN,SA,SG	Carex comosa	B,PR
Caragana jubata	B,HU,KL	Carex crinita	B,PR
Caragana microphylla	B,EL,FW,LN,N,SA	Carex dallii	SG
Caragana pekinensis	B	Carex dipsacea	B,HP,SA
Caragana pygmaea	B,LN,SA,SG	Carex disticha	B,SG
Caragana rosea	B,LN,SA	Carex elata 'Aurea'	B,HP
Caragana spinosa	SG	Carex flacca	B,JE,SA
Caralluma foetida	DV	Carex flagellifera	AP,B,HP,SG
Caralluma rogersii	DD	Carex flava	B,G,JE,SG
Caralluma russelliana	DV	Carex folliculata	B,JE
Caralluma sp mix	C	Carex 'Frosted Curls'	B,P,PM,SA
Carapa grandiflora	B	Carex gracilis	G,SA
Carapa procera	B	Carex grayi	B,DE,G,HP,JE,KL,SA,SG
Cardamine alpina ex Tyrol	G	Carex hirta	B
Cardamine asarifolia	B,CG	Carex hispida	C,HP
Cardamine bipinnata	VO	Carex lacustris	B,PR
Cardamine bulbifera	B,C,I,KL	Carex leersiana	B,JE
Cardamine carnea	KL	Carex lupilina	B,PR
Cardamine heptaphylla	B,C,G,HP	Carex lurida	B,JE
Cardamine hirsuta	B	Carex macrocephala	B,JE,SA
Cardamine kitaibelii	B	Carex media	SG
Cardamine oligosperma	B,DD	Carex megalandra	KL
Cardamine opizii	SG	Carex melanathiformis	SG
Cardamine polyphylla	C	Carex montana	KL
Cardamine pratensis	B,C,CN,CO,JE,SU	Carex muhlenbergii	B,PR
Cardamine trifolia	HP	Carex muricata	SG
Cardaria draba	B,SG	Carex muricata ssp pairaei	SG
Cardiocrinum cordatum	B,CG	Carex muskingumensis	AP,B,G,HP,JE,KL,SA,T
Cardiocrinum giganteum	AP,B,C,G,JE,LG,P,PA,	Carex nigra	B,JE
	PL,RS,SA,SC,SG,T	Carex obnupta	AB,B
Cardiocrinum giganteum v yunnanense	C	Carex otrubae	B,G,SG
Cardiocrinum glehnii	C,DD,SA,SG	Carex ovalis	HP
Cardiospermum grandiflorum	B	Carex paniculata	B,JE
Cardiospermum halicacabum	B,C,DE,G,HP,JO,KS,PI,	Carex pendula	AP,B,C,DD,E,G,HP,LA,
	PK,V		JE,SA,SC,SG
Carduncellus mitissimus	B,G,SC	Carex petriei	AP,B,G,HP,SA,SC,SS

CAREX

Carex prairea	B,PR
Carex pseudocyperus	AP,B,G,JE,SA,SC
Carex remota	B,JE,SG
Carex retrorsa	B,PR
Carex rhyncophysa	SG
Carex riparia	B,JE,SA,SG
Carex riparia 'Variegata'	B
Carex rostrata	CG
Carex scoparia	B,PR
Carex secta	AP,B,HP,SA,SG
Carex secta v tenuiculmis	B,HP,JE,SC
Carex sempervirens ssp tatrorum	SG
Carex solandri	B
Carex sp China	SG
Carex sp 'Majken'	JE
Carex sp orange/green	SZ
Carex spissa	SZ
Carex sprengellii	PR
Carex stipata	B,PR
Carex stricta	B,PR
Carex sylvatica	B,G,JE,SA
Carex tenuisecta 'Bronzina'	B
Carex testacea	AP,B,C,HP,P,SC
Carex trifida	B,HP,SA,SG
Carex tuckermani	B,PR
Carex tumulicola	SZ
Carex umbrosa	B,JE
Carex vesicaria	SG
Carex vulpina	B,JE
Carex vulpinoidea	B,PR
Carica chrysopetala	B
Carica goudoutiana	B
Carica papaya	B,C,EL,G,LN,RE,SA,TT,V
Carica papaya 'Ceylon'	B
Carica papaya 'Coorg Honeydew'	B,EL,SA
Carica papaya dw	B
Carica papaya 'Mammoth'	B
Carica papaya 'Ranchi'	B
Carica papaya 'Red'	B,CA,EL
Carica papaya 'Solo'	B,C,CA
Carica papaya 'Sunrise'	B
Carica papaya 'Sunset'	B
Carica papaya 'Waimanolo'	B
Carica papaya 'Washington'	B
Carica pentagona	B
Carica pubescens	B
Carica quercifolia	B,CG
Carica stipulata	B
Cariniana pyriformis	B
Carissa bispinosa	B,WA
Carissa carandas	B,EL
Carissa edulis	B,SI,WA
Carissa grandiflora see C.macrocarpa	
Carissa haematocarpa	B,SI
Carissa macrocarpa	B,C,CA,FW,KB,O,SA, SI,VE,WA
Carissa spinarum	B
Carlina acanthifolia	AP,B,C,JE,SA,T
Carlina acaulis	B,BS,G,HP,HU,SC,T
Carlina acaulis bronze form	B,C,G,JE,SA
Carlina acaulis caulescens see C.a. ssp simplex	
Carlina acaulis ssp simplex	B,C,JE,SA,SC,SG,V
Carlina vulgaris	B,C,G,JE,SA,SG
Carlina vulgaris 'Silver Star'	B,JE,SA
Carlina vulgaris ssp intermedia	B
Carlina vulgaris ssp vulgaris	CG

Carludovica palmata	B,C,CA,EL,SA,SG
Carmichaelia aligera	B,SA,SS
Carmichaelia angustata	CG
Carmichaelia arborea	SG
Carmichaelia australis see C.arborea	
Carmichaelia enysii	AP,B,SC,SS
Carmichaelia glabrata	B,SS
Carmichaelia grandiflora	B,SS
Carmichaelia kirkii	B,SS
Carmichaelia monroi	B,SA,SS
Carmichaelia ovata	B
Carmichaelia petriei	B,SG,SS
Carmichaelia rivulata	B,SS
Carmichaelia robusta	B,SS
Carmichaelia subulata	G,SG
Carmichaelia violacea	SA
Carmona retusa	B
Carnegiea euphorbioides	CG
Carnegiea gigantea	B,C,CH,DV,HU,Y
Carpanthea pomeridiana	B,C,DT,DV,F,KB,SG,SI,Y
Carpanthea pomeridiana 'Golden Carpet'	J,SE,V
Carpentaria acuminata	B,C,CA,EL,HA,N,O,SA
Carpenteria californica	AP,B,C,CA,HP,SA,VE
Carpha alpina	B,SS
Carpinus betulus	B,C,CA,FW,I,LN,N,SA, VE
Carpinus bitrilus	CG
Carpinus caroliniana	B,FW,G,LN,N,SA
Carpinus caucasica	FW,LN,N,SA
Carpinus cordata	B,CG,FW,LN,SA
Carpinus coreana	B,N
Carpinus fargesii see C.laxiflora v macrostachya	
Carpinus japonica	B,LN,SA
Carpinus laxiflora	B,FW,N,SA
Carpinus laxiflora Korean form	N
Carpinus laxiflora v macrostachya	B,C
Carpinus orientalis	B,FW,LN,N,SA
Carpinus polyneura	B,C,FW,N
Carpinus schisiensis	N
Carpinus turczaninowii	B,C,FW,LN,N,SA
Carpinus viminea	B,FW,N
Carpobrotus aequilaterus	B
Carpobrotus deliciosus	B,SI
Carpobrotus edulis	B,C,DV,SA,SI
Carpobrotus edulis v parviflora	B,SI
Carpobrotus glaucescens	B
Carpobrotus muirii	B,SI
Carpobrotus quadrifidus	B,SI
Carpobrotus rossii	B
Carpobrotus sauerae	B,SA,SI
Carpobrotus virescens	B,NI
Carpodetus serratus	B,SS
Carrierea calycina	B
Carruanthus caninus	DV
Carruanthus peersii	B
Carthamus lanatus	G
Carthamus tinctorius	BY,C,CP,HU,KS,SG,SU, TH,V
Carthamus tinctorius 'Fire Tuft'	DE
Carthamus tinctorius 'Goldtuft'	BS,CO,KI,ST
Carthamus tinctorius 'Grenade'	C
Carthamus tinctorius 'Grenade' s-c	B,L
Carthamus tinctorius 'Kinko' orange	B,BS,CN,MO
Carthamus tinctorius 'Lasting Orange'	BS,DE,DT,PK,SK
Carthamus tinctorius 'Lasting White'	BD,BS,C,PK
Carthamus tinctorius 'Lasting Yellow'	BS,PK,SK

CARTHAMUS

Carthamus tinctorius 'Orange & Cream'	T
Carthamus tinctorius 'Orange-Gold'	U
Carthamus tinctorius 'Shiro' yellow	B,BS,CN,MO
Carthamus tinctorius 'Zanzibar'	B
Carum carvi	CG,CN,CP,HP,HU,KS,SG
Carya aquatica	B,LN,SA
Carya cathayensis	B,LN,SA
Carya cordiformis	B,LN
Carya glabra	B,LN,SA
Carya hunanesis	B
Carya illinoiensis	B,FW,LN,SA,VE
Carya illinoiensis Imp	B,FW
Carya laciniosa	B,CG,FW,LN,SA
Carya myristicaeformis	B,LN,SA
Carya ovata	B,CA,FW,LN,SA,VE
Carya texana	B
Carya tomentosa	B,LN,SA
Caryopteris 'Blue Beard'	PK
Caryopteris incana	AP,SA,SC,SZ
Caryopteris incana dw	SZ
Caryopteris mongolica	LN,SA
Caryopteris odorata	B,C
Caryopteris x bungei	T
Caryopteris x clandonensis	E,SA
Caryopteris x clandonensis new hybrids	B
Caryopteris x cland. 'Worcester Gold'	E
Caryota cummingii	O
Caryota maxima	O
Caryota mitis	B,C,CA,EL,O,SA
Caryota no	O
Caryota ochlandra	B,CA,O,SA
Caryota rumphiana	O
Caryota urens	B,CA,EL,O,SA
Casimiroa edulis	B
Casimiroa tetrameria	B
Cassia abbreviata ssp beareana	SI
Cassia absus	B
Cassia afrofistula	B
Cassia afrofistula 'Beareana'	B
Cassia angustifolia	EL,O
Cassia arborescens	B
Cassia artemisoides	CA,DD,SZ
Cassia australis	EL,HA,SA
Cassia barclayana	O
Cassia bauhinoides	SW
Cassia brewsteri	B,EL,HA,NI,O
Cassia candolleana	EL,HA,O,SA
Cassia carnaval	WA
Cassia corymbosa see Senna	
Cassia covesii	SW
Cassia emarginata	DD
Cassia eremophylla	CA,EL,HA,SA
Cassia fasciculata	HW,PR
Cassia fistula	B,CA,DV,EL,HA,HU,O, RE,SA,TT
Cassia glauca	EL,HA,SA
Cassia grandis	B,EL,HA,HU,O,RE,SA, TT
Cassia hebecarpa	C,CP,PR
Cassia helmsii	C
Cassia javanica	B,EL,HA,HU,O,SA,WA
Cassia 'John Bull'	B
Cassia laevigata	EL,SG,WA
Cassia leptophylla	B,CA,HU
Cassia marginata	EL,HA,O,SA
Cassia marilandica	JE,PK,PR,SA,SC

Cassia moschata	B
Cassia multijuga	EL,HA,O,SA
Cassia nodosa	B,CA,EL,HA,HU,O,SA
Cassia occidentalis	EL,O
Cassia odorata prostrata	SZ
Cassia pumila	B
Cassia renigera	B,EL,HA,O,SA
Cassia reticulata	RE,TT
Cassia roxburghii	B
Cassia siamea	WA
Cassia spectabilis	EL,LN,O,RE,SA,WA
Cassia sturtii	C,CA,EL,HU,JE,SA,VE
Cassia tomentella	B
Cassine aethiopica	B,SI,WA
Cassine crocea	B,SI
Cassine transvaalensis	B,WA
Cassinia aculeata	B,HA
Cassinia arcuata	B,EL,HA,NI,SA
Cassinia aureonitens	AU
Cassinia laevis	B,NI
Cassinia leptophylla	B,SS
Cassinia longifolia	HA
Cassinia quinquefaria	B,HA
Cassinia uncata	B,NI
Cassinopsis ilicifolia	B,KB,SI
Cassiope hypnoides	C
Cassiope stellerana	VO
Cassipoe pectinata AC1709	X
Cassipoe pectinata AC1867	X
Cassytha filiformis	B
Castalis nudicaulis	B,SI
Castalis tragus	B,SI
Castalis tragus v pinnatifida	B,SI
Castanea crenata	VE
Castanea dentata	B,LN,SA
Castanea mollissima	B,FW,LN,SA
Castanea sativa	B,EL,HA,LN,SA,VE,WA
Castanopsis cuspidata	SA
Castanopsis eyeri	B,SA
Castanopsis sclerophylla	SA
Castanopsis sempervirens	AB,SA
Castanopsis tibetana	B,SA
Castanospermum australe	B,CA,EL,HA,O,SA,WA
Castanospora alphandii	B
Castellanosia caineana	DV,Y
Castilla elastica	B,SA
Castilleja coccinea	AV,B,PR
Castilleja foliolosa	B
Castilleja haydeni	B,RM
Castilleja hispida	NO
Castilleja indivisa	B
Castilleja integra	AB,B,SW
Castilleja linariifolia	B
Castilleja martinii	B
Castilleja miniata	C,JE,KL,NO,RM,SC
Castilleja miniata v miniata	B
Castilleja rhexifolia	NO
Castilleja sessiflora	B,PR
Castilleja stenantha	B
Castilleja sulphurea	B,RM
Casuarina acuaria	B
Casuarina acutivalvis	B
Casuarina campestris	B
Casuarina corniculata	B
Casuarina cristata	B,EL,HU,NI,SA
Casuarina cristata ssp cristata	HA,O

CASUARINA

Casuarina cunninghamiana	B,CA,EL,FW,HA,LN,NI, O,SA,VE,WA
Casuarina decaisneana	B,EL,HA,SA
Casuarina decussata	B
Casuarina distyla	B,SA
Casuarina equisetifolia	B,CA,EL,HA,LN,NI,O, SA,VE,WA
Casuarina equisetifolia v incana	B,NI
Casuarina erecta	B
Casuarina fraserana	B
Casuarina glauca	B,CA,EL,HA,NI,O,SA, WA
Casuarina helmsii	B
Casuarina huegeliana	B
Casuarina humilis	B
Casuarina inophloia	B
Casuarina lehmanniana	B,HA
Casuarina littoralis see Allocasuarina	
Casuarina luehmannii	B
Casuarina monilifera	B
Casuarina muellerana	B
Casuarina nana	B,C,SA
Casuarina paludosa	B,SA
Casuarina pauper	B,NI,O
Casuarina pinaster	B
Casuarina pusilla	B
Casuarina rigida	B
Casuarina scleroclada	B
Casuarina sp mix	C,EL
Casuarina stricta see Allocasuarina verticillata	
Casuarina tesselata	B
Casuarina thuyoides	B
Casuarina torulosa	B,VE
Casuarina trichodon	B
Casuarina verticillata	B
Catalpa bignonioides	B,C,CG,FW,G,HA,HU, LN,N,SA,VE
Catalpa bungei	G,LN,SA
Catalpa ovata	B,CG,EL,LN,SA,SG,VE
Catalpa speciosa	B,CA,CG,EL,FW,G,LN, N,SA,VE
Catananche caerulea	w.a.
Catananche caerulea 'Alba'	C,CN,HP,JE,KS
Catananche caerulea 'Bicolor'	HP,MA,T
Catananche caerulea 'Major'	AP,HP
Catananche 'Stargazer'	PL,SE
Catapodium rigidum	HP
Catasetum violascens	B
Catharanthus lanceus	SI
Catharanthus 'Morning Mist'	BD
Catharanthus pusillus	B
Catharanthus roseus	B,C,EL,FR,HA,KI,SA
Catharanthus roseus 'Albus'	B
Catharanthus roseus 'Apricot Delight'	B,BS,MO,PK,SK,T
Catharanthus roseus 'Cooler' s-c	B,BS,CA,MO,PK,SK,T
Catharanthus roseus 'Grape Cooler' mix	BD,BS,CA,MO,SK
Catharanthus roseus 'Ice Cool Mix'	MO,SE
Catharanthus roseus 'Kermesina'	B
Catharanthus roseus 'Little Blanche'	B,CA
Catharanthus roseus 'Little Bright Eyes'	B,CA
Catharanthus roseus 'Little Delicata'	B,CA
Catharanthus roseus 'Little Linda'	B,CA
Catharanthus roseus 'Little Pinkie'	B,CA
Catharanthus roseus 'Little' Series mix	BU,CA,DE,PI
Catharanthus roseus 'Magic Carpet' mix	J,V
Catharanthus roseus mix	BS

Catharanthus roseus mix tall	HU
Catharanthus roseus 'Ocellatus Albus'	B
Catharanthus roseus 'Pacifica' mix	BS,MO,PK,SK
Catharanthus roseus 'Pacifica' s-c	CL,PK,SK,T
Catharanthus roseus 'Parasol'	B,CA,PK,SK
Catharanthus roseus 'Passion'	PK
Catharanthus roseus 'Petit'	F
Catharanthus roseus 'Pretty In Series'	B,BS,CA,MO
Catharanthus ros. 'Terrace Salmon Pink'	PL
Catharanthus roseus 'Terrace Vermillion'	PL,T
Catharanthus roseus 'Tropicana' mix	BS,C,CA,CL,MO,SE,T
Catharanthus ros.'Tropicana.' s-c, mix	CA,SK
Cathartolinum catharticum	SG
Catophractes alexandri	B,SI
Catopsis sessiliflora	B
Cattleya aurantiaca	CG
Cattleya maxima	B
Catunaregam spinosa	B
Cautleya spicata	BS
Ceanothus americanus	B,PR,SG
Ceanothus arboreus	C
Ceanothus 'Burkwoodii'	HP
Ceanothus cordulatus	B,NO
Ceanothus crassifolius	B
Ceanothus cuneatus	B,CA,LN,NO,SA
Ceanothus cyaneus	B
Ceanothus greggii	B
Ceanothus griseus	B
Ceanothus gr. horizontalis 'Yankee Point'	HP
Ceanothus impressus	B,HP,SC
Ceanothus integerrimus	B,C,EL,FW,LN,NO,SA
Ceanothus lemmonii	NO
Ceanothus leucodermis	B,SW
Ceanothus megacarpus	B
Ceanothus ovatus	B,PR
Ceanothus prostratus	B,FW,LN,NO,SA
Ceanothus 'Puget Blue'	HP
Ceanothus ramulosus	B
Ceanothus sanguineus	B,C,EL,FW,LN,NO,SA
Ceanothus spinosus	B
Ceanothus thyrsiflorus	B,HP
Ceanothus thyrsiflorus v repens	C,HP
Ceanothus tomentosus	B
Ceanothus velutinus	B,HP,LN,NO
Ceanothus x delileanus	HP
Cecropia palmata	B
Cedrela chinensis	SA
Cedrela mexicana	B
Cedrela microcarpa	B,WA
Cedrela montana	B
Cedrela odorata	B,RE
Cedrela serrata	B
Cedrela tonduzzi	B
Cedronella canariensis	AP,B,BH,C,CN,CP,G,HP, SG
Cedronella triphylla see C.canariensis	
Cedrus atlantica 'Argentea'	B,FW,LN,VE
Cedrus atlantica f glauca	B,C,CA,EL,FW,LN,N, V,VE
Cedrus atlantica see C.libani ssp a.	
Cedrus brevifolia see C.libani ssp b.	
Cedrus deodara	B,BH,C,CA,EL,FW,HA, LN,N,SA,SG,VE,WA
Cedrus deodara 'Aurea'	B
Cedrus libani	B,C,CA,FW,LN,N,SA,VE
Cedrus libani ssp atlantica	B,CA,EL,FW,HA,LN,SA,

CEDRUS

	VE
Cedrus libani ssp brevifolia	B,FW,N,SA,SG,VE
Cedrus libani ssp stenocoma	B,FW
Ceiba pentandra	B,DV,EL,HA,RE,SA
Celanthe sylvatica	SI
Celastrus orbiculatus	B,C,DE,FW,LN,SA,SG
Celastrus scandens	B,C,CA,FW,LN,PR,SA, SG
Celmisia allanii	AP,PM
Celmisia alpina	AP,B,SS
Celmisia angustifolia	AP,AU,B,SC,SS
Celmisia angustifolia (Mt.Hutt form)	PM
Celmisia angustifolia (s.leaf form)	PM
Celmisia armstrongii	B,SS
Celmisia bellidioides	AP,B,SC,SS
Celmisia coriacea	HP,KL
Celmisia dallii	B,PM,SS
Celmisia densiflora	AP,AU,B,SC,SS
Celmisia discolor	B,SC,SS
Celmisia du-rietzii	B,SC,SS
Celmisia glandulosa	B,SS
Celmisia gracilenta	AP,B,KL,SC,SG,SS
Celmisia graminifolia	B,SS
Celmisia haastii	AP,AU,PM,SS
Celmisia hectorii	AU,B,SC,SS
Celmisia hookeri	AP,B,C,SC,SS
Celmisia incana	KL,PM,SC
Celmisia laricifolia	B,SS
Celmisia lateralis	B
Celmisia longifolia	AP,G,HP,PM,SC,SG
Celmisia lyallii	AU,B,SC,SS
Celmisia mackauii	B,SA
Celmisia monroi	AP,PM,SC
Celmisia petiolata	B,SS
Celmisia prorepens	B,SS
Celmisia semicordata	AP,AU,B,C,PM,SA,SS
Celmisia sericophylla	PM,SG
Celmisia sessiliflora	B,SC,SS
Celmisia spectabilis	AP,AU,B,PM,SC,SS
Celmisia spectabilis v argentea	SG
Celmisia spectabilis v magnifica	B,PM,SC,SS
Celmisia stricta	AU
Celmisia traversii	B,PM,SS
Celmisia viscosa	AU,B,SC,SS
Celmisia walkeri	AU,B,SC,SG,SS
Celmisia webbiana see C.walkeri	
Celosia argentea	B,G
Celosia argentea cristata 'Bombay Purple'	CL,MO,O
Celosia argentea cristata 'Bombay' s-c	B
Celosia argentea 'Sparkler Carmine'	C
Celosia 'Charm' mix	BS
Celosia cristata	DD,FR,SD
Celosia cristata 'Chief' mix	JO,PK,SK
Celosia cristata 'Chief' s-c	C,DE
Celosia cristata 'Coral Garden'	C,KS
Celosia cristata 'Crest' s-c	B
Celosia cristata 'Empress Blend'	SK
Celosia cristata 'Fireglow'	PK,SK
Celosia cristata 'Jewel Box'	BS,J,KS,SE,SK,T
Celosia cristata 'Kurume Corona'	KS
Celosia cristata nana	PI,V
Celosia cristata 'Prestige Scarlet'	PK,SK
Celosia cristata 'Toreador'	B,DE
Celosia cristata 'Treasure Chest'	PK
Celosia floribunda	DD
Celosia 'Olympia' mix	BS,CL,L,MO

Celosia 'Olympic' s-c	B
Celosia plumosa	BY,CA,KI,PI,V
Celosia plumosa 'Apricot Brandy'	B,BS,CA,DE,PK,SE,SK
Celosia plumosa 'Castle' mix	BS,PK,SK,TU
Celosia plumosa 'Castle' s-c	B,BS,PI,PK,SK
Celosia plumosa 'Century' mix	B,BD,BS,C,CL,MO,PK, S,SK,T,VY
Celosia plumosa 'Century' s-c	BS,CL,MO,PK,SK,TE
Celosia plumosa 'Dw Crown'	BS
Celosia plumosa 'Dw Geisha'	BS,D,SE
Celosia plumosa 'Fairy Fountains'	BD,BS,KS,MO,PI
Celosia plumosa 'Fontana' mix	BS
Celosia plumosa 'Fontana' s-c	B
Celosia plumosa 'Forest Fire'	B,BU,SD
Celosia plumosa 'Forest Fire' imp	B
Celosia plumosa 'Golden Triumph'	B
Celosia plumosa 'Kewpie' Series s-c,mix	SK
Celosia plumosa 'Kimono' mix	BS,CL,CO,DE,J,KI,L, MO,PK,S,SK,T,YA
Celosia plumosa 'Kimono' s-c	BS,SK
Celosia plumosa 'Lilliput' mix	BS
Celosia plumosa mix	FR,J
Celosia plumosa 'Rondo'	CL
Celosia plumosa 'Sparkler' s-c	PI,SK
Celosia spicata 'Flamingo Feather'	BS,C,CA,CO,HU,JO,KI, KS,L,MO,PI,S,SK,T,V
Celosia spicata 'Flamingo Pink Feather'	B,CA,DI,U
Celosia spicata 'Flamingo Purple Feather'	B,BS,C,KS,MO,PK,SE
Celosia spicata 'New Look'	DE,F,SK
Celosia spicata 'Pink Candle'	PK,SK
Celosia spicata 'Xanthippe'	B
Celosia thompsonii 'Magnifica'	BS
Celtis africana	B,BH,C,KB,SI,WA
Celtis australis	B,C,CA,EL,HA,LN,SA, VE,WA
Celtis caucasica	B,LN,SG
Celtis chinensis	EL,SA
Celtis glabrata	SA
Celtis juliana	B,FW,LN
Celtis laevigata	B,LN,SA
Celtis occidentalis	B,C,CA,CG,FW,LN,NO, SA,VE
Celtis reticulata	B,LN,NO
Celtis sinensis	B,C,CA,FW,LN,V,WA
Celtis tournefortii	B,SA
Cenarrhenes nitida	B
Cenchrus ciliaris	B,EL
Cenchrus ciliaris 'Biloela'	B
Cenchrus ciliaris 'Gayndah'	B
Cenchrus ciliaris 'Molopo'	B
Cenchrus ciliaris 'Numbank'	B
Cenchrus ciliaris 'U.S.A.'	B
Cenchrus incertus	B
Cenchrus setigerus	B
Cenia turbinata	B,SI
Centaurea americana	B,SD,SW,SZ
Centaurea americana 'Aloha'	B,PK
Centaurea americana 'Jolly Joker'	C,HU
Centaurea americana 'Lilac Charm'	B
Centaurea atropurpurea	AP,CG,SG
Centaurea bella	HP,KL,SC
Centaurea calcitrapa	B
Centaurea cheiranthifolia v purpurascens	VO
Centaurea cineraria	B,G,JE
Centaurea collina	B
Centaurea crocodylum	B

CENTAUREA

Centaurea cyanus — AB,AP,B,BU,C,CA,CN,C O,DD,DI,F,FR,G,HP,HW, LA,SD,SG,SU,TE,TH,TU
Centaurea cyanus 'Baby Blue' — B,BD,BS,L,MO
Centaurea cyanus 'Baby Pink' — B
Centaurea cyanus 'Ball Giant mix' — M
Centaurea cyanus 'Ball Series' s-c — B,BS,DE,F,V
Centaurea cyanus 'Black Boy' — B
Centaurea cyanus 'Blue Boy' — B,BS,BU,CN,DE,JO, KS,MO
Centaurea cyanus 'Blue Diadem' — B,D,S,T
Centaurea cyanus 'Blue Double' — BD,BS,BY,CO,J,KI,ST, TU,YA
Centaurea cyanus 'Deep Damson' — SE
Centaurea cyanus Dw — HU
Centaurea cyanus 'Emperor William' — B,BH
Centaurea c. 'Extra Early Dutch Dbl Blue' — BY
Centaurea cyanus 'Florence Lavender' — B,CL
Centaurea cyanus 'Florence' mix — BD,CL,D,DT,J,MO,SE,U
Centaurea cyanus 'Florence' pink — B,BS,CL,D,KS,MO,O, S,V
Centaurea cyanus 'Florence' pink/white — U
Centaurea cyanus 'Florence' red — B,BS,CL,D,KS,MO,U
Centaurea cyanus 'Florence' violet — B,CL,MO
Centaurea cyanus 'Florence' white — B,BS,CL,D,KS,MO,O, PI,S,V
Centaurea cyanus 'Frosted Queen' mix — SK
Centaurea cyanus 'Frosty' mix — DE,F,J,JO,KS,S,V
Centaurea cyanus 'Jubilee Gem' — B,DN,L,S,SK,T
Centaurea cyanus 'King Size' mix — C
Centaurea cyanus 'King Size' s-c — B
Centaurea cyanus 'Mauve Queen' — B,F
Centaurea cyanus 'Midget' mix — F,S,VY
Centaurea cyanus 'Midget' s-c — F
Centaurea cyanus mix choice — BY,C,JO
Centaurea cyanus mix cut fl — T
Centaurea cyanus mix tall — F,HU
Centaurea cyanus mix tall dbl — BD,BS,CO,J,KI,KS,L, R,S,SE,ST,TU,U,YA
Centaurea cyanus mix tall dbl p.s — S
Centaurea cyanus 'Pinkie' — B,BS,CN,MO
Centaurea cyanus 'Polka Dot' — BD,BS,BY,C,CL,CO, DN,F,KI,KS,MO,PI,PK,S, SE,SK,VH,VY
Centaurea cyanus 'Red Boy' — B,BS,BU,BY,CN,DE,MO
Centaurea cyanus 'Snowman' — B,BS,BY,C,KS,MO
Centaurea cyanus tall dbl s-c — BD,BY
Centaurea cyanus tall strains s-c, mix — SK
Centaurea cyanus 'Victoria Blue' — B
Centaurea cyanus 'Victoria White' — B
Centaurea cyanus wild dw — B
Centaurea cynaroides see Leuzea centauroides
Centaurea dealbata — B,BS,C,CN,HP,JE,MO, SA,T
Centaurea fischeri see C. cheiranthifolia v purpurascens
Centaurea jacea — B,HU,JE,SG,V
Centaurea kotschyana — HP
Centaurea macrocephala — AP,B,BS,C,G,HP,HU,JE, KI,KS,MO,P,RS,SA,SC, SG,SK,ST,SU,T,V
Centaurea micranthos — B
Centaurea montana — AB,AP,B,BH,BS,C,CG, CN,DE,E,G,HP,I,JE,MO, PI,PK,SA,SK,T,V
Centaurea montana alba — B,HP,JE,SA
Centaurea montana 'Ochroleuca' — E

Centaurea moschata see Amberboa
Centaurea nervosa — C
Centaurea nigra — B,C,CN,CO,HU,JE,LA, SA,SG,TU
Centaurea nigra ssp nemoralis — CG
Centaurea nigra v rivularis — B,JE,SA
Centaurea nigrofimbria — VO
Centaurea orientalis — B,G,JE,SA
Centaurea ornata — I
Centaurea paniculata v henryi — B
Centaurea phrygia — AP,B,HP,SG,T
Centaurea pulcherrima — AP,B,C,F,G,HP,JE,SA
Centaurea pulchra 'Major' see Leuzea centauroides
Centaurea rothrockii — B,SW,T
Centaurea rupestris — B,G,JE
Centaurea ruthenica — B,CG,G,SG
Centaurea sadlerana — SG
Centaurea scabiosa — B,C,CG,CN,G,HP,LA,JE, SA,SG,TH
Centaurea scabiosa alba — B,NS
Centaurea scabiosa 'Alpestris' — B
Centaurea scilloides — HP
Centaurea sibirica — SG
Centaurea simplicicaulis — AP,HP
Centaurea sosnovskyi — VO
Centaurea sp — KL
Centaurea triumfettii — VO
Centaurea uniflora — AP,CG
Centaurea uniflora ssp nervosa — AP,B,F,JE,SC
Centaurium chloodes see C.confertum
Centaurium confertum — AP,B,C,G,KL,SC,SG
Centaurium erythraea — B,BH,C,CN,DD,G,HP,JE, LA,SA,SC
Centaurium muhlenbergii — B
Centaurium pulchellum — B,DV,SG
Centaurium scilloides — AP,B,C,G,SC,T
Centella asiatica — B
Centranthus albus — HP,JD
Centranthus angustifolius — B,C
Centranthus calyptrata — B,KS,SG
Centranthus calyptrata — DI
Centranthus macrosiphon — B,V
Centranthus macr. 'Tumbling Spurs' — F
Centranthus ruber — AB,AP,B,C,CN,DD,E,G, HP,HU,L,PK,PM,SU,TH
Centranthus ruber 'Albus' — AP,B,E,G,HP,HU,JE, KS,MA,SA
Centranthus ruber 'Betsy' — B,BS,L
Centranthus ruber 'Coccineus' — E,G,JE,MO,SA,SK
Centranthus ruber red — S
Centranthus ruber 'Rosenrot' — JE
Centranthus ruber 'Roseus' — B,C,SE
Centranthus ruber 'Snowcloud' — C,CN,L,SE
Centranthus ruber 'Star' — T
Centrosema pubescens — B
Cephalanthera rubra — B
Cephalanthus occidentalis — B,C,FW,LN,PR,SA
Cephalaria alpina — AP,B,C,G,HP,HU,JE,SA
Cephalaria alpina 'Nana' — HP
Cephalaria dipsacoides — AP,CG,G
Cephalaria galpiniana ssp simplicior — B,SI
Cephalaria gigantea — AP,B,BS,C,CL,G,HP,HU, I,JD,JE,MO,P,PL,SA, SC,SG,T
Cephalaria leucantha — AP,B,C,T
Cephalaria natalensis — B,SI

CEPHALARIA

Cephalaria oblongifloia	B,SI
Cephalaria tchihatchewii	HP,SG
Cephalipterum drummondii	B,C,NI,O
Cephalipterum drummondii white	B,NI
Cephalipterum f major	O
Cephalipterum f minor	O
Cephalocereus chrysacanthus	B,BC,DV
Cephalocereus palmeri	DV
Cephalocereus royenii	B
Cephalocereus senilis	B,DV,Y
Cephalocleistocactus schattatianus	DV,Y
Cephalophora aromatica	B,DD,SG
Cephalophyllum alstonii	B,C,DV,KB,Y
Cephalophyllum aureorubrum	B,DV,KB,Y
Cephalophyllum caespitosum	B,DV,SI
Cephalophyllum caespitosum v spissum	B
Cephalophyllum compactum	B
Cephalophyllum diversiphyllum	B,DV
Cephalophyllum franciscii	B,DV,Y
Cephalophyllum gracile	B,DV
Cephalophyllum loreum	B
Cephalophyllum parvibracteatum	B,DV
Cephalophyllum pillansii	B,DV,Y
Cephalophyllum procumbens	DV
Cephalophyllum pulchrum	B
Cephalophyllum purpureo-album	B
Cephalophyllum regale	DV
Cephalophyllum sp mix	C,KB
Cephalophyllum spongiosum	B,DV,GC
Cephalophyllum staminodiosum	B
Cephalophyllum subulatoides	B,DV
Cephalosphaea usumbanensis	B,SA
Cephalotaxus chinensis	SA
Cephalotaxus fortunei	A,B,CG,EL,FW,LN,SA
Cephalotaxus harringtonia	B,CG
Cephalotaxus harringtonia v drupacea	A,B,C,FW,SA
Cephalotaxus oliveri	B
Cephalotaxus sinensis	B,EL,LN
Cerastium alpinum	AP,KL,SG
Cerastium alpinum ssp lanatum	AP,B,G,JE,KL,RM,SC
Cerastium arabidis	B,SI
Cerastium articum edmonstonii	SG
Cerastium arvense	B,JE
Cerastium biebersteinii	C,HU,JE,SA
Cerastium boissieri	SG
Cerastium brachypetalum	SG
Cerastium fontanum	B
Cerastium grandiflorum	B,JE
Cerastium lineare	VO
Cerastium ponticum	B
Cerastium sp	KL
Cerastium tomentosum	B,BD,BS,BY,DE,F,HP,J,K L,L,MO,PI,PK,S,SA,SC, SG,ST,SU,T,TH,U,V,VY
Cerastium tomentosum v columnae	B,C,CN,KS
Cerastium tom. v columnae 'Silberteppich'	BS,HU,JE,SK
Cerastium tomentosum 'Yo-Yo'	CL
Cerasus mahaleb	SG
Cerasus maximowiczii	SG
Ceratoides lanata	NO
Ceratonia siliqua	B,C,CA,EL,FW,HA,KL, KS,LN,O,SA,VE,WA
Ceratopetalum apetalum	B,HA,O
Ceratopetalum gummiferum	B,C,EL,HA,NI,O,SA,SH, WA
Ceratotheca triloba	AP,B,BH,G,KB,SI

Ceratotheca triloba 'Alba'	B,KB
Ceratotheca triloba mauve	B,C,KB
Ceratozamia hildae	O
Ceratozamia latifolia	O
Ceratozamia mexicana	O
Ceratozamia robusta	O
Cerbera manghas	B
Cercidiphyllum japonicum	B,C,CA,CG,EL,FW,LN, N,SA,VE
Cercidium floridum	CA,SA
Cercidium microphyllum	B,CA
Cercidium praecox	CA,DD
Cercis canadensis	A,AP,B,CA,DE,EL,FW, HU,LN,N,NO,SA,SC,VE
Cercis chinensis	AP,B,C,CA,EL,FW,LN,SA
Cercis gigantea	SA
Cercis occidentalis	A,AB,B,C,CA,DD,FW, HU,LN,NO,SA
Cercis siliquastrum	A,AP,B,C,CA,CG,EL,FW, G,HP,JD,LN,O,RH,SA, SC,VE,WA
Cercis siliquastrum 'Afghan'	SA
Cercis siliquastrum f albida	B,C,FW,N,SA
Cercis yunnanensis	SG
Cercocarpus betuloides	CA,HU
Cercocarpus ledifolius	B,C,LN,NO,SA
Cercocarpus montanus	AB,B,C,LN,NO,SA
Cercocarpus montanus v glaber	B
Cereus aethiops	B,CH,DV
Cereus azureus	B
Cereus chalybaeus	DV
Cereus cochabambensis	B,DV,Y
Cereus comarapanus	B,DV,Y
Cereus forbesii see C.validus	
Cereus grandicostatus	B,CH
Cereus hankeanus	B,DV,GC
Cereus jamacura	B,CH,DV,Y
Cereus peruviana x azureus	Y
Cereus peruviana see C.uruguayanus	
Cereus peruvianus spiral	HU
Cereus sp mix	C,Y
Cereus uruguayanus 'Monstrosus'	B,DV,GC,HU,Y
Cereus uruguayanus 'Peruvianus'	B,CH,DD,DV,HU,Y
Cereus validus	B,CH,DV,GC,Y
Cereus xanthocarpus	B,BC,DV,Y
Cerinthe glabra	AP,B,C,G,HP,JE,SA
Cerinthe major	AP,DI,HP,T
Cerinthe major v purpurascens	AP,F,HP,KS,MA,P,PL, SZ,T
Cerinthe minor	B,HP
Cerochlamys pachyphylla	B
Cerochlamys pachyphylla v albiflora	B
Ceropegia ampliata	B,C
Ceropegia linearis ssp woodii	B,SI
Ceropegia sp	SI
Ceropegia stapeliformis	B,CF
Ceropegia stapeliformis v serpentina	B
Ceroxylon quindiuense	B
Cestrum aurantiacum	AP,HP
Cestrum auriculatum	B
Cestrum diurnum	B
Cestrum nocturnum	B,C,CA,DD,HA,HU,SA
Cestrum parqui	B
Cestrum sp 'Hual de Noche'	B,HU
Chaenactis alpina	B,RM
Chaenactis douglasii	B,RM

CHAENACTIS

Chaenactis fremontii	B
Chaenactis glabriuscula	B
Chaenactis xantiana	B
Chaenomeles cathayensis	C,CG,NG,SG
Chaenomeles japonica	A,B,CG,FW,LN,RS,SA,V
Chaenomeles sp & cv mix	C
Chaenomeles speciosa	C,CA,CG,LN,N,SA,VE
Chaenomeles x californica	C
Chaenorrhinum glareosum	AP,B,HP,SC
Chaenorrhinum minus	B
Chaenorrhinum origanifolium	AP,G,KL,SG
Chaerophyllum aromaticum	SG
Chaerophyllum bulbosum	B,DD
Chaerophyllum hirsutum	G,SG
Chaerophyllum hirsutum 'Roseum'	B,HP,P
Chaerophyllum prescottii	SG
Chaerophyllum temulentum	B,SG
Chaetosciadium trichospermum	B
Chamaebatiaria millefolium	B,SW
Chamaecereus see Echinopsis chamaecereus	
Chamaecrista fasciculata	B
Chamaecyparis funebris see Cupressus	
Chamaecyparis lawsoniana	AB,B,BS,C,DD,EL,FW,H A,LN,RH,SA,SG,VE,WA
Chamaecyparis lawsoniana 'Allumii'	B,BS,C,RS,SG
Chamaecyparis lawsoniana 'Argentea'	B,CG,EL,FW,SA
Chamaecyparis lawsoniana 'Aurea'	B,EL,SA
Chamaecyparis lawsoniana 'Blue Jacket'	RS
Chamaecyparis lawsoniana 'Ellwoodii'	KL
Chamaecyparis lawsoniana 'Fletcheri'	B
Chamaecyparis laws. 'Pendula Glauca'	B,EL,SA
Chamaecyparis lawsoniana 'Pyramidalis'	B,FW,SA
Chamaecyparis l. 'Triumf Van Boskoop'	B,FW
Chamaecyparis nootkatensis	LN,RH
Chamaecyparis obtusa	B,C,EL,FW,LN,SA
Chamaecyparis pisifera	B,FW,LN,RH,SA
Chamaecyparis pisifera 'Filifera'	B
Chamaecyparis pisifera 'Plumosa Aurea'	CG
Chamaecyparis pisifera 'Squarrosa'	CG
Chamaecyparis thyoides	RH
Chamaecyparis thyoides 'Glauca'	B,C,FW,SA
Chamaecytisus austriacus	SG
Chamaecytisus hirsutus	G,KL,SG
Chamaecytisus palmensis	B
Chamaecytisus proliferus	DD,EL,HA,HU,O,SA,VE
Chamaecytisus purpureus	KL
Chamaecytisus rochelii	SG
Chamaecytisus ruthenicus	G,SG
Chamaedaphne calyculata	B
Chamaedorea cataractarum	B,CA,EL,O
Chamaedorea costaricana	B,CA,O,SA
Chamaedorea elegans	B,HA,EL,O,SA,SK,V
Chamaedorea elegans collinia	CA
Chamaedorea ernesti-augusti	CA,O
Chamaedorea erumpens	B,EL,O
Chamaedorea 'Florida'	B,CA
Chamaedorea geonomiformis	B,O
Chamaedorea glaucifolia	B,EL
Chamaedorea metallica h. see C.microspadix	
Chamaedorea microspadix	B,CA,EL,SA
Chamaedorea neurochlamys	O
Chamaedorea oblongata	B,CG,EL,SA
Chamaedorea pacaya	B
Chamaedorea radicalis	B,EL,O,SA
Chamaedorea seifritzii	B,C,CA,EL,HA,O
Chamaedorea stolonifera	B

Chamaedorea tenellaa	B,O
Chamaedorea tepejilote	B,CA,CG,EL,HU,O,SA
Chamaelaucium megalopetalum	O
Chamaelaucium micranthum uncinatum	O
Chamaelaucium uncinatum	EL,HA,O,SH
Chamaelopsis mix	CH,Y
Chamaemelum caucasicum	KL,VO
Chamaemelum nobile	AP,B,BY,CG,CN,CP,DI, JE,KS,SA,SG,T,TH
Chamaenerion see Epilobium	
Chamaerops excelsa h. see Trachycarpus fortunei	
Chamaerops humilis	B,C,CA,EL,FW,O,SA,V, VE
Chamaescilla corymbosa	B,C,NI
Chamaescilla corymbosa v latifolia	B,NI
Chamaescilla spiralis	B,NI
Chamaespartium sagittale see Genista sagittalis	
Chambeyronia macrocarpa	B,CA
Chamelaucium conostigmum	B,NI
Chamelaucium megalopetalum	B,NI
Chamelaucium micranthum	B,NI
Chamelaucium uncinatum	B,C,NI,SA
Chamerion angustifolium	SG
Chasmanthe aethiopica	AP,B,C,KB,SI
Chasmanthe bicolor	B,C,G,MN,RU
Chasmanthe floribunda	B,C,KB,RU,SI
Chasmanthe floribunda v duckitti	RU,SI
Chasmanthium latifolium	B,C,CP,DE,G,JE,LG,NT, SA,SC
Chasmatophyllum braunsii	B,DV
Chasmatophyllum musculinum	B,DV
Cheesmania latisiliqua	B,SS
Cheiranthera filifolia	B,NI
Cheiranthus see Erysimum	
Cheiranthus x kewensis	BH
Cheiridopsis aspera	B
Cheiridopsis aurea	B,DV,GC,SI,Y
Cheiridopsis borealis	Y
Cheiridopsis brownii	B
Cheiridopsis brownii v robusta	B,DV
Cheiridopsis candidissima see C.denticulata	
Cheiridopsis caroli-schmidtii	B,DV
Cheiridopsis cigarettifera	B,DV,SI
Cheiridopsis cuprea	B,DV,Y
Cheiridopsis denticulata	B,DV,KB,SI,Y
Cheiridopsis derenbergiana	DV
Cheiridopsis dilatata	B
Cheiridopsis duplessii	B,DV,SI,Y
Cheiridopsis excavata	B,DV,KB
Cheiridopsis herrei	B
Cheiridopsis imitans	B
Cheiridopsis marlothii	B,DV,SI,Y
Cheiridopsis meyeri v minor	B
Cheiridopsis peculiaris	B,DV,SI,Y
Cheiridopsis pillansii	B,DV,KB,SI,Y
Cheiridopsis pillansii v crassa	B
Cheiridopsis purpurea	B
Cheiridopsis robusta	B,DV,KB
Cheiridopsis roodiae	B,Y
Cheiridopsis rostrata	B,SI
Cheiridopsis schlechteri	B,DV,KB
Cheiridopsis sp mix	C,KB
Cheiridopsis speciosa	B
Cheiridopsis turbinata	B
Cheiridopsis vanbredai	B
Cheiridopsis vanzylii	B,DV,KB,SI,Y

CHEIRODENDRON

Cheirodendron trigynum	DD
Chelidonium japonicum	B,P,SC
Chelidonium majus	C,CG,CN,CP,DD,G,HP, HU,JE,RH,SG
Chelidonium majus fl.pl.	AP,B,C,CP,HP,JE,P
Chelidonium majus 'Laciniatum'	AP,CG
Chelidonium majus 'Laciniatum fl.pl.'	HP,NG
Chelidonium majus semi-plena	SG
Chelone glabra	B,HP,JE,NT,PR,SA
Chelone lyonii	B,JE,NT,SA
Chelone obliqua	AP,B,BS,CG,F,G,HP, JE,SA,T
Chenopodium album	AB,B,CP,DD,HU
Chenopodium album v edulis	DD
Chenopodium ambrosioides	AB,B,C,CN,CP,DD,HU, KS
Chenopodium atro-virens	B
Chenopodium berlandieri 'Chual'	B
Chenopodium berlandieri 'Huazontle'	B,DD
Chenopodium berlandieri 'Quelite'	B
Chenopodium berlandieri v nuttaliae	B
Chenopodium bonus-henricus	B,CN,DD,HU,SG,TH
Chenopodium botrys	B,C,CP,DD,HU,PI,SG
Chenopodium botrys 'Green Magic'	B
Chenopodium capitatum	B,HU,SG
Chenopodium desertorum	B,NI
Chenopodium foliosum	B,C,DD,T
Chenopodium giganteum	B,C,CP,DD,HU,T
Chenopodium murale	B,DD
Chenopodium nuttaliae	B
Chenopodium quinoa	B,C,DD,KS
Chenopodium quinoa Andean Hybrids	B,HU,T
Chenopodium quinoa hyb	B,DD
Chenopodium sp	AP,DD
Chenopodium urbicum	B
Chiastophyllum oppositifolium	AP,B,C,DV,G,HP,KL,P, SA,SC,VO
Chiastophyllum oppos. 'Goldtropfchen'	JE,PK
Chileorebutia aerocarpa	BC
Chileorebutia napina	BC
Chiliotrichum diffusum	AR
Chilopsis linearis	B,CA,RS,SA,SW
Chilopsis linearis dk purple	B
Chimaphila japonica	KL
Chimaphila umbellata	B,C,NO
Chimonanthus praecox	AP,B,BS,C,CA,CG,DD, EL,FW,G,HA,N,SA
Chionanthus foveolata	B
Chionanthus retusus	B,C,CA,EL,FW,SA
Chionanthus virginicus	B,C,CA,EL,FW,G,LN,SA
Chionochloa beddiei	B,SA
Chionochloa conspicua	B,C,SA,SS
Chionochloa flavescens	AP,B,C,SA,SS
Chionochloa pallens	AP,B,SS
Chionochloa rigida	AP,B
Chionochloa rubra	AP,B,SC,SS
Chionodoxa forbesii	AP,B,G,KL
Chionodoxa luciliae h. see C.forbesii	
Chionodoxa sardensis	AP,B,G,KL,SC
Chionohebe pulvinaris	B,SS
Chiranthodendron pentadactylon	B
Chirita caliginosa	C
Chirita lavandulacea	SG
Chirita micromusa	C
Chirita sericea	C
Chironia baccifera	B,BH,KB

Chironia linoides ssp linoides	B
Chironia melampyrifolia	B,SI
Chironia ?peglerae	B,SI
Chironia purpurascens ssp humilis	B,SI
Chloris barbata	B
Chloris gayana	HA
Chloris gayana 'Callide'	B,EL
Chloris gayana 'Katambora'	B,EL
Chloris gayana 'Mbah'	B
Chloris gayana 'Pioneer'	B,EL
Chloris gayana 'Samford'	B
Chloris truncata	HA
Chlorogalum pomeridianum	B,HU,MN
Chlorophytum capense	B,SI
Chlorophytum crassinerve	B,SI
Chlorophytum inornatum	B
Chlorophytum krookianum	B,KB<SI
Chlorophytum macrophyllum	B
Chlorophytum orchidastrum	B,SG
Choisya arizonica	B,SW
Chondrilla juncea	B
Chondropetalum ebracteatum	B,SI
Chondropetalum hookerianum	B,SI
Chondropetalum mucronatum	B,SI
Chondropetalum sp nova	SI
Chondropetalum tectorum	B,KB,O,SA,SI
Chordospartium stevensonii	AP,B,C,SA,SC,SS
Chorisia insignis	B,EL,SA
Chorisia speciosa	B,CA,DV,EL,HA,SA,WA, Y
Chorispora bungeana	VO
Chorizema aciculare	B,NI
Chorizema cordatum	B,NI,O,RS,SA
Chorizema dicksonii	B,C,NI,SA
Chorizema diversifolium	B,NI,O,SA
Chorizema ilicifolium	B,C,NI,O,RS,SA
Chorizema nervosum	B,NI
Chorizema reticulatum	B,NI
Chorizema rhombeum	B,NI,SA
Chosena arbutifolia	SG
Chosmanthe floribunda	CG
Christella patens v lepida	B
Christia vespertilionis	B
Chrysalidocarpus ankaizinensis	B
Chrysalidocarpus cabadae	B,CA,O
Chrysalidocarpus catechu	HA
Chrysalidocarpus decipiens	B,EL
Chrysalidocarpus fibrosus	O
Chrysalidocarpus lucubensis	CA,O,SA
Chrysalidocarpus lutescens	B,DD,EL,HA,O,SA,VE
Chrysalidocarpus lutescens (g)	B,N
Chrysalidocarpus madagascariensis	B
Chrysalidocarpus mad. v lucubensis	O
Chrysalidocarpus monimony	O
Chrysalidocarpus tsaravotsira	O
Chrysanthemoides incana	B,SI
Chrysanthemoides monilifera	B,SI
Chrysanthemum anserinifolium	HP
Chrysanthemum 'Antwerp Star'	C
Chrysanthemum arcticum L. see Arctanthemum	
Chrysanthemum carinatum	AB,B,HW,SG
Chrysanthemum car. annual special mix	FR,S
Chrysanthemum carinatum 'Bridal Robe'	S
Chrysanthemum carinatum 'Chameleon'	B
Chrysanthemum carinatum 'Court Jesters'	C,DT,T
Chrysanthemum car. Dunnettii Choice mix	SK

CRYSANTHEMUM

Chrysanthemum car. 'Dunnettii Luteum'	B,KS
Chrysanthemum car. 'Flame Shades'	B
Chrysanthemum carinatum 'John Bright'	B
Chrysanthemum carinatum 'Merry Mix'	BU,C,CA
Chrysanthemum carinatum 'Polar Star'	B,KS,T
Chrysanthemum cinerariifolium see C.Tanacetum	
Chrysanthemum coronarium	CA,CP,G,SD,SG
Chrysanthemum cor. 'Cream Bonnet'	B
Chrysanthemum coronarium fl.pl.	BS,BY
Chrysanthemum cor. 'Golden Bonnet'	B
Chrysanthemum cor. 'Golden Gem'	B,T
Chrysanthemum cor. 'Golden Glory'	B
Chrysanthemum cor. 'Primrose Gem'	B,T
Chrysanthemum corymbosum see C.Tanacetum	
Chrysanthemum discoideum	B
Chrysanthemum f1 'Fanfare'	BS,C,CA,CL,DE,DT,F, FR,JE,L,MO,PL,T
Chrysanthemum f1 'Fashion mix'	C,DE,SE
Chrysanthemum f1 'Super Jet'	D
Chrysanthemum gruppenstolz	SG
Chrysanthemum Incurved fl, mix	C
Chrysanthemum indicum 'Cascade'	DT
Chrysanthemum i. 'Charm Early Fash. Mix'	T
Chrysanthemum i. f1 'Autumn Glory Mix'	BS,CA,CL,DT,MO,PK, SE,SK,U
Chrysanthemum i. Spiders/Spoons imp	T
Chrysanthemum Korean Hybrids	B,BS,BY,C,D,F,JE,MO, SA
Chrysanthemum macrophyllum see C.Tanacetum	
Chrysanthemum multicaule	B,C,SK,V
Chrysanthemum multicaule 'Goblin'	BS,DT,MO
Chrysanthemum multicaule 'Gold Plate'	BS
Chrysanthemum multicaule 'Moonlight'	BS,F,MO,T
Chrysanthemum nipponicum see Nipponanthemum	
Chrysanthemum nivellii 'Snowstorm'	T
Chrysanthemum 'Rainbow'	BS,D,KI,SU
Chrysanthemum sebatense	B
Chrysanthemum sebatense 'Silver Carpet'	C
Chrysanthemum segetum	B,C,CN,CO,G,LA,SU, TH,TU,Z
Chrysanthemum segetum 'Eastern Star'	B
Chrysanthemum segetum 'Eldorado'	B
Chrysanthemum segetum 'German Flag'	B
Chrysanthemum segetum 'Gloria'	B
Chrysanthemum segetum 'Helios'	B
Chrysanthemum segetum 'Paradiso'	B
Chrysanthemum segetum 'Prado'	C
Chrysanthemum spider type, mix	C
Chrysanthemum spray forms	PT
Chrysanthemum tianschanicum	SG
Chrysanthemum 'Tricolor'	BS,BY,D,DE,F,KI,M,U
Chrysanthemum x spectabile 'Annette'	B
Chrysanthemum x spectabile 'Cecilia'	B
Chrysanthemum x spectabile 'Mogul'	B
Chrysobalanus icaco	B
Chrysocephalum apiculatum	B,NI,O
Chrysocoma ciliata	B,SI
Chrysocoma coma-aurea	B,BH,C,HP,KB,SI
Chrysocoma sp	SI
Chrysolepis chrysophylla	SA
Chrysolidocarpus lutescens	RE
Chrysophyllum cainito	B,RE,SA
Chrysophyllum oliviforme	B
Chrysopog gryllus	B,JE
Chrysopsis mariana	JE
Chrysopsis villosa see Heterotheca	

Chrysosplenium alternifolium	B,C,JE
Chrysothamnus friedrichsthaliana	C
Chrysothamnus hyb mix	C
Chrysothamnus nauseosus	B,C,CA,LN,NO,SA
Chrysothamnus naus. ssp bernardinus	B
Chrysothamnus viscidiflorus	LN,NO
Chrysothamnus viscidiflorus ssp pumilus	B
Chrysothemis villosa	C
Chytranthus macrobotrys	B
Cibotium chamissoi	B
Cibotium glaucum	B
Cicerbita alpina	B,C,JE
Cicerbita plumieri	HP
Cichorium intybus	AP,B,C,CA,CN,CO,CP, HP,HW,JE,KS,LA,SA, SG,TH
Cichorium intybus 'Roseum'	HP
Cicuta maculata	B,PR
Cilia capitata	SG
Cima mexicana	B
Cimicifuga americana	B,C,G,JE,SA
Cimicifuga cordifolia	SA
Cimicifuga dahurica	C,JE,SA
Cimicifuga foetida	JE,SG
Cimicifuga japonica	B,SG
Cimicifuga racemosa	B,C,CG,HU,SA,SC,SG,T
Cimicifuga ramosa 'Atropurpureum' see C.simplex	
Cimicifuga ramosa see C.simplex v s. 'Pritchard's Giant'	
Cimicifuga rubifolia	B,C,G,JE
Cimicifuga simplex	B,C,DD,JE
Cimicifuga simplex Atropurpurea Group	AP,B,G,JE,PA,SA,T
Cimicifuga simplex 'Brunette'	HP
Cimicifuga simplex v s. 'Pritchard's Giant'	B,G,JE,SA
Cinchona pubescens v succirubra	B
Cineraria fl hyb see Pericallis	
Cineraria saxifraga	B
Cineraria see Senecio	
Cinnamonum camphora	CA,EL,FW,LN,WA
Cipadessa baccifera	B,EL
Cipocereus minensis	CH,DV
Circaea alpina	SG
Circaea lutetiana	B,C,JE
Cirsium acaule	AP,B,C,G,JE,KL
Cirsium arvense	B
Cirsium brachycephalum	B
Cirsium candelabrum	HP
Cirsium canum	B,G,SG
Cirsium carolinianum	B
Cirsium discolor	B
Cirsium dissectum	B
Cirsium eriophorum	AP,B,G,SC,SG
Cirsium flodmanii	SG
Cirsium helenoides see C.heterophyllum	
Cirsium heterophyllum	B,C,HP,JE,SA,SG
Cirsium japonicum	AP,B,CN,F,SA,SC,V
Cirsium japonicum 'Lilac Beauty'	B
Cirsium japonicum 'Pink Beauty'	B,BS,C,CL,DE,JE,KS, MO
Cirsium japonicum 'Rose Beauty'	B,BS,C,CL,DE,HP,JE,KS, L,MO
Cirsium japonicum 'Snow Beauty'	B
Cirsium japonicum 'Strawberry Ripple'	U
Cirsium japonicum 'White Puff'	JE
Cirsium kamtschaticum	SG
Cirsium muticum	B
Cirsium oleraceum	B,C,SG

CIRSIUM

Cirsium palustre	B
Cirsium rivulare atropurpureum	HP
Cirsium setosum	SG
Cirsium spinosissimum	AP,B
Cirsium tall pink/rose beauty	T
Cirsium texanum	B
Cirsium undulatum	B
Cirsium vulgare	B
Cissampelos tropaeolifolia	B
Cissus antarctica	B,C,CA,EL,HA,NI,O,SA,
	SH,V
Cissus hypoglauca	B,C,EL,HA,NI,O,SH
Cissus quadrangularis	B,EL,SI
Cissus rhombifolia	B,CA,EL,O
Cissus saundersii	DV
Cissus setosa	B
Cissus sp	SI
Cistus albidus	B,G,HP,SA,SG,VE
Cistus clusii	SA
Cistus creticus	B,LN,RH,SC,T
Cistus creticus ssp incanus	AP,B,C,CA,LN,SA,VO
Cistus crispus hort see C.x pulverulentus	
Cistus heterophyllus	RH
Cistus hirsutus	SG
Cistus incanus see C.creticus ssp incanus	
Cistus incanus ssp corsicus see C.creticus	
Cistus ladanifer	AP,B,DD,G,HP,LN,SA,
	SC,SD,SG
Cistus ladanifer v sulcatus	P
Cistus laurifolius	AP,B,C,CG,EL,G,HP,JE,
	RH,SA,SC,SG,VE
Cistus libanotis	SA
Cistus mix vars	T
Cistus monspeliensis	AP,B,C,CG,G,HP,SA,
	SC,SG,VE
Cistus palhinhae see C.ladanifer v sulcatus	
Cistus parviflorus	HP,KL,RH,SG
Cistus populifolius	AP,C,HP,SA,SC,SG
Cistus psilosepalus	AP,G,RH,SC,SG
Cistus salviifolius	AP,B,C,CG,EL,G,HP,HU,
	SA,SC,SG,VE
Cistus 'Silver Pink'	AP,C
Cistus sp Portugal	SG
Cistus symphytifolius	AP,SA
Cistus varius	SG
Cistus villosus see C.creticus	
Cistus x dansereaui 'Decumbens'	SG
Cistus x lusitanicus see C.x dansereaui	
Cistus x obtusifolius	HP
Cistus x pulverulentus	SA,VE
Citharexylum fruticosum	B
Citrullus colocynthis	B
Citrullus ecirrhosus	B,SI
Citrullus lanatus	B,SI
Citrullus lanatus v citroides	B
Citrullus metuliferus	SI
Citrullus mucosospermus	B
Citrullus vulgaris	B
Citrus aurantifolia	B
Citrus aurantium	LN
Citrus calomondin see x Citrofortunella microcarpa	
Citrus citrange	SA
Citrus 'Citronelle'	B,EL,SA
Citrus hystrix	B
Citrus jambhiri	B,SA
Citrus kumquat see Fortunella margarita	

Citrus limequat	SA
Citrus limetta	B
Citrus limettoides	B
Citrus limon	B
Citrus limon 'Villa Franca'	B
Citrus macrophylla	SA
Citrus maxima	B
Citrus medica	B
Citrus reticulata	LN
Citrus sinensis	B
Citrus sinensis 'Washington'	B
Citrus sp	RE
Citrus trifoliata	FW,VE
Citrus volkamericna	LN,SA,VE
Citrus x limonia	LN
Citrus x paradisi see C. x tangelo	
Citrus x tangelo	B
Citrus x tangelo 'Golden Special'	B
Cladanthus arabicus	B,J
Cladanthus arabicus 'Criss-Cross'	C
Cladium mariscus	B,C,JE
Cladrastis lutea	B,C,FW,LN,N,SA,VE
Cladrastis sinensis	LN,SA
Clarisia racemosa	B
Clarkia amoena	AB,AP,B,CA,DD,DI,PI,
	SG
Clarkia amoena 'Aurora'	B,HU
Clarkia amoena 'Azaleaflora'	B,BS,BY,C,CL,DT,F,FR,
	HU,KI,L,M,MO,R,S,T,TE,
	U,VH,YA
Clarkia amoena 'Bornita Mix'	F,T
Clarkia amoena 'Dream Double'	BS,KI
Clarkia amoena 'Dw Gem'	BS,MO
Clarkia amoena f1 'Grace Lavender'	B
Clarkia amoena f1 'Grace Lavender Eye'	B
Clarkia amoena f1 'Grace' mix	BS,C,CA,CL,D,JO,KI,
	MO,PK
Clarkia amoena f1 'Grace' s-c	B,PK
Clarkia amoena f1 'Satin' mix	BS,C,CL,D,DT,MO,PK,
	S,SK,T,YA
Clarkia amoena f1 'Satin' s-c	SE,T
Clarkia amoena 'Furora'	B
Clarkia amoena 'Gloriana'	B
Clarkia amoena 'Lilac Lady'	V
Clarkia amoena 'Memoria'	B
Clarkia amoena mix dw	BS
Clarkia amoena mix dw bedding	D,DT,F
Clarkia amoena mix dw selected	S,TU
Clarkia amoena mix single	BS,DN,FR,SU
Clarkia amoena 'Precious Gems'	S,SE
Clarkia amoena 'Schamini'	F,SE
Clarkia amoena ssp lindleyi	SG
Clarkia amoena ssp whitneyi	B,SZ
Clarkia amoena 'Vivid'	HU
Clarkia bottae	B,DI,G
Clarkia bottae 'Amethyst Glow'	T
Clarkia bottae 'Lady in Blue'	T
Clarkia bottae 'Lilac Blossom'	BS,C,CO,HU,J,KI,U,VY
Clarkia bottae 'Lilac Pixie'	F,PK
Clarkia bottae 'Pink Joy'	S,V
Clarkia breweri	B
Clarkia breweri 'Pink Ribbons'	C
Clarkia concinna	B
Clarkia Crown mix	CO
Clarkia dbl delight	KI
Clarkia 'Dbl Nain Cherie Sweetheart'	T

CLARKIA

Clarkia deflexa	AB,B
Clarkia 'Dwarf Asterix'	U
Clarkia imbricata	B
Clarkia 'Jewel' dw	J
Clarkia 'Kelvedon Glory'	C
Clarkia mix	SK
Clarkia mix dw show	C,M,VY
Clarkia mix imp dw	T
Clarkia mix single	CO,FR,TU
Clarkia mix tall dbl	BS,MO,SK
Clarkia 'Monarch' dw mix	C,SK
Clarkia 'Passion for Purple'	S
Clarkia pulchella 'Alba'	V
Clarkia pulchella 'Filigree'	D,F
Clarkia pulchella mix	J,S,SG
Clarkia pulchella mix dbl choice	BY,C,F,L
Clarkia pulchella 'Snowflake'	B,T
Clarkia purpurea	B,SW,SZ
Clarkia 'Rosy Morn re-selected'	C
Clarkia rubicunda	B,BS,T
Clarkia rubicunda 'Lilacina'	F
Clarkia rubicunda shamini	PL,T
Clarkia 'Salmon Princess' dw	B,BS,C,F,MO,PL,T
Clarkia sp	T
Clarkia speciosa ssp immaculata	SZ
Clarkia 'Sybil Sherwood'	B,BS,C,MO,S
Clarkia tenella	AP,B,SZ
Clarkia tenella 'Blue Magic'	C,F
Clarkia unguiculata	AB,B,BD,C,CG,G,HU,
	SG,ST,V
Clarkia unguiculata 'Apple Blossom'	B,C,T,V
Clarkia unguiculata 'Brilliant' dbl	S
Clarkia unguiculata 'Chieftain'	C
Clarkia unguiculata 'Enchantress'	DT
Clarkia unguiculata 'Love Affair'	D
Clarkia unguiculata mix dbl	BS,BU,J,M,TU,U,VH
Clarkia unguiculata mix dbl special	DT,VY
Clarkia unguiculata 'Rhapsody'	S
Clarkia unguiculata 'Royal Bouquet'	B,T
Clarkia unguiculata 'Salmon Queen'	C
Clarkia 'White Bouquet' dbl	BS
Clausena anisata	B,SI
Clausena domesticum	B
Clausena lansium	B,EL
Claytonia australasica see Neopaxia	
Claytonia lanceolata	B,RM
Claytonia megarrhiza	B,RM,SW
Claytonia megarrhiza v nivalis	AP,SC
Claytonia nivalis	I
Claytonia perfoliata	B,CN,TH
Claytonia sibirica	AP,C,CG,JE,SA
Cleistanthus collinus	B
Cleistocactus angosturensis	B,BC,DV,Y
Cleistocactus aureispinus	B
Cleistocactus azarensis	DV
Cleistocactus baumannii	B,CH,DV,Y
Cleistocactus baumannii v flavispinus	B,DV,Y
Cleistocactus brookei	BC,CH,DV,Y
Cleistocactus bruneispinus	DV
Cleistocactus buchtienii	B,DV,Y
Cleistocactus candelilla	B,DV,Y
Cleistocactus chacoanus	B,Y
Cleistocactus hildegardiae v flavirufus	Y
Cleistocactus jujuyensis	DV
Cleistocactus luribayensis	B,DV,Y
Cleistocactus parviflorus	B,Y

Cleistocactus potosinus	DV,Y
Cleistocactus ritteri	B
Cleistocactus rojoi	DV
Cleistocactus samaipatanus	B
Cleistocactus smaragdiflorus	B
Cleistocactus sp mix	C,CH,DV,Y
Cleistocactus strausii	B,BC,C,CH,Y
Cleistocactus tarijensis	B,DV,Y
Cleistocactus tolimanensis	DV
Cleistocactus tupizensis	B,DV,Y
Cleistocactus vallegrandensis	DV,Y
Cleistocactus villamontesii	DV,Y
Cleistocactus viridiflorus	DV,Y
Cleistocactus vulpis cauda	CH,Y
Clematis addisonii	AP,BR,G,HP,IC,SC
Clematis aethusifolia	BR,CG,HP,IC,SA,SC
Clematis afoliata	AU,B,C,SS
Clematis akeboides h. see C.orientalis	BR,G
Clematis aljonushka	BR
Clematis alpina	AP,B,C,DV,FW,G,HP,IC,J
	E,KL,PL,SA,SC,SE,T,VO
Clematis alpina 'Alba'	KL
Clematis alpina blue	IC
Clematis alpina fl.pl	KL
Clematis alpina 'Frances Rivis'	AP,B,BR,C,HP,IC,SC
Clematis alpina 'Pamela Jackman'	BR,IC,SC
Clematis alpina pink	IC
Clematis alpina 'Rosea'	KL
Clematis alpina 'Rubra'	B,JE
Clematis alpina 'Ruby'	AP,BR,IC
Clematis alpina ssp sibirica	AP,HP,IC,KL,RS,SG
Clematis alpina 'Willy'	IC
Clematis annamieke	BR
Clematis apiifolia	B,KL
Clematis arabella	BR
Clematis aristata	AR,AU,B,EL,HA,HP,HU,
	NI,O,SA,SH
Clematis aristata cw Tasmania	IC
Clematis aristata x gentianoides	AR
Clematis armandii	AP,B,HP,SC,SG
Clematis australis	B,SC,SS
Clematis balearica	HP
Clematis balearica 'Freckles'	RS
Clematis barbellata	BR,SC
Clematis 'Bill Mackenzie'	AP,B,BR,C,RM,RS,SC,T
Clematis brachiata	B,BH,KB,SI
Clematis brachyura	IC
Clematis brevicaudata	CG,SA,SG
Clematis buchananiana	B,C,CG,SA
Clematis campaniflora	AP,B,BR,C,CG,G,HP,I,
	IC,JE,N,PL,SC,SG
Clematis chiisanensis	N,SC
Clematis chrysocoma	BR,G
Clematis cirrhosa	SA,SC
Clematis cirrhosa balearica 'Freckles'	AP,BR
Clematis cirrhosa 'Wisley Cream'	BR
Clematis coactilis	BR,IC
Clematis columbiana	B,C,IC,KL,NO,SC
Clematis columbiana v tenuiloba	B,RM
Clematis connata	C
Clematis crispa	BR,CG,G,HP
Clematis crispa cw W.Virginia	IC
Clematis cunninghamii	AR
Clematis cylindrica	BR
Clematis 'Duchess of Albany'	BR
Clematis 'Etoile Rose'	BR

CLEMATIS

Clematis fargesii see C.potaninii	
Clematis fauriei x sibirica 'Pansy'	IC
Clematis flammula	AP,B,BH,BR,C,CG,JE, LN,RS,SA,SC
Clematis flammula rotundiflora	BR
Clematis florida 'Sieboldii'	HP
Clematis foetida	B
Clematis forsteri	AP,B,PM,SA,SC
Clematis forsteri petriei	BR
Clematis fruticosa	SA
Clematis fusca	AP,BR,IC,SG
Clematis fusca (In Vladivostok) cult	IC
Clematis fusca v kamtschatica	IC
Clematis fusca v mandschurica	IC
Clematis fusca violacea	BR
Clematis fusijamana	IC
Clematis gentianoides	BR,HP,SC
Clematis glauca	B,IC,SG
Clematis glauca akeboides	AP
Clematis glaucophylla	AP,BR,IC
Clematis glycinoides	B,C,EL,HA,NI,O,SA
Clematis glycinoides cw Australia	IC
Clematis 'Gravetye Beauty'	BR
Clematis 'Helios'	B,BS,MO,T
Clematis heracleifolia	AP,B,CG,G,HP,JE,SA
Clematis heracleifolia v davidiana	BR,HP,IC
Clematis hexapetala	BR,IC,SG
Clematis hiliariae	BR
Clematis hirsutissima	AP,B,C,NO,SC
Clematis hookeriana	B,C
Clematis Hybrids	BH,C,KL,PL,SE
Clematis indivisa	AP,AR,FW,HP,IC,SS
Clematis integrifolia	AP,B,BR,C,CG,G,HP,IC, JD,JE,KL,RS,SA,SG,T
Clematis integrifolia 'Alba'	AP,BR
Clematis integrifolia 'Olgae'	BR,G,IC
Clematis integrifolia (Prannohybrid blue)	IC
Clematis integrifolia (Prannohybrid red)	IC
Clematis integrifolia 'Rosea'	AP,B,BR,HP,IC
Clematis integrifolia v viticella 'Eriostemon'	IC
Clematis intricata	BR,HP,IC
Clematis ispahanica	BR
Clematis japonica	G
Clematis 'Kermisina'	BR,IC
Clematis kirilowii	CG,IC
Clematis koreana	BR,G
Clematis koreana v fragrans	IC
Clematis koreana yellow	AP,BR,KL,SC
Clematis ladakhiana	BR
Clematis lasiantha	AP,B,RS,SW
Clematis ligusticifolia	B,C,CG,EL,HU,IC,LN, NO,SA
Clematis 'Lunar Lass'	AP,BR,PM
Clematis mackaui	CG
Clematis macropetala	AP,B,C,G,HP,IC,PL,SA, SC,SG
Clematis macropetala hyb	JE
Clematis macropetala 'Jan Lindmark'	IC
Clematis macropetala 'Maidwell Hall'	AP,HP,SG
Clematis macropetala 'Rosy o' Grady'	BR,IC
Clematis mandschurica	AP,B,BR,CG,RS,SG
Clematis marata	AP,B,SA,SS
Clematis marmoraria	AP,AU,G,HP,PM,SC
Clematis marmoraria hyb	AP,PM,SC
Clematis mauritiana	B
Clematis microphylla	B,C,EL,HA,NI,O,RS,SA

Clematis 'Minuet'	AP,BR,IC
Clematis monroi	CG
Clematis montana	B,BR,EL,G,HP,KL,SA,V
Clematis montana 'Elizabeth'	B
Clematis montana 'Rosea'	KL
Clematis montana 'Snowflake'	B
Clematis montana v rubens	B,BR,C,IC,PL,SC
Clematis montana v wilsonii	BR,IC
Clematis montana 'Warwickshire Rose'	HP
Clematis napaulensis	B,BR,C,CG,IC,SA,SC
Clematis 'Nelly Moser'	AP,B,KL
Clematis obscura	IC
Clematis occidentalis	B,LN,SA,SG
Clematis occidentalis v dissecta	IC
Clematis occidentalis v grosseserrata	IC
Clematis ochroleuca	AP,BR,HP
Clematis orientalis	B,C,BR,HP,RS,SA,SG
Clematis orientalis 'Burford Variety'	BR
Clematis 'Pagoda'	BR
Clematis paniculata see C.indivisa	
Clematis parviflora	BR
Clematis patens	B
Clematis petriei	AP,B,PM,SC,SS
Clematis petriei x marmoraria	AP,HP,KL
Clematis pitcherii	AP,BR,G,IC,SZ
Clematis potaninii	AP,B,BR,HP,IC,KL,P,SC
Clematis potaninii 'Souljet'	CG,SC
Clematis potaninii v potaninii	AP,G,HP,LG
Clematis pubescens	B,C,NI,O
Clematis purpureostriata x aljonushka	BR
Clematis quadribracteolata	AP,B,SS
Clematis recta	AP,B,BR,C,CG,G,HP,IC, JD,JE,N,SA,SC,SG
Clematis recta 'Purpurea'	AP,B,BR,G,HP,JD,JE, LG,RS,SA,SC,SG
Clematis rehderiana	AP,BR,DV,E,G,HP,SC,SG
Clematis serratifolia	B,BR,G,HP,IC,SA,SC
Clematis sibirica see C.alpina ssp s.	
Clematis simsii see C.pitcheri	
Clematis songarica	RS
Clematis sp	C,NI,PL
Clematis sp Ecuador	RS
Clematis speciosa	SG
Clematis stans	C,CG,G,HP,I
Clematis 'Sun Star'	SE,U
Clematis tangutica	AP,B,BR,BS,C,CG,DT, EL,F,FW,G,HP,HU,IC,JE, KL,LG,LN,N,PL,S,SA, SC,SG,T,V
Clematis tangutica 'Aureolin'	IC
Clematis tangutica 'Radar Love'	BD,C,L,PK
Clematis tangutica vernayi	IC
Clematis 'Tentel'	IC
Clematis tenuiloba	SG
Clematis terniflora	AU,B,BR,CG,FW,JE,PK, RS,SA,SC,SG
Clematis terniflora v robusta see C.terniflora v t.	
Clematis terniflora v t.	SG
Clematis texensis	AP,B,G,HP,KL,SC,SZ
Clematis tibetana	AP,B,CG,HP,RS,SC
Clematis tibetana ssp vernayi	AP,B,BR
Clematis tubulosa	CG
Clematis versicolor	AP,B,BR,G,SC
Clematis viorna	AP,BR,CG,G,HP,IC,RS, SZ
Clematis virginiana cw (ligusticifolia?)	IC

CLEMATIS

Clematis virginiana h. see C.vitalba	
Clematis viscosa	CG
Clematis vitalba	A,AB,B,BR,C,C,CG,EL,G, HP,JE,LN,PR,RS,SA,SG, TH,VE,Z
Clematis viticella	AP,B,BH,BR,BS,CA,CG, DT,EL,FW,G,HP,IC,JE,KI, KL,LN,N,SA,SC,ST
Clematis wilsonii	IC
Clematis x aromatica	HP
Clematis x clematopsis	B,SI
Clematis x durandii	BR
Clematis x eriostemon	BR
Clematis x eriostemon 'Hendersonii'	HP,RS,SG
Clematopsis scabiosifolia	B,C,KB,SA,SI
Clematopsis sp	SI
Cleome angustifolia	B,SI
Cleome foliosa	B,SI
Cleome gynandra	B
Cleome hassleri	JO,SD,SK
Cleome hassleriana	AB,B,BY,C,DI,EL,G,HW, J,PK,RH,SG,TE,TH,V
Cleome hassleriana 'Cherry Queen'	B,C,PK,T
Cleome hassleriana 'Colour Fountain'	BD,BS,DE,F
Cleome hassleriana 'Helen Campbell'	B,C,DE,HU,KS,SK,T
Cleome hassleriana mix	HU,VY
Cleome hassleriana pink	HU
Cleome hassleriana 'Pink Queen'	B,BS,C,PK,SK,SU,V
Cleome hassleriana 'Rose Queen'	B,BD,BS,DE,MO,PI,SK, TE
Cleome hassleriana 'Violet Queen'	B,C,DE,HU,PI,PK,SD, SK,T,TE,V
Cleome hassleriana 'White Queen'	PI,PK,TE,V
Cleome hirta	B,SI
Cleome isomeris	B
Cleome lutea	B
Cleome marshallii	B
Cleome monophylla	B
Cleome rosea	B
Cleome serrulata	B,SG,SW
Cleome serrulata 'Orchid Festival'	B
Cleome sp	SI
Cleome spinosa see C.hassleriana	
Cleome viscosa	B,C,HU,NI,SA
Cleretum papulosum	B,KB
Cleretum papulosum v schlechteri	B,KB,SI
Clerodendrum colebrookianum	B
Clerodendrum floribundum	B
Clerodendrum glabrum	B,SI
Clerodendrum kaempferi	B
Clerodendrum speciosum	B,CG
Clerodendrum thomsonae	B
Clerodendrum tomentosum	B,EL,NI,O,SA
Clerodendrum trichotomum	B,C,CG,EL,FW,LN,SA, SG,VE
Clerodendrum trichotomum v fargesii	CG,NG
Clethra acuminata	B,FW
Clethra alnifolia	B,FW,HP,SA
Clethra alnifolia 'Rosea'	B
Clethra arborea	B,SG
Clethra barbinervis	A,AP,B,FW,LN,SA
Clethra delavayi AC1869	X
Clethra tomentosa	CG
Cleyera japonica	B,FW,LN,SA
Clianthus formosus	C,DD,DI,F,HA,HU,NI,O, SA,T,VE

Clianthus puniceus	B,C,CG,HP,HU,SA,SC, SG,SS,V,VE
Clianthus puniceus albus	B,C,HP,SA
Clianthus puniceus v roseus	AU,C
Cliffortia cuneata	B,SI
Cliftonia monophylla	AP,B
Clinopodium vulgare	B,C,CN,G,LA,SG,SU
Clintonia andrewsiana	AP,HP
Clintonia udensis	SC,SG
Clintonia uniflora	B,C,NO
Clitoria mariana	B,RS,SW
Clitoria ternatea	B,C,DD,EL,HU,SA
Clitoria ternatea fl.pl. 'Blue Sails'	RS,T
Clitoria ternatea fl.pl. 'Lady Blue'	PL
Clitoria ternatea fl.pl. 'Lady White'	PL
Clitoria ternatea semi-dbl	B
Clitoria ternatea 'Ultra Alba'	B
Clitoria ternatea 'Ultra Marina'	B
Clivia gardenii	B,CF
Clivia hybrids	C,CA,HA
Clivia miniata	B,CF,DV,KB,O,SA,SC,SI
Clivia miniata 'Aurea'	B
Clivia miniata 'Citrina'	PL
Clivia miniata hyb California	B,EL
Clivia miniata hyb new	B
Clivia miniata 'Mammoth'	B
Clivia miniata salmon shades	PL
Clivia miniata twice fl	PK
Clivia miniata Twins	B
Clivia nobilis	CF
Clusia major	B
Cneoridium dumosum	B
Cneorum tricoccon	AP,CG,NG,SC,SG,SZ
Cnicus benedictus	B,CN,CP,PO,SG,SU,TH
Cobaea scandens	B,BS,BY,C,CO,D,DE,DI, DT,EL,F,FR,HP,HU,J,KI, KS,L,PI,PL,MO,S,SA, SK,ST,T,TH,V
Cobaea scandens f alba	B,BS,C,MO,PL,SE,T
Coccinea rehmannii	SI
Coccinia grandis	B
Coccinia palmata	B,SI
Coccinia quinqueloba	B,SI
Coccinia rehmannii	B,DD,SI
Coccoloba uvifera	B,C,CA,SA,T
Coccothrinax alexandri	B
Coccothrinax alta	B,CA,EL,O
Coccothrinax argentata	B,CA,O
Coccothrinax argentea	C,O,SA
Coccothrinax bermudezii	B
Coccothrinax crinita	B,O
Coccothrinax cupularis	B
Coccothrinax fragrans	B,O
Coccothrinax littoralis	B
Coccothrinax miraguama	B,O
Coccothrinax miraguama ssp roseocarpa	B
Coccothrinax rigida	B
Coccothrinax salvatoris	B
Cochemiea halei	BC
Cochemiea maritima	Y
Cochemiea pondii	DV
Cochemiea poselgeri	BC,DV,Y
Cochemiea setespina	DV,Y
Cochisea robbinsorum	DV
Cochlearia anglica	B
Cochlearia glastifolia	B

70

COCHLEARIA

Cochlearia officinalis	B
Cochlospermum fraseri	B,NI,O,SA
Cochlospermum religiosum	B
Cochlospermum vitifolium	B,DD,RE,SA
Cocos nucifera	B
Cocos weddelliana see Lytocaryum weddellianum	
Codariocalyx motorius	B
Coddia rudis	B
Codiaeum bonplandianus	B
Codiaeum californicus	B
Codiaeum glabellus	B
Codiaeum macrostachys	B
Codiaeum megalobotrys	B,SI
Codiaeum megalocarpus	B
Codiaeum sylvaticus	B,SI
Codiaeum variegatum hyb	B
Codonanthe crassifolia	B
Codonocarpus cotinifolius	B,C,NI
Codonocarpus pyramidalis	B,NI
Codonopsis bhutanica	AP,KL,SC
Codonopsis bulleyana	AP,B,P
Codonopsis cardiophylla	AP,SC,SG
Codonopsis clematidea	AP,B,BS,C,F,G,HU,JE,KI,
	KL,NG,P,PM,RS,SA,SC,
	SG,ST,T,V,VO
Codonopsis convolvulacea	AP,SC,SG
Codonopsis cordifolia	KL
Codonopsis dicentrifolia	AP,CG,SC
Codonopsis lanceolata	AP
Codonopsis mollis	B,C,HU,JE,SA,SC
Codonopsis ovata	AP,C,CG,G,KL,PM,SG
Codonopsis pilosula	AP,B,C,DD,G,KL,RS,SA
Codonopsis rotundifolia	AP,G,SC
Codonopsis rotundifolia v angustifolia	RS
Codonopsis sp	KL
Codonopsis tabulosa	C
Codonopsis tangshen	AP,P,PO,RS,SC
Codonopsis ussuriensis see C.lanceolata	
Codonopsis vinciflora	AP,C,SC
Codonopsis viridiflora	AP,B,F
Codonopsis viridis	BS,C,PL
Coeloglossum viride	CG
Coffea arabica	B,BS,BY,CA,CG,EL,FR,
	HA,MO,SG
Coffea arabica 'Nana'	B,C,CA,SA,V
Coffea sp	RE
Coffea sp & cvs	B
Coix lacryma-jobi	AB,BS,C,CG,DD,DE,G,
	HU,SG,SK,SU,V
Cola acuminata	B
Cola digitata	B
Cola urceolata	B
Colchicum alpinum	AP,SC,SG
Colchicum atropurpureum	AP,G
Colchicum atticum	AR
Colchicum autumnale	AP,AR,B,C,G,HU,JE,KL,
	MN,PM,PO,SA,SC
Colchicum autumnale striatum	SG
Colchicum balansae	AR
Colchicum baytopiorum	AP,AR,B,G,SC
Colchicum baytopiorum PB224 Turkey	MN
Colchicum bivonae	AP,AR,NG
Colchicum bornmuelleri	AP,G,PM
Colchicum cilicium	B,JE
Colchicum corsicum	AP,AR,B,C,LG,MN,NG
Colchicum cupanii	AR,B

Colchicum cupanii MS969 Italy	MN
Colchicum cupanii MS977 Italy	MN
Colchicum cupanii S.L163 Evvia	MN
Colchicum cupanii S.L454 Greece	MN
Colchicum cupanii v bertolonii	B
Colchicum cupanii v bertolonii S.L259	MN
Colchicum cupanii v bertolonii C.R.	MN
Colchicum cupanii v pulverulentum	B
Colchicum cupanii v pulverulentum C.R.	MN
Colchicum decaisnei	AR
Colchicum giganteum	AP,B,CG,MN
Colchicum hungaricum	KL
Colchicum kotschyi	AR,B,MN
Colchicum levieri	B
Colchicum levieri MS937 France	MN
Colchicum longiflorum	B
Colchicum lusitanicum v algeriense	B
Colchicum lusitanicum v algeriense C.R.	MN
Colchicum lusitanicum v algeriense C.R.	MN
Colchicum lusitanicum v algeriense C.R.	MN
Colchicum lusitanicum v algeriense C.R.	MN
Colchicum luteum	AP,BS
Colchicum macrophyllum	AP,AR,B,CG,JE,SC
Colchicum micranthum ABS 4512	NG
Colchicum neapolitanum C.R. (longifl.)	MN
Colchicum parnassicum	AR
Colchicum pelopponesiacum S.L191 Gr.	MN
Colchicum psaridis S.L200 Greece	MN
Colchicum pusillum	B,SC
Colchicum pusillum MS699 Crete	MN
Colchicum pusillum MS745 Crete	MN
Colchicum pusillum MS803 Crete	MN
Colchicum soboliferum	AR
Colchicum sp & hyb mix	C,NG
Colchicum sp ?neapolitanum Yugoslavia	MN
Colchicum sp nova S.B.L122 Jordan	MN
Colchicum speciosum	AP,B,G,MN,PM,SC,SG
Colchicum speciosum 'Album'	AP,NG
Colchicum speciosum atropurpurea	NG
Colchicum speciosum JCA Iran	MN
Colchicum speciosum PF dwarf	MN
Colchicum speciosum v bornmuelleri	CG,MN
Colchicum speciosum v illyricum see C.giganteum	
Colchicum triphyllum	AR
Colchicum troodii L/Cu105 Cyprus	MN
Colchicum umbrosum	AP,KL,MN
Colchicum variegatum	AR,B
Coldenia procumbens	B
Coleocephalocereus goebelianus	B,CH
Coleocephalocereus pluricostatus	B,BR
Coleogyne ramosissima	B
Coleonema album	B,SI
Coleonema pulchellum	B,KB,SA,SI
Coleonema pulchrum	B,SI
Coleostephus myconis 'Goblin'	B
Coleostephus myconis 'Moonlight'	B
Coleostephus myconis 'Sunlight'	B
Coleus see Solenostemon	
Collections 'Wedding Bouquet'	U
Colletia ferox	B,SA
Colletia hystrix	B,HP,SA,SG
Colletia spinosa	SA
Collinsia bicolor see C.heterophylla	
Collinsia grandiflora	B
Collinsia heterophylla	AB,B,C,CA,HP,KS,RS,
	SW,V

COLLINSIA

Collinsia heterophylla 'Blushing Bride'	T
Collinsia heterophylla 'Pink Surprise'	B
Collinsia verna	NT
Collomia biflora	B,C,HP
Collomia coccinea 'Neon'	B,T
Collomia grandiflora	AP,B,HP,P,SC
Collomia involucrata	SG
Collybia velutipes d.m.p	B
Colobanthus acicularis	B,SC,SS
Colobanthus apetalous v alpinus	B,SS
Colobanthus sp	KL
Colocasia affinis	B
Colocasia affinis v jenningsii	C
Colocasia esculenta	B
Colocasia gigantea	SG
Colophospermum mopane	B,SI,WA
Colpias mollis	B,SI
Colpoon compressum	B,BH,SI
Colpothrinax wrightii	B
Colquhounia coccinea	B,SA
Colquhounia mollis	B,SA
Colubrina arborescens	B
Colubrina asiatica	B
Columnea kienastiana	B
Colutea arborescens	A,AP,B,C,CA,DD,FW,G,
	HP,HU,LN,SA,SC,SG,VE
Colutea cilicia	HP
Colutea istria	G,HP,SG
Colutea laxmannii	SG
Colutea orientalis	HP,SA
Colutea persica	AP,HP
Colutea x media	AP,HP,JD,KL
Colvillea racemosa	B,EL,HA,HU,SA,SI
Comarum see Potentilla	
Combretum aculeatum	B
Combretum apiculatum	B,SI,WA
Combretum bracteosum	B,SI
Combretum caffrum	B,KB,SI
Combretum collinum	B,SI
Combretum collinum ssp gazense	B,SI
Combretum collinum ssp ondogense	B,SI
Combretum elaeagnoides	B,SI
Combretum erythrophyllum	B,KB,SI,WA
Combretum hereroense	B,SA,SI
Combretum imberbe	B,SI
Combretum kraussii	B,KB,SI,WA
Combretum micranthum	B
Combretum microphyllum	B,SI,WA
Combretum molle	B,SI,WA
Combretum obovatum	B,SI
Combretum padoides	B,SI,WA
Combretum zeyheri	B,SI,WA
Comesperma calymega	B,NI
Comesperma ciliatum	B,NI
Comesperma ericinum	B
Comesperma virgatum	B,NI
Commelina attenuata	B
Commelina benghalensis	B
Commelina Coelestis Group	AP,B,C,G,HP,JE,SA,SG
Commelina Coelestis Gr 'Sleeping Beauty'	C,F,KS
Commelina dianthifolia	AP,B,DD,HP,KL,SC,SW,
	T,W
Commelina graminifolia	B,JE
Commelina tuberosa	AP,C,G,HP,JE,RS,SC,SG
Commelina tuberosa 'Alba'	HP
Commelina virginica	C,G

Commersonia bartramia	B
Commicarpus pentandrus	B
Commiphora neglecta	B,SI
Commiphora pyracanthoides	B,SI
Compositae 'Flor Olorosa'	B
Compositae 'Hoja Del Pescado'	B
Compositae 'Oreja De Perro'	B
Compositae 'Palo De Sal'	B
Compositae 'Santa Teresa Montes'	B
Conandron ramondioides	C
Conandron ramondioides v nana	C
Conanthera bifolia	B,DD,MN
Condalia globosa v pubescens	B
Conicosia communis	DV
Conicosia elongata	SI
Conicosia pugioniformis	B,DV,KB,SI,Y
Conioselinum schugnanicum	SG
Conium maculatum	B,G,SG
Conoclinium coelestinum	B
Conophytum altum	B,DV,SI
Conophytum ampliatum	DV
Conophytum angelicae	B,DV
Conophytum apiatum	B,KB
Conophytum bergeri	DV
Conophytum bilobum	B,DV,KB,SI
Conophytum breve	B,SI
Conophytum brevisectum	DV
Conophytum brevitubum	DV
Conophytum calculus	B,DV,SI,Y
Conophytum christiansenianum	DV
Conophytum concavum	B,BC,DV
Conophytum conradii	DV
Conophytum crassum	SI
Conophytum cupreatum	B,DV
Conophytum dissimile	SI
Conophytum ectypum	DV
Conophytum elishae	B,DV,SI
Conophytum ernianum	DV
Conophytum ficiforme	DV
Conophytum frutescens	DV
Conophytum fulleri	DV
Conophytum giftbergense	B,DV
Conophytum gracile	B,DV
Conophytum kennedyi	DV
Conophytum lavisianum	DV
Conophytum limpidum	DV
Conophytum linearilucidum	DV
Conophytum marginatum	DV
Conophytum meyerae	B,DV,KB
Conophytum minusculum v leipoldtii	SI
Conophytum minutiflorum	DV
Conophytum minutum	B,DV,SI,Y
Conophytum minutum v pearsonii	B,SI
Conophytum mundum	DV
Conophytum novicium	DV
Conophytum obcordellum f mundum	B,Y
Conophytum obcordell. ssp ceresianum	B,SI
Conophytum obcord. ssp obcordellum	SI
Conophytum ornatum	B
Conophytum peersii	DV
Conophytum pellucidum	BC,DV
Conophytum pellucidum 'Pardicolor'	B,BC
Conophytum pillansii	B,DV,SI,Y
Conophytum pluriforme	DV
Conophytum praesectum	B,KB
Conophytum quaesitum	B,BC,DV

CONOPHYTUM

Conophytum rostratum	DV
Conophytum ruschii	DV
Conophytum saxetanum	DV
Conophytum smorenskaduense	DV
Conophytum sp	DV,GC,SI,Y
Conophytum sp, ssp, v	B
Conophytum speciosum	DV
Conophytum subfenestratum	B,DV,SI
Conophytum suprenum	DV
Conophytum truncatum	B,SI
Conophytum umdausense	B,DV
Conophytum uvaeforme	B,DV,Y
Conophytum uvaeforme v hillii	BC
Conophytum uvaeforme v subincanum	B,SI
Conophytum uvaeforme v uvaeforme	SI
Conophytum variabile	DV
Conophytum velutinum	B,BC,DV
Conopodium majus	B,HP
Conospermum amoenum	B,O
Conospermum bracteosum	B,NI
Conospermum brownii	B
Conospermum caerulescens	B,NI
Conospermum caeruleum	B,NI,O,SA
Conospermum densiflorum	B
Conospermum distichum	B,NI
Conospermum huegelii	B,NI,O
Conospermum incurvum	B,NI,O,SA
Conospermum mitchellii	B
Conospermum stoechadis	B,NI,O
Conospermum triplinervium	B,NI,SA
Conospermum triplinervium v minor	B,NI,O
Conostomium sp	SI
Conostylis sp	B
Conothamnus aureus	B,NI
Conringia orientalis	SG
Consolida ajacis	AB,AP,B,C,G,SD,SG,T
Consolida ajacis 'Bell Blue'	BY
Consolida ajacis dbl/single	TH
Consolida ajacis dwarf	B,BD,BS,KI,KS,ST,TU,V
Consolida ajacis earlybird Resistant	B
Consolida ajacis 'Exquisite Pink'	BY
Consolida ajacis hyacinth fl dw	BS,BY,CN,D,DE,F,MO, T,U
Consolida ajacis hyacinth fl tall	B,BD,BS,CN,D,KI,KS, L,MO,R,T,TU,V
Consolida ajacis 'Lilac Spire'	BY
Consolida ajacis 'Miss California'	BY
Consolida ajacis 'Rosamund'	BY
Consolida 'Audace'	M
Consolida 'Blue Rocket'	V
Consolida 'Blue Spire'	BY,L,SK,SU
Consolida 'Cloud Blue'	B,C,DI,J,JO,KS,YA
Consolida 'Cloud Snow'	C,D,JO
Consolida 'Earlibird' s-c,mix	SK
Consolida 'Eastern Blues'	B
Consolida 'Formula Mix'	L
Consolida 'Frosted Skies'	B,BS,DT,F,MO,PL,SE, T,U,V
Consolida giant	CO,DE
Consolida 'Imperial' mix	BS,BU,BY,CA,D,DE,DN, DT,F,J,JO,KI,KS,PI,PK, SE,ST,SU,U,VH,VY,YA
Consolida 'Imperial' pastels	DI
Consolida 'Imperial' s-c	B,BS,CA,DE,JO,KS,PK,T
Consolida Improved	T
Consolida 'King' s-c,mix	BY,SK

Consolida minus	B
Consolida orientalis	CG
Consolida 'Q Series' s-c	B
Consolida 'Regal' s-c	BS
Consolida regalis	AP,CG,G,SG
Consolida 'Rocket'	CO,HW,MC,S,Z
Consolida 'Rosalie'	L,SK
Consolida 'Salmon'	L,SK
Consolida 'Sky Blue'	D
Consolida Stock fl special mix	BS,DE,S
Consolida 'Sublime' mix	BS,CN,MO,T
Consolida 'Sublime' s-c	B,BS,CN,MO,T
Consolida 'White Spire'	BY,L
Convallaria majalis	B,C,JE,SG
Convallaria majalis v keiskei	SG
Convallaria majalis v rosea	NG
Convolvulus althaeoides	B,SA
Convolvulus arvensis	B
Convolvulus betonicifolius	B
Convolvulus cantabricus	B,C,JE,SA
Convolvulus capensis	B,SI
Convolvulus chilensis	B,HP,P
Convolvulus dorycnium	B
Convolvulus erubescens	B,HU,NI
Convolvulus major mix	BS,D,S
Convolvulus pentapetaloides	B
Convolvulus remotus	RS
Convolvulus sabatius	AP,HP,SG,T
Convolvulus scamonia	SG
Convolvulus sepium	SG
Convolvulus siculus	SG
Convolvulus sp	SI
Convolvulus 'Star of Yelta'	PL,T
Convolvulus tricolor	B,BS,C,CO,D,DI,DT,F,FR, G,J,KS,PI,SU,TH,W,V
Convolvulus tricolor choice mix	BD,HU
Convolvulus tricolor 'Ensign Blue'	S,PL,T
Convolvulus tricolor 'Ensign Dark Blue'	S
Convolvulus tricolor 'Ensign' mix	HU,S,KS,T
Convolvulus tricolor 'Ensign Red'	F,KS,PL,SE,T
Convolvulus tricolor 'Ensign Rose'	PK,T
Convolvulus tricolor 'Ensign Royal'	B,BD,C,F,KS,PK,SE,V
Convolvulus tricolor 'Ensign White'	KS,T
Convolvulus tricolor 'Erecta Blue Flash'	B,C
Convolvulus tricolor 'Erecta Red Flash'	B
Convolvulus tricolor 'Flagship'	F,SE
Convolvulus tricolor 'Rainbow Flash'	T
Convolvulus tricolor red	B
Conyza canadensis	B
Conyza cardaminifolia	B,DD
Cooperia see Zephyranthes	
Coopernookia polygalacea	B,NI
Copaifera langsdorfii	B
Copaifera mildbraedii	B
Copernicia alba	B
Copernicia baileyana	O
Copernicia cerifera	CA
Copernicia glabrescens ssp glabrescens	B
Copernicia glabrescens ssp hav.	B
Copernicia hospita	B
Copernicia pruinifera	O
Copiapoa alticostata	DV
Copiapoa barquitensis	DV
Copiapoa bridgesii	B,BC
Copiapoa cinerascens	DV
Copiapoa cinerea	DV

COPIAPOA

Copiapoa cinerea v albispina	DV
Copiapoa cinerea v columna-alba	DV
Copiapoa cinerea v gigantea	B
Copiapoa coquimbana	B,DV
Copiapoa cupreata	B
Copiapoa echinoides	Y
Copiapoa gigantea	DV
Copiapoa grandiflora	Y
Copiapoa haseltoniana	DV
Copiapoa haseltoniana v paposo	DV
Copiapoa humilis	B,CH,DV,Y
Copiapoa hypogaea	B,CH,DV,GC,Y
Copiapoa lembcke	B
Copiapoa longispina	B,Y
Copiapoa magnifica	B
Copiapoa marginata	B
Copiapoa militaris	DV
Copiapoa montana	B
Copiapoa multicolor	B
Copiapoa pseudocoquimbana	B
Copiapoa pseudocoquimbana v vulgata	B
Copiapoa serpentisulcata	DV
Copiapoa sp mix	C
Copiapoa tenuissima	B,CH,DV,Y
Copiapoa wagenknechtii	B
Coprinus comatus d.m.p	B
Coprosma acerosa see C.brunnea	
Coprosma antipoda	B
Coprosma areolata	B
Coprosma atropurpurea	B,SS
Coprosma brunnea	B,SC,SS
Coprosma cheesemanii	B,CG,SS
Coprosma colensoi	B,SS
Coprosma crassifolia	B
Coprosma crenulata	B,SS
Coprosma depressa	B,SS
Coprosma grandifolia	B
Coprosma hirtella	B,HA,NI
Coprosma lucida	B,SS
Coprosma macrocarpa	B
Coprosma nitida	B,C,O
Coprosma parviflora	B,SS
Coprosma petriei	B,SS
Coprosma propinqua	B,SS
Coprosma pseudocuneata	B,SS
Coprosma pumila	B,SS
Coprosma quadrifida	B,NI,O
Coprosma repens	B,CA,EL,SA
Coprosma rhamnoides	AP
Coprosma rigida	B
Coprosma robusta	B,SA
Coprosma rotundifolia	B,SS
Coprosma rugosa	B,SA,SS
Coprosma serrulata	B,SS
Coprosma sp	AP,AU
Coptis japonica	B,C
Corallocarpus bainesii	B,SI
Corallocarpus dissectus	B,KB,SI
Corallorhiza maculata	NO
Corallorhiza ssp	NO
Corallorhiza striata	NO
Corallospartium crassicaule	B,SS
Corchorus aestuans	B
Corchorus walcottii	B,NI
Cordia abyssinica	B
Cordia alliodora	B

Cordia amplifolia	B
Cordia boussieri	B,EL,SA
Cordia caffra	B,SI
Cordia dentata	B
Cordia dichotoma	B,NI
Cordia myxa	B
Cordia obliqua	B
Cordia sebestena	B,DD,EL,SA
Cordia sinensis	B,SI
Cordia subcordata	B
Cordia superba	B,EL
Cordia wallichii	B
Cordyla africana	B,WA
Cordyla madagascariensis	B
Cordyline australis	AP,B,BS,C,CA,CL,DV, EL,HA,HP,MO,O,SA,SS, T,VE,YA
Cordyline australis 'Purple Tower'	T
Cordyline australis 'Purpurea'	B,C,CA,EL,HA,O,SA,VE
Cordyline australis 'Red Robyn'	B,SA
Cordyline banksii	B,C,SA,SS
Cordyline banksii 'Purpurea'	B
Cordyline baueri	B
Cordyline baueri 'Purpurea'	B
Cordyline bicolor	B,EL,SA
Cordyline fruticosa	B,DV,EL,HA,SA,SH
Cordyline fruticosa 'Bicolor'	B,EL
Cordyline fruticosa 'Hawaiian Red'	SA
Cordyline fruticosa 'Hawaiian Ti'	B,CA
Cordyline fruticosa hybrids	C,EL,O,T
Cordyline fruticosa pink special	B,CA
Cordyline fruticosa red dw	B
Cordyline fruticosa 'Rubra'	B
Cordyline fruticosa 'Tricolor'	EL,SA
Cordyline fruticosa 'Variegata'	B,CA,SA
Cordyline fruticosa white	B
Cordyline indivisa	AU,B,BS,BY,C,CA,DE, DV,EL,FW,KI,MO,O,SA, SK,SS,ST,VE,X
Cordyline petiolaris	B,EL,O,SA
Cordyline pumilio	B,SA,SC
Cordyline rubra	B,EL,HA
Cordyline stricta	B,C,EL,HA,O,SA
Cordyline terminalis see C.fruticosa	
Cordyline trilocular	B
Coreopsis 'American Dream'	F,PA,PL,T
Coreopsis auriculata 'Cutting Gold' see 'Schnittgold'	
Coreopsis auriculata 'Schnittgold'	CL,JE
Coreopsis auriculata 'Sonnenkind'	C,DE,JE,SA
Coreopsis basalis 'Gold King'	B,C
Coreopsis basalis 'Golden Crown'	B,KS
Coreopsis bigelovii	B
Coreopsis gigantea	B
Coreopsis grandiflora	AP,B,BS,BY,CG,CN,CO, FR,G,HP,KI,KL,SG,ST
Coreopsis grandiflora 'Domino'	JE
Coreopsis grandiflora 'Early Sunrise'	B,BD,BS,CL,D,DE,DT,F, HP,J,JE,KI,KS,L,MO,PK, PL,R,S,SE,SK,T,TU,V,VY
Coreopsis grandiflora 'Louis D'or'	B
Coreopsis grandiflora 'Mayfield Giants'	B,BD,BS,L,MO,SK,T,V
Coreopsis grandiflora 'Roi Soleil'	JE
Coreopsis grandiflora 'Tetra Giants'	JE
Coreopsis lanceolata	AB,B,C,CA,CG,G,HP, HW,JE,JO,NT,PR,SG
Coreopsis lanceolata 'Baby Gold'	B,SK

74

COREOPSIS

Coreopsis lanceolata 'Brown Eyes'	SK
Coreopsis lanceolata maroon	SD
Coreopsis lanceolata 'Sterntaler'	B,JE,SA
Coreopsis lanceolata 'Sunburst'	B,BS,BU,BY,C,DE,JE,KI,PI,VH
Coreopsis 'Mardi Graz'	J
Coreopsis maritima	B
Coreopsis palmata	B,G,JE,PR,SG
Coreopsis pygmaea	KL
Coreopsis radiata 'Tiger Stripes'	DT
Coreopsis rosea	JE,KL
Coreopsis rosea 'Sunray'	AP,B,BD,BS,BY,C,CA,G,HU,JE,MO,SA,SK
Coreopsis stillmanii 'Golden Fleece'	B,C
Coreopsis tinctoria	AB,B,CA,CN,DD,G,HP,HW,KS,NT,SD,SG,TE,V
Coreopsis tinctoria 'Double Golden'	B
Coreopsis tinctoria dwarf	C,J,T
Coreopsis tinctoria 'Fiery Beam'	C
Coreopsis tinctoria 'Gold Star'	B,BS,D
Coreopsis tinctoria 'Mahogany Midget'	B,BS,D,DT,F,SK
Coreopsis tinctoria tall	C,HU
Coreopsis 'Treasure Trove'	U
Coreopsis tripteris	B,C,JE,PR
Coreopsis verticillata	AV,B,HP
Coreopsis verticillata 'Moonbeam'	AP,HP
Corethrogyne californica	B
Coriaria arborea	B,SG
Coriaria kingiana	B,SA,SG
Coriaria microphylla	B,SG
Coriaria myrtifolia	SA,SG
Coriaria nepalensis	SG
Coriaria pottsiana	SG
Coriaria pteridoides N.Zealand	SG
Coriaria ruscifolia	SG
Coriaria sarmentosa	B,SG
Coriaria sinica	B,SA
Coriaria terminalis v xanthocarpa	AP,C,HP,I,KL,NG,SC,SG
Coridothymus capitatus	B
Corispermum hyssopifolium	CG
Corispermum nitidum	B
Cornus alba	A,B,C,CG,DD,FW,LN,SA,VE
Cornus alba 'Sibirica'	B,FW,LN,SA
Cornus alternifolia	B,CA,CG,FW,LN,SA
Cornus amomum	B,FW,LN,SA
Cornus amomum obliqua	PR
Cornus australis	LN,SG
Cornus baileyi see C.stolonifera 'Baileyi'	
Cornus bretschneideri	SA
Cornus canadensis	A,AB,AP,B,BS,C,CA,CG,FW,JE,LN,NO,SA,SG,T
Cornus capitata	B,C,CG,FW,HA,LN,SA
Cornus controversa	A,B,C,CA,EL,FW,LN,SA,VE
Cornus darvasica	SG
Cornus drummondii	LN,SA
Cornus florida	A,B,C,CA,EL,FW,LN,NO,SA,VE
Cornus florida f rubra	B,C,FW,LN,N,SA,VE
Cornus florida 'Variegated'	B,FW
Cornus hongkongensis	B,FW
Cornus kousa	B,DE,EL,FW,G,LN,SA,VE
Cornus kousa 'Milky Way'	B,LN,SA
Cornus kousa v angustata	B,FW,LN,N,SA
Cornus kousa v chinensis	A,B,C,CA,EL,FW,LN,N,SA,VE
Cornus kousa v chinensis Imp	B,FW
Cornus kousa weeping form	B
Cornus macrophylla	B,FW,LN
Cornus mas	A,B,C,CG,DD,EL,FW,HP,LN,SA,SG,VE
Cornus mas variegata	C
Cornus nuttallii	AB,B,C,CA,FW,LN,N,NO,SA,VE
Cornus obliqua	SG
Cornus officinalis	EL,FW,LN,SA,VE
Cornus pumila	CG
Cornus racemosa	B,CG,FW,G,LN,SA
Cornus rugosa	B,SA
Cornus sanguinea	A,B,C,CG,FW,LN,SA,VE
Cornus sessilis	B
Cornus stolonifera	AB,B,C,CG,FW,LN,NO,PR,SA,SG
Cornus stolonifera 'Baileyi'	CG
Cornus stricta	B
Cornus suecia	C
Cornus walteri	B,C,EL,LN,SA
Corokia cotoneaster	B,C,CG,SA,SS
Corokia x virgata	AP,B,C,SA
Coronilla cappadocica see C.orientalis	
Coronilla coronata	AP,B,SC
Coronilla emerus see Hippocrepis	
Coronilla minima	AP,B,G,KL,SC
Coronilla orientalis	AP,SC,SG
Coronilla vaginalis	AP,B,G,KL
Coronilla valentina ssp glauca	AP,C,HP,SA
Coronilla valentina ssp valentina	SG
Coronilla varia	B,C,DI,FW,JE,KS,PK,SA,VE
Corryocactus melanotrichus	B,DV,Y
Corryocactus melanotrichus v caulescens	DV,Y
Corryocactus quadrangularis	B
Corryocactus tarijensis	DV,Y
Corryocactus urmiriensis	B,DV,Y
Cortaderia argentea see C.selloana	
Cortaderia fulvida	B,C
Cortaderia richardii	B,HP,SC,SG
Cortaderia selloana	B,BD,C,CN,HP,JE,KI,L,LN,SA,ST,SU,T,V,VE
Cortaderia selloana 'Pink Feather'	BD,BY,CA,CL,DE,EL,L,MO,PK,SK
Cortaderia selloana 'Rosea'	B,C,JE,SA,V,VE
Cortaderia selloana 'Sunningdale Silver'	PK
Cortaderia selloana 'White Feather'	BY,CA,CL,CN,DE,EL,F,MO,PK,SK
Cortaderia toetoe	SA
Cortusa matthioli	AP,B,CG,G,HP,KL,SA,SG
Cortusa matthioli 'Alba'	AP,B,G,JE,KL,SC
Cortusa matthioli f pekinensis	AP,B,C,G,JE,SC,SG
Cortusa pekinensis	CG
Cortusa turkestanica	AP,B,CG,G,HP,SC,SG
Cortusa turkestanica 'Alba'	P
Coryanthera flava	NI,O
Corycium magnum	B
Corydalis alpestris	VO
Corydalis aquae-gelidae	B,DD
Corydalis aurea	B,SC,SW
Corydalis bracteata	SG
Corydalis caseana	B,SW
Corydalis cava	AP,C,G,JE,KL,SA,SC
Corydalis cava albiflora	AP,NG

CORYDALIS

Corydalis cheilanthifolia	AP,B,C,G,I,JE,P,RH,SG,T
Corydalis conorhiza	VO
Corydalis flexuosa	AP,SC
Corydalis fumariifolia	AP,PM
Corydalis incisa	B
Corydalis intermedia	B
Corydalis latiloba	AR
Corydalis lutea	AP,B,BS,C,CG,CL,CN,F, G,I,JE,MO,P,RH,SA,T,TH
Corydalis nobilis	B,C,CG,G,JE,SA
Corydalis ochotensis	B,P
Corydalis ochroleuca	B,C,CG,G,I,JE,KL,P,PM, RH,SC,SG,T
Corydalis ophiocarpa	AP,B,C,P
Corydalis rosea	AP,C,MN,SC
Corydalis saxicola	AP,B,PM
Corydalis sempervirens	AP,B,C,CG,HP,NG,P,PM, RM,SC,T
Corydalis sempervirens 'Alba'	AP,B,P
Corydalis smithiana	AP,NG
Corydalis solida	AP,C,F,G,JE,PM,SC
Corydalis solida f transsilvanica	KL
Corydalis solida MS881 Spain	MN
Corydalis tenela	VO
Corydalis tomentella	AP,C,I,KL,SC
Corydalis wendelboi	AR
Corydalis wilsonii	AP,B,I,JE,SC,SG
Corylopsis goloana	CG
Corylopsis pauciflora	B,CG,N,SA
Corylopsis platypetala see C.sinensis v calvescens	
Corylopsis sinensis	B,N
Corylopsis spicata	AP,N,SG
Corylus americana	B,FW,LN
Corylus avellana	B,C,FW,LN,SA,VE
Corylus chinensis	LN,SA
Corylus colurna	B,FW,LN,SA,VE
Corylus cornuta	B,G,LN,SA,SG
Corylus heterophylla	B,LN,SA,SG
Corylus mandschurica	LN,SA
Corylus maxima	LN,SA
Corymbium africanum	B,SI
Corymbium glabrum	B,SI
Corymbium laxum ssp laxum	B,SI
Corymbium theileri	B,SI
Corynanthera flava	B,C,O,SA
Corynephorus canescens	B,C,HP,JE,SA
Corypha elata	O
Corypha umbraculifera	B,O
Corypha utan	B
Coryphantha andreae	B,Y
Coryphantha asterias	DV
Coryphantha bergerana	B
Coryphantha bumammma v bianca	B,Y
Coryphantha calipensis	B,DV,Y
Coryphantha chihuahuensis	B
Coryphantha clava	B,DV
Coryphantha compacta	BC,DV
Coryphantha cornifera	B,DV,Y
Coryphantha delaetiana	B,Y
Coryphantha durangensis	B
Coryphantha echinoidea	B
Coryphantha echinus	B,DV
Coryphantha echinus SB377	Y
Coryphantha erecta	B
Coryphantha gladiispina	B,Y
Coryphantha greenwoodii	B

Coryphantha hendricksoni	B
Coryphantha hesteri	DV
Coryphantha indensis	B
Coryphantha macromeris	B,DV
Coryphantha maiz-tablasensis	B,DV,Y
Coryphantha nickelsae	B
Coryphantha obscura SB714	Y
Coryphantha pallida	B,Y
Coryphantha palmeri	B,BC,DV,Y
Coryphantha pectinata	Y
Coryphantha poselgeriana	DV
Coryphantha poselgeriana v valida	B
Coryphantha potosina	B
Coryphantha pseudechinus	B,DV
Coryphantha pulleineana	B
Coryphantha pusilliflora	B
Coryphantha pycnacantha	B
Coryphantha radians	B,DV,Y
Coryphantha ramillosa	B
Coryphantha recurvata	B
Coryphantha retusa	B,Y
Coryphantha roederana	B
Coryphantha scheeri	B
Coryphantha scheeri v robustispina	B
Coryphantha scheeri v valida	B
Coryphantha sp mix	B,Y
Coryphantha sulcata	B,DV,Y
Coryphantha sulcolanata	B,DV,Y
Coryphantha unicornis	B,Y
Coryphantha vaupeliana	B
Coryphantha villarensis	B
Coryphantha voghtherriana	DV
Cosmelia rubra	B
Cosmidium burridgeanum 'Brunette'	BS,DT,F,KS,U
Cosmos atrosanguineus	B,HP
Cosmos bipinnatus	AV,AP,DD,G,HW,SG,SP
Cosmos bipinnatus 'Candy Stripe'	B,BS,DE,HU,KS,L,MO, PK,SE
Cosmos bipinnatus 'Collarette'	KS
Cosmos bipinnatus 'Daydream'	B,BD,BS,DT,F,KS,MO, PK,SK,T,V
Cosmos bipinnatus 'Dazzler'	C,DE,DI,PI,SK
Cosmos bipinnatus 'Early Wonder'	PK
Cosmos bipinnatus 'Frosty Rose'	J
Cosmos bipinnatus giant series	B
Cosmos bipinnatus 'Gloria'	T
Cosmos bipinnatus 'Hinomaru'	PI
Cosmos bipinnatus 'Imperial Pink'	PK,S,SK
Cosmos bipinnatus 'Klondyke Sunny Red'	HU
Cosmos bipinnatus 'Picotee'	B,BS,DI,DT,F,JO,PL,SE, SK,T
Cosmos bipinnatus 'Pied Piper Red'	B,BS,MO,PI,T
Cosmos bipinnatus 'Psyche Mix'	JO,PI,T,TE
Cosmos bipinnatus 'Purity'	B,C,DE,KS,PI,T
Cosmos bipinnatus 'Sea Shells'	BD,BS,C,D,DE,DT,F,HU, J,JO,KS,L,MO,PI,PK,PL, S,SD,SE,SK,T,TE,V,VY
Cosmos bipinnatus 'Sensation Dazzler'	SK
Cosmos bipinnatus 'Sensation Early' mix	w.a.
Cosmos bipinnatus 'Sensation Early' s-c	B,HU,JO
Cosmos bipinnatus 'Sensation Pinkie'	DI,SK
Cosmos bipinnatus 'Sensation Radiance'	SK
Cosmos bipinnatus 'Sonata Dw White'	B,BD,C,CL,D,KS,MO,O, PK,PL,SK,T
Cosmos bipinnatus 'Sonata' mix	BS,CL,D,DT,F,J,KS,L,M, MO,PI,PK,PL,S,SE,SK,

76

COSMOS

	T,U,V,VY
Cosmos bipinnatus 'Sonata' s-c	BS,CL,MO,PI,PL
Cosmos bipinnatus 'Sweet Dreams'	PL,SE
Cosmos bipinnatus 'Versailles'	C,JO,KS,L,PK,PL,SK,T
Cosmos bipinnatus 'Versailles' s-c	B,C,DE,JO,PI,PK,SK
Cosmos bipinnatus white	DI
Cosmos bipinnatus 'Yellow Garden'	B,DI,PI
Cosmos diversifolius	SG
Cosmos 'Gazebo'	T
Cosmos 'Polidor' mix	SK
Cosmos sp	SZ
Cosmos sp 'Montes'	HU
Cosmos sp perennial	HP
Cosmos sulphureus	AB,AP,G,HW,SG,TE
Cosmos sulphureus 'Bright Lights'	BS,BU,DE,DT,KS,L,
	PK,TE,VY
Cosmos sulphureus 'Diablo'	B,G
Cosmos sulphureus 'Ladybird Dwarf mix'	BS,CL,CO,DE,KI,MO,PI,
	PK,SK,T,TU,VH
Cosmos sulphureus 'Ladybird Dwarf' s-c	B,BS,CL,DE,MO,SK,T
Cosmos sulphureus 'Lemon Twist'	B,PK,T
Cosmos sulphureus 'Sunny Gold'	CA,S,T,V
Cosmos sulphureus 'Sunny Red'	B,CA,S,T
Cosmos sulphureus 'Sunset'	B,C,DD,DE,PI,SD,V
Costus afer	B
Costus barbatus	B
Costus cuspidatus	B
Costus guanaiensis v macrostrobilus	B
Costus guanaiensis v tarmicus	B
Costus igneus see C.cuspidatus	
Costus lima	B
Costus lucanusianus	B,EL
Costus malortieanus	B
Costus pictus	B
Costus speciosus	B,C,EL,SA
Costus spicatus	B
Costus spiralis	B
Cotinus coggygria	A,B,C,CA,EL,FW,G,HP,
	LN,SA,VE
Cotinus coggygria 'Grace'	HP
Cotinus coggygria 'Notcutt's Variety'	HP
Cotinus coggygria Purpureus Group	B,EL,FW,SA
Cotinus obovatus	SA
Cotoneaster acuminatus	LN,SG
Cotoneaster acutifolius	B,EL,FW,LN,SA,VE
Cotoneaster adpressus	SG
Cotoneaster adpressus v praecox see C.nanshan	
Cotoneaster amoenus	RH,SG
Cotoneaster apiculatus	B,CA,CG,LN,SA
Cotoneaster armenus	SG
Cotoneaster ascendens	SG
Cotoneaster assamensiss	SG
Cotoneaster astrophoros	SG
Cotoneaster bacillaris	SG
Cotoneaster Bonsai mix	C
Cotoneaster bullatus	B,FW,LN,RH,SA,SG,VE
Cotoneaster bullatus f floribundus see C.bullatus	
Cotoneaster buxifolius f vellaeus see C.astrophoros	
Cotoneaster cambricus	SG
Cotoneaster cavei	SG
Cotoneaster cinerascens	SG
Cotoneaster cochleatus of gdns	SG
Cotoneaster dammeri	AP,B,LN,SG
Cotoneaster dielsianus	B,CA,FW,LN,RH,SA,SG
Cotoneaster diganthus	CG
Cotoneaster divaricatus	B,FW,LN,SA,SG

Cotoneaster duthianus	SG
Cotoneaster ellipticus	SG
Cotoneaster falconeri	SG
Cotoneaster faveolatus	CG,SG
Cotoneaster franchettii	B,C,EL,FW,LN,RH,SA,
	SG,VE,WA
Cotoneaster franchettii v cinerascens	B,FW,RH
Cotoneaster frigidus	NG,SG
Cotoneaster glaucophyllus	B,RH,SG
Cotoneaster glaucophyllus v microphyllus	HP,SG
Cotoneaster glaucophyllus v serotinus	RH
Cotoneaster harrovianus	RH
Cotoneaster hebephyllus	RH
Cotoneaster horizontalis	AP,B,CA,EL,FW,HP,KL,
	LN,SA,SG,VE
Cotoneaster horizontalis 'Prostratus'	AP,B,FW
Cotoneaster horizontalis 'Saxatilis'	AP,RS
Cotoneaster hupehensis	LN,SG
Cotoneaster ignavus	SG
Cotoneaster induratus	SG
Cotoneaster integerrimus	LN,SA,SG
Cotoneaster integrifolius	B,SA,SG,V
Cotoneaster kitaibelii	SG
Cotoneaster kweischoviensis	SG
Cotoneaster lacteus	B,CA,LN,RH,SA,VE,WA
Cotoneaster lindleyi	SG
Cotoneaster linearifolius	B,FW
Cotoneaster lucidus	B,LN,SA,SG
Cotoneaster marquandii	SG
Cotoneaster melanocarpus	LN,RH,SG
Cotoneaster melanocarpus v altaicus	SG
Cotoneaster melanocarpus v laxiflorus	SG
Cotoneaster melanocarpus x multiflorus	SG
Cotoneaster multiflorus	B,FW,LN,SA
Cotoneaster multiflorus v calocarpus	B,FW,SG
Cotoneaster nanshan	B,CA,FW,SA,SG
Cotoneaster niger	RS
Cotoneaster nitidus	AP,SG
Cotoneaster obscurus	SG
Cotoneaster oliganthus	SG
Cotoneaster pannosus	B,C,EL,SG,VE,WA
Cotoneaster perpusillus	B,FW
Cotoneaster polyanthemus	SG
Cotoneaster procumbens	SG
Cotoneaster przewalskii	SG
Cotoneaster racemiflorus	B,SG
Cotoneaster racemiflorus v nummularius	B,FW,SG
Cotoneaster racemiflorus v songoricus	SG
Cotoneaster racemiflorus v veitchii	B,FW
Cotoneaster roborovskii	SG
Cotoneaster roseus	SG
Cotoneaster rotundifolius	SG
Cotoneaster salicifolius	AP,B,CA,FW,LN,RH,SA,
	VE
Cotoneaster salicifolius v floccosus	B
Cotoneaster salicifolius v rugosus of gdns	B,FW
Cotoneaster sandakphuensis	SG
Cotoneaster saxatilis	SG
Cotoneaster scandinavicus	SG
Cotoneaster shansiensis	SG
Cotoneaster sikangensis	SG
Cotoneaster simonsii	B,LN,SA,SG
Cotoneaster sp China	SG
Cotoneaster sp mix	C
Cotoneaster splendens	SG
Cotoneaster staintonii	SG

COTONEASTER

Cotoneaster suavis	SG
Cotoneaster tomentosus	SG
Cotoneaster veitchii	SG
Cotoneaster wardii	RH,SG
Cotoneaster x watereri	B
Cotoneaster zabellii	CG,SG
Cotoneaster zeravschanicus	SG
Cotula alpina	B,P
Cotula barbata	B,KI
Cotula coronopifolia	AP,B,SI
Cotula hispida	B,I,JE,SC,SI
Cotula sp	SI
Cotula turbinata 'Select'	B
Cotula 'Yellow Marbles'	BS,C,CO
Cotyledon adscandens	CG
Cotyledon barbeyi	B,CG,DV,KB,SI,Y
Cotyledon campanulata	B,SI
Cotyledon grandiflorum	DV
Cotyledon luteosquamata	DV
Cotyledon orbiculata	B,BH,C,DV,HP,KB,Y
Cotyledon orbiculata v flanaganii	B,KB,Y
Cotyledon orbiculata v oblonga	DV,KB,SI,Y
Cotyledon orbiculata v oblonga red	B,KB
Cotyledon orbiculata v oblonga yellow	B,KB
Cotyledon orbiculata v orbiculata	B,KB,SI
Cotyledon orbiculata v spuria	KB
Cotyledon paniculata see Tylecodon paniculatus	
Cotyledon papillaris	B,KB
Cotyledon sp mix	BH,C,SI
Cotyledon teretifolia	Y
Cotyledon umbilicus	B
Cotyledon undulata see C. orbiculata v oblonga	
Cotyledon velutina	B,DV,SI,Y
Cotyledon wallichii see Tylecodon papillaris ssp wallichii	
Couroupita guianensis	B
Coursetia glandulosa	SA
Cowania mexicana	B,LN,SW
Cowania mexicana v stansburiana	B,LN
Cowania stansburiana	C,EL,NO,SA
Crabbea reticulata	B
Crabia zimmermannii	B,WA
Crambe abyssinica	B,DD,KS
Crambe abyssinica 'Funfare'	B
Crambe abyssinica 'Serenata'	C
Crambe cordifolia	AP,B,C,CG,CN,G,HP,JE, P,PK,SA,SG,T
Crambe maritima	AP,B,C,CN,DD,HP,JE, SA,SG
Crambe maritima 'Lily White'	B
Crambe tatarica	B,C,CG,JE,SG
Craspedia globosa	BS,CA,CN,CO,DE,DI,DT, HA,HU,JO,KI,KS,L,MO, NI,PK,S,ST,SU,T,U,V
Craspedia incana	AP,B,SC,SS
Craspedia lanata	AP,B,SS
Craspedia uniflora	B,PM,SG,SS
Crassula acinaciformis	B,SI
Crassula alba v alba	B,SI
Crassula arborescens	B,DV,SI
Crassula arborescens v arborescens	B,SI
Crassula barklyi	B
Crassula capensis v capensis	B,SI
Crassula capitella	B,SI
Crassula ciliata	B,SI
Crassula coccinea	B,SI,Y
Crassula columnaris	B,DV,SI,Y

Crassula cultrata	B,DV,KB,Y
Crassula cymosa	B,SI
Crassula dejecta	B,DV,KB,SI,Y
Crassula dependens	B,SI
Crassula dichotoma	B,SI
Crassula dubia	B,DV,Y
Crassula falcata see C. perfoliata v minor	
Crassula fascicularis	B,SI
Crassula lactea	SG
Crassula lanceolata ssp lanceolata	B,SI
Crassula lanuginosa	SG
Crassula multicava	B,KB,SI,Y
Crassula multiflora	B,KB,SI,Y
Crassula muscosa tetragona	SG
Crassula muscosa v pseudolicopodioides	SG
Crassula muscosa v purpurii	SG
Crassula natalensis	B,SI
Crassula nudicaulis	DV,KB,Y
Crassula nudicaulis v nudicaulis	B,SI
Crassula obtusa	SI
Crassula obvallata	B,DV,Y
Crassula orbicularis	B,SI
Crassula ovata	B,C,DV,KB,SA,SI,Y
Crassula pellucida ssp marginalis	B,KB,SI,Y
Crassula peploides	B,RM
Crassula perfoliata	Y
Crassula perfoliata v minor	B,C,DV,KB,SG,SI,Y
Crassula perfoliata v perfoliata	B,KB
Crassula perforata	B,SI
Crassula pruinosa	B,SI
Crassula pubescens ssp radicans	B,KB,Y
Crassula rogersii	B,DV,KB,Y
Crassula rubricaulis	B,KB,SI,Y
Crassula rupestris	B,SI
Crassula sarcocaulis	AP,B,SC,SI
Crassula sarcocaulis ssp rupicola	Y
Crassula saxifraga	B,SI
Crassula scabra	B,KB,SI
Crassula sp mix	C,SG,SI,Y
Crassula swaziensis	B,SI
Crassula tetragona	B,Y
Crassula tetragona ssp acutifolia	B,KB,Y
Crassula tetragona ssp robusta	B,SA,Y
Crassula tomentosa	B,SI
Crassula vaginata	B,SI
Crataegus alemanniensis	SG
Crataegus alemanniensis 'Lacinata'	SG
Crataegus alemanniensis v orientobaltica	SG
Crataegus altaica	LN,SG
Crataegus ambigua	LN,SG
Crataegus apiifolia	B
Crataegus apiomorpha	SG
Crataegus armena	SG
Crataegus arnoldiana	LN,SA,SG
Crataegus azarolus	A,B,C,LN,SA
Crataegus basilica	SG
Crataegus beata	SG
Crataegus brachyacantha	B
Crataegus calpodendron	NG,SG
Crataegus canadensis	SG
Crataegus canbyi	NG,SG
Crataegus caucasica	SG
Crataegus cerronis	LN,SA
Crataegus champlainensis	NG
Crataegus chlorosarca	B,HP,SA,SG
Crataegus coccinea	LN,SA

CRATAEGUS

Crataegus coccinoides	B,LN,NG
Crataegus coleae	SG
Crataegus columbiana	B,C,LN,NO,SA
Crataegus crus-galli	B,C,CA,EL,FW,LN,NG, SA
Crataegus crus-galli 'Inermis'	B,FW
Crataegus dahurica	SG
Crataegus delawarensis	SG
Crataegus densiflora	SG
Crataegus douglasii	A,AB,B,C,LN,NO,SA,SG
Crataegus ellwangerana	NG
Crataegus faxonii	SG
Crataegus fecunda	SG
Crataegus flabellata	SG
Crataegus foetida	SG
Crataegus gravis	SG
Crataegus grayana	SG
Crataegus hajastana	SG
Crataegus horrida	SG
Crataegus horrida v aboriginum	SG
Crataegus intricata	B,C,FW,LN
Crataegus iracunda	SG
Crataegus iracunda v populnea	SG
Crataegus irrasa	SG
Crataegus jackii	NG
Crataegus jesupii	SG
Crataegus jonesiae	C,NG
Crataegus korolkowii	SG
Crataegus laciniata	LN,NG,SA
Crataegus laevigata	A,B,FW,KL,LN,SA,SG
Crataegus laevigata 'Rosea'	B
Crataegus laneyi	SG
Crataegus laurentiana	SG
Crataegus lettermanii	SG
Crataegus lindmanii	SG
Crataegus macrantha	SG
Crataegus macrantha 'Scimitar'	C
Crataegus macrosperma	NG,SG
Crataegus maximowiczii	LN,SG
Crataegus mollis	A,B,C,FW,LN,SG
Crataegus monogyna	A,AB,B,FW,LN,SA,SG, VE
Crataegus nigra	SG
Crataegus orientalis see C.laciniata	
Crataegus osiliensis	SG
Crataegus pedicellata	SG
Crataegus pennsylvanica	SG
Crataegus pentagyna	B,SG
Crataegus persimilis 'Prunifolia'	NG
Crataegus phaenopyrum	B,C,FW,LN,SA,WA
Crataegus pinnatifida	B,LN,SG
Crataegus pinnatifida major	SA
Crataegus polyclada	NG
Crataegus praecoqua	SG
Crataegus pringlei	SG
Crataegus pringlei v exclusa	SG
Crataegus prona	SG
Crataegus pruinosa	SG
Crataegus pseudoheterophylla	SG
Crataegus pubescens	B,EL,LN,WA
Crataegus punctata	B,FW,LN,SA,SG
Crataegus punctata f aurea	NG,SG
Crataegus putnamiana	SG
Crataegus roanensis	SG
Crataegus russanovii	SG
Crataegus sanguinea	SG

Crataegus sanguinea v chlorocarpa	SG
Crataegus scabrida	SG
Crataegus sonangensis AC1617	X
Crataegus sp mix	C,DD
Crataegus stankovii	SG
Crataegus stevenii	SG
Crataegus submollis	LN,NG,SG
Crataegus suborbiculata	SG
Crataegus succulenta	B,LN
Crataegus tanacetifolia	C
Crataegus tomentosa	NG
Crataegus turcomanica	SG
Crataegus uniflora	B
Crataegus vailliae	SG
Crataegus viridis 'Winter King'	B,LN
Crataegus vulsa	B
Crataegus x calycina	SG
Crataegus x curonica	SG
Crataegus x degenii	SG
Crataegus x dsungarica	SG
Crataegus x dunensis	SG
Crataegus x kyrtostyla	SG
Crataegus x luzinii	SG
Crataegus x maritima	SG
Crataegus x ovalifolia	SG
Crataegus x persimilis	SG
Crataegus x prunifolia	B,C,LN,SA
Crataegus x schneideri	SG
Cratageus oxycantha see C. laevigata	
Craterocapsa tarsodes	B,SI
Craterostigma plantagineum	B,SI
Craterostigma wilmsii	B,SA,SI
Crateva magna	B
Cremanthodium arnicoides	KL
Cremanthodium elisii	KL
Cremanthodium helianthus	KL
Cremanthodium nepalense	KL
Cremanthodium retusum	SG
Crepis aurea	AP,B,G,KL,SC,T
Crepis biennis	B,NS
Crepis capillaris	B
Crepis 'Coconut Ice'	U
Crepis conyzifolia	SG
Crepis conyzifolia ssp conyzifolia	SG
Crepis incana	AP,HP,I,PA,SC
Crepis nana	B,RM
Crepis paludosa	SG
Crepis pygmaea	B,C
Crepis rhoeadifolia	B
Crepis rubra	AP,BS,C,D,DE,F,HP,KI, KS,RH,S,SC,SE,TU,W
Crepis rubra 'Alba'	B,KS
Crepis rubra 'Rosea'	B,J,SG,V
Crepis sancta	B
Crepis sibirica	SG
Crepis vesicaria	SG
Crescentia alata	B,RE,TT
Crescentia cujete	B,SA
Crinodendron hookerianum	B,P,PL,SG
Crinum asiaticum	B,G
Crinum asiaticum v japonicum	C
Crinum bulbispermum	B,RU,SG
Crinum lineare	CF
Crinum macowanii	RU
Crinum moorei	B,RU
Crinum pedunculatum	B,C,EL,HA,O

CRINUM

Crinum x powellii	B	Crocus longiflorus Italy Coll Ref	MN
Crithmum maritimum	B,C,JE	Crocus malyi	AR
Crocosmia aurea	B,SI	Crocus michelsonii	AR
Crocosmia Bressingham Hybrids	C	Crocus minimus	AP,B,KL
Crocosmia 'Emberglow'	B	Crocus napolitanus	CG,SG
Crocosmia hyb	BS,SA,T,W	Crocus nevadensis	AR
Crocosmia 'Lucifer'	AP,B,C,E,LG,MA,PA,PM	Crocus niveus	AP,AR,B
Crocosmia masonorum	AP,C,G,I,JE,SC,T	Crocus niveus MS Greece	MN
Crocosmia 'Orangerot'	JE	Crocus nudiflorus	AP,B,C,CG,SC
Crocosmia paniculata	B,I,SA,SI	Crocus olivieri	AR
Crocosmia pottsii	B,SI	Crocus oreocreticus	AR
Crocosmia 'Solfatarre'	B,I	Crocus pallasii	AR,PM
Crocosmia variegata	B	Crocus pallasii ssp dispathaceus	JE
Crocosmia x crocosmiiflora	E	Crocus pallasii v haussnechtii S.B.L146	MN
Crocus abantensis	B,JE,SC	Crocus paschei	AR
Crocus adanensis	AR	Crocus pulchellus	AP,G,PM,SG
Crocus aleppicus	B	Crocus pulchellus M.T4582 Turkey	AP,MN
Crocus aleppicus Coll Ref	MN	Crocus reticulatus	AR
Crocus angustifolius	AP,G,SC	Crocus robertianus	AR
Crocus antalyensis	AR	Crocus scepusiensis	CG
Crocus asumaniae	AR,JE	Crocus scharojanii	VO
Crocus banaticus	AP,G,PM,SC	Crocus serotinus ssp ?clusii PB209	MN
Crocus baytopiorium	JE,SC	Crocus serotinus ssp clusii PB375	MN
Crocus biflorus aff ssp artvinensis	AR	Crocus serotinus ssp salzmannii	AR
Crocus biflorus ssp biflorus	AP,B	Crocus serotinus ssp salzmannii Coll Ref	MN
Crocus biflorus ssp biflorus Coll Ref	MN	Crocus serotinus v serotinus PB167 Port.	MN
Crocus biflorus ssp isauricus	AR	Crocus ?serotinus v serotinus S.F237	MN
Crocus biflorus ssp melantherus	AR	Crocus sieberi 'Cedric Morris'	NG
Crocus biflorus ssp nubigena	AR	Crocus sieberi ssp sublimis	AR
Crocus biflorus ssp pulchricolor	AR	Crocus sp mix	AP,C,KL,MN,NG
Crocus biflorus ssp punctatus	KL	Crocus speciosus	AP,B,CG,G,PM,SC
Crocus boryi	AR,SC	Crocus speciosus 'Albus'	B,MN
Crocus byzantinus	CG	Crocus speciosus ssp xantholaimos	AR
Crocus cambessedesii	AR,B,MN	Crocus thomasii	AR,MN
Crocus cancelatus ssp cancelatus	KL	Crocus tommasinianus	AP,B,C,CG,KL,SC
Crocus cancellatus	AR,CG	Crocus tommasinianus PF6584 Yugo.	MN
Crocus cancellatus ssp mazziaricus	AR,B,MN	Crocus tournefourtii	AR
Crocus cartwrightianus	AR	Crocus veluchensis	AR
Crocus caspius	AR	Crocus vernus ssp albiflorus	AP,B,C
Crocus chrysanthus	AP,B,SC	Crocus vernus ssp vernus	AP,AR,JE,SC
Crocus chrysanthus 'Advance'	B	Crocus versicolor	AR
Crocus chrysanthus 'Ladykiller'	B	Crossandra infundibuliformis	B,BS,PK,SA
Crocus cvijicii	AR	Crossandra spinescens	SI
Crocus dalmaticus	CG	Crotalaria barnabassii	B
Crocus danfordiae	AR,KL	Crotalaria benthamiana	B,NI
Crocus etruscus MS949 Italy	MN	Crotalaria brachycarpa	B,SI
Crocus flavus see C. flavus ssp f.		Crotalaria capensis	B,KB,SI
Crocus flavus ssp f. M.T4578 Turkey	MN	Crotalaria 'Chepil De Burro'	B,HU
Crocus flavus ssp flavus	AP,AR,B,CG,SC,SG	Crotalaria cunninghamii	B,C,NI,O,SA
Crocus fleischeri	AP,CG,G,SC	Crotalaria eremaea	B
Crocus gargaricus ssp gargaricus	AR	Crotalaria globifera	B,SI
Crocus goulimyi	AP,AR,B,G,MN,SC	Crotalaria grahamiana	B,EL
Crocus hadriaticus	AP,B,SC	Crotalaria incana	DD
Crocus hadriaticus S.L470 Greece	MN	Crotalaria juncea	B
Crocus hyemalis S.B.L124 Jordan	MN	Crotalaria laburnifolia	B
Crocus imperati ssp imperati 'De Jager'	KL	Crotalaria longirostrata	B,HU
Crocus imperatii ssp suaveolens MS962	MN	Crotalaria longirostrata 'Chapil'	HU
Crocus karduchorum	AR	Crotalaria medicaginea	B,NI
Crocus kotschyanus	AP,AR,B,CG,G,SC,SG	Crotalaria meyerana	B
Crocus kotschyanus ssp cappadocicus	AR	Crotalaria novae-hollandiae	B,NI,O
Crocus kotschyanus ssp suworowianus	AR	Crotalaria pallida	B,HU
Crocus kotschyanus Turkey Coll Ref	MN	Crotalaria paniculata	B
Crocus kotschyanus v leucopharynx	AP,SG	Crotalaria retusa	B
Crocus laevigatus	AR	Crotalaria sagittalis	B,PR
Crocus leichtlinii	AR	Crotalaria semperflorens	B,EL,O,SA
Crocus longiflorus	AP,AR,B	Crotalaria sessiliflora	B

CROTALARIA

Crotalaria sp	SI
Crotalaria spectabilis	HU
Crotalaria verrucosa	B
Croton megalobotrys	WA
Croton megalocarpus	SA
Croton sylvaticus	KB,WA
Crowea angustifolia	B,NI,O,SA
Crowea angustifolia v dentata	B,NI,O
Cruciata laevipes	B
Crupina crupinastrus	B
Cryptandra arbutiflora	B,NI
Cryptanthus sp	B
Cryptocarya glaucescens	B
Cryptocarya liebertiana	B
Cryptocarya mackinnoniana	O
Cryptocarya wyliei	B,KB
Cryptolepis oblongifolia	B
Cryptomeria japonica	B,C,CA,CG,EL,FW,G,HA,
	LN,N,RH,SA,T,V,VE,WA
Cryptomeria japonica 'Lobbii'	B,FW
Cryptomeria japonica v sinensis	B,LN,SA
Cryptostegia grandiflora	B,C,EL,SA
Cryptostephanus vansonii	B,RU
Cryptotaenia japonica atropurpurea	AP,HP
Crysophyllum mexicanum	B
Ctenium concinnum	B,SI
Ctenolepis garcinii	B
Cucubalus baccifer	B,G,NS
Cucumis aegyptica	BH
Cucumis africanus	HU
Cucumis dipsaceus	B,HU
Cucumis metuliferus	B,C,HU,SA,SI
Cucumis myriocarpus	B,SI
Cucumis saggitatus	B,SI
Cucumis zeyheri	B,SI
Cucurbita digitata	SA
Cucurbita ficifolia	HU
Cucurbita foetidissima	HU
Cucurbita ornamental gourd	BS,BY,C,CN,D,DD,DT,
	F,FR,G,JO,KI,KS,L,PK,
	SG,SU,V,VH
Cucurbita orn. 'Choose Your Weapons.'	T
Cucurbita orn.l gourd 'Crown of Thorns'	BS,JO
Cucurbita ornamental gourd 'Large Bottle'	B,JO,T
Cucurbita ornamental gourd 'Luffa'	PK,T
Cucurbita ornamental gourd small fruited	BS,D,T,U
Cucurbita ornamental gourd 'Turks Turban'	B,BS,JO,T
Cucurbita ornamental gourd warted	BS
Cudrania tricuspidata	B,C
Cumarinia odorata	B,BC,Y
Cunninghamia konishii	SA
Cunninghamia lanceolata	B,C,EL,LN,N,SA
Cunonia capensis	B,KB,LN,O,SA,SI,WA
Cupaniopsis anacardioides	B,CA,HA,NI,O,SA
Cuphea 'Dynamite'	SK
Cuphea hyssopifolia	CG,G
Cuphea ignea	B,BD,BS,C,CL,EL,G,J,
	KI,L,PK,SA,U,V
Cuphea lanceolata	SG
Cuphea lanceolata 'Firefly'	C,EL
Cuphea llavea see C.x purpurea	
Cuphea miniata see C.x purpurea	
Cuphea platycentra	BY,CA,DE,MO
Cuphea x purpurea	B,DI,EL,F,HP,T
Cupressus anjouce	CG
Cupressus arizonica	B,C,CA,CG,DV,EL,FW,

	HA,LN,SA,VE
Cupressus arizonica v glabra	B,CA,HA,RH,WA
Cupressus arizonica v nevadensis	B
Cupressus arizonica v stephensonii	B
Cupressus bakeri	B,LN,SA
Cupressus chengiana	B
Cupressus duclouxiana	B,SG
Cupressus funebris	B,C,EL,FW,HA,LN,RH,
	SA,SG,WA
Cupressus glabra see C.arizonica v glabra	
Cupressus goveniana	B,EL
Cupressus goveniana v pygmaea	B,SA
Cupressus guadalupensis ssp forbesii	B,SA
Cupressus himalaica ssp darjeelingensis	B
Cupressus knightiana	CG
Cupressus lusitanica	B,CA,CG,DV,EL,LN,SA,
	WA
Cupressus lusitanica v benthamii	B,FW
Cupressus macnabiana	B,SA
Cupressus macrocarpa	A,B,BS,C,CA,EL,FW,
	HA,HU,LN,SA,VE
Cupressus meridionalis	DV
Cupressus sargentii	B,SA
Cupressus semp. v semp. see C.'Stricta'	
Cupressus sempervirens	B,DV,EL,FW,HA,HP,KL,
	LN,RH
Cupressus sempervirens cereiformis	B
Cupressus sempervirens f horizontalis	B,CA,EL,FW,LN,SA,VE,
	WA
Cupressus sempervirens pyramidalis see C.s.'Stricta'	
Cupressus sempervirens 'Stricta'	B,C,CA,EL,FW,LN,SA,
	SC,VE,WA
Cupressus torulosa	B,C,EL,FW,HA,LN,SA,
	WA
Cupressus torulosa AC1408	X
Cupressus torulosa 'Cashmeriana'	C,FW,HA,N,SA
Cupulanthus bracteolasus	AU
Curcuma inodora	B
Curtisia dentata	B,SI
Cuscuta campestris	B
Cuscuta chinensis	B
Cussonia natalensis	B
Cussonia paniculata	B,C,DV,KB,O,SA,SI,Y,
	WA
Cussonia paniculata v sinuata	B
Cussonia spicata	B,CA,DV,KB,O,SI,WA,Y
Cyamopsis tetragonolobus	B,DD
Cyanella alba	B,RU,SI
Cyanella hyacinthoides	AP,B,RU,SI
Cyanella lutea	B,RU,SI
Cyanella orchidiformis	B,G,RU,SI
Cyanotis foecunda	B,SI
Cyanotis somaliensis	SG
Cyanotis speciosa	SI
Cyathea australis	B,C,EL,HA,SA
Cyathea brownii	B,EL
Cyathea cooperi	B,EL,HA,SA
Cyathea cunninghamii	B,C
Cyathea dealbata	B,C,SA
Cyathea leichardtiana	B,HA,SA
Cyathea medullaris	B,C,SA
Cyathea smithii	B,SA
Cyathodes colensoi	B,C,SS
Cyathodes empetrifolia	B
Cyathodes fasciculata see Leucopogon fasciculatus	
Cyathodes glauca	B,O

81

CYATHODES

Cyathodes juniperina	B,SS
Cyathodes parviflora	B,HA,O
Cyathodes pumila	B,SS
Cybistax donnell-smithii	B
Cycas angulata	O
Cycas arenticola	O
Cycas armstrongii	B,EL,O,SA
Cycas arnhemica	O
Cycas basaltica	B,O
Cycas brunnea	O
Cycas 'Bynoe/Fog Bay'	O
Cycas cairnsiana	B,O,SA
Cycas calcicola	B,C,O
Cycas canalis	O
Cycas circinalis	B,CA,O
Cycas conferta	B,O
Cycas couttsiana	O
Cycas furfuracea	B,O
Cycas guizhouensis	B
Cycas kennedyana see C.papuana	
Cycas 'Kimbleton'	O
Cycas lane-poolei	B
Cycas 'Lichfield Park'	O
Cycas machonochii	B,O
Cycas 'Marlborough Blue'	C
Cycas media	B,C,EL,HA,SA,O
Cycas megacarpa	C,O
Cycas neo-calidonicae	O
Cycas nitida	B
Cycas normanbyana	B,EL
Cycas ophiolitica	O
Cycas orientalis	O
Cycas panzhihuaensis	B
Cycas papuana	B,EL,HA
Cycas pectinata	O
Cycas platyphylla	O
Cycas 'Port Keats'	O
Cycas pruinosa green & blue	B,O
Cycas revoluta	B,C,CA,CG,EL,HA,LN, O,SA,VE
Cycas riamensis	O
Cycas rumphii	B,EL,O
Cycas segmentifida	B
Cycas sp mix	T
Cycas sylvestris	O
Cycas taiwaniana	B,CA
Cycas thouarsii see C.rumphii	
Cycas wadei	O
Cyclamen africanum	AP,AR,AS,B,C,CG,JW, LG,P,PM,SC,SG
Cyclamen africanum JCA855	MN
Cyclamen africanum S.L277 Tunisia	MN
Cyclamen africanum x hederifolium	JW
Cyclamen 'Albadonna'	B,BS,MO
Cyclamen balearicum	AP,AR,AS,C,G,JW,KL, MN,NH,SC
Cyclamen balearicum 'Silvery Leaf forms'	C,JW
Cyclamen 'Cantorial' mix o-p	CL
Cyclamen 'Cardinal'	B,BS,MO
Cyclamen 'Cascade'	J
Cyclamen 'Christmas Scarlet'	U
Cyclamen cilicium	AP,AR,AS,B,C,CG,CT, JE,JW,KL,LG,MN,N,PL, PM,SC,SG
Cyclamen cilicium f album	AP,C,CT,JW,KL,PM,SC
Cyclamen cilicium v cilicium	SG

Cyclamen cilicium v intaminatum	AP,SG
Cyclamen coum	w.a.
Cyclamen coum best patterns	AR,AS,CT,JW
Cyclamen coum 'Broadleigh Silver'	CT
Cyclamen coum dark nose	AR
Cyclamen coum f albissimum	AP,B,C,G,JE,SE
Cyclamen coum f albiss. 'Golan Heights'	JW
Cyclamen coum 'Linett Jewel'	CT
Cyclamen coum 'Linett Rose'	CT
Cyclamen coum mass fl	CT
Cyclamen coum mass fl clear light pink	CT
Cyclamen coum mass fl deep rich pink	CT,PL
Cyclamen coum mass fl white	CT
Cyclamen coum 'Maurice Dryden'	AP,AS,CT,JW,SC
Cyclamen coum 'Meaden's Crimson'	CT
Cyclamen coum mix show	C
Cyclamen coum Nymans Strain	AS
Cyclamen coum Pewter Group	AP,AR,AS,C,JW,PM,SE, SG
Cyclamen coum 'Rubrum'	B,JE,SC
Cyclamen coum silver leaf	AP,AR,B,CT,G,JE,JW,PL
Cyclamen coum 'Silver Star'	CT
Cyclamen coum ssp caucasicum	AP,B,C,G,NG,PM,SC,SG
Cyclamen coum ssp coum	SG
Cyclamen coum ssp elegans	JW
Cyclamen coum 'Turkish Princess'	CT
Cyclamen creticum	AP,AS,G,JW
Cyclamen creticum x balearicum	JW
Cyclamen creticum x repandum	JW
Cyclamen cyprium	AP,AR,AS,B,C,JW,MN, PL,SC
Cyclamen cyprium E.S.	AP,JW
Cyclamen 'Dainty Ballerina'	BS
Cyclamen 'Dresden' mix	CL
Cyclamen 'Esprit' mix	BS,D,J,MO
Cyclamen 'Esprit' s-c	B,BS,MO
Cyclamen f1 'Butterfly'	L,SK
Cyclamen f1 'Dart' s-c	YA
Cyclamen f1 'Dressy' s-c,mix	BS
Cyclamen f1 'Fairytales Mix'	BS,YA
Cyclamen f1 'Firmament' mix	BS,S
Cyclamen f1 'Firmament' s-c	BS
Cyclamen f1 'Graduation'	BS
Cyclamen f1 'Halios' s-c,mix	B,BS,MO
Cyclamen f1 'Laser' mix	CL
Cyclamen f1 'Miracle' mix	BS,CL,PK
Cyclamen f1 'Miracle' s-c	CL
Cyclamen f1 'New Wave'	BS,CL
Cyclamen f1 'Petite Wonder' mix	BS
Cyclamen f1 'Romance' s-c, mix	BS
Cyclamen f1 'Sierra' mix	BS,CA,CL,SK
Cyclamen f1 'Sierra' s-c	CL,SK
Cyclamen f1 'Zodiac'	BS,L
Cyclamen 'Fancy free'	O-P
Cyclamen 'Fringed' o-p	CL
Cyclamen graecum	AP,AR,B,C,CG,JW,P, PL,SC,SG
Cyclamen graecum f album	AR,AS,JW
Cyclamen graecum Greece	MN
Cyclamen graecum MS772 Crete	MN
Cyclamen graecum pink	AS
Cyclamen graecum S.L165/2 Evvia	MN
Cyclamen graecum silvery leaf	JW
Cyclamen green leaf form	C
Cyclamen hederifolium	w.a.
Cyclamen hederifolium 'Album'	AP,AR,AS,B,BS,C,G,JW,

CYCLAMEN

	P,PL,PM,RS,SA,SG,T
Cyclamen hederifolium 'Bowles' Apollo'	AP,AR,C,NG
Cyclamen hederifolium 'Island' scented	C,NG
Cyclamen hederifolium mix	AP,BS,C,SE,T
Cyclamen hederifolium 'Perlenteppich'	CT,JE
Cyclamen hederifolium pewter leaf	AR
Cyclamen hederifolium 'Rosenteppich'	JE
Cyclamen hederifolium 'Roseum'	AS,B,BS,PL,SA
Cyclamen hederifolium sagittate leaf	JW
Cyclamen hederifolium scented fl	AR,JW
Cyclamen hederifolium 'Silver Arrows'	AR
Cyclamen hederifolium 'Silver Cloud'	AP,C,CT,NG
Cyclamen hederifolium silver leaf	AP,AR,JW,KL,SC
Cyclamen hederifolium 'Silver Swan'	NG
Cyclamen hederifolium 'White Apollo'	AR
Cyclamen hederifolium x africanum	AP,JW
Cyclamen hederifolium x graecum	JW
Cyclamen inaminatum pink	NG
Cyclamen intaminatum	AP,AR,AS,G,HW,JW, NG,SC
Cyclamen intaminatum marked leaf cw	AS,JW
Cyclamen intaminatum silvery leaf	JW
Cyclamen libanoticum	AP,AR,AS,B,C,HW,JW, P,PL,SC
Cyclamen lightly marked leaf form	C
Cyclamen miniature	BY
Cyclamen mirabile	AP,AS,B,C,G,JE,JW,MN
Cyclamen mix autumn fl.	CT
Cyclamen mix blended	BS
Cyclamen mix hardy sp	C,CL,PK
Cyclamen mix new giants	BS,BY
Cyclamen mix scented	BS,D,MO,S
Cyclamen mix winter fl.	CT
Cyclamen neapolitanum see C.hederifolium	
Cyclamen parviflorum	AP,C,HW,JW,SC
Cyclamen 'Pastel Compacta' mix	YA
Cyclamen 'Pastel Decora' mix	YA
Cyclamen persicum	AP,AR,AS,BD,CG,FR, G,JW,KL,SC,V
Cyclamen persicum 'Benary's Special'	C
Cyclamen persicum crimson	AR
Cyclamen persicum 'Crown' mix	KI,ST
Cyclamen persicum g. 'Flamenco Frills'	T
Cyclamen persicum g. 'Fringed & Ruffled'	T
Cyclamen persicum g. 'Fuzzy Wuzzy'	T
Cyclamen persicum g. 'Gold Medal'	T
Cyclamen persicum g. 'Pink Delight'	T
Cyclamen persicum 'Mozart'	V
Cyclamen persicum Polunin	MN
Cyclamen persicum polypetalum	C
Cyclamen persicum Rhodes	MN
Cyclamen persicum S.L55 Jordan	MN
Cyclamen persicum v album	C,D
Cyclamen persicum 'Victoria'	B,PL,T
Cyclamen persicum wild form	C
Cyclamen 'Poppet'	U
Cyclamen pseudibericum	AP,AR,AS,B,C,G,HW,JE, JW,NG,PL,PM,SC
Cyclamen pseudib. & ps. 'Roseum' mix	CT
Cyclamen pseudibericum pale pink	AR
Cyclamen pseudibericum 'Roseum'	AS,JW
Cyclamen pseudib. Van Tubergen's Variety	NG
Cyclamen purpurascens	AP,AR,AS,B,C,CT,G, JE,JW,SA,SC,T,V
Cyclamen purpurascens 'Lake Garda'	AS
Cyclamen purpurascens silver leaf	NG

Cyclamen repandum	AP,AS,B,C,CT,G,JE,JW, KL,PL,SC,SE
Cyclamen repandum 'Album'	AP,AS,JW,NG
Cyclamen repandum PB111 Italy	MN
Cyclamen repandum 'Pelops' see C. r. ssp pelonnesiacum f p.	
Cyclamen repandum ssp pelon. f p.	AS
Cyclamen repandum ssp pelop.	AP,AR,C,CT,JW
Cyclamen rep. ssp pel. Balearic Hybrids	C
Cyclamen repandum ssp rhodense	AR,AS,C,JW
Cyclamen repandum vividum	AP,C,JW
Cyclamen repandum x balearicum	AP,AS,JW
Cyclamen rholfsianum	AP,AS,C,G,JW,MN,SC
Cyclamen 'Rose Beauty'	B,BS,MO
Cyclamen 'Rubin'	B,BS,MO
Cyclamen 'Salmon Beauty'	B,BS,MO
Cyclamen 'Scentsation' mix	C,T
Cyclamen 'Schone Helena'	BS,C,KI,MO
Cyclamen silver leaf scented	U
Cyclamen silvery leaf form	BS,C,MO
Cyclamen starter pack	CT
Cyclamen 'Super Puppet' mix	S
Cyclamen 'Tiny Mites'	BS,T
Cyclamen 'Treasure Chest'	C,S
Cyclamen 'Treasure Trove'	J,T
Cyclamen 'Triumph Special'	S
Cyclamen trochopteranthum	AP,AS,C,CG,G,HW,JW, PM,SC
Cyclamen 'Wellensiek'	C
Cyclamen x saundersii	JW
Cyclamen x wellensiekii	AS
Cyclanthera 'Fat Baby'	C
Cyclanthera 'Lady's Slipper'	C
Cyclanthera pedata	B,CG
Cyclanthus bipartitus	B
Cyclopia intermedia	B,SI
Cyclopia maculata	B,SI
Cyclopia sp	SI
Cyclosorus pennigera	B
Cycnium racemosum	B
Cydonia japonica see Chaenomeles speciosa	
Cydonia oblongata	LN,SA
Cylindrophyllum comptoni	SI
Cylindropuntia acanthocarpa	DV
Cylindropuntia fulgida	DV
Cymbalaria aequitrilobata	SG
Cymbalaria hepaticifolia	CG
Cymbalaria muralis	AP,B,C,G,HP,JE,SA,TH
Cymbalaria pallida	B
Cymbidium aloifolium	B
Cymbidium canaliculatum	B
Cymbidium suave	B
Cymbopogon ambiguus	B,NI,SA
Cymbopogon bombycinus	B,NI,SA
Cymbopogon citratus	B,CN,PL,TH
Cymbopogon excavatus	B,BH,SI
Cymbopogon flexuosus	B
Cymbopogon martinii	B,BH
Cymbopogon nardus	B
Cymbopogon obtectus	B,NI,SA
Cymbopogon refractus	HA
Cymopterus multinervatus	SW
Cynanchum floribundum	B,NI
Cynanchum laeve	B
Cynanchum obtusifolium	B
Cynanchum vincetoxicum	B
Cynara baetica ssp maroccana	NG

CYNARA

Cynara cardunculus	AP,B,C,CG,CN,CP,DD, HP,JE,SC,SA,T,V	Cyphostemma juttae	B,CH,KB,SI,Y
Cynara scolymus	CG,CN,DD,FW,G,SA	Cyphostemma sandersonii	B,SI
Cynara scolymus 'Brittany Blue'	C	Cypripedium calceolus	AP,B,G,KL
Cynodon dactylon	B,EL,FR	Cypripedium macranthum	AP,SC
Cynodon dactylon 'Numex Sahara'	B	Cypripedium montanum	NO
Cynoglossum amabile	AB,AP,DN,HP,PI,SD,TE	Cyrilla racemiflora	B,FW,SA
Cynoglossum amabile 'Avalanche'	B,KS,T	Cyrostachys renda	CA
Cynoglossum amabile blue	BH,BY,DI,S,SC	Cyrtanthus brachyscyphus	AP,B,G,SI
Cynoglossum amabile 'Blue Bird'	BS,L	Cyrtanthus breviflorus	AR,B,C,CF,SI
Cynoglossum amabile 'Firmament'	AP,B,DE,J,KS,SK	Cyrtanthus clavatus	B,CF,SI
Cynoglossum amabile 'Mystery Rose'	B,BS,D,J,KS,MO,T	Cyrtanthus elatus	B,CF,SI,SG
Cynoglossum amabile pink	BH,DI	Cyrtanthus elatus x montanus	B,SI
Cynoglossum amabile 'Shower Blue'	B,T,V	Cyrtanthus euculus	B
Cynoglossum amabile 'Shower Pink'	V	Cyrtanthus helictus	B,SI
Cynoglossum creticum	B	Cyrtanthus herrei	B
Cynoglossum dioscoridis	AP,HP	Cyrtanthus loddigiesanus	B,CF
Cynoglossum glochidiatum	HP	Cyrtanthus mackenii	C,SI
Cynoglossum macrostylum	SG	Cyrtanthus mackenii v mackenii	B
Cynoglossum nervosum	AP,B,G,HP,JE,SG	Cyrtanthus macowanii	SG
Cynoglossum officinale	AP,B,CN,G,HP,HU,JE, SA,SC,SG	Cyrtanthus obliquus	B,CF,SI
		Cyrtanthus obrienii	B,SI
Cynoglossum viridiflorum	SG	Cyrtanthus ochroleucus	B,SI
Cynoglossum wallichii	B,DD	Cyrtanthus sanguineus	B,SI
Cynoglossum zeylanicum	AP,HP	Cyrtanthus sp/hyb	RU,SI
Cynosurus cristatus	B	Cyrtanthus speciosus see C.elatus	
Cynosurus echinatus	SG	Cyrtanthus spiralis	CF,SI
Cypella coelestis	AP,KL,SZ	Cyrtanthus suaveolens	B,SI
Cypella herbertii	AP,B,C,CG,G,KL,MN,SC	Cyrtanthus tuckii v viridilobus	B,C,SI
Cypella plumbea	AP	Cyrtomium acculeatum	B
Cyperus alternifolius see C.involucratus		Cyrtomium caryotideum	B
Cyperus compactus	SA	Cyrtomium falcatum	B,EL,SA,SC
Cyperus corymbosus	B	Cyrtomium falcatum 'Rochefordianum'	B
Cyperus eragrostis	HP,JE,SA	Cyrtomium fortunei	B,G
Cyperus esculentus v sativus	B,HU	Cyrtostachys lakka	B,O,SA
Cyperus fuscus	B,NS	Cyrtostachys lakka g	B
Cyperus glaber	CL,JE,SA	Cyrtostachys renda	EL,RE
Cyperus gymnocaulos	B,NI	Cysticapnos vesicaria	B,SI
Cyperus involucratus	B,BS,BY,C,CA,CL,DE, MO,SA,SG,SK	Cytharexylum subflavescens	B
		Cytisus alpinus	VE
Cyperus involucratus nanus	B,CA,SA	Cytisus austriacus	SA
Cyperus longus	B	Cytisus battandieri	AP,C,G,HP,N,SA,SC,T
Cyperus nanus v compactus	B,C	Cytisus decumbens	B
Cyperus natalensis	SG	Cytisus emeriflorus	B,SG
Cyperus obtusiflorus v sphaerocephalus	SI	Cytisus grandiflorus	C
Cyperus papyrus	B,C,CA,DE,DV,G,HP, JE,SA,SG,V	Cytisus hyb mix	D,DT,L,S,V
		Cytisus maderensis see Genista	
Cyperus profiler	B	Cytisus mix choice	BS
Cyperus reflexus	HA	Cytisus mix new hybrids	BS,BY,C,CL,KI
Cyperus schweinitz	PR	Cytisus 'Monarch' mix	BD,BS,C,CN,MO
Cyperus ustulatus	B,SA	Cytisus monspessulanus see Genista monspessulana	
Cyperus 'Zumila'	B	Cytisus multiflorus	B,C,SA,VE
Cyphia elata	B,SI	Cytisus nigricans	B,SA,SG
Cyphia longifolia	B,SI	Cytisus procumbens	SG
Cyphia phyteuma	SI	Cytisus scoparius	A,B,C,CA,CP,EL,FR,FW, HP,LN,SA,SG,VE
Cyphia sp	SI		
Cyphia volubilis	B,SI	Cytisus scoparius f andreanus	B
Cyphomandra betacea	B,C,CA,CG,DD,EL,O, SA,SG,TT	Cytisus scoparius southern	C
		Cytisus sessilifolius	B,SC,SG
		Cytisus striatus	SG
Cyphomandra betacea 'Fragrans'	B	Cytisus supranubius	C
Cyphomandra betacea 'Large Fruit'	B	Cytisus x praecox	KL
Cyphomandra betacea 'Red Fruit'	B	Cytronium falcatum	CG
Cyphomandra betacea 'Virus-free Red'	B	Daboecia cantabrica	C,RH,SC
Cyphomandra hartwegii	B	Daboecia cantabrica hyb	C,JE
Cyphophoenix nucele	B	Dacrycarpus dacrydoides	B,SA
Cyphostemma bainesii	B,CH,DV	Dacrydium cupressinum	B

DACRYODES

Dacryodes edulis	B	Dahlia 'Morada'	B
Dactylis glomerata	B	Dahlia 'Naranja'	B,HU
Dactylis glomerata 'Currie'	B	Dahlia 'Phantom of The Opera'	DE
Dactylis pokygama	B	Dahlia 'Piccolo' mix	J,PK
Dactylis sp Spain	SG	Dahlia pinnata	B,SG
Dactyloctenium aegyptium	B	Dahlia 'Pompon' mix	BY,C,CO,D,DT,F,KI,L,
Dactyloctenium radulans	B,NI		MO,PK,R,S,ST,T,U
Dactylopsis digitata	B,C,DV,Y	Dahlia 'Promenade' hyb	BS
Dactylorhiza fuchsii	AP,HP,I,SC	Dahlia 'Redskin' mix	BD,BS,BY,C,CL,CN,CO,
Dactylorhiza 'Lydia'	I		DE,F,J,MO,PI,PL,S,SE,
Dactylorhiza maculata	AP,CG,G,PO,SC		SU,T,TE,TU,V,VH,YA
Dactylorhiza majalis	CG,KL,SC	Dahlia 'Rigoletto'	BS,DE,F,M,PK,S,SE
Dactylorhiza sambucina	B	Dahlia 'Sangria'	U
Dactylorhiza sp/hyb hardy	C	Dahlia scapigera	CG
Daemonorops mollis	B	Dahlia sherffii	B,P,MN,SW
Dahlia 'Bambino' mix	T	Dahlia sherffii x coccinea	B
Dahlia Bedding	BS,PT	Dahlia Southbank Hybrids	CL
Dahlia 'Bishop of Llandaff'	SZ	Dahlia 'Sunny Yellow'	CL
Dahlia 'Cactus' mix	BS,BY,C,DT,F,KI,L,MO,	Dahlia Unwin's Dw Hybrids	B,BS,BY,CA,DE,DT,J,KI,
	ST,T,V,VH		L,MC,MO,PI,ST,TU,U,V,
Dahlia 'Calico' mix	SK		YA
Dahlia 'Cocktail' mix	BS	Dais cotinifolia	B,C,KB,SA,SI,WA
Dahlia 'Collarette Dandy'	BS,BY,C,CL,D,KI,L,SE,	Dalanum ladanum	SG
	SU,T	Dalbergia armata	B
Dahlia 'Coltness' hyb mix	BD,BS,BY,C,CL,CO,D,F,	Dalbergia assamica	HA
	MO,S,ST,T,TU,U,VH,YA	Dalbergia greveana	B
Dahlia 'Dandy'	MO,SK	Dalbergia latifolia	B,EL,HA
Dahlia 'Dapper' mix	BS	Dalbergia melanoxylon	B
Dahlia 'Decorative' mix	BD,BS,F,KI,PK,R,SE,ST	Dalbergia obovata	B,KB,SI
Dahlia 'Delight' mix	VY	Dalbergia paniculata	B
Dahlia 'Diablo' c.s	MO	Dalbergia purpurascens	B,SI
Dahlia 'Diablo' mix	BD,BS,C,CL,D,DT,F,	Dalbergia retusa	B,RE,SA
	J,L,MO,SK,YA	Dalbergia sissoo	B,CA,HA,HU,SA
Dahlia 'Dw Amore'	D	Dalbergiella nyasae	B,SI
Dahlia Dw dbl quilled	S	Dalea candida	B
Dahlia 'Dw Delight'	D,DT	Dalea commosum	JE,SA
Dahlia Dw hyb dbl	D,F	Dalea exile	DD
Dahlia Dw hyb semi-dbl	BU,C,FR,T	Dalea formosa	SW
Dahlia 'Early Bird' mix	BS,C,CL,CN,DN,KI,	Dalea gattingeri	B
	MO,YA	Dalea greggii	SW
Dahlia 'Exhibition'	M,PT	Dalea purpurea	B,C,DD,HU,JE,PR,SA
Dahlia f1 'Sunny Red'	BS	Dalea searlsiae	SW
Dahlia f1 'Sunny Yellow'	BS,C	Dalea spinosa	SA,SW
Dahlia f2 'Sunny White'	B,BS,MO	Dalea 'Toronjil'	B,HU
Dahlia 'Figaro'	CN,F,J,L,MO,PK,R,SE,	Dalea villosum	B,PR
	SK,T,U,V	Damaeonorops mollis	B,O
Dahlia 'Figaro' imp	BS,CL,DT,KI,MO,YA	Damasonium alisma	SG
Dahlia 'Figaro' s-c	B,BS,CL,MO,SK,U	Dampiera sacculata	B,NI
Dahlia 'Fresco'	CA	Danae racemosa	B,SA
Dahlia 'Giant Decorative' hyb special dbl	BY,C,DT,MO	Danthonia californica	B
Dahlia 'Hammett'	YA	Danthonia decumbens	B
Dahlia 'Harlequin mix'	J,SK	Danthonia longifolia	B
Dahlia 'Heirloom Border Dahlias'	T	Danthonia pallida	B
Dahlia hortensis	DD,SD	Danthonia sp	HA
Dahlia imperialis	B,HU	Danthonia spicata	B
Dahlia 'Masterpiece mix' dbl	J	Daphne acutiloba	KL
Dahlia merckii	AP,CG,KL,SG	Daphne albowiana	AP,G,HP,KL,NG,SC
Dahlia 'Mignon' mix	BD,BS,G,MO,V	Daphne alpina	AP,B,C,CG,HP,KL,SA,SC
Dahlia 'Mignon' s-c	B,T	Daphne altaica	KL
Dahlia 'Mistral' mix	BS	Daphne arbuscula	VO
Dahlia mix Dw border	S	Daphne blagayana	B,SA
Dahlia mix giant hybrids	T	Daphne caucasica	KL
Dahlia mix lg fl dbl	SK	Daphne circassica	VO
Dahlia mix mammoth fl	S	Daphne cneorum	B,G,SA
Dahlia mix Showpiece Hybrids	PL,T	Daphne giraldii	AP,AR,B,C,G,HP,JE,KL,
Dahlia 'Monarch' mix	BS		NG,PL,PO,SC,SG

DAPHNE

Daphne glomerata	VO	Datura sanguinea see Brugmansia	
Daphne gnidium	B,C,SA	Datura stramonium	AP,B,BS,C,CN,CP,DV,
Daphne kosanini	KL		G,KL,LG,SG,SU,W
Daphne laureola	AP,B,CG,G,HP,PO	Datura stramonium v inermis	B,C
Daphne laureola ssp philippi	HP	Datura suavelolens see Brugmansia	
Daphne maloniana	VO	Datura un-named v	C
Daphne mezereum	AP,AR,B,BS,C,CG,EL,	Datura violacea	DV
	G,HP,JE,KL,LG,LN,NG,	Datura violacea plena	DV
	P,PO,SA,SC,SG,VE	Datura wrightii	DI,SZ
Daphne mezereum f alba	AP,AR,B,C,G,HP,KL,NG,	Daubenya aurea	AR,B,RU,SI
	P,SC,SG	Daubenya aurea v aurea	RU
Daphne mezereum v rubra	AP,KL,NG	Daubenya aurea v coccinea	B,RU
Daphne oleoides	AP,B,CG,G,HP,KL,NG,	Daucus carota	B,C,CN,CP,DD,HP,HW,
	RM,SA,SC,VO		KS,LA,NS,NT,SG,TH,Z
Daphne oleoides v glandulosa	NG	Daucus carota v carota	HU
Daphne papyracea	B,EL	Daucus littoralis	B
Daphne retusa see D. tangutica Retusa Group		Davallia fejeensis	B
Daphne sericea	AP,CG	Davallia pyxidata	SG
Daphne striata	AP,B,C,SC	Davallia solida	SG
Daphne tangutica	AP,AR,C,G,HP,NG,PM,	Davallia tyermannii	B,SG
	SC,SG,W	Davidia involucrata	B,C,CA,EL,FW,LN,N,SA,
Daphne tangutica Retusa Group	HP,KL		VE
Daphniphyllum macropodum	LN,SA	Davidia involucrata v vilmoriana	G
Darlingia darlingiana	B,O	Davidsonia pruriens	B
Darlingia ferruginea	O	Daviesia acicularis	B,C,HA,NI
Darlingtonia californica	B,BA,C,DV,HU,SC,Y	Daviesia angulata	B,NI
Darmera peltatum	B,C,G,HP,JE,P,RH,SA,T	Daviesia benthamii	B,NI
Darwinia diosmoides	B,NI,SA	Daviesia cordata	B,NI,O,SA
Darwinia purpurea	B	Daviesia corymbosa	B,EL,HA,NI
Dasispermum suffruticosum	B,BH,SI	Daviesia flexuosa	B,NI
Dasylirion durangensis	B	Daviesia genistifolia	B,HA
Dasylirion heteiacanthium	B	Daviesia horrida	B,NI
Dasylirion leiophyllum	B,SW	Daviesia juncea	B,NI
Dasylirion longissimum	B,C,SA	Daviesia latifolia	B,EL,HA,HU,NI
Dasylirion texanum	BC	Daviesia longifolia	B,NI
Dasylirion wheeleri	B,BC,CA,DV,NO,SA,SW	Daviesia mimosoides	B,HA,NI
Dasypogon bromeliifolius	B,DD,NI,O,SA	Daviesia pectinata	B
Datisca cannabina	B,C,SG	Daviesia polyphylla	B,NI
Datisca glomerata	B,DD	Daviesia revoluta	B,C,NI
Datura ceratocaula	B	Daviesia rhombifolia	B,NI
Datura discolor	B	Daviesia teretifolia	B,NI
Datura 'Double Blackcurrant Swirl'	T	Daviesia ulicifolia	B,HA,NI
Datura fastuosa 'Cherub'	BS,DT,F	Daviesia umbellulata	B,NI
Datura golden dbl	B,SE	Daviesia virgata	B,HA
Datura inoxia	AP,B,BS,C,CP,DT,DV,HP,	Daviesia wyattiana	B,NI
	HU,LG,N,PIT,V	Decaisnea fargesii	A,AP,B,C,CG,FW,G,SA,
Datura inoxia s-c	PL		SG
Datura inoxia ssp inoxia	B	Deckenia nobilis	B,O
Datura 'La Fleur Lilac'	B,C,T	Decodon verticillatus	B,PR
Datura 'Lavender'	SE	Degenia velebitica	AP,G,KL,SC,SG
Datura lilac single	C	Deinbollia oblongifolia	B
Datura metel	B,C,CP,F	Delairea odorata	B
Datura metel 'Belle Blanche'	B,C,F,U	Delonix adansioides	SI
Datura metel 'Black'	B,HU	Delonix boivinii	SI
Datura metel 'Cornucopea'	B	Delonix elata	B
Datura metel dbl lavender	HU	Delonix pumila	SI
Datura metel dbl purple	HU	Delonix regia	B,C,CA,DD,DV,EL,FW,
Datura metel dbl white	HU		HA,HU,LN,O,RE,SA,SG,
Datura metel dbl yellow	HU		SI,T,TT,WA
Datura metel fl pl 'Petticoat'	JE		
Datura metel 'Golden Queen'	B,DI	Delosperma abyssinica	B,SI
Datura metel mix	HU	Delosperma annulare	B
Datura metel triple yellow	B,HU	Delosperma ashtonii	AP,B,KB,KL,SI
Datura meteloides see D.inoxia		Delosperma bosseranum	B,DV
Datura purple dbl	B,C,DI	Delosperma cooperi	B,C,DV,JE,SC
Datura quercifolia	AP,B	Delosperma echinatus	SG
		Delosperma floribundum	B,SI

DELOSPERMA

Delosperma guthriei	DV
Delosperma hallii	B
Delosperma harazianum	AP,B
Delosperma littorale	B,SI
Delosperma lydenburgense	B,C,KB,SI,Y
Delosperma madagascariensis	DV
Delosperma minimum	B,KB
Delosperma nalurense	DV
Delosperma pergamentaceum	B
Delosperma pruinosum	B,KB
Delosperma rogersii	B,KB,SI,Y
Delosperma sp	C,SI,T
Delosperma sutherlandii	B,DV,JE,Y
Delosperma uncinatum	B,KB,SI,Y
Delphinium altaicum	CG
Delphinium amabile	SW
Delphinium ambiguum see Consolida ajacis	
Delphinium andersonii	SW
Delphinium andesicola	AP,B,RS,SW
Delphinium anthriscifolium	KL
Delphinium Astolat Group	B,BS,C,CL,DE,JE,JO, MO,PK,SA,SK
Delphinium barbeyi	B,SW
Delphinium Belladonna Group Imp	T
Delphinium Belladonna Group mix	HP,MO,PL,SA,SE
Delphinium Belladonna Group s-c	BS
Delphinium Belladonna Streichen Strain	BS
Delphinium bicolor	B,SW
Delphinium 'Bitter Chocolate' mix	PL
Delphinium Black Knight Group	B,BS,BY,C,CA,CL,DE,JE, MO,PK,SA,SK
Delphinium Blue Bird Group	B,BS,BY,C,CA,CL,JE, MO,PK,SA,SK
Delphinium 'Blue Dawn'	B,JE
Delphinium Blue Fountains Group	BS,BY,C,DE,F,J,KS,M, MO,U
Delphinium 'Blue Jay'	B,BS,JE,MO,SA,SK
Delphinium 'Blue Pygmy'	B,T
Delphinium 'Blue Shadow'	B
Delphinium Blue Springs Group	BS,CG,FR,JE,MO,V
Delphinium brunonianum	AP,C,G,I,KL,SC
Delphinium bulleyanum	G,SC,SG
Delphinium Cameliard Group	B,BS,CL,E,JE,MO,SA
Delphinium cardinale	B,C,HP,JE,SA,SW
Delphinium card. 'Beverley Hills' scarlet	PK
Delphinium card. 'Beverly Hills Salmon'	F,PK,U
Delphinium carolinianum	RS
Delphinium 'Casa Blanca'	B,C,DE,JE,SA,T
Delphinium cashmerianum	AP,CG,G,HP,SC,SG
Delphinium caucasicum	SG,VO
Delphinium 'Centurion Sky Blue'	CL,F,MO,O,U
Delphinium 'Centurion White'	F
Delphinium chamissonsis	SG
Delphinium cheilanthum	B,HP,T
Delphinium 'Cliveden Beauty'	B,BS,JE
Delphinium Connecticut Yankees Group	C,DE,DN,JE,PK,S
Delphinium cottage gdn mix	P
Delphinium Crown mix	BS,KI,ST,VH
Delphinium cuneatum	SG
Delphinium delavayi	B,HP
Delphinium 'Delphi' s-c	BS,PL
Delphinium dipterocarpum	B,SG
Delphinium drepanocentrum	SG
Delphinium 'Dw. Blue Heaven'	T
Delphinium 'Dw. Pacific' mix	D
Delphinium 'Dw. Snowhite'	T

Delphinium Dw 'Temple Bells'	PL
Delphinium elatum	B,CG,G,HP,JE,SA,SC,SG
Delphinium exaltatum	B,C,G,HP,JE
Delphinium f2 'Dreaming Spires'	BS,D,F,J,MO,SE,V
Delphinium f2 'Moody Blues'	DI
Delphinium fissum	B
Delphinium Foerster's Hybrids	C,JE
Delphinium Galahad Group	B,BS,BY,C,CA,CL,DE,JE, MO,PK,SA,SK
Delphinium geranifolium	B,SC,SW
Delphinium glareosum	AP,HP
Delphinium glaucum	B,C,HP,SG
Delphinium grandiflora ACE1606	NG
Delphinium grandiflorum	AP,B,G,HP,PM,RM,RS, SC,SG
Delphinium grandiflorum 'Blauer Zwerg'	AP,C,G,HP,JE,SC
Delphinium grandiflorum 'Blue Butterfly'	AP,B,BS,C,DI,HP,KI,KL, PK,S,SC,SE,ST
Delphinium grandiflorum 'Blue Mirror'	B,C,F
Delphinium grand. 'Butterfly Compactum'	B,DI,JE
Delphinium grandiflorum 'Butterfly' mix	T
Delphinium grandiflorum 'Butterfly' s-c	B
Delphinium grand. 'Gentian Blue Dw'	B
Delphinium grandiflorum 'Sky-blue Dw'	B,J,SA
Delphinium grandiflorum 'Snow-white Dw'	B,V
Delphinium Guinevere Group	B,BS,BY,C,CA,CL,DT, JE,MO,PK,SA,SK
Delphinium hybridum special mix	S
Delphinium 'Karl Foerster'	T
Delphinium King Arthur Group	B,BS,BY,C,CA,CL,DE,JE, MO,PK,SA,SK
Delphinium Lancelot Group	B,C,JE
Delphinium likiangense	AP,HP,KL
Delphinium luteum	AP,RS
Delphinium 'Magic Fountains Crystal' mix	BS
Delphinium 'Magic Fountains' mix	BD,BS,CL,CN,CO,DT,F, JE,KI,MA,MO,PK,S,SE, SK,T,TU,VY,YA
Delphinium 'Magic Fountains' s-c	B,BS,JE,L,MO,PK,PL, SK
Delphinium 'Magic Fountains' white	B,JE,MO,PL,SK
Delphinium 'Manhattan'	BS
Delphinium menziesii	AP,B,DD,KL,SC
Delphinium mix finest cvs	BL
Delphinium mix finest cvs dw	BL
Delphinium nelsonii	B,RM,SW
Delphinium nudicaule	AP,B,BS,C,CN,F,HP,JE, MO,SA,SC,SG
Delphinium nuttallianum	B,C,NO,SW
Delphinium occidentale	NO,RS
Delphinium orfordii	AP,HP
Delphinium 'Oriental Blue'	B,F
Delphinium oxysepalum	AP,CG,G,HP,KL,SC,SG
Delphinium 'Pacific Clear Springs' mix	BS,JE,KI,M,U
Delphinium 'Pacific Deluxe mix'	JE
Delphinium Pacific Giants 'Round Table'	BD,C,CN,DE,DT,JE,JO, KS,MO
Delphinium Pacific Hyb mix	w.a.
Delphinium parishii	B
Delphinium parryi	AP,B,SC,SW
Delphinium Percival Group	B,C,JE
Delphinium peregrinum	B
Delphinium 'Pink Dream'	V
Delphinium pogonanthum	RS
Delphinium przewalskii	AP,PM,SC
Delphinium pylzowii	AP,B,HP,KL,RS,SC,SG

DELPHINIUM

Delphinium requienii	AP,C,CG,HP,LG,MA,RS, SC,T
Delphinium requienii 'Variegata'	B,P
Delphinium retropilosum	SG
Delphinium rose & pink	SE
Delphinium scaposum	B,RS,SW
Delphinium schmalhausenii	CG
Delphinium scopulorum	B,DD,RS,SW
Delphinium 'Seafoam'	PL,SE
Delphinium semibarbatum	AP,B,BS,C,CN,D,F,G,HP, MO,PK,PL,RS,SA,SE,T
Delphinium S.thern Noblemen Gr.,s-c h-p	AP
Delphinium speciosum	B,SC
Delphinium staphisagria	AP,B,CG,HP,LG,NG
Delphinium 'Steichen'	B,BS,DT
Delphinium Summer Skies Group	AP,B,BS,BY,CA,CL,JE, MO,PK
Delphinium tatsienense	AP,G,HP,KL,RS,SC,SG
Delphinium tatsienense 'Album'	AP,HP,KL,RS
Delphinium 'Tom Pouce' Series s-c	B,BS,MO
Delphinium triste	CG,SG
Delphinium trolliifolium	DD
Delphinium vestitum	B
Delphinium villosum	B
Delphinium virescens	B,PR
Delphinium virescens wootoni	B,RS,SW
Delphinium x bellamosum	B,BS,JE,SA
Delphinium x cultorum	AP,G,SG
Dendranthema mongolicum	G,SG
Dendranthema zawadskii	G,HP,SG
Dendrobium canaliculatum	B
Dendrocalamus giganteus	B,EL,SA
Dendrocalamus strictus	B,DV,SA
Dendrocereus nudiflorus	B
Dendromecon rigida	B,SW
Dendrophthoe falcata	B
Denmoza rhodacantha	B,BC,DV,Y
Dentaria see Cardamine	
Derris robusta	DD
Deschampsia caespitosa	B,C,DE,HP,JE,NO,SA,SG
Deschampsia caespitosa 'Goldtau'	HP
Deschampsia flexuosa	B,C,PM,SA
Deschampsia flexuosa 'Tatra Gold'	HP
Deschampsia rubra	B
Descurainia pinnata	B
Descurainia sophia	SG
Desfontainea spinosa	SA
Desmanthus illinoensis	B,HU,PR
Desmanthus virgatus	B
Desmodium calycantha	SA
Desmodium canadense	B,KL,PR,SA
Desmodium canescens	B,PR
Desmodium elegans	B,SA,SG
Desmodium gangeticum	HU
Desmodium glutinosum	B,PR
Desmodium illinoiense	B
Desmodium intortum	B
Desmodium paniculatum	B
Desmodium pulchellum	B
Desmodium rensonii	B,HU
Desmodium tortuosum	DD
Desmodium triflorum	B
Desmodium uncinatum	B
Desmoschoenus spiralis	B
Deuterocohnia longipetala	CG
Deutzia scabra	B

Deutzia sp CNW1108	X
Dialium englerianum	SI
Dialium pachyphyllum	B
Dialium schlechteri	B
Dianella brevipedunculata	B
Dianella caerulea	AU,B,HA,NI,SA
Dianella caerulea v protensa	B,NI
Dianella congesta	B
Dianella ensifolia	G
Dianella intermedia	B
Dianella intermedia v norfolkensis	SG
Dianella laevis	B,HA
Dianella nigra	AU,B,SA,SC,SG,SS
Dianella revoluta	AU,B,HA,NI
Dianella revoluta v revoluta	RS
Dianella sp	SG
Dianella tasmanica	AR,AU,B,C,CG,MN,T
Dianthus acicularis	KL
Dianthus albus	T
Dianthus Allwoodii Alpinus Group	AL,AP,B,BD,BS,C,CG, CL,D,DE,G,GI,GO,HP,JE, KL,MO,PK,SA,SC,T
Dianthus alpinus	AP,B,BS,CG,G,HP,J,JE, JO,KI,KL,S,SA,ST,VH
Dianthus alpinus 'Albus'	KL
Dianthus alpinus 'Joan's Blood'	AP,I,SC
Dianthus amurensis	AP,B,G,HP,JE,KL,P
Dianthus amurensis 'Siberian Blue'	U
Dianthus anatolicus	AP,B,C,G,JE,SC,SG
Dianthus arenarius	AP,B,BD,BY,C,CL,HP,JE, KL,KS,L,SA,SC,SG
Dianthus arenarius 'White Maiden'	SK
Dianthus armeria	AP,B,C,G,HP,KL,NS,SC, SU,TH
Dianthus barbatus	AB,AP,AV,B,DD,G,HP,I,J E,KL,LG,PI,SG,V,VH
Dianthus barbatus 'Albus'	C,MO
Dianthus barbatus Auricula-Eyed	BD,BS,BY,CL,CN,D,F, KI,MO,SU,T,TH,TU,YA
Dianthus barbatus 'Beauty' s-c & mix	BS,BY,MO
Dianthus barbatus 'Bright Eyes'	CN,D
Dianthus barbatus 'D.T.Brown's' mix	BS
Dianthus barbatus dbl mix	BD,BS,CN,TH,TU,V,VH
Dianthus barbatus 'Diadem'	BS
Dianthus barbatus 'Diadem' Imp	BS,MO
Dianthus barb. 'Dunnets Dark Crimson'	BS,BY,HU,MO
Dianthus barbatus 'Duplex Super Dbl' mix	BS,DT,L,YA
Dianthus barbatus 'Early Bird' mix	YA
Dianthus b barbatus f1 'Hollandia' mix	B,BS,JO,MO,PK
Dianthus b. f1 'Hollandia' s-c Homeland	B,PK
Dianthus barbatus fl pl 'Blaupunkt' mix	JE
Dianthus barbatus fl pl mix	BU,C,CO,FR,JE,MO
Dianthus barbatus fl pl nanus	B,JE
Dianthus barbatus 'Forerunner'	D,KS
Dianthus barbatus 'Gemstones'	BS,KI
Dianthus barbatus 'Harlequin'	B,BS,F,KS,SE,T
Dianthus barbatus 'Homeland'	B,C
Dianthus barbatus 'Indian Carpet'	B,BS,BY,CL,CO,D,J,JE, KI,KS,L,MO,R,ST,T,U,V, YA
Dianthus barbatus 'Kurokawa Extra Early'	C
Dianthus barbatus 'M's Giant Single' mix	M
Dianthus barbatus 'M's Super Double' mix	M
Dianthus barbatus 'Messenger'	BS,CL,CN,MO,SK,TU
Dianthus barbatus 'Midget'	SK
Dianthus barbatus mix dw	I,U

DIANTHUS

Dianthus barbatus mix special	D,DT,MO
Dianthus barbatus 'Monarch'	F,SK
Dianthus barbatus 'New Era' mix	C,T
Dianthus barbatus Nigrescens Group	BS,C,HP,TH
Dianthus barbatus 'Oeschberg'	B,BS,C,HU,JE,KI
Dianthus barbatus 'Pink Beauty'	BS
Dianthus barbatus 'Pinnochio' mix	T
Dianthus barbatus 'Prelude' s-c	B
Dianthus barbatus 'Prettiness'	KI
Dianthus barbatus 'Roundabout' mix	BD,BS,C,CL,D,F,I,J, MO,SK,T,YA
Dianthus barbatus 'Scarlet Beauty'	BS,BY,C,MO
Dianthus barbatus single mix	BD,BS,C,F,FR,HU,J, ST,TH,TU
Dianthus barbatus single super mix	CL
Dianthus barbatus single/dbl mix	VY
Dianthus barbatus 'Snow White'	BY
Dianthus barbatus 'Soham Glory' dbl	BY
Dianthus barbatus 'Sooty'	B,P,T
Dianthus barbatus ssp compactus	CG
Dianthus barbatus 'Standard Albus'	B
Dianthus barbatus 'Standard Series' s-c	B
Dianthus barbatus 'Summer Beauty'	BS
Dianthus barbatus tall mix	DN,KS,SK
Dianthus barbatus tall scarlet	KS
Dianthus barbatus tall white	BS,KS
Dianthus barbatus 'Eminent Victorians'	TH
Dianthus barbatus 'Unwins Choice' mix	U
Dianthus barbatus 'Wee Willie' mix	BS,BU,BY,C,CL,DE,M, MO,PI,SK,TU,VY,YA
Dianthus barbatus x superbus	G
Dianthus basuticus	SI
Dianthus basuticus ssp basuticus	B,SI
Dianthus biflorus	SG
Dianthus brevicaulis	G
Dianthus brevicaulis brevicaulis	KL
Dianthus caesius see D.gratanianopolitanus	
Dianthus caespitosus	B,KB,SI
Dianthus callizonus	B,KL
Dianthus campestris	G,SG
Dianthus capitatus	SG
Dianthus carthusianorum	AP,B,C,CG,G,HP,HU,JE, SA,SC,SG,V
Dianthus carthusianorum v humilis	B,KL
Dianthus caryophyllus	B,CG
Dianthus cary. 'Chabaud Enchantment'	D
Dianthus cary. 'Chabaud Giant Dble' mix	BD,BS,CA,CL,FR,GO, J,KI,L,M,PI,R,SE,SK,SU T,U,V,VH
Dianthus c. 'Chabaud Giant Super Claudia'	MO
Dianthus c. 'Chabaud Giant Superb' mix	BY,C,CO,DT,S,ST
Dianthus caryophyllus 'Chabaud' s-c	FR,SK
Dianthus caryophyllus choice dbl mix	F
Dianthus caryophyllus 'Clove Pinks'	KS
Dianthus cary. 'Double Triumph' mix	BS,C
Dianthus caryophyllus 'Du Tyrol'	AL,B
Dianthus caryophyllus dw dbl	BS
Dianthus caryophyllus 'Dw Fragrance'	AL,BD,BS,BU,BY,CA, DE,DT,F,MO,R,SK,SU,TE
Dianthus caryophyllus 'Enfant De Nice'	BD,BS,CL,FR,MO,SK
Dianthus caryophyllus English Giants mix	PK
Dianthus caryophyllus f1 'Knight'	BS,KI,S
Dianthus caryophyllus f1 'Lillipot' mix	BS,C,L,MO,SE,SK,T
Dianthus caryophyllus f1 'Lillipot' s-c	B,BS,CA,CL,MO,SK,T
Dianthus caryophyllus f1 'Luminette' mix	T
Dianthus caryophyllus f1 'Minarette'	KI

Dianthus caryophyllus f1 'Mini Spice Mix'	BS,F
Dianthus caryophyllus f1 'Mini Spice' s-c	BS,SK
Dianthus caryophyllus f1 'Monarch' mix	CA,CL,PK,U
Dianthus caryophyllus f1 'Monarch' s-c	CL
Dianthus caryophyllus fl pl 'Orion'	SG
Dianthus caryophyllus 'Floristan'	BS,D,DTJ,L,MO,U
Dianthus caryophyllus 'Floristan Red'	T
Dianthus cary. 'Grenadin Dark Red'	B,JE
Dianthus caryophyllus 'Grenadin' mix	BS,JE,PK,SK,V
Dianthus cary. 'Grenadin Pale Gold'	B,JE,SK
Dianthus caryophyllus 'Grenadin Pink'	B,JE,SK
Dianthus caryophyllus 'Grenadin Scarlet'	B,JE,SK
Dianthus caryophyllus 'Grenadin White'	B,HU,JE,SK
Dianthus caryophyllus Hardy Border mix	AL,BD,BS,BY,CL,GI,KI, M,MO,ST,U
Dianthus caryophyllus 'King of the Blacks'	C,HU,SK,V
Dianthus caryophyllus 'Margarita'	BS,KI
Dianthus caryophyllus 'Peach Delight'	T
Dianthus cary. Perpetual Choice mix	AL,BS,BY,C,GI,KI,ST
Dianthus caryophyllus picotee	AL
Dianthus caryophyllus Rainbow dbl blend	SK
Dianthus caryophyllus 'Red Riding Hood'	T
Dianthus caryophyllus 'Sprite'	KI
Dianthus caryophyllus 'Stripes & Picotees'	BS,F,SE,T
Dianthus caryophyllus superb	BS,TU
Dianthus caryophyllus 'Tige de Fer'	BS
Dianthus caryophyllus 'Trailing'	BS,DI,DT,F,KS,PL,SE, T,V,VH
Dianthus caryophyllus 'Vienna' mix	BS,CL,JE,MO,SK
Dianthus chinensis	BU,CO,FR,J,SC,SG,SE,V
Dianthus chinensis 'Baby Doll'	BD,BS,BY,CL,D,DE, DT,F,J,KI,M,MO,PK,S, SK,TU,V
Dianthus chinensis 'Black/White Minstrels'	BS,DI,DT,KS,PL,SE,T
Dianthus chinensis 'Chianti'	B,BD,MO
Dianthus chinensis dbl mix	BS,BY,D,FR,KI,ST,TH, VH
Dianthus chinensis f1 'Carpet Mix'	BS,MO,SK,YA
Dianthus chinensis f1 'Carpet Persian'	BS,C,R,SK
Dianthus chinensis f1 'Carpet' s-c	BS,MO,SK
Dianthus chinensis f1 'Festival Carmine'	B,BS,MO,SK
Dianthus chin. f1 'Festival Cherry Picotee'	B,BS,MO,SK
Dianthus chinensis f1 'Fire Carpet'	BS,MO,T
Dianthus chinensis f1 'First Love'	BS,L
Dianthus chinensis f1 'Ideal Carmine'	B,BS,MO,SK,YA
Dianthus chin. f1 'Ideal Cherry Picotee'	B,BS,MO,SK,YA
Dianthus chinensis f1 'Ideal Crimson'	B,BS,MO,SK,YA
Dianthus chinensis f1 'Ideal' Mix	BS,MO,PK,SK,TU,YA
Dianthus chinensis f1 'Ideal Pink'	BS,MO,YA
Dianthus chinensis f1 'Ideal Raspberry'	YA
Dianthus chinensis f1 'Ideal Red'	PK,YA
Dianthus chinensis f1 'Ideal Rose'	B,BS,MO,SK,YA
Dianthus chinensis f1 'Ideal Violet'	B,BS,MO,PK,SK,YA
Dianthus chinensis f1 'Ideal Violet Picotee'	B,BS,MO,SK,YA
Dianthus chinensis f1 'Magic Charms'	BS,C,CA,CL,DT,L,MO, SK,YA
Dianthus chinensis f1 'Magic Charms' s-c	B,BS,CL,MO,SK
Dianthus chinensis f1 'Miss Japan Series'	B,BS
Dianthus chinensis f1 'Panda' mix	CL
Dianthus chinensis f1 'Panda' s-c	CL
Dianthus chinensis f1 'Parfait Raspberry'	B,BS,CA,CL,F,KI,L, MO,O,SK,VY
Dianthus chinensis f1 'Parfait Strawberry'	B,BS,CA,CL,F,L,MO, SK,U,VY
Dianthus chinensis f1 'Pink Flash'	U
Dianthus chinensis f1 'Princess' mix	CA,CL,D,S,SK

DIANTHUS

Dianthus chinensis f1 'Princess' s-c	CA,CL,SK
Dianthus c. f1 'Rosemarie Velvet Lavender'	B,BS,MO
Dianthus chinensis f1 'Rosemarie White'	BS
Dianthus chinensis f1 'Snowfire'	BS,CL,CO,KI,L,S,U
Dianthus chinensis f1 'Telstar' mix	BS,L,M,MO
Dianthus chinensis f1 'Telstar' s-c	B,BS,DE,MO
Dianthus chinensis 'Heddewigii,Dbl'	BS,TH
Dianthus chinensis 'Heddewigii,Dbl Gaiety'	BS,DE,DN,F,SK,VY
Dianthus chin. 'Heddewigii,dbl Salmon'	B
Dianthus chinensis 'Heddewigii Frosty'	T
Dianthus chin. 'Heddewigii,Snowball Dble'	B
Dianthus chinensis 'Merry-go-round'	B,C,CA,F
Dianthus chinensis mix superb single	BS
Dianthus chinensis 'Splendour'	T
Dianthus chinensis 'Welcome Crimson'	B,BS,MO
Dianthus chinensis 'White Carpet'	B
Dianthus chin. x D.barbatus f1 'Telstar mix'	J
Dianthus ciliatus ssp dalmaticus	B
Dianthus cinnabarinus see D.biflorus	
Dianthus 'Colour Magician'	BS,O
Dianthus cruentus	B,G,JE,SC
Dianthus cruentus ssp tauricus	SG
Dianthus deltoides	AL,AP,B,BS,C,CG,CN,
	CO,G,HP,HU,J,KI,KL,LG,
	SA,SC,SG,ST,SU,TH,V
Dianthus deltoides 'Albus'	AP,B,BS,C,CN,G,HP,JE,
	MO,RM,RS,SA,SC,TH
Dianthus deltoides 'Arctic Fire'	B,BS,C,JE,MO,PK,PL,
	SA
Dianthus deltoides 'Bicolor'	B
Dianthus deltoides 'Brilliancy'	B,BD,BS,BY,CN,JE,MO,
	SA,T
Dianthus deltoides 'Brilliant'	AP,B,C,CG,HP,JE,KL,L,
	PI,SC
Dianthus deltoides 'Broughty Blaze'	B
Dianthus deltoides 'Erectus'	AP,B,BD,BS,JE,MO
Dianthus deltoides f2 'Canta Libre'	BS,C,CL,JO,MO
Dianthus deltoides 'Fanal'	SA
Dianthus deltoides 'Leuchtfunk'	AP,B,BS,BY,C,CL,JE,KI,
	KL,MO,SC,VY
Dianthus deltoides 'Lueur'	B,JE
Dianthus deltoides 'Microchip'	AP,B,CL,SC
Dianthus deltoides 'Nelli'	B,JE
Dianthus deltoides 'Pacino'	MO
Dianthus deltoides 'Red Maiden'	SK
Dianthus deltoides 'Roseus'	B,JE
Dianthus deltoides 'Rubin'	KL
Dianthus deltoides 'Samos'	B,JE,SC
Dianthus deltoides 'Starburst'	D
Dianthus deltoides 'Steriker'	B
Dianthus deltoides 'Vampire'	B
Dianthus deltoides 'Wisley Variety'	B
Dianthus deltoides 'Zing'	B,PK
Dianthus drenowskianus	KL
Dianthus erinaceus	AP,C,SC,SG
Dianthus f1 'Diamond' mix	YA
Dianthus 'Fenbows Nutmeg Clove'	T
Dianthus ferrugineus	VO
Dianthus fragrans	HP
Dianthus fragrant village pinks	AL
Dianthus freynii	B,KL,SG
Dianthus furcatus	AP,B,G
Dianthus gallicus	B,KL,SG
Dianthus giganteus	B,G,HP,SC,SG
Dianthus giganteus ssp banaticus	SG
Dianthus glacialis	AP,B,C,G,JE,KL,SC

Dianthus glacialis ssp gelidus	KL
Dianthus gratianopolitanus	AL,AP,B,BS,BY,C,HP,JE,
	KL,L,MO,PI,RM,SA,SC,
	SG,SK,SU,TH
Dianthus gratianopolitanus 'Grandiflora'	B,HU,JE
Dianthus gratianopolitanus red, dk eye	B,JE
Dianthus gratianopolitanus rose	CL
Dianthus gratianopolitanus 'Rosefeder'	B,JE
Dianthus gratianopolitanus 'Splendens'	B,JE
Dianthus gratianopolitanus 'Star Cushion'	B
Dianthus gratianopolitanus 'Sternkissen'	JE
Dianthus haematocalyx	AP,CG,SC
Dianthus hoeltzeri	B
Dianthus hungaricus	AP,B,CG,SC,SG
Dianthus hybrida 'Rainbow Loveliness'	B,BS,DI,DT,J,JO,PL,S,
	SE,T,U
Dianthus 'Ideal Dp Violet'	SK
Dianthus 'Ideal Fuchsia'	SK
Dianthus 'Ideal' Pearl	PK,SK
Dianthus 'Ipswich Pinks'	BD,T
Dianthus japonicus 'Ginza' mix	C
Dianthus japonicus 'Ginza' red	B,BS,MO
Dianthus japonicus 'Ginza' white	B,BS,MO
Dianthus knappii	AL,AP,B,BS,C,CG,F,G,H
	P,HU,JE,KL,MO,NG,P,P
	K,PL,S,SA,SC,SE,T,U,V
Dianthus kusnetzovii	VO
Dianthus 'Lady Seymour'	SE
Dianthus lilaceus	CG
Dianthus lumnitzeri	CG,G,SC
Dianthus lusitanus	CG,G,KL
Dianthus membranaceus	BS
Dianthus 'Microchips'	AP,B,JE,KL,SC
Dianthus microlepis	KL
Dianthus microlepis f albus	AL,FR
Dianthus mix gdn pinks	P
Dianthus mix select	JD
Dianthus mix sm	AP,B,C,G,HP,JE,KL,SA,
Dianthus monspessulanus	AP,CG,KL,SC
Dianthus monspessulanus ssp sterbergii	B,JE,KL
Dianthus myrtinervius	B,G,JE
Dianthus nardiformis	
Dianthus neglectus see D.pavonius	
Dianthus nitidus of gdns	B,JE,KL,SC
Dianthus pallens	SG
Dianthus pavonius	AP,B,CG,G,JE,KL,RM,
	SA,SC,VO
Dianthus pavonius hyb	PM
Dianthus petraeus	AP,B,C,G,JE,SG
Dianthus petraeus ssp integer	AP,B,SC
Dianthus petraeus ssp noeanus	B,G,RM,SC,SG
Dianthus petraeus ssp orbelicus	CG
Dianthus petraeus v bebius	B
Dianthus pinifolius	B,G
Dianthus pinifolius ssp lilacinus	B,G
Dianthus plumarius	AB,AP,B,CG,F,G,HP,JE,
	KL,KS,PL,SA,SG,TH,V
Dianthus plumarius Ballad blend	SK
Dianthus plumarius fl pl 'Albus'	B,G,JE
Dianthus plum. fl pl 'Nanus Pink Shades'	B,JE
Dianthus plumarius fl pl 'Roseus'	B,JE
Dianthus plumarius fl pl 'Spring Charm'	JE
Dianthus plumarius 'Highland Hybrids'	BS,T
Dianthus plumarius 'Lumnitzeri'	B,KL
Dianthus plumarius mix dbl	D
Dianthus plumarius mix single	BS,CL,DT,HU,MO

DIANTHUS

Dianthus plumarius 'Sonata'	T
Dianthus plumarius 'Spring Beauty'	BD,BS,BY,C,HU,KI,L,
	MO,SK,U
Dianthus plumarius ssp praecox	B,KL
Dianthus plumarius ssp regis-stephani	B
Dianthus pontederae	AP,B,CG,JE,KL,SG
Dianthus pontederae giganteiformis	SG
Dianthus pungens	B,SA,SG
Dianthus pyrenaicus	AP,CG,KL
Dianthus 'Queen of Henri'	AP
Dianthus seguieri	AP,B,C,CG,HP,SC,SG
Dianthus serotinus	AP,B,C,G,SC
Dianthus shinanensis	AP,HP,SG
Dianthus 'Shrimp'	BS,MO
Dianthus simulans	KL
Dianthus sp	AP,BH,G,KL,SG,SI
Dianthus sp rock gdn mix	BS,C
Dianthus speciosus	SG
Dianthus spiculifolius	G,HP,KL,SG
Dianthus squarrosus	AP
Dianthus strictus v bebius	JE
Dianthus subacaulis	AP,B,C,G,JE,SC,SG
Dianthus superbus	AP,B,C,CG,DV,G,HP,JE,
	RM,SA,SC,SG
Dianthus superbus alpestris	SG
Dianthus superbus 'Arc En Ciel'	B
Dianthus superbus 'Crimsonia'	B
Dianthus superbus 'Primadonna'	B,JE,PK
Dianthus superbus 'Snowdonia'	B
Dianthus superbus 'Spooky'	B
Dianthus superbus ssp longicalycinus	AP,B
Dianthus sup. ssp longicalycinus f albus	B
Dianthus superbus ssp speciosus	B
Dianthus superbus Super Fantasy mix	T,V
Dianthus sylvestris	AP,B,CG,G,JE,KL,SA,
	SG,VO
Dianthus sylvestris ssp siculum	B
Dianthus sylvestris ssp tergestinus	B,JE
Dianthus sylvestris strictus	KL
Dianthus tatrea	CG
Dianthus tenuifolium	AP,B,CG,G,KL
Dianthus tianschanicus	SG
Dianthus tristis	CG,KL
Dianthus 'Twinkletoes'	S
Dianthus uralensis	SA
Dianthus versicolor	SG
Dianthus viscidus	SG
Dianthus webbianus	CG
Dianthus x arvernensis	B,G,JE,SC
Dianthus x roysii	AP,B,C,JE,KL
Dianthus zeyheri	B,BH,KB,SI
Diapensia lapponica	C
Diapensia obovata	VO
Diascia barberae	AP,B,SI,V
Diascia barberae 'Apricot Queen'	B,C
Diascia barberae 'Pink Queen'	B,BD,BS,C,CL,D,DT,F,
	MO,PK,PL,S,SE,U
Diascia elongata	B,SI
Diascia integerrima	B,SI
Diascia longicornis	B,SI
Diascia sp	SI
Diastema affine	B
Dicentra 'Bacchanal'	B,P
Dicentra chrysantha	B,C
Dicentra eximia	AP,B,C,DE,HU,JE,PL,SA
Dicentra formosa	AB,AP,B,C,HP,JE,SA,SG

Dicentra formosa 'Luxuriant'	G,
Dicentra formosa ssp formosa	SG
Dicentra macrocapnos	AP,B,HP,RS
Dicentra ochroleuca	B
Dicentra peregrina	AP,B,JE,SC
Dicentra peregrina 'Alba'	B,JE,KL,SC
Dicentra scandens	AP,B,C,G,HP,JE,P,SA
Dicentra sp China	SG
Dicentra spectabilis	w.a.
Dicentra spectabilis f alba	AP,B,BS,CN,DE,EL,G,
	HP,JE,MO,PL,SA,SC,T
Dicentra torulosa	AP,HP,T
Dicentra uniflora 'White Heart'	C
Dicerma biarticulatum	B
Dicerocaryum eriocarpum	B,SI
Dicerocaryum senecioides	B,SI
Dicerocaryum zanguebarium	B,DD
Dichanthium aristatum	B
Dichanthium sericeum	B,HA,NI
Dichelostemma capitatum	B,SW
Dichelostemma ida-maia	AP,G,LG
Dichelostemma multiflorum	B,Sg
Dichelostemma pulchellum	B,SC,SW
Dichodon cerastoides	SG
Dichondra micrantha	B,PK
Dichondra repens	BS,CA,DI,FR,HA,MO
Dichopogon capillipes	B,NI
Dichopogon strictus	AP,B,NI
Dichorisandra thyrsiflora	B
Dichrostachys cinerea	B,SI
Dichrostachys spicata	B,NI
Dicksonia antarctica	B,C,EL,G,HA,N,SA,SH
Dicksonia fibrosa	B,C,SA
Dicksonia squarrosa	B,C
Dicliptera suberecta	HP
Dicoma anomala	B,SI
Dicoma grandididieri	B,SI
Dicoma zeyheri	C,KB
Dicranopteris linearis	B
Dicranostigma franchetianum	AP,B,G,SG
Dicranostigma franchetianum 'Aristocrat'	C,HU
Dicranostigma lactucoides	KL,SC,W
Dicranostigma leptopodum	B,CG
Dicrastylis exsuccosa v elliptica	B,NI
Dicrastylis fulva	B,NI
Dicrastylis microphylla	B,NI
Dicrocaulon spissum	B
Dictamnus albus	AP,BS,C,CG,CN,FW,G,
	HP,JD,JE,KL,MO,RM,
	RS,SA,SC,SG,T,TH,U
Dictamnus albus 'Albiflorus'	G,JE,KL
Dictamnus albus v caucasicus	KL
Dictamnus albus v purpurea	AP,B,BS,BY,DE,FW,G,
	P,HU,JD,LG,MO,PO,RS,
	SC,SG,T
Dictamnus fraxinella see D.albus v purpurea	
Dictamnus mix	C
Dictyolimon macrorrhabdos	KL,SC,SG
Dictyosperma album	B,C,CA,EL,SH
Dictyosperma album v rubrum	CA,O
Didelta carnosa	B,SI
Didelta spinosa	B,SI
Didiera madagascariensis	B,SI
Didiscus see Trachymene	
Didymaotus lapidiformis	B,C,DV,SI,Y
Didymochlaena truncatula	B

91

DIERAMA

Dierama argyreum	B,P,SI
Dierama 'Candy Stripe' (V)	P
Dierama cooperi	SZ
Dierama dracomontanum	AP,B,C,LG,P,SA,SC,SI
Dierama erectum	B,SI
Dierama floriferum	SI
Dierama galpinii	B,SI
Dierama hyb dw	C
Dierama igneum	B,P,SA,SI
Dierama latifolium	B,P,SI
Dierama medium	B,C,SI
Dierama mossii	B,SI
Dierama pauciflorum	B,SI
Dierama pendulum	AP,B,C,KB,RU,SC,SI
Dierama pendulum robustum	SZ
Dierama pulcherrimum	AP,B,C,G,HU,I,JE,LG,N, P,PA,PL,RH,SA,SG,V,X
Dierama pulcherrimum dk purple	SZ
Dierama pulcherrimum 'Donard' hyb	AP,C,P,PL,SC,T
Dierama pulcherrimum ex- Slieve Donard	SZ
Dierama pulcherrimum 'Silver Dawn'	SZ
Dierama pulcherrimum 'Snowbells'	B,P
Dierama reynoldsii	B,SI
Dierama robustum	B,SI
Dierama robustum x dubium	B,SI
Dierama sp	AP,BH,RU
Dierama trichorhizum	B,SI
Diervilla x splendens	B
Dietes bicolor	B,BH,CA,EL,HA,O,RU, SA,SI
Dietes butcheriana	B,KB,O,RU,SI
Dietes flavida	B
Dietes grandiflora	AP,B,DV,KB,MN,RU,SC, SE,SI,T
Dietes iridioides	AP,B,CA,G,HA,KB,O,RU, SA,SC,SG,SI
Dietes robinsoniana	AU
Dietes vegeta	WA
Digitalis alba	SA,SU
Digitalis ambigua see D.grandiflora	
Digitalis 'Campanulata alba'	DG
Digitalis cariensis	C
Digitalis ciliata	AP,HP
Digitalis davisiana	AP,B,G,HP,PL,RS,SA,SC
Digitalis dubia	AP,B,C,HP,P,SA,SC,SG
Digitalis ferruginea	AP,B,C,CN,CP,DG,F,G,H, P,HU,LG,NG,PI,SA,T,TH
Digitalis ferruginea 'Gigantea'	B,DG,JE
Digitalis ferruginea 'Yellow Herald'	B,C,DG,JE
Digitalis 'Flashing Spires' (V)	P
Digitalis fontanesii	HP
Digitalis 'Glory of Roundway'	DG
Digitalis grandiflora	w.a.
Digitalis grandiflora 'Carillon' dw	AP,B,BS,C,DG,HP,HU, JE,KI,KS,RS,SA,SE,ST
Digitalis grandiflora lamarkii	T
Digitalis heywoodii see D.purpurea ssp h.	
Digitalis 'John Innes Tetra'	B,DG,F,HP,KS,PL,T
Digitalis laevigata	AP,B,C,DG,F,HP,JE,NG, RS,SA,SC
Digitalis laevigata ssp graeca	C,HP,T
Digitalis lamarckii hort see D.lanata	
Digitalis lanata	AP,B,BS,C,CN,CP,DG,E, F,G,HP,HU,JE,KI,LG,P, PL,RH,RS,SA,SC,SG, SU,T,V

Digitalis lanata 'Berggold'	B
Digitalis lanata 'Krajovy'	B
Digitalis leucophragma S3198	E
Digitalis lutea	AP,B,BY,C,CN,CP,DG,E, F,G,HP,HU,JD,JE,KL,LG, MA,NG,P,PL,RH,SA,SC, SG,SU,T,W
Digitalis lutea Brickell's form	HP,NG
Digitalis Marshalls superior hybrids	M
Digitalis micrantha	C
Digitalis mix selected	BY,CO,P,S
Digitalis obscura	AP,B,C,DG,HP,HU,JD, JE,P,PL,SA,SC,SG,T,V,W
Digitalis parviflora	AP,B,C,DG,F,G,HP,JE, LG,NG,P,PL,SA,SC,SG,T
Digitalis purpurea	w.a.
Digitalis purpurea 'Chedglow' (V)	NS
Digitalis purpurea Excelsior Group	AP,BD,BS,C,CL,CN,D,F, HP,HU,J,KI,KS,L,MO,PI, PK,R,S,SA,SK,ST,SU,T, TU,U,V,Y
Digitalis purpurea Excelsior Group Purple	B,PI,SG
Digitalis purpurea Excelsior Group red	B,C,JE
Digitalis purpurea f albiflora	AP,B,C,CN,DG,F,HP,JD, JE,KS,L,P,PL,SC,T,TH,V
Digitalis purpurea 'Fairy'	B
Digitalis purpurea Foxy Group	B,BD,BS,BY,C,CL,CO, DG,D,DE,DT,F,HP,HU,JE, JO,KI,KS,MO,PI,PK,SA, SD,SE,SG,SK,TU
Digitalis purpurea Giant Spotted Group	B,BS,DG,DT,F,L,MO,PL
Digitalis purpurea Glittering Prizes Group	HP,SE,T,V
Digitalis purpurea Gloxinoides Group	BU,P,JE,SA
Digitalis purpurea Gloxin. Gr. 'The Shirley'	B,BS,C,DE,HU,T
Digitalis purpurea 'Isabellina'	B
Digitalis purpurea 'Monstrosa'	B
Digitalis purpurea peloric	F,T
Digitalis purpurea 'Primrose'	F,PL
Digitalis purpurea ssp heywoodii	B,DG,E,G,HP,P,PL,RM, SC,T
Digitalis purpurea ssp purpurea	B,SA
Digitalis purpurea 'Strawberry Crush'	SE
Digitalis purpurea 'Sutton's Apricot'	AP,B,BD,BS,C,CN,DG,F, G,HP,HU,I,JE,KI,KS,L, MO,NS,P,PK,PL,S,SA, SE,ST,T,V
Digitalis schischkinii	C
Digitalis sibirica	AP,G,HP,RS,SC
Digitalis sp brown fl	PM
Digitalis sp & forms mix	C,DI,P
Digitalis thapsi	AP,B,DG,HP,JE,P,RS,SG
Digitalis trojana	AP,HP
Digitalis viridiflora	AP,B,BS,C,DG,F,G,HP, HU,JE,KL,LG,P,PL,RS, SA,SC
Digitalis x mertonensis	AP,B,C,CN,DG,F,HP,HU, I,G,JE,KS,L,P,PK,PL,SA, SC,SG,T
Dilatris corymbosa	B,SA,SI
Dilatris ixioides	B,SI
Dilatris pillansii	B,SI
Dilatris viscosa	B,SI
Dillenia indica	B,C,EL,SA
Dillwynia cinerascens	B,NI
Dillwynia floribunda	HA,NI,SA
Dillwynia floribunda v floribunda	B

DILLWYNIA

Dillwynia floribunda v teretifolia	HA
Dillwynia glaberrima	B,HA
Dillwynia juniperinum	B,HA,HU
Dillwynia phylicoides	B
Dillwynia retorta	B,HA,NI
Dillwynia uncinata	B,NI
Dimorphotheca aurantiaca see D.sinuata	
Dimorphotheca cuneata	B,SA,SI
Dimorphotheca hybrida giant mix	T
Dimorphotheca 'Irish Linen'	U
Dimorphotheca minor	SG
Dimorphotheca montana	B,SA,SI
Dimorphotheca pluvialis	AP,B,BU,C,KB,SG,SI,TU
Dimorphotheca pluvialis 'Glistening White'	B,BS,C,J,S,SE,T
Dimorphotheca pluvialis mix special	S
Dimorphotheca pluvialis 'Tetra Polar Star'	B,T,V
Dimorphotheca sinuata	B,BS,BY,C,CA,CO,D,DE, DT,F,FR,J,KB,KI,KS,L, MO,PK,SG,SI,ST,SU
Dimorphotheca sinuata 'Apollo'	V
Dimorphotheca sinuata hyb Imp	C
Dimorphotheca sinuata 'Orange Glory'	B
Dimorphotheca sinuata 'Salmon Queen'	B,DT,SE,T,V
Dimorphotheca sinuata 'Starshine'	T,PK,V
Dimorphotheca sinuata 'Sunshine Hybrids'	U
Dimorphotheca sinuata 'Tetra Goliath'	B
Dinteranthus inexpectatus	B,DV
Dinteranthus microspermus	DV
Dinteranthus microsp. ssp puberulus	B,SI,Y
Dinteranthus pole-evansii	B,C,DV,GC,SI,Y
Dinteranthus puberulus	B,DV,KB
Dinteranthus vanzylii	B,DV,Y
Dinteranthus wilmotianus	B,DV,KB,SI,Y
Dinteranthus wilmotianus ssp impunctata	B
Dionaea muscipula	AP,B,C,CA,DV,G,PK,SE, T
Dionysia aretioides	B,JE
Dionysia involucrata	AP,B,JE,SC
Dioon edule	B,C,CA,EL,HU,SA
Dioon edule 'Queretaro'	O
Dioon edule 'Rio Verde'	O
Dioon edule 'Tamaulipas'	O
Dioon edule v edule	O
Dioon edule v palma solo	O
Dioon mejiae	B,O
Dioon rzedowskii	O
Dioon spinulosum	CA,EL,O
Dioscorea cotinifolia	B,SI
Dioscorea dregeana	C,DV,SI
Dioscorea elephantipes	B,BH,C,CH,DV,SI,Y
Dioscorea hastifolia	B,DV
Dioscorea japonica	B,DD,HU
Dioscorea oppositifolia	B
Dioscorea sp	SI
Dioscorea sylvatica	B,SA,SI
Dioscorea villosa	B,PR,SG
Diosma hirsuta	B,SI
Diosporum lanuginosum	B
Diospyros armata	SA
Diospyros austroafricana	B,KB,SI
Diospyros dichrophylla	B,KB,SI
Diospyros digyna	B
Diospyros discolor	B
Diospyros ebenum	B
Diospyros exsculpta	B
Diospyros ferrea	B

Diospyros glabra	B,SI
Diospyros kaki	C,CA,EL,FW,LN,SA,VE
Diospyros lotus	A,B,C,CA,FW,LN,SA,VE
Diospyros lycioides	BH,SI
Diospyros lycioides ssp guerkei	B,KB,SI
Diospyros lycioides ssp lycioides	B,KB
Diospyros mannii	B
Diospyros melanoxylon	B
Diospyros mespiliformis	B,WA
Diospyros ramulosa	B,SI
Diospyros rhombifolia	B,FW,LN
Diospyros simii	B,C,KB,SI
Diospyros sp mix	BH
Diospyros virginiana	A,B,C,CA,CG,DE,EL,FW, LN,SA,VE
Diospyros whyteana	B,BH,C,KB,SI
Dipcadi fulvum	B
Dipcadi fulvum S.F90 Morocco	MN
Dipcadi marlothii	B,SI
Dipcadi serotinum	AP,B,CG,G,KL,LG,SA,SC
Dipcadi serotinum MS877 France	MN
Dipcadi serotinum S.L449/1 Spain	MN
Dipcadi serotinum v lividum	B
Dipcadi serotinum v lividum A.B.S4409	MN
Dipcadi serotinum v lividum S.F230 Spain	MN
Dipcadi serotinum v lividum S.F279/1	MN
Dipcadi serotinum v lividum S.F322	MN
Dipcadi viride	B,SC,SI
Diphylleia cymosa	AP,B,NG
Diphysa robinoides	B
Diplarrhena latifolia	AR,AU,B,SC
Diplarrhena moraea	AP,B,C,HP,HU,KL,NI,SG
Diplocyclos palmatus	B,SG
Diploglottis campbellii	B
Diploglottis cunninghamii	B
Diploglottis diphyllostegia	B
Diplolaena angustifolia	B,C,NI,O,SA
Diplolaena dampieri	B,NI
Diplolaena microcephala	B
Diplopeltis eriocarpa	B,NI
Diplopeltis huegelii	B,NI,SA
Diplorhynchus condylocarpon	B
Diplosoma luckhoffii	B
Diplotaxis erucoides	B
Diplotaxis muralis	G,SG
Dipogon lignosus	B,SA,SI
Dipsacus fullonum	AB,AP,B,BH,BS,BY,C, CN,CO,CP,G,HP,HU,JE, KI,LA,MO,S,SA,SC,SG, ST,SU,TH,TU,V,W,Z
Dipsacus fullonum v alba	B,HU
Dipsacus gmellinii	SG
Dipsacus inermis	C,HP
Dipsacus japonicus	B,SG
Dipsacus laciniatus	B,G
Dipsacus pilosus	AP,B,JE,SG
Dipsacus sativus	B,FI,JE,SA
Dipsacus sylvestris see D.fullonum	
Dipterronia sinensis	B,LN,N,SA,SG
Dirca palustris	B
Disa atricapilla	B,SI
Disa cardinalis	B
Disa caulescens	B,SI
Disa cornuta	B,SI
Disa crassicornis	B,SI
Disa fasciata	B,SI

93

DISA

Disa ferruginea	B,SI
Disa racemosa	B
Disa uniflora	B,C,SI
Disa x kewensis	B
Disanthus cercidifolius	B,FW
Discaria toumatou	B,SS
Dischisma ciliatum	B,SI
Dischisma sp	SI
Discocactus alteolens	B,DV
Discocactus crystallophilus	B,DV
Discocactus griseus	B,DV
Discocactus horstii	B,DV
Discocactus insignis	B,DV
Discocactus insignis HU347	Y
Discocactus latispinus	DV
Discocactus magnimammus	B,DV
Discocactus nigrisaetosus	B,DV
Discocactus placentiformis v alteolens	Y
Discocactus pugionanthus	B,CH,DV
Discocactus sp nova HU coll ref	DV
Discocactus subviridigriseus	B,DV
Diselma archeri	O
Disperis capensis	B
Disphyma clavellatum	B,DD,DV,SA
Disphyma crassifolium	DV,NI
Disporum hookeri	C,NO
Disporum smithii	AP,B,HP,PM,SC
Disporum trachycarpum	B,C,NO,SG,SW
Dissotis canescens	B,C,KB,SI
Dissotis debilis	B,SI
Dissotis princeps	B,C,EL,KB,SI
Dissotis princeps v princeps	B,SI
Dissotis princeps white	B,KB
Dissotis senegambiensis	B,SI
Dissotis sp	SI
Distylium racemosa	LN,SA
Dithyrea wislizenii	B
Diuris concinna	B
Diuris corymbosa	B
Diuris magnifica	B
Dizygotheca see Schefflera	
Doatia novazelandae	AU
Dodecatheon alpinum	AP,B,KL,SW
Dodecatheon clevelandii	AP,B,SC,SW
Dodecatheon clevelandii ssp insulare	AP,SG
Dodecatheon conjugens	AP,B,C,RM,SC,SW
Dodecatheon cusickii see D. pulchellum ssp c.	
Dodecatheon dentatum	AP,HP
Dodecatheon ellisae	B,SW
Dodecatheon hendersonii	AP,B,HP,KL,SC,SG
Dodecatheon jeffreyi	AP,B,CG,G,NO,SC,SG
Dodecatheon jeffreyi 'Red Light'	C,JE
Dodecatheon littorale	KL
Dodecatheon meadia	AP,B,BD,BS,C,CG,D,G,
	HP,HU,JE,KL,L,LG,MO,
	NT,PA,PL,PR,SA,SC,ST,
	SU,TH
Dodecatheon meadia f album	AP,B,G,HP,JE,KL,SC
Dodecatheon meadia 'Goliath'	B,C,JE
Dodecatheon meadia mix	JE
Dodecatheon meadia red	B,C,G,JE,PA
Dodecatheon pulchellum	AB,AP,B,CG,HP,JE,KL,
	NO,PR,RM,SG,SC,SW
Dodecatheon pulchellum 'Red Wings'	AP,B,HP,P,SC
Dodecatheon pulchellum ssp cusikii	KL
Dodecatheon sp	KL

Dodecatheon tatrandum see D.jeffreyi	
Dodonaea angustifolia	B,HA,SI,WA
Dodonaea angustifolia 'Purpurea'	WA
Dodonaea aptera	B,NI
Dodonaea baueri	B,NI
Dodonaea boroniifolia	B,EL
Dodonaea ceratocarpa	B,NI
Dodonaea concinna	B
Dodonaea coriacea	B,NI
Dodonaea cuneata	EL,HA
Dodonaea divaricata	B,NI
Dodonaea eriocarpa	B
Dodonaea falcata	B
Dodonaea filifolia	B
Dodonaea 'Giant Lantern'	B,EL
Dodonaea hackettiana	AU,B,NI
Dodonaea hirsuta	B,NI
Dodonaea humilis	B,NI
Dodonaea lanceolata	B,NI
Dodonaea lobulata	B,HA,NI
Dodonaea madagascariensis	B
Dodonaea multijuga	B,NI
Dodonaea oxyptera	B,NI
Dodonaea peduncularis	B,NI
Dodonaea petiolaris	B,NI
Dodonaea physocarpa	B
Dodonaea pinifolia	B,NI
Dodonaea ptarmicaefolia	B,NI
Dodonaea rigida	B,NI
Dodonaea rupicola	B,NI
Dodonaea sinuolata	B,EL
Dodonaea stenozyga	B,NI
Dodonaea triangularis	B,NI
Dodonaea triquetra	B,EL,HA,NI
Dodonaea truncatiales	B,NI
Dodonaea viscosa	EL,HA,NI,O,SA,VE,WA
Dodonaea viscosa 'Purpurea'	B,CA,EL,HA,SA,VE
Dodonaea viscosa ssp viscosa	B
Dodonaea viscosa v linearis	B
Dolichandrone spathacea	B,EL
Dolichoglottis lyallii	B,SS
Dolichoglottis scorzoneroides	AP,B,SS
Dolichos lablab see Lablab purpurascens	
Dolichothele albescens	DV
Dolichothele decipiens	DV
Dolichothele longimamma	DV
Dolichothele melaleuca	DV
Dolichothele saffordii	DV
Dolichothele sphaerica	DV
Dombeya autumnalis	B,KB,SI
Dombeya burgessiae	B,C,EL,KB,SA,SI
Dombeya cacuminum	SI
Dombeya calantha	B,EL,SA
Dombeya cymosa	B,SI
Dombeya goetzenii	B
Dombeya macranthae	SI
Dombeya natalensis	DV
Dombeya pulchra	B,SI
Dombeya rotundifolia	B,SI,WA
Dombeya tiliacea	B,KB,SI
Dombeya wallichii	B
Dombeya x cayeuxii	CG
Donatia novaezelandiae	B,SS
Doronicum austriacum	AP,B,HP,KL,P,SC,SG
Doronicum catarractae	C,HP
Doronicum columnae	AP,J

94

DORONICUM

Doronicum grandiflorum	B,JE,SG,ST
Doronicum 'Little Leo'	B,BS,PL,U
Doronicum orientale	AP,B,CN,G,HP,JE,KI,KL, SA,SC,V
Doronicum orientale 'Finesse'	B,C,JE
Doronicum orientale 'Goldcut'	B,BS,JE,MO
Doronicum orientale 'Magnificum'	B,BS,BY,C,CL,CN,D,HU ,JE,L,MO,SA,SK
Doronicum pardalianches	B,G,JE,SG
Doronicum plantagineum	AP,HP,SG
Doronicum styriacum	SG
Dorotheanthus bellidiformis	B,BY,C,CN,CO,D,DN,DV, F,FR,HU,J,KB,KS,L,M, PI,R,SK,ST,TU,U,V,VH,Y
Dorotheanthus bellidiformis p.s	J
Dorotheanthus bellidiformis 'Sparkles'	S
Dorotheanthus bellidiformis ssp bellid.	SI
Dorotheanthus bidouwensis	B
Dorotheanthus booysenii	B
Dorotheanthus 'Cape Sunshine'	U
Dorotheanthus 'Gelato Dark Pink'	B,CL,MO,SE
Dorotheanthus 'Gelato White'	B,C,CL,MO
Dorotheanthus gramineus	B,C,CG,DV,F,KB,SI,Y
Dorotheanthus 'Harlequin' mix	DT,J
Dorotheanthus 'Lunette'	B,BD,BY,C,CL,D,DT,F,KI, MO,PL,S,SK,V,VH
Dorotheanthus 'Magic Carpet'	BD,BS,CL,KI,MO,SE, SU,T,YA
Dorotheanthus maughanii	B,SI
Dorotheanthus oculatus	DV
Dorotheanthus 'Pomeridiana Sunshine'	D
Dorotheanthus rourkei	B,SI
Dorotheanthus sp	SI
Dorstenia carnulosa	Y
Dorstenia foetida	Y
Doryanthes excelsa	B,C,DD,EL,HA,O,SA,SH
Doryanthes palmeri	B,RS
Doryopteris pedata	B,SA
Doryphora sassafras	B
Dovea macrocarpa	B,SI
Dovyalis caffra	B,EL,KB,SA,SI,WA
Dovyalis hebecarpa	B
Dovyalis zeyheri	B,SI
Downingia elegans	C,G
Downingia yina v major	B,DD
Draba aizoides	AP,B,BD,BS,C,CG,CL, CN,JE,KL,L,MO,SA,SC, SG,VO
Draba alpina	B,SC
Draba alpina v glacialis	SG
Draba arabisans	KL
Draba asprella	B,SW
Draba athoa	KL
Draba athoa f leiocarpa	KL
Draba borealis	B,JE,KL,SG
Draba bruniifolia	AP,B,G,JE,KL
Draba bryoides see D. rigida v b.	
Draba bucegi	KL
Draba cappadocica	AP,KL,SC
Draba condensata	KL
Draba crassifolia	SG
Draba cretica	KL
Draba cuspidata	KL
Draba daurica see D.glabella	
Draba dedeana	AP,C,G,KL,SC,SG
Draba dedeana v mauii	SG

Draba densifolia	AP,SC,SG
Draba dubia	AP,B,C
Draba fladnizensis	SG
Draba glabella	KL,SC,SG
Draba gracilis	KL
Draba haynaldii	KL
Draba helleriana	B,SW
Draba hispanica	AP,B,JE,KL,RM,SC,SG
Draba hoppeana	KL
Draba imbricata see D. rigida v imbricata	
Draba incana	SC,SG
Draba incana Stylaris Gr.	KL
Draba incerta	AP,KL,SG
Draba kitadakensis	KL
Draba kotschyi	KL
Draba languinosa	SG
Draba lasiocarpa	AP,B,G,JE,KL,SC
Draba linearis	SG
Draba loiseleurii	AP,B,G,JE,SG
Draba longisiliqua	AP,I,KL,SC
Draba mix rock gdn	C,JE
Draba muralis	CG,VO
Draba nivalis	KL
Draba norvegica	AP,G,KL,SC,SG
Draba oligosperma	AP,B,G,KL,RM,SC,SG
Draba ossetica v racemosa	VO
Draba parnassica	B,KL
Draba paysonii	B,KL
Draba paysonii v treleasei	KL
Draba polytricha	AP,SC,SG
Draba ramosissima	JE
Draba rigida	AP,KL,SG
Draba rigida v bryoides	KL,VO
Draba rigida v imbricata	KL
Draba rosularis	KL,VO
Draba sachalinensis	KL
Draba sakurai	AP,B,G,JE
Draba scabra	VO
Draba sendtneri	SG
Draba sp	KL
Draba sphaeroides cusikii	KL
Draba stellata	B
Draba stylaris see D. incana Stylaris Gr.	
Draba supranivalis	VO
Draba tomentosa	AP,G,SC,SG,VO
Draba ussuriensis	
Draba ventosa	AP,I,KL,SC,SG
Draba x salomonii	KL
Draba zapettii	KL
Dracaena draco	B,C,CA,CG,CL,DV,EL, HA,O,SA,T,V,VE,WA
Dracaena fragrans	B
Dracaena fragrans 'Massangeana'	B,CA
Dracaena hookeriana	B,CF,SA,SI
Dracaena indivisa see Cordyline	
Dracaena multiflora	B
Dracaena thalioides	CG
Dracaena umbraculifera	B
Dracocephalum argunense	AP,KL,SC,T
Dracocephalum austriacum	B,KL,SG
Dracocephalum botryoides	B,KL
Dracocephalum 'Dragon Heather'	U
Dracocephalum forrestii	SC,SG
Dracocephalum grandiflorum	AP,B,JE,KL,SA,SG
Dracocephalum imberbe	B,HP,RM,T
Dracocephalum mairei see D.renatii	

DRACOCEPHALUM

Dracocephalum moldavica	AP,B,C,CG,CN,DD,G,HU, PI,SG,SU,T,TH,V
Dracocephalum mold. 'Dragonhead Blue'	KS
Dracocephalum moldavica 'Snow Dragon'	B,PI
Dracocephalum nutans	B,C,JE,KL,SC,SG
Dracocephalum parviflorum	DD
Dracocephalum purdomii	SG
Dracocephalum renatii	KL,SG
Dracocephalum ruyschiana	AP,B,C,G,JE,SA,SG
Dracocephalum ruyschiana 'Blue Drips'	F
Dracocephalum scrobiculatum	T
Dracocephalum speciosum	KL
Dracocephalum tanguticum	B,JE
Dracocephalum wallichi	AP,HP,KL
Dracocephalum wendeloi	AP,HP
Dracophilus dealbatus	B,DV
Dracophilus delaetianus	B,DV
Dracophilus montis-draconis	B,DV
Dracophilus proximus	B,DV,SI,Y
Dracophyllum acerosum	B,SS
Dracophyllum kirkii	B,SS
Dracophyllum latifolium	B
Dracophyllum longifolium	B,SS
Dracophyllum milliganii	AR
Dracophyllum pronum	B,SS
Dracophyllum ruyscianum	HP
Dracophyllum traversii	B,SS
Dracopis amplexicaulis	B,HU,NT,SD
Dracunculus muscivorus	B
Dracunculus vulgaris	AP,B,C,G,JE,SC
Drakaea glyptodon	B
Drapetes dieffenbachii	B,SS
Dregea sinensis	SZ
Dregea volubilis	B
Drimia altissima	B,SI
Drimia elata	B,C,SI
Drimia robusta	B,SI
Drimys lanceolata	A,AU,B,C
Drimys winterii	A,B,SA
Drosanthemum ambiguum	DV
Drosanthemum bellum	B,KB,SI,Y
Drosanthemum bicolor	B,KB,SI,Y
Drosanthemum eburneum	B
Drosanthemum floribundum	B,C,KB,SI,Y
Drosanthemum godmaniae	B
Drosanthemum hallii	B
Drosanthemum hispidum	B,SI,Y
Drosanthemum intermedium	DV,Y
Drosanthemum marinum	DV
Drosanthemum micans	B,KB,SI,Y
Drosanthemum sp mix	C,Y
Drosanthemum speciosum	C
Drosanthemum striatum	B,KB,SI,Y
Drosanthemum subalbum	B
Drosanthemum tuberculiferum	B,KB,SI,Y
Drosera admirabilis	B,DV
Drosera affinis	DV
Drosera alba	B
Drosera aliciae	B,C,DV,SI
Drosera andersoniana	B
Drosera androsacea	B,DV
Drosera anglica	B,DV,SI
Drosera arcturi	B,SS
Drosera auriculata	B,DV
Drosera banksii	B
Drosera binata	B,C,CG,DV,SI

Drosera binata v kopuatai	DV
Drosera binata v multifida	B,DV,Y
Drosera brevifolia	B,DV
Drosera bulbosa	B,DV
Drosera bulbosa ssp bulbosa	B,NI
Drosera bulbosa ssp major	B
Drosera burkeana	B,DV
Drosera burmanni	B,DV
Drosera 'California Sunset'	DV
Drosera capensis	B,C,CG,DV,SC,SG,SI,Y
Drosera capensis narrow lf	DV
Drosera capensis red	DV,Y
Drosera capensis white form	DV,HP
Drosera capillaris	B,DV
Drosera caucasica	CG
Drosera cistiflora	B,C,DV,SI
Drosera coccicaulis	B,DV
Drosera coccicaulis x D.'Magaliesberg'	B
Drosera collinsiae	B,DV
Drosera communis	B,SG
Drosera cuneifolia	B,DV
Drosera curvispata	DV
Drosera dielsiana	B,DVY
Drosera dielsiana x D.'Magaliesberg'	B
Drosera dilatato-petiolaris	B
Drosera ericksonae	B,DV
Drosera erythrogyne	B,DV
Drosera erythrorhiza	B,C,DV,NI
Drosera erythrorhiza ssp collina	B
Drosera erythrorhiza ssp magna	B
Drosera erythrorhiza ssp squamosa	B
Drosera esmereldae	B,DV
Drosera falconeri	B,DV
Drosera falconeri x D.dilatato-petiolaris	B
Drosera filiformis	DV
Drosera filiformis v filiformis	B
Drosera filiformis v tracyi	B
Drosera 'Floating'	B
Drosera formosa	DV
Drosera gigantea	B,DV
Drosera gigantea ssp geniculata	B
Drosera glabripes	B,DV,SI
Drosera glanduligera	B,DV,NI
Drosera graminifolia	B,DV
Drosera graniticola	B,DV
Drosera hamiltonii	B,DV
Drosera heterophylla	B,DV
Drosera hilaris	B,DV,SI
Drosera hirtella	B
Drosera huegelii	B,DV
Drosera indica	B,DV
Drosera intermedia	B,DV,SI
Drosera kaieteurensis	B,DV
Drosera lanata	B
Drosera linearis	B
Drosera lovelae	DV
Drosera lowriei	B,DV
Drosera macrantha	B,DV
Drosera macrantha Gravel Form	B
Drosera macrantha ssp planchonii	B
Drosera macrophylla	B
Drosera macrophylla ssp monantha	B
Drosera madagascarensis	B,DV
Drosera menziesii ssp	B
Drosera modesta	B
Drosera montana	B,CG,DV

DROSERA

Drosera natalensis	DV
Drosera neesii	DV
Drosera 'Negamoto'	DV
Drosera nitidula ssp omissa	DV
Drosera ordensis	B,DV
Drosera pallida	DV
Drosera pauciflora	DV
Drosera peltata	B,C,DV
Drosera petiolaris	B,DV
Drosera planchonii	C
Drosera pulchella	DV
Drosera pygmaea	B,CG,DV
Drosera regia	B,DV
Drosera rotundifolia	B,DV,G,SI
Drosera salina	DV
Drosera sp mix	C
Drosera sp,ssp, v, hyb	B
Drosera spathulata	DV,Y
Drosera spatulata v kansai	DV
Drosera stenopetala	B,CG,DV
Drosera stolonifera	B,DV,NI
Drosera trinervia	B,DV,SI
Drosera venusta	DV
Drosera villosa	DV
Drosera whittakeri	B,C
Drosera zeheri	DV
Drosophyllum lusitanicum	B,CG,DV
Dryadanthe tetrandra	VO
Dryandra arborea	B,NI
Dryandra arctotidis	B,NI,O
Dryandra armata	B,C,NI,O
Dryandra ashbyi	B,NI,O
Dryandra baxteri	B,EL,NI,O,SA
Dryandra bipinnatifida	B,NI
Dryandra calophylla	B,NI,O
Dryandra carduacea	B,NI,O
Dryandra carlinoides	B,NI,O
Dryandra cirsioides	B,NI,O
Dryandra comosa	B,NI,O
Dryandra conferta	B,NI,O
Dryandra cuneata	B,EL,NI,O,SA
Dryandra drummondii	B,NI,O
Dryandra erythrocephala	B,NI,O
Dryandra ferruginea	B,NI,O
Dryandra foliosissima	B,NI,O
Dryandra formosa	B,C,EL,NI,O,SA
Dryandra fraseri	B,NI,O
Dryandra hewardiana	B,NI,O
Dryandra horrida	B,NI,O
Dryandra kippistiana	B,NI,O
Dryandra longifolia	B,NI
Dryandra mucronulata	B,EL,NI,O
Dryandra nivea	B,EL,NI,O
Dryandra nobilis	B,EL,NI,O
Dryandra obtusa	B,NI,O
Dryandra polycephala	B,EL,NI,O
Dryandra praemorsa	B,EL,NI,O
Dryandra preissii	B,NI,O
Dryandra proteoides	B,NI,O
Dryandra pteridifolia	B,EL,NI,O
Dryandra pulchella	B,NI,O
Dryandra quercifolia	B,C,EL,NI,O,SA
Dryandra seneciifolia	B,NI,O
Dryandra serra	B,NI,O
Dryandra serratuloides	B,NI,O
Dryandra sessilis	B,EL,NI,O

Dryandra shuttleworthiana	B,NI,O
Dryandra speciosa	B,EL,NI,O,SA
Dryandra speciosa 'Tammin'	B
Dryandra stuposa	B,EL,NI,O
Dryandra subpinnatifida	B,NI,O
Dryandra tenuifolia	B,NI,O
Dryandra tridentata	B,NI,O
Dryandra vestita	B,NI,O
Dryas caucasica	KL,VO
Dryas drummondii	AP,B,JE,KL,SC,SG
Dryas integrifolia	B,SG
Dryas octopetala	AP,B,BS,C,G,HP,I,JE,KI,
	KL,RM,SA,SC,SG,ST
Dryas octopetala 'Minor'	KL
Dryas octopetala ssp hookeriana	B,SG
Dryas x suendermannii	AP,B,G,HP,SC
Drymophila cyanocarpa	B,NI,SC
Dryopteris Cristata Gr.	KL
Dryopteris erthrosora	N
Dryopteris filix-mas	C
Drypetes sepiaria	B
Dterocarya hupehensis	B
Duchesnea indica	AP,B,F,JE,KL,SC,SG
Duchesnea indica 'Harlequin'	P
Dudleya albiflora	B
Dudleya brittonii	B
Dudleya caespitosa	B
Dudleya candida	B
Dudleya cymosa	AP,B,SC
Dudleya farinosa	DV
Dudleya pulverulenta	B
Dudleya saxosa v collomiae	B
Dudleya viridicata	DV
Dugaldia hoopesii	KL
Dunalia australis	B,HP,PL,SE
Duranta erecta	B,C,CA,HA,O,SA,WA
Duranta erecta 'Alba'	B
Duranta erecta 'Variegata'	B
Duranta repens see D.erecta	
Durio zibethinus	B
Duschekia fruticosa	SG
Duvalia polita v transvaalensis	B,SI
Duvalia pubescens	B,SI
Duvernoia adhatodoides	KB,SI
Dyckia altissima	B
Dyckia brevifolia	B,DV
Dyckia encholiroides	B,BC,DV
Dyckia floribunda	B,EL,SA
Dyckia fosterana	B
Dyckia frigida	B
Dyckia glomerata	B
Dyckia goiana	B
Dyckia leptostachya	B,EL
Dyckia maritima	B
Dyckia marnier-lapostollei estevesii	BC
Dyckia rariflora	B
Dyckia remotiflora	B
Dyckia sulphurea	B,CG,DV,EL
Dyckia tuberosa	B
Dyckia velascana	B,DV
Dyerophytum africanum	B,SI
Dypsis nodifera	B,SI
Dypsis pinnatifrons	B,EL,O
Dysoxylum fraseranum	B
Dysoxylum muelleri	B
Dysoxylum rufum	O

DYSOXYLUM

Dysoxylum spectabile	B
Dysphania rhadinostachys	B,NI
Dyssodia tenuiloba	KL
Eberlanzia spinosa	B,DV,Y
Ebracteola montis-moltkei	B,DV,Y
Ecballium elaterium	AP,B,CG
Ecbolium ligustrinum	B
Eccremocarpus scaber	AP,B,BS,BY,C,EL,G,HP,I, KI,KL,LG,MO,N,PI,SA, SC,SG,X
Eccremocarpus scaber Anglia Hybrids s-c	T
Eccremocarpus scaber apricot	LG
Eccremocarpus scaber 'Carnival Time'	F
Eccremocarpus scaber cherry red	C
Eccremocarpus scaber f aureus	AP,NG,SC
Eccremocarpus scaber f carmineus	SC,SG,W
Eccremocarpus scaber f roseus	AP,I
Eccremocarpus scaber 'Fireworks'	AP,U
Eccremocarpus scaber orange	B
Eccremocarpus scaber 'Tresco Gold'	B,EL
Eccremocarpus scaber 'Tresco' mix	C,D,DT,EL,J,JO,PK,S,V
Eccremocarpus scaber 'Tresco Rose'	B,EL
Eccremocarpus scaber 'Tresco Scarlet'	B,SC
Eccremocarpus scaber yellow	P
Ecdeiocolea monostachya	B,HU,NI,O
Echeandia flavescens	B,SW
Echeandia flavescens v stenocarpa	B,SW
Echeveria affinis	B
Echeveria carnicolor	B,DV
Echeveria chihuahuaensis	B
Echeveria dactylifera	DV
Echeveria laui	BC,CH,DV,Y
Echeveria lilacina	BC
Echeveria paniculata	B
Echeveria peacockii	B,C,CN,MO,T,U
Echeveria rubromarginata	B
Echeveria sp mix	C,CH
Echeveria strictiflora	B
Echeveria strictiflora v nova	B
Echeveria tolimanensis	B,DV
Echeveria walpoleana	B
Echinacea angustifolia	AB,B,CN,DD,HU,JE,LN, PO,PR,SD,SG,TH
Echinacea atrorubens	B
Echinacea laevigata	B
Echinacea pallida	AB,B,BH,C,CN,CP,G,HP, HU,HW,JE,PR,SA,SD,T
Echinacea paradoxa	B,JE,PR,SD,T
Echinacea purpurea	w.a.
Echinacea purpurea 'Alba'	AP,B,JE
Echinacea purpurea 'Bravado'	B,D,PK
Echinacea purpurea 'Brilliant Star'	C,S,SK
Echinacea purpurea hyb	T
Echinacea purpurea 'Leuchtstern'	B,JE,SA
Echinacea purpurea Lustre Hybrids	B
Echinacea purpurea 'Magnus'	B,HP,JE,LG,T
Echinacea purpurea 'Pink Flamingo'	J,PL,V
Echinacea purpurea 'Satellite Mix'	U
Echinacea purpurea 'White Swan'	AP,DE,DI,F,HP,J,JO,KS, PA,PK,PL,PM,SA,SK,T,V
Echinacea simulata	B
Echinacea tennessiensis	AB,B,HP
Echinocactus coahuilense	B,BC,GC,Y
Echinocactus electracanthus	B
Echinocactus grusonii	B,C,CH,DV,Y
Echinocactus horizonthalonius	B,BC,DV,Y

Echinocactus hyb	GC
Echinocactus ingens	DV
Echinocactus mix	C,T,Y
Echinocactus parryi	B
Echinocactus platyacanthus	B,DV,Y
Echinocactus polycephalus	B,DV
Echinocactus senile	Y
Echinocactus senile f aureum	BC
Echinocactus sp /hyb mix	C,SO,Y
Echinocactus texensis	B,BR,C,DV,Y
Echinocactus xeranthemoides	B
Echinocereus adustus	B
Echinocereus adustus v schwarzi	B,BC
Echinocereus berlandieri	B,CH,DV,Y
Echinocereus boyce-thompsonii	Y
Echinocereus brandegeei	B
Echinocereus bristolii	B
Echinocereus bristolii v pseudopectinatus	B,BC
Echinocereus castaneus	Y
Echinocereus chisoensis	B,BC
Echinocereus chisoensis v fobeanus	B
Echinocereus chloranthus	B,DV,Y
Echinocereus chloranthus v cylindricus	B
Echinocereus chloranthus v cyl. 'Corelli'	B
Echinocereus chloranthus v neocapillus	B
Echinocereus chloranthus v nov	B
Echinocereus cinerascens v septentr.	B
Echinocereus coccineus	B,BC,DV
Echinocereus coccineus v arizonica	B
Echinocereus coccineus v arizonicus	B
Echinocereus coccineus v guerneyi	B
Echinocereus coccineus v paucispinus	B
Echinocereus conglomeratus	B
Echinocereus cucumis	DV
Echinocereus cylindricus	B
Echinocereus dasyacanthus	B,DV,Y
Echinocereus dasy. v neomexicanus	B
Echinocereus davisii	B,BC,DV,Y
Echinocereus delaetii	B
Echinocereus engelmannii	B,DV,Y
Echinocereus engelmannii v acicularis	B
Echinocereus engelmannii v bonkerae	B,BC
Echinocereus engel. v boyce-thompsonii	B
Echinocereus engel. v chrysocentrus	B,BC,CH
Echinocereus engelmannii v fasciculatus	B
Echinocereus engelmannii v variegatus	B
Echinocereus enneacanthus	B,DV,Y
Echinocereus enn. sarissophorus	BC
Echinocereus enneacanthus v brevispinus	B
Echinocereus fasciculatus	B,DV,Y
Echinocereus fendleri	B,BC,DV,RM
Echinocereus fendleri v kuenzleri	B
Echinocereus fendleri v rectispinus	B,DV
Echinocereus fitchii	B,DV,Y
Echinocereus fitchii v albertii	B
Echinocereus fitchii v armatus	B
Echinocereus floresii	Y
Echinocereus fobeanus	DV
Echinocereus gentryi	DV,GC,Y
Echinocereus gonacanthus	DV
Echinocereus grandis	B,BC
Echinocereus knippelianus	B,DV,Y
Echinocereus knippelianus v kruegeri	B,DV
Echinocereus knippelianus v reyesi	B,DV
Echinocereus kohresii	DV
Echinocereus laui	B,CH,DV

ECHINOCEREUS

Echinocereus ledingii	B
Echinocereus leonensis	B
Echinocereus longisetus	B
Echinocereus luteus	DV
Echinocereus maritimus	B
Echinocereus melanocentruus	Y
Echinocereus moricallii	DV
Echinocereus neo-mexicanus	Y
Echinocereus nicholae	DV
Echinocereus nicholii	B
Echinocereus ochoterenae	B,DV,Y
Echinocereus octacanthus	B,Y
Echinocereus palmeri	B
Echinocereus pamanesiorus	B,DV
Echinocereus papillosus	B
Echinocereus papillosus v angusticeps	B,DV
Echinocereus parkeri	B
Echinocereus parkerii	B
Echinocereus pectinatus	B,C,DV
Echinocereus pectinatus rigidissimus	CH
Echinocereus pectinatus v wenigeri	B
Echinocereus pentalophos v procumbens	Y
Echinocereus pentalophus	B,Y
Echinocereus perbellus	DV
Echinocereus polyacantha	B
Echinocereus polyacanthus	B
Echinocereus polyacanthus v densus	B
Echinocereus poselgeri	B
Echinocereus primolanata	B
Echinocereus primolanatus	B
Echinocereus pulchellus	B,DV,Y
Echinocereus pul. v amoenus 'Albiflorus'	B
Echinocereus pulchellus v sharpei	DV
Echinocereus pulchellus v weinbergii	B
Echinocereus purpureus	Y
Echinocereus reichenbachii	B,BC,DV,Y
Echinocereus reichenbachii v albispinus	B,DV
Echinocereus reichenbachii v baileyi	B,DV,Y
Echinocereus reichenbachii v caespitosus	B
Echinocereus reichenbachii v castaneus	B
Echinocereus reichenb. v oklahomensis	DV
Echinocereus reichenbachii v perbellus	B,BC
Echinocereus rigidissimus	DV,Y
Echinocereus rigidissimus v rubrispinus	Y
Echinocereus rigidissimus v rufispinus	GC
Echinocereus rigidissimus vars	B
Echinocereus roetteri	B
Echinocereus rufispinus	B
Echinocereus russanthus	B,DV
Echinocereus russanthus sp Nova	BC
Echinocereus russanthus v cowperi	B
Echinocereus russanthus v fiehnii	BC
Echinocereus russanthus 'Weedenii'	B
Echinocereus sarissophorus	DV
Echinocereus scheeri	B
Echinocereus scheeri obscuriensis	BC
Echinocereus schmollii	B,Y
Echinocereus sciurus	B,DV
Echinocereus sciurus v floresii	B
Echinocereus scopulorum	DV
Echinocereus sp mix	C,CH,T,Y
Echinocereus spinigemmatus	B,DV
Echinocereus stoloniferus	B
Echinocereus stramineus	B,CH,DV
Echinocereus stramineus parkeri	BC
Echinocereus stramineus v ochoterenae	B

Echinocereus subinermis	B,Y
Echinocereus subinermis v luteus	DV
Echinocereus triglochidiatus	DV
Echinocereus trigloch. v gonacanthus	DV
Echinocereus trigloch. v mohavensis	B,BC,Y
Echinocereus viereckii	B
Echinocereus viereckii v morricalii	B
Echinocereus viridiflorus	B,BR,CH,DV,RM,Y
Echinocereus viridiflorus montanus	BC
Echinocereus websterianus	B,C,DV
Echinocereus x lloydi	B
Echinocereus x roetteri	B
Echinochloa crus-galli	SG,T
Echinochloa crus-galli v frumentacea	B
Echinocystis lobata	B,PR,SG
Echinofossulocactus see Stenocactus	
Echinomastus acunensis	DV
Echinomastus acunensis /neolloydia	B,DV
Echinomastus dasyacanthus	B,BC,DV
Echinomastus durangensis	B
Echinomastus durangensis v minor	B
Echinomastus erectocentrus	B,DV
Echinomastus intertextus	B,BC,DV
Echinomastus johnsonii	B
Echinomastus johnsonii v lutescens	B
Echinomastus laui	B
Echinomastus macdowellii	DV
Echinomastus mariposensis	B
Echinomastus unguispinus	B
Echinomastus warnockii	B
Echinops adenocaulos	B
Echinops bannaticus	B,G,HP,SG
Echinops bannaticus 'Blue Globe'	JO
Echinops bannaticus 'Blue Glow'	B,C,DE,JE,SA
Echinops bannaticus 'Taplow Blue'	B,HU
Echinops exaltatus	HP,SG,T
Echinops giganteus	HP
Echinops latifolius	SG
Echinops ritro	w.a.
Echinops ruthenicus	SG,T
Echinops setifer	B
Echinops sphaerocephalus	AB,AP,B,C,DE,G,HP,HU, JE,SA,SG
Echinops sphaerocephalus 'Arctic Glow'	JE
Echinops strigosus	T
Echinopsis ancistrophora	B,Y
Echinopsis ancist. ssp cardenasiana	B
Echinopsis aurea	Y
Echinopsis backebergii	B
Echinopsis b.i v hertrichiana 'Allegriana'	B
Echinopsis backebergii v larae	B
Echinopsis boiyubensis	B
Echinopsis bridgesii	DV,Y
Echinopsis bruchii	B,Y
Echinopsis camarapana	B
Echinopsis camarguensis	B,Y
Echinopsis camarguensis v robustior	B
Echinopsis cardenasia	BC,CH,DV,Y
Echinopsis chacoana	B,Y
Echinopsis cinnabarina	B,Y
Echinopsis cinnabarina v draxleriana	B
Echinopsis cinnabarina v walterspeilii	B
Echinopsis cochabambensis	B
Echinopsis cordobensis	Y
Echinopsis denudatum	Y
Echinopsis eyriesii	B,Y

ECHINOPSIS

Echinopsis ferox	B,Y
Echinopsis ferox v longispina	B,BC
Echinopsis grandiflora v inermis	Y
Echinopsis herbasii	B
Echinopsis histrichoides	Y
Echinopsis huascha	B,Y
Echinopsis huottii	B
Echinopsis hyb	B,BC
Echinopsis hyb 'New Abbeybrook' f1 & f2	T
Echinopsis hyb new Holly Gate	C
Echinopsis hyb Paramount	GC
Echinopsis ibicuatensis	B
Echinopsis lageniformis	B,Y
Echinopsis leucantha	B,BC,DV,Y
Echinopsis lotii	DV,Y
Echinopsis macrogona	B,Y
Echinopsis mairanana	DV
Echinopsis mamillosa	B,DV,Y
Echinopsis mammilosa v kermesina	B
Echinopsis melanopotamica	DV
Echinopsis minuana	DV
Echinopsis mirabilis	B,G
Echinopsis multiplex see E.oxygena	
Echinopsis obrepanda	B,Y
Echinopsis obrepanda v calorubra	B,Y
Echinopsis obrepanda v mizquensis	B
Echinopsis pachanoi	B,Y
Echinopsis pachanoi x peruvianus	B
Echinopsis pasacana	B,Y
Echinopsis pentlandii	B,Y
Echinopsis pentlandii v hardeniana	B
Echinopsis peruvianus	B
Echinopsis rhodotricha	B,BC,DV,Y
Echinopsis rubriflora	Y
Echinopsis schickendantzii	B,BC,Y
Echinopsis schwantesii	Y
Echinopsis shaferi	DV,Y
Echinopsis silvestrii	B,DV
Echinopsis smrzianus	B
Echinopsis sp mix	C,Y
Echinopsis spachiana	B,BC,Y
Echinopsis spiniflora	B,DV,Y
Echinopsis subdenudata	B
Echinopsis tapecuna v tropica	B
Echinopsis tarijensis	B
Echinopsis terscheckii	B,Y
Echinopsis thionantha	B,Y
Echinopsis turbinata	B,DV
Echinopsis validus	B,Y
Echinopsis vallegrandensis	B
Echinopsis werdermanii	B,Y
Echium aculeatum	SA
Echium albicans	SA
Echium angustifolium	B
Echium boisseri	SA
Echium candicans	B,C,CA,HU,SA,SC,T,VE
Echium fastuosum see E.candidans	
Echium giganteum	SA
Echium hyb mix	BY,CO,KI,SU
Echium italicum	B,JE
Echium lycopis	DD,SA
Echium nervosum	B
Echium pininana	B,C,P,SA,SG,T
Echium plantagineum	DD
Echium plantagineum bedder mix	J,S,V
Echium plantagineum 'Blue Bedder Dw'	B,BD,BS,BY,C,DE,KS,

	L,MO,S,T
Echium plantagineum Crown hybrids	BS
Echium plantagineum dw hybrids	D,F,KS,L,PI,T,TU,V
Echium plantagineum 'Moody Blues'	U
Echium plantagineum white bedder dw	B
Echium russicum	AP,B,JE,SA
Echium simplex	B
Echium sp	DI
Echium virescens	SA
Echium vulgare	AP,B,C,CG,CN,CP,DD,
	G,HP,HU,JE,P,SA,SC,
	SD,SG,SP,TH
Echium vulgare Drake's Form	B,D
Echium vulgare dw hyb	C
Echium wildpretii	AP,B,C,CA,SG
Echium wildpretii x pininana hyb	C,HP
Edible fungus nutrient substrate	B
Edithcolea grandis	B
Edmondia pinifolia	B,SI
Edmondia sesamoides	B,SI
Edraianthus caricius	KL
Edraianthus coris	KL
Edraianthus dinaricus	KL
Edraianthus graminifolius	AP,B,C,CG,G,HP,JE,KL,
	SC,SG,VO
Edraianthus graminifolius albus see E.gr. ssp niveus	
Edraianthus graminifolius ssp niveus	B,JE,KL,SC
Edraianthus horwatii	KL
Edraianthus jugoslavicus	CG
Edraianthus kitaibeli	CG,G
Edraianthus parnassicus	KL
Edraianthus pumilio	AP,B,CG,G,JE,KL,RM
Edraianthus serbicus	AP,B,G,KL,PM,SG
Edraianthus serpyllifolius	AP,HP
Edraianthus tenuifolius	AP,B,C,G,KL,SC,SG
Edraianthus wettsteinii	VO
Ehretia dicksonii	LN,SA
Ehretia pubescens	B
Ehretia rigida	B,EL,SI
Ehrhata thunbergii	B,SI
Einadia nutans	B
Ekebergia capensis	B,SI,WA
Ekebergia pterophylla	B,KB,WA
Elaeagnus angustifolia	A,B,C,CA,EL,FW,HP,HU,
	LN,NO,SA,VE
Elaeagnus commutata	A,B,C,FW,LN,NO,SA,
	SG,VE
Elaeagnus macrophylla	B
Elaeagnus multiflora	A,B,CG,SA,VE
Elaeagnus philippinensis	DD
Elaeagnus pungens	B,C,CA
Elaeagnus umbellata	A,B,C,FW,HP,HU,LN,
	NO,SA,VE
Elaeagnus umbellata 'Cardinal'	B
Elaeis guineensis	B,CA,O,SA
Elaeis oleifera	B
Elaeocarpus angustifolius	B,HA,O
Elaeocarpus dentatus	B
Elaeocarpus foveolatus	O
Elaeocarpus grandis	WA
Elaeocarpus hookerianus	B
Elaeocarpus reticulatus	B,C,HA,NI
Elaeocarpus reticulatus 'Flamingo'	B,EL
Elaeocarpus reticulatus pink	B,HA
Elaphoglossum villosum	SG
Elegia caespitosus	B,SI

ELEGIA

Elegia capensis	B,KB,O,SA,SI	Empodium namaquensis	B,RU
Elegia cuspidata	B,C,KB,O,SI	Empodium plicata	RU
Elegia equisetacea	B,SA,SI	Encelia californica	B,CA
Elegia fenestrata	B	Encelia farinosa	B,CA,SA,SW
Elegia filacea	B,SI	Encelia virginensis	B
Elegia grandis	B,SI	Encephalartos ferox	CF
Elegia grandispicata	B,SI	Encephalartos friderici-guilielmi	B
Elegia sp	BH	Encephalartos lebomboensis	CF
Elegia thyrsoidea	SI	Encephalartos lehmanii	CF
Eleiotis monophylla	B	Encephalartos longifolius	CF
Eleocharis acicularis	B,PR	Encephalartos natalensis	CF
Eleocharis mamillata	KL	Encephalartos trispinosus	CF
Elephantopus tomentosus	B	Encephalartos villosus	CF
Elettaria cardamomum	SA	Encephalocarpus sp	O
Eleusine coracana	B,DD,HU	Encephalocarpus strobiliformis	BC,DV
Eleutherine latifolia	C	Enchylaena tomentosa	B,C,NI,SA
Eleutherococcus henryi	B,CG	Enchylaena tomentosa v tomentosa	AU
Eleutherococcus lasiogyne	B	Endiandra palmerstonii	O
Eleutherococcus senticosus	C,EL,KL,LN,SA	Endiandra sieberii	B
Eleutherococcus sessiliflorus	B,DD,LN,SA,SG	Engelhardia roxburghiana	B
Eleutherococcus sieboldianus	SG	Enicostema axillare	B
Elisanthe noctiflora	SG	Enkianthus campanulatus	AP,B,C,FW,KL,LN,SA,
Elmera racemosa	AP,SC		SG,X
Elsholtzia ciliata	B,G,SG	Enkianthus campanulatus v palibinii	B,C,FW,N,SA
Elsholtzia cristata	CG	Enkianthus cernuus v rubens	G,N
Elsholtzia densa	B	Enkianthus chinensis	B,FW,N,SA
Elsholtzia fruticosa	SA	Enkianthus chinensis C&H7084	X
Elsholtzia stauntonii	AP,B,C,G,JE,SA	Enneapogon avenaceus	B,NI
Elymus arenarius see Leymus		Enneapogon intermedius	B,NI
Elymus canadensis	B,DD,JE,NO,PR,SA	Enneapogon nigricans	B,NI
Elymus caninus	SG	Enneapogon oblongus	B,NI
Elymus condensatus	B,CA,SA	Ensete ventricosum	B,BS,BY,C,CA,FW,PK,
Elymus fibrosus	SG		RE,SA,ST,T,V,VE,WA
Elymus glaucus h see E.hispidus		Entada abyssinica	B,SI
Elymus hispidus	AB,AP,B,C,CA,DD,HP	Entada gigas	B
Elymus magellanicus	AP,B,CG,E,HP,SC	Entada pusaetha	B
Elymus mutabilis	SG	Entandrophragma caudatum	B,SI,WA
Elymus pycnanthus	B	Entandrophragma excelsum	B
Elymus riparius	B,PR	Entelea arborescens	B,SA
Elymus sibiricus	SG	Enterolobium contortisiliquum	B,WA
Elymus tenuis	E	Enterolobium cyclocarpum	B,DD,RE,TT
Elymus trachycaulos	B	Enterolobium timbouva	EL,SA
Elymus trichophora	SG	Enteropogon dolichostachyus	B
Elymus villosus	B,PR	Epacris obtusifolia	B,NI
Elymus virginicus	B,DE,PR	Ephedra equisetina	LN,SA
Elytrigia repens	SG	Ephedra monosperma	B,SC,SG
Elytropus chilensis	SA	Ephedra nevadensis	B,BH,C,CP,DD,HU,LN,
Embothrium coccineum	AU,AP,B,C,SA,SC		NO
Embothrium coccineum Lanceolatum Gr.	C,HP	Ephedra rupestris	SZ
Embothrium grandifolium	B	Ephedra tweediana	SZ
Emilia atriplicifolia	B,PR	Ephedra viridis	AB,B,C,CP,LN,NO
Emilia coccinea	B,SG,T	Epiblema grandiflorum	B
Emilia coccinea 'Golden Magic'	B	Epidendrum ibaguense	B
Emilia coccinea 'Scarlet Magic'	B,PK	Epidendrum imatophyllum	B
Emilia glabra	B	Epidendrum nocturnum	B
Emilia hastata	SG	Epidendrum parkinsonianum	B
Emilia muhlenbergii	PR	Epidendrum rigidum	B
Emilia robusta	SG	Epidendrum secundum	B
Emilia sonchifolia mix	C	Epidendrum warasii	B
Emilia suaveolens	G,PR	Epilobium anagallidifolium	B
Eminium spiculatum	JE	Epilobium angustifolium	AB,B,BS,G,HU,JE,NO,
Emmenopterys henryi	B,EL,LN,SA		PR,SA,SG
Empetrum nigrum	B,C,JE,PO,SA,SG	Epilobium angustifolium f album	AP,B,C,HP,JE,P
Empetrum rubrum	AR	Epilobium angustifolium 'Stahl Rose'	HP
Empetrum sibiricum	VO	Epilobium cana see Zauschneria californica ssp cana	
Empleureum unicapsularis	B,BH	Epilobium caucasicum	VO

EPILOBIUM

Epilobium chloriifolium	B
Epilobium cinereum	SG
Epilobium crassum	AP,B,C,G,SC,SS
Epilobium dodonaei	AP,B,BS,C,G,HP,JE,SA, SC,SG,T
Epilobium fleischeri	AP,B,G,HP,JE,KL,NG,SA
Epilobium glabellum of gdns	HP
Epilobium glandulosum	B,PR
Epilobium hirsutum	B,JE
Epilobium hirsutum album	HP
Epilobium hyemalis	SG
Epilobium lanceolatum	B
Epilobium leptophyllum	B
Epilobium luteum	SC
Epilobium melanocaulon	B,SS
Epilobium microphyllum see Zauschneria californica ssp cana	
Epilobium montanum	B,SG
Epilobium nummularifolius	B
Epilobium obcordatum	AP,C,KL
Epilobium paniculatum v jucundum	SZ
Epilobium parviflorum	B,SG
Epilobium pedunculare	SG
Epilobium pynostachyum	B,SS
Epilobium rostratum	B,SS
Epilobium tasmanicum	AP,B,P
Epilobium tetragonum	B,SG
Epipactis atrorubens	CG
Epipactis gigantea	B,G,HU,SC
Epipactis helleborine	B,CG
Epipactis palustris	AP,B,CG,G,SC
Epiphyllum hyb mix	C,CH,DV,T
Epiphyllum thomasianum	B,DV,HU
Episcia hyb mix	C
Epithelantha bokei	B
Epithelantha dickisoniae	DV
Epithelantha greggii	B,BC
Epithelantha micromeris	B,DV
Epithelantha micromeris v neomexicana	BC
Epithelantha neomexicana	DV
Epithelantha pachyrhiza	B,DV
Epithelantha unguispina	DV
Equisetum laevigatum	B
Equisetum palustrum	CG
Eragrostis abyssinica	L,MO
Eragrostis brownii	HA
Eragrostis capensis	B,SI
Eragrostis cilianensis	B
Eragrostis curvula	C,CA,HA,JE,SA
Eragrostis elegans	DE
Eragrostis eriopoda	B,NI
Eragrostis falcata	B
Eragrostis interrupta	B
Eragrostis nutans	B
Eragrostis setifolia	B,NI
Eragrostis spectabilis	B,PR
Eragrostis tef	B,C,DD
Eragrostis tenella	B,T
Eragrostis trichodes	DE,JE,NO,SA
Eranthis cilicica	AP,AR,B,G,PM,SC
Eranthis hyemalis	AP,B,BS,BY,C,CO,F,G, KI,KL,MA,SA,SC,SU,TH
Eranthis hyemalis Ciliciaca Group	NG
Ercilla volubilis	SA
Eremaea beaufortioides	AU,B
Eremaea fimbriata	B
Eremaea pauciflora	B,NI
Eremaea purpurea	B,NI
Eremaea violacea	B
Eremocrinum albomarginatum	B
Eremophila alternifolia	B,NI
Eremophila bignoniiflora	B,NI
Eremophila cuneifolia	B,NI
Eremophila densifolia	B,EL,NI
Eremophila desertii	B,NI
Eremophila divaricata	B,NI
Eremophila duttonii	B,NI,SA
Eremophila foliosissima	B,NI
Eremophila freelingii	B,NI
Eremophila gilesii	B,EL,NI
Eremophila glabra	B,NI
Eremophila ionantha	B,NI,SA
Eremophila laanii	B,NI
Eremophila longifolia	B,EL,NI,O
Eremophila macdonnellii	B,NI
Eremophila maculata	B,C,EL,NI,O,SA
Eremophila pachyphylla	B,NI
Eremophila polyclada	B,NI
Eremophila racemosa	B,NI
Eremophila scoparia	B,NI
Eremophila serrulata	B,NI
Eremophila spectabilis	B,NI,SA
Eremophila youngii	B,NI
Eremurus altaicus	SG
Eremurus bungei see E.stenophyllus ssp st.	
Eremurus Erfo Hybrids	C,JE
Eremurus himalaicus	AP,AR,B,G,RH,SC,SG
Eremurus hybrids	D,DE,F,SC
Eremurus olgae	B,G,SA
Eremurus regelii	KL
Eremurus robustus	AP,AR,B,C,G,JE,KL,RH, RS,SC
Eremurus Ruiter Hybrids	AP,B,E
Eremurus Shelford hyb	AP,BS,C,KI,PK,SA
Eremurus sp white	KL
Eremurus spectabilis	AR,B,G
Eremurus stenophyllus	AR,B,C,CG,G,SC,T
Eremurus stenophyllus Cathedral Mix	T
Eremurus stenophyllus ssp stenophyllus	AP,G,JE,MN,SG
Eremurus stenophyllus x 'Perfectus'	B,JE,SA
Eremurus tauricus	G,JE,SA,SG
Erepsia anceps	B,SI
Erepsia bracteata	B,SI
Erepsia inclaudens	B,SI
Erepsia mutabilis	B
Erepsia sp	SI
Eriachne aristidea	B,NI
Eriachne benthamii	B
Erianthus contortus	B,JE,SA
Erianthus giganteus	NT
Erianthus ravennae	AV,B,C,CA,DE,JE,SA
Erianthus strictus	B,JE,NT
Erica abietina	B,SI
Erica acuta	B,SI
Erica affinis	B,SI
Erica alopecurus	B,SI
Erica arborea	B,C,JE,RH,SA
Erica ardens	B,SI
Erica atrovinosa	B,SI
Erica australis	SA
Erica axilliflora	B
Erica baccans	B,CG,KB,O,SI
Erica bauera	B,O,SI

ERICA

Erica bergiana	B,KB,SI
Erica bergiana 'Major'	B,SI
Erica bicolor	B
Erica blandfordia	B,SI
Erica blenna	B,SI
Erica brachialis	B,Kb,O,SI
Erica bracteolaris	B,SI
Erica breviflora	B,SI
Erica caffra	B,KB,O,SI
Erica calcareophila	B,SI
Erica cameronii	B,SI
Erica carnea	B,RH
Erica cerinthoides	B,SI
Erica chrysocodon	B,SI
Erica ciliaris	RH
Erica cinerea	B,RH,SI
Erica coccinea	B,KB,O,SI
Erica colorans	B,SI
Erica conferta	B,SI
Erica conica	B,SI
Erica coriifolia	B,SI
Erica cruenta	B,SI
Erica cubica	B,SI
Erica curviflora	B,KB,O
Erica curvirostris	B,KB,O
Erica daphniflora	B,SI
Erica deliciosa	B,SI
Erica demissa	B,O,SI
Erica densifolia	B,O
Erica denticulata	B,SI
Erica diaphana	B,KB,O
Erica discolor	B,C,KB,O,SI
Erica elimensis	B,SI
Erica fastigiata	B,SI
Erica filamentosa	B
Erica filipendulina	B,SI
Erica foliaceae	B
Erica formosa	B,KB,O,SI
Erica gallorum	B
Erica georgica	B,SI
Erica gibbosa	B,KB,O,SI
Erica gilva	B,KB,O
Erica glandulosa	B,KB,O,SI
Erica glauca v elegans	B,SI
Erica glauca v elegans 'Alba'	B,SI
Erica glauca v glauca	B,SI
Erica glomiflora	B,KB,O,SI
Erica glutinosa	B,SI
Erica goatcheriana	B,SI
Erica gracilis	B,SI
Erica grandiflora	B,O,SI
Erica grandiflora v exsurgens	B,SI
Erica hebecalyx	B,KB,O
Erica heliophila	B,SI
Erica hibbertia	B,SI
Erica hirtiflora	B,KB,O,SI
Erica holosericea	B,SI
Erica imbricata	B,KB,O,SI
Erica inflata	B,SI
Erica infundibuliformis	B,SI
Erica junonia v minor	B,SI
Erica laeta	B,O,SI
Erica lanipes	B,SI
Erica lateralis	B,KB,O,SI
Erica leucotrachela	B,KB,O
Erica longifolia	B,O,SI

Erica lucida	B,KB,O
Erica lutea	B,O
Erica mammosa	B,C,KB,O,SI
Erica marifolia	B,SI
Erica mauritanica	B
Erica maximiliani	B
Erica melanthera	B,SI
Erica monsoniana	B
Erica multumbellifera	B,SI
Erica nana	B,O,SI
Erica nudiflora	B,SI
Erica oatesii	B,SI
Erica oblongiflora	B,O
Erica onosmiflora	B,SI
Erica oresigena	B,SI
Erica parilis	B,SI
Erica parviflora	B
Erica patersonia	B,KB,O,SI
Erica pectinifolia	B,SI
Erica perspicua	B,O,SI
Erica petraea	B,SI
Erica phylicifolia	B
Erica physodes	B,SI
Erica pillansii	B
Erica pinea	B,C,KB,O
Erica plukenetii	B,SI
Erica polifolia	B,SI
Erica porteri	B,SI
Erica praecox	B
Erica propinqua	B,KB,O
Erica pulchella	B,SI
Erica quadrangularis	O,SI
Erica racemosa	B,SI
Erica regerminans	B
Erica regia	B,SI
Erica savillea	B,SI
Erica savillea v grandiflora	B,SI
Erica scabriuscula	B,SI
Erica selaginifolia	B,SI
Erica senilis	B
Erica sessiliflora	B,O,SI
Erica sitiens	B,O
Erica sp mix	C,KB,O,SI,VE
Erica sparsa	KB,O,SI
Erica speciosa	B,KB,O,SI
Erica sphaerocephala	B,KB,SI
Erica spheroidea	O,SI
Erica straussiana	B
Erica subdivaricata	B
Erica subulata	SI
Erica syngenesia	B
Erica taxifolia	B,KB,O,SI
Erica tenella	B,SI
Erica tenuis	B
Erica terminalis	B,C,RH
Erica tetralix	B,C,JE,RH,SA
Erica thomae	B
Erica thunbergii	SI
Erica triflora	B,SI
Erica tumida	B,SI
Erica urna-viridis	B,SI
Erica vagans	RH
Erica ventricosa	SI
Erica verecunda	B,SI
Erica versicolor	B,KB,O,SI
Erica verticillata of gdns	B,KB,O,SI

ERICA

Erica vestita	B,SI
Erica viridescens v viridescens	B,KB,O
Erica viscaria v decora	SI
Erica walkeria	B,SI
Ericameria parishii	B
Erigeron acer	B,CN
Erigeron acris	SG
Erigeron alascanus	KL
Erigeron alpinus	AP,B,G,HP,KL,SC,VO
Erigeron andicola	SG
Erigeron atticus	AP,B,G,KL
Erigeron aurantiacus	B,BS,C,CL,MO,N,G,JE, KI,VO
Erigeron aurantiacus hyb	SA
Erigeron aureus	KL
Erigeron aureus 'Canary Bird'	AP,C,HP,PM
Erigeron 'Azure Beauty'	T
Erigeron 'Azure Fairy'	B,BS,C,CL,JE,L,MO,SA
Erigeron bellidifolius	SG
Erigeron 'Betty Black'	KL
Erigeron 'Blue Beauty'	B,BD,JE,PK,SA
Erigeron borealis	AP,HP,KL,SC
Erigeron canadensiss	SG
Erigeron chrysopsidis	KL
Erigeron chrysopsidis 'Grand Ridge'	AP,G,PM,SC
Erigeron compositus	AP,C,G,HP,KL ,SC,SG
Erigeron compositus 'Rocky'	AP,B,BS
Erigeron compositus v discoideus	AP,B,SG
Erigeron compositus v glabratus	SG
Erigeron elegantulus	B,KL
Erigeron flettii	AP,G,HP,I,KL,SC
Erigeron frigidus	KL
Erigeron gaudinii	B
Erigeron glabellus	AP,SC,SG
Erigeron glabratus	AP,HP
Erigeron glaucus	AP,B,C,G,HP,JE,SC
Erigeron glaucus 'Albus'	B,JE
Erigeron howellii	KL
Erigeron humilis	AP,KL,SC,SG
Erigeron hyb pink	FR
Erigeron hybridus x 'Strahlenriese'	SG
Erigeron 'Jewel' mix	T
Erigeron 'Jewel' pink	B,BD,BS,BY,C,CL,D
Erigeron karvinskianus	AP,B,DV,G,FR,HP,I,L, MA,SC
Erigeron karvinskianus 'Blutenmeer'	JE
Erigeron linearis	B,KL
Erigeron lonchophyllus	KL
Erigeron melanocephalus	B,RM
Erigeron montanensis	KL
Erigeron multiradiatus	SC,SG
Erigeron nanus	AP,B,G,SC
Erigeron neglectus	KL
Erigeron oreganus	KL
Erigeron peregrinus	KL
Erigeron philadelphicus	HP
Erigeron pinnatisectus	AP,B,HP,KL,RM
Erigeron polymorphus	KL
Erigeron 'Profusion'	BS,BY,C,CL,CO,D,DT,F, J,KI,MO,PK,SK,SU,T, U,V,YA
Erigeron pulchellus	AP,B
Erigeron pumilis	AP,SG
Erigeron pyrenaeus h see E.alpinus	
Erigeron roylei	SG
Erigeron simplex	AP,HP,SC,SG

Erigeron sp	BH,KL
Erigeron speciosus Blue Shades	B,BY
Erigeron speciosus 'Grandiflorus'	DE,HU,JE,V
Erigeron speciosus 'Lilac Beauty'	B
Erigeron speciosus ssp macranthus	B
Erigeron trifidus	C,JE,KL,SC
Erigeron tweedyi	AP,HP
Erigeron unalaschkensis	SG
Erigeron uniflorus	AP,B,KL,SC,SG,VO
Erigeron ursinus	B,RM
Erinus alpinus	AP,B,BS,BY,C,CL,CN, G,HP,I,JE,KL,L,MO,RH, RM,SA,SC,T,W
Erinus alpinus 'Albus'	AP,B,C,G,HP,I,JE,KL,SC
Erinus alpinus 'Carmineus'	KL
Erinus alpinus 'Dr.Hahnle'	AP,B,C,G,JE,SC
Eriobotrya deflexa	B,CA,SA
Eriobotrya japonica	B,C,CA,G,LN,SA
Eriocactus see Parodia	
Eriocephalus africanus	B,BH,KB,SA,SI
Eriocephalus duttonii	SA
Eriocephalus ericoides	B,BH,SI
Eriocephalus ionantha	SA
Eriocephalus nivea	SA
Eriocephalus racemosus	B,BH
Eriocephalus sp	BH,SI
Eriocephalus spectabilis	SA
Eriocereus bonplandii	DV,Y
Eriocereus jusbertii see Harrisia jusbertii	
Eriocereus pomenensis	DV,Y
Eriodictyon californicum	B
Eriodictyon crassifolium	B
Eriodictyon lanatum	B
Eriodictyon trichocalyx	B
Eriodictyon trichocalyx v lanatum	SW
Eriogonum arborescens	B,SA
Eriogonum caespitosum	B,RM
Eriogonum cinereum	B
Eriogonum corymbosum 'San Rafael'	B,RM
Eriogonum fasciculatum	C,CA,DD,JE,NO
Eriogonum fasciculatum ssp fasciculatum	B
Eriogonum flavum v piperi	B,RM
Eriogonum giganteum	B,C,CA
Eriogonum heracleoides	NO
Eriogonum jamesii	AP,B,RM
Eriogonum jamesii v jamesii	B,RM
Eriogonum marifolium	B,RM
Eriogonum niveum nanum	I
Eriogonum ovalifolium	AP,B,RM,SC,SG
Eriogonum ovalifolium v nivale	KL
Eriogonum parvifolium	B
Eriogonum rosense	B,RM
Eriogonum saxatile	AP,B,SC,SG
Eriogonum sphaerocephalum	SG
Eriogonum umbellatum	AP,B,HP,JE,NO,SG
Eriogonum umbellatum ex 'Alturas Red'	B,RM
Eriogonum umbellatum ssp subaridum	KL
Eriogonum umbellatum v proliferum	B,RM
Eriogonum umbellatum v subalpinum	NO,SG
Eriogonum umb. v umb. ex Kannah Creek	RM
Eriophorum alpinum	B
Eriophorum angustifolium	B,G,HP,JE,SC
Eriophorum polystachon	SG
Eriophorum sp	PR
Eriophorum vaginatum see Scirpus fauriei v vaginatus	
Eriophyllum confertiflorum	B,CA,SA

ERIOPHYLLUM

Eriophyllum lanatum	AP,B,BS,DD,G,HP,JE, KI,NO,SA,SC,SG
Eriophyllum lanatum 'Bella'	JE
Eriophyllum lanatum 'Pointe'	B,BS,C,JE,MO,SG
Eriophyllum stoechadifolium	B
Eriosema distinctum	B
Eriosema salignum	B
Eriosema squarrosum	B,SI
Eriospermum abyssinicum	B,SI
Eriospermum mackenii	B,SI
Eriospermum natalense	B,SI
Eriospermum porphyrovalve	SI
Eriospermum sp	SI
Eriospermum tenellum	B,SI
Eriostemon australasius	B,EL,HA,SH
Eriostemon difformis v difformis	HA
Eriostemon spicatus	B,EL,NI,SA
Eriosyce aurata	DV
Eriosyce ceratistes	DV
Eriosyce ceratistes v mollesensis	DV
Eriosyce ceratistes v santiagoensis	DV
Eriosyce ceratistes v tulahuen	DV
Eriosyce ceratites v combarbela	DV
Eriosyce ceratites v Huatalame	DV
Eriosyce ceratites v Saladillo	DV
Eriosyce ihotzkyanae	BC,DV
Eriosyce sandillon	BC,DV
Eriosyce sp mix	C
Eritrichium aretioides	B,RM
Eritrichium canum	AP,C,KL,RM,SG
Eritrichium caucasicum	KL,VO
Eritrichium kamtschaticum	VO
Eritrichium nanum	B,C,CG,KL,SC
Eritrichium nanum 'Himmelsherold'	JE
Eritrichium rupestre see E.canum	
Eritrichium sibiricum	AP,KL,P,SC
Eritrichium strictum see E.canum	
Eritrichium terglouense	VO
Eritrichium tianshanicum	VO
Ermania parryoides	VO
Erodium botrys	CG
Erodium carvifolium	AP,B,HP,RM
Erodium castellanum	AP,CG,G,HP,SC
Erodium ciconium	CG
Erodium cicutarium	AP,B,CG,SG
Erodium cicutarium ssp cicutarium	CG
Erodium danicum	CG
Erodium gruinum	AP,B,C,G,HP,P,SC
Erodium guttatum	KL
Erodium hirtum	B,CG
Erodium malacoides	CG
Erodium manescavii	AP,B,C,G,HL,HP,JE,P, PL,SA,SC
Erodium moschatum	CG
Erodium pelargoniiflorum	AP,B,CG,HP,P,SC
Erodium petraeum	HP
Erodium telavivense	B
Erodium trifolium	AP,C,HP,I
Eromophila nivea	SA
Eruca sativa	B,DD,SG,TH
Eruca vesicaria	B,CN,CP
Erucaria hispanica	B
Ervatamia angustisepala	B
Erymophyllum ram. ssp involucratum	B,NI,O
Erymophyllum ramosum ssp ramosum	B,NI,O
Erymophyllum tenellum	O

Eryngium agavifolium	AP,B,C,DV,G,HP,JE,KL, LG,NG,P,SA,SC,SG,T
Eryngium alpinum	AP,B,C,FR,G,HP,J,KL, PA,SC,T
Eryngium alpinum 'Blue Dwarf'	PA
Eryngium alpinum 'Blue Lace'	B
Eryngium alpinum 'Etiole Bleu'	B,C,JE,SA,U,V
Eryngium alpinum 'Superbum'	AP,B,BS,C,CL,CN,D,F, HP,HU,JE,KI,KS,L,MO, PL,SA,ST
Eryngium amethystinum	AP,B,C,CG,DE,F,HP,JE, SA,SC,SG
Eryngium anethipteum	CG
Eryngium aquaticum	SG
Eryngium biebersteinianum see E.caucasicum	
Eryngium billardieri	B
Eryngium bourgatii	AP,B,BS,C,CG,CL,CN, G,HP,J,JE,LG,MO,P, RS,SA,SC,SG,VO
Eryngium bourgatii 'Oxford Blue'	NG,PA,SA
Eryngium caeruleum	CG,G,HP,SC
Eryngium campestre	B,C,CG,JE,SA,SG
Eryngium canigallii	CG
Eryngium caucasicum	AP,B
Eryngium creticum	HP
Eryngium dichotomum	B
Eryngium eburneum	HP,T
Eryngium foetidum	B,CP,DD,HU
Eryngium giganteum	AP,B,C,G,HP,HU,JE,LG, PA,PK,RH,SA,SC,SE,T
Eryngium gig. 'Miss Willmott's Ghost'	C,G,P,PL,PM,SA,SC,SG
Eryngium glaciale	VO
Eryngium horridum	B,P,SA
Eryngium hybrid	SZ
Eryngium maritimum	AP,B,C,CN,G,HP,JE,KL, PL,SA,SC,TH
Eryngium pandanifolium	P,SA
Eryngium pandanifolium v lassauxii	HP
Eryngium planum	AP,B,BH,BS,C,CL,CN, HP,HU,JE,JO,KL,KS, MO,P,PK,SA,SC,SG,SU
Eryngium planum 'Azureum'	B
Eryngium planum 'Blaukappe'	B,C,JE
Eryngium planum 'Fluela'	AP,SA
Eryngium planum 'Seven Seas'	B
Eryngium planum 'Tetra Petra'	B
Eryngium 'Silver Ghost'	P
Eryngium sp mix	AP,BY,C,P,PA,T
Eryngium spinalba	B,C,HP,JE
Eryngium tricuspidatum	C,G,HP,JE,SA
Eryngium variifolium	AP,B,HP,JE,P,SA,SG,T
Eryngium x oliverianum	AP,C,HP,SA
Eryngium x tripartitum	AP,C,F,G,HP,JE,SA,SC
Eryngium x zabelii	HP
Eryngium yuccifolium	B,C,CG,CP,F,G,HP,JE, NT,P,PR,RH,SA,SG
Erysimum 'Apricot Delight'	B
Erysimum bedder golden	B,BS,BY,CL,CN,J,L, MO,U
Erysimum bedder mix	BS,CL,F,L,M,MO,R,S, T,U,VH
Erysimum bedder orange	B,BS,BY,CL,CN,J,KI, L,M,MO,S,ST,T,U
Erysimum bedder primrose	B,BS,BY,CL,CN,J, L,M,MO,S,V
Erysimum bedder scarlet	B,BS,BY,CL,CN,J,L,M,

ERYSIMUM

	MO,S,T,U
Erysimum 'Blood Red'	B,BD,BS,CL,D,F,J,KI,M,
	MO,S,ST,SU,T,TU,V,
	VH,YA
Erysimum 'Bredon'	AP,HP
Erysimum capitatum	AP,B,HP,SC,SW
Erysimum caricum	KL
Erysimum 'Carmine King'	BS
Erysimum cheiri	AB,AP,B,C,CO,DE,F,
	HP,IG,SG,SU,TH
Erysimum 'Cloth Of Gold'	B,BD,BS,C,CL,D,F,HU,
	KI,M,MO,S,ST,T,TU,VH
Erysimum concinnum see E.suffrutescens	
Erysimum 'Covent Garden'	B,C,HU
Erysimum Crown	BS
Erysimum 'D.T.Brown's Special'	BS
Erysimum dbl dw branching	L,T
Erysimum 'Eastern Queen'	VH
Erysimum 'Ellen Wilmot'	PL
Erysimum f1 'Prince' dw mix/s-c	PL
Erysimum 'Fair Lady'	BD,BS,C,CL,CN,F,HU,
	J,KI,L,M,MC,MO,SU,T,
	TU,U,V
Erysimum 'Fire King'	B,BD,BS,BY,C,CL,KI,
	MO,S,ST,SU,TU,VH,YA
Erysimum 'Fire King Imp'	D
Erysimum gelidum	KL
Erysimum giant pink	B,BD,BS,MO
Erysimum 'Glasnost Mix'	T
Erysimum 'Gold King'	BS
Erysimum 'Golden Monarch'	B,BD,BS,CL,MO,YA
Erysimum golden yellow	BY,J
Erysimum 'Goliath'	B,BS
Erysimum grandiflorum	CG
Erysimum 'Harlequin'	BS,D,MO
Erysimum helveticum	AP,B,G,HP,JE,KL,PM,
	SC,SG
Erysimum helveticum ssp wahlenbergii	SG
Erysimum hieraciifolium	B,G,JE
Erysimum hieraciifolium 'Golden Gem'	B,G,I,KL,MO,PL,V
Erysimum hybridum 'Marengo'	F
Erysimum 'Indian Carpet' dw	BY
Erysimum 'Ivory White'	BS,CL,S,TU,U,YA
Erysimum kotschyanum	KL
Erysimum 'Lemon Delight'	B
Erysimum leptostylum	SG
Erysimum linifolium	AP,B,BS,C,HP,KI,L,
	MO,SU
Erysimum linifolium 'Little Kiss' Series	T
Erysimum linifolium 'Little Kiss White'	PK
Erysimum linifolium 'Variegatum'	B
Erysimum mix dbl, dw	BS,C
Erysimum mix dbl, tall	C
Erysimum mix fine	C,CN
Erysimum mix single	BS,CO,J,ST,Z
Erysimum mix Soham special	BY
Erysimum mix special stock	BS,D
Erysimum mix super	CL,MO
Erysimum 'Moonlight'	AP,PM,SC
Erysimum mutabilis	B
Erysimum nivale	B,RM
Erysimum ochroleucum	B
Erysimum odoratuum	AP,SG
Erysimum 'Orange King'	BS
Erysimum 'Orange Monarch'	B
Erysimum pastel shades	D

Erysimum perofskianum	AP,B,KL,SA
Erysimum perofskianum 'Gold Shot'	B,BS,C,PK
Erysimum 'Persian Carpet'	BS,BY,CN,CO,KI,L,
	MO,S,ST,TU,YA
Erysimum 'Pink Monarch'	YA
Erysimum 'Plantworld Series'	B,P
Erysimum 'Primrose Dame'	BS,KI,SU
Erysimum 'Primrose Monarch'	B,BD,CL,MO,TU
Erysimum 'Prince Golden'	CL,D,S,SK
Erysimum 'Prince' mix	BD,BS,CL,D,F,MO,S,SK
Erysimum 'Prince Orange'	CL,D,S,SK
Erysimum 'Prince Primrose'	CL,D,S,SK
Erysimum 'Prince Red'	CL,D,S,SK
Erysimum 'Prince Violet'	CL,D,S,SK
Erysimum pulchellum	KL
Erysimum pulchellum ssp korabense	KL
Erysimum pumilum	AP,B,C,JE
Erysimum 'Ruby Gem'	B,BD,BS,BY,CL,DT,KI,
	MO,S,YA
Erysimum saxosum	KL
Erysimum 'Scarlet Emperor'	B,BD,BS,BY
Erysimum scoparium	AP,B,P
Erysimum semperflorens	C
Erysimum 'Siberian'	CO
Erysimum 'Simplicity mix'	BS,KI
Erysimum 'Spring Jester'	D
Erysimum suffrutescens	AP,B,C,HP,SC,T
Erysimum 'Sulphur Delight'	B
Erysimum 'Tom Thumb' mix	BS,C,CL,CO,DT,J,KI,
	L,MO,R,ST,TU,V
Erysimum torulosum	HP
Erysimum 'Turkish Bazaar'	B,JE
Erysimum 'Vulcan'	B,BS,BY,C,CL,J,KI,MO,
	YA
Erysimum 'Vulcan' Imp	D
Erysimum wahlenbergii	SG
Erysimum wheeleri	B,C,HP,SC,SG,SW,T
Erysimum white	BY
Erysimum 'White Dame'	B,BD,BS,MO,T,VH
Erysimum x allionii	BS,BY,D,F,G,HP,J,JE,
	KI,PI,PK,SK,SU,TU,V
Erysimum x allionii imp	BS,L
Erysimum x allionii orange	B,BS,CN,DE,ST
Erysimum x allionii 'Orange Queen'	CL
Erysimum x allionii 'Spring Tapestry'	J,V
Erysimum 'Yellow Bird'	B,JE
Erythea armata	C,SA,VE
Erythea edulis	SA,VE
Erythrina abyssinica	B,SA
Erythrina amazonica	B
Erythrina americana	B,HU
Erythrina berteroana	B,RE,SA,TT
Erythrina caffra	B,CA,LN,SA,SI,WA
Erythrina cobanensis	DD
Erythrina corallodendrum	B,C,DD,FW,HU,VE
Erythrina crista-galli	B,C,CA,CG,DD,DE,DV,
	EL,FW,HA,HU,JE,N,O,
	SA,SC,SG,T,V,VE,WA
Erythrina dominguezii	B,EL
Erythrina edulis	B
Erythrina falcata	B
Erythrina flabelliformis	B,CA,DD,HU,SW
Erythrina folkersii	B,DD
Erythrina fusca	B,DD,RE,SA,SG,TT
Erythrina guatemalensis	DD
Erythrina herbacea	B,EL

ERYTHRINA

Erythrina humeana	B,DD,LN,SA,SI,WA
Erythrina indica see E.variegata	
Erythrina lanceolata	B
Erythrina latissima	B,SI,WA
Erythrina livingstoniana	B,SA
Erythrina lysistemon	B,C,EL,RE,SA,TT,WA
Erythrina macrophylla	DD
Erythrina poeppigiana	B,HU,RE,SA
Erythrina princeps see E.humeana	
Erythrina rubrinervia	B
Erythrina senegalensis	B
Erythrina smithiana	B
Erythrina speciosa	B
Erythrina speciosa v rosea	B,EL
Erythrina stricta	C
Erythrina tahitensis	DD
Erythrina tajamulcensis	DD
Erythrina tholloniana	DD
Erythrina variegata	B,CA,DD,EL,HA,SA,V
Erythrina verna	B
Erythrina vespertilio	B,C,EL,HA,HU,NI,O,SA
Erythrina zeyheri	B,SI
Erythrochiton brasiliense	CG
Erythronium californicum	AP,AR,G,LG,NG,SC
Erythronium californicum 'White Beauty'	AP,B,G,I,LG,PA
Erythronium caucasicum	VO
Erythronium citrinum	AR
Erythronium citrinum v roderickii	AR
Erythronium 'Citronella'	B
Erythronium dens canis 'Rose Queen'	CT
Erythronium dens-canis	AP,AR,B,C,CG,G,JE, KL,SA,SC
Erythronium dens-canis v nivale	KL
Erythronium grandiflorum	AB,AP,AR,B,C,JE,NO, SA,SW
Erythronium grandiflorum ssp grand.	RM
Erythronium helenae	AR
Erythronium hendersonii	AP,AR,B,G,KL,NG,SC
Erythronium howellii	AR,NG
Erythronium japonicum	AR,B
Erythronium japonicum Japan	PH
Erythronium klamathense	AR
Erythronium montanum	AB,B,C,JE
Erythronium multiscapoideum	AP,AR,G,NG,SC
Erythronium nudopetalum	AR
Erythronium oregonum	AP,B,JE,NG,PA,SC
Erythronium oregonum ssp leucandrum	AR
Erythronium pluriflorum	AR
Erythronium purpurascens	AR,B
Erythronium pusaterii	AR
Erythronium revolutum	AP,AR,B,JE,LG,SC,SG
Erythronium revolutum v johnsonii	AP,LG,NG,SC,SG
Erythronium revolutum v smithii	C
Erythronium sibericum	AP,AR,B,NG
Erythronium sibiricum Russua	PH
Erythronium sp mix	AP,C,PA,SC
Erythronium tuolumnense	AR
Erythrophleum africanum	B,SI
Erythrophleum chlorostachys	B,NI,O
Erythrophleum fordii	B
Erythrophysa alata	B,SI
Erythroxylon coca	CG
Escallonia alpina	SA
Escallonia florida	SA
Escallonia rosea	SA
Eschscholzia aurantiaca	PI,PK

Eschscholzia Ballerina 'Masquerade'	PL
Eschscholzia caespitosa	AP,B,SC
Eschscholzia caespitosa 'Sundew'	AP,B,C,DI,HU,J,KS,PM, T,V
Eschscholzia californica	AB,AP,AV,B,C,CA,DD,DI, DN,G,HW,J,PK,PM,RH, SG,TH,VH
Eschscholzia cal., 8 varieties sep.pack	B
Eschscholzia californica 'Alba'	B,C,HU,KS
Eschscholzia californica 'Apricot Bush'	F
Eschscholzia californica 'Apricot Chiffon'	B,C,DI,F,KS,PK
Eschscholzia californica 'Apricot Flambeau'	DT,SE,T
Eschscholzia californica 'Aurantiaca'	KS,PK
Eschscholzia cal. 'Aurantiaca Orange King'	B,HU
Eschscholzia californica 'Ballerina' mix	BS,BY,C,DT,HU,KS,L,T
Eschscholzia californica 'Brilliant' mix	BU
Eschscholzia californica 'Carmine King'	B,DT,KS
Eschscholzia californica cream	DI,SZ
Eschscholzia californica 'Dalli'	B,BS,C,CL,D,J,O,T,U,V
Eschscholzia californica 'Golden Values'	F
Eschscholzia californica 'Golden West'	B,DI
Eschscholzia californica 'Inferno'	F,PL,SE,T
Eschscholzia californica 'Ivory Castle'	B,C
Eschscholzia californica 'Jersey Cream'	PL,SE
Eschscholzia californica 'Mahogany Red'	B
Eschscholzia californica 'Mikado'	B,F,SE
Eschscholzia californica 'Milky White'	T
Eschscholzia californica 'Mission Bells'	BD,BS,C,CO,DE,DN,KI, SK,ST,SU,T,TU,VY
Eschscholzia californica mix single	BY,DT,F,HU
Eschscholzia californica mix special	S,SK
Eschscholzia cal. 'Monarch Art Shades'	C,F,T,U
Eschscholzia californica 'Moonglow'	T
Eschscholzia californica 'Orange'	DI,KS
Eschscholzia californica pink	T
Eschscholzia californica 'Prima Ballerina'	F
Eschscholzia californica 'Purple Gleam'	B,C,DI,HU,KS,TE,V
Eschscholzia californica 'Purple Violet'	T
Eschscholzia californica 'Red Chief'	B,C,DI,HU,TE
Eschscholzia californica 'Rose Bush'	F,KS
Eschscholzia californica 'Rose Chiffon'	DI,F,PK,SE,T
Eschscholzia cal. 'Sugared Almonds'	SE
Eschscholzia californica 'Thai Silk Apricot'	B
Eschscholzia californica 'Thai Silk Fire'	B
Eschscholzia californica 'Thai Silk' mix	D,J,PK,T,TE,VY
Eschscholzia californica 'Thai Silk Orange'	B
Eschscholzia californica 'Thai Silk Rose'	B
Eschscholzia cal. Unwins superb mix	U
Eschscholzia californica v maritima	SG
Eschscholzia lobbii	SG
Eschscholzia lobbii 'Moonlight'	F
Eschscholzia mexicana	B,SG,SW
Eschscholzia pulchella	SG
Escobaria aguirreana	B
Escobaria albicolumnaria	B,DV
Escobaria asperispina	DV
Escobaria bibeana	BC
Escobaria chaffeyi	B,BC,DV,Y
Escobaria chihuahuensis	DV
Escobaria cubensis	B
Escobaria dasyacantha	B,DV
Escobaria duncanii	B,DV
Escobaria emskoetteriana	DV,Y
Escobaria gigantea	DV
Escobaria guadalupensis	DV
Escobaria hesteri	B

ESCOBARIA

Escobaria laredoi	B,DV
Escobaria leei	B
Escobaria lloydii	B,DV
Escobaria minima	B,BC,Y
Escobaria missouri. v asperispina	B
Escobaria missouri. v caespitosa	B
Escobaria missouriensis	B,DV
Escobaria muehlbaueriana	DV
Escobaria nellieae	DV
Escobaria orcuttii	B
Escobaria orcuttii v koenigii	B,DV
Escobaria orcuttii v macraxina	B
Escobaria organensis	B
Escobaria robbinsorum	B
Escobaria roseana	B,BC,DV,Y
Escobaria runyonii	B,DV
Escobaria sandbergii	B
Escobaria sneedii	B,BC
Escobaria tuberculosa	B,DV
Escobaria tuberculosa v varicolor	B
Escobaria villardii	B,DV
Escobaria vivipara	B,DV,Y
Escobaria vivipara v arizonica	B,DV,Y
Escobaria vivipara v desertii	B
Escobaria vivipara v kaibabensis	B,DV
Escobaria vivipara v neomexicana	B
Escobaria vivipara v radiosa	B
Escobaria vivipara v rosea	B
Escobaria vivipara v zilziana	B
Escobaria zilziana	B,DV
Escobaria zilziana chariacantha	BC
Escontria chiotilla	B
Esobe gooseberry	B
Espeletia sp	KL
Espostoa baumanii	DV
Espostoa bella	DV
Espostoa cantaensis	CH,Y
Espostoa churinensis	B,BC,Y
Espostoa hylea	B,BC,DV
Espostoa lanata	B,C,DV,Y
Espostoa lanata rubrispina	B,BC,DV
Espostoa lanata v sericata	DV
Espostoa laticornua	B,DV,Y
Espostoa melanostele	B,DV
Espostoa melanostele v churinensis	DV
Espostoa mirabilis	B,CH,DV
Espostoa mirabilis v primigena	Y
Espostoa nana	B,DV,Y
Espostoa procera	DV
Espostoa ritteri	B,CH,DV,Y
Espostoa ruficeps	DV
Espostoa sp mix	C
Espostoa superba	DV
Etlingera elatior	B,RE
Etlingera hieroglyphica	B
Eucalyptus acaciiformis	B,C,EL,HA,NI
Eucalyptus accedens	B,EL,NI
Eucalyptus acies	AU,B,NI
Eucalyptus acmenioides	B,C,EL,HA,NI,O
Eucalyptus 'Affinis'	B,NI
Eucalyptus agglomerata	AU,B,EL,HA,NI,O
Eucalyptus aggregata	B,C,EL,HA,O,SA,SH,VE
Eucalyptus alba	B,HA,NI,O,VE
Eucalyptus albens	B,EL,HA,NI
Eucalyptus albida	B,NI
Eucalyptus alpina	B,C,HA,NI,O,VE

Eucalyptus amplifolia	EL,HA
Eucalyptus amplifolia v amplifolia	B,NI
Eucalyptus amplifolia v sessiliflora	B,NI
Eucalyptus amygdalina	AU,B,EL,HA,NI,O,SA,VE
Eucalyptus anceps	B,NI,O
Eucalyptus andrewsii	B,NI
Eucalyptus andrewsii ssp andrewsii	O
Eucalyptus andrewsii ssp campanulata	B,NI
Eucalyptus angulosa	B,CA,EL,NI
Eucalyptus angustissima	B,NI
Eucalyptus annulata	B,EL,NI
Eucalyptus apiculata	B,NI
Eucalyptus arachnaea	B,NI
Eucalyptus archeri	B,EL,HA,NI,O,RH,SA,VE
Eucalyptus argillacea	B,NI
Eucalyptus argophloia	B,NI
Eucalyptus arnhemensis	B,NI
Eucalyptus aromaphloia	B,HA,NI,O
Eucalyptus aspera	B,NI
Eucalyptus astringens	B,EL,HA,NI,VE
Eucalyptus australiana	VE
Eucalyptus 'Baby Blue'	CA,VE
Eucalyptus baileyana	B
Eucalyptus bakeri	B,HA
Eucalyptus balladoniensis	AU,B,NI
Eucalyptus bancroftii	B,EL,NI,O
Eucalyptus banksii	B,NI
Eucalyptus bauerana	B,EL
Eucalyptus baxteri	B,EL,NI
Eucalyptus behriana	B,C,NI
Eucalyptus benthamii	B
Eucalyptus beyeri	B,NI
Eucalyptus bicostata	EL,HA,SA,SH,VE
Eucalyptus bigalerita	B,NI,O
Eucalyptus blakelyi	B,C,EL,HA,NI
Eucalyptus blaxlandii	AU
Eucalyptus bleeseri	B,NI,O
Eucalyptus bosistoana	B,EL,HA,NI
Eucalyptus botryoides	AU,B,C,CA,EL,FW,HA, NI,O,SA,VE,WA
Eucalyptus botryoides v nana	B,EL,NI,O
Eucalyptus brachycorys	B,NI
Eucalyptus brachyphylla	B,NI
Eucalyptus brassiana	B,NI
Eucalyptus brevifolia	B,NI,O
Eucalyptus bridgesiana	B,C,EL,HA,NI,O,SA,SH, VE,WA
Eucalyptus brockwayi	B,NI,O
Eucalyptus brookerana	B,EL,NI,O
Eucalyptus brownii	B,NI
Eucalyptus brunnea	B
Eucalyptus buprestium	B,NI
Eucalyptus burdettiana	AU,B,EL,HA,HU,NI
Eucalyptus burgessiana	B,NI
Eucalyptus burracoppinensis	B,NI,O
Eucalyptus caesia	AU,C,EL,HA,HU,SA
Eucalyptus caesia ssp caesia	B,NI,O
Eucalyptus caesia ssp magna	NI,O
Eucalyptus caesia ssp magna c.s	B
Eucalyptus caesia weeping	B,EL,SA
Eucalyptus calcareana	B,NI
Eucalyptus calcicola	AU,B,EL
Eucalyptus caleyi	B,NI,O
Eucalyptus caliginosa	B,HA
Eucalyptus 'Callanii'	B,NI
Eucalyptus calophylla	B,CA,EL,HA,NI,O,SA,

EUCALYPTUS

	VE,WA
Eucalyptus calophylla 'Rosea'	B,EL,HA,NI,O,VE
Eucalyptus calycogona	B,C,NI,O,VE
Eucalyptus camaldulensis	B,CA,EL,FW,HA,HU,
	LN,NI,O,SA,VE,WA
Eucalyptus camaldulensis ssp subcinerea	HA
Eucalyptus camaldulensis v brevirostris	B,NI
Eucalyptus camaldulensis v obtusa	EL,HA,NI,O
Eucalyptus camaldulensis x rudis	AU,B
Eucalyptus cambageana	B,NI
Eucalyptus camfieldii	B,NI
Eucalyptus campaspe	B,EL,HA,NI,O,VE
Eucalyptus camphora	B,HA,NI,O,SA
Eucalyptus canaliculata	B,HA,NI
Eucalyptus cannonii	AU
Eucalyptus capillosa ssp capillosa	B,NI
Eucalyptus capillosa ssp polyclada	B,NI
Eucalyptus capitellata	B,NI
Eucalyptus carnei	B
Eucalyptus celastroides	B
Eucalyptus celastroides ssp virella	B,NI
Eucalyptus centralis	B,NI
Eucalyptus cephalocarpa	B,NI,O,VE
Eucalyptus ceratocorys	B,NI
Eucalyptus cinerea	B,C,CA,CP,EL,GO,HA,
	HU,LN,NI,O,PK,SA,SH,
	VE,WA
Eucalyptus cinerea 'Pendula'	B,EL,VE
Eucalyptus cinerea ssp cephalocarpa	HA
Eucalyptus citriodora	B,BS,BY,C,CA,CL,CN,CP,
	DE,EL,FW,HA,HU,KS,
	LN,MO,N,NI,O,SA,T,VE,
	WA
Eucalyptus cladocalyx	B,CA,EL,HA,LN,NI,O,
	SA,VE,WA
Eucalyptus cladocalyx 'Nana'	AU,B,CA,EL,HA,NI,O,SA
Eucalyptus clelandi	B,NI
Eucalyptus cloeziana	B,EL,HA,HU,NI,O,VE
Eucalyptus cneorifolia	AU,B,EL,HA,NI
Eucalyptus coccifera	AU,B,C,EL,HA,HU,LN,
	N,NI,O,SA,SH,VE
Eucalyptus concinna	AU,B,NI
Eucalyptus conferruminata	AU,B,EL,NI
Eucalyptus confluens	B,NI
Eucalyptus conglobata	B,EL,NI
Eucalyptus conglomerata	B,EL
Eucalyptus conica	B,NI
Eucalyptus Conservatory mix	U,V
Eucalyptus consideniana	B,C,HA,NI
Eucalyptus coolabah	B
Eucalyptus cooperana	B,NI
Eucalyptus cordata	AU,B,C,CA,EL,HA,NI,
	O,SA,SH,VE
Eucalyptus cornuta	AU,B,C,CA,EL,NI,SA
Eucalyptus coronata	B,NI
Eucalyptus corrugata	B,EL,NI
Eucalyptus cosmophylla	B,C,EL,HA,NI
Eucalyptus crebra	B,EL,HA,NI,O,SA,SH
Eucalyptus crenulata	B,EL,HA,NI,O,SA,VE
Eucalyptus crucis	AU,EL,HU,SA
Eucalyptus crucis ssp crucis	B,NI,O
Eucalyptus curtisii	B,EL,HA,NI,O
Eucalyptus cyanophylla	B,NI
Eucalyptus cylindriflora	B,NI
Eucalyptus cylindrocarpa	B,NI
Eucalyptus cypellocarpa	B,C,EL,HA,NI,O,SA

Eucalyptus dalrympleana	AU,B,C,CA,EL,HA,LN,
	N,NI,O,SA,VE
Eucalyptus dalrympleana ssp heptantha	B,NI
Eucalyptus dawsonii	B,NI
Eucalyptus dealbata	B,EL,HA,NI
Eucalyptus deanei	B,CA,HA,NI,O,VE
Eucalyptus debeuzevillei see E.pauciflora ssp d	
Eucalyptus decaisniana	B
Eucalyptus decipiens	B,NI,O
Eucalyptus decorticans	B,HA,NI
Eucalyptus decurva	AU,B,NI
Eucalyptus deglupta	B,CA,O
Eucalyptus delegatensis	AU,B,C,EL,HA,NI,O,SA,
	VE
Eucalyptus dendromorpha	B
Eucalyptus desmondensis	B,EL,NI,O
Eucalyptus dicromophloia	B,NI
Eucalyptus dielsii	B,NI
Eucalyptus diptera	B,EL,NI
Eucalyptus diversicolor	B,CA,EL,NI,O,WA
Eucalyptus diversifolia	AU,B,EL,HA,NI,VE
Eucalyptus dives	AU,B,EL,HA,LN,NI,O,
	SA,VE,WA
Eucalyptus doratoxylon	B,NI
Eucalyptus drepanophylla	B,EL,O
Eucalyptus drummondii	B,NI
Eucalyptus drysdalensis	B,NI
Eucalyptus dumosa	AU,B,EL,HA,NI
Eucalyptus dundasii	B,NI,O
Eucalyptus dunnii	B,EL,HA,NI,O
Eucalyptus dwyeri	B,C,EL,NI
Eucalyptus ebbanoensis	B,NI
Eucalyptus effusa	B,NI
Eucalyptus elata	B,CA,EL,HA,LN,NI,O,
	WA
Eucalyptus elata andreana	SH
Eucalyptus eremophila	AU,B,CA,EL,HA,NI,O,SA
Eucalyptus eremophila red	NI,SA
Eucalyptus erythranda	NI,O
Eucalyptus erythrocorys	AU,B,C,CA,EL,HA,NI,O,
	SA
Eucalyptus erythronema	AU,B,C,EL,HA,NI,O
Eucalyptus erythronema red	EL,NI,HA
Eucalyptus erythronema v marginata	B,NI,O
Eucalyptus erythronema v m. yellow fl	AU,B,NI
Eucalyptus eudesmioides ssp eud.	B,NI
Eucalyptus eugenioides	B,EL,HA,NI
Eucalyptus ewartiana	B,NI
Eucalyptus exilis	B,NI
Eucalyptus eximia	B,EL,HA,NI
Eucalyptus eximia v nana	B,C,EL,HA,NI,O,SA,SH,
	VE
Eucalyptus exserta	B,EL,HA,NI,VE
Eucalyptus falcata	B,NI
Eucalyptus famelica	B,NI
Eucalyptus fasciculosa	B,HA,NI
Eucalyptus fastigata	AU,B,EL,HA,LN,NI,O,VE
Eucalyptus ferruginea	B,NI
Eucalyptus fibrosa	B,EL,NI
Eucalyptus fibrosa ssp fibrosa	HA
Eucalyptus fibrosa ssp nubila	B,NI
Eucalyptus ficifolia	B,C,CA,EL,HA,HU,NI,
	O,PK,SA,VE,WA
Eucalyptus fl mix	C,EL
Eucalyptus flavida	B,NI
Eucalyptus flocktoniae	AU,B,EL,NI,O

EUCALYPTUS

Eucalyptus foecunda	AU,B,EL,HA,NI
Eucalyptus formanii	B,NI
Eucalyptus forrestiana	B,C,CA,EL,HA,HU,O,SA
Eucalyptus forrestiana ssp dolichorhyncha	B,NI,O
Eucalyptus forrestiana ssp stoatei	B
Eucalyptus fraseri	B,NI
Eucalyptus fraxinoides	AU,B,C,EL,HA,LN,NI,O, WA
Eucalyptus froggattii	B,NI
Eucalyptus Frost Resistant Sp Mix	BS,T
Eucalyptus fruticetorum	C,NI,VE
Eucalyptus gamophylla	AU,B,C,EL,NI,O,SA
Eucalyptus gardneri	AU,B,EL,HA,NI,O
Eucalyptus georgei	B,NI
Eucalyptus gillenii	B,NI
Eucalyptus gillii	AU,B,EL,HA,NI,SA,VE
Eucalyptus gittinsii	B,NI
Eucalyptus glaucescens	AU,B,C,EL,HA,NI,O,SA, SH
Eucalyptus globoidea	B,EL,HA,LN,NI,WA
Eucalyptus globulus	B,BD,BS,BY,C,CA,CL, CN,CP,EL,FW,HU,L,LN, MO,NI,O,RE,SA,SH,V, VE,WA
Eucalyptus globulus ssp bicostata	B,HA,NI,O
Eucalyptus globulus ssp globulus	B,HA,O
Eucalyptus globulus ssp glob. 'Compacta'	B,CA,EL,HA,O,SA,VE
Eucalyptus globulus ssp maidenii	B,HA,NI,O
Eucalyptus gomphocephala	AU,B,CA,EL,HA,LN, NI,O,SA,VE,WA
Eucalyptus gongylocarpa	B,NI
Eucalyptus goniantha ssp goniantha	B,NI
Eucalyptus goniocalyx	B,EL,HA,NI,O,VE
Eucalyptus gracilis	B,EL,HA,NI
Eucalyptus grandis	B,CA,EL,HA,LN,NI,O, VE,WA
Eucalyptus gregsoniana	AU,B,C,EL,HA,HU,NI, O,RH,SA,SH
Eucalyptus griffithsii	B,NI
Eucalyptus grossa	B,C,EL,HA,NI,RE,SA
Eucalyptus guilfoylei	B,NI
Eucalyptus gullickii	EL,SH
Eucalyptus gummifera	B,EL,HA,NI,O
Eucalyptus gunnii	AU,BD,BS,BY,C,CA,CN, EL,F,HA,KI,L,LN,MO,N, NI,O,SA,SH,VE,YA
Eucalyptus gunnii clean seed	B,CL,VE
Eucalyptus gunnii 'Silver Drop'	T
Eucalyptus haemastoma	B,EL,HA,HU,NI
Eucalyptus haematoxylon	B,NI
Eucalyptus halophila	B,NI
Eucalyptus henryi	B
Eucalyptus herbertiana	B
Eucalyptus hypochlamydea ssp hyp.	B,NI
Eucalyptus incerata	B,NI
Eucalyptus incrassata	B,EL,HA,NI
Eucalyptus indurata	B,NI
Eucalyptus intermedia	B,HA,NI,O
Eucalyptus intertexta	B,HA,NI,O
Eucalyptus jacksonii	B,NI
Eucalyptus johnstonii	AU,B,C,EL,NI,O,SA,VE
Eucalyptus jucunda	B,NI
Eucalyptus jutsonii	B,NI
Eucalyptus kartzoffiana	B,HA
Eucalyptus kessellii	B,NI
Eucalyptus kingsmillii	B,NI

Eucalyptus kitsoniana	B,C,EL,HA,NI
Eucalyptus kochii ssp kochii	B,NI
Eucalyptus kochii ssp plenissima	B,NI,O
Eucalyptus kondinensis	B,HA,NI,O
Eucalyptus kruseana	AU,B,CA,EL,HA,HU,NI, O,SA,SH,VE
Eucalyptus kybeanensis	AU,B,C,NI
Eucalyptus laeliae	B,NI
Eucalyptus laevopinea	AU,B,NI
Eucalyptus lane-poolei	B,NI,O
Eucalyptus lansdowneana	AU
Eucalyptus lansdown. ssp albopurpurea	B,EL,HU,NI,O
Eucalyptus lansdown. ssp lansdowneana	B,NI,O
Eucalyptus laophila	AU
Eucalyptus largiflorens	B,EL,HA,NI,VE
Eucalyptus lateritica	B,NI
Eucalyptus lehmannii	AU,B,CA,EL,HA,NI,O, VE,WA
Eucalyptus leptocalyx	AU,B,NI
Eucalyptus leptophleba	HA
Eucalyptus leptophylla	AU,B,NI
Eucalyptus leptopoda	B,NI
Eucalyptus lesouefii	B,EL,NI
Eucalyptus leucophloia	B,NI
Eucalyptus leucoxylon	AU,CA,EL,HA,HU,SA
Eucalyptus leucoxylon rosea	CA,EL,HA,SA,VE
Eucalyptus leucoxylon ssp leucoxylon	B,NI,O
Eucalyptus leucoxylon ssp megalocarpa	B,HA,NI,O,SA
Eucalyptus leucoxylon ssp petiolaris	B,NI
Eucalyptus leuc. ssp pruinosa 'Rosea'	B,NI,O
Eucalyptus leuc. v macrocarpa rosea	HA
Eucalyptus leuhmanniana	HA
Eucalyptus ligulata	AU
Eucalyptus ligustrina	B,NI
Eucalyptus linearis	C,CA
Eucalyptus 'Little Boy Blue'	B,EL,SA,SH
Eucalyptus littorea	AU
Eucalyptus livida	B,NI
Eucalyptus longicornis	B,NI
Eucalyptus longifolia	B,EL,NI
Eucalyptus loxophleba	B
Eucalyptus loxophleba ssp gratiae	B,NI
Eucalyptus loxophleba ssp lissophloia	B,NI
Eucalyptus luehmanniana	B,EL,NI
Eucalyptus macarthurii	AU,B,EL,HA,NI,O,SA, WA
Eucalyptus mackintii	B,NI
Eucalyptus macrandra	AU,B,EL,NI,O
Eucalyptus macrocarpa	B,C,CA,EL,HA,NI,O,SA, T,VE
Eucalyptus macrocarpa ssp elachantha	B,NI
Eucalyptus macrorhyncha	EL,HA
Eucalyptus macrorhyncha ssp cannonii	B,NI
Eucalyptus macrorhyncha ssp macro.	B,NI
Eucalyptus maculata	B,CA,EL,HA,NI,O,WA
Eucalyptus maidenii	EL,SA,VE,WA
Eucalyptus mannensis	B,HA,NI
Eucalyptus mannifera	EL,HA,SH
Eucalyptus mannifera ssp maculosa	B,EL,HA,NI,O
Eucalyptus mannifera ssp mannifera	B,NI
Eucalyptus mannifera ssp praecox	B
Eucalyptus marginata	B,NI,O,VE
Eucalyptus marginata v thalassica	B,NI
Eucalyptus mckieana	B,NI
Eucalyptus megacarpa	B,NI
Eucalyptus megacornuta	B,EL,HU,NI

EUCALYPTUS

Eucalyptus melanophloia	B,EL,HA,NI,SH,VE
Eucalyptus melanoxylon	B,NI
Eucalyptus melliodora	B,CA,EL,HA,NI,VE,WA
Eucalyptus merrickiae	B
Eucalyptus micranthera	B,NI
Eucalyptus microcarpa	B,EL,HA,NI
Eucalyptus microcorys	B,CA,EL,HA,NI,SA,WA
Eucalyptus microtheca	AU,B,CA,EL,HA,NI,O
Eucalyptus miniata	B,NI
Eucalyptus misella	B,NI
Eucalyptus mitchelliana	B,O
Eucalyptus moluccana	B,EL,HA,NI,O
Eucalyptus 'Moon Lagoon'	B,NI,O
Eucalyptus moorei	B,EL,HA,NI,SH
Eucalyptus moorei nana	AU,B,C,EL,N,O,SA
Eucalyptus morrisii	B,HA,NI
Eucalyptus muellarana	B,C,CA,EL,HA,LN,NI,WA
Eucalyptus neglecta	B,NI,O,SA
Eucalyptus nesophila	VE
Eucalyptus newbeyi	B,NI
Eucalyptus nicholii	B,C,CA,EL,HA,NI,O,SA, VE
Eucalyptus nigra	B,NI
Eucalyptus nigrifunda	B,NI
Eucalyptus niphophila see E.pauciflora ssp n.	
Eucalyptus nitens	AU,B,C,CA,EL,HA,NI,O, SA,VE,WA
Eucalyptus nitida	B,C,EL,NI,O,SA
Eucalyptus nortonii	B,HA,NI
Eucalyptus notabilis	B,NI
Eucalyptus nova-anglica	B,EL,HA,NI,O,SA,SH,VE
Eucalyptus nutans	B,CA,EL,HA,HU,NI,O,SA
Eucalyptus obliqua	B,EL,HA,LN,NI,O,SA, WA
Eucalyptus oblonga	B,NI
Eucalyptus obtusiflora	B,EL,NI,O,SA
Eucalyptus occidentalis	AU,B,EL,HA,NI,O,VE
Eucalyptus occidentalis v stenantha	B,NI
Eucalyptus ochrophloia	B,NI,O,VE
Eucalyptus odontocarpa	B,NI
Eucalyptus odorata	B,HA,NI
Eucalyptus oldfieldii	B,NI
Eucalyptus oleosa	EL,HA,NI,VE
Eucalyptus oleosa v oleosa	B,EL
Eucalyptus olsenii	AU,HA,NI
Eucalyptus orbifolia	AU,B,CA,EL,HU,NI,O,SA
Eucalyptus oreades	AU,B,CA,EL,NI,O,WA
Eucalyptus orgadophila	B,NI
Eucalyptus ovata	EL,HA,NI,O
Eucalyptus ovata v ovata	B
Eucalyptus ovularis	B,NI
Eucalyptus oxymitra	AU,B,EL,HA,NI
Eucalyptus pachycalyx	B,NI
Eucalyptus pachyloma	B,NI
Eucalyptus pachyphylla	AU,B,EL,NI,O,VE
Eucalyptus paniculata	B,EL,HA,LN,NI,WA
Eucalyptus papuana	B,CA,EL,NI,O
Eucalyptus parramattensis	B,HA,NI
Eucalyptus parvifolia	B,C,CA,EL,HA,O,RH,SA, VE
Eucalyptus patellaris	B
Eucalyptus patens	B,NI
Eucalyptus pauciflora	B,C,CA,EL,HA,SH
Eucalyptus pauciflora 'Pendula'	B,EL,HU,SA,X
Eucalyptus pauciflora ssp debeuzevillei	AU,B,NI,SA
Eucalyptus pauciflora ssp niphophila	AU,B,BS,C,CA,CN,EL,

	HA,HU,MO,N,NI,O,RH, SA,T,VE
Eucalyptus pauciflora ssp pauciflora	AU,NI,O
Eucalyptus pellita	B,EL,NI,O
Eucalyptus peltata	B,NI
Eucalyptus pendens	B
Eucalyptus perfoliata	B,NI
Eucalyptus perriniana	AU,B,C,EL,HU,N,NI,O, RH,SA,SH,VE,X
Eucalyptus petraea	B,NI
Eucalyptus phaeotricha	HA
Eucalyptus phoenicia	AU,B,NI
Eucalyptus pileata	B,NI
Eucalyptus pilligaensis	B,NI
Eucalyptus pilularis	B,EL,HA,NI,O
Eucalyptus pimpiniana	B,NI
Eucalyptus piperita	B,EL,HA,HU,NI,O
Eucalyptus piperita ssp urceolaris	B,HA,NI
Eucalyptus planchoniana	B,EL,HA,NI,O
Eucalyptus platycorys	B,NI
Eucalyptus platyphylla	B
Eucalyptus platypus	AU,B,CA,EL,HA
Eucalyptus platypus v heterophylla red fl	EL,NI
Eucalyptus platypus v platypus	NI,O
Eucalyptus pluricaulis ssp porphyrea	B,NI,O
Eucalyptus polita	B,NI
Eucalyptus polyanthemos	B,C,CA,EL,HA,HU,LN, NI,O,SA,SH,VE,WA
Eucalyptus polybractea	B,EL,NI
Eucalyptus polycarpa	B,NI,O
Eucalyptus populnea	B,EL,HA,NI,O,VE
Eucalyptus populnea x crebra 'Rariflora'	B
Eucalyptus porosa	B,HA,NI
Eucalyptus porrecta	B,NI
Eucalyptus preissiana	AU,B,EL,HA,NI,O,VE
Eucalyptus preissiana x staeri	B,NI
Eucalyptus propinqua	B,HA,NI,VE
Eucalyptus pruinosa	B,NI
Eucalyptus pryoriana	AU,B,EL,HA,NI
Eucalyptus pseudoglobulus	EL,HA,SA
Eucalyptus pterocarpa	B,NI
Eucalyptus ptychocarpa	B,EL,HA,NI,O
Eucalyptus pulchella	AU,B,EL,HA,NI,O
Eucalyptus pulverulenta	AU,B,C,CA,EL,HA,HU, NI,O,SA,SH,VE
Eucalyptus pumila	B,NI
Eucalyptus punctata	B,EL,HA,LN,NI,VE,WA
Eucalyptus punctata v didyma	B,NI
Eucalyptus punctata v longistrata	B,HA,NI
Eucalyptus pyriformis	B,EL,NI,O
Eucalyptus pyriformis pink fl	NI
Eucalyptus pyrocarpa	B,NI
Eucalyptus quadrangulata	B,EL,NI
Eucalyptus racemosa	EL,NI,VE
Eucalyptus radiata	AU,C,CA,EL,HA,SA,SH
Eucalyptus radiata ssp radiata	B,NI,O
Eucalyptus radiata ssp robertsonii	B,NI
Eucalyptus radiata v australiana	B,EL,NI,O
Eucalyptus raveretiana	B,EL,NI
Eucalyptus recondita	B,NI
Eucalyptus redacta	B,NI
Eucalyptus redunca	B,NI
Eucalyptus regnans	B,C,EL,HA,HU,LN,NI, O,SA,VE
Eucalyptus remota	B,NI
Eucalyptus resinifera	B,CA,EL,HA,LN,NI,O,

111

EUCALYPTUS

	SA,VE
Eucalyptus rhodantha	AU,B,NI,O
Eucalyptus rigens	B,NI
Eucalyptus rigidula	B,NI
Eucalyptus risdonii	AU,B,C,EL,HA,N,NI,O, SA,SH,VE
Eucalyptus robertsoni	VE
Eucalyptus robusta	AU,B,CA,EL,HA,LN,NI, O,SA,VE,WA
Eucalyptus rodwayi	AU,B,EL,NI,O
Eucalyptus rossii	B,C,EL,HA,NI
Eucalyptus rubida	B,C,EL,HA,NI,O,SA,SH, WA
Eucalyptus rudis	AU,B,CA,EL,FW,NI,O
Eucalyptus rugosa	B,NI,O
Eucalyptus rummeryi	B,NI,WA
Eucalyptus salicola	B,NI
Eucalyptus saligna	B,CA,EL,HA,HU,LN,NI, O,SA
Eucalyptus salmonophloia	B,EL,HA,NI,O
Eucalyptus salubris	AU,B,EL,HA,NI,O,VE, WA
Eucalyptus salubris v glauca	B,HU,NI
Eucalyptus sargentii	AU,B,NI,O,VE
Eucalyptus sclerophylla	B,EL,NI
Eucalyptus scoparia	B,EL,HA,NI,O,SA,SH
Eucalyptus seeana	B,EL,HA,NI
Eucalyptus sepulcralis	B,NI,O
Eucalyptus sessilis	B,NI
Eucalyptus setosa	AU,B,NI,O
Eucalyptus sheathiana	B,NI
Eucalyptus shirleyi	B,NI
Eucalyptus siderophloia	B,EL,HA,NI,VE
Eucalyptus sideroxylon	AU,B,CA,EL,HA,HU,NI, O,SA,VE,WA
Eucalyptus sideroxylon 'Rosea'	B,CA,EL,HA,NI,SA,VE
Eucalyptus sideroxylon ssp tricarpa	B,EL,HA,NI
Eucalyptus sieberi	AU,B,EL,HA,NI,O,SA
Eucalyptus signata	B,EL,HA,NI
Eucalyptus 'Silver Dollar'	JO,VY
Eucalyptus 'Silver Plate'	CL,JO
Eucalyptus 'Silver Spoon'	B
Eucalyptus similis	B,NI
Eucalyptus smithii	B,CA,EL,HA,LN,O,SA, WA
Eucalyptus socialis	B,EL,HA,NI,O
Eucalyptus sp mix	C,S
Eucalyptus sp mix dw	C
Eucalyptus sp mix foliage	O
Eucalyptus sp mix tropical	C
Eucalyptus spathulata	B,CA,EL,HA,NI,O
Eucalyptus spathulata v grandiflora	B,NI
Eucalyptus staeri	B,NI
Eucalyptus staigerana	B,NI
Eucalyptus steedmanii	AU,B,EL,HA,NI
Eucalyptus stellulata	AU,B,C,CA,EL,HA,LN,N, NI,O,SA,SH
Eucalyptus stoatei	EL,HA,NI,O
Eucalyptus stowardii	B,NI
Eucalyptus striaticalyx	B,NI
Eucalyptus stricklandii	AU,B,C,EL,HA,NI,O,VE
Eucalyptus stricta	B,C,EL,HA,NI,SA
Eucalyptus stricta v subcampanulata	B,NI
Eucalyptus sturgissiana	B,C,EL,NI,O,SH
Eucalyptus subcrenulata	AU,B,C,EL,NI,O,SA
Eucalyptus talyuberlup	AU,B,NI

Eucalyptus tenuipes	B,HA,NI
Eucalyptus tenuiramis	AU,B,C,EL,NI,O,SA
Eucalyptus tereticornis	B,CA,EL,HA,LN,NI,O,VE
Eucalyptus terminalis	B,NI
Eucalyptus tessellaris	B,HA,NI,O
Eucalyptus tetragona	B,EL,NI,O,SH
Eucalyptus tetraptera	AU,B,C,EL,HA,HU,O
Eucalyptus tetr. x angulosa 'Erythrandra'	B
Eucalyptus tetrodonta	B,NI
Eucalyptus thozetiana	B,NI
Eucalyptus 'Tinghaensis'	B,NI
Eucalyptus todtiana	B,EL,NI
Eucalyptus torelliana	B,EL,HA,NI,O
Eucalyptus torquata	AU,B,C,CA,EL,HA,HU, NI,O,RE,SA,WA
Eucalyptus torq. x woodwardii 'Torwood'	AU,B,EL,NI,O
Eucalyptus 'Trabuti'	B,CA
Eucalyptus trachyphloia	B,HA,NI
Eucalyptus transcontinentalis	AU,B,EL,NI,VE
Eucalyptus 'Tricarpa'	B
Eucalyptus triflora	O
Eucalyptus trivalvis	B,NI
Eucalyptus uceolaris	O
Eucalyptus umbra	EL,HA
Eucalyptus umbra ssp umbra	B,NI
Eucalyptus uncinata	AU,B,NI
Eucalyptus urnigera	B,C,EL,NI,O,SA,VE
Eucalyptus urophylla	B,CA
Eucalyptus vernicosa	AU,B,EL,O
Eucalyptus victrix	B,NI
Eucalyptus viminalis	B,C,CA,EL,HA,HU,NI,O, SA,VE,WA
Eucalyptus viminalis ssp cygnetensis	B,NI
Eucalyptus viridis	B,CA,EL,HA,NI,SA,VE
Eucalyptus wandoo	B,EL,NI,O,VE
Eucalyptus watsoniana	B,NI
Eucalyptus websterana	AU,B,SA
Eucalyptus websterana ssp norsemanica	B,NI,O
Eucalyptus whitei	B,NI
Eucalyptus willisii	B,NI
Eucalyptus woodwardii	AU,B,EL,HA,NI,O,RE,SA
Eucalyptus woollsiana	B,NI
Eucalyptus xanthonema	B,NI
Eucalyptus yalatensis	B,NI
Eucalyptus youmanii	B,EL,NI,O,SA
Eucalyptus youngiana	B,NI,O
Eucalyptus yumbarrana	AU,B,NI
Eucalyptus zygophylla	B
Euclea acutifolia	B
Euclea lancea	B,SI
Euclea natalensis	B,KB
Euclea pseudabenus	B,BH,SI
Euclea racemosa	B,SI
Euclea undulata	B,BH,SI
Euclidium syriacum	DD
Euclinia longiflora	B
Eucnide bartonioides	B,CG,T
Eucodonia mix hyb/var	C
Eucomis autumnalis	B,C,DV,KB,SA,SI
Eucomis bicolor	AP,B,C,E,G,PM,SI
Eucomis bicolor v alba	C,G
Eucomis comosa	C,G,LG,SG
Eucomis montana	B,SI
Eucomis pole-evansi	B,G,SC,SI
Eucomis regia	B,SI
Eucommia ulmoides	B,C,CA,EL,FW,LN,SA

EUCRYPHIA

Eucryphia cordifolia	N,SA
Eucryphia glutinosa	AU,N,SA,SG
Eucryphia lucida	B,N,O,SA
Eucryphia moorei	B,SA
Eugenia aggregata	B
Eugenia bracteata	B
Eugenia brasiliensis	B
Eugenia buxifolia	B
Eugenia cumini	HA
Eugenia leuhmannii	B,HA,O
Eugenia myrtifolia	CA,HA,O,SA,SH
Eugenia reinwardtiana	B
Eugenia stipitata	B
Eugenia uniflora	B,CA,HA
Eugenia uniflora 'Adams Concord'	B
Eugenia uniflora 'My Fancy'	B
Eugenia uvalha	B
Eugenia victoriana	B
Eulophia clavicornis	B,SI
Eulophia livingstoniana	B
Eulophia sp	SI
Eulychnia acida	DV
Eulychnia castanea	DV,Y
Eulychnia iquiquensis	DV
Eulychnia longispina	DV
Eulychnia spinibarbis	DV
Eulychnia spinibarbis v esmeralda	DV
Eulychnia spinibarbis v ovalle	DV
Eulychnia taltalensis	DV
Eulychnia totoralensis	DV
Euonymus alatus	AP,B,CA,FW,G,LN,RH, SA,SG
Euonymus alatus compactus	SG
Euonymus americanus	B,FW
Euonymus atropurpureus	B,SG
Euonymus bungeanus	LN,SA
Euonymus bungeanus 'Pink Lady'	B
Euonymus bungeanus v semi-persistens	NG
Euonymus cornutus quinquecornutus	AP,HP,NG
Euonymus europaeus	AP,B,C,CA,CG,FW,LN, RH,SA,SG,VE
Euonymus europaeus 'Albus'	SG
Euonymus europaeus 'Red Cascade'	HP
Euonymus europaeus v intermedius	RH
Euonymus fortunei	B,FW
Euonymus fortunei v vegetus	B
Euonymus fortunei v vegetus Sarcoxi	B
Euonymus hamiltonianus	B
Euonymus hamiltonianus ssp maackii	LN,SG
Euonymus hamilt. ssp sieboldianus	B,C,FW,NG,RH,SA,SG
Euonymus japonicus	B,CG
Euonymus latifolius	AP,B,CG
Euonymus leiophloeus	SG
Euonymus maximowiczianus	SG
Euonymus myrianthus	B,RH
Euonymus oxyphyllus	AP,C,SC
Euonymus phellomanus	AP,SA,SC,SG
Euonymus planipes	AP,B,C,FW,G,HP,RH,SA
Euonymus sachalinensis h. see E.planipes	
Euonymus sacrosanctus	SG
Euonymus verrucosus	LN,SG
Euonymus verrucosus c.w.	HP
Euonymus yedoensis see E.hamiltonianus ssp sieboldianus	
Eupatorium altissimum	B,PR
Eupatorium aromaticum	AP,HP
Eupatorium cannabinum	B,C,CG,CO,G,HP,HU,JE, LA,SA,SC,SG
Eupatorium coelestinum	JE,PR
Eupatorium dubium	B
Eupatorium greggii	SW
Eupatorium hyssopifolius	B,PR
Eupatorium ligustrinum	HP,SA
Eupatorium maculatum see E.purpureum ssp maculatum	
Eupatorium madrense	HP
Eupatorium perfoliatum	AB,B,CP,DD,JE,JO,P,PR, SA
Eupatorium purpureum	AB,AP,B,BS,C,CN,CP, DD,DE,G,HP,HU,JE,KI, NT,SA,SC,SG,TH
Eupatorium purpureum ssp maculatum	AB,B,CP,HP,JE,SG
Eupatorium purp. ssp mac. 'Atroppm'	B,HP,JE,PR,SA,T
Eupatorium purp. ssp maculatum 'Glow'	B
Eupatorium 'Queen of the Meadow'	DE
Eupatorium rotundifolium	C,PR
Eupatorium rugosum	AP,B,C,G,HP,JE,SC,SG
Eupatorium semiserratum	B
Eupatorium sordida	B
Eupatorium triplinerve	AP,HP
Eupatorium urticaefolium	KL
Euphorbia amygdaloides	B,JE,RH,SA
Euphorbia amygdaloides 'Purpurea'	B,HP,JE,P,SA,T
Euphorbia amygdaloides v robbiae	AP,B,HP,P,RH,SA
Euphorbia angularis	SG
Euphorbia antiquorum	B,CG
Euphorbia balsamifera	DV
Euphorbia bothii	CH
Euphorbia brittingeri	B,CG,G
Euphorbia caducifolia	DV
Euphorbia canariensis	B,DV
Euphorbia caput-medusae	B,DV
Euphorbia characias	B,C,F,HP,JE,RH,SA
Euphorbia characias dw	SZ
Euphorbia characias 'Portuguese Velvet'	HP
Euphorbia characias ssp wulfenii	AP,B,DV,F,HP,JE,P,RH, SZ,T,W
Euphorbia char. ssp wulfenii 'Jimmy Platt'	C,NG
Euphorbia ch. ssp wulf. 'John Tomlinson'	C,HP,NG
Euphorbia char. ssp wulf. 'Lambrook Gold'	HP,W
Euphorbia ch. ssp wulf. 'Lambrook Yellow'	HP
Euphorbia ch. ssp wulf. Margery Fish Gr.	HP
Euphorbia clandestina	B,DV
Euphorbia clava	B,DV
Euphorbia clavarioides v truncata	B,SI
Euphorbia cognata	HP
Euphorbia confinalis	DV
Euphorbia cooperi	DV
Euphorbia coralloides	B,C,G,HP,JE,P,SA,SC
Euphorbia cornigera	B,JE,P,SA
Euphorbia corollata	B,JE,PR
Euphorbia cotinifolia	B
Euphorbia cyathophora	B,J,KS,V
Euphorbia cyparissias	B,C,F,JE,SA,W
Euphorbia decaryi	DV
Euphorbia didieroides	DV
Euphorbia donii	HP
Euphorbia drummondii	B,NI
Euphorbia dulcis	HP
Euphorbia dulcis 'Chameleon'	B,HP,P,SC
Euphorbia enopla	CH,DV
Euphorbia evansii	DV
Euphorbia exigua	CG
Euphorbia ferox	CH,DV

EUPHORBIA

Euphorbia fischerana	SG	Euphorbia symmetrica	DV
Euphorbia 'Golden Foam'	B,P	Euphorbia tirucallii	SG
Euphorbia grandialata	B,DV,SA,SI	Euphorbia triangularis	B,DV
Euphorbia grandicornis	B,C	Euphorbia trigona	SG
Euphorbia graniticola	DV	Euphorbia tuberculata	B
Euphorbia griffithii	B,JE	Euphorbia tuberculatoides	B,Y
Euphorbia griffithii 'Dixter'	HP	Euphorbia variegata see E.marginata	
Euphorbia griffithii 'Fireglow'	AP,B,HP,P	Euphorbia villosa	B
Euphorbia hamata	Y	Euphorbia virgata	HP
Euphorbia helioscopia	B,CG	Euphorbia virosa	B
Euphorbia heterophylla of gdns see E.cyathora		Euphorbia wallichii	HP,JE,SC,T
Euphorbia hirta	B	Euphorbia wallichii T&M form	T
Euphorbia horrida	CH	Euphrasia cockayniana	B,SS
Euphorbia hyberna	AP,B,P	Euphrasia monroi	B,SS
Euphorbia ingens	B,HU	Euphrasia salisburgensis	SG
Euphorbia ipecacuanha	CG	Eurea lacinata	RE
Euphorbia jacquemontii	HP	Eurotia lanata	B,LN
Euphorbia komponii	SI	Eurya japonica	CG
Euphorbia lathyris	AB,AP,B,BH,BS,C,CA, C	Eurya marginata	CG
	P,G,HP,HU,JE,KI,SA,SG	Eurycorymbus cavalieri	B
Euphorbia leucocephala	B,C	Euryops abrotanifolius	B,SI
Euphorbia lophogona	SG	Euryops candollei	B,SI
Euphorbia louwii	B,SI	Euryops chrysanthemoides	B,SI
Euphorbia 'Magic Flute'	U	Euryops decumbens	B,SI
Euphorbia marginata 'Early Snow'	B,J,VY	Euryops lateriflorus	B,SI
Euphorbia marginata 'Kilimanjaro'	B,JO	Euryops laxus	B,SI
Euphorbia marginata 'Late Snow'	B	Euryops linearis	B,KB
Euphorbia marginata 'Snow Top'	B,PI,PK	Euryops othonoides	B,SA,SI
Euphorbia marginata 'Summer Icicle'	B,BD,BS,DE,MO,T,VH	Euryops pectinatus	B
Euphorbia marginata (V)	B,BS,BY,C,DI,HU,HW,	Euryops speciosissimus	B,SI
	KS,L,S,SG,SK,V	Euryops tegetoides	B,SI
Euphorbia mellifera	AP,B,C,HP,NG,P,SA,SZ	Euryops tenuissimus	B,SA,SI
Euphorbia milii	B	Euryops transvaalensis	B,SI
Euphorbia mix	C,P	Euryops tysonii	B,SI
Euphorbia mix Border sp/Fl Arranging	T	Euryops virgineus	B,C,KB,SI
Euphorbia multiceps	B,SI	Euryops wagnerii	B,SI
Euphorbia myrsinites	AP,B,BS,C,CL,CN,F,FG,	Eustoma exaltatum	B,SW
	HP,HU,JE,MO,PK,SA,	Eustoma f1 'Blue Line'	DI
	SC,SG,SK,SZ	Eustoma f1 'Do-Re-Mi'	DI,PL
Euphorbia nicaeensis	B,C,HP,JE,SA,SZ	Eustoma f1 dw pink	SK
Euphorbia obesa	B,BC,DV,SA,SI,Y	Eustoma f1 dw white	SK
Euphorbia palustris	B,G,HP,JE,SA	Eustoma f1 'White Palace'	PL
Euphorbia palustris 'Zauberflote'	C	Eustoma grandiflorum	EL,V
Euphorbia pendula	SG	Eustoma grandiflorum dbl edge mix	T
Euphorbia pentagona	DV	Eustoma grandiflorum dbl pink picotee	SE
Euphorbia pilosa	B	Eustoma grandiflorum f1 'Blue Lisa'	BS,DI,PI
Euphorbia pinea	SA	Eustoma grandiflorum f1 'Echo' mix	C,PK,SK
Euphorbia pithyusa	B,P	Eustoma grandiflorum f1 'Echo' s-c	C,DE,PK,T
Euphorbia platyphyllos	B,CG,SG	Eustoma grandiflorum f1 'Heidi'	C,D,DI,MO,PK,S,SK
Euphorbia polychroma	AP,B,BD,BS,C,CL,CN,	Eustoma grandiflorum f1 'Mermaid Blue'	CL,DE,SK
	DE,F,G,HP,HU,JE,MO,	Eustoma grandiflorum f1 'Yodel' mix	C
	PK,SA,SK,V	Eustoma grandiflorum f1 'Yodel' s-c	C
Euphorbia polygona	DV	Eustoma grandiflorum f1 'Mermaid Mix'	T
Euphorbia pseudocactus	B,DV	Eustoma grandiflorum f1 'Mickey Mix'	T
Euphorbia pulcherrima 'Santa Catarina'	B,HU	Eustoma grandiflorum f1 'Mix'	T
Euphorbia ramipressa	SG	Eustoma grandiflorum f1 'Red Glass'	PK
Euphorbia regis-jubae	C,DV,SA	Eustoma grandilforum dbl primrose	SE
Euphorbia rigida	B	Eustoma grandilforum 'Rainy Orange'	PL,SE
Euphorbia schillingii	HP,SA	Eustoma grandilforum 'Rainy Pink'	PL
Euphorbia schoenlandii	B,C,DV,GC,SI,Y	Eustoma russelianum see E.grandiflorum	
Euphorbia seduduniensis	SG	Eustrephus latifolius	B,EL,HA,HU,SA
Euphorbia seguieriana	B,CG,JE,SA	Eutaxia epacridioides	B,NI
Euphorbia sikkimensis	AP,B,HP,P	Eutaxia parvifolia	B,NI,SA
Euphorbia sp	SI	Euterpe dominicana	B
Euphorbia sp succulent mix	C	Euterpe edulis	B,EL,O,SA
Euphorbia spinosa	JE	Euterpe globosa	B

EUTERPE

Euterpe macrospadix	B,O,RE
Euterpe oleracea	B,CA
Evodia daniellii	DD
Evodiopanax innovans	CG
Evolvulus alsinoides	B
Evolvulus arizonicus	B,SW
Exacum affine	BS,BY,KI
Exacum affine 'Midget' blue	BD,BS,C,CL,J,L,MO,PK, SK
Exacum affine 'Midget' white	B,BD,BS,C,CL,MO,SK
Exacum best blue Imp	YA
Exacum best rose	U
Exacum best white Imp	YA
Exacum pedunculatum	B
Exacum 'Sweet Star'	U
Exacum 'Tiddywinks'	BS
Exocarpos bidwillii	B,SS
Exocarpos sparteus	B,NI
Exochorda giraldii	B,SA
Exochorda giraldii v wilsonii	B,FW
Exochorda racemosa	B,CG,FW,JD,SA
Exochorda serratifolia	SA
Exochorda x macrantha	HP
Fadogia agrestis	B
Fadogia caessneri	B
Fagara zanthoxyloides	B
Fagonia mollis	B
Fagopyrum esculentum	DE,G,KS,SU
Fagopyrum tataricum	CG,DD
Fagraea berterana	B,DD
Fagus asplenifolia	VE
Fagus crenata	B,FW,LN,N,SA
Fagus engleriana	B,EL,LN
Fagus grandifolia	B,FW,LN,SA
Fagus longipetiolata	B
Fagus lucida	B,FW,N
Fagus mosenaica	B,FW
Fagus orientalis	B,FW,SA
Fagus sylvatica	B,C,CA,EL,FW,LN,SA,VE
Fagus sylvatica 'Atropurpurea'	B,C,FW,LN,N,RS,SA,VE
Fagus sylvatica heterophylla	N
Faidherbia albida	B,SA,SI,WA
Falcaria vulgaris	B
Falcatum variegatum	CG
Fallopia aubertii see F.baldschuanica	
Fallopia baldschuanica	C
Fallopia cuspidatum	B
Fallopia cuspidatum v compactum	B
Fallopia dumetorum	B
Fallugia paradoxa	AP,B,DD,LN,NO,RM,SA, SW
Fargesia murieliae	AP,HP,JE
Faroa axillaris	B
Farsetia aegyptica	B
Fascicularia bicolor	SA
Fatsia japonica	AP,B,BS,C,CG,CL,FW,KI, LG,MO,N,S,SG,SK,ST, T,VE
Faucaria albidens	B
Faucaria bosscheana	B,CH,DV,Y
Faucaria britteniae	B,CH,DV,Y
Faucaria candida	B
Faucaria felina ssp felina	B,KB
Faucaria felina v jamesii	B
Faucaria hooleae	B,KB
Faucaria kingiae	B

Faucaria longidens	DV
Faucaria lupina	B
Faucaria mix	KB,Y
Faucaria paucidens	B,DV
Faucaria peersii	B
Faucaria plana	B
Faucaria speciosa	B
Faucaria subintegra	B,CH,DV,Y
Faucaria tigrina	B,DV,SI
Faucaria tuberculosa	B,DV,SI,Y
Faurea saligna	B,SI
Faurea speciosa	B,KB
Fedia cornucopiae	B,C,G,HP,SZ
Feijoa see Acca	
Felicia aethiopica	B,C,SA,SI
Felicia aethiopica ssp aethiopica	B
Felicia amelloides	DE,HP,KL
Felicia amelloides 'Read's White'	HP
Felicia australis	B,SI
Felicia bergeriana	B,S,SE,T
Felicia bergeriana 'Cub Scout'	C,KS
Felicia dregei	B,SI
Felicia dubia	B,KB
Felicia echinata	B,KB,SA,SI
Felicia elongata	B,SI
Felicia filifolia	B,BH,SI
Felicia fruticosa	B,SI
Felicia heterophylla	AP,B,CO,EL,KB,SG,SI
Felicia heterophylla blue/rose mix	T
Felicia heterophylla 'Spring Marchen'	B,BS,CL
Felicia heterophylla 'The Blues'	BD,BS,C,KS,L,MO,S,V
Felicia heterophylla 'The Rose'	B,BD,BS,C,KS,MO,V
Felicia hyssopifolia	B,SI
Felicia minima	B,SI
Felicia petiolata	AP,HP
Felicia quinquenervia	B,SI
Felicia rosulata	AP,KL,SG
Felicia sp	AP,SI
Felicia tenella	B,EL,SI
Felicia uliginosa	AP,SC
Fendlera rupicola	B,SW
Fenestraria aurantiaca	DV
Fenestraria aurantiaca f rhopalophylla	B,DV,SI,Y
Fenestraria aurantiaca f rhop 'Fireworth'	B,SI
Fenestraria aurantiaca f rhop. hybs.	B
Fenestraria rhodaphylla see F.aurantiaca f r.	
Fenestraria sp mix	C
Feretia aeruginescens	B,SI
Ferocactus acanthodes of gdns see F.cylandraceus	
Ferocactus corniferus	B
Ferocactus covillei	DV
Ferocactus cylindraceus	B,CH,DV,Y
Ferocactus cylindraceus tortulospinus	BC
Ferocactus cylindraceus v eastwoodiae	B,DV,Y
Ferocactus cylindraceus v lecontei	B,DV,Y
Ferocactus diguettii	B
Ferocactus echinde	B,DV
Ferocactus echidne v aurispina	GC,Y
Ferocactus emoryi	B,CH,Y
Ferocactus flavispinus	B
Ferocactus flavovirens	B,DV,Y
Ferocactus gatesii	B,DV,Y
Ferocactus glaucescens	B,BC,DV,Y
Ferocactus gracilis	B,CH,DD,DV
Ferocactus gracilis San Fernando	Y
Ferocactus gracilis v coloratus	B,BC,Y

115

FEROCACTUS

Ferocactus hamatacanthus	B,DV,Y
Ferocactus herrerae	B,CH,DV,Y
Ferocactus histrix	B,CH,DV,Y
Ferocactus horridus	DV
Ferocactus latispinus	B,BC,CH,DV,Y
Ferocactus latispinus v flavispinus	DV,Y
Ferocactus latispinus v spiralis	B,Y
Ferocactus lindsayi	B
Ferocactus macrodiscus	B,BC,DV
Ferocactus mathssonii	DV
Ferocactus novilis	B,DV
Ferocactus orcuttii	DV,Y
Ferocactus peninsulae	B,DV
Ferocactus peninsulae v santa-maria	B
Ferocactus peninsulae v townsendianus	B
Ferocactus pilosus	B,GC,Y
Ferocactus pringlei	DV
Ferocactus rectispinus	B,BC,Y
Ferocactus robustus	B,DV,Y
Ferocactus santa-maria	B
Ferocactus schwarzii	CH,Y
Ferocactus sinuatus	B
Ferocactus sinuatus v papyracanthus	B
Ferocactus sp mix	C,CH,Y
Ferocactus stainesi	B,CH,DV
Ferocactus stainesii v pilosus	DV
Ferocactus townsendianus	DV
Ferocactus viridescens	B,BC,CH,DV,Y
Ferocactus wislizenii	B,DV,Y
Ferraria crispa	AP,C,MN,RU,SC,SZ
Ferraria crispa ssp crispa	B,SI
Ferraria densepunctulata	B,RU
Ferraria divaricata	B,SI
Ferraria ferrariola	B,SI
Ferraria sp	SI
Ferraria undulata see F.crispa	
Ferula asafoetida	C,DD
Ferula 'Cedric Morris'	NG
Ferula communis	B,C,HP,JE,SA,SG
Ferula sadlerana	B,SA,SG
Ferula soogarica	SG
Festuca altissima	SG
Festuca amethystina	B,C,CA,G,HP,JE,SA,SC
Festuca arizonica	NO
Festuca elatior	B
Festuca elatior 'Demeter'	B
Festuca gautieri	B,G,JE,SA,SG
Festuca gigantea	B,HP,JE,SA,SG
Festuca glauca	B,BD,CA,CN,DE,HP,JE,
	KI,L,NO,SA,V
Festuca glauca 'Elijah Blue'	HP,I,P,PM
Festuca glauca 'Meerblau'	KL
Festuca glauca 'Seeigel'(Sea Urchin)	B
Festuca glauca select	JE
Festuca idahoensis	B,NO
Festuca incrassata	B
Festuca juncifolia	B
Festuca longifolia	B,CA
Festuca mairei	B,G,SA
Festuca megalura	B,CA
Festuca novae-zelandiae	JE,SA,SS
Festuca occidentalis	B,SA
Festuca ovina	B,CA,HP,FR,JE,NO
Festuca ovina glauca	AV,C,HU,PK,SC,SK
Festuca ovina v novae-zelandiae	B
Festuca pratensis	B,SG

Festuca pseudovina	B,SG
Festuca pulchella	JE
Festuca punctoria	AP,G,PM
Festuca rubra	B,CA,FR,SG
Festuca rubra 'Ensylva'	B
Festuca rubra ssp commutata	B
Festuca rubra ssp commutata 'Frida'	B
Festuca rubra ssp littoralis	B
Festuca rubra ssp rubra	B
Festuca rubra v pruinosa	B
Festuca scoparia see F.gautieri	
Festuca tatrae	SG
Festuca tenuifolia	B
Festuca valesiaca	SG
Festuca valesiaca 'Silbersee'(Silver Sea)	I
Festuca valesiaca v glaucantha	B,HP,JE,SA
Fibigia clypeata	AP,B,BS,C,CN,G,HP,HU,
	JD,JE,MO,SC,SG
Fibigia triquetra	KL
Ficalhoa laurifolia	B
Ficinia radiata	B,SI
Ficus auriculata	B
Ficus benghalensis	B,C,CA,DV,EL,HA,SA
Ficus benjamina	B,C,CA,DV,EL,HA,O,SA,
	VE
Ficus benjamina v nuda	B
Ficus burtt davyi 'Cango'	B,KB
Ficus burtt-davyi	B,KB,SI
Ficus capensis	C
Ficus carica	B,G,LN,SA
Ficus cordata	B,C
Ficus cordata ssp salicifolia	B,SI
Ficus coronata	B
Ficus craterostoma	B,SI
Ficus elastica	B,EL,KI,SA
Ficus elastica 'Decora'	B,BS,C,CA,L,MO,PK
Ficus fraseri	B
Ficus glumosa	B,SI
Ficus hillii	B,EL,O,SA
Ficus hispida	B,SI
Ficus ingens	B,SI
Ficus lutea	B,SI
Ficus lyrata	B
Ficus macrophylla	B,C,EL,HA,O,SA,VE
Ficus microcarpa	B,HA
Ficus natalensis	B,C,KB
Ficus nigropunctata	B,SI
Ficus obliqua	B,EL,HA
Ficus obliqua v obliqua	O
Ficus palmeri	CA,DD,DV
Ficus petiolaris	B,CH,DV,Y
Ficus platypoda	B
Ficus platypoda v nana	O
Ficus pumila	B
Ficus racemosa	B,EL,HA,SA
Ficus religiosa	B,CA,DV,EL,HA,LN,SA,
	VE
Ficus ruginosa	B,O
Ficus sp mix	C,T
Ficus superba v henneana	B
Ficus sur	B,KB,SI
Ficus sycomorus	B,SI
Ficus thonningii	B,KB,SI
Ficus virens	B,EL,O
Ficus virens ssp sublanceolata	B
Ficus watkinsoniana	B,HA,O

FILIPENDULA

Filipendula camtschatica	SG
Filipendula palmata	B,G,SG
Filipendula rubra	B,JE
Filipendula ulmaria	AP,B,BS,C,CN,CO,DE,G,
	HU,JE,KI,KS,LA,SA,SG,
	TH,TU
Filipendula ulmaria 'Aurea'	G,HP
Filipendula vulgaris	AP,B,C,CN,DD,G,JE,KL,
	LA,PK,SA,SC,SG,SU,TH
Filipendula vulgaris 'Multiplex'	HP
Filipendula vulgaris plena	SG
Firmiana simplex	B,C,CA,LN,SA,VE,WA
Fitzroya cupressoides	SA
Flacourtia indica	B,WA
Flacourtia jangomans	B,EL,HA,SA
Flaveria australasica	B,NI
Flemingia macrophylla	B
Flemingia strobilifera	B
Flindersia australis	B,HA,NI,O,SA
Flindersia brayleyana	B,O
Flindersia maculosa	B,O
Flindersia schottiana	B
Flindersia xanthoxyla	B,NI,O
Fockea edulis	B,C,DV,SI
Fockea sp	SI
Foeniculum dulce	CN,CP,DD
Foeniculum vulgare	AP,B,CN,DD,G,HP,LA,
	SG,TH
Foeniculum vulgare 'Purpureum'	AP,B,CN,CP,E,G,HP,JE,
	KS,PK,SA,SG
Foeniculum vulgare 'Smokey'	AP,B,T
Foeniculum vulgare v giganteum	DD
Foeniculum 'Bronze' see F. v. Purp.	CP,KS,SG
Fokea edulis	CF
Fokienia hodginsii	B,C,SA
Fontanesia fortunei	SA
Forchammeria watsonii	DD
Forestiera neomexicana	B,LN,SA
Forestiera segregata	B
Forstera sedifolia	AP,B,SS
Forstera tenella	B,SS
Forsythia giraldiana	B,CG
Forsythia japonica	B
Forsythia suspensa	B,SA
Fortunella crassifolia	B
Fortunella japonica	B
Fortunella margarita	SA
Fosterella penduliflora	B,DV
Fosterella villosula	DV
Fothergilla major	B,SA
Fouquieria burragei	B
Fouquieria columnaris	B
Fouquieria diguetii	B,DD,DV
Fouquieria macdougalii	DV
Fouquieria splendens	B,BC,C,CA,CH,DV,SA,
	SW,Y
Foveolina tenella	B,SI
Fragaria vesca	B,C,CN,JE,TH,V
Fragaria vesca 'Reugen'	B,HU
Fragaria virginiana	B
Frailea castanea	B
Frailea columbiana	Y
Frailea dadakii	DV
Frailea friedrichii	B,Y
Frailea fulvolanata	DV
Frailea gigantea	DV

Frailea gracillima	DV
Frailea grahliana	B,Y
Frailea horstii	B,BC,DV
Frailea horstii v fecotrigensis	DV
Frailea knippeliana	B
Frailea lepida	B,BC,DV
Frailea magnifica	B,DV
Frailea mammifera	B,DV,Y
Frailea matoana	DV,Y
Frailea phaeodisca	DV
Frailea pseudograhliana	B,Y
Frailea pseudopulcherrima	Y
Frailea pulcherimma see F.pygmaea	
Frailea pumila	B,Y
Frailea pygmaea	B,DV,Y
Frailea pygmaea v aurea	B,Y
Frailea pygmaea v boyansis	B,Y
Frailea pygmaea v lorencoensis	B,Y
Frailea pygmaea v phaeodisca	B,Y
Frailea schilinzkyana	B
Frailea schlosseriana	DV
Frailea sp mix	C
Frailea ybatense	B,DV,Y
Francoa appendiculata	AP,B,C,HP,SC
Francoa ramosa	B,C,HP,SC
Francoa ramosa alba	HP
Francoa sonchifolia	AP,B,C,G,HP,I,JE,KL,LG,
	P,RH,SA,SC,SG
Francoa sonchifolia 'Alba'	HP
Francoa sonchifolia Rogerson's Form	HP
Francoa sonchifolia T&M Form	T
Frangula alnus	SG
Frankenia connata	B,NI
Frankenia laevis	SG
Frankenia serpyllifolia	B,NI
Franklinia alatamaha	B,FW,SA
Frasera albicaulis	B
Frasera fastigiata	NO
Frasera parryi	B
Frasera speciosa	B,HU,SW
Fraxinus americana	B,C,CA,CG,EL,FW,HA,
	LN,SA,VE
Fraxinus angustifolia	B,EL,HA,LN,SA,SG,WA
Fraxinus angustifolia 'Raywood'	B
Fraxinus anomala	B,LN,SW
Fraxinus bungeana	B,EL,LN,SA
Fraxinus caroliniana	B
Fraxinus chinensis	B,EL,LN,SA
Fraxinus cuspidata v macropetala	B,SW
Fraxinus dipetala	B
Fraxinus excelsior	A,B,C,CA,EL,FW,LN,SA,
	VE
Fraxinus excelsior 'Jaspidea'	SG
Fraxinus excelsior 'Pendula'	B,RS
Fraxinus griffithii	B,EL,HA
Fraxinus insularis	B,EL
Fraxinus latifolia	AB,B,CA,CG,LN,NO
Fraxinus mandshurica	B,EL,LN,SA,SG
Fraxinus micrantha	B,FW
Fraxinus ornus	A,B,C,CA,FW,HA,LN,SA,
	VE
Fraxinus pallisus	CG
Fraxinus pennsylvanica	B,C,EL,LN,NO,SG,WA
Fraxinus pennsylvanica v lanceolata see F. p. v subintegerrima	
Fraxinus pennsylvanica v subintegerrima	CA,FW,SA
Fraxinus potamophila	CG

FRAXINUS

Fraxinus uhdei	B,CA
Fraxinus velutina	B,C,CA,EL,LN,SA,WA
Fraxinus velutina v coriacea	B
Freesia alba of gdns	AP,B,CG,KB,RU,SI
Freesia andersonii	MN
Freesia blue	BS
Freesia caryophyllacea	B,SI
Freesia corymbosa	B
Freesia elimensis	B,C,RU,SC,SI
Freesia fergusonae	B,MN,RU
Freesia hyb florist	B
Freesia hyb fragrant	U
Freesia hyb mix	BY,D,FR,VH
Freesia laxa	B,SI
Freesia leichtlinii	RU
Freesia mix Super Giants	C,CL,F,M,PK,T
Freesia mix Superior	J,V
Freesia muirei	MN
Freesia occidentalis	B,RU
Freesia 'Olympiade' mix	SK
Freesia 'Parigo's' mix	BD,MO
Freesia 'Parigo's' s-c	BS
Freesia refracta alba	AP,C
Freesia 'Royal Crown'	KI,L,YA
Freesia 'Royals' mix	S
Fremontodendron 'California Glory'	HP
Fremontodendron californicum	AP,B,C,CA,EL,G,HP,HU, JE,KL,SA
Fremontodendron mexicanum	B,CA,CG,SA,VE
Freylinia lanceolata	B
Freylinia tropica	BH
Frithia pulchra	B,DV,PK,SI,Y
Frithia pulchra v minor	B
Fritillaria acmopetala	AP,AR,B,C,CG,G,KL,LG, MN,PA,PM,SC
Fritillaria acmopetala dark form	AR
Fritillaria acmopetala ssp wendelboi	AR
Fritillaria affinis	AB,AP,AR,B,CG,DD,JE, KL,LG,NG,NO,SC
Fritillaria agrestis	AR
Fritillaria alburyana	AR
Fritillaria alfredae ssp glaucoviridis	AR
Fritillaria argolica	AR
Fritillaria armena	AR
Fritillaria atropurpurea	B,SW
Fritillaria aurea	AP,AR,PM,SC
Fritillaria aurea x pinardii	AR
Fritillaria biflora	AP,AR,LG,NG
Fritillaria bithynica	AP,AR,B,CG,KL,LG,MN, PM,SC,SG
Fritillaria bucharica	AR
Fritillaria camschatcensis	AP,AR,B,CG,G,NG,PL
Fritillaria carica	AR
Fritillaria caucasica	AP,AR,CG,KL,SC,VO
Fritillaria chlorantha	AR
Fritillaria citrina see F.bithynica	
Fritillaria colina	KL,VO
Fritillaria conica	AR
Fritillaria crassifolia	AP,AR,LG,PM,SC,VO
Fritillaria crassifolia ssp kurdica	AP,AR,B,CG,JE,LG,PM
Fritillaria davisii	AP,AR,CG,G,NG,PM,SC
Fritillaria drenovskii	AR
Fritillaria eastwoodiae	AR
Fritillaria eduardii	AR,KL
Fritillaria ehrhartii	AR
Fritillaria elwesii	KL

Fritillaria epirotica	AP,NG,PM
Fritillaria fleischeriana	KL
Fritillaria forbesii	AR
Fritillaria galatica	KL
Fritillaria gibbosa	AR
Fritillaria glauca	AR,NG
Fritillaria gracilis	CG,KL,SC
Fritillaria graeca	AP,AR,G,KL,LG,NG,SC
Fritillaria graeca ssp graeca	KL
Fritillaria graeca ssp thessala	AP,C,G,LG,PM,SC
Fritillaria gussichiae	AP,AR,CG,G,KL
Fritillaria hermonis	AR
Fritillaria hermonis ssp amana	AP,AR,CG,G,NG,SC
Fritillaria imperialis	AP,AR,B,CG,G,JE,KL, LG,RH,SC
Fritillaria imperialis 'Fasciata'	CG
Fritillaria imperialis 'Lutea'	AP,CG,KL,PM,SC
Fritillaria involucrata	AP,AR,B,CG,G,KL,LG, NG,PM,SC
Fritillaria kittaniae	AR
Fritillaria kotschyana	AR
Fritillaria kurdica	CG,KL
Fritillaria lanceolata see F.affinis	
Fritillaria latifolia	AR,KL,PM,SC,VO
Fritillaria latifolia v nobilis see F.latifolia	
Fritillaria liliacea	AP,AR,NG
Fritillaria lusitanica	AP,AR,CG,G
Fritillaria maximowiczii	SG
Fritillaria meleagris	AP,AR,B,C,CG,CN,CO, DV,G,I,JE,KL,LG,MN,N, NG,PA,PM,RH,SA,SC, SG,SU,T,TH
Fritillaria meleagris 'Aphrodite'	KL
Fritillaria meleagris f alba	AP,B,G,JE,KL,LG,PM,SG
Fritillaria meleagris 'Jupiter'	PM
Fritillaria meleagris 'Poseidon'	PM
Fritillaria meleagris 'Saturnus'	KL,PM
Fritillaria meleagris 'Triton'	KL
Fritillaria messanensis	AP,B,C,G,LG,PM,SC
Fritillaria messanensis Greece	MN
Fritillaria messanensis ssp gracilis	AP,AR,CG,G,SC
Fritillaria messanensis ssp gussichiae	CG
Fritillaria messanensis ssp messanensis	KL
Fritillaria michailovskyi	AP,AR,B,C,G,JE,KL,LG, PM,SC
Fritillaria micrantha	AR
Fritillaria minima	AR
Fritillaria mix	P
Fritillaria montana	AP,AR,KL,NG
Fritillaria nigra h see F. pyrenaica	
Fritillaria obliqua	AR
Fritillaria orientalis	AP,AR,C,NG
Fritillaria pallidiflora	AP,AR,C,CG,G,JE,KL, LG,N,NG,PM,SC,SG
Fritillaria persica	AP,AR,JE,KL,LG,SC
Fritillaria pinardi	AP,AR,CG,KL,SC
Fritillaria pinetorum	AR
Fritillaria pluriflora	AR
Fritillaria pontica	AP,AR,B,C,G,JE,KL,LG, MN,NG,PA,PM,SC
Fritillaria pontica v substipelata	NG
Fritillaria pudica	AP,AR,B,CG,JE,KL,NO, SW
Fritillaria purdyi	AR
Fritillaria pyrenaica	AP,B,C,CG,G,LG,KL,NG, SA,SC

FRITILLARIA

Fritillaria pyrenaica lutea	AP,NG
Fritillaria raddeana	AP,AR,B,G,KL,LG,NG
Fritillaria recurva	AR
Fritillaria recurva v coccinea	AR
Fritillaria reuteri	AR
Fritillaria rhodocanakis	AP,AR,G,PM
Fritillaria rixii	AR
Fritillaria roderickii	AR
Fritillaria roylei	NG
Fritillaria ruthenica	AP,AR,G,KL,NG,SC,SG
Fritillaria sewerzowii	AR
Fritillaria sibthorpiana	AR
Fritillaria sp	KL
Fritillaria sp & forms mix	AP,C,G,SC
Fritillaria spetsiotica	AR
Fritillaria stribrnyi	AR,KL
Fritillaria thessala	CG
Fritillaria thessala ssp ionica	AR
Fritillaria tubiiformis	AP,AR,B,C,CG,G,JE,SC
Fritillaria tuntasia	AP,AR,NG
Fritillaria uva-crispa	KL
Fritillaria uva-vulpis	AP,CG,G,MN,PM,SC
Fritillaria verticillata	PA
Fritillaria viridea	AR
Fritillaria walujawii	PM,SC
Fritillaria whitallii	AP,AR,PM,SC
Froelichia floridana	B,CG,PR,SG
Fuchsia 'Ballerina' mix	J,T
Fuchsia boliviana	C,SG
Fuchsia 'Crown Supreme'	BS
Fuchsia excorticata	B,C,SA,SS
Fuchsia f1 'Chimes'	BD,D,F,KI,M,MO,PK,S, SE,SK,T,U
Fuchsia f1 'Florabelle'	BD,C,CA,CL,D,DI,DT,J, L,M,MO,O,PI,PK,S,SE, T,V,YA
Fuchsia 'Fete Florale'	B,BD,PL,T,U
Fuchsia 'Flucia Montes'	B,HU
Fuchsia 'Fuchsoides'	SE
Fuchsia 'Fuseedia' f2	T,U
Fuchsia hyb mix	BY,C,FR,JE,V
Fuchsia loxensis red form	B
Fuchsia magellanica	B,C,G,JE,SA
Fuchsia mix Supreme	CO
Fuchsia procumbens	AP,B,C,HP,I,SC,SG,SS
Fuchsia regia	SG
Fumana ericoides	SG
Fumana procumbens	B,C,G,JE,SC,SG
Fumana thymifolia	B
Fumaria bastardii	CG
Fumaria officinalis	B,C,SG
Funastrum crispum	B,DD
Furcraea foetida	SA
Furcraea longaeva	SA
Gagea fibrosa	AR
Gagea granulose	SG
Gagea mauretanica	AP,B
Gagea mauretanica A.B.S4376 Morocco	MN
Gagea villosa	KL
Gahnia aspera	B,EL,HA,NI
Gahnia clarkei	B
Gahnia grandis	AU,B
Gahnia melanocarpa	B,HA,NI
Gahnia microstachya	B
Gahnia setifolia	B
Gahnia sieberana	AP,AU,B,EL,HA,NI,SA

Gahnia subaequiglumis	AU,B,EL,HA,SA
Gaillardia aristata see G.x grandiflora	
Gaillardia 'Gaiety'	C,DI
Gaillardia 'Lollipops'	U
Gaillardia mix dbl	FR
Gaillardia 'Monarch Mix'	SK,U
Gaillardia pulchella	AV,B,CA,DD,G,HW,NT, SD,SG,SW,V
Gaillardia pulchella dbl mix	T
Gaillardia pulchella 'Lorenziana' dbl mix	HU,SK
Gaillardia pulchella 'Picta'	B,C
Gaillardia pulchella 'Red Plume'	B,BS,D,F,L,PI,PK,SE,SK, T
Gaillardia pulchella 'Sherbet Plume'	U
Gaillardia pulchella 'Yellow Plume'	B,BS,D,L,PK
Gaillardia 'Summer Fire'	U
Gaillardia x grandiflora	AP,AV,B,C,FR,HP,HW,JE, KS,NO,PI,SC,SG
Gaillardia x grandiflora 'Aurea Pura'	B
Gaillardia x grandiflora 'Bremen'	B,JE,SA
Gaillardia x grandiflora 'Burgunder'	B,BS,CN,G,JE,MO,PL, SA,T,W
Gaillardia x grandiflora 'Dazzler'	B,BD,BS,CN,DE,JE,KI, MO,R,ST
Gaillardia x grandiflora dw	FR,SA
Gaillardia x grandiflora 'Fackelschein'	B,C,F,JE,PK,U
Gaillardia x grandiflora 'Goldkobold'	B,JE,PK,T
Gaillardia x grandiflora hyb giant	BS,BY,CL,D,DT,MO
Gaillardia x grandiflora hyb new	BD,CN,L
Gaillardia x grandiflora hyb reselected	T
Gaillardia x grandiflora 'Indian Yellow'	T
Gaillardia x grandiflora 'Kobold'	AP,B,BD,BS,C,CL,CN,D, HP,HU,JE,KI,KL,MO,PK, S,SE,SK,ST
Gaillardia x grandiflora 'Maxima Aurea'	JE,SA
Gaillardia x grandiflora mix	BS,CO,DE,F,J,KI,PK,TU, V
Gaillardia x grandiflora 'Tokajer'	B,DE,JE,T
Gaillardia x grandiflora 'Wirral Flame'	PA
Galactites tomentosa	AP,B,HP,P
Galanthus allenii	B
Galanthus caucasicus	G,NG
Galanthus elwesii	AP,B,JE,KL,NG,SC
Galanthus elwesii 'Cassaba'	NG
Galanthus fosteri	AR
Galanthus gracilis	B,JE,NG
Galanthus ikariae ssp ikariae 'Seer Sucker'	NG
Galanthus nivalis	AP,AR,B,G,JE,KL,PM, SC,SG
Galanthus nivalis S.forms	NG
Galanthus plicatus	AP,NG
Galanthus plicatus ssp byzantinus	NG
Galanthus plicatus 'Warham'	NG
Galanthus reginae-olgae	AR,NG
Galanthus sp & hyb mix	C,CT,NG
Galatella biflora	SG
Galaxia ciliata	B,RU
Galaxia fugacissima	B,RU,SI
Galaxia luteoalba	B,SI
Galaxia ovata	B,RU,SC,SI
Galaxia variabilis	B,SI
Galaxia versicolor	B,RU,SI
Galega officinalis	AP,B,BS,C,CN,G,HP,JE, KI,SA,SC,SG,TH
Galega officinalis 'Alba'	AP,B,C,CN,G,HP,LG
Galega officinalis 'Bicolor'	B,HP,T,V,W

GALEOPSIS

Galeopsis ladanum	B
Galeopsis segetum	SG
Galeopsis speciosa	AP,B
Galeopsis tetrahit	B,LA
Galium aparine	AB,B,SG
Galium boreale	B,PR,SG
Galium mollugo	B,JE,LA,SG
Galium odoratum	B,JE,SA,SG
Galium palustre	B
Galium saxatile	B
Galium schultesii	SG
Galium triflorum	SG
Galium uliginosum	SG
Galium verum	B,C,CN,HP,HU,JE,LA, SA,SG,TH,TU,V,Z
Gallito rojo	B
Galphimia glauca	B,C,EL,SA
Galpinia transvaalica	B,C,Kb,SA,SI,WA
Galtonia alba	KL
Galtonia candicans	AP,B,BH,C,CG,G,JE,KL, LG,NG,RH,RU,SA,SC, SG,SI
Galtonia princeps	AP,B,C,G,LG,NG,SC,SG
Galtonia sp	KL,SI
Galtonia viridiflora	AP,B,C,G,JE,KL,NG,PL, RH,SC,SE,SI,T,V
Garcinia sp	B
Gardenia augusta	C,CA,FW,SA
Gardenia augusta cvs	B
Gardenia carinata	B,EL
Gardenia cornuta	B,C,KB,SI,WA
Gardenia coronaria	DV
Gardenia jasminoides see G.augusta	
Gardenia resiniflua	B,SI
Gardenia sp mix	BH
Gardenia spathulifolia	B,C,EL
Gardenia ternifolia	B
Gardenia ternifolia ssp jovis-tonantis	B,SI
Gardenia thunbergii	B,C,CA,EL,KB,LN,O,RE, SA,SI,WA
Gardenia volkensii	WA
Gardenia volkensii ssp volkensii	B,SI
Garidella nigellastrum 'Blue Butterflies'	B
Garidella nigellastrum 'Summer Stars'	T
Garrya buxifolia	B,SA
Garrya elliptica	A,C,SA,SG
Garrya fremontii	B,C,SG
Garrya wrightii	B
Garuleum sp	SI
Gasteria acinacifolia	B,CF,DV,KB,SI,Y
Gasteria armstrongii	DV,Y
Gasteria batesiana	B,KB
Gasteria baylissiana	B,DV,KB,SI,Y
Gasteria bicolor	CF,DV,KB,SI,Y
Gasteria bicolor ssp bicolor	B
Gasteria bicolor ssp liliputana	B,SI
Gasteria brachyphylla	SI,Y
Gasteria brachyphylla ssp brachyphylla	B
Gasteria carinata	B
Gasteria croucheri	B,SI
Gasteria disticha	B,DV,SI,Y
Gasteria ellaphieae	B,KB,SI
Gasteria excelsa	B,DV
Gasteria huttoniae	B
Gasteria maculata	DV
Gasteria marmorata	DV

Gasteria nitida	SI
Gasteria nitida v armstrongii	B,SI
Gasteria obliqua	SI
Gasteria pulchra	B,CF,KB
Gasteria rawlinsonii	B,KB
Gasteria sp mix	C,Y
Gasteria transvaalensis	B
Gasteria vlokii	B,DV,SI,Y
Gastrococos crispa	B
Gastrolobium sp	B
Gaultheria adenothrix	AP,B,G,SC
Gaultheria antipoda	B,CG,SA,SS
Gaultheria crassa	AU,B,C,CG,SS
Gaultheria cuneata	SG
Gaultheria depressa	AU,SA,SC,SS
Gaultheria fragrantissima	NO
Gaultheria hispida	AU,B,C,O,SA
Gaultheria itoana	G
Gaultheria macrostigma	B,SA,SS
Gaultheria miqueliana	AP,B,JE,SG
Gaultheria nana	B,SS
Gaultheria ovalifolia see G.fragrantissima	
Gaultheria paniculata	B,SA
Gaultheria parvifolia	B
Gaultheria parvula	AU
Gaultheria procumbens	B,C,FW,JE,PO,SA,VE
Gaultheria pumila	SA
Gaultheria rupestris	B
Gaultheria shallon	A,AB,B,C,CA,FW,G,JE, LN,NO,SA
Gaultheria shallon 'Select'	B
Gaultheria sp (white fruits) CNW487	X
Gaultheria tasmanica	B
Gaura biennis	AP,B,G,PR
Gaura coccinea	B
Gaura lindheimeri	BS,C,G,HP,JE,KI,SA,T
Gaura lindheimeri 'The Bride'	AP,B,BS,F,HP,J,JO,MO,V
Gaura longiflora	PR
Gaura parviflora	KL,SG
Gaussia maya	B
Gaussia princeps	B
Gazania 'Chansonette'	B,BS,BY,CA,D,DT,F,J, MO,PK,U,V
Gazania 'Daybreak Bright Orange'	B,D,O,U
Gazania 'Daybreak' mix	BD,BS,CL,DT,MO,PI,R, SK,TU
Gazania 'Daybreak Series' s-c	B,BS,CA,CL,L,MO,S,SK, U,YA
Gazania Harlequin Hybrids	T
Gazania hyb mix	FR
Gazania krebsiana	AP,B,SA,SI
Gazania krebsiana 'Orange Peacock'	B,F
Gazania liechtensteinii	B,SI
Gazania 'Mini-Star' mix	BD,BS,C,CA,CL,DE,DT, F,KI,MO,S,SE,SK,T,YA
Gazania 'Mini-Star' s-c	B,BS,CL,MO
Gazania 'Mini-Star' white	B,BS,C,CL,MO
Gazania 'Orange Surprise'	S
Gazania rigens	B,DD
Gazania rigens Bronze Red	B
Gazania rigens 'Grandiflora'	B
Gazania rigens Red Shades	B
Gazania rigens v uniflora	B
Gazania sp	SI
Gazania splendens	BS,CA,CO,KI,SG,ST
Gazania 'Sundance Mix'	T

GAZANIA

Gazania 'Sunshine' mix	C,CA,EL,F,KS,PK,SE
Gazania 'Sunshine' s-c	BD
Gazania 'Sunshine White'	B
Gazania Suttons Hybrids mix	S
Gazania 'Talent' mix	BS,C,CL,D,DT,L,MO,PK, S,T,TU,YA
Gazania 'Talent' yellow	B,BS,CL,MO
Geijera linearifolia	B,NI
Geijera parviflora	B,CA,EL,HA,NI,O,SA
Geissorhiza aspera	B,MN,RU,SC,SI
Geissorhiza bonae-spei	B
Geissorhiza brevifolia	RU
Geissorhiza brevifolia pink	RU
Geissorhiza carinatus	RU
Geissorhiza ceresianus	RU
Geissorhiza confusa	B,SI
Geissorhiza corrugata	RU
Geissorhiza darlingensis	B,KB,RU,SI
Geissorhiza gracilis	RU
Geissorhiza heterostyla	AP,B,RU,SI
Geissorhiza humilis	B,SI
Geissorhiza imbricata	B,RU
Geissorhiza inaequalis	B,MN,RU
Geissorhiza inflexa	B,RU,SI
Geissorhiza involutus	RU
Geissorhiza longifolia	B,SI
Geissorhiza mathewsii	B
Geissorhiza monantha	B,KB,RU,SC
Geissorhiza ornithogaloides	B,SI
Geissorhiza ovalifolia	B,SI
Geissorhiza ovata	B
Geissorhiza purpureolutea	B
Geissorhiza radians	B,C,RU,SI
Geissorhiza sp	SI
Geissorhiza splendidissima	B,KB,RU,SC,SI
Geissorhiza stellatus	RU
Geissorhiza tenella	B,SI
Geissorhiza tulbaghensis	B,RU,SI
Geissorhiza vaginatus	RU
Geissorhiza viridiflorus	RU
Gelasine azurea see G.coerulea	
Gelasine azurea v orientalis	MN
Gelasine coerulea	AP,C,MN,SC
Gelasine elongata	B
Gelasine elongata v orientalis	B
Gelasine uruguainensis v orientalis	B
Geleznowia verrucosa	B,NI,O
Gelsemium sempervirens	B
Genipa americana	B
Genista aethnensis	AP,B,C,FW,HP,SA,T
Genista florida	SA,SG
Genista germanica	B
Genista hispanica ssp occidentalis	B
Genista horridum	SA
Genista maderensis	B,SA
Genista monspessulana	B,HP,SA,SC,SG
Genista radiata	SG,VO
Genista sagittalis	AP,B,C,DE,JE,KL,SA,SG
Genista scorpius	SA
Genista tenera	SG
Genista tinctoria	A,AP,B,C,FW,G,HA,HP, HU,JE,KL,RS,SA,SG
Genista tinctoria 'Royal Gold'	KL
Genista umbellata	SA
Genlisea filiformis	B,DV
Genlisea sp	B

Genlisea violacea	B,DV
Gentaurium tenuiflorum	B
Gentiana acaulis	w.a.
Gentiana acaulis 'Blue Gem'	J
Gentiana acaulis v angustifolia	HU
Gentiana affinis	AP,B,HP,KL,NO,SC,SW
Gentiana alba	B
Gentiana algida	B,F,JE,RM,SW
Gentiana alpina	B,C,VO
Gentiana amarella	C
Gentiana andrewsii	AP,B,DV,G,HU,JE,PR,SC
Gentiana andrewsii 'Cream'	B,HU
Gentiana angulosa	C
Gentiana angustifolia	AP,B,HP,JE,KL,PK,SG
Gentiana angustifolia 'Alba'	KL
Gentiana angustifolia 'Frei Hybrid'	JE
Gentiana asclepiadea	AP,B,C,DE,F,G,HP,JD,JE, KL,P,PA,RH,RS,SA,SG,T
Gentiana asclepiadea 'Knightshayes'	C,HP
Gentiana asclepiadea 'Nymans'	C,G,I
Gentiana asclepiadea 'Phyllis'	AP,B,P
Gentiana asclepiadea 'Pink Cascade'	HP
Gentiana asclepiadea 'Rosea'	KL
Gentiana asclepiadea turquoise	BS,C,KI
Gentiana asclepiadea v alba	AP,B,C,G,HP,JE,KL,P, SC,SG
Gentiana asclepiadea 'Whitethroat'	P
Gentiana axiliflora	CG,KL
Gentiana bavarica	AP,B,C,JE,KL
Gentiana bavarica ssp subcaulis	CG,VO
Gentiana bellidifolia	AP,B,SS
Gentiana bigelovii	CG,G,SC
Gentiana bisetaea	KL
Gentiana boissieri	VO
Gentiana brachyphylla	AP,B,C,CG,JE,KL,SC,VO
Gentiana bracteosa	SG
Gentiana burseri	AP,CG,G,SG
Gentiana burseri v villarsii	AP,B,CG,SG
Gentiana cachemirica	AP,DV,KL,SC,SG
Gentiana calycosa	NO
Gentiana campestris	B,CG
Gentiana catesbaei	C
Gentiana ciliata	KL
Gentiana clusii	AP,B,BS,C,CG,G,JE,KL, SC,VO
Gentiana clusii f alboviolacea	B,G,JE
Gentiana clusii 'Rosea'	KL
Gentiana clusii v caulescens	KL
Gentiana clusii v rochelii	VO
Gentiana corymbifera	B,C,CG,SA,SS
Gentiana cruciata	AP,B,BS,CG,DV,G,HP, HU,JE,KI,KL,SC,SG
Gentiana cruciata ssp phlogifolia	B,CG,KL,SG
Gentiana dahurica	AP,B,BS,C,CG,G,HP,HU, JE,SA,SG
Gentiana dalmatica	SG
Gentiana decumbens	AP,B,BS,HP,RS,SC
Gentiana dendrologii	CG,SG
Gentiana dentosa	DV
Gentiana dimilensis	VO
Gentiana dinarica	AP,B,C,JE,KL,SC
Gentiana divisa	CG,SC
Gentiana fetisowii	AP,CG,DV,G,SG
Gentiana flavida	PR,SG
Gentiana freyniana	B,G,KL,SC,SG
Gentiana froelichii	KL,VO

GENTIANA

Gentiana gelida	AP,B,G,RM,SC,SG
Gentiana germanica	B,CG
Gentiana gracilipes	AP,B,C,CG,DV,G,JE,SC
Gentiana gracilis 'Alba'	KL
Gentiana grombczewskii	SG
Gentiana grossheimii	AP,B,G,P,SC
Gentiana hybrid white/blue	KL
Gentiana imbricata	JE
Gentiana kesselringii see G.walujewii	
Gentiana kochiana see G. acaulis	
Gentiana kurroo	AP,B,C,JE
Gentiana lagodechiana see septemfida v lagodechiana	
Gentiana loderi	KL
Gentiana lutea	AP,B,C,CG,CN,F,G,HP,
	JE,KL,P,PO,SA,SC,SG
Gentiana macrophylla see G.burseri v villarsii	
Gentiana makinoi	DE,G,RS
Gentiana makinoi 'Alba'	B,JE
Gentiana makinoi 'Royal Blue'	B,SA
Gentiana montana	B,SS
Gentiana 'Moorcroftiana'	DV,T
Gentiana newberryi	AP,CG
Gentiana nivalis	B,CG
Gentiana oliverei	AP,B,KL,SC,SG
Gentiana orbicularis	KL,VO
Gentiana ornata	CG
Gentiana oschtenica	KL<VO
Gentiana pannonica	AP,CG,G,KL,SC,SG
Gentiana paradoxa	AP,B,G,KL,P,RM,SC
Gentiana paradoxa 'Blauer Herold'	B,JE
Gentiana parryi	AP,B,KL,SC,SG,SW
Gentiana phlogifolia see G.cruciata	
Gentiana pneumonantha	AP,B,C,CG,HP,JE,KL,SA,
	AP,HP
Gentiana przewalskii	AP,HP
Gentiana puberulenta	AP,B
Gentiana punctata	B,C,DV,F,G,JE,SG
Gentiana purpurea	AP,B,C,CG,G,HU,JE,SA,
	SC,VO
Gentiana purpurea 'Nana'	AP,B,C,JE
Gentiana pyrenaica	B
Gentiana quinquefolia	PR
Gentiana rochelii	SG
Gentiana saponaria	B,CG,SG
Gentiana saxosa	AP,CG,HP,KL,P,SC,SG
Gentiana scabra	AP,CG,G,SC
Gentiana scabra v buergeri	AP,B,C
Gentiana septemfida	AP,B,BS,C,CG,DE,DV,F,
	G,HP,I,KI,KL,MO,PK,
	RM,SC,SG,ST,W
Gentiana septemfida flatifolia	SG
Gentiana septemfida v lagodechiana	AP,B,C,CL,CN,HP,JE,
	KL,SA,SC,SG,T,V
Gentiana septemfida v l. 'Hascombensis'	AP,SC
Gentiana septemfida v lagodechiana select	B,JE
Gentiana serotina	B,SS
Gentiana sino-ornata 'Blauer Edelstein'	JE
Gentiana sino-ornata new hyb	B
Gentiana siphonantha	AP,B,DV,G,SC
Gentiana sp	KL,SG
Gentiana sp mix	AP,C,I,SC
Gentiana speciosa	C
Gentiana straminea	AP,B,G,JE,KL,SG
Gentiana 'Strathmore'	HP
Gentiana tenuifolia	B,C,SA
Gentiana tergestina	C,VO
Gentiana terglouensis	AP,B,C

Gentiana thermalis	RM
Gentiana tianschanica	AP,KL,SC,SG
Gentiana tibetica	AP,B,BS,CG,DV,G,HP,JE,
	SC,SG
Gentiana triflora	AP,B,HP,P,SC
Gentiana triflora 'Alba'	B,P,SC
Gentiana triflora v japonica	B,JE,SC
Gentiana triflora v japonica 'Alba'	B,C,SC
Gentiana triflora v montana	HP,KL
Gentiana triflora v montana 'Alba'	KL
Gentiana trinervis	B,P
Gentiana utriculosa	B,CG
Gentiana verna	AP,B,BS,C,G,HP,JE,KL,
	RM,SA,SC,SG,VO
Gentiana verna ssp angulosa see G.v. ssp balcanica	
Gentiana verna ssp balcanica	B,G,I,JE,KL,SC,VO
Gentiana verna ssp tergestina	KL
Gentiana waltonii	I
Gentiana walujewii	AP,B,I,KL,SA,SC,SG
Gentiana wutaiensis	AP,B,CG,HP,SC,SG
Gentiana x hascombensis see G.septemfida v l. 'Hascombensis'	
Gentiana x hexafarreri	B,JE,P
Gentiana x oliviana	KL
Gentianella amarella	KL
Gentianella campestris	B
Gentianella detonsa elegans	SW
Gentianella germanica	B,DV,G
Gentianella lutescens	SG
Gentianella quinquefolia	B
Gentianella tenella	AP,B
Gentianella utriculosa	B
Gentianopsis crinita	AP,B,PR
Gentianopsis detonsa v elegans	B
Geonoma congesta	B,SA
Geonoma schottiana	B
Geranium albanum	AP,CG,HP,SA
Geranium albiflorum	HP
Geranium andersonii	B
Geranium aristatum	AP,B,CG,HP,JE,P,SA,SC
Geranium asphodeloides	AP,B,C,CG,G,HL,HP,P
Geranium asphodeloides ssp crenophilum	HP
Geranium asphodeloides White form	HP
Geranium bicknelli	SG
Geranium biuncinatum	AP,B,P,SC
Geranium bohemicum	BS,C,CG,HL,HP,P,SC,T
Geranium 'Brookside'	T
Geranium caffrum	AP,HP,P,SC
Geranium canariense	B,HP,P
Geranium carolinianum	CG
Geranium cinereum	AP,CG,SC
Geranium cinereum v subcaulescens	VO
Geranium clarkei 'Kashmir Blue'	HP
Geranium clarkei 'Kashmir Purple'	HL,HP
Geranium clarkei 'Kashmir White'	HP
Geranium collinum	C,HP
Geranium columbinum	B,CG
Geranium dalmaticum	AP,CG,HP,SC
Geranium dissectum	B,C,SU
Geranium divaricatum	SG
Geranium donianum	KL
Geranium endressii	AP,C,CG,DE,HP,KL
Geranium endressii hybs	B,JE
Geranium erianthum	AP,B,CG,G,HP,P,SG
Geranium eriostemon see G.platyanthum	
Geranium farreri	AP,B,CG,HP,KL,P,SC
Geranium fremontii	B,CG,HP,RM,SC

GERANIUM

Geranium gracile	AP,B,HP,P	Geranium pratense 'Silver Queen'	AP,C,HL,P
Geranium gymnocaulon v pumilum	VO	Geranium pratense striatum	AP,SG
Geranium h. see Pelargonium		Geranium procurrens	C
Geranium harveyi	P	Geranium psilostemon	AP,B,C,DE,HL,HP,JD,JE,
Geranium himalayense	HL,HP		P,PL,SC
Geranium himalayense 'Gravetye'	AP,B,P	Geranium psilostemon 'Bressingham Flair'	HP
Geranium himalayense 'Plenum'	B	Geranium pulchrum	B,HP,P,SI
Geranium ibericum	B,HP,JE,KL,RS,SG	Geranium purpureum	CG
Geranium incanum	AP,B,BH,C,CF,DV,HP,	Geranium pusillum	B,CG
	KB,SC,SI	Geranium pylzowianum	HP
Geranium incanum v multifidum	AP,HP	Geranium pyrenaicum	AP,B,C,CG,DV,HP,SA,
Geranium incanum white	B,SI		SC,SG,T
Geranium kishtvariense	C	Geranium pyrenaicum 'Bill Wallis'	AP,B,HP,P
Geranium lambertii	HP	Geranium pyrenaicum f albiflorum	AP,B,HP,P
Geranium lanuginosum	AP,CG,HP,P	Geranium reflexum	CG,G,HP
Geranium libani	AP,HP,NG	Geranium regelii	AP,SC
Geranium lucidum	B,CG,HP,P	Geranium renardii	AP,HP
Geranium luganense	CG	Geranium richardsonii	AP,B,P,SG
Geranium macrorrhizum	AP,B,C,CG,DE,G,HP,JE,	Geranium rivulare	B,P
	SA,SG	Geranium robertianum	AP,B,C,CG,CN,DE,SA,
Geranium macrorrhizum 'Album'	C,HP,SC,SG		SU,TH
Geranium macrorrhizum 'Bevan's Variety'	B,P	Geranium robertianum 'Album'	KL
Geranium macr. 'Ingwersen's Variety'	AP,C,HP	Geranium robertianum 'Celtic White'	B,HL,HP,P
Geranium macrorrhizum purple-red	JE	Geranium robustum	AP,B,HP,P,PL,SI
Geranium maculatum	AB,AP,B,G,HP,JE,PO,	Geranium rotundifolium	CG
	PR,SG	Geranium rubescens	C,G,HP,P
Geranium maderense	AP,B,BH,C,DD,DI,DV,	Geranium ruprechtii	AP,B,HP,P,VO
	HP,P,SA,SC,SG	Geranium sanguineum	AP,B,BD,BS,C,CG,CL,
Geranium mix border vars	T		CN,DE,F,G,HP,JE,L,MO,
Geranium mix hardy	C,HL,JE,P,PL		P,PL,PM,SA,SC,SG,SU,
Geranium molle	AP,B,CG		T,TH
Geranium napuligerum h. see G.farreri		Geranium sanguineum 'Album'	AP,HP,RM
Geranium nepalense	CG,SA	Geranium sanguineum 'Cedric Morris'	PL
Geranium nepalense v thunbergii	B,JE	Geranium sanguineum 'Nanum'	B,JE,SC
Geranium nervosum	B,P,SG	Geranium sanguineum 'Sara'	HL
Geranium 'Nimbus'	B,C,P	Geranium sanguineum v lancastriense	C,KL
Geranium nodosum	AP,B,HP,JE	Geranium sanguineum v striatum	AP,B,G,HL,HP,I,JE,PL,
Geranium ocellatum	CG,P		SC,SG
Geranium orientalitibeticum	AP,HP	Geranium sanguineum 'Vision'	C,PK
Geranium ornithopodon	B,SI	Geranium sessiliflorum	B,CG,SC,SS
Geranium palmatum	AP,B,C,CG,D,HP,P,SC	Geranium sessiliflorum 'Nigricans'	AP,B,HP,P,SC
Geranium palustre	G,HP,SG	Geranium sessiliflorum 'Rubrum'	B,P
Geranium 'Pastel Clouds'	B,P	Geranium sibiricum	B,CG
Geranium 'Persian Carpet'	B,P	Geranium sinense	AP,B,HP,P,SC
Geranium phaeum	AP,B,C,CG,F,G,HL,HP,JE,	Geranium sp	SG,SI
	P,PL,SA,SC,T	Geranium 'Splish Splash'	BS,MO
Geranium phaeum 'Album'	AP,HP,SG	Geranium striatum	P
Geranium phaeum 'Lily Lovell'	HP	Geranium swatense	HP
Geranium phaeum 'Samobar'	HP	Geranium sylvaticum	B,C,CG,DE,F,G,HP,JE,
Geranium phaeum v lividum	HP		SA,SC,SG
Geranium 'Philippe Vapelle'	P	Geranium sylvaticum 'Album'	AP,HP
Geranium platyanthum	B,HP,P,SC,SG	Geranium sylvaticum 'Amy Doncaster'	HP
Geranium platypetalum	CG,HP,SG	Geranium sylvaticum 'Baker's Pink'	HP
Geranium polyanthes	HP	Geranium sylvaticum 'Mayflower'	B,HP,P
Geranium pratense	AP,B,BS,C,CG,CN,CO,	Geranium sylvaticum white & lace veins	C
	DE,F,G,HL,HP,JE,KI,LA,	Geranium thunbergii	AP,B,CG,HP,I,P,SG
	P,PL,SA,SC,SG,SU,TH,	Geranium transbaicalicum	C,HP
	V,Z	Geranium traversii	AP,B,P,SC,SS
Geranium pratense albiflorum	AP,B,C,CG,G,HL,HP,JE,	Geranium traversii 'Chocolate Pot'	PL
	P,SC,SG	Geranium traversii v elegans	HP
Geranium pratense 'Galactic	C	Geranium tuberosum	B,HP
Geranium pratense hyb 'Spinners'	C	Geranium versicolor	AP,B,C,G,HP,P
Geranium pratense 'Mrs Kendall Clarke'	AP,B,C,G,HL,SC	Geranium viscosissimum	AP,B,C,HP,JE,NO,SG
Geranium pratense pale azure	C,HL	Geranium wallichianum	AP,C
Geranium pratense 'Rose Queen'	B,HL,P	Geranium wallichianum 'Buxton's Variety'	AP,B,C,G,HL,HP,PL,SC,T
Geranium pratense roseum	HP	Geranium 'Wargrave Pink'	C

GERANIUM

Geranium wilfordii	CG
Geranium 'Winscombe'	B,P
Geranium wlassovianum	CG
Geranium x magnificum	HP
Geranium x monacense	HP
Geranium x oxonianum	AP,C,HP,P
Geranium x oxonianum 'Claridge Druce'	AP,C,HL,G
Geranium x oxonianum 'Thurstonianum'	AP,HL
Geranium yesoense v nipponicum	KL
Gerardia tenuifolia	PR
Gerbera 'Blackheart' mix	T
Gerbera 'Californian Giants' mix	DE,J,SE,V
Gerbera cordata	C
Gerbera crocea	B,SI
Gerbera 'Dw Pandora' mix	T
Gerbera 'Dw Parade' mix	J,V
Gerbera f1 'Festival' mix	SK,YA
Gerbera f1 'Mardi Gras' mix	T
Gerbera f1 'Masquerade Mix'	YA
Gerbera f1 'Skipper'	CL
Gerbera f1 'Tempo' dw mix	BS,C,CA,CL,MO,SK
Gerbera 'Festival' s-c, mix	SK
Gerbera hyb mix	FR
Gerbera Jameson's Hybrids	B,BD,BS,BY,C,CA,CL,F,
	KI,L,MO,S
Gerbera jamesonii 'Rainbow' s-c/mix	PK
Gerbera kunzeana	KL
Gerbera mix florist strain	CA
Gerbera nivea	KL
Gerbera sp	SI
Gerbera tomentosa	B,SI
Gesneria cardinalis see Sinningia	C
Gesneria christii	C
Gesneria cuneifolia 'Quebradillas'	C
Gesneria macrantha compacta	CL,L
Gesneria 'Sundrop'	C
Gesneriads sp & hyb mix	C
Gessorhiza schinzii	SI
Gethyllis sp	RU
Geum album	CG
Geum aleppicum	AP,B,G,PR,RS,SG
Geum 'Borissii'	AP,B,HP,JE,P,SA,SG,T
Geum bulgaricum	CG,KL
Geum calthaefolium	B,HP,P,SC
Geum canadense	B
Geum chiloense	G,HP,KL<SC,T
Geum coccineum	KL
Geum 'Dingle Apricot'	HP
Geum glaciale	KL
Geum 'Gold Ball' see 'Lady Stratheden'	
Geum japonicum	B,SC
Geum 'Lady Stratheden'	AP,B,BD,BS,C,CL,CN,
	CO,DE,DT,F,HP,J,JE,KI,
	L,MO,SA,SK,ST,SU,V
Geum leiospermum	AP,P,SC
Geum 'Lionel Cox'	HP
Geum macrophyllum	AP,B,C,JE,KL,SC,SG
Geum macrophyllum perincisum	SG
Geum magellanicum see G.parviflorum	
Geum 'Marika'	HP
Geum montanum	AP,B,BD,BS,C,CG,G,HP,
	JE,KL,MO,RS,SA,SG,T
Geum 'Mrs. J.Bradshaw'	AP,B,BD,BS,BY,C,CL,C
	N,CO,DE,F,G,HP,HU,J,J
	KI,L,MO,S,SA,ST,SU,V
Geum 'Mrs. J.Bradshaw' Imp	BS,DT,SK

Geum parviflorum	AP,B,C,G,HP,P,RS,SS
Geum pentapetalum	VO
Geum peruvianum	SG
Geum pyrenaicum	AP,B,G,JE,KL,SC,SG
Geum quellyon see G. chiloense	
Geum reptans see Sieversia	
Geum rhodopeum	B
Geum rivale	AP,B,C,CG,CN,G,HP,JD,
	JE,LA,RH,SA,SC,SG,SU
Geum rivale 'Album'	AP,HP,SC,T
Geum rivale islandicum	KL
Geum rivale 'Leonard's Variety'	B,HP,P
Geum scarlet & gold	D
Geum talbotianum	AR
Geum triflorum	AP,B,HP,JE,NO,PR,SG
Geum triflorum v campanulatum	AP,HP
Geum triflorum v ciliatum	B
Geum Two Ladies	BD,SE,U
Geum uniflorum	B,SS
Geum urbanum	AB,AP,B,C,CN,DD,G,JE,
	LA,SA,SC,SG,TH,Z
Geum x intermedium	AP,HP,SA
Gevuina avellana	B,SA
Gibbaeum album	B,DV,SI,Y
Gibbaeum comptonii	B,DV,Y
Gibbaeum cryptopodium	B,DV,SI,Y
Gibbaeum dispar	B,DV,SI,Y
Gibbaeum esterhuyseniae	B
Gibbaeum geminum	B
Gibbaeum gibbosum	B
Gibbaeum haagei	DV,Y
Gibbaeum heathii	B,DV,SI,Y
Gibbaeum pachypodium	DV
Gibbaeum petrense	B,DV,Y
Gibbaeum pilosulum	B,DV
Gibbaeum pubescens	B,SI
Gibbaeum schwantesii	B
Gibbaeum shandii	B,DV
Gibbaeum velutinum	B,DV,Y
Gilia achilleifolia	B,C
Gilia aggregata see Ipomopsis	
Gilia capitata	B,C,DD,G,J,KS,SC,V
Gilia capitata abrontanifolia	AP,T
Gilia capitata 'Alba'	B
Gilia diegensis	B
Gilia leptantha	B,DD,G,KS
Gilia leptantha ssp purpusii	B
Gilia longiflora	SW
Gilia milefoliata	SG
Gilia rigidula	B,SW
Gilia rubra	C,HU,V
Gilia subnuda	B,SW
Gilia tenuituba	B,SW
Gilia thurberi	B,SW
Gilia tricolor	AB,B,BS,G,HU,J,KS,SG,
	T,V
Gilia tricolor 'Snow Queen'	B,V
Gillenia trifoliata	AP,B,C,G,HP,I,JE,SG,T
Gingidia montana	B,SC,SS
Ginkgo biloba	A,AB,BS,C,CA,CG,DD,
	EL,FW,HA,HU,LN,N,SA,
	T,V,VE,WA
Gladiolus abbreviatus	RU,SI
Gladiolus alatus	RU,SI
Gladiolus alatus v alatus	B,KB,RU
Gladiolus alatus v meliusculus	B,KB,RU

GLADIOLUS

Gladiolus anatolicus	AR
Gladiolus angustus	B,RU,SI
Gladiolus antakiensis	AR
Gladiolus aurantiacus	B,C,SI
Gladiolus aureus	B,KB
Gladiolus bonae-spei	B,SI
Gladiolus brevifolius v brevifolius	B,SI
Gladiolus callianthus	AP,B,G
Gladiolus cardinalis	AR,B,RU,SI
Gladiolus carinatus	KB,SI
Gladiolus carinatus ssp carinatus	B,RU
Gladiolus carinatus ssp parviflorus	B,RU,SI
Gladiolus carmineus	B,RU,SC,SI
Gladiolus carneus	B,C,CG,KB,RS,RU,SA, SC,SI
Gladiolus carneus v albidus	B,RU,SC
Gladiolus carneus v macowanii	B,RU
Gladiolus caryophyllaceus	B,RU,SC,SI
Gladiolus caucasicus	VO
Gladiolus ceresianus	B,SI
Gladiolus citrinus	B,SI
Gladiolus citrinus x alatus	SI
Gladiolus communis	AP,B,G,LG,SC
Gladiolus communis ssp byzantinus	C,I
Gladiolus communis ssp byzantinus C.R.	MN
Gladiolus crassifolius	B,SA,SI
Gladiolus cunonius	B,RU,SI
Gladiolus dalenii	B,RU,SA,SI
Gladiolus debilis	B
Gladiolus ?dubius S.F301 Spain	MN
Gladiolus ecklonii	B,SI
Gladiolus equitans	B,SA,SI
Gladiolus exilis	B,SI
Gladiolus floribundus	SI
Gladiolus floribundus ssp floribundus	AP,B
Gladiolus fourcadei	SI
Gladiolus garnieri	AP,B
Gladiolus gracilis	KB,SI
Gladiolus gracilis ssp gracilis	B,RU,SI
Gladiolus gracilis v latifolius	B,KB,RU,SC,SI
Gladiolus gueinzii	B,RU,SI
Gladiolus huttonii	B,KB,RU
Gladiolus hyalinus	B,RU,SI
Gladiolus illyricus	AP,B,BS,G,JE,KL,MN, SC,SG
Gladiolus imbricatus	AP,B,CG,G,JE,KL,MN, SC,SG
Gladiolus italicus	AP,B,C,CG,G,JE,KL,SC
Gladiolus kamiesbergensos	B,SI
Gladiolus kotschyanus	AR,MN,RS
Gladiolus liliaceus	B,KB,RU,SA,SI
Gladiolus longicollis	B,SI
Gladiolus maculatus	RU
Gladiolus maculatus ssp meridionalis	AR
Gladiolus maculatus v maculatus	B
Gladiolus marlothii	B,RU,SI
Gladiolus monticola	B,RU,SI
Gladiolus nerineoides	SI
Gladiolus ochroleucus	RU,SC
Gladiolus ochroleucus v macowanii	B,SI
Gladiolus ochroleucus v ochroleucus	B,SI
Gladiolus odoratus	B,RU,SI
Gladiolus oppositiflorus ssp salmoneus	B,SI
Gladiolus orchidiflorus	B,RU,SI
Gladiolus palustris	AP,B,G,JE,KL,SA,SC
Gladiolus pappei	B,SI

Gladiolus patersonii	B,RU,SI
Gladiolus permeabilis	B,RU
Gladiolus permeabilis v wilsonii	B,RU,SI
Gladiolus Primulinus Hybrids	C
Gladiolus priorii	B,KB,RU,SI
Gladiolus pritzelii	B,RU,SI
Gladiolus punctulatus	B,RU,SI
Gladiolus quadrangulus	B,RU,SI
Gladiolus recurvus	B,RU,SI
Gladiolus rogersii	BH,KB,RU
Gladiolus rogersii v rogersii	B,SI
Gladiolus saccatus	B,SI
Gladiolus saundersii	B,SI
Gladiolus scullyi	B,RU,SI
Gladiolus segetum see G.italicus	
Gladiolus sericeo-villosus	B,SI
Gladiolus sp	SI
Gladiolus splendens	B
Gladiolus stefaniae	AR,B,SI
Gladiolus tenellus	B,RU,SI
Gladiolus teretifolius	B,SI
Gladiolus tristis	AP,AR,B,KB,LG,RU,SI
Gladiolus tristis v concolor	AP,B,C,SI
Gladiolus undulatus	B,SI
Gladiolus uysiae	B,SI
Gladiolus venustus	B,SI
Gladiolus vigilans	B,SI
Gladiolus violaceo-lineatus	B,SI
Gladiolus virescens	AP,SI
Gladiolus virescens v virescens	B,SI
Gladiolus watermeyeri	B,RU,SI
Gladiolus watsonius	B,RU,SI
Glandulicactus see Sclerocactus	
Glandulicactus wrightii	B,Y
Glaucidium palmatum	AP,B,CG,HP,JE,KL,SA,
Glaucium corniculatum	B,C,G,HP,P,SA,SC
Glaucium elegans	P
Glaucium fimbrilligerum	KL
Glaucium flavum	AP,B,C,CG,CP,G,HP,JE,N G,SA,SC,SG,SU,T,TH,W
Glaucium flavum aurantiacum see G.flavum f fulvum	
Glaucium flavum f fulvum	AP,B,BS,C,HP,JE,KI
Glaucium grandiflorum	B
Glaucium vitellianum	W
Glechoma hederacea	B,C,JE
Gleditsia caspica	B,CA,LN,SA
Gleditsia chinensis	SA
Gleditsia japonica	B,LN,SA
Gleditsia macrantha	SA
Gleditsia sp	KL
Gleditsia triacanthos	A,B,C,CA,EL,FW,G,HA, HU,LN,NO,SA,SG,VE, WA
Gleditsia triacanthos f inermis	B,EL,FW,HA,HU,LN,N, SA,VE
Gleditsia triacanthos f inermis imp	B,FW
Gleditsia triacanthos v sinensis	B
Gliricidia sepium	B,DD,EL,HA,HU,LN,RE, SA,TT
Glischrocaryon aureum	B,NI
Globba marantiana	C
Globba winitii	B
Globularia cordifolia	AP,B,BS,C,CG,G,HP,JE, KI,KL,SA,SC,SG
Globularia incanescens	AP,B,RM,SC
Globularia meridionalis	KL

GLOBULARIA

Globularia nana see G.repens
Globularia nudicaulis | AP,B,C,JE,SA,SC
Globularia punctata | AP,B,G,JE,KL,SC,SG,T
Globularia repens | B,C,KL,SC,VO
Globularia sp | KL
Globularia trichosanthes | AP,KL,SC,SG
Globularia vulgaris | HA,SG
Glochidion ferdinandi | B
Glochidion sinicum | SA
Gloriosa mix dbl | BS
Gloriosa mix single | BS
Gloriosa superba | B,C,CF,EL,O,RU,SA,SE, SI,T,V
Gloriosa superba 'Carsonii' | C
Gloriosa superba 'Lutea' | C
Gloriosa superba 'Rothschildiana' | AP,B,C,CA,EL,G,KL,SA
Gloriosa superba 'Simplex' | B,SC,SG
Gloriosa verschuuri | C
Glottiphyllum arrectum | SG
Glottiphyllum depressum | B,SI
Glottiphyllum fragrans | B,KB,SI
Glottiphyllum herrei | B,KB
Glottiphyllum linguiforme | DV,Y
Glottiphyllum longum | B,CG,KB,SI
Glottiphyllum muirii | B
Glottiphyllum nelii | B,KB,SG,Y
Glottiphyllum oligocarpum | B,DV,KB,Y
Glottiphyllum parvifolium | B,DV,KB,SG
Glottiphyllum platycarpum | SG
Glottiphyllum pygmaeum | B,KB
Glottiphyllum regium | B
Glottiphyllum salmii | B,Kb
Glottiphyllum semicylindricum | B
Glottiphyllum sp mix | C,KB
Gloxinia Crown mix | BS,KI
Gloxinia cvs mix h-p | BL
Gloxinia f1 'Avanti' | YA
Gloxinia f1 hyb 'Brocade' | C,CA,CL,L,PK,T
Gloxinia f1 hyb 'Empress' mix | BS,CL,D,DT,L,MO,SK,T
Gloxinia f1 hyb 'Fanfare' mix | CL
Gloxinia f1 hyb 'Glory' mix | CL,SK
Gloxinia f1 hyb 'Glory' s-c | CL
Gloxinia f1 hyb 'Gregor Mendal' | BS
Gloxinia f1 hyb 'Ultra' mix | C
Gloxinia f2 hyb 'Jester' mix | BS,J,SE,T,V
Gloxinia mix giant fl | BY,PK
Gloxinia perennis | B,C
Gloxinia racemosa | C
Glumicalyx flanaganii | B,SI
Glumicalyx goseloides | B,SI
Glumicalyx montanus | B,SI
Glumicalyx nutans | B,SI
Glyceria canadensis | B,PR
Glyceria fluitans | B
Glyceria grandis | B,PR
Glyceria maxima | B,JE,SA
Glyceria striata | B,PR
Glycine canescens | B,NI
Glycine max | DD
Glycine tabacina | B,NI
Glycosmis pentaphylla | B
Glycyrrhiza acanthocarpa | B,DD
Glycyrrhiza echinata | A,B,C,HU,JE
Glycyrrhiza glabra | A,B,BH,C,CP,G,JE,LN, PO,SA
Glycyrrhiza lepidota | B,PR,SG

Glycyrrhiza uralensis | SG
Glyptostrobus pensilis | B
Gmelina arborea | B,C,EL,LN,RE,SA,WA
Gmelina asiatica | B
Gmelina leichardtii | B,EL,O
Gmelinii v japonica | CG
Gnaphalium 'Fairy Gold' see Helichrysum thianschanicum 'Goldkind'
Gnaphalium nitidulum | B,SS
Gnaphalium obtusifolium | PR
Gnaphalium supinum | KL
Gnaphalium sylvaticum | B
Gnaphalium traversii | B,SS
Gnetum gnemon | B
Gnidia squarrosa | B
Gochnatia arborescens | DD
Godetia see Clarkia
Gomphocarpus fruticosus | B,JE,SI,SG
Gomphocarpus physocarpa | B,C,SI
Gomphocarpus rostratus | B,SI
Gompholobium aristatum | B
Gompholobium baxteri | B,NI
Gompholobium capitatum | B,NI
Gompholobium confertum | B,NI
Gompholobium knightianum | B,NI,SA
Gompholobium latifolium | B,C,DD,HA,NI,SA
Gompholobium marginatum | B,NI
Gompholobium ovatum | B,NI
Gompholobium polymorphum | AU,B,NI
Gompholobium preissii | B,NI
Gompholobium scabrum | B,NI
Gompholobium shuttleworthii | B,NI
Gompholobium tomentosum | B,NI
Gompholobium venustum | B,NI
Gompholobium villosum | B,NI
Gompholobium virgatum | B,HA,NI
Gomphostigma virgatum | B,SI
Gomphrena affinis | B,NI,O
Gomphrena canescens | B,NI,O,SA
Gomphrena cunninghamii | B,NI,O
Gomphrena decumbens | B
Gomphrena diffusa | B
Gomphrena dispersa 'Pink Pinheads' | BS,C,KS
Gomphrena globosa | BS,CG,DD,DT,F,FR,GO, KI,L,PI,SD,SU,V
Gomphrena globosa 'Aurea-superba' | B,HU
Gomphrena globosa 'Buddy Purple' | DE,SK
Gomphrena globosa 'Choice Soft Pink' | B
Gomphrena globosa 'Dwarf Buddy' | B,BS,C,KS,T
Gomphrena globosa 'Dwarf Cissy' | B,KS
Gomphrena globosa 'Dwarf Dolly' cs | B
Gomphrena globosa 'Gemini Mix' | D
Gomphrena globosa 'Gnome' s-c | B,PI,PK,SK
Gomphrena globosa 'Gnome' white | B,PK,SK
Gomphrena globosa 'Lavender Lady' | B,BS,DE,PK
Gomphrena globosa mix tall | DE
Gomphrena globosa 'Q formula mix' | C,KI
Gomphrena globosa 'Q Lavender Lilac' | C
Gomphrena globosa 'Q Lilac' | B
Gomphrena globosa 'Q Pink' | B,C
Gomphrena globosa 'Q Purple' | B,C
Gomphrena globosa 'Q Rose' | B,C
Gomphrena globosa 'Q White' | B,C,DE
Gomphrena globosa 'Rose Bicolour' | B,JO,KS,PK
Gomphrena globosa rose pink imp | PK
Gomphrena globosa s-c | HU,JO,KS
Gomphrena globosa 'Sunburst' mix | BD,BS,MO

GOMPHRENA

Gomphrena globosa 'Sunburst' s-c	BS,MO
Gomphrena globosa white	HU,JO,PK
Gomphrena haageana	C
Gomphrena haageana 'Orange Globe'	B,C,CO,DE,JO,KS,SG
Gomphrena 'Pixie'	U
Gomphrena 'Strawberry Fields'	B,BS,C,DE,DI,HU,JO,KI, KS,PI,PK,U,V
Goniolimon speciosum	AP,SG
Goniolimon tataricum	B,BD,C,CG,CL,GO,JE, KS,PK,SA,SG,V
Goniolimon tataricum v angustifolium	BY,CA,CN,DE,HU,JO, SK,T
Goniolimon tataricum 'Woodcreek'	B,SK
Goniophlebium subauriculatum	B,SG
Goodenia havilandii	B,NI
Goodenia incana	B,NI
Goodenia pinnatifida	B,NI
Goodenia pterygosperma	B,NI
Goodenia scaevolina	B,NI,O,SA
Goodenia scapigera	B,NI,O
Goodenia stelligera	B,NI
Goodenia viscida	B
Goodenia watsonii	B,NI
Goodia latifolia	AU,B,DD,EL,HA,NI,SA
Gordonia axillaris	B
Gordonia lasianthus	B
Gorteria diffusa	B,SI
Gorteria personata	B,SI
Gossypioides kirkii	B,SI
Gossypium arboreum	B,DD,SG
Gossypium australe	B,NI
Gossypium barbadense	B
Gossypium bickii	B,NI
Gossypium davidsonii	DD
Gossypium herbaceum	C,DE,FR,V
Gossypium herbaceum africanum	B,SI
Gossypium hirsutum	B,C
Gossypium hirsutum 'Peruvian Brown'	B
Gossypium h. v punct. 'Hopi Short Staple'	B
Gossypium nanking	B
Gossypium robinsonii	B,NI,SA
Gossypium soilana	B
Gossypium sturtianum	B,EL,NI,O,SA
Gossypium thurberi	B
Gossypium tomentosum	B
Graptopetalum bellum	B,C,DV,SE,V,Y
Grass, Alsike Clover	CD
Grass, Bowling Green	YA
Grass, Centipede	PK
Grass, Chalky Soil	CO,SU
Grass, Cocksfoot	CD
Grass, Creeping Red Fescue	CD
Grass, Dryland Pasture	BU
Grass, Early Bite	CD
Grass, Economy Irrigated Pasture	BU
Grass, 'Evergreen'	ST
Grass, Exposed Clay Subsoil	CO,PR
Grass, Gallop Mixture	CD
Grass, Herbal mix	CO
Grass, Horse Leys	CD
Grass, Intensive Dairy Graze	CD
Grass, Landscape	CA,YA
Grass, lawn mix, All-purpose	BY,D
Grass, lawn mix, Fine	CO,KI,PK,ST,TU,YA
Grass, lawn mix, Hardwearing	BY,CD,D
Grass, lawn mix, Ornamental	AV,BD,BS,BY,CD,D,DT,

	KI,T,TU,V
Grass, lawn mix, Practical	KI
Grass, lawn mix, Shady	CA,D,KI,PK,TU
Grass, Light Land	CD
Grass, Loam/Alluvial Soil	CO
Grass, Low Maintenance mix	CO
Grass, Lucerne	CD
Grass, Maximum D-Value	CD
Grass, Maximum Early	CD
Grass, Maximum Yield	CD
Grass, Meadow Fescue	CD
Grass, Meadow Sedge Short	PR
Grass, Meadow Sedge Tall	PR
Grass, Medium to Heavy Soil	SU
Grass, Nature's Choice	BU
Grass, Over-Seeding Mix	CD
Grass, Paddock mix	BY,CO,KI
Grass, Permanent	CD
Grass, Playground/Football	BU,ST
Grass, Pochon High Clover Ley	CD
Grass, Prairie short	PR
Grass, Prairie tall	PR
Grass, Quick Bulk	CD
Grass, Quickturf	YA
Grass, Red Clover	CD
Grass, Red Clover Ley	CD
Grass, Ryegrass	CD,ST
Grass, Sainfoin	CD
Grass, Sandy Soil	CO,SU
Grass, Set-Aside Mixtures	CD
Grass, Sportsturf	ST,YA
Grass, Suburban	YA
Grass, Timothy	CD
Grass, Tufflawn mix	CA,CO
Grass, Under Trees mix	CO
Grass, Westerwolds Bulk	CD
Grass, Wet Soil	CO
Grass, White Clover	CD
Grass, Woodland	PR,SU
Grass, Woods Edge Savanna Short	PR
Grass, Woods Edge Savanna Tall	PR
Grass, Your Own Mix	CD
Grass/Wildflower mix, Butterfly Meadow	YS
Grass/Wildflower mix, Hedgerow mixes	YS
Grass/Wildflower mix, The Bluebell Wood	YS
Grass/Wildflower mix, The Country Lane	YS
Grasses, Ornamental	BY,CA,CO,F,J,PK,SK,ST, VY
Gratiola officinalis	B,C,G,JE
Grayia spinosa	B
Greenovia aizoon	DV
Greenovia aurea	C
Grevillea agrifolia	B,O
Grevillea annulifera	O
Grevillea aquifolium	HU,O
Grevillea baileyana	B
Grevillea banksii	B,HA,SA,SH
Grevillea banksii 'Alba'	B,EL,HA,O,SA
Grevillea banksii 'Forsterii'	EL,HU,NI,O,VE
Grevillea bipinnatifida	B,NI,O
Grevillea biternata	O
Grevillea brownii	O
Grevillea candelabroides	B,NI,O
Grevillea 'Coochin Hills'	HA,O
Grevillea crithmifolia	B,NI,O
Grevillea decurrens	B,EL

GREVILLEA

Grevillea didymobotrya	B,NI
Grevillea drummondii	B,NI
Grevillea dryandri	B,EL,O
Grevillea endlicherana	B,NI,O
Grevillea eriobotrya	B,NI,O
Grevillea eriobotryoides	B
Grevillea eriostachya	B,O
Grevillea excelsior	O
Grevillea fasciculata	O
Grevillea floribunda	O
Grevillea formosa	EL,O
Grevillea glauca	B,NI,O,SA
Grevillea goodii ssp decora	B,NI,O
Grevillea goodii ssp goodii	B,NI,O
Grevillea hakeoides	B
Grevillea heliosperma	O
Grevillea hookerana	B,NI,O
Grevillea insignis	O
Grevillea integrifolia	O
Grevillea juncifolia	B,NI,O
Grevillea leucopteris	B,NI,O
Grevillea monticola	B,NI,O
Grevillea nudiflora	B,NI,O
Grevillea paradoxa	B,NI,O
Grevillea petrophiloides	B,NI,O
Grevillea pilulifera	B,NI,O
Grevillea plurijuga	B,NI,O
Grevillea polybotrya	B,NI,O
Grevillea pteridifolia	B,NI,O
Grevillea pterosperma	B,NI,O
Grevillea pulchella	B,NI,O
Grevillea pyramidalis	B,NI,O
Grevillea quercifolia	B,NI,O
Grevillea ramosissima	O
Grevillea refracta	B,NI,O
Grevillea robusta	B,BS,BY,C,CA,CL,DE, DV,EL,FW,HA,KI,LN, MO,NI,O,RE,S,SA,SH, SK,T,TT,V,VE,WA
Grevillea 'Sandra Gordon'	B,HA
Grevillea sp mix	C,EL
Grevillea stenobotrya	B,HA,NI,O
Grevillea stenostachya	B
Grevillea striata	B,HA,NI,O
Grevillea synapheae	B,NI
Grevillea teretifolia	B,NI,O
Grevillea venusta	O
Grevillea whiteana	B,EL
Grevillea wickhamii	B,EL,NI,O
Grevillea wilsonii	B,NI,O
Grewia asiatica	B
Grewia bicolor	B,SI
Grewia breviflora	B,NI
Grewia caffra see G.occidentalis	
Grewia carpinifolia	B
Grewia flava	SI
Grewia flavescens	SI
Grewia flavescens v flavescens	B,KB
Grewia hirsuta	B
Grewia occidentalis	B,C,CA,KB,SI
Grewia oppositifolia	B,EL,SA
Grewia polygama	B,NI
Grewia retinervis	B,SI
Grewia robusta	B,KB
Greyia flanaganii	B,KB
Greyia radlkoferi	B,KB,SI

Greyia sutherlandii	B,C,SI
Gridelis squarrosa	KL
Grielum grandiflorum	B,SI
Grielum humifusum	B,SI
Grielum sp	SI
Grindelia aphanactis	B,DD
Grindelia chiloensis	HP
Grindelia integrifolia	B
Grindelia nana	B
Grindelia oregana	AB
Grindelia robusta	B,G,JE,SA,SG
Grindelia stricta ssp venulosa	B
Griselina littoralis	B,SA,SS
Gronophyllum microcarpum	O
Gronophyllum ramsayi	O
Guaiacum officinale	B
Guaiacum sanctum	B
Guaicam coulteri	SA
Guazuma ulmifolia	B
Guibourtia coleosperma	B,SI
Guichenotia ledifolia	B,C,NI,SA
Guichenotia macrantha	B,NI,SA,SC
Guizotia abyssinica	B
Gulubia costata	O
Gundelia tournefortii	B,JE
Gunnera flavida	B,C,P,SA
Gunnera magellanica	AR,B,P
Gunnera manicata	B,BS,C,CN,G,HU,JE, MO,N,SA,T
Gunnera monoica	B
Gunnera perpensa	B,SI
Gunnera prorepens	B,P,PM,SC
Gunnera tinctoria	B,HU,JE,SA,SG
Gunniopsis quadrifida	B,NI
Gutierrezia sarothrae	B
Guzmania sp	B
Gymnadenia conopsea	B,CG
Gymnadenia odoratissima	B
Gymnelaea lanceolata	B
Gymnocactus beguinii	B,DV,Y
Gymnocactus gielsdorfianus	Y
Gymnocactus horripilus	B,DV
Gymnocactus knuthianus	B,DV
Gymnocactus saueri	DV
Gymnocactus subterraneus v zaragosae	B
Gymnocactus viereckii	B,DV
Gymnocactus viereckii LAU1159	CH,Y
Gymnocactus viereckii v major	B,DV
Gymnocactus viereckii v major LAU730	Y
Gymnocalycium achirasense	DV,Y
Gymnocalycium alboareolatum	B
Gymnocalycium amershauseri	DV
Gymnocalycium andreae	DV,Y
Gymnocalycium andreae v grandiflorum	DV,Y
Gymnocalycium andreae v longispinum	B
Gymnocalycium anisitsii	B,DV,Y
Gymnocalycium asterium	DV
Gymnocalycium baldianum	B,DV,Y
Gymnocalycium baldianum x venturianum	CH
Gymnocalycium bayrianum	B,BC
Gymnocalycium bicolor	B
Gymnocalycium bicolor v simplex	Y
Gymnocalycium bodenbenderianum	B,DV,Y
Gymnocalycium bozsingianum	B,Y
Gymnocalycium brachypetalum	DV
Gymnocalycium bruchii	DV,Y

GYMNOCALYCIUM

Gymnocalycium bruchii /g.lafaldense	B,CH,Y
Gymnocalycium buenekeri	Y
Gymnocalycium calochlorum	B,DV
Gymnocalycium calochlorum v proliferum	B,Y
Gymnocalycium capillaensis	B,DV
Gymnocalycium cardenasianum	B,DV,Y
Gymnocalycium carminanthum	Y
Gymnocalycium castellanosii	B,Y
Gymnocalycium chiquitanum	B,Y
Gymnocalycium chubutense	B,DV,Y
Gymnocalycium comaropense	B,DV
Gymnocalycium damsii	B,DV
Gymnocalycium damsii f De Robore	DV
Gymnocalycium damsii f De Salinas	DV
Gymnocalycium damsii v centrispinum	Y
Gymnocalycium damsii v rotundulum	DV,Y
Gymnocalycium damsii v tucavocense	B,BC,DV,Y
Gymnocalycium deeszianum	B,Y
Gymnocalycium delaetii	B,DV
Gymnocalycium denudatum	B
Gymnocalycium denud. v wagnerianum	B
Gymnocalycium doppianum	Y
Gymnocalycium erinaceum	DV
Gymnocalycium eurypleurus	B,DV,Y
Gymnocalycium eytianum	B,DV
Gymnocalycium ferrari	B,DV,Y
Gymnocalycium friedrichii	B,DV
Gymnocalycium fried. v angustostriatum	DV
Gymnocalycium fucarocence	CH,DV
Gymnocalycium gibbosum	B,DV,Y
Gymnocalycium gibbosum v ferox	Y
Gymnocalycium gibbosum v nigrum	Y
Gymnocalycium gibbosum v nobile	DV,Y
Gymnocalycium gibb. v pleuricostatum	Y
Gymnocalycium gibb. v schlumbergeri	Y
Gymnocalycium glaucum	DV,GC,Y
Gymnocalycium guerkeanum	Y
Gymnocalycium hamatum	Y
Gymnocalycium henisii	B,DV
Gymnocalycium horridispinum	B,Y
Gymnocalycium hossei	Y
Gymnocalycium hossei v longispinum	Y
Gymnocalycium hybopleurum	B,DV
Gymnocalycium hyptiacanthum	Y
Gymnocalycium intermedium P113	DV
Gymnocalycium intertextum	Y
Gymnocalycium joossenianum	B,DV
Gymnocalycium kieslingii	DV
Gymnocalycium knollii WO66	DV
Gymnocalycium kozelskyanum	B,DV,Y
Gymnocalycium lagunillasense	BC
Gymnocalycium leptanthum	B,DV
Gymnocalycium marquezii	B,GC,DV,Y
Gymnocalycium marsoneri	Y
Gymnocalycium mazanense	B,DV,Y
Gymnocalycium megatae	B,Y
Gymnocalycium michoga	B
Gymnocalycium mihanovichii	B,DV,Y
Gymnocalycium mihanovichii f caespitosa	DV
Gymnocalycium mih. f Yeredangue	DV
Gymnocalycium mih. v albiflorum	DV
Gymnocalycium mih. v filadelfiense	DV
Gymnocalycium mih. v friedrichii	DV,Y
Gymnocalycium mih. v friedr. f albiflorum	Y
Gymnocalycium mih. v pirarettaense	DV,Y
Gymnocalycium mihanovichii v robustior	DV,Y

Gymnocalycium mih. v rysanekianum	DV
Gymnocalycium mih. v stenogorum	DV
Gymnocalycium mih. v sten. f albiflorum	Y
Gymnocalycium millaresii	DV
Gymnocalycium mix	Y
Gymnocalycium monvillei	B,Y
Gymnocalycium moserianum	B,DV,Y
Gymnocalycium mostii	B,Y
Gymnocalycium multiflorum	B,DV,Y
Gymnocalycium nidulans	B,DV
Gymnocalycium nigriareolatum	DV
Gymnocalycium ochoterenae	B
Gymnocalycium ochoterenae FR734	Y
Gymnocalycium och. v variispinum	Y
Gymnocalycium oenanthemum	Y
Gymnocalycium ourselianum	DV,Y
Gymnocalycium parvulum	DV
Gymnocalycium pflanzii	B,DV,Y
Gymnocalycium pflanzii v albipulpa	Y
Gymnocalycium pflanzii v eytianum	DV
Gymnocalycium piltziorum	DV
Gymnocalycium platense	DV,Y
Gymnocalycium platygonum	DV
Gymnocalycium proliferum	DV
Gymnocalycium pseudoragonesii	DV
Gymnocalycium pseudostriglianum	DV
Gymnocalycium pungens	B,DV,Y
Gymnocalycium quehlianum	B,DV,Y
Gymnocalycium quelianum v triacanthum	DV
Gymnocalycium ragonesii	B,DV,Y
Gymnocalycium riograndense	B
Gymnocalycium riojense	DV,Y
Gymnocalycium ritterianum	Y
Gymnocalycium saglione	B,DV,Y
Gymnocalycium saglione v albispinum	Y
Gymnocalycium saglione v logispinum	DV
Gymnocalycium saglione v tilcarense	Y
Gymnocalycium schickendantzii	B,BC,DV,Y
Gymnocalycium schickendantzii v. delaetii	Y
Gymnocalycium schroederianum	B,DV
Gymnocalycium schuetzianum	Y
Gymnocalycium sigelianum	DV
Gymnocalycium sp mix	C,CH,Y
Gymnocalycium spegazzini	B,BC,DV,Y
Gymnocalycium speg. v halonius	DV
Gymnocalycium stellatum	B,DV,Y
Gymnocalycium stellatum v albispinum	Y
Gymnocalycium stellatum v cinerium	Y
Gymnocalycium stellatum v kleinianum	DV
Gymnocalycium stellatum v paucispinum	B,DV,Y
Gymnocalycium striglianum	Y
Gymnocalycium stuckertii	B,DV,Y
Gymnocalycium sutterianum	DV,Y
Gymnocalycium tilcarense	BC,DV
Gymnocalycium tillianum	B,Y
Gymnocalycium tudae	B,DV,Y
Gymnocalycium uruguayense	B
Gymnocalycium vallegrandense	Y
Gymnocalycium valnicekianum	B,DV,GC
Gymnocalycium vatteri	B,DV
Gymnocalycium vatteri one-spine form	DV
Gymnocalycium wagnerianum	Y
Gymnocalycium weissianum	B,Y
Gymnocalycium zegarrae	B,DV,Y
Gymnocereus amazonicus	Y
Gymnocladus chinensis	EL,LN,SA

GYMNOCLADUS

Gymnocladus dioica	
A,B,C,FW,HU,LN,SA,SG,VE	
Gynandriris cedarmontana	B,RU,SI
Gynandriris pritzeliana	B,SI
Gynandriris setifolia	AP,B,MN,RU,SC,SI
Gynandriris sisyrinchium	SG
Gynandriris sisyrinchium Coll Ref	MN
Gynandriris sisyrinchium v purpurea CF.	MN
Gynandriris sisyrinchium v purpurea S.F7	MN
Gynandriris sp	RU
Gynura scandens	SG
Gypsophila altissima	B,HP
Gypsophila bicolor	CG,SG
Gypsophila bungeana	VO
Gypsophila cerastioides	AP,B,HP,KL,RM,T,V
Gypsophila elegans	C,FR,HW,J,SG,SK,U,V
Gypsophila elegans 'Carmine & Rose'	T
Gypsophila elegans 'Carminea'	B,BS
Gypsophila elegans 'Colour Blend'	D
Gypsophila elegans 'Covent Garden'	w.a
Gypsophila elegans 'Crimson'	B,DE,L,SE,TE
Gypsophila elegans 'Lady Lace'	B,JO
Gypsophila elegans mix Imp	BD,T
Gypsophila elegans 'Rose Charm'	VH
Gypsophila elegans 'Rosea'	B,BD,BS,BY,CA,CN,DE, F,KI,KS,MO,PI,SG,SK, ST,U
Gypsophila elegans 'Snowflake'	PK
Gypsophila elegans 'White Elephant'	B,D,DT
Gypsophila elegans white giant	BY,DE,T
Gypsophila elegans 'White Monarch'	B,F
Gypsophila fastigiata ssp arenaria	B
Gypsophila 'Kermesina'	C
Gypsophila latifolia alba	SG
Gypsophila muralis	B,CA,CG,DD
Gypsophila muralis 'Garden Bride'	B,BD,BS,CL,MO,SE,SK, T,U,YA
Gypsophila muralis 'Gypsy'	B,BS,F,PK,SK,T,VY
Gypsophila muralis 'Pink Sugar Dot'	B,JO
Gypsophila pacifica	B,BS,C,CA,DE,GO,JE,KI, KS,MO,PK,SA
Gypsophila pacifica 'Rose'	U
Gypsophila paniculata	AB,AP,B,BS,C,CO,CP, DD,DI,G,JE,KI,KS,L,LN, MO,PI,PK,S,SA,SG,ST, SU,T,TH
Gypsophila paniculata dbl	DT,GO,KS,L,M,S,SK
Gypsophila paniculata 'Diamond Spray'	U
Gypsophila paniculata 'Flocon De Neige'	B,BH,BS,BY,C,CL,CN, D,DE,F,HP,JE,JO,MO, PI,PK,SE,T,V,VY
Gypsophila paniculata 'Perfecta'	PK
Gypsophila paniculata 'Virgo'	B
Gypsophila paniculata 'White Delight'	BS
Gypsophila patrinii	SG
Gypsophila petraea	KL
Gypsophila repens	AP,B,BS,C,CG,G,JE,KL, SC,SG,SK,V
Gypsophila repens alba	B,BD,BS,CL,CN,HU,MO, SA
Gypsophila repens 'Rosea'	AP,B,BD,BS,C,CL,CN, HP,HU,JE,L,MO,PI,SA,T
Gypsophila silenoides	T
Gypsophila 'Snow Fountain'	F,SK
Gypsophila tenuifolia	AP,SC
Gypsophila tenuifolia v gracilipes	B
Gyrocarpus americanus	B,NI,WA
Gyrostemon ramulosus	B,NI
Gysophila petraea	KL
Haageocereus acranthus	DV
Haageocereus albispinus	DV
Haageocereus aureispinus	DV,Y
Haageocereus chosicensis	Y
Haageocereus chrysacanthus	DV,Y
Haageocereus fortalazensis	DV
Haageocereus lachayensis	B
Haageocereus olowinskianus	Y
Haageocereus pachystele	DV
Haageocereus pectinatus	DV
Haageocereus pluriflorus	DV
Haageocereus pseudoacranthus	DV,Y
Haageocereus pseudomelanostele	DV
Haageocereus salmonoides	DV
Haageocereus sp mix	C
Haageocereus subtilispina	Y
Haageocereus versicolor	Y
Haastia recurva	B,SS
Haastia sinclairii	B,SS
Haberlea rhodopensis	AP,B,G,JE,KL,PA,SC
Hablitzia tamnoides	B,C
Habranthus andersonii see H.tubispathus	
Habranthus 'Argentine Pink'	C
Habranthus gracilifolius	AP,B,I,LG,MN,SC
Habranthus robustus	AP,B,G,LG,MN,SG
Habranthus tubispathus	AP,B,C,CG,G,I,LG,MN, NG,PM,SC,SG
Habranthus tubispathus cupreus	AP
Habranthus tubispathus Cutler 4/41	MN
Habranthus verecunda	I
Hackelia floribunda	G,SG
Hacquetia epipactis	AP,B,HP,SC
Haemanthus albiflos	B,CF,RU,SG
Haemanthus amarylloides	B
Haemanthus coccineus	B,CF,RU
Haemanthus humilis ssp humilis	B,RU
Haemanthus pubescens v leipoldtii	RU
Haemanthus pubescens v pubescens	RU
Haemanthus sanguineus	B,RU
Haemanthus sp	RU
Haematoxylum brasiletto	B
Haematoxylum campechianum	B
Haemodorum laxum	B,NI,SA
Haemodorum paniculatum	B,NI
Haemodorum planifolium	AU,HA
Haemodorum simplex	B,NI
Haemodorum spicatum	B,NI
Hakea adnata	B,NI,O
Hakea amplexicaulis	B,NI,O
Hakea angustifolia	B
Hakea arborescens	B,NI,O
Hakea bakeriana	HA
Hakea baxteri	B,O
Hakea brachyptera	B,NI,O
Hakea brooksiana	B,NI,O
Hakea brownii	B,NI
Hakea bucculenta	AU,B,C,EL,NI,O,SA
Hakea ceratophylla	B,NI,O
Hakea cinerea	B,NI,O
Hakea clavata	B,NI,O
Hakea commutata	B,NI,O
Hakea conchifolia	B,O
Hakea coriacea	B,NI,O

HAKEA

Hakea corymbosa	B,NI,O
Hakea costata	B,NI,O
Hakea crassifolia	B,NI,O
Hakea cucullata	B,NI,O
Hakea cyclocarpa	B,NI,O
Hakea cycloptera	NI,O
Hakea dactyloides	B,EL,HA,NI,O
Hakea decurrens	B,NI,O
Hakea elliptica	B,NI,O
Hakea epiglottis	B,NI,O
Hakea erecta	B,NI,O
Hakea eriantha	B,HA,NI,O
Hakea erinacea	B,NI,O
Hakea eyreana	B,NI,O
Hakea ferruginea	B,NI,O
Hakea flabellifolia	B,NI,O
Hakea florulenta	B,NI,O
Hakea francisiana	B,EL,NI,O
Hakea gibbosa	B,EL,HA,NI,O,SA
Hakea gilbertii	B,NI
Hakea grammatophylla	B,HA,NI,O
Hakea incrassata	B,NI,O
Hakea invaginata	B,NI
Hakea lasianthoides	B,NI
Hakea laurina	AU,B,CA,EL,HA,NI,O, SA,VE
Hakea lehmanniana	B,NI,O
Hakea leucoptera	B,EL,HA,NI,O
Hakea lissocarpha	B,NI,O
Hakea lissosperma	AP,AU,B,EL,HA,NI,O,SA
Hakea lorea	B,O
Hakea macraeana	O
Hakea macrocarpa	B,NI
Hakea meisnerana	B,NI
Hakea microcarpa	AU,B,HA,O
Hakea minyma	B,NI,O
Hakea multilineata	B,EL,NI,O
Hakea neurophylla	B,NI,O
Hakea nitida	B,NI,O
Hakea nodosa	O
Hakea obliqua	B,NI,O
Hakea obliqua v brooksiana	B
Hakea obtusa	B,NI,O
Hakea oldfieldii	B,NI
Hakea oleifolia	B,NI
Hakea orthorrhyncha	B,EL,NI,O
Hakea pandanicarpa	B,NI,O
Hakea petiolaris	B,NI,O
Hakea platysperma	B,EL,NI,O
Hakea plurinervia	B,NI,O
Hakea preissii	B,NI,O
Hakea prostrata	B,NI,O
Hakea purpurea	B,HA,O
Hakea pycnoneura	B,NI,O
Hakea recurva	B,NI,O
Hakea rostrata	B,NI,O
Hakea ruscifolia	B,NI
Hakea salicifolia	B,C,HA,NI,O,SA,VE
Hakea saligna	WA
Hakea scoparia	B,NI,O
Hakea sericea see H.lissosperma	
Hakea smilacifolia	B,NI,O
Hakea sp mix	C
Hakea stenocarpa	B,NI,O
Hakea stenophylla	B
Hakea strumosa	B,NI,O

Hakea suaveolens	B,CA,HA,NI,O,VE
Hakea sulcata	B,NI,O
Hakea teretifolia	B,EL,HA,NI,O
Hakea teretifolia r-v	EL,HA
Hakea trifurcata	B,NI,O
Hakea ulicina	B,NI,O
Hakea undulata	B,EL,NI,O
Hakea varia	B,NI,O
Hakea varia v florida	B
Hakea verrucosa	B,NI,O
Hakea victoriae	AU,B,EL,NI,O
Haleria corniculata	AP,P
Halesia carolina	B,C,CG,FW,LN,SA,VE
Halesia diptera	B,LN,SA
Halesia monticola	B,FW,N,SA
Halesia monticola f rosea	B
Halesia monticola v vestita	HP
Halgania argyrophylla	B
Halgania cyanea	B,NI
Halimium atriplicifolium	SA,SZ
Halimium lasianthum	CG
Halimium ocymoides	SA,SG
Halimodendron halodendron	LN,SA
Halleria elliptica	B,SI
Halleria lucida	B,KB,SI
Halmoorea trispatha	B
Haloragis erecta	B
Haloragis erecta 'Wellington Bronze'	B,C,P
Haloragodendron glandulosum	B,NI
Halosarcia pergranulata	B,NI
Haloxylon ammodendron	B,LN
Haloxylon persicum	B,DD,LN
Hamamelis japonica	B,C,FW,LN,SA,T
Hamamelis japonica arborea	N,SG
Hamamelis mollis	B,C,CA,FW,G,LN,SA,VE
Hamamelis mollis 'Pallida'	G,N
Hamamelis vernalis	B,FW,LN,SA
Hamamelis virginiana	A,B,C,CA,CG,EL,FW,LN, NO,SA,VE
Hamamelis x intermedia	B,N
Hamatocactus harnatacanthus see Ferocactus	
Hamatocactus setispinus see Thelocactus	
Hamatocactus sinuatus	B,Y
Hamelia patens	B,EL,SA
Hannonia hesperidum	AR,B
Hannonia hesperidum S.F.273 Morocco	MN
Haplocarpha scaposa	B,SC,SI
Haplopappus brandegii see Erigeron aureus	
Haplopappus glutinosus	AP,G,HP,I,SC,SG
Haplopappus juncifolius	KL
Haplopappus linearifolius	B
Haplopappus lyallii see Tonestus	
Haplopappus pinifolius	B
Haplopappus RB 94063	I
Haplopappus rehderii	AP,B,HP
Haplophytum crooksii	B,SW
Hardenbergia comptoniana	AP,B,C,DI,EL,HU,NI,O, RS,SA,SC,V,VE
Hardenbergia violacea	AP,B,EL,HA,NI,O,SA,SH, T,VE
Hardenbergia violacea 'White Crystal'	B,HA
Hardwickia binata	B
Harpagophytum procumbens	B,SI
Harpagophytum zeyheri	B,SI
Harpephyllum caffrum	B,C,CA,CL,EL,HA,O,SA, SI,WA

HARPULLIA

Harpullia pendula	B,EL,HA,O,SA
Harrimaniella see Cassiope	
Harrisia bonplandii	B,BC,DVY
Harrisia brookii	B
Harrisia eriophora	B
Harrisia guelichii	DV
Harrisia jusbertii	Y
Harrisia martinii	DV
Harrisia pomanensis	B,DV
Hartogiella schinoides	B,SI
Harungana madagascariensis	B,SI
Haworthia angolensis	B,SI
Haworthia arachnoidea	B
Haworthia attenuata	B,SI
Haworthia bolusii	B,SI
Haworthia comptoniana	B,SI
Haworthia decipiens	B
Haworthia emelyae	B,SI
Haworthia emelyae v multifolia	B
Haworthia herbacea	SI
Haworthia koelmaniorum	B,SI
Haworthia longiana	SI
Haworthia maughanii	B,DV
Haworthia mutica	B,SI
Haworthia nigra	SI
Haworthia pappilosa	DV
Haworthia pumila	B,CH,DV,SI,Y
Haworthia pygmeae	B,SI
Haworthia reinwardtii v olivaceae	DV
Haworthia reticulata v reticulata	B,SI
Haworthia retusa	B,SI
Haworthia sp mix	C,Y
Haworthia truncata	B,CH,DV
Haworthia unicolor	DV
Haworthia xiphiophylla	B,SI
Hebe acutiflora	CG
Hebe albicans	AP,B,SG
Hebe allanii	B,C
Hebe amplexicaulis	B,SS
Hebe barkeri	B
Hebe 'Bowles Variety'	HP
Hebe 'Brill Blue'	HP
Hebe buchananii	B
Hebe canterburiensis	B,SS
Hebe 'Carl Teschner' see H.'Youngii'	
Hebe chathamica	B,SS
Hebe ciliolata	B,SS
Hebe coarctata	B,SS
Hebe cupressoides	B,SS
Hebe dieffenbachii	B,SS
Hebe epacridea	B,C,SS
Hebe haastii	B,SS
Hebe hectoris	B
Hebe hulkeana	AP,B,C,SA,SC,SS
Hebe lavaudiana	C
Hebe lyallii see Parahebe	SG
Hebe lycopodioides	B,G,SS
Hebe macrantha	AP,B,SS
Hebe ochracea	B,SS
Hebe odora	B,SC,SS
Hebe pimeleoides	B,SG,SS
Hebe pimelioides v 'Glaucocaerulea'	B,SS
Hebe pimelioides v minor	B,SS
Hebe pinguifolia	B,SS
Hebe raoulii	AP,SA,SC,SS
Hebe raoulii v raoulii	B
Hebe rauolii v macgaskillii	B,C
Hebe recurva	B,SA,SS
Hebe salicifolia	B,LG
Hebe sp mix	B
Hebe speciosa	B,C,SA
Hebe stricta	SA
Hebe stricta v stricta	B
Hebe subalpina	B,SG,SS
Hebe tetrasticha	B,SS
Hebe topiaria	B,SS
Hebe toriganii	CG
Hebe traversii	B,SG,SS
Hebe vernicosa	B,SS
Hebe 'Youngii'	AP,HP
Hebenstretia comosa	B,SI
Hebenstretia comosa 'Attraction'	B,HU,V
Hebenstretia dentata	B,C,SI
Hebenstretia dura	B,SI
Hebenstretia fastigiosa	B,SI
Hebenstretia sp	SI
Hectorella caespitosa	B,SS
Hedeoma nana	B,DD
Hedeoma pulegioides	B,C,CP
Hedera colchica	SG
Hedera helix	B,LN,SA,VE
Hedera helix ssp poetarum	C,NG
Hedera hibernica	SA
Hedycarya arborea	B
Hedychium coccineum	B
Hedychium coccineum v aurantiacum	B
Hedychium coronarium	B
Hedychium flavescens	B,EL,SA
Hedychium flavum	B
Hedychium gardneranum	B,HP,SG
Hedychium horsfieldii	SG
Hedychium mix	BS
Hedychium roxburghii	B,EL
Hedychium sp	SG,V
Hedychium spicatum	B
Hedyotis crouchiana	B,NI
Hedysarum alpinum	SG
Hedysarum arcticum	SG
Hedysarum boreale	NO
Hedysarum boreale ssp mackenzii	SG
Hedysarum boreale v boreale	SG
Hedysarum boutignyanum	B
Hedysarum caucasicum	VO
Hedysarum consanguineum	SG
Hedysarum coronarium	AP,B,BS,C,HP,HU,KI,SA, T,TH,V
Hedysarum ferganense	SG
Hedysarum flavescens	SG,VO
Hedysarum hedysaroides	AP,B,JE,KL,SA
Hedysarum neglectum	SG
Hedysarum obscurum	C
Hedysarum occidentale	NO
Hedyscepe canterburyana	B,EL,O
Hegemone lilacina	VO
Heimia myrtifolia	B,EL
Heimia salicifolia	B,C,CP,DD,HU,I
Helenium amarum	B,T
Helenium amarum 'Sunny Boy'	B
Helenium autumnale	B,BS,CN,DE,DT,F,G,HP, JE,PR,SC,SG,TH
Helenium autumnale hybrids new	B,JE
Helenium autumnale 'Praecox'	B,JE

HELENIUM

Helenium autumnale Sunshine Hybrid	T
Helenium bigelovii	B,SA
Helenium flexuosum	B
Helenium hoopesii	AP,B,BD,BS,C,CL,CN, CO,DE,HP,JE,KI,MO,SA, SG,ST
Helenium puberulum	SZ
Helenium 'Rotgold'	B,BD,BY,C,CL,D,HU, JE,JO,L,MO,SA
Heliabravoa chende	DV,Y
Helianthella quinquenervis	B,HP,JE
Helianthella uniflora	C,NO
Helianthemum apenninum	B,C,CG,G,JE,SA,SG
Helianthemum apenninum v roseum	B,CG,SG
Helianthemum canadense	B
Helianthemum canum	AP,B,RS,SC
Helianthemum canum ssp baleanum	KL
Helianthemum caput-felis	CG
Helianthemum Choice mix	SU
Helianthemum Crown mix	KI
Helianthemum grandiflorum	SG
Helianthemum hybridum	B,T
Helianthemum mix	BS,HP,I,MO,S
Helianthemum mix rock gdn	CL
Helianthemum numm. ssp obscurum	CG
Helianthemum nummalarium Sunshine	F
Helianthemum nummularium	B,BS,BY,C,CG,CN,D,G, HP,J,JE,PO,SA,ST,U,V
Helianthemum nummularium hybrids new	B
Helianthemum nummularium mutabile	DE,DV,HU,JE,L,SK
Helianthemum n. 'Rhodanthe Carneum'	HP
Helianthemum numm. ssp grandiflorum	B,JE,KL
Helianthemum nuttallii	SG
Helianthemum oelandicum ssp alpestre	AP,B,JE
Helianthemum ovatum see H.nummalarium ssp obscurum	
Helianthemum pilosus	B
Helianthemum salicifolius	B
Helianthemum scoparium	B,SW
Helianthemum scoparium v aldersonii	B
Helianthemum sp	KL
Helianthemum stipulatum	B
Helianthocereus antezanae	DV,Y
Helianthocereus bertramianus	DV,Y
Helianthocereus crassicaulis	Y
Helianthocereus escayachensis	DV,Y
Helianthocereus grandiflorus	DV,Y
Helianthocereus herzogianus	DV,Y
Helianthocereus huascha	Y
Helianthocereus narvaecensis	Y
Helianthocereus orurensis	Y
Helianthocereus pasacana	Y
Helianthocereus poco	DV,Y
Helianthocereus poco v fricianus	DV,Y
Helianthocereus randallii	DV,Y
Helianthus angustifolius	B,JE
Helianthus angustifolius divaricatus mix	HU
Helianthus annuus	AB,AV,B,C,HW,PR,SG, TH
Helianthus annuus 'African Sunset'	SE
Helianthus annuus 'Apache Brown Striped'	B
Helianthus annuus 'Autumn Beauty'	AB,B,C,DE,FR,GO,HU ,J,JO,KS,PI,VY
Helianthus annuus 'Big Smile' dw	B,BS,CO,D,JO,MO,PL, SE,SK,TE
Helianthus annuus 'Discovery' mix	SD
Helianthus annuus Dwarf	B,DD

Helianthus annuus 'Evening Sun'	AB,B,C,DI,HU,KS,SD,TE
Helianthus annuus f1 'Full Sun' pollenless	B
Helianthus annuus f1 'Moonbright'	BS,CA,JO,MO,PI,VY
Helianthus annuus f1 'Sunbeam'	Bs,CA,DE,DI,JO,KS,MO, SK,T,V
Helianthus annuus f1 'Sunbright'	B,BS,CA,DE,L,JO,MO, TE,VY,
Helianthus annuus f1 'Sunrich Lemon'	JO,SK,VY
Helianthus annuus f1 'Sunrich Orange'	BS,JO,SK
Helianthus annuus f1 'Sunspot'	BD,BS,C,CL,KS,MO,PK, SE,SK,T,VY
Helianthus annuus 'Floristan'	B,BD,BS,C,KS,L,MO,PI, PK,PL,TE,VY
Helianthus annuus 'Full Sun'	S
Helianthus annuus 'Giant Single'	B,BD,BS,BY,C,CO,D,DE, DT,F,J,KI,KS,L,M,MO, PK,S,ST,T,TE,TU,U,V, VH,VY
Helianthus annuus 'Gloriosa'	SD
Helianthus annuus 'Gloriosa Red'	AB,B
Helianthus annuus 'Gold Bouquet'	M
Helianthus annuus 'Gold & Silver'	F
Helianthus annuus 'Hallo'	B,KS
Helianthus annuus 'Havasupai Striped'	B
Helianthus annuus 'Henry Wilde'	B,C,DE,KS
Helianthus annuus 'Holiday'	B,BS,C,FR,JO,KS
Helianthus annuus 'Hopi Black Dye'	B
Helianthus annuus 'Incredible' dw	B,BS,DE,F,KI,ST,V
Helianthus annuus 'Israeli Single'	SD
Helianthus annuus 'Lemon Moon'	B,V
Helianthus annuus 'Lemon Queen'	DI,F,JO
Helianthus annuus lg fl mix	PK
Helianthus annuus 'Mammoth Grey Stripe'	BU,DE,DN,PI
Helianthus annuus 'Mammoth Russian'	C,DI,JO,SD,SK,VY
Helianthus annuus 'Mane Golden'	B,DD,SD
Helianthus annuus 'Mane Yellow'	B,DD
Helianthus annuus mix	DT,PK,PL,SK,SP
Helianthus annuus 'Moonwalker'	B,BS,SE,T,V
Helianthus annuus 'Music Box'	BD,BS,C,D,HU,J,KI,KS, M,MO,PI,SP,T,TE,TU, U,VH
Helianthus annuus 'Orange Double'	BS
Helianthus annuus 'Orange Sun'	B,T
Helianthus annuus 'Oranges and Lemons'	DI
Helianthus annuus 'Pacino'	B,BS,C,F,JO,MO,PL,TE, U,VY
Helianthus annuus 'Pastiche'	C,SE,T,VH
Helianthus annuus 'Piccolo'	PK
Helianthus annuus 'Prado Red'	B,BD,T,TE,V
Helianthus annuus 'Prado Yellow'	B,BD,T
Helianthus annuus 'Primrose'	PI
Helianthus annuus 'Red Sun'	B,HU,SE,TE
Helianthus annuus 'Sole d'Oro'	PI
Helianthus annuus 'Sonja'	B,BD,BS,C,CA,DT,F,HU, JO,KS,MO,PI,PK,SK,VY
Helianthus annuus 'Stars'	U
Helianthus annuus 'Stella'	B,DT
Helianthus annuus 'Summer Days'	F
Helianthus annuus 'Sunburst'	F,S,T
Helianthus annuus 'Suncross'	DI
Helianthus annuus 'Sungold'	B,BS,BY,C,DE,F,JO,KS, L,PK,TE,V,VY
Helianthus annuus 'Sunray Yellow'	PL
Helianthus annuus 'Sunshine'	SD
Helianthus annuus 'Taiyo'	B,C,DE,HU,T,U,VH
Helianthus annuus 'Tarahumara White'	B,SD

HELIANTHUS

Helianthus annuus 'Teddy Bear' dw	B,BD,BS,C,CL,DN,DT, F,K,MO,PK,SK,ST,TE,U, VY
Helianthus annuus 'The Sun'	B
Helianthus annuus 'Tiger's Eye' mix	SD
Helianthus annuus 'Titan'	F
Helianthus annuus 'Tohoku Yae'	JO
Helianthus annuus 'Valentine'	B,BD,BS,HU,J,JO,KS, L,MO,PK,SE,T,TE
Helianthus annuus 'Velvet Queen'	B,C,F,JO,KS,SE,T,VY
Helianthus annuus 'Velvet Tapestry'	PK,SE
Helianthus annuus 'Zebulon'	B
Helianthus argophyllus	B,DD
Helianthus atrorubens	B,NT
Helianthus debilis	C,KS
Helianthus debilis 'Italian White'	B,DE,JO,PK,T,V
Helianthus debilis miniature mix	DE
Helianthus debilis 'Piccolo'	KS
Helianthus debilis ssp cucumerifolius	BS,CO,V
Helianthus debilis 'Vanilla Ice'	B,BD,BS,C,CO,DE,HU, MO,PI,SE
Helianthus divaricatus	JE
Helianthus 'Endurance'	SD
Helianthus giganteus	B
Helianthus 'Golden Hedge'	BS
Helianthus grosse-serratus	B,PR
Helianthus hirsuta	B,PR
Helianthus maximiliani	AV,B,C,HU,JE,JO,NO, PK,PR,SA,SD
Helianthus mix	SP
Helianthus mollis	B,JE,PR
Helianthus nuttalii	B,C,HU,JE
Helianthus occidentalis	B,JE,PR
Helianthus simulans	NT
Helianthus strumosus	B,JE
Helianthus x laetiflorus	B,C,JE,PR
Helianthus yellow dbl	FR
Helichrysum adenocarpum	B,SI
Helichrysum albidum	O
Helichrysum allioides	B,SI
Helichrysum appendiculatum	B,SI
Helichrysum arenarium	B,C,JE,KL,SA,SG
Helichrysum argyrosphaerum	SI
Helichrysum aureonitens	B,SI
Helichrysum aureum ssp aureum	B,SI
Helichrysum basalticum	AP,B,RM
Helichrysum bellidioides	AP,B,PM,SC,SS
Helichrysum bellidioides prostratum	SG
Helichrysum bellum	B,G,PM,RM
Helichrysum bracteatum see Bracteantha bracteata	
Helichrysum cassinianum	BS,KI,HI,PK,T
Helichrysum cassinianum 'Gabriele'	C
Helichrysum cassinianum 'Pink Bedder'	U
Helichrysum cassinianum 'Rose Beauty'	BD,BS,J,KS,MO
Helichrysum cassinianum 'Tanner's Pride'	BS,MO,T
Helichrysum confertifolium	B,SI
Helichrysum cooperi	B,SI
Helichrysum dasyanthum	B,C,KB,SI
Helichrysum davenportii	C,NI
Helichrysum dendroidum	HA
Helichrysum depressum	B,SS
Helichrysum diosmifolium see Ozothamnus diosmifolius	
Helichrysum felinum	B,SI
Helichrysum filicaule	B,SS
Helichrysum foetidum	B,SI
Helichrysum glomeratum see H. aggregatum	

Helichrysum grandiflorum	B,SI
Helichrysum heldreichii	AP,I
Helichrysum herbaceum	B,SI
Helichrysum hookeri see Ozothamnus	
Helichrysum italicum	AP,B,C,G,JE
Helichrysum lepidophyllum	CG,NI,O
Helichrysum leucopsideum	B,NI
Helichrysum lindleyii	B,O
Helichrysum marginatum	B,SI
Helichrysum milfordae	AP,G,I,SC
Helichrysum nitens	B,SI
Helichrysum orientale	I,SG
Helichrysum pandurifolium	B,SI
Helichrysum petiolare	B,HP,SI
Helichrysum petiolare 'Limelight'	B
Helichrysum petiolare 'Variegatum'	B
Helichrysum podolepideum	C,NI
Helichrysum scorpioides	AP,HP,SG,O
Helichrysum semipapposum	B,NI,O
Helichrysum sessiloides	I,KL,SC
Helichrysum setosum	C,T
Helichrysum sibthorpii	AP,I,KL,SC
Helichrysum sp	SC,SI,T
Helichrysum splendidum	SC
Helichrysum stoechas	B,C
Helichrysum subulifolium	AU,C,D,NI,U
Helichrysum subulifolium 'Golden Sun'	B,BS,J,MO,PK,T
Helichrysum 'Summer Solstice'	T
Helichrysum sutherlandii	B,SI
Helichrysum thianschanicum	G,HP,SA,SC
Helichrysum thianschanicum 'Goldkind'	B,BS,C,CL,D,JE,KI,MO, U,V
Helichrysum 'Tom Thumb' mix	J
Helichrysum trilineatum	B,SI
Helichrysum umbraculigerum	B,SI
Heliconia aemygdiana ssp transandina	B
Heliconia bihai	B,CA
Heliconia bourgaeana	B
Heliconia caribaea	B
Heliconia chartacea	B
Heliconia longiflora	B
Heliconia platystachys	B
Heliconia schiedeana	B,CA
Heliconia sclerotricha	B
Heliconia stricta 'Dwarf Jamaican'	B
Heliconia wagnerana	B,RE,SA
Helicteres isora	B,EL
Helictotrichon sempervirens	B,G,HP,JE,SA
Helinus integrifolius	B,SI
Helionopsis orientalis	C
Heliophila carnosa	B,SI
Heliophila coronopifolia	KB
Heliophila longifolia	AP,B,C,SI
Heliophila longifolia 'Atlantis'	B
Heliophila longifolia 'Blue Bird'	B,F
Heliophila longifolia 'Mediterranean Blue'	V
Heliophila rigidiuscula	B,SI
Heliophila scoparia	B,SI
Heliophila sp	SI
Heliopsis helianthoides	B,JE,PI,PR,SG
Heliopsis helianthoides v scabra	HP
Heliopsis hel. v scabra New Hybrids mix	C,JE
Heliopsis hel. v scabra 'Sommersonne'	B,BS,C,CL,D,DE,HP,HU, JE,KI,KS,L,MO,SK,V
Heliopsis mix border vars	T
Heliopsis orientalis flavida	SA

HELIOPSIS

Heliopsis scabra	HU,SA
Heliopsis scabra 'Goldspitz'	T
Heliotropium arborescens	B,CN,DI,HU,TH,TU,V
Heliotropium arborescens 'Marine'	B,BD,BS,BY,C,CL,DE,
	F,HU,J,JO,KI,L,MO,PI,
	PL,S,SK,T,YA
Heliotropium arborescens 'Mini-Marine'	B,BS,D,MO,PK,T
Heliotropium europaeum	B,CG
Heliotropium f1 'Blue Wonder'	BS
Heliotropium indicum	B
Heliotropium mix finest	C
Heliotropium paniculatum	B,HU,NI
Heliotropium 'Regale' mix	BS,CO,DE,KI
Heliotropum europaeum	B
Helipterum argyropsis	B
Helipterum muelleri 'Snowflake'	B
Helipterum sandfordii	B,BS,J,KI,KS,MO,SU
Helipterum stipitatum	HA,NI,O
Helleborus abchasicus WM9611	NG
Helleborus argutifolius	AP,AR,AS,B,BS,BY,C,C
	G,CT,F,G,HP,I,JE,KL,LG,
	PL,PH,RH,SA,SC,SG,W
Helleborus argutifolius (V)	AS
Helleborus Ashwood garden hyb	AP,AS
Helleborus atrorubens	AR,AS,NG,PH
Helleborus atrorubens f cupreus	B
Helleborus bocconei	C
Helleborus corsicus see H.argutifolius	
Helleborus croaticus	AR,B,JE,PH,SA
Helleborus croaticus WM9731	AS,NG
Helleborus cyclophyllus	AP,B,C,CT,HP,JE,NG,PH,
	SA,T
Helleborus dumetorum	AP,AR,B,C,JE,PH
Helleborus dumetorum Coll Ref WM	NG
Helleborus dumetorum Cool Ref WM	AS
Helleborus dumetorum ssp atrorubens	B,JE,SC
Helleborus ex 'Andromeda'	AR
Helleborus ex 'Cassandra'	AR
Helleborus ex 'Cosmos'	AR
Helleborus ex 'Electra'	AR
Helleborus ex guttatus hyb	AR
Helleborus ex 'Inca'	AR
Helleborus ex 'Katinka'	AR
Helleborus ex 'Orion'	AR
Helleborus ex 'Sirius'	AR
Helleborus ex 'Titania'	AR
Helleborus ex 'Zodiac' hyb	AR
Helleborus ex 'Zuleika'	AR
Helleborus foetidus	AP,B,BS,C,CG,CT,G,HP,
	JE,KL,MN,PH,PL,PO,
	SA,SC,SG,T,W
Helleborus foetidus Bowles Cabbage Stalk	NG
Helleborus foetidus England	MN
Helleborus foetidus 'Gertrude Jekyll'	HP,NG,PH
Helleborus foetidus 'Gold Leaf'	NG
Helleborus foetidus 'Pontarlier'	PH
Helleborus foetidus 'Ruth'	AR,NG,PH
Helleborus foetidus 'Sienna'	AR,NG,PH
Helleborus foetidus 'Sopron'	AP,AR,CT,NG,PH
Helleborus foetidus 'Tros-os-Montes'	PH
Helleborus foetidus (v)	PH
Helleborus foetidus 'Wester Flisk'	AP,AR,AS,B,C,CT,HP,
	JE,PH,SC
Helleborus guttatus	CG,SC
Helleborus lividus	AP,AR,B,C,HP,MN,PH
Helleborus lividus Majorca	AS
Helleborus mix winter fl. imp	T
Helleborus multifidus	AR,C,JE,KL,SA
Helleborus multifidus ssp bocconei	AP,AR,AS,NG
Helleborus multifidus ssp bocconei lt	PH
Helleborus multifidus ssp hercegovinus	PH
Helleborus multifidus ssp istriacus	AR,AS,NG,PH
Helleborus multifidus ssp multifidus	AS,B,NG,PH
Helleborus niger	w.a.
Helleborus niger 'Grandiflorus'	B
Helleborus niger 'Maximus'	B,JE
Helleborus niger ssp macranthus	B,C,JE,SA
Helleborus niger ssp macranthus 'Roseus'	B,C,JE,SA
Helleborus niger 'Sunrise' Coll Ref WM	AS,NG,PH
Helleborus niger 'Sunset'	PH
Helleborus odoratus Ukraine	NG
Helleborus odoratus WM9643	NG
Helleborus odorus	AP,AR,AS,B,C,CG,F,
	JE,KL,PH
Helleborus orientalis h	AP,AR,AS,B,BS,C,G,HP,
	JE,KL,MA,SA,SC,SE,T
Helleborus orientalis h 'Amethyst'	NG
Helleborus orientalis h best picotees	NG
Helleborus orientalis h clear colours	CT
Helleborus orientalis h dark	AR,PH
Helleborus orientalis h 'Eric's Best'	NG
Helleborus orientalis h 'Good Blue'	C
Helleborus orientalis h 'Helen Ballard' mix	AP,P,PH
Helleborus orientalis h mix	AP,AR,PL
Helleborus orientalis h Netta's Famous	NG
Helleborus orientalis h Netta's Pink	NG
Helleborus orientalis h new hybrids	B,JE
Helleborus orientalis h s-c	B,C,CT,JD,JE,NG,PH
Helleborus orientalis h selected forms	P
Helleborus orientalis h Spot,Speck,Picotee	AR,CT,PH
Helleborus orientalis h ssp guttatus	AP,AR,B,JD,SC,T
Helleborus orientalis h ssp orientalis	JE
Helleborus orientalis h Stripey Child	NG
Helleborus orientalis h 'Sylvia'	NG
Helleborus orientalis h Unspotted	PH
Helleborus orientalis h 'Ushba'	AP,KL,NG
Helleborus orientalis h Very Best mix	NG
Helleborus orientalis h white	C,CT,G
Helleborus orientalis h WM9602	NG
Helleborus orientalis ssp abchasicus	AR,B,JD
Helleborus orientalis/caucasicus	NG,PH
Helleborus Pedigree mix	C
Helleborus purpurascens	AP,AR,AS,B,C,F,JE,KL,
	NG,PH,SASC,
Helleborus purpurascens pale gr	NG
Helleborus sp	JD
Helleborus sp fragrant	P
Helleborus sp mix	PA
Helleborus Thoroughbred mix	C
Helleborus torquatus	AP,AR,AS,B,HP,NG,PH
Helleborus torquatus hyb	AR,G
Helleborus torquatus WM9744	NG
Helleborus vesicarius	AR,B,JE,PH
Helleborus viridis	AP,B,C,G,HP,JD,JE,NG,
	PK,SA
Helleborus viridis MS473 Spain	MN
Helleborus viridis ssp occidentalis	B,HP,PH
Helleborus x sternii	AP,B,C,CT,G,HP,JD,JE,
	P,PH
Helleborus x sternii Blackthorn Strain Gr.	AP,AR,AS,HP,SC
Helleborus x sternii 'Boughton Beauty'	AP,AS,C,NG
Heloniopsis orientalis	AR

HELONIOPSIS

Heloniopsis orientalis v flavida	C
Hemerocallis citrina	B,KL,SC
Hemerocallis 'Corky'	HP
Hemerocallis dumortieri	NG,SG
Hemerocallis esculenta	NG
Hemerocallis 'Frans Hals'	HP
Hemerocallis fulva	B,TH
Hemerocallis 'Golden Chimes'	AP,HP
Hemerocallis hyb mix	AP,C,HU,SC
Hemerocallis hybrids new	B,BS,JE
Hemerocallis hybrids new miniature	BS,C,CA,CL,JE,L,MO, OK
Hemerocallis Lilioasphedelus Russ	PH
Hemerocallis lilioasphodelus	AP,B,C,CA,G,HP,JE,SG
Hemerocallis lilioasphodelus minor	SG
Hemerocallis middendorffii v esculenta	SG
Hemerocallis middendorfii	AP,SG
Hemerocallis middendorfii v exaltata	B,JE
Hemerocallis minor	B,G,SG
Hemerocallis mix novelties	BS,CA,CL,F,MO
Hemerocallis Park's Economy mix	PK
Hemerocallis Saxton's Tetraploid Hybrids	PK
Hemerocallis 'Stella d'Oro'	HP
Hemerocallis 'Summer Trumpets'	U
Hemerocallis thunbergii	KL
Hemerocallis 'Whichford'	E
Hemerocallis yezoensis	SA
Hemiandra pungens	B,NI,SA
Hemidesmus indicus	B
Hemigenia eutaxoides	AU
Hemigenia pritzelii	B,NI
Hemigenia ramosissima	B,NI
Hemigenia sericea	B,NI
Hemionitis arifolia	B
Hemiphragma heterophyllum	SG
Hemispherica 'Helani Tulip Ginger'	B
Hemitelia smithii	C
Hemizygia canescens	B,BH,SI
Hemizygia obermeyerii	B,BH,SI
Hemizygia sp	B,SI
Hemizygia transvaalensis	BH,SI
Hepatica nobilis	AP,B,C,CG,G,SC,SG
Heracleum dissectum	SG
Heracleum lanatum	HU,JE,SG
Heracleum lehmannianum	B,C,HP,JE
Heracleum mantegazzianum	B,I,JE
Heracleum maximum	PR
Heracleum minimum	SC,SG
Heracleum sibiricum	SG
Heracleum sphondylium	B,C,DD,LA,HU,SG
Heracleum sphondylium ssp montanum	B
Heracleum sphondylium v roseum	B,NS
Heracleum stevenii	SG
Herbertia lahue	AP,B,MN
Herbertia lahue ssp amoena	C
Herbertia platensis	AP,C,SC
Herbertia pulchella	AP,LG,SC
Herbertia tigridioides	C
Hereroa fimbriata	B,KB
Hereroa herrei	B
Hereroa hesperantha	B
Hereroa incurva	B,DV
Hereroa muirii	B,SG
Hereroa odoratum	B,C,Y
Hereroa puttkameriana	B,DV
Hereroa sp	SI

Hereroa teretifolia	B,KB
Hereroa uncipetala	B
Hermannia althaeifolia	B,SI
Hermannia disermifolia	B,SI
Hermannia grandiflora	B,SA,SI
Hermannia hyssopifolia	B,SI
Hermannia multiflora	B,SI
Hermannia pinnata	B,SI
Hermannia saccifera	B,C,SA,SI
Hermannia ssp	SI
Hermannia stricta	BH,SA,SI
Hermas villosa	B
Hermbstaedtia glauca	B,SI
Hermodactylus tuberosus	AP,AR,B,RS
Hermodactylus tuberosus B.S348 Italy	MN
Hermodactylus tuberosus Crete	MN
Hermodactylus tuberosus Greece	MN
Herniaria glabra	B,BS,C,CL,CN,JE,MO, SA
Herpolirion novae-zelandiae	B,SS
Herrania pulcherrima	B
Herrea elongata	B
Herreanthus meyeri	DV
Herreanthus meyeri v rex	B,Y
Herschelianthe graminifolia	B,SI
Hesperaloe funifera	B
Hesperaloe parviflora	B,DV,HU,SA,SW
Hesperaloe parviflora 'Rubra'	B,CA
Hesperaloe pavia	B
Hesperantha angusta	B
Hesperantha bachmannii	B,G,KB,RU,SA,SC,SI
Hesperantha baurii	AP,B,SC,SI,SZ
Hesperantha cucullata	AP,B,C,G,RU,SC,SI
Hesperantha erecta	B,RU
Hesperantha falcata	AP,B,G,RU,SC,SI
Hesperantha geminata	B,SI
Hesperantha humilis	B,SI
Hesperantha latifolia	B,KL,RU,SI
Hesperantha luticola	RU
Hesperantha monantha	RU
Hesperantha pauciflora	AP,B,MN,RU,SI
Hesperantha purpurea	RU
Hesperantha rivulicola	B
Hesperantha sp	SC,SI
Hesperantha vaginata	B,C,KB,RU,SA,SI
Hesperantha woodii	B,SI
Hesperis lutea see Sisymbrium luteum	
Hesperis matronalis	w.a.
Hesperis matronalis 'Purpurea'	B,C,CN,DE,JO
Hesperis matronalis v albiflora	AP,B,C,CN,DE,HP,JE, JO,T
Hesperis steviniana	B,C,HP,T
Hesperocallis undulata	B,SW
Hesperocallis undulata dwarf	SW
Hesperochiron pumilus	B,SC,SW
Hessia brevifolia	RU
Hessia chapinii	B
Hessia discifera	B
Hessia dregeana	B
Hessia gemmata	B
Hessia unguiculata	B
Hessia zeyheri	B
Heterodendron oleifolium	B,NI
Heterolepis aliena	B,KB,SA,SI
Heterolepis peduncularis	B,SI
Heteromorpha arborescens	B,BH,SI

HETEROMORPHA

Heteromorpha trifoliata	B,DV,KB,SI
Heteropappus altaicus	AP,B,C,HP,SG
Heteropogon contortus	B
Heteropterys nitida	B
Heteropterys salicifolia	B,EL
Heteropyxis natalensis	B,BH,KB,SI,WA
Heterospathe elata	B,O
Heterospathe philippensis	O
Heterotheca camporum	B,PR
Heterotheca graminifolia	NT
Heterotheca mariana	NT
Heterotheca pumila	RM
Heterotheca rutterii	KL
Heterotheca subaxillaris	B
Heterotheca villosa	AP,B,DD,G,JE,KL,SA,SG
Hetropyxis natalensis	O
Heuchera americana	B,HP,JE,PA
Heuchera americana 'Dale's Strain'	JE
Heuchera 'Autumn Leaves'	P
Heuchera bracteata	AP,SG
Heuchera Bressingham Hybrids	AP,B,BS,C,D,DE,EL,HU, JE,KI,L,MO,PI,PK,SA, SK,T
Heuchera chlorantha	AP,HP,SG
Heuchera cylindrica	AP,B,HP,JE,KL,NO,PA, SA,SC,SG
Heuchera cylindrica 'Greenfinch'	AP,B,C,G,HP,P,PL,T
Heuchera 'Emperor's Cloak'	B,P
Heuchera 'Firefly'	B,BS,C,CL,EL,MO
Heuchera 'Green Ivory'	B,HP
Heuchera hallii	B,KL,RM
Heuchera hartwegii	SG
Heuchera himalayensis	SG
Heuchera hybrida	B
Heuchera micrantha	AB,B,DV,SC
Heuchera micrantha 'Palace'	SA
Heuchera micrantha v diversifolia	SG
Heuchera micrantha v div. 'Purple Palace'	AP,B,BS,C,CL,D,DE,EL, F,G,HP,HU,MO,P,PK,T, U,V
Heuchera mic. v div. 'Purple Palace Select'	JE
Heuchera parvifolia	B
Heuchera pilosa	B,SG
Heuchera 'Pluie De Feu'	B
Heuchera pubescens	B,DV,SG
Heuchera pubescens 'Alba'	HP
Heuchera pulchella	B,RM,SC,T
Heuchera 'Red Spangles'	HP
Heuchera richardsonii	B,JE,PR,SG
Heuchera richardsonii v grayana	DV
Heuchera sanguinea	AB,B,BS,BY,CN,DV,G, HP,HU,S,SG,SW,V
Heuchera sanguinea crimson	SA,SK
Heuchera sanguinea 'Fackel'	SA
Heuchera sanguinea 'Sioux Falls'	B,JE
Heuchera sanguinea 'Splendens'	B,JE
Heuchera sanguinea super Hyb	CL
Heuchera sanguinea 'White Cloud'	B,C,EL,JE
Heuchera 'Titania'	B
Heuchera 'Widar'	B,JE
Heuchera x brizoides	KL
Heuchera x pruhoniciana Dr.Sitar's Hyb	B,C,D,T
Hevea brasiliensis	B
Hewittia sublobata	B
Hexaglottis lewisiae	B,RU
Hexaglottis longifolia	B,SI

Hexalobus crispiflorus	B
Hibbertia amplexicaulis	B,NI,SA
Hibbertia aurea	B
Hibbertia commutata	B,NI
Hibbertia cuneiformis	B,NI
Hibbertia hypericoides	B,NI
Hibbertia lasiopus	B,NI
Hibbertia ovata	B,NI
Hibbertia scandens	B,C,EL,HA,NI,O
Hibbertia serrata	B,NI,SA
Hibbertia vaginata	B,NI
Hibiscadelphus giffardianus	B
Hibiscus acetosella 'Red Shield'	B,HU
Hibiscus 'Baltimore' mix	JE
Hibiscus biseptus	B,SW
Hibiscus calyphyllus	B,SI
Hibiscus cameronii	B
Hibiscus cannabinus	B,C,CG
Hibiscus 'Charles September'	B
Hibiscus coccineus	B,C,CG,EL,HU,JE,SC,SA
Hibiscus 'Cooperi'	B
Hibiscus coulteri	B,RS,SW
Hibiscus denisonii	B
Hibiscus denudatus	RS
Hibiscus denudatus v involucellatus	B,SW
Hibiscus diversifolius	B,C,DV,KB,SI
Hibiscus elatus	B
Hibiscus engleri	B,SI
Hibiscus f1 'Disco Belle' mix	BS,C,CA,CL,DE,DT,JE, MO,PK,T,V
Hibiscus f1 'Disco Belle Pink'	JE,PK
Hibiscus f1 'Disco Belle Red'	B,CA,DE,JE,PK
Hibiscus f1 'Disco Belle White'	B,CA,DE,JE,PK
Hibiscus f1 'Les Belles'	D
Hibiscus f1 'Southern Belle' mix	BD,BS,BY,C,DE,EL,JE, MO,PK,SK
Hibiscus fragilis	B
Hibiscus genevii	B
Hibiscus 'Gina Marie'	B
Hibiscus grandiflora	FS
Hibiscus hamabo	B,EL
Hibiscus 'Harvest Moon'	B
Hibiscus insignus	B,EL
Hibiscus 'Joan Kinchen'	B
Hibiscus lasiocarpos	B
Hibiscus ludwigii	B,EL,SI
Hibiscus makinoi	B
Hibiscus manihot see Abelmoschus	
Hibiscus meersianus	B
Hibiscus militaris	B,C,PR
Hibiscus moscheutos	AP,B,FW,HU
Hibiscus mutabilis	B,C,EL,HU,SA
Hibiscus 'Okinawan'	B
Hibiscus ovalifolius	B
Hibiscus panduriformis	B,C,NI,SA
Hibiscus paramutabilis	B,FW
Hibiscus pedunculatus	B,SI
Hibiscus praeteritus	B,SI
Hibiscus pusillus	B,C,SI
Hibiscus radiatus	B
Hibiscus rockii	B
Hibiscus 'Ross Estey'	B
Hibiscus sabdariffa	B,C,DD,EL
Hibiscus schizopetalus	B
Hibiscus sororius	B
Hibiscus sp	LG,SI

HIBISCUS

Hibiscus surattensis	B
Hibiscus syriacus	A,AP,B,CA,EL,FW,G,HP, HU,LN,N,SA,VE
Hibiscus syriacus v album	B,C,SA
Hibiscus syriacus 'Woodbridge'	C
Hibiscus taiwanensis	B,EL
Hibiscus tiliaceus	B,CA,EL,HA,NI,O,SA, SI,WA
Hibiscus trionum	AP,B,C,DD,DE,EL,G,HP, KL,NI,RS,SA,SI,SZ,W
Hibiscus trionum 'Simply Love'	B,BD,BS,C,MO,PK,T
Hibiscus trionum 'Sunnyday'	AP,B,T
Hibiscus trionum 'Vanilla Ice'	AP,U,V
Hibiscus vitifolius	B
Hicksbeachia pinnatifolia	B
Hieracium albiflorum	B,HU
Hieracium alpinum	AP,B,JE,SG
Hieracium amplexicaule	RH
Hieracium argenteum	SG
Hieracium aurantiacum see Pilosella aurantiaca	
Hieracium bombycinum see H.mixtum	
Hieracium bupleuroides	SG
Hieracium canadense	B,PR
Hieracium chondrillifolium	B,G,JE
Hieracium intybaceum	B,G,JE
Hieracium islandicum	HP
Hieracium korschynskyi	SG
Hieracium lanatum	AP,B,C,G,HP,RH,SC,SG
Hieracium longipilum	B,PR
Hieracium maculatum	AP,HP,I,PM,RH,SC
Hieracium maculatum 'Leopard'	B,G,JE,SA
Hieracium mixtum	AP,HP,JE,SC,SG
Hieracium murorum	KL
Hieracium pilosella see Pilosella officinarum	
Hieracium prenanthoides	SG
Hieracium ssp	LA
Hieracium tomentosum	JE
Hieracium umbellatum	B,JE,SG
Hieracium villosum	AP,B,C,G,HP,I,JE,KL,SA, SC,SG,V
Hieracium vulgatum	B
Hieracium waldsteinii	AP,HP
Hieracium wetteranum	SG
Hierochloe alpina	SG
Hierochloe occidentalis	B
Hierochloe odorata	G,HU,SG
Hilaria jamesii	B
Hilaria rigida	B
Hildewintera aureispina	BC,Y
Hippeastrum 'Appleblossom'	B
Hippeastrum bicolor	B
Hippeastrum elwesii	AP,C
Hippeastrum hyb mix	AP,B,C,HU,SG
Hippeastrum picotee	B
Hippeastrum 'Red Lion'	B
Hippeastrum sp BCW 5038	AP,SC
Hippeastrum 'United Nations'	B
Hippeastrum vittatum	B,SA
Hippeastrum vittatum f1 hyb s-c	B
Hippeastrum white, red striped	C
Hippia frutescens	B,BH,SI
Hippobroma see Laurentia	
Hippocrepis comosa	B,SU
Hippocrepis emurus	AP,B,C,G,JD,SA,VE
Hippophae rhamnoides	A,B,C,DD,FW,LN,SA, SG,VE

Hippophae salicifolia	LN,SA
Hiptage benghalensis	B
Hirpicium alienatum	B,SI
Hirpicium armerioides	B,SI
Hirpicium linearifolium	B,SI
Hoffmanseggia jamesii	B
Hohenbergia augusta	B
Hohenbergia disjuncta	B
Hohenbergia megalantha	B
Hohenbergia membranostrobilis	B
Hohenbergia portoricensis	B
Hohenbergia ridleyi	B
Hohenbergia stellata	B
Hoheria angustifolia	B,SA,SS
Hoheria glabrata	B,SS
Hoheria lyallii	AP,B,HP,LG,SS
Hoheria populnea	B,SS
Holacantha emoryi	B
Holarrhena pubescens	B
Holcus lanatus	B
Holodiscus discolor	AB,B,C,FW,HP,LN,NO, SA,SG
Holodiscus dumosus	B,FW,NO,SW
Holoschoenus romanus ssp holosch.	B
Holothrix sp	SI
Holubia saccata	B,SI
Homalanthus populifolius	B
Homeria breyniana see H.collina	
Homeria collina	AP,B,C,G,MN,RU,SC,SZ
Homeria comptonii	B,KB,SI
Homeria cookii	B,SI
Homeria elegans	B,KB,RU,SI
Homeria flaccida	B
Homeria marlothii	AP,B,MN
Homeria miniata	B,SI
Homeria ochroleuca	B,KB,RU,SI
Homeria pendula	B,SI
Homeria ramosissima	B,SI
Homeria sp	SI
Homeria tricolor	B,SI
Homogyne alpina	B,G,SG
Honkenya peploides	B,DD
Hoodia bainsii	B,SI
Hoodia gordonii	B,C,Y
Hoodia lugardii	B,SI
Hoodia sp	SI
Hoplophyllum spinosum	B,SI
Hordelymus europaeus	B
Hordeum brachyantherum	B,CA
Hordeum brevisubulatum	SG
Hordeum californicum	B
Hordeum distichum	B
Hordeum jubatum	AP,B,C,CA,HP,KI,KL,MO, SC,SG,SU,T,V
Hordeum junceum	AP,P
Hordeum murinum	B
Hordeum polystichum	B
Hordeum pyrenaicum	SG
Hordeum secalinum	B
Hordeum vulgare 'Kanzaki'	B
Horminum pyrenaicum	AP,B,G,HP,I,JE,KL,P,SA
Horridocactus aconcaguensis	Y
Horridocactus andicolus	DV
Horridocactus andicolus v andacolensis	DV
Horridocactus atroviridis	DV
Horridocactus choapenensis	BC

HORRIDOCACTUS

Horridocactus curvispinus	DV	Humulus japonicus	B,BH,BS,BY,C,DE,SG,V
Horridocactus curvispinus petorcensis	BC	Humulus lupulus	B,C,CG,CN,DT,JE,SA,SG
Horridocactus heinrichianus Tambillos	BC	Humulus lupulus 'Aureus'	B
Horridocactus limariensis	DV	Humulus scandens	SA
Horridocactus lissocarpus	DV	Hunnemania fumariifolia	PI
Horridocactus nigracans	DV	Hunnemannia fumariifolia	DI
Horridocactus odoriflorus	DV	Hunnemannia fumariifolia 'Sunlite'	B,KS,T
Horridocactus robustus	DV	Hupocalyptus colutioides	BH
Horridocactus tuberisulcatus	Y	Hura crepitans	B
Horridocactus woutersiana	DV	Hurungana madagascariensis	B
Hosta American crosses	PK	Hutchinsia see Thlaspi	
Hosta 'Buckshaw Blue'	HP	Hyacinthella acutiloba	AR
Hosta caerulea	B,FW,G	Hyacinthella atchleyi	AR
Hosta elata	DE,JE,SG	Hyacinthella azurea	RM
Hosta fortunei	B,C	Hyacinthella glabrescens	KL
Hosta fortunei f aurea	CG	Hyacinthella heldreichii	KL
Hosta 'Francis Williams'	HP	Hyacinthella hispida	AR
Hosta 'Gingko Craig'	HP	Hyacinthella lazulina	AR
Hosta gracillima	AP,SC,SG	Hyacinthoides hispanica	AP,B,C,G,KL,SC
Hosta kikuti	KL	Hyacinthoides hispanica 'La Grandesse'	KL
Hosta lancifolia 'Minima'	KL	Hyacinthoides hispanica MS467 Portugal	MN
Hosta minor	B,C,JE	Hyacinthoides hispanica 'Rose'	KL
Hosta mix decorative foliage	PL,T,V	Hyacinthoides hispanica v algeriense	B
Hosta montana	B	Hyacinthoides hispanica v algeriense C.R.	MN
Hosta New Hybrids	B,BS,JE,SA	Hyacinthoides hispanica v algeriense C.R.	MN
Hosta plantaginea	B,DE	Hyacinthoides italica	KL
Hosta rectifolia	DE,JE	Hyacinthoides non-scripta	AP,AR,B,C,CN,CO,DD,K
Hosta setosa	KL		I,LA,LG,PA,SA,SU,TH,Z
Hosta sieboldiana	AP,B,BS,C,G,HP,SG,T	Hyacinthoides non-scripta pink	RS
Hosta sieboldiana 'Elegans'	B,BD,C,DE,HP,JE,L,SA	Hyacinthoides reverchonii	AR
Hosta sieboldii	DT,F,JE,SG	Hyacinthoides vincentina white	AR
Hosta sp mix	AP,C,FW,I,J,N,PA	Hyacinthus orientalis ssp chionophilus	AR
Hosta 'Tall Boy'	B	Hyacinthus tabrizianus	NG
Hosta tokudama	G	Hyalosperma cotula	B,NI,O
Hosta 'True Blue'	PM	Hyalosperma glutinosum	B
Hosta undulata	SA	Hyalosperma glutinosum ssp venustum	NI,O
Hosta ventricosa	AP,B,C,DE,E,HU,JE,PK,	Hyalosperma praecox	B,NI,O
	SA,SC,SG,T	Hybanthus calycinus	B,NI
Houstonia longifolia	B,PR	Hybanthus enneaspermus	B
Hovea acanthoclada	B,NI	Hybanthus floribundus	B,C,NI,SA
Hovea acutifolia	B,EL,HA,NI	Hybanthus floribundus ssp adpressus	B,NI
Hovea chorizemifolia	B,NI	Hydrangea arborescens	B,CG
Hovea elliptica	B,C,EL,HA,NI,SA	Hydrangea aspera ssp sargetiana	B
Hovea lanceolata	B,HA,SA	Hydrangea aspera Villosa Group	SA,SG
Hovea linearis	B,SA	Hydrangea bretschneideri	FW
Hovea longifolia	B	Hydrangea heteromalla	B,SG
Hovea pungens	B,NI,SA	Hydrangea heteromalla AC1342	X
Hovea purpurea v rosmarinifolia	B	Hydrangea heteromalla AC1886	X
Hovea rosmarinifolia	HA,NI	Hydrangea heteromalla Bretschneideri Gr	SA
Hovea trisperma	B,NI	Hydrangea heteromalla CNW376	X
Hovenia acerba	B	Hydrangea indochinensis	SG
Hovenia dulcis	A,B,C,CG,EL,FW,LN,SA	Hydrangea macrophylla	B
Howea belmoreana	B,CA,EL,HA,O,SA	Hydrangea paniculata	B,HP,SA
Howea forsterana	B,CA,EL,HA,O,SA,SH,T	Hydrangea petiolaris	B,C,FW,SA
Hoya australis	B	Hydrangea quercifolia	B,C,FW,SA
Hoya australis ssp bandaensis	B	Hydrangea sargentiana see H.aspera ssp sargetiana	
Hoya carnosa	B	Hydrangea sp CNW818	X
Hoya purpureofusca	B,C	Hydrangea sp CNW871	X
Huernia hystrix	B,SI	Hydrangea sp CNW885	X
Huernia pillansii	B	Hydrangea villosa see H.aspera Villosa Group	
Huernia quinta	SI	Hydrastis canadensis	B,DD,SG
Huernia whitesloaneana	B,SI	Hydriastele wendlandiana	B,EL,O
Huernia zebrina v magniflora	B,SI	Hydrophilus rattrayii	B
Hugonia mystax	B	Hydrophyllum canadense	HP
Hugueninia tanacetifolia	B,CG	Hydrophyllum capitatum	B,SW
Hugueninia tanacetifolia v suffruticosa	C,JE	Hygrophila auriculata	B

HYLOMECON

Hylomecon japonicum	AP,HP,JE,KL,SC
Hymenaea courbaril	B,RE,SA
Hymenocallis littoralis	B,JE
Hymenocallis 'Sulphur Queen'	B
Hymenocardia ulmoides	B,SI
Hymenodictyon floribundum	B,SI
Hymenogyne glabra	B,SI
Hymenolepis parviflora	B,SI
Hymenorebutia mix	Y
Hymenosporum flavum	AP,B,C,CA,EL,HA,HP, HU,NI,O,SA,SC,SH,WA
Hymenoxis lyallii 'Alba'	KL
Hymenoxis scaposa	KL
Hymenoxis torreyana	B,KL
Hymenoxys grandiflora see Tetraneuris	
Hymenoxys subintegra	AP,KL,SG
Hyophorbe indica	O
Hyophorbe lagenicaulis	B,CA,EL,O
Hyophorbe verschaffelti	B,CA,EL,O,SA
Hyoscyamus albus	B,C,G,HU,SA
Hyoscyamus aureus	AP,SA
Hyoscyamus niger	AP,B,C,CN,G,SG,TH
Hypericum aethiopicum	B,SI
Hypericum androsaemum	AP,B,C,E,G,HP,JE,LA, SA,SG
Hypericum andros. 'Gladys Brabazon'	C
Hypericum archibaldii	HP
Hypericum ascyron	B,JE,SC,SG
Hypericum athoum	AP,G,I,SC
Hypericum balearicum	SG
Hypericum buckleyi	AP,I
Hypericum calycinum	AP,B,BD,BS,BY,C,CA, CL,CN,DE,HA,JE,L,MO, SA,SK,TH
Hypericum canariense	C
Hypericum cerastoides	AP,B,I,JE,KL,RH,SC,SG
Hypericum choisianum	SG
Hypericum cistifolium	B
Hypericum coris	AP,B,C,G,HP,I,JE,RH,SC
Hypericum delphicum	I
Hypericum erectum	KL
Hypericum forrestii	RH
Hypericum fragile h see H.olympicum f minus	
Hypericum galioides	B
Hypericum henryi ssp henryi	B
Hypericum henryi ssp uraloides	RH
Hypericum 'Hidcote'	RS
Hypericum hircinum	B,RH
Hypericum hirsutum	B,SG
Hypericum hyssopifolium	B,C,JE,RH
Hypericum japonicum	B,SS
Hypericum kamtschaticum	AP,RH
Hypericum kiusianum v yakusimense	AP,B,KL,P,SC
Hypericum kouytchense	RH,SA
Hypericum lalandii	B,SI
Hypericum lancasteri	SG
Hypericum linarifolium	B
Hypericum maculatum	B,CG
Hypericum montanum	B,SG
Hypericum olympicum	AP,B,C,G,HP,I,JE,KL,RH, SA,SC,SG,T
Hypericum olympicum f minus	B,C,CG,JE,SG
Hypericum olymp. f uniflorum 'Citrinum'	AP,B,CL,HP,JE,L,MO
Hypericum olympicum 'Grandiflorum' see H.o. f uniflorum	
Hypericum orientale	AP,B,JE,KL,SC
Hypericum pallens	SG

Hypericum patulum	B,CP,JE
Hypericum perforatum	AP,B,C,CN,CP,DD,G,HP, LA,JE,RH,SC,SG,TH
Hypericum perforatum 'Pharma'	B
Hypericum perforatum 'Topas'	B
Hypericum polyphyllum 'Grandiflorum' see H.olympicum f uniflorum	
Hypericum polyphyllum see H. olympicum f minus	
Hypericum proliferum	B,JE
Hypericum pseudohenryi	RH
Hypericum pseudopetiolatum v yakusimanum see H.kiusianum v y.	
Hypericum ptarmicaefolium	VO
Hypericum pulchrum	AP,B,JE
Hypericum punctatum	B,CP,PR
Hypericum pyramidatum	PR
Hypericum repens	I
Hypericum revolutum	B,C,SI
Hypericum richeri	B
Hypericum roeperianum	B
Hypericum sp	KL,SG
Hypericum sp 2m shrubs CNW769	X
Hypericum sp CNW848	X
Hypericum sp coll Murren	W
Hypericum subsessile	SG
Hypericum tenuicaule	SG
Hypericum tetrapterum	AP,B,G,JE,LA,SU
Hypericum triquetrifolium	B
Hypericum uralum	C
Hypericum x inodorum	RH
Hypericum x inodorum 'Albury Purple'	E,HP
Hypericum x inodorum 'Elstead'	HP
Hypericum yakusimense see H.kiusianum v y.	
Hypericum yezoense	P
Hypertelis salsoloides	B,SI
Hyphaena coriacea	SA
Hyphaene coriacea	B,CA,O
Hyphaene natalensis hybrid	O
Hyphaene petersiana	O
Hyphaene shadron	B
Hyphaene shatan	B
Hypocalymma angustifolium	B,NI,O,SA
Hypocalymma robustum	B,NI,O
Hypocalymma strictum	B,NI
Hypocalymma xanthopetalum	B
Hypocalyptus sophoroides	B,SA,SI
Hypochoeris radicata	B,C
Hypochoeris uniflora	AP,B,JE,KL,SA,SC
Hypodiscus aristatus	B,SI
Hypodiscus synchrolepis	B,SI
Hypoestes aristata	B
Hypoestes phyllostachya	BY,C,KI
Hypoestes phyllostachya 'Arctic White'	BS
Hypoestes phyllostachya 'Confetti' mix	S,T,YA
Hypoestes phyllostachya 'Confetti' pink	SK
Hypoestes phyllostachya 'Confetti Red'	B,BS,CA,MO,SK,YA
Hypoestes phyllostachya 'Confetti Rose'	B,BS,CA,MO,SK,YA
Hypoestes phyllostachya 'Confetti White'	B,BS,CA,MO,SK,YA
Hypoestes phyllo. 'Confetti Wine Red'	B,BS,CA,MO,SK,YA
Hypoestes phyllostachya 'Desert Pink'	BS,MO
Hypoestes phyllo. 'Pink Splash' select	B,BS,CA,CL,HA,J,L, MO,PK,T,V
Hypoestes phyllo. 'Red Splash' select	BS,CL,MO,PK,SK
Hypoestes phyllo. 'Rose Splash' select	B,BS,CL,HA,MO,SK
Hypoestes phyllostachya 'Splash' mix	L,PI,PK
Hypoestes phyllo. 'White Splash' select	B,BS,CA,CL,HA,MO,PK
Hypoestes 'Splash' s-c	B,BS,CA,CL,HA,MO,PK, SK

HYPOXIS

Hypoxis angustifolia	AP,B,SI	Ilex aquifolium 'Bacciflava'(Fructo Luteo)	C
Hypoxis aquatica	B,SI	Ilex aquifolium variegated	C
Hypoxis capensis	B,SI	Ilex canariensis	SA
Hypoxis colchicifolia	B,SI	Ilex cassine	B
Hypoxis decumbens .	CG	Ilex chinensis see I.purpurea	
Hypoxis hemerocallidea	B,C,SI	Ilex cornuta	B,CA,FW,LN,SA
Hypoxis hirsuta	B,PR	Ilex crenata	B,FW,SA
Hypoxis hygrometrica	AP,G,PM,SC	Ilex decidua	B,FW,LN,SA
Hypoxis obtusa	RU	Ilex geniculata	SG
Hypoxis rigidula	B,SI	Ilex glabra	B,FW
Hypoxis sp	BH,SI	Ilex laevigata	SG
Hypoxis villosa	B	Ilex latifolia	B,LN
Hypoxis woodii	B,SI	Ilex mitis	B,KB,SI,WA
Hyptis emoryi	B,SA	Ilex montana	B,FW,LN
Hyptis suaveolens	B	Ilex opaca	B,C,FW,LN,NO,SA
Hyssopus fergonensis	SG	Ilex paraguariensis	B
Hyssopus officinalis	AP,B,CN,CP,DD,G,HP,	Ilex pedunculosa	B
	HU,KS,RH,SA,SG,TH	Ilex pernyi	G,SG
Hyssopus officinalis f albus	AP,B,CN,E,G,HP,JE,SA	Ilex purpurea	B,EL,LN,SA
Hyssopus officinalis f roseus	AP,B,CN,HP,JE,P,SA	Ilex serrata	B,FW
Hyssopus officinalis 'Ruber'	E	Ilex verticillata	B,FW,LN,NO,SA,SG
Hyssopus officinalis 'Sprite Blue'	B	Ilex vomitoria	B,FW,LN,SA
Hyssopus officinalis 'Sprite Pink'	B	Ilex x altaclarensis	RH,SG
Hyssopus officinalis 'Sprite Snow'	B	Ilex x altaclerensis 'Golden King'	HP
Hyssopus officinalis ssp aristatus	CN,G,HP,RH,SG	Iliamna rivularis see Sphaeralcea	
Hyssopus officinalis v canescens	B	Iliamna see Sphaeralcea	
Hystrix patula	AP,B,G,HP,JE,KL,PR,SA	Illicium anisatum	B,SA
Iberis amara	B,BH,DI,G,SG	Imitaria muirii	B
Iberis amara 'Empress' hyacinth fl	B,DE,KS	Impatiens auricoma 'African Queen'	DI
Iberis amara 'Iceberg'	B,C,J,VY	Impatiens Baby mix	J
Iberis amara 'Iceberg Superior'	B,BS,MO	Impatiens balfourii	B,CG,HU,SG
Iberis amara 'Mount Hood'	B	Impatiens balsamina	B,C,CG,G,SG
Iberis amara 'White Pinnacle'	B	Impatiens balsamina bush fl	BS,CO,HU,ST
Iberis coronaria hyacinth fl	DT,PI,T	Impatiens balsamina camellia fl mix	BD,BS,BY,D,DE,F,FR,
Iberis crenata	T		J,MO,PI,SK,T,V
Iberis Crown mix	BS	Impatiens balsamina 'Carambole' mix	PK
Iberis 'Fantasia'	S	Impatiens balsamina dw dbl mix	MO
Iberis gibraltarica	AP,B,BD,BS,BY,C,CN,	Impatiens balsamina gardenia fl	DE
	CO,HU,JE,KI,L,MO,SA	Impatiens balsamina 'Tom Thumb'	BD,BS,C,D,DE,DT,L,
Iberis hybrida	B		MO,SE,SK,T,YA
Iberis mix special	BY,CO,DT,L	Impatiens balsamina 'Topknot' mix	BS,D,MO,R
Iberis saxatilis	B,C,JE	Impatiens balsamina 'Topknot' s-c	B,BS,DE
Iberis sempervirens pink	S	Impatiens brachcentra	CG
Iberis sempervirens 'Schneeflocke'	AP,B,C,FR,JE,KS,SE,	Impatiens burtonii	B,DD
	T,U,VY	Impatiens capensis	B,PR
Iberis sempervirens white	BY,CA,CG,CL,D,JE,KI,	Impatiens cristata	CG
	KL,L,MO,PK,S,SA,SC,	Impatiens 'Dazzler Violet Star'	T
	SK,ST,SU,TU,V	Impatiens dwarf mix	CO,PI,SU,VH
Iberis 'Spangles'	KI	Impatiens edgeworthii	C,HP
Iberis umbellata	AB,BH,FR,G,SG,TH	Impatiens f1 'Accent Apricot'	CA,CL,M,SK,U,VH
Iberis umbellata 'Fairy' mix	BD,BS,BU,C,CA,D,DE,	Impatiens f1 'Accent Blush Pink'	SK
	DN,F,J,M,MO,S,SE,SU,	Impatiens f1 'Accent Bright Eye'	CA,DT,PK,SK
	T,U,V,VY	Impatiens f1 'Accent' Burgundy	PI,PK,SK
Iberis umbellata 'Flash' mix	C,F,J,KS,SK,T	Impatiens f1 'Accent Burgundy Star'	B,BS,CA,CL,MO,PK,SK
Iberis umbellata 'Flash' s-c	B,BS,MO	Impatiens f1 'Accent Carmine'	CA
Iberis umbellata 'Flash White'	B,KS	Impatiens f1 'Accent' coral	SK
Iberis umbellata super mix	C	Impatiens f1 'Accent' cranberry	SK
Iberis white giant hyacinth fl	SK	Impatiens f1 'Accent Dp Pink'	CA
Ibervillea sonorae	B,DV,HU	Impatiens f1 'Accent Lavender Blue'	CA,CL,D,DT,M,PK,SK,
Ibicella lutea	B,DV,G		VH
Ichnocarpus frutescens	B	Impatiens f1 'Accent Lilac'	CA,SK
Ichnolepsis tuberosa	DV	Impatiens f1 'Accent' mix	BS,CL,D,DE,F,J,M,S,SE,
Idesia polycarpa	B,C,CA,EL,G,LN,SA		SK
Idria columnaris	HU	Impatiens f1 'Accent Mystic' mix	CA,SK
Ilex aquifolium	A,AB,B,C,CA,EL,FW,G,	Impatiens f1 'Accent Orange'	CA,SK
	KL,LN,RH,SA,VE	Impatiens f1 'Accent Orange Star'	BS,B,CA,CL,MO,SK

IMPATIENS

Impatiens f1 'Accent' Pastel mix	CA,PK,SK
Impatiens f1 'Accent Pink'	CA,CL,D,M,PI,PK,SK,VH
Impatiens f1 'Accent Red'	BS,CA,CL,D,DT,M,PK,SK,VH
Impatiens f1 'Accent Red Star'	B,CA,CL,MO,SK
Impatiens f1 'Accent Rose'	BS,CA,CL,D,SK
Impatiens f1 'Accent Rose Star'	B,CA,CL,MO,PK
Impatiens f1 'Accent Salmon'	CA,CL,D,PK,SK
Impatiens f1 'Accent Scarlet'	CA,SK
Impatiens f1 'Accent' Star mix	CA,DE,PK,SK
Impatiens f1 'Accent Sunrise' mix	CA,SK
Impatiens f1 'Accent Violet'	BS,CA,CL,D,PK,SK
Impatiens f1 'Accent Violet Star'	B,CA,CL,MO,SK
Impatiens f1 'Accent White'	CA,CL,D,DE,M,PI,PK,SK,VH
Impatiens f1 'Bellizzy Colourballs' dbl mix	C,FR
Impatiens f1 'Blitz Jumbo'	D,SK
Impatiens f1 'Blitz' mix	BS,J,SK,U
Impatiens f1 'Blitz' s-c	BS,CA,SE,SK
Impatiens f1 'Blue Satin'	DI
Impatiens f1 'Blush'	DI
Impatiens f1 'Bright Shades'	U
Impatiens f1 'Bruno'	D,F
Impatiens f1 'Busy Lizzie Accents'	M
Impatiens f1 'Carnival Salmon'	YA
Impatiens f1 'Carousel' mix dbl	D,DI,MO,S
Impatiens f1 'Chelsea Girl'	F
Impatiens f1 'Cherry Blush'	U,V
Impatiens f1 'Circus'	F
Impatiens f1 'Dble Confection' mix	BS,DT,J,MO,PL,SK,T,U
Impatiens f1 'Dble Confection' s-c	SE,T
Impatiens f1 'Deco Burgundy'	B,BS,CL,SK
Impatiens f1 'Deco Crystal'	B,BS,CL,SK,U
Impatiens f1 'Deco Daydream'	D
Impatiens f1 'Deco' mix	BS,CA,CL,DT,KI,M,MO,SK,ST,YA
Impatiens f1 'Deco' s-c	B,BS,CL,MO,SK
Impatiens f1 'Deco Tri-colour'	CA,SK
Impatiens f1 'Emperor Mixed'	U
Impatiens f1 'Expo' mix	D,F,S
Impatiens f1 'Expo Picotee'	F
Impatiens f1 'Expo' s-c	MO,YA
Impatiens f1 'Eye-Eye' mix	D
Impatiens f1 'Florette Stars' mix	BS,J,TU
Impatiens f1 'Futura' mix	BS,CA
Impatiens f1 'Imp' mix	M
Impatiens f1 'Impact' mix	BS,C
Impatiens f1 'Impact's-c	BS,C
Impatiens f1 'Impulse Appleblossom'	BD
Impatiens f1 'Lavender Blush'	U
Impatiens f1 'Lilac Pearl'	T,U
Impatiens f1 'Mega Orange Star'	B,BS,C,CA,CL,D,L,MO,O,SE,T,U,YA
Impatiens f1 mix special	DT
Impatiens f1 'Mosaic Lilac'	CL,D,DI,DT,PI,PK,SE,SK,T,U
Impatiens f1 'Mystic'	U
Impatiens f1 'Neon'	U
Impatiens f1 'New Guinea Borneo Bold'	BS
Impatiens f1 'New Guinea Spectra'	BD,BS,C,CA,CL,DT,F,J,KI,L,M,MO,PK,R,S,SE,SK,T,U,V,YA
Impatiens f1 'New Guinea Tango'	B,BS,C,CA,CL,D,DE,DT,FR,J,KI,L,MO,PK,SE,T,V
Impatiens f1 'Novette Star' mix	D,S
Impatiens f1 'Pantomime'	F
Impatiens f1 'Petticoat'	V
Impatiens f1 'Plum Sorbet'	U
Impatiens f1 'Pride'	PK
Impatiens f1 'Revue' s-c	V
Impatiens f1 'Rosette' mix	BD,BS,F,KI,L,MO,SE
Impatiens f1 'Starbright'	BD,BS,CL,CO,F,KI,L,M,MO,R,SE,U,V,YA
Impatiens f1 'Sunrise' mix	DT
Impatiens f1 'Super Elfin Apricot'	B,BS,CL,MO,SK,YA
Impatiens f1 'Super Elfin Blue Pearl'	B,BS,CA,CL,KI,MO,S,SE,SK,YA
Impatiens f1 'Super Elfin Blush'	B,BS,CA,CL,MO,SK,YA
Impatiens f1 'Super Elfin' Carmine	SK
Impatiens f1 'Super Elfin Cherry'	B,BS,CA,CL,KI,MO,SK,YA
Impatiens f1 'Super Elfin Coral'	B,BS,CA,CL,MO,SK,YA
Impatiens f1 'Super Elfin Lavender'	B,BS,CL,MO,SK,YA
Impatiens f1 'Super Elfin Lilac'	B,BS,CL,SK,MO,YA
Impatiens f1 'Super Elfin Lipstick'	B,BS,CA,CL,F,SK,MO,YA
Impatiens f1 'Super Elfin' Melon	SK
Impatiens f1 'Super Elfin' mix	BD,BS,CA,CL,CN,D,F,J,KI,L,R,S,SE,ST,TU,VH,SK,MO,YA
Impatiens f1 'Super Elfin Mother of Pearl'	F
Impatiens f1 'Super Elfin Orange'	B,BS,CA,CL,KI,MO,SK,YA
Impatiens f1 'Super Elfin Pastel'	BD,BS,CA,CL,DT,J,KI,MO,S,V,YA
Impatiens f1 'Super Elfin Pearl'	B,BS,CA,CL,F,MO,SK,YA
Impatiens f1 'Super Elfin Pink'	B,BS,CA,CL,KI,MO,SK,YA
Impatiens f1 'Super Elfin Red'	B,CA,CL,KI,MO,S,SK
Impatiens f1 'Super Elfin Red Velvet'	B,CA,CL,F,MO,SK,YA
Impatiens f1 'Super Elfin Rose'	B,BS,CA,CL,MO,S,SK,YA
Impatiens f1 'Super Elfin Salmon'	B,BS,CL,KI,MO,SK,YA
Impatiens f1 'Super Elfin Salmon Blush'	B,BS,CL,MO,S,YA
Impatiens f1 'Super Elfin Scarlet'	B,BS,CA,CL,SK,MO,YA
Impatiens f1 'Super Elfin Twilight'	CA
Impatiens f1 'Super Elfin Violet'	B,BS,CA,CL,MO,SK,YA .
Impatiens f1 'Super Elfin White'	B,BS,CA,CL,KI,S,SK,MO,YA
Impatiens f1 'Swirl Coral'	B,BS,CA,MO,PK,S,SE,SK
Impatiens f1 'Swirl' mix	BS,CL,M,MO,S,SE,SK,T,VH,U,YA
Impatiens f1 'Swirl Peach'	B,BS,CA,MO,PK,SE,SK
Impatiens f1 'Swirl Pink'	B,BS,CA,MO,PK,SE,SK,YA
Impatiens f1 'Symphony Red Star'	F
Impatiens f1 'Tempo Burgundy'	B,BS,L,T,U
Impatiens f1 'Tempo' mix	BD,BS,CA,CL,L,MO,SK,T,VY
Impatiens f1 'Tempo Pastel' mix	CA,SA
Impatiens f1 'Tempo Salsa' mix	SK
Impatiens f1 'Tempo Series' s-c	B,BS,DT,F,L,MO,SK,T,VY
Impatiens f1 'Unwins Pride Mix'	U
Impatiens f1 'Unwins Pride Red Glow'	U
Impatiens f1 'Unwins Pride Tahiti'	U
Impatiens f1 'Wedgewood' mix	SK
Impatiens f2 'Dainty Maid'	D
Impatiens f2 'Imagination' mix	CL
Impatiens f2 mix dwarf	BS,L,S
Impatiens f2 mix economy	SK
Impatiens f2 'Safari'	B,BS,CN,F,J,KI,MO,R,

IMPATIENS

	TU,V,YA
Impatiens 'Fruit Salad'	U
Impatiens 'Gem'	BS
Impatiens glandulifera	B,C,CG,G,HU,KL,SG
Impatiens glandulifera alba	CG
Impatiens hochstatteri	DV
Impatiens hochstetteri ssp hochstetteri	B,SI
Impatiens 'Holstii' hyb	BS
Impatiens hyb	FR,I
Impatiens hyb 'Rainbow Shower'	B
Impatiens Improved formula mix	BS
Impatiens 'Little Lizzie'	BS,KI,MC,ST
Impatiens 'Mosaic Rose'	D,U
Impatiens 'New Guinea Firelake Original'	PL
Impatiens niamniamensis	B
Impatiens noli-tangere	AP,B,SG
Impatiens oncidioides 'Malaysia Gold'	T
Impatiens pallida	B,PR
Impatiens platypetala	C
Impatiens scabrida	AP,CG,HP
Impatiens sodenii	NG
Impatiens sylvicola	B,SI
Impatiens textori	B,C
Impatiens 'Victoria Rose'	DI,U
Impatiens walleriana	B,CG,SG,SI
Impatiens walleriana 'Sultani'	C,TH
Impatiens walleriana 'Sultani Scarlet'	BS,KI,PI,ST
Impatiens zombensis	B,SI
Imperata cylindrica	G,HA,NI
Imperata cylindrica v major	B
Incarvillea arguta	AP,C,HP
Incarvillea compacta	AP,B,G,HP,KL,NG,RM, SC,SG
Incarvillea delavayi	AP,B,BS,C,CG,CL,DD, G,HP,HU,JD,JE,KI,KL, L,LG,MO,PL,PM,S,SA, SC,SG,T,TH,X
Incarvillea delavayi alba	AP,B,C,G,HP,JE,P,PL,SA
Incarvillea mairei	AP,B,CG,HP,JE,SA,SG
Incarvillea mairei 'Nyoto Sama'	SC
Incarvillea mairei v grandiflora	AP,B,CG,G,KL,SC,SG
Incarvillea olgae	AP,B,G,JE,RM,SA,SG
Incarvillea sinensis	AP,HP,SC
Incarvillea sinensis 'Alba'	HP
Incarvillea sinensis 'Cheron'	AP,B,BS,C,D,DT,HP,MO, T,V
Incarvillea sin. ssp variabilis f prizewalskii	SG
Incarvillea 'Snowtop'	AP,HP
Incarvillea sp	AP,SC,SG
Indigofera amblyantha	B,C,EL,HU,SA
Indigofera aspalathoides	B
Indigofera australis	AU,B,C,EL,HA,NI,O,SA, SH
Indigofera brevidens	B,NI
Indigofera cylindrica	BH,C
Indigofera cytisoides	B,SA,SI
Indigofera decora	B
Indigofera dosua	B
Indigofera enneaphylla	B
Indigofera filicaulis	B,SI
Indigofera filifolia	B,BH,SI
Indigofera foliosa	B,SI
Indigofera frutescens	B,DD,KB,SI
Indigofera glabra	B
Indigofera hedyantha	B,SI
Indigofera heterantha	AP,B,C,SA,G

Indigofera hilaris	B,SI
Indigofera hirsuta	B,HU
Indigofera kirilowii	AP,LN,SA
Indigofera langebergensis	B,SI
Indigofera linifolia	B,NI
Indigofera linnaei	B
Indigofera monophylla	B,NI
Indigofera natalensis	B,KB,SI
Indigofera pendula	SG
Indigofera pseudotinctoria	AP,B,C,CA,EL,LN,SA
Indigofera sp	SI
Indigofera suffruticosa	B,DD
Indigofera tinctoria	B,C,CP,EL
Indigofera trita	B,NI
Indigofera woodii	B,SI
Indoneesiella echioides	B
Inga edulis	B
Inga fuillei	B
Inga spectabilis	B
Inula acaulis	AP,KL,SC,VO
Inula britannica	B,SG
Inula candida	B,JE
Inula conyzae	B
Inula ensifolia	AP,B,BS,C,CG,G,HP,I,JE, KL,MO,SC,SG,V
Inula ensifolia 'Compacta'	AP,B,G,SC
Inula ensifolia 'Mediterranean Sun'	U
Inula ensifolia 'Star Gold'	CL
Inula ensifolia 'Star Oriental'	CL
Inula germanica	B
Inula grandiflora	DD,KL,PA,PS,VO
Inula helenium	AP,B,BS,C,CN,CP,DD,G, HP,HU,JE,RS,SA,SG,TH
Inula helenium 'Goliath'	B,C
Inula hirta	B,G,JE
Inula hookeri	AP,G,HP,SC
Inula magnifica	AP,B,C,CG,DD,G,HP,HU, JE,SA,SC,SG
Inula montana	B
Inula oculus-christi	B
Inula orientalis	AP,B,C,F,G,HP,SA,T
Inula orientalis 'Grandiflora'	B,JE
Inula pulicaria	B
Inula racemosa	AP,B,HP
Inula racemosa 'Sonnenspeer'	JE
Inula rhizocephala	AP,B,G,JE,KL,SC
Inula royleana	AP,B,G,HP,SA,SC
Inula salicina	B,SG
Inulanthera calva	B,SI
Iochroma cyanea	B
Ionopsidium acaule	B,C,J,MO,T,V
Iostephane heterophylla	B,SW
Ipheion uniflorum	AP,B,G
Ipheion uniflorum 'Album'	PM
Ipheion uniflorum 'Froyle Mill'	AP,PM
Ipomoea aculeatum	DI
Ipomoea adenioides	B,SI
Ipomoea alba	B,C,EL,F,HU,KS,PK,T
Ipomoea albivenia	B,SI
Ipomoea andersonii	T
Ipomoea arborescens	B
Ipomoea batatas	B
Ipomoea brasiliensis	C,HU,SI
Ipomoea cairica	B
Ipomoea carnea	B,C
Ipomoea carnea ssp fistulosa	B

IPOMOEA

Ipomoea coccinea	AP,B,C,SG,SW
Ipomoea costata	B,C,EL,HU,NI,SA
Ipomoea dbl blue picotee	SE
Ipomoea Hawaiian Woodrose	CA
Ipomoea hederacea	B,CG,G,HU,SG
Ipomoea hederacea 'Roman Candy'	T
Ipomoea heterophylla	B
Ipomoea holubii	CG
Ipomoea kituensis	DD
Ipomoea leptophylla	B,SC
Ipomoea leptotoma	B,SW
Ipomoea lobata	AP,B,C,CG,CL,DI,DT,F, G,HP,J,KS,L,MO,PI,PK, S,SA,V
Ipomoea lobata 'Citronella'	B,BS,DT,PK,SE,T,U
Ipomoea lobata 'Exotic Love'	CO,HU,JO,SE
Ipomoea lobata 'Mexican Fiesta'	U
Ipomoea mix colour	T
Ipomoea mix dw picotee	SK
Ipomoea mix variegated leaf	BS,PK
Ipomoea mix Zebra Stripes	PL
Ipomoea muelleri	B,HU,NI,SA
Ipomoea murucoides 'Pajaro Bobo'	HU
Ipomoea nil	B,C,KS
Ipomoea pennata	C,RS
Ipomoea pes-caprae	EL,SA
Ipomoea pes-tigridis	B
Ipomoea platensis	B,CH,Y
Ipomoea platycodon fl picotee	T
Ipomoea platycodon fl white	T
Ipomoea pubescens	B
Ipomoea purpurea	AP,B,BU,C,CG,F,HP,PG, PK,SG,T,W
Ipomoea purpurea 'Kniola's Purple-black'	B
Ipomoea quamoclit	AP,B,EL,F,HP,SA,V
Ipomoea quamoclit 'Cardinalis'	DE,PI,PK
Ipomoea 'Quebraplata'	B,HU
Ipomoea sepiaria	B
Ipomoea setosa v campanulata	B,HU
Ipomoea sp 'Quebraplatita Azul'	B,HU
Ipomoea sp 'Quebraplatita Roja'	B,HU
Ipomoea sp 'Quebraplatita Rosa'	B,HU
Ipomoea trichocarpa	B,HU
Ipomoea tricolor	AB,DD,DE,G,HP,SK,V, VY
Ipomoea tricolor 'Blue Star'	B,JO
Ipomoea tricolor 'Cardinal'	BS,S
Ipomoea tricolor 'Crimson Rambler'	B,F,JO,PG
Ipomoea tricolor 'Early Call'	PI,T,U
Ipomoea tricolor 'Flying Saucers'	B,D,F,PI
Ipomoea tricolor 'Heavenly Blue'	w.a.
Ipomoea tricolor 'Magenta Climber'	B
Ipomoea tricolor mini sky blue	SE,T
Ipomoea tricolor mix	FR,J,SE,TE
Ipomoea tricolor 'Moonflower'	BD,PG,PI,SE
Ipomoea tricolor 'Pearly Gates'	B,BS,CA,DE,HU,JO,PI, PK,SK,V
Ipomoea tricolor 'Scarlet O'Hara'	B,BS,BY,C,CA,DE,HU,L, MO,PG,PI,PK,SK
Ipomoea tricolor 'Scarlet Star'	T
Ipomoea tricolor 'Sunrise Serenade'	B
Ipomoea tricolor 'Super Garland'	C
Ipomoea villosa	B
Ipomoea violacea	SG
Ipomoea x multifida	B,C,NO,RM,SW
Ipomopsis aggregata	AB,B,C,NO,RM,SW

Ipomopsis aggregata arizonica	B,SW
Ipomopsis aggregata v macrosiphon	B,SW
Ipomopsis globularis	B,RM
Ipomopsis longiflora	B
Ipomopsis rubra	AP,B,HW,KS,SZ,V
Ipomopsis rubra 'Red Arrow'	B
Ipomopsis spicata	B
Iriartea deltoides	B
Iriartea gigantea	B,O,RE
Iriartea ventricosa	B
Iris aphylla	B,G,JE
Iris aphylla ssp bohemica	KL
Iris aphylla ssp hungarica	B
Iris attica	AP,MN
Iris aucheri	AR
Iris barbata	JE
Iris barbata elatior hyb	G
Iris barbata nana new hybrids	JE
Iris biglumis see I.lactea	
Iris bracteata	AP,I,SC
Iris bucharica h see I.orchioides	
Iris bulleyana	AP,B,JE,SA,SC
Iris bulleyana AC1601	X
Iris California Hybrids	AP,HP,PL,SC,T
Iris carthaliniae	G,SG
Iris caucasica	AR
Iris chrysographes	AP,B,G,JE,KL,LG,SC,SG
Iris chrysographes 'Black Forms'	AP,B,C,EL,F,LG,PA,SC
Iris chrysographes 'Black Knight'	T
Iris chrysographes forrestii	PL
Iris chrysographes hyb	I,SC
Iris clarkei	AP,B,G,JE,SC,SG
Iris cretensis see I. unguicularis ssp c.	
Iris crocea	B
Iris cycloglossa	AR,B,RM
Iris decora	AP,B,G,SC
Iris delavayi	AP,B,CG,DD,G,I,NG,SC
Iris demetri	SG
Iris dichotoma	CG,SG
Iris douglasiana	AP,B,C,CG,JE,LG,SC
Iris ensata	AP,B,CA,G,HU,JE,KL,P,P K,SA,SC,SG
Iris ensata hyb	BS,JE,L,SA
Iris ensata new hybrids	B
Iris ensata Prize Winning mix	P
Iris foetidissima	AP,B,C,CG,CN,G,I,JE,KL, LG,PO,RH,RS,SA,SC, SG,TH,W
Iris foetidissima 'Citrina'	AP,C,NG,SC,SG
Iris forrestii	AP,B,CG,G,I,JE,SA,SC
Iris fulva	B
Iris germanica cvs mix	C
Iris germanica 'Florentina'	B,CG
Iris 'Gordon'	KL
Iris gracilipes	B
Iris graminea	AP,B,C,G,JE,KL,LG,NG, SA,SC
Iris graminea ssp pseudocyperus	B
Iris hartwegii	B
Iris 'Hercules'	KL
Iris histroides 'J.S.Dijt'	KL
Iris histroides 'Major'	KL
Iris hoogiana	B,G
Iris humilis	CG,SG
Iris hymenospatha	AR
Iris innominata 'Broadleigh Rose'	P

IRIS

Iris innominata hyb	AP,HP,I,SG
Iris J437	P
Iris japonica	B,SG
Iris kaempferi see I.ensata	
Iris kamaonensis	B,JE,SG
Iris kerneriana	AP,CG,G,NG,SC
Iris kolpakowskiana	AR
Iris lactea	AP,G,PH,SC,SG
Iris lactea v hyacinthiana	HP
Iris lacustris	KL
Iris laevigata	AP,B,CG,G,JE,SA,SC,SG
Iris laevigata f alba	B,JE
Iris latifolia	AP,B,G,JE,LG,RS,SC
Iris latifolia LG340 Spain	MN
Iris linifolia	AR
Iris longipetala	B
Iris luriola	CG
Iris lutescens	AP,C,JE,MN,SC
Iris lutescens B.S337 Italy	MN
Iris lutescens B.S389 France	MN
Iris lutescens L/E171 Spain	MN
Iris lutescens MS515 France	MN
Iris lutescens MS524 Spain	MN
Iris lutescens 'Nana'	B
Iris maackii	B,DD,G,SA,SG
Iris macrosiphon	AP,PM,SC
Iris magnifica	AP,AR,B,G,JE,KL,LG,PM
Iris magnifica f alba	AP,KL,NG
Iris magnifica x willmottiana	AR
Iris missouriensis	AB,AV,B,C,G,JE,RM,SA, SC,SG,SW
Iris missouriensis v arizonica	B,SW
Iris musulanica	SG
Iris neglecta	CG
Iris nicolai	AR
Iris notha	G,SG
Iris orchioides	AP,AR,B,G,LG,SC,SG
Iris orientalis	AP,B,G,JE,SC
Iris oristata	B
Iris Pacific Coast hyb see I.Californian hyb	
Iris palaestina	B
Iris pallida	AP,B,CG,JE,SA
Iris paradoxa f choschab	B,JE
Iris persica	AR
Iris plicata	CG
Iris polakii	B,CG,SG
Iris prismatica	AP,B,CG,DD,KL,SC,SG
Iris prismatica alba	KL
Iris pseudacorus	AP,B,C,CG,CN,DD,EL,G, HU,I,JE,KL,LA,LG,PO, RH,SA,TH
Iris pseudacorus 'Alba'	B,JE
Iris pseudacorus aureus	PM
Iris pseudacorus new hybrids	B
Iris pseudacorus new vars	JE
Iris pseudacorus 'Sulphur Queen'	B
Iris pumila	AP,B,JE,SC
Iris purpureobractea	PM
Iris regius uzziae S.B.L160 Jordan	MN
Iris reichenbachii	AP,B,JE,SC
Iris reticulata	AP,B,G,KL,SC
Iris reticulata 'Sevan'	KL
Iris ruthenica	AP,B,CG,G
Iris sanguinea	AP,B,CG,G,JE,SA,SG
Iris sanguinea 'Snow Queen'	B,G,JE,SA
Iris sari	B,JE

Iris setosa	AP,B,DD,G,JE,KL,NO, RH,SA,SC,SG,VO
Iris setosa 'Alba'	G,I,P,SG
Iris setosa 'Blue Light'	B,BD,BS,C,CL,HU,JE, KL,L,MO,PK,SK,ST
Iris setosa major	I
Iris setosa ssp canadensis	AP,B,CG,G,HP,JE,KL, SA,SC,SG
Iris setosa v arctica	AP,G,P
Iris setosa v nana see I.setosa canadensis	
Iris sibirica	AP,B,CG,DD,EL,G,HU, JE,KL,LG,RH,RS,SA,SG
Iris 'Sibirica Alba'	AP,B,G,JD,JE,KL,SA,SG
Iris sibirica cult mix	C
Iris sibirica ex 'Flight of Butterflies'	RM
Iris sibirica new hybrids	AP,JE,SA,T
Iris sibirica Plant World hyb	C,P
Iris sibirica 'Red Flare'	T
Iris sibirica 'Soft Blue'	HP
Iris sibirica v artica	SG
Iris sibirica v rimouski	SG
Iris sikkimensis	AP,CG,SC
Iris sintenisii	AP,B,CG,G,JE,KL,NG,SG
Iris sp mix	AP,C,EL,JE,P,PL,SC
Iris spuria	AP,B,G,JE,KL,SC,SG
Iris spuria maritima	AP,I
Iris spuria ssp muselmanica	SA,SG
Iris spuria v halophila	AP,CG,G,MN,SC,SG
Iris stenophylla	AR
Iris suaveolens	AP,B,JE,PM
Iris subbiflora	CG
Iris tectorum	AP,B,G,JE,KL,SC
Iris tenax	AB,AP,B,C,CG,G,JE,NO, SA,SC
Iris tigrida	SG
Iris tingitana v fontanesii A.B.S4211	MN
Iris tingitana v fontanesii A.B.S4452	MN
Iris unguicularis ssp carica	AR
Iris unguicularis ssp cretensis	CG,KL,SC
Iris uniflora	SG
Iris variegata	AP,B,G,JE,SA
Iris ventricosa	SG
Iris versicolor	AP,B,G,JE,KL,PM,PR, SA,SC,SG
Iris versicolor 'Kermesina'	B,JE
Iris vicaria	AR
Iris virginica	AP,B,G
Iris virginica v shrevei	V,PR
Iris wilmottiana	AR
Iris wilsonii	AP,CG
Iris winogradowii	AP,B
Iris x monnieri	B,JE,MN,SA
Iris x sambucina	B
Iris xiphium	B,MA
Iris xiphium B.S411 Portugal	MN
Iris xiphium MS437 Portugal	MN
Iris xiphium MS502 Spain	MN
Irvingia gabonensis	B
Irvingia grandifolia	B
Irvingia smithii	B
Irvingia wombulu	B
Isatis glauca	B,C,JE
Isatis lusitanica	B
Isatis tinctoria	AP,C,CN,CP,DD,G,HP,JE, LA,KS,NS,RH,SA,SG,TH
Ischryolepis ocreata	B,SI

ISCHRYOLEPIS

Ischryolepis subverticillata	B,SI
Iseilema membranaceum	B,NI
Islaya copiapoides Challa	DV
Islaya islayensis	Y
Islaya islayensis Ilo	DV
Islaya krainziana Africa	DV
Islaya mollendensis	Y
Islaya solitaria	Y
Islaya sp mix	C,DV
Islaya unguispina	DV
Isolatocereus dumortiera	CH
Isolepis canariensis	SA
Isolepis cernua	B,SG
Isolepis nodosa	B,NI
Isomeris arborea	B,SZ
Isoplexis canariensis	AP,CG,G,HP,SC,SG
Isoplexis canariensis ssp lamarkii	SG
Isoplexis sceptrum	C,T
Isopogon alcicornis	B,NI
Isopogon anemonifolius	B,C,EL,HA,NI,O,SA,SH
Isopogon anethifolius	B,EL,HA,NI,O,SA,SH
Isopogon attenuatus	B,NI
Isopogon axillaris	B,NI
Isopogon baxteri	B,NI,O
Isopogon buxifolius	B,NI,O
Isopogon cuneatus	B,NI,O
Isopogon divergens	B,NI,O
Isopogon dubius	B,NI,O
Isopogon formosus	B,EL,NI,O,SA
Isopogon latifolius	B,NI
Isopogon polycephalus	B,NI,O
Isopogon scabriusculus	B,NI
Isopogon sphaerocephalus	B,NI,O
Isopogon teretifolius	B,NI,O
Isopogon tridens	B
Isopogon trilobus	B,NI,O
Isopogon villosus	O
Isopyrum thalictroides	B,JE
Isotoma axillaris see Solenopsis	
Isotropis cuneifolia	B,NI,SA
Itea illicifolia	G,SA
Itea virginica	B,FW,SA
Iva hayesiana	B
Ixerba brexioides	B
Ixia campanulata	B
Ixia capillaris	B,RU,SI
Ixia conferta	B,RU
Ixia conferta v ochroleuca	B,KB
Ixia dubia	B,KB,RU,SI
Ixia flexuosa	AP,B,KB,RU,SA,SI
Ixia frederickii	B,KB
Ixia latifolia v angustifolia	B,SI
Ixia lavender pink	C
Ixia maculata	B,C,KB,RU,SI
Ixia marginifolia	B,RU,SI
Ixia odorata	B,RU,SI
Ixia patens	RU
Ixia pauciflora	B,RU
Ixia polystachya	B,RU,SI
Ixia pumilio	C
Ixia rapunculoides	B,KB,RU,SI
Ixia scillaris	B,SI
Ixia sp	AP,RU,SC,SI
Ixia thomasiae	B,RU,SI
Ixia trifolia	B,SI
Ixia vanzijliae	B,RU

Ixia viridiflora	AP,B,C,KB,PL,RU,SA,SI
Ixiochlamys cuneifolia	B,NI
Ixiodia achillaeoides ssp achilaeoides	O
Ixiodia achillaeoides ssp alata	O
Ixiodia achillaeoides ssp arenicola	O
Ixiolirion album	KL
Ixiolirion tataricum	AP,B,CG,G,JE,KL,PA,SC
Ixiolirion tataricum Ledebourii Gr	B,G
Ixora arborea	B
Ixora coccinea	B
Ixora pavetta	B
Ixora pusilla	SG
Jacaranda acutifolia	B
Jacaranda caucana	B,EL
Jacaranda copaia	B
Jacaranda mimosifolia	B,BS,BY,C,CA,CG,CL,D E,DV,EL,HA,HU,KI,LN,O, RE,SA,ST,T,TT,V,VE,WA
Jacaranda obtusifolia	B
Jacksonia furcellata	B,NI
Jacksonia lehmannii	B,NI
Jacksonia scoparia	B,DD,EL,HA,HU,NI,SA
Jacksonia sternbergiana	B,NI
Jacksonia thesioides	B,NI
Jacobsenia hallii	B
Jacobsenia kolbei	B,DV
Jacquemontia pentantha	B
Jacquemontia pringlei	B,SW
Jacquinia pungens	B
Jagera pseudorhus	B,O
Jaltomata edulis	DD
Jamesia americana	B,SW
Jasione amethystina see J. crispa ssp a.	
Jasione crispa	AP,B,JE,SC,T,VO
Jasione crispa ssp amethystina	KL,VO
Jasione crispa ssp crispa	SG
Jasione heldreichii	AP,C,HP,I,SC,SG
Jasione laevis	AP,B,CG,CN,G,HP,KL, SA,SC,SG
Jasione laevis 'Blaulicht'(Blue Light)	BS,C,CL,HP,JE,L,MO,V
Jasione laevis 'Blue Buttons'	B
Jasione montana	AP,B,BS,C,CG,CN,JE,KI, KL,RS,SC,SU,TH
Jasione perennis see J.laevis	
Jasminum abyssinicum	SI
Jasminum 'Angustifolium'	B
Jasminum beesianuum	SG
Jasminum floridum	B
Jasminum fruticans	CG,SA,VE
Jasminum humile 'Revolutum'	B,SA
Jasminum lineare	B
Jasminum mesnyi	B
Jasminum nudiflorum	SA
Jasminum officinale	B,CA,I,SA
Jasminum polyanthum	B
Jatropha cinerea	B,DD
Jatropha curcas	B,DV,EL,HU,SA,SI
Jatropha gossypifolia	B,CH,DV,EL
Jatropha macrocarpa	DV
Jatropha macrorrhiza	B,SW
Jatropha multifida	B,DV
Jatropha panduriifolia	B
Jatropha podagrica	B,DV,EL
Jatropha tanjorensis	B
Jeffersonia diphylla	AP,B,CG,G,KL,SC
Jeffersonia dubia	AP,HP,KL

JENSENOBOTRYΛ

Jensenobotrya lossowiana	B
Johnsonia lupulina	B,C,NI
Johnsonia pubescens	B
Jovellana sinclairii	B,HP
Jovibarba hirta	B
Jovibarba hirta ssp arenaria	B
Jovibarba hueffellii	AP,B,JE,SC
Jovibarba sobolifera	B
Jubaea chilensis	B,CA,CG,EL,O,SA,VE
Jubaeopsis caffra	B
Juglans ailanthifolia	B,FW,LN,SA,SG
Juglans ailanthifolia v cordiformis	B,FW,SA
Juglans alanchanum	B
Juglans californica	B
Juglans cathayensis	LN,SA
Juglans cinerea	B,CG,FW,LN,SA
Juglans hindsii	B,FW,LN,SA
Juglans major	B,SA
Juglans mandshurica	B,FW,LN,SA,SG
Juglans microcarpa	B,LN,SA,WA
Juglans neotropica	B
Juglans nigra	B,CA,CG,EL,FW,HA,LN, SA,VE,WA
Juglans nigra imp	FW
Juglans regia	B,C,CA,FW,N,SA,VE,WA
Juglans regia hardy carpathian	B,FW,LN
Juglans regia Imp	B,FW
Juncus antarcticus	B,SS
Juncus brachycarpus	B,PR
Juncus compressus	B,SG
Juncus conglomeratus	B
Juncus decipiens 'Curly-Wurly'	DE,JE
Juncus effusus	AP,B,C,CG,JE,PR,SA,SG
Juncus ensifolius	AP,B,C,G,JE,SA,SC
Juncus inflexus	A,B,JE,SA,SG
Juncus interior	B,PR
Juncus nodosus	B,PR
Juncus pallidus	B,NI
Juncus tenuis	B,PR,SG
Juncus torreyi	B,PR
Juncus usitanus	HA
Juncus xiphoides	B,HU
Juniperus cedrus	B
Juniperus chinensis	B,C,CA,EL,FW,LN,SA,V
Juniperus communis	A,B,C,EL,FW,HU,LN,PO, SA,SG,VE
Juniperus communis bush form	B,FW
Juniperus communis ssp nana	CG,SG
Juniperus communis v depressa	B,PO
Juniperus conferta	HA,SA,SG
Juniperus davurica	SA
Juniperus deppeana	B
Juniperus deppeana v glauca	B
Juniperus deppleana v pachyphlaea	C,FW,HU,SA
Juniperus excelsa	B,LN,SA
Juniperus flaccida	B,CA,LN
Juniperus foetidissima	B,LN,SA
Juniperus formosana	B,EL,FW,LN,SA
Juniperus horizontalis	B,C,FW,LN,SA
Juniperus monosperma	B,FW,SA
Juniperus nana	B,FW,SA
Juniperus occidentalis	AB,LN
Juniperus osteosperma	B,LN
Juniperus oxycedrus	B,LN,SA,VE
Juniperus pachyphloea see J.deppleana	
Juniperus phoenicea	B,CG,LN,SA,SG,VE

Juniperus pinchotii	B
Juniperus rigida	B,EL,LN,SA,V
Juniperus rigida prostrata	SA
Juniperus sabina	B,SA,SG
Juniperus sabina v tamariscifolia	CG
Juniperus scopulorum	B,C,EL,FW,LN,NO,SA
Juniperus scopulorum 'Glauca'	B
Juniperus silicicola	B,CA,LN,SA
Juniperus squamata 'Meyeri'	CG
Juniperus thurifera	SA
Juniperus virginiana	A,B,C,CA,CG,EL,FW,HU, LN,SA,SG,VE
Juniperus vulgaris	B,LN
Juno bucharica	KL
Juno orchioides	KL
Juno vicaria	kL
Jurinea alata	B,JE
Jurinea ceratocarpa v depressa	KL
Jurinea coronopifolia	VO
Jurinea mollis	B,C,JE
Jurinea moschus ssp moschus	VO
Jurinea moschus ssp pinnatissecta	VO
Jurinea subacaulis	VO
Jurinella see Jurinea	
Justicia aconitiflora	B
Justicia adhatoda	B
Justicia betonica	B,SA
Justicia carnea	B
Justicia prostrata	B
Juttadinteria albata	B,SI
Juttadinteria ausensis	B
Juttadinteria decumbens	B
Juttadinteria deserticola	B
Juttadinteria kovismontana	B
Juttadinteria simpsoni	B,DV,SI
Juttadinteria suavissima	B,DV
Juttadinteria tetrasepala	B,SI
Kadsura japonica	CG
Kalanchoe ballyi	DV
Kalanchoe blossfeldiana	CG
Kalanchoe blossfeldiana 'Pot Gold Hyb'	T
Kalanchoe blossfeldiana Swiss hyb mix	C,J,S,V
Kalanchoe blossfeldiana 'Tetra Vulcan'	B,BD,BS,CL,MO
Kalanchoe blossf. 'Tom Thumb Scarlet'	BS,L
Kalanchoe blossf. 'Tom Thumb Yellow'	B
Kalanchoe brachyloba	B,KB,Y
Kalanchoe brasiliensis	DV
Kalanchoe grandiflora	DV
Kalanchoe lanceolata	B,SI
Kalanchoe laxiflora	DV
Kalanchoe lugardii	CG,DV
Kalanchoe paniculata	B,KB,SI
Kalanchoe rotundifolia	B,CH
Kalanchoe sexangularis	B,SI
Kalanchoe somaliensis	DV
Kalanchoe sp mix	C,EL
Kalanchoe streptantha	DV
Kalanchoe thyrsiflora	B,CH,GC,KB,SI,Y
Kalimerus incisa	AP,C,G
Kallstroemia grandiflora	SW
Kallstroemia platyptera	C
Kalmia angustifolia	B,C,FW,SA,SG
Kalmia latifolia	B,C,CG,FW,HU,LN,NO, SA,VE
Kalmia latifolia 'Rubra'	B,C,EL,FW,VE
Kalmia latifolia white	B,FW

KALMIA

Kalmia microphylla	B,RM
Kalmia polifolia	CG
Kalmia sp mix	T
Kalopanax septemlobus	B,CG,G,LN,SA
Karomia speciosa ssp speciosa	SI
Keckiella antirrhinoides	CG
Keckiella antirrhinoides ssp antirrhinoides	B
Keckiella antirrhinoides ssp microphylla	B,SW
Keckiella cordifolia	B,SW
Keckiella ternata	B,SW
Kedrostis africana	AP,B,DV,SI
Kedrostis punctata	B,CH
Keetia gueinzii	B
Kennedia beckxiana	B,C,EL,NI,O,PL,SA
Kennedia carinata	B,NI
Kennedia coccinea	AU,B,C,DV,EL,NI,O,SA,VE
Kennedia eximia	B,C,HA,NI,O
Kennedia glabrata	B
Kennedia macrophylla	B,HA,NI,O
Kennedia microphylla	B,NI
Kennedia nigricans	B,C,EL,HA,HU,NI,O,PL,SA,SH
Kennedia prorepens	B,NI
Kennedia prostrata	AU,B,C,EL,HA,HU,NI,O,SA,SH
Kennedia retrorsa	B,NI
Kennedia rubicunda	AU,B,C,CA,EL,HA,HP,NI,O,SA,SH,VE
Kennedia sp mix	C
Kensitia pillansii	B
Kentranthus see Centranthus	
Keraudrenia integrifolia	B,NI
Kernera boissieri	KL
Kerria japonica	A,B,FW,LN,SA
Kerria japonica 'Albescens'	B
Keteleeria davidiana	B,CG,EL,SA
Keteleeria evelyniana	B,EL
Khadia acutipetala	B,SI
Khadia sp	SI
Khaya anthotheca	B,SA
Khaya madagascariensis	B,SI
Khaya nyasica	B,EL,LN,SA,WA
Khaya senegalensis	B
Kickxia elatine	SG
Kickxia elatine ssp elatine	CG
Kickxia sieberi	B
Kigelia africana	B,C,SI,WA
Kigelia pinnata	CA,EL,HA,O,RE,SA
Kiggelaria africana	B,EL,KB,LN,SA,SI,WA
Kirengeshoma palmata	AP,B,JE,SA,SC
Kirkia acuminata	B,EL,LN,SA,SI,WA
Kirkia wilmsii	B,SI,WA
Kirkianella novae-zelandiae	B,SS
Kissenia capensis	B,SI
Kitaibela vitifolia	AP,B,C,G,HP,HU,JD,JE,PL,SA,SC
Kleinedoxa gabonensis	B
Kleinhovia hospita	B
Kleinia fulgens	B,SI
Kleinia grandiflora	B
Kleinia longiflora	B,DD
Knautia arvensis	B,C,CG,CN,CO,DD,G,HP,HU,JE,LA,SA,TH,TU
Knautia macedonica	AP,B,C,G,HP,I,JD,JE,P,PL,RS,SA,SC,SE,T
Knautia macedonica 'Melton Pastels'	B,PK,PL,T
Knautia saragavensis 'Pink Stars'	B,C
Knightia excelsa	B,SA
Kniphofia baurii	B,SI
Kniphofia 'Border Ballet'	JE,PL,U
Kniphofia brachystachya	B,SI
Kniphofia breviflora	B,SI
Kniphofia buchananii	B,SI
Kniphofia caulescens	B,HP,P,SI
Kniphofia citrina	B,HP,JE,SG,SI
Kniphofia Crown hybrids	BS,N
Kniphofia 'Earliest of All'	HP
Kniphofia ensifolia	AP,B,G,JE,RH
Kniphofia Express Hybrids	JE
Kniphofia 'Fairyland'	BS,C,DT,HP
Kniphofia foliosa	B,RH
Kniphofia galpinii	KL
Kniphofia hirsuta	B,SI
Kniphofia hybrid	B,CG,HP,KI,SA
Kniphofia hybrida mix	BD,BY,C,F
Kniphofia hybrids dw	AP,HP
Kniphofia ichopensis	B,SC,SI
Kniphofia laxiflora	B,KB,SI
Kniphofia linearifolia	B,C,SC,SI,T
Kniphofia littoralis	B,SI
Kniphofia natalensis	RH
Kniphofia northiae	B,LG,SI
Kniphofia Pfitzer's Hybrids mix	BS,SK
Kniphofia praecox	B,SC,SI
Kniphofia pumila	B,G
Kniphofia ritularis	B,SI
Kniphofia rooperi	B,C,SI
Kniphofia 'Royal Castle'	B,HU,V
Kniphofia sarmentosa	B,SI
Kniphofia sp	SI
Kniphofia splendida	SI
Kniphofia stricta	B,SI
Kniphofia thompsonii v snowdenii	RH
Kniphofia triangularis	C,JE,RH,SG
Kniphofia triangularis hyb	JE
Kniphofia triangularis ssp triangularis	B,SI
Kniphofia typhoides	B,SI
Kniphofia tysonii	B,SI
Kniphofia uvaria	B,CG,CN,EL,G,HP,J,RH,SI
Kniphofia uvaria new hybrids	B,CA,DE,EL,JE,CL,L,MO,T
Kniphofia uvaria special hybrids	T
Kniphofia uvaria v grandiflora	B,JE
Knowltonia capensis	B,SI
Knowltonia sp	SI
Knowltonia vesicatoria	BH
Kochea laniflora	B
Kochia see Bassia	
Koeleria cristata see K.micrantha	
Koeleria glauca	AP,B,BS,C,CA,G,HP,JE,SA,SC
Koeleria macrantha	B,DD,DE,JE,NO,PR,SA,SG
Koelreuteria bipinnata	B,CA,EL,LN
Koelreuteria integrifolia	FW,LN,SA
Koelreuteria paniculata	A,AP,B,C,CA,CG,DV,EL,W,G,HA,HU,LN,N,O,SA,SC,VE
Kolkwitzia amabilis	B,C,CG,EL,FW,HP,KL,LN,N,SA,SG,T,VE

148

KOROLKOWIA

Korolkowia sewerzowii	KL	Lachenalia gillettii	B,RU,SC
Kosteletskya virginica	JE,NT	Lachenalia haarlemensis	B,RU,SI
Krainzia guelzowiana	DV	Lachenalia hirta	B,RU,SI
Krainzia guelzowiana v splendens	DV	Lachenalia isopetala	B,SI
Krainzia longiflora	BC,DV	Lachenalia juncifolia	B,RU
Kraussia floribunda	B,BH,C	Lachenalia kliprandensis	B,SI
Kuhnia eupatorioides	B,PR	Lachenalia latifolia	B,RU,SC
Kunzea ambigua	B,C,EL,HA,NI,O,SA	Lachenalia liliiflora	AP,B,KB,MN,RU,SI
Kunzea baxteri	AU,B,C,EL,HA,NI,O,SA	Lachenalia longibracteata	B,RU
Kunzea capitata	AU,B,C,EL,HA,NI,O,SH	Lachenalia marginata	RU
Kunzea ericifolia	B,NI	Lachenalia mathewsii	AP,B,DV,KB,RU,SI
Kunzea ericoides	AU,B,HA,NI,SA,SH,SS	Lachenalia mediana	B,RU,SC,SI
Kunzea flavescens	B,NI,O	Lachenalia minima	B,RU
Kunzea 'Mauve Mist'	B,EL	Lachenalia mutabilis	AP,B,RU,SI
Kunzea micromera	B,NI	Lachenalia namaquensis	B,C,KB,O,RU,SI
Kunzea opposita	B	Lachenalia namibiensis	B,KB,O,RU
Kunzea parvifolia	B,C,EL,HA,NI,O,SA,SH	Lachenalia orchioides	RU,SC
Kunzea pomifera	B	Lachenalia orchioides v glaucina	B,SI
Kunzea preissiana	B,NI	Lachenalia orchioides v glaucina var.1	B
Kunzea pulchella	B,NI	Lachenalia orchioides v glaucina var.2	B
Kunzea recurva	B,NI,O	Lachenalia orchioides v orchioides	B,RU,SI
Kunzea sp mix	C	Lachenalia orthopetala	B,DV,KB,O,RU,SI
Labichea lanceolata	SA	Lachenalia pallida	AP,B,DV,KB,RU,SC,SI
Labichea lanceolata ssp brevifolia	B,NI	Lachenalia pallida blue	B,RU
Labichea lanceolata ssp lanceolata	B,NI	Lachenalia pallida yellow	KB
Labichea punctata	B,NI	Lachenalia patula	B,KB,SI
Lablab fabiiformis	B	Lachenalia peersii	B,DV,KB,SI
Lablab lignosus	C	Lachenalia polyphylla	B,SI
Lablab purpureus	C,DE,F,HU,JO,PI,PK,SK	Lachenalia purpureo-caerulea	B,C,DV,KB,MN,RU,SI
Lablab purpureus cvs	B	Lachenalia pusilla	B,C,RU,SI
Laburnum alpinum	B,FW,HP,LN,SA,SG	Lachenalia pustulata	B,C,DV,KB,RU,SI
Laburnum anagyroides	A,AB,B,CG,FW,HP,KL,	Lachenalia pustulata white	B,KB,RU
	LN,SA,SG	Lachenalia reflexa	AP,B,C,KB,MN,RU,SC,SI
Laburnum anagyroides 'Quercifolium'	SG	Lachenalia rosea	B,G,RU,SC
Laburnum mix bonsai types	C	Lachenalia rubida	B,RU,SI
Laburnum watereri	SA	Lachenalia salteri	B
Laburnum watereri x 'Vossii'	B,EL,FW	Lachenalia sp	AP,KB,MN,RU,SI
Laccospadix australasica	B,EL,HA,O,SA	Lachenalia splendida	AP,B,DV,KB,RU,SI
Lachenalia alba	B,SI	Lachenalia thomasiae	B,RU,SI
Lachenalia algoensis	B,RU,SC	Lachenalia trichophylla	B
Lachenalia aloides	B,DV,RU,SC,SI	Lachenalia undulata	B,RU,SI
Lachenalia aloides 'Nelsonii'	B	Lachenalia unicolor	B,C,HU,KB,MN,RU,SI
Lachenalia aloides v aurea	B	Lachenalia unifolia	B,RU,SI
Lachenalia aloides v luteola	B	Lachenalia unifolia wrightii	B,SI
Lachenalia aloides v quadricolor	AP,B,RU	Lachenalia van rhynsdorp form	B
Lachenalia aloides v vanzyliae	RU	Lachenalia variegata	B,DV,RU,SI
Lachenalia ameliae	B,RU	Lachenalia violacea	B,RU,SA,SI
Lachenalia arbuthnotiae	B,KB,RU,SI	Lachenalia viridiflora	B,C,O,RU,SI
Lachenalia attenuata	B,SI	Lachenalia zebrina f zebrina	B,SI
Lachenalia bachmannii	B,KB,RU	Lachenalia zeyheri	B,MN,RU,SI
Lachenalia bulbifera	B,RU,SA,SC,SI	Lachenostylis hirta	B,SI
Lachenalia bulbifera 'Agulhas' form	B,RU	Lachnospermum imbricatum	B,SI
Lachenalia bulbifera orange	RU	Lachnostachys eriobotrya	B,NI,SA
Lachenalia bulbifera red	RU	Lactuca perennis	AP,B,HP,SC
Lachenalia capensis	B,RU	Lactuca saligna	B,NS
Lachenalia carnosa	B,RU,SA,SI	Lactuca sativa v angustana	B
Lachenalia comptonii	B,RU,SI	Lactuca sativa v asparagina	B
Lachenalia concordiana	B,SI	Lactuca serriola	B,SG
Lachenalia congesta	B,RU,SI	Lactuca virosa	B,SG
Lachenalia contaminata	B,C,DV,KB,RU,SI	Lafoensia punicifolia	B
Lachenalia elegans	AP,B,MN,RU,SI	Lagenaria siceraria	DD,KS,V
Lachenalia elegans v elegans	RU	Lagenaria siceraria 'Apache Dipper Gourd'	B
Lachenalia elegans v flava	RU	Lagenaria siceraria 'Hernandez Snake'	HU
Lachenalia elegans v suaveolens	B,RU	Lagenaria siceraria 'Hopi Rattle Gourd'	B
Lachenalia fistulosa	AP,B,C,O,RU,SI	Lagenaria siceraria 'Long Dipper Gourd'	B,HU,JO
Lachenalia framesii	B,RU	Lagenaria sic. 'Mayo Gooseneck Gourd'	B

LAGENARIA

Lagenaria siceraria 'O'odham Dipper'	B
Lagenaria sic. 'O'odham Small Bilobal'	B
Lagenaria sic. 'Peyote Ceremonial Gourd'	B
Lagenaria sic. 'San Juan Snake Gourd'	B
Lagenaria sic. 'S. Domingo Dipper Gourd'	B
Lagenaria siceraria v clavatina	SG
Lagenaria sic. 'Yaqui Deer Dance Rattle'	B
Lagenaria sphaerica	B,SI
Lagenophora cuneata	B,SS
Lagerstroemia archerana	B,EL,HA
Lagerstroemia duperreana	B
Lagerstroemia floribunda	B,EL,HA,SA
Lagerstroemia flos reginae	EL,HA,SA
Lagerstroemia indica	B,CA,DE,EL,FW,HA,JE, LN,SA,VE,WA
Lagerstroemia indica 'Alba'	B,JE
Lagerstroemia ind. 'Basham's Party Pink'	B
Lagerstroemia indica 'Little Chief'	BS,EL,HA,T
Lagerstroemia lanceolata	EL,HA,SA
Lagerstroemia loudonii	B
Lagerstroemia microcarpa	B
Lagerstroemia mix supersonic	PK
Lagerstroemia reginae	B
Lagerstroemia rosea	HA
Lagerstroemia speciosa	B,CA,DD,RE
Lagerstroemia thorellii	EL,HA,SA
Lagerstroemia villosa	B,EL
Lagopsis marubiastrum	VO
Lagotis glauca	VO
Lagunaria patersonii	B,C,CA,EL,HA,HU,LN, NI,O,SA,WA
Lagurus ovatus	AP,B,C,CG,CL,DE,F,G,J, JO,KI,KS,MO,PK,SG, SK,T,U,V,VY
Lagurus ovatus florist select	B
Lagurus ovatus 'Nanus'	B
Lallemantia canescens	B,HP,RM
Lamarchea hakeifolia	B,NI
Lamarckia aurea	B,HU
Lamarckia aurea 'Golden Shower'	C
Lambertia formosa	B,EL,HA,NI,O,SA
Lambertia multiflora	B
Lambertia propinqua	B,NI,O
Lamiastrum see Lamium	
Lamium album	B
Lamium eriocephalum	B,RM
Lamium galeobdolon	B,HP,JE,SU
Lamium maculatum	B,C,JE
Lamium moschatum	B
Lamium purpureum	B,JE
Lamium tomentosum	VO
Lamourouxia dasyantha	B
Lampranthus amoenus	B,KB,SA,SI,Y
Lampranthus aureus	B,C,SI,Y
Lampranthus bicolor	B,SI
Lampranthus blandus	B
Lampranthus cedarbergensis	B,SI
Lampranthus copiosus	B,KB,SI,Y
Lampranthus corolliflorus	B,SI
Lampranthus deltoides	B,KB,SG,SI,Y
Lampranthus emarginatus	B,DV,SI
Lampranthus explanatus	B,SI,Y
Lampranthus falcatus	B,SI
Lampranthus franciscii	B
Lampranthus glaucus	B,SI
Lampranthus haworthii	B,SI .
Lampranthus hoerleianianus	B,SI
Lampranthus maximilianus	B,SI
Lampranthus multiradiatus	B,KB,SA,SI,Y
Lampranthus primavernus	B,KB,SI,Y
Lampranthus promontorii	B
Lampranthus roseus	B,KB,SI,Y
Lampranthus scaber	B,SI
Lampranthus sp mix	C,T
Lampranthus spectabilis	B,C,SA
Lampranthus stayneri	B
Lampranthus tegens	B,SI,Y
Lampranthus violaceus	B,SI,Y
Lanaria lanata	B,SI
Lannea coromandelica	B
Lansium domesticum	B
Lantana camara	B,EL,JE,SA,SC,SG,VE
Lantana camara hyb	G,PK,T
Lantana camara v splendens	B
Lantana Crown hybrids	BS,KI
Lantana hybrida nana mix	BY,C,DE,HU
Lantana lilacina	B
Lantana montevidensis	B,CA
Lapageria rosea	B,C,DD,P,PL,SA,SE,T
Lapageria rosea v albiflora	PL
Lapeirousia anceps	AP,B,G,HP,RU,SI
Lapeirousia arenicola	B,SI
Lapeirousia corymbosa	B,RU,SI
Lapeirousia cruenta see Anomatheca laxa	
Lapeirousia divaricata	AP,B,SC,SI
Lapeirousia fabricii	B,RU,SI
Lapeirousia jacquinii	AP,B,DV,G,KB,RU,SA,SI
Lapeirousia laxa see Anomatheca laxa	
Lapeirousia laxa v alba	C
Lapeirousia micrantha	B,SI
Lapeirousia neglecta	B,SI
Lapeirousia oreogena	B,RU,SA,SC,SI
Lapeirousia plicata	B,RU,SI
Lapeirousia pyramidalis	B,RU,SI
Lapeirousia silenoides	B,RU,SA,SI
Lapeirousia sp	SI
Lapidaria margaretae	B,BC,DV,SI,Y
Laportea canadensis	B,DD
Lappula squarrosa	SG
Lapsana communis	B,CG,CN,TH
Lapsana communis 'Inky' (V)	B,NS
Lardizabala biternata	B,SA
Larix decidua	B,C,CA,EL,FW,LN,RH, SA,SG,VE
Larix decidua v sudetica	B,VE
Larix gmelinii	B,FW,LN,RH,SA,SG
Larix gmelinii v olgensis	B
Larix kaempferi	B,C,CG,FW,G,LN,N,RH, SA,SG,T,VE
Larix laricina	AP,B,FW,HP,LN,SG
Larix leptolepis	CA
Larix lyallii	LN,NO
Larix occidentalis	AB,B,C,FW,LN,NO,SA
Larix olgensis	LN,SA
Larix pricipis	SA
Larix sibirica	B,FW,LN,SA,SG
Larix sukaczewii	LN,SA
Larix x czekanowskii	SG
Larix x marschlinsii	VE
Larrea tridentata	B,HU,SA
Laserpitium gallicum	B,HP,JE
Laserpitium halleri	B

LASERPITIUM

Laserpitium hispidum	SG
Laserpitium latifolium	B,HP,JE,SG
Laserpitium siler	B,G,JE
Lasiopetalum baueri	B,NI
Lasiopetalum behrii	B,NI,SA
Lasiopetalum bracteatum	B,NI
Lasiopetalum indutum	B,NI
Lasiopetalum schulzenii	B,NI
Lasiospermum bipinnatum	B,KB<SI
Lasthenia glabrata	B
Latania loddigesii	B,CA,O
Latania lontaroides	B,O
Latania verschaffeltii	B,O
Lathraea clandestina	AP,NG
Lathyraea squamaria	CG
Lathyrus angulatus	B,RS
Lathyrus angustifoliius RB94068	P
Lathyrus annuus	B,BS,PG,RS
Lathyrus annuus 'Mrs.Rosamund Penney'	B,BS,PG
Lathyrus annuus red	BS,PG,RS
Lathyrus aphaca	B,RS,SG
Lathyrus articulatus	B,BS,PG,RS
Lathyrus aureus	AP,B,C,HP,LG,NG,SC,SG
Lathyrus belinensis	B,PG
Lathyrus blepharicarpus	B
Lathyrus chilensis	C
Lathyrus chloranthus	AP,B,BS,C,HP,HU,MS, NG,PG,PL,RS
Lathyrus chloranthus 'Lemonade'	T
Lathyrus cirrhosus	HP
Lathyrus clymenum	AP,B,BS,CG,PG,PL,RS
Lathyrus clymenum articulatus see L.articulatus	
Lathyrus clymenum 'Chelsea'	B,BS,PG
Lathyrus davidii	KL,NG
Lathyrus filiformis	B,RS,SC
Lathyrus fremontii h. see L.laxiflorus	
Lathyrus gmelinii	B,JE,SA
Lathyrus gorgonii	PG
Lathyrus grandiflorus	B,C,G,HP,JE,NG,SA
Lathyrus heterophyllus	BS,C,F,HP,JE,NG,PG,SA
Lathyrus hierosolymitanus	B,PG,RS
Lathyrus hirsutus	B,BS,PG,PL
Lathyrus japonicus	B,G,KL,SA,SC
Lathyrus laetiflorus v alefeldii	B,RS
Lathyrus laevigatus	AP,B,JE
Lathyrus latifolius	w.a
Lathyrus latifolius 'Albus'	AP,BS,G,HP,JD,LG,SC
Lathyrus latifolius 'Apple Blossom'	B,PG
Lathyrus latifolius 'Bishop's Pink'	B,BS
Lathyrus latifolius deep pink	B,BS,RS
Lathyrus latifolius finest mix	BO,JE
Lathyrus latifolius pale pink	HP,I,LG,PG,RS
Lathyrus latifolius 'Pearl' mix	BS,DE,JO,KS
Lathyrus latifolius (Pearl Pink) 'Rose Perle'	B,BS,BY,C,DI,JD,JE,SA
Lathyrus latifolius 'Pearl Red'	B,BS,BY,C,JE,KS
Lathyrus latifolius 'Pearl White'	AP,B,BS,BY,C,DI,G,I,JE, KS,LG,P,PG,PL,SA,T
Lathyrus latifolius 'Pink Blush'	P
Lathyrus latifolius purple	B,BS,PG
Lathyrus latifolius splendens	PL
Lathyrus latifolius two tone pink	I
Lathyrus laxiflorus	AP,B,BS,HP,KL,NG,P,PG
Lathyrus linifolius v montanus	B,G,HP,SC
Lathyrus luteus	B,C
Lathyrus maritimus	AB,B,C,FW,NG,SG
Lathyrus miniature unknown	C

Lathyrus mix bushy & climbing sp	T
Lathyrus nervosus	B,C,HP,PG,PL,SE,SG
Lathyrus neurolobus	B,RS
Lathyrus niger	AP,B,CG,HP,JE,NS,RS, SA
Lathyrus nissolia	B,G,RS
Lathyrus ochrus	AP,B,BS,CG,NG,PG,RS
Lathyrus odoratus	AP,B,LG,SC,SG
Lathyrus odoratus 'Aerospace'	B,BS,KI
Lathyrus odoratus 'Air Warden'	B,BD,BS,BY,KI,M,MO, PG
Lathyrus odoratus 'Alan Titchmarsh'	B,BO,BS,DS,KI,SB,TU, WO
Lathyrus odoratus 'Alan Williams'	B,BS,KI,MS
Lathyrus odoratus 'Alastair'	WO
Lathyrus odoratus 'Alice Hardwick'	B,BO,BS,KI
Lathyrus odoratus 'America'	B,BO,BS,C,DS,DT,F,PG, TH
Lathyrus odoratus 'American Beauty'	L
Lathyrus odoratus 'Angela Ann'	B,BS,DS,KI,MS,PG,SB
Lathyrus odoratus 'Annabelle'	BO,T
Lathyrus odoratus 'Anne Gregg'	B,SB,WO
Lathyrus odoratus 'Anne Vestry'	BS
Lathyrus odoratus 'Annie B Gilroy'	B,BS,PG,TH
Lathyrus odoratus 'Annie Good'	B,BS,DS,KI,PG
Lathyrus odoratus 'Anniversary'	B,BS,DS,KI,MS,PG,SB, T,WO
Lathyrus odoratus 'Anthea Turner'	T
Lathyrus odoratus 'Antique Fantasy Mix'	T
Lathyrus odoratus 'Apricot Queen'	DS
Lathyrus odoratus 'Apricot Sprite'	B,BS,KI,SB
Lathyrus odoratus 'Arbor Low'	BS,KI
Lathyrus odoratus 'Arthur Hellyer'	U
Lathyrus odoratus 'Ascot'	B,BS,SB
Lathyrus odoratus 'Avon Beauty'	BS
Lathyrus odoratus 'Balcony Bride'	PL
Lathyrus odoratus 'Ballerina'	M
Lathyrus odoratus 'Balmoral'	B,SB
Lathyrus odoratus 'Band Aid'	B,BS,KI,SB,U
Lathyrus odoratus 'Barry Dare'	U
Lathyrus odoratus 'Batheaston'	BS,KI,PG,WO
Lathyrus odoratus 'Beacon'	BS
Lathyrus odoratus 'Beaujolais'	B,BD,BS,D,KI,MO,S, TU,WO
Lathyrus odoratus 'Beauty Queen'	BS
Lathyrus odoratus 'Benjamin Townsend'	B,BS,PG
Lathyrus odoratus 'Bert Boucher'	BS
Lathyrus odoratus 'Bijou'	BS,BU,CA,DT,F,KI,PI, SK,T
Lathyrus odoratus 'Black Diamond'	B,BS,BY,KI,PG
Lathyrus odoratus 'Black Knight'	B,BS,C,F,PG,TH
Lathyrus odoratus 'Black Prince'	BS,KI,WO
Lathyrus odoratus 'Blanche Ferry'	B,BS,PG,TH
Lathyrus odoratus 'Blaze'	BS
Lathyrus odoratus 'Blue Danube'	BO,BS,BY,KI,T,U,WO
Lathyrus odoratus 'Blue Heaven'	BS,KI
Lathyrus odoratus 'Blue Ice'	M
Lathyrus odoratus 'Blue Mantle'	BS
Lathyrus odoratus 'Blue Riband'	BS
Lathyrus odoratus 'Blue Triumph'	BO,BS
Lathyrus odoratus 'Blue Velvet'	B,BD,BS,KI,MO,PG
Lathyrus odoratus 'Blushing Bride'	BS,KI
Lathyrus odoratus 'Bolton's Unequalled'	BO
Lathyrus odoratus 'Bouquet mix'	BS,D,DT,F,KI,M,S,SE
Lathyrus odoratus 'Bouquet' s-c	S
Lathyrus odoratus 'Cupani's Original 1699'	B,BS,PG

LATHYRUS

Lathyrus odoratus 'Brampton'	PG
Lathyrus odoratus 'Brian Clough'	B,BS,DS,KI,M,MS,SB, U,WO
Lathyrus odoratus 'Bridget'	U
Lathyrus odoratus 'Bristol Cream'	BS,KI
Lathyrus odoratus 'Buccaneer'	B,BS,KI,PG
Lathyrus odoratus 'Burnished Bronze'	BS,KI,MS
Lathyrus odoratus 'Burpee's Patio mix'	MS
Lathyrus odoratus 'Busby'	B,BS,C,PG,T,TH
Lathyrus odoratus 'Butterfly'	B,BS,PG
Lathyrus odoratus Bygones see Old fashioned	
Lathyrus odoratus 'Cambridge Blue'	B,BS,KI,PG,U
Lathyrus odoratus 'Candy Frills'	BO
Lathyrus odoratus 'Candyman'	F
Lathyrus odoratus 'Captain of The Blues'	B,BS,PG,TH
Lathyrus odoratus 'Captain Scott'	BO,WO
Lathyrus odoratus 'Carlotta'	BS,BY,J,KI,WO
Lathyrus odoratus 'Cascade'	L
Lathyrus odoratus 'Catherine'	B,BS,SB,U
Lathyrus odoratus 'Celebration'	SB
Lathyrus odoratus 'Champagne Bubbles'	U,WO
Lathyrus odoratus 'Charles Unwin'	SB,U
Lathyrus odoratus 'Charlie's Angel'	B,BS,DS,KI,MS,PG,U
Lathyrus odoratus 'Charlotte Riley'	BS,PB,G
Lathyrus odoratus 'Chatsworth'	T
Lathyrus odoratus 'Chesire Blue'	B,BS,MS,PG,TH
Lathyrus odoratus children's mix	PG
Lathyrus odoratus 'Claire Elizabeth'	BO,BS,KI,WO
Lathyrus odoratus 'Colin Unwin'	B,SB,U
Lathyrus odoratus collections	BO,BY,D,DS,KI,SB,U
Lathyrus odoratus 'Columbus'	U
Lathyrus odoratus 'Comet'	U
Lathyrus odoratus 'Concorde'	BS,KI
Lathyrus odoratus 'Continental'	BD,BS,CL,CN,KI,KS,MO
Lathyrus odoratus 'Corinne'	BO,BS,KI
Lathyrus odoratus 'Countess Cadogan'	B,BS,PG,TH
Lathyrus odoratus 'Countess of Radnor'	PG
Lathyrus odoratus 'Cream Beauty'	BS,BY,DE
Lathyrus odoratus 'Cream Delight'	BS
Lathyrus odoratus 'Cream Southbourne'	B,BO,BS,DS,KI,PG,SB, T,U,WO
Lathyrus odoratus 'Cream Triumph'	WO
Lathyrus odoratus 'Cubar Edge'	BS
Lathyrus odoratus 'Cupani'	C,DT,F,PG,TH
Lathyrus odoratus 'Cupid Pink'	B,BS,DS
Lathyrus odoratus 'Cupid Pink Imp'	CL,S,V
Lathyrus odoratus 'Cuthbertson'	AB,B,BS,F,SK
Lathyrus odoratus 'Daily Mail'	U
Lathyrus odoratus 'Daleman'	BO
Lathyrus odoratus 'Daphne'	L,U
Lathyrus odoratus 'Dawn'	MS
Lathyrus odoratus 'Dean's Scarlet'	BO,BS,KI,WO
Lathyrus odoratus 'Denis Compton'	BO,BS,KI,WO
Lathyrus odoratus 'Denise Tanner'	BS,PG
Lathyrus odoratus 'Diamond Wedding'	B,BS,KI,PG,WO
Lathyrus odoratus 'Diana'	BS,U
Lathyrus odoratus Dobies Giant Waved	D
Lathyrus odoratus 'Dolly Varden'	B,PG
Lathyrus odoratus 'Donna Jones'	B,BS,PG
Lathyrus odoratus 'Dorothy Dee'	DS
Lathyrus odoratus 'Dorothy Eckford'	BO,BS,BY,C,DS,MS,PG, TH
Lathyrus odoratus 'Douglas McArthur'	L
Lathyrus odoratus 'Dr. Robert Uvedale'	PG
Lathyrus odoratus 'Dragonfly'	B,BS,PG,TH
Lathyrus odor. 'Duchess of Roxburghe'	WO
Lathyrus odoratus 'Duke of York'	C,PG
Lathyrus odoratus 'Dynasty'	B,BS,KI,MS,PG,WO
Lathyrus odoratus 'Early Spencer'	DE
Lathyrus odoratus 'Eckford's Mix'	DT
Lathyrus odoratus 'Eclipse'	BS,DS,MS
Lathyrus odoratus 'Edward Unwin'	U
Lathyrus odoratus 'Edwardian Collection'	U
Lathyrus odoratus 'Elaine Paige'	B,BS,SB
Lathyrus odoratus 'Elegance'	B,SB
Lathyrus odoratus 'Elizabeth'	PG
Lathyrus odoratus 'Elizabeth Taylor'	B,BD,BO,BS,BY,J,KI, MO,PG,TU
Lathyrus odoratus 'Ella'	BS
Lathyrus odoratus 'Ena Margaret'	BS
Lathyrus odoratus 'Esther Rantzen'	B,BS,KI,SB
Lathyrus odoratus 'Ethel Grace'	B,BO,BS,MS,PG
Lathyrus odoratus 'Eva Bridger'	DS
Lathyrus odoratus 'Evening Glow'	BS,KI
Lathyrus odoratus 'Evensong'	U
Lathyrus odoratus 'Exhibition Coll.' 10 pk	U
Lathyrus odoratus 'Explorer'	BS,D,DT,F,PK,SK
Lathyrus odoratus 'Fairy Queen'	B,BS,PG,TH
Lathyrus odoratus 'Fanny Adams'	PG
Lathyrus odoratus 'Fantasia' mix	F,S,T
Lathyrus odoratus 'Fatima'	BS,KI,U
Lathyrus odoratus 'Felicity Kendal'	B,BS,KI,SB,WO
Lathyrus odoratus 'Fiona'	BS
Lathyrus odoratus 'Firebrand'	BS,KI
Lathyrus odoratus 'Firecrest'	BO,BS,KI,T
Lathyrus odoratus 'Fireglow'	BS
Lathyrus odoratus 'First Lady'	BS,KI,WO
Lathyrus odoratus 'Flagship'	J
Lathyrus odoratus 'Flashlight'	BS
Lathyrus odoratus 'Flora Norton'	B,BO,BS,BY,F,PG,PL,TH
Lathyrus odoratus 'Floral Tribute'	T
Lathyrus odoratus 'Floriana'	V
Lathyrus odoratus 'Fl. Arrangers' Blend'	T,U
Lathyrus odoratus 'Fragrantissima'	T
Lathyrus odoratus 'Frolic'	BS,KI
Lathyrus odoratus 'Gaiety'	BO,BS,KI
Lathyrus odoratus 'Galaxy' mix	BO,BS,BY,CL,D,DI,F, KI,M,MO,R,S,ST,YA,U
Lathyrus odor. 'Gardener's Favourite' 5 pk	U
Lathyrus odoratus 'Geoff Hamilton'	DS
Lathyrus odoratus 'Geranium Pink'	B,BD,BY,J,MO
Lathyrus odoratus 'Geranium Pink Imp.'	BS,KI
Lathyrus odoratus 'Giant Exhibition Mix'	SE
Lathyrus odoratus 'Giant Hybrids Mix'	BS
Lathyrus odoratus giant late heat-resist	PK
Lathyrus odoratus 'Giant Waved Mix'	CN,J,V
Lathyrus odoratus 'Gipsy Queen'	B,BO,BS,KI,PG
Lathyrus odoratus 'Glow'	U
Lathyrus odoratus 'Gorleston'	BO
Lathyrus odoratus 'Grace Of Monaco'	B,BS,KI,SB
Lathyrus odor. 'Grand.Scented' s-c, mix	BY
Lathyrus odoratus 'Grayson Grand. 300's'	PG
Lathyrus odoratus 'Grayson's Heritage'	BS,PG
Lathyrus odoratus 'Great Expectations'	BS,KI
Lathyrus odoratus 'Hampton Court'	B,BS,KI,SB
Lathyrus odoratus 'Hanslope Gem'	BS,KI
Lathyrus odoratus 'Harvest Time'	BS
Lathyrus odoratus 'Harvey's Blush'	BS,KI
Lathyrus odoratus 'Hazel Tasker'	BS
Lathyrus odoratus 'Henry Eckford'	B,BS,C,PG,TH
Lathyrus odoratus 'Her Majesty'	U
Lathyrus odoratus 'Herald'	BS,WO

LATHYRUS

Lathyrus odoratus 'Hillbury'	WO
Lathyrus odoratus 'Holymoorside'	PG
Lathyrus odoratus 'Honeymoon'	BS,DS,KI,MS,TU
Lathyrus odoratus 'Hunters Moon'	BS,KI,TU
Lathyrus odoratus 'Ice Butter Grandiflora'	BS,KI
Lathyrus odoratus 'Ice Cream'	J
Lathyrus odoratus 'Ice Raspberry'	BS
Lathyrus odoratus 'Ice Strawberry'	BS
Lathyrus odoratus 'Ice Vanilla Grandiflora'	BS,KI
Lathyrus odoratus 'Indigo King'	B,BS,PG,TH
Lathyrus odoratus 'Ivory Queen'	BS,PG
Lathyrus odoratus 'Jacqueline O'Brien'	BO
Lathyrus odoratus 'Janet Scott'	B,BO,BS,C,DS,F,PG,TH
Lathyrus odoratus 'Jayne Amanda'	BO,BS,KI,MS
Lathyrus odoratus 'Jet Set'	BS,D,F,J,S
Lathyrus odoratus 'Jill Walton'	B,MS
Lathyrus odoratus 'Jilly'	B,BS,DS,KI,MS,PG,SB, U,WO
Lathyrus odoratus 'Jimmy Young'	U
Lathyrus odoratus 'John Ness'	BS
Lathyrus odoratus 'Joker'	BO,BS,KI,WO
Lathyrus odoratus 'Judy Gaunt'	PG
Lathyrus odoratus 'Judyth Macleod'	PG
Lathyrus odoratus 'Juliana'	BS
Lathyrus odoratus 'Karen Louise'	BS,CO
Lathyrus odoratus 'Karen Reeve'	BS,DS,MS,PG
Lathyrus odoratus 'Ken Colledge'	U
Lathyrus odoratus 'King Edward VII'	B,BO,BS,BY,C,DS,F,PG, TH
Lathyrus odoratus 'King of Mauves'	BS,KI,WO
Lathyrus odoratus 'King's Bounty'	BS,KI
Lathyrus odoratus 'King's Bride'	BS,KI
Lathyrus odoratus 'King's Cloak'	BS,KI
Lathyrus odoratus 'King's Frill'	BS
Lathyrus odoratus 'Kingfisher'	B,BS,PG,TH
Lathyrus odoratus 'Kings Reach'	BS,KI
Lathyrus odoratus Kings' Scented Coll.	KI
Lathyrus odoratus Kings' Special	KI
Lathyrus odoratus 'Kiri Te Kanawa'	B,SB
Lathyrus odoratus 'Kiwi Bicolours Mix'	BS,DT,F,YA
Lathyrus odoratus 'Knee-Hi'	BO,BS,BY,C,DE,DN,KI, KS,L,ST
Lathyrus odoratus 'Lady Diana'	BS,KI
Lathyrus odoratus 'Lady Fairburn'	BS,KI,WO
Lathyrus odoratus 'Lady Grisel Hamilton'	B,BS,C,F,PG,TH
Lathyrus odoratus 'Lady Penny'	BO
Lathyrus odoratus 'Lady Serena James'	BY,PG
Lathyrus odoratus 'Lady Turral'	B,BS,PG
Lathyrus odoratus 'Larkspur'	BS,BY,KI
Lathyrus odoratus 'Laura'	DS
Lathyrus odoratus 'Leamington'	B,BD,BS,BY,D,J,KI,M, MO,PG,S
Lathyrus odoratus 'Liberty Belle'	PG
Lathyrus odoratus 'Lilac Queen'	PG
Lathyrus odoratus 'Lilac Ripple'	B,BS,PG,PL,T
Lathyrus odoratus 'Lilac Silk'	BO,BS,KI,WO
Lathyrus odoratus 'Lilac Time'	B,BS,KI,SB
Lathyrus odoratus 'Little Sweetheart'	BS,BY,KI,KS,V
Lathyrus odoratus 'Liz Bolton'	BO,BS
Lathyrus odoratus 'Lizbeth'	B,BS,DS,KI,MS,PG
Lathyrus odoratus 'Lord Nelson'	B,BO,BS,C,PG,PL,TH
Lathyrus odoratus 'Louise'	BS,T
Lathyrus odoratus 'Love Match'	D
Lathyrus odoratus 'Lovejoy'	B,BO,BS,KI,PG
Lathyrus odoratus 'Lucy'	B,SB
Lathyrus odoratus 'Lustre'	BS
Lathyrus odoratus 'Macmillan Nurse'	U
Lathyrus odoratus 'Maggie May'	T
Lathyrus odoratus 'Majesty'	BS
Lathyrus odoratus 'Mammoth' mix	BD,BS,C,CN,DN,KI,MO, PI,SK
Lathyrus odoratus 'Mammoth' s-c	BS
Lathyrus odoratus 'Margot'	BO,BS
Lathyrus odoratus 'Marguerite'	WO
Lathyrus odoratus 'Marilyn Barlow'	PG
Lathyrus odoratus 'Marion'	BS,KI,MS,WO
Lathyrus odoratus 'Marmalade'	PL
Lathyrus odoratus 'Mars'	SE,U
Lathyrus odoratus 'Marti Caine'	MS
Lathyrus odoratus 'Mary Malcolm'	BO
Lathyrus odoratus 'Mary Rose'	BO
Lathyrus odoratus 'Matucana'	B,BS,BY,DI,DS,JD,PG, PL,SE,T
Lathyrus odoratus 'Maudie Best'	BS,KI
Lathyrus odoratus 'Mauve Queen'	PG
Lathyrus odoratus 'Maytime'	WO
Lathyrus odoratus 'Memories'	T
Lathyrus odoratus 'Midnight'	B,BS,KI,SB,U,WO
Lathyrus odoratus 'Midnight Star'	PL
Lathyrus odoratus 'Milestone'	BS,U
Lathyrus odoratus 'Miss Truslove'	B,BS,KI,PG
Lathyrus odoratus 'Miss Willmott'	B,BS,F,PG,TH
Lathyrus odoratus mix, 10 Varieties	T
Lathyrus odoratus mix Unwins stripes	U
Lathyrus od. mix superscented Old Fash.	BS,U
Lathyrus odoratus mix waved standards	YA
Lathyrus odoratus 'Mixed Ripples'	WO,T
Lathyrus odoratus 'Mollie Rilstone'	B,BS,DS,KI,MS,PG,T
Lathyrus odoratus 'Monarch's Diamond'	WO
Lathyrus odoratus 'Morning Rose'	DS,WO
Lathyrus odoratus 'Mr. President'	PG
Lathyrus odoratus 'Mrs Bernard Jones'	B,BO,BS,DS,MS,PG,SB, TU,U,WO
Lathyrus odoratus 'Mrs C Kay'	B,BS,KI,PG
Lathyrus odoratus 'Mrs Collier'	B,BO,BS,C,DS,F,MS,PG, PL,TH
Lathyrus odoratus 'Mrs R Bolton'	B,BD,BS,BY,KI,M,MO, PG,S
Lathyrus odoratus 'Mrs Walter Wright'	BO,BS,TH
Lathyrus odoratus multiflora mix	BS,CA
Lathyrus odoratus 'Myrtle Mann'	BS,KI
Lathyrus odoratus 'Nacre'	PG
Lathyrus odoratus 'Nancy Colledge'	U
Lathyrus odoratus 'Nanette Newman'	B,BS,KI,SB,
Lathyrus odoratus 'Nelly Viner'	B,BS,PG
Lathyrus odoratus 'Nimbus'	U
Lathyrus odoratus 'Noel Edmonds'	B,BS,KI,SB,WO
Lathyrus odoratus 'Noel Sutton'	B,BD,BO,BS,BY,D,DS,J, KI,M,MO,MS,S,SB,WO
Lathyrus odoratus 'Nora Holman'	B,BS,DS,KI,MS,PG
Lathyrus odoratus 'North Shore'	BS,PL,T
Lathyrus odoratus 'Oban Bay'	BO
Lathyrus odoratus 'Old Spice' mix	C,DE,F,J,M,SE,VY
Lathyrus odoratus 'Old Times'	U
Lathyrus odoratus Old-Fashioned mix	C,CO,D,HP,J,KI,MC,MS, PG,PL,SB,ST,V,VH
Lathyrus odoratus Old-Fashioned Scented	S,TU
Lathyrus odoratus 'Orange Dragon'	BO,BS
Lathyrus odoratus 'Orange Surprise'	BS,BY,KI,T
Lathyrus odoratus 'Our Harry'	BS
Lathyrus odoratus 'Our Jenny'	BO
Lathyrus odoratus 'Ouse Valley'	BS,DS,KI

LATHYRUS

Variety	Codes
Lathyrus odoratus 'Painted Lady'	AP,B,BS,BY,C,DS,DT,F,K I,MS,PG,PL,SE,SU,T,TH
Lathyrus odoratus 'Pall Mall'	BS,KI
Lathyrus odoratus 'Pamela'	KI,MS
Lathyrus odoratus 'Patio'	BS,D,F,KI,S,U
Lathyrus odoratus 'Patio Collection' 6 pk	U
Lathyrus odoratus 'Peach Sundae'	BS
Lathyrus odoratus 'Pearl'	PG
Lathyrus odoratus 'Pearl's Buck'	L
Lathyrus odoratus 'Peerless Pink'	BS
Lathyrus odoratus 'Percy Thrower'	B,BO,BS,DS,KI,SB,WO
Lathyrus odoratus 'Perfume Delight'	B,BS,KI,KS,PI,VY
Lathyrus odoratus 'Phantom of The Opera'	SE
Lathyrus odoratus 'Philip Miller'	B,BS,PG
Lathyrus odoratus 'Phoebe'	BO
Lathyrus odoratus 'Pink Bouquet'	U
Lathyrus odoratus 'Pink Expression'	U
Lathyrus odoratus 'Pink Leamington'	BS
Lathyrus odoratus 'Pink Pageant'	PL
Lathyrus odoratus 'Pluto'	BO,BS
Lathyrus odoratus 'Pocahontas'	PG
Lathyrus odor. 'Pois de Senteur Sauvage'	BS,PG
Lathyrus odoratus 'Powdered Lady'	PL
Lathyrus odoratus 'Pre-Sp. Grandiflora'	PG
Lathyrus odoratus 'Premier Collection'	DT
Lathyrus odoratus 'Pretty in Pink'	U
Lathyrus odoratus 'Pretty Polly'	BO,BS,KI
Lathyrus odoratus 'Prima Donna'	B,BS,C,PG,TH
Lathyrus odoratus 'Prince Edward of York'	B,BS,C,PG,TH
Lathyrus odoratus 'Princess Elizabeth'	B,BD,BS,BY,J,KI,MO, PG,S
Lathyrus odoratus 'Princess Juliana'	U
Lathyrus odoratus 'Princess of Wales'	C,DS
Lathyrus odoratus 'Prize Strain'	T
Lathyrus odoratus 'Pulsar'	U
Lathyrus odoratus 'Purple Prince'	B,BS,C,PG
Lathyrus odoratus 'Purple Velvet'	BS
Lathyrus odoratus 'Queen Alexandra'	B,BO,BS,PG,PL,TH
Lathyrus odoratus 'Queen Mother'	DS,MS
Lathyrus odoratus 'Queen of the Isles'	B,BS,C,PG,TH
Lathyrus odoratus 'Quito'	B,BS,C,PG
Lathyrus odoratus 'Razamataz'	PG
Lathyrus odoratus 'Red Arrow'	B,BS,DS,PG,SB,U,WO
Lathyrus odoratus 'Red Ensign'	BO,BS,DS,KI
Lathyrus odoratus 'Remembrance'	B,SB
Lathyrus odoratus 'Restormal'	B,BS,DS,KI,MS,PG
Lathyrus odoratus Rockery Sweet Peas	PL
Lathyrus odoratus 'Romance'	S
Lathyrus odoratus 'Rosalind'	U
Lathyrus odoratus 'Rosalyn Morris'	BS
Lathyrus odoratus 'Rosemary Padley'	BO,BS
Lathyrus odoratus 'Rosemary Verey'	T
Lathyrus odoratus 'Rosina'	B,MS,SB,WO
Lathyrus odoratus 'Rosy Frills'	BS,KI,U
Lathyrus odoratus 'Roy Castle'	BO
Lathyrus odoratus 'Roy Phillips'	BS,WO
Lathyrus odoratus 'Royal Baby'	U,WO
Lathyrus odoratus 'Royal Blue'	B,BS,C,V
Lathyrus odoratus 'Royal Crimson'	BS,C
Lathyrus odoratus 'Royal Family' mix	BD,BU,C,CA,CN,DE, HU,J,MO,PK,VY
Lathyrus odoratus 'Royal Flush'	BO,BS
Lathyrus odoratus 'Royal Lavender'	B,BS,C,J,KS
Lathyrus odoratus 'Royal Maroon'	B,BS,J
Lathyrus odoratus 'Royal Navy Blue'	B,BS,C,J,T,V
Lathyrus odoratus 'Royal Pink'	J,V
Lathyrus odoratus 'Royal Rose Pink'	B,BS,C
Lathyrus odoratus 'Royal Scarlet'	B,BS,C,J
Lathyrus odoratus 'Royal Wedding'	B,BS,DS,KI,MS,PG,SB, T,TU,U,WO
Lathyrus odoratus 'Royal White'	B,BS,C,J,KS,V
Lathyrus odoratus 'Royals mix' multiflora	AB,BS,CL,JO,S,SE,KS, YA
Lathyrus odoratus 'Ruffled mix'	BS
Lathyrus odoratus 'Sandringham'	B,BS,KI,SB
Lathyrus odoratus 'Sarah'	B,BS,KI,SB
Lathyrus odoratus Scented coll	CO,DS,FR,SB,KI
Lathyrus odoratus 'Scented Coll.' 8 pk	U
Lathyrus odoratus 'Sea Wolfe'	BS,DS,KI
Lathyrus odoratus 'Selana'	WO
Lathyrus odoratus 'Senator'	B,BS,PG,TH
Lathyrus odoratus 'Sheila Mcqueen'	BS,U
Lathyrus odoratus 'Shirley Pink'	BS,KI
Lathyrus odoratus 'Shirley Temple'	L
Lathyrus odoratus 'Sicilian Fuchsia'	B,BS,MS,PG,TH
Lathyrus odoratus 'Sicilian Pink'	BO
Lathyrus odoratus 'Silver Jubilee'	WO
Lathyrus odoratus 'Skylon'	BS
Lathyrus odoratus small coll	CO
Lathyrus odoratus 'Snoopea'	BO,BS,BY,CO,DS,KI,SU, T,TU,VH
Lathyrus odoratus 'Snow White'	PG
Lathyrus odoratus 'Snowdonia Park'	BS,KI
Lathyrus odoratus 'Sonia'	BO,WO
Lathyrus odoratus 'South Atlantic'	BS,BY,KI
Lathyrus odoratus 'Southampton'	B,BO,BS,PG,WO
Lathyrus odoratus 'Southbourne'	BO,BS,D,KI,U,WO
Lathyrus odoratus 'Special Collection'	BS,DT
Lathyrus odoratus special mix, 50 vars	SB
Lathyrus o. special mix tall Spencer vars	S
Lathyrus odoratus Spencer choice mix	BD,BY,C,CL,DT,KI,MS
Lathyrus o Spencer special highly scented	BY,MS,PG
Lathyrus odoratus Spencer types s-c	B,BS
Lathyrus odoratus Spencer waved	BS,CO,KI,MO,R,ST,TU, VH
Lathyrus odoratus 'Splendour'	BS
Lathyrus odoratus 'Steve Davis'	BS,KI,U
Lathyrus odoratus 'Stylish'	B,BD,BS,J,KI,MO
Lathyrus odoratus 'Su Pollard'	B,BS,KI,SB
Lathyrus odoratus 'Summer Breeze'	SE,T
Lathyrus odoratus summer fl mix	SK
Lathyrus odoratus 'Sunsilk'	WO
Lathyrus odor. 'Super Start Special' c.s	U
Lathyrus odoratus 'Superfine'	WO
Lathyrus odoratus 'Supersnoop'	BD,DN,J,KS,MO,SB,ST, VY,YA
Lathyrus odoratus 'Swan Lake'	B,BS,BY,J,KI,M,PG
Lathyrus odoratus 'Sylvia'	U
Lathyrus odoratus 'Sylvia Mary'	BO,BS
Lathyrus odoratus tall	F
Lathyrus odoratus 'Tell Tale'	BS,KI
Lathyrus odoratus 'Terry Wogan'	BS,BY,KI,M,TU,U,WO
Lathyrus odoratus 'The Doctor'	BS,KI,U
Lathyrus odoratus 'The Exhibitor's Coll.'	KI,S,ST
Lathyrus odor. 'The Small Grower Coll.'	KI,ST
Lathyrus odoratus 'The York Pea'	B,BS,PG
Lathyrus odoratus 'Thomas Bradley'	U
Lathyrus odoratus 'Titan'	B,SB
Lathyrus odoratus Top 6	V
Lathyrus odoratus 'Tovah Martin'	PG
Lathyrus odoratus 'Treasure Island'	L
Lathyrus odoratus 'Uncle Albert'	PG

LATHYRUS

Lathyrus odoratus 'Unique'	B,BS,PG
Lathyrus odoratus Unwins hyb mix	U
Lathyrus o. Unwins striped 'Butterfly' mix	C
Lathyrus odoratus 'Velvet Night'	BS
Lathyrus odoratus 'Vera Lynn'	BS,KI
Lathyrus odoratus 'Victorian Collection'	PL,TH
Lathyrus odoratus 'Violet Queen'	B,BS,PG,TH
Lathyrus odoratus 'Virginia'	PG
Lathyrus odoratus 'W.J.Unwin'	U
Lathyrus odoratus 'Welcome'	B,BS,BY,J,KI,PG,TU
Lathyrus odoratus 'White Ensign'	B,BD,BS,BY,KI,MO
Lathyrus odoratus 'White Royal'	J
Lathyrus odoratus 'White Supreme'	B,BO,BS,DS,KI,MS,PG, SB,T
Lathyrus odoratus wild form	C
Lathyrus odoratus 'Willies Red'	BS
Lathyrus odoratus 'Wiltshire Ripple'	BS,KI,T,V
Lathyrus odoratus 'Windsor'	U
Lathyrus odoratus 'Wings'	T
Lathyrus odoratus 'Winner'	BS,KI,WO
Lathyrus odoratus 'Winston Churchill'	B,BD,BS,BY,D,J,KI,MO, PG,S
Lathyrus odoratus 'Winter Elegance' s-c	B,BS,MO,VY
Lathyrus odoratus 'Wisteria'	BS
Lathyrus odoratus 'Xenia Field'	BO,BS,KI
Lathyrus odoratus 'Yankie Doodle'	PG
Lathyrus odoratus 'Yardley'	BS,KI
Lathyrus odoratus 'Yasmin Khan'	B,BO,BS,KI,PG,PL,WO
Lathyrus palustris	B,C,JE
Lathyrus perennial mix	SK
Lathyrus pisiformis	SG
Lathyrus pratensis	B,BS,C,PG,RS,SG,SU
Lathyrus pubescens	NG
Lathyrus roseus	B
Lathyrus rotundifolius	AP,C,HP,NG,RS,SC
Lathyrus sativus	AP,B,BS,C,F,G,HP,I,NG, PG,PL,RS,SE,SZ,T,W
Lathyrus sativus mix	PG
Lathyrus sativus v albo-azureus	B,PG
Lathyrus sativus v albus	B,C,NG,PG
Lathyrus sativus v azureus see L sativus	
Lathyrus sp mix	PL
Lathyrus sp purple	P
Lathyrus sphaericus	RS
Lathyrus splendens	B,SA
Lathyrus stoechas v albiflora	C
Lathyrus sylvestris	AP,B,C,CG,CO,F,HP,LG, NG,NS,P,PG,SA,SG,SU
Lathyrus 'Tickled Pink'	T
Lathyrus tingitanus	AP,B,BS,C,DS,F,HP,I,KL, LG,NG,PG,PL,RS,T
Lathyrus tingitanus 'Flame'	RS
Lathyrus tingitanus 'Harmony'	BS,PB,G
Lathyrus tingitanus mix	BS
Lathyrus tingitanus roseus	AP,B,BS,DS
Lathyrus tingitanus salmon pink form	C,NG
Lathyrus tuberosus	B,C,G,LG,KL,SG
Lathyrus venetus	B,JE
Lathyrus venosus	B,SG
Lathyrus vernus	AP,B,BS,C,CG,F,G,HP,JD ,JE,KL,NG,P,PG,SA,SG
Lathyrus vernus 'Alboroseus'	AP,C,HP,NG
Lathyrus vernus 'Caeruleus'	HP
Lathyrus vernus cyaneus	B,RS
Lathyrus vernus f roseus	B,HP,JD
Lathyrus vernus 'Flaccidus'	HP

Lathyrus vernus forms mix	C
Lathyrus vernus 'Rosenelfe'	HP,JE
Lathyrus vernus v albus	AP,SG
Lathyrus vestitus	B,SC
Launea angustifolia	B,JE
Laurelia novae-zelandiae	B
Laurelia sempervirens	SA
Laurentia axillaris see Solenopsis	
Laurocerasus officinalis	SG
Laurophyllus capensis	B,SI
Laurus nobilis	A,B,C,CA,FW,LN,N,SA, VE
Lavandula angustifolia	AP,B,BD,C,CG,CP,DV,EL, FW,G,HU,KL,KS,RH, RM,SA,SG,T,TH,VE
Lavandula angustifolia 'Hidcote'	AP,B,BD,BS,C,CL,CN, EL,G,HP,JE,L,MO,PL, SA,T,TU,YA
Lavandula angustifolia 'Lady'	B,BD,BS,C,CL,CN,D,JE, KS,MO,PL,S,SE,SK,T
Lavandula angustifolia 'Loddon Pink'	HP
Lavandula angustifolia 'Munstead'	w.a.
Lavandula angustifolia 'Nana Alba'	AP,B,E,G,HP,KL,NG,RS
Lavandula angustifolia 'Rosea'	AP,B,C,CN,G,HP,JE,KL, PL,RS
Lavandula angustifolia 'Royal Purple'	HP
Lavandula canariensis	AP,B,BH,RS
Lavandula cretica	I
Lavandula dentata	B,G,KS,RS
Lavandula hybrida	SG
Lavandula 'Imperial Gem'	HP
Lavandula lanata	AP,B,C,CN,HP,RS,SA,VO
Lavandula latifolia	B,CG,CN,SG,JE
Lavandula luiserii	BH
Lavandula mix Dw vars	C,CN
Lavandula multifida	B,BH,DD,G,RS,SG
Lavandula multifida dentata	SA
Lavandula officinalis/spica see angustifolia	
Lavandula pedunculata	P
Lavandula pinnata	HP,SA,SG
Lavandula ssp mix	KS
Lavandula stoechas	AP,B,BS,C,CN,DD,F,G,H P,JE,RS,SA,SG,T,VE
Lavandula stoechas f leucantha	B,HP,RS
Lavandula stoechas ssp pedunculata	AP,B,BH,CG,HP,SA,SC
Lavandula viridis	AP,B,BH,C,CG,DD,HP,P
Lavatera arborea	B,C,DD,SA,SG
Lavatera arborea 'Variegata'	AP,B,C,G,HP,P,SG
Lavatera assurgentiflora	B,DD
Lavatera 'Barnsley'	HP
Lavatera 'Bredon Springs'	HP
Lavatera cachemiriana	AP,B,G,HP,HU,SG,T
Lavatera 'Candy Floss'	HP,I
Lavatera maritima	B,SA
Lavatera oblongifolia	SA
Lavatera olbia	B,CG
Lavatera plebeia	B,NI,RS
Lavatera punctata	B
Lavatera 'Snowcap'	I
Lavatera sp	KL
Lavatera tauricensis	HP,T
Lavatera thuringiaca	AP,B,HP,JE,NG,SA,SG,V
Lavatera thuringiaca 'Ice Cool'	AP
Lavatera thuringiaca 'Rose'	T
Lavatera triloba	SA
Lavatera trimestris	AP,BS,FR,G,HW,R,SD,

LAVATERA

Lavatera trimestris 'Beauty' mix	SG,T,V
	BS,CL,D,MO,PI,S,VY
Lavatera trimestris 'Beauty Pink'	B,BS,CL,DI,F,HP,J,JO,
	MO,T,U,V
Lavatera trimestris 'Beauty Rose'	B,BS,CL,MO,T
Lavatera trimestris 'Beauty Salmon'	BS,C,MO
Lavatera trimestris 'Beauty White'	B,BS,CL,MO
Lavatera trimestris 'Loveliness'	B,BS,BY,CO,HU,KI,S,ST,
	T,VH
Lavatera trimestris 'Mont Blanc'	AP,B,BD,BS,BY,CO,D,
	DE,DT,F,G,HU,J,JO,KI,
	KS,L,PK,S,SK,ST,SU,T,
	TU,U,V,VH,VY,YA
Lavatera trimestris 'Mont Rose'	PK
Lavatera trimestris 'Parade' mix	BD,BS,C,DT,F,KS,M,
	PL,SE,U
Lavatera trimestris 'Pastel' mix	J
Lavatera trimestris 'Ruby Regis'	B,BD,BS,C,F,KS,PK,T,
	TU,V,VY,W
Lavatera trimestris 'Silver Cup'	B,BD,BS,BY,C,CO,D,DI,
	DT,F,G,HU,J,JO,KI,KS,L,
	PI,S,SK,ST,SU,T,TU,U,
	V,VY,YA
Lavatera trimestris 'Tanagra'	B,BS,DE
Lavatera trimestris 'White Cherub'	D,T
Lavigera macrocarpa	B
Lawrencella davenportii	B,NI,O
Lawrencia berthae	B,NI
Lawrencia viridigrisea	B,NI
Lawsonia inermis	B,BH,EL,SA
Lawsoniana inermis v alba	HU
Laxmannia gracilis	B,NI
Laxmannia minor	B,NI
Laxmannia paleacea	B,NI
Layia chrysanthemoides	B
Layia platyglossa	AB,B,C,CA,D,SG,T,V
Lebeckia plukenetiana	B,SI
Lebeckia sericea	B,SI
Lebeckia simsiana	B
Lecythis minor	B
Lecythis pisonis	B
Ledebouria cooperi	B,SI
Ledebouria marginata	B,SI
Ledebouria ovalifolia	AP,B,SI
Ledebouria socialis	AP,SG
Ledum groenlandicum	G,X
Ledum palustre	KL,SG
Leea coccinea see L.guineensis	
Leea guineensis	B,CA,EL,SA
Leea guineensis v rubra	B
Leea indica	B,EL
Leea rubra	CA,SA
Leersia oryzoides	B,PR
Legousia 'Blue Carpet'	S
Legousia pentagonia	T
Legousia speculum-veneris	B,HP
Leibnitzia anandria	SG
Leibnitzia kunzeana	KL
Leipoldtia amplexicaulis	B
Leipoldtia britteniae	B
Leipoldtia jacobseniana	B
Leipoldtia weigangiana	B
Lemaireocereus eburneus	B,DV,Y
Lemaireocereus griseus	BC
Lemaireocereus montanus	B,Y
Lemaireocereus pruinosus	Y

Lemaireocereus thurberi see Stenocactus	
Lenophyllum guttatum	B
Lenophyllum reflexum	B
Lens culinaris	DD
Lens culinaris 'Masoor'	B
Lens culinaris 'O'odham Lentil'	B
Lens culinaris 'Tarahumara Pink'	B
Lens esculenta	C
Lentinus edodes d.m.p	B
Leonotis leonurus see L.ocymifolia	
Leonotis nepetiifolia	B,HU,SZ
Leonotis ocymifolia	AB,AP,B,BH,C,DD,G,KB,
	SA,SI
Leonotis ocymifolia ssp ocymifolia	B,SI
Leonotis ocymifolia ssp raineriana	B,SI
Leonotis ocymifolia white	B,KB
Leonotis 'Staircase'	BS,C,F
Leontodon autumnalis	B,CG,JE,LA
Leontodon hispidus	B,C,G,SG
Leontodon hispidus ssp glabratus	SG
Leontodon hispidus ssp hispidus	SG
Leontodon montanus	VO
Leontodon rigens	JE
Leontodon sp	KL
Leontopodium alpinum	w.a.
Leontopodium alpinum ssp nivale	AP,B,KL,VO
Leontopodium alpinum ssp pamiricum	KL
Leontopodium discolor	B,G,SC
Leontopodium fauriei	KL,SC
Leontopodium jacotianum	AP,B
Leontopodium leontopodiodes	B,C,G,SC,SG.VO
Leontopodium linearifolia	CG
Leontopodium nivale see L. alpinum ssp n.	
Leontopodium ochroleucum	VO
Leontopodium ochroleucum v campestre	B,G,JE,KL,SC,SG
Leontopodium palibinianum see L. ochroleucum v campestre	
Leontopodium soulei	AP,G,JE,KL,SC,SG
Leontopodium sp	KL
Leontopodium stracheyi	CG
Leontopodium wilsonii	B,KL
Leonurus cardiaca	B,C,CG,CN,CP,DD,G,HP,
	HU,JE,SA,SG,TH
Leonurus sibiricus	AP,DD,F,G,HP,SG,T
Leonurus tataricus	SG
Leopoldia maritima S.L258 Tunisia	MN
Leopoldia tenuiflora see Muscari tenuiflorum	
Lepechinia fragrans	B
Lepidagathis cristata	B
Lepidium attraxa	SG
Lepidium campestre	B,SG
Lepidium densiflorum	SG
Lepidium fremontii	B
Lepidium leptopetalum	B,NI
Lepidium menziesii	B
Lepidium pholidogynum	B,NI
Lepidium ruderale	BS,C,MO
Lepidium sativum	B,DD,KL
Lepidium strongylophyllum	B,NI
Lepidospartium squamatum	B
Lepidosperma costale	B
Lepidothamnus laxifolius	B,SS
Lepidozamia hopei	O
Lepidozamia peroffskyana	B,C,EL,O
Lepisanthes tetraphylla	B
Leptadenia reticulata	B
Leptarrhena pyrolifolia	B,C

156

LEPTINELLA

Leptinella atrata	B,SS
Leptinella dendyii	AP,B,SS
Leptinella pectinata	B,SS
Leptinella pyrethrifolia	B,SS
Leptinella squalida	B
Leptodactylon californicum	B,SW
Leptodermis pilosa AC1439	X
Leptomeria empetriformis	B
Leptopteris superba	B
Leptosema chambersii	B,NI
Leptosiphon hyb	C,V
Leptosiphon Rainbow mix	D
Leptosiphon 'Stardust Hybrids' mix	T
Leptospermum arachnoides	AU,B,HA,NI,O
Leptospermum 'Beach'	B
Leptospermum brachyandrum	B,EL,HA,NI,O
Leptospermum brevipes	B,HA,NI
Leptospermum continentale	AU,HA
Leptospermum 'Copper Glow'	EL,SH
Leptospermum coriaceum coastal strain	B,NI
Leptospermum emarginatum	B,HA
Leptospermum epacridoideum	B,EL,HA,NI,SA
Leptospermum erubescens	AU,B,NI
Leptospermum glaucescens	B,NI
Leptospermum grandiflorum	AU,B,EL,HA,NI,O,RH,SA
Leptospermum horizontalis	EL,HA
Leptospermum juniperinum	AU,B,EL,HA,NI
Leptospermum laevigatum	AU,B,CA,EL,HA,NI,O,SA
Leptospermum lanigerum	AU,B,EL,HA,HP,NI,O,RH
Leptospermum lanigerum v macrocarpum	HA
Leptospermum liversidgei	B,EL,RH,NI,O,SA
Leptospermum macroc. 'Copper Sheen'	B
Leptospermum microcarpum	B
Leptospermum micromyrtus	RH
Leptospermum minutifolium	AU,B,NI,O
Leptospermum myrsinoides	B,HA,NI
Leptospermum myrtifolium	AU,B,HA,NI
Leptospermum nitidum	AU,B,EL,NI,O,SA
Leptospermum obovatum	AU,B,EL,HA,NI,SG
Leptospermum oligandrum	B,NI
Leptospermum parvifolium	HA
Leptospermum petersonii	C,HA,NI,O,RE,SA,SH
Leptospermum peter. ssp lanceolatum	B,NI
Leptospermum polyanthum	AU
Leptospermum polygalifolium	B,HA,NI,O,SA
Leptospermum polygal. 'Copper Glow'	O
Leptospermum rotundifolium	B,EL,HA,NI,O,SA,SH,VE
Leptospermum rotundifolium 'Jervis Bay'	B,EL,NI
Leptospermum rotundif. 'Pink Beauty'	B,EL,SH
Leptospermum rotundifolium v alba	B,EL
Leptospermum rupestre	AU,B,HA,NI,O
Leptospermum rupestre 'Roseum'	B
Leptospermum scoparium	AP,AU,B,HA,NI,O,RH, SS,WA
Leptospermum scoparium 'Horizontalis'	B
Leptospermum scoparium 'Roseum'	B,EL,SA
Leptospermum scoparium v nanum	C,I
Leptospermum scoparium v nicholsii	C,SC
Leptospermum scoparium v rotundifolium	HA,O
Leptospermum scoparium v scoparium	HU
Leptospermum semibaccatum	B,EL,HA,NI
Leptospermum sp mix	C
Leptospermum speciosum	B,NI
Leptospermum spinescens	B,NI
Leptospermum squarrosum	AU,B,EL,HA,NI,O
Leptospermum trinervium	AU,B,HA,NI

Leptospermum trivalvum	B,HA
Leptospermum whiteii	HA
Leschenaultia biloba	B,O,SA
Leschenaultia floribunda	B,C,SA
Leschenaultia formosa	B,O,SA
Leschenaultia linarioides	B
Leschenaultia macrantha	AU,B,O
Lespedeza bicolor	A,B,C,DD,EL,FW,HU,LN, SG
Lespedeza bicolor japonica	SA
Lespedeza capitata	B,PR
Lespedeza cuneata	B,LN
Lespedeza thunbergii	B,G,HP,HU,LN,SA,SG
Lespedeza virginica	B,PR
Lesquerella alpina	KL
Lesquerella arctica	AP
Lesquerella fendleri	AP,B,SW
Lesquerella gordonii	B
Lesquerella intermedia	B,SW
Lesquerella purpurea	B,SW
Lesquerella purshii	KL
Lessertia diffusa	B,SI
Lessertia perennans	B,SI
Lessertia sp	SI
Lessertia spinescens	B,SI
Leucadendron album	B,O,SI
Leucadendron arcuatum	B,KB,O
Leucadendron argenteum	B,C,EL,KB,O,SA,SI
Leucadendron barkerae	B,SI
Leucadendron brunioides	B,O,SI
Leucadendron chamelaea	B,KB,O,SI
Leucadendron cinereum	B,SI
Leucadendron comosum	B,SI
Leucadendron conicum	B,KB
Leucadendron coniferum	B,EL,KB,O,SI
Leucadendron corymbosum	B,SI
Leucadendron daphnoides	B,EL,O,SI
Leucadendron discolor	B,EL,O,SI
Leucadendron dregei	B,SI
Leucadendron dubium	B,SI
Leucadendron elimense	B
Leucadendron elimense ssp elimense	O,SI
Leucadendron elimense ssp salteri	O
Leucadendron eucalyptifolium	B,KB,O,SI
Leucadendron flexuosum	B,SI
Leucadendron floridum	B,O
Leucadendron galpinii	B,EL,O,SA,SI
Leucadendron gandogeri	B,O,SI
Leucadendron hypophyllocarpodendron	SI
Leucadendron lanigerum	B,SI
Leucadendron laureolum	B,EL,KB,O,SI
Leucadendron laxum	B,SI
Leucadendron levisanus	B,SI
Leucadendron linifolium	B,EL,SI
Leucadendron loeriense	B,KB,O
Leucadendron loranthifolium	B,KB,SI
Leucadendron macowanii	B,O
Leucadendron meridianum	B,O,SI
Leucadendron microcephalum	B
Leucadendron modestum	B,KB,O,SI
Leucadendron nervosum	B,EL,SI
Leucadendron nobile	B,SI
Leucadendron platyspermum	B,SI
Leucadendron procerum	B,SI
Leucadendron pubescens	B,SI
Leucadendron pubibracteolatum	SI

LEUCADENDRON

Leucadendron remotum	B,SI
Leucadendron roodii	B
Leucadendron rubrum	B,EL,O,SI
Leucadendron salicifolium	B,KB,SI
Leucadendron salignum	B,EL,KB,O,SA,SI
Leucadendron sessile	B,EL,KB,O,SI
Leucadendron sheliae	B
Leucadendron sp mix	C,KB,V
Leucadendron spissifolium ssp fragrans	B,KB,SI
Leucadendron spissifolium ssp natalense	KB
Leucadendron spissifolium ssp oribinum	SI
Leucadendron spissifolium ssp phillipsii	B,KB,O
Leucadendron spissifolium ssp spissif.	SI
Leucadendron stellare	B,KB,SI
Leucadendron strobolinum	B,KB,O,SI
Leucadendron teretifolium	B,O,SI
Leucadendron thymifolium	B,O,SI
Leucadendron tinctum	B,EL,KB,O,SI
Leucadendron uliginosum ssp uliginosum	B,KB,O,SI
Leucadendron verticillatum	B,SI
Leucadendron xanthoconus	B,KB,O,SI
Leucaena cunninghamii	B,EL,HA,SA
Leucaena glauca	EL,SA
Leucaena 'Guaje'	DD
Leucaena 'Guaje Costeno'	B,HU
Leucaena latisiliqua	B,C,CA,EL,LN,O,RE,WA
Leucaena latisiliqua 'K636'	B,WA
Leucaena latisiliqua 'K8'	B,EL,HA
Leucaena latisiliqua 'Peru'	B
Leucaena leucocephala see L.latisiliqua	
Leucaena salvadorensis	B
Leucaena shannoni	B
Leucanthemella serotinum	JE
Leucanthemopsis alpina	B,C,JE,KL,RM,SA,SC, SG,VO
Leucanthemopsis pectinata	SG,VO
Leucanthemum maximum h see L.x superbum	
Leucanthemum paludosum	C,D,PI,T,V
Leucanthemum paludosum 'Giganteum'	B
Leucanthemum paludosum 'Snowland'	B,BS,CL,KI,MO,PK,SK
Leucanthemum paludosum 'Sterling'	B
Leucanthemum paludosum 'White Ring'	B,L
Leucanthemum vulgare	B,C,CN,CO,G,HP,JE,LA, SA,SG,TH,V
Leucanthemum vulgare 'Maikonigin'	B,DE,DN,JE,V
Leucanthemum vulgare 'May Empress'	B
Leucanthemum vulgare 'Paris White'	U
Leucanthemum vulgare 'Rhine View'	B,JE
Leucanthemum waldsteinii	SG
Leucanthemum x superbum	AB,AV,B,BU,F,HP,HU,JE, PK,SD,SG,SU,T,TH,TU, VH,Z
Leucanthemum x superbum 'Alaska'	B,BS,BU,CA,DE,F,JE,JO, PI,SA,SK
Leucanthemum x superbum 'Amelia'	B
Leucanthemum x superb. 'Antwerp Star'	B,C
Leucanthemum x superbum 'Coconut Ice'	BS,KI
Leucanthemum x s. 'Diener's Dbl Giants'	B
Leucanthemum x sup. 'Etoile D'anvers'	B
Leucanthemum x superbum 'Exhibition'	B
Leucanthemum x superbum f1 'Nordlicht'	B,JE
Leucanthemum x sup. f1 'Snow Lady'	B,BD,BS,C,CA,CL,F,JE,L ,MO,PK,S,SE,SK,VY,YA
Leucanthemum x superbum f1 'Starburst'	B,T
Leucanthemum x superb. fl pl 'Snowdreft'	B,JE
Leucanthemum x s. 'Little Silver Princess'	B,BD,C,D,JE,S,SA,SK,V

Leucanthemum x sup. 'Marconi' dbl	B,SK
Leucanthemum x sup. 'Mayfield Giant'	B,CO,KI
Leucanthemum x sup. 'Northern Lights'	T
Leucanthemum x superbum 'Polaris'	B,BS,C,JE
Leucanthemum x sup. 'Rijnsburg Glory'	B,JE
Leucanthemum x sup. 'Snow Banquet'	PK,SE
Leucanthemum x superbum 'Supra'	B,JE
Leucanthemum x sup. 'White Iceberg'	BS,BY,KI
Leucanthemum x sup. 'White Knight'	B,BS
Leucas aspera	B
Leucas sp	SI
Leuchtenbergia principis	B,BC,C,CH,DV,GC,Y
Leucochrysum albicans	O
Leucochrysum fitzgibbonii	B,HA,NI,O
Leucochrysum molle	B,NI,O
Leucocoryne ixioides	B
Leucocoryne ixioides 'The Bride'	B
Leucocoryne narcissoides	B
Leucocoryne new hybrids	B
Leucogenes grandiceps	AP,B,SS
Leucogenes leontopodium	SC
Leucojum aestivum	AP,B,G,JE,KL,MN
Leucojum autumnale	AP,AR,LG,NG,SC,SG
Leucojum autumnale v oporanthum	AP,B,G
Leucojum autumnale v oporanthum MS.	MN,PM
Leucojum autumnale v pulchellum	B,PM,SC
Leucojum autumnale v pulchellum A.B.S.	MN
Leucojum nicaeensis	AP,AR,C,G,NG,PM,SG
Leucojum roseum	AP,AR,I,NG,PM,SC
Leucojum tingitanum	AR
Leucojum trichophyllum	AP,B,LG
Leucojum trichophyllum B.S.409 Portugal	MN
Leucojum trichophyllum B.S.449/1	MN
Leucojum vernum	AP,AR,B,C,G,JE,KL,PM,
Leucojum vernum Nancy Lindsay's form	NG
Leucojum vernum v carpathicum	AP,B,G,NG,SC
Leucophyta brownii	AU,B,NI,O
Leucopogon capitellatus	B,NI
Leucopogon ericioides	HA
Leucopogon fasciculatus	B,C
Leucopogon fraseri	AU,SS
Leucopogon nutans	B,NI
Leucopogon obovatus	B,NI
Leucopogon ovalifolius	B,NI
Leucopogon propinquus	B,NI
Leucopogon pulchellus	B
Leucopogon rubicundus	B,NI
Leucopogon strictus	B,NI
Leucopogon suaveolens	B
Leucopogon verticillatus	B,C,NI
Leucorchis albida	CG
Leucosidea sericea	B,SI
Leucospermum bolusii	B,EL,O,SI
Leucospermum catherinae	B,O,SI
Leucospermum conocarpodendon	B
Leucospermum conocarp. ssp conocarp.	O,SI
Leucospermum cordifolium	B,EL,KB,O,SA,SI,V
Leucospermum cordifolium x patersonnii 'High Gold'	B,SI
Leucospermum cord. 'Yellow Bird' o-p.	B,SI
Leucospermum cuneiforme	B,KB,O,SI
Leucospermum erubescens	B,KB,O,SI
Leucospermum formosum	B,KB,O,SI
Leucospermum glabrum	B,EL,KB,O,SI
Leucospermum glabrum 'Helderfontein'	B,SI
Leucospermum grandiflorum	B,KB,SA,SI
Leucospermum guenzii	B,O,SI

LEUCOSPERMUM

Leucospermum hyb mix	O
Leucospermum incisum	B
Leucospermum lineare 'Ballerina'	B,SI
Leucospermum muirii	B,EL,KB,O,SI
Leucospermum oleifolium	B,KB,O
Leucospermum patersoni	O
Leucospermum praecox	B,KB,SI
Leucospermum praemorsum	B,SI
Leucospermum reflexum	B,KB,O
Leucospermum reflexum 'Rocket'	O
Leucospermum reflexum v luteum	B
Leucospermum 'Scarlet Ribbon'	B,EL,SI
Leucospermum sp mix	C,KB,V
Leucospermum 'Tango'	SI
Leucospermum tottum	B,KB,O
Leucospermum vestitum	B,SI
Leucothe axillaris	B,FW,LN
Leucothoe catesbaei of gdns	B,C,FW
Leucothoe grayana	B,FW
Leucothoe racemosa	B,FW
Leuzea australis	B,NI
Leuzea carthamnoides	KL
Leuzea centauroides	B,HP,SG
Leuzea conifera	AP,B,HP,SA,SC
Leuzea rhapontica	B,G,JE
Levenhookia chippendalei	B,NI
Levenhookia pulcherrima	B
Levenhookia pusilla	B,NI
Levenhookia stipitata	B
Levisticum officinale	B,CN,CP,DD,G,HP,HU, KS,SA,SC,SG,TH
Levisticum officinale 'Magnus'	B
Lewisia Ashwood Hybrids	AP,AS
Lewisia 'Ashwood Strain'	AP,AS,C,D,S,SC
Lewisia 'Ballet Royale'	PL,SE
Lewisia Birch hybrids	C,I
Lewisia brachycalyx	AP,AS,B,C,G,KL,SG,SW
Lewisia brachycalyx pink	B,SC,SW
Lewisia cantelovii	AP,AS,C,KL,SC
Lewisia cantelovii o-p	FH
Lewisia columbiana	AP,AS,C,CG,G,I,JE,KL
Lewisia columbiana alba	AS
Lewisia columbiana hyb o-p	FH
Lewisia columbiana 'Rosea'	AP,AS,SC,SG
Lewisia columbiana ssp rupicola	AP,AS,KL,SC
Lewisia columbiana ssp wallowensis	AP,AS,CG,KL,SC
Lewisia congdonii	AP,AS,SG
Lewisia cotyledon	AP,AS,B,BP,BS,BY,CG, CL,CN,G,KL,L,P,PA,PM, RM,SC,SG
Lewisia cotyledon ex Brannan Bar MB	AS
Lewisia cotyledon f alba	AP,B,JE,KL,SC,SG
Lewisia cotyledon 'Fransi'	AP,B,JE
Lewisia cotyledon hyb	AP,CG,HP,JE,SC,SG
Lewisia cotyledon hyb o-p	FH
Lewisia cotyledon hyb selected	PM
Lewisia cotyledon 'Praline'	JE
Lewisia cotyledon 'Regenbogen'	BS,C,JE
Lewisia cotyledon 'Rondo'	JE
Lewisia cotyledon 'Soranda Hybrids' resel.	B,J,PK,V
Lewisia cotyledon 'Sunset Strain'	AP,B,BD,BS,CG,G,JE, MO,SA,SC
Lewisia cotyledon v heckneri	AP,B,CG,JE,SC,SG
Lewisia cotyledon v howellii	AP,AS,KL,SC,SG
Lewisia Howellii Hybrids	BS,T
Lewisia leeana	AS,G,SC

Lewisia longipetala	AP,AS,G,I,KL,SC,SG
Lewisia longiscapa	AS
Lewisia mix	CH,JE
Lewisia mix rock garden	U
Lewisia nevadensis	AP,B,BS,C,CG,DV,G,HP, JE,KL,PM,SA,SC
Lewisia nevadensis bernadina see L.n.	
Lewisia nevadensis o-p	FH
Lewisia nevadensis rosea	AP,AS,SC
Lewisia oppositifolia	AP,AS,KL,SC
Lewisia oppositifolia richeyi	AS
Lewisia pygmaea	AP,AS,B,C,CG,DV,G,HU ,I,JE,KL,RM,SC,SW
Lewisia pygmaea 'Alba'	KL
Lewisia rediviva	AP,AS,B,C,JE,KL,NO,SC, SP,SW
Lewisia rediviva alba	AP,SC
Lewisia rediviva ex alba	AS
Lewisia rediviva Jolon Strain	AP,AS
Lewisia rediviva o-p	FH
Lewisia 'Rose Splendour'	AP
Lewisia serrata	AP,AS
Lewisia sierrae	AP,AS,B,G,HP,I,JE,KL
Lewisia triphylla	AP,B,C,G,KL,RM,SC
Lewisia tweedyi	AP,AS,B,C,G,JE,KL,PL, SC,SG
Lewisia tweedyi 'Alba'	AP,AS,G,SC
Lewisia tweedyi 'Elliotts Variety'	AS
Lewisia tweedyi ex lemon form	AS
Lewisia tweedyi 'Lovedream'	B,C,JE
Lewisia tweedyi 'Rosea'	AP,AS,SC
Lewisia 'White Splendour'	AS,I
Leycesteria crocothyrsos	AP,B,P
Leycesteria formosa	B,C,HP,JE,P,RH,SA,SG,T
Leymus arenarius	B,C,CA,DE,JE,SA
Leymus condensatus	B
Leymus secalinus	B
Leyssera gnaphaloides	SI
Leyssera sp	SI
Lhotzkya see Calytrix	
Liatris aspera	B,HU,JE,PR,T
Liatris cylindracea	B,CG,JE,PR
Liatris earleyi	B
Liatris elegans	B,JE
Liatris graminifolia	B
Liatris ligulistylis	B,CG,JE,PR
Liatris microcephala	NT
Liatris punctata	B,NO,PR,RM
Liatris pycnostachya	B,C,CG,DE,G,HU,HW, JE,NO,PR,SA,SG,T
Liatris scariosa	B,G
Liatris scariosa 'Alba'	JE
Liatris scariosa 'Gracious'	T
Liatris scariosa 'September Gory'	JE
Liatris spicata	AB,AP,B,BS,CL,CO,EL, G,HP,HU,HW,JE,L,LG, KI,KL,KS,NT,PI,PR,SA, SG,SU,TH,TU
	KL
Liatris spicata f montana	
Liatris spicata 'Floristan Violet'	B,BS,C,CN,HU,JE,MO, PK
Liatris spicata 'Floristan White'	B,BS,C,CN,G,JE,KI,MO, PK
Liatris spicata 'Kobold'	B,BS,C,CN,DE,EL,G,JE, MO,PK,PM,SA,SK,U,V
Liatris spicata 'Picador'	DE,JE

LIATRIS

Liatris spicata 'Purple Torch'	B
Liatris spicata voilet	BY,SA
Liatris spicata white	KL,SA
Liatris spicata 'White Torch'	B
Liatris squarrosa	B,NT,PR
Libanotis pyrenaica	SG
Libertia caerulescens	AP,C,P
Libertia formosa	AP,B,C,HP,RH,SC,SG
Libertia grandiflora	AP,AU,B,C,HP,I,JE,MN, RS,SA
Libertia ixioides	AP,B,HP,SA,SC,SG,SS
Libertia peregrinans	AP,B,C,HP
Libertia peregrinans 'Gold Leaf'	P
Libertia pulchella	AP,AU
Libocedrus decurrens see Calocedrus	
Libocedrus plumosa	B
Licuala grandis	B,C,CA,EL,O,SA,VE
Licuala pacifica	B
Licuala paludosa	B
Licuala ramsayi	B,EL,O,SA
Licuala spinosa	B,CA,EL,O,Re,SA
Lignocarpus carnosulus	B,SS
Ligousia pentagonia	B
Ligularia altaica	AP,SG
Ligularia amplexicaulis	B
Ligularia clivorum see L.dentata	
Ligularia dentata	B,C,HP,HU,JE,PI,SA,SG
Ligularia dentata 'Dark Beauty'	B,C,JE,SA
Ligularia dentata 'Desdemona'	AP,B,HP,P,SC,SG
Ligularia dentata 'Othello'	HP,T
Ligularia fischeri	B,JE,SC
Ligularia glauca	SG
Ligularia 'Gregynog Gold'	HP
Ligularia heterophylla	VO
Ligularia hodgsonii	B,SA
Ligularia japonica	AP,B,JE
Ligularia lapathifolia	KL
Ligularia macrophylla	KL,SG
Ligularia przewalskii	AP,B,C,DE,G,HP,JE,L, SA,SC,T
Ligularia sachalinensis	G,HP,SC,SG
Ligularia sibirica	B,CG,G,JE,KL,SG,VO
Ligularia stenocephala	AP,B,JE
Ligularia 'The Rocket'	AP,HP
Ligularia veitchiana	AP,B,HP,SG
Ligularia wilsoniana	B,G
Ligusticum ferrulaceum	B
Ligusticum hultenii	DD
Ligusticum lucidum	HP
Ligusticum mutellinum	DD
Ligusticum porteri	AB,B
Ligusticum scoticum	B,G,NS,PO,SG
Ligustrum acutissimum	CG
Ligustrum chenaultii	SA
Ligustrum ibota	B,LN,WA
Ligustrum japonicum	B,C,CA,LN,SA,VE
Ligustrum lucidum	B,C,G,HU,LN,SA,WA
Ligustrum obtusifolium	B,LN,SA
Ligustrum ovalifolium	B,SA
Ligustrum sinense	B,SA,VE
Ligustrum tschonoskii	CG
Ligustrum vulgare	B,LN,SA,SG,VE
Lilium albanicum	LG
Lilium alexandrae	LG
Lilium amabile	LG,SC
Lilium amabile v luteum	C,LG

Lilium armenum	KL
Lilium Asiatic hub s-c	B
Lilium Asiatic hyb mix	C,HU,PK
Lilium Asiatic hyb mix h-p	T
Lilium auratum	B,LG
Lilium 'Bright Star'	B
Lilium brownii	LG
Lilium bulbiferum	AP,AR,CG,G,SC
Lilium bulbiferum ssp bulbiferum	B
Lilium bulbiferum v croceum	B,G,JE,LG,SC
Lilium callosum	LG
Lilium canadense	AP,B,G,HU,LG,SC
Lilium candidum	AP,AR,C,G,JE,LG
Lilium candidum L/Y Yugoslavia	MN
Lilium carniolicum	JE,KL,LG,VO
Lilium cernuum	AP,LG,SC
Lilium chalcedonicum	LG
Lilium Chinese Trumpet hybrids	PK
Lilium columbianum	AB,AP,B,C,G,HU,JE,NO
Lilium concolor v partheneion	PM
Lilium concolor v strictum	B,HU
Lilium dauricum	AP,LG
Lilium dauricum v alpinum	LG
Lilium davidii	AP,B,C,LG,SC
Lilium davidii v willmottiae	AP,B,C,DE,HP,JE,LG
Lilium duchartrei	AP,G,LG,SC
Lilium formosanum	AP,B,C,DD,G,HU,LG,SC
Lilium formosanum 'Little Snowwhite'	B,C,KL,SC
Lilium formosanum 'Little Snowwhite' h-p	T
Lilium formosanum v pricei	AP,AR,G,HP,HU,LG,P, PA,RS,SC,SG
Lilium grayi	LG
Lilium hansoniii	AP,G,LG,NG,SC
Lilium henryi	AP,B,C,G,HU,LG,SC
Lilium humboldtii	B,LG
Lilium humboldtii bloomerianum	SW
Lilium hyb Aurelian mix	AP,C
Lilium hyb Aurelian 'Reflexed Yellow'	C
Lilium hyb - bulbiferum x 'Brismark'	B
Lilium hyb - martagon x pumilum	B
Lilium hybrids	G,LG
Lilium japonicum	LG
Lilium kelleyanum	LG
Lilium kelloggii	LG
Lilium kesselringianum	KL,VO
Lilium 'Kiwi Fanfare'	C
Lilium lancifolium	AP,CG,KL,LG,SC
Lilium lancifolium fl.pl.	AP,B,C,P
Lilium lankongense	AP,LG,SC
Lilium ledebourii	AP,AR,LG,NG,SC
Lilium leichtlinii v maximowiczii	C
Lilium leucanthum v centifolium	C,G,LG
Lilium Lily World sp & cvs mix	LG,SC
Lilium longiflorum	LG,SC
Lilium longiflorum f1 hyb 'Snow Trumpet'	B,BD,C,CL,MO,PK,T
Lilium longiflorum Trumpet hybrids	B,V
Lilium 'Mabel Violet' o-p	C
Lilium mackliniae	AP,B,KL,LG,P,SC
Lilium maculatum	LG
Lilium martagon	AP,AR,B,C,CG,DV,G,I, JE,KL,LG,MN,N,P,PL, PM,RS,SA,SC,SG,T,V
Lilium martagon 'Glisten'	SG
Lilium martagon hyb mix	AP,SC,T
Lilium martagon Russia	PH
Lilium martagon v album	AP,AR,B,C,G,JE,KL,LG,

LILIUM

	MN,PL,RS,SC,SG
Lilium martagon v cattaniae	AP,G,HP,KL,LG,SC,SG
Lilium martagon v dalmaticum	NG
Lilium medeoloides	B,G,SC
Lilium michiganense	B,PR
Lilium monadelphum	AP,AR,B,C,G,JE,KL,LG,
	NG,PL,SC,SG,VO
Lilium nanum	AP,B,G,LG,SC
Lilium nepalense	C
Lilium pardalinum	B,G,LG
Lilium parryi	AP,B,LG
Lilium parvum	LG,SG
Lilium pensylvanicum	SG
Lilium philadelphicum	AP,PR,SG
Lilium philippinense	AR,B,C,EL,LG
Lilium pomponium	AP,B,C,G,LG,PM,SC,SG
Lilium pumilum	AP,B,C,HU,JE,LG,RS,SG
Lilium pyrenaicum	AP,B,C,G,JE,KL,LG,NG,
	SA,SC,SG
Lilium regale	AP,B,BS,BY,C,CL,G,HU,
	JE,KI,KL,LG,MA,N,RS,
	PL,SA,SC,SG,T
Lilium regale 'Album'	AP,G,HP,LG
Lilium regale 'Pink Picotee'	T
Lilium rubellum	B,LG,SC
Lilium sacchalinense	SA
Lilium sargentiae	LG,SG
Lilium sp mix	PA,T
Lilium speciosum v clivorum	AR
Lilium speciosum v speciosum	LG
Lilium sulphureum	LG
Lilium superbum	B,LG,SC
Lilium szovitsianum see L.monadelphum	
Lilium tigrinum see L.lancifolium	
Lilium Trumpet Hyb mix h-p	T
Lilium Trumpet Hyb New Zealand s-c mix	C
Lilium Trumpet mix o-p	HU
Lilium Trumpets 'Wyoming' mix	C
Lilium umbellatum	B,SW
Lilium washingtonianum	B,C
Lilium x aurelianense 'Copper King'	C
Lilium x aurelianense 'First Love'	C
Lilium x formolongo 'White Horn'	PI
Lilium x testaceum	B
Limnanthes douglasii	w.a.
Limnanthes douglasii v sulphurea	B,C
Limonia acidissima	B
Limonium aureum 'Sahin's Gold'	B,PK
Limonium bellidifolium	AP,I,PK,SC
Limonium bellidifolium 'Spangle'	B,CA,HU
Limonium binervosum	SG
Limonium bonduelli	B,C,T
Limonium caspia 'Dazzling Blue'	B,SA,U
Limonium cosyrense	AP,I,SC
Limonium dregeanum 'Confetti'	B
Limonium dregeanum 'Stardust'	B,CA
Limonium dumosum see Goniolimon tataricum v angustifolium	
Limonium Excellent Series s-c,mix	CA
Limonium fortunei 'Confetti'	C,T
Limonium gmelinii	B,C,DE,G,HU,JE,KS
Limonium gmelinii hungaricum	SA
Limonium gougetianum	AP,G,HP,JE,SC
Limonium latifolium see L.platyphyllum	
Limonium longifolium	B,SI
Limonium meyeri	SG
Limonium minutum	AP,G,KL,PM,SC

Limonium mix	M,VY
Limonium otolepis 'Lavender Lace'	B,C
Limonium otolepis 'Select'	T
Limonium 'Party Pinks'	U
Limonium peregrinum	B,SI
Limonium perezii	B,CA,CN,JE,KS,MO,PK,
	SA,SC,T,V
Limonium perezii 'Atlantis'	B
Limonium perezii 'Blue Seas'	JO
Limonium platyphyllum	AP,B,BY,C,DE,DT,HP,JE,
	JO,KI,KS,L,PK,SA,SK,
	SU,T,VY
Limonium pruinosum	B
Limonium puberulum	B
Limonium purpuratum	B,SI
Limonium ramosissimum	C
Limonium sinensis	JE
Limonium sinensis 'Stardust'	CL,KI,MO
Limonium sinuatum	AB,B,BU,CL,PI,SU
Limonium sinuatum 'American Beauty'	B,C,HU,JO,PI,SK,T
Limonium sinuatum 'Apricot'	C,HU,PI
Limonium sinuatum 'Apricot Beauty'	B,BY,T
Limonium sinuatum 'Art Shades mix'	CO,J,ST,TU,V,VH
Limonium sinuatum 'Art Shades' s-c	KI
Limonium sinuatum 'Azure'	T
Limonium sinuatum 'Beidermeier mix'	D,J,T,V
Limonium sinuatum 'Blue Peter'	CL
Limonium sinuatum 'Blue River'	B,MO
Limonium sinuatum 'Chamois'	B,SK
Limonium sinuatum 'Compindi'	C,HU
Limonium sinuatum 'Compindi Rose'	C
Limonium sinuatum 'Forever Blue'	B
Limonium sinuatum 'Forever Gold'	B,BD,CL,DI,KS,MO,O,
	SK
Limonium sinuatum 'Forever Happy'	KS
Limonium sinuatum 'Forever Lavender'	B,KS
Limonium sinuatum 'Forever' mix	C,F,T
Limonium sinuatum 'Forever Moonlight'	B,BS,DT,KS,T
Limonium sinuatum 'Forever Pink'	B
Limonium sinuatum 'Forever Rose'	B,KS
Limonium sinuatum 'Forever Silver'	B,KS
Limonium sinuatum 'Formula mix' s-c	D,T
Limonium sinuatum 'Fortress' mix	MO
Limonium sinuatum 'Gold Coast'	B,BY,C,CL,PI,SK,T
Limonium sinuatum 'Heavenly Blue'	BY,CL,JO,PI,SK
Limonium sinuatum hyb mix	U
Limonium sinuatum 'Iceberg'	B,BY,C,CL,HU,JO,PI,SK,
	T,V
Limonium sinuatum 'Kaleidoscope' s-c	YA
Limonium sinuatum 'Lavender'	C,KS
Limonium sinuatum 'Market Blue'	T
Limonium sinuatum 'Market Rose'	SK
Limonium sinuatum 'Midnight Blue'	B,BY,C,HU,JO,PI,SK
Limonium sinuatum mix special	F,S
Limonium sinuatum 'Pacific' mix	C,CA,DE,HU,KS,SK
Limonium sinuatum 'Pacific' s-c	B,CA,DE,JO,KS,SK
Limonium sinuatum 'Pacific' white	B,CA,SK
Limonium sinuatum 'Petite Bouquet' mix	BD,C,CA,CL,CO,KI,KS,
	MO,PK,R,SK,TU
Limonium sinuatum 'Petite Bouquet' s-c	KS,SK
Limonium sinuatum 'Purple Monarch'	BY,C,T
Limonium sinuatum 'Q' mix	BS,DT
Limonium sinuatum 'Q' s-c	B,L
Limonium sinuatum 'Q' white	B
Limonium sinuatum 'Rainbow' mix	BY
Limonium sinuatum 'Rose Light'	B,BY,C,CL,HU,JO,PI,V

LIMONIUM

Limonium sinuatum 'Salmon Shades'	KS
Limonium sinuatum 'Sky Blue'	C,HU
Limonium sinuatum soft pastel mix	BS,C,KS,MO,SE,SK,T,U
Limonium sinuatum 'Soiree' imp s-c	PK
Limonium sinuatum 'Sunset Shades Mix'	B,BD,C,CA,CL,DT,F,JO, KS,MO,PI,PK,SE,SK,T, V,VY
Limonium sinuatum 'Turbo' s-c, mix	BS,SK
Limonium sinuatum 'Twilight'	BY,C,PI
Limonium speciosus 'Blue Diamond'	JE
Limonium 'Sunburst Dark Blue'	MO,S
Limonium 'Sunburst Golden'	U
Limonium 'Sunburst' mix	MO,S
Limonium 'Sunburst Pale Blue'	MO,S
Limonium 'Sunburst' pastel mix	BS
Limonium 'Sunburst Rose'	MO,S
Limonium 'Sunburst' s-c	BS
Limonium 'Sunburst White'	MO,S
Limonium 'Sunburst Yellow'	MO,S
Limonium suworowii see Psylliostachys	
Limonium tetragonum see L.dregeanum	
Linanthus floribundus	B
Linanthus grandiflorus	AB,AP,B,C,HU,KS,SC
Linanthus grandiflorus 'Princess Blush'	V
Linanthus nuttallii	B,JE,SW
Linaria aeruginea	AP,C,RS,SC
Linaria aeruginea ssp nevadensis	AP,HP,SG
Linaria alpina	AP,B,BS,C,CG,G,HP,JE, KL,RS,SA,SC,SG,T
Linaria alpina hyb	I
Linaria amethystea	B
Linaria anticaria	T
Linaria broussonetii	C
Linaria canadense	HU
Linaria dalmatica	HP
Linaria genistifolia	AP,B,CG,HP,KL,T
Linaria genistifolia ssp dalmatica	AP,B,C,G,JE,SC,SG
Linaria glacialis	VO
Linaria halaeva	B
Linaria joppensis	B
Linaria maroccana	AB,AP,B,I,KS
Linaria maroccana 'Excelsior Mixed'	J,V
Linaria maroccana 'Fairy Bouquet Mixed'	B,BY,C,CO,D,DE,DN, DT,F,HU,KI,L,PK,S,SU, T,TU,U
Linaria maroccana 'Fantasy' s-c, mix	F,PL
Linaria maroccana 'Fantasy' s-c p.s.	B
Linaria maroccana 'Northern Lights Mix'	B,HU,KS,PI,T
Linaria nevadensis	KL
Linaria nevadensis 'Elfin Delight'	CG,V
Linaria nevadensis 'Gemstones'	T
Linaria perenne dw	KL
Linaria perenne ssp extraaxillare	KL
Linaria purpurea	AP,B,BS,C,HP,JE,NS, SA,SC,SU,V,W
Linaria purpurea 'Alba' see L.p. 'Springside White'	
Linaria purpurea 'Bowles' Mauve'	B
Linaria purpurea 'Canon Went'	AP,B,BH,BS,C,HP,JE, NS,PK,SA,SC,T
Linaria purpurea 'Rev. C.E.Bowring'	B,PK
Linaria purpurea 'Springside White'	B,HP,JE,SA
Linaria repens	B,G,HP,HU,JE
Linaria reticulata 'Aureopurpurea'	B,T
Linaria reticulata 'Flamenco'	C,J
Linaria 'Sue'	HP
Linaria supina	AP,B,G,JE,SC

Linaria tonzigii	B,CG
Linaria triornithophora	AP,B,G,HP,P,T
Linaria tristis	KL
Linaria vulgaris	B,C,CN,CO,F,HP,JE,LA, SA,SG,TH,V
Lindelofia anchusoides	HP
Lindelofia longiflora	AP,B,G,HP,JE,SA
Lindera benzoin	A,B,DD,FW,LN,SA
Lindera glauca	LN,SA
Lindera obtusiloba	B,EL,FW,LN,N,SA
Lindheimera texana	B,KS,PK,T
Lindmania penduliflora	DV
Linnaea borealis	B,C
Linospadix minor	B,O,SA
Linospadix monostachya	B,C,EL,HA,O,SA
Linum africanum	B,SI
Linum alpinum	JE,SA
Linum arboreum	AP,SC
Linum austriacum	G,KL,W
Linum bienne	B
Linum capitatum	AP,B,JE,KL,SC
Linum cariense	VO
Linum dolmiticum	B,HP,JE
Linum flavum	AP,B,BS,BY,HU,MO,SC
Linum flavum 'Compactum'	AP,B,C,CL,G,JE,SA,SC, SG,SK,T
Linum flavum v comp. 'Golden Cushion'	V
Linum Gemmel's Hybrid	JE
Linum grandiflorum	G,HW,SG
Linum grandiflorum 'Album'	T
Linum grandiflorum 'Bright Eyes'	B,C,J,KS,T,TU,V
Linum hirsutum	AP,B,JE,SA
Linum komarovii 'Blue Ice'	T
Linum lanuginosum	VO
Linum lewisii	HU,NO,SG,SW,W
Linum marginale	RS
Linum monogynum	AP,B,C,SC,SS
Linum narbonense	AP,B,C,G,HP,JE,SA,SC
Linum narbonense 'Heavenly Blue'	T
Linum perenne	AP,AV,B,BS,BU,C,CN, CO,DD,DT,G,HP,HU,HW, JD,JE,KI,KL,KS,L,SA, SC,SG,SK,TH,V
Linum perenne album	AP,B,C,CG,CN,HP,HU, JE,SA,TH
Linum perenne 'Blau Saphir'	B,BD,BS,BY,C,CL,DE, JE,MO,PK,S,SA,T,TU
Linum perenne 'Bryce Canyon'	B,HU
Linum perenne 'Diamant'	B,BD,BS,C,JE,KI,KS, MO,SA,T
Linum perenne 'Himmelszelt'	B,JE
Linum perenne 'Jewels Mix'	U
Linum perenne ssp alpinum	AP,B,C
Linum perenne ssp lewisii	AB,AP,B,C,HP,PI,RS
Linum pubescens	B
Linum rhodopeum	SG
Linum rigidum	RM
Linum rubrum	AB,AP,B,BS,BY,C,CA, CO,D,DN,HU,KI,KS,L, PI,ST,T,V
Linum scarlet	DT,J,S,U
Linum sp	P,SI
Linum suffruticosum ssp salsoloides	AP,B,C,JE,SC
Linum sulcatum	B,PR
Linum tauricum	B,JE
Linum trigynum	CG

LINUM

Linum usitatissimum	B,BS,C,CP,DD,G,HU,KS, SG,V,W
Linum usitatissimum cvs	B
Linum virginianum	B
Liparia splendens	B,SI
Lippia dulcis	B,C,CP
Liquidambar acalycina	B
Liquidambar formosana	B,EL,FW,LN,N,SA
Liquidambar styraciflua	A,B,BS,C,CA,CG,EL,FW, HA,HU,LN,N,SA,T,VE, WA
Liriodendron chinense	B,FW,LN,SA
Liriodendron tulipifera	A,C,CA,CG,EL,FW,HA, LN,RH,SA,VE
Liriope muscari	B,C,CA,SA
Liriope muscari 'Big Blue'	JE
Liriope muscari 'Gigantea'	B,CA,SA
Lisianthus coronaria	DD
Listera ovata	B
Litchi chinensis	B,CA
Lithocarpus densiflorus	B,CA,LN,SA
Lithocarpus sclerophylla	B
Lithodora arvensis	SG
Lithops alpina	CG
Lithops aucampiae	B,CH,DV,SI
Lithops aucampiae 'Kuruman'	B,DV,Y
Lithops aucampiae ssp aucampiae	DV,Y
Lithops aucampiae ssp eunicae v eu. C48	Y
Lithops aucampiae ssp eu. v fluminalis C54	Y
Lithops aucampiae ssp euniceae	B,DV
Lithops aucampiae v fluminalis	B,BC,DV
Lithops aucampiae v koelemanii	B,DV
Lithops aucampiae v koele.i C16 & C256	Y
Lithops aucampiae v 'Kuruman'	Y
Lithops bromfieldii	B,DV
Lithops bromfieldii v br. C40,C41 & C348	Y
Lithops bromfieldii v glaudinae	B,DV
Lithops bromfieldii v glaud. C116 & C382	Y
Lithops bromfieldii v insularis	B,DV
Lithops bromfieldii v insularis C42 & C57	Y
Lithops bromfieldii v insularis 'Sulphurea'	B,DV
Lithops bromfieldii v ins. 'Sulphurea' C362	Y
Lithops bromfieldii v mennellii	B,DV
Lithops bromfieldii v menn. C44 & C283	Y
Lithops comptonii	B,DV,SI
Lithops comptonii v comp. C125 & C347	Y
Lithops comptonii v weberi	B,DV,Y
Lithops dinteri	B,CG,DV
Lithops dinteri 'Dintergreen'	DV,Y
Lithops dinteri ssp d. v brevis C84 & C268	Y
Lithops dinteri ssp dinteri v dinteri C206	Y
Lithops dinteri ssp friederichii	B,DV,Y
Lithops dinteri ssp multipunctata	B,BC,DV,Y
Lithops dinteri v brevis	B,DV
Lithops divergens	B,DV,CG
Lithops divergens v amethystina	B,BC,DV,Y
Lithops divergens v div. C202 & C269	Y
Lithops dorotheae	B,DV,Y
Lithops elevata	CG
Lithops erniana	B
Lithops erniana v witputzensis /l.kara.ssp	B
Lithops francisci	B,CG,DV,Y
Lithops fulleri v brunnea	B
Lithops fulleri v rouxii	B
Lithops fulleri v rouxii /julii ssp fu.v.rou.	B
Lithops fulleri vars	B

Lithops fulviceps	B,CG,SI
Lithops fulviceps v aurea	B,DV,Y
Lithops fulviceps v fulviceps	DV,Y
Lithops fulviceps v fulviceps 'Lydiae'	B,DV,Y
Lithops fulviceps v lactinea	B,DV,Y
Lithops gesinae	B,CG,DV,SI
Lithops gesinae v annae	B,DG,KB,Y
Lithops gesinae v gesinae C207	Y
Lithops geyeri	B,CG,DV,KB,Y
Lithops gracilidelineata	B,BC,CG,DV
Lithops gracil. ssp brandbergensis	B,DV,Y
Lithops gracil. ssp gracil 'Fritz White Lady'	DV,Y
Lithops gracilidelineata ssp gracil v gr. c. r.	DV,Y
Lithops gracilidelineata v waldroniae	B,DV,Y
Lithops hallii	B,BC,CG,SI
Lithops hallii brown form	B,DV,Y
Lithops hallii 'Salicola Reticulata'	B,DV,Y
Lithops hallii 'Salicola Reticulata' grey f.	DV
Lithops hallii v hallii coll ref	DV,Y
Lithops hallii v ochracea	B,DV,Y
Lithops hallii v och.'Gr. Soapstone' C111A	DV,Y
Lithops hallii v white form	B
Lithops harlequin	CH
Lithops helmutii	B,CG,DV,KB,Y
Lithops herrei	B,DV,Y
Lithops herrei v 'Translucens'	B,DV,Y
Lithops hookeri see L.turbiniformis	
Lithops hookeri see L.turbiniformis	
Lithops julii	B,CG,SI
Lithops julii 'Pallid'	B
Lithops julii 'Reticulata'	B
Lithops julii ssp fulleri	B,BC,DV,KB,Y
Lithops julii ssp fulleri 'Fullergreen'	DV
Lithops julii ssp fulleri v brunnea	B,DV,Y
Lithops julii ssp fulleri v rouxii	B,DV,Y
Lithops julii ssp julii	DV,KB,Y
Lithops julii ssp julii 'Chrysocephala'	B,DV,Y
Lithops julii ssp julii 'Fuscous'	B
Lithops julii ssp julii 'Littlewoodii'	B,DV,Y
Lithops julii ssp julii 'Reticulata'	Y
Lithops karasmontana	B,CG
Lithops karasmontana 'Jacobseniana'	B,DV,Y
Lithops karasmontana 'Mickbergensis'	B,DV,Y
Lithops karasmontana 'Opalina'	B,Y
Lithops karasmontana 'Signalberg'	B,DV,Y
Lithops karasmontana ssp bella	B,DV,Y
Lithops karasmontana ssp eberlanzii	B,DV,Y
Lithops kar. ssp eberl.i 'Avocado Cream'	B,DV,Y
Lithops karas. ssp eberlanzii 'Erniana'	B,DV,Y
Lithops kar. ssp eberlanzii 'Witputzensis'	B,DV,Y
Lithops karasmontana ssp karas v karas	KB,Y
Lithops karasmontana ssp karasmontana	DV
Lithops karasmontana v aiaisensis	B,DV,Y
Lithops karasmontana v lerichiana	B,DV,Y
Lithops karasmontana v tischerii	B,DV,Y
Lithops kunjasensis	CG
Lithops lesliei	B,CG,DV,SI
Lithops lesliei 'Albiflora'	B,DV,Y
Lithops lesliei 'Albinica'	B,DV,KB,Y
Lithops lesliei 'Kimberley'	B,DV,Y
Lithops lesliei 'Luteoviridis'	B,DV,Y
Lithops lesliei 'Maraisii'	B,DV,Y
Lithops lesliei 'Pietersburg'	B,DV,Y
Lithops lesliei 'Prince Albert'	B
Lithops lesliei ssp burchellii	B,DV,Y
Lithops lesliei ssp lesliei	DV,Y

LITHOPS

Lithops lesliei 'Storms Albinigold'	DV,Y
Lithops lesliei v hornii	B,DV,Y
Lithops lesliei v mariae	B,DV,Y
Lithops lesliei v minor	B,DV,Y
Lithops lesliei v minor 'Witblom'	B,DV,Y
Lithops lesliei v rubrobrunnea	B,DV,Y
Lithops lesliei v venteri	B,DV,Y
Lithops lesliei 'Warrenton'	B,DV,Y
Lithops marginata	CG
Lithops marmorata	B,SI
Lithops marmorata 'Diutina'	B,DV,Y
Lithops marmorata 'Framesii'	B,CH,DV,Y
Lithops marmorata ssp marmorata	CH,DV,Y
Lithops marmorata 'Umdausensis'	B
Lithops marmorata v elisae	B,DV,KB,Y
Lithops meyeri	B,DV,KB,Y
Lithops naureeniae	B,DV,Y
Lithops olivacea	B,CH
Lithops olivacea v nebrownii	B,DV,Y
Lithops olivacea v olivacea	DV,KB,Y
Lithops optica	B,DV,SI,Y
Lithops optica 'Maculata'	B,Y
Lithops optica 'Rubra'	B,CH,DV,Y
Lithops otzeniana	B,CH,DV,Y
Lithops Pebble Plants mix	SK,T
Lithops pseudotruncatella	B,DV,SI
Lithops pseudotruncatella 'Alpina'	B,DV,Y
Lithops pseudotruncatella 'Mundtii'	B,DV,Y
Lithops pseudotruncatella pallid form	B,DV
Lithops pseudotruncatella ssp archerae	B,DV,Y
Lithops pseudotruncatella ssp dendritica	B,DV,Y
Lithops pseudotruncatella ssp d. 'Farinosa'	B,DV,Y
Lithops pseudotr. ssp d. 'Pulmonuncula.'	B,DV,Y
Lithops pseudotr. ssp groendraaiensis	B,DV,Y
Lithops pseudotr. ssp pseudo v pseudo	KB,Y
Lithops pseudotruncatella ssp volkii	B,CG,DV,Y
Lithops pseudotruncatella v elisabethiae	B,DV,Y
Lithops pseudotruncatella v riehmerae	B,DV,Y
Lithops pseudotruncatella Witkop form	DV,Y
Lithops pseudotruncortella v alpina	SG
Lithops rugosa	CG
Lithops ruschiorum	B
Lithops ruschiorum 'Nellii'	B,DV,Y
Lithops ruschiorum v lineata	B,DV
Lithops ruschiorum v ruschiorum coll ref	DV,Y
Lithops salicola	B,DV,KB,SI,Y
Lithops salicola Maculate form	B,DV,Y
Lithops schwantesii	B,BC,DV
Lithops schwantesii grey form	B,DV,Y
Lithops schwantesii 'Gulielmi'	B,DV,Y
Lithops schwantesii 'Kubisensis'	B,DV,Y
Lithops schwantesii ssp gebseri	B,Y
Lithops schwantesii ssp sch v sch	Y
Lithops schwantesii ssp schwantesii	DV
Lithops schwantesii 'Triebneri'	B,DV,KB
Lithops schwantesii v marthae	B,DV,Y
Lithops schwantesii v rugosa	B,DV,KB,Y
Lithops schwantesii v urikosensis	B,DV,Y
Lithops schwantesii v urik. 'Christinae'	B,DV,Y
Lithops schwantesii v urik. 'Kunjasensis'	B,DV,Y
Lithops schwantesii v urik. 'Nutupsdrift'	DV
Lithops sp mix	C,DV,FR,J,KB,L,PK,SI, SO,Y
Lithops steineckiana	B,DV,Y
Lithops 'Sunstone'	CH
Lithops 'Talisman'	B,CH
Lithops terricolor	B,DV,KB,SI,Y
Lithops terricolor 'Localis'	B,Y
Lithops terricolor 'Peersii'	B,DV,Y
Lithops terricolor 'Prince Albert'	B,Y
Lithops terricolor 'Silver Spurs'	DV,Y
Lithops turbiniformis v dabneri	B,DV,Y
Lithops turbiniformis v elephina	B,DV,Y
Lithops turbiniformis v hookeri	DV,Y
Lithops turb. v hookeri vermiculate form	B,DV,Y
Lithops turbiniformis v lutea	B,DV,Y
Lithops turbiniformis v marginata	B,DV,Y
Lithops turbiniformis v marginata cerise	B,DV,Y
Lithops turbiniformis v marginata red-br.	B,DV,Y
Lithops turbiniformis v subfenestrata	B,DV,Y
Lithops turb. v subfen. 'Brunneoviolacea'	B,DV,Y
Lithops turbiniformis v susannae	B,DV,Y
Lithops vallis-mariae	B,DV
Lithops vallis-mariae 'Margarethae'	B
Lithops vallis-mariae v groendraaiensis	B
Lithops verruculosa	B,DV,SI
Lithops verruculosa 'Inae'	B,DV,Y
Lithops verruculosa v glabra	B,DV,Y
Lithops verruculosa v verruculosa	Y
Lithops villetii	B
Lithops villetii ssp deboeri	DV,Y
Lithops villetii ssp villetii	DV,Y
Lithops villetii v kennedyi	B,DV,Y
Lithops viridis	B,DV
Lithops werneri	B,DV,Y
Lithospermum canescens	B
Lithospermum caroliniense	B,JE
Lithospermum erythrorhizon	B,CG
Lithospermum incisum	B
Lithospermum officinale	AB,AP,G,KL,PO,SG
Litsea leefeana	O
Littonia modesta	AP,B,C,MN,RU,SG,SI
Living Stones /Succulents exc Lithops	C
Livistona alfredii	B,C,NI,O,SA
Livistona australis	B,C,CA,EL,HA,O,SA,VE
Livistona benthamii	O
Livistona chinensis	B,C,CA,EL,FW,HA,O,SA
Livistona decipiens	B,CA,EL,HA,O,SA
Livistona drudei	O
Livistona eastonii	B,O
Livistona humilis	B,O,SA
Livistona inermis	B,O
Livistona jenkensiana	B,HA,O,SA
Livistona loryphylla	B,O
Livistona mariae	B,EL,HA,O
Livistona muelleri	B,EL,O
Livistona rigida	B,EL,O
Livistona robinsoniana	O
Livistona rotundifolia	B,CA,EL,O,SA
Livistona saribus	B,CA,O,RE
Livistona 'Victoria River'	B,O
Lloydia serotina	B,C,RM,SW
Loasa triphylla	B,DV,SG,T
Loasa triphylla v volcanica	AP,B,C,I,SG
Lobelia anatina	B,HP,SW,T,V
Lobelia cardinalis	AP,B,BH,C,CG,CP,DV, HU,HW,JE,NT,PR,SA, SK,SW,T,W
Lobelia cardinalis 'Alba'	HP
Lobelia cardinalis multiflora	B,SW
Lobelia chamaepitys	B,SI
Lobelia comosa	B,CG,KB,SA,SI

LOBELIA

Variety	Code
Lobelia 'Complexion'	T
Lobelia 'Compliment Blue'	B,BS,CA,D,JE,KI,MO, SK,YA
Lobelia 'Compliment Deep Red'	B,BS,CA,CL,JE,MO
Lobelia 'Compliment' mix	BS,CL,J,MO,PK,U
Lobelia 'Compliment Scarlet'	B,BS,CA,CL,JE,KI,MO, SK,V,YA
Lobelia coronopifolia	B,SI
Lobelia erinus	FR,I
Lobelia erinus blue	FR
Lobelia erinus 'Blue Gown'	BS,BY
Lobelia erinus 'Blue Moon'	PK,T
Lobelia erinus 'Blue Pearl'	B,BD,L
Lobelia erinus 'Blue Stone'	PK,U
Lobelia erinus 'Blue Wings'	D
Lobelia erinus 'Cambridge Blue'	B,BD,BS,BY,C,CA,CL, CN,CO,D,F,J,KI,L,M,MO, R,SE,SK,ST,T,TU,V,VH, YA
Lobelia erinus 'Cambridge Blue' c.s	DT,MO,S,SK
Lobelia erinus 'Cascade Blue'	B,BS,BY,F,J,SE,SK,T,U,V, YA
Lobelia erinus 'Cascade' blue p.s	SK
Lobelia erinus 'Cascade Crimson'	T
Lobelia erinus 'Cascade' lavender p.s	SK
Lobelia erinus 'Cascade Lilac'	B,D,SE,SK,T,VH,YA
Lobelia erinus 'Cascade' mix	BD,BS,BY,CO,DE,DT,F, HU,J,KI,KS,L,M,MC,PL, R,S,SE,SK,ST,T,U,V,VH, YA
Lobelia erinus 'Cascade' mix p.s	BD,MO,SK,U,YA
Lobelia erinus 'Cascade Red'	B,BS,BY,D,F,J,S,SK,T,V, YA
Lobelia erinus 'Cascade' red p.s	SK
Lobelia erinus 'Cascade Rose'	B,SK
Lobelia erinus 'Cascade' rose p.s	SK
Lobelia erinus 'Cascade Ruby'	B,BS,U,YA
Lobelia erinus 'Cascade Sapphire'	B,BD,CL,D,F,KI,L,S,SE, SK,ST,U
Lobelia erinus 'Cascade Sapphire' p.s	SK,YA
Lobelia erinus 'Cascade White'	B,BS,SE,SK,T,YA
Lobelia erinus 'Cascade' white p.s	SK
Lobelia erinus 'Cobalt Blue'	B,BD,BS,F,KI,MO,SK,TH
Lobelia erinus 'Cobalt Blue' p.s.	SK
Lobelia erinus 'Colour Cascade' mix p.s	SK
Lobelia erinus 'Crystal' c.s	S
Lobelia erinus 'Crystal Palace'	w.a.
Lobelia erinus 'Crystal Palace' p.s	BD,DT,MO,S,SK,YA
Lobelia erinus 'Early Dwarf Blue Mink'	B
Lobelia erinus 'Early Dwarf Snow Mink'	B
Lobelia erinus 'Emperor William'	B,BD,BS,CL,L,T,TH
Lobelia erinus 'Fountains Blue'	B,BD,C,CL,CN,CO,D,DT ,KS,MO,PK,TU
Lobelia erinus 'Fountains Crimson'	B,BD,BS,C,CL,CN,DT,F, KS,MO,PK,TU
Lobelia erinus 'Fountains Lilac'	B,BD,BS,C,CL,CN,D,DT, F,KS,M,MO,PK,TU,V
Lobelia erinus 'Fountains' mix	BS,C,CL,CN,D,DT,F,KI,M C,MO,PK,SE,ST,SU,TU
Lobelia erinus 'Fountains Rose'	B,BD,BS,C,CL,CN,D,DT, MO,PK,TU
Lobelia erinus 'Fountains' Select	CL
Lobelia erinus 'Fountains White'	B,BD,BS,C,CL,CN,CO, D,DE,DT,F,KS,MO,PK,S, TU,V,VY
Lobelia erinus 'Half Moon'	M
Lobelia erinus 'Hamburgia'	B
Lobelia erinus 'Kaleidoscope'	U
Lobelia erinus 'Lilac Time'	B
Lobelia erinus 'Mixed Shades' p.s	D
Lobelia erinus 'Mrs.Clibran'	AB,B,BD,BS,C,CL,CN, J,KI,L,MO,S,SE,SK,TH, V,YA
Lobelia erinus 'Mrs.Clibran Imp'	D,DT,F,T,U
Lobelia erinus 'Mrs.Clibran' p.s	MO,SK,YA
Lobelia erinus 'Palace Blue'	B,MO,YA
Lobelia erinus 'Palace Blue Eye'	B,F,MO
Lobelia erinus 'Palace Royal'	B,MO
Lobelia erinus 'Palace White'	B,MO
Lobelia erinus 'Paper Moon'	PK
Lobelia erinus 'Rainbow' mix	SK
Lobelia erinus 'Rapid Blue' p.s	D
Lobelia erinus 'Rapid White' p.s	D
Lobelia erinus 'Regatta Blue Splash'	BS,CL,D,DT,F,MO,PL, SE,T
Lobelia erinus 'Regatta Lilac'	B,BS,C,CL,MO,PL,YA
Lobelia erinus 'Regatta Marine Blue'	B,BS,C,CL,F,JO,MO,YA
Lobelia erinus 'Regatta Midnight Blue'	B,BS,CL,MO
Lobelia erinus 'Regatta' mix	BS,C,CL,DT,L,MO,PL, VY,YA
Lobelia erinus 'Regatta Rose'	B,MO
Lobelia erinus 'Regatta Sky Blue'	B,BS,C,CL,MO,YA
Lobelia erinus 'Regatta White'	B,BS,CL,MO
Lobelia erinus 'Regattas' multi-p.s	SK
Lobelia erinus 'Ripples'	U
Lobelia erinus 'Riviera Blue Eyes'	B,BS,CL,L,MO,SK
Lobelia erinus 'Riviera Blue Splash'	B,BS,CL,DT,F,KI,KS,L, MO,PK,SE,SK,T,U,YA
Lobelia erinus 'Riviera Lilac'	B,BS,C,CL,DT,F,KI,KS,L, MO,SE,SK,T,TU,V,YA
Lobelia erinus 'Riviera Lilac' c.s	D,S,SE
Lobelia erinus 'Riviera Marine Blue'	B,BS,CL,MO,SK
Lobelia erinus 'Riviera Midnight'	B,BS,CL,MO,SK,YA
Lobelia erinus 'Riviera' mix	BD,BS,CL,DT,MO,PL, VY,YA
Lobelia erinus 'Riviera Sky Blue'	B,BS,C,CL,D,KS,MO,SK, YA
Lobelia erinus 'Riviera White'	B,BS,CL,L,MO,SK
Lobelia erinus 'Rivieras' multi-p.s	SK
Lobelia erinus 'Rosamond'	B,BD,BS,BY,C,CL,CN, DT,F,J,KI,L,MO,PI,R,SE, SK,ST,T,TU,U,V,YA
Lobelia erinus 'Rosamond' p.s	SK,YA
Lobelia erinus 'Sapphire'	B,BY,C,CA,DN,DT,F,FR, J,M,MO,R,TU,V,VH,VY
Lobelia erinus 'Sapphire' p.s	BD,MO
Lobelia erinus 'Sky Blue'	CL
Lobelia erinus 'Snowball'	BD,BS,M,R,T,YA
Lobelia erinus 'Snowball' p.s	YA
Lobelia erinus 'String of Pearls'	BD,BS,BY,C,CN,F,J,KI, L,M,MO,R,SE,ST,T,TU, V,VH,YA
Lobelia erinus 'String of Pearls' p.s	BD,MO,S,YS
Lobelia erinus 'Sutton's Blue'	B
Lobelia erinus 'White Lady'	B,BS,BY,CA,CL,CN,CO, D,F,J,KI,MO,PI,SE,SK, ST,TH,TU,U,V,VH
Lobelia erinus 'White Lady' c.s	DT,MO,S,SK
Lobelia erinus 'White Perfection'	BS,DT,L,TH
Lobelia excelsa	C
Lobelia f1 'Fan Cinnabar Pink'	JE
Lobelia f1 'Fan Cinnabar Rose'	B,BS,CL,CO,D,DE,DT,

LOBELIA

	JO,KI,MO
Lobelia f1 'Fan Deep Red'	B,BS,C,CL,DE,JE,JO,KI,
	MO
Lobelia f1 'Fan' Mix	DT,L,T
Lobelia f1 'Fan Orchid Rose'	BS,CL,JO,MO
Lobelia f1 'Fan Scarlet'	B,BS,CL,JE,MO,O,S,SE,
	U,YA
Lobelia f1 'Fan Scarlet & Cinnabar Rose'	T
Lobelia heterophylla	B,NI
Lobelia holstii	B,SA
Lobelia inflata	AB,B,C,CN,CP,HU,PO,
	PR
Lobelia laxifolia v angustifolia	B,HU
Lobelia 'Light Blue Basket'	S
Lobelia linnaoides	B,SC,SS
Lobelia lutea	B,C,SI
Lobelia pinifolia	B,SI
Lobelia 'Queen Victoria'	AP,B,BD,BS,BY,C,CL,
	CN,DE,DT,F,HP,HU,I,KI,
	L,MO,R,T
Lobelia rhombifolia	B,NI
Lobelia rhytidosperma	B,NI
Lobelia roughii	B,SC,SS
Lobelia sessilifolia	B,C,HP,JE,P,SA,SG
Lobelia siphilitica	AB,AP,B,BS,C,CG,CN,
	CP,DD,HP,HU,KI,LG,
	NT,P,PR,SA,SG,T,W
Lobelia siphilitica 'Blue Select'	B,JE,T
Lobelia siphilitica f albiflora	B,C,G,JE,NT,SA
Lobelia sp	I,SI
Lobelia spicata	B,PR
Lobelia splendens 'Blinkfeuer'	B
Lobelia splendens 'Elmfeuer'	B,JE
Lobelia tenuior	B,NI,O
Lobelia tenuior 'Blue Wings'	B,C,J,T
Lobelia tupa	B,C,DD,HP,HU,NG,P,
	SA,SZ,T
Lobelia tupa 'Candelabra'	PL
Lobelia valida	B,C,HP,KB,SA,SI
Lobelia valida 'African Skies'	B
Lobelia valida 'Blue Ribbons'	V
Lobelia valida 'South Seas'	T
Lobelia x gerardii	G,T
Lobelia x gerardii 'Vedrariensis'	B,BD,BS,CN,HP,JE,MO,
	SA,SC
Lobelia x speciosa hyb	T
Lobelia x speciosa 'Pink Flamingo'	B,C,F,T,V
Lobivia acanthophlegma	B,DV,Y
Lobivia acanthophlegma v oligotricha	B
Lobivia acanthophlegma v patula	Y
Lobivia anccastii	DV
Lobivia arachnacantha v torecillasensis	Y
Lobivia argentea	DV
Lobivia atrovirens	B
Lobivia atrovirens v ritteri	B
Lobivia aurantiaca	Y
Lobivia aurea	B,BC,DV
Lobivia aurea v leucomalla	B
Lobivia aurea v mazanense	DV
Lobivia aurea v schaferi	B
Lobivia backebergii	DV
Lobivia binghamiana	Y
Lobivia breviflora	Y
Lobivia bruchii	DV
Lobivia caineana	B
Lobivia cardenasiana	B,Y

Lobivia chrysantha	B,Y
Lobivia cinnabarina	DV
Lobivia cinnabarina see Echinopsis	
Lobivia cintiensis	B,DV,Y
Lobivia crassicaulis	DV
Lobivia cruciaureispina	DV
Lobivia culpinensis	Y
Lobivia cylindracea	Y
Lobivia draxleriana	DV,Y
Lobivia drijveriana	DV,Y
Lobivia einsteinii v aureiflora	B
Lobivia emmae	Y
Lobivia famatimensis	DV,Y
Lobivia famatimensis v leucomalla	Y
Lobivia famatimensis v setosa	Y
Lobivia ferox	DV,Y
Lobivia ferox see Echinopsis	
Lobivia formosa	DV
Lobivia glauca v paucicostata	Y
Lobivia guinesensis	Y
Lobivia haageana v chrysantha	Y
Lobivia haagei	B
Lobivia haematantha	Y
Lobivia haematantha v amblayensis	B
Lobivia haematantha v densispina	B
Lobivia haematantha v elongata	B
Lobivia haematantha v kuehnrichii	B
Lobivia haematantha v rebutioides	B
Lobivia hertrichiana	B
Lobivia hertrichiana v laui	B
Lobivia higginsiana	DV
Lobivia horrida	B,DV,Y
Lobivia incuensis	DV
Lobivia jajoiana	B,Y
Lobivia jajoiana v fleischerana	B,Y
Lobivia jajoiana v nigrostoma	B
Lobivia jajoiana v paucicostata	B
Lobivia lateritia	B,Y
Lobivia laui	DV
Lobivia leucorhodon	DV,Y
Lobivia longispina	Y
Lobivia mairiae	DV
Lobivia marsoneri	B
Lobivia marsoneri iridescens	BC
Lobivia maximilliana	DV,Y
Lobivia maximilliana v caespitosa	B
Lobivia maximilliana v charazanensis	B
Lobivia maximilliana v corbula	B
Lobivia maximilliana v intermedia	B
Lobivia maximilliana v westii	B
Lobivia mistiensis	DV
Lobivia multicostata	Y
Lobivia napina	Y
Lobivia obrepanda	Y
Lobivia oligotricha	DV,Y
Lobivia omasuyana	DV,Y
Lobivia oyonica	Y
Lobivia pachycantha	Y
Lobivia peeslianum	Y
Lobivia pentlandii	DV,Y
Lobivia pentlandii see Echinopsis	
Lobivia pugionacantha v rossii	B
Lobivia pusilla	Y
Lobivia pusilla v flaviflora	DV
Lobivia pygmaea	B
Lobivia rossii	Y

LOBIVIA

Lobivia rossii v salmonea	DV,Y
Lobivia saltensis	B
Lobivia saltensis v pseudocachensis	B
Lobivia sanguiniflora	B
Lobivia schieliana v quiabayensis	B
Lobivia schreiteri	B
Lobivia silvestri	DV
Lobivia sp mix	C,Y
Lobivia steinmannii	B
Lobivia steinmannii v costata	B
Lobivia sublimiflora v krausii	Y
Lobivia tegeleriana	B
Lobivia tenuispina	B,DV,Y
Lobivia thionantha	B
Lobivia thionantha v aurantiaca	B
Lobivia thionantha v glauca	B
Lobivia tiegelana	DV,Y
Lobivia tiegelana v cinnabarina	B
Lobivia tiegelana v pusilla	B
Lobivia tiegelana v ruberrima	DV,Y
Lobivia varians	DV
Lobivia wegheiana	Y
Lobivia winteriana	DV
Lobivia wrightiana	B
Lobivia wrightiana v winteriana	Y
Lobivia zecheri	B
Lobivopsis Paramount Hybrids	Y
Lobostemon fruticosus	B,BH,KB
Lobostemon montanus	BH
Lobostemon sp	SI
Lobularia 'Aphrodite' mix	BS,DT,F,SE
Lobularia 'Apricot Shades'	SE,T
Lobularia 'Delight Purple' s-c	CL
Lobularia 'Easter Basket'	DT,SK
Lobularia 'Golf'	CL,F,PL
Lobularia 'Little Dorrit'	F,J,M
Lobularia maritima	B,SG,TH
Lobularia maritima 'Basket' Series s-c	SK
Lobularia maritima 'Carpet Of Snow'	AB,B,BS,BU,C,CA,D,DE, DT,F,J,JO,KI,L,MO,PI,R, S,SE,SK,ST,T,U,V,VH
Lobularia maritima 'Creamery'	B,BD,BS,CL,F,KS,MO
Lobularia maritima 'Easter Bonnet' dp pink	B,BS,D,YA
Lobularia maritima 'Easter Bonnet' mix	BD,BS,D,J,L,M,MO,PK, SE,TU,V,VY,YA
Lobularia maritima 'Easter Bonnet' s-c	B,BS,MO,PK,YA
Lobularia maritima 'Minimum'	B,BS,BY,D,L
Lobularia maritima 'Minimum' Imp	BS
Lobularia maritima 'Navy Blue'	B,SK
Lobularia maritima 'New Apricot'	B,BD,BS,L,MO
Lobularia maritima 'New Lemon'	B,BD,BS,MO
Lobularia maritima 'New Purple'	B,BD,BS,L,MO
Lobularia maritima 'New Red'	B,BD,BS,F,MO
Lobularia maritima 'New Salmon'	B,BD,BS,MO
Lobularia maritima 'Rosario'	B,BS,L,MO
Lobularia maritima 'Rosie O'Day'	B,BD,BS,BU,BY,C,CA, CL,CN,DN,DT,J,KI,L, MO,R,S,SK,TU,V,YA
Lobularia maritima 'Royal Carpet'	B,BS,C,CA,D,DN,DT,F,J, KI,MO,O,PI,SK,ST,V,VY
Lobularia maritima 'Snow Crystals'	B,BD,BS,CA,CL,CN,D, DT,F,L,MO,O,S,SE,SK, T,U,YA
Lobularia maritima 'Snowcloth'	B,BS,DN,F,KS,M,MO, PK,SK,TE,YA,VY
Lobularia maritima 'Snowcloth' Imp	BS

Lobularia maritima 'Snowdrift'	B,BD,BS,CL,KS,MO,S
Lobularia maritima ssp benthamii	B
Lobularia maritima 'Violet Queen'	B,BS,BY,CL
Lobularia maritima 'Wonderland Purple'	B,BS,CA,SK,YA
Lobularia maritima 'Wonderland Rose'	CA,SK,VY
Lobularia maritima 'Wonderland White'	B,BS,CA,SK
Lobularia 'Morning Mist'	S
Lobularia 'Oriental Night'	AB,BS,C,D,DE,J,JO,S,T
Lobularia 'Pastel Carpet'	BD,BS,BU,C,CL,DE,KI, KS,MC,MO,T
Lobularia 'Rosebud'	BS
Lobularia 'Sweet White'	T
Lobularia 'Tiny Tim'	B,MO
Lobularia 'Trailing Rosy Red'	BS,DT,F,T
Lobularia 'Treasure Trail'	PL
Lobularia 'White Carpet'	BY
Lobularia 'Wonderland' mix	BS,MO,VY
Lobularia 'Wonderland' s-c	BS,MO
Lodoicea maldivica	B
Logania obovata	B,NI
Logania stenophylla	B,NI
Loiseleuria procumbens	AP,B,C,JE
Lolium multiflorum	B
Lolium multiflorum 'Barcoo'	B
Lolium multiflorum 'Paroa'	B
Lolium perenne	B,FR
Lolium perenne 'Gator'	B
Lolium perenne 'Hermes'	B
Lolium perenne 'Kangaroo Valley'	B
Lolium perenne 'Loretta'	B
Lolium perenne 'Lorina'	B
Lolium perenne 'Matilda'	B
Lolium perenne 'Victorian'	B
Lomandra hastilis	B,NI
Lomandra longifolia	AU,B,EL,HA,NI,SA
Lomandra obliqua	B
Lomatia frazeri	B,HA,NI,O,SA
Lomatia ilicifolia	HA
Lomatia myricoides	AU,B,HA,O,SA
Lomatia silaifolia	B,O
Lomatia tinctoria	B
Lomatium californicum	B,DD
Lomatium dissectum	AB,B,DD,NO
Lomatium macrocarpum	B,DD,NO
Lomatium nudicaule	AB,B,DD
Lomatium triternatum	B,DD,NO
Lomatium utriculatum	B,DD
Lonas annua	B,CN,DE,PI,PK
Lonas annua 'Gold Rush'	B,BS,CL,CO,KI,L,MO
Lonas annua 'Golden Yellow'	J,JO,V
Lonas inodora	BS,BY,C,D,KI,KS,MO, SK,SU,T
Lonchocarpus capassus	B,SI,WA
Lonchocarpus eriocalyx	B,SI
Lonchocarpus sericeus	B
Lonchostoma monogynum	B,SI
Lonicera albiflora	B,SW
Lonicera alpigena	B,G,SG
Lonicera altmannii	B
Lonicera canadensis	SG
Lonicera caprifolium	KL
Lonicera chamissoi	DD
Lonicera chrysantha latifolia	SG
Lonicera chrysantha v longipes	SG
Lonicera ciliosa	AB,B,C,NO
Lonicera demissa	B

LONICERA

Lonicera dioica	B,HP,SG
Lonicera edulis	LN,SG
Lonicera etrusca	B,SA,SG
Lonicera fragrantissima	B
Lonicera gibbiflora	SG
Lonicera glabra	B
Lonicera henryi	SG
Lonicera hispidula	B,SG
Lonicera involucrata	AB,B,N,SG
Lonicera japonica	B,CA,EL,FW,LN,SA
Lonicera korolkowii	SG
Lonicera maackii	B,CG,FW,LN,SA,SG
Lonicera maackii f podocarpa	B,FW,HP,LN
Lonicera maximowiczii	SG
Lonicera maximowiczii v sachalinensis	SG
Lonicera morrowii	SG
Lonicera nigra	AP,G,SG
Lonicera pallasii	SG
Lonicera periclymenum	B,CN,CO,RS,TH
Lonicera periclymenum 'Serotina'	B
Lonicera pileata	SG
Lonicera praeflorens	B
Lonicera pseudochrysantha	SG
Lonicera pyrenaica	NG,VO
Lonicera ruprechtiana	NG,SG
Lonicera sempervirens	B
Lonicera strusca	CG
Lonicera tatarica	B,C,FW,LN,SA,SG
Lonicera trichosantha	SG
Lonicera utahensis	NO
Lonicera vesicaria	SG
Lonicera x heckrottii	KL
Lonicera xylosteum	AP,B,CG,LN,NG,SA,SG
Lopezia racemosa	P,V
Lopezia racemosa 'Pink Brush'	C,HU
Lopezia racemosa 'Pretty Rose'	B
Lophocereus schottii see Pachycereus	
Lophocereus see Pachycereus	
Lophomyrtus obcordatus	B
Lophomyrtus x ralphii	B
Lophophora diffusa	B,Y
Lophophora echinata v diffusa	CH,DV,GC
Lophophora frichii	CH,DV,Y
Lophophora williamsii	B,CH,DV,T,Y
Lophophora williamsii v decipiens	DV
Lophospermum erubescens	AP,B,C,D,G,HP,J,JE,P,S, SC,SG,V
Lophostemon confertus	B,C,CA,DD,EL,HA,HU, LN,NI,O,SA,WA
Loranthus europaeus	B
Loropetalum chinense	B,C,LN,SA
Lotononis bainesii	B
Lotononis corymbosa	B,SI
Lotus alpinus	VO
Lotus berthelotii	B
Lotus corniculatus	AB,AP,B,C,CN,CO,G,HP, HU,JE,LA,SA,SC,SU,TH
Lotus corniculatus 'Kalo'	B
Lotus creticus	B
Lotus cruentus	B,NI
Lotus discolor	B,SI
Lotus formosissimus	SZ
Lotus frondosus	SG
Lotus herbaceus	B
Lotus hirsutum	AP,B,C,HP,I,JD,JE,SA

Lotus maritimus	AP,B,C,SC,SG
Lotus pentaphyllum	SG
Lotus rigidus	DD
Lotus scoparius	B,CA
Lotus sessilifolius	B
Lotus tetragonolobus	FW,G
Lotus uliginosus	B,C
Lotus wrightii	B
Loxanthocereus eulalianus	B
Loxostylis alata	B,SI,WA
Luchea candica	B
Luculia grandifolia	B
Luculia gratissima v rosea	B,EL,SA
Luculia tsetensis	B,EL,SA
Ludwigia alternifolia	B,HU,PR
Ludwigia hexapetala	B
Ludwigia octovalvis	B
Luffa acutangula	HU
Luffa aegyptica	CP,DD,HU,KS
Luffa cylindrica	C,CA,CG,EL,FR,HA,SA, SG
Luffa operculata	B
Luma apiculata	B,SA
Lunaria annua	AP,BD,BH,C,CN,DD,DE, DI,DT,E,F,FR,G,HP,JE, JO,L,KI,KL,KS,PI,S,SA, ST,SU,T,TH,V,VY
Lunaria annua 'Atrococcinea'	B
Lunaria annua mix	AB,BY,CO,D,HU,J,KS, MO,PK,T,TU
Lunaria annua 'Munstead Purple'	B
Lunaria annua 'Sissinghurst White'	B,KS
Lunaria annua v albiflora	AP,B,C,E,HP,SA,SK,T,V
Lunaria annua v Variegata Purple'	AP,B,C,HP,T
Lunaria annua 'Variegata White'	AP,B,C,HP,HU,JD,MA
Lunaria annua violet	B,HU
Lunaria biennis see L.annua	
Lunaria rediviva	AP,B,BH,C,G,HP,JE,LG, NG,RS,SA,SG
Lupinus albicaulis	AB,B,DD,NO
Lupinus albifrons	AP,B,HP,KL
Lupinus albifrons v douglasii	NG
Lupinus albus	B,C
Lupinus angustifolius	B,RS
Lupinus angustifolius blue	B
Lupinus angustifolius 'Chittick'	B
Lupinus angustifolius 'Illyarrie'	B
Lupinus angustifolius 'Yandee'	B
Lupinus arboreus	AB,AP,B,BS,BY,CG,CN, HP,JE,KI,LN,P,SA,SC,T
Lupinus arboreus 'Barton-on-Sea'	B,NS
Lupinus arboreus blue	P
Lupinus arboreus hyb mix	C,D,MO
Lupinus arboreus wild form	A,C,E,JE,SA,SG
Lupinus arcticus	AP,SC,SG
Lupinus argenteus	NO,SA
Lupinus benthami	B
Lupinus bicolor	B
Lupinus Carnival mix	JE
Lupinus caudatus	B
Lupinus chamissonis	HP,NG
Lupinus 'Chandelier'	B,BS,BY,C,CL,JE,KI,MO, SA,SU
Lupinus 'Chepilillo'	B,HU
Lupinus cruickshankii 'Pink Javelin'	T
Lupinus densiflorus v aureus	B,RS

168

LUPINUS

Lupinus elegans	CG
Lupinus excubitus v austromontanus	B
Lupinus 'Gallery' Blue	B,BS,JE,L,MO,SA,SK
Lupinus 'Gallery' mix	BD,BS,C,CL,CN,J,JE,L, MO,PL,SK,T,U,YA
Lupinus 'Gallery' Pink	B,BS,JE,L,MO,SA,SK
Lupinus 'Gallery' Red	B,BS,JE,L,MO,PL,SA, SK
Lupinus 'Gallery' White	B,BS,JE,L,MO,PL,SA, SK
Lupinus 'Gallery' Yellow	B,BS,JE,L,MO,SA,SK
Lupinus hartwegii	V
Lupinus hartwegii 'Biancaneve'	F,PL,T
Lupinus hartwegii 'King' mix	DE
Lupinus hartwegii ssp cruickshankii	F,RS
Lupinus hartwegii ssp cruicksh. 'Sunrise'	BS,B,MO,PL,PK,SE,T, TU
Lupinus hirsutissimus	B,CG
Lupinus latifolius	B,C,DD
Lupinus latifolius v parishii	B,SZ
Lupinus laxiflorus	NO
Lupinus lepidus	JE
Lupinus lepidus 'Panache Bleu'	B
Lupinus lepidus v lepidus	B
Lupinus littoralis	AP,B,HP,JE,SA,SC,SG
Lupinus longifolius	B
Lupinus 'Lulu' mix	BS,BY,C,MO,S,T
Lupinus luteus	B,BS,C,LG,RS,T,TH
Lupinus micranthus	SG
Lupinus microcarpus	B,P
Lupinus mutabilis	SG
Lupinus 'My Castle'	B,BS,BY,C,CL,DE,JE,KI, MO,SA,SU
Lupinus nanus	AP,B,CG,KL,SC,V
Lupinus nanus 'Pixie Delight' mix	B,C,D,DN,F,KS,S,T,V
Lupinus 'Noble Maiden'	B,BS,BY,C,CL,DE,KI,KS, MO,SA,ST
Lupinus nootkatensis	HP,SC,SG
Lupinus palaestinus	B
Lupinus perennis	A,AB,B,HW,JE,PR,SA
Lupinus pilosus see L.varius ssp orientalis	
Lupinus polyphyllus	AB,AV,B,C,CG,DD,FW, HP,LA,SG,SP
Lupinus polyphyllus 'Band of Nobles' s-c	T
Lupinus polyph. Band of Nobles Series	C,CL,DT
Lupinus polyphyllus 'Flamme Rouge'	B,BS,JE,ST
Lupinus polyphyllus 'Garden Gnome'	BS,C,CO,JE,ST,SU,TU
Lupinus polyphyllus Minarette Group	BS,J,JE,L,PK,SA,V
Lupinus Russell Hyb	w.a.
Lupinus Russell Hyb dw	B,D,SA
Lupinus Russell reselected	D
Lupinus sericeus	B,C,JE,NO,RS,SA
Lupinus subcarnosus	C
Lupinus succulentus	AB,B,CA,RS,SA
Lupinus texensis	AP,B,CA,F,HW,KS,RS, SG,T
Lupinus 'The Chatelaine'	B,BS,BY,C,CL,DE,HP,JE, KI,MO,SA
Lupinus 'The Governor'	B,BS,BY,C,CL,DE,JE, KI,MO,SA
Lupinus 'The Page'	B,BS,BY,C,CL,DE,JE, KI,MO,SA
Lupinus varius	B,F
Lupinus varius ssp orientalis	B
Lupinus versicolor	AP,HP,P,SC
Lupinus versicolor hyb	P

Luzula albida	SA
Luzula alpinopilosa	B,JE,SG
Luzula glabrata	B
Luzula luzuliodes	B,G,JE,SG
Luzula nivea	AP,B,C,CL,G,HP,JE,PA, SA,SC
Luzula pallescens	SG
Luzula parviflora	SG
Luzula rufa	B,SS
Luzula spicata	KL
Luzula sylvatica	B,DE,G,HP,SA
Luzula sylvatica 'Marginata'	SA
Luzula sylvatica 'Select'	JE
Luzula ulophylla	AP,B,G,JE,KL,SC,SS
Luzuriaga marginata	AR
Luzuriaga radicans	B,SA
Lychnis alpina	AP,B,BS,C,CG,CL,CN, DV,G,HP,HU,JE,KL,MO, SA,SC,SG
Lychnis alpina alba	AP,HP,KL,SC,SG
Lychnis alpina 'Drake's Form'	B
Lychnis alpina 'Rosea'	AP,B,SC
Lychnis alpina v oelandica	CG
Lychnis apetala	B,RM
Lychnis 'Blue Angel'	BD,BS,J,KS,MO
Lychnis Brilliant mix	S
Lychnis chalcedonica	w.a.
Lychnis chalcedonica apricot	AP,HP
Lychnis chalcedonica 'Carnea'	HP
Lychnis chalcedonica 'Morgenrot'	JE
Lychnis chalcedonica 'Raureif'	JE
Lychnis chalcedonica 'Rosea'	AP,B,C,G,HP,PL,RH,SG
Lychnis chalcedonica 'Summer Sparkle'	U,V
Lychnis chalcedonica v albiflora	AP,B,BD,C,CN,G,HP,MO, PL,SC,SG,SK
Lychnis chalcedonica 'Valetta'	PL
Lychnis 'Cherry Blossom'	KS
Lychnis cognata	AP,HP
Lychnis coronaria	AB,AP,B,BS,C,CN,CP,D D,EL,HP,HU,I,JE,KL,KS, PA,PI,RH,SC,SG,SU,TH
Lychnis coronaria Alba Group	AP,B,C,CN,G,HP,I,JE, MA,PA,RH,RS,SC,SG,T
Lychnis coronaria 'Angel's Blush'	AP,B,HP,HU,PL,PK
Lychnis coronaria Atrosanguinea 'Cerise'	T
Lychnis coronaria Atrosanguinea Group	AP,B,HP,KS,SC,T
Lychnis coronaria 'Flottbek'	JE
Lychnis coronaria Oculata Group	AP,B,BS,C,HP,KS
Lychnis 'Dancing Ladies' mix	C,PK,T,V
Lychnis flos-cuculi	AP,B,C,CN,CO,G,HP,JE, LA,SA,SC,SG,SU,TH,V,Z
Lychnis flos-cuculi dw form	NG
Lychnis flos-cuculi 'Little Robin'	AP
Lychnis flos-cuculi 'Nana'	AP,C,HP,JE,SC
Lychnis flos-cuculi v albiflora	B,C,HP,I
Lychnis flos-jovis	AP,B,BH,C,HP,JE,KL,SA, SC,SG,Z
Lychnis flos-jovis 'Alba'	C,BH,HP,I
Lychnis flos-jovis 'Peggy'	BS,C,JE
Lychnis fulgens	SG
Lychnis Heavenly mix	J
Lychnis miqueliana	AP,C,RS,SC,SG
Lychnis 'Molten Lava'	B,BD,BS,CL,D,DT,F,HP, MO,S,SE
Lychnis oculata	C,F,KS
Lychnis oculata candida	KS

LYCHNIS

Lychnis 'Rose Angel'	BD,BS,J,KS,MO
Lychnis 'Rose Pearl'	BS
Lychnis 'Royal Celebration'	D
Lychnis sieboldii	AP,SC,SG
Lychnis sp	KL,PA
Lychnis sp 'Terry's Pink'	JE
Lychnis viscaria	AP,B,C,G,HP,JE,KL,RH,
	SA,SC,SG
Lychnis viscaria alba	B,G,HP,SG
Lychnis viscaria 'Firebird'	B,JE,SA
Lychnis viscaria 'Snowbird'	JE,SA
Lychnis viscaria 'Splendens'	AP,HP
Lychnis viscaria 'Splendens Plena'	B,HP,SG
Lychnis viscaria ssp atropurpurea	B,JE,SG
Lychnis wilfordii	AP,B,HP,KL,P
Lychnis x arkwrightii	AP,C,G,HP,SC
Lychnis x arkwrightii 'Orange Zwerg'	C,JE
Lychnis x arkwrightii 'Vesuvius'	AP,B,BD,BS,C,DE,EL,G,
	HP,JE,MO,PK,SA,T
Lychnis x haageana	C,G,HP,I,JE,KL,L,RS,SC
Lychnis x haageana new hyb	B,DE,SA
Lychnis x walkeri 'Abbotswood Rose'	HP
Lychnis yunnanensis	AP,B,C,G,HP,JE,KL,SA,
	SC,SG
Lycium barbarum	A,SA
Lycium chinense	DD,HU,LN,SA
Lycium exsertum	B,HU
Lycium ferocissimum	B,KB
Lycium pallidum	B
Lycopus europaeus	B,CN,CP,DD,LA,SA,
	SG,TH
Lycopus exaltatus	B
Lycoris sanguinea	B
Lycoris squamigera	B
Lygodium japonicum	SG
Lygodium scandens	CG
Lymania alvimii	B
Lymania smithii	B
Lyonothamnus floribundus	CA
Lyonothamnus floribundus v asplenifolius	B,SA
Lyperanthus nigricans	B,NI,SA
Lyperanthus serratus	B
Lysichiton americanus	AP,C
Lysichiton camtschatcensis	AP,HP
Lysiloma bahamensis	B
Lysiloma candida	DD
Lysiloma divaricata	DD
Lysiloma microphylla	B,SA
Lysiloma thornberi	CA
Lysimachia atropurpurea	B,HP,JE,MA,P
Lysimachia atropurpurea 'Geronimo'	C
Lysimachia barystachys	B,JE
Lysimachia ciliata	B,HP,JE,SA,SG
Lysimachia clethroides	B,C,G,HP,JE,SA,SG
Lysimachia clethroides 'Lady Jane'	C,T
Lysimachia clethroides MW159R	X
Lysimachia clethroides MW82R	X
Lysimachia ephemerum	AP,B,CG,G,HP,JE,SA,T
Lysimachia hybrida	B,PR
Lysimachia japonica minutissima	I,KL,P
Lysimachia lichiangensis	AP,B,C,G,HP,MA,P,SG
Lysimachia minoricensis	B,HP,JE,P,SA,T
Lysimachia nemorum	B,HP
Lysimachia punctata	AP,B,BS,C,CL,CN,DE,
	HP,HU,JE,KI,MO,SA,
	SG,SU,T,V

Lysimachia pyramidalis	SG
Lysimachia quadriflora	B,PR
Lysimachia terrestris	B
Lysimachia verticillaris	HP
Lysimachia vulgaris	B,C,CN,CP,G,HP,JE,RH,
	SA,SG,TH
Lysinema ciliatum	B,NI
Lysiphyllum carronii	B,O
Lysiphyllum cunninghamii	B,O
Lysiphyllum gilvum	B,NI
Lysiphyllum hookeri	B,O
Lythrum salicaria	B,BH,BS,C,CN,CO,F,G,
	HP,JE,KI,LA,SG,TH,V,Z
Lythrum salicaria red hyb	B,C,JE
Lythrum salicaria 'Rosy Gem'	B,BS,C,CL,CN,DE,MO,
	SA
Lythrum salicaria x 'Robert'	D
Lythrum virgatus	B
Lythrum x hybrida	T
Lytocaryum weddellianum	B,CA,EL,O
Lytocaryum weddellianum g	B
Maackia amurensis	A,B,C,DD,EL,FW,LN,N,
	SA,SG
Maackia amurensis v buergeri	B
Maackia chinensis	B,FW,N
Maba chrysocarpa	B
Macadamia integrifolia	B,CA,O,RE
Macadamia integrifolia 'Beaumont'	B
Macadamia integrifolia 'Mullimbimby Marvel'	B,EL
Macadamia ternifolia	B,EL,SA
Macadamia tetraphylla	B,O
Macademia integrifolia	CA
Macaranga kilimandscharica	B,SA
Macfadyena unguis-cati	B,C,HU,SA
Machaeranthera bigelovii	B
Machaeranthera tanacetifolia	B,DD,T
Machaeranthera tortifolia	B,HU
Machaerina sinclairii	CG
Machaerocereus gummosus	B
Machairophyllum albidum	B,KB,Y
Mackaya bella	B,CG,EL,KB,SI
Mackaya gangetica	B
Macleania popenoei	B
Macleaya cordata	B,C,G,HP,JE,MA,SA,SG
Macleaya frutescens	CG
Macleaya microcarpa	HP,T,W
Maclura pomifera	A,B,C,FW,HU,LN,SA,VE,
	WA
Macropidia fuliginosa	B,O
Macropiper excelsum	B,SS
Macroptilium atropurpureum	B
Macrotomia echioides see Arnebia pulchra	
Macrotyloma axillare	B
Macrotyloma uniflorum	B
Macrozamia communis	B,C,CA,EL,HA,NI,O,SA,
	SH
Macrozamia conferta	O
Macrozamia cranei	O
Macrozamia crassifolia	O
Macrozamia diplomera	O
Macrozamia douglasii	O
Macrozamia dyeri see M.riedlei	
Macrozamia fawcettii	B,O
Macrozamia fearnsdei	O
Macrozamia flexuosa	O
Macrozamia fraseri	B,NI,O

MACROZAMIA

Macrozamia heteromera	B,O
Macrozamia heteromera blue	O
Macrozamia hyb	B
Macrozamia johnsonii	O
Macrozamia lomandroides	O
Macrozamia lucida	B,EL,NI,O
Macrozamia macdonnellii	B,O
Macrozamia machinii	O
Macrozamia miquellii	B,C,EL,HA,NI,O,SH
Macrozamia moorei	B,EL,HA,O,SA
Macrozamia mountperriensis	B,O
Macrozamia 'Northern Pilliga'	O
Macrozamia occidua	O
Macrozamia parcifolia	O
Macrozamia pauli-guilielmi	EL,HA,O
Macrozamia pauli-guilielmi ssp p-g cit	B
Macrozamia platyrachis	O
Macrozamia plurinervia	O
Macrozamia riedlei	B,C,EL,NI,O,SA
Macrozamia secunda	B,O
Macrozamia 'Southern Pilliga'	O
Macrozamia spiralis	B,C,EL,HA,NI,O,SA
Macrozamia stenomera	O
Macrozamia viridis	O
Madhuca longifolia	B
Madia elegans	B,C,DT,SZ
Madia sativa	B,HU
Maerua cafra	B,SI
Maerua juncea	B
Maerua oblongifolia	B
Maerua schinzii	B,SI
Maesa lanceolata	B,SI
Maesopsis eminii	B
Magnolia acuminata	B,FW,LN,SA
Magnolia biondii	EL,LN,SA
Magnolia campbellii	HP,X
Magnolia campbellii	X
Magnolia campbellii v alba	X
Magnolia 'Charles Raffil'	X
Magnolia cylindrica	EL,N,X
Magnolia dawsoniana 'Clarke's Variety'	X
Magnolia delavayi	SA
Magnolia denudata	AP,B,EL,FW,LN,N,SA,X
Magnolia 'Frank Gladney'	X
Magnolia 'Galaxy'	X
Magnolia grandiflora	B,C,CA,CG,EL,FW,LN,N, SA,VE,WA
Magnolia hypoleuca 1995	X
Magnolia kobus	A,B,C,FW,G,LN,SA
Magnolia liliflora	FW,LN,SA
Magnolia macrophylla	B,C,CA,FW,LN,SA
Magnolia 'Manchu Fan'	X
Magnolia officinalis	EL,SA
Magnolia 'Pickards Opal'	X
Magnolia sargentiana v robusta	X
Magnolia sarg. v r. Caerhays dk form	X
Magnolia sieboldii	AP,B,C,EL,FW,HP,LN,N, SA,SC,SG,X
Magnolia sinensis	AP,C,N,SC
Magnolia 'Spectrum'	X
Magnolia sprengeri	SA
Magnolia stellata	B,FW,KL,N,SA
Magnolia tripetala	B,C,CG,FW,LN,NG
Magnolia virginiana	A,B,C,CA,CG,EL,LN,SA
Magnolia 'Wada's Picture Giant'	X
Magnolia wilsonii	AP,B,C,HP,N,SC,SG,T,X

Magnolia wilsonii 1995	X
Magnolia x highdownensis	AP,C
Magnolia x soulangeana	B,C,CG,DV,FW,LN,N,SA, VE,X
Magnolia x soulangeana 'Alba Superba'	X
Magnolia x soulangeana 'Alexandrina'	X
Magnolia x soulangeana 'Brozzoni'	X
Magnolia x soulangeana 'Lennei'	B,N,SA
Magnolia x soulangeana 'Lennei Alba'	X
Magnolia x soul. 'Robusta' (Nymans form)	X
Magnolia x soulangeana 'Rustic Rubra'	N
Mahonia aquifolium	A,AB,B,C,CA,CG,DD,EL, FW,HP,LN,NO,SA,SG,VE
Mahonia fremontii	SA
Mahonia haematocarpa	B
Mahonia japonica	A,B,SA,VE
Mahonia japonica 'Bealei'	B,CA,SA
Mahonia lomariifolia	B,C,CA,SA
Mahonia nervosa	A,B,C,FW,G,LN,SA,SG
Mahonia nevinii	B
Mahonia 'Pinnacle' pinnata of gdns	SA
Mahonia pumila	SA
Mahonia repens	A,B,C,CA,CG,DD,FW,G, LN,SA
Maianthemum bifolium	AP,B,C,JE,SG
Maianthemum kamtschaticum	SG
Maihuenia patagonica	B,DV
Maihuenia poeppigii	B,DV,P,Y
Maireana aphylla	B,NI
Maireana appressa	B,NI
Maireana astrotricha	B,NI
Maireana atkinsiana	B
Maireana brevifolia	B,HA,NI,SA
Maireana carnosa	B,NI
Maireana convexa	B,NI
Maireana eriantha	B,NI
Maireana erioclada	B,NI
Maireana georgei	B,HA,NI
Maireana melanocoma	B,NI
Maireana pentatropis	B,NI
Maireana platycarpa	B,NI
Maireana polypterygia	B,NI
Maireana pyramidata	B,HA,NI
Maireana schistocarpa	B,NI
Maireana tomentosa	B,NI
Maireana triptera	B,NI
Maireana turbinata	B,NI
Maitenus boaria	SA
Maitenus disticha	SA
Malacothamnus densiflorus	B,HU
Malaxis spicata	B
Malcolmia maritima	AB,BS,C,D,DT,F,J,KI,KS, PK,SU,T,U
Malcomia maritima	BS,BY,D,HU,S,T,TH,TU
Maleophora crocea	DV,SI,Y
Maleophora crocea v purpureocrocea	Y
Maleophora lutea	DV,SI
Malephora crocea	B,Y
Malephora crocea v purpureo-crocea	B,Y
Malleostemon hursthousei	B,NI,SA
Malleostemon roseus	B,NI
Mallotus japonicus	CG
Mallotus philippensis	B
Mallotus rhamnifolius	B
Malope trifida	B,HU
Malope trifida grandiflora 'Choice' mix	C,CO,F,T

MALOPE

Malope trifida mix	G,J,KS,PI,PL,S,V
Malope trifida 'Pink Queen'	B,DI,F,KS,PK,T
Malope trifida 'Red Queen'	B
Malope trifida 'Tetra Vulcan'	B,C,DT,G,T
Malope trifida 'White Queen'	B,C,KS,T
Malosma laurina	B
Malpighia coccigera	B
Malpighia glabra	B
Malpighia punicifolia	DD
Malus angustifolia	B,LN
Malus baccata	B,C,EL,FW,LN,NO,SA, SG
Malus baccata v mandshurica	B,FW,LN
Malus 'Bittenfelder'	B,FW,LN,SA,VE
Malus brevipes	NO
Malus communis	CA,LN,SA,VE
Malus coronaria	B,LN
Malus domestica	FW
Malus domestica 'Delicious'	LN,SA
Malus domestica ssp cerasifera	SG
Malus domestica ssp prunifolia	SG
Malus floribunda	B,C,FW,N,SA
Malus honanensis	B,EL,LN,SA
Malus hupehensis	B,CA,EL,FW,LN,SA,SG
Malus hupehensis 'Rosea'	B,FW
Malus hyb small fruited	T
Malus kansuensis	LN,SG
Malus mandschurica	SG
Malus micromalus	B,EL,FW,LN
Malus mix	C
Malus prunifolia	B,EL,LN,SA,SG
Malus pumila 'Antonovka'	B,FW,LN,SA
Malus pumila northern prov.(u.s.a.)	B
Malus sargentii	B,FW,SA,SG
Malus sieboldii	FW,LN,SA
Malus sieboldii v arborescens	B,FW
Malus sp	SG
Malus sylvestris	B,FW,LN,SA
Malus toringoides	B,FW,LN,N,SG
Malus x zumi	B,FW,LN
Malus x zumi v calocarpa	B,FW,LN
Malus yunnanensis	SG
Malva alcea	AP,B,G,JE
Malva alcea v fastigiata	AP,B,C,HP,HU,JE,PK,SA
Malva crispa see M.verticillata	
Malva fastigiata	DD
Malva 'Gibbortello'	B,HP,P
Malva mix	DI
Malva moschata	AP,B,C,CN,G,HP,JE,KL, LA,PK,PL,SC,SG,TH,V, VY,Z
Malva moschata alba	AP,B,C,CN,G,HP,HU,I, JE,KS,LG,NG,P,PL,RS, SA,SC,SG,U,VY
Malva moschata 'Pirouette'	HL,T,V
Malva moschata rosea	AP,B,HP,HU,KS,PI,SA,T
Malva neglecta	B,C,SA,SG
Malva officinalis	SG
Malva parviflora	B
Malva pusilla	SG
Malva robusta	SG
Malva sp	KL
Malva sylvestris	AP,B,BS,C,CG,CN,CO, G,HP,JE,LA,SA,SG
Malva sylvestris 'Brave Heart'	B,C,HP,P,T
Malva sylvestris 'Highnam'	NS

Malva sylvestris mauritania purple	HU
Malva sylvestris mauritiana	AP,B,F,G,HP,HU,JE,KS, SA,V,VY
Malva sylvestris mauritiana 'Bibor Felho'	AP,T
Malva sylvestris mauritiana 'Moravia'	B
Malva sylvestris 'Zebrina'	B,C,DT,F,G,HP,KS,PK, PL,SE,SK,T,V
Malva verticillata	DD,SG
Malva verticillata 'Crispa'	B,C
Malva 'Windsor Castle'	PL,SE
Malvastrum coromandelianum	B
Malvastrum lateritium	HP
Malvastrum lateritum 'Blossom Pink'	PL
Malvastrum peruvianum	SG
Malvaviscus 'Fire Darts'	B
Mammea africana	B
Mammea americana	B
Mammilaria affinis	DV
Mammilaria alamensis	Y
Mammilaria albata sanciro	BC
Mammilaria albiarmata	B
Mammilaria albicans	B,DV,Y
Mammilaria albicoma	B,DV
Mammilaria albilanata	B,DV
Mammilaria angelensis	B
Mammilaria arida	CH,DV,Y
Mammilaria armillata	B,Y
Mammilaria aureilanata	B
Mammilaria aureilanata v. alba	B
Mammilaria aurihamata	B,Y
Mammilaria backebergiana	B,DV,Y
Mammilaria backebergiana v ernestii	B,Y
Mammilaria barbata	B,GC
Mammilaria baumii	B,DV
Mammilaria baxteriana	B,DV,Y
Mammilaria beiselii	DV
Mammilaria bella	B
Mammilaria bicornuta	Y
Mammilaria blossfeldiana	B,BC,DV
Mammilaria blossfeldiana v shurliana	DV
Mammilaria bocasana	B,CH,DV,Y
Mammilaria bocasana LAU 1182	Y
Mammilaria bocasana v Ed Hummel	Y
Mammilaria bocasana v multilanata	Y
Mammilaria bocasana v roseiflora	CH,DV,Y
Mammilaria bocensis	B,Y
Mammilaria bombycina	B,BC,CH,DV,Y
Mammilaria boolii	B,CH,DV,Y
Mammilaria brandegeei	B,Y
Mammilaria brauneana	DV,Y
Mammilaria bravoae	DV
Mammilaria bucareliensis	DV
Mammilaria bucareliensis v bicornuta	DV
Mammilaria bullardiana	B
Mammilaria caerulea	BC
Mammilaria calacantha	B
Mammilaria camptotricha	CH
Mammilaria canalensis	B,CH,Y
Mammilaria candida	B,DV
Mammilaria candida v caespitosa	B
Mammilaria capensis (m.armillata)	B,Y
Mammilaria capensis pallida	BC
Mammilaria carmenae	B,DV,GC,Y
Mammilaria carnea	B,DV,Y
Mammilaria carretii	B,BC
Mammilaria casoi	DV

172

MAMMILARIA

Mammilaria celsiana	B,CH,DV,Y	Mammilaria glassii siberiensis	BC
Mammilaria centraliplumosa	B	Mammilaria glassii v nominis dulcis	Y
Mammilaria centricirrha see M. magnimamma		Mammilaria goodridgii	B,BC
Mammilaria cerralboa	B	Mammilaria graessneriana	B
Mammilaria chionocephala	B,DV,Y	Mammilaria grahamii	B,Y
Mammilaria coahuilensis	B	Mammilaria grahamii f oliviae	B
Mammilaria collina	B,DV,Y	Mammilaria guelzowiana	B,CH,Y
Mammilaria collinsii	B,DV	Mammilaria guelzowiana v splendens	Y
Mammilaria columbiana	B,CH,DV,Y	Mammilaria guerreronis	B
Mammilaria compressa	B,Y	Mammilaria guerrocephala	DV
Mammilaria confusa	Y	Mammilaria gummifera	B,CH,Y
Mammilaria cowperae	DV,Y	Mammilaria haageana	B,DV,Y
Mammilaria craigii	DV	Mammilaria haageana f conspicua	B
Mammilaria crassior	BC	Mammilaria haageana v schmollii	B
Mammilaria crinita	B	Mammilaria hahniana	B,CH,DV,Y
Mammilaria crucigera aff	B	Mammilaria hahniana v albiflora	B
Mammilaria dawsonii	CH,DV	Mammilaria hahniana v woodsii	B
Mammilaria dealbata see M.haageana		Mammilaria halbingeri	BC
Mammilaria decipiens	B	Mammilaria halei	B
Mammilaria deherdtiana v dodsonii	B	Mammilaria hamilton-hottea	DV
Mammilaria densispina	B,DV,Y	Mammilaria haynii	Y
Mammilaria denudata (m.lasiacantha)	B,DV,Y	Mammilaria heeriana	CH,DV
Mammilaria dioica	B,Y	Mammilaria heidiae	B,Y
Mammilaria discolor	B,DV	Mammilaria hernandezii	Y
Mammilaria discolor f. esperanzaensis	B	Mammilaria herrerae	B
Mammilaria dixanthocentron	B,BC,DV,Y	Mammilaria herrerae v. albiflora	B
Mammilaria dixanthocentron f flavicentra	B	Mammilaria heyderi	B,CH
Mammilaria dumetorum	B	Mammilaria heyderi v applanata	B,Y
Mammilaria duoformis	B	Mammilaria heyderi v bullingtoniana	B,BC
Mammilaria durispina	B	Mammilaria heyderi v hemispherica	B,Y
Mammilaria duwei	B,DV,Y	Mammilaria hidalgensis	DV
Mammilaria egregia	B	Mammilaria hirsuta	Y
Mammilaria elegans	B,DV,Y	Mammilaria huitzilopochtli	B,DV
Mammilaria elongata	B,Y	Mammilaria huitzilopochtli v niduliformis	BC
Mammilaria elongata mix forms	Y	Mammilaria humboldtii	DV,Y
Mammilaria elongata v. echinata /-aria	B	Mammilaria hutchisoniana	B,DV,GC,Y
Mammilaria erectacantha	B	Mammilaria ingens	DV
Mammilaria eriacantha	Y	Mammilaria insularis	B,Y
Mammilaria ernestii	DV	Mammilaria jaliscana	B
Mammilaria erythrosperma	B	Mammilaria johnstonii	B,DV,Y
Mammilaria eschauzieri	Y	Mammilaria johnstonii v guaymensis	B,Y
Mammilaria esseriana	Y	Mammilaria johnstonii v sancarlensis	B,BC,DV
Mammilaria estebanensis	B	Mammilaria karwinskiana	B,DV,Y
Mammilaria euthele	Y	Mammilaria kelleriana	Y
Mammilaria evermanniana	B,Y	Mammilaria kewensis	B,Y
Mammilaria fasciculata	DV	Mammilaria kladiwae	BC,CH,DV,Y
Mammilaria felicis	Y	Mammilaria klissingiana	B,DV
Mammilaria fera-rubra	Y	Mammilaria knebeliana	B
Mammilaria fittkaui	B,CH,GC,Y	Mammilaria kunthii	DV,Y
Mammilaria flavicentra	B	Mammilaria kunzeana	DV
Mammilaria flavovirens	DV	Mammilaria lasiacantha	B,DV
Mammilaria formosa	B	Mammilaria laui LAU1044	Y
Mammilaria fraileana	B,DV,Y	Mammilaria lenta	B,DV
Mammilaria freudenbergeri	BC	Mammilaria leucantha	B
Mammilaria fuscata	B,Y	Mammilaria lewisiana	B,BC
Mammilaria fuscohamata	Y	Mammilaria lindsayii	B,Y
Mammilaria garessii	B	Mammilaria lloydii	B,DV,Y
Mammilaria gasseriana	B	Mammilaria longicoma	DV,Y
Mammilaria gasterantha	B,BC,Y	Mammilaria longiflora	B,Y
Mammilaria gaumeri	B,Y	Mammilaria longiflora v stampferi	B,Y
Mammilaria geminispina	B,CH,DV,Y	Mammilaria longimamma	B
Mammilaria gigantea	B,Y	Mammilaria louisae	B,DV,Y
Mammilaria gilensis	B,GC,Y	Mammilaria macrocarpa	B
Mammilaria ginsa maru	CH,DV,Y	Mammilaria magallanii	B
Mammilaria glareosa	B	Mammilaria magallanii v hamatispina	B
Mammilaria glassii	B,CH,DV,Y	Mammilaria magallanii v hamat. 'Chica'	B

MAMMILARIA

Mammilaria magnifica	B,DV,Y	Mammilaria parkinsonii	B,CH,GC,Y
Mammilaria magnifica v minor	B	Mammilaria pectinifera	B,Y
Mammilaria magnimamma	B,CH,DV,Y	Mammilaria peninsularis	B,GC,Y
Mammilaria magnimamma v bockii	B	Mammilaria pennispinosa	B,BC,DV,GC,Y
Mammilaria magnimamma v macrantha	Y	Mammilaria pennispinosa v nazasensis	B,DV
Mammilaria mainiae	B,BC	Mammilaria perbella	B,CH,Y
Mammilaria mammilaris	B,CH	Mammilaria petrophila	B
Mammilaria maritima	B	Mammilaria petterssonii	B,Y
Mammilaria marksiana	B,DV,Y	Mammilaria phitauiana	B
Mammilaria martinezii	GC,Y	Mammilaria picta	B
Mammilaria mathildae	B	Mammilaria pilcayensis	DV,Y
Mammilaria matudae	B,DV,GC,Y	Mammilaria pilcayensis v chrysothele	Y
Mammilaria matudae v serpentiformis	B	Mammilaria pilispina	B
Mammilaria matudae v spinosior	B	Mammilaria pilosa	B
Mammilaria mazatlanensis	B,Y	Mammilaria pitcayensis	C,CH
Mammilaria mazatlanensis v monocentra	Y	Mammilaria plumosa	B,CH,DV,GC,Y
Mammilaria mazatlanensis v patonii	B	Mammilaria polyedra	B
Mammilaria meiacantha	B	Mammilaria polythele	B
Mammilaria meigiana	B	Mammilaria poselgeri	B
Mammilaria melaleuca	Y	Mammilaria pottsii	B
Mammilaria melanocentra	B,Y	Mammilaria preissnitzii	BC
Mammilaria mercadensis	B,Y	Mammilaria pringlei	B,DV,Y
Mammilaria meridiorosei	B,DV	Mammilaria prolifera	B
Mammilaria meyranii	B,CH,DV	Mammilaria prolifera v texana	B
Mammilaria meyranii v michoacana	B,Y	Mammilaria pseudoperbella	B,DV,GC,Y
Mammilaria microcarpa	B,DV,Y	Mammilaria purpurascens	Y
Mammilaria microcarpa v arizonica	Y	Mammilaria pygmaea	B,Y
Mammilaria microcarpa v auricarpa	B,Y	Mammilaria recurva	DV
Mammilaria microhelia	B,DV,Y	Mammilaria rekoi	B,DV,Y
Mammilaria microhelia v microheliopsis	Y	Mammilaria rekoi v aureispina	B,Y
Mammilaria microheliopsis	DV	Mammilaria rekoi v leptacantha	B
Mammilaria microthele	B	Mammilaria rettigiana	B,DV
Mammilaria miegeana	DV	Mammilaria rhodantha	B,DV,Y
Mammilaria mitlensis	B	Mammilaria rhodantha v flavispina	DV
Mammilaria moellerana	B,DV,Y	Mammilaria rhodantha v ruberrima	B
Mammilaria mollendorffiana	B	Mammilaria ritterana	B,DV
Mammilaria monancistracantha	Y	Mammilaria rosamonte	Y
Mammilaria montensis	B	Mammilaria roseoalba	B,Y
Mammilaria morganiana	B,Y	Mammilaria roseocentra	B
Mammilaria morricalii	B,DV	Mammilaria rubrograndis	B,DV
Mammilaria muehlenpfordtii	B	Mammilaria rubrum	B
Mammilaria multidigitata	B,Y	Mammilaria ruestii	B,DV,Y
Mammilaria multiseta	BC	Mammilaria saetigera	B,DV,Y
Mammilaria mundtii	B	Mammilaria sanluisensis	DV
Mammilaria mystax	B,BC,CH,Y	Mammilaria santaclarensis	Y
Mammilaria nana	B,Y	Mammilaria scheidweileriana	DV,Y
Mammilaria nana v 'Trichacantha'	B	Mammilaria schiedeana	B,CH,Y
Mammilaria napina	B,BC	Mammilaria schiedeana f plumosa	B
Mammilaria nejapensis	B,BC,CH,Y	Mammilaria schumannii see Bartschella	
Mammilaria neomystix	Y	Mammilaria scrippsiana	B,Y
Mammilaria neopalmeri	B,Y	Mammilaria scrippsiana v. autlanensis	B
Mammilaria neopotosina	B	Mammilaria sempervivi	B,Y
Mammilaria neoschwarziana	B	Mammilaria senilis	B
Mammilaria neumanniana	DV	Mammilaria setispina	B
Mammilaria nivosa	B,DV	Mammilaria sheldonii	B,Y
Mammilaria nolascana	DV	Mammilaria sheldonii f inaiae	B
Mammilaria nunezii	DV	Mammilaria simplex	BC
Mammilaria obconella	B	Mammilaria sinistrohamata	B,DV
Mammilaria obscura	B	Mammilaria slevinii	B,DV,Y
Mammilaria occidentalis	B	Mammilaria solisioides	B,BC
Mammilaria ochoterenae	DV	Mammilaria sonorensis	B,Y
Mammilaria ocotillensis	CH	Mammilaria sonorensis v 'Tesopacensis'	B
Mammilaria ortiz-rubiona	Y	Mammilaria sp	C,CH,DV,FR,T,Y
Mammilaria oteroi	B,DV,Y	Mammilaria sphaerica	B
Mammilaria pachycylindrica	B	Mammilaria spinosissima	B,CH,DV,GC,Y
Mammilaria painteri	B,DV,Y	Mammilaria spinosissima v auricoma	B

MAMMILARIA

Mammilaria standleyi	B
Mammilaria supertexta	B,BC
Mammilaria surculosa	B
Mammilaria swinglei	B,DV
Mammilaria tayloriorum	B
Mammilaria tepexicensis	BC
Mammilaria tetracantha v galeottii	B
Mammilaria tetrancistra	B,BC
Mammilaria thornberi	B
Mammilaria tiegeliana	Y
Mammilaria tlalocii	B
Mammilaria tolimensis	Y
Mammilaria uncinata	B,Y
Mammilaria vagaspina	DV
Mammilaria varieaculeata	Y
Mammilaria vaupelii	B,DV
Mammilaria vaupelii v flavispina	B
Mammilaria vetula	B
Mammilaria viereckii	B,Y
Mammilaria viperina	B
Mammilaria virginis	B
Mammilaria viridiflora	B,Y
Mammilaria vonwyssiana	DV
Mammilaria wagnerana / m. obscura	B
Mammilaria weingartiana	B
Mammilaria wicoxii	DV
Mammilaria wiesingeri	B,Y
Mammilaria wildii	B
Mammilaria winterae	B,DV
Mammilaria woburnensis	DV
Mammilaria wohlschlageri	B
Mammilaria woodsii	DV
Mammilaria wrightii	B,DV,Y
Mammilaria wrightii v wilcoxii	Y
Mammilaria wrightii v wolfii	B
Mammilaria xaltianguensis	B,Y
Mammilaria yucatanensis	B,BC,Y
Mammilaria zacatecasensis	B,DV
Mammilaria zahniana	Y'
Mammilaria zeilmanniana	B,CH,DV,GC,SO,Y
Mammilaria zeilmanniana v alba	CH,BC,Y
Mammilaria zephyranthoides	B,BC
Mammilaria zeyeriana	B
Mammilaria zuccariniana	B
Mammilloydia candida	Y
Mammilloydia candida v rosea	Y
Mammilopsis senilis	DV,Y
Mandevilla laxa	B,C,DI,EL,FW,HP,SA,T
Mandragora autumnalis	B,JE
Mandragora officinarum	AP,B,HP,JE,NG,SA,SC
Manfreda maculata	B
Manfreda virginica	B,HU
Mangifera foetida	B
Mangifera indica	B,CA
Mangifera indica 'Manzana'	B
Manihot esculenta	B,C
Manihot glaziovii	B
Manihot palmata	CG
Manilkara hexandra	B
Manilkara roxburghiana	B
Manilkara sapota	SA
Manilkara zapodilla	B,CA,RE
Manochlamys albicans	B,SI
Mansoa alliacea	B
Manulea altissima	B,KB
Manulea benthamiana	B,SI

Manulea corymbosa	B,SI
Marah fabaceus	B
Marah macrocarpus	B
Maresia pulchella	B
Margaretha weisei	B
Marginatocereus marginatus see Stenocereus	
Marginatocereus marginatus see Stenocereus	
Margyricarpus pinnatus	AP,B,SG
Marica gracilis	MN
Markhamia acuminata	B,EL,SA
Markhamia lutea	B
Markhamia obtusifolia	B,SA,SI
Markhamia zanzibarica	B,SI
Marojejea beranitso	B
Marojejea darianii	B,EL
Marojejya insignis	B,EL
Marrubium incanum	B,JE,SA
Marrubium peregrinum	B
Marrubium supinum	C,HP
Marrubium vulgare	AP,B,CN,CP,DD,G,HU, JE,KS,SA,SG,TH
Marrubium vulgare 'Green Pompon'	C,T
Marrubium vulgare 'Pompon'	B,JE
Marsiprospermum grandiforum	AU
Martynia annua	B
Massonia depressa	AP,B,DV,RU,SC,SI
Massonia pustulata	AP,B,SC,SI
Massonia sp	DV,RU,SI
Matelea sp	B
Matricaria grandiflora 'Gold Pompoms'	T
Matricaria grandiflora 'Pincushion'	C
Matricaria inodorum 'Bridal Robe'	C,T
Matricaria matricarioides	B,CP
Matricaria nigellifolia	B,SI
Matricaria perforata	SG
Matricaria recutita	B,HU
Matricaria recutita 'Bodegold'	B,BD
Matricaria sp	KL
Matteuccia struthiopteris	B,C,KL
Matthiola arborescens	AP,HP
Matthiola aspera	B
Matthiola bicornis	BS,BY,DN,HU,PI,SK,TH
Matthiola bicornis 'Hansens' mix	MO
Matthiola bicornis 'Miracle' mix	MO
Matthiola 'Caesar' s-c, mix	BS
Matthiola 'East Lothian Stocks' mix	BD,BY,C,D,S
Matthiola fruticulosa	AP,B
Matthiola 'Goldcut Rosy Red'	PL
Matthiola incana	AP,B,DI,CG,CO,I,J,NS, SC,ST,TH,VH
Matthiola incana Anthony Series s-c, mix	BS,CN
Matthiola incana 'Austral' mix	YA
Matthiola incana 'Batavia' apple-blossom	B,SE,T,V
Matthiola incana 'Beauty of Nice'	BD,BS,MO
Matthiola incana 'Brompton' mix	BD,BS,BY,C,CL,CN,DT, F,KI,L,M,MO,R,SU,T,TU, U,YA
Matthiola incana 'Brompton' s-c	BY
Matthiola incana 'Cheerful'	PK
Matthiola incana 'Cinderella' dark blue	B,BS,CL,MO
Matthiola incana 'Cinderella' mix	BS,CL,D,J,L,MO,S,T,YA
Matthiola incana 'Cinderella' s-c	B,BS,CL,MO,T
Matthiola incana 'Cleopatra' mix	BS,CN
Matthiola incana 'Double Flash' s-c	B
Matthiola incana 'Floral Delight'	SE
Matthiola incana 'Forcing Wonder'	L

MATTHIOLA

Matthiola incana 'Giant Column' s-c	B,T
Matthiola incana 'Giant Excelsior Col.r' mix	BS,BY,C,CN,JO,PI,U,YA
Matthiola inc. 'Giant Exc. Valour' s-c, mix	B,BS
Matthiola incana 'Giant Imperial mix'	C,F,PK,SE
Matthiola incana 'Giant Perfection mix'	BS,DE,S,U
Matthiola incana 'Gladiator' s-c, mix	BS
Matthiola incana 'Happistock' mix	T
Matthiola incana 'Imperial Crown'	BS
Matthiola incana 'Legacy mix'	BS,DT,MO,SE,T
Matthiola incana 'Mammoth Exc. Col.' wh.	B,BY
Matthiola incana 'Midget Series'	BS,KI,SK
Matthiola incana mix	S
Matthiola incana 'Nordic' s-c	YA
Matthiola incana 'Pacific Column' mix	CL
Matthiola incana 'Park' mix	MO,U
Matthiola incana 'Park' s-c	B
Matthiola incana 'Queen Astrid'	BS
Matthiola incana 'Record Series' mix	CL
Matthiola incana 'Regal' mix	J,V
Matthiola incana 'Sentinel' mix	B,BS,MO
Matthiola incana 'Sentinel' s-c	B,BS,MO
Matthiola incana 'Seven Week' mix	C,CA,DE
Matthiola incana special mix	M
Matthiola incana 'Superb Bedding mix'	S
Matthiola incana 'Tartan' mix	CL
Matthiola incana 'Ten Week' 100% dbl	KI
Matthiola incana 'Ten Week' mix	BD,BS,BY,C,CA,CL,CN, CO,D,DN,FJ,KI,L,M,MO, R,SK,ST,TU,U,V,VY,YA
Matthiola incana 'Tristar' s-c, mix	BS
Matthiola incana 'Viking' s-c	B
Matthiola incana white perennial	C
Matthiola 'Little Gem' mix	PL
Matthiola longipetala	B
Matthiola longipetala ssp bicornis	AP,BS,C,CO,D,FJ,KI,KS, L,S,ST,SU,T,TU,V,VH
Matthiola 'Midget' s-c, mix	SK
Matthiola mix florist strain	CA
Matthiola sinuata	B
Matthiola 'Starlight Scentsation'	T,U
Matthiola tricuspidata	B
Matucana aureiflora	B
Matucana aureiflora v elata	B
Matucana caespitosa	B
Matucana haynei	DV
Matucana hystrix	Y
Matucana madisoniorum	B
Matucana madisoniorum v horridispinum	B
Matucana multicolor	DV
Matucana oreodoxa	B
Matucana paucicostata	B
Matucana paucicostata 'Senilis'	B
Matucana ritteri	B
Matucana roseo-alba	B,Y
Matucana variabilis	B,DV
Matucana weberbaueri	B,DV,Y
Matucana weberbaueri v flammels	Y
Matucana winteri	B
Maughaniella luckhoffii	DV,GC,Y
Maurandella antirrhiniflora	AP,B,NG,SG,SW,T
Maurandella antirrhiniflora 'Coccinea'	B,C
Maurandya barclayana	AP,B,C,CG,DI,HP,P,SC, SG,T
Maurandya barclayana alba	HP,SG
Maurandya erubescens see Lophospermum	
Maurandya purpusii	SC,SG

Maurandya 'Red Dragon'	B,P
Maurandya scandens	AP,B,SC,SE,V
Maurandya scandens	AP,C,HP
Maurandya scandens 'Amethyst Pink'	PL,SE
Maurandya scandens 'Bride's White'	EL
Maurandya scandens 'Jewel MIx'	PL,T
Maurandya scandens 'Joan Loraine'	B,BD,MO
Maurandya scandens 'Mystic Rose'	B,BD,MO,PK,SE
Maurandya scandens 'Pink Ice'	EL,I
Maurandya scandens s-c	B
Maurandya scandens 'Sky Blue'	B,EL
Maurandya scandens 'Snowwhite'	B,PL
Maurandya scandens 'Summer Snow'	B,BD,MO
Maurandya scandens 'Violet Glow'	EL,PL,SE
Maurandya wislizenii	B,HU,SW
Maxillaria crassifolia	B
Maxillaria tenuifolia	B
Maytenus acuminata	B,SI
Maytenus bachmannii	B,KB
Maytenus boaria	B,C,CA,LN
Maytenus capitatus	B,SI
Maytenus emarginata	B
Maytenus heterophylla	B,KB,SI
Maytenus oleoides	B,SI
Maytenus procumbens	B,SI
Maytenus undata	B,SI
Mazus pumilio	B
Mazus radicans	B
Mazus reptans	AP,B,JE,SC
Meconopsis aculeata	AP,B,KL,PL,PO,SC
Meconopsis baileyi see M.betonicifolia	
Meconopsis betonicifolia	w.a.
Meconopsis betonicifolia Harlow Carr strain	HP
Meconopsis betonicifolia v alba	AP,B,C,G,HP,JE,P,PL,SA, SC,SE,T
Meconopsis betonicifolia x integrifolia	KL
Meconopsis cambrica	w.a.
Meconopsis cambrica dbl yellow	P
Meconopsis cambrica fl.pl	AP,B,C,HP,PM,SC
Meconopsis cambrica 'Frances Perry'	AP,B,C,G,HP,NG,NS,P, PL,PM,SC,T
Meconopsis cambrica 'Muriel Brown'	AP,B,HP,P
Meconopsis cambrica 'Rubra'	AP,JE,SA
Meconopsis cambrica v aurantiaca	AP,B,C,HP,I,JE,SA,SC
Meconopsis cambrica v aurantiaca fl.pl.	AP,B,JE,P,PL,SC
Meconopsis delavayi CLD1093	LG
Meconopsis dhwoji	AP,HP,SC,SG
Meconopsis grandis	AP,B,C,G,HP,JE,KL,LG,P, PL,SA,SC,SE,SG,T
Meconopsis grandis alba	HP
Meconopsis horridula	AP,B,G,HP,JE,LG,P,PL, SA,SC,SG
Meconopsis horridula fl.pl.	B,P
Meconopsis horridula prattii	SG
Meconopsis horridula prattii AC1613	X
Meconopsis horridula prattii AC1644	X
Meconopsis integrifolia	AP,B,HP
Meconopsis mix	JE
Meconopsis napaulensis	AP,B,BS,C,CG,HP,JE,P,P L,PM,SA,SC,SE,SG,T,X
Meconopsis napaulensis (pink)	PL,SC,SE
Meconopsis paniculata	AP,B,C,HP,P,SC,SG
Meconopsis pseudointegrifolia	AP,PL,X
Meconopsis punicea	AP,HP,KL,LG,PL,SC
Meconopsis quintuplinervia	AP,HP,KL,PL,SC,SG
Meconopsis regia	AP,B,C,G,HP,JE,PL,SC,T

MECONOPSIS

Meconopsis regia bicolor	B,P	Melaleuca cornucopiae	B,NI
Meconopsis robusta	AP,SC,SG	Melaleuca crassifolia	CA
Meconopsis simplicifolia	AP,B,LG,PL,SC	Melaleuca cucculata	B,NI
Meconopsis sp mix	AP,PL,SC,T	Melaleuca cuneata	B
Meconopsis superba	AP,B,C,HP,JE,PL,SA,SG	Melaleuca cuticularis	AU,B,NI,O
Meconopsis villosa	AP,B,C,HP,JE,P,PL,,SG	Melaleuca decora	AU,B,HA,NI
Meconopsis x beamishii	HP,SG	Melaleuca decussata	B,C,CA,EL,HA,NI,O
Meconopsis x macrantha	HP	Melaleuca densa	B,NI
Meconopsis x musgravei	SG	Melaleuca depressa	B
Meconopsis x sheldonii	AP,HP,PL	Melaleuca diosmatifolia	B,CA,NI
Meconopsis x sheld. Crewdson Hybrids	AP,C,HP	Melaleuca diosmatifolia	B,HA,NI
Medicago arabica	SG	Melaleuca eleuterostachya	B,NI
Medicago arborea	SA	Melaleuca elliptica	AU,B,CA,EL,HA,NI,O,SA
Medicago falcata	SG	Melaleuca ericifolia	AU,B,C,CA,EL,HA,NI,O,
Medicago lupulina	B,C,SG		SA
Medicago minima	SG	Melaleuca ericifolia nana	B,EL,HA,NI,SA
Medicago orbicularis	B	Melaleuca erubescens see M.diosmatifolia	
Medicago sativa	B,C,DD,SU	Melaleuca filifolia	AU,B,DD,NI
Medicago sativa cvs	B	Melaleuca fulgens	AU,B,EL,HA,NI,O
Medicago scutellata	B	Melaleuca fulgens ssp steedmanii	AU,B
Medicago tornata 'Tornafield'	B	Melaleuca fulgens v corrugata	B,NI
Medinilla magnifica	B,EL,SA	Melaleuca gibbosa	B,NI
Mediolobivia aureiflora	Y	Melaleuca glaberrima	B,NI,O
Mediolobivia aureiflora v albilongiseta	Y	Melaleuca globifera	B
Mediolobivia aureiflora v rubriflora	Y	Melaleuca glomerata	B,HA,NI
Mediolobivia chameleon	Y	Melaleuca halmaturorum	B,EL,HA,NI
Mediolobivia christinae	DV,Y	Melaleuca halmaturorum ssp cymbifolia	B
Mediolobivia diersiana	Y	Melaleuca hamulosa	B,NI
Mediolobivia elegans	Y	Melaleuca holosericea	AU,B,NI
Mediolobivia eucaliptana	DV,Y	Melaleuca huegelii	AU,B,CA,EL,HA,NI,SA
Mediolobivia gracilispina FR1118	Y	Melaleuca hypericifolia	AU,B,EL,HA,HP,NI,SH
Mediolobivia haefneriana	Y	Melaleuca incana	B,EL,HA,NI,O
Mediolobivia huarinensis	DV	Melaleuca irbyana	B,HA
Mediolobivia ithyacantha	Y	Melaleuca lanceolata	B,EL,HA,NI,O
Mediolobivia mudanensis	Y	Melaleuca lanceolata ssp lanceolata	AU
Mediolobivia multicostata	DV	Melaleuca lanceolata ssp occidentalis	B,NI
Mediolobivia orurensis v haagei	DV	Melaleuca lasiandra	B
Mediolobivia pectinata	DV,Y	Melaleuca lateriflora	B,NI
Mediolobivia pectinata v digitiformis	Y	Melaleuca lateritia	B,EL,HA,HU,NI,O,SH
Mediolobivia pectinata v neosteinmannii	Y	Melaleuca laxiflora	B,NI
Mediolobivia pygmaea	DV,Y	Melaleuca leptospermoides	B,NI
Mediolobivia ritteri	DV,Y	Melaleuca leucadendron	B,CA,EL,HA,LN,NI,O
Megacodon sp	DV	Melaleuca linariifolia	AU,B,CA,EL,HA,NI,O,
Megacodon violescens	DV		SH,VE
Meiostemon tetrandus	B,SI	Melaleuca macronychia	AU,B,EL,NI
Melaleuca acerosa	AU,B,NI,O	Melaleuca megacephala	B,HA,NI
Melaleuca acuminata	AU,B,CA,HA,NI,O	Melaleuca microphylla	B,NI
Melaleuca alternifolia	AU,B,C,EL,HA,HU,NI,O	Melaleuca nematophylla	C,EL,O
Melaleuca arcana	B	Melaleuca nesophila	AU,B,CA,EL,HA,NI,O,VE
Melaleuca argentea	B,HA,NI	Melaleuca nodosa	AU,B,EL,HA,NI,O
Melaleuca armillaris	AU,B,C,CA,EL,HA,NI,O	Melaleuca oldfieldii	B,NI
Melaleuca baxteri	B	Melaleuca parviflora	DV
Melaleuca biconvexa	B,HA,NI	Melaleuca pauciflora see M.biconvexa	
Melaleuca bracteata	B,C,CA,HA,HU,NI,O	Melaleuca pauperiflora	B,NI
Melaleuca brevifolia	AU,B,HA,NI	Melaleuca pentagona	AU,B,NI
Melaleuca brevifolia 'Neglecta'	B,NI	Melaleuca platycalyx	AU,B,NI
Melaleuca calycina ssp dempta	B,NI	Melaleuca preissiana	B,EL,NI
Melaleuca capitata	B,EL,SH	Melaleuca pulchella	B,HA,HU,NI,O
Melaleuca cardiophylla	B,NI	Melaleuca pungens	B,NI
Melaleuca cardiophylla v parviflora	B,NI	Melaleuca pustulata	B,NI
Melaleuca ciliosa	B,NI	Melaleuca quadrifaria	B,NI
Melaleuca citrina	B,NI,O	Melaleuca quinquenervia see M.viridiflora v rubiflora	
Melaleuca coccinea	B,NI,O	Melaleuca radula	B,HA,NI
Melaleuca coccinea ssp coccinea	AU	Melaleuca rhaphiophylla	B,NI
Melaleuca conothamnoides	B,EL,NI,O	Melaleuca scabra aff 'Concinna'	B,NI
Melaleuca cordata	B,NI	Melaleuca scabra 'Bicolor'	B,NI

MELALEUCA

Melaleuca sheathiana	B,NI
Melaleuca sieberi	B,HA,NI
Melaleuca sp mix	C
Melaleuca spathulata	AU,B,EL,HU,NI,SA
Melaleuca spicigera	B,NI
Melaleuca squamea	AU,B,CA,HA,NI
Melaleuca squarrosa	AU,B,C,EL,HA,NI,SA,SH
Melaleuca steedmanii	HA
Melaleuca striata	B,NI
Melaleuca stypheloides	B,CA,EL,HA,NI,O
Melaleuca suberosa	B,NI
Melaleuca subfalcata	B,NI
Melaleuca tamariscina	B,EL
Melaleuca teretifolia	B,NI
Melaleuca thymifolia	AU,B,EL,HA,HU,NI,O,
	SH,VE
Melaleuca thymoides	AU,B,EL,NI
Melaleuca thyoides	B,NI
Melaleuca trichophylla	B,NI
Melaleuca trichostachya	B,HA,NI
Melaleuca uncinata	B,HA,NI
Melaleuca undulata	B,NI
Melaleuca viminea	B,NI
Melaleuca violacea	AU,B,NI,O
Melaleuca viridiflora	B,EL,NI
Melaleuca viridiflora 'Red Cloud'	B,EL
Melaleuca viridiflora v rubiflora red	B,NI
Melaleuca viridiflora v rubriflora	B,EL,HA,NI
Melaleuca wilsonii	AU,B,EL,HA,HU,NI,O,SA
Melampodium paludosum	AP,C,S,V
Melampodium paludosum 'Derby'	PK
Melampodium paludosum 'Showstar'	B,BS,CL,DE,JO,MO,SK
Melandrium zawadskii see Silene	
Melanthium virginicum	PR
Melasphaerula ramosa	AP,B,C,G,HP,MN,RU,SI
Melastoma sanguineum	B,EL
Melhania oblongifolia	B,NI
Melia azedarach	B,C,CA,DV,EL,FW,HA,
	HU,LN,RE,SA,TT,VE
Melia azedarach 'Floribunda'	B
Melia azedarach 'Umbraculiformis'	B,WA
Melia azedarach v australasica	B,NI,O
Melia composita	DD
Melia toosendan	B,CA,CG,LN,SA
Melianthus comosus	B,SA,SI
Melianthus major	B,C,SA,SI,SZ
Melianthus minor	B,SA,SI
Melianthus pectinatus	B,SA,SI
Melianthus sp	BH,SI
Melianthus villosus	SA
Melica altissima	HP,SG
Melica altissima 'Atropurpurea'	B,G,HP,JE,P,SA,SC,T
Melica ciliata	AP,B,C,CA,CG,DE,G,HP,
	JE,SG,SA,SC,T
Melica imperfecta	B
Melica nutans	B,G,HP,JE,SA
Melica torreyana	B
Melica transsilvanica	B,JE,KL,SA,SC
Melica transsilvanica atropurpurea	AP,SA
Melica uniflora	B,JE,SA
Melica uniflora f albida	NG,SG
Melica uniflora variegata	I
Melicoccus bijugatus	B
Melicope elleryana	B,NI,O,SA
Melicope ternata	B
Melicytus alpinus	AU,B,SS

Melicytus crassifolius	AU,B,CG,SG,SS
Melicytus lanceolatus	B,C,SA
Melicytus obovatus	B,SS
Melicytus ramiflorus	B,C
Melilotus alba	B,C,G,LA,SG,SU
Melilotus altissima	B,SG
Melilotus officinalis	B,C,PO,SG
Melilotus officinalis albus	AB,HP
Melilotus suaveolens	SG
Melinis neriglume	SZ
Melinis repens	B,JO,SA,SI,SK
Melinus minutiflora	B
Meliosma parviflora	CG
Melissa officinalis	A,B,CN,CP,DD,G,HP,HU,
	KS,RH,TH
Melittis melisophyllum	B,C,HP,I,JE,SA
Melocactus amazonicus	DV,Y
Melocactus amoenus	B,DV
Melocactus arcuatispinus	B
Melocactus azulensis	B,DV
Melocactus azureus	B,CH,DV,Y
Melocactus bahiensis	B,DV,Y
Melocactus broadwayi	DV
Melocactus caesius	B,BC,Y
Melocactus canescens	Y
Melocactus collineus	DV
Melocactus concinnus	B
Melocactus conoideus	B,DV
Melocactus conoideus V form	DV
Melocactus curvispinus	B,DV,Y
Melocactus delessertianus	B,Y
Melocactus depressus	Y
Melocactus disciformis	DV
Melocactus ernestii	B,CH,DV,Y
Melocactus glaucescens	B
Melocactus glauxianus	DV
Melocactus grisoleoviridis	B
Melocactus guitarta	B
Melocactus holguinensis	BC
Melocactus incuensis HU166	DV
Melocactus itaberensis	Y
Melocactus lenselinkianus	DV
Melocactus loboguerreroi	B
Melocactus longispinus	Y
Melocactus macrodiscus v minor see M.zehntneri	
Melocactus matanzanus	B,DV,Y
Melocactus maxonii	B,Y
Melocactus melocactoides	DV,Y
Melocactus morrochapensis	Y
Melocactus neglectus	B
Melocactus neglectus v diamantinensis	B
Melocactus neryi	B,Y
Melocactus oreas	B,Y
Melocactus pachyacanthus	DV
Melocactus peruvianus	G,Y
Melocactus rubrisaetosus HU137	BC
Melocactus rubrispinus	DV,Y
Melocactus ruestii	Y
Melocactus salvadorensis	B,Y
Melocactus saxicola	Y
Melocactus seminudus	DV
Melocactus sp	BC,Y
Melocactus uebelmannianus	Y
Melocactus violaceus	BC
Melocactus zehntneri	B,Y
Melochia corchorifolia	B

MELOCHIA

Melochia nodiflora	B
Melochia tomentosa	DD
Melothria pendula	B,DD,HU
Memecylon umbellatum	B
Menispermum canadense	B
Menispermum dahuricum	LN,SA,SG
Menodora juncea	B
Mentha aquatica	A,B,C,DV,TH
Mentha arvensis	SG
Mentha longifolia	A,B,C,JE
Mentha longifolia ssp capensis	B,KB,SI
Mentha longifolia ssp wissii	B,KB,SI
Mentha pulegium	C,CN,CP,DI,GO,HU,SA, TH
Mentha requienii	B
Mentha spicata	C,CN,JE
Mentha spicata 'Crispa'	B,G,TH
Mentha spicata viridis	KS,SA,TH
Mentha suaveolens	A,B
Mentha suaveolens 'Variegata'	B
Mentha x piperita	B,C,DV,HU,JE,KS,SA,TH
Mentha x piperita f citrata	B,T
Mentzelia decapetala	B
Mentzelia laevicaulis	B,DD,NO,SC
Mentzelia lindleyi	AP,B,C,CA,D,HU,J,PL,S, T,V
Mentzelia pumila	B
Menyanthes trifoliata	B,C
Menziesia pentandra	KL
Mercurialis perennis	B
Merendera filifolia A.B.S4665 Morocco	MN
Merendera filifolia S.F300 Spain	MN
Merendera montana	AP,AR,B,G,SA,SC,VO
Merendera montana MS900/1 Spain	MN
Merendera montana MS909 Spain	MN
Merendera montana MS913/3 Spain	MN
Merendera montana S.F221 Spain	MN
Merendera pyrenaica see M. montana	
Merendera trigyna	AP,AR,PM
Merremia aurea	DD
Merremia kentrocaulos	B,SI
Merremia sibirica	B,HU
Merremia tridentata	B
Merremia tuberosa	B,C,DD,HU
Mertensia arizonica	B
Mertensia asiatica	AP,B,JE,P
Mertensia ciliata	B,KL
Mertensia maritima	AP,B,HP,P,PO,SC
Mertensia primuloides	KL
Mertensia pulmonarioides	P
Mertensia sibirica	AP,B,HP,PL,SC
Mertensia simplissima	AP,B,HP,P
Mertensia virginica see M.pulmonarioides	
Mertensia viridis	B,RM,SW
Merxmuellera arundinacea	B,SI
Meryta sinclairii	B,SA
Mesembryanthemum crystallinum	B,DV
Mesembryanthemum guerichianum	B,DV,SI
Mesembryanthemum nodiflorum	B,DV
Mesembryanthemum pellitum	B
Mesembryanthemum speciosum	SI
Mesomelaena tetragona	B,NI
Mespilus germanica	B,C,FW,LN,SA,SG,VE
Mesua ferrea	B,EL
Metalasia cephalotes	B,SI
Metalasia muricata	B,KB,SI

Metasequoia glyptostroboides	B,C,CA,CG,DD,EL,FW, LN,N,SA,VE
Metrosideros angustifolia	B,SI
Metrosideros excelsus	B,C,CA,DV,HA,LN,SA, WA
Metrosideros fulgens	B,SS
Metrosideros robusta	B
Metrosideros tomentosus see M.excelsus	
Metrosideros umbellata	B,SS
Metroxylon rumphii	B
Meum athamanticum	B,G,HP,JE,PO,SA,SC
Meyerophytum meyeri	B
Mibora minima	KL
Michauxia campanuloides	C,G,HP,SE,T
Michauxia tchihatcheffii	PL,SE,T,V
Michelia champaca	B,C,EL,HA,SA,WA
Michelia doltsopa	B
Michelia figo	B,LN,SA
Michelia maudiae	B,SA
Michelia sinensis	B,FW,SA
Michelia wilsonii see M.sinensis	
Micranthocereus auri-azureus	B,DV
Micranthocereus densiflorus	B,DV,Y
Micranthocereus polyanthus	B,Y
Micranthocereus streckerii	B,Y
Micranthocereus villianus	B
Micranthus alopecuroides	B,SI
Micranthus junceus	B,SI
Micranthus tubulosus	B,SI
Microlaena avenacea	B
Microlaena stipoides	HA
Microlepia speluncae	SA
Microloma sagittatum	B
Micromeles alnifolia	SG
Micromeria dalmatica	B
Micromeria 'Emperor's Mint'	B,CN
Micromeria fruticosa	B
Micromeria thymifolia	AP,B,C,JE
Micropterum papulosum	DV,Y
Micropterum pinnatifidum	DV
Micropterum schlechteri	B,C,DV,Y
Microseris lanceolata	KL
Microseris ringens	HP,NG,SA
Microseris ringens 'Girandole'	AP,B,BS,KI,T
Microsorium punctatum	SG
Microsperma tasseloides 'Golden Tassel'	B
Microsteris gracilis	DD
Microtis media ssp densiflora	B
Microtis oliganthus	B,SS
Microtis unifolia	B,SS
Mila caespitosa	B,DV
Mila caespitosa v churinensis	B,DV
Mila cereoides	B
Mila fortalezensis	B
Mila maritima	B
Mila nealeana	B
Mila pugionifera	B
Milicia excelsa	AP,B,HP
Milium effusum	AP,B,C,G,HP,I,JE,P,SA, SC,SG
Milium effusum 'Aureum'	
Milla biflora	B,SW
Milletia sutherlandii	KB
Millettia dura	B,EL
Millettia grandis	B,SI,WA
Millettia laurentii	B

MILLETTIA

Millettia ovalifolia	B,EL,SA
Millingtonia hortensis	B
Mimetes cucullatus	B,O,SI
Mimosa biuncifera	B,HU
Mimosa dysocarpa	B
Mimosa hostilis	B
Mimosa intsia	B
Mimosa pigra	B,WA
Mimosa polycarpa	B
Mimosa pudica	w.a.
Mimosa quitoense	B
Mimosa scabrella	B,HU,RE
Mimosa tenuiflora	B
Mimosa xantii	DD
Mimulus 'Andean Nymph' forms	AP,B,BS,C,CL,HP,MO, SC,SE,T,V
Mimulus aurantiacus	AP,B,CA,SW
Mimulus 'Bonfire'	BS
Mimulus brevipes	B,SW
Mimulus cardinalis	AP,B,C,CG,EL,G,HP,JE, SA,SC,SG,SW,
Mimulus cardinalis 'Siskiyou Gold'	B
Mimulus cardinalis 'Whitecroft Scarlet'	B,BS,MO,SC
Mimulus 'Crown Jewels'	BS,KI
Mimulus extra choice mix	F
Mimulus f1 Calypso	B,BD,BS,CL,D,DT,MO, R,S,SE,SK,T
Mimulus f1 'Magic' mix	CL,D,F,J,L,MO,TU,YA
Mimulus f1 'Magic Pastel' mix	BS,DT,J,MO,S
Mimulus f1 'Magic' s-c	B,CL,MO,YA
Mimulus f1 Malibu	BD,BS,C,D
Mimulus f1 Malibu 92	M
Mimulus f1 Malibu orange	S
Mimulus f1 Malibu Sunshine	U
Mimulus f1 'Mystic' mix	CL,PK,VY
Mimulus f1 'Mystic' with spots	YA
Mimulus f1 'Mystic' with spots p.s.	YA
Mimulus f1 'Sparkles'	U
Mimulus f1 'Viva'	B,BS,C,D,F
Mimulus guttatus	AB,AP,B,C,CG,G,HP,JE, SA,SG
Mimulus guttatus 'Richard Bush'	B,HP,P
Mimulus guttatus (V) see M.g. 'Richard Bush'	
Mimulus 'Highland Fling'	BD,BS,CN,MO
Mimulus 'Highland Series' s-c	B,BS,CN,MO
Mimulus lewisii	AP,B,C,G,HP,JE,NO,SA, SC,SG,T
Mimulus longiflorus	B
Mimulus luteus	B,C,G,HP,JE,KL,PI,SA, SC,T,TH
Mimulus luteus 'Tigrinus Grandiflorus'	BS,C,CO,DE,HU,JE,KI, L,ST,SU,V
Mimulus 'Magic' mix p.s	MO
Mimulus minima	B,JE
Mimulus mix shade loving	T
Mimulus pictus	SZ
Mimulus primuloides	B,G,SW
Mimulus puniceus	B,CA
Mimulus 'Queen's Prize'	AP,BS,DT,HP
Mimulus ringens	AP,B,C,EL,G,HP,HU,JE, P,PR,SA,SC
Mimulus 'Roter Kaiser'	B,JE,T
Mimulus tilingii	AP,B,EL,HP,JE,SC
Mimusops coriacea	B,EL
Mimusops elengi	B,EL,HA,LN,SA
Mimusops hexandra	B,EL,HA,SA

Mimusops obovata	B
Mimusops obtusifolia	B
Mimusops zeyheri	B
Mina see Ipomoea	
Minuartia capillacea	AP,B,JE,RS
Minuartia circassica	KL
Minuartia kashmirica	AP
Minuartia langii	SG
Minuartia laricifolia	AP,B,C,G,JE
Minuartia laricifolia ssp kitaibelii	KL
Minuartia macrocarpa	VO
Minuartia obtusiloba	B,RM
Minuartia recurva	AP,B,KL
Minuartia recurva ssp oreina	B
Minuartia rimarium	VO
Minuartia stellata	KL
Minuartia striata	KL
Minuartia verna	AP,B,C,I,JE,KL,SG
Minulus gracilus	SI
Minuria denticulata	B,NI,SA
Minuria leptophylla	B,NI
Mirabilis dichotoma	B
Mirabilis hirsuta	SG
Mirabilis jalapa	AB,AP,BU,C,DI,EL,F,G, HU,KS,LG,PI,RH,S,SG, SK,TH,V
Mirabilis jalapa 4 0' Clock Special	DE,JO,T
Mirabilis jalapa 'Afternoon Delight'	U
Mirabilis jalapa Crown mix	BS
Mirabilis jalapa 'Fellow's Pastels'	B,HU
Mirabilis jalapa prov.	B
Mirabilis jalapa red	B,G
Mirabilis jalapa rose	B,G
Mirabilis jalapa Teatime	BD,BS,DT,F,MO
Mirabilis jalapa white	B,G
Mirabilis jalapa yellow	B,G
Mirabilis longiflora	B
Mirabilis multiflora	B,SW
Mirabilis pumila	B
Mirabilis sp	DD
Mirabilis viscosa	F
Mirbelia dilatata	B,NI,SA
Mirbelia pungens	B,NI,SA
Miscanthus nepalensis	B
Miscanthus sinensis	AV,B,C,CA,DE,HP,JE,PK, SA,SC
Miscanthus sinensis 'Flamingo'	AP,HP
Miscanthus sinensis hyb late	B,JE,V
Miscanthus sinensis hyb new	B,C,JE,SA
Miscanthus sinensis 'Zebrinus'	AV,B
Miscanthus transmorrisonensis	B,DE,JE
Misopates orontium	B
Mitchella repens	B
Mitella breweri	AP,B,HP,MA,P,SC,SG
Mitella caulescens	SG
Mitella pentandra	SG
Mitraria coccinea	SA
Mitrophyllum clivorum	B,KB
Mitrophyllum grande	B
Mitrophyllum ripense	B
Modiola caroliniana	B,HU
Moehringia muscosa	AP,B,SC
Moehringia pendantra	CG
Molinia arundinacea	DE,JE,SA
Molinia caerulea	B,CA,DE,JE,SA,SG
Molinia caerulea ssp arundinacea	B

MOLINIA

Molinia caerulea variegata	HP,I	Montinia caryophyllacea	B,SI
Mollugo disticha	B	Montonoa bipinnatifida	B
Mollugo pentaphylla	B	Montonoa grandiflora	B
Mollugo verticillata	B	Monvillea diffusa	DV
Molopospermum peloponnesiacum	AP,B,C,JE,SA	Monvillea pugionifera	DV
Moltkia petraea	AP,B,BS,C,G,JE,SA,SG	Monvillea vallegrandensis	DV,Y
Moltkia suffriticosa	CG,SC	Moraea algoensis	B,RU
Molucella laevis	w.a.	Moraea alticola	B,LG,NG,SI
Momordica balsamina	SI	Moraea ardesiaca	SI
Momordica charantia	HU	Moraea aristata	AP,B,KB,RU,SI
Momordica cochinchinensis	B	Moraea atropunctata	B,RU,SI
Momordica rostrata	Y	Moraea bellendenii	AP,B,RU,SC
Monadenia bracteata	B	Moraea bicolor	SA,SG
Monadenia ophrydea	B,SI	Moraea bipartita	B,KB,RU
Monarda astromontana	BS	Moraea bituminosa	AP,B,RU,SI
Monarda austromontana	B,G,HP,HU,SW,T	Moraea ciliata	B,RU,SA,SI
Monarda balsamina	SG	Moraea cooperi	B,SI
Monarda bradburniana	B,G,JE	Moraea crispa	B
Monarda bradburniana ssp russeliana	F	Moraea falcifolia	B,SI
Monarda 'Cambridge Scarlet'	CG,HP,T	Moraea fugax	AP,B,RU,SA,SC,SI
Monarda citriodora	B,BS,CN,CP,DD,DE,F,G,	Moraea fugax yellow	B,KB,MN,RU
	HU,HW,JE,KS,PI,SA,T,	Moraea gawleri	B,MN,RU,SI
	TH	Moraea gigandra	B,SI
Monarda didyma	B,BY,CN,DD,DE,EL,G,H	Moraea gracilenta	B,RU
	P,KI,KL,SA,SG,ST,TH,V	Moraea gramnicola	B,SI
Monarda didyma 'Alba'	B,C,JE,SA	Moraea huttonii	AP,B,SC,SI
Monarda didyma 'Croftway Pink'	HP	Moraea inconspicua	B,SI
Monarda didyma 'Fishes'	HP	Moraea insolens	B,KB,SI
Monarda didyma 'Goldmelisse'	JE	Moraea iridioides see Dietes	SA
Monarda didyma hyb new	B,PL	Moraea loubseri	AP,B,G,MN,RU
Monarda didyma mix vars	BS,JE	Moraea lurida	B,SI
Monarda didyma 'Panorama'	B,BD,BS,C,CL,D,DT,F,H	Moraea macrocarpa	B,KB,SI
	U,J,JE,L,MO,PK,SE,SK	Moraea macronyx	B,SI
Monarda didyma 'Red Bergamot'	B,CO,F,JE,V	Moraea moggii	AP,C
Monarda didyma 'Violacea'	B	Moraea natalensis	AP,SC,SG
Monarda fistulosa	AB,B,C,CN,CP,G,HU,JE,	Moraea neglecta	B,KB
	KL,PR,SG	Moraea neopavonia	B
Monarda 'Lambada'	B,BS,C,JO,PL,SA,U	Moraea papilionacea	AP,B,SC,SI
Monarda menthifolia	B,SW,T	Moraea polyanthes	AP,B,G,RU,SI
Monarda mix superb	T	Moraea polystachya	AP,B,BH,RU,SC
Monarda 'Pisces'	HP	Moraea ramosissima	B,SI
Monarda punctata	B,C,CP,DI,HP,HU,JE,	Moraea reticulata	B,SI
	PR,SW,T	Moraea robusta	B,SI
Monarda 'Squaw'	HP	Moraea serpentina	B,RU,SI
Monardella lanceolata	B,SW	Moraea sp	SI
Monardella macrantha ssp nana	B	Moraea sp mix	AP,C,SI
Monardella nana nana	SW	Moraea spathulata	AP,B,CF,HP,MN,P,RU,SI
Monardella odoratissima	B,DD,JE,SW,T	Moraea stricta	AP,B,SI
Monilaria chrysoleuca v polita	B	Moraea tortilis	B
Monilaria chrysoleuca v salmonea	B	Moraea tricolor	B,RU
Monilaria moniliformis	B,DV,SI,Y	Moraea tricolor white	RU
Monilaria pisiformis	B,DV,Y	Moraea tricuspidata	AP,B,SI
Monimia rotundifolia	B	Moraea trifida	B,SI
Monochather paradoxa	B	Moraea tripetala	B,HP,RU,SI,SZ
Monocostus uniflorus	B	Moraea unguiculata	B,SI
Monolena primuliflora	CG	Moraea vegeta	AP,B,RU,SC,SI
Monopsis debilis	B,SI	Moraea villosa	B,C,KB,RU,SA,SC,SI
Monopsis decipiens	B,SI	Moricandia arvensis	B,C,T
Monopsis lutea see Lobelia		Moricandia nitens	B
Monopsis sp	SI	Morina kokanica	SG
Monopsis unidentata	B,SI	Morina longifolia	AP,B,BS,C,G,HP,JD,JE,
Monsonia emarginata	B,SI		KL,P,SA,SC,SG,T
Monstera deliciosa	B,C,CA,EL,HA,LN,PK,SA	Morina persica	AP,B,C,G,HP,JE,SA,SG
Monstera deliciosa 'Seidel'	B	Morinda citrifolia	DD,NI
Monstera deliciosa 'Tauer Strain'	B,CL	Morinda coreia	B
Monstera friedrichsthalii	B	Moringa drouhardii	B,DV,SI

MORINGA

Moringa monilifera	BH
Moringa oleifera	B,CA,DD,SA,VE
Moringa ovalifolia	B
Moringa pterygosperma	EL,SA,WA
Morus alba	A,C,CA,FW,LN,N,NO,SA, SG,VE
Morus alba v tatarica	A,B,FW,LN,SA
Morus australis	B,SG
Morus nigra	A,B,C,FW,LN,N,SA,VE
Morus rubra	B,FW,LN
Mucizonia sedoides	VO
Mucuna bennettii	B,SA
Mucuna derringiana	DD,LN,SA
Mucuna Florida speckled	HU
Mucuna gigantea	DD
Mucuna pruriens	B
Mucuna pruriens v utilis	B
Mucuna sempervirens	B
Muehlenbeckia axillaris h see M.complexa	
Muehlenbeckia complexa	AU,B,SS
Muhlenbergia dumosa	SA
Muhlenbergia lindheimeri	SZ
Muhlenbergia mexicana	B,JE
Muhlenbergia rigens	B,SZ
Mukia maderaspatana	B,DD,NI
Mundia spinosa	B,C
Mundulea sericea	B,SI,WA
Muntingia calabura	B
Murdannia simplex	B,SI
Murraya exotica see M.paniculata	
Murraya koenigii	B,BH
Murraya paniculata	B,C,CA,EL,HA,O,SA,SG
Musa acuminata	B
Musa baccara	B
Musa balbisiana	B
Musa basjoo	C
Musa bicolor	B
Musa coccinea see M.uranoscopus	
Musa ensete see Ensete ventricosum	
Musa ornata	B,SG
Musa sp	RE,SE,T
Musa troglodytarum	B
Musa uranoscopus	B,C,CA,EL,SA
Musa velutina	B,C,CG,EL,FW,SA,SG, VE
Musa violacea	B,BS,C,EL,FW,SA
Musa x paradisiaca	B,BS,CG
Musa zebrina (invalid name)	CA,RE,SA,SG
Muscari anatolicum	AR
Muscari armeniacum	AP,B,G,KL,RH,SC,SG
Muscari aucheri	AP,AR,B,KL,NG,RH,SG
Muscari aucheri bi-color form	NG
Muscari azureum	B,G,KL,NG,RH
Muscari azureum 'Album'	KL
Muscari 'Baby's Breath'	NG
Muscari botryoides	AP,B
Muscari botryoides f album	SG
Muscari bourgaei Turkey	AR,MN
Muscari caucasicum	AR
Muscari comosum	AP,AR,B,C,CG,G,NG,SG
Muscari comosum A.B.S4368 Morocco	MN
Muscari comosum 'Album'	NG
Muscari comosum LG163 Spain	MN
Muscari comosum 'Plumosum'	KL
Muscari conicum	G,SG
Muscari grandiflorum v populeum A.B.	MN

Muscari grandifolium	AR
Muscari inconstrictum S.L15 Jordan	MN
Muscari inconstrictum S.L20 Jordan	MN
Muscari inconstrictum S.L56/1 Jordan	MN
Muscari kerneri	NG
Muscari latifolium	AP,AR,B,G,HU,JD,KL, MN,NG,SA,SC
Muscari longipes	AR
Muscari macrocarpum	AR
Muscari mcbeathianum	AR
Muscari mirum	AR
Muscari muscarimi	AP,AR,JE
Muscari neglectum	AP,B,C,CG,KL,SC,SG
Muscari neglectum B.S349 Italy	MN
Muscari neglectum bucharicum	NG
Muscari pallens	AP,KL,NG
Muscari pallens alba	NG
Muscari pseudomuscari	AP,AR,MN,NG,SC
Muscari pseudomuscari B.S.B.E842 Iran	MN
Muscari racemosum see M.neglectum	
Muscari sp	AP,C,KL,SC
Muscari spritzenhoferi MS707 Crete	MN
Muscari spritzenhoferi SL702 Crete	MN
Muscari steupii	SG
Muscari tenuiflorum	AR,KL,SC,SG
Muscari tenuiflorum S.L90 Jordan	MN
Muscari tubergenianum see M.aucheri	
Mussaenda incana	B,EL
Mutisia coccinea	SG
Mutisia decurrens	AP,SA
Mutisia ilicifolia	AP,B,C,HP,NG,P,SA,SC
Mutisia latifolia	B,P
Mutisia 'Maiden's Blush'	U
Mutisia oligodon	AP,SA,SC,T
Mutisia retusa see M.spinosa v pulchella	
Mutisia spinosa	AP,HP,NG,SA,SC
Mutisia spinosa v pulchella	SA,SC
Mutisia subulata	B,P
Myagrum perfoliatum	CG
Myoporum acuminatum see M.tenuifolium	
Myoporum apiculatum	B
Myoporum caprarioides	B
Myoporum insulare	B,EL,HA,NI,SA,WA
Myoporum laetum	B,SA,SC
Myoporum parviflorum	SG
Myoporum platycarpum	B,NI
Myoporum serratum	B
Myoporum tenuifolium	B,EL,HA,NI,SA
Myoporum tetrandrum	B,NI
Myosotidium hortensia	B,HP,SC,SS,T
Myosotis alpestris	AB,AP,B,CG,FR,G,KL, SC,SG,VO
Myosotis alpestris blue	DI,FR
Myosotis alpestris 'Little Boy Blue'	BY
Myosotis alpestris 'Pink Posies'	B,P
Myosotis alpestris tall s-c	KS
Myosotis alpestris white	DI
Myosotis arvensis	B,C,CP,SU
Myosotis australis	AP,AU,B,SC,SS
Myosotis azorica 'Maria Luisa'	B
Myosotis blue dw	J
Myosotis blue light	KI
Myosotis 'Blue Spire'	BS
Myosotis colensoi	B,SC
Myosotis 'Compindi'	BS,D,DT
Myosotis dissitiflora 'Blue-Bird'	B,PI

MYOSOTIS

Myosotis explanata	AP,B
Myosotis macrantha	B,SS
Myosotis 'Magnum' mix	MO
Myosotis mix	F,J
Myosotis 'Nina' s-c	BS
Myosotis palustris see M.scorpioides	
Myosotis pygmaea v minutiflora	B,SS
Myosotis rakiura	AP,B,SG,SS
Myosotis rose pink	D
Myosotis scorpioides	B,C,JE,SA
Myosotis scorpioides 'John Beaty'	HP
Myosotis scorpioides 'Pinkie'	B,P
Myosotis sp	AP,SG
Myosotis stricta	SG
Myosotis sylvatica	B,DN,HP,R,SG,ST,TH, TU,V
Myosotis sylvatica 'Ball Blue'	B,BS,CL,CN,D,MO,SK, SU,T,V,YA
Myosotis sylvatica 'Ball Marine'	B
Myosotis sylvatica 'Ball Pink'	B
Myosotis sylvatica 'Ball Snow'	B
Myosotis sylvatica 'Blue'	B,CO,U
Myosotis sylvatica 'Blue Basket'	B,BS,CL,HU,MO
Myosotis sylvatica 'Bobo' s-c	B,L,VY
Myosotis sylvatica 'Carmine King'	B,BS,T
Myosotis sylvatica f lactea	HP
Myosotis sylvatica 'Indigo Compacta'	B,BS,CL,F,MO,VY
Myosotis sylvatica 'Music'	B,BS,CL,KI,MO
Myosotis sylvatica 'Pompadour'	B,BS,MO
Myosotis sylvatica 'Princess' s-c	B,BY
Myosotis sylvatica 'Rosie'	B,BY,U
Myosotis sylvatica 'Rosylva'	B,BS,C,CL,DE,MO,O,T,U
Myosotis sylvatica 'Royal Blue'	B,BS,BY,CL,J,MO,S,VH
Myosotis sylvatica 'Royal Blue Imp'	T
Myosotis sylvatica 'Snow Queen'	B
Myosotis sylv. 'Spring Symphony Blue'	DE,S
Myosotis sylv. 'Spring Symphony' mix	S
Myosotis sylvatica 'Ultramarine'	B,BS,C,KS,MO
Myosotis sylvatica Unwins special mix	U
Myosotis sylvatica 'Victoria Dw Azurea'	B,BD,BS,C,CL,CN,MO
Myosotis sylvatica 'Victoria Dw' mix	BD,BS,C,KI,T,V,YA
Myosotis sylvatica 'Victoria Dw Rosea'	B,BD,BS,C,CL,CN,MO, SK
Myosotis sylvatica 'Victoria Dw White'	B,BD,BS,C,CL,CN,MO, SK
Myosotis sylvatica white	B,C
Myosotis traversii	AU,B,SC,SS
Myosurus minimus	B
Myrcianthes leucoxyla	B
Myrciaria cauliflora	B
Myrciaria edulis	B
Myrciaria floribunda	B
Myrciaria glomerata	B
Myrianthus arboreus	B
Myrica californica	AB
Myrica cerifera	A,B,C,CA,FW,LN,NO,SA
Myrica cordifolia	BH
Myrica gale	B,PO,SG
Myrica pensylvanica	A,B,C,FW,NG,SA
Myrica rubra	B,EL,FW,LN
Myricaria trunciflora	SA
Myriocephalus guerinae	NI,O
Myriocephalus stuartii	B,C,NI,O
Myrospermum sousanum	B
Myroxylon balsamum	B,EL,SA
Myrrhis odorata	AP,B,C,CG,CN,E,HP,HU,

	JE,LA,SA,SC,TH
Myrsine africana	B,KB,LN,SI,WA
Myrsine australis	B
Myrsine divaricata	B,SS
Myrsine nummularia	B,SS
Myrsiphyllum asparagoides	B,SI
Myrsiphyllum scandens	B,SI
Myrtillocactus geometrizans	B,BC,DV,GC,Y
Myrtillocactus geom. v grandiareolatus	DV,Y
Myrtus communis	A,B,C,CA,CG,CN,CP,E L,HP,LN,SA,SG,T,V,VE
Myrtus communis 'Compacta'	B,C,CA
Myrtus communis ssp tarentina	B,SG
Myrtus lechleriana see Anomyrtus luma	
Myrtus luma see Luma apiculata	
Nageia nagi	B
Namaquanthus vanheerdii	B,Y
Nananthus broomii	B,DV
Nananthus transvaalensis	B,DV
Nananthus vittatus	B
Nananthus wilmaniae	B,DV
Nandina domestica	AP,B,C,CA,CG,EL,FW, HA,LN,N,RM,SA,SG,VE
Nandina domestica 'Pygmaea'	CA,N,SA
Nandina domestica 'Richmond'	B
Nandina domestica v leucocarpa	B,C
Nani petiolata	B
Napaea dioica	B,G,PR
Narcissus albidus ssp.kesticus S.F 70	MN
Narcissus albidus v occidentalis S.F.15	MN
Narcissus apertus	B
Narcissus assoanus	AP,AR,KL,PM,SG
Narcissus assoanus ssp minutus MS570	MN
Narcissus assoanus ssp requienii B.S481	MN
Narcissus atlanticus	AR,MN
Narcissus bertolonii	CG
Narcissus bicolor	AR,MN
Narcissus bujei	AR
Narcissus bulbocodium	AP,B,CG,G,KL,RH,SC
Narcissus bulb. genuinus x albidus S.B.	MN
Narcissus b. genuinus x albidus S.B.L268	MN
Narcissus bulbocodium 'Golden Bells'	AP
Narcissus bulbocodium 'Nylon'	PM
Narcissus bulbocodium ssp citrinus	AP,KL
Narcissus bulbocodium ssp filifolius	AP
Narcissus bulbocodium ssp genuinus S.F.	MN
Narcissus bulbocodium ssp mairei A.B.S.	MN
Narcissus bulbocodium ssp mix	AP,MN
Narcissus bulbocodium ssp nivalis	AP,AR
Narcissus bulbocodium ssp obesus	AP,PM,SC
Narcissus bulbocodium ssp obesus h.	MN
Narcissus bulbocodium ssp obesus MS.	MN
Narcissus bulbocodium ssp praecox	AR
Narcissus bulb. ssp romieuxii 'Atlas Gold'	PM
Narcissus bulb. ssp rom.'Treble Chance'	PM
Narcissus bulbocodium ssp tenuifolius	AP,AR,PM
Narcissus bulb. ssp tenuifolius S.B.214 .	MN
Narcissus bulb. ssp viriditubus Coll Ref	AP,MN
Narcissus bulb. ssp vulgaris MS.412 Sp.	MN
Narcissus bulbocodium 'Taffeta'	B
Narcissus bulbocodium v conspicuus	AP,B,KL,SC
Narcissus bulbocodium v conspicuus S.F.	MN
Narcissus bulbocodium v graellsii	AR,KL
Narcissus bulbocodium v pallidus	AR
Narcissus calcicola	AP,CG,SC
Narcissus cantabricus clusii	AP

NARCISSUS

Narcissus cantabricus foliosus	AP
Narcissus cantabricus ssp cantabricus	AP,AR,PM,SC
Narcissus cant. ssp cantabricus MS.424	MN
Narcissus cant. ssp cantabricus S.F.395	MN
Narcissus cant. ssp eualbidus S.F.354/2	MN
Narcissus cantabricus ssp monophyllus	AP
Narcissus cant. ssp monophyllus Coll Ref	MN
Narcissus cantabricus tananicus	AP
Narcissus cantabricus v petunioides	AP,AR
Narcissus citrinus ssp belinensis B.S391	MN
Narcissus citrinus ssp belinensis MS579	MN
Narcissus citrinus ssp citrinus MS567	MN
Narcissus citrinus ssp citrinus MS577	MN
Narcissus citrinus ssp graellsii MS399	MN
Narcissus cordubensis	AR,MN
Narcissus cupularis	AP,AR
Narcissus cyclameanus	AP
Narcissus cyclamineus	AR
Narcissus elegans ssp elegans A.B.S.4301	MN
Narcissus eugeniae	AR
Narcissus 'Far North' mix	C
Narcissus fernandesii	AP,AR
Narcissus fernandesii Coll Ref	MN
Narcissus hedreanthus	AP
Narcissus hedreanthus MS543 Spain	MN
Narcissus hispanicus	AR
Narcissus hispanicus ssp bujei MS853	MN
Narcissus hisp. ssp pinetorum B.S470	MN
Narcissus humilis ssp humilis S.F.14	MN
Narcissus hum. ssp mauretanica S.F.268	MN
Narcissus jacquemondii	AR
Narcissus jonquilla	AP,B,RS,SC
Narcissus jonquilla B.S420 Spain	MN
Narcissus juncifolius see N.assoanus	
Narcissus longispathus	AR,MN
Narcissus luteolentus S.S127 Spain	MN
Narcissus minor	AP,B,NG,SC
Narcissus nevadensis	AR
Narcissus nobilis	AR
Narcissus nobilis v leonensis	AR
Narcissus nobilis v primigenius MS905	MN
Narcissus obvallaris	AR
Narcissus pallidiflorus ssp macrolobus	MN
Narcissus pallid. ssp pallidiflorus B.S442	MN
Narcissus pallid. ssp pallidiflorus B.S482	MN
Narcissus pallid. ssp pallidiflorus MS576	MN
Narcissus papyraceus	AP,AR,MN,SC
Narcissus papy. ssp papyraceus PB Port.	MN
Narcissus papy. ssp papyraceus S.B.L48	MN
Narcissus perez-chiscanoi MS560	MN
Narcissus poeticus	C,JE,SG
Narcissus poeticus v recurvus	B
Narcissus pseudonarcissus	AP,B,C,CO,SC,SG,Z
Narcissus pseudon. moschatus MS 840	MN
Narcissus pseudonarcissus Trade	MN
Narcissus readinganorum MS434 Spain	MN
Narcissus requienii see N.assoanus	
Narcissus romieuxii	AR
Narcissus romieuxii HC2522 ex Morocco	LG
Narcissus romieuxii mesatlanticus	AP
Narcissus r. ssp albidus v zaianicus f albus	MN
Narcissus romieuxii ssp riffanus B8928	MN
Narcissus romieuxii v rifanus	AP,AR
Narcissus romieuxii zaianicus	AP,AR
Narcissus rupicola	AP,AR,KL,PM,SC,SG
Narcissus rupicola ssp marvieri	AP,AR

Narcissus rupicola ssp watieri	AP,AR
Narcissus scaberulus	AP
Narcissus serotinus	AP
Narcissus serotinus Coll Ref	MN
Narcissus serotinus ssp grandiflorus C. R.	MN
Narcissus serot. ssp orientalis S.L487	MN
Narcissus sp mix	MN
Narcissus tazetta	AR,G
Narcissus taz. ssp grandicrenatus PB103	MN
Narcissus triandrus ssp pallidulus	AR,MN
Narcissus triandrus ssp triandrus	AP,AR,G,RS
Narcissus triandrus ssp triandrus MS915	MN
Narcissus triandrus ssp triandrus PB376	MN
Narcissus triandus	AP
Narcissus viridiflorus MS498 Spain	MN
Narcissus viridiflorus MS500 Spain	MN
Narcissus viridiflorus MS639 Spain	MN
Narcissus watieri	AP,PM,SC
Narcissus zaianicus	AP
Narcissus zaianicus Coll Ref	MN
Narcissus zaianicus lutescens	AP
Narcissus z. v albus S.B.L85 see N.romieuxii ssp albidus v z. f albus	
Nardus stricta	B,C
Narthecium ossifragrum	B,C,G,JE,SC
Nassella trichotoma	E,HP
Nasturtium officinale	B,CN,TH
Nauclea orientalis	B,NI,O,SA
Nebelia fragarioides	B,SA,SI
Nebelia paleacea	B,SI
Nebelia sphaerocephala	SA
Nectandra globosa	B
Nectaroscordum siculum	AP,B,C,G,I,JD,LG,PA, SC,SG,T
Nectaroscordum siculum ssp bulgaricum	AP,C
Nelia schlechteri	B
Nelumbo lutea	B
Nelumbo nucifera	C,SA,V
Nelumbo nucifera 'Alba Grandiflora'	B
Nemastylis tenuis pringlei	B,HP,SW
Nemcia capitata	B,NI
Nemcia coriacea	B,NI
Nemcia ilicifolia	B,NI,SA
Nemcia reticulata	B,NI
Nemcia spathulata	B,NI
Nemesia caerulea	B,HP,P,PM,SI
Nemesia caerulea 'Pallida'	B,BS,DT,F,PK,T
Nemesia 'Carnival' mix	w.a
Nemesia cheiranthus	B,SI
Nemesia f1 'Nebula'	YA
Nemesia floribunda	B,SG
Nemesia 'Funfair'	CT
Nemesia 'Galaxy' mix	BS,DT,L,MO,YA
Nemesia ligulata	SI
Nemesia melissifolia	CG,SG
Nemesia mix dw	FR
Nemesia nana compacta 'Orange King'	T
Nemesia sp	SI
Nemesia 'St.George'	J
Nemesia strumosa	AB,B,KB,SI
Nemesia strumosa 'Blue Gem'	B,BS,T,V
Nemesia strumosa 'Blue & White'	SE,SK
Nemesia strumosa 'Danish Flag'	B,BD,BS,DT,KI,L,MO
Nemesia strumosa 'Fire King'	B,DE,F,SE
Nemesia strumosa 'KLM'	BD,BS,C,CL,DT,F,J,KI, KS,L,MO,T,U,V,YA
Nemesia strumosa 'KLM' p.s	B

NEMESIA

Nemesia strumosa 'Mello White'	T
Nemesia strumosa 'National Ensign'	F,KS,PK
Nemesia strumosa 'Orange Prince'	B,BS,CL,MO,PI
Nemesia strumosa 'Pastel Shades'	DT,F,U
Nemesia strumosa 'Red Ensign'	CL
Nemesia strumosa 'Red & White'	C,SE,SK,T
Nemesia strumosa 'Snow Princess'	B,D,KS
Nemesia strumosa Unwins Hybrids	U
Nemesia 'Tapestry' mix	T,VH
Nemesia 'Triumph' mix	BS,BY,F,J,KI,TU
Nemesia versicolor	B,CG,KB,SG,SI
Nemesia versicolor 'Blue Bird'	B
Nemopanthus mucronatus	B,LN
Nemophila atomaria 'Snowstorm'	B,C,KS,L,PL,SE,T,V
Nemophila 'Freckles'	B,BD,BS,MO
Nemophila insignis see N.menziesii	
Nemophila maculata 'Five Spot'	AB,AP,B,BS,C,DE,DT,F, HW,J,KS,L,MO,T,U,V,VY
Nemophila menziesii	AB,B,BD,BS,C,CA,CO,D, DE,DI,DN,DT,F,HU,HW, JS,KI,KS,L,MO,SK,ST, SU,T,TH,V,VY
Nemophila parviflora	HU
Nemophila 'Penny Black'	B,BD,BS,C,DI,DT,KS, MO,PL,SE,T,V
Neobakeria angustifolia	RU,SI
Neobinghamia climaxacantha	B,Y
Neobinghamia sp Rio Lurin	DV
Neobinghamia viligera	B,DV
Neobuxbaumia euphorbioides	B,Y
Neobuxbaumia polylopha	B,Y
Neobuxbaumia tetetzo	B
Neocardenasia herzogiana	B,DV,Y
Neocardenasia palos blancos	DV
Neochilenia aerocarpa	Y
Neochilenia aspillagai	Y
Neochilenia atroviridis	DV
Neochilenia caditayensis v flaviflorus	DV
Neochilenia carrizalensis	DV
Neochilenia chorosensis	DV
Neochilenia crispa	DV,Y
Neochilenia deherdtiana	BC,DV
Neochilenia dimorpha	DV
Neochilenia eriosyzoides	DV
Neochilenia esmeralda	DV
Neochilenia flavida	DV
Neochilenia floccosa	Y
Neochilenia fusca	DV
Neochilenia glaucescens	BC
Neochilenia intermedia	DV
Neochilenia jussieui	DV
Neochilenia kunzei	DV
Neochilenia lembckei	DV
Neochilenia lissocarpa v luteospina	DV
Neochilenia neohankeana	DV
Neochilenia nigrihorrida	DV
Neochilenia nigriscoparia	DV
Neochilenia odieri	DV
Neochilenia odoriflora	DV,Y
Neochilenia pajalonensis	DV
Neochilenia paucicostata	DV,Y
Neochilenia pilispina	DV
Neochilenia reichii	DV
Neochilenia setosiflora	DV
Neochilenia sp mix	C,Y
Neochilenia subikii	BC,DV

Neochilenia taltalensis	DV,Y
Neochilenia vanbaelii	DV
Neochilenia wagenknechtii	DV,Y
Neochilenia wagenknechtii v napina	Y
Neodypsis baronii	B,EL,O
Neodypsis darianii	B
Neodypsis decaryi	B,CA,EL,HA,O
Neodypsis lastelliana	B,CA,EL,O
Neodypsis leptocheilos	B,EL,O
Neogomesia agavioides	DV
Neohenricia sibbetti	B
Neolitsea dealbata	O
Neolloydia conoidea	B
Neolloydia conoidea v grandiflora	B
Neolloydia conoides	B
Neolloydia dasyacantha	B
Neolloydia intertexta	B
Neolloydia odorata	Y
Neolloydia schmiedickeana	B,DV,Y
Neomarica gracilis	B
Neonicholsonia watsonii	B,O,SA
Neopatersonia uitenhagensis	B
Neopaxia australasica	B,SS
Neophlolga pink crown shaft	CA
Neoporteria atrispinosa	B,DV,Y
Neoporteria cachtayensis	DV
Neoporteria castaneoides	Y
Neoporteria cephalophora	Y
Neoporteria chilensis	DV
Neoporteria clavata	DV
Neoporteria coimasensis	B,DV,Y
Neoporteria coimasensis Las Coimas	DV
Neoporteria crispa	DV,Y
Neoporteria curvispina	Y
Neoporteria dimorpha	DV
Neoporteria engleri	DV
Neoporteria esmeraldana	Y
Neoporteria floccosa	DV
Neoporteria fusca	Y
Neoporteria gerocephala	B,DV
Neoporteria gracilis	Y
Neoporteria heracantha	DV
Neoporteria illapelensis	DV
Neoporteria laniceps	DV
Neoporteria litoralis see N.subgibbosa	
Neoporteria microsperma	DV,Y
Neoporteria multicolor	B,DV,Y
Neoporteria napina v mitis	Y
Neoporteria nidus f senilis	DV,Y
Neoporteria nigrihorrida	DV,Y
Neoporteria odoriflora	DV,Y
Neoporteria paucicostata	DV,Y
Neoporteria pilispina	DV
Neoporteria pseudolaniceps	DV,Y
Neoporteria senilis Ovalle	DV
Neoporteria sp	B,DV
Neoporteria sp mix	CH,Y
Neoporteria subgibbosa	B,DV,Y
Neoporteria subgibbosa v intermedia	DV
Neoporteria subgibbosa v orientalis	DV
Neoporteria taltalensis	B,Y
Neoporteria vexatus v horridus	DV
Neoporteria wagenknechtii	B,Y
Neoporteria woutersiana	DV
Neoraimondia arequipensis	B,DV
Neoraimondia aticensis	DV

NEORAIMONDIA

Neoraimondia roseiflora	DV,HU
Neoraimondia roseiflora v churinensis	DV
Neoregelia sp	B
Nepenthes khasiana	B,C
Nepenthes pervillei	B,DV
Nepenthes sp & hyb	B
Nepenthes ventricosa	B,C
Nepeta camphorata	B,C,CP,DD,HP,SG,T,V
Nepeta cataria	AP,B,C,CN,CP,DD,F,HP,
	HU,JE,KS,SA,SG,T
Nepeta cataria 'Citriodora'	B,C,CN,CP,DD,G,HP,JE,
	P,PL,T,V
Nepeta clarkei	B,HP,JE,SA
Nepeta govanianaa	HP
Nepeta grandiflora	AP,BH,C,G,HP,SG,SZ,T
Nepeta italica	SG
Nepeta kokanica	B,SG
Nepeta lanceolata	B,C,HU
Nepeta latifolia	B,HP,P
Nepeta mussinii see N.racemosa	
Nepeta nawaschinii	SG
Nepeta nepetella	AP,CG,G,HP,KL,SC
Nepeta nervosa	AP,B,C,CN,F,G,HP,JE,PL,
	SA,SC,SG
Nepeta nervosa 'Blue Carpet'	B,PK
Nepeta nuda	AP,SG
Nepeta parnassica	AP,B,HP,P
Nepeta racemosa	BD,BS,BY,C,CL,CN,D,
	DE,DT,F,HP,HU,KI,L,
	MO,SA,SG,ST,T,V
Nepeta sibirica	AP,B,BH,CG,HP,JE,SA,
	SG
Nepeta sibthorpii	AP,SZ
Nepeta 'Six Hills Giant'	HP,P
Nepeta sp woolly	B,P,SG
Nepeta stewartiana	AP,B,P
Nepeta subsessilis	AP,B,G,HP,JE,NG,P,SG,
	SZ
Nepeta sulphurea	SG
Nepeta teydea	B,SZ
Nepeta transcaucasica	SG
Nepeta troodii	P
Nepeta tuberosa	AP,G,HP,NG,P,SZ
Nepeta x faassenii	AP,B,G,HP,JE,KS
Nepeta x faassenii 'Alba'	B,JE
Nepeta x faassenii 'Select'	B,JE
Nephelium lappaceum	B
Nephrolepis cordata	B
Nephrolepis cordata compacta	SA
Nephrolepis cordifolia	B,SG
Nephrolepis cordifolia 'Plumosa'	B,SA
Nephrolepis exaltata	B,SA,SG
Nephrolepis exaltata 'Bornstedt'	B,SA
Nephrolepis exaltata 'Erecta'	B
Nephrolepis exaltata 'Fluffy Ruffles'	SG
Nephrolepis exaltata 'Teddy Junior'	SG
Nephrolepis exaltata 'Whitmanii'	CG,SG
Nephrolepis imbricata	B,SA
Neptunia dimorphantha	B,NI
Neptunia monosperma	B,NI
Neptunia oleracea	B
Neptunia plena	C
Nerine angulata	B,RU
Nerine bowdenii	B,C
Nerine bowdenii Fenwick's Variety	PM
Nerine filamentosa	B,MN,RU

Nerine filifolia	B,CF,MN,RU
Nerine humilis	B,RU
Nerine humilis v tulbaghensis	B
Nerine krigei	B,CF,RU
Nerine masionorum	B,RU
Nerine sarniensis	B,RU
Nerine undulata	B,RU
Nerium oleander	C,CA,EL,HA,HP,HU,G,
	JE,SA,VE
Nerium oleander 'Fiesta' s-c	B,CA
Nerium oleander mix	B,C
Nerium oleander 'Variegata'	B
Nertera balfouriana	B,SS
Nertera depressa	SS
Nertera granadensis	B
Nestegis cunninghamii	B
Nestegis lanceolata	B
Neurachne alopecuroides	B,NI
New Mexico Native Shrub Seed	AV
Newcastelea sp	B,NI
Newtonia buchananii	B,SI
Newtonia hildebrantii	B,SI
Nicandra physaloides	AB,AP,B,BS,C,CO,CP,F,
	G,HP,HU,I,KL,P,PI,SG,
	SZ,T,TH,V
Nicandra physaloides 'Alba'	AP,B,C,P
Nicandra physaloides 'Black Pod'	B,HU
Nicandra physaloides lg fl	T
Nicandra rustica	CP
Nicotiana acuminata	B
Nicotiana affinis see N.alata	
Nicotiana alata	AB,BD,BS,CO,D,DV,G,
	HP,PK,S,SD,SG,TH
Nicotiana alata grandiflora	C,V
Nicotiana alata 'Lumina'	JO
Nicotiana alata o-p	CL,MO
Nicotiana alata 'Sweet White'	B,BY,HU
Nicotiana alata 'Tabaco Blanco'	B
Nicotiana antennaria	B
Nicotiana 'Bedder Crimson'	B,BS,DE
Nicotiana 'Bedder White'	B,BS,DE,DI
Nicotiana 'Breakthrough Mix'	T
Nicotiana 'Canasta'	BD
Nicotiana 'Crimson King'	SK
Nicotiana 'Daylight Sensation'	BY,SK
Nicotiana 'Evening Fragrance'	S
Nicotiana f1 'Domino Crimson'	BS,CL,D,L,MO,PK,SK
Nicotiana f1 'Domino Lime Green'	BS,CL,D,DT,F,L,M,MO,
	PK,SK,YA
Nicotiana f1 'Domino' mix	BD,BS,BY,CL,D,DT,F,J,
	L,M,MO,PK,R,S,SE,SK,
	T,TU,U,VY,YA
Nicotiana f1 'Domino Picotee'	MO,PK
Nicotiana f1 'Domino' Pink Bicolour	BS,CL,L,MO,SK
Nicotiana f1 'Domino Purple'	BS,CL,MO,PK,SK
Nicotiana f1 'Domino Purple/wh eye'	MO,SK
Nicotiana f1 'Domino Red'	BS,CL,MO,PK,SK,YA
Nicotiana f1 'Domino Rose Picotee'	SK
Nicotiana f1 'Domino' s-c p.s	MO,U
Nicotiana f1 'Domino Salmon Pink'	BS,CL,D,DT,F,L,M,MO,
	PK,PL,S,SE,SK,T,U,V,YA
Nicotiana f1 'Domino White'	CL,D,DT,F,L,M,MO,PK,
	SK,T,YA
Nicotiana f1 'Gnome'	BS
Nicotiana f1 'Heaven Scent'	BS
Nicotiana f1 'Hippy'	D,S

NICOTIANA

Nicotiana f1 'Merlin Magic' — F
Nicotiana f1 'Merlin' s-c, mix — SK
Nicotiana f1 'Merlin Salmon Pink' — BS,MO
Nicotiana f1 'Metro' mix — BS,KI
Nicotiana f1 'Nicki' mix — BS,CL,JO,SK
Nicotiana f1 'Nicki' s-c — BS,DE,SK,T
Nicotiana f1 'Starship Burgundy' — MO
Nicotiana f1 'Starship Lime Green' — B,BS,CL,MO
Nicotiana f1 'Starship' mix — BS,MO
Nicotiana f1 'Starship Pink' — B,BS,CL,MO
Nicotiana f1 'Starship Red' — B,BS,CL,MO
Nicotiana f1 'Starship Rose Pink' — B,BS,CL,MO
Nicotiana f1 'Starship White' — B,BS,CL,MO
Nicotiana f1 'VIP' s-c — C
Nicotiana f2 'Mannequin' mix — BS
Nicotiana f2 'Roulette' — BS,D,DT,F,J,KI,L,MO,YA
Nicotiana f2 'Tinkerbells' — BS
Nicotiana f2 'Top Arts' — BS
Nicotiana 'Fragrant Cloud' — SE,T
Nicotiana 'Fragrant Delight' — B
Nicotiana fruticosa — DV
Nicotiana glauca — B,C,CP,DV,HU,JE,SG
Nicotiana glutinosa — DV
Nicotiana 'Havana Appleblossom' — BS,CL,D,DI,DT,F,M,MO, O,PK,R,SE,T,U,V,VH,YA
Nicotiana 'Havana Appleblossom' p.s — YA
Nicotiana 'Havana' mix — T
Nicotiana 'Havana Series' s-c — BS,F,MO,YA
Nicotiana hyb f1 mix — FR
Nicotiana knightiana — AP,B,C,NG,P,RS
Nicotiana langsdorfii — AP,B,C,DD,DV,F,G,HU, KS,MA,P,PL,SG,T,V
Nicotiana langsdorfii 'Cream-Splash' (V) — B,P
Nicotiana 'Lime Green' — B,BD,BS,BY,CO,DI,DT, F,J,KI,L,MO,S,SE,ST,T, V,VH
Nicotiana 'Lime Green Unwins Strain' — U
Nicotiana longiflora — DV,SG
Nicotiana megalosiphon — DV,SG
Nicotiana 'Merlin Peach' — D,U
Nicotiana 'Mop-Cap' — P
Nicotiana noctiflora — HP
Nicotiana paniculata — DV,SG
Nicotiana pink and purple — DI
Nicotiana repanda — DV
Nicotiana rustica — AB,AP,B,C,DD,DV,HU ,PL,PR,RS,SG,T
Nicotiana rustica cvs — B
Nicotiana sanderae — DV,SG
Nicotiana 'Sensation' mix — BD,BS,CO,D,DE,F,J, KI,MO,PI,PK,ST,T,TU, SU,V,VH
Nicotiana 'Shade Star' — PI
Nicotiana suaveolens — SZ
Nicotiana sylvestris — AP,BH,BS,C,DI,DT,F,G, HP,HU,I,JO,KS,L,PK,PL, RH,SC,SD,SG,T,TH,V
Nicotiana sylvestris 'Only The Lonely' — B,BD,BS,C,MO,PI,TE
Nicotiana tabacum — AB,B,BS,CP,DD,DV,HU, SG,SU
Nicotiana tabacum 'Burley' tn90 — B,C,HU
Nicotiana tabacum cvs — AB,B,BS,HU
Nicotiana tabacum 'Virginian' — B,V
Nicotiana 'Tania' red,dw — B
Nicotiana trigonophylla — B,DD
Nicotiana velutina — B,DD

Nicotiana white scented — SK
Nidorella auriculata — SI
Nidularium angraensis — B
Nidularium sp — B
Nierembergia caerulea 'Mont Blanc' — B,BS,CL,CN,D,DE,F,KI, MO,O,PK,SE,SK,T,V
Nierembergia caerulea 'Purple Robe' — B,C,CN,DE,MO,PI,PK, SK,T,V
Nierembergia caerulea v violacea — B,SC
Nierembergia caerulea 'White Robe' — BS,C
Nierembergia solanacea — B
Nigella arvensis — B
Nigella ciliaris — B
Nigella ciliaris 'Pinwheel' — KS
Nigella damascena — AB,AP,B,BH,BY,DD,DI,F R,G,I,JO,KL,RH,SG,TH, VO
Nigella damascena 'Albion' — B
Nigella damascena 'Blue Cambridge' — B
Nigella damascena 'Blue Midget' — KS
Nigella damascena 'Blue Oxford' — B,BS,T
Nigella damascena 'Dw Moody Blue' — T
Nigella damascena f nana — SG
Nigella damascena fl pl mix — C
Nigella damascena 'Miss Jekyll Dark Blue' — B,BD,BS,CN,DE,KS,MO
Nigella damascena 'Miss Jekyll' mix — AP,DE,KS,V
Nigella damascena 'Miss Jekyll Rose' — B,BD,BS,KS,MO
Nigella damascena 'Miss Jekyll Sky Blue' — AP,B,BS,C,CO,D,DI,DT,F, HU,J,KI,KS,L,S,ST,SU,T
Nigella damascena 'Miss Jekyll White' — B,BD,BS,DE,HU,KS,MO, T
Nigella damascena 'Mulberry Rose' — B,C,DI,SK,T,V
Nigella damascena 'Persian Indigo' — B,KS
Nigella damascena 'Persian Jewels' — B,BD,BS,BY,C,CN,CO,D, DE,DT,F,G,HU,J,KI,KS, L,M,PI,PK,S,SK,ST,SU,T ,TU,U,V,VY
Nigella damascena 'Persian Red' — B,SE
Nigella damascena 'Persian Violet' — B
Nigella damascena 'Shorty Blue' — B,BS,C,KI,MO
Nigella damascena white — BY,DI
Nigella hispanica — B,BS,BY,CN,G,MO,NG, T,TH,V
Nigella hispanica 'Curiosity' — C,DI,KS
Nigella hispanica 'Exotic' — PI
Nigella orientalis — AP,BH,NG,RH
Nigella orientalis 'Transformer' — B,BS,BY,C,CN,F,HU,JO, KI,MO,PI,T,V
Nigella sativa — B,C,CN,HU,KS,SG
Nigella sp mix — F
Nigritella nigra — CG
Nipponanthemum nipponicum — B,JE
Nissolia fruticosa — CG
Nitraria billardieri — B,NI,SA
Nitraria schoberi — HU
Nivenia binata — B,SI
Nivenia corymbosa — B,SI
Nivenia stokoei — B,SI
Nolana humifusa — B,BS,C,DT,KS
Nolana humifusa sky blue — PK,SK
Nolana napiformis — B,SC
Nolana paradoxa — AB,AP,SC,SG
Nolana paradoxa 'Blue Bird' — B,BD,BS,BY,C,CO,D, DE,DT,F,HU,KI,KS,L, MO,S,T,U,V
Nolana paradoxa 'Little Bells' — B,BS,MO

NOLANA

Nolana paradoxa 'Shooting Star'	D,S,V
Nolana paradoxa 'Snow Bird'	B,BD,BS,D,KS,MO,PK, S,T,U,V
Nolina beldingii	B,DV
Nolina bigelowii	B,DV,SA,SW
Nolina durangensis	B
Nolina gracilis	B,O,SA
Nolina greenii	DV
Nolina guatemalensis	B,CA,EL,O,SA
Nolina lindheimeri	DV
Nolina microcarpa	B,CH,DV,HU,SA,SW
Nolina parryi	B
Nolina recurvata	B,CA,DV,EL,HA,LN,O,SA ,T
Nolina sp mix	C
Nolina stricta	B,CA,DV,HA,O
Nolina texana	B,O,RS
Nomocharis aperta	AP,LG,SC,SG
Nomocharis farreri	KL
Nomocharis mairei see N. pardanthina	
Nomocharis mix	KL,P
Nomocharis oxypetala v insigne	SG
Nomocharis pardanthina	AP,G,KL,N,SC
Nomocharis pardanthina f punctulata	AP,PM,SC
Nomocharis saluenensis	AP,SC,SG
Nonea aurea	NG
Nonea pulla	B,JE
Normanbya normanbyi	B,CA,EL,HA,O
Noronhia emarginata	B
Nothofagus alessandri	B,SA
Nothofagus alpina	B,C,SA
Nothofagus antarctica	B,C,SA
Nothofagus cunninghamii	B,N,O,SA
Nothofagus dombeyi	B,C,SA
Nothofagus fusca	B
Nothofagus obliqua	B,C,N,SA
Nothofagus procera see N.alpina	
Nothofagus pumilio	B,N,SA
Nothofagus truncata	B
Notholirion bulbiferum	AP,B,LG,SC
Notholirion campanulatum	AP,C,SC
Notholirion macrophyllum	AP,B,SC
Nothoscordum bivalve	SG
Nothoscordum gracile	AP,CG,G,HP,I,KL,SC
Nothoscordum gr. v macrocarpum Cutler	MN

Nothoscordum inodorum see N.gracile

Nothoscordum minarum yellow Argentina	MN
Nothoscordum sp Castillo 8264 Argentina	MN
Nothoscordum texanum	B,SW
Notobasis syriaca	B
Notocactus see Parodia	
Notospartium carmichaeliae	AP,B,SC,SS,SW
Notospartium glabrescens	B,SS,SW
Notospartium torulosum	B,SS,SW
Notothlaspi australe	SS
Notothlaspi rosulatum	B,SS,SW
Novosieversia glacialis	VO
Nuphar lutea	B,SA
Nuxia congesta	B,SI,WA
Nuxia floribunda	B,LN,SI,WA

Nuxia oppositifolia	B,SI
Nuytsia floribunda	B,EL,NI,O,SA
Nyctanthes arbortristis	B,EL,HA,SA
Nycteranthus noctiflorum	B
Nylandtia spinosa	B,SI
Nymania capensis	B,C,SI
Nymphaea capensis	C
Nymphaea lotus v dentata	C
Nymphaea micrantha	C
Nymphaea 'Sir Galahad'	C
Nypa fruticans	B
Nyssa aquatica	B,EL,FW,LN,SA
Nyssa ogeche	B
Nyssa sinensis	B,FW,LN,SA
Nyssa sylvatica	B,C,CA,CG,EL,FW,HA, LN,N,SA,VE
Obregonia denegrii	B,BC,C,CH,DV,GC,Y
Ochna kirkii	SG
Ochna natalita	B,SI
Ochna obtusata v gamblei	B
Ochna pulchra	B,WA
Ochna serrulata	B,C,CA,EL,HA,SA,SG,SI
Ochroma lagopus	B,RE
Ochrosia sandwichensis	B
Ocimum adscendens	B
Ocimum americanum	B,DD,SI
Ocimum basilicum	CP,DD
Ocimum basilicum 'Dark Opal'	BS,BY,C,CN,CO,HU,ST,T
Ocimum basilicum micranthemum	B
Ocimum basilicum 'Ruffles' green	B,CN
Ocimum basilicum 'Ruffles' purple	B,CN,L,S,T
Ocimum canum See O.americanum	
Ocimum gratissimum	B,SI
Ocimum kilimandscharicum	CP,DD
Ocimum micranthum	CP
Ocimum sp	SI
Ocimum tenuiflorum	CP
Ocimum viride	CP
Ocotea usumbarensis	B,SA
Odontites lutea	B
Odontites verna	B
Odontites vulgaris	B,SG
Odontophorus angustifolius	B
Odontophorus marlothii	B,SI
Odontophorus nanus	B
Oedera capensis	SI
Oedera imbricata	B
Oemleria cerasiformis	AB,B,C,CG,HP,SA
Oenanthe aquatica	B
Oenanthe crocata	B,G
Oenanthe silaifolia	B
Oenothera acaulis	AP,C,F,HP,KL,NG,SC, SG,SZ
Oenothera acaulis 'Aurea'	AP,B,HP,JE,SC
Oenothera albicaulis	SW
Oenothera 'Apricot Delight'	B,P
Oenothera argillicola	AP,B
Oenothera berlandieri see O.speciosa 'Rosea'	
Oenothera biennis	AB,B,BY,C,CN,CP,DD, E,HP,HU,I,JE,LA,PR,SD, SG,TH,TU
Oenothera biennis 'Saguin'	B
Oenothera brachycarpa	AP,B,HP,SW
Oenothera brevipes	B,RS,SW
Oenothera caespitosa	AP,B,BS,C,HP,J,JE,RS, SC,SG,SW,V

OENOTHERA

Oenothera cardiophylla	B,SW	Olea europaea	B,C,CA,EL,FW,HU,LN,
Oenothera cheiranthifolia	EL		N,SA,T,V,VE
Oenothera 'Colin Porter'	B,C,HP,P	Olea europaea ssp africana	BH,C,KB,SI,WA
Oenothera deltoides	B,SW	Olea exasperata	B,SI
Oenothera d. v howellii 'Antioch Dunes'	T	Olea hochstetteri	B
Oenothera drummondii	B	Olearia albida	AU,B
Oenothera elata	B,SW	Olearia allomii	B
Oenothera elata ssp hookeri	AP,B,C,DD,JE,SW	Olearia arborescens	B
Oenothera erythrosepala see O.glaziouana		Olearia axillaris	B,HA,NI,O
Oenothera flava	SC,SG	Olearia cheesemanii	B,HP,SS
Oenothera flava ssp taraxacoides	B,SW	Olearia ciliata	B,NI,O
Oenothera fruticosa	G,HP,SG	Olearia colensoi	B
Oenothera fruticosa 'Fireworks'	AP,HP	Olearia cymbifolia	CG
Oenothera fruticosa ssp glauca	AP,B,C,G,HP,HU,JE,SA,	Olearia frostii	HP,RS
	SC,SG	Olearia furfuracea	B,CG
Oenothera fruticosa 'Sundrops'	BH	Olearia gravis	B,NI
Oenothera fruticosa 'Youngii'	JE	Olearia ilicifolia	B,SS
Oenothera glabrescens	SG	Olearia insignis	HP
Oenothera glaziouana	AP,B,BH,C,CA,CN,E,F,G,	Olearia lacunosa	B,SS
	HP,HU,JE,KI,SA,SC,SG,	Olearia lessoniana	B
	SZ,V	Olearia lirata	AU,HA
Oenothera hartweggii	B,SW	Olearia lyallii	B
Oenothera hookeri see O.elata ssp hookeri		Olearia macrodonta	AP,B,SC,SG,SS
Oenothera kunthiana	AP,HP,JE,RH,RS,SC	Olearia magniflora	B,NI
Oenothera lamarckiana see O.glaziouana		Olearia microphylla	HA,O
Oenothera 'Lemon Sunset'	HP,T,V	Olearia moschata	B,SS
Oenothera macrocarpa	AP,B,BD,BS,C,CG,CL,	Olearia myrsinoides	SG
	CN,DE,DT,F,HP,HU,HW,	Olearia nummarifolia	AP,B,HP,I,SS
	I,J,JE,KL,KS,L,MO,PK,	Olearia paniculata	B,SC,SS
	SA,SC,SG,SK,V	Olearia passerinoides	B,NI
Oenothera missouriensis see O.macrocarpa		Olearia paucidentata	B,NI
Oenothera mollis	B,P	Olearia phlogopappa	AU
Oenothera 'Moonlight'	HP,I	Olearia phlogopappa 'Comber's Pink'	AP,HP
Oenothera neomexicana	SW	Olearia pimeleoides	B,NI,O
Oenothera nuttalli	HP	Olearia ramosissima	B,NI
Oenothera odorata h see O.glaziouana		Olearia rudis	B,NI
Oenothera pallida	B,DI,HU,JE,KS,SA,SW,T	Olearia sp	AU
Oenothera pallida 'Innocence'	BS,C,CO,KI,L,S	Olearia tilicifolia	B
Oenothera perennis	AP,B,G,HP,I,JE,KL,SG	Olearia traversii	B,SW
Oenothera pilosella	SG	Olearia virgata	B,CG,SW
Oenothera pumila see O. perennis		Olearia virgata v lineata	B,HP
Oenothera rosea	AP,B,CG,G,HP,KL	Olearia x haastii	CG,G,SC
Oenothera 'Siskyou'	HP	Olearia x mollis	HP
Oenothera sp	AP,BH,SC,SZ,T	Olearia x scilloniensis	HP
Oenothera speciosa	B,BS,CA,DE,DT,HP,HW,	Olinia emarginata	B,C,KB
	JE,JO,PK,SC	Olinia ventosa	B,KB
Oenothera speciosa pink	B,KS,T	Olnea tesota	SA
Oenothera speciosa 'Rosea'	HP,HU	Olsynium douglasii	B,JE,SC,SG
Oenothera speciosa 'Silky Orchid'	F	Olsynium douglasii album	HP
Oenothera stricta	AP,B,HP,I,RH,SC,SG	Olsynium filifolium	HP
Oenothera stricta 'Sulphurea'	AP,HP	Olympisciadum caespitosum	B,RM
Oenothera syrticola	B,JE	Omalanthus populifolius	B,HA,O
Oenothera tetragona see O.fruticosa ssp glauca		Omalotheca norvegica	SG
Oenothera tetragona v fraseri see O.f. ssp glauca		Omalotheca sylvatica	SG
Oenothera texensis	HP	Omphalodes cappadocica	P
Oenothera versicolor	HP	Omphalodes kuzinskyana	B,PM
Oenothera versicolor 'Sunset Boulevard'	B,BS,MO,P,T	Omphalodes linifolia	AP,B,C,HP,I,LG,NG,SC,V
Oenothera 'Wedding Bells'	U	Omphalodes lojkae	KL,VO
Oenothera xylocarpa	SZ	Omphalodes verna	HP
Oldenburgia arbuscula	KB	Oncidium altissimum	B
Oldenlandia herbacea	B	Oncidium cebolleta	B
Oldenlandia umbellata	B	Oncidium macranthum	B
Olea africana	EL,LN,SA	Oncidium sphacelatum	B
Olea capensis	SA	Oncoba spinosa	B,WA
Olea capensis ssp macrocarpa	WA	Oncosiphon grandiflorum	B,SI
Olea cuspidata	FW	Oncosiphon grandiflorum 'Pincushion'	B

ONCOSPERMA

Oncosperma tigillarium	B,O
Onixotis triquetrum	B,MN,RU,SI
Onobrychis sibirica	SG
Onobrychis viciifolia	AP,B,C,DD,G,HP,LA,SG, SU
Onoclea sensibilis	B,PR
Ononis alopecuroides	B
Ononis arvensis	SG
Ononis cenisia see O.cristata	
Ononis cristata	B
Ononis fructicosa	C,SA
Ononis natrix	B,G,KL,SC
Ononis repens	AP,B,KL
Ononis rotundifolia	AP,C,G,HP,JE,SA,SC,SG
Ononis speciosus	SA
Ononis spinosa	B,BS,G,JE,KI,SA,SG,SU
Onopordum acanthium	AP,C,CN,CP,G,HP,JE, KI,P,PK,SA,SC,SG,ST, SU,T,TH
Onopordum acaulon	SA
Onopordum nervosum	AP,B,BS,C,HP,SC
Onosma arenaria	G
Onosma brignetii	SG
Onosma echioides	SC,SG
Onosma helvetica	SC,SG
Onosma heterophylla	SG
Onosma nanum	AP,KL,SC,SG
Onosma rupestre	SG
Onosma salteri	HP
Onosma seranschinica	B,JE
Onosma sericeum	B,RM
Onosma sp	KL
Onosma stellulatum	B,C,G,JE,SA,SG
Onosma taurica	AP,HP
Onosma tornensis	B,G
Onosmodium mollis	B,PR
Onychium japonicum	B
Oophytum nanum	B,DV,Y
Oophytum oviforme	B,C,DV,SI,Y
Opercularia echinocephala	B,NI
Operculicarya decaryi	B,DV
Operculina brownii	B,NI
Ophiopogon jaburan	B,CA,SC
Ophiopogon jaburan 'Vittatus'	B
Ophiopogon planiscapus 'Nigrescens'	AP,B,C,HP,JE,PL,SA
Ophrys apifera	B
Ophrys holosericea	B
Ophthalmophyllum australe	DV
Ophthalmophyllum dinteri	B,BC,Y
Ophthalmophyllum friedrichiae	Y
Ophthalmophyllum haramoepense	B,DV
Ophthalmophyllum herrei	B,DV
Ophthalmophyllum latum	B,DV,Y
Ophthalmophyllum littlewoodii	B
Ophthalmophyllum longum	B,DV
Ophthalmophyllum lysiae	DV
Ophthalmophyllum maughanii	B,DV
Ophthalmophyllum mix	Y
Ophthalmophyllum praesectum	B,DV,Y
Ophthalmophyllum pubescens	B
Ophthalmophyllum schlechteri	B,DV,Y
Ophthalmophyllum schuldtii	B
Ophthalmophyllum triebneri	B,DV
Ophthalmophyllum vanheerdei	DV
Ophthalmophyllum verrucosum	B,BC,DV
Oplismenus compositus	B

Oplopanax horridus	AB,B,SG
Opuntia alta	B
Opuntia amyclaea	DV
Opuntia anacantha	DV
Opuntia arizonica	BC
Opuntia atrispina	B
Opuntia basilaris	B,CH,DV
Opuntia bermichiana	BC
Opuntia carreana	DV
Opuntia caudata	DV
Opuntia chakensis	DV
Opuntia chisosensis	B
Opuntia chlorotica	B,CH,DV
Opuntia chlorotica v santa-rita	B
Opuntia cintiensis	DV
Opuntia clavata	B
Opuntia cochenillifera	B
Opuntia compressa	B,JE,PR
Opuntia compressa v rafinesqui	B
Opuntia cuerva	DV
Opuntia decumbens	B
Opuntia dulcis	BB,C
Opuntia engelmannii v alta	DV
Opuntia erinacea	B,CH,DV
Opuntia ficus-indica	B,C,DV,JE
Opuntia ficus-indica v dillei	B
Opuntia imbricata	B
Opuntia imbricata v vexans	B
Opuntia inamoena	DV
Opuntia inamoena v chapeoensis	DV
Opuntia invicta	B,DV
Opuntia itapetala	DV
Opuntia joconostele	B
Opuntia kleinia	B
Opuntia laetivirens	DV
Opuntia leptocaulis	B
Opuntia leucotricha	B,CH
Opuntia lindheimeri see O.linguiformis	
Opuntia linguiformis	B
Opuntia loomisii aff	B
Opuntia mackensii	B,BC
Opuntia macrocentra	B,BC,DV
Opuntia macrorhiza	B
Opuntia microdasys	B
Opuntia microdasys v rufida	B
Opuntia mieckleyi	DV
Opuntia mix winter hardy	C,HU,JE
Opuntia nopalea	B,DV
Opuntia oricola	B
Opuntia otaviana	DV
Opuntia palmadora	DV
Opuntia palmadora v chapoensis	DV
Opuntia phaeacantha	B,BC,DV,JE
Opuntia phaeacantha v albispina	BC
Opuntia phaeacantha v brunnea	B
Opuntia phaeacantha v camanchica	B,DV
Opuntia phaeacantha v charlestonensis	BC
Opuntia phaeacantha v discata	BC,DV,G
Opuntia phaeacantha v major	B,DV
Opuntia phaeacantha v minor	BC
Opuntia phaeacantha v nigracans	DV
Opuntia phaeacantha v rubra	BC
Opuntia phaeacantha v tortispina	BC
Opuntia pilifera	B
Opuntia polyacantha	B
Opuntia polyacantha v hystricina	B

OPUNTIA

Opuntia polycantha juniperina	BC,G
Opuntia quimilo	B,DV
Opuntia rhodantha	BC
Opuntia rhodantha salmonea	BC
Opuntia robusta	B
Opuntia rosea	B
Opuntia sanguinicula	B,DV
Opuntia sp mix	C,CH
Opuntia spinosior	B
Opuntia spinulifera	B
Opuntia stenopetala	B
Opuntia stricta	B
Opuntia strigil	B
Opuntia sulphurea	B
Opuntia tardospina	BC
Opuntia tortispina	B
Opuntia tuna	B
Opuntia velutina	B
Opuntia viridiflora	B
Opuntia whipplei	B
Orbea tapscottii	B,SI
Orbea variegata	B,DV,KB,SI
Orbea woodii	B,SI
Orbeanthus hardyi	B,SI
Orbeopsis caudata	B,DD
Orbeopsis caudata ssp rhodesiaca	B,SI
Orbeopsis lutea	B,SI
Orbeopsis lutea ssp lutea	B,SI
Orbeopsis melanantha	B,SI
Orbignya polysticha	B
Orchis mascula	AP,B,CG,SC
Orchis militaris	B
Orchis morio	B
Orchis sancta	B
Orchis sp	KL
Oreobilus pectinatus	B,SS,SW
Oreocereus aequatorialis	B
Oreocereus arboreus	Y
Oreocereus aurantiacus	B
Oreocereus celsianus	B,DV
Oreocereus culpinensis	DV,Y
Oreocereus fossulatus	B,DV,Y
Oreocereus giganteus	B,BC,Y
Oreocereus gracilis	B
Oreocereus haynei	B
Oreocereus haynei vars	B
Oreocereus hendriksenianus	B,DV,Y
Oreocereus hendriksenianus v densilanatus	Y
Oreocereus hendriksenianus v gracilior	B,DV,Y
Oreocereus intertexta	B
Oreocereus lecoriensis	DV
Oreocereus magnificus	B,DV,Y
Oreocereus maximus	B,DV,Y
Oreocereus neocelsianus	DV,Y
Oreocereus potosinus	B,DV,Y
Oreocereus seracata	Y
Oreocereus sp mix	C,Y
Oreocereus trollii	B,BC,DV,Y
Oreocereus trollii v mayor	Y
Oreocereus urmiriensis	B,DV,Y
Oreomyrrhis colensoi	B,SS,SW
Oreopanax xalapensis	B,HU
Oriana sylvicola	B,O
Orianopsis appendiculata	B,O
Origanum acutidens	B,RM
Origanum creticum	T
Origanum laevigatum	BH,C,I,JE,T
Origanum laevigatum album	T
Origanum laevigatum 'Herrenhausen'	PA
Origanum laevigatum 'Hopley's'	I,PA,T
Origanum 'Rosenkuppel'	HP
Origanum rotundifolium	AP,SC
Origanum vulgare 'Aureum'	B
Origanum vulgare 'Gold Tip' (V)	B
Origanum vulgare ssp hirtum	AP,B,CG,SG
Origanum vulgare v album	JE
Origanum vulgare v prismaticun	SG
Orites acicularis	B
Orites diversifolia	B,O
Orixa japonica	SA
Orlaya grandiflora	AP,B
Ormocarpum kirkii	B,SI
Ormosia henryi	B
Ornithogalum arabicum	SA
Ornithogalum arcuatum	AP,G,MN
Ornithogalum comosum	B
Ornithogalum conicum ssp strictum	B,SI
Ornithogalum dubium	B,O,RU,SA,SI,T
Ornithogalum exscapum	AP,MN
Ornithogalum fimbriatum	PM
Ornithogalum fimbrimarginatum	B,RU
Ornithogalum glandulosum	B,RU
Ornithogalum graminifolium	B,RU,SI
Ornithogalum hispidum	B,RU,SI
Ornithogalum longibracteatum	AP,B,CG,G,RU,SC,SG,SI
Ornithogalum maculatum	AP,B,C,RU,SI
Ornithogalum magnum	C,G,KL,MN
Ornithogalum montanum	AP,B,SG
Ornithogalum multifolium	B,RU,SC,SI
Ornithogalum narbonense	KL,NG,RS,SA,SC
Ornithogalum nutans	AP,B,SG
Ornithogalum pilosum	B,RU
Ornithogalum polyphyllum	B,RU
Ornithogalum prasinum	B,RU
Ornithogalum pruinosum	B,RU,SI
Ornithogalum pyramidale	AP,B,C,G,HP,KL,SG
Ornithogalum pyramidalis aff S.L93 Jordan	MN
Ornithogalum pyrenaicum	AP,B,C,DD,JE,KL,NG, PA,SA,SC
Ornithogalum pyrenaicum A.B.S4368A Morocco	MN
Ornithogalum pyrenaicum v flavescens	AP,G,MN
Ornithogalum rogersii	B
Ornithogalum saundersiae	AP,B,SC,SI
Ornithogalum secundum	B,SI
Ornithogalum sessiliflorum A.B.S4619 Morocco	MN
Ornithogalum sibthorpii see O. sigmoideum	
Ornithogalum sigmoideum	KL
Ornithogalum sp	G,SI,Y
Ornithogalum spicatum B.S404 Portugal	MN
Ornithogalum suaveolens	B,RU,SI
Ornithogalum tenuifolium ssp tenuifolium	KB
Ornithogalum thyrsoides	B,C,KB,O,RU,SA,SC,SI
Ornithogalum umbellatum	AP,B,C,CG,JE,KL,SG
Ornithogalum unifolium	B,RU
Ornithogalum xanthochlorum	B,SI
Ornithoglossum viride	B,RU,SI
Ornithopus compressus 'Pitman'	B
Ornithopus compressus 'Uniserra'	B
Ornithopus sativus	CG
Ornothogalum arianum	SG
Ornothogalum fischerianum	SG
Ornothogalum gussonei	SG

OROBANCHE

Orobanche hederae	AP,C,G,HP,NG	Ourisia macrophylla	HP,JE,P,SC
Orobanche ramosa	SG	Ourisia macrophylla v lactea	SG
Orostachys iwarenge	DV	Ourisia sessilifolia	B,SS,SW
Oroxylum indicum	B,DD	Owenia acidula	B,EL,NI,SA
Oroya peruviana	B,Y	Owenia reticulata	B,NI
Orphium frutescens	B,C,KB,SA,SI	Oxalis acetosella	B
Orphium frutescens select	B	Oxalis corniculata	B
Orthocarpus purpurascens	B	Oxalis deppei see O.tetraphylla	
Orthophytum foliosum	B	Oxalis lactea	B,SS,SW
Orthopterum coeganum	B	Oxalis megalorrhiza	AP,B
Orthosiphon labiatus	B,SI,SZ	Oxalis oregana	B,G
Orthrosanthus chimboracensis	AP,B,SC,SZ	Oxalis purpurea	B
Orthrosanthus chimb. v centroamericanus	HU	Oxalis stricta	B
Orthrosanthus laxus	AP,AU,NI,P,SA,SC,SG	Oxalis tetraphylla	B,G
Orthrosanthus multiflorus	B,C,KL,NI,SC	Oxalis tetraphylla 'Iron Cross'	B
Orthrosanthus polystachyus	AU,NI,P	Oxalis valdiviensis	P
Orychophragmus violaceus	B,T	Oxipolis rigidior	B
Oryza sativa	SG	Oxydendrum arboreum	A,B,C,FW,HU,I,LN,N,SA,
Oryzopsis hymenoides	B,CA,DD,NO		VE
Oscularia caulescens	C	Oxylobium arborescens	B,HA,NI
Osmanthus fragrans	B,C,EL,LN,SA	Oxylobium ellipticum	AU,B,NI
Osmanthus heterophyllus	B	Oxylobium ilicifolium	B,EL,HA,NI
Osmaronia see Oemleria		Oxylobium lanceolata	NI,SA
Osmitopsis asteriscoides	B,SI	Oxylobium microphyllum	B,NI
Osmitopsis osmitoides	B,SI	Oxylobium procumbens	B,HA,NI
Osmorhiza chilensis	B,HU	Oxylobium robustum	B,NI
Osmorhiza claytonii	B,PR	Oxypetalum caeruleum see Tweedia caerulea	
Osmunda regalis	B,N,SC	Oxyria digyna	A,AP,B,C,HP,I,RM,SG
Osteocarpum acropterum ssp acropterum	B,NI	Oxytropis amethystea	B
Osteocarpum acrop. ssp dipterocarpum	B,NI	Oxytropis campanulata	SG
Osteomelis schwerinae v microphylla	SG	Oxytropis campestris	AP,B,G,JE,KL,SA,SC,SG
Osteospermum acutifolium	SI	Oxytropis campestris v gracilis	AP,B,RM
Osteospermum barberiae h see O.jucundum		Oxytropis campestris v johannensis	SG
Osteospermum clandestinum	B,SI	Oxytropis chionobia	VO
Osteospermum ecklonis	AP,B,F,SA,SC,SI	Oxytropis deflexa	B,RM
Osteospermum hyoseroides	C	Oxytropis foucadi	VO
Osteospermum hyoseroides Pot Pourri	BS,F,J,U	Oxytropis gaudinii	CG
Osteospermum hyseroides	SI	Oxytropis halleri	AP,KL,SC,SG
Osteospermum jucundum	AP,b,I,SG,SI	Oxytropis kamtschatica	VO
Osteospermum oppositifolium	B,SA,SI	Oxytropis lagopus	AP,B
Osteospermum pinnatum	B,SI	Oxytropis lambertii	B,KL,RM,SA
Osteospermum 'Silver Sparkler' (V)	B	Oxytropis lapponica	JE
Osteospermum 'Sky & Ice'	B,BD,BS,MO	Oxytropis middendorffii	SG
Osteospermum sp	SI	Oxytropis monticola	SG
Osteospermum 'Starshine'	C	Oxytropis myriophylla	SG
Osteospermum tripterus 'Gaiety'	B,BD,DD,PK	Oxytropis parryi	B,RM
Ostrowskia magnifica	B,SC	Oxytropis pilosa	B,SC
Ostrya carpinifolia	B,CG,FW,LN,N,SA,VE	Oxytropis podocarpa	B,RM
Ostrya japonica	B,C,EL,LN,N,SA	Oxytropis revoluta	VO
Ostrya virginiana	B,FW,G,LN,N,SA	Oxytropis setida	CG
Osyris quadripartita	SA	Oxytropis songorica	SG
Otholobium fruticans	B,SI	Oxytropis splendens	RM,SG
Otholobium hirtum	B,SI	Oxytropis strobilacea	SG
Otholobium obliquum	B,SI	Oxytropis teres	SG
Otholobium sp	SI	Oxytropis urumovii	AP,KL,SG
Otholobium striatum	B	Oxytropis viscida	B,RM,SG
Othonna arborescens	B,DV,SA,SI	Ozoroa mucronata	B,SI
Othonna cheirifolia	AP,SC	Ozothamnus diosmifolius	B,HA,O
Othonna cuneata	B	Ozothamnus hookeri	AP,HP,I
Othonna filicaulis	B,DV,SI	Ozothamnus lepidophyllus	B,NI
Othonna lepidocaulis	B,SI	Ozothamnus rosmarinifolius	HP
Othonna lobata	B,DV	Ozothamnus selago	B,SG,SS
Othonna sp	SI	Pachira aquatica	B,EL
Ourisia caespitosa	AP,B,SS,SW	Pachira fendleri	B
Ourisia crosbyi	HP	Pachira insignis	B
Ourisia macrocarpa	B,SS,SW	Pachira quinatum	SA

PACHYCARPUS

Pachycarpus campanulatus	B,SI	Paeonia japonica h. see P. lactiflora	
Pachycarpus grandiflorus	B,SI	Paeonia kartalinika	PH
Pachycarpus sp	SI	Paeonia lactiflora	G,HP,KL,PH,SA,SG
Pachycereus chrysomalus	BC	Paeonia lactiflora hyb	B,JE,PH
Pachycereus hollianus	B	Paeonia lagodechiana	PH
Pachycereus pecten-aboriginum	B,DV,HU	Paeonia lithophila	AR
Pachycereus pringlei	B,DD,DV,Y	Paeonia lutea see P.delavayi v lutea	
Pachycormus discolor	DV	Paeonia mascula	AP,B,CG,G,HP,JE,KL,LG,
Pachycymbium rogersii	B,SI		NG,SC,SG
Pachygone ovata	B	Paeonia mascula ssp arietina	CG,PH,SC,SG
Pachyphragma macrophyllum	AP,C,HP	Paeonia mascula ssp mascula	AP,B,CG,KL,PH,PM
Pachyphytum compactum	B	Paeonia mascula ssp russii	AP,NG,PH
Pachypleurum mutellinoides	SG	Paeonia mascula ssp triternata	CG,NG,PH,SC
Pachypodium baronii	B,O,SI	Paeonia mlokosewitschii	AP,AR,B,C,CG,G,HP,JD,
Pachypodium baronii v windsorii	B,DV		JE,KL,NG,PH,SC,SG
Pachypodium bispinosum	BC,CF,SI	Paeonia moutan	SA
Pachypodium decaryi	B,O	Paeonia obovata	AP,AR,B,G,HP,PH,SA
Pachypodium densiflorum	B,BC,DV,O	Paeonia obovata v alba	AP,HP
Pachypodium geayi	B,CA,DV,O,SI	Paeonia officinalis	AP,B,C,CG,G,PH,SA,SG
Pachypodium horombense	B,O	Paeonia officinalis ssp banatica	AP,B,CG,JE,KL,SG
Pachypodium lamerei	B,CA,CH,DV,O,SA,V	Paeonia officinalis ssp humilis see P.o. ssp macrocarpa	
Pachypodium lealii	B,O	Paeonia officinalis ssp macrocarpa	AP,HP,SC,SG
Pachypodium namaquanum	B	Paeonia officinalis ssp villosa	AP,CG,HP
Pachypodium rosulatum	B,CH,DV,O,V	Paeonia papaveracea	SA
Pachypodium rutenbergianum	DV	Paeonia peregrina	AP,B,CG,G,JE,PH,SA,SG
Pachypodium rutenb. v meridionale	DV	Paeonia potaninii see P. delavayi Potaninii Gr	
Pachypodium saundersii	B,CA,O,SI	Paeonia ruprectii	PH
Pachyrhizus erosus	DV	Paeonia special border mix	T
Pachyrhizus tuberosus	B	Paeonia steveniana	AR
Pachysandra terminalis	B	Paeonia suffruticosa	AP,C,EL,FW,G,HP,LN,PH
Pachystegia insignis	AP,B,DD,SA,SC,SG,SS	Paeonia suffruticosa Chinese Hybrids	AR
Pachystegia minor	AP	Paeonia suffruticosa ssp rockii	AR,HP
Pachystegia rufa	AU,B,SC,SS	Paeonia tenuifolia	B,CG,G,HP,JE,KL,PH,SG
Pachystigma sp	SI	Paeonia tenuifolia ssp biebersteiniana	PH,SG
Packera aurea	B	Paeonia tenuifolia ssp lithophila	PH
Packera fendleri (Senecio)	B,RM	Paeonia tomentosa	AR,PH,SG
Packera paupercula	B	Paeonia veitchii	AP,B,CG,G,HP,JE,PH,
Padus asiatica	SG		SA,SC,SG
Padus avium	SG	Paeonia veitchii alba	B,HP,PH
Padus maackii	SG	Paeonia veitchii v woodwardii	AP,AR,G,HP,SC,SG
Padus virginiana x P. avium	SG	Paeonia wittmanniana	KL
Paederota bonarota	KL	Paeonia wittmanniana macrophylla	PH
Paederota lutea	VO	Paeonia wittmanniana nudicarpa	PH,SG
Paeonia anomala	AP,AR,B,G,HP,KL,PH,SG	Palafoxia hookerana	B
Paeonia anomala v intermedia	SG	Palisota barteri	CG
Paeonia arborea	CG	Palisota bracteosa	SG
Paeonia beresovskii	HP,KL	Paliurus spina-christi	B,C,LN,SA,VE
Paeonia broteroi	AP,AR,CG,G,HP,PH,SG	Palura paniculata	B
Paeonia brownii	B,NO,PH	Pamburus missionis	B
Paeonia brownii maroon sepal	PH	Pamianthe peruviana	B,PL
Paeonia californica	B,PH,SW	Panax ginseng	LN,SA
Paeonia cambessedesii	AP,AR,HP,KL,MN,NG,	Panax ginseng (st)	JE,SA
	PH,SC,SG	Panax japonicus	B
Paeonia caucasica see P.mascula ssp mascula		Panax quinquefolius	CG
Paeonia chamaeleon	AP,PH	Pancratium canariense	SA
Paeonia coriacea	AP,PH,SA	Pancratium maritimum	AP,B,C,CG,JE,T
Paeonia daurica	AR	Pancratium maritimum Tunisia	MN
Paeonia delavayi	AP,B,C,CG,G,HP,I,JD,	Pancratium tenuifolium	B
	LG,NG,P,PH,SA,SC	Panda oleosa	B
Paeonia delavayi Potaninii group	AP,HP	Pandanus aquaticus	O
Paeonia delavayi v ludlowii	AP,B,C,HP,JD,JE,LG,	Pandanus basedowii	O
	P,PH,SA,SC,SG	Pandanus furcatus	O
Paeonia delavayi v lutea	AP,G,HP,N,X	Pandanus montana	O
Paeonia emodi	AP,B,HP,PH,SC	Pandanus spiralis	O,SA
Paeonia European sp,ex botanic gdns mix	PH	Pandanus tectorius	B
Paeonia hybridum	B,SG	Pandanus utilis	B,CA

PANDANUS

Pandanus vandermeerchii	B
Pandorea doratoxylon see pandorana	
Pandorea jasminoides	AU,B,C,DV,EL,HA,HP, NI,O,SA,SC,SE,SH,T
Pandorea pandorana	AU,B,C,EL,HA,NI,O,PL, SA,SC,SH
Panicum antidotale	B
Panicum capillare	B
Panicum coloratum 'Bambatsi'	B
Panicum coloratum v makarikariense	B
Panicum decompositum	B,HA,NI
Panicum hamil	B
Panicum maximum 'Colonaio'	B
Panicum maximum v trichoglume	B
Panicum miliaceum	B,I,SG
Panicum miliaceum 'Violaceum'	B,BS,C,DE,EL,MO,SU, T,V
Panicum miliaceum 'Violaceum Rubra'	DE
Panicum psilopodium	B
Panicum ruderale	B
Panicum sonorum 'Guarijio'	B
Panicum turgidum	B
Panicum virgatum	B,CA,NO,NT,PR,SA
Panicum virgatum red hyb	JE,SA
Papaver aculeatum	B,SI
Papaver alboroseum	AP,HP,KL,SC,SG
Papaver alpinum	AP,B,BD,BS,C,CL,CN, DV,G,HU,I,J,JE,KL,L, MO,S,SA,SC,SG,T,V
Papaver alpinum ssp kerneri	CG
Papaver alpinum ssp sendteri	CG
Papaver alpinum ssp tataricum	KL
Papaver amurense	KL
Papaver anomalum	B,HP,HU,JE,RS
Papaver anomalum album	AP,B,G,HP,NG,T
Papaver argemone	B,C,CG,DV
Papaver atlanticum	AP,B,C,DV,G,HP,HU,JE, SA,SC,SG
Papaver atlanticum dbl form	C,HP
Papaver atlanticum semi-pl	B
Papaver bracteatum see P.orientale v bracteatum	
Papaver burseri	AP,B,CG,G,HP,I,JE,SC
Papaver carmeli	B,DV
Papaver commutatum	AB,AP,B,C,D,DI,J,KS,L G,P,PL,PM,SC,SE,T,V,W
Papaver corona-snacti-stephanii	KL
Papaver croceum	VO
Papaver dahlianum	KL
Papaver 'Danebrog Laced'	T,TE
Papaver degenii	T
Papaver dubium	B,C,CG,F,G,HP,HU,LA, SG
Papaver ecoanense	AP,T
Papaver 'Eighth Wonder'	SE
Papaver f1 'Summer Blaze'	F
Papaver fauriei	AP,C,G,KL,RM,SC,SG
Papaver fauriei 'Pacino'	AP,BS,C,CN,F,JE,MO
Papaver florist pod	HU
Papaver fugax	HP
Papaver heldreichii see P.spicatum	
Papaver hybridum	CG
Papaver kerneri	KL,VO
Papaver kluanense	AP,B,C,KL,RM
Papaver laciniatum 'Aigrette'	T
Papaver laciniatum carmine	B
Papaver laciniatum crimson	B,C,PL,T

Papaver laciniatum 'Crimson Feathers'	DI
Papaver laciniatum fimbriatum	W
Papaver laciniatum fl.pl.	JE
Papaver laciniatum 'Fluffy Ruffles' mix	C,DI,KS,PI
Papaver laciniatum lilac	B
Papaver laciniatum mix	PL
Papaver laciniatum pink	B,PL,T
Papaver laciniatum pink dark	W
Papaver laciniatum pink dbl	W
Papaver laciniatum rose	B,T
Papaver laciniatum 'Rose Feathers'	C,DI
Papaver laciniatum salmon	B,PL,T
Papaver laciniatum 'White Swansdown'	B,C,DI,PL,T
Papaver Ladybird hyb	B,P
Papaver lapponicum	AP,SC,SG
Papaver lateritium	AP,C,DV,G,HP
Papaver lateritium fl.pl	B,HP,HU
Papaver lisae	KL,VO
Papaver microcarpum	VO
Papaver mix single/dbl	SP
Papaver miyabeanum of gnds see fauriei	
Papaver nordhagianum	SG
Papaver nudicaule	AB,AP,CA,DV,KL,SK
Papaver nudicaule 'Artists Glory'	BS,MO
Papaver nudicaule 'Aurora Borealis'	B
Papaver nudicaule 'Ballerina mix'	J,V
Papaver nudicaule Constance Finnis Gr.	HP
Papaver nudicaule 'Delight' mix	BY
Papaver nudicaule deluxe mix	JE
Papaver n. 'Dobies Sunbeam Art Shades'	D
Papaver nudicaule dwarf	B,F,SA
Papaver nudicaule 'Excelsior'	B
Papaver nud. f1 'Champagne Bubbles'	AP,B,BD,BS,C,CL,DE, JO,KS,MO,U,VY
Papaver nudicaule f1 'Illumination'	C
Papaver nudicaule f1 'Matador'	C
Papaver nudicaule f1 'Summer Breeze'	BD,CL,D,J,MO,S
Papaver nudicaule f1 'Summer Breeze' s-c	JE
Papaver nudicaule f2 'Wind Song' mix	B
Papaver nudicaule f2 'Windsong' s-c	JE,SA
Papaver n. Gartenzwerg Gr./Gdn Gnome	BS,C,CL,JE,L,MO,T
Papaver nudicaule 'Gartford Giants'	B,BU,DE,DN,PI
Papaver nudicaule 'Giant Coonara' mix	U
Papaver nudicaule 'Giganteum'	SA,ST
Papaver nudicaule 'Giganteum Matador'	B,JE
Papaver nudicaule hybridum	CG
Papaver nudicaule 'Kelmscott Giants'	B,BS
Papaver nudicaule lge fl special	S
Papaver nudicaule Meadhome Strain	HP
Papaver nudicaule 'Meadow Pastels'	B,BD,C,JE,SA,T,VH
Papaver nudicaule of gdns	AP,AV,B,CO,G,HP,KI,SC, SG,VH
Papaver nudicaule 'Oregon Rainbows'	B,T
Papaver nudicaule 'Pacino'	AP,B,CL
Papaver nudicaule 'Partyfun'	B,C,CL,JE,MO,PK,SK
Papaver nudicaule 'Red Sails'	B,D,F,SE,T,U,V
Papaver nudicaule 'Rubro Aurantiacum'	SG
Papaver nudicaule 'Ruffled Chief'	B
Papaver nudicaule 'San Remo'	B,DT,HU,JE,SA
Papaver nudicaule 'Sea Shanty'	PL
Papaver nudicaule v croceum	KL
Papaver nudicaule 'Wonderland' mix	BS,C,CA,CO,JE,KI,SK,T
Papaver nudicaule 'Wonderland Orange'	B,BS,JE
Papaver nudicaule 'Wonderland Pink'	B,BS,JE
Papaver nudicaule 'Wonderland White'	B,BS,DI,JE
Papaver nudicaule 'Wonderland Yellow'	B,BS,JE

PAPAVER

Papaver 'Orange Chiffon' i-s h	DI
Papaver oreophilum	CG
Papaver orientale	AP,B,BY,CG,DE,DI,DN, FR,G,HP,KI,KL,PI,SK, ST,TU,W
Papaver orientale 'Allegro'	AP,BD,BS,CL,MO,PK, SA,SK,T,V
Papaver orientale 'Allegro Vivace'	U
Papaver orientale 'Beauty Of Livermere'	AB,AP,B,BS,DE,JE,SU
Papaver orientale 'Benary's Special' mix	C,KS
Papaver orientale 'Brilliant'	B,DE,F,HU,JE,SA,V
Papaver orientale carneum	B,DE,HP,HU,JE,SA
Papaver orientale 'Chelsea Pensioner'	JD
Papaver orientale 'Choir Boy'	PL
Papaver orientale fl.pl. red shades	B,JE
Papaver orientale 'Haremstraum'	JE
Papaver orientale hyb mix	AP,B,KI
Papaver orientale 'Marcus Perry'	HP
Papaver orientale mix	BH,F,HP,HU,P,PM,S,SG
Papaver orientale mix border vars	T
Papaver orientale 'Nana Allegro'	B,J,JE,L
Papaver orientale 'Pizzicato'	B,BD,BS,C,CL,D,DT,F, HU,JE,KS,M,MO,O,PK, S,SA,SK,T,U,V,VY,YA
Papaver orientale 'Prince of Orange'	SA
Papaver or. 'Princess Victoria Louise'	B,JE,KS,SA
Papaver orientale 'Queen Alexandra'	B,JE,SA
Papaver orientale 'Royal Wedding'	C,JE
Papaver orientale 'Salmon Glow'	JD
Papaver orientale 'The Cardinal'	PL
Papaver orientale v bracteatum	AP,B,G,KL,SC,T,VO
Papaver paeony	BS,F,S,TU
Papaver paeony fl 'Summer Fruits'	T
Papaver paeony 'Flemish Antique'	F
Papaver paeony 'Guinness'	F
Papaver paeony 'Oase'	B,C,CO,PK
Papaver paeony 'Peony Black'	AP,B,C,DT,KS,PL,SE,T,V
Papaver paeony 'Peony' mix	DE,T,U
Papaver paeony 'Peony Pink Chiffon'	AP,C
Papaver paeony 'Peony' s-c	B,F,KS,T
Papaver paeony 'Peony White Cloud'	B,BS,C,CO,HU,KI,KS, PK,SE,T
Papaver paeony pink/red	HU
Papaver paeony 'Taffeta'	D
Papaver 'Patty's Plum'	HP
Papaver persicum	SA,SG
Papaver pilosum	AP,B,C,DV,F,G,HP,JE, SA,SC,SG
Papaver pilosum 'Orange Crepe'	KS
Papaver pyrenaicum	DV
Papaver radicatum	AP,B,C,G,JE,SC,SG
Papaver radicatum pink form	AP,C
Papaver radicatum white form	C
Papaver rhaeticum	AP,B,C,CG,DV,G,JE, KL,SA,SC
Papaver rhoeas	AB,AP,B,BD,CA,CN,CO, DD,DI,DV,E,G,HW,JO, LA,PI,PL,SC,SD,SG,TH, TU,V,W
Papaver rhoeas 'American Legion'	B,DE
Papaver rhoeas 'Angel Wings'	B,F,KS
Papaver rhoeas 'Angels Choir'	B,BD,MO,PK,T
Papaver rhoeas 'Cedric Morris'	AP,RS
Papaver rhoeas 'Fairy Wings'	DI,J
Papaver rhoeas mix dbl	BH,C,J,V
Papaver rhoeas mix selected single	F,S

Papaver rhoeas 'Mother of Pearl'	PK,PL,SE,T,V,VH
Papaver rhoeas 'Shirley'	AB,BD,BS,BU,BY,CN, CO,DE,Di,DN,DT,F,FR, HU,J,JO,KI,L,MO,PI, SK,ST,SU,T,TE,V,VY
Papaver rhoeas 'Shirley Ryburgh Hyb dbl'	SK
Papaver rhoeas wild	HU
Papaver rupifragum	AP,B,C,CG,DV,HP,JE,P ,RS,SA,SC,SG,T,V
Papaver rupifragum fl.pl.	AP,C,HP,PL
Papaver rupifragum 'Tangerine Gem' dbl	BS
Papaver schinzianum	SG
Papaver sendtneri	AP,B,C,G,JE,KL,SC,Tj
Papaver somniferum	AB,AP,B,CG,G,I,KI,KL, L,P,PK,SD,SG,ST,TH,W
Papaver somniferum 'Breadseed'	B,DD
Papaver somniferum 'Carnation' mix	SD
Papaver somniferum 'Danish Flag'	AP,B,C,F,KL,PL,S,SE,V
Papaver somniferum dbl pink	B,CG
Papaver somniferum dbl purple	B,SZ
Papaver somniferum dbl scarlet	B,SZ
Papaver somniferum 'Giganteum'	B,BD,BS,DE,MO
Papaver somniferum 'Hen & Chickens'	B,BD,BS,C,CN,CO,KS, MO,NG,SE,T
Papaver somniferum 'Igor'	B,NS
Papaver somniferum 'Maximum'	B,C,KS
Papaver somniferum 'Minimum'	B,C,KS,MO
Papaver somniferum mix	CG,SZ
Papaver somniferum mix purple	DD
Papaver somniferum 'Pepperbox'	B
Papaver somniferum 'Raj Red'	B,DD
Papaver somniferum single lilac	B
Papaver somniferum single white	B
Papaver somniferum v lucinata	SG
Papaver sp, forms & cult	B,BH,C,RM
Papaver spicatum	AP,B,C,DV,HP,JD,PL, SC,T
Papaver spicatum spicatum	SG
Papaver suaveolens mix	KL
Papaver subpiriforme	B
Papaver syriacus	B
Papaver 'The Clown'	SK
Papaver triniifolium	AP,B,C,HP,KL,NG,SC
Papaver 'Victoria Cross'	DT
Pappea capensis	B,WA
Paradisea liliastrum	AP,B,C,G,HP,KL,MN,RS, SA,SC,T
Paradisea liliastrum 'Major'	JE
Paradisea lusitanicum	AP,B,C,G,HP,JE,P,SC
Paragonia pyramidata	B
Parahebe catarractae	AP,SG
Parahebe decora	AP,B,SA,SC,SS
Parahebe derwentiana	AU
Parahebe linifolia	B,SC,SS
Parahebe lyallii	AP,B,SG,SS
Parahebe perfoliata	AU,AP,B,HP,P
Parajubaea torallyi	B
Paranomus bracteolaris	B,SI
Paranomus reflexus	B,O
Paranomus spicatus	B,SI
Paraquilegia anemonoides CNW522	X
Paraserianthes lophantha	B,C,EL,HA,HP,JE,NI,O, SA,SG
Parentucellia viscosa	B
Parinari curatelifolia	B,SA
Parinari excelsa	B

195

PARIS

Paris polyphylla	B,SG
Paris quadrifolia	B,C,G,HP,JE,KL,PO,SC
Parkia africana	B
Parkia biglandulosa	B,CG,SA
Parkia pedunculata	B
Parkinsonia aculeata	B,C,CA,DD,EL,FW,HA, LN,SA,VE,WA
Parkinsonia africana	B,SI
Parkinsonia florida	B
Parmentiera cereifera	B,EL,SA
Parmentiera edulis	B,EL
Parnassia laxmannii	VO
Parnassia nubicola	B
Parnassia palustris	AP,B,C,JE,KL,SC,SG
Parnassia sp	SG
Parochetus africana	LG
Parodia acutus	B,Y
Parodia acutus v lourencoensis	B
Parodia agnetae	B,Y
Parodia agnetae v aureispinus	B
Parodia alamoensis	DV
Parodia allosiphon	B,DV
Parodia amplicostatus	Y
Parodia arachnites	Y
Parodia arechavaletai	DV,Y
Parodia arechavaletai f estonica platen	DV
Parodia arechavaletai v aureus	B,Y
Parodia arechavaletai v limiticola	B,Y
Parodia arechavaletai v nanus	Y
Parodia arnostianus	B,Y
Parodia aureicentra	B,DV
Parodia aureispina	B,CH,DV,GC,Y
Parodia aurisetus	B,Y
Parodia aurisetus v longispinus	B
Parodia ayopayana	DV
Parodia betaniana	B
Parodia bilbaoensis	Y
Parodia blaauwianus	B
Parodia bommeljei	B,Y
Parodia brevihamatus f conjugens	B
Parodia buenekeri	B
Parodia buenekeri v conjugens	B
Parodia buenekeri v intermedia	B
Parodia buiningii	B,DV,Y
Parodia cacapavanus HU11	Y
Parodia caespitosus	B
Parodia camargensis	B,BC,CH,DV,Y
Parodia camargensis v castanea	B
Parodia camblayana	B,DV
Parodia campestrae	B
Parodia carambeiensis	DV,Y
Parodia caraparina	B
Parodia cardenasii	B,SG
Parodia cardenasii v applanata	B
Parodia carrerana	B,DV,Y
Parodia catamarcensis	DV,Y
Parodia catarinensis	B
Parodia chrysacanthios	B,CH,DV,Y
Parodia chrysocomus v rubrispinus	B
Parodia claviceps	B,CH,DV,Y
Parodia cobrensis	B
Parodia comarapana	B,BC,DV
Parodia commutans	B,DV
Parodia concinna	B,DV,Y
Parodia concinna f Casupe	DV
Parodia concinna f tolomban	B

Parodia concinna v cunarpiruensis	B,DV,Y
Parodia concinna v flavispinus	B,Y
Parodia concinna v gibberulus	DV
Parodia concinna v joadii	B
Parodia concinna v nigrispinus	DV
Parodia concinna v parviflorum	B,DV
Parodia concinna v piriapolisensis	B
Parodia concinna v wotthuysianus	DV
Parodia concinnoides HU77	DV
Parodia corynodes	B,Y
Parodia crassigibbus	B,BC,DV,Y
Parodia cufajata	DV
Parodia culpinensis	B
Parodia dextrohamata	BC
Parodia elegans	DV
Parodia eremiticus	B,DV,Y
Parodia erinacea	B,DV,Y
Parodia erubescens	B,DV
Parodia erythracanthus	DV,Y
Parodia erythrantha	B,Y
Parodia escayechensis	B,DV,Y
Parodia eugeniae	B,DV,Y
Parodia faustiana	B
Parodia ferrugineus	B,DV,Y
Parodia floricomus	B,DV,Y
Parodia floricomus v flavispinus	B
Parodia floricomus v rubrispinus	B,BC,Y
Parodia floricomus v spinosissimus	Y
Parodia floricomus v velenovsky	B
Parodia formosa	DV
Parodia fricii	Y
Parodia fuscus	DV,Y
Parodia gibberulus	DV
Parodia glaucinus	B
Parodia glaucinus v depressus	B,BC
Parodia glaucinus v gracilis	B
Parodia glischrocarpa	B
Parodia globularis	B,Y
Parodia gracilis	B,DV,Y
Parodia graessneri	B
Parodia graessneri v albisetus	B
Parodia graessneri v flaviflorus	B
Parodia grossei	B,Y
Parodia haselbergii	B,CH
Parodia hausteiniana	DV
Parodia herteri	B,DV,Y
Parodia horstii	B,BC,DV,Y
Parodia incomptus	B,Y
Parodia intermedius	B,Y
Parodia laetivirens	B,DV
Parodia laui	B,Y
Parodia lecoriensis	B,DV
Parodia lecoriensis v longispina	DV
Parodia leninghausii	B,CH,Y
Parodia leucocarpa	Y
Parodia linkii	B,DV
Parodia linkii f Sao Paulo des Missiones	DV
Parodia linkii v buenekeri	B
Parodia linkii v guaibensis	B,DV,Y
Parodia maassii	B,DV,Y
Parodia maassii v albescens	B,DV,Y
Parodia maassii v intermedia	B,Y
Parodia maassii v multispina	B,DV,Y
Parodia maassii v potosina	DV
Parodia maassii v rectispina	B,DV,Y
Parodia macroacanthus	B,Y

PARODIA

Parodia magnifica	B,Y	Parodia pampeanus	DV
Parodia mairanana	B,GC,Y	Parodia paraguyensis	CH
Parodia mammulosa	B,CH,DV,Y	Parodia parvula Lau427	DV
Parodia mammulosa f Wichadero WRA40	DV	Parodia patagonicus	DV
Parodia mammulosa 'Lemon Ball'	T	Parodia pauciareolatus	B
Parodia mammulosa v albispinus	B	Parodia paulus	DV,Y
Parodia mammulosa v arapayensis	DV	Parodia penicillata	B,DV,Y
Parodia mammulosa v arbolitoensis	B	Parodia penicillata v fulviceps	DV
Parodia mammulosa v brasiliensis	B,DV,Y	Parodia penicillata v nivosa	B,Y
Parodia mammulosa v curtinensis	B	Parodia potosina	DV,Y
Parodia mammulosa v erubescens	DV	Parodia procera	B
Parodia mammulosa v gracilior	B,Y	Parodia pseudorutilans	B
Parodia mammulosa v gracilispinus	DV	Parodia punae	B
Parodia mammulosa v hircinus	DV	Parodia purpureus v meugelianus	B
Parodia mammulosa v marmarajensis	DV	Parodia rauschii	DV,Y
Parodia mammulosa v masollerensis	B,Y	Parodia rechensis	B
Parodia mammulosa v meldiensis	B,Y	Parodia riojensis	B
Parodia mammulosa v multiflorus	B	Parodia ritteri	B,DV
Parodia mammulosa v nigrispinus	B	Parodia ritteri v cintiensis	DV
Parodia mammulosa v pampeanus	B	Parodia ritterianus	Y
Parodia mammulosa v paucicostatus	B,DV,Y	Parodia roseoluteus	B,DV,Y
Parodia mammulosa v rubrispinus	B,Y	Parodia rubida	B,DV,Y
Parodia mammulosa v tureczakianus	BC	Parodia rubistaminea	B
Parodia mannii	B,DV,Y	Parodia rubriflora	B
Parodia maxima	B,DV,Y	Parodia rutilans	B,DV,Y
Parodia megalanthus	B	Parodia sanagasta	B,DV,Y
Parodia megapotamicus	B,DV,Y	Parodia sanguiniflora see P.microsperma	
Parodia megapotamicus v alacriportanus	DV	Parodia schlosseri	B,DV
Parodia megapotamicus v crucicentrus	B	Parodia schuetziana	B,Y
Parodia mercedesiana	B	Parodia schumannianus	B,DV,Y
Parodia microsperma	B,CH,DV,GC,SG,Y	Parodia schumannianus v brevispinus	Y
Parodia microthele	B	Parodia scopa	B,CH,DV,Y
Parodia militaris	B	Parodia scopa v brasiliensis	DV
Parodia minimus	B,Y	Parodia scopa v brunispinus	B
Parodia muegelianus	B,DV,Y	Parodia scopa v candida	DV
Parodia mueller-melchersii	B,DV	Parodia scopa v daenikerianus	B,DV,Y
Parodia mueller-melchersii v caveraensis	DV	Parodia scopa v elachisanthus	B,DV,Y
Parodia mueller-melchersii v gracilispinus	DV	Parodia scopa v erythinus	B,DV
Parodia mueller-melchersii v longispinus	B,DV	Parodia scopa v glauserianus	B
Parodia mueller-moelleri	B,DV,Y	Parodia scopa v longispinus	B,DV,Y
Parodia multicostata	B,Y	Parodia scopa v murielii	B,Y
Parodia multicostatus	Y	Parodia scopaoides	B,DV
Parodia muricatus	B	Parodia securituberculatus	B,Y
Parodia mutabilis	B,Y	Parodia sellowii	B
Parodia neoarechavaletai v kovarikii	B	Parodia sessiliflora	B,Y
Parodia nigrispina	DV	Parodia setispinus	B,DV
Parodia nilsonii	DV	Parodia setosa	B
Parodia nivosa	B,Y	Parodia sotomayorensis	B
Parodia notabilis	B,DV,Y	Parodia sp	C,CH,DV,Y
Parodia ocampoi	Y	Parodia splendens	DV,Y
Parodia oropezana	DV	Parodia steumeri	B,DV,Y
Parodia orthacanthus	B,DV	Parodia stockeringii v semicylindricus	DV
Parodia ottonis	B,CH,DV,Y	Parodia subterranea	B,BC
Parodia ottonis 1266B	Y	Parodia subtilihamata	B,Y
Parodia ottonis v blossfeldianus	B	Parodia succineus	B,DV
Parodia ottonis v campestrensis	DV	Parodia succineus v albispinus	B,DV,Y
Parodia ottonis v janousekianus	B,DV,Y	Parodia sulphureus	B
Parodia ottonis v nugualensis	B,Y	Parodia suprema	B,DV,Y
Parodia ottonis v paraguayensis	B,DV	Parodia tabularis	B,DV,Y
Parodia ottonis v rufispinus	B	Parodia tabularis v nigrispinus	B,Y
Parodia ottonis v schuldtii	B	Parodia tabularis v splendens	Y
Parodia ottonis v tenuispinus	B	Parodia tabularis v tolomban	DV
Parodia ottonis v tortuosus	B	Parodia tarabucina	B
Parodia ottonis v vencluianus	B	Parodia taratensis	Y
Parodia otuyensis	B	Parodia tilcarensis	B
Parodia oxycostatus	B	Parodia tuberculosi-costata	DV

PARODIA

Parodia turececkianus	DV
Parodia uebelmanniana	B,BC,CH,DV,Y
Parodia uebelmannianus v flaviflorus	B
Parodia uhligiana	DV
Parodia vanvleitii v antonianus	B,DV
Parodia vanvlietii	B,DV,Y
Parodia vanvlietii v gracilior	B,DV,Y
Parodia vanvlietii v rubrispinus	B
Parodia variicolor	DV,Y
Parodia vatteri	DV
Parodia veenianus	B,DV,Y
Parodia veerbekianus	B,Y
Parodia vorwerkiana see P.erinacea	
Parodia warasii	B,BC,CH,Y
Parodia weberiana	B
Parodia werdermannianus	B,DV,Y
Parodia winkleri	B,DV
Parodia yamparaezi	B
Parodia yunpiensis	B,Y
Paronychia argentea	B
Paronychia fastigiata	B
Paronychia kapela	JE,SA,SC
Paronychia kapela ssp serpyllifolia	B,C
Paronychia sp	KL
Parrotia persica	B,FW,LN,SA
Parrotiopsis jacquemontiana	B,CG,G,SA
Parsonsia capsularis	B,SS,SW
Parsonsia columella	B
Parsonsia eucalyptophylla	HA
Parsonsia heterophylla	B,C,SW
Parsonsia multiflora	B
Parsonsia praemorsa	B
Parsonsia schrankii	B
Parsonsia sepium	B
Parsonsia spinifex	B
Parsonsia ureus	B
Parsonsia ventricosa	B,NI,SA
Parsonsia zeylanica	B
Parthenium integrifolium	B,C,CP,JE,PR
Parthenocissus henryae	B,SA
Parthenocissus quinquefolia	A,C,CA,EL,F,FW,LN,SA, VE
Parthenocissus tricuspidata	B,C,FW,LN,SA,V
Parthenocissus tricuspidata 'Veitchii'	BS,BY,CA,KI,S,SA,VE
Paspalum ciliatifolium	PR
Paspalum dilatatum	B,EL,HA
Paspalum notatum	B
Paspalum plicatulum 'Bryan'	B
Paspalum plicatulum 'Rodd's Bay'	B
Paspalum wettsteinii	B
Passerina falcifolia	B,SI
Passerina vulgaris	B,SI
Passiflora actinia	B
Passiflora adenopoda	B
Passiflora 'Adularia'	B,NP,T
Passiflora alata	B,C,EL,NP,SA,T
Passiflora alata 'Shannon'	B,NP
Passiflora 'Amethyst'	B,NP
Passiflora ampullacea	B,C,EL,T
Passiflora anfracta	B
Passiflora antioquiensis	B,T
Passiflora arida v cerralbensis	DD
Passiflora aurantia	B,NP
Passiflora auriculata	B,NP
Passiflora biflora	B,NP
Passiflora bryonoides	CG,NG

Passiflora caerulea	w.a.
Passiflora caerulea 'Constance Elliott'	B,NP
Passiflora capsularis	B,C,EL,NP,SA,SG
Passiflora cinnabarina	B,C,DV,EL,NI,O,SA
Passiflora citrina	B,NP
Passiflora coccinea	B,EL,NP,PL,SA,SE,T,V
Passiflora coriacea	B,NP
Passiflora coriacea cw Costa Rica	NP
Passiflora cuneata	B,NP
Passiflora decaisneana	B,NP
Passiflora edulis	AP,B,BS,C,CA,CN,DD, DV,FW,HA,HU,NP,O,SA, T,V,VE
Passiflora edulis f flavicarpa	B,CA,NP
Passiflora edulis f flavicarpa 'Golden Giant'	B,EL
Passiflora edulis 'Hawaiian Gold'	B,HA
Passiflora edulis yellow	C
Passiflora eichleriana	CG
Passiflora filipes	NP
Passiflora flavicarpa	EL,SA
Passiflora foetida	B,C,CG,EL,SA
Passiflora foetida hirsuta	B,NP
Passiflora foetida hirsutissima	B,NP
Passiflora foetida orinocensis	NP
Passiflora gibertii	B,NP
Passiflora gracilis	B,C,EL,NP,T
Passiflora guatemalensis	B,NP
Passiflora hahnii	B,C
Passiflora helleri	B
Passiflora herbertiana	B,C,NP
Passiflora incarnata	AP,B,CG,EL,NP,T
Passiflora indica	B
Passiflora involucrata	B
Passiflora kalbreyerii	B,NP
Passiflora laurifolia	B,NP,SA
Passiflora ligularis	B,C,EL,NP,SA,T,TT
Passiflora lindeniana	B,C,NP
Passiflora lutea	B
Passiflora maliformis	B,C,EL,NP,SA,T
Passiflora manicata	B,C,NP
Passiflora mixta	B,C,NP
Passiflora mollissima	B,C,EL,FW,HA,HU,O, PL,SA,SE,T,V
Passiflora morifolia	B,C,EL,NP,SA
Passiflora 'Norfolk'	B
Passiflora oerstedii	B,C,NP
Passiflora organensis marmorata hyb	NP
Passiflora pallens	B,NP
Passiflora Passion Fruits of The World	T
Passiflora phoenicia hyb	B,NP
Passiflora platyloba	B,C,NP
Passiflora puncata hyb	B,NP
Passiflora quadrangularis	B,C,EL,HU,NP,O,SA,T,V
Passiflora quadrifolia	B,NP
Passiflora racemosa	B,NP
Passiflora rubra	B,C,EL,NP
Passiflora rubra pink fruited	NP
Passiflora sanguinolenta	B,NP
Passiflora seemanii	B,EL,NP,SA
Passiflora serratifolia	B,NP
Passiflora serrulata	B,NP
Passiflora sp mix	C,RE,T
Passiflora suberosa	B,C,CG,NP
Passiflora subpeltata	B,C,DD,EL,NP,SA,SE,T
Passiflora 'Sunburst'	B
Passiflora tetandra	B

PASSIFLORA

Passiflora tridactylites	B,NP
Passiflora vitifolia	B,C,T
Passiflora vitifolia 'Scarlet Flame'	B,NP
Passiflora warmingii	CG
Passiflora x exoniensis	CG
Passiflora x hyb	B
Passiflora x kewensis	B
Passiflora x piresii	B,NP
Passiflora zamorana	B,C
Pastinaca sativa	B,C,LA,SG
Pastinaca sativa ssp pratensis	B
Pastinaca sativa ssp sylvestris	SG
Patersonia fragilis	AR,HA
Patersonia glabrata	AP,B,EL,HA,NI
Patersonia juncea	B,NI
Patersonia longifolia	B,EL
Patersonia occidentalis	AU,B,C,EL,NI,SA
Patersonia sericea	B,HA,NI
Patersonia umbrosa	B,NI,SA
Patersonia umbrosa 'Xanthina'	B
Patrinia gibbosa	AP,B,C,G,JE,KL,SA
Patrinia intermedia	KL,SG
Patrinia scabiosifolia	B,KL,JE,PK,SG
Patrinia scabiosifolia MW250R	X
Patrinia triloba	JE
Paulownia elongata	B,C,HU,LN,SA
Paulownia fargesii	X
Paulownia fortunei	B,EL,LN,N,SA
Paulownia sp	SG
Paulownia tomentosa	AB,AP,B,C,CA,CG,DD, EL,FW,G,HA,HP,HU,LN, N,SA,T,VE
Pavetta lanceolata	B,SI
Pavetta revoluta	B,SI
Pavetta zeyheri	B,KB
Pavonia brasiliensis	B,HU
Pavonia columella	SI
Pavonia hastata	B,NI,SA
Pavonia missionum	B,SG
Pavonia praemorsa	B,C,SG,SI,SZ
Pavonia schrankii	B
Pavonia spinifex	B,SG
Pavonia urens	B,SI
Pavonia zeylanica	B
Pedalium murex	B
Peddiea africana	B,KB
Pedicularis bracteata	DD
Pedicularis bracteata v flavida	B
Pedicularis canadensis	AP,B,PR
Pedicularis centranthera	SW
Pedicularis foliosa	C,SG
Pedicularis groenlandica	AB,B,C,HU,NO,RM
Pedicularis kerneri	CG
Pedicularis lanceolata	B,PR
Pedicularis palustris	B
Pedicularis procera	HU
Pedicularis sudetica	SG
Pedilanthus macrocarpus	B
Pedilanthus tithymaloides	SG
Pediocactus simpsonii	B,DV
Pediocactus simpsonii v minor	B,DV
Pediocactus simpsonii v nigrispinus	B
Pediocactus simpsonii v robustior	B
Peganum harmala	B,C,CP
Pegolettia baccharidifolia	B
Pelargonium abrotanifolium	B

Pelargonium acetosum	B,CF,G,SI
Pelargonium acraeum	B,CF
Pelargonium album	B
Pelargonium alchemilloides	B,CF,DV,G,I,SC,SI
Pelargonium alchemilloides dk zoned lf	CF
Pelargonium alchemilloides white	CF
Pelargonium alternans	B,CF,SI
Pelargonium antidysentericum	B,SI
Pelargonium appendiculatum	B,CF,SI
Pelargonium aridum	B,CF,CH,DV,G,SI,Y
Pelargonium auritum	B,CF,SI
Pelargonium auritum v auritum	MN
Pelargonium australe	AP,AR,B,C,G,HP,MN,SC
Pelargonium 'Baby Butterflies'	PL
Pelargonium barklyi	B,MN
Pelargonium betulinum	B,KB
Pelargonium betulinum purple	B,C,DV,SI
Pelargonium bowkeri	B,SI
Pelargonium caffrum	B,SI
Pelargonium campestre	CF
Pelargonium candicans	B,CF,DV,SI
Pelargonium capitatum	AP,AU,B,C,CF,DV,G,HU, KB,SI,Y
Pelargonium carnosum	B,CF,CH,DV,GC,MN,SI,Y
Pelargonium caucalifolium v convolvulifol.	B
Pelargonium caylae	B
Pelargonium ceratophyllum	B
Pelargonium chamaedrifolium	B,CF,SC,SI
Pelargonium citronellum	B,C,DV,SI
Pelargonium columbinum	B
Pelargonium cordifolium	B,C,CF,SI
Pelargonium coronopifolium	B,SI
Pelargonium cortusifolium	B
Pelargonium 'Country Garden'	CO,KI,MC,ST
Pelargonium crassicaule	B
Pelargonium crispum	B,SI
Pelargonium crithmifolium	B,CF,MN
Pelargonium cucullatum	BH,C,CF,DV
Pelargonium cucullatum ssp cucullatum	B,SI
Pelargonium cucullatum ssp strigifolium	SI
Pelargonium dasyphyllum	B,G,SI
Pelargonium denticulatum	B,CF,G,SI
Pelargonium desertorum	B
Pelargonium dichondrifolium	B,CF,SI
Pelargonium dipetalum	B
Pelargonium dolomiticum	B,CF,SI
Pelargonium echinatum	B,SI
Pelargonium elegans	B,CF,SI
Pelargonium elongatum	B,CF,HP,SI
Pelargonium endlicherianum	AP,AR,B,G,JE,PM
Pelargonium engleranum	B,SI
Pelargonium exhibens	B,CF,DV,SI
Pelargonium exstipulatum	B,BH,SI
Pelargonium f1 'Apollo' mix	BS
Pelargonium f1 'Atlanta' s-c, mix	BS
Pelargonium f1 'Avanti' mix	BS,KI
Pelargonium f1 'Avanti' s-c	BS,T,YA
Pelargonium f1 'Breakaway Red'	B,BD,BS,CL,D,F,MO,PK, S
Pelargonium f1 'Breakaway Red' p.s	S
Pelargonium f1 'Breakaway Salmon'	B,BD,BS,CL,MO,PK,S,T
Pelargonium f1 'Cascade Salmon'	BS
Pelargonium f1 'Century' mix	BS,CL,F
Pelargonium f1 'Century' s-c	BS,B,CL,F,MO
Pelargonium f1 'Challenge'	BS,J
Pelargonium f1 'Cheerio Cherry'	BS,U

PELARGONIUM

Pelargonium f1 'Cheerio Series' s-c, mix	BS
Pelargonium f1 'Cherie'	BS,J
Pelargonium f1 'Cherry Diamond'	BS
Pelargonium f1 'Classic Scarlet'	T
Pelargonium f1 'Container Mix'	DT
Pelargonium f1 'Dynamo' s-c	BS
Pelargonium f1 'Elite' mix	BS,CL,PK,SK
Pelargonium f1 'Elite Red'	B,BD,BS,BU,CL,J,L,MO,PK,SK
Pelargonium f1 'Elite' s-c	BS,CL,J,PK,SK
Pelargonium f1 'Eyes Right'	BS,PL,T
Pelargonium f1 'Freckles'	PK
Pelargonium f1 'Gala'	J
Pelargonium f1 'Gala White'	U
Pelargonium f1 'Geronimo'	BS
Pelargonium f1 'Hollywood Star'	BD,BS,J,KI,T,U,YA
Pelargonium f1 'Horizon Deep Scarlet'	S
Pelargonium f1 'Horizon' mix	BS,L
Pelargonium f1 'Horizon Series' s-c	BS,YA
Pelargonium f1 'Ivy Leaved Mix'	U
Pelargonium f1 'Leo'	U
Pelargonium f1 'Maverick' mix	BS,CL,DT,MO,SK
Pelargonium f1 'Maverick' s-c	BS,CL,MO,SK
Pelargonium f1 'Maverick Star'	BD,BS,CL,MO,PK,S,SE,SK
Pelargonium f1 'Multibloom Bright Rose'	B,BS,C,CA,CL,MO,SK,U
Pelargonium f1 'Multibloom Collection'	M,U
Pelargonium f1 'Multibloom Lavender'	B,BS,CA,CL,MO,PK,SK
Pelargonium f1 'Multibloom' mix	BS,BY,C,CA,CL,F,M,MO,PK,SE,SK,U
Pelargonium f1 'Multibloom Pink'	B,BS,C,CA,CL,MO,PK,SK
Pelargonium f1 'Multibloom Red'	B,BS,CA,CL,MO,PI,PK,SK
Pelargonium f1 'Multibloom Salmon'	B,BS,C,CA,CL,DT,M,MO,PK,SK,T
Pelargonium f1 'Multibloom Scarlet'	B,BS,C,CA,CL,DT,M,MO,SK
Pelargonium f1 'Multibloom Scarlet Eye'	B,BS,C,CA,CL,MO,PK,SK
Pelargonium f1 'Multibloom White'	B,BS,C,CA,CL,M,MO,PK,SK
Pelargonium f1 'Musical Mix'	BS
Pelargonium f1 'Mustang'	SK
Pelargonium f1 'Orange Appeal'	B,BD,BS,CA,CL,D,DT,F,KI,L,MO,O,PK,S,SK,U
Pelargonium f1 'Orange Blaze'	J
Pelargonium f1 'Orbit' mix	BS,BU,CA,CN,L,MO,PK,PL,SK
Pelargonium f1 'Orbit' s-c	B,BS,CA,CN,MO,PK,SK
Pelargonium f1 'Orbit White'	B,BS,CN,MO,PK,S,SK
Pelargonium f1 'Pulsar Series' mix	BS,MO
Pelargonium f1 'Pulsar Series' s-c	BS,MO
Pelargonium f1 'Raspberry Ripple'	BS,CL,DT,F,L,MO,SE,SK,T,U
Pelargonium f1 'Ringo 2000' mix	VY
Pelargonium f1 'Ringo 2000' s-c	BS,SK
Pelargonium f1 'Sensation' mix	BS,D,J,L,KI,MO,S,SE,U
Pelargonium f1 'Sensation' mix s.st.	S
Pelargonium f1 'Sensation' s-c	B,L,MO,SE
Pelargonium f1 'Sheba'	U
Pelargonium f1 'Signal Orange'	YA
Pelargonium f1 'Solo'	YA
Pelargonium f1 'Sprinter' mix	BS,CA,J,M,ST,TU
Pelargonium f1 'Sprinter Series' s-c	BS,KI
Pelargonium f1 'Startel' mix	T
Pelargonium f1 'Summer Showers' ivy lf	BD,BS,BY,C,CA,CL,CO,D,DT,F,KI,L,MO,PK,PL,SE,SK,ST,T,TU,VH,VY
Pelargonium f1 'Summer Showers' s-c	CL,MO,PK
Pelargonium f1 'Summertime Lilac'	BS,CL,D,MO,T
Pelargonium f1 'Sundance Orange-scarlet'	BS
Pelargonium f1 'Sundance Salmon-rose'	BS,SE,T
Pelargonium f1 'Tango Orange'	BS,PL,T
Pelargonium f1 'Tornado Lilac Cadix'	BS,MO,SE,SK,T,U
Pelargonium f1 'Tornado White Felix'	BS,MO,SE,SK,T,U
Pelargonium f1 'Unwins Special Mix'	U
Pelargonium f1 'Venus'	BS,DT,F,MO,PL,U
Pelargonium f1 'Video' mix	BD,CL,D,J,MO,S,SE,U,YA
Pelargonium f1 'Video' mix supastart	S
Pelargonium f1 'Video' s-c	B,BD,BS,MO
Pelargonium f1 'Vogue Appleblossom'	T
Pelargonium f1 'White Star'	BD
Pelargonium f2 'Bambi'	DT,KI,ST,VH
Pelargonium f2 'Border Series' s-c	T
Pelargonium f2 'Cabaret'	BS,CL,L,MO
Pelargonium f2 'Capri' mix	BS
Pelargonium f2 'Carioca Mix'	BY,T
Pelargonium f2 deep rose	J
Pelargonium f2 deep salmon	J
Pelargonium f2 'Fleuriste'	BS
Pelargonium f2 hyb choice mix	C,DT
Pelargonium f2 'Lucky Break'	BS,J,M,SE,T,U
Pelargonium f2 'Lucky Charm'	BD,BS,CN,MO,R
Pelargonium f2 'Lustre Series' s-c, mix	BS,YA
Pelargonium f2 'Matisse'	F
Pelargonium f2 'Mr. Stripey'	S
Pelargonium f2 'Paintbox'	BD,BS,CN,MO,PI,SE,TU
Pelargonium f2 'Palette'	YA
Pelargonium f2 'Pastorale'	D,S
Pelargonium f2 'Picasso'	BS
Pelargonium f2 'Pinto' mix	BS,D,SK
Pelargonium f2 'Pinto' s-c	BS,SK
Pelargonium f2 'Scarlet Border'	VH
Pelargonium f2 scarlet red	J
Pelargonium f2 SG75 mix	BS
Pelargonium f2 'Speckles'	BS,J,PL
Pelargonium f2 'Sprite'	CL
Pelargonium f2 'Stardust'	BS,D,PL
Pelargonium f2 'Torbay Colour Mix'	S
Pelargonium f2 'Torbay Colour Mix' p.s	S
Pelargonium f2 'Vista Pale Salmon'	S
Pelargonium f2 'Vista Red'	D,S
Pelargonium f2 'Vista Rose'	D,S
Pelargonium f2 'Vista Salmon'	D
Pelargonium f2 'Vista White'	D,S
Pelargonium ferulaceum	DV
Pelargonium fissifolium	B
Pelargonium Florist Strain	BS
Pelargonium frutetorum	B
Pelargonium fruticosum	B,CF,G,SI
Pelargonium fulgidum	B,CF,SI
Pelargonium gibbosum	B,DV
Pelargonium glutinosum	B,C,SI
Pelargonium glutinosum carneum	CF
Pelargonium grandiflorum	B
Pelargonium graveolens	B,C,CF,DV,SI
Pelargonium greytonense	B,DV,SI
Pelargonium griseum	B
Pelargonium grossularoides	B,C,HU,SC,SI
Pelargonium grossularoides v anceps	DV

PELARGONIUM

Pelargonium hirtum	B,CF,MN,SI
Pelargonium hispidum	B,CF,SI
Pelargonium hyb mix	FR
Pelargonium hystrix	SI
Pelargonium incrassatum	B,C,SI
Pelargonium inquinans	B,G
Pelargonium iocastum	B,SI
Pelargonium ionidiflorum	B
Pelargonium klinghardtense	B
Pelargonium laevigatum	B
Pelargonium lanceolatum	B
Pelargonium laxum	B,CF
Pelargonium lobatum	B
Pelargonium longicaule ssp longicaule	B,SI
Pelargonium longifolium	B,SI
Pelargonium luridum	B,SI
Pelargonium luteolum	B
Pelargonium madagascariense	C,CF,HP
Pelargonium magenteum	B,SI
Pelargonium minimum	B,SI
Pelargonium mix scented	C,DI
Pelargonium mollicomum	B,CF,SI
Pelargonium 'Multibloom Orange'	U
Pelargonium multibracteatum	B,CF,SI
Pelargonium multicaule	C,CF
Pelargonium multicaule ssp multicaule	B,SI
Pelargonium mutans	SI
Pelargonium myrrhifolium	SI
Pelargonium myrr. v coriandrifolium	B
Pelargonium myrrhifolium v myrrhifolium	B
Pelargonium namaquense	MN,SI
Pelargonium nanum	B,SI
Pelargonium oblongatum	B,SI
Pelargonium odoratissimum	B,CF,DV
Pelargonium odoratissum apple scent lvs	DV
Pelargonium oreophilum	B
Pelargonium ovale	B,SI
Pelargonium ovale ssp veronicifolium	B
Pelargonium panduriforme	B,CF,SI
Pelargonium papilionaceum	B,CF,G,SI
Pelargonium patulum	B,SI
Pelargonium peltatum	B,CF,RI,SI
Pelargonium praemorsum ssp praem.	B,SI
Pelargonium pseudoglutinosum	B
Pelargonium pulchellum	B
Pelargonium pulverulentum	CF
Pelargonium quercetorum	AR
Pelargonium quercifolium	B,CF,DV,SG,SI
Pelargonium quinquelobatum	B,CF,DV,G,SC,SI
Pelargonium radens	B,C,CF,DV,G,SI
Pelargonium radulifolium	B
Pelargonium rapaceum	B,SI
Pelargonium reniforme	B,CF
Pelargonium ribifolium	B,CF
Pelargonium 'Ripple' mix	T
Pelargonium 'Rosy Sunset'	U
Pelargonium scabrum	B,SI
Pelargonium schizopetalum	CF
Pelargonium senecioides	B,SI
Pelargonium sericifolium	B
Pelargonium sidoides	B,CF,G
Pelargonium South Africa mix	C
Pelargonium sp	BH,DV,PK,SI
Pelargonium sp aromatic	SI
Pelargonium stipulaceum	B
Pelargonium sublignosum	B

Pelargonium suburbanum	CF,DV
Pelargonium suburb. ssp bipinatifidum	B
Pelargonium suburb. ssp suburbanum	B,SI
Pelargonium tenuicaule	B,SI
Pelargonium ternatum	B,SI
Pelargonium 'Tetra Scarlet'	PK
Pelargonium tetragonum	B,CF,SI
Pelargonium tomentosum	B,G,KS,SI
Pelargonium tongaense	B,CF,DV,SI
Pelargonium tragacanthoides	B
Pelargonium transpaarense	CF
Pelargonium transvaalense	B,DV
Pelargonium tricolor mauve	SI
Pelargonium tricolor white & red	B,SI
Pelargonium trifidum	B,SI
Pelargonium triste	B,C,CF,DV,SI
Pelargonium vitifolium	AP,B,BH,C,CF,DV,G,SI
Pelargonium worcesterae	B,CF
Pelargonium World's Top 6 mix	PL,T
Pelargonium xerophyton	B
Pelargonium zonale	B,CF,FR,SI
Pelargonium zonale f1 'Hallo Purple'	C
Pelargonium zonale f1 'Hallo White'	C
Pelargonium zonale f1 'Sprinter' 'Hallo'	C
Pelargonium zonale hyb mix	CF,FR
Pelecyphora asseliformis	B
Pelecyphora pseudopectinatus	CH,DV
Pelecyphora pseudopectinatus v rubriflora	DV
Pelecyphora strobiliformis	B
Pelecyphora valdeziana	DV
Pelecyphora valdeziana v albiflora	DV
Peliostemon virgatum	B
Pellaea atropurpurea	G,SG
Pellaea calomelanos	B
Pellaea falcata	B,HA
Pellaea hastata see P.calomelanos	
Pellaea rotundifolia	B,SA,SG
Pellaea viridis	B
Pellaea viridis hastata	SA
Peltoboykinia tellimoides	AP,B,JE,SA
Peltoboykinia watanabei	AP,C,I,SC
Peltophorum africanum	B,C,DD,EL,HU,KB,LN, SA,SI,WA
Peltophorum dubium	B,CA,CG
Peltophorum ferrugineum	B,EL,HA,LN,O,SA
Peltophorum inerme	DV
Peltoyne purpurea	B
Peniocereus greggii	B
Pennisetum alopecuroides	B,C,DE,HA,,JE,PK,SA
Pennisetum alopecuroides v viridescens	B,JE,SA
Pennisetum americanum	B,SG
Pennisetum clandestinum	DI
Pennisetum clandestinum 'Whittet'	B
Pennisetum flaccidum	B,JE
Pennisetum orientale	AP,B,C,DE,HP,JE,SA,SC
Pennisetum purpureum	SG
Pennisetum ruppelii see P.setaceum	
Pennisetum setaceum	B,C,CA,DE,JO,MO,PK, SK,V
Pennisetum villosum	B,CA,G,DE,HP,JO,MO, SG,V
Penstemon acuminatus	NO
Penstemon albertinus	AP,B,KL,RM
Penstemon albidus	KL
Penstemon albomarginatus	B,SW
Penstemon alpinus	AP,B,C,CG,JE,SC

PENSTEMON

Penstemon aluviorum	CG
Penstemon ambiguus	B,JE,NO,SW
Penstemon 'Andenken an Friedrich Hahn'	C,JE
Penstemon angustifolius	AP,B,C,NO,RM,SC,SW
Penstemon antirrhinoides see Keckiella	
Penstemon aridus	AP,B,G,RM,SW
Penstemon arizonicus see P.whippleanus	
Penstemon attenuatus	NO
Penstemon auriberbis	B,RM
Penstemon azureus	B,CG,G,SA,SC,SG
Penstemon baccharifolius	B,SW
Penstemon barbatus	AP,B,BS,G,KL,NO,RH, RM,S,SC,SW,T,TH
Penstemon barbatus 'Coccineus'	B,C,G,JE,PK,SA
Penstemon barbatus 'Petite Bouquet'	B,BD,BS,F,MO,PL
Penstemon barbatus praecox nanus	AP,B,C,DE,SA
Penstemon barbatus praecox nan. 'Rondo'	BS,JE,PK,SK
Penstemon breviflorus	B
Penstemon bridgesii	B,SA,SW
Penstemon caesius	B
Penstemon caespitosus	AP,B,RM
Penstemon californicus	CG
Penstemon calycosus	B,I
Penstemon 'Cambridge Mix'	C,CN,DT,MO,SE,T,U,V
Penstemon campanulatus	AP,B,CG,G,JE,SA,SC, SG,SW,T
Penstemon camp. v chihuahuaensis	B,SW
Penstemon cardinalis	CG,SZ
Penstemon cardinalis v regalis	B,SW
Penstemon cardwellii	AP,B,C,CG,G,KL,SC
Penstemon centranthifolius	B,CG,SW
Penstemon clevelandii	B,SW
Penstemon clutei	T
Penstemon cobaea	B,JE,SC
Penstemon comarrhenus	B,SW
Penstemon confertus	AP,CG,JE,SC,SG
Penstemon crandallii	SC
Penstemon cyananthus	B,C,CG,JE,NO,SA,SW
Penstemon dasyphyllus	B,SW
Penstemon davidsonii	KL
Penstemon davidsonii ssp praeteritus	B,RM
Penstemon davidsonii v menziesii	AP,CG,G
Penstemon deustus	B,C,NO,SG
Penstemon digitalis	AP,B,C,G,HW,JD,JE,PR, SA,SC
Penstemon digitalis 'Albus'	T
Penstemon digitalis 'Husker's Red'	AP,B,C,DE,F,G,JE,JO,P, PK,PL,RM,SA,SC,SE
Penstemon digitalis x calycosus	CG
Penstemon douglasii	CG
Penstemon 'Dw Salmon Red'	B
Penstemon eatonii	B,C,HU,JE,NO,RM,SA, SW
Penstemon eriantherus	AP
Penstemon eriantherus v eriantherus	B,RM,SG
Penstemon eriantherus v redactus	B,RM
Penstemon euglaucus	SG
Penstemon fendleri	B,SW
Penstemon flowersii	B,RM
Penstemon fremontii	B,RM
Penstemon fruticosus	B,C,NO,SC,SG
Penstemon fruticosus v scouleri	AP,B,C,JE
Penstemon fruticosus v scouleri 'Albus'	AP,JE,P
Penstemon gentianoides	B
Penstemon glaber	AP,B,JE,KL,SC
Penstemon glaber v alpinus	CG
Penstemon glandulosus	NO
Penstemon globosus	NO
Penstemon gloxinoides hyb new mix	CL
Penstemon gloxinoides 'Sensation' mix	C,D,SE,T
Penstemon gormanii	AP,CG,I,SC,SG
Penstemon gracilis	AP,B,JE,PR,SG
Penstemon gracilis	KL
Penstemon grandiflorus	AB,AP,B,KL,PR,RM,T
Penstemon grinnellii ssp grinnellii	B
Penstemon grinnellii ssp scrophularoides	B
Penstemon hallii	AP,B,KL,RM
Penstemon hartwegii 'Earlibird'	B,T
Penstemon hartwegii finest mix	PK
Penstemon hartwegii giganteus mix	HU
Penstemon hartwegii 'Scarlet Queen'	BS,C,DT,F,PL
Penstemon hartwegii 'Skyline'	BS,V
Penstemon heterophyllus	AP,B,CG,G,SC,SW
Penstemon heterophyllus 'Blue Gem'	I
Penstemon heterophyllus 'True Blue'	SE
Penstemon heterophyllus 'Zuriblau'	G,HP,JE,SA,SG
Penstemon hirsutus	AP,B,CG,F,G,JE,KL,P,SC
Penstemon hirsutus v pygmaeus	AP,B,C,G,KL,RM,SC
Penstemon hirsutus v pygmaeus albus	SG
Penstemon hirsutus v pygmaeus atropp.	P
Penstemon humilis	AP,B,JE,SC
Penstemon hyacinth fl	F
Penstemon hyb choice	BY
Penstemon hyb Crown	BS
Penstemon hyb giant	BS,CO,KI,MO,ST,SU
Penstemon jamesii	AP,B,CG,KL,RM,SG,SW
Penstemon 'Jingle Bells'	BS,MO
Penstemon kunthii see P.campanulatus	
Penstemon labrosus	B,SW
Penstemon laetus ssp roezlii	KL,SG
Penstemon laevis	B,SW
Penstemon laricifolius	AP,B,RM
Penstemon laricifolius v laricifolius	AP,B,RM
Penstemon laxifolius	B
Penstemon leiophyllus	B,SW
Penstemon linarioides	B,G,RM,SW
Penstemon linarioides ssp coloradoensis	AP,B,RM
Penstemon lyallii	AP,B,C,P,SC,SG
Penstemon menziesii menziesii	SG
Penstemon menziesii 'Microphyllus'	RS
Penstemon menziesii see P.davidsonii v menziesii	
Penstemon mix giant	FR
Penstemon mix lge Fl	BD,BS,S
Penstemon montanus	AP,B,SC
Penstemon neomexicanus	AP,B,SW
Penstemon newberryi	AP,B,CG,G,SG
Penstemon newberryi f humilior	RS
Penstemon nitidus	AP,B,RM
Penstemon nudiflorus	B,SW
Penstemon oliganthus	B,SW
Penstemon ophianthus	B,SW
Penstemon ovatus	AP,B,C,JE,P,SA,SC,SG,T
Penstemon pachyphyllus	B,SW
Penstemon pallidus	B,CG,HU,PR,SC
Penstemon palmeri	B,CA,CG,HU,NO,SA,SW
Penstemon 'Papal Purple'	C,P
Penstemon parryi	B,JE,SW
Penstemon parryi x superbus	SW
Penstemon paysoniorum	B,RM
Penstemon PCHA148	P
Penstemon perfoliatus	CG
Penstemon petiolatus	SW

PENSTEMON

Penstemon pinifolius	AP,B,G,JE,KL,NO,SW
Penstemon pinifolius 'Mersea Yellow'	AP,JE,KL
Penstemon platyphyllus	B,SW
Penstemon Prize Strain	DT,L
Penstemon procerus	AP,B,C,JE,KL,NO,RM, SG
Penstemon pseudospectabilis	B,NO,SW
Penstemon pubescens see P.hirsutus	
Penstemon pumilus	RM
Penstemon pygmaea	CG
Penstemon 'Rainbow' mix	C
Penstemon ramaleyi	RM
Penstemon ramosus	B,SW
Penstemon rattani	AP,B
Penstemon richardsonii	AP,B,C,G,HP,JE,SC
Penstemon roezlii see P.laetus v roezlii	
Penstemon rupicola	AP,KL,SC,SG
Penstemon rydbegii	AP,NO,SW
Penstemon 'Schoenholzeri'(Firebird)	B,P
Penstemon scouleri see P.fruticosus v scouleri	
Penstemon secundiflorus	AP,CG,RM
Penstemon sepalulus	B,SW
Penstemon serrulatus	AB,AP,B,C,CG,G,JE,SG
Penstemon 'Six Hills'	KL
Penstemon smallii	AP,B,HU,NT
Penstemon sp	AP,KL,LN,RS,SC,T
Penstemon sp dw alpine mix	Pl
Penstemon speciosus v kennedyi	AP,RM
Penstemon spectabilis	B,SW
Penstemon stenophyllus	B,SW
Penstemon strictus	AP,B,BS,C,DE,F,JE,KI, KL,NO,RM,SA,SC,SG, ST,SW,T
Penstemon subglaber	B,HU
Penstemon subulatus	B,SW
Penstemon superbus	B,SW
Penstemon tenuis	B
Penstemon teucrioides	AP,RM
Penstemon thompsoniae	AP,B,SW
Penstemon thurberi	B,DD,SW
Penstemon triphyllus	AP,NO
Penstemon un-named sp	T
Penstemon utahensis	B,JE,KL,SA,SC,SW
Penstemon utahensis 'Alba'	B,JE,SA
Penstemon venustus	AP,B,C,CG,JE,NO,SC
Penstemon Victorian mix	U
Penstemon virens	AP,RM
Penstemon virgatus	AP,RM,SA
Penstemon virgatus ssp arizonicus	AP,B,SC,SW
Penstemon virgatus ssp putus	B,SW
Penstemon virgatus ssp virgatus	B,SW
Penstemon watsonii	B,SW
Penstemon whippleanus	AP,B,CG,G,JE,KL,NO, RM,SA,SC,SW
Penstemon wilcoxii	NO
Penstemon wislizenii	B,MA,SW
Penstemon x edithae	P
Pentachondra pumila	AU,B,SS,SW
Pentaclethra macrophylla	B
Pentadiplandra brazzeana	B
Pentaglottis sempervirens	HP
Pentagonia grandiflora aff	B
Pentanisia sp	SI
Pentapeltis peltigera	B,NI
Pentaphylloides davurica	SG
Pentaphylloides fruticosa	SG

Pentarrhinum insipidum	B,SI
Pentas Egyptian Star Red	PL
Pentas lanceolata New Look	C,CL,D,J,MO,PK
Pentas New Look s-c	B,C
Penthorum sedoides	B,DV,PR,SG
Pentzia elegans	BH
Pentzia grandiflora	B,KB,KS
Pentzia incana	B,SI
Pentzia pilulifera	B,SI
Pentzia 'Pincushion'	B,BS,KI,SU
Pentzia sp	SI
Pentzia suffruticosa	B,BH,C,SI
Peperomia maculosa	C
Peperomia pellucida	B
Peperomia retusa	B,SI
Pereskia acutifolia	B
Perezia multiflora	SG
Perezia recurvata	AP,AU,KL,PM
Pergularia daemia v daemia	B,SI
Pericallis 'Amigo'	B,BS,MO
Pericallis 'Brilliant'	CL
Pericallis 'Chloe'	CL
Pericallis 'Cindy'	CL,D
Pericallis 'Cupid'	BS,SK
Pericallis 'Daruma'	B
Pericallis 'Dutch Master'	B
Pericallis 'Erfut' dw finest mix	C,CA
Pericallis f1 'Grandiflora Nana Elite'	SK
Pericallis 'Feltham Star'	B
Pericallis 'Gay' mix	V
Pericallis 'Giant Rainbow'	B
Pericallis hybridus 'Dw. British Beauty'	T
Pericallis 'Jubilee'	BD,BS,MO
Pericallis lanata	HP,RS
Pericallis 'Melody Picotee'	SE
Pericallis 'Meteor'	YA
Pericallis mix hyb	FR
Pericallis 'Palette' mix	FR
Pericallis 'Rasse Moll'	BS
Pericallis 'Royalty'	CL
Pericallis 'Sandor' s-c,mix	B,L
Pericallis 'Sox Blue'	YA
Pericallis 'Sox Pink'	YA
Pericallis 'Spring Glory'	BS,FM
Pericallis 'Star Wars'	B,CL,MO,YA
Pericallis 'Starbright'	U
Pericallis 'Starlet' mini mix	C,MO
Pericallis 'Supernova'	YA
Pericallis 'Tourette' mix	CA
Pericalymma elliptica	B,NI
Perideridia kelloggii	DD
Perideridia parishii	B
Perilla frutescens	CP,DD
Perilla frutescens 'Atropurpurea'	B,CP,KI,KS,PK
Perilla frutescens 'Macrobiotic'	B
Perilla frutescens v crispa	B,YA
Perilla frutescens v crispa laciniata	C,CL,MO
Periploca graeca	C,CG,HP,NG,SA,T
Perityle incana	B
Perotis indica	B
Perovskia atriplicifolia	B,DE,JE,SA
Persea americana	B,LN
Persicaria bistorta	AP,B,C,HU,JE,SA,SG
Persicaria bistorta 'Superba'	B,HP
Persicaria bistortoides	B
Persicaria capitata	I,JO

PERSICARIA

Persicaria capitata 'Afghan'	C,J
Persicaria capitata 'Victory Carpet'	B,BS,D,MO,PK,SK
Persicaria macrophyllum	B
Persicaria milletii	B,HP,JE,SA
Persicaria orientale	B,C,DI
Persicaria virginiana	B
Persicaria virginiana 'Variegatum'	B
Persoonia caleyi	B,EL,NI,O
Persoonia comata	B,NI,O
Persoonia cornifolia	B,EL,NI,O
Persoonia curvifolia	O
Persoonia elliptica	B,NI,O
Persoonia gunnii	B,NI,O
Persoonia laevis	B,EL,HA,NI,O,SA
Persoonia lanceolata	B,O
Persoonia linearis	B,EL,HA,NI,O
Persoonia longifolia	B,NI,O
Persoonia mollis	HA
Persoonia oxycoccoides	HA
Persoonia pinifolia	B,EL,HA,NI,O,SA
Persoonia saccata	B,NI
Persoonia sylvatica	HA
Persoonia teretifolia	B,NI,O
Persoonia tortifolia	B,NI,O
Persoonia virgata	B,HA
Perymenium strigillosum	B
Petalostemon see Dalea	
Petalostigma pubescens	B,NI
Petalostigma quadriloculare	B,NI
Petalostylis labicheoides	B,HA,NI
Petasites albus	CG,G,SG
Petasites frigidus	B,DD
Petasites frigidus v palmatus	AB
Petasites hybridus	B,JE,SA,SG
Petasites rubellus	SG
Petiveria sp	SG
Petopentia natalensis	B
Petrea volubilis	B,C,CA,DD,SA
Petrocoptis glaucifolia	AP,B,G,JE,SC
Petrocoptis pyrenaica	AP,B,HP,KL,SC
Petrocoptis pyrenaica ssp glaucifolia	HP
Petrophile biloba	AU,B,NI,O
Petrophile canescens	AU,B,NI,O
Petrophile carduacea	B,NI
Petrophile divaricata	B,NI,O
Petrophile diversifolia	B,NI,O,SA
Petrophile ericifolia	B,NI
Petrophile fastigiata	B,NI
Petrophile heterophylla	B,NI
Petrophile incurvata	B,NI
Petrophile linearis	B,NI
Petrophile longifolia	B,NI,O
Petrophile macrostachya	B,NI
Petrophile pulchella	B,HA,NI,O
Petrophile scabriuscula	B,NI
Petrophile serruriae	B,NI,O
Petrophile sessilis	B,EL,HA,NI,O,SA
Petrophile shuttleworthiana	B,NI
Petrophile squamata	B,NI
Petrophile striata	B,NI
Petrophile teretifolia	B,NI
Petrophile trifida	B
Petrophytum caespitosum	AP,B,JE,KL,RM,SC,SW
Petrophytum cinerascens	AP,I
Petrorhagia nanteuillii	B,NS,TH
Petrorhagia prolifera	AP,CG,SG
Petrorhagia saxifraga	AP,B,BS,BY,C,G,HP,I, JE,KI,KL,MO,SA,SC,SG
Petroselinum crispum	B,CP,DD,TH
Petteria ramentacea	B,HP,SA
Petunia axillaris	SG
Petunia axillaris 'Rainmaster'	DI,F
Petunia 'Babylon Pink'	R
Petunia 'Babylon Purple'	R
Petunia 'California Girl'	CL
Petunia 'Cavalcade' mix	BS
Petunia 'Cloud Snow'	B,BS,CL,KI
Petunia 'Coral Satin'	BS
Petunia 'Dreams' mix p.s	MO
Petunia 'Electra'	BS
Petunia f1 'Birthday Celebration'	S
Petunia f1 Blue & White Lace	U
Petunia f1 'Brass Band'	BS
Petunia f1 'Buttercream'	SE,U
Petunia f1 'Chiffon Morn'	DT,SE,SK,V,VY
Petunia f1 'Devon Cream' mix	SE,U
Petunia f1 'Eagle' p.s.	YA
Petunia f1 'Explorer' s-c	YA
Petunia f1 Global Grandiflora	T
Petunia f1 grandiflora 'Starburst'	BY
Petunia f1 mix Unwins fine	U
Petunia f1 'Niagara Mix'	D,L
Petunia f1 'Petunia Collection'	U
Petunia f1 'Pink Passion Mix'	U
Petunia f1 'Polo Rose Flare'	U
Petunia f1 'Prism Sunshine'	BS,DT,M,S,T,U,YA
Petunia f1 'Reflections' mix	BS,J,KI
Petunia f1 'Rose Star'	KI
Petunia f1 'Serene' mix	S
Petunia f1 'Starfire' mix	J
Petunia f1 'Strawberry Tart'	D
Petunia f1 'Summer Morn'	D
Petunia f1 'Summer Serenade'	J,TU
Petunia f1 'Summer Stars'	T,U
Petunia f1 'Summertime Carpet'	F
Petunia f1 'Super Magic'	BS,CA,KI
Petunia f1 'Traum Series'	V
Petunia f1 'Victoria Falls Mix'	U
Petunia f1 'Wave Pink'	DT,SE,SK,T,U,VY
Petunia f1 'Wave Pink' p.s	D
Petunia f1 'Wave Purple'	DT,PI,S,SE,SK,T,U,VY
Petunia f1 'Wave Purple' p.s	D
Petunia f1 'White Swan'	T
Petunia f2 Balcony Choice	BS,DT,F
Petunia f2 'Carnival'	BS,KI,VH
Petunia f2 Colorama Bedding	B,BD,BS,DN,DT,L,MO, VY
Petunia f2 Compact Choice	BS,S
Petunia f2 'Fancy Pants'	D,S
Petunia f2 'Stars & Stripes'	BS,F
Petunia 'Festival' mix	CL
Petunia 'Frosty' s-c,mix	BS
Petunia 'Galaxy' mix	BS,YA
Petunia 'Glitters'	BS
Petunia grandiflora 'Calypso'	BU
Petunia grandiflora 'Countdown' s-c/mix	PK
Petunia grandiflora f'Polaris' mix	BS,R
Petunia grandiflora f1 'Aladdin' mix	DT,F,MO,SK
Petunia grandiflora f1 'Aladdin' s-c	B,BS,MO,SK
Petunia grandiflora f1 'All Double Dwarf'	C
Petunia grandiflora f1 'Ballet'	BU
Petunia grandiflora f1 'Blue Danube'	SK

PETUNIA

Petunia grandiflora f1 'Caprice' — SK
Petunia grandiflora f1 'Cascade' dbl s-c — B,BS,CA,DT,F,MO,PK, SK,T
Petunia grandiflora f1 'Cherry Frost' — SK
Petunia grandiflora f1 'Cloud Blue' — B,BS,BU,KI,MO
Petunia grandiflora f1 'Cloud' mix — BS,CL,KI,MO
Petunia grandiflora f1 'Cloud Orchid' — B,BS,CL,KI,MO
Petunia grandiflora f1 'Cloud Pink' — B,BS,BU,CL,KI,MO
Petunia grandiflora f1 'Cloud Red' — B,BS,BU,CL,KI,MO,SK
Petunia grandiflora f1 'Cloud Rose' — B,BS,CL,MO
Petunia grandiflora f1 'Cloud Salmon' — B,BS,CL,KI,MO
Petunia grandiflora f1 'Cloud Snow' — SK
Petunia grandiflora f1 'Daddy' mix — BD,BS,CA,CL,D,DT,F, J,KI,L,M,MO,SE,SK,YA
Petunia grandiflora f1 'Daddy' s-c — BS,CL,F,MO,SE,SK,T,VH
Petunia grandiflora f1 'Dreams' mix — BS,DT,J,KI,MO,SK,T
Petunia grandiflora f1 'Dreams' s-c — BS,L,MOSK,
Petunia grandiflora f1 'Duet' — SK
Petunia grandiflora f1 'Express Series' — CL
Petunia grandiflora f1 'Falcon Blue Imp' — B,BS,MO
Petunia grandiflora f1 'Falcon Burgundy' — B,BS,MO,SK
Petunia grandiflora f1 'Falcon' coral — SK
Petunia grandiflora f1 'Falcon' dp rose — SK
Petunia grandiflora f1 'Falcon Lilac' — B,BS,MO,SK
Petunia grandiflora f1 'Falcon Mid-blue' — B,BS,MO,S,SK
Petunia grandiflora f1 'Falcon' mix — BS,MO,S,SK
Petunia grand. f1 'Falcon Pastel Salmon' — S,SK
Petunia grandiflora f1 'Falcon Pink Morn' — B,BS,MO,SK
Petunia grandiflora f1 'Falcon Pink Veined' — B,BS,CA,SK
Petunia grandiflora f1 'Falcon' plum vein — SK
Petunia grandiflora f1 'Falcon Red' — B,BS,MO,S,SK
Petunia grandiflora f1 'Falcon Red Morn' — B,BS,CA,F,MO,S,SK
Petunia grandiflora f1 'Falcon' red star — SK
Petunia grandiflora f1 'Falcon' red veined — SK
Petunia grandiflora f1 'Falcon Red/White' — B,BS,CA,MO
Petunia grandiflora f1 'Falcon Rose' — B,BS,CA,MO,SK
Petunia grandiflora f1 'Falcon Salmon' — B,BS,CA,MO,S,SK
Petunia grandiflora f1 'Falcon' white — SK
Petunia grandiflora f1 'Flamenco' — SK
Petunia grandiflora f1 'Frost Blue' — S
Petunia grandiflora f1 'Frost Mix' — F
Petunia grandiflora f1 'Frost Red' — F
Petunia grandiflora f1 Giant Victorious Mix — F
Petunia grandiflora f1 Glorious dbl mix — BD,BS,BU,DT,KI,MO, YA,SK
Petunia grandiflora f1 'Happiness' — SK
Petunia grandiflora f1 Harmony mix — CL
Petunia grandiflora f1 'Hulahoop' mix — BS,DT,L,MO,PK,SK,YA
Petunia grandiflora f1 'Hulahoop' s-c — BS,MO,PK,SK,YA
Petunia grandiflora f1 'Ice Series' — BS,CL
Petunia grandiflora f1 'Lady Purple' — C,T
Petunia grandiflora f1 'Lyric' — SK
Petunia grandiflora f1 mix — FR
Petunia grandiflora f1 picotee mix — BS,C,D,J,KI,MO,SE, ST,T,TU
Petunia grandiflora f1 picotee s-c — BS,CA
Petunia grandiflora f1 'Pirouete Purple' — BS,CL,D,MO,PK,SK
Petunia grandiflora f1 'Pirouete Rose' — CL,D,MO,PK,SK
Petunia grandiflora f1 'Plum Vein' — SK
Petunia grandiflora f1 'Polaris' s-c — BS
Petunia grandiflora f1 'Polaris' veined s-c — BS
Petunia grandiflora f1 'Razzle Dazzle' — BS,CA,CO,D,J,KI,MO,S
Petunia grandiflora f1 'Sonata' — SK
Petunia grandiflora f1 'Storm Lavender' — B,BS,CL,KS,MO,O,PK, S,SE,SK,U
Petunia grandiflora f1 'Storm' mix — U

Petunia grandiflora f1 'Storm Pink' — B,BS,CL,MO,SK,U
Petunia grandiflora f1 'Storm Salmon' — B,BS,MO,SK
Petunia grandiflora f1 'Storm Snow White' — B,BS,U
Petunia grandiflora f1 'Super Cascade' dbl — BD,BS,CA,CO,DT,F,KI, KS,M,MC,MO,SE,SK, ST,T,U,YA
Petunia grandiflora f1 'Ultra' mix — BD,MO
Petunia grandiflora f1 'Ultra' mix p.s — BD,MO
Petunia grandiflora f1 'Ultra Series' s-c — BS,CA,CN,MO,SK
Petunia grandiflora f1 'Ultra Star' mix/s-c — BS,CA,MO,SK,T
Petunia grandiflora f1 'Valentine' — SK
Petunia grandiflora f1 'Aladdin' Series p.s — MO
Petunia grandiflora f2 'Colour Parade' — BS,C,CA,MO,SK
Petunia grandiflora 'Flash' — BS,CA
Petunia grandiflora special mix — CL,UDT
Petunia grandiflora 'Yellow Magic' — BS,R,SK
Petunia grandiflora f1 'Falcon White' — B,BS,CA,MO,S
Petunia Highlight — BS
Petunia hybrida — SG
Petunia hybrida dw mix — HU
Petunia integrifolia — B
Petunia Kentucky old-fashioned — HU
Petunia 'Marshmallow' — BS,F,T
Petunia 'Mercury' — BS
Petunia milliflora f1 'Dreamcoat' — BS
Petunia milliflora f1 'Fantasy Blue' — BS,CL,D,MO,S,SE,SK
Petunia milliflora f1 'Fantasy Crystal' — BS,CL,D,KS,MO,S,SK
Petunia milliflora f1 'Fantasy Ivory' — BS,CL,D,KS,MO,S,SE, SK
Petunia milliflora f1 'Fantasy' mix — BS,C,CL,D,DT,F,KI,KS, J,MO,S,SE,SK,TU,U,VY
Petunia milliflora f1 'Fantasy Pink' — BS,CL,D,MO,S,SK
Petunia milliflora f1 'Fantasy Pink Morn' — BS,CL,D,KS,MO,PI,S, SE,SK,U
Petunia milliflora f1 'Fantasy Red' — BS,CL,D,MO,S,SE,SK,U
Petunia milliflora f1 'Fantasy Salmon' — BS,CL,D,MO,S,SE,SK
Petunia mix dw bedding — D
Petunia multiflora f1 'Bonanza' — BS,BU,J,KI,L,MO,R,SK, TU,V,YA
Petunia multiflora f1 'Carpet Buttercream' — BS,D,MO
Petunia multiflora f1 'Carpet' mix — BS,D,DT,F,J,L,MO,S,SE
Petunia multiflora f1 'Carpet' s-c — BS,F,L,MO,T
Petunia multiflora f1 'Celebrity' mix — BS,BU,CA,F,L,MO,PK, SE,SK,VY,YA
Petunia multiflora f1 'Celebrity' mix p.s — MO
Petunia multiflora f1 'Celebrity' s-c — BS,DT,F,MO,PK,SE,SK, T,YA
Petunia multiflora f1 'Cherry Tart' mix — J,SK
Petunia multiflora f1 dbl mix — FR,M,PK
Petunia multiflora f1 Delight mix dbl — CA,F,J,SE,T
Petunia multiflora f1 'Duo' mix dbl — BD,BS,CL,D,DT,F,KI, MO,S,SE,T,U,YA
Petunia multiflora f1 'Duo Series' s-c — BS,CL,MO,SE
Petunia multiflora f1 formula mix — C,DT,S,SE,ST
Petunia multiflora f1 'Frenzy Series' s-c — CL
Petunia multiflora f1 'Garden Party' mix — BS,J,MO
Petunia mult. f1 'Garden Party' s-c/ mix — BS
Petunia multiflora f1 'Heavenly Lavender' — CL,MO,SE,SK
Petunia multiflora f1 'Honey Bunch imp' — SK
Petunia mult. f1 'Horizon Laven. Sunrise' — DT
Petunia multiflora f1 'Joy' mix — BS,M,MO,SE
Petunia multiflora f1 'Joy' s-c — BS,BU,M
Petunia multiflora f1 'Merlin Picotee' mix — BS,CL,DT,KI,MO,SK, T,U,YA
Petunia multiflora f1 'Merlin' s-c — BS,MO,SK,YA
Petunia multiflora f1 'Mirage' mix — BS,CN,DT,F,MO

PETUNIA

Petunia multiflora f1 'Mirage Reflections'	BD,D,MO,S	Phacelia campanularia	AP,B,BS,BY,C,CA,CG,D,
Petunia multiflora f1 'Mirage Reflect.' p.s	BD,MO		DI,HU,J,KI,KS,MO,S,
Petunia multiflora f1 'Mirage Series' s-c	BS,CN,D,F,MO,YA		SK,SU,TH,TU,U,V
Petunia multiflora f1 'Pastel Salmon'	T	Phacelia campanularia 'Blue Wonder'	PK
Petunia multiflora f1 'Pearl Series'	BS,KI,MO	Phacelia cicutaria	B
Petunia multiflora f1 'Peppermint'	SK	Phacelia distans	B
Petunia multiflora f1 'Plum dbl'	SK	Phacelia grandiflora	B
Petunia multiflora f1 'Plum Pudding'	D,MO,S,U	Phacelia linearis	CG
Petunia multiflora f1 'Plum' s-c	BS,BU,MO,T	Phacelia minor	B
Petunia multiflora f1 'Polo Mix'	BS,T	Phacelia parryi	B,SW,V
Petunia multiflora f1 'Polo' s-c	BS	Phacelia parryi 'Royal Admiral'	PK
Petunia mult. f1 'Primetime Series' s-c	CA,CL,F,SK	Phacelia 'Sea Seventeen'	F
Petunia multiflora f1 'Resisto' mix	CL,CO,DT,J,KI,ST,TU	Phacelia sericea	AP,B,KL,RM,SC,SW
Petunia multiflora f1 'Satin & Silk'	S	Phacelia tanacetifolia	AB,B,BS,C,CG,CO,DD,
Petunia multiflora f1 'Stars'	SE,T		DI,FR,HU,KS,SC,SG,SP,
Petunia multiflora f1 'Summer Sun'	T		SU,V
Petunia multiflora f2 'Confetti' mix	F	Phacelia viscida	B
Petunia multiflora f2 Crown	BS,BY	Phaenocoma prolifera	B,C,SA,SI
Petunia multiflora f2 deluxe blend	BS,C,CL,MO	Phaeomeria magnifica pink	C
Petunia multiflora f2 mix	YA	Phagnalon helichrysoides	AP,B,I
Petunia multiflora f2 'Mosaic' mix	BS	Phagnalon rupestre	B
Petunia multiflora f2 'Star' mix	BS	Phagnalon saxatile	B,I
Petunia multiflora f2 super mix	BS	Phalaris aquatica cvs	B
Petunia multiflora o-p 'Celestial Rose'	C	Phalaris aquatica cw	B,HU
Petunia multiflora o-p 'Fire Chief'	C	Phalaris arundinacea	B,CA,HU,JE,SA
Petunia multiflora o-p 'Snowball'	C	Phalaris arundinacea 'Feesey'	I
Petunia multiflora 'Pow-Wow'	BU	Phalaris californica	B,HU
Petunia multiflora single mix	BS,R	Phalaris canariensis	B,C,CA,CN,DD,DE,JO,
Petunia multifora f2 'Rainbow'	J,KI,MC,PI,ST,SU,T,		MO,PI,SG,SU,V
	TU,VH	Phalaris minor	B
Petunia 'Nana Compacta Mix'	C,CO,J,V	Pharnaceum sp	SI
Petunia old-fashioned Shenandoah	HU	Phaseolus caracalla	DI
Petunia 'Orange Bells'	BS	Phaseolus sp	B,DD,JO
Petunia Pan-American all-dbl	BY	Phaseolus vulgaris	B,KL
Petunia Patio Collection	U	Phebalium filifolium	B
Petunia 'Peach Morn'	T	Phebalium tuberculosum	SA
Petunia 'Pearly Wave'	T	Phebalium tuberc. ssp tuberculosum	B,NI
Petunia pendula mix	BS,C,FR	Phellandrum aquaticum	SG
Petunia Pendulina mix	F	Phellodendron amurense	A,C,CG,EL,FW,LN,RE,
Petunia picotee red	CL,S		SA
Petunia 'Resisto' dw	BS	Phellodendron chinense	B
Petunia 'Rosette' mix	CL	Phellodendron lavallei	B,DD
Petunia 'Rosy Wave'	T	Phellodendron sachalinense	B
Petunia sp	AB,AP	Phemeranthus calycinus	B
Petunia 'Stardust' mix	BS	Phemeranthus longipes	B
Petunia 'Superbissima' mix	BS,FR	Pherosphaera hookerana	B
Petunia 'Vogue'	U	Philadelphus coronarius	B
Peucedanum austriacum	SG	Philadelphus inodorum	B
Peucedanum caffrum	B,SI	Philadelphus lewisii	B,C,LN,NO,SG
Peucedanum capense	B,SI	Philadelphus microphyllus	B,SW
Peucedanum ferulaceum	B,SI	Philadelphus new hyb	B
Peucedanum galbanum	B,SI	Philadelphus tenuifolius MW127R	X
Peucedanum morisonii	SG	Philippicereus castaneus	Y
Peucedanum officinalis	B,JE	Phillyrea angustifolia	LN,SA,VE
Peucedanum oreoselinum	SG	Phillyrea latifolia	SA,SG,VE
Peucedanum ostruthium	B,G,HP,JE,SA	Phillyrea media see P.latifolia	
Peucedanum ruthenicum	SG	Philodendron adamantinum	B
Peucedanum sp	SI	Philodendron 'Angra Dos Reis'	B,EL
Peucedanum thodei	B,SI	Philodendron 'Barryi'	B
Peucedanum venutum	B	Philodendron bipinnatifidum	B,BS,CA,CL,EL,HA,SA
Peucedanum verticillare	B,G,HP,JE,SA	Philodendron bipinnatifidum 'Compactum'	B
Peucephyllum schottii	B	Philodendron bipinnatifidum 'Sao Paolo'	B
Pfeiffera ianthothele	DV,Y	Philodendron bipinnatifidum 'Uruguay'	B
Pfeiffera multigona	Y	Philodendron cannifolium	B,EL,HA
Phacelia bipinnatifida	AP,KL,NT	Philodendron colombianum	B
Phacelia bolanderi	AP,B,DD,HP,SZ	Philodendron cordatum	B,EL

PHILODENDRON

Philodendron crassinervium	B
Philodendron cymbispathum	B
Philodendron eichleri	B
Philodendron erubescens	B
Philodendron 'Evansii'	B,CA
Philodendron eximium	B
Philodendron fragrans	B,EL
Philodendron giganteum	B
Philodendron hastatum of gdns	B,CA,HA
Philodendron hyb	B
Philodendron imbe	B,CA,EL
Philodendron lundii	B,CA,CL,EL
Philodendron mamei	B
Philodendron martianum	B
Philodendron mello-barretoanum	B
Philodendron ornatum	B
Philodendron pseudoradiatum	B
Philodendron radiatum	B
Philodendron rubrinervum	B
Philodendron saxicolum	B
Philodendron scandens	B
Philodendron scandens ssp oxycardium	B
Philodendron selloum	CA,EL,MO,SA,SK
Philodendron speciosum	B
Philodendron tuxla	B,CA,EL,HA
Philodendron undulatum	B
Philodendron wendlandii	B
Philodendron williamsii	B
Philotheca slasolifolia	HA
Phlebodium see Polypodium	
Phleum arenarium	B
Phleum hirsutum	SG
Phleum phleoides	B,SG
Phleum pratense	B,C,DE,SA,SG
Phleum pratense ssp bertolonii	B
Phlomis cashmeriana	B,C,HP,JE,SA
Phlomis chrysophylla	SA,SG
Phlomis crinita	SA
Phlomis fruticosa	B,BH,BS,C,HP,HU,JE, SA,SC,SG
Phlomis herba-venti	B,SG
Phlomis italica	AP,HP
Phlomis longifolia	SA
Phlomis lychnitis	B,SA
Phlomis purpurea	B,SA
Phlomis russeliana	AP,B,BS,C,F,G,HP,JE,KI, P,SA,SC,SG,SZ,T
Phlomis samia h see P.russeliana	
Phlomis tuberosa	AP,B,G,HP,JE,SA,SC,SG
Phlomis viscosa see P.russeliana	
Phlox amoena h see P.x procumbens	
Phlox carolina	B
Phlox carolina 'Bill Baker'	HP
Phlox decussata	BY,CO,KI,ST
Phlox decussata hyb	BS,SK
Phlox divaricata	B,SC
Phlox drummondii	B,BY,CG,HW,PI,R,SG, TH
Phlox drummondii 'African Sunset'	B,BS,C,CO,J,KI,KS, MO,PL,S,TU,U
Phlox drummondii 'Beauty' mix	BS,BU,C,CA,CL,DE, DN,L,MO,S,SE,VY,YA
Phlox drummondii 'Blue Beauty'	BS,V
Phlox drummondii 'Bright Eyes'	D,S,SE
Phlox drummondii 'Brilliancy'	F
Phlox drummondii 'Cecily'	F,PK

Phlox drummondii 'Chanal'	B,BS,C,CL,D,DT,J,KI,KS, MO,YA
Phlox drummondii Choice mix	BD,C
Phlox drummondii 'Coral Reef'	BS,DT,F,PK,SE
Phlox drummondii 'Crystal' Series	B,BS,MO
Phlox drummondii 'Dolly' s-c	B,SK
Phlox drummondii 'Dolly' Series mix	BS,MO,SK
Phlox drummondii dw mix	FR,J,SK,ST,V
Phlox drummondii dw s-c	SK
Phlox drummondii f2 'Ethnie' mix	B,BS,CL,DE,MO
Phlox drummondii 'Fantasy' mix	BD,BS,CN,DT,F,MO,SE
Phlox drummondii 'Globe' mix	SK
Phlox drummondii 'Grandiflora Brilliant'	C
Phlox drummondii 'Grandiflora Cinnabar'	B
Phlox drummondii 'Grandiflora Coccinea'	B
Phlox drummondii 'Grandiflora Leopoldii'	B,DT
Phlox drummondii 'Grandiflora' mix	BS,SK,TU
Phlox drummondii 'Hazy Days'	D
Phlox drummondii lge fl	CO,DT,S
Phlox drummondii 'Masterpiece'	BS,KI,ST
Phlox drummondii 'Nana Compacta Mix'	BS,KI,SU
Phlox drummondii 'Palona'	BS,DT,F,MO
Phlox drummondii 'Phlox of Sheep'	B,BD,BS,KS,MO,T,V
Phlox drummondii 'Promise Peach'	B,BS,C,MO
Phlox drummondii 'Promise Pink'	B,BS,MO,PK,U
Phlox drummondii 'Tapestry'	D,F
Phlox drummondii 'Twinkles'	B,BD,BS,BY,C,DE,DT,J, KI,KS,L,MO,SK,SV,V
Phlox drummondii 'Twinkling Stars'	D,F,VY
Phlox nivalis	B
Phlox paniculata	AP,C,G,HP,PK,SA,V
Phlox paniculata new hybrids	B,BS,CN,DE,JE,L
Phlox pilosa	B,JE,PR
Phlox stolonifera	B
Phlox 'Tutti Frutti'	U
Phlox viscida	NO
Phlox x arendsii newest hybrids	JE
Phlox x procumbens	B
Phoenix acaulis	B,EL,HA,O,SA
Phoenix canariensis	B,C,CA,CG,DD,EL,FW, HA,HP,O,S,SA,V,VE,WA
Phoenix dactylifera	B,C,CA,EL,FW,HA,O,SA, VE,WA
Phoenix dactylifera 'Midjool'	B,EL
Phoenix hanceana	B,O
Phoenix hyb	B
Phoenix loureiri	DV
Phoenix paludosa	B,O
Phoenix pusilla	B,O
Phoenix reclinata	B,C,CA,EL,HA,O,SA,SI, VE
Phoenix roebelinii	B,C,CA,EL,HA,O,RE,SA, SG,VE
Phoenix rupicola	B,C,CA,EL,HA,O,SA
Phoenix sylvestris	B,CA,DV,EL,SA
Pholiota aegerita d.m.p	B
Pholistoma auritum	B
Phormium colensoi see P.cookianum	
Phormium cookianum	A,AP,AU,B,C,HP,LG,SA, SC,SG,VE
Phormium cookianum hyb pink striped	B
Phormium cookianum ssp hookeri	HP
Phormium cookianum 'Tricolor'	B,SA
Phormium 'Dazzler'	HP
Phormium 'Sundower'	HP
Phormium tenax	A,AP,B,C,CA,DV,EL,HA,

PHORMIUM

	HP,JE,RH,SA,SG,SS,VE
Phormium tenax 'Bronze'	B,C,CA
Phormium tenax Purpureum Group	B,BS,C,EL,HA,HP,KI,SA, T,VE
Phormium tenax 'Purpureum Select Red'	B
Phormium tenax 'Rainbow'	EL,T
Phormium tenax 'Red Edge'	C
Phormium tenax 'Variegatum'	AP,B,BS,CA,EL,HA,HU, N,SA,SC,VE
Phormium tenax 'Yellow Wave'	C,HP,PM
Photinia amphidoxa	SG
Photinia arbutifolia	B,C,CA,SA,SG
Photinia davidiana	B,SA
Photinia davidsoniae	C,LN,SG
Photinia lasiogyna	SG
Photinia melanocarpa	SG
Photinia serratifolia	B,CA,HA,LN,SA,WA
Photinia villosa	LN,SG
Phragmites australis	C,HA,JE,SA
Phuopsis stylosa	B,BS,C,G,HP,JE,KI,SA, SC,SG,V
Phygelius aequalis	AP,B,HP,SA,SG,SI
Phygelius aequalis 'Yellow Trumpet'	AP,B,HP,JE
Phygelius capensis	AP,B,C,CG,DE,G,HP,JE, SA,SI
Phygelius x rectus 'African Queen'	C,HP,PL
Phyla nodiflora	B
Phylica buxifolia	B,SI
Phylica callosa	B,SI
Phylica cryptandroides	B,SI
Phylica ericifolia	BH
Phylica oleifolia	SI
Phylica plumosa	B,C,SA,SI
Phylica pubescens	KB
Phylica purpurea	B,KB
Phylica sp mix	BH
Phylica stipularis	B,SI
Phyllacne colensoi	B,SS
Phyllanthus acidus	B
Phyllanthus amarus	B
Phyllanthus calycinus	B,NI,SA
Phyllanthus emblica	B,HA
Phyllanthus grandifolius	SG
Phyllanthus polyphyllus	B
Phyllanthus reticulatus	B
Phyllobolus sp	SI
Phyllocarpus septentrionalis	B
Phyllocladus alpinus	B
Phyllocladus aspleniifolius	O,SA
Phyllocladus aspleniifolius v alpinus	AU
Phyllocladus trichomanoides	B
Phyllodoce caerulea	C,SC
Phyllodoce empetriformis	NO
Phyllostachys edulis	B
Phyllostachys pubescens	SA
Phymaspermum acerosum	B,KB
Phymatocarpus maxwellii	AU,B,NI
Physalis alkekengi	AB,B,C,CG,CL,DD,DI,F, HU,PK,SG,VY
Physalis alkekengi 'Pygmaea'	B
Physalis edulis	BH,BS
Physalis franchetii	BD,BH,BS,BY,C,CO,D, DE,DT,GO,J,JE,JO,KI, MO,PI,SK,TH,U
Physalis franchetii 'Gigantea'	CN,JE,L,S,SA,SU,V
Physalis heterophylla	B

Physalis ixocarpa	B,CG,CP
Physalis minima	B
Physalis peruviana	B,C,DD,SG,ST
Physalis peruviana 'Gigantea'	DD,T
Physalis peruviana 'Goldenberry'	DD
Physalis philadelphica	W
Physalis philadelphica 'Purple De Milpa'	B
Physalis phil. 'Tepehuan Tomatillo'	B
Physalis pruinosa	B,DD
Physalis subglabrata	B
Physaria acutifolia	B,SW
Physaria alpestris	AP,C
Physaria newberryi	B,SW
Physocarpus capitatus	DD
Physocarpus malvaceus	NO
Physocarpus opulifolius	B,C,FW,PR,SA,SG
Physocarpus ribesifolius	SG
Physochliana orientalis	AP,JE
Physoplexis comosa	AP,C,G,JE,KL,SC
Physopsis lachnostachya	B,HU,NI
Physostegia digitalis	B
Physostegia virginiana	AB,B,BS,DD,HP,KI,PR, SA,KI,T,TH
Physostegia virginiana 'Alba'	AP,CG,G,HP,JE,SA,SC, SG,SK
Physostegia virginiana grandiflora 'Rosea'	CN,JE,MO
Physostegia virginiana New Hybrids	B
Physostegia virginiana 'Rose Crown'	B,C,DE,F
Physostegia virginiana 'Rose Spire'	B,SK
Physostegia virginiana 'Schneekrone'	B,BS,C,CL,CN,D,DE, DT,F,HP,HU,JE,L,MO, PK,U,V
Physostegia virginiana speciosa	B,PR
Physostegia virginiana 'Summer Snow'	HP,T
Physostegia virginiana 'Vivid'	PK
Physostegia virginiana 'White Spire'	B
Phytelephas macrocarpa	B
Phyteuma balbisii see P.cordatum	
Phyteuma betonicifolium	B,C,G,SC
Phyteuma charmelii	AP,B,C,G,HP,KL,SC
Phyteuma cordatum	AP,C,SG
Phyteuma globulariifolius	B
Phyteuma hemisphaericus	AP,B,C,CG,HP,JE,SC,VO
Phyteuma nigrum	AP,C,G,HP,HU,JE,KL, RM,SA,SC,SG
Phyteuma orbiculare	AP,B,CG,G,JE,KL,SA,SG
Phyteuma ovatum	B,HP
Phyteuma scheuchzeri	AP,B,C,CG,G,JE,KL,SG
Phyteuma scheuchzeri ssp scheuchzeri	CG
Phyteuma sieberi	AP,CG,G,SC,VO
Phyteuma spicatum	AP,B,C,CG,DV,G,HU,I, JE,SG
Phyteuma spicatum 'Caeruleum'	B,JE
Phytolacca acinosa	AP,C,HU,JE
Phytolacca americana	B,C,CN,DV,HP,HU,JE, KL,RH,SA,Y
Phytolacca americana 'Yellow Berry'	B
Phytolacca dioica	B,C,DV,EL,LN,SA,VE, WA,Y
Phytolacca mexicana	SA
Phytolacca polyandra	B,HP
Piaranthus punctatus	B,C,Y
Picea abies	B,C,CG,EL,FW,LN,NO, SA,VE
Picea ajanensis	LN,SG
Picea asperata	B,CA,CG,EL,FW,LN,SA,

PICEA

	SG	Pilosocereus fulvilanatus	B,DV
Picea breweriana	B,C,FW,N,LN,SA,T,VE	Pilosocereus glaucescens	B,Y
Picea cembra	A	Pilosocereus glaucochrous	Y
Picea engelmannii	AB,B,C,CA,DD,EL,FW,	Pilosocereus luetzelburgii	Y
	LN,NO,SA,VE	Pilosocereus magnificus	B,DV,Y
Picea excelsa	BY,EL,LN,MO	Pilosocereus multicostatus	DV
Picea glauca	A,B,C,EL,FW,LN,SA,SG,	Pilosocereus pachycladus	DV,Y
	VE	Pilosocereus palmeri	DV,Y
Picea glauca 'Densata'	B,C,CA,FW,LN,SA	Pilosocereus pentaedrophorus	Y
Picea glauca v albertiana	B,FW,LN	Pilosocereus royenii	DV,Y
Picea glehnii	B,FW,LN,N,SA,SG	Pilosocereus werdermannianus	DV
Picea jezoensis	B,EL,FW,LN,N,SA,SG	Pimelea ammocharis	B,NI
Picea jezoensis v hondoensis	B,FW,LN,N,SA	Pimelea argentea	B,NI
Picea koraiensis see P.koyamae		Pimelea brevistyla	B,NI
Picea koyamae	B,C,EL,LN,SG	Pimelea ciliata	B,NI
Picea likiangensis	B,EL,FW,LN	Pimelea cocinna	B,SS
Picea lutzii	FW	Pimelea ferruginea	B,O
Picea mariana	B,C,FW,LN,SA	Pimelea floribunda	B,NI
Picea meyeri	B,CA,EL,FW,LN,N,SA	Pimelea glauca	B,NI,SA
Picea morinda	FW,HA	Pimelea holroydii	B,NI,SA
Picea obovata	B,FW,LN,SA	Pimelea imbricata	B,NI
Picea obovata v caerulea	B,FW,N	Pimelea imbricata ssp piligera	B,NI
Picea omorika	B,C,FW,LN,N,SA,VE	Pimelea imbricata v baxteri	B,NI
Picea omorika 'Fassei'	CG	Pimelea lehmanniana	B,NI
Picea orientalis	B,C,FW,LN,SA,VE	Pimelea linifolia	HA
Picea pungens	AB,B,NO,SG	Pimelea longiflora	B,NI,SA
Picea pungens f glauca	B,BS,C,CA,CG,EL,FW,	Pimelea microcephala	HA
	LN,N,SA,T,VE	Pimelea oreophylla	B,SS
Picea purpurea	B,EL,FW,LN	Pimelea physodes	B,C,NI,O,SA
Picea rubens	B,FW,LN,SA	Pimelea rosea	B
Picea schrenkiana	SA	Pimelea spectabilis	B,NI,O,SA
Picea schrenkiana ssp tianschanica	B,EL,FW,LN	Pimelea suaveolens	B,NI,O
Picea sitchensis	AB,B,C,EL,FW,LN,SA,VE	Pimelea sylvestris	B,NI,SA
Picea smithiana	B,CG,DD,LN,N,SA	Pimelea traversii	B,SS,SW
Picea wilsonii	B,CA,EL,FW,LN,SA	Pimenta dioica	B,CA
Picea x lutzii	B	Pimenta racemosa	B
Pickeringia montana	SA	Pimpinella anisum	B,BH,CN,CP,HU,KS
Picrasma quassioides	B,SA	Pimpinella major	B,HP,SG
Picris echioides	B,LA,NS	Pimpinella major 'Rosea'	AP,HP,LG
Picris echioides 'Teras'	B	Pimpinella saxifraga	B,C,CP,DD,G,JE,SA,SG
Picris hieracioides	SG	Pinanga barnesii	B,O
Pieranthus punctatum	CH	Pinanga coronata	B,O
Pieris floribunda	B,FW,KL,LN,SA	Pinanga dicksonii	B
Pieris formosa	RH,SG	Pinanga insignis	B,CA,O
Pieris japonica	B,C,CA,CG,FW,LN,RH,	Pinanga javana	B,O
	SA,VE	Pinanga kuhlii	CA,EL,O,RE,SA
Pieris japonica 'Yakushimanum'	B	Pinanga maculata	B,O
Pieris sp CNW377	X	Pinanga patula	B,O
Pigafetta filaris	O	Pinckneya pubens	B
Pilea involucrata	B,C,CA,SA	Pinellia ternata	AP,HP
Pilea involucrata 'Silver Tree'	B	Pinellia tripartita	AP,G,PM
Pileanthus filifolius	B	Pinguicula 'Agarra Mosca Violeta'	B,HU
Pileanthus peduncularis	B,O	Pinguicula agnata	B
Piliostigma thonningii	B,SI	Pinguicula alpina	B,C
Pillansia templemanii	B,SI	Pinguicula caerulea	B,DV
Pilosella aurantiaca	AP,B,C,CN,G,HP,HU,I,J	Pinguicula corsica	B,DV
	E,KL,NS,SA,SC,SU,T,TH	Pinguicula grandiflora	AP,B,DV,G,KL,PM,SC,Y
Pilosella officinarum	B,G,HU,JE,SC,SG,SU	Pinguicula grandiflora f pallida	B,DV
Pilosocereus alensis	B,DV,Y	Pinguicula grandiflora ssp grandiflora	B
Pilosocereus arrabidae	BC	Pinguicula grandiflora ssp rosea	B
Pilosocereus aurilanatus	DV,Y	Pinguicula gypsicola	B
Pilosocereus azureus	B,BC,DV,Y	Pinguicula ionantha	B
Pilosocereus bradei	BC,Y	Pinguicula jaumavensis	B
Pilosocereus braduii v horstii	DV	Pinguicula leptoceras	C
Pilosocereus brasiliensis ML407	BC	Pinguicula longifolia ssp longifolia	B
Pilosocereus chryostelle	B	Pinguicula lusitanica	B,DV

209

PINGUICULA

Pinguicula lutea — B
Pinguicula moranensis 'Cantil Del Tambor' — B
Pinguicula moranensis 'La Vuelta' — B
Pinguicula potosiensis — B
Pinguicula primuliflora — B,DV
Pinguicula villosa — RS
Pinguicula vulgaris — AP,B,C,CG,DV,SG,VO
Pinguicula vulgaris f bicolor — B
Pinguicula westonii — DV
Pinus albicaulis — B,FW,LN,N,NO
Pinus aristata — B,C,CA,FW,HU,LN,N, NO,SA,VE
Pinus armandii — B,C,CA,EL,FW,LN,SA
Pinus attenuata — B,CA,FW,LN,SA,VE
Pinus austriaca see P.nigra ssp nigra
Pinus ayacahuite — B,CA,SA
Pinus balfouriana — B,LN
Pinus banksiana — B,FW,HP,LN,N,SA
Pinus brutia see P.halepensis ssp brutia
Pinus brutia ssp eldarica — B
Pinus bungeana — B,C,CA,EL,FW,LN,SA
Pinus canariensis — B,C,CA,FW,HA,LN,SA, VE
Pinus caribaea — CA,SA
Pinus caribaea v bahamensis — B
Pinus caribaea v caribaea — B,LN,VE
Pinus caribaea v hondurensis — B,FW,LN
Pinus cembra — B,CA,CG,EL,FW,HU,LN, N,SA,VE
Pinus cembra ssp sibirica — B,LN,SA
Pinus cembra ssp sibirica 'Glauca' — B,FW
Pinus cembroides — B,DD,HU,LN
Pinus cembroides edulis see P.edulis
Pinus cembroides monophylla — FW,N,SA
Pinus cembroides remota — FW
Pinus clausa — B
Pinus contorta — B,CA,LN,NO,SA
Pinus contorta v contorta — AB,FW,VE
Pinus contorta v latifolia — AB,B,DD,EL,FW,LN,SA, SG,VE
Pinus contorta v murrayana — B,FW,LN
Pinus coulteri — B,C,CA,EL,FW,HU,LN, N,SA
Pinus densa — B
Pinus densiflora — B,C,CA,EL,FW,G,HU,LN, N,SA,VE
Pinus echinata — B,CA,FW,LN,SA,VE
Pinus edulis — AB,B,CA,DD,EL,FW,HU, LN,NO,VE
Pinus edulis v fallax — B
Pinus eldarica — CA,EL,FW,LN,SA,VE
Pinus elliottii — B,CA,EL,FW,LN,SA,WA
Pinus elliottii v elliottii — VE
Pinus engelmannii — B,EL,LN,SA
Pinus flexilis — AP,B,C,FW,G,LN,NO,SA
Pinus flexilis v reflexa — FW
Pinus gerardiana — A,FW,HA,LN,SA
Pinus glabra — B,CA,FW,LN
Pinus greggii — B,SA
Pinus halepensis — B,C,CA,CG,EL,FW,G,HA, KL,LN,SA,SG,VE,WA
Pinus halepensis reg — SA
Pinus halepensis ssp brutia — B,CA,CG,FW,LN,SA,VE
Pinus heldreichii — B,FW,LN,SA
Pinus incinata prostrata — CG
Pinus jeffreyi — B,CA,FW,LN,SA,VE

Pinus kesiya — B,LN,SA
Pinus khasyana — CA
Pinus koraiensis — A,CA,EL,FW,HU,LN,N, SA,SG
Pinus lambertiana — AB,B,CA,EL,FW,LN,SA, VE
Pinus laricio salzmannii — VE
Pinus leucodermis see P.heldreichiiv l.
Pinus massoniana — B,CA,EL,LN,N,SA,VE
Pinus maximartinezii — B,LN
Pinus maximinoi — B,LN
Pinus merkusii — B,SA
Pinus michoacana — LN,SA,VE
Pinus monophylla — B,CA,LN
Pinus montezumae — B,CA,EL,FW,LN,N,SA
Pinus monticola — AB,B,C,DD,FW,LN,NO, SA,VE
Pinus mugo — B,FW,LN,V,VO
Pinus mugo forms mix — N
Pinus mugo rostrata — FW
Pinus mugo ssp uncinata — B,CG,KL,SA
Pinus mugo v mughus see P.mugo v mugo
Pinus mugo v mugo — AP,B,CA,DV,EL,FW,HU, LN,SA,VE
Pinus mugo v pumilio — B,C,CA,EL,FW,LN,SA, T,VE
Pinus muricata — B,C,CA,FW,LN,SA,VE
Pinus nelsonii — LN,SA
Pinus nigra — CA,CG,EL,FW,LN,N
Pinus nigra poiretana — FW
Pinus nigra ssp laricio — B,FW,LN
Pinus nigra ssp nigra — B,CG,LN,SA,VE
Pinus nigra v austriaca see P.nigra ssp n.
Pinus nigra v calabrica — B,LN,SA,VE
Pinus nigra v caramanica see P.nigra ssp laricio
Pinus nigra v corsicana — LN,SA,VE
Pinus nigra v maritima — B,C
Pinus nigra v pyramidalis — B,FW,LN
Pinus nigra 'Villetta Barrea' — B
Pinus oocarpa — B,CA,LN,SA
Pinus pallasiana — LN,SA
Pinus pallassiana — SG
Pinus palustris — B,C,CA,FW,LN,SA,VE
Pinus parviflora — B,C,CA,EL,FW,HU,LN, N,SA,T,V,VE
Pinus parviflora f glauca — KL,X
Pinus patula — B,C,CA,EL,FW,HA,LN, SA,VE,WA
Pinus peuce — B,FW,LN,SA,SG
Pinus pinaster — B,C,CA,EL,FW,HA,LN, N,SA,SG,VE
Pinus pinea — A,B,C,CA,EL,FW,HA,KS, LN,N,SA,T,VE
Pinus pithyusa — B,LN,SA
Pinus ponderosa — AB,B,C,CA,DD,EL,FW, HU,LN,NO,SA,VE
Pinus ponderosa 'Rosebud' — B,FW
Pinus ponderosa ssp scopulorum — B,FW,SA
Pinus ponderosa timber — B
Pinus pseudostrobus — B,LN
Pinus pumila — B,C,CA,DD,EL,FW,HU, LN,N,SA,SG,VE
Pinus radiata — B,C,CA,EL,FW,HA,HU, LN,RH,SA,VE,WA
Pinus resinosa — B,FW,HP,LN,SA,VE
Pinus rigida — B,C,CA,FW,G,LN,SA

PINUS

Pinus roxburghii	B,CA,FW,HA,HU,LN,SA,WA
Pinus sabiniana	AB,B,CA,EL,FW,LN,SA
Pinus serotina	B,FW,SA
Pinus siberica glauca see P.cembra ssp s.'Glauca'	
Pinus sibirica	A,FW,LN,SG
Pinus sp mix	C
Pinus strobiformis	B,LN,SA
Pinus strobus	B,C,CA,CG,EL,FW,LN,N,SA,VE
Pinus sylvestris	B,C,CA,CG,EL,FW,LN,N,NO,SA,SG,VE
Pinus sylvestris v mongolica	B,EL,SA
Pinus sylvestris v rigensis	B
Pinus szemaonensis	B,EL,LN
Pinus tabuliiformis	B,C,EL,FW,LN,SA
Pinus taeda	B,CA,EL,FW,LN,SA
Pinus taiwanensis	EL,LN,SA
Pinus tecunumanii	B
Pinus tenuifolia	VE
Pinus thunbergii	B,C,CA,EL,FW,G,HU,LN,N,SA,T,V,VE
Pinus torreyana	B,CA,FW,LN,SA
Pinus uncinata see P.mugo ssp uncinata	
Pinus virginiana	B,CA,FW,LN,SA
Pinus wallichiana	B,CG,FW,LN,N,SC,VE
Pinus yunnanensis	B,EL,FW,LN,N,SA
Piper angustifolium	B
Piper augustum	B
Piper concepsionis	B
Piper guineense	B
Piper marginatum	B
Piper nigrum	B,RE,SA
Piptanthus nepalensis	AP,B,C,CG,HP,SA,SG
Pisolithus tinctorius	B
Pisonia umbellifera	B
Pistacia atlantica	B,CA,EL,LN,SA,VE
Pistacia chinensis	B,C,CA,EL,FW,HA,LN,SA
Pistacia lentiscus	SA,VE
Pistacia palaestina	B
Pistacia terebinthus	B,CG,SA,SG,VE
Pistacia texana	B
Pistacia vera	B,EL,LN,SA,VE
Pitcairnea angustifolia	DV
Pitcairnea carnea	DV
Pitcairnia andreana	CG
Pitcairnia corallina	B
Pitcairnia decidua	B
Pitcairnia flammea	B,DV
Pitcairnia flammea v floccosa	B
Pitcairnia heterophylla	B,SG
Pitcairnia integrifolia	B,DV
Pitcairnia morelii	B
Pitcairnia seidelii	B
Pitcairnia xanthocalyx	CG
Pithecellobium arboretum	B
Pithecellobium dulce	B,DD,EL,HA,LN,SA
Pithecellobium flexicaule	B,CA,CG,HU
Pithecellobium mangense	B
Pithecellobium mexicanum	DD
Pithecellobium saman	EL,SA
Pittosporum bicolor	B,NI,O,SA
Pittosporum crassifolium	B,C,CA,LN,SA,VE,WA
Pittosporum eugenoides	B,C,CA,O,SA
Pittosporum phillyreoides	B,C,CA,EL,HA,NI,O,SA

Pittosporum ralphii	B,C,CG,SA
Pittosporum revolutum	B,EL,HA,NI,O
Pittosporum rhombifolium	B,CA,EL,HA,NI,O,SA
Pittosporum tenuifolium	B,C,CA,HP,SA,SG,SS,VE
Pittosporum tenuifolium ssp colensoi	B
Pittosporum tobira	B,C,CA,CG,EL,FW,LN,O,SA,VE
Pittosporum turneri	CG
Pittosporum undulatum	B,BS,BY,C,CA,EL,HA,LN,NI,O,WA
Pittosporum viridiflorum	B,CA,LN,SA,SI,WA
Pityrodia loxocarpa	B,NI,SA
Pityrodia terminalis	B
Placospermum coriaceum	O,SA
Plagianthus divaricatus	B,C
Planchonella australis	B
Planchonella costata	B
Plantago affra	B
Plantago antartica	SG
Plantago argentea	B,C,HP,SG
Plantago asiatica 'Variegata'	AP,B,E,G,P
Plantago coronopus	B,G,KL,SG
Plantago grandiflora	P
Plantago insularis	B,CA,SG
Plantago lagopus	B
Plantago lanceolata	B,JE,LA,SG
Plantago lanceolata 'Ballydowling Varieg'	NS
Plantago latifolia 'Atropurpurea'	JE,SA
Plantago major	B,C,DD,SG,SI
Plantago major 'Atropurpurea' see P.m. 'Rubrifolia'	
Plantago major B&L12649	NG
Plantago major 'Frills'	NS
Plantago major 'Karmozijn'	E
Plantago major 'Rosularis'	B,C,E,G,HP,SC,TH
Plantago major 'Rosularis' Bowles variety	P
Plantago major 'Rubrifolia'	AP,B,BH,C,DD,E,G,HP,RH,SC,T
Plantago maritima	SC,SG
Plantago media	C,HP,SG,SU,TH
Plantago nivalis	AP,G,HP,JE,KL,P,SC,SG
Plantago patagonica	B
Plantago psyllium	B,DD
Plantago purshii	B,PR
Plantago raoulii	AP,KL,NG
Plantago salsa	SG
Plantago sempervirens	B,HP,SC
Plantago squalida	SG
Plantago triandra	P
Platanthera bifolia	B,SC,SG
Platanus acerifolia	CA,WA
Platanus mexicana	B
Platanus occidentalis	B,CA,FW,LN,SA
Platanus orientalis	B,C,CA,FW,HA,LN,SA
Platanus orientalis v digitata	HA
Platanus racemosa	B,CA,LN
Platanus racemosa v wrightii	CA,DV
Platanus wrightii	B,WA
Platanus x hispanica	B,SA
Platycarya strobilacea	LN,SA
Platycerium alcicorne h see bifurcatum	
Platycerium andinum	B
Platycerium bifurcatum	B,EL,SA
Platycerium elephantotis	DV
Platycerium grande h see P.superbum	
Platycerium hillii	B,DV
Platycerium mixed	C

PLATYCERIUM

Platycerium ridleyi	DV
Platycerium stemaria	DV
Platycerium superbum	B,EL,SA,SG
Platycerium wilhelminae-reginae	SA
Platycladus orientalis see Thuja	
Platycodon dk & light blue mix	HU
Platycodon f1 'Sentimental Blue'	B,BS,C,CL,HP,JE,KL,
	MO,PK,SK
Platycodon grandiflorus	AB,AP,BS,C,CG,CN,DV,
	G,HP,I,J,KL,LG,MO,PI,
	SC,SG,T,TH
Platycodon grandiflorus 'Alpinum'	B
Platycodon gr. apoyama 'Misato Purple'	JE
Platycodon grandiflorus 'Blaue Glocke'	JE
Platycodon grandiflorus f albus	AP,B,G,JE,KL,SG
Platycodon grandiflorus f apoyama	AP,G,KL,SC
Platycodon grandiflorus f1 'Astra Blue'	JE,YA
Platycodon grandiflorus f1 'Astra Pink'	JE,YA
Platycodon grandiflorus f1 'Astra White'	JE,YA
Platycodon grandiflorus 'Florist Blue'	B,C,HU,SA
Platycodon grandiflorus 'Florist' mix	C
Platycodon grandiflorus 'Florist Pink'	B,C,SA
Platycodon grandiflorus 'Florist White'	B,C,SA
Platycodon grandiflorus 'Fuji Blue'	JE,PK
Platycodon grandiflorus 'Fuji' mix	DE,PK,V
Platycodon grandiflorus 'Fuji Pink'	G,JE,PK
Platycodon grandiflorus 'Fuji White'	JE,PK,T
Platycodon grandiflorus 'Hakone Blue'	JE
Platycodon grandiflorus 'Hakone White'	JE
Platycodon grandiflorus hyb mix	JE
Platycodon grandiflorus 'Komachi'	B,PK,SK
Platycodon grandiflorus mariesii	AP,B,BS,C,CG,CN,G,HP,
	JE,KI,KL,SC,SU
Platycodon grandiflorus mariesii album	B,SC
Platycodon grandiflorus 'Mini Blue'	B
Platycodon grandiflorus 'Mini White'	B
Platycodon grandiflorus MW89R	X
Platycodon grandiflorus 'Park's Dble Blue'	B,C,PK
Platycodon grandiflorus 'Perlmutterschale'	B,JE,KL,T
Platycodon grandiflorus pumilum	KL
Platycodon grandiflorus 'Pygmy Blue'	D,S,T
Platycodon grandiflorus roseum	KL
Platycodon grandiflorus roseus	AP,HP
Platycodon grandiflorus 'Zwerg'	HP,JE
Platylobium formosum	B,HA
Platymiscium pinnatum	B
Platysace compressa	B,NI
Platystemon californica	SG,T,V
Plectranthus ciliatus	B,C,SI
Plectranthus dolichopodus	B,SI
Plectranthus ecklonii	B,SI
Plectranthus ecklonii 'Erma'	B,KB,SI
Plectranthus ecklonii 'Medleywood'	B,KB,SI
Plectranthus ecklonii tall blue	B,KB
Plectranthus ecklonii 'Tommy'	B,SI
Plectranthus elegantulus	B,SI
Plectranthus ernstii	B,SI
Plectranthus fruticosus	B,BH,SI
Plectranthus fruticosus 'James'	B,KB,SI
Plectranthus grallatus	B,SI
Plectranthus hadiensis	B,SI
Plectranthus hadiensis v tomentosus	B,SI
Plectranthus had. v tomentosus 'Carnegie'	KB
Plectranthus hereroensis	B,BH
Plectranthus hereroensis 'Witpoortjie'	KB
Plectranthus laxiflorus	B,SI

Plectranthus mandalensis	B,SI
Plectranthus oertendahlii	B
Plectranthus rehmannii	B,KB,SI
Plectranthus sp mix	BH,C
Plectranthus spicatus	SI
Plectranthus spicatus 'Nelspruit'	B,KB
Plectranthus verticillatus	B,SI
Plectranthus zuluensis	SI
Plectritis congesta	DD
Pleioblastus auricomus	B
Pleioblastus humilis v pumilus	B
Pleioblastus pygmaeus	B
Pleioblastus variegatus	B
Pleiogynium cerasiferum	EL,HA
Pleiogynium timorense	B,NI,O,SA
Pleione formosana	B,G
Pleione forrestii	B
Pleione limprichtii	AP,G,KL
Pleione 'Oriental Grace'	B
Pleione 'Shantung Ridgeway'	B
Pleione 'Versailles'	B,SC
Pleiospilos bolusii	B,DV,SI,Y
Pleiospilos compactus	B,DV,KB,SI
Pleiospilos compactus ssp canus	B,SI
Pleiospilos compactus ssp minor	B,DV
Pleiospilos compactus ssp sororius	B,DV
Pleiospilos dekenahii	DV
Pleiospilos dimidiatus	SG
Pleiospilos fergusonae	B,CH,DV,SG,Y
Pleiospilos hilmari	DV
Pleiospilos leipoldtii	DV
Pleiospilos magnipunctatus	DV,SG
Pleiospilos nelii	B,CH,DV,SI,Y
Pleiospilos prismaticus	DV
Pleiospilos rouxii	DV
Pleiospilos simulans	B,DV,SI,Y
Pleurospermum brunonis	HP
Pleurostemon uralense	SG
Pleurothallis grobyi	B
Pleurotus eryngii d.m.p	B
Pleurotus ostreatus d.m.p	B
Pluchea purpurascens	B
Plukenetia volubilis	B
Plumbago auriculata	B,BS,BY,C,CA,CL,CN,
	DE,EL,FW,HA,HP,JE,KI,
	PK,PL,SA,ST,T,V,VE
Plumbago auriculata 'African Queen'	PL
Plumbago capensis see P.auriculata	
Plumbago tristis	B,SI
Plumbago zeylanica	B
Plumeria frangipanni alba	B,SA,T
Plumeria frangipanni rubra	SA
Plumeria hyb	CA
Plumeria 'New Hawaiian'	B
Plumeria rubra	B,C,G,V
Plumeria rubra v acutifolia	C,DV
Pneumonanthe asclepiadea	SG
Poa alpina	G,JE,NO,SG
Poa alpina v nodosa	B,C,SA
Poa alpina v vivipara	AP,B,KL
Poa angustifolia	SG
Poa annua	B
Poa attenuata	SG
Poa canbyi	NO
Poa chaixii	B,JE,SA,SC
Poa cita	B,SS

POA

Poa colensoi	B,SS
Poa compressa	B
Poa labillardieri	B,HA
Poa laxa	SG
Poa leptocoma ssp paucispicula	SG
Poa lindsayii	SS
Poa nemoralis	B,FR,SA
Poa poiformis	B
Poa pratensis	FR,SG
Poa sandbergii	NO
Poa scabrella	CA
Poa sclerophylla	SS
Poa sibirica	SG
Poa sieberiana	HA
Poa trivialis	B
Podalyria biflora	B,SI
Podalyria calyptrata	B,BH,C,DD,EL,KB,LN, SA,SI,WA
Podalyria canescens	B,SI
Podalyria sericea	B,BH,C,DD,KB,SA,SI
Podalyria sp	SI
Podocarpus elatus	B,EL,HA,O,SA
Podocarpus elongatus	B,KB,SI
Podocarpus falcatus	HA,KB,SI,WA
Podocarpus glacilior	CA
Podocarpus henkelii	B,CA,SI,WA
Podocarpus latifolius	B,SI,WA
Podocarpus macrophyllus	B,CA,LN,SA
Podocarpus macrophyllus 'Maki'	B,CA,FW
Podocarpus nagi	CA
Podocarpus nivalis	B,SS
Podocarpus rumphii	B
Podocarpus salignus	B,SA
Podocarpus totara	B
Podolepis auriculata	B,NI,O
Podolepis canescens	B,NI
Podolepis gracilis	B,NI,O
Podolepis jaceoides	B,NI,O
Podolepis nutans	B,NI,O
Podophyllum aurantiacum	SG
Podophyllum emodi see P.hexandrum	
Podophyllum hexandrum	AP,B,CG,G,HP,JE,KL,RS, SA,SC,SG,T
Podophyllum hexandrum 'Majus'	AP,HP,KL
Podophyllum hexandrum v chinense	HP,SG
Podophyllum peltatum	AP,B,CG,JE
Podospermum laciniatum	CG
Podotheca gnaphalioides	B,NI
Podranea brycei	B
Podranea ricasoliana	B,SI
Pogostemon heyneanus	B
Polanisia dodecandra	B
Polanisia uniglandulosa	DD
Polaskia chichipe	B,Y
Polemonium acutifolium	SG
Polemonium acutifolium 'Album'	B,JE
Polemonium archibaldii	HP
Polemonium boreale	AP,HP,KL
Polemonium brandegei	AP,HP,KL
Polemonium brandegei ssp mellitum	AP,B,P
Polemonium caeruleum	AB,AP,B,BS,C,CN,DD, G,HP,I,JE,KI,KL,KS,PA, PK,SA,SC,SG,SU,TH,VH
Polemonium caeruleum ssp amygdalinum	HP
Polemonium caeruleum ssp c. f album	AP,B,C,CN,DT,F,G,HP,JE, KL,PL,SA,SC,T,V

Polemonium caeruleum v album see P.c. ssp c.f album	
Polemonium caeruleum v himalayanum	AP,B,HP
Polemonium caeruleum 'White Pearl'	B,BS,C,HU,MO
Polemonium carneum	BS,C,HP,JE,KL,SA,SC
Polemonium carneum 'Apricot Delight'	B,BS,CN,HP,MO,T,V
Polemonium cashmerianum	AP,B,C,HP,HU,JE,SG,T, W
Polemonium cashmerianum album	B,C,JE
Polemonium caucasicum	SG
Polemonium delicaticum	AP,G,RM,SG
Polemonium elegans	B,KL
Polemonium filicinum	SG
Polemonium foliosissimum	AP,B,G,HP,JE,SW
Polemonium foliosissimum 'Album'	B
Polemonium foliosissimum v flavum	HP
Polemonium 'Golden Showers' (V)	B,P
Polemonium mellitum	C
Polemonium nipponicum	AP,HP
Polemonium pauciflorum	AP,B,C,DT,F,G,HP,JD,JE, KL,P,PL,PM,RS,SA,SC, SE,SG,SW
Polemonium pauciflorum silver leaf form	HP,T
Polemonium pauciflorum ssp hinckleyi	HP
Polemonium pulcherrimum	AP,B,C,HP,KL,NO,P,SC, SG,SW
Polemonium pulcherrimum 'Tricolor'	HP
Polemonium racemosum	KL
Polemonium reptans	AP,B,C,G,PO,PR,SA,SC
Polemonium reptans 'Album' see P.r. 'Virginia White'	
Polemonium reptans 'Blue Pearl'	B,BS,C,DE,HP,HU,JE, MO,S,SK,V
Polemonium reptans 'Virginia White'	B,HP
Polemonium scopulinum	B,HP,SW
Polemonium sp	KL
Polemonium viscosum	AP,B,HP,KL,RM,SC,SW
Polemonium x richardsonii	B,G,HP
Polemonium yezoense	AP,HP
Polemonium yezoense 'Purple Rain'	B,P
Polianthes nelsonii	B,SW
Polianthes tuberosa 'The Pearl'	B
Pollia japonica	B,C
Polyalthia longifolia 'Pendula'	B,O
Polyalthia nitidissima	B,NI
Polyalthia obtusifolia	B,EL
Polyalthia suberosa	B
Polycalymma stuartii	B,NI
Polycarpaea aurea	B
Polycarpaea longiflora	B
Polygala alpestris	B,VO
Polygala alpicola	VO
Polygala amoenissima	VO
Polygala chamaebuxus	B,C
Polygala fruticosa	BH
Polygala hottentotta	B,SI
Polygala major	VO
Polygala myrtifolia	B,SA,SI,VE
Polygala senega	B,PR
Polygala virgata	B,BH,C,SA,VE
Polygonatum biflorum	B,JE
Polygonatum falcatum variegatum	CG
Polygonatum hirtum	B,JE,NG
Polygonatum humile	B,JE
Polygonatum maximoviczii	SA
Polygonatum multiflorum h see P.x hybridum	
Polygonatum odoratum	C,G,JE,KI,SA,SG,ST
Polygonatum odoratum v thunbergii	B,JE

213

POLYGONATUM

Polygonatum sibiricum	SG
Polygonatum verticillatum	B,JE,SA,SG
Polygonatum x hybridum	B,G,JE,SA,T
Polygonum alpinum	B,CG,SG
Polygonum angustifolium	SG
Polygonum arenarium	B
Polygonum bistorta see Persicaria	
Polygonum convolvulus	B
Polygonum dibotrys	B
Polygonum divaricatum	SG
Polygonum fagopyrum	B
Polygonum filiforme	G,HU,JE,SC
Polygonum filiforme 'Variegatum'	AP,JE
Polygonum lapathifolium	B
Polygonum sachalinense	B,DD,FW
Polygonum saggittatum	B,PR
Polygonum see also Persicaria/Fallopia	
Polygonum tataricum	B
Polygonum tinctorium	C,CP
Polygonum viviparum	AP,B,C,JE,SA
Polygonum weyrichii	B,DD,JE,SG
Polymeria ambigua	B,NI
Polymnia uvedalya	B
Polypodium aureum	B
Polypodium aureum 'Mandaianum'	B,SG
Polypodium aureum v areolatum	B,SA,SG
Polypodium punctatum	B
Polypodium vulgare	B,G
Polypogon monspeliensis	B,C,MO,PI,V
Polypompholyx multifida	B,DV
Polyscias elegans	B,EL,O,SA
Polyscias fulva	B
Polyscias murrayi	B,EL,O
Polystichum erythrosora	B
Polystichum munitum	B,C,G,HU
Polystichum setiferum	G,N
Polystichum tsussimense	B,G
Polytaenia nuttallii	B,PR
Polyxena ensifolia	AP,B,RU,SC,SI
Polyxena odorata	SC,SI
Polyxena sp	RU,SI
Pomaderris elliptica	AU,B,NI
Pomaderris hamiltonii	B
Pomaderris kumeraho	B,SA
Pomaderris myrtilloides	B,NI
Pomaderris obcordata	AU,B,C,NI
Pomaderris phylicifolia	B
Pomaderris rugosa	B
Pomaderris sp	HA
Poncirus trifoliata	A,B,C,EL,G,LN,SA,SG
Pongamia pinnata	B,EL,HA,O,SA
Pontederia cordata	JE
Pontederia cordata 'Alba'	JE
Populus alba	B,SA
Populus balsamifera	SG
Populus canescens	SA
Populus fremontii	B
Populus nigra	SA
Populus suaveolens	SG
Populus tremula	B,CA,FW,LN,NO,SA,SG
Porophyllum ruderale	AB,DD
Porophyllum ruderale ssp macrocephalum	B
Portea fosteriana	B
Portea kermesiana	B
Portea kermesiana v rubra	B
Portea leptantha	B

Portea petropolitana	B
Portea petropolitana v extensa	B
Portea petropolitana v noettigii	B
Portulaca cryptopetala	CG,Y
Portulaca cyanosperma	DV,Y
Portulaca dbl mix	B,BS,BU,C,D,DE,DN, F,FR,MO,PI,PK,TU,VY
Portulaca dbl mix imp	CA,HU,S,SK
Portulaca f1 hyb 'Sundial' mix	BS,CA,CL,DT,F,MO,PI, R,S,SE,SK,U,YA
Portulaca f1 hyb 'Sundial' s-c	BS,PL,SE,SK,T,U
Portulaca f2 hyb 'Calypso'	BD,BS,CL,J,MO,SK,V
Portulaca f2 hyb 'Kariba'	B,C,T
Portulaca f2 'Sundance'	CA,D
Portulaca foliosa	B
Portulaca grandiflora	B,BY,CG,CO,DE,DV,KI, SG
Portulaca grandiflora 'Afternoon Delight'	PK
Portulaca grandiflora 'Cloudbeater' mix	T
Portulaca grandiflora 'Swan Lake'	B,T
Portulaca marginata	B,DV,SG
Portulaca 'Minilace' mix	BS
Portulaca mix single	C,FR,HU
Portulaca mundula DJF1350	Y
Portulaca oleracea	B,CG,CN,DD,DV,HU,NI
Portulaca 'Patio Gems'	U
Portulaca philippii	Y
Portulaca pilosa	B,DV,NI
Portulaca sp	SI
Portulaca 'Sundial Mango'	T
Portulacaria afra	B
Posoqueria latifolia	B
Potentilla alba	AP,SG
Potentilla alchemilloides	AP,B,SG
Potentilla andicola	AP,HP
Potentilla argentea	AP,B,BS,C,G,HP,JE,SA, SG
Potentilla argentea v calibra	JE
Potentilla arguta	AP,B,KL,PR,SG
Potentilla argyrophylla see P. atrosanguinea v argyrophylla	
Potentilla atrosanguinea	AP,B,C,F,G,HP,JE,PL,RH, SA,SC,SG,T,V
Potentilla atrosanguinea v argyrophylla	B,F,HP,JE,KL,SA,T
Potentilla aurea	B,F,HP,JE,KL,SA,SC
Potentilla aurea ssp chrysocraspeda	KL
Potentilla biflora	VO
Potentilla calabra	AP,B
Potentilla caulescens	VO
Potentilla cinerea	SG
Potentilla cinerea ssp velutina	VO
Potentilla clusiana	VO
Potentilla crantzii	AP,B,C,G,JE,SC,SG
Potentilla dbl French hybrids	PK
Potentilla dickinsii	KL
Potentilla diversifolia	RM,SG
Potentilla divina	KL,VO
Potentilla erecta	B,C,CN,HP,JE,SA,SC
Potentilla 'Etna'	B,D,HP,P
Potentilla fissa	KL
Potentilla fragiformis see P.megalantha	
Potentilla fruticosa	G,KL,LN,SA
Potentilla fruticosa v pyrenaica	B
Potentilla fulgens see P.lineata	
Potentilla glandulosa ssp pseudorupestris	SG
Potentilla gracilis	B,C,HP,JE,KL,SA,SC,SG
Potentilla grandiflora	AP,B,JE,KL,SA,SC

POTENTILLA

Potentilla haynaldiana	KL	Prasophyllum cypochilum	B
Potentilla 'Herzblut'	JE	Prasophyllum drummondii	B
Potentilla hippiana	G,SG	Prasophyllum regium	B
Potentilla hyb	B	Pratia angulata	B,SC,SG,SS
Potentilla hyb, dbl	C	Pratia macrodon	B,SS
Potentilla hyparctica	AP,SC,SG	Pratia puberula	SG
Potentilla hyparctica v nana	KL	Premna serratifolia	B
Potentilla inquinans	SG	Prenanthes alba	PR
Potentilla lineata	B	Prenanthes purpurea	SG
Potentilla lutea	C	Prenanthes racemosa	B
Potentilla megalantha	AP,B,C,DE,G,HP,JE,KL,	Prenia sladeniana	B,SI
	PL,RM,SA,SC,SG,T	Prenia sp	SI
Potentilla 'Melton Fire'	AP,B,BS,G,T,V	Priestleya laevigata	B,KB
Potentilla 'Monsieur Rouillard'	T	Priestleya myrtifolia	B
Potentilla multifidiformis	KL	Primula acaulis see P.vulgaris	
Potentilla nepalensis	AP,CN,HP,RH,SC,SG	Primula 'Alaska'	BS,CL
Potentilla nepalensis 'Helen Jane'	B,HP	Primula algida	AP,CG,G,KL,VO
Potentilla nepalensis 'Miss Willmott'	AP,B,BD,BS,C,CL,DE,	Primula All Sorts	U
	DT,F,G,HP,JE,KI,KL,L,	Primula alpicola	AP,B,C,CG,FH,JE,P,SA,
	MO,P,PK,PL,SA,SC,T		SC,SG
Potentilla nepalensis red	B,JE	Primula alpicola alba	CR,SC
Potentilla nepalensis 'Roxana'	AP,B,HP,JE	Primula alpicola mix	FH
Potentilla neumanniana	B,KL,SA	Primula alpicola v luna	HP
Potentilla nitida	AP,B,KL,SC	Primula alpicola v violacea	AP,B,CG,CR,FH,HP,JE,G
Potentilla nivalis	G,KL,RM,SC,SG	Primula alpicola white & yellow	FH
Potentilla norvegica	B,JE,SG	Primula alpine mix	J
Potentilla oweriniana	KL,VO	Primula amoena see P.elatior ssp meyeri	
Potentilla palustris	B,C,G,HP,NS,SA,SC,SG	Primula angustifolia	B,SW
Potentilla pamirica	AP,KL	Primula anisodora	CG,P,SC
Potentilla pectinata	KL	Primula aurantiaca	AP,CG,CR,HP
Potentilla pectinisecta	B,SG	Primula auricula	AP,BD,BS,C,CO,CR,D,
Potentilla pedata	HP		FH,FW,G,HP,HU,J,JE,
Potentilla pensylvanica	JE,SA		KL,LG,MO,R,RM,S,SC,
Potentilla pulvinaris	KL		TH,U,V,VO
Potentilla pyrenaica	AP,SA	Primula auricula alpine mix	FH,L,NG,SA,ST,V,W
Potentilla recta	AP,B,F,G,HP,JE,SC,SG	Primula auricula 'Alpine Pastures' h-p	CR
Potentilla recta 'Alba'	B,C,F,HP,PL	Primula auricula Beckfoot Strain	CR
Potentilla recta 'Citrina' see P.r. pallida		Primula auricula dbl	BP,CR,P,PL
Potentilla recta 'Macrantha' see P.r. 'Warrenii'		Primula auricula 'Douglas Prize Mix'	T
Potentilla recta pallida	AP,E,HP,I	Primula auricula hyb	AP,C
Potentilla recta v sulphurea see P.r. pallida		Primula auricula mix	BP,F,FH,M,NG,W
Potentilla recta 'Warrenii'	AP,B,BS,C,CL,G,HP,I,SA,	Primula auricula 'Old Irish Blue' h-p	CR
	SG	Primula auricula 'Old Yellow Dusty Miller'	CR
Potentilla rupestris	AP,B,G,HP,JE,KL,SA,SG	Primula auricula pubescens	SA
Potentilla salesovianum	SG	Primula auricula show mix	AS,FH,NG
Potentilla sp	KL,SC,T	Primula auricula ssp bauhinii	B,C,CR,JE
Potentilla speciosa	AP,B,C,JE,RM,SC,VO	Primula Barnhaven Blues Gr (PR)	B,BP
Potentilla sterilis	B	Primula Barnhaven Gold (PR)	B,BP
Potentilla strigosa	SG	Primula Barnhaven Traditional Gr	BP
Potentilla tergemina	SG	Primula bayernii	KL,VO
Potentilla thurberi	AP,B,C,HP,JE,SC,SW	Primula beesiana	AP,B,BS,C,CG,CR,F,FH,
Potentilla thurberi 'Monarch's Velvet'	B,BS,HP,L,MO,PK,PL,		G,HP,JE,KI,KL,P,SA,SC,
	SE,T		SG,SU
Potentilla tridentata see Sibbaldiopsis		Primula Beidermeier	BS
Potentilla verna see P. neumanniana		Primula bellidifolia	B,BP,CG,G,SC
Potentilla villosa see P.crantzii		Primula 'Bellissima'	PK
Potentilla 'White Queen'	B,BS,MO	Primula 'Bergfruhling' Mix (PR)	FH
Poterium see Sanguisorba		Primula 'Bergfruhling' s-c (PR)	FH
Pothomorphe peltata	B	Primula bi-colours s-c	MO
Pourouma cecropiifolia	B,RE,SA	Primula Bolton's selected giants (PO)	BO
Pouteria caimito	B	Primula boveana	FH,SC
Pouteria campechiana	B	Primula 'Boys n' Girls' (PO)	BP
Pouteria obovata	B	Primula 'Brotwell Gold'	KL
Pouteria sapota	B,CA	Primula 'Brown's Special Strain' (PO)	BS
Pouteria sericea	B	Primula bulleyana	AP,B,BS,C,CG,CR,DV,
Prasophyllum colensoi	B,SW		FH,HP,I,JE,KI,P,SA,SG,T

PRIMULA

Primula 'Bumbles' (PO)	C	Primula elatior 'Alba'	B,JE
Primula burmanica	AP,B,BS,CR,I,JE,KL,SG	Primula elatior 'Aurea'	B,JE
Primula 'Butterscotch' (PR)	BP	Primula elatior cordifolia	SG
Primula Candelabra Hyb T&M	T,V	Primula elatior deep-blue primrose	W
Primula Candelabra Hybrids	AP,C,CG,FH,HP,J,JE,KL,	Primula elatior 'Gigantea' mix	JE
	PL,PM,SC,W	Primula elatior 'Grandiflora' mix	JE
Primula candelabra 'Oriental Sunrise'	B,BP	Primula elatior hyb	FH
Primula candelabra 'PW Rainbows'	P	Primula elatior hyb red colours	JE
Primula 'Candy Pinks' (PR)	B,BP	Primula elatior 'Old Curiosity'	F
Primula capitata	AP,B,CG,FH,SA,SC,SG	Primula elatior 'Paris 90'	F
Primula capitata AC1725	X	Primula elatior 'Selected Blues'	F
Primula capitata ssp mooreana	B,BP,C,CR,FH,JE,SC	Primula elatior ssp intricata	CG,FH,SC
Primula Carnation Victorians Gr (PO)	BP	Primula elatior ssp leucophylla	I
Primula cashmeriana	SA	Primula elatior ssp meyeri	KL,SC,SG,VO
Primula 'Casquet'	BP	Primula elatior ssp pallasii	AP,SC,SG,W
Primula cernua	FH,SC	Primula elatior 'Victorian Mauve'	F
Primula cernua ex F.Cabot coll	FH	Primula elatior 'Vierlander Gold'	B,JE
Primula 'Charisma'	CL	Primula elatior x P.juliae	W
Primula Chartreuse Gr (PO)	B,BP,BS,F	Primula Elizabethan strain	CR
Primula chionantha	AP,B,BS,C,CR,FH,HP,	Primula elliptica	KL
	JE,KI,SA,SC,T	Primula ellisae	CR
Primula chionantha Sinopurpurea Group	AP,B,CR,HP,JE,SG,W	Primula English Spring Trio	C
Primula chungensis	AP,B,BS,C,CR,HP,JE,PL,	Primula 'Eskimo' mix	BS,R
	SA,SC,SG	Primula European hyb mix	FH
Primula chungensis 'Red Hugh'	SG	Primula Exhibition Giants (PO)	BD,MO
Primula clusiana	AP,KL,VO	Primula Exotic Collection mix	BS,T
Primula cockburniana	AP,B,C,CR,F,FH,G,HP,	Primula Exotic Collection s-c	BS
	JE,RM,SC,SG,W	Primula f1 Bi-colour s-c	BS,KI
Primula concholoba	AP,CR,FH,SC	Primula f1 'Bright Lights'	U
Primula conspersa	SG	Primula f1 'Can Can'	BS
Primula cortusoides	AP,B,JE,SA,SC	Primula f1 'Concorde' s-c (PO)	YA
Primula, Cowichan 'Black Eyed Reds'	CR	Primula f1 'Corona' (PR)	BS
Primula, Cowichans 'Amethyst'	B,BP	Primula f1 Countrywide	S
Primula, Cowichans blue	B,BP	Primula f1 'Crescendo' mix (PO)	BS,CN,MO,PK
Primula, Cowichans garnet	B,BP,C	Primula f1 'Crescendo' s-c (PO)	BS,CL,D,DTJ,JE,MO,R,
Primula, Cowichans mix	BP,PL,SC,W		S,T,U,YA
Primula, Cowichans 'Venetian'	B,BP	Primula f1 'Dania' mix	MO,SK,U,YA
Primula, Cowichans yellow	B,BP	Primula f1 'Dania Series' s-c	YA
Primula Crown mix	BS	Primula f1 'Daniella' s-c	YA
Primula cusickii	NO	Primula f1 'Danova' mix	SK
Primula daonensis	AP,CG,KL,SC,SG	Primula f1 'Danova Series' s-c, mix	BS,MO,YA
Primula darialica	AP,CG,G	Primula f1 'Dreamer'	BS,MO
Primula Daybreak Gr (PO)	B,BP	Primula f1 'Encore' mix	J
Primula dbl (PR)	BP,CR	Primula f1 'Fama'	BS,MO,R
Primula denticulata	AP,B,BD,BY,C,CG,CN,C	Primula f1 'Fantasia' (PO)	BS
	R,DT,DV,HP,I,J,JE,KI,KL	Primula f1 'Finesse' mix	BS,CL,D,J,L,MO,V,YA
	,PL,S,SC,SG,SU,T,V,YA	Primula f1 'Flamina' (PR)	BS
Primula denticulata blue selection	B,FH,JE	Primula f1 Garden Pride mix	J
Primula denticulata Grandiflora Hybrids	B,JE	Primula f1 'Harlequin' mix (PO)	F,J
Primula denticulata hyb	L,S,ST	Primula f1 'Husky' mix	CL,S
Primula denticulata lilac	BY,CL,MO	Primula f1 'Jackpot' mix	S
Primula denticulata mix	BP,BS,BY,CL,FH,KL,MO	Primula f1 'Lovely'	BS,CL,D,MO
Primula denticulata mix dk colours	B,FH,JE	Primula f1 'Lucento'	BS,MO
Primula denticulata 'Ronsdorf'	B,C	Primula f1 'Magnus' (PO)	PK
Primula denticulata 'Ruby'	B,BS,BY,C,CG,CL,FH,	Primula f1 'Mascara' (PR)	BS
	JE,MO,PL	Primula f1 'Meteor Series' s-c	YA
Primula denticulata 'Snowball'	C	Primula f1 'Miranda'	YA
Primula denticulata v alba	B,BP,BS,C,CG,CL,FH,	Primula f1 'Pacific Bicolour Shades' (POO	BS,SK
	JE,KL	Primula f1 'Pageant'	BS,CL,KI,L,MO,SE
Primula denticulata white	MO	Primula f1 'Pastel'	BS,MO
Primula 'Desert Sunset' (PO)	B,BP	Primula f1 picotee mix	SK
Primula 'Easterbloom' s-c	B	Primula f1 'Prominent' s-c & mix	BS
Primula elatior	AP,B,C,CG,CN,CO,CR,	Primula f1 'Rainbow' mix (PO)	BS,CL,EL,L,MO
	F,FR,G,HP,HU,I,JE,KL,	Primula f1 'Rainbow' s-c (PO)	BS,CL,EL
	P,PL,PM,RM,SA,SC,SG,	Primula f1 'Rapido' (PR) s-c,mix	BS
	SU,V,W	Primula f1 'Riviera'	BS,YA

216

PRIMULA

Name	Code
Primula f1 'Serenade' s-c, mix	BS
Primula f1 Show mix	BS,S
Primula f1 Show s-c	BS
Primula f1 'Silver Lining'	T
Primula f1 'Spectrum' mix	L
Primula f1 'Spectrum' s-c	T
Primula f1 'Spring Rainbow' (PO)	D,S
Primula f1 'Supreme'	BS,MO
Primula f1 'Titania'	YA
Primula f1 'Wanda' mix	BS,D,DT,J,R,SE,t,U,YA
Primula f1 'Wanda' s-c	BS,JE,FH
Primula farinosa	AP,B,C,CG,CR,DV,FH,G, JE,KL,SA,SC,SU,TH
Primula farinosa ex Bavaria	FH
Primula farinosa ex JCA786.600	FH
Primula fasciana	CG
Primula 'Fire Dance' (PO)	B,BP
Primula firmipes	AP,CG,G,SG
Primula flaccida	AP,FH
Primula Flamingo Gr (PO)	B,BP,BS
Primula floribunda v isabellina	W
Primula florindae	AP,B,BS,C,CG,CR,FH,G, HP,HU,I,JE,KI,KL,P,PL, SA,SC,SG,T,W
Primula florindae hyb	BP,FH
Primula florindae hyb orange	C,KL
Primula florindae Keilour Hybrids	B,JE
Primula florindae red & orange	B
Primula florindae red shades	C,FH,JE,SC
Primula florindae 'Ruby'	B
Primula Flower Arranger's (PO)	BP
Primula 'Fondant Creams'	U
Primula forrestii	AP,SC,SG,W
Primula forrestii AC1422	X
Primula 'Forza'	CL
Primula frondosa	AP,B,C,FH,G,HP,JE,SA, SG,W
Primula Galaxy mix (PO)	YA
Primula Galligaskins Gr (PO)	BP
Primula geraniifolia	SC,SG
Primula 'Gigha'(Winter White) (PO)	BP
Primula glaucesens	CG,SC
Primula glaucesens ssp calycina	C,CR
Primula glomerata	AP,CR,PL
Primula glutinosa	CG,CR
Primula 'Gold Lace Doctor's Delight'	CR
Primula Gold Laced Gr (PO)	B,BP,BS,CR,DT,F,FH,G, NG,P,SE,T,W
Primula Grand Canyon Gr (PO)	B,BP
Primula grandis	AP,CG,SC,SG
Primula halleri	AP,B,CG,CR,FH,G,JE,KL, SA,SC
Primula 'Harbour Lights' (PO)	B,BP
Primula Harlow Carr hyb	C,CR
Primula Harvest Yellows Gr (PO)	B,BP
Primula helodoxa	C,CG,CR,JE,P,SA,SC, SG,T,W
Primula heucherifolia	AP,SC,SG
Primula hirsuta	AP,B,C,CR,FH,G,JE,KL, SA,SC,VO
Primula Hose in Hose	BP
Primula hyb Dobies colours	D
Primula hyb h-p (PR)	W
Primula hyb Marshall's giant	M
Primula hyllopana	CG
Primula incana	SG

Name	Code
Primula Indian Reds Gr (PO)	B,BP
Primula Inshriach Hybrids	C,CG,P
Primula integrifolia	B,C,CR,JE,SA,VO
Primula involucrata ssp yargonensis	B,CG,FH,JE,SC,SG
Primula ioessa	CR,G
Primula Jack in Green Gr (PO)	BP
Primula Jack in Green & Hose in Hose mix	P
Primula Jackanapes Gr (PO)	BP
Primula Jackanapes-on-Horseback	BP
Primula japonica	AP,BD,BS,CG,CN,G,HP, KL,L,RM,SA,SC,SG
Primula japonica 'Alba'	B,CR,G,JE
Primula japonica 'Carminea'	B,JE
Primula japonica 'Fuji'	AP,HP,P
Primula japonica 'Glowing Embers'	FH
Primula japonica 'Hall Barn Ripple'	CR
Primula japonica 'Miller's Crimson'	AP,B,BP,BS,C,CR,HP, JE,KL,P,SA,SC
Primula japonica mix	AP,B,PM,S,T
Primula japonica mix deluxe	JE
Primula japonica mix hyb	C,MO,SC
Primula japonica 'Postford White'	AP,B,BP,CR,G,HP,P,SG
Primula japonica red forms	AP,FH
Primula japonica 'Valley Red'	AP,CG,CR,SC
Primula japonica white forms	FH
Primula 'Jazz Parade' (PR)	BS
Primula jesoana	AP,SC,SG
Primula Jewel Group	M
Primula juliae	B,JE,SC
Primula kewensis	AP,FH,SC,W
Primula kewensis 'Mountain Spring'	CL,FH
Primula kewensis 'Thurgold'	B,BD,BS,BY,C
Primula latifolia	AP,B,CR,SC,VO
Primula laurentiana ex Great Wassi see P.mistassinica v macropoda	
Primula Limelight Gr (PO)	BP
Primula 'Little Egypt' (PO)	B,BP
Primula littoniana see P.vialii	
Primula longiflora see P. halleri	
Primula luteola	AP,B,C,F,JE,SG
Primula macrocalyx	G,SG,VO
Primula macrophylla	AP,C,CR,SC
Primula malacoides 'Ballerina mix'	CL,FH
Primula malacoides 'Benary's special mix'	C
Primula malacoides 'Bright Eyes'	T
Primula malacoides Classic mix	BS
Primula malacoides f1 'Prima mix'	MO,YA
Primula malacoides 'Lollipops mix'	YA
Primula malacoides mix	BD,BS,J,L,MO,SK,U
Primula malacoides mix special	BS,BY,S
Primula malacoides white dbl	PI
Primula 'Mardigras' (PR)	KI,ST
Primula marginata	AP,B,CR,G,KL,SC
Primula Marine Blues Gr (PO)	BP
Primula M's Giant Fenland Strain (PO)	M
Primula melanops	HP,SC,SG
Primula 'Mexico' (PO)	B,BP
Primula Midnight Gr (PO)	B,BP
Primula minima	AP,B,CR
Primula mistassinica alba	FH
Primula mistassinica v macropoda	AP,FH
Primula mix choice	PI
Primula mix giant superb	S,T
Primula mix hardy sp	BS,BY,C,DT,F,MO,PL, SE,T
Primula mix lg fl (PO)	C,CO,F,J,T,TU,VH
Primula mix (PR)	BD,FH,TU

PRIMULA

Primula mix superb (PO)	CR,D,DT,U	Primula reidii	AP,B,BP
Primula miyabeana	SC	Primula reidii hyb	AP,FH
Primula modesta v faurieae	AP,FH,HP	Primula reidii hyb white	FH
Primula mollis	B,P,SC	Primula reidii v williamsii alba	AP,HP
Primula 'Morning Star'	CL	Primula 'Repeat Performance'	PL,SE
Primula 'Mother's Day'	BS,BY,VH	Primula 'Reverie' (PO)	B,BP
Primula muscarioides	AP,FH,KL,SC	Primula rosea	AP,CG,CN,CR,FH,G,KL
Primula Mystery Packet	BP	Primula rosea 'Gigas'	B,G,JE
Primula New Pinks Gr (PO)	BP	Primula rosea 'Grandiflora'	B,BD,BS,C,CL,JE,KI,L,
Primula nivalis	KL		MO,SA,SC,T
Primula nivalis v farinosa	VO	Primula 'Rosetta Jones Strain' dbl (PR)	C,FH,PL,SE
Primula nutans	CG	Primula 'Rumba' mix (PO)	CL
Primula obconica	KI,L,V,YA	Primula rusbyi	AP,B,SC,SW
Primula obconica 'Blue Agate'	T	Primula Rustic Reds Gr (PO)	B,BP
Primula obconica 'Chartres' o-p	CL	Primula saxatilis	AP,B,BP,CG,FH,G,JE,SG
Primula obconica Crown mix	BS	Primula scandinavica	AP,C,FH,KL,SC,W
Primula obconica deep blue	C	Primula scotica	AP,B,C,CR,FH,SC,SG,T
Primula obconica f1 'Ariane'	CL,FH,MO	Primula secundiflora	AP,B,C,CG,CR,HP,JE,SA,
Primula obconica f1 'Cantata' mix	CL,MO,S		SC,SG
Primula obconica f1 'Cantata' red & wh	PL	Primula sieboldii	AP,CR,FH,G,HP,JE,KL
Primula obconica f1 'Juno Series'	CA	Primula sieboldii 'Dancing Ladies'	B,BP
Primula obconica f1 'Libre' mix	CL,D,PK,SK	Primula sieboldii 'Galaxy'	BP
Primula obconica f1 'Pink Velvet' mix	CL	Primula sieboldii 'Manakoora'	B,BP
Primula obconica 'Fashbender Blue'	BS	Primula sieboldii 'Pago-Pago'	BP,G
Primula obconica fimbriata	BS	Primula sieboldii 'Tah-ni'	BP
Primula obconica finest mix	C,J,ST	Primula sieboldii 'Winter Dreams'	B,BP
Primula obconica 'Freedom mix'	J	Primula sikkimensis	AP,B,BS,CG,CR,FH,HP,
Primula obconica 'Gigantea Galaxy mix'	BS,YA		JE,KI,KL,SA,SC,SG
Primula obconica 'Gigantea' mix	BY,MO	Primula sikkimensis Coll Ref	AP,X
Primula obconica mix Suttons formula	S	Primula sikkimensis crimson & gold	FH
Primula obconica 'Queen of the Market'	C	Primula sikkimensis hyb	FH
Primula obconica 'Red Agate'	C	Primula sikkimensis sect CNW137	X
Primula obconica special formula	CL	Primula sikk. sp candel. section AC1474	X
Primula obconica 'Swift' o-p	CL	Primula sikk. sp candel. section AC1789	X
Primula 'Oranges and Lemons' (PO)	BP	Primula sikkimensis sp muscaroides section AC1952	X
Primula Osiered Amber Gr (PR)	B,BP	Primula sikkimensis 'Tilman No.2'	CR
Primula 'Pacific Blue' (PO)	BS,KI,MO	Primula sikkimensis v hopeana	CG
Primula 'Pacific Giants' mix (PO)	BS,BY,CL,CN,F,J,KI,L,M,	Primula Silver Dollar strain mix (PO)	BP
	MO,R,SE,SK,SU,TU,U,	Primula sinensis	FH
	YA	Primula sinensis f1 'Fanfare'	BS,MO,YA
Primula 'Pacific Giants' s-c (PO)	B,BD,BS,MO	Primula sinensis single superb mix	J,S
Primula palinuri	KL,SG	Primula sinoplantaginea	CR,HP,SC
Primula pallasii	SG	Primula sinopurpurea see P.chionantha Sinopurpurea Gr	
Primula Pantaloons Gr (PO)	BP	Primula smithiana	C,CR,JE,SA,SC,SG
Primula 'Paris '90' (PO)	BP	Primula Southbank Strain (PO)	CL
Primula parryi	B,JE,SW	Primula sp nivalis section	SG
Primula pavianae	CG	Primula sp yellow	KL
Primula pedemontana	AP,B,CG,SC	Primula spectabilis	AP,CG,KL
Primula petiolaris	B,C	Primula 'Spectrum Bi-colour'	BS
Primula Pheasant Eye blue	PL	Primula specuicola	B,SW
Primula poissonii	AP,G,HP,SC,W,X	Primula spice shades (PO)	B,BP
Primula poissonii Coll Ref	AP,X	Primula 'Spring Parade'	F
Primula polyneura	AP,B,BP,C,CR,FH,HP,JE,	Primula 'Sunset Shades'	JE
	SA,SC,SG,W	Primula 'Supra'	CL
Primula prolifera	AP,G,HP,PL,SG,X	Primula Tartan Reds Gr	B,BP
Primula prolifera v smithiana	B	Primula tinted shades (PO)	BP
Primula 'Prominent' mix	MO	Primula 'Torino'	SE
Primula pubescens	AP,B,CR,DT,G	Primula Traditional Gr Yellows	B,BP
Primula pulverulenta	AP,B,BP,C,CG,CR,D,FH,	Primula Triumph mix (PO)	BY
	G,HP,JE,L,P,PA,SA,SC,	Primula ussuriensis	KL
	SG,V,W	Primula venusta	KL
Primula pulverulenta Bartley Hybrids	BP,CG,HP,SC	Primula veris	w.a.
Primula 'Quantum Series'	CL	Primula veris 'Beckfoot Tudor Cowslips'	CR
Primula 'Ramona' (PO)	B,BP	Primula veris 'Coronation Cowslip'	BP,CR
Primula 'Regal' mix (PO)	KI	Primula veris hyb mix	AP,B,C,FH
Primula 'Regency' mix	R	Primula v. ssp canescens exJCA 790.203	FH

218

PRIMULA

Primula veris ssp columnea	AP,B,C,G,JE
Primula veris ssp macrocalyx	AP,SG
Primula veris ssp veris v ampliata	SG
Primula veris Sunrise/Sunset shades	B,PL
Primula veris Switzerland	FH
Primula verticillata	AP,FH,SC,SG
Primula verticillata ssp boveana	SG
Primula verticillata v simensis	SG
Primula vialii	w.a.
Primula Victorian Fuchsia (PO)	BP
Primula Victorians mauve (PO)	B,BP
Primula Victorians mix (PO)	BP
Primula Victorians muted (PO)	BP
Primula Victorians old rose(PO)	B,BP
Primula Victorians Valentine (PO)	BP
Primula Victorians Violet(PO)	B,BP
Primula villosa	AP,CR
Primula viscosa	C,JE,SA
Primula vivid shades (PO)	BP
Primula vulgaris	w.a.
Primula vulgaris 'Ernst Benary' mix	BS,DT,L,MO
Primula vulgaris 'Ernst Benary' s-c	BS,JE
Primula vulgaris f1 'African-violet' dp blue	B
Primula vulgaris f1 'Apple-blossom'	B
Primula vulgaris f1 'Birdseye' pink,rose	B
Primula vulgaris f1 'Joker' mix	BS,C,KI,MO
Primula vulgaris f1 'Joker' s-c	BS,MO
Primula vulgaris f1 'Orient Star'	BS,C,MO
Primula vulgaris 'Harbinger'	B,BP
Primula vulgaris 'Harmony'	BP
Primula vulgaris 'Langdon's Blue'	B
Primula vulgaris 'Osterblute' s-c	JE
Primula vulgaris 'Potsdam'	C
Primula vulgaris Select Series	B
Primula vulgaris Selection Blue	JE
Primula vulgaris Selection mix	JE
Primula vulgaris Selection Red	JE
Primula vulgaris Selection White	JE
Primula vulgaris Selection Yellow	JE
Primula vulgaris Springtime mix	BP
Primula vulgaris 'True Blue'	T
Primula waltonii	AP,CR,SG
Primula 'Wanda Blue Moon' (PRO	CR
Primula 'Wanda Cornish Primrose'	CR
Primula 'Wanda Ember Shadows' (PR)	CR
Primula 'Wanda Lilac Time' (PR)	CR
Primula 'Wanda' mix	C,T,V
Primula 'Wanda Red Riding Hood' (PR)	CR
Primula 'Wanda Rosie-Posie' (PR)	CR
Primula 'Wanda' s-c	MO
Primula 'Wanda Snow Shadows' (PR)	CR
Primula 'Wanda' supreme mix	BS,CL,EL,MO,PL,T
Primula Wanda x pruhonica	PL
Primula wilsonii	AP,C,SC,SG
Primula wulfeniana	KL,VO
Primula x bullesiana	B,BS,C,CG,DT,FH,G,JE, L,SA,SC
Primula x chunglenta	B,JE,SC
Primula x juliana see P.x pruhonicensis	
Primula x 'McWatts Cream'	HP
Primula x polyantha	HP
Primula x pruhonicensis	KL
Primula x pruhonicensis blue	BP
Primula x pruhon. f1 'Bergfruhling' s-c	JE
Primula x pruhonicensis 'Fireflies'	B,BP,W
Primula x pruhonicensis 'Footlight Parade'	BP

Primula x pruhonicensis mix	B,BP,FH
Primula x pruhonicensis red	B,BP
Primula x pruhonicensis s-c	BP
Primula x pruhonicensis yellow	BP
Primula x pubescens	KL
Primula x pubescens Boothman's Variety	AP,FH
Primula x pubescens 'Exhibition' s-c	JE
Primula x pubescens 'Gigantea'	B,JE
Primula x pubescens hyb	AP,CN,FH,JE
Primula x pubescens 'Pink Denim'	CR
Primula yargongensis see P.involucrata ssp y.	
Prinsepia sinensis	B,C,FW,LN,SA,SG
Prinsepia uniflora	LN,SA
Printzia polifolia	B,SI
Prismatocarpus fruticosus	B,SI
Pritchardia grandis	B
Pritchardia hillebrandii	B
Pritchardia pacifica	B,CA,EL,O,SA
Pritchardia pacifica g	B
Pritchardia thurstonii	B,CA,O
Pritchardia thurstonii g	B
Pritzelago alpina	B
Proboscidea fragrans	B
Proboscidea louisianica	B,CP,DV,G
Proboscidea parviflora v hohokamiana	B
Proboscidea parv. v hohokamiana paiute	B
Proboscidea parviflora v parviflora	B
Proboscidea parviflora v sinaloensis	B
Proboscidea sp	CP
Pronaya fraseri	B,NI
Prosopis chilensis see P.glandulosa	
Prosopis glandulosa	B,CA,LN,SA
Prosopis juliiflora	B,CA,LN,SA,VE,WA
Prosopis pubescens	B,CA,HU
Prostanthera baxteri	B,NI,SA
Prostanthera campbellii	AU
Prostanthera cuneata	AP,HP,SG
Prostanthera lasianthos	B,EL,HA,NI,O,P,SA
Prostanthera nivea	B,HP,SA
Prostanthera striatiflora	B,NI
Protasparagus densiflorus ssp meyersii	SI
Protasparagus natalensis	SI
Protasparagus sp	SI
Protasparagus subulatus	SI
Protasparagus virgatus	SI
Protea acaulos	B,SI
Protea acuminata	B,SI
Protea amplexicaulis	B,O,SI
Protea angolensis	B,SI
Protea angustata	B,SI
Protea arborea	B
Protea aristata	B,KB
Protea aurea	C,SI
Protea aurea ssp aurea	B,KB,O
Protea aurea ssp potbergensis	B,KB
Protea burchellii	B,DV,O,SI
Protea caffra	B,SI
Protea canaliculata	B,SI
Protea collection of 4	C
Protea compacta	B,DV,EL,O,SA,SI,V,VE
Protea convexa	B,SI
Protea cordata	B,C,SI
Protea coronata	B,DV,KB,O,SI
Protea cynaroides	B,C,CA,CF,DV,EL,O,SA, SI,V,VE
Protea cynaroides cvs	B

PROTEA

Protea effusa	B,SI	Prununs prostrata	JE
Protea eximia	B,C,DV,EL,KB,O,SA,SI,V	Prunus africana	B,WA
Protea gaguedi	B,SI	Prunus americana	FW,LN,NO,SA
Protea grandiceps	B,EL,KB,O,SA,SI,V	Prunus amygdalus see P.dulcis	
Protea humiflora	B,SI	Prunus armeniaca	B,CA,LN,VE
Protea hyb	O,SI	Prunus armeniaca cvs	B,SA
Protea lacticolor	B,O,SI	Prunus armeniaca v ansu	B,FW,LN
Protea lacticolor x mundi	SI	Prunus avium	B,C,FW,LN,SA,VE
Protea laevis	B,SI	Prunus avium sylvestris	FW
Protea lanceolata	B,DV,SI	Prunus besseyi	B,FW,LN,N,NO,SA,SG
Protea laurifolia	B,EL,O,SA,SI	Prunus capuli see P.salicifolia	
Protea lepidocarpodendron	B,O,SI	Prunus caroliniana	B,CA,FW,LN,SA
Protea longifolia	B,C,DV,O,SI	Prunus cerasifera	A,B,C,LN,SG,VE
Protea lorifolia	B,SI	Prunus cerasifera myrobalum	FW,SA
Protea magnifica	B,C,EL,O,SI,V	Prunus cerasifera ssp divaricata	LN,RS
Protea magnifica 'Cedarberg'	B	Prunus davidiana	B,C,FW,LN,SA
Protea magnifica 'Koo'	B	Prunus domestica	LN,SA
Protea mundii	B,DV,KB,O,SI	Prunus dulcis	LN,SA,VE
Protea namaquana	B,SI	Prunus emarginata	AB,NO
Protea nana	B,O,SA,SC,SI,VE	Prunus fasciculata	NO
Protea neriifolia	B,CA,DV,EL,KB,O,SA, SI,V	Prunus fremontii	B
		Prunus fruticosa	B,LN,SG
Protea neriifolia cream	C	Prunus glandulosa	B,LN,SA
Protea nitida	B,O,SI	Prunus ilicifolia	B,CA,SA
Protea obtusifolia	B,CA,DV,EL,KB,O,SI,V	Prunus incisa	FW,N
Protea pendula	B,SI	Prunus instititia	SA
Protea pudens	B	Prunus jamasakura	B
Protea pulchra	B,C	Prunus laurocerasus	B,C,LN,SA
Protea punctata	B,KB,O,SI	Prunus laur. 'Schipkaensis Macrophylla'	C
Protea recondita	B,SI	Prunus leveillana v pendula	FW
Protea repens	B,C,EL,KB,O,SI,V	Prunus lusitanica	LN,SA
Protea repens white	B,KB	Prunus lyonii	B,CA,LN,SA
Protea roupelliae	B,KB,SI	Prunus maackii	B,C,DD,FW,LN,N,SA,SG
Protea rubropilosa	B,KB,SI	Prunus mahaleb	A,AP,B,C,CA,FW,LN,SA, VE
Protea scabra	B,SI		
Protea scolopendrifolia	B,SI	Prunus mandshurica	B,C,FW,LN,N,SA
Protea scolymocephala	B,C,KB,O,SI	Prunus maritima	B,FW,LN
Protea sp mix	KB,T	Prunus mume	FW,LN,N,SA
Protea speciosa	B,O,SI	Prunus nana	SG
Protea stokoei	B	Prunus nemaguard	FW
Protea subulifolia	B,SI	Prunus nemared	FW
Protea subvestita	B,SI	Prunus nigra	B
Protea sulphurea	B,O,SI	Prunus padus	A,B,C,FW,LN,SA,SG,VE
Protea susannae	B,KB,O,SA,SI	Prunus pendula 'Pendula Rosea'	B,FW,SA
Protea venusta	B,KB,SI	Prunus pensylvanica	FW,LN,SA,SG
Protea witzenbergiana	B,SI	Prunus persica	C,CA,FW,SA
Protea witzenbergiana x pendula	B,SI	Prunus persica 'Montclar'	VE
Protorhus longifolia	B	Prunus persica 'Rubira'	VE
Prumnopitys andina	B,SA	Prunus persica 'Saint Julien' no.2	VE
Prumnopitys ferruginea	B,SS	Prunus persica sylvestris	VE
Prumnopitys taxifolia	B,SS	Prunus prostrata	B,LN
Prunella grandiflora	AP,B,G,HP,JE,KL,PA,PK, SA,SC,SG	Prunus prostrata v discolor	FW,N
		Prunus pubigera	C
Prunella grandiflora 'Alba'	B,HP,JE,SA	Prunus pumila	B,SG
Prunella grandiflora 'Blue Loveliness'	P	Prunus salicifolia	B,C
Prunella grandiflora 'Pagoda'	B,C,I,JE,T,U,V	Prunus salicina	B,FW,LN,SA
Prunella grandiflora 'Pink Loveliness'	HP,P,RS	Prunus salicina v mandshurica	B,LN
Prunella grandiflora 'Rosea'	B,SG	Prunus sargentii	B,FW,SA
Prunella grandiflora 'Rubra'	JE	Prunus serotina	A,B,C,FW,LN,SA,VE
Prunella grandiflora ssp pyrenaica	SG	Prunus serotina ssp capuli	WA
Prunella hyssopifolia	RH	Prunus serrula	FW
Prunella laciniata	AP,HP,SG	Prunus serrulata	B,FW,LN,SA,VE
Prunella vulgaris	AB,C,CN,CP,DD,HU,JE, LA,SA,SG	Prunus sp mix	C
		Prunus spinosa	A,B,C,LN,SA,SG,VE
Prunella vulgaris alba	AP,HP	Prunus tangutica	LN,SA
Prunella x webbiana see P.grandiflora		Prunus tenella	A,B,FW,KL,LN,N,SA

PRUNUS

Prunus tomentosa	B,CA,FW,G,HP,LN,NO, SA,SG
Prunus triloba	B,C,LN,SA
Prunus triloba v plena	C
Prunus virginiana	AB,B,C,HP,LN,NO,SA, SG
Prunus virginiana melanocarpa	FW,LN
Prunus virginiana 'Schubert'	B,FW,LN
Prunus x subhirtella	B,FW,SA
Prunus x subhirtella 'Pendula' h see P.pendula 'Pendula Rosea'	
Prunus x yedoensis	B,FW,SA
Psammophora longifolia	B
Psammophora modesta	B
Psammophora nissenii	B
Psathyrostachys juncea	SG
Pseudarthria hookeri	B,SI
Pseudarthria viscida	B
Pseudocydonia sinensis	B
Pseudoespostoa melanostele	Y
Pseudoespostoa melanostele v inermis	Y
Pseudofumaria see Corydalis	
Pseudognaphalium luteoalbum	B,NI
Pseudognaphalium obtusifolium	B
Pseudolachnostylis maprouneifolia	B,SI,WA
Pseudolarix amabilis	B,C,FW,LN,N,SA
Pseudolobivia ancistrophora	Y
Pseudolobivia arachnacantha	DV
Pseudolobivia aurea	DV,Y
Pseudolobivia aurea v dobeana	BC
Pseudolobivia aurea v fallax	Y
Pseudolobivia aurea v grandiflora	Y
Pseudolobivia callichroma	BC,DV
Pseudolobivia calorubra pojoensis	BC
Pseudolobivia cardenasianum	BC,DV
Pseudolobivia imperialis	DV
Pseudolobivia kermesina	DV
Pseudolobivia kratochviliana	Y
Pseudolobivia leucorhodantha	Y
Pseudolobivia longispina	Y
Pseudolobivia longispina v nigra	Y
Pseudolobivia obrepanda	Y
Pseudolobivia polyancistra	DV
Pseudolobivia pusilla v aureiflora	DV
Pseudolobivia tapecuana	BC
Pseudolobivia torrecillasensis	DV,Y
Pseudolobivia torrecill. v saipinensis	DV
Pseudolobivia vallegrandis	DV
Pseudomuscari see Muscari	
Pseudopanax arboreus	B,SA
Pseudopanax colensoi	SS
Pseudopanax colensoi v ternatus	C
Pseudopanax crassifolius	B,SA
Pseudopanax crassifolius v trifoliatus	B
Pseudopanax ferox	B,SA
Pseudopanax laetus	B
Pseudopanax lessonii hybrids	B,SA
Pseudophoenix sargentii	B,CA
Pseudosamanea guachepele	B
Pseudosbeckia swynnertonii	B,SI
Pseudotsuga macrocarpa	B,CA,LN,SA
Pseudotsuga menziesii	B,C,CA,DD,EL,FW,G,KL, LN,NO,SA,SG,VE
Pseudotsuga menziesii 'Caesia'	B,FW,LN,SA,SG
Pseudotsuga menziesii v glauca	B,C,CA,FW,LN,SA,SG, VE
Pseudotsuga menziesii 'Viridis'	B,BU,FW

Pseudotsuga sinensis	B,EL
Pseudowintera colorata	B
Psidium angulatum	B
Psidium cattleyanum see P.littorale v longipes	
Psidium friedrichsthalium	B,RE
Psidium guajava	B,DD,EL,HA,LN,RE,SA, TT
Psidium guajava 'Beaumont'	B,EL
Psidium guajava v pyriferum	B,C
Psidium guajava v pyriferum 'Bromar'	B
Psidium guajava white	B,EL
Psidium guajava 'Winter Wonder'	B,EL
Psidium guineense	B
Psidium littorale	SG
Psidium littorale lucidum	CA
Psidium littorale v littorale	B,HU
Psidium littorale v littorale 'Gold'	B
Psidium littorale v longipes	B,C,CA,HA,HU,SA,SG
Psidium sartorium	B
Psilanthus bengalensis	B
Psilostrophe sparsiflora	B
Psilostrophe tagetina	AP,DD,T
Psoralea aphylla	B,SI
Psoralea australasica	B,NI
Psoralea bituminosa	B,SA
Psoralea cuspidata	B,PR
Psoralea esculenta	B,PR
Psoralea lachnostachys	B,NI
Psoralea leucantha	B,NI
Psoralea macrostachya	B
Psoralea parva	B,NI
Psoralea physodes	DD
Psoralea pinnata	B,BH,C,KB,SA,SI
Psoralea pustulata	B,NI
Psoralea tenuiflora	B
Psorothamnus spinosus	B
Psychotria capensis	B,C,KB,SI
Psychotria viridis	B
Psychotria zombamontana	B,SI
Psydrax obovata	B,SI
Psylliostachys suworowii	AB,B,BY,C,CL,CN,GO, HP,JO,KI,KS,L,MO,PI, PK,S,SG,SK,SU,V,VY
Psylliostachys suworowii 'Pink Pokers'	T
Ptaeroxylon obliquum	B,SI,WA
Ptelea trifoliata	B,C,FW,G,HP,LN,N,RS, SA,T
Pteleopsis myrtifolia	B,SI
Pteris argyraea	B,SA
Pteris cretica	SG
Pteris cretica 'Albo-lineata'	B,SA,SG
Pteris cretica major	SA
Pteris cretica 'Mayii'	B,SA
Pteris cretica multifida	SA
Pteris cretica 'Parkeri'	B,SA,SG
Pteris cretica 'Rivertoniana'	B,SA
Pteris cretica 'Rowerii'	B,SA
Pteris cretica 'Tricolor'	B
Pteris cretica v alexandrae	SG
Pteris cretica 'Wimsettii'	B,SA
Pteris ensiformis	B,SA,SG
Pteris ensiformis 'Evergemiensis'	B
Pteris longifolia	B,SA,SG
Pteris multifida	B
Pteris multifida 'Ouvardii'	B
Pteris quadriaurita 'Faurei'	B

PTERIS

Pteris tremula	B,SA
Pteris umbrosa	B
Pteris umbrosa 'Berlin'	B
Pteris vittata	B
Pterocarpus angolensis	B,C,SA,SI,WA
Pterocarpus indicus	B
Pterocarpus lucens	B
Pterocarpus marsupium	B,EL,HA,SA
Pterocarpus rotundifolius	B,SI,WA
Pterocarpus santalinus	B
Pterocarya fraxinifolia	A,B,LN,RS,SA,SG,VE
Pterocarya hupehensis	B,LN
Pterocarya stenoptera	B,LN,SA
Pterocaulon sphacelatum	B,NI
Pterocelastrus echinatus	B,SI
Pterocelatrus tricuspidatus	B,SI
Pteroceltis tartarinowii	B,SA
Pterocephalus hookeri Coll Ref	AP,I
Pterocephalus perennis	AP,B,HP,JE
Pterocephalus perennis ssp perennis	AP,G,I
Pterocephalus plumosus	B
Pterodiscus ngamicus	B,SI
Pterogodium catholicum	SI
Pterogodium magnum	SI
Pterolobium hexapetalum	B
Pteronia camphorata	B,BH,SI
Pteronia glauca	B,SI
Pteropogon humboldtianum	B,C,O,T
Pteropyrum olivieri	VO
Pterospermum acerifolium	B,EL,HA
Pterospermum suberifolium	B
Pterospora andromeda	NO
Pterostylis barbata	B
Pterostylis nana	B
Pterostylis nana 'Gnangarra'	B
Pterostylis recurva	B
Pterostyrax corymbosa	SA
Pterostyrax hispida	AP,B,CG,G,SA,X
Pterostyrax psilophylla	B,SA
Pterygota alata	B
Ptilostemon afer	AP,B,C,CG,FH,G,HP,JE,
Ptilostemon chamaepeuce	AP,CG
Ptilotrichium spinosum see Alyssum	
Ptilotus aervoides	B,NI
Ptilotus astrolasius	B,NI
Ptilotus auriculifolius	B,NI,SA
Ptilotus axillaris	B,NI
Ptilotus calostachyus	B,NI,SA
Ptilotus carinatus	B,NI
Ptilotus clementii	B,NI,SA
Ptilotus exaltatus	AU,B,HA,NI,O,SA
Ptilotus exaltatus semi-lunatus	HA
Ptilotus gomphrenoides	B,NI
Ptilotus helipteroides	AU,B,NI,O
Ptilotus macrocephalus	B,NI
Ptilotus manglesii	B
Ptilotus obovatus	B,NI,O,SA
Ptilotus polakii	B,NI
Ptilotus polystachyus	AU,B,NI
Ptilotus rotundifolius	B,NI,O,SA
Ptychoraphis augusta	RE
Ptychosperma elegans	B,CA,EL,HA,O,SA
Ptychosperma macarthurii	B,CA,EL,HA,O,RE,SA
Ptychosperma microcarpa hyb	B,O
Puccinellia ciliata 'Menemen'	B
Puccinellia distans	B,NO

Puccinellia festuciformis	CG
Pueraria lobata	A,C,FW,LN,SA
Pulicaria crispa	B
Pulicaria dysenterica	B,C,G,LA
Pulicaria vulgaris	B
Pulmonaria angustifolia	B
Pulmonaria mollissima	JE,SA,SG
Pulmonaria officinalis	B,C,DE,G,HP,JE,SA
Pulsatilla alba	AP,B,KL,SC,SG,VO
Pulsatilla albana	AP,B,G,KL,RS,SC,VO
Pulsatilla albana v albana	KL
Pulsatilla albana v violacea	KL
Pulsatilla alpina	AP,B,BS,B,C,CG,CN,G,H
	P,JE,KI,KL,SA,SG,SU,T
Pulsatilla alpina alba	DV
Pulsatilla alpina ssp apiifolia	AP,B,BS,CN,G,HP,J,JE,K
	I,KL,PL,SA,SC,SG,T,VO
Pulsatilla alpina ssp sulphurea see P.a.apiifolia	
Pulsatilla ambigua	AP,B,G,KL,RS,SC
Pulsatilla armena	CG
Pulsatilla aurea	KL,VO
Pulsatilla australis	KL
Pulsatilla balearica	KL
Pulsatilla bungeana	KL
Pulsatilla campanella	VO
Pulsatilla dahurica	AP,SC,SG
Pulsatilla georgica	KL
Pulsatilla grandis	JE
Pulsatilla halleri	AP,B,C,CG,G,JE,KL,NG,
	P,RS,SC,T
Pulsatilla halleri ssp grandis	AP,B,C,G
Pulsatilla halleri ssp slavica	AP,AR,G,HP,SC,SG
Pulsatilla halleri ssp taurica	AR,B,JE
Pulsatilla montana	AP,AR,B,C,CG,JE,SC,SG
Pulsatilla multifida	KL
Pulsatilla myrrhidifolia	B
Pulsatilla occidentalis	AB,AP,B,C,JE,KL,SC
Pulsatilla patens	AP,B,C,G,NO,PR,RM,
	SC,SG,SW
Pulsatilla pratensis	AP,B,CG,G,NG,SC,SG
Pulsatilla pratensis ssp nigricans	AP,B,G,HP,JE,SC
Pulsatilla rubra	KL
Pulsatilla slavica	KL
Pulsatilla slavica 'Rubra'	KL
Pulsatilla sp	KL
Pulsatilla sulphurea	C,SE,V
Pulsatilla tenuiloba	SG
Pulsatilla turkzaninovii	AP,SG
Pulsatilla vernalis	AP,B,C,G,HP,JE,SA,SC
Pulsatilla vulgaris	w.a.
Pulsatilla vulgaris 'Blaue Glocke'	JE
Pulsatilla vulgaris 'Eve Constance'	AP,I
Pulsatilla vulgaris f alba	AP,B,BS,C,CN,G,HP,JE,
	KL,PL,SC
Pulsatilla vulgaris Fringed mix	AP,C,D,KL,P,SC,SE,T
Pulsatilla vulgaris Fringed red	KL,PM
Pulsatilla vulgaris 'Gotlandica'	AP,HP,SC,SG
Pulsatilla vulgaris Heiler Hybrids	C,F,JE
Pulsatilla vulgaris mix	AP,J,P,S,T,V
Pulsatilla vulgaris 'Papageno'	AP,BS,G,JE,PL,SC
Pulsatilla vulgaris pink	NG
Pulsatilla vulgaris red & blue	N
Pulsatilla vulgaris 'Rode Klokke'	AP,G,JE,SC,SE
Pulsatilla vulgaris 'Rubra'	AP,B,BS,C,FH,G,HP,KL,
	MO,RS,SA,SG,PL
Pulsatilla vulgaris ssp grandis	B,KL

PULSATILLA

Pulsatilla vulgaris 'Violacea'	B
Pulsatilla vulgaris 'White Swan'	AP,HP
Pulsatilla zimmermanii	RH
Pultenaea acerosa	B,NI
Pultenaea blakelyi	B,HA
Pultenaea canaliculata v latifolia	B,NI
Pultenaea cunninghamii	HA
Pultenaea daphnoides	B,EL,NI,SA
Pultenaea daphnoides v obcordata	B,NI
Pultenaea ericifolia	B,NI
Pultenaea euchila	B,HA,NI
Pultenaea flexilis	B,HA
Pultenaea foliolosa	HA
Pultenaea juniperina	B,HA,NI
Pultenaea microphylla	B,HA,NI,SA
Pultenaea microphylla v cinerescens	B,NI
Pultenaea myrtoides	B,NI
Pultenaea obcordata	B,NI
Pultenaea paleacea v paleacea	B,NI
Pultenaea polifolia	B,EL,NI
Pultenaea reticulata	B,NI
Pultenaea retusa	B,HA,NI
Pultenaea rosmarinifolius	B,HA,NI
Pultenaea scabra	B
Pultenaea skinneri	B,NI
Pultenaea tenuifolia	B,NI
Pultenaea villosa	AU,B,EL,HA,NI,SA
Pultenaea villulosa	B
Pultenaea viscosa	B,EL,HA,NI
Punica granatum	C,CA,DV,EL,HA,KL,LN, SA,V,VE
Punica granatum 'Minima'	B,EL,SA
Punica granatum purple	HU
Punica granatum v nana	B,BD,BS,BY,C,CA,CG, EL,HA,JE,MO,N,SA,SG, V,VE
Punica granatum v nana 'Orange Pygmy'	B
Pupalia lappacea	B
Purshia tridentata	B,C,LN,NO
Puschkinia scilloides	AP,B,G,KL,SC
Puschkinia scilloides 'Alba'	AP,B,KL
Puschkinia scilloides Pol5328	MN
Puschkinia scilloides v libanotica	HP
Putterlickia pyracantha	B,SI
Puya alpestris	B,C,CA,HP,HU
Puya berteroniana see alpestris	
Puya chilensis	B,SA
Puya coerulea	B,P
Puya coquimbensis	SA
Puya mirabilis	B,BC,C,DV,EL,SA,SG,W, Y
Puya mirabilis v tucumana	DV
Puya sp mix	C
Pycnanthemum flexuosum	B,C
Pycnanthemum incanum	B,NT
Pycnanthemum pilosum	B,C,CN,G,JE,PR
Pycnanthemum pycnanthemoides	B,C,CP
Pycnanthemum tenuifolium	CP,PR
Pycnanthemum virginianum	B,DD,PR
Pycnosorus chrysantha	O
Pycnosorus globosus	NI,O
Pycnostachys coerulea	BH,SI
Pycnostachys glomerata	B
Pycnostachys reticulata	B,KB,SI
Pycnostachys urticifolia	B,KB,SI
Pygmaecereus bylesianus	B,BC

Pyracantha angustifolia	B,C,EL,HA,SA,WA
Pyracantha aurantiaca	B
Pyracantha coccinea	B,C,EL,FW,LN,SA,SG, WA
Pyracantha coccinea 'Lalandei'	B,C,CA,FW,WA
Pyracantha crenatoserrata	B
Pyracantha crenulata	B,SA,WA
Pyracantha rogersiana	B
Pyracantha rogersiana 'Flava'	B
Pyracantha sp AC1469	X
Pyracantha 'Waterer's Orange'	HP
Pyracantha yunnanensis	CA
Pyrethrum radicans see Leucanthemopsis pectinata	
Pyrethrum roseum see Tanacetum coccineum	
Pyrola asarifolia	C,NO
Pyrola media	KL
Pyrola minor	SG
Pyrola norvegica	C
Pyrola picta	NO
Pyrola rotundifolia	CG
Pyrola secunda	C,NO
Pyrrhocactus andicolus	DV
Pyrrhocactus andreaeana	B
Pyrrhocactus atrispinosus	B
Pyrrhocactus bulbocalyx	B,DV,Y
Pyrrhocactus cachytayensis	DV,Y
Pyrrhocactus catamarcensis	B,DV,Y
Pyrrhocactus choapensis Illapel	DV
Pyrrhocactus curvispinus v alicahue	DV
Pyrrhocactus curv. v combarbelensis	DV
Pyrrhocactus curvispinus v petorcensis	DV
Pyrrhocactus curvispinus v putaendo	DV
Pyrrhocactus curvispinus v santiagoensis	DV
Pyrrhocactus dubius	B,DV,Y
Pyrrhocactus echinus	DV,Y
Pyrrhocactus engleri	DV
Pyrrhocactus eriosyzoides	DV
Pyrrhocactus floccosus	DV
Pyrrhocactus garabentai	DV
Pyrrhocactus gracilis	DV
Pyrrhocactus horridus	DV
Pyrrhocactus intermedius	Y
Pyrrhocactus megliolli	B
Pyrrhocactus paucicostatus	DV
Pyrrhocactus paucicostatus v viridis	DV
Pyrrhocactus pichidangue	DV
Pyrrhocactus pilispinus	DV
Pyrrhocactus robustus	DV
Pyrrhocactus saxifraga	DV
Pyrrhocactus sp	DV
Pyrrhocactus strausianus	B,DV,Y
Pyrrhocactus taltalensis	DV
Pyrrhocactus tuberisulcatus	B,DV
Pyrrhocactus umadeave	DV,Y
Pyrrhocactus umadeave v marayesensis	B,BC
Pyrrosia rupestris	HA
Pyrus betulifolia	B,FW,LN,SA,VE
Pyrus calleryana	A,B,CA,FW,LN,SA,VE
Pyrus communis	B,CA,FW,LN,SA,VE
Pyrus communis 'Bartlett'	B,FW,LN
Pyrus communis v kirschensaller	LN,VE
Pyrus pyrifolia	B,CA,FW,LN,SA,SG
Pyrus salicifolia	SA
Pyrus ussuriensis	B,CA,FW,LN,SA,SG
Qualea paraensis	B
Quaqua sp	SI

QUARARIBEA

Quararibea mestonii	B
Quercus acutissima	B,EL,FW,HA,LN,N,SA, WA
Quercus agrifolia	B,CA,LN,SA
Quercus alba	B,CA,FW,LN,SA
Quercus arizonica	B
Quercus bicolor	B,CA,EL,FW,HA,LN,N, SA
Quercus canariensis	B,LN,SA,WA
Quercus castaneifolia	B,LN,N,SA
Quercus cerris	B,C,EL,FW,HA,LN,SA, SG,VE,WA
Quercus chapmanii	B
Quercus chrysolepis	B,CA,LN,SA
Quercus coccifera	B,VE
Quercus coccinea	B,CA,EL,FW,LN,N,SA
Quercus costaricensis	B
Quercus dentata	B,LN,SA
Quercus douglasii	B,CA,EL,HA,LN,SA
Quercus dumosa	B,CA,LN,SA
Quercus durata	B
Quercus ellipsoidalis	B,LN,SA
Quercus emoryi	B
Quercus engelmannii	B,CA,EL
Quercus faginea	LN,SA
Quercus falcata	B,LN,SA
Quercus falcata v pagodifolia	B,LN,SA
Quercus frainetto	LN,SA,SG
Quercus gambellii	B,LN,SA
Quercus garryana	B,CA,LN,SA
Quercus georgiana	B
Quercus glandulifera	B
Quercus glauca	B,SA
Quercus hemispherica	B
Quercus hypoleucoides	B
Quercus ilex	A,B,C,CA,EL,HA,LN,N, SA,VE,WA
Quercus ilex v rotundifolium	VE
Quercus ilicifolia	B,FW,N,SA
Quercus imbricaria	B,LN,SA
Quercus incana	B,SA
Quercus ithaburensis	LN,SA
Quercus kelloggii	B,CA,LN,SA
Quercus laevis	B
Quercus laurifolia	B,CA,LN,SA
Quercus leucotrichophora	B,WA
Quercus liaotungensis	SA
Quercus lobata	B,CA,EL,HA,LN,SA
Quercus lusitanica	EL,HA,SA
Quercus lyrata	B,FW,LN,SA
Quercus macedonica	SA
Quercus macrocarpa	B,CA,EL,FW,HA,LN,N, SA,WA
Quercus marilandica	B,LN,SA
Quercus mexicana	B,WA
Quercus michauxii	B,LN,SA
Quercus mongolica	SA,SG
Quercus muehlenbergii	B,FW,LN,SA
Quercus myrsinifolia	B,SA
Quercus myrtifolia	B
Quercus nigra	B,LN,SA,WA
Quercus nuttallii	B,LN,SA
Quercus oblongifolia	B
Quercus palustris	B,CA,EL,FW,HA,LN,N, SA,VE,WA
Quercus petraea	B,LN,SA,SG

Quercus phellos	B,CA,FW,LN,N,SA
Quercus phillyreoides	B,N,SA
Quercus polymorphus	LN,SA
Quercus prinoides	B
Quercus prinus	B,FW,LN,SA
Quercus pubescens	B,SA,SG,VE
Quercus pyrenaica	EL,SA
Quercus reticulata	B
Quercus robur	B,C,EL,FW,HA,LN,N, SA,WA
Quercus robur f fastigiata	B,EL,FW,LN
Quercus rubra	B,CA,FW,HA,LN,N,SA, VE,WA
Quercus rugosa	B,WA
Quercus sadlerana	B
Quercus shumardii	B,CA,FW,LN,SA
Quercus stellata	B,LN,SA
Quercus suber	B,CA,EL,HA,LN,N,SA, VE,WA
Quercus trojana	SG
Quercus vacciniifolia	SA
Quercus variabilis	B,LN,SA
Quercus velutina	B,FW,LN,SA
Quercus virginiana	B,CA,LN,SA
Quercus wislizenii	B,CA,LN,SA
Quesnelia augusto-coburgii	B
Quesnelia blanda	B
Quesnelia humilis	B
Quesnelia liboniana	B
Quesnelia marmorata	B
Quesnelia quesneliana	B
Quesnelia seideliana	B
Quesnelia testuda	B
Quillaja saponaria	B,SA
Quinoa	CO,DD,JO
Quisqualis indica	B
Rabdosiella calycina	B,KB,SI
Rabiea albinota	B,DV
Rabiea albipunctata	B,DV,SI
Rabiea difformis	DV,Y
Rabiea lesliei	B
Radermachera frondosa	B,EL
Radermachera sinica	B,C,CA,EL,HA,O,PK,SA
Radermachera sinica 'Jumbo'	B,S
Radermachera xylocarpa	B
Radyera farragei	B,NI,SA
Radyera urens	B,SI
Rafinesquia californica	HU
Rafinesquia neomexicana	B
Rafnia amplexicaulis	B,SI
Rafnia capensis	B,SI
Raimondia quinduensis	B
Ramonda myconi	AP,B,C,CG,G,HP,I,JE, KL,P,PL,PM,SC,SG,T
Ramonda myconi v alba	KL
Ramonda nathaliae	AP,B,G,JE,VO
Ramonda serbica	AP,B,G,JE,KL,SC,SG,VO
Randia dumetorum	B
Randia formosa	B
Randia megacarpa	B,DD
Ranunculus abortinus	B
Ranunculus aconitifolius	AP,B,C,HP,JE,SA,SC
Ranunculus acris	B,CO,LA,SU,V
Ranunculus acris 'Citrinus'	AP,B,G,HP,P
Ranunculus acris 'Stevenii'	HP
Ranunculus adoneus	KL

RANUNCULUS

Ranunculus alpestris	B,C,SC,VO	Raoulia australis h see R.hookeri	
Ranunculus amplexicaulis	AP,B,JE,SC,SG	Raoulia glabra	AP,B,SC,SG,SS
Ranunculus aquatilis	B	Raoulia hookeri	AP,B,HP,SC,SG,SS
Ranunculus arvensis	B	Raoulia monroi	SC
Ranunculus asiaticus 'Elfin'	BS	Raoulia subsericea	AP,B,SC,SS
Ranunculus asiaticus f1 'Accolade' s-c	CL	Raoulia tenuicaulis	B,PM,SS
Ranunculus as. f1 'Bloomingdale' mix	BS,C,CA,DE,DT,J,MO,	Rapanea howitteana	SA
	PL,SK,T,V	Rapanea melanophloeos	B,SI,WA
Ranunculus as f1 'Bloomingdale' s-c	B,BS,MO,YA	Raphia gigantica	B
Ranunculus asiaticus giant mix	BS,CO,KI	Raphiolepis clara	CA
Ranunculus asiaticus S.L18 Jordan	MN	Raphiolepis ovata	CA
Ranunculus baurii	B,SI	Raphiolepsis indica	CA,EL,HA,LN,SA
Ranunculus bulbosus	B,SG	Raphiolepsis umbellata	EL,SA
Ranunculus calandrinioides	AP,SC,SG	Raphiolepsis umbellata v ovata	C,HA
Ranunculus calandrinioides S.F137	MN	Raphionacme hirsuta	B,SI
Ranunculus cortusifolius	AP,HP,SG,SZ	Ratibida columnaris	AV,B,HU,HW,JE,SA
Ranunculus cortusifolius Canaries	MN	Ratibida columnifera	AB,AP,B,C,DD,HP,HW,
Ranunculus crenatus	KL,VO		PR,SC,SD,V
Ranunculus crithmifolius	AU,B,SS	Ratibida columnifera f pulcherrima	B,JE
Ranunculus dbl mix	C	Ratibida pinnata	B,DD,G,HP,HW,JE,PR
Ranunculus enysii	AU,B,SS	Ratibida tagetes	B
Ranunculus eschscholtzii	B,G,SG	Rauvolfia caffra	B,SA,SI,WA
Ranunculus ficaria	B	Rauvolfia serpentina	B
Ranunculus flammula	B,G,JE,SG	Rauvolfia tetraphylla	B,EL
Ranunculus gelidus	VO	Rauvolfia verticillata	B,EL
Ranunculus glacialis	B,JE,SA,SC	Rauwenhoffia leichardtii	B
Ranunculus godleyanus	AU	Ravenala madagascariensis	B,C,CA,EL,O,VE
Ranunculus gouanii	KL	Ravenea glauca	B
Ranunculus gracilipes	B,SS	Ravenea madagascariensis	B,EL,SA
Ranunculus gramineus	AP,B,G,HP,JE,KL,P,PM,	Ravenea rivularis	B,CA,EL,HA,O,SI
	SA,SC	Razania japonica	KL
Ranunculus grandis	SG	Reaumuria hirtella	B
Ranunculus haastii	AU,B,SS	Rebutia albiareolata	B,DV,Y
Ranunculus helenae	VO	Rebutia albida	DV,Y
Ranunculus hispid	PR	Rebutia albipilosa	B,DV
Ranunculus illyricus	KL	Rebutia alegraiana	Y
Ranunculus insignis	AP,B,P,SC,SS	Rebutia almeyeri	Y
Ranunculus lappaceus	AP,KL,SC	Rebutia archibuiningiana	B
Ranunculus lingua	HP	Rebutia arenacea	B,DV,Y
Ranunculus lingua 'Grandiflorus'	B,P	Rebutia aureicentra	Y
Ranunculus lojkae	VO	Rebutia aureispina	B
Ranunculus lyallii	AP,AU,B,C,SA,SS	Rebutia bicolorispina	DV
Ranunculus marginatus	B	Rebutia breviflora	Y
Ranunculus monroi	B,SS	Rebutia buiningiana	Y
Ranunculus montanus	AP,B,VO	Rebutia cajasensis	B
Ranunculus multifidus	B,SI	Rebutia calliantha	B,DV,Y
Ranunculus nepalensis	B	Rebutia canaletas	B
Ranunculus nivicola	B,KL,P	Rebutia candiae	B,DV,Y
Ranunculus occidentalis	SG	Rebutia chrysacantha	B,Y
Ranunculus ophioglossifolius	B,NS,SG	Rebutia cintiensis	B
Ranunculus parnassifolium	AP,B,JE,KL,SC,VO	Rebutia corroana	B,Y
Ranunculus pensylvanicus	B,PR	Rebutia crispata	B,DV
Ranunculus platanifolius	B,KL,SG	Rebutia curvispinus	CH,DV
Ranunculus polyanthemos	AP,SC	Rebutia cylindrica	DV,Y
Ranunculus pyrenaeum	B,C,JE,SA,SC,SG	Rebutia deminuta	B
Ranunculus repens	B	Rebutia densipectinata	B
Ranunculus rhomboideus	B,PR	Rebutia donaldiana	B,CH,Y
Ranunculus sceleratus	B	Rebutia erinacea	DV,Y
Ranunculus scutatus	VO	Rebutia erinacea v catarinensis	B,Y
Ranunculus seguieri	B,KL	Rebutia erinacea v catarirensis	Y
Ranunculus sericophyllus	B,SS	Rebutia espinosae	DV
Ranunculus sp ex Morocco	AP	Rebutia fiebrigii	B,DV
Ranunculus sp mix	SC	Rebutia fiebrigii v densiseta	B
Ranunculus thora	AP,B,JE,KL	Rebutia fiebrigii v nivosa	B
Ranunculus 'Victoria' mix	CA	Rebutia flavissima	DV,Y
Raoulia apice-nigra	B,SS	Rebutia flavistyla	B,CH,DV

REBUTIA

Rebutia frankiana	Y
Rebutia frankii	B
Rebutia fulviseta	B,CH
Rebutia glomeriseta	Y
Rebutia glomerispina	DV,Y
Rebutia graciliflora	B,Y
Rebutia graciliflora v borealis	B
Rebutia gracilispina	B
Rebutia grandiflora	B,BC,Y
Rebutia hediniana	B
Rebutia heliosa	B
Rebutia heliosa v cajasensis	B
Rebutia hoffmannii	CH,DV
Rebutia HS13	BC
Rebutia HS189	BC
Rebutia ithyacantha	B
Rebutia jujuyana	B
Rebutia kariusiana	DV,Y
Rebutia knuthiana	DV
Rebutia krahnii	Y
Rebutia krainziana	B,CH,DV,Y
Rebutia krainziana albiflora	BC
Rebutia krainziana v rubiginosa	Y
Rebutia kupperana	B
Rebutia kupperiana v spiniflora	B
Rebutia lanata	B
Rebutia lateritia KK1519	Y
Rebutia lauii	B
Rebutia lepida	Y
Rebutia longigibba	B
Rebutia lucida	Y
Rebutia makusii v longispina	DV
Rebutia mammillosa v australis	Y
Rebutia mammillosa v orientalis	CH,DV,Y
Rebutia mammilosa	DV
Rebutia margarethae	Y
Rebutia marsoneri	B,DV,Y
Rebutia marsoneri v brevispina	B
Rebutia marsoneri v vatteri	Y
Rebutia maxima	B
Rebutia menesesii	B,DV,Y
Rebutia menesesii v kamiensis	Y
Rebutia middendorfii	SA
Rebutia miniscula	B,BC,CH,DV
Rebutia miniscula f kariusiana	B
Rebutia miniscula ssp grandiflora	Y
Rebutia miniscula v knuthiana	Y
Rebutia minuscula	B,Y
Rebutia minuscula v bruneoaurantiaca	Y
Rebutia minuscula v densispina	B
Rebutia minuscula v rosea	Y
Rebutia multispina	B,Y
Rebutia muscula see R.fiebrigii	
Rebutia narvaecensis	B
Rebutia neocumingii	DV
Rebutia nitida	B
Rebutia patericalyx	DV,Y
Rebutia pilosa	B
Rebutia platygona	Y
Rebutia poecilantha	B,DV
Rebutia polymorpha	Y
Rebutia potosina	B
Rebutia pseudodeminuta	B
Rebutia pseudodeminuta v schneideriana	B
Rebutia pseudodeminuta v schumanniana	B
Rebutia pseudokrainziana	Y

Rebutia pulquinensis	B,DV
Rebutia pulquinensis v mairananensis	B,Y
Rebutia pygmaea	CH,DV
Rebutia ritteri	B
Rebutia robustispina	B
Rebutia salmonea	CH
Rebutia sanguinea	BC
Rebutia scheiliana	DV
Rebutia senilis	B,DV,Y
Rebutia senilis v cana	Y
Rebutia senilis v chrysacantha	B
Rebutia senilis v elegans	B,Y
Rebutia senilis v erecta	B
Rebutia senilis v gracilis	Y
Rebutia senilis v iseliana	B,CH,DV
Rebutia senilis v kesselringiana	B,BC,DV
Rebutia senilis v kessel. 'Rose Of York'	B,DV
Rebutia senilis v lilacino-rosea	Y
Rebutia senilis v longiflora	B
Rebutia senilis v luteospina	B
Rebutia senilis v schieliana	B,Y
Rebutia senilis v stuemeri	B,DV,Y
Rebutia sp Lau 974	DV
Rebutia sp mix	C,CH,FR,SO,Y
Rebutia sp Ue 924	Y
Rebutia spegazziniana	B
Rebutia spinosissima	B
Rebutia steinbachii	DV
Rebutia steinbachii v polymorpha	B
Rebutia steinbachii v violaciflora	Y
Rebutia sucrensis	B
Rebutia tamboensis	B
Rebutia tarijensis	DV
Rebutia tiraquensis	DV
Rebutia tiraquensis v electracantha	B,Y
Rebutia tuberculosa v chrysacantha	DV,Y
Rebutia tuberosa	B
Rebutia vanbaelii	DV,Y
Rebutia vatteri	CH,DV
Rebutia violaciflora see R.minuscula	
Rebutia violaciflora v knuthiana	Y
Rebutia vorwerkii	Y
Rebutia wessneriana	B,DV
Rebutia wessneriana v beryllioides	B
Rebutia xanthocarpa	B,CH,DV,Y
Rebutia xanthocarpa pink form	DV
Rebutia xanthocarpa v citricarpa	B
Rebutia xanthocarpa v coerulescens	B
Rebutia xanthocarpa v cristata	DV
Rebutia xanthocarpa v dasyphrissa	B,Y
Rebutia xanthocarpa v salmonea	B,DV,Y
Rebutia xanthocarpa v splendens	DV,Y
Rebutia xanthocarpa v violaciflora	B
Rechsteinaria leucotricha see Sinninga canescens	
Rechsteineria leucotricha	T
Rechsteineria see Sinningia	
Rechsteineria speciosa	DV
Reclamation ground cover,grasses	B
Regelia ciliata	B,NI,SA
Regelia cymbifolia	B,NI
Regelia inops	B,NI
Regelia megacephala	B,NI
Regelia velutina	B,NI,SA
Rehmannia angulata see R.elata	
Rehmannia elata	AP,B,BS,C,CL,CN,E,F,G,HP,JE,MO,SA,SC,V

REHMANNIA

Rehmannia elata 'Popstar'	T
Rehmannia glutinosa	C
Rehmannia sp	RS
Reinhardtia gracilis	O
Reinhardtia simplex	B,SA
Reissantia indica	B
Relhania pungens	B,SI
Renealmia alpina	B
Reseda alba	B,G,HP,NG,SC,SG,V
Reseda complicata	VO
Reseda lutea	B,C,CN,CO,G,LA,RH,SG
Reseda luteola	B,C,CN,CP,HP,LA,RH,TH
Reseda muricata	B
Reseda odorata	BH,BY,CN,CP,DE,DI,F,J,
	JO,KI,KS,SE,SK,ST,SU,
	TH,TU,U
Reseda odorata 'Alba'	JO,KS
Reseda odorata 'Fragrant Beauty'	T
Reseda odorata 'Grandiflora'	AB,B,C,HU
Reseda odorata 'Machet'	B,C,D,V
Reseda odorata 'Red Monarch'	B
Reseda orientalis	B
Reseda stenostachya	B
Restio bifarius	B,SI
Restio fimbriatus	O
Restio gracilis	B
Restio pachystachyus	B,SI
Restio quadratus	B,SI
Restio tetraphyllus	AU,B,EL,SA
Restio tetraphyllus ssp meiostachys	O
Restio tremulus	B,NI,O
Retama monosperma	B,C,FW,HP,SA,VE
Retama raetam	B,SA
Retama raetam v judaica	B
Retama spaerocarpa	C,SA
Rhadamanthus namibensis	B,SI
Rhagodia baccata	B,HU,NI
Rhagodia preissii	B
Rhamnus alaternus	SA,VE
Rhamnus alnifolia	NO
Rhamnus alpinus	G
Rhamnus californicus	B,CA,LN
Rhamnus carolinianus	B,FW,LN,SA
Rhamnus catharticus	B,C,FW,LN,SA,SG,VE
Rhamnus davurica	LN,SG
Rhamnus frangula	A,B,FW,LN,SA,VE
Rhamnus frangula 'Columnaris'	B,FW
Rhamnus japonicus	NG
Rhamnus koraiensis	B
Rhamnus lycioides	SA
Rhamnus microcarpa	VO
Rhamnus pallasii	KL,VO
Rhamnus prinoides	B,KB,SI,WA
Rhamnus pumila	B,KL
Rhamnus purshianus	AB,B,NO
Rhamnus saxatilis	VO
Rhamnus saxatilis ssp saxatilis	SG
Rhamnus sp	KL
Rhaphidophora decursiva	B
Rhaphiolepis indica	B
Rhaphiolepis indica 'Clara'	B
Rhaphiolepis umbellata	B
Rhaphiolepis umbellata v integerrima	CG
Rhaphiolepis x delacourii	B
Rhaphithamnus spinosus	C,SA
Rhapidophyllum hystrix	CA

Rhapis excelsa	B,CA,EL,O,SA
Rhapis subtilis	B,O
Rhaponticum carthamoides	CG,KL,SG
Rhaponticum chamarense	SG
Rhaponticum orientale	SG
Rhaponticum serratuloides	SG
Rheedia macrophylla	B
Rheedia madruno	B
Rheedia magnifolia	B
Rheum alexandrae AC1569	X
Rheum altaicum	SG
Rheum australe	B,CG,DD,JE,SA
Rheum compactum	B,SG
Rheum emodi see R.australe	
Rheum Himalayan Green	HU
Rheum palmatum	BS,CG,HP,SC,T
Rheum palmatum 'Atropurpureum' see R.p. 'Atrosanguineum'	
Rheum palmatum 'Atrosanguineum'	B,HP,JE,P,PA,PM
Rheum palmatum 'Bowles Crimson'	AP,B,BS,MO
Rheum palmatum red	SA
Rheum palmatum rubrum	HP
Rheum palmatum v tanguticum	B,CN,JE,P,SA
Rheum palmatum v tang. red selection	JE
Rheum rhabarbarum	DD
Rheum rhaponticum	B,JE
Rheum tataricum	C
Rheum tibeticum	B,JE
Rheum undulatum	SG
Rheum x cultorum see R.x hybridum	
Rheum x hybridum 'Glaskin's Perpetual'	B
Rheum x hybridum 'Victoria'	B
Rhexia virginica	AP,B,C,JE
Rhigozum brevispinosum	B,SI
Rhigozum obovatum	B,KB,SI
Rhinanthus angustifolius	B
Rhinanthus minor	B,C,CN,LA,RS,SU
Rhinanthus serotinus ssp grandiflorus	B
Rhinephyllum broomii	AP,B,DV,SC,SG
Rhinephyllum macradenium	B
Rhinephyllum muirii	B
Rhinopetalum bucharicum	KL
Rhinopetalum stanatherum	KL
Rhipsalis baccifera	Y
Rhipsalis cappiliformis	SG
Rhipsalis cereucula	DV
Rhipsalis clavata	SG
Rhipsalis coralloides	DV
Rhipsalis fasciculata	CH,DV
Rhipsalis heptagona	SG
Rhipsalis horrida	CH,DV
Rhipsalis houlletiana	SG
Rhipsalis mesembrianthemoides	SG
Rhipsalis roseana	DV
Rhipsalis sp mix	C,CH
Rhipsalis teres	DV
Rhipsalis warmingiana	DV
Rhodanthe 'Baby Sun'	BS,U
Rhodanthe charsleyae	B,NI,O
Rhodanthe chlorocephala 'Alba'	KS
Rhodanthe chlorocephala 'Bonnie'	B,D,KS,M
Rhodanthe chlorocephala 'Brilliant'	B,KS
Rhodanthe chlorocephala dbl mix	BS,BY,CO,FR,J,L,KI,PI,
	SK,ST,SU,T,TU
Rhodanthe chlorocephala dbl s-c	B,T
Rhodanthe chlorocephala dbl white	C
Rhodanthe chlorocephala giant mix	KS

RHODANTHE

Rhodanthe chlorocephala 'Goliath' — B,F,PK
Rhodanthe chlorocephala semi-dbl — U
Rhodanthe chlorocephala special — S
Rhodanthe chlorocephala ssp chlorocephala — B,O
Rhodanthe chlorocephala ssp roseum — B,BS,C,CN,F,HA,NI,O, R,SG,SU,TE,V
Rhodanthe citrina — B,O
Rhodanthe 'Ebony Rouge' — SE
Rhodanthe floribunda — B,NI,O
Rhodanthe manglesii — AB,B,BS,C,CO,D,HA, HU,J,KI,L,MO,NI,O, TU,V,VY
Rhodanthe manglesii 'Maculata Album' — B,C,KS,MO,NI
Rhodanthe manglesii 'Maculatum' mix — BS,C
Rhodanthe mang. 'Maculatum Roseum' — B,C,DI,KS,MO
Rhodanthe manglesii 'Pinky' — BS,U
Rhodanthe manglesii 'Timeless Rose' — B,C,PK
Rhodanthe manglessii 'Maculata' rose — BY
Rhodanthe mix giant fl dbl — DE
Rhodanthe 'Pierrot' — DI,PL,U
Rhodanthe polygalifolia — B,NI,O
Rhodanthe Sensation Giants mix — JO,VY
Rhodanthe sterilescens — B,NI,O
Rhodanthe stricta — B,NI,O
Rhodanthe 'Tetred' — C
Rhodiola coccinea — VO
Rhodiola himalensis v ishidae — B
Rhodiola kirilovii — B,CG,DV
Rhodiola linearifolia — VO
Rhodiola pachyclados see Sedum
Rhodiola pinnatifida — SG
Rhodiola primuloides v pachyclada — B
Rhodiola rhodantha — B,KL,SC
Rhodiola rosea — AP,B,C,I,JE,SC,SG
Rhodiola semenowii — HP,VO
Rhodiola stephanii — DV
Rhodochiton atrosanguineum — AP,B,BS,C,CL,D,DT,EL, F,G,HP,HU,J,JO,MO,PK, PL,S,SA,SE,SG,T

Rhodocoma arida — B,SI
Rhodocoma gigantea — B,SI
Rhododendron adenogynum — B,FW
Rhododendron aff sororium KR4278 — X
Rhododendron aganniphum — B,FW
Rhododendron aganniphum AC1831 — X
Rhododendron agastum — B,FW
Rhododendron albiflorum — B,FW
Rhododendron albrechtii — CG,SG
Rhododendron albrechtii h-p — X
Rhododendron alutaceum — DV,X
Rhododendron ambiguum — B,FW,SG,X
Rhododendron angustinii — SG
Rhododendron anhweiense — X
Rhododendron anthosphaerum — B,FW
Rhododendron anthosphaerum AC1852 — X
Rhododendron anthosphaerum AC1910 — X
Rhododendron arboreum — B,C,FW,SA
Rhododendron argentium — DV
Rhododendron aritum AC1374 — X
Rhododendron asterochnoum Leibo — X
Rhododendron asterochnoum Yunnan — X
Rhododendron atlanticum — B,FW,SA
Rhododendron augustinii — N
Rhododendron aureum — B,FW,VO
Rhododendron aureum MW10R — X
Rhododendron auriculatum — X

Rhododendron auritum — X
Rhododendron austrinum — B
Rhododendron Azalea mix — HU
Rhododendron balfourianum AC1575 — X
Rhododendron barbatum — SA
Rhododendron basilicum — DV
Rhododendron beesianum — B,FW,SA
Rhododendron beesianum Coll. Ref — X
Rhododendron bergii Coll Ref — X
Rhododendron brachyanthum Coll Ref — X
Rhododendron brachycarpum — DV,SG
Rh. brachycarpum ssp fauieri MW306R — X
Rh. brach. ssp fauieri MW327R pink — X
Rhododendron brachycarpum v tigerstedii — FW,X
Rhododendron bureavii — SG
Rhododendron bureavii Coll Ref — X
Rhododendron burmanicum — CG
Rhododendron calendulaceum — B,FW
Rhododendron californicum — C
Rhododendron calostrotum — DV
Rhododendron calostrotum AC3011 — X
Rhododendron cal. ssp riparium CC7563 — X
Rhododendron campanulatum — SA
Rhododendron campanulatum TW34 — X
Rhododendron camtschaticum — AP,B,G,JE,KL,SC,VO
Rhododendron carolinianum see R.minus v minus Carolinianum Gr
Rhododendron catawbiense — B,SA
Rhododendron catawbiense 'Album' — B,FW
Rhododendron catawbiense hyb — C,FW
Rhododendron cat. 'Roseum Varieties' — B
Rhododendron catawbiense v compactum — B,FW
Rhododendron caucasicum — VO
Rhododendron cephalanthum — B,FW
Rh. cf rufosquamosum KR4270 — X
Rhododendron cf veitchianum Coll Ref — X
Rhododendron chrysanthum see R. aureum
Rhododendron ciliicalyx — B,CG,FW
Rhododendron clementinae AC1950 — X
Rhododendron colletum Coll Ref — X
Rhododendron concinnum (Tower Court) — SG,X
Rhododendron coriaceum — CG
Rhododendron coriaceum AC1921 — X
Rhododendron crinigerum — B,FW
Rhododendron cubittii — CG
Rhododendron cuneatum AC1493 — X
Rhododendron cvs — B
Rhododendron cyanocarpum — B,FW
Rhododendron cyanocarpum AC1352 — X
Rhododendron dalhousieae v rhabdotum — C,X
Rhododendron dauricum — B,FW,SG
Rhododendron davidsonianum — B,CG,DV,FW
Rhododendron davidsonianum AC2081 — X
Rhododendron decatros — B,FW
Rhododendron decorum — B,FW,SG,X
Rhododendron decorum CNW602 — X
Rhododendron decorum Coll Ref — X
Rhododendron degronianum — B,FW,X
Rhododendron deg. ssp heptamerum — DV,X
Rhododendron delavayi — CG
Rhododendron delavayi AC911 — X
Rhododendron delavayi CNW994 — X
Rhododendron delavayi Coll Ref — X
Rhododendron denudatum AC1143 — X
Rhododendron denudatum C&H7118 — X
Rh. diaprepes (Garg.) x R. Walloper x1328 — X
Rh. diaprepes (Garg.) x R. Walloper x1331 — X

RHODODENDRON

Rhododendron dichroanthum AC3079 X
Rhododendron discolor see R. fortunei ssp d.
Rh. d. seedling x R. 'Bisciut Box' h-p 1994 X
Rhododendron doshongense cf AC1729 X
Rhododendron edgeworthii CG,X
Rhododendron ellipticum CG
Rhododendron 'Exbury' hyb B,FW
Rhododendron excellens C&H7180 X
Rhododendron eximeum X
Rhododendron faberi B,FW
Rhododendron facetum KR3986 X
Rhododendron fargesii see R.oreodoxa v fargesii
Rhododendron fastigiatum MF96156 X
Rhododendron faucium KR3465 X
Rhododendron fauriei see R.brachycarpum ssp f.
Rhododendron ferrugineum AP,B,C,DV,FW,G,JE,KL, SA,SC
Rhododendron ferrugineum X
Rhododendron fictolacteum Coll Ref X
Rhododendron floccigerum AC1898 X
Rhododendron fortunei B,DV,EL,FW,SA,X
Rhododendron fortunei f1 Lu Shan B,FW,N
Rhododendron fortunei f1 Lu Shan h-p C
Rhododendron fortunei ssp discolor B,FW,KL,SA,X
Rh. fortunei ssp discolor Houlstonii Gr DV,X
Rhododendron fulvum B,FW
Rhododendron fumidum CNW1048 X
Rhododendron fumidum CNW944 X
Rhododendron fumidum CNW974 X
Rhododendron Gable Hybrids mix FW
Rhododendron 'Ghent' hyb B,FW
Rhododendron glaucopeplum Coll Ref X
Rhododendron glaucophyllum C,SG
Rhododendron glischrum B,FW
Rhododendron gongshanensis B,FW
Rhododendron grande AP,X
Rhododendron gratum AC3009 X
Rhododendron 'Gwillt King' h-p X
Rhododendron 'Gwillt King' o-p X
Rhododendron 'Gwillt King' x penjerrick X
Rhododendron habrotrichum CG
Rhododendron haematodes FW
Rhododendron heliolepis B,FW
Rhododendron heliolepis Coll Ref X
Rhododendron heliolepis sp CNW998 X
Rh. heliolepis v fumidum AC2069 X
Rhododendron hemsleyanum B,FW,X
Rhododendron hippophaeoides Coll Ref X
Rhododendron hirsutum B,JE,KL,X
Rhododendron honanense B,FW
Rhododendron houlstonii see R.fortunei ssp discolor Houlstonii Gr
Rhododendron huianum EGM330 X
Rhododendron hunnewellianum CG
Rhododendron hyb mix C
Rhododendron impeditum 'Album' KL
Rhododendron imperator CC7530 X
Rhododendron intermedium X
Rhododendron irroratum B,FW
Rhododendron irroratum sp CNW362 X
Rhododendron irroratum sp CNW363 X
Rhododendron irroratum sp CNW365 X
Rhododendron irroratum sp CNW392 X
Rhododendron irroratum sp CNW395 X
Rhododendron irroratum sp CNW555 X
Rhododendron irroratum sp CNW568 X
Rhododendron irroratum sp CNW674 X

Rhododendron irr. ssp pogonostylum CG
Rhododendron japonicum B,FW,N
Rhododendron jununegig B,FW
Rhododendron kaempheri albiflorum X
Rhododendron 'Kermesinum' KL
Rhododendron kesselringii X
Rhododendron 'Knap Hill' hyb C,FW
Rhododendron kotschyi see R.myrtifolium
Rhododendron lacteum B,FW
Rhododendron latouchae CG
Rhododendron lepidotum TW40 X
Rhododendron leptothrium B,FW
Rhododendron leptothrium KR4028 X
Rhododendron leucaspis SG
Rhododendron linearifolium B
Rhododendron litiense MF96155 X
Rhododendron luteum B,FW,G,KL,N,RH,SC,VO
Rhododendron macabeanum X
Rhododendron macrophyllum AB,B,CG,FW
Rhododendron maddenii SG
Rhododendron madennii Coll Ref X
Rhododendron makinoi B,FW,X
Rhododendron mallotum X
Rhododendron maximum B,FW,HU,SA
Rhododendron metternichii see R.degronianum ssp heptamerum
Rhododendron micranthum B,FW,LN
Rhododendron microphyton AC20990 X
Rhododendron minus FW,SA,SG,X
Rhododendron mix N
Rhododendron mix bonsai N
Rhododendron mix deciduous N
Rhododendron Modern Hybrids B
Rhododendron molle B,FW,KL
Rhododendron mollicomum CG
Rhododendron mollis hyb B,BS,C,F,FW,SA
Rh. monosematum CNW956 see R.pachytrichum Monosematum
Rhododendron montroseanum white X
Rhododendron morii CG,X
Rhododendron moupinense N
Rhododendron mucronata hyb B
Rhododendron mucronulatum B,FW,G,LN,SA,SG
Rhododendron mucronulatum MW109R X
Rhododendron mucronulatum MW242R X
Rhododendron myrtifolium DV
Rhododendron neriifolium Coll Ref X
Rhododendron nipponicum AP,SC,X
Rhododendron nudiflorum see R.periclymenoides
Rhododendron nuttallii X
Rhododendron nuttallii KR4255 X
Rhododendron obtusa arnoldiana FW
Rhododendron obtusa hyb B
Rhododendron obtusa kaempferi hyb B,FW
Rhododendron Obtusum Group X
Rhododendron occidentale B,FW,SA
Rhododendron 'Old Spice' X
Rhododendron oreodoxa v fargesii B,FW,SA
Rh. oreodoxa v fargesii aff AC1104 X
Rhododendron oreotrephes B,FW,SG
Rhododendron oreotrephes KR4113 X
Rhododendron pachypodum CG
Rhododendron pachypodum AC1993 X
Rh. pachytrichum Monosematum Gr C.R. X
Rhododendron pentaphyllum X
Rhododendron periclymenoides B
Rhododendron phaeochrysum B,FW
Rh. phaeochrysum v levistratum AC1757 X

RHODODENDRON

Rh. pogonostylum see R.irroratum ssp p.
Rhododendron polylepis — X
Rhododendron ponticum — B,FW,SA,VO
Rhododendron poukhanense see R.yedoense v p.
Rhododendron primulifolium AC1745 — X
Rhododendron procumbens — FW,SA
Rhododendron prunifolium — B
Rhododendron pubocostatum AC2051 — X
Rhododendron pumilum — AP,G,SG
Rhododendron purdomii — LN
Rhododendron racemosum — DV,X
Rhododendron racemosum CNW789 — X
Rhododendron reticulatum — B,SA,X
Rhododendron rex ssp arizelum — B,FW
Rhododendron rex ssp rex C&H7003 — X
Rhododendron rhabdotum see R. dalhousieae v r.
Rhododendron ririei — CG
Rhgododendron rosea — B,FW,SA
Rhododendron rothschildii AC1868 — X
Rh. roxieanum v oreonanstes AC1750 — X
Rhododendron rubiginosum — B,DV,FW,SG
Rhododendron rubiginosum CNW 1143 — X
Rhododendron rubiginosum CNW 381 — X
Rhododendron rubiginosum CNW 683 — X
Rhododendron rubiginosum Coll Ref — X
Rhododendron rushforthii KR2357A — X
Rhododendron russatum aff AC1538 — X
Rhododendron saluenense — B,FW
Rhododendron sanguineum Coll Ref — X
Rhododendron scabrifolium — B,FW
Rhododendron scabrum — X
Rhododendron schlippenbachii — B,C,CG,FW,G,KL,LN,SA
Rhododendron schlippenbachii MW157R — X
Rhododendron scottianum see R.pachypodum
Rhododendron selense — B,FW
Rhododendron selense AC1756 — X
Rhododendron selense? CNW6120 — X
Rh. selense ssp dasycladum AC1943 — X
Rh. selense ssp jucundum Coll Ref — X
Rhododendron serotinum — X
Rhododendron sichotense MW243R — X
Rhododendron sidereum — B,FW
Rhododendron sidereum AC3056 — X
Rhododendron siderophyllum — B,FW
Rhododendron siderophyllum AC2094 — X
Rh. siderophyllum aff CNW1112 — X
Rh. sikangense aff CNW1060 — X
Rh. sikangense v exquisetum AC2066 — X
Rh. sikangense v exquisitum CNW967 — X
Rhododendron simsii — B,FW,LN
Rhododendron sinogrande — B,FW,X
Rhododendron sinogrande Coll ref — X
Rh. sinonuttallii-excellens AC1996 — X
Rhododendron smirnowii — B,DV,FW,SC
Rhododendron souliei — B,FW
Rh. 'Southern Cross' x R. 'Bisciut Box' h-p — X
Rhododendron sp AC2016 — X
Rh. sp lapponicum series AC1539 — X
Rhododendron sp mix — C
Rh. spaeroblastum v wumengense C.R. — X
Rhododendron sperabile — B,FW
Rh. sperabile whiesiense AC1915 — X
Rh. sphaeroblastum v wumengense C.Ref — X
Rhododendron spiciferum v album C.Ref — X
Rhododendron spilotum — X
Rhododendron stewartianum — B,FW

Rhododendron strigillosum EGM305 — X
Rhododendron subsect. Parishia KR4013 — X
Rhododendron sutchuenense — KL,X
Rhododendron taggianum — CG
Rhododendron tapetiforme AC1754 — X
Rhododendron tashiroi — CG
Rhododendron traillianum — B,FW
Rhododendron trichocladum CNW612 — X
Rhododendron trichocladum CNW622 — X
Rhododendron trichocladum CNW841 — X
Rhododendron trichocladum CNW880 — X
Rhododendron trichocladum Coll Ref — X
Rhododendron trichostomum Coll Ref — X
Rhododendron triflorum — X
Rhododendron uvarifolium — B,FW
Rhododendron uvarifolium CNW382 — X
Rhododendron uvarifolium Coll Ref — X
Rhododendron valentinum aff C&H7186 — X
Rhododendron vaseyi — B,FW,SA,SG,X
Rhododendron vernicosum — B,FW
Rhododendron vernicosum C&H7009 — X
Rhododendron vernicosum C&H7027 — X
Rhododendron vernicosum Coll Ref — X
Rhododendron viridescens CC7557 — X
Rhododendron viscosum — B,FW
Rhododendron wadanum — CG,X
Rhododendron wardii — B,FW,SG,X
Rhododendron wardii Coll Ref — X
Rhododendron wardii puralbum cf C.Ref — X
Rhododendron wardii v litiense AC1874 — X
Rhododendron weyrichii — X
Rhododendron wightii — DV
Rhododendron williamsianum — B,FW
Rhododendron x halense — KL
Rhododendron xanthocodon — X
Rhododendron yakushimanum — B,C,CG,FW,N,SA,SG,X
Rhododendron yedoense v poukhanense — B,FW,SA
Rhododendron yunnanense — B,FW,SG
Rhododendron yunnannse AC1417 — X
Rhododendron zaleucum — DV
Rhodohypoxis baurii — B,SI
Rhodohypoxis mix — AP,C,I
Rhodomyrtus tomentosa — B,EL,HA,SH
Rhodophiala advena — AR
Rhodophiala andicola — P
Rhodophiala pratensis — AR
Rhodosphaera rhodanthema — B,HA,O
Rhodothamnus chamaecistus — KL
Rhodotypos kerrioides see R.scandens
Rhodotypos scandens — AP,B,C,CG,FW,HP,LG, NG,SA,SC,SG

Rhoeo discolor see Tradescantia
Rhoicissus digitata — B,C,KB,O,SA,SI
Rhoicissus tomentosa — B,KB,SI
Rhombophyllum dolabriforme — B,DV,KB
Rhombophyllum nelii — B,Y
Rhopaloblaste augusta — B
Rhopalostylis baueri — B,CA,HA,O,SA
Rhopalostylis cheesmanii — O
Rhopalostylis sapida — B,CA,EL,HA,O,SA,SS
Rhopalostylis sapida g — B
Rhus angustifolia — B,SI
Rhus aromatica — B,CA,CG,FW,LN,SA
Rhus batophylla — B,KB,SI
Rhus burchellii — B,SI
Rhus chinensis — B,LN,SA

RHUS

Rhus chirindensis	B,KB,SI,WA	Ribes pubescens	SG
Rhus choriophylla	B,SW	Ribes sanguineum	AB,B,C,HP,LN,NO,VE
Rhus ciliata	B,SI	Ribes speciosum	B,SG
Rhus copallina	B,C,FW,LN,NT,SA	Ribes viscosissimum	NO
Rhus coriaria	LN,SA	Ribes x holosericeum	SG
Rhus crenata	B,SI	Richea alpina	AR
Rhus dentata	B,SI	Richea dracophylla	AU,B,C,NI,P,O,SA
Rhus discolor	B,SI	Richea pandanifolia	AR,B,O
Rhus erosa	B,SI	Richea scoparia	AR,B
Rhus glabra	A,B,C,CA,FW,LN,NO,NT, SA	Richea sprengelioides	AR
		Ricinocarpus pinifolius	B,HA,NI
Rhus glauca	B,SI	Ricinocarpus tuberculatus	B,NI,O
Rhus gueinzii	B,KB	Ricinodendron heudelotii	B
Rhus incisa	B,SI	Ricinus communis	B,CG,DD,EL,G,HU,PI,SA
Rhus integrifolia	B,C,CA,NO	Ricinus communis 'Carmencita'	B,BS,C,DE,HU,JO,L,MO,
Rhus laevigata	B,SI		T,YA
Rhus lancea	B,BH,CA,KB,SI,WA	Ricinus communis 'Carmencita Pink'	B,BS,C,JO,MO,T
Rhus laurina	CA	Ricinus communis 'Gibsonii'	B,BS,C,SA,V
Rhus leptodictya	B,LN,SI,WA	Ricinus communis 'Higuerilla Roja'	B,HU
Rhus lucida	B,SI	Ricinus communis 'Impala'	B,D,SA,T
Rhus megalismontana	B,SI	Ricinus communis purple	B,G,Sg
Rhus microphylla	B,SW	Ricinus communis 'Sanguineus'	B,BS,DE,HU,SG,SK
Rhus ovata	B	Ricinus communis v cambodgensis	SG
Rhus pallens	B,SI	Ricinus communis v rugosus	SG
Rhus pendulina	B,KB,SI,WA	Ricinus communis 'Zanzibarensis'	B,BS,BY,C,CP,FR,HU,
Rhus populifolia	B,SI		MO,SA,SG,SK,V
Rhus potaninii	B,LN,SA,SG		
Rhus punjabensis v sinica	B	Ricinus sp purple New Zealand	CP
Rhus pyroides	B,SI,WA	Ricinus vars mix	SK
Rhus succdanea	B,CG,LN,SA	Ricotia lunaria	B
Rhus transvaalensis	B,KB	Ridolfia segetum	B,DD
Rhus trilobata	B,C,CA,CG,FW,LN,NO, SA,SG	Ripogonum scandens	B
		Rivea corymbosa	HU
Rhus typhina	A,B,C,CA,FW,HU,LN,NT SA	Rivea hypocrateriformis	B
		Rivina humilis	DV
Rhus typhina 'Dissecta'	CG	Rivinea aurantiaca	SG
Rhus undulata	B	Rivinea laevis	SG
Rhus undulata v celastroides	B,SI	Robinia hispida v fertilis	B,C,EL,FW,LN,SA,SH
Rhus undulata v undulata	SI	Robinia neomexicana	B,C,SA,SW
Rhus vernicflua	B,CG,LN,SA,SG	Robinia pseudoacacia	A,AB,B,C,CA,CG,DD,EL,
Rhynchelytrum see Melinis			FR,FW,HA,HP,HU,LN,N,
Rhynchocalyx lawsonoides	B,SI		NO,SA,SG,T,VE,WA
Rhynchosia capitata	B	Robinia pseudoacacia 'Pusztavacs'	VE
Rhynchosia minima	B,NI	Robinia x ambigua	KL
Rhynchosia phaseoloides	B,HU	Roceocereus mizquiensis	B
Rhynchosia pyramidalis	DD	Roceocereus tephracanthus	B
Rhynchosia sordida	B,SI	Rodgersia aesculifolia	B,BS,C,G,JE,SA,SC
Rhynchosia texana	SA	Rodgersia henrici hyb	B,JE,SA
Rhytidophyllum tomentosum	B	Rodgersia hyb new	B,C,JE
Ribes alpinum	A,B,LN,NO,SA,SG	Rodgersia hyb red	B,JE
Ribes alpinum 'Pumilum'	SG	Rodgersia pinnata	AP,B,BS,C,F,JE,SA,SG,T
Ribes altissima	SG	Rodgersia pinnata CNW865	X
Ribes aureum h see R.odoratum		Rodgersia pinnata 'Superba'	C,HP,JE,P
Ribes cereum	G,LN,NO	Rodgersia pinnata v elegans	B,C
Ribes diacatha	SG	Rodgersia podophylla	B,G,JE
Ribes divaricatum	AB	Rodgersia sambucifolia	B,JE,SA
Ribes fasciculatum	G,SG	Rodgersia sp AC1563	X
Ribes fasciculatum v chinense	B	Rodgersia sp mix	T
Ribes glandulosum	SG	Roella ciliata	B,SI
Ribes komarowii	SG	Roella compacta	B,SI
Ribes latifolium	DD,SG	Roella maculata	B,SI
Ribes magellanicum	SA	Roella triflora	B,SI
Ribes nigrum	LN,SA,SG,VE	Roemeria refracta	B
Ribes odoratum	AP,B,LN,NO,SA,SG	Rogeria longifolia	B,SI
Ribes oxyacanthoides	SG	Rollinia deliciosa	B
Ribes petraeum	B,G,SG	Rollinia mucosa	B
		Romanzoffia californica	SG

ROMANZOFFIA

Romanzoffia sitchensis	P
Romneya coulteri	C,CA,EL,HP,JE,PL,SA,T
Romneya coulteri coulteri	B,SW
Romneya coulteri v trichocalyx	B,SW
Romularia hirsuta	SA
Romularia tetragona	SA
Romulea amoena	AR,B,RU,SI
Romulea atrandra	AR,KB
Romulea atrandra ssp atranda	B,RU,SI
Romulea austinii	B
Romulea bifrons	AP
Romulea bifrons Coll Ref	MN
Romulea bulbicodium	AP,AR,C,SC,SG
Romulea bulbicodium B.S345 Italy	MN
Romulea bulbicodium (violet)	MN
Romulea bulbocodium v crocea	AR
Romulea campanuloides	B,LG,MN,RU,SC,SI
Romulea citrina	AP,B,RU,SI
Romulea clusiana	MN,SC
Romulea clusiana S.F327 Morocco	MN
Romulea columnae	AP,G,SC
Romulea columnae A.B.S4610 Morocco	MN
Romulea columnae Spain	MN
Romulea columnae v saccodoana	MN
Romulea crocea L/T19 Turkey	MN
Romulea cruciata	B,RU,SI
Romulea cruciata v cruciata	B,RU
Romulea cruciata v intermedia	RU
Romulea dichotoma	B,SI
Romulea diversiformis	AR,B,RU,SI
Romulea engleri	MN
Romulea eximia	B,RU,SI
Romulea flava	AP,B,KB,RU,SC,SI
Romulea flava v minor	B,SI
Romulea flava white	B,RU
Romulea gaditana PB206 Portugal	MN
Romulea gigantea	B,RU
Romulea hirsuta	RU
Romulea hirsuta ssp zeyheri	B,RU,SI
Romulea hirsuta v cuprea	RU
Romulea hirsuta v hirsuta	B,RU,SI
Romulea hirta	AP,AR,B,RU,SC,SI
Romulea hirta S.Africa	MN
Romulea kamisensis	B,RU,SI
Romulea komsbergensis	AR,B,RU,SI
Romulea leipoldtii	B,RU,SC,SI
Romulea ligustica v rouyana A.B.S4313	MN
Romulea linaresii	AP,G,SC
Romulea linaresii C.E.H626 Yugoslavia	MN
Romulea linaresii Corsica	MN
Romulea linaresii L/Sa 65 Sardinia	MN
Romulea linaresii ssp graeca	AR
Romulea luteoflora	AR,B,SC,SI
Romulea macowani v alticola	AP,MN,SC
Romulea macowanii v oreophila	B,SI
Romulea minutiflora	AP,B,RU
Romulea monadelpha	B,KB,RU,SI
Romulea montana	B
Romulea monticola	AR,B,RU,SI
Romulea monticola S.Africa	MN
Romulea multiscapata	AP,RU
Romulea namaquensis	B,RU
Romulea nivalis	AP,HP
Romulea obscura	B,RU
Romulea obscura v campestris	B
Romulea obscura v obscura	B,RU,SC

Romulea pearsonii	AR,B,SI
Romulea pratensis	AP,B,G,RU,SC
Romulea pratensis S.Africa	MN
Romulea ramiflora	AP,MN
Romulea ramiflora S.F63 Morocco	MN
Romulea requienii	AP,G,LG,SC
Romulea rosea	AP,B,C,G,RU,SC
Romulea rosea v australis	B,RU
Romulea rosea v reflexa	B,RU
Romulea rosea v rosea	B,RU
Romulea rosea v speciosa	AP,B,RU
Romulea sabulosa	AP,B,MN,RU,SC,SI
Romulea saldanhensis	AP,AR,B,MN,RU,SC,SI
Romulea schlechteri	B,SI
Romulea setifolia	B,RU,SI
Romulea setifolia v aggregata	B,RU
Romulea sladenii	AR,B,RU,SI
Romulea sp	AP,KL,RU,SC,SI
Romulea sp A.B.S4421 Morocco	MN
Romulea sp MS465 Spain	MN
Romulea sp S.F383 Morocco	MN
Romulea sp S.L12 Jordan	MN
Romulea stellata	B,RU,SI
Romulea subfistulosa	B,RU,SI
Romulea syringodeoflora	AR,B,SI
Romulea tabularis ·	AP,B,C,G,RU,SI
Romulea tempskyana	AP,MN
Romulea tetragona	AR,B,RU,SI
Romulea thodei	AP,PM,SC
Romulea tortuosa	RU
Romulea tortuosa v aurea	AR,B,SI
Romulea tortuosa v tortuosa	AP,B,SI
Romulea toximontana	B,RU
Romulea triflora	B,RU,SI
Romulea unifolia	B,SI
Romulea zahnii	AP,MN,SC
Rooksbya euphorbioides see Neobuxbaumia	
Roridula dentata	B
Rorippa islandica	DD
Rorippa nasturtium-aquatica	DD
Rosa achburensis	SG
Rosa acicularis	AP,B,FW,LN,SG
Rosa alpina see R.pendulina	
Rosa arizonica	B,SW
Rosa arkansana	B,FW,LN,PR
Rosa arvensis	B,LN
Rosa bella	B,SG
Rosa blanda	B,LN,PR,SG
Rosa bracteata	HU
Rosa brunonii	B,HP,LN
Rosa californica	B,SW
Rosa canina	B,C,CN,FW,HU,LN,RS, SA,SG,TH,VE,Z
Rosa canina inermis	VE
Rosa carolina	B,LN,SA
Rosa carpatica	KL
Rosa chinensis	CN,HU,LN,PK,SA,V
Rosa chinensis 'Angel Wings'	B,BS,U
Rosa corymbifera	CG
Rosa davidii	B,LN,SA
Rosa davurica	LN,SA,SG
Rosa dumalia	CG,G,SG
Rosa eglanteria see R.rubiginosa	
Rosa filipes	RH
Rosa filipes 'Kiftsgate'	C
Rosa forrestiana	SG

ROSA

Rosa 'Fru Dagmar Hastrup'	C
Rosa gallica	C
Rosa 'Geranium' moyesii hyb	C
Rosa glauca	AP,B,C,FW,G,HP,LN,RH, SC,SG
Rosa gymnocarpa	B,C,LN,NO,SG
Rosa hemsleyana	CG,SG
Rosa laevigata	EL,LN
Rosa laxa	B,SA,VE
Rosa laxa alba	SG
Rosa longiscupis cf AC1828	X
Rosa macrophylla	AP,C,X
Rosa majalis	RS,SG
Rosa maracandica	SG
Rosa marrettii	SG
Rosa maximowicziana	SG
Rosa moschata	BH,C,LN,SA
Rosa moyesii	A,AP,B,C,CG,HP,LG,LN, RH,SA,SC,SG
Rosa moyesii AC1586	X
Rosa moyesii fargesii	SG
Rosa multibracteata	CG,SG
Rosa multiflora	B,C,KL,LN,SA,SG
Rosa multiflora inermis	B,CA,FW,VE
Rosa multiflora 'Nana'	B
Rosa multiflora thorny	B,CA,FW
Rosa nitidula	B,G,SG
Rosa nutkana	AB,B,C,LN,NO,SG
Rosa obtusifolia	SG
Rosa old fashioned roses mix	C
Rosa palustris	B
Rosa pendulina	B,C,CG,SG
Rosa pfanders	LN,VE
Rosa pimpinellifolia	B,C,CG,G,KL,LN,SA, SC,SG,VE
Rosa pimpinellifolia 'Altaica'	SG
Rosa polyantha Fairy Rose dw	B,BD,BS,BY,C,DE,J,KI, L,MO,ST,T
Rosa pomifera see R.villosa	
Rosa primula	B,C,FW
Rosa pteracantha AC1557	X
Rosa roxburghii	C,G,SG
Rosa rubiginosa	A,B,C,FW,G,HP,LN,PO, SA,VE
Rosa rugosa	A,AB,AP,BD,BH,C,CA, FW,HP,HU,LN,RH,SA, SC,SG,VE
Rosa rugosa 'Alba'	B,C,FW,LN,SA,SG,VE
Rosa rugosa rubra	B,FW,LN,SA,VE
Rosa 'Schmids Ideal'	LN,VE
Rosa sericea	AP,LN,SA,SG
Rosa sericea v omeiensis AC1658	X
Rosa setigera	B,PR
Rosa soulieana	C
Rosa sp	BH,C,KL,T
Rosa spinosissima see R.pimpinellifolia	
Rosa stellata erlansoniae	B,SW
Rosa subcanina	RS
Rosa subcollina	RS
Rosa sweginzowii	AP,C,SG
Rosa tomentosa	RS
Rosa ultramontana	SG
Rosa villosa	B,CG,DD,LN,RS,SG
Rosa virginiana	B,C,FW,G,LN,SA,SG
Rosa vosagiaca	RS
Rosa wichurana	B,CG,FW,LN,SA

Rosa woodsii	B,C,FW,LN,NO,SA,SG
Rosa x alba	RS
Rosa x damascena	B
Rosa xanthina	B,HU,LN,SA
Rosa xanthina f hugonis	B,FW,LN,SA
Roscoea alpina	AP,B,BS,C,G,JE,P,SA,SC
Roscoea alpina pink	P
Roscoea cautleoides	AP,B,C,G,JE,P,RH,SG
Roscoea humeana	G,SC,SG
Roscoea purpurea	AP,B,C,G,JE,SC,SG,T
Roscoea purpurea v procera see R.purpurea	
Roscoea scillifolia	AP,NG
Roseocereus tephracanthus	B,Y
Roseocereus tephracanthus v mizquens	B,Y
Rosmarinus officinalis	B,CG,CN,DD,SA,SG,TH, VE
Rosmarinus officinalis Prostratus Group	B,G,HP
Rosmarinus officinalis v albiflorus	B
Rostkovia magellanica	AU
Rosularia muratdaghensis	KL
Rosularia sempervivum	AP,KL,RM
Rosularia spathulata h see R.sempervivum ssp galaucophylla	
Rothia indica	B
Rothmannia capensis	B,C,KB,O,SA,SI,WA
Rothmannia globosa	B,C,HA,KB,O,SA,SI,WA
Rothmannia manganjae	B,EL
Rothmannia sp mix	BH
Rothmannia urcelliformis	B,SI
Rottboellia myurus	B
Roystonea elata	B,O
Roystonea lenis	B
Roystonea oleracea	B,CA,EL,O
Roystonea regia	B,C,CA,EL,HA,O,RE,VE
Roystonea stellata	B
Roystonea violacea	B
Rubia peregrina	B
Rubia tinctoria	B
Rubus alleghaniensis	B
Rubus caesius	SG
Rubus chamaemorus	B,C,PO
Rubus cockburnianus	SG
Rubus crataegifolius	SG
Rubus deliciosus	HP
Rubus discolor	DD
Rubus fruticosus	B,LN
Rubus glaucus	B
Rubus idaeus	B,DD,NO,SG
Rubus illecebrosus	SG
Rubus laciniatus	NO
Rubus leucodermis	AB,NO
Rubus ludwigii	B,SI
Rubus niveus	C
Rubus odoratus	SG
Rubus parviflorus	AB,AU,B,NO
Rubus parvus	B
Rubus phoenicolasius	B,DD,SG
Rubus procerus	B
Rubus rosifolius	B,SI
Rubus saxatilis	B,C
Rubus schmidelioides	B,SS
Rubus spectabilis	AB,C,NO
Rubus ursinus	AB,B,NO
Rudbeckia amplexicaulis	HW
Rudbeckia californica	T
Rudbeckia fulgida	B,G,TH
Rudbeckia fulgida v dearnii	JE

RUDBECKIA

Rudbeckia fulgida v speciosa	B,C,F,JE,PM,SA
Rudbeckia fulgida v sullivanti 'Goldsturm'	B,BS,CL,CN,D,DD,DE,
	G,HU,JE,L,MO,NT,P,PA,
	PK,SA,SK,T,U,V
Rudbeckia fulgida wild	HU
Rudbeckia hirta	AB,AP,AV,B,C,CA,DI,FR,
	G,HP,HW,JO,NT,PR,RI,
	SG
Rudbeckia hirta All Sorts Mix	T
Rudbeckia hirta 'Autumn Leaves'	B,DE
Rudbeckia hirta 'Becky' mix	BD,BS,J,KI,KS,M,MO,
	PK,SE,SK,T,U
Rudbeckia hirta 'Giant Dbl Daisy'	B,BD,BS
Rudbeckia hirta 'Gloriosa Dbl Daisy'	C,F,J,KI,L,MO,RI,SD,
	SG,SK,T,V
Rudbeckia hirta 'Goldilocks'	B,BS,CA,CL,D,DT,F,M,
	MO,PK,PL,S,SE,SK,SU,
	T,TU,V
Rudbeckia hirta 'Indian Summer'	B,BS,CA,CL,DT,HU,JO,
	KS,MO,PI,PK,SK,VY
Rudbeckia hirta 'Irish Eyes'	B,BS,C,KI,PL,SK,ST,T
Rudbeckia hirta 'Kelvedon Star'	T
Rudbeckia hirta 'Marmalade'	B,BS,BY,CA,CL,CO,D,
	DT,F,J,KI,L,MO,PI,S,SK,
	T,YA
Rudbeckia hirta mix dk dbl	HU
Rudbeckia hirta 'My Joy'	B,BS
Rudbeckia hirta 'Rustic Dwarf'	AP,B,BD,BS,BY,C,CL,
	CO,D,DT,F,HU,J,JO,KI,L,
	MO,PI,R,S,ST,SU,T,TE,
	U,VH,VY,YA
Rudbeckia hirta 'Sonora'	C,D,F,SE,V
Rudbeckia hirta 'Toto'	B,BS,CL,D,MO,PI,PK,
	PL,T,U
Rudbeckia hirta x pulcherrima	T
Rudbeckia laciniata	B,HP,JE,PR,SA
Rudbeckia maxima	B,JE,SA
Rudbeckia occidentalis	AP,B,HP,JE,SA
Rudbeckia occidentalis 'Green Wizard'	B,HP,MO,P,PK,SE,T
Rudbeckia purpurea see Echinacea	
Rudbeckia ritida 'Herbstsonne'	T
Rudbeckia subtomentosa	B,JE,PR
Rudbeckia triloba	B,DD,G,HU,JE,NT,PR
Ruellia humilis	AP,B,PR
Ruellia morongii	C
Ruellia prostratus	B
Ruellia tuberosa	B,EL
Rulingia platycalyx	B,NI
Rumex acetosa	B,CN,CP,DD,G,KS,SU
Rumex acetosa 'Blonde De Lyon'	B
Rumex acetosa 'Nobel'	B
Rumex acetosella	B,CN,HU,JE
Rumex alpestris	SG
Rumex alpinus	CG
Rumex altissimus	B,PR
Rumex aquaticus	CG,SG
Rumex confertus	SG
Rumex conglomeratus	B,SG
Rumex cordatus	B,SI
Rumex crispus	B,CP,DD,SG
Rumex cyperus	B
Rumex hydrolapathum	B,C,JE
Rumex hymenosepalus	B
Rumex lunaria	SA
Rumex maritimus	B,SG
Rumex obtusifolius	B

Rumex patienta	B,DD
Rumex rubrifolius	HP
Rumex sagittatus	B,SI
Rumex sanguineus	AP,B,C,CG,HP,I,PA,SG
Rumex sanguineus ssp viridus	B,JE
Rumex sanguineus v sanguineus	HP
Rumex scutatus	B,CN,SG
Rumex sibiricus	SG
Rumex sp	SI
Rumex stenphyllus	SG
Rumex thyrsiflorus	SG
Rumex venosus	B,DD,SG
Rumex verticillatus	B,PR
Rumex woodii	B,SI
Rumohra adiantiformis	B
Rupicapnos africana	AP,PM,SC
Ruschia caroli	B,SI
Ruschia concinna	B,SI
Ruschia cupulata	DV
Ruschia dualis	B,DV,SI
Ruschia elevata	B,DV
Ruschia fredericii	DV
Ruschia fulleri	B
Ruschia gemina	B,KB
Ruschia gracillima	B
Ruschia indurata	B,DV
Ruschia intrusa	B
Ruschia lineolata	B,DV,KB,SI
Ruschia macowanii	B,DV,SI
Ruschia macrocarpa	DV
Ruschia marianae	B,SI,Y
Ruschia maxima	B,DV,KB,SI,Y
Ruschia misera	SI
Ruschia multiflora	B,KB,SI
Ruschia pulchella	B,SI
Ruschia pulvinaris	B
Ruschia pungens	B,SI
Ruschia pygmaea	B,DV,SI,Y
Ruschia rigidicaulis	B,SI
Ruschia rubricaulis	B
Ruschia rupicola	B
Ruschia salteri	B
Ruschia sarmentosa	DV
Ruschia schlechteri	DV
Ruschia schneiderana	B,DV
Ruschia solida	B,SI
Ruschia sp	C,SI
Ruschia stenophylla	DV
Ruschia strubeniae	B,KB,SI
Ruschia subpaniculata	B,SI
Ruschia tumidula	B,SI
Ruschia uncinata	B,SI
Ruscus aculeatus	B,LN,NG,SA,VE
Ruspolia hypocrateriformis	B,EL,SI
Russelia equisetiformis	B
Ruta corsica	SC,SG
Ruta graveolens	AP,B,C,CN,CP,G,HP,HU,
	KL,KS,SA,SC,SG,TH
Ruta graveolens 'Variegata'	B,HP,P,T
Ruta graveolens 'Variegata Harlequin'	B,C
Ruta sp Spain	SG
Rutidosis helichrysoides	B,NI
Ruttya ovata	B
Sabal blackburniana	B,CG
Sabal causiarum	B,CA,EL,O,RE,SA,TT
Sabal etonia	B

SABAL

Sabal mauritiiformis	O
Sabal mexicana	B,CA,DV,EL,HA,O,SA
Sabal minor	B,C,EL,HA,O,SA,SG
Sabal palmetto	B,CA,EL,HA,HU,O,SA
Sabal princeps	B,EL,O
Sabatia angularis	B,C,JE
Saccharum officinarum	B
Saccharum officinarum v nigra	B
Saccharum spontaneum	B
Sacropeterium spinosum	B
Sagina saginoides	C
Sagina subulata	B,BS,C,CL,CN,FR,HU,JE ,MO,PK,SA,T,V
Sagittaria latifolia	B,JE,PR
Sagittaria sagittifolia	B,C,JE,SA
Saintpaulia 'Carnival' mix	J,V
Saintpaulia diplotricha	C
Saintpaulia f1 'Classic' mix	PK
Saintpaulia f1 'Fantasy'	PK
Saintpaulia f1 'Fantasy Teacup'	PK
Saintpaulia f1 'Fantasy' (V)	PK
Saintpaulia 'Fairytale' s-c	B,BS,MO
Saintpaulia 'Fondant Creams' mix	V
Saintpaulia hyb (V) leaf	C
Saintpaulia ionantha	C
Saintpaulia 'Mistral' mix	CL
Saintpaulia 'Rainbow Falls' mix	T
Saintpaulia selection	F
Saintpaulia 'Virginia'	C
Salacca zalacca	B
Salacia chinensis	B
Salacia senegalensis	B
Salazaria mexicana	B,SW
Salix alba	B,SA
Salix caprea	B,SA
Salix cinerea	B
Salix fragilis	B
Salix retusa	B,KL
Salix tschuktschorum ssp kamtschatica	VO
Salmea 'Palito De Chile'	B,HU
Salpiglossis 'Batik'	U
Salpiglossis 'Emperor' mix	BS
Salpiglossis f1 'Casino' mix	BS,CL,DE,DT,L,MO,PK, SE,T,U,YA
Salpiglossis f1 'Festival' mix	D,S
Salpiglossis f1 'Flamenco' mix	F
Salpiglossis f1 'Royale' mix	BS
Salpiglossis f1 'Splash' mix	BS,DE
Salpiglossis f1 'Triumph' mix	S
Salpiglossis f2 'Bolero'	BD,BS,C,F,J,KI,L,MO,PI, SK,T,TU,V
Salpiglossis f2 'Carnival'	D,S
Salpiglossis f2 hyb	BY
Salpiglossis grandiflora mix	HU
Salpiglossis sinuata	AB,B,DE,TH
Salpiglossis sinuata f1 'Chocolate Pot'	DT,F,T
Salpiglossis sinuata f1 'Chocolate Royale' see Choc. Pot	
Salpiglossis sinuata 'Gloomy Rival'	B,C
Salpiglossis sinuata 'Kew Blue'	B,T
Salpiglossis 'Superbissima'	DT
Salsola kali	SG
Saltera sarcocolla	B
Salvia aethiopis	AP,B,C,DD,G,HP,PV,SA, SZ
Salvia africana-caerulea	B,SI
Salvia africana-lutea	B,BH,KB,SI

Salvia algeriensis	HP,PV
Salvia 'Amethyst Blue'	BS,KI
Salvia amplexicaulis	B,G,JE,SA,SZ
Salvia apiana	B,C,CA,CP,DD,HU,KS
Salvia apiana apiana	SW
Salvia argentea	AP,B,BH,BS,C,CG,E,F,G, HP,JE,SA,SC,SG,SW,T
Salvia arizonica	B,SG,SW
Salvia aucheri	PV
Salvia aurita	BH
Salvia austriaca	AP,B,G,HP,PV,SZ
Salvia azurea	B,C,CP,HP,HW,NO,SA
Salvia azurea ssp pitcheri	B
Salvia azurea v grandiflora	B,HU,SD
Salvia barrelieri	AP,D,HP,PV,SA
Salvia bertolonii see S.pratensis Bertolonii Gr	
Salvia bicolor see S.barrelieri	
Salvia bulleyana	AP,C,HP,JE,NG,P,PV,SA, SC,SG,T
Salvia cacalcifolia	B,HP
Salvia campanulata	AP,HP
Salvia canariensis	AP,SZ
Salvia candelabrum	CG,T
Salvia candidissima	RM
Salvia canescens	PM
Salvia cardinalis see S.fulgens	
Salvia carduacea	B,SW
Salvia chamaedryoides	DD
Salvia cleistogama	SC,T
Salvia 'Cleopatra' mix	CO,KI,MC
Salvia clevelandii	B,BH,C,CA,HU,KS,SW
Salvia clevelandii 'Winifred Gilman'	SZ
Salvia coahuilensis	SZ
Salvia coahuilensis hyb	SZ
Salvia coccinea	AP,B,C,CG,CP,DD,G,HP, HU,HW,NT,SA,SD,SG
Salvia coccinea 'Cherry Blossom'	T
Salvia coccinea 'Coral Nymph'	AP,B,BS,D,EL,HP,J,KS, MO,PK,PV,V
Salvia coccinea 'Lady In Red'	B,BS,C,CA,CL,D,DE,J, JE,JO,MO,O,PK,T,U,V
Salvia coccinea 'Pink Pearl'	B,DI
Salvia coccinea 'Red Indian'	B
Salvia coccinea 'Rosea'	PV
Salvia coccinea 'Snow Nymph'	B,BS,KS,MO,PK
Salvia coccinea 'Starry Eyed'	KS,V
Salvia coccinea v bicolor	C,CP
Salvia coccinea 'White Dove'	B
Salvia columbariae	AB,B,C,DD,SW
Salvia cyanescens	HP,PV
Salvia darcyi	AP,SZ
Salvia davidsonii	B,SW
Salvia dentata	B,SI
Salvia deserta see S.x sylvestris	
Salvia disermas	AP,B,BH,SI
Salvia divinorum	B,DD
Salvia dolichantha	AP,PV
Salvia dolomitica	B,SI
Salvia dorrii	B,RM
Salvia elegans	B,SW
Salvia eremostachya	B,SW
Salvia farinacea	B,BH,F,G,HU,RH,SA,SD
Salvia farinacea 'Blue Bedder'	B,BS,BY,DE,DI,KI,KS,PI
Salvia farinacea 'Cirrhus'	BS,MO,PL
Salvia far. 'Delft, Porcelain/Warwick Coll.'	T
Salvia farinacea 'Mini Victoria'	SK

SALVIA

Salvia farinacea 'Reference'	B,BS,C,CN,MO
Salvia farinacea 'Rhea'	B,BS,CL,MO
Salvia farinacea 'Silver'	C,JO,PK
Salvia farinacea 'Strata'	B,BS,CL,D,DI,DT,J,JO,
	KS,MO,O,PI,PK,PL,PV,
	S,SE,SK,T,U,YA
Salvia farinacea 'Victoria'	BD,BS,CA,CL,CN,CO,D,
	DE,DT,KI,J,JO,L,MO,PK,
	PV,S,SK,ST,SU,T,V,VY
Salvia farinacea 'Victoria Blue'	B,C,S,SE
Salvia farinacea 'Victoria White'	B,BD,BS,CL,CN,S
Salvia farinacea white	DI,MO,SK
Salvia 'Flamex'	BS
Salvia forskaohei	AP,B,C,G,HP,P,PV,SA,SZ
Salvia fruticosa	B,HP,PV,SA
Salvia fulgens	B,SW
Salvia gesneriiflora	B
Salvia glutinosa	AP,B,BH,CP,G,HP,JE,PV,
	SA,SC,SG
Salvia greggii x lycioides	HP,SZ
Salvia haematodes see S.pratensis Haematodes Gr	
Salvia henryi	B,SW
Salvia hians	AP,B,HP,JE,SC,SG,SZ,T
Salvia hispanica	PV
Salvia hispanica 'Chia'	BH,HU
Salvia horminum see S. viridis	
Salvia icterina	B
Salvia involucrata 'Boutin'	B
Salvia involucrata 'Hidalgo'	SZ
Salvia iodantha	B,SW
Salvia judaica	AP,PV,SA
Salvia jurisicii	AP,B,BS,CG,G,HP,JE,KI,
	KL,RM,SA,SC,SG,T,VO
Salvia lanceolata see S.reflexa	
Salvia lavandulifolia	AP,B,CP,G,SA
Salvia leucantha	B
Salvia leucophylla	B,P,SW
Salvia 'Little Tango'	DE
Salvia lycioides h see S.greggii x lycioides	
Salvia lyrata	AP,B,BH,C,CP,HP,HU,
	NO,PV
Salvia madrensis	B,SW
Salvia 'Melba'	BS
Salvia mellifera	B,CA,KS,PV,SW
Salvia meryame 'Mint Sauce' coll Mt. Kil.	P
Salvia mexicana	AP,B,HP,SZ
Salvia microphylla	B,HP,RH,SA,SZ
Salvia microphylla grahamii	SZ
Salvia microphylla v microphylla	HP
Salvia microphylla v neurepia see S. microphylla v m.	
Salvia microphylla v wislezenii	B,SW
Salvia moelleri	P
Salvia mohavensis	B,SW
Salvia moorcroftiana	AP,HP,SG,SZ,T
Salvia moricana	BS,DT
Salvia multicaulis	HP
Salvia multifida	PV
Salvia munzii	B,SW
Salvia namaensis	BH
Salvia napifolia	PV
Salvia nemorosa	AP,B,CG,G,HP,HU,JE,SA
Salvia nemorosa 'Amethyst'	PV
Salvia nemorosa rose	SA
Salvia nemorosa 'Rosenwein'	B,JE
Salvia nemorosa ssp tesquicola	SG,T
Salvia nilotica	AP,HP,PV,SZ

Salvia nubicola	HP,PV,SA,SZ
Salvia nutans	B,CG,G
Salvia officinalis	B,CN,CP,DD,DV,G,HP,
	HU,JE,KS,SA,TH,VE
Salvia officinalis 'Albiflora'	B,HP,P
Salvia officinalis 'Latifolia'	B
Salvia officinalis Purpurascens Gr	B
Salvia officinalis 'Rosea'	PV
Salvia officinalis v minor ssp alba	BH,JE
Salvia 'Orange Zest'	T
Salvia palaestina	SZ
Salvia patens	AP,B,BD,BS,C,D,DE,G,
	HP,MO,PM,SA,SC,TH
Salvia patens 'Cambridge Blue'	AP,HP,SC,SZ,T
Salvia patens 'Chilcombe'	HP,NG
Salvia patens 'Lavender Lady'	HP
Salvia patens 'Oxford Blue'	B,HP
Salvia patens Varsity mix	PL
Salvia pratensis	AP,B,C,CN,CP,G,HP,JE,
	RH,SA,T,V
Salvia pratensis 'Baumgartenii'	B
Salvia pratensis Bertolonii Group	AP,B,HP,JE,PV,SA
Salvia pratensis dumetorum	PV
Salvia pratensis Haematodes Group	AP,B,C,CP,F,G,HP,JE,PV,
	RH,T
Salvia pratensis 'Haematodes Indigo'	B,JE
Salvia przewalskii	AP,G,HP,PV,SA,SC
Salvia recognita	AP,B,HP,JE,PV,SC,SZ
Salvia 'Red Rose'	BS
Salvia reflexa	AP,B,PV,SI
Salvia regeliana	AP,B,HP,P,PV
Salvia 'Renaissance'	BS
Salvia repens	C,PV
Salvia repens v repens	B,CP,SI
Salvia reptans	AP,SZ
Salvia ringens	AP,B,G,HP,JE,PV
Salvia roborowskii	PV
Salvia roemeriana	AP,HP,SZ
Salvia rugosa	PV
Salvia ryparia	PV
Salvia scabiosifolia	AP,HP
Salvia scabra	AP,BH,PV,SZ
Salvia 'Scarlet O' Hara'	BS,KI
Salvia sclarea	AP,B,C,CG,CN,CP,E,F,G,
	HP,HU,JE,JO,KS,PV,RH,
	SA,SC,SG,TH,V
Salvia sclarea 'Alba'	PV
Salvia sclarea v turkestanica	AP,B,C,CP,G,HP,MA,PL,
	RH,SA,SG,SC,SZ,T
Salvia somalensis	PV,SZ
Salvia sonomensis	B,SW
Salvia sp	AP,SI,SZ
Salvia sp ACE1157	HP
Salvia sp mix	BH,SC
Salvia spathacea	SW,SZ
Salvia splendens	SG,TH
Salvia splendens 'Blaze Of Fire'	B,BD,BS,BY,CA,CL,CN,
	CO,D,F,J,KI,L,M,MO,R,
	S,SE,ST,SU,T,U,V,VH,YA
Salvia splendens 'Bonfire'	BD,PI,SK
Salvia splendens 'Carabiniere'	BS,CL,CN,KI,MO,S,SK,
	YA
Salvia splendens 'Carabiniere Series' s-c	CA,PI
Salvia splendens collection	U
Salvia splendens 'Coral Nymph'	CL,S
Salvia splendens 'Dress Parade'	C,CA,M,S

236

SALVIA

Salvia splendens 'Fire & Ice'	SK
Salvia splendens 'Firecracker'	D
Salvia splendens 'Flare'	DT,M,PK,S,SK
Salvia splendens 'Fuego'	BS,CA
Salvia splendens 'Fury'	CL
Salvia splendens 'Hotline'	PK
Salvia splendens 'Inferno' dw	B
Salvia splendens 'Maestro'	BS,CL,MO,SK,YA
Salvia splendens mix dw	FR
Salvia splendens 'Phoenix Dark Salmon'	B,BD,BS,MO
Salvia splendens 'Phoenix' mix	BD,BS,CL,D,DT,J,MO, SE,T,V,VH
Salvia splendens 'Phoenix Purple'	BD,BS,MO
Salvia splendens 'Phoenix Red'	BS,D,MO
Salvia splendens 'Piccolo Salmon' dw	B
Salvia splendens 'Piccolo Scarlet' dw	B
Salvia splendens 'Purple Beacon'	BS
Salvia splendens 'Rambo'	BS,D,MO
Salvia splendens 'Red Arrow'	B,BS,DT,J,MO,SE,SK, T,TU
Salvia splendens red dw	FR
Salvia splendens 'Red Riches'	BS,MO,YA
Salvia splendens 'Red River'	S
Salvia splendens 'Red Rum'	YA
Salvia splendens red tall	FR
Salvia splendens 'Red Vista'	SK
Salvia splendens 'Ryco'	SK
Salvia splendens 'Salsa' s-c	DI,SK
Salvia splendens 'Salsa Scarlet Bicolour'	BS,MO,SE,SK
Salvia splendens 'Salsa Series' mix	CL,S,SK
Salvia splendens 'Scarlet King'	BS,F,L,MO
Salvia splendens 'Scarlet Queen'	BS,MO,SK
Salvia splendens 'Scarlet Signal'	F
Salvia splendens 'Sizzler Burgundy'	BS,MO,SK,T
Salvia splendens 'Sizzler Lavender'	MO,SK
Salvia splendens 'Sizzler' mix	BS,CL,MO,SK,U,YA
Salvia splendens 'Sizzler Orchid'	MO,SK
Salvia splendens 'Sizzler Pink'	SK
Salvia splendens 'Sizzler Plum'	SK
Salvia splendens 'Sizzler Purple' dw	B,BS,MO,SK
Salvia splendens 'Sizzler Red'	MO,SK
Salvia splendens 'Sizzler Rose'	SK
Salvia splendens 'Sizzler Rose Bicolor'	U
Salvia splendens 'Sizzler Salmon'	BS,KI,MO,SK
Salvia splendens 'Sizzler White'	MO,SK
Salvia splendens 'Sky & Ice'	SK
Salvia splendens 'Splendissima'	T
Salvia splendens 'St. John's Fire'	C,SK,VY
Salvia splendens 'Vanguard'	BS,CL,CN,KI,MO
Salvia splendens 'Volcano'	BS
Salvia staminea	AP,HP,PV,SZ
Salvia stenophylla	AP,B,CP,HP,PV
Salvia stepposa	PV,SG
Salvia tachiei	AP,RH
Salvia taraxacifolia	AP,SZ
Salvia tesquicola see S.nemorosa ssp t.	
Salvia tiliacea	SA
Salvia tiliifolia	B,C,CP,DD,G,HU,PV,SD, SG
Salvia tingitana	PV
Salvia tomentosa	PV
Salvia 'Top Series'	EL
Salvia transsylvanica	AP,B,G,HP,JE,PV,RH,SA, SZ,T
Salvia trijuga	PV
Salvia turkestanica	P
Salvia uliginosa	AP,B
Salvia vaseyi	B,SW
Salvia verbenaca	AP,B,C,DD,HP,SU
Salvia verticillata	AP,B,F,G,HP,JE,KL,P,PV, SA,SC,SG
Salvia verticillata 'Alba'	B,C,HP,JE,PV
Salvia verticillata 'Purple Rain'	HP
Salvia virgata	HP,PV
Salvia viridis	AP,B,BY,C,CN,EL,F,G,HP, I,J,KS,L,PI,SG,TH
Salvia viridis 'Blue Bird'	SK,V
Salvia viridis 'Blue Monday'	B,KS
Salvia viridis 'Bouquet' mix	BS,CO,KI,S,V
Salvia viridis 'Claryssa' mix & s-c	T
Salvia viridis 'Colour Blend'	D,JO
Salvia viridis 'Monarch Art Shades'	BS,M,MO,U
Salvia viridis 'Oxford Blue'	BS,C,HU,JO
Salvia viridis 'Pink Sundae'	B,BS,C,DE,HU,JO,KS
Salvia viridis 'Tricolour'	DT,SK
Salvia viridis 'White Swan'	B,HU,KS,SK
Salvia viscosa	AP,HP,PV,SZ
Salvia x jamensis	HP,SZ
Salvia x superba	AP,B,C,HP,RM,SG
Salvia x sylvestris	SA,SG
Salvia x sylvestris 'Blaukonigin'	BS,C,CL,F,JE,MO,PK,T,V
Salvia x sylvestris 'Blue Princess'	B,EL
Salvia x sylvestris 'Mainacht' (May Night)	HP,SG
Salvia x sylvestris 'Rose Princess'	B,EL,PK
Salvia x sylvestris 'Rose Queen'	AP,B,BS,C,HP,JE,MO,T
Samanea saman	CA,DV,EL,HU,O,RE,SA, TT
Sambucus caerulea	A,AB,B,FW,LN,NO,SA
Sambucus caerulea v neomexicana	B
Sambucus canadensis	B,LN,SA
Sambucus ebulus	B,C,G,SG
Sambucus glauca see caerulea	
Sambucus hybridum	B
Sambucus latipinna	B
Sambucus nigra	A,B,BH,FW,HU,LN,PO, SA,SU,VE
Sambucus pubens	B
Sambucus racemosa	A,B,C,DD,FW,LN,SA,SG, VE
Sambucus racemosa 'Sutherland Gold'	SG
Sambucus racemosa v arborescens	AB
Sambucus sibirica	SG
Sambucus sieboldiana v coreana	SG
Sambucus wightiana see S.javanica	
Sandersonia aurantiaca	AP,B,C,G,SA,SC,SI,T
Sandersonia aurantiaca Dutch Selection	B
Sandoricum koetjepe	B
Sanguinaria canadensis	AP,B,G,JE,KL,PO,SA,T
Sanguisorba alpina	SG
Sanguisorba canadensis	B,SC
Sanguisorba dodecandra	B,G
Sanguisorba minor	G,HU,JE,KS,LA,NO,SA
Sanguisorba minor ssp muricata	B
Sanguisorba officinalis	C,G,HU,JE,LA,SA,SG
Sanguisorba parviflora	SG
Sanguisorba tenuifolia	B,C,G,JE,SG
Sanicula europaea	B,JE,PO
Sansevieria aethiopica	B
Sansevieria hyacinthoides	B
Sansevieria roxburghiana	B
Sansevieria stuckyi	CG
Sansevieria zeylanica	B,C

SANTALUM

Santalum acuminatum	B,DD,EL,HA,NI,O,SA
Santalum album	B,EL,HA
Santalum spicatum	B,EL,NI,O,SA
Santolina canescens	SA
Santolina chamaecyparissus	B,BH,C,DE,G,JE,PK,SA, T
Santolina chamaecyparissus 'Silver Glade'	U
Santolina pectinata	SG
Santolina pinnata	B,BD,CN,JE
Santolina pinnata ssp neapolitana	B,BH,BS,CL,HP,L,MO, SA
Santolina pinnata ssp neap. 'Sulphurea'	HP
Santolina rosmarinifolia	B,G,JE,SA
Santolina tomentosa see S.pinnata ssp neapolitana	
Sanvitalia 'Carpet' s-c	SK
Sanvitalia procumbens	B,BS,C,CG,CL,D,DD, DT,HU,L,MO,SG
Sanvitalia procumbens 'Gold Braid'	BS,CO,DE,KI,V
Sanvitalia procumbens 'Irish Eyes'	B,BD,BS,MO
Sanvitalia procumbens 'Mandarin Orange'	B,BD,BS,MO,PK,SK,V
Sanvitalia procumbens single yellow	JO,PI
Sapindus drummondii	B,EL,SA
Sapindus laurifolia	B
Sapindus mukorossi	B,HA,LN,SA,WA
Sapindus 'Pipe Negro'	B
Sapindus saponaria	B
Sapium sebiferum	B,C,CA,EL,FW,HA,LN, SA
Saponaria caespitosa	AP,B,G,JE,KL,PM,RH, SC,VO
Saponaria calabrica	B
Saponaria calabrica select	C
Saponaria chlorifolia	RM
Saponaria lutea	AP,B,C,CG,G,JE,KL,SG
Saponaria ocymoides	AP,B,BD,BH,BS,BY,C, CL,CN,CO,DV,HP,I,J, JE,KI,KL,KS,L,MO,PI, SA,SC,SG,SK,ST,T,V
Saponaria ocymoides 'Snow Tip'	B,BY,JE
Saponaria officinalis	A,AP,B,BH,C,CG,CN,CP, EL,G,HH,HP,HU,JE,KS, SA,SG,TH
Saponaria officinalis 'Rosea Plena'	B,HP
Saponaria pulvinaris see S. pumilio	
Saponaria pumilio	B,C,JE,KL,VO
Saponaria splendens	B
Saponaria vaccaria	SU,TU
Saponaria vaccaria 'Alba'	MO,YA
Saponaria vaccaria 'Pink Beauty'	BD,BS,BY,C,CN,DE,J, JO,L,MO,T,YA
Saponaria vaccaria 'White Beauty'	BD,BS,CN
Saponaria x olivana	B,G,HP
Saraca indica	B,C,CA,HA,SA
Saraca thaipingensis	B
Sarcocapnos enneaphylla	AP,PM
Sarcocaulon camdeboense	CF
Sarcocaulon crassicaule	B
Sarcocaulon l-heritieri	SI
Sarcocaulon van der rietiae	CF
Sarcocaulon vanderietae	B
Sarcocephalus xanthoxylon	B.DD
Sarcochilus falcatus	B
Sarcococca confusa	AP,B,CA,HP,SA
Sarcococca hookeriana	CG,LN,SA,SG
Sarcococca ruscifolia	B,CA,JE,SA
Sarcopoterium spinosum	B

Sarcostemma viminale	B,SI
Sarracenia alata	B,C,DV
Sarracenia alata hyb	B
Sarracenia flava	B,BA,DV,HP
Sarracenia flava hyb	B
Sarracenia flava v atropurpurea	B
Sarracenia leucophylla	B,BA,C,DV
Sarracenia leucophylla hyb	B
Sarracenia minor	B,C,DV
Sarracenia Nat. Coll. Hyb non-anon. mix	BA,C
Sarracenia oreophila	B,BA,C,DV
Sarracenia oreophila hyb	B
Sarracenia oreophila x courtii	DV
Sarracenia psittacina	B,C,DV
Sarracenia purpurea	AP,B,BA,C,DV,G,HP
Sarracenia purpurea hyb	B,T
Sarracenia purpurea ssp gibbosa	B
Sarracenia purpurea ssp purpurea	B
Sarracenia purp. ssp purp. heterophylla	B,C
Sarracenia purpurea ssp venosa	B,DV
Sarracenia purpurea ssp venosa hyb	B
Sarracenia rubra	B,DV
Sarracenia rubra hyb	B
Sarracenia sp & hyb mix	C
Sarracenia x catesbei	DV
Sarracenia x courtii hyb	B,DV
Sarracenia x mitchelliana	B
Sarracenia x rehderi	B
Sassafras albidum	B,LN,SA
Sassafras tsumu	B,LN,SA
Satureja alternipilosa	JE
Satureja biflora	B,BH,G
Satureja caerulea	B
Satureja calamintha	HU
Satureja hortensis	B,CG,CN,CP,DD,HU,SG, TH
Satureja montana	B,CN,CP,G,JE,SA,SG,TH
Satureja montana ssp illyrica	G,JE,SG
Satureja nepeta	SG
Satyrium carneum	B,SI
Satyrium coriifolium	B,SI
Satyrium erectum	B,SI
Satyrium longicauda v longicauda	B,SI
Satyrium macrophyllum	B,SI
Satyrium pumilum	B,SI
Sauromatum venosum	KL
Saussurea amara	SG
Saussurea controversa	SG
Saussurea deltoides	KL
Saussurea gnaphalodes	VO
Saussurea grandiflora	I
Saussurea heteromala	B,G
Saussurea japonica	SG
Saussurea pseudotilesii	SG
Saussurea pygmaea	B,VO
Saussurea riederi v insularis	SG
Saussurea sacchaliensis	SA
Saussurea tilesii	SG
Saxegothaea conspicua	B,SA
Saxifraga aizoides	AP,CG,JE,SC,SG
Saxifraga aizoon see S.paniculata	
Saxifraga aphylla	VO
Saxifraga aretioides	KL
Saxifraga aspera	AP,B,G,JE,SC
Saxifraga biflora	B,C,JE
Saxifraga boryi	SG

SAXIFRAGA

Saxifraga bronchialis	B,SG,SW
Saxifraga bronchialis ssp austromontana	RM
Saxifraga bryoides	DV
Saxifraga burserana	AP,B
Saxifraga caesia	AP,B,C,KL,SC,SG
Saxifraga caespitosa	AP,HP,KL,RM
Saxifraga callosa	AP,G,KL,SC
Saxifraga callosa v albertiana	AP,SC,SG
Saxifraga callosa v australis	B,C
Saxifraga callosa v lantoscana see S.callosa v australis	
Saxifraga camposii	B
Saxifraga carpatica	DV
Saxifraga cartilaginea	VO
Saxifraga cebennensis	AP,B,I,KL,SC,SG
Saxifraga cernua	VO
Saxifraga cherlerioides	C,VO
Saxifraga chrysosplenifolia see S.rotundifolia ssp c.	
Saxifraga cochlearis	G,SC,SG
Saxifraga cochlearis 'Minor'	B,JE
Saxifraga columnaris	KL,VO
Saxifraga conifera	SG
Saxifraga continentalis	CG
Saxifraga cordifolia rotundifolia	CG
Saxifraga cortusifolia v fortunei see s.fortunei	
Saxifraga corymbosa	AP,DV
Saxifraga cotyledon	AP,DV,KL,SC,SG
Saxifraga cotyledon 'Islandica'	JE
Saxifraga cotyledon 'Montafonensis'	CG,SC
Saxifraga cotyledon norvegica	SG
Saxifraga cotyledon 'Pyramidalis'	B,G,JE
Saxifraga crustata	AP,DV,RM,VO
Saxifraga cuneifolia	AP,B,G,HP,SC
Saxifraga cuneifolia v subintegra	SG
Saxifraga cuneifolia variegata	HP
Saxifraga cymbalaria	AP,DV,I,SC
Saxifraga demissa	KL
Saxifraga densa see S.cherlerioides	
Saxifraga desoulavyi	KL,VO
Saxifraga diapensioides	VO
Saxifraga dinikii	KL,VO
Saxifraga 'Elf'	HP
Saxifraga Encrusted mlx	AP,BS,BY,SC
Saxifraga exarata	B,JE,VO
Saxifraga exarata ssp moschata	VO
Saxifraga ferdinandi-coburghi	G,RM,VO
Saxifraga ferdinandi-coburghi v pravislawii	SG
Saxifraga flagellaris	VO
Saxifraga Flower Carpet	KI
Saxifraga fortunei	B,G,JE
Saxifraga frederici-augusta ssp grisebachii	B,VO
Saxifraga fred.i-augusta ssp gris. 'Wisley'	KL
Saxifraga frederici-augusti ssp grisebachii	AP,JE,PM,SC,SG,VO
Saxifraga funstonii	VO
Saxifraga globulifera	DV
Saxifraga granulata	AP,B,C,CG,CN,DV,G, JE,SG,SU,TH
Saxifraga 'Gregor Mendel'	B,G
Saxifraga grisebachii see S.frederici-a. ssp g.	
Saxifraga hostii	AP,B,C,CG,G,HP,JE
Saxifraga hostii ssp hostii	CG
Saxifraga huetiana	C
Saxifraga hybrids	VO
Saxifraga hypnoides	AP,B,SC
Saxifraga juniperifolia	VO
Saxifraga kabschia mix	AP,G
Saxifraga kolenatiana	VO

Saxifraga kotschyi	VO
Saxifraga latepetiolata	SG
Saxifraga lingulata see S.callosa	
Saxifraga longifolia	AP,B,G,JE,KL,SC,VO
Saxifraga luteoviridis	AP,KL,RM,SC,SG
Saxifraga manschuriensis	AP,B,JE
Saxifraga marginata	AP,B,CG,DV,G,JE,SC
Saxifraga marg. ssp marg. v coryophylla	KL
Saxifraga merkii	VO
Saxifraga mertensiana	AP,B,P
Saxifraga mix rock garden	JE,T
Saxifraga mix silver varieties	I,PL
Saxifraga mix sm rosette varieties	JE
Saxifraga mix sp & vars	T,VO
Saxifraga moschata f pygmaea see S. exarata ssp m	
Saxifraga Mossy Varieties mix	AP,BD,BS,BY,C,CL,D,DE ,I,J,KI,L,MO,S,U
Saxifraga mutata	AP,B,C,DV,JE
Saxifraga nathorstii	KL
Saxifraga nelsoniana	AP,G,SG
Saxifraga nevadensis	SG
Saxifraga nivalis	
Saxifraga oppositifolia	AP,B,BS,C,CG,G,JE,KL, SC,SG,VO
Saxifraga oppositifolia 'Latina'	B,C,JE
Saxifraga oppositifolia 'Splendens'	AP,SC
Saxifraga oppositifolia 'Theoden'	KL
Saxifraga paniculata	AP,B,C,CL,CN,DE,DV,G, HP,JE,KL,MO,RM,SA, SC,SG
Saxifraga paniculata ex 'Minutissima'	RM
Saxifraga paniculata hirtifolia	SG
Saxifraga paniculata ssp brevifolia	B,G,JE,SC
Saxifraga paniculata v sturmiana	CG
Saxifraga pedemontana	AP,PM
Saxifraga pensylvanica	B,G,PR
Saxifraga pentadactylis	CG
Saxifraga 'Peter Pan'	KL
Saxifraga poluniniana	KL
Saxifraga probynii	SG
Saxifraga pseudo-pallida	KL
Saxifraga pubescens ssp iratiana	PM
Saxifraga punctata see S.nelsoniana	
Saxifraga retusa	KL
Saxifraga rosacea	B,SG
Saxifraga rotundifolia	AP,B,G,JE,SA,SC,SG
Saxifraga rot. ssp chrysospleniifolia	B
Saxifraga sachalinensis	KL
Saxifraga sancta	B,G
Saxifraga sarmentosa see S.stolonifera	
Saxifraga scardica	KL,VO
Saxifraga scleropoda	KL,VO
Saxifraga sempervivum	AP,B,DV,JE,KL,RM,VO
Saxifraga serpyllifolia ssp chrysantha	RM
Saxifraga spathularis	JE,RH,SG
Saxifraga squarrosa	VO
Saxifraga stellaris	B,C,JE,SC
Saxifraga stenophylla	VO
Saxifraga stolizkae	KL
Saxifraga stolonifera	B,JE
Saxifraga stribryni	AP,DV,G,KL,PM,SC
Saxifraga tridactylites	DV
Saxifraga trifurcata	B,BD,BS,C,CN,DV,G,HP, JE,KL,MO,RH,SA,T,TH
Saxifraga umbrosa	
Saxifraga u. v primuloides 'Clarence Elliott'	AP,B,C,G,JE,SC

239

SAXIFRAGA

Saxifraga vandellii	AP,B,C
Saxifraga virginensis	B,JE
Saxifraga 'White Pixie'	AP
Saxifraga 'Whitehill'	AP
Saxifraga x apiculata see S.'Gregor Mendel'	
Saxifraga x arendsii	AP,B,C,CN,KL,R,SA
Saxifraga x arendsii 'Floral Carpet'	B,BS,DE,JE,MO,V
Saxifraga x arendsii 'Manteau Pourpre'	B,BS,MO
Saxifraga x arendsii 'Purpurteppich'	BS,JE
Saxifraga x arendsii 'Schneeteppich'	B,BS,JE,MO
Saxifraga x urbium	HP,RH
Saxifraga x wehrhahnii	KL
Scabiosa africana	B,KB,SI
Scabiosa albanensis	B,SI
Scabiosa alpina see Cephalaria alpina	
Scabiosa argentea	B
Scabiosa atropurpurea	DD,DI,HP,PK,SG
Scabiosa atropurpurea 'Ace of Spades'	T
Scabiosa atropurpurea 'Black Knight'	B
Scabiosa atropurpurea 'Blue Cockade'	B
Scabiosa atropurpurea 'Fire King'	B
Scabiosa atropurpurea Imperial mix	BD,JO
Scabiosa atropurpurea mix dw dbl	B,F,MO,T
Scabiosa atropurpurea 'Nana'	B
Scabiosa atropurpurea 'Oxford Blue'	B,DE
Scabiosa atropurpurea 'Salmon Queen'	B
Scabiosa atropurpurea 'Snowmaiden'	B
Scabiosa atropurpurea tall	PI,V
Scabiosa Black Widow/Satchmo see Chile Black	
Scabiosa canescens	SG
Scabiosa caucasica	B,BY,CG,HP,SC,SG,T, TH,VO
Scabiosa caucasica 'Clive Greaves'	HP
Scabiosa caucasica 'Compliment'	B,FE
Scabiosa caucasica 'Fama'	B,BS,C,CL,CN,D,DE,HP, JE,MO,PK,PL,SK,T
Scabiosa caucasica 'Goldingensis'	B,BS,BY,CN,MO,SA
Scabiosa caucasica 'House's Hybs'	B,BS,C,CL,CN,D,DT,HP, JE,KI,L,MO,SA,SE,ST, TU,YA
Scabiosa caucasica hyb giant	SK
Scabiosa caucasica 'Lavender Blue'	CL,DE,FR
Scabiosa caucasica 'Miss Wlmott'	HP
Scabiosa caucasica 'Perfecta Alba'	B,C,DE,JE,PL
Scabiosa caucasica 'Perfecta Blue'	B,JE,PL,V
Scabiosa caucasica 'Perfecta Dark Lavender'	B
Scabiosa caucasica 'Perfecta Lilac'	B
Scabiosa caucasica 'Spielarten'	B,JE
Scabiosa 'Chile Black'	AP,G,HP,P,PL
Scabiosa columbaria	AP,C,CG,CN,HP,JD,JE, LA,SA,SC,SG,SI,TH
Scabiosa columbaria lilac	B
Scabiosa columbaria 'Nana'	B,JE,RH,SC
Scabiosa columbaria v ochroleuca	AP,B,C,G,HP,JE,PL,SA, SC,SG
Scabiosa cretica	AP,HP,SC,T
Scabiosa drakensbergensis	B,SI
Scabiosa farinosa	AP,C,SC,SG
Scabiosa fischeri	AP,HP,SG
Scabiosa gigantea see Cephalaria	
Scabiosa graminifolia	AP,B,C,G,HP,JE,KL,LG, NG,RH,SC,SG,SZ
Scabiosa hyb border	U
Scabiosa incisa	B,KB,SI
Scabiosa japonica	AP,C,HP
Scabiosa japonica v alpina	AP,B,C,G,JE,KL,P
Scabiosa lucida	AP,B,C,G,HP,JE,KL,SG
Scabiosa minoana	HP
Scabiosa mix dbl lg fl	S,TU
Scabiosa mix dw	BD,BS,CO
Scabiosa mix finest	SK
Scabiosa mix giant hyb	C,D,J,KI
Scabiosa ochroleuca see S.columbaria v o.	
Scabiosa perfecta	SA
Scabiosa perfecta alba	SA
Scabiosa 'Pink Lace'	C
Scabiosa prolifera	AP,B,T
Scabiosa rhizantha	B
Scabiosa rumelica see Knautia macedonica	
Scabiosa silenifolia	SG
Scabiosa sp	AB,AP
Scabiosa stellata	AB,B,D,DE,G,JO,KS,SD
Scabiosa stellata 'Paper Moon'	BS,C,DE,F,J,S,SU,T,U,V
Scabiosa stellata 'Ping-pong'	BS,CL,CO,KI,L,MO,PI, PK,SU,TE,TU
Scabiosa 'Sunburst' s-c	BS
Scabiosa tall dbl	BS,CO,ST
Scabiosa triandra	G,HP,SG,T
Scabiosa x hybrida	B
Scadoxus membranaceus	B
Scadoxus multiflorus	B
Scadoxus multiflorus ssp katherinae	B,C,CG,RU,SG
Scadoxus puniceus	B,CF,DV,PL,RU
Scaevola calendulacea	B,HA,NI
Scaevola calliptera	B,NI
Scaevola crassifolia	B,C,NI,SA
Scaevola fasciculata	B,NI
Scaevola frutescens	B
Scaevola frutescens v sericea	B,CA
Scaevola globulifera	B,NI
Scaevola koenigii	B
Scaevola nitida	B,NI
Scaevola pilosa	B,NI
Scaevola platyphylla	B,NI
Scaevola plumieri	B
Scaevola spinescens	B,NI
Scaevola stenophylla	B,NI
Scaevola taccada	B
Scaevola thesioides	B,NI
Scandix pecten-veneris	B,C,G,NS
Sceletium sp	KB
Sceletium subvelutinum	DV
Sceletium tortuosum	B,SI
Scheelea butyraceae	B
Scheelia rostrata	B,O
Schefflera actinophylla	B,C,CA,CL,EL,HA,O,SA, SK,V,VE
Schefflera actinophylla compacta	B,CA
Schefflera arboricola	B,BS,C,CA,CL,DE,EL, HA,SA
Schefflera digitata	AU,B
Schefflera elegantissima	B,C,HA,SA
Schefflera pueckleri	B
Schefflera venulosa	B,EL,SA
Schima argentea see s.wallichii ssp noronhae v superba	
Schima wallichii	B,LN,SA
Schinus molle	B,C,CA,EL,FW,HA,LN, SA,SG,VE,WA
Schinus patagonicus	AP,SA
Schinus terebinthifolius	B,C,CA,EL,HA,LN,SA, WA
Schinziophyton rautenenii	SI

SCHISANDRA

Schisandra chinensis	A,C,DD,KL,LN,PL,SA, SG
Schisandra grandiflora	B
Schivereckia doerfleri	AP,B,JE,KL,SC
Schivereckia podolica	AP,B,C,JE
Schizachyrium scoparium	B,C,DE,JE,KL,NO,PR,SA
Schizanthus 'Angel Wings' mix	B,C,DN,F,HU,PI,TE
Schizanthus candidus	B,P
Schizanthus dbl mix	VH
Schizanthus 'Dr. Badger'	BS,C,CO,DE,KI,ST,V
Schizanthus Dw Bouquet mix	FR,T
Schizanthus f2 'Disco'	T
Schizanthus 'Gay Pansies'	F
Schizanthus gilliesii	RS
Schizanthus grahamii	AP,B,KL,SZ
Schizanthus 'Hit Parade'	B,BS,C,BY,CL,MO,PK,S, SK,YA
Schizanthus hookeri	AP,B,P,RS,SG
Schizanthus 'Hot Lips'	PL
Schizanthus hyb lge fl	J
Schizanthus 'My Lovely'	D
Schizanthus 'Pierrot'	U
Schizanthus pinnatus 'Lilac Time'	B
Schizanthus 'Star Parade'	B,BS,C,CL,D,DT,F,J,L, MO,S,SK,T
Schizanthus 'Sweet Lips'	T
Schizanthus x wisetonensis	AB,BS,BY,TH
Schizobasis intricata	B,SI
Schizocodon soldanelloides see Shortia	
Schizolobium parahybum	B,DD,EL,HA,RE,SA,TT
Schizonepeta multifida	SG
Schizopetalon walkeri	B,C,F,RS,T
Schizophragma hydrangeoides	HP,SA
Schizostylis coccinea	AP,B,PL,SA,SI
Schizostylis coccinea alba	AP,B,SG
Schizostylis coccinea 'Major'	C
Schizostylis coccinea 'Sunrise'	B,P
Schkuhria pinnata	B
Schkuhria pinnata 'Starry Skies'	C
Schlumbergera hyb mix	AP,CH
Schlumbergera 'Noel' hyb	C,T
Schoenia cassiniana	AU,NI,O
Schoenia cassiniana 'Rose Beauty'	B
Schoenia filifolia ssp subulifolia	AU,B,HU,NI,O
Schoenia macivorii	B,NI,O
Schoenoplectus lacustris tabernaemontani	B,JE
Schoenus pauciflorus	B,SS
Scholtzia involucrata	B,NI
Scholtzia laxiflora	B,NI
Scholtzia oligandra	B,NI
Scholtzia spathulata	B,NI
Schotia afra	B,EL,HA,SI,WA
Schotia brachypetala	B,C,EL,HA,LN,SA,SI,WA
Schotia kaffra	SA
Schotia latifolia	B,EL,LN,SA,SI,WA
Schrankia uncinata	PR
Schrebera alata	B,EL,WA
Schwantesia acutipetala	B,DV
Schwantesia herrei f major	B
Schwantesia herrei v minor	B
Schwantesia marlothii	B
Schwantesia pillansii	B,DV
Schwantesia ruedebuschii	B,DV
Schwantesia speciosa	B
Schwantesia triebneri	B,DV
Sciadopytis verticillata	B,C,FW,LN,SA,VE

Scilla allionii	MN
Scilla autumnalis	AP,AR,CG,G,MN,NG,SC
Scilla autumnalis Corfu	MN
Scilla autumnalis Greece	MN
Scilla autumnalis MS495 Gibraltar	MN
Scilla autumnalis MS771 Crete	MN
Scilla autumnalis Spain	MN
Scilla autumnalis v fallax A.B.S4345	MN
Scilla autumnalis v gracillima S.L382	MN
Scilla baurii	B,SI
Scilla bifolia	AP,AR,B,C,G,JE,SG
Scilla bifolia 'Rosea'	AP,B,SC
Scilla bithynica	AR
Scilla cilicica H.Wollin Cyprus	MN
Scilla gruilhuberi	AP,G,MN
Scilla hohenackeri	AR,PM
Scilla hohenackeri B.S.B.E811	MN
Scilla intermedia A.B.S.4410 Morocco	MN
Scilla intermedia A.B.S.4427 Morocco	MN
Scilla intermedia A.B.S.4449 Morocco	MN
Scilla intermedia S.F383 Morocco	MN
Scilla lilio hyacinthus	AR
Scilla lingulata S.F281 Morocco	MN
Scilla litardierei	AP,AR,B,G,KL,MN,SG
Scilla mauretanica S.F65 Morocco	MN
Scilla melaina	AR
Scilla messeniaca	AR,NG
Scilla mischenkoana	AP,G,KL,MN
Scilla monophylla	AP,MN
Scilla morisii Cyprus	MN
Scilla morrisii	AR
Scilla natalensis	B,C,RU,SI
Scilla nervosa	B,RU,SI
Scilla non-scripta see Hyacinthoides	
Scilla numidica S.L288 Tunisia	MN
Scilla obtusifolia A.B.S4395 Morocco	MN
Scilla obtusifolia MS509 Spain	MN
Scilla obtusifolia S.B.L41/4 Morocco	MN
Scilla obtusifolia S.F280 Morocco	MN
Scilla obtusifolia S.L252 Tunisia	MN
Scilla obtusifolia v glauca S.L375 Morocco	MN
Scilla persica	AP,MN
Scilla persica B.S.B.E1054	MN
Scilla peruviana	AP,B,C,CG,G,NG,SA,SC
Scilla peruviana 'Alba'	B,SC
Scilla peruviana v elegans	MN
Scilla peruviana v gattefossei	AP,MN
Scilla peruviana v ifnense S.F56 Morocco	MN
Scilla peruviana v venusta	MN
Scilla pratensis see S.litardieri	
Scilla ramburei	MN,PM
Scilla scilloides	AP,B,G,PM,SC
Scilla siberica	AP,B,G,KL,SC
Scilla siberica 'Alba'	AP,B,KL,SC
Scilla siberica Polunin25 Lebanon	MN
Scilla siberica 'Spring Beauty'	B
Scilla verna	AP,AR,B,DV,G,SA,SC
Scilla verna aff MS467 Portugal	MN
Scilla villosa S.L310 Tunisia	MN
Scilla vincentii MS442 Portugal	MN
Scilla vincentii VH702 Portugal	MN
Scilla vincentii VH719 Portugal	MN
Scirpoides holoschoenus	B,JE,SA
Scirpus acutus	AB,B,PR
Scirpus atrovirens	B,DE,PR
Scirpus cyperinus	B,PR

SCIRPUS

Scirpus fauriei v vaginatus	B,G,JE
Scirpus mucronatus	B,JE,SA
Scirpus paludosus	B
Scirpus robustus	B
Scirpus sylvaticus	B,JE,SA
Scirpus validus	PR
Scleranthus biflorus	AP,C,G,P,SC
Scleranthus biflorus 'Brockiei'	B
Scleranthus biflorus 'Uniflorus'	AP,B,SG,SS
Sclerocactus brevihamatus	B
Sclerocactus cloveriae	DV
Sclerocactus cloveriae v reevesii	DV
Sclerocactus glaucus	B
Sclerocactus glaucus SB141	Y
Sclerocactus heilii	B
Sclerocactus intermedius	DV
Sclerocactus mesae-verdae	B
Sclerocactus parviflorus	B,DV
Sclerocactus polyancistrus	B
Sclerocactus pubispinus	B
Sclerocactus scheeri	B,DV,Y
Sclerocactus schleseri	B
Sclerocactus spinosior	B,DV
Sclerocactus tobuschii	B
Sclerocactus uncinatus	B,DV,Y
Sclerocactus uncinatus v wrightii	Y
Sclerocactus wetlandicus	B
Sclerocactus whipplei	B,DV
Sclerocactus whipplei intermedis	CH
Sclerocactus wrightiae	B
Sclerocarya birrea	B,SA
Sclerocarya birrea ssp caffra	B,C,SI
Sclerocarya caffra	WA
Sclerochiton harveyanus	B
Sclerolaena diacantha	B,NI
Sclerolaena eurotioides	B,NI
Sclerolaena microcarpa	B,NI
Sclerostegia tenuis	B,NI
Scletium concavum	SI
Scoliopus begelovii	AR
Scoliopus hallii	NG
Scolopendrium see Asplenium	
Scolymus see Cynara	
Scoparia dulcis	B
Scopelogena gracilis	B,DV
Scopelogena veruculata	B
Scopolia carniolica	B,G,JE
Scorzonera austriaca	B,SG
Scorzonera hispanica	B,SG
Scorzonera humilis	B,HP
Scorzonera papposa	B
Scorzonera radiata	SG
Scorzonera rosea	KL
Scorzonera sp	RM
Scrophularia auriculata	B,HP
Scrophularia californica	B,DD
Scrophularia canina ssp hoppei	C
Scrophularia glabrata	B
Scrophularia grandiflora	B,JE,SG
Scrophularia lanceolata	B
Scrophularia nodosa	AP,B,C,CG,G,LA,JE,SA, SC,SG
Scrophularia nodosa tracheliodes	NS
Scutellaria albida	CG,G
Scutellaria alpina	AP,B,C,G,HP,JE,KL,SA, SC,SG

Scutellaria alpina 'Arcobaleno'	JE
Scutellaria alpina Fairy Carpet Mix	F
Scutellaria alpina Greencourt Form	AP
Scutellaria altissima	AP,B,BS,C,G,HP,JE,P,SA
Scutellaria baicalensis	AP,DD,G,JE,RM,SC,SG, T
Scutellaria columnae	HP
Scutellaria galericulata	B,CN,TH
Scutellaria incana	B,G,JE
Scutellaria lateriflora	B,CN,CP,DD,HP
Scutellaria minor	B,KL
Scutellaria novae zelandiae	AP,B,P,SC
Scutellaria orientalis	AP,B,HP,SC
Scutellaria orientalis v pinnatifida	G,JE
Scutellaria rubicunde	SG
Scutellaria salviifolia	KL,RM
Scutellaria scordiifolia	AP,HP
Scutellaria tessellata	B,SW
Scutellaria tournefortii	NG
Scutellaria woronowii	SG
Scutia myrtina	B,WA
Sebaea cf sedoides	B,SI
Sebaea exacoides	B,SI
Sebaea minutiflora	B,SI
Sebaea sp	SI
Sebaea spathulata	SI
Sebastiana chamaelea	B
Secale cereale 'Tetra Pectus Rye'	B
Secamone alpini	B
Secamone sp	DV
Securidaca longipedunculata	B,EL,SA,WA
Securinega leucopyrus	B
Securinega suffruticosa	B,LN,SG
Sedum acre	B,BD,BS,BY,C,CL,CN, JE,KI,L,MO,SA,SK,ST,V
Sedum aizoon	AP,B,DV,G,HP,I,JE,SA, SG
Sedum aizoon 'Aurantiacum' see S.aizoon 'Euphorbioides'	
Sedum aizoon 'Euphorbioides'	T
Sedum album	AP,B,DV,HP,JE,KL,SG
Sedum anacampseros	B,C,DV
Sedum anglicum	DV
Sedum anopetalum see S.ochroleucum	
Sedum arenarium	DV
Sedum borissovae	DV,SG
Sedum brevifolia	DV
Sedum camtschaticum	KL
Sedum caucasicum	DV
Sedum cauticola	KL
Sedum cepaea	DV
Sedum Crown mix	BS
Sedum dasyphyllum	AP,B,DV,KL
Sedum 'Dragon's Blood' see S.spurium 'Schorbluser Blut'	
Sedum ewersii	AP,B
Sedum fabaria	B
Sedum floriferum see S.kamtschaticum	
Sedum forsterianum see S.rupestre	
Sedum 'Herbstfreunde'	KL
Sedum hirsutum	DV
Sedum hirsutum ssp baeticum	SG
Sedum hispanicum	CG
Sedum hybridum	B,DV,SG
Sedum hyperaizoon	DV
Sedum kamtschaticum	AP,B,C,DV,HP,JE,SA,SG
Sedum kamtschaticum 'Tricolor'	CG
Sedum kamtschaticum v ellacombianum	DV,G,JE

242

SEDUM

Sedum kamtschaticum v middendorffianum see S.middend.	
Sedum lanceolatum	B,JE
Sedum lydium	DV,KL
Sedum maximum	DV
Sedum maximum v caucasicum	DV
Sedum middendorffianum	B,DV,SG
Sedum mix rock garden	SK,T
Sedum ochroleucum	B,DV
Sedum oreganum	B,C,DV,JE
Sedum pachyclados	KL
Sedum pallescens	SG
Sedum pallidum	DV
Sedum pilosum	AP,DV,G,KL,SC
Sedum popuifolium	B,DV,JE
Sedum purpureum	SG
Sedum reflexum see S.rupestre	
Sedum rubens	B,DV
Sedum rupestre	B,BS,C,CG,CL,CN,DV, HU,I,JE,MO,SG,SU
Sedum sartorianum	DV
Sedum sartorianum v stribrnyi	DV
Sedum sediforme	B,CG,DV
Sedum selskianum	B,BS,CL,DV,SA
Sedum sempervivoides	B,G,JE,KL,SC
Sedum sexangulare	DV
Sedum 'Silver Moon'	I
Sedum sp mix	BD,BS,C,CA,CL,CN,D, DE,JE,L,MO,PK
Sedum spathulifolium	B,C,JE
Sedum spathulifolium ssp pruinosum	P
Sedum spectabile	DV
Sedum spectabile 'Autumn Beauty'	B
Sedum spurium	B,CG,DV,SG
Sedum spurium 'Coccineum'	B,BS,C,CL,CN,HU,JE, MO,S,SA,T,V
Sedum spurium 'Schorbluser Blut'	SK
Sedum stelliferum	SC
Sedum stenopetalum	SG
Sedum stoloniferum	B,DV
Sedum takesimense	DV
Sedum tatarinowii	DV
Sedum telephium	A,AP,B,DV,SC,SG,T
Sedum telephium 'Purpureum'	B
Sedum telephium ssp fabaria see S.fabaria	
Sedum telephium ssp maximum	AP,B,DV,G,JE,SG
Sedum tenuifolium	DV
Sedum urvillei	DV
Sedum villosum	C,G,SC
Selaginella selaginoides	B
Selago corymbosa	B,SI
Selago serrata	B,SI
Selago sp	SI
Selago spuria	B,SI
Selago thunbergii	B
Selenicereus grandiflorus	DV
Selenicereus pteranthus	DV
Selenicereus tesudo	B,DV,Y
Selinum carvifolia	B,CG,HP
Selinum tenuifolium see S.wallichianum	
Selinum wallichianum	B,HP,JE,SA,SC
Semiaquilegia adoxoides	AP,HP
Semiaquilegia adoxoides fl.pl.	KL
Semiaquilegia ecalcarata	AP,B,C,CG,G,HP,HU,JD, JE,KL,P,PL,SA,SC,SG
Semiaquilegia ecalcarata dw early	B,P
Semiaquilegia ecalcarata 'Flore Pleno'	AP,C,HP

Semiaquilegia simultrix see S. ecalcarata	
Semiarundinaria fastuosa	HP
Semnanthe lacera	B,DV,SI
Sempervivum alatuum	SG
Sempervivum arachnoideum	B,C,CG,RM,SC,SG,VO
Sempervivum arach. ssp tomentosum	B,JE,SG
Sempervivum atlanticum	SG
Sempervivum ballsii	SG
Sempervivum ciliosum	RM,SG
Sempervivum grandiflorum	AP,C,CG
Sempervivum guiseppii	SG
Sempervivum Hyb New American	T
Sempervivum marmoreum	SC,SG
Sempervivum montanum	B,CG,DV,SG
Sempervivum montanum braunii	SG
Sempervivum montanum striatum	SG
Sempervivum octopodes apelalum	SG
Sempervivum pitonii	SG
Sempervivum pumilum	VO
Sempervivum ruthenicum	B
Sempervivum sp & hyb mix	C,HP,HU,I,SK,V,W
Sempervivum sp mix	BS,CN,DE,F,J,KI,L,MO, PK,R,SA,SK,ST,TH
Sempervivum tectorum	B,C,CG,DV,I,JE,SG
Sempervivum tectorum glaucum	SG
Sempervivum thompsonianum	SG
Sempervivum vincentii	B,SG
Sempervivum winter hardy vars	JE
Sempervivum wulfenii	AP,B,DV,SG
Sempervivum zeleborii	SG
Senecio abrotanifolius	AP,KL,SC,SG,VO
Senecio aizoides	SG
Senecio alpinus	JE,SA,SG
Senecio anethifolius	B,NI
Senecio angulatus	B,SI
Senecio arcticulatus	SG
Senecio arcticus	SG
Senecio barbatus	B,SI
Senecio brachypodus	B,SI
Senecio cakilefolius	B,SI
Senecio canabifolius	SG
Senecio candoleanus	VO
Senecio canus	SG
Senecio capitatus	VO
Senecio carniolicus	SG
Senecio chrysanthemoides see Euryops	
Senecio cineraria	B,HP,SG
Senecio cineraria Berlin Market strain	DE
Senecio cineraria 'Candicans'	AR,AU,B,BS,BY,L,MO
Senecio cineraria 'Cirrus'	B,BS,BY,CA,CL,CN,D, DT,F,MO,PK,SK,T,U,YA
Senecio cineraria 'Diamond'	BS,FR,SA
Senecio cineraria 'Dwarf Silver'	D
Senecio cineraria New Look	DE
Senecio cineraria 'Silver Dust'	w.a.
Senecio cineraria 'Silver Dust' p.s	B,BD,CL,MO
Senecio cineraria 'Silver Lace'	B,SK
Senecio cineraria 'Silver Queen'	PK
Senecio cinerascens	B,SI
Senecio coleophyllus	B,SI
Senecio confusus	B
Senecio cordatus	B,G
Senecio coronatus	B,SI
Senecio doria	B,HP,JE
Senecio doronicum	B,JE,SA
Senecio douglasii	B

SENECIO

Senecio dregeanus	B,SI
Senecio elegans	B,C,KB,SI
Senecio elegans white	B,KB
Senecio erucifolius	SG
Senecio fremontii v blitoides	RM
Senecio glastifolius	B,KB,SI
Senecio grandifolius	SG
Senecio gregorii	B,NI,O
Senecio harbourii	RM
Senecio helminthioides	B,SI
Senecio integrifolius	KL,SG,VO
Senecio jacobaea	B,SG
Senecio jacobaea 'Elegans'	B
Senecio joppensis	B
Senecio kleinia	C,DV
Senecio korabense	VO
Senecio lautus	B,O
Senecio leucophyllus	VO
Senecio littoralis	AR
Senecio macroglossus	B,SI
Senecio macrospermus	B,SI
Senecio magnificus	B,NI,O,SA
Senecio nemorensis	B,JE,SA,SG
Senecio nemorensis v fuchsii	B,JE
Senecio plattensis	B,PR
Senecio platylepis	B,DD
Senecio pleistocephalus	B,SI
Senecio polyodon	AP,B,HP,P
Senecio primulaefolius	VO
Senecio pseudoarnica	KL,SG
Senecio pulcher	HP
Senecio pyroglossus	VO
Senecio radicans	SG
Senecio resedifolius	SG
Senecio scandens	AP,HP,P
Senecio serpens	SG
Senecio smithii	HP
Senecio soldanella	RM
Senecio sp	SC,SI
Senecio speciosus	HP,SI
Senecio subalpinus	SG
Senecio sylvaticus	B
Senecio tanguticus see Sinacalia tangutica	
Senecio tournefortii	VO
Senecio tournefortii v granatensis	VO
Senecio triangularis	B,DD
Senecio umbrosus	SG
Senecio vernalis	B
Senecio vulgaris	B
Senna aciphylla	B,NI
Senna alata	B,C,FW,HA,HU,O,SA,SK
Senna armata	B
Senna artemisoides	AU,C,DV,HA
Senna artemisoides ssp artemisoides	B,NI,O
Senna artemisoides ssp circinnata	B,NI
Senna artemisoides ssp coriacea	B,NI
Senna artemisoides ssp filifolia	B,NI,O
Senna artemisoides ssp hamersleyensis	B,NI
Senna artemisoides ssp helmsii	B,NI,O
Senna artemisoides ssp oligophylla	B,NI,O
Senna artemisoides ssp petiolaris	B,NI
Senna artemisoides ssp sturtii	B,NI,O
Senna artemisoides ssp zygophylla	B,NI
Senna atomaria	B
Senna auriculata	B
Senna barclayana	B,NI,O

Senna candolleana	B
Senna corymbosa	C,HU,JE,V,VE
Senna costata	B,NI
Senna covesii	B
Senna didymobotrya	B,C,G,HA,JE,O,SA,VE
Senna glutinosa ssp chatelainiana	B,NI,O
Senna glutinosa ssp ferraria	B,NI
Senna glutinosa ssp glutinosa	B,NI,O
Senna glutinosa ssp luerssenii	B,NI,O
Senna glutinosa ssp pruinosa	B,NI,O
Senna hebecarpa	B
Senna hirsuta	B
Senna hirsuta v glaberrima	B
Senna marilandica	B,HP
Senna multijuga	B
Senna notabilis	B,NI,O
Senna occidentalis	B
Senna odorata	AU,B,NI,O
Senna pallida	B
Senna pendula v glabrata	B
Senna petersii	B
Senna planitiicola	AU,B,NI
Senna pleurocarpa v angustifolia	B,NI
Senna pleurocarpa v pleurocarpa	B,NI,O
Senna reticulata	B
Senna roemerana	B
Senna septemtrionalis	B
Senna siamea	B,HA,O,RE,SA
Senna spectabilis	B
Senna sturtii	B
Senna surattensis	B,CA
Senna venusta	B,NI,O
Senna x floribunda	B,HA,O,SA
Sequoia sempervirens	A,AB,B,C,CA,CG,DD,EL, FW,LN,N,NO,SA,T,V,VE, WA
Sequoiadendron giganteum	A,AB,B,C,CA,CG,DD,EL, FW,HU,LN,N,NO,SA,VE
Serenoa repens	B,CA,SA
Sericanthe andongensis	B,SI
Seriphidium canum	B,C,LN,NO,SA
Seriphidium maritimum	B,HP
Seriphidium palmeri	B
Seriphidium tridentatum	B,C,NO,SA
Seriphidium tripartitum v rupicola	B
Seriphidium vallesiacum	B
Seronoa repens	C,O
Seronoa repens blue	O
Serratula centauroides	SG
Serratula radiata	B
Serratula seoanii	HP,I,SC
Serratula tinctoria	AP,B,G,HP,JE,SG
Serratula tinctoria ssp macrocephala	AP,B,C
Serratula wolfii	G,SC,SG
Serruria adscendens	B,SI
Serruria cygnaea	SI
Serruria elongata	B,SI
Serruria flava	O
Serruria florida	B,C,O,SI,V
Serruria hybrid	SI
Serruria pedunculata	B,SI
Serruria phylicoides	B,SI
Sesamum alatum	B,SI
Sesamum capense	B,SI
Sesamum indicum	C,CN,HU
Sesamum indicum 'Thai Black'	B,DD

SESAMUM

Sesamum indicum 'Turkish'	B,DD	Sida subspicata	B,NI
Sesamum sp	SI	Sidalcea campestris	B,DD
Sesamum triphyllum	B,SI	Sidalcea canadensis	B
Sesbania aculeata	B	Sidalcea candida	AP,B,C,HP,KL,P,SC
Sesbania agyptica	EL,SA	Sidalcea candida 'Bianca'	JE,SA
Sesbania bispinosa	B	Sidalcea 'Croftway Red'	HP
Sesbania cannabina	AU,B,NI,SA	Sidalcea Crown	BS
Sesbania cannabina v sericea	B,NI	Sidalcea cusickii	SZ
Sesbania formosa	B,C,NI,O,SA	Sidalcea 'Elsie Heugh'	AP,HP
Sesbania grandiflora	B,DD,EL,HA,HU,O,SA -	Sidalcea hyb special	BY,T
Sesbania punicea	B,EL,G,SA	Sidalcea malviflora	AP,B,HP,KL
Sesbania sesban	B,O	Sidalcea malviflora Pink Hybrid	B,SA,U
Sesbania tripetii	B,C,EL,HU,SA,SC	Sidalcea malviflora Stark's Hybrids	C,JE,SA
Sesbania versicaria	B	Sidalcea neomexicana	B,JE,SA
Seseli buchtormense	SG	Sidalcea 'Party Girl'	AP,BD,BS,C,CL,CN,CO,
Seseli gummiferum	AP,B,JE		G,HP,JE,KI,KS,L,MO,SA,
Seseli ledebourii	SG		ST,T,V
Seseli libanotis	G,SG	Sidalcea 'Purpetta'	C,G,JE
Sesleria hueffleriana	B,JE	Sidalcea 'Rosaly'	JE
Sesleria sadlerana	B,JE,SA	Sidalcea 'Rosanna'	C,JE
Sessilistigma radians	B,RU	Sidalcea 'Rose Queen'	HP
Setaria anceps 'Kazungula'	B	Sidalcea rosea	HP
Setaria anceps 'Nandi'	B	Sideritis glacialis	VO
Setaria anceps 'Narok'	B	Sideritis hyssopifolia	AP,B,KL,SC,SG,SZ,VO
Setaria annual vars	MO	Sideritis montana	B
Setaria chevalieri	B	Sideritis syriaca	AP,B,HP,JE,SC
Setaria glauca	B,V	Sideritis syriaca ssp syriaca	T
Setaria italica	DD,JO,SG	Sideritis taurica	SZ
Setaria italica 'Hairy'	B	Sideroxylon inerme	B
Setaria italica 'Macrocheata'	B,BS,C,DE,JO	Sideroxylon tempisque	B,SA
Setaria italica 'Polydactyla'	B	Siegfriedia darwinoides	B,NI
Setaria italica 'White Wonder'	B,SD	Sieversia reptans	AP,B,BS,C,G,I,JE,SA,
Setaria macrostachya	B,MO		SC,VO
Setaria palmifolia	B,CA,SA	Silaum silaus	B
Setaria pumila	AP,SA	Silene acaulis	B,C,HP,JE,KL,RM,SA,
Setaria sphacelata	SI		SC,VO
Setaria viridis	B	Silene acaulis pedunculata	SG
Seticereus chlorocarpus	DV,Y	Silene acaulis ssp bryoides	B,CG
Seticereus icasagonus v oehmeanus	DV	Silene acaulis ssp exscapa see S.acaulis ssp bryoides	
Seticereus icosagonus	DV,Y	Silene aegyptiaca	B
Seticereus microspermus	DV	Silene alba see S.latifolia	
Setiechinopsis mirabilis	CH,SG,Y	Silene alpestris	AP,B,C,G,HP,JE,KL,SA,
Severinia buxifolia	B		SC,SG
Shepherdia argentea	B,FW,LN,NO,SA,SG	Silene argaea	AP,KL,RM
Shepherdia canadensis	A,B,FW,LN,NO,SA	Silene armeria	AP,B,C,G,HP,HU,HW,KL,
Shortia soldanelloides	A,B,KL,SC		PI,SC,VY
Shortia uniflora	B	Silene armeria compacta 'None-so-pretty'	B,BD,BS,MO
Sibbaldia parviflora	VO	Silene armeria 'Electra'	B,J,SK,U
Sibbaldia pauciflora	SG	Silene asterias	AP,B,C,G,HP,JE,SC,T,VO
Sibbaldia procumbens	B,G,JE,SC	Silene 'Balletje Balletje'	B,BS,C,KI
Sibbaldia semiglabra	VO	Silene bellidifolia	B
Sibbaldiopsis tridentata	AP,B,JE,KL	Silene bellidioides	B,BH,KB,SI,T
Sibiraea laevigata	SG	Silene boryi	VO
Sicana odorifera	B,C	Silene burchellii	AP,B,SI
Sida acuta	B	Silene campanula	T
Sida cordata	B	Silene caroliniana	KL
Sida cordifolia	B	Silene caryophylloides ssp echinus	SG,VO
Sida cordifolium	SI	Silene ciliata	KL
Sida echinocarpa	B,NI	Silene ciliata v graefferi	SG
Sida filicaulis	B	Silene clandestina	B,SI
Sida filiformis	B,NI	Silene coeli-rosa 'Blossom' s-c	B,T
Sida goniocarpa	B,NI	Silene coeli-rosa 'Blue Pearl'	B,V
Sida ovata	B,SI	Silene coeli-rosa nana 'Angel' mix	C,T,V
Sida petrophila	B,C,NI	Silene coeli-rosa nana 'Blue Angel'	B,C,DI,T
Sida rohlenae	B,NI	Silene coeli-rosa nana 'Rose Angel'	B,C,V
Sida schimperiana	B	Silene coeli-rosa 'Rose'	B,SD

SILENE

Silene compacta	AP,B,HP,JE,SA	Silene uniflora 'White Bells'	AP,BS,HP
Silene conica h.	B,C,EL,KS	Silene vallesia	AP,C,HP,JE
Silene delavayi	AP,PM,SC	Silene virginica	AP,B,C,G,JE
Silene dichotoma	B	Silene viscosa	SG
Silene dinarica	AP,SC,SG	Silene vulgaris	AP,B,C,CN,HP,JE,KS,LA,
Silene dioica	AP,B,C,CN,CO,DD,G,HP,		SA,SG,TH
	JE,LA,SA,SC,SG,TU,V	Silene vulgaris	SG
Silene dioica et alba	W	Silene vulgaris ssp alpina see S.uniflora ssp prostrata	
Silene dioica 'Graham's Delight'	AP,B,P	Silene vulgaris ssp gloriosa	SG
Silene elisabethae	AP,B,C,G,JE,KL,SC	Silene vulgaris ssp macrocarpa	SG
Silene falcata	RM	Silene vulgaris ssp maritima see S.uniflora	
Silene fimbriata	HP,JD,JE,LG,NG	Silene waldensteinii	AP,B,JE,SG,VO
Silene gallica	B,NS,SG	Silene wallichiana see S.vulgaris	
Silene gallica ssp quinquevulnera	AP,SC	Silene zawadskii	AP,B,BS,HP,JE,KL,SG
Silene hookeri	AP,B,C,HP,JE,SC	Silphium dentatum	NT
Silene italica	G,NS	Silphium integrifolium	B,DD,G,JE,PR,SG
Silene keiskii	AP,SG	Silphium laciniatum	B,C,HU,JE,PR
Silene laciniata	AP,B,KL,SC,SW	Silphium perfoliatum	AP,B,G,HP,JE,PR
Silene lagascae	CG	Silphium terebinthinaceum	B,JE,PR
Silene latifolia	AP,B,C,CG,CN,HP,LA,	Silphium trifoliatum	B
	JE,SA,SG,SU	Silybum eburneum	B,DD,SG
Silene lerchenfeldiana	KL	Silybum marianum	AP,B,C,CG,CN,CP,DD,E,
Silene maritima see S.uniflora			G,HP,HU,JE,PA,PO,SA,
Silene multinerva	B		SC,SG,SU,TH
Silene muscipula	SG	Silybum marianum 'Adriana'	B,PL
Silene nemoralis	HP	Silybum marianum album	HP
Silene nigrescens	HP,KL,SC,SG	Simarouba glauca	B
Silene noctiflora	AP,B,C,G,HP,SC,TH	Simmondsia chinensis	AB,B,C,CA,EL,FW,LN,O,
Silene nutans	AP,B,G,HP,JE,SA,SG		SA
Silene obtusifolia	SG	Sinacalia tangutica	C,JE,SA
Silene orientalis see S.compacta		Sinningia canescens	B,BC,C,DV,SG,Y
Silene otites	B,SG	Sinningia cardinalis	B,BC,DV,SA
Silene otites ssp hungarica	B	Sinningia cardinalis v compacta	C
Silene palaestina	B	Sinningia 'Diego'	D
Silene pendula	F,I	Sinningia eumorpha	C
Silene pendula 'Alba'	B	Sinningia f1 'Empress' mix	B
Silene pendula 'Compacta'	AP,BS,SC,T,V	Sinningia hyb mini, Cindy-ella	C
Silene pendula 'Compacta Peach Blossom'	B,BS,D,DI,DT,KS,MO,SE	Sinningia hyb mini mix	C,PK,T
Silene pendula 'Compacta Snowball' fl pl	BS,C,KS,MO,T	Sinningia speciosa f1 'Carmen'	T
Silene pendula 'Compacta Triumph'	B	Sinningia speciosa hyb new	B
Silene pendula 'Rosea'	B,DI	Sinningia verticillata	B,SA
Silene pendula 'Ruberrima'	B	Sinocalycanthus chinensis	B,FW
Silene petersonii	RM	Sinocrassula indica	SG
Silene 'Pink Pirouette'	T	Sinojackia xylocarpa	B,LN,SA
Silene primulaeflora	BH	Sinowilsonia henryi	SA
Silene procumbens	SG	Siphonochilus kirkii	B,SI
Silene pusilla	AP,B,G,JE,KL,SC	Sison amomum	B
Silene regia	B,C,HP,JE,PR	Sisymbrium altissimum	B
Silene rupestris	B,VO	Sisymbrium loeselii	SG
Silene saxifraga	AP,B,G,JE,SC,SG	Sisymbrium luteum	B,C,JE
Silene schafta	AP,B,BS,C,CG,CL,DE,	Sisymbrium officinale	B
	DV,G,HP,J,KI,KL,MO,	Sisyndite spartea	B,SI
	SA,SC,SG,T	Sisyrinchium angustifolium	B,HP,KL,NO
Silene schafta 'Splendens'	B,JE	Sisyrinchium angustifolium album	HP,KL
Silene schmuckeri	KL	Sisyrinchium arenarium	MN
Silene scouleri v pauciflora	B,JE	Sisyrinchium arizonicum	B,SW
Silene sibirica	KL	Sisyrinchium atlanticum	AP
Silene sp	SG,SI	Sisyrinchium bellum see S.idahoense v bellum	
Silene stellata	B,PR	Sisyrinchium bermudianum see S.angustifolium	
Silene stenophylla	VO	Sisyrinchium californicum	AP,B,DD,DE,G,HP,I,KL,
Silene thessalonica	B,P		PM,SA,SC,SG
Silene undulata	B,SI	Sisyrinchium californicum Brachypus Gr.	AP,HP,MO
Silene uniflora	AP,B,C,E,G,HP,SA,SG,T	Sisyrinchium campestre	B,C,JE,PR,SG
Silene uniflora 'Robin White Breast'	AP,BS,C,CL,JE,L,MO	Sisyrinchium campestre albiflorum	B,PR
Silene uniflora 'Rosea'	AP,SG	Sisyrinchium chilense	AP,I
Silene uniflora ssp prostrata	B	Sisyrinchium commutatum	AP,B,P

SISYRINCHIUM

Sisyrinchium convolutum	C,HP,SC,SG
Sisyrinchium cuspidatum see S.arenarium	
Sisyrinchium demissum	B,SW
Sisyrinchium depauperatum	AP,HP,SC
Sisyrinchium douglasii see Olsynium	
Sisyrinchium elmeri	B,SC
Sisyrinchium filifolium see Olsynium	
Sisyrinchium graminoides	AP,B,BS,CG,F,HP,JE,RH, RS,SA,SC,SG,T
Sisyrinchium graminoides 'Album'	AP,B,G,HP,JE,P,SC,T
Sisyrinchium idahoense v bellum	AB,AP,B,BS,C,CA,CL, DD,G,HP,HU,JE,KL,KS, L,MO,SA,SG,SW,U
Sisyrinchium idahoense v bellum 'Album'	KL
Sisyrinchium inflatum	NO
Sisyrinchium iridifolium see S.micranthum	
Sisyrinchium littorale	AP,B,JE,KL,RS
Sisyrinchium longipes	SW
Sisyrinchium macrocarpum	AP,B,G,HP,MN,PM,SG
Sisyrinchium macrocephalum	AV
Sisyrinchium micranthum	AP,B,HP,JE,SC,SG
Sisyrinchium mix	AP,P
Sisyrinchium montanum	AP,B,G,SC,SG
Sisyrinchium montanum v crebum	SG
Sisyrinchium 'Mrs. Spivey'	AP,I,SC
Sisyrinchium patagonicum	AP,C,G,HP,KL,RS,SC,SG
Sisyrinchium 'Pole Star'	AP,C,KL
Sisyrinchium 'Raspberry'	HP
Sisyrinchium sp	AP,C,JE,KL,P,SC,T
Sisyrinchium striatum	AP,B,BS,C,E,F,G,HP,I,JE, LG,P,PM,RH,SA,SC,SG, SZ,T,TH
Sisyrinchium tenuifolium	B,SC
Sitanion hystrix	B,DE,NO
Sium sisarum	B,CN,DD
Skiatophyllum tripolium	B,KB
Skimmia japonica	B,HP,RH,SA,SG
Smelowskia calycina	RM
Smilacina japonica	B
Smilacina racemosa	AP,B,C,G,HP,JE,LG,NO, SA,SC,SG,SW,T
Smilacina stellata	B,C,NO,SG,SW
Smilacina trifolia	SG
Smilax aspera	B,CA,CL,DE,L,NG
Smilax bona-nox	B
Smilax herbacea	B,HU
Smilax laurifolia	B
Smilax mersiphyllum	SK
Smilax zarsaparilla	B
Smithiantha zebrina	C
Smodingium argutum	B,WA
Smyrnium olusatrum	A,B,C,CN,DD,HP,LA,SA, SG,TH
Smyrnium perfoliatum	AP,C,CG,HP,JD,MA,NG, PA,SA,SG,T
Soehrensia bruchii	Y
Soehrensia formosa	Y
Soehrensia grandis	Y
Soehrensia korethroides	Y
Solanaceae 'Miltomate Criollo'	B,HU
Solanaceae 'Miltomate Montes'	B,HU
Solanaceae 'Miltomate Vallisto'	B
Solandra maxima	B
Solanum abutiloides 'Jade Chalice'	PL
Solanum aculeatissimum	B,DD
Solanum atropurpureum	B,HU

Solanum aviculare	AP,AU,B,HU,NI,SA,SG
Solanum biflorum	CG
Solanum burbankii	DD
Solanum capsicastrum	B,T
Solanum carolinense	B
Solanum carstellatum	CG
Solanum centrale	B,NI
Solanum cithrifolium	SG
Solanum coactiliferum	B
Solanum crispum	HP
Solanum crispum 'Glasnevin'	I
Solanum crispum 'Variegatum'	HP
Solanum diversiflorum	B,NI
Solanum douglasii	HU
Solanum dulcamara	B,HU,PO,SG
Solanum elaeagnifolium	B
Solanum ferocissimum	B,NI
Solanum gabrielae	B,NI
Solanum giganteum	B,SI
Solanum gilo	B,DD
Solanum hindsianum	B,DD
Solanum hirsutissimum	B
Solanum horridum	B,NI
Solanum integrifolium	B,HU
Solanum japonense	B
Solanum jasminoides album	HP
Solanum khasianum	B
Solanum kitagawae	SG
Solanum laciniatum	AU,B,C,HP,P,SA
Solanum lasiophyllum	B,NI,SA
Solanum macrocarpum	DD
Solanum madagascariensis	DV
Solanum mammosum	B,EL
Solanum maritimum	HU
Solanum mauritianum	B,C
Solanum melanocerasum	B
Solanum melongena	B
Solanum melongena 'Diamond'	B,DD
Solanum melongena 'Golden Eggs'	B,C,EL,L
Solanum melongena v insanum	B
Solanum melongena 'White Eggs'	PK
Solanum muricatum	B
Solanum nigrum	B,CP,SG
Solanum opacum	HU
Solanum persicum	SG
Solanum petrophilum	B,NI
Solanum phlomoides	B,NI
Solanum pseudocapsicum	SI,V
Solanum pseudocapsicum 'Ballad'	CL
Solanum pseudocapsicum 'Balloon'	B,YA
Solanum pseudocapsicum 'Big Boy'	B
Solanum pseudocapsicum 'Capital'	CL
Solanum pseudocapsicum 'Cherry Ripe'	BS,SK
Solanum pseudocaps. 'Covent Garden'	BS
Solanum pseudocapsicum 'Dw Red'	D
Solanum pseudocapsicum 'Harlequin'	B
Solanum pseudocapsicum 'Joker'	B,BD,BS,HU,J,L,MO,YA
Solanum pseudocaps. 'New Patterson'	B,C
Solanum pseudocapsicum 'Pearl'	BS
Solanum pseudocapsicum 'Pinocchio'	BS
Solanum pseudocapsicum 'Xmas Cherry'	SK
Solanum ptycanthum	B
Solanum pyrenacantha	DV
Solanum quitoense	B,C,RE,SA,TT
Solanum rigescens	B,SI
Solanum seaforthianum	B,C,EL,HU

SOLANUM

Solanum sessiflorum	B
Solanum simile	B,HU,NI
Solanum sisymbrifolium	HP,HU,T
Solanum sturtianum	B,NI
Solanum surattense	B
Solanum torvum	B
Solanum trilobatum	B
Solanum umbelliferum	T
Solanum viarum	B
Solanum wrightii	B
Solanum x burbankii	B
Solanum xanthocarpum	B
Solanum xantii	B,HU
Soldanella alpina	AP,B,C,CG,G,HP,JE,KL, SA,SC,T
Soldanella carpatica	AP,DV,KL,VO
Soldanella hungarica	B,KL,SC
Soldanella minima	B,KL
Soldanella montana	AP,B,CG,G,JE,KL,P,SC
Soldanella pusilla	B,C,G,JE
Solena amplexicaulis	B
Solenomelus pedunculatus	AP,AR,B
Solenomelus sisyrinchium	AP,P
Solenopsis axillaris	AU,B,C,DT,F,HP,P,R,V
Solenopsis axillaris alba	AP,B,C,HP,P
Solenopsis axillaris 'Fantasy Blue'	D
Solenopsis axillaris pink	B,P,S
Solenopsis axillaris 'Stars Blue'	B,CL,J,L,MO,PK,PL,SE, T,U
Solenopsis axillaris 'Stars Mix'	SE
Solenopsis axillaris 'Stars Shooting'	MO,PK,T
Solenopsis axillaris 'Stars White'	B,CL,D
Solenopsis axillaris 'White Charm' see 'Stars'	
Solenopsis 'Starlight Pink'	T,U
Solenostemon 'Black Dragon'	BS,DT,F
Solenostemon 'Brilliant' mix	PK
Solenostemon 'Camelot'	F
Solenostemon 'Carefree'	B,BS,CA,DT,L,MO
Solenostemon 'Color Pride'	C
Solenostemon f1 'Dragon Sunset/Volcano'	T,V
Solenostemon 'Fairway'	C,D,PK
Solenostemon 'Fashion Parade' mix	J,M,SE,SK,U
Solenostemon 'Festive Dance'	C
Solenostemon 'Fiji' mix	CA
Solenostemon 'Flame Dancers'	F
Solenostemon frederici	SG
Solenostemon hyb superb mix	DT
Solenostemon hypocrateriformis	B,C
Solenostemon 'Midway' mix	DE
Solenostemon 'Milky Way'	BS
Solenostemon mix dw	FR
Solenostemon 'Nottingham Lace'	SE
Solenostemon petraea	B
Solenostemon 'Prize Strain'	BS
Solenostemon 'Prize Strain Imp'	T
Solenostemon 'Rainbow' mix	BD,BU,C,D,J,L,MO,PI, S,SK
Solenostemon 'Rainbow Striped'	SK
Solenostemon rotundifolius	B
Solenostemon 'Sabre'	B,BS,BY,CL,MO
Solenostemon 'Salmon Lace'	C
Solenostemon 'Scarlet Poncho'	U
Solenostemon 'Rainbow Masterblend'	B,BS,DE
Solenostemon 'Seven Dwarfs' mix	SK
Solenostemon 'Superfine Rainbow' mix	BS,C
Solenostemon 'Top Crown'	BS,CO,KI,ST
Solenostemon 'Vindaloo'	U
Solenostemon 'Volcano'	C
Solenostemon 'Wizard Golden'	SK,U
Solenostemon 'Wizard' mix	BS,BY,CA,CL,MO,R,S, SK,T,U,YA
Solenostemon 'Wizard Rose'	CA,SK
Solenostemon 'Wizard Scarlet'	DT,SK,U
Solenostemon 'Wizard Velvet'	C,CA,SK
Solidago alpina	VO
Solidago caesia	G,KL,NT
Solidago canadensis	AB,B,HP,JE,NO,SA
Solidago canadensis 'Golden Baby'	B,BS,C,CL,CN,DE,J,JE, L,MO,PK,U,V
Solidago canadensis 'Yellow Springs'	BS,CO,KI,SU
Solidago cutleri	AP,C,JE,SC
Solidago flexicaulis	B,PR
Solidago gigantea	CG,JE
Solidago glomerata	B,C,G,JE
Solidago graminifolia	B,G,PR
Solidago hispida	G,SG
Solidago juncea	B
Solidago missouriensis	B,G,SC,SG
Solidago multiradiata	AP,KL,RM
Solidago nemoralis	B,NT,PR
Solidago odora	B,G,NT
Solidago 'Perkeo'	B
Solidago riddellii	B,CG,PR,SG
Solidago rigida	B,G,JE,PR,SG
Solidago rigida v humilis	SG
Solidago rugosa	G,NT
Solidago sempervirens	B,NT
Solidago spathulata nana	SC
Solidago speciosa	B,JE,NT,PR
Solidago sphacelata	NT
Solidago spiraefolia	SG
Solidago tenuifolia	B
Solidago uliginosa	G,JE
Solidago ulmifolia	B,PR
Solidago virgaurea	AP,B,CG,CN,G,JE,SA, SC,SG,SU,TH
Solidago Virgaurea ssp alpestris	KL
Solidago virgaurea ssp gigantea	CG
Solidago virgaurea ssp minuta	AP,G,JE,KL,SC,SG
Solisia pectinata	BC,DV
Sollya heterophylla	C,CA,EL,HA,HU,NI,O, PL,SA,SC,SH,T
Sollya heterophylla pink	NI,SA
Sollya parviflora	B
Sonchus acaulis	SA
Sonchus arboreus	SA
Sonchus arvensis	B
Sonchus asper	B
Sonchus congestus	SA
Sonchus oleraceus v glabrescens	B
Sonchus palustris	B,G
Sophora arizonica	B,HU
Sophora chrysophylla	B,DD
Sophora davidii	B,LN,SA
Sophora formosa	B,SW
Sophora japonica	A,C,CA,EL,FW,HA,LN,N, SA,T,VE,WA
Sophora macrocarpaa	SA
Sophora microphylla	B,C,N,SA,SS
Sophora mollis	C
Sophora prostrata	B,SS
Sophora secundiflora	B,C,CA,HU,SA

248

SOPHORA

Sophora sp	SI
Sophora stenophylla	B,SW
Sophora tetraptera	AP,B,C,EL,HA,NI,SA,SS, T
Sophora tetraptera 'Otari Gnome'	B
Sophora tomentosa	B,HU,SA
Sopubia cana	B,SI
Sopubia mannii tenuifolia	B,SI
Sorbaria kirilowii	B,SA
Sorbaria rhoifolia MW315R	X
Sorbaria sorbifolia	LN,SA,SG
Sorbaria sorbifolia f incerta	SG
Sorbaria sp Russia	SG
Sorbaria tomentosa v angustifolia	SA
Sorbus adanii	NG
Sorbus alnifolia	B,EL,FW,LN,NG,SA
Sorbus americana	B,FW,LN,SA,SG
Sorbus amurensis	SG
Sorbus anglica	B,NS,SG
Sorbus aria	A,B,C,FW,LN,SA,VE
Sorbus aria 'Majestica'	X
Sorbus aucuparia	A,AP,B,C,EL,FW,LN,NO, SA,SC,SG,VE
Sorbus aucuparia 'Fastigiata'	AB,B,FW,LN,NO,SA,SG
Sorbus aucuparia 'Rossica'	SG
Sorbus aucuparia ssp sibirica	SG
Sorbus aucuparia v edulis	SG
Sorbus bakonyensis	SG
Sorbus bristoliensis	B,NS,SG
Sorbus cascadensis	NG,SG
Sorbus cashmiriana	AP,C,G,HP,N,NG,SC,SG
Sorbus chamaemespilus	C
Sorbus commixta	B,EL,FW,LN,N,NG,SA, SG
Sorbus commixta v rufoferruginea	SG
Sorbus danubialis	B
Sorbus decora	AP,HP,LN,NG,SG
Sorbus decora mougeotii	SG
Sorbus decora rupicola	SG
Sorbus decora v nana see S.aucuparia 'Fastigiata'	
Sorbus devoniensis	B,SG
Sorbus discolor h. see S.commixta	
Sorbus domestica	A,B,C,FW,SA,SG,VE
Sorbus epidendron	SG
Sorbus erubescens	SG
Sorbus essertiauna	SA
Sorbus folliolosa	SG
Sorbus forrestii	AP,HP,NG,SG
Sorbus fruticosa	AP,HP,NG,SC,SG
Sorbus graeca	SG
Sorbus hibernica	SG
Sorbus hupehensis	B,FW,N,NG,SC,SG
Sorbus insignis	SG
Sorbus intermedia	A,B,FW,LN,RS,SA,VE
Sorbus 'Joseph Rock'	AP,C,N
Sorbus koehneana h. see S.fruticosa	
Sorbus kusnetzovii	SG
Sorbus lancastriensis	B
Sorbus latifolia	B,G,LN
Sorbus laxiflora	SG
Sorbus leptophylla	SG
Sorbus leyana	SG
Sorbus maderensis	SG
Sorbus megalocarpa	N,SG
Sorbus meliosmifolia	SG
Sorbus microphylla	SG
Sorbus minima	SG
Sorbus mougeotii	B,SG
Sorbus munda	SG
Sorbus 'Pink Pearl'	SG
Sorbus pogonpetala	SG
Sorbus pohuashanensis h see S.x kewensis	
Sorbus porrigentiformis	SG
Sorbus poteriifolia	SG
Sorbus prattii	SC,SG
Sorbus pseudofennica	SG
Sorbus randaiensis	SG
Sorbus reducta	AP,HP,N,NG,SC,SG
Sorbus rehderiana	SG
Sorbus rockii	NG
Sorbus rupicola	B,G,SG
Sorbus scalaris	SG
Sorbus scopulina h. see S. aucuparia 'Fastigiata'	
Sorbus setschwanensis	SC,SG
Sorbus sibirica	SG
Sorbus simonkaiana	SG
Sorbus sitchensis	LN,NO,SG
Sorbus sp	AP,NG,SG
Sorbus takhtajanii	SG
Sorbus torminalis	A,B,FW,LN,SA,VE
Sorbus vestita	SG
Sorbus vexans	B,NS
Sorbus vilmorinii	AP,HP,SC,SG
Sorbus wardii	SG
Sorbus x hybrida Norway	SG
Sorbus x kewensis	B,EL,LN,SA,SG
Sorbus x thuringiaca 'Decurrens'	SG
Sorghastrum avenaceum	B,CA,DE,JE,NT,PR,SA
Sorghastrum avenaceum 'Indian Steel'	B,JE
Sorghastrum avenaceum 'Ne-54'	B
Sorghastrum nutans see S.avenaceum	
Sorghum bicolor	B,PI,PK,SD,VY
Sorghum caffrorum	SG
Sorghum carneum v nigrum	B,BS,PI,SU,T,V
Sorghum sudanense	B
Sorghum timorense	B
Sorghum vulgare	C,CP,DD,JO
Sowerbaea juncea	AP,B,HA,NI
Sowerbaea laxiflora	B,NI
Sparaxis bulbifera	AP,B,KB,RU,SC,SI
Sparaxis 'Colour Mill'	B,BD,BS,HU,L,MO,S
Sparaxis elegans	B,RU,SI
Sparaxis fragrans	B,RU
Sparaxis fragrans purple	RU
Sparaxis fragrans ssp acutiloba	KB,RU
Sparaxis fragrans ssp grandiflora	B,RU,SI
Sparaxis fragrans v fimbriata	RU
Sparaxis fragrans v violacea	RU
Sparaxis fragrans yellow	RU
Sparaxis grandiflora see S.fragrans	
Sparaxis parviflora	B,MN,RU,SC,SI
Sparaxis pillansii	SI
Sparaxis sp	SC,SI
Sparaxis tricolor	AP,B,KB,RU,SA,SI
Sparaxis variegata	AP,B,G,RU,SC
Sparaxis variegata v meterlekampiae	B
Sparaxis villosa	AP,B,KB,RU,SC,SI
Sparganium erectum	B,C,JE,SA,SG
Sparganium eurycarpum	B,PR
Sparmannia africana	B,C,SA,SI,WA
Sparmannia ricinocarpa	B,SI
Spartina cynosuroides	B,JE,SA

SPARTINA

Spartina pectinata	B,DE,JE,PR,SA
Spartium junceum	B,C,CA,FW,G,HP,LN,SA, SC,VE
Spathiphyllum floribundum 'Mauna Loa'	B,CA
Spathiphyllum 'Tasson'	B,CA
Spathiphyllum wallisii	B
Spathodea campanulata	B,CA,DD,EL,HA,HU,O, RE,SA,WA
Spergula arvensis	B
Spergularia nicaeensis	SG
Spergularia rubra	B,C,JE,SA
Spergularia rupicola	AP,B
Spermacoce hispida	B
Spermacoce ocymoides	B
Spermacoce pusilla	B
Sphaeralcea ambigua	AP,HU,RM,SW
Sphaeralcea coccinea	B,C,JE,NO,RM,SA,SC
Sphaeralcea fendleri venusta	AP,B,HP,SW,SZ,T
Sphaeralcea grossularoides	NO
Sphaeralcea incana	PL,T
Sphaeralcea 'Los Brisas'	T
Sphaeralcea munroana	C,HP,NO
Sphaeralcea remota	C,PR
Sphaeralcea rivularis	HP,JE
Sphaeralcea subhastata	B
Sphaeranthus indicus	B
Sphaerolobium alatum	B,NI,SA
Sphaerolobium grandiflorum	B,NI
Sphaerolobium medium	B,NI
Sphaerolobium scabriusculum	B,NI
Sphaerolobium vimineum	B,NI
Sphaeromeria capitata	RM
Sphaerophysa salsula	SG
Sphallerocarpus gracilis	SG
Sphalmanthus aridum	B,SI
Sphalmanthus delus	B
Sphalmanthus noctiflorus	B,SI
Sphalmanthus prasinus	B
Sphalmanthus sp	SI
Sphedamnocarpus pruriens	B,SI
Sphenotoma gracilis	B,C,NI
Spilanthes acmella	DD,HU
Spiloxene canaliculata	RU
Spiloxene capensis	RU
Spiloxene linearis	B,SI
Spiloxene scullyii	RU
Spiloxene serrata	RU
Spinifex littoreus	B
Spinifex sericeus	HA
Spiraea alba	B,PR,SG
Spiraea alpina	SG
Spiraea aquilegifolia	SG
Spiraea bella	SG
Spiraea betulifolia	NO,SG
Spiraea bumaldii	SA
Spiraea chamaedrifolia	SG
Spiraea crenata	SG
Spiraea douglasii	AB,B,C,FW,NO,SG
Spiraea humilis	SG
Spiraea hypericifolia	SG
Spiraea japonica	SG
Spiraea margaritae	SG
Spiraea media	SG
Spiraea nipponica 'Snowmound'	B
Spiraea salicifolia	SG
Spiraea sericea	SG

Spiraea sp China	SG
Spiraea stevenii	VO
Spiraea tomentosa	PR
Spiraea trilobata	SG
Spiraea ussuriensis	SG
Spiraea x schinaboukii	SG
Spiraea x vanhouttei	SG
Spiranthes aestivalis	B
Spiranthes ovalis	B
Spirea densiflora	NO
Spodiopogon sibiricus	B,DE,G,JE
Spondias dulcis	B
Spondias mangifera	B
Spondias mombin	B,RE
Spondias pinnata	B
Spondias purpurea	B
Sporobolus airoides	B,NO
Sporobolus aspera	B,PR
Sporobolus cryptandrus	B,NO,PR
Sporobolus heterolepis	B,DE,JE,PR,SA
Spraguea umbellata	AP,SC
Sprekelia formosissima	B
Sprengelia incarnata	B,NI
Sprengelia sprengelioides	B,NI
Spyridium globulosum	B,C,NI
Spyridium rotundifolium	B,NI
Staavia dodii	B
Staavia glutinosa	B
Staberoha aemula	B,SI
Staberoha distachyos	B,SI
Stachys albotomentosa	SZ
Stachys alopecurus	KL
Stachys alpina	B,G,KL,SG
Stachys annua	AP,B
Stachys betonica see S.officinalis	
Stachys bicolor	KL
Stachys byzantina	w.a.
Stachys candida	I,SC
Stachys coccinea	AP,HP,P,SW
Stachys cretica	AP,B,C,HP
Stachys discolor	HP
Stachys germanica	B,C,G,SA
Stachys grandiflora see S.macrantha	
Stachys iva	AP,RM
Stachys lanata see S.byzantina	
Stachys linearis	B
Stachys macrantha	AP,B,G,HP,KL,RS,SA, SC,SG,T,VO
Stachys macrantha 'Robusta'	HP
Stachys macrantha 'Rosea'	HP
Stachys macrantha 'Superba'	BH,F,HP,JE,PK
Stachys minor	RM
Stachys monierii	AP,B,F,G,HP,JE,KL,P,SA
Stachys nivea	VO
Stachys officinalis	AP,B,C,CO,CP,DD,G,HP, HU,I,JE,LA,SA,SG,TH
Stachys officinalis nana	CP
Stachys palustris	B,SG
Stachys pillansii	SG
Stachys recta	AP,B,G,SG
Stachys rigida	B,SW
Stachys sylvatica	B,G,HU,JE,LA,SA,SU
Stachys sylvatica 'Husker's Variety'	B,P
Stachys thireri	SC,T
Stachytarpheta indica	C
Stachytarpheta jamaicensis	B

STACHYTARPHETA

Stachytarpheta mutabilis	C
Stackhousia huegelii	B,NI,SA
Stackhousia pubescens	B,NI
Staehelina uniflosculosa	AP,HP
Stanleya integrifolia	C
Stanleya pinnata	B,SW
Stapelia ambigua	CG
Stapelia asterias	Y
Stapelia desmetiana	B
Stapelia dummeri	SI
Stapelia flavirostris see S.grandiflora	
Stapelia gemniflora	CG
Stapelia gettliffei	B,DD,SI
Stapelia glanduliflora	B,SI
Stapelia grandiflora	B,DV
Stapelia hirsuta	B,SI
Stapelia kwebensis	B,SI
Stapelia leendertziae	SC
Stapelia lepida	CG
Stapelia longipedicellata	SI
Stapelia nobilis	B,DD,SI
Stapelia pilansii	CG
Stapelia schinzii	B,DV,SI
Stapelia sp	AP,C,SI
Stapelia tapscottii	DV
Stapelia villettii	DV
Staphylea bumalda	SA
Staphylea colchica	B,HP,SG
Staphylea holocarpa	SA
Staphylea pinnata	A,AP,B,G,HP,LN,SA
Staphylea trifolia	A,B,FW,LN,SA,SG
Stauntonia hexaphylla	C
Stayneria neilii	B
Steganotaenia araliacea	B,SI
Steirodiscus tagetes	B,C,SI
Steirodiscus tagetes 'Goldilocks'	B,BS,MO,SK,T
Stellaria graminea	B,SG
Stellaria holostea	B,C,CN,JE,SA,SU,TH
Stellaria media	AB,B,DD
Stellaria nemorum	SG
Stemmadenia donnell-smithii	B,RE
Stemodia floribunda	B,NI
Stenactis annua	B
Stenocactus acroacanthus	Y
Stenocactus albatus	B,DV,Y
Stenocactus anfractuosus	Y
Stenocactus caespitosus	Y
Stenocactus confusus	Y
Stenocactus coptonogonus	B,Y
Stenocactus crispatus	B,DV,Y
Stenocactus dicroanthus	Y
Stenocactus erectocentrus	B
Stenocactus guerraianus	Y
Stenocactus heteracanthus	Y
Stenocactus hookeri	BC,DV
Stenocactus kellerianus	Y
Stenocactus lamellosus see S.crispatus	
Stenocactus multicostatus	B,DV,Y
Stenocactus obvallatus	BC,DV
Stenocactus ochoterenaus	B,DV,Y
Stenocactus pentacanthus	DV
Stenocactus phyllacanthus	B
Stenocactus phyllacanthus v tricuspidatus	B
Stenocactus sp mix	C,Y
Stenocactus tetracanthus	BC
Stenocactus tricuspidatus	Y

Stenocactus violaciflorus	B,DV,Y
Stenocactus zacatecasensis	B,DV,Y
Stenocarpus sinuatus	C,CA,EL,HA,NI,O,SA, SH,WA
Stenocereus eruca	CH
Stenocereus pruinosus	B
Stenocereus stellatus	B
Stenocereus thurberi	B,DV
Stenochlaena tenuifolia	SG
Stenoglottis longifolia	B
Stenomesson aurantiacum	B,C
Stenomesson raui	B,C
Stenomesson sp 'White Parasol'	C
Stenopetalum filifolium	B,NI
Stenotus acaulis	Y
Stephanocereus leucostele	Y
Stephanotis floribunda	B,C,CA,DD,EL,HA,PK, PL,SA,SE,T,VE
Sterculia africana	B,SI
Sterculia alata	EL,HA,SA
Sterculia apetala	B
Sterculia discolor	C
Sterculia foetida	B
Sterculia murex	B,WA
Sterculia quinqueloba	B,SI
Sterculia rupestris	C
Stereospermum euphoroides	B,SI
Sternbergia candida	AR,B,JE
Sternbergia clusiana	AP,B,JE
Sternbergia colchicifolia	AP,B,G,PM
Sternbergia fischeriana	B,JE
Sternbergia lutea	AP
Sternbergia lutea Angustifolia Gr	B,SC
Sternbergia lutea Angustifolia Gr S.L469	MN
Sternbergia lutea v graeca MS802 Crete	MN
Sternbergia lutea v sicula Coll Ref	MN
Sternbergia sicula	AP,B,G
Sternbergia sicula 'Graeca'	B
Stetsonia coryne	B,CH,DV,Y
Stetsonia coryne v procera	DV,Y
Stevia rebaudiana	B
Stewartia gemmata	B,FW
Stewartia grandiflora	FW,SA
Stewartia malacodendron	B
Stewartia monadelpha	B,FW,LN,SA
Stewartia ovata	B,FW,SA
Stewartia ovata v grandiflora	B
Stewartia pseudocamellia	B,C,FW,HP,LN,SA
Stewartia pseudocamellia Koreana group	B,FW,N,SA
Stewartia sinensis	B,FW,SA
Stictocardia beraviensis	B,C
Stilbe vestita	B
Stipa arundinacea	C,E,HP,RH
Stipa badachshanica	SG
Stipa barbata	AP,B,BS,G,JE,SA
Stipa barbata 'Silver Feather'	C
Stipa brachytricum	JE,SA
Stipa brandisii	SG
Stipa calamagrostis	AP,B,HP,JE,SA
Stipa capillata	B,G,HP,JE,SA,SC,SG
Stipa cernua	B
Stipa comata	B,NO
Stipa coronata	B
Stipa elegantissima	AP,B,NI,SA,SZ
Stipa extremiorientalis	B,JE,SA
Stipa gigantea	AP,B,G,HP,JE,SA

STIPA

Stipa grandis	B,JE,SA	Streptocarpus f1 'Bandwagon'	BS
Stipa joannis	KL	Streptocarpus f1 'Concord'	BS,EL,MO,S
Stipa juncea	B	Streptocarpus f1 'Goodhope'	J,V
Stipa lepida	B	Streptocarpus f1 'Lipstick'	T
Stipa lessingiana	SG	Streptocarpus f1 'Melody'	D
Stipa nitida	B,NI	Streptocarpus f1 'Royal' mix	CL,F,L,SE,T,YA
Stipa nodosa	B	Streptocarpus f1 'Windowsill Magic'	T
Stipa pennata	AP,C,JE,KL,SA,SC,SG,T	Streptocarpus f2 'Fiesta'	J,T,V
Stipa pulcherrima	G,SG	Streptocarpus fanniniae	B,C,SI
Stipa pulcherrima 'Windfeder'	JE	Streptocarpus fasciatus	B,C,SI
Stipa pulchra	B,CA	Streptocarpus floribundus	B,C,SI
Stipa ramosissima	SZ	Streptocarpus formosus	B,C,SI
Stipa robusta	B,HU	Streptocarpus gardenii	B,C,DV,SI
Stipa semibarbata	B,NI	Streptocarpus goetzei	DV
Stipa sp	KL	Streptocarpus grandis	B,C,DV,SI
Stipa spartea	DE,PR	Streptocarpus haygarthii	B,CG,DV,SI
Stipa splendens	SG	Streptocarpus hyb mix	B,BS,BY,C,ST
Stipa tenacissima	B,C,G,JE,SA,V	Streptocarpus insignis	DV
Stipa tenuifolia	AP,HP	Streptocarpus johannis	B,SI
Stipa tenuissima	C,HP,HU,JE,SA,SG	Streptocarpus kentaniensis	B,C
Stipa ucrainica	B,JE,SG	Streptocarpus kentaniensis white	C
Stipa viridula	B,G,PR	Streptocarpus kirkii	B,DV
Stipagrostis raddiana	B	Streptocarpus 'Merrivale' mix	C
Stirlingia latifolia	B,EL,NI,O,SA	Streptocarpus modestus	B,C,SI
Stirlingia simplex	B,NI	Streptocarpus nobilis	DV
Stirlingia tenuifolia	B,NI	Streptocarpus pentherianus	B,C,SI
Stoebe plumosa	B,BH	Streptocarpus polyanthus	C,SI
Stoeberia littlewoodii	B,KB	Streptocarpus polyanthus ssp comptonii	B,KB,SI
Stokesia laevis	B,BS,C,G,HP,JE,NT,SA,T	Streptocarpus polyanthus ssp polyanthus	B,SI
Stokesia laevis alba	B,HP,PL,SA,SE	Streptocarpus primulifolius	B,DV,SI
Stokesia laevis 'Blue Star'	HP,PL	Streptocarpus prolixus	SI
Stokesia laevis 'Mischung'	JE	Streptocarpus rexii	B,C,DV,SG,SI
Stokesia laevis 'Traumeri'	C,HP,JE	Streptocarpus saundersii	B,SI
Stokesia laevis 'Wyoming'	HP	Streptocarpus saxorum	B
Stomatium latifolium	Y	Streptocarpus sp	SI
Stomatium loganii	B	Streptocarpus trabeculatus	B,C,SI
Stomatium niveum	B,DV,SI	Streptocarpus 'Wahroonga' mix	C
Stomatium pyrodorum	B	Streptocarpus wendlandii	B,C,CG,SI
Stomatium sp	SI	Streptocarpus 'Wiesmoor' hyb	C
Strangea cynanchocarpa	B	Streptocarpus wilmsii	B
Strelitzia juncea	B,C,CA,CF,O,SI	Streptoglossa decurrens	B,NI
Strelitzia nicolai	B,C,CA,CG,DV,EL,HA,O,	Streptopus amplexifolius	B,C,G,JE,NO
	SA,SI,VE	Streptopus roseus	B,NG
Strelitzia reginae	B,CA,CF,CG,DD,DV,EL,	Streptosolen jamesonii	B
	FR,HA,KB,LN,O,PK,PL,	Striga asiatica	G
	S,SA,SI,V,VE	Strobilanthes atropurpurea	G
Strelitzia reginae dw	T	Strombocactus disciformis	B,C,CH,DV,Y
Strelitzia reginae 'Mandela's Gold'	B,KB,SI	Strombosia globulifera	B
Streptocalyx floribundus	B	Strophanthus kombe	C
Streptocalyx longifolius	B	Strophanthus speciosus	B,C,KB,SI
Streptocalyx poeppigii	B	Stropharia ferrii d.m.p	B
Streptocarpella see Streptocarpus		Strumaria chaplinii	RU
Streptocarpus 'Blue Angel'	PK	Strumaria karooica	RU
Streptocarpus bolusii	B,SI	Strumaria picta	RU
Streptocarpus candidus	B,C,SI	Strumaria rubella	B
Streptocarpus caulescens	DV,HP	Strumaria salteri	B,RU
Streptocarpus caulescens ssp pallens	B,SI	Strumaria tenella	B,RU
Streptocarpus compressus	B,SI	Strumaria truncata	B,RU
Streptocarpus confusus ssp confusus	B,SI	Strumaria watermeyeri	B,RU
Streptocarpus cooperi	B,C,DV	Strychnos cocculoides	B,SI
Streptocarpus Crown Hybrids	KI	Strychnos colubrina	B
Streptocarpus cyaneus	B,SI	Strychnos decussata	B
Streptocarpus cyaneus ssp polackii	B,SI	Strychnos madagascariensis	B,SI
Streptocarpus cyaneus v roseoalbus	B,SI	Strychnos nux-vomica	B
Streptocarpus dunii	B,DV,SI	Strychnos potatorum	B,SI
Streptocarpus eylesii	B,SI	Strychnos wallichiana	B

STYLIDIUM

Stylidium affine	AU,B,NI,SA
Stylidium albolilacinum	B
Stylidium amoenum mauve	B
Stylidium articulatum	B,NI
Stylidium brunonianum	B,NI,SA
Stylidium brunonianum v minor	B,NI
Stylidium calcaratum	B,NI
Stylidium canaliculatum	B
Stylidium caricifolium	B,NI
Stylidium caricifolium v nungarinense	B,NI
Stylidium ciliatum	B
Stylidium cordifolium	B
Stylidium crassifolium	B,C,NI
Stylidium curtum	B
Stylidium dichotomum	B,NI
Stylidium diuroides ssp diuroides	B
Stylidium diversifolium	B,NI
Stylidium elongatum	B,NI
Stylidium glandulosum	B
Stylidium graminifolium	AU,B,HA,NI
Stylidium guttatum	B
Stylidium hispidum	B,NI
Stylidium imbricatum	B,NI
Stylidium junceum	B,NI
Stylidium laricifolium	B,HA,NI
Stylidium macranthum	B,C,NI
Stylidium merrallii	B
Stylidium mimeticum	B
Stylidium multiscapum	B
Stylidium muscicola	B
Stylidium pedunculatum v ericksonae	B
Stylidium piliferum	B
Stylidium piliferum ssp minor	B
Stylidium piliferum ssp piliferum	B
Stylidium pilosum	B
Stylidium plantagineum	B,NI
Stylidium pubigerum	B,NI
Stylidium rigidifolium	B
Stylidium schizanthum	B
Stylidium schoenoides	B,NI
Stylidium soboliferum	B
Stylidium spathulatum	B,NI
Stylidium spathulatum ssp acuminatum	B
Stylidium spinulosum	B,NI
Stylidium tepperianum	B
Stylobasium spathulatum	B,EL,NI,SA
Stylomecon heterophyllum	B,C
Stylophorum diphyllum	AP,B,BS,C,G,HP,JE,RM
Stylophorum lasiocarpum	AP,B,C,G,HP,JE,SC
Stylosanthes fruticosa	B
Stylosanthes guianensis 'Cook'	B
Stylosanthes guianensis 'Graham'	B
Stylosanthes guianensis 'Oxley'	B
Stylosanthes hamata 'Verano'	B
Stylosanthes scabra 'Fitzroy'	B
Stylosanthes scabra 'Seca'	B
Stypandra caespitosa	HA
Stypandra glauca	HA
Stypandra imbricata	B
Styphelia pulchella aff	B,NI
Styphelia tenuiflora	B,NI
Styrax americanum	B,CA,FW,LN,SA
Styrax confucus	B,FW
Styrax hemslyanus	HP,SA
Styrax japonicus	B,C,FW,LN,N,SA,SG,VE
Styrax obassia	B,C,FW,LN,N,SA,X

Styrax odoratissimum	SA
Styrax officinale	C,LN,SA
Styrax officinale v californicum	B
Styrax serrulata	SA
Submatucana aureiflora	B,DV
Submatucana caespitosa	DV,Y
Submatucana calliantha	DV
Submatucana celendiensis	DV
Submatucana huagalensis	DV
Submatucana intertexta	DV,Y
Submatucana madisoniorum	B,DV,Y
Submatucana madisoniorum v asterium	DV
Submatucana oreodoxa	DV
Submatucana paucicostata	Y
Submatucana paucispina	DV
Submatucana senilis	DV
Submatucana tubercolosa	Y
Submatucana weberbaueri	DV
Succisa pratensis	AP,C,CN,CO,G,HP,LA,JE, SA,SC,SG,TH
Succisa pratensis dw	KL
Succisella petteri	CG
Sulcorebutia see Rebutia	Y
Suregada angustifolia	B
Sutera aurantiaca	B,SI
Sutera carvalhoi	B,SI
Sutera grandiflora	B,SI
Sutera sp	SI
Sutera tristis	B,SI
Sutherlandia frutescens	AP,B,BH,C,EL,G,HP,HU, KB,PL,SA,SI,T,WA
Sutherlandia frutescens prostrata	AP,SC
Sutherlandia microphylla	B,BH,SI
Sutherlandia montana	B,SI
Sutherlandia sp	BH,SC,SI
Swainsona burkittii	B,NI
Swainsona canescens	B,NI
Swainsona cyclocarpa	B,NI
Swainsona fissimontana	B,NI
Swainsona formosa see Clianthus	
Swainsona galegifolia	B,EL,HA,HU,O,SA
Swainsona greyana ssp greyana	B,NI
Swainsona kingii	B,NI
Swainsona maccullochiana	B,NI,O,SA
Swainsona microcalyx	O
Swainsona murrayana	B,NI
Swainsona novae-zelandiae	B,SS
Swainsona phacoides	B
Swainsona procumbens	B,O,SA
Swainsona pterostylis	B,NI
Swainsona pubescens	O
Swainsona stenodonta	B,NI
Swainsona stipularis	B,DD,NI,O,SA
Swainsona swainsonoides	B,NI
Swainsona tephrotricha	RS
Swainsona viridis	B,NI
Swartzia madagascariensis	B,SI
Swertia albomarginata	RM
Swertia aucheri	SG
Swertia bimaculata	B
Swertia canadensis	KL
Swertia longifolia	SG
Swertia perennis	AP,B,C,DV,JE,SA,SW
Swertia perennis ssp alpestris	SG
Swertia petiolata	SG
Swietenia humilis	B,SA

SWIETENIA

Swietenia macrophylla	B,LN,SA
Swietenia mahagoni	B,C,CA,EL,HA,LN,RE,SA
Swinglia glutinosa	B
Syagrus cocoides	B
Syagrus flexuosa	B
Syagrus romanzoffianum	B,C,CA,EL,HA,N,O,SA, VE,WA
Syagrus romanzoffianum 'Silver Queen'	CA
Syagrus schizophylla	B
Symphoricarpos albus	A,AB,B,C,CG,FW,HP,LN, NO,SA,SG
Symphoricarpos albus v laevigatus	B,RS
Symphoricarpos mollis	NO
Symphoricarpos occidentalis	B,FW,LN,SG
Symphoricarpos orbiculatus	B,C,FW,LN,SA
Symphoricarpos oreophilus	B,LN,NO,SG
Symphyandra armena	AP,B,G,JE,P,RS,SC,SE, SG,T,V
Symphyandra cretica	AP,T
Symphyandra hoffmannii	AP,B,C,CG,G,HP,JE,KL, P,RS,SA,SC,SG,T
Symphyandra ossetica	P
Symphyandra pendula	AP,B,C,G,HP,JE,KL,RS
Symphyandra wanneri	AP,C,G,HP,JE,KL,P,SG
Symphyandra zanzegura	AP,HP,RH,SC
Symphytum officinale	B,CN,JE,TH
Symphytum officinale white fl.	A
Symphytum orientale	A
Symphytum x uplandicum	B,CN,HP,SA
Symplocos paniculata	B
Synaphea acutiloba	B,NI,O
Synaphea petiolaris	B,NI
Syncarpha affinis	B
Syncarpha argyropsis	B
Syncarpha canescens	B,SI
Syncarpha eximia	B,SI
Syncarpha milleflora	B,SI
Syncarpha paniculata	B,SI
Syncarpha speciosissima	B,KB,SI
Syncarpha variegata	B,SI
Syncarpha vestita	B,KB,SI
Syncarpia glomulifera	B,C,EL,HA,LN,NI,O,SA, WA
Syncarpia hillii	B,LN,WA
Syncarpia laurifolia see S.glomulifera	
Syncolostemon macranthus	B,SI
Syncolostemon rotundifolius	B,KB
Synecanthus warscewicdanus	SA
Synedrella nodiflora	B
Syneilesis aconitifolia	B
Syngonium podophyllum	CA,SA
Syngonium podophyllum 'Emerald Gem'	B
Syngonium podophyllum 'Variegatum'	B
Syngonium reticulatum	B
Syngonium vellozianum	B
Synnotia see Sparaxis	
Synsepalum dulcificum	B,SA
Synsepalum subcordatum	B
Synthyris missurica v magna	RM
Synthyris reniformis	AP,B
Syragus romanzoffianum	O
Syringa amurensis japonica see S.reticulata	
Syringa amurensis see S.reticulata ssp amurensis	
Syringa josikaea	B,FW,LN,SA,SG
Syringa josikaea 'Pallida'	B
Syringa komarowii	B

Syringa oblata	B,CA,EL,FW,LN,SA
Syringa pekinensis	C
Syringa pubescens	C
Syringa reflexa	LN
Syringa reticulata	B,FW,LN
Syringa reticulata ssp amurensis	B,EL,FW,LN,SA,SG
Syringa reticulata ssp pekinensis	B,FW,SA
Syringa taiwania flouseana	SA
Syringa velutina of gdns	SA
Syringa villosa	B,C,CA,CG,FW,LN,SA
Syringa vulgaris	A,B,C,CA,FW,LN,SA,VE
Syringa vulgaris 'Alba'	B
Syringa wolfii	B,C,FW,LN,SG
Syringa x prestoniae	B
Syringodea longituba	B,RU,SI
Syzygium aqueum	B
Syzygium australis	SA,WA
Syzygium cordatum	B,SI,WA
Syzygium cumini	B,DD,SA
Syzygium forte ssp forte	B
Syzygium francisii	B,O
Syzygium guineense	B,SA
Syzygium jambos	B
Syzygium legatii	WA
Syzygium luehmannii	B
Syzygium maire	B
Syzygium malaccense	B
Syzygium moorei	B,O
Syzygium oleosum	B
Syzygium paniculatum	B
Syzygium samarangense	B
Syzygium wilsonii ssp cryptophlebia	B
Syzygium wilsonii ssp wilsonii	B
Tabebuia argentea	B,CA,EL,SA
Tabebuia chrysantha	B,EL,RE,SA
Tabebuia chrysotricha	B,CA,EL,SA
Tabebuia guayacan	B,SA
Tabebuia heterophylla	B
Tabebuia impetiginosa	B,CA,SA
Tabebuia ochracea	B,SA
Tabebuia pallida	B,CA
Tabebuia pentaphylla	CA
Tabebuia rosea	B,C,EL,RE,SA
Tabebuia roseoalba	B
Tabebuia serratifolia	B,EL
Tabernaemontana divaricata	B
Tabernaemontana elegans	B,SI,WA
Tabernaemontana sananho	B
Tacca chantrieri	B,C,EL,SA,T
Tacca nivea	B,C,PL
Tacitus bellus see Graptopetalum	
Taenidia integerrima	B,PR
Tagetes dw lg fl yellow	FR
Tagetes erecta	B,DD,G,SD,SG,TH,VH
Tagetes erecta 'Calando' mix	BS,DT,J,L,MO,YA
Tagetes erecta 'Calando' s-c	BS
Tagetes erecta 'Crackerjack' mix	AB,BD,BS,BU,BY,CA,CL, CN,DN,DT,F,KI,L,MO,PI, S,SK,SU,T,TE,TU,U,VY, YA
Tagetes erecta 'Crush' mix	DE,SE
Tagetes erecta 'Cupid' mix dw	BS,C,MO
Tagetes erecta 'Excel Orange'	SK
Tagetes erecta f1 'Antigua Series' mix	BS,CL,MO,PK,SE,SK
Tagetes erecta f1 'Antigua Series' s-c	BS
Tagetes erecta f1 'Ball Mix'	V

TAGETES

Tagetes erecta f1 'Ball Orange'	V
Tagetes erecta f1 'Ball Yellow'	V
Tagetes erecta f1 'Beau Brummell'	B
Tagetes erecta f1 'Beau Geste'	B
Tagetes erecta f1 'Discovery' mix	BS,CA,MO,PK,T,YA
Tagetes erecta f1 'Discovery Orange'	B,BS,L,MO,PK,R,SK,T,V Y,YA
Tagetes erecta f1 'Discovery Yellow'	B,BS,L,MO,PK,R,SK,T, VY,YA
Tagetes erecta f1 'Dubloon'	BS,CA,DE,SK
Tagetes erecta f1 'Eagle' dbl	BS,CA,DE,SK
Tagetes erecta f1 'Excel Gold'	CL,M,SK
Tagetes erecta f1 'Excel' mix	CL,M,U
Tagetes erecta f1 'Excel Primrose'	CL,M,SK
Tagetes erecta f1 'Galore Gold'	B,BS,MO,PK,S,SK
Tagetes erecta f1 'Galore' mix	BS,MO
Tagetes erecta f1 'Galore Yellow'	B,BS,MO,PK,SK
Tagetes erecta f1 'Gay Ladies'	KI,MO,S
Tagetes erecta f1 'Gold Coins' mix	BS,CA,JO,L,SK,U
Tagetes erecta f1 'Gold 'n' Vanilla'	SE,T
Tagetes erecta f1 'Inca Gold'	B,BS,CA,CL,CN,D,DT, L,MO,PK,S,SE,SK,T,YA
Tagetes erecta f1 'Inca' mix	BS,C,CA,CL,CN,D,DT, F,J,KI,L,MO,PK,S,SE, SK,ST,T,TU,YA
Tagetes erecta f1 'Inca Orange'	B,BS,BY,CA,CL,CN,D, DT,L,MO,PK,S,SE,SK,T, U,YA
Tagetes erecta f1 'Inca Yellow'	B,BS,BY,CA,CL,CN,D, DT,L,MO,PK,S,SE,SK,T, U,YA
Tagetes erecta f1 'Jubilee Golden'	B,BS,MO,PK,SK
Tagetes erecta f1 'Jubilee Mix'	BS,BU,D,MO,PK,SK,U
Tagetes erecta f1 'Jubilee Orange'	B,BS,MO,PK,SK
Tagetes erecta f1 'Jubilee Yellow'	B,MO,PK,SK
Tagetes erecta f1 'Lady First'	CA,MO,PI,SK
Tagetes erecta f1 'Lady Gold'	B,BD,BS,MO
Tagetes erecta f1 'Lady Orange'	B,BS,CA,MO,SK
Tagetes erecta f1 'Lady Yellow'	B,BS,SK
Tagetes erecta f1 'Marvel' mix	BS,F,MO,SK
Tagetes erecta f1 'Marvel' s-c	B,BS,MO,SK
Tagetes erecta f1 'Marvellous' mix	D
Tagetes erecta f1 'Perfection Colour Blend'	CL,D,F,HU,PK
Tagetes erecta f1 'Perfection Gold'	CL,D,SK,U
Tagetes erecta f1 'Perfection Orange'	CL,D,F,SK
Tagetes erecta f1 'Perfection Yellow'	CL,D,F,SK
Tagetes erecta f1 'Sumo' mix	BS,KI,S,T
Tagetes erecta f1 'Sumo' s-c	BS,YA
Tagetes erecta f1 'Voyager Orange'	B,MO
Tagetes erecta f1 'Voyager Yellow'	B,MO
Tagetes erecta f1 'Yellow Galore'	S
Tagetes erecta 'Galore' orange	SK
Tagetes erecta 'Golden Age'	MO
Tagetes erecta 'Golden Age' dwarf	B,BY,KI
Tagetes erecta 'Golden Trumpets'	B
Tagetes erecta 'Guys & Dolls' mix	BS,BU,CA,CL,PK
Tagetes erecta 'Hawaii'	HU
Tagetes erecta 'Hawaii' (xanthophyll)	B,BS,BY
Tagetes erecta 'Hunter's Moon'	T
Tagetes erecta 'Luxor' mix	BS,MO
Tagetes erecta mix dbl	CO,J
Tagetes erecta 'Moonbeam'	T,VH
Tagetes erecta 'Pineapple Crush'	CA
Tagetes erecta 'Pinwheel'	DD
Tagetes erecta 'Pumpkin Crush'	CA
Tagetes erecta 'Rhapsody'	D

Tagetes erecta 'Sahara'	F
Tagetes erecta 'Snowbird'	BS
Tagetes erecta 'Snowdrift'	B
Tagetes erecta 'Sovereign Gold'	SK
Tagetes erecta 'Sunset Giants'	BS,C,F,KI,M,MC,ST
Tagetes erecta 'Sunspot' mix	CL,D,T
Tagetes erecta 'Superjack' mix	BS,R
Tagetes erecta 'Superjack Orange'	S
Tagetes erecta tall dbl orange	B
Tagetes erecta tall dbl yellow	B
Tagetes erecta 'Treasure Trove' mix	CL,DE
Tagetes erecta white	ST
Tagetes erecta 'White Snowdrift'	DI
Tagetes f1 'Galore' s-c	PK
Tagetes f1 'Vanilla'	CL,DT,F,KI,KS,L,MO,PL, R,SE,V,U,YA
Tagetes filifolia	B,HU
Tagetes 'Hunters Moon'	T
Tagetes lacera	DD
Tagetes lemmoni	AP,B,KS,SW
Tagetes lucida	B,DD,HU,KS
Tagetes lucida 'Pericon'	HU
Tagetes lunulata	B,DD,KS
Tagetes Marigold Package Deal	T
Tagetes minuta	BH,C,CN,CO,DD,SD,SU, TH
Tagetes patula	AB,B,G,JE,SG,SU,TH
Tagetes patula 'Alamo Series'	CL
Tagetes patula 'Anigua' s-c	SK
Tagetes patula 'Aurora' mix	SK
Tagetes patula 'Aurora Primrose'	U
Tagetes patula 'Aurora Series' s-c	BS,CL,DT,MO,PK,SK
Tagetes patula 'Bolero'	B,MO,U,V,VY
Tagetes patula 'Bonanza Bee'	B,BD,BS,MO,SK
Tagetes patula 'Bonanza Deep Orange'	B,BD
Tagetes patula 'Bonanza Flame'	B,BD,BS,MO
Tagetes patula 'Bonanza Gold'	B,BD,BS,MO,SK
Tagetes patula 'Bonanza Harmony'	B,BD,BS,MO,SK
Tagetes patula 'Bonanza Orange'	B,BD,BS,MO,SK
Tagetes patula 'Bonanza Series' mix	CA,PI,SK
Tagetes patula 'Bonanza Yellow'	B,BD,BS,MO,SK
Tagetes patula 'Bonita' mix	BSC,DT,F,J,KI,MO,T,VH, YA
Tagetes patula 'Bonita' s-c	BS
Tagetes patula 'Boy,golden'	B,BS,CL,CN,D,MO,VY, YA
Tagetes patula 'Boy,harmony'	B,BS,CA,CL,CN,D,MO, VY,YA
Tagetes patula 'Boy o Boy mix'	BS,BY,CA,CL,CN,D,DT, F,J,L,R,KI,MC,MO,S,SE, SG,ST,SU,T,TU,V,VY,YA
Tagetes patula 'Boy,orange'	B,BS,BY,CA,CL,CN,D, F,L,MO,S,T,V,VY,YA
Tagetes patula 'Boy Spry'	CA,VY
Tagetes patula 'Boy,yellow'	B,BS,BY,CA,CL,CN,D, L,MO,SK,T,V,VY,YA
Tagetes patula 'Brocade' mix	CA
Tagetes patula 'Brocade Red'	B,BS,MO,S
Tagetes patula 'Brocade Spanish'	AB,B,BS,BY,CL,KI,M, MO,SD,SK,SU,TU
Tagetes patula 'Butterscotch'	BS
Tagetes patula 'Calico'	B,BS,MO
Tagetes patula 'Carmen'	B,MO
Tagetes patula 'Centenary'	D
Tagetes patula 'Champion Mixed'	BS,KI
Tagetes patula 'Champion' s-c	BS

TAGETES

Name	Code
Tagetes patula Choice Single	SU
Tagetes patula 'Crested Series'	BS,D,YA
Tagetes patula 'Dainty Marietta'	B,BS,CN,D,L,MO
Tagetes patula 'Del Sol'	B,MO
Tagetes patula 'Disco Flame'	B,BS,CL,DE,MO,SK
Tagetes patula 'Disco Golden'	B,BS,CL,DE,MO,SK
Tagetes patula 'Disco Marietta'	B,BS,CL,MO,S,SK
Tagetes patula 'Disco' mix	BS,CA,CL,CO,DT,KI,L, MO,PK,R,SK,TU,YA
Tagetes patula 'Disco Orange'	B,BS,CL,MO,SK
Tagetes patula 'Disco Red'	B,BS,CL,MO,PI,S,SK
Tagetes patula 'Disco Yellow'	B,BS,CL,MO,SK
Tagetes patula 'Espana Granada'	B,BS,MO,SK
Tagetes patula 'Espana' mix	BD,J,MO,SK
Tagetes patula 'Espana Ole'	B,BS,MO
Tagetes patula 'Espana Red Marietta'	B,BS,MO,SK
Tagetes patula 'Fantasia' mix	S
Tagetes patula 'Favourite' mix	BS,DT,J,L,MO,S,T,U,V
Tagetes patula 'Fiesta'	B,MO
Tagetes patula 'Fireflame'	T
Tagetes patula 'French Candy'	SK
Tagetes patula 'Garden Gate' mix	BS,CL,DT,KI,L,MO
Tagetes patula 'Gate,golden'	B,BS,CL,DT,KI,L,MO, SK,T,VY
Tagetes patula 'Gate,orange'	B,BS,CL,DT,L,MO
Tagetes patula 'Gate,yellow'	B,BS,CL,DT,L,MO
Tagetes patula 'Golden Days'	KI,ST
Tagetes patula 'Goldfinch'	D,MO,S,U,YA
Tagetes patula 'Goldie'	S
Tagetes patula 'Granada'	YA
Tagetes patula 'Gypsy Sunshine'	T
Tagetes patula 'Harlequin'	PL,SE
Tagetes patula 'Harmony'	KS
Tagetes patula 'Hero Bee'	YA
Tagetes patula 'Hero Flame'	B,BS,L,MO,SK,YA
Tagetes patula 'Hero Gold'	B,BS,DT,L,MO,SK,YA
Tagetes patula 'Hero Harmony'	B,BS,L,MO,SK,YA
Tagetes patula 'Hero' mix	BS,DT,L,MO,PI,PK,SK, YA
Tagetes patula 'Hero Orange'	B,BS,DT,L,MO,SK,YA
Tagetes patula 'Hero Red'	B,BS,L,YA
Tagetes patula 'Hero Spry'	B,BS,L,MO,SK,YA
Tagetes patula 'Hero Yellow'	B,BS,L,SK,YA
Tagetes patula 'Honeycomb'	BY,C,CL,D,F,J,MO,S,SK, T,V,YA
Tagetes patula 'Instant'	BS
Tagetes patula 'Jacket,orange'	B,BS,CL,D,J,M,MO,YA
Tagetes patula 'Jacket,yellow'	B,BS,CL,D,F,J,M,MO,U, YA
Tagetes patula 'Janie Series'	CA,SK
Tagetes patula 'Juliette'	BS,F
Tagetes patula 'Legion of Honour'	BS,C,KI
Tagetes patula 'Lemon Drop'	CA,SE,SK
Tagetes patula 'Lilliput Orange Flame'	C
Tagetes patula 'Little Hero' s-c, mix	SK
Tagetes patula 'Marionette Mix'	U
Tagetes patula 'Mischief' mix	BS,D
Tagetes patula 'Mischief' s-c	BS
Tagetes patula mix dw dbl	BU,BY,CO,F,J,TU
Tagetes patula 'Mr. Majestic'	BS,MO,T
Tagetes patula 'Naughty Marietta'	B,BS,BY,CL,CN,D,DT, F,J,KI,MO,ST,T,U,YA
Tagetes patula 'Orion'	B
Tagetes patula 'Pascal'	BS
Tagetes patula 'Petite' mix	BS,BU,DN,KI,M,PI,S
Tagetes patula 'Petite' s-c	BS
Tagetes patula 'Pinwheel'	SD
Tagetes patula 'Pinwheel' dbl	SD
Tagetes patula 'Queen Bee'	B,BS,S,VH,YA
Tagetes patula 'Queen Sophia'	BS,BU,BY,CA,S,U
Tagetes patula 'Red Cherry'	B,F,MO,SE,YA
Tagetes patula 'Red Marietta'	BD,BS,D,DD,F,MO,YA
Tagetes patula 'Romania Bronze'	SG
Tagetes patula 'Royal Crested' mix	BS,CL,KI,J,MO,S,YA
Tagetes patula 'Royal Crested' s-c	B,BS,U
Tagetes patula 'Royal King'	BS,D,MO,SK
Tagetes patula 'Rusty Red'	BS
Tagetes patula 'Safari Bolero'	B,BS,CL,DT,L,MO,SK, YA
Tagetes patula 'Safari Gold'	B,BS,CL,L,MO,SK,YA
Tagetes patula 'Safari' mix	BS,CL,DT,F,J,L,MO,SK, YA
Tagetes patula 'Safari Orange'	B,BS,CL,L,MO,SK,YA
Tagetes patula 'Safari Primrose'	B,BS,CL,D,DT,L,MO
Tagetes patula 'Safari Queen'	B,BS,CL,L,MO,SK,YA
Tagetes patula 'Safari Scarlet'	B,BS,CL,L,MO,PL,SK, YA
Tagetes patula 'Safari Tangerine'	B,BS,CL,D,G,L,MO,O, SK,U,YA
Tagetes patula 'Safari Yellow'	B,BS,CL,KI,L,MO,SK,YA
Tagetes patula 'Silvia'	BS,BY,D
Tagetes patula 'Sophia Classic'	M
Tagetes patula 'Sophia' mix	BS,CG,CL,D,F,J,JO,PI, PK,S
Tagetes patula 'Sophia' s-c	BS,D,T
Tagetes patula 'Sparky'	BS,D,DT,MO,PI
Tagetes patula 'Spice'	BS
Tagetes patula 'Striped Marvel'	KS,T
Tagetes patula 'Sunny'	B
Tagetes patula 'Suzanna'	SG
Tagetes patula 'Tall Scotch Prize'	DT
Tagetes patula 'Tangerine'	B,BS,BY,J,V
Tagetes patula 'Tanja'	BS,MO,YA
Tagetes patula 'Tiger Eyes'	B,BS,CO,F,KI,M,MO,SE, T,VH
Tagetes p.'Tripl. Crested Fr. Anem. Fl' s-c	SK
Tagetes patula 'Troubadour' yellow	SK
Tagetes patula 'Valencia' golden-orange	B,MO
Tagetes patula 'Winner' orange	D,MO,S,U
Tagetes pumila 'Mandarin Imp'	MO
Tagetes pusilla	B
Tagetes 'Safari Red'	PL
Tagetes sp 'Bruxe'	HU
Tagetes tenuifolia	DD,SG
Tagetes tenuifolia 'Carina'	BY,C
Tagetes tenuifolia 'Carina Osena'	C
Tagetes tenuifolia 'Gem Golden'	B,BS,C,CL,CN,CO,DT,F, J,KI,L,MO,PI,S,ST,T,U, V,VH,YA
Tagetes tenuifolia 'Gem Lemon'	BS,C,CL,CN,D,DI,DT,F, GO,J,KI,KS,L,MO,R,S, ST,T,TE,U,V,VH,VY,YA
Tagetes tenuifolia 'Gem' mix	BS,JO,TU
Tagetes tenuifolia 'Gem Orange'	L,V,YA
Tagetes tenuifolia 'Gem Tangerine'	B,BS,C,CL,D,DT,F,KI, KS,MO,R,S,SK,TE,VY
Tagetes tenuifolia 'Golden Ring'	BS,BY
Tagetes tenuifolia 'Lemon Star'	B,BS,PI
Tagetes tenuifolia 'Little Giant'	SK
Tagetes tenuifolia 'Lulu'	BS,BY,M,SK
Tagetes tenuifolia 'Luna'	YA
Tagetes tenuifolia 'Ornament'	C,HU,L

TAGETES

Tagetes tenuifolia 'Paprika'	B,F,J,M,T,V
Tagetes tenuifolia 'Starfire'	BS,C,CL,CN,F,HU,J,KI, KS,L,M,MO,PK,S,T,TU, V,VH,YA
Tagetes tenuifolia 'Sundance'	U
Tagetes tenuifolia 'Tessy Gold'	B,BS,DT
Tagetes tenuifolia 'Ursula'	D
Tagetes triploid 'Beau' s-c, mix	BS,MO
Tagetes triploid 'Little Nell'	B,BS,CL,MO
Tagetes triploid 'Nell Gwyn'	B,BD,BS,CL,MO
Tagetes triploid 'Seven Star'	B,BS,D,MO,T
Tagetes triploid 'Solar Series' s-c, mix	B,BS,CL,MO
Tagetes triploid 'Super Star'	BS,KI
Tagetes triploid 'Super Star Orange'	U
Tagetes triploid 'Suzie Wong'	B,CL,MO,T
Tagetes triploid 'Trinity' mix	T
Tagetes triploid 'Zenith' mix	BS,CL,L,MO,SK
Tagetes triploid 'Zenith' s-c	B,BS,CL,D,MO,PK,SK, U,YA
Tagetes tubiflora	B
Talinum angustissimum	B
Talinum appelachianum	DV
Talinum aurantiacum	B,SW
Talinum brevifolium	B,SW
Talinum caffrum	B,DV,Y
Talinum calycinum	AP,B,HU
Talinum confertiflorum	DV
Talinum napiforme	DV
Talinum okanoganense	AP,I,KL,RM,SC
Talinum paniculatum	AP,B,C,DV,G,KL
Talinum parviflorum	DV
Talinum parvulum	DV
Talinum portulacifolium	B,DV
Talinum punae	DV
Talinum rugospermum	B,JE,SC
Talinum sediforme	DV
Talinum sp	DV,Y
Talinum spinescens	AP,C,I,RM,SC
Talinum teretifolium	AP,B,DV,KL,SC
Talinum 'Zoe'	I
Tamarindus indica	B,DD,EL,HA,HU,RE,SA, TT
Tamarix aphylla	B
Tamarix chinensis	LN,SA
Tamarix gallica	B,C,FW,SA,VE
Tamarix parviflora	CG
Tamus communis	B,C,G,SG
Tanacetum balsamita	B
Tanacetum balsamita ssp balsamita	SG
Tanacetum boreale	SG
Tanacetum cinerariifolium	B,C,CN,CP,JE,KS,SD
Tanacetum coccineum	B,C,FR,HP,SG
Tanacetum coccineum 'Duro'	B,JE
Tanacetum coccineum 'James Kelway'	B,PK,SA,SC
Tanacetum coccineum Robinson's Giant Fl	C,DT,L,MO,SE,SK
Tanacetum coccineum Robinson's mix	CN,DE,JE,PI,PK,SA
Tanacetum coccineum Robinson's s-c	B,BS,CN,JE,SA,T
Tanacetum coccineum 'Silver Princess'	B,BS
Tanacetum coccineum single giant	BD,BS,V
Tanacetum corymbosum	AP,B,C,HP,JE,RS,SC,SG
Tanacetum densum ssp amani	AP,RM
Tanacetum hultenii	B,DD
Tanacetum hyb lge fl	BS,S,ST
Tanacetum karelinii	VO
Tanacetum macrophyllum	B,C,HP,JE
Tanacetum mix dbl	BY,J,PK,V

Tanacetum mix single	BY,CO,D,J,TU
Tanacetum mix superb	T
Tanacetum niveum	B,C,CP,HP,T
Tanacetum parthenium	AP,B,C,CN,CP,DD,DI, HP,HU,JE,KS,LA,SA,SG, TH,YA
Tanacetum parthenium 'Alba'	CP
Tanacetum parthenium 'Aureum'	B,BY,C,CN,CP,G,HP,I,SZ, TH
Tanacetum parthenium 'Ball's Dbl White'	B,D,DE,PI
Tanacetum parthenium 'Butterball'	B,BS,D,DT,F,MO,T,U
Tanacetum parthenium 'Fortuna'	B
Tanacetum parthenium 'Gold Ball'	B,BS,BY,C,CL,D,DE,DT, J,KI,L,MO,PI,S,TU,V,YA
Tanacetum parthenium 'Goldball Imp'	B
Tanacetum parthenium 'Golden Moss'	B,BS,CL,MO,T
Tanacetum parthenium 'Perfection'	B
Tanacetum parthenium plenum	HP,I
Tanacetum parthenium 'Princess Daisy'	B
Tanacetum parthenium 'Rotary'	B
Tanacetum parthenium 'Roya'	B
Tanacetum parthenium 'Salome'	B
Tanacetum parthenium 'Santana'	BS,CL,F,MO,PK,T
Tanacetum parthenium 'Santana Yellow'	B,BS,CL,MO
Tanacetum parthenium 'Selma Star'	B,BS,KI,ST
Tanacetum parthenium 'Silverball'	B,BS,BY,CO,KI,TU
Tanacetum parthenium 'Snowball'	B,BD,BS,C,DT,JO,L,MO, SK,V
Tanacetum parth. 'Tetra White Wonder'	B,SK
Tanacetum parthenium 'Tom Thumb'	SG
Tanacetum parthenium 'Variegatum'	B
Tanacetum parthenium 'White Bonnet'	HP
Tanacetum parthenium 'White Star'	B,BL,CL,MO,SK,VY,YA
Tanacetum ptarmiciflorum	BS,S,SG,YA
Tanacetum ptarmiciflorum 'Silver Feather'	BY,CL,J,L,MO,PI,T
Tanacetum roseum	C,CP,DI
Tanacetum roseum 'Duro'	C
Tanacetum roseum King Size	CL,F
Tanacetum 'Selma Tetra'	BS,MO
Tanacetum 'Snow Dwarf'	U
Tanacetum 'Snow Puffs'	D
Tanacetum vulgare	A,B,C,CN,G,GO,HP,HU, JE,KS,LA,SA,SG,TH
Tanacetum vulgare 'Gold-sticks'	B
Tanacetum 'White Gem'	S
Tanquana archeri	B,KB
Tanquana hilmarii	B,Y
Tanquana prismatica	B
Tapeinochilus ananassae	B
Taraxacum magellanicum	B,G,SS
Taraxacum montanum	KL
Taraxacum officinale	AB,CN,DD
Taraxacum officinale album	NS,SG
Taraxacum rubifolium	SZ
Taraxacum serotinum	B
Taraxacum sp	AP,SG
Tarchonanthus camphoratus	B,BH,KB,SI
Tarenna asiatica	B
Tarenna zimbabwensis	B,SI
Tavaresia barklyi	B,SI
Taxodium ascendens see T.distichum v imbricatum	
Taxodium distichum	B,C,CA,CG,EL,FW,LN, N,SA,VE,WA
Taxodium distichum v imbricatum	B,CA,SA
Taxodium dist. v imbricatum 'Nutans'	B
Taxodium mucronatum	B,CA,EL,HA,LN,SA

TAXUS

Taxus baccata	A,B,C,CA,FW,G,KL,LN, SA,VE
Taxus baccata 'Dovastoniana'	CG
Taxus baccata 'Erecta'	B
Taxus baccata 'Fastigiata'	B,SA,VE
Taxus baccata pyramidalis	FW
Taxus brevifolia	AB,B,C,DD,LN,NO
Taxus chinensis	B,C,FW,SA
Taxus cuspidata	B,DD,EL,FW,SA,V
Taxus cuspidata 'Capitata'	B,FW,LN
Taxus mairei	LN,SA
Taxus x media 'Hicksii'	B
Taxus x media 'Kelseyi'	B
Tecoma capensis	B,EL,SA,SI,SG
Tecoma stans	B,C,CA,DD,DV,EL,HA, JE,LN,O,SA,SW,WA
Tecoma stans 'Trovadora'	HU
Tecoma x smithii	B,EL
Tecomanthe hillii	B,EL
Tecomanthe speciosa	C
Tecomaria capensis	C,CA
Tecophilaea cyanocrocus	AR
Tecophilaea cyanocrocus 'Leichtlinii'	AR
Tectaria incisa	B
Tectona grandis	B,C,CA,EL,HA,LN,RE,SA
Teesdaliopsis conferta	CG,SC
Telekia speciosa	AP,B,C,CG,G,HP,HU,,JE, P,SA,SC,T
Telekia speciosissima	B,G,SG
Telephium imperata	B,C,SC
Telesonix jamesii see Boykinia	
Teline see Genista	
Tellima grandiflora	AP,B,C,G,HP,HU,I,JE,P, RH,SA,SC,SG
Tellima grandiflora odorata group	AP,E,HP
Tellima grandiflora odorata 'Howell'	T
Tellima grandiflora Rubra Group	E,HP,SG
Telopea mongaensis	B,EL,O,SA
Telopea oreades	B,C,EL,HA,NI,O,SA
Telopea speciosissima	AU,B,C,EL,HA,NI,O,SA, SI,V
Telopea truncata	B,C,N,O,SA
Teloxys aristata	B,C,V
Templetonia biloba	B,NI
Templetonia egena	B,NI
Templetonia hookeri	B,NI
Templetonia neglecta	B,NI
Templetonia retusa	AU,B,C,EL,NI,O,SA
Templetonia stenophylla	B,NI
Tenicroa filifolia	B,RU
Tephrocactus alexanderi	DV
Tephrocactus alexanderi v bruchii	BC,DV
Tephrocactus articulatus	DV
Tephrocactus articulatus polyacanthus	BC
Tephrocactus articulatus v atrispinus	DV
Tephrocactus articulatus v papyracanthus	DV
Tephrocactus articulatus v syringacanthus	DV
Tephrocactus asplandii	BC,DV
Tephrocactus bolivianus	DV
Tephrocactus camachoi	DV
Tephrocactus chilecitoensis	CH,DV
Tephrocactus crispicrinitus	DV
Tephrocactus floccosus	DV
Tephrocactus floccosus v ovoides	DV
Tephrocactus glomeratus	CH,DV
Tephrocactus ignescens	DV

Tephrocactus kuenrichii	DV
Tephrocactus mistiensis	DV
Tephrocactus noodtiae	DV
Tephrocactus rauhii	DV
Tephrocactus syringacanthus	CH
Tephrosia candida	B,SI
Tephrosia eriocarpa	B,NI,SA
Tephrosia flammea	B,NI
Tephrosia glomeruliflora	B
Tephrosia grandiflora	B,BH,SI
Tephrosia maxima	B
Tephrosia polystachya	B,SI
Tephrosia purpurea	B
Tephrosia rosea	B,NI,SA
Tephrosia sp	SI
Tephrosia uniovulata	B,NI
Tephrosia villosa	B
Tephrosia virginiana	B,DD,PR
Tephrosia vogelii	B,HU,SI
Teramnus labialis	B
Terminalia amazona	B,SA
Terminalia arjuna	B,CA,LN
Terminalia arostrata	B,NI,O
Terminalia bellirica	B
Terminalia brownii	B
Terminalia canescens	B,NI,SA
Terminalia carpentariae	B,NI
Terminalia catappa	B,EL,HA,RE,SA
Terminalia cunninghamii	B,NI
Terminalia ferdinandiana	B,NI,O
Terminalia ivorensis	B
Terminalia lucida	B
Terminalia mantaly	B,SI
Terminalia mollis	B,SI
Terminalia petiolaris	B,NI
Terminalia phanerophlebia	B,KB
Terminalia platyphylla	B,NI
Terminalia platyptera	B
Terminalia porphyrocarpa	B,NI
Terminalia prunioides	BH
Terminalia randii	B,SI
Terminalia sericea	B,SI,WA
Terminalia sericocarpa	B,EL,O
Terminalia stuhlmannii	B,SI
Terminalia supranitifolia	B,NI
Terminalia trichopoda	B,SI
Ternstroemia gymnanthera see T.japonica	
Ternstroemia japonica	B,C,CA,EL,LN,SA
Testudinaria elephantipes see Dioscorea	
Tetracarpidium conophorum	B
Tetracentron sinense	B,SG
Tetraclinis articulata	B
Tetradenia riparia	B,BH,SI
Tetradium danielli	B,C,FW,NG,SA,VE
Tetradium elleryana	B,HA,RE,SA
Tetradium fraxinifolia	C
Tetradium hupehensis	SA
Tetraganolobus purpureus	AP,CG
Tetragonia decumbens	B,SI
Tetragonia diptera	B,NI
Tetragonia eremaea	B,NI
Tetragonia tetragonioides	B,CG,DD
Tetragonolobus see Lotus	C,SC,SG
Tetranema roseum	B,SG
Tetranema roseum 'Violetta'	C
Tetraneuris acaulis	B,RM,SG

TETRANEURIS

Tetraneuris grandiflora	B,JE,KL,RM,SW
Tetraneuris torreyana	RM
Tetrapanax papyrifer	B,C,HA,SA
Tetrapathaea tetrandra see Passiflora	
Tetrarrhena laevis	B,NI
Tetraselago wilmsii	B,SI
Tetratheca confertifolia	B,NI
Tetratheca hirsuta	B,NI
Tetratheca setigera	B,NI
Tetratheca virgata	B,NI
Teucrium arduinii	C,I,SC
Teucrium asiaticum	AP,HP,SC,SG
Teucrium botrys	B,KL
Teucrium canadense	AB,B,CP,PR
Teucrium chamaedrys	AP,B,BS,C,CG,CL,CN,JE,
	MO,SA,SC,T,TH
Teucrium flavum	AP,B,C,G,JE,SC,SZ
Teucrium flavum grandiflorum	T
Teucrium fruticans	HP
Teucrium granatense	VO
Teucrium hyrcanicum	AP,B,C,CP,E,G,HP,P,SC
Teucrium massiliense	B,C,CP
Teucrium montanum	AP,B,C,SC
Teucrium polium	AP,B,C,JE,S
Teucrium polium 'Aureum'	B,I
Teucrium pyrenaicum	G,SA,SG,VO
Teucrium racemosum v racemosum	B,NI
Teucrium rotundifolium	VO
Teucrium scorodonia	B,C,CN,CP,E,HU,JE,NS,
	SA,SG
Teucrium scorodonia 'Crispum'	SC
Thalictrum alpinum	AP,B,G,SC
Thalictrum aquilegiifolium	AP,B,BS,CN,DT,EL,G,HP,
	HU,JE,KI,MO,PK,SA,SC,
	SG,SU
Thalictrum aquilegiifolium hyb new	B,C,CL,F,T,V
Thalictrum aquilegiifolium 'Purpureum'	B,JE,SA
Thalictrum aquilegiifolium v album	AP,B,G,HP,JE,SA
Thalictrum chelidonii	HP,SA,SC,SG
Thalictrum dasycarpum	B,JE,PR
Thalictrum delavayi	AP,B,BS,C,CN,G,HP,JE,
	MA,MO,SA,SC,T,TH
Thalictrum delavayi 'Album'	HP,NG,SC
Thalictrum del. album 'Sternenhimmel'	JE
Thalictrum dioicum	B,PR
Thalictrum dipterocarpum see T.delavayi	
Thalictrum fendleri	B,CG
Thalictrum flavum	AP,G,HP,SA,SG,T
Thalictrum flavum ssp flavum	B,JE
Thalictrum flavum ssp glaucum	AP,B,C,HP,HU,JE,P,SG
Thalictrum foetidum	B,HU,JE,SC,SG
Thalictrum isopyroides	SG
Thalictrum javanicum	B,SC
Thalictrum lucidum	AP,B,C,G,HP,JE
Thalictrum minus	AP,B,C,CG,DE,G,HP,SA,
	SC,SG
Thalictrum minus adiantifolium	B,G,HP,JE,SA
Thalictrum minus ssp minus	JE
Thalictrum orientale	AR
Thalictrum petaloideum	G,SG
Thalictrum polycarpum	B,DD
Thalictrum polygamum	B,HP,SG
Thalictrum rochebrunianum	AP,B,G,HP,JE,SA,SC
Thalictrum simplex	SG
Thalictrum sp	AP,HP,SC,SG
Thalictrum speciosissimum see T.flavum ssp glaucum	

Thalictrum tuberosum	AR
Thalictrum venulosum	SG
Thamnocalamus spathaceus h see Fargesia murieliae	
Thamnochortus bachmannii	B,SI
Thamnochortus cinereus	B,BH,SI
Thamnochortus insignis	B,C,KB,O,SI
Thamnochortus lucens	SI
Thamnochortus platypteris	B,SI
Thamnochortus rigidus	B,SI
Thamnochortus sp nova	SI
Thamnochortus spicigerus	B,O,SI
Thamnosma montana	SA,SW
Thapsia garganica	SA
Thaspium trifoliatum	B,PR
Thea sinensis see Camellia	
Thelesperma burridgeanum	B
Thelesperma burridgeanum 'Brunette'	C,HU
Thelocactus bicolor	B,DV,Y
Thelocactus bicolor v bolansis	B,DV,Y
Thelocactus bicolor v flavidispinum	B
Thelocactus bicolor v pottsii	B,Y
Thelocactus bicolor v schottii	B,DV,Y
Thelocactus bicolor v texensis	DV
Thelocactus bicolor v tricolor	Y
Thelocactus bolensis	B
Thelocactus bueckii	B
Thelocactus conothele	B,Y
Thelocactus conothele v argenteus	B
Thelocactus conothele v aurantiacus	B
Thelocactus flavidispinus	DV,Y
Thelocactus fossulatus	DV
Thelocactus hastifer	B
Thelocactus heterochromus	B
Thelocactus hexaedrophorus	B,DV
Thelocactus hexaedrophorus v fossulatus	B,Y
Thelocactus krainzianus	Y
Thelocactus leucacanthus	B,DV,Y
Thelocactus leucacanthus v schmollii	B
Thelocactus lloydii	B,Y
Thelocactus lophothele	Y
Thelocactus lophothele v longispinus	Y
Thelocactus macdowellii	B,BC,GC
Thelocactus matudae	B
Thelocactus nidulans	DV,Y
Thelocactus paradensis	Y
Thelocactus rinconensis	B,CH,DV,Y
Thelocactus saussieri albiflora	BC
Thelocactus schwarzii	B,DV
Thelocactus setispinus	B,SG,Y
Thelocactus setispinus v hamatus	B
Thelocactus setispinus v setaceus	B
Thelocactus sp mix	C,CH,Y
Thelocactus tulensis	B,Y
Thelocactus wagnerianus	Y
Thelymitra antennifera	Y
Thelymitra benthamiana	B,NI
Thelymitra campanulata	B
Thelymitra flexuosa	B
Thelymitra graminea	B
Thelymitra holmesii	B
Thelymitra ixioides	B
Thelymitra longifolium	B,SS
Thelymitra nuda white	B
Thelypteris dentata	B
Themeda pilbara	B
Themeda triandra	B,EL,HA,NI,SA

THEMEDA

Themeda triandra japonica	B,JE
Theobroma cacao	B
Theobroma gilleri	B
Thereianthus spicatus	B,SI
Thermopsis barbata	HP
Thermopsis caroliniana see T.villosa	
Thermopsis fabacea see T.lupinoides	
Thermopsis lanceolata	B,BS,C,HP,JE,KI,SA,SG, U,V
Thermopsis lupinoides	B,DD,HP,JE,SC,SG
Thermopsis macrophylla	B
Thermopsis mollis	HP
Thermopsis montana see rhombifolia	
Thermopsis rhombifolia	AP,B,C,HP,JE,NO,SA, SG,T
Thermopsis villosa	AP,B,C,HP,JD,JE,KL,NT, SG
Thesium alpinum	SG
Thespesia acutiloba	B
Thespesia populnea	B,DV,EL,HA,RE,SA
Thevetia neriifolia see T.peruviana	
Thevetia peruviana	B,C,CA,EL,FW,HA,HU, RE,SA,VE
Thevetia peruviana 'Alba'	B
Thevetia thevetoides	CA,DD
Thinopyrum intermedium	DE
Thladiantha speciosa	B
Thlaspi alpestre	AP,B,G
Thlaspi alpestre 'Krodde'	C
Thlaspi alpina	KL,VO
Thlaspi alpina ssp brevicaulis	KL
Thlaspi alpinum	AP,C,CG,G,JE,KL,SA,SC
Thlaspi arvense	B,CG,LA,SG
Thlaspi bellidifolium	KL
Thlaspi bulbosum	AP,KL,SC,SG
Thlaspi ceratocarpum	B
Thlaspi fendleri	B,SW
Thlaspi jankae	KL
Thlaspi lilacina	RM
Thlaspi montanum	AP,B,G,RM,SC
Thlaspi montanum v montanum	KL
Thlaspi perfoliatum	CG
Thlaspi praecox	KL
Thlaspi rotundifolium	AP,B,C,JE,KL,NG,SA,VO
Thlaspi stylosum	KL
Thomasia angustifolia	B,NI
Thomasia glutinosa	B,NI
Thomasia macrocarpa	B
Thomasia quercifolia	B,NI
Thomasia triphylla	B,NI
Thorncroftia succulenta	B,KB,SI
Thounidium decandrum	B
Threlkeldia diffusa	B,NI
Thrinax compacta	B
Thrinax excelsa	B
Thrinax morrisii	B,O,SA
Thrinax parviflora	B,C,CA,O,SA
Thrinax radiata	B,EL
Thrincia tuberosa	B
Thrixanthocereus blossfeldiorum	DV,Y
Thryallis glauca	B
Thryptomene aspera ssp glabra	B,NI
Thryptomene baeckeacea aff	B,NI
Thryptomene calycina	B
Thryptomene johnsonii	B,NI,SA
Thryptomene kochii	B,NI

Thryptomene maisoneum	B
Thryptomene mucronulata	B,NI
Thryptomene racemulosa	B,NI
Thuja compacta	DV,EL,HA
Thuja occidentalis	A,B,C,CA,FW,KL,LN,SA, SG,VE
Thuja occidentalis 'Aurea'	KL
Thuja occidentalis 'Cristata'	CG
Thuja occidentalis 'Fastigiata'	B
Thuja occidentalis 'Filiformis'	CG
Thuja occidentalis 'Malonyana'	KL
Thuja occidentalis 'Pyramidalis'	SA
Thuja occidentalis 'Rosenthallii'	CG
Thuja occidentalis 'Wareana'	CG
Thuja orientalis	B,C,CA,CG,EL,FW,HA, LN,SA,VE,WA
Thuja orientalis 'Aurea'	B,C,EL,FW,SA,VE
Thuja orientalis 'Aurea Nana'	B,C,FW,SA,VE
Thuja orientalis 'Beverleyensis'	B
Thuja orientalis 'Pyramidalis'	B,DV,FW,SA,VE
Thuja orientalis 'Sieboldii'	B
Thuja orientalis v compacta (nana)	B,C,FW,LN,SA,VE
Thuja plicata	A,AB,B,C,CA,CG,FW,LN, NO,SA,VE
Thuja standishii	LN,SG
Thujopsis dolobrata	CG,SA
Thunbergia alata	AP,B,BS,BY,C,CA,CO, DE,DN,EL,HU,J,KI,KS,L, PI,R,S,SA,SK,ST,TH,jVH
Thunbergia alata 'Susie' mix	BD,BS,CA,CL,D,DT,F,M, MO,PK,SE,SK,T,U,V,YA
Thunbergia alata 'Susie Orange'	SK,V
Thunbergia erecta	B
Thunbergia fragrans	B
Thunbergia grandiflora	B,PL,SA
Thunbergia grandiflora 'Alba'	B
Thunbergia kirkii	B
Thunbergia lancifolia	B,C
Thunbergia natalensis	B,SI
Thuranthos basuticum	B,SI
Thymophylla tenuiloba	B,BD,BS,DT,G,KS,L,MO, PK,SG
Thymophylla tenuiloba 'Golden Cascade'	J,SK
Thymophylla tenuiloba 'Shooting Star'	BS,C,CL,DE,F
Thymus adamovicii	SG
Thymus argaeus	T
Thymus caespititius	B
Thymus camphorata	SG
Thymus carnosus	B
Thymus 'Coconut'	B
Thymus comosus	AP,B,SC,T
Thymus doerfleri 'Bressingham Pink'	B
Thymus hirsutus	KL
Thymus longiflorus	SA
Thymus 'Longwood'	B
Thymus marschallianus see T.pannonicus	
Thymus mastichiana	AP,SA,SC
Thymus polytrichus	B
Thymus polytrichus ssp arcticus	B,SG,SU
Thymus pseudolanuginosus	B
Thymus pulegioides	B,C,JE
Thymus pulegioides albiflora	SG
Thymus richardii ssp nitidus	SG
Thymus serpyllum	B,BD,BS,BY,C,CL,CN, DE,DI,HU,J,JE,L,MO,S, SA,T,TH,V,VE

THYMUS

Thymus serpyllum 'Aureus'	B
Thymus serpyllum coccineus	B
Thymus serpyllum 'Minor'	B
Thymus sp	AP,SG
Thymus thracicus	B
Thymus vulgaris 'Silver Posie'	B
Thymus x citriodorus	B,C
Thymus x citriodorus cvs	B
Thymus zygis	SA
Thysanotus dichotomus	B,NI
Thysanotus manglesianus	B,NI
Thysanotus multiflorus	B,NI,SA
Thysanotus thyrsoideus	B,NI
Tiarella cordifolia	AP,HP,SC
Tiarella polyphylla	AP,B,G,HP,P
Tiarella polyphylla 'Filigran'	BS,JE
Tiarella sp	PA
Tiarella wherryi	AP,B,C,CG,HP,HU,JE, NT,SA
Tibouchina granulosa	B,SE
Tibouchina holosericea	B
Tibouchina mix	EL,SA
Tibouchina mutabilis	B
Tibouchina paratropica	SG
Tibouchina sellowiana	B
Tibouchina urvilleana	B
Tigridia chrysantha	B,SW
Tigridia dugesii	B,SW
Tigridia durangense	B,SC,SW
Tigridia multiflora	B,SW
Tigridia pavonia	AP,B,DD,KL,LG,SC,T
Tilia americana	A,B,CA,EL,FW,LN,SA
Tilia amurensis	B,LN,SA,SG
Tilia argentea see T.tomentosa	
Tilia cordata	A,B,C,FW,LN,SA,SG,VE
Tilia dasystyla	LN,SA
Tilia japonica	SA
Tilia mandschurica	LN,SA
Tilia miqueliana	C
Tilia mongolica	LN,SA
Tilia oliveri	B,LN,SA
Tilia platyphyllos	A,B,FW,LN,SA,SG,VE
Tilia sibirica	SG
Tilia tomentosa	A,B,C,CG,FW,LN,SA,VE
Tillandsia aeranthos	B
Tillandsia anceps	B
Tillandsia balbisiana	B
Tillandsia bulbosa	B
Tillandsia capitata v rubra	B
Tillandsia dura	B
Tillandsia gardneri	B
Tillandsia geminiflora	B
Tillandsia geminiflora v gigantea	B
Tillandsia geminiflora v incana	B
Tillandsia juncea	B
Tillandsia loliacea	B
Tillandsia lorentziana	B
Tillandsia mallemontii	B
Tillandsia paraensis	B
Tillandsia pohliana	B
Tillandsia polystachia	B
Tillandsia pruinosa	B
Tillandsia punctulata	B
Tillandsia regnellii	B
Tillandsia remota	B
Tillandsia rubida	B

Tillandsia schiedeana	B
Tillandsia schiedeana v minor	B
Tillandsia schreiteri	B
Tillandsia seideliana	B
Tillandsia setacea	B
Tillandsia simulata	B
Tillandsia spiculosa	B
Tillandsia spiculosa v ustulata	B
Tillandsia streptocarpa	B
Tillandsia stricta	B
Tillandsia tenuifolia	B
Tillandsia tricholepis	B
Tillandsia vernicosa	B
Tillandsia vestita	B
Tillandsia viridiflora	B
Tillandsia xerographica	B
Tillandsia xiphioides	B
Tinnea barbata	B,SI
Tinnea rhodesiana	B,SI
Tinospora smilacina	B
Tipuana tipu	C,CA,EL,HA,LN,O,SA, VE,WA
Titanopsis calcarea	AP,B,DV,SG,SI,Y
Titanopsis fulleri	B,DV,SI,Y
Titanopsis hugo-schlechteri	B,DV,SI,Y
Titanopsis hugo-schlechteri v alboviridis	B
Titanopsis luckhoffii	DV
Titanopsis luederitzii	B,DV
Titanopsis primosii	B,DV,Y
Titanopsis schwantesii	B,DV,SI
Titanopsis sp mix	C,Y
Tithonia 'Arla'	B,HU
Tithonia 'Fiesta del Sol'	F
Tithonia rotundifolia	AB,B,G,SD,SG,V
Tithonia rotundifolia 'Goldfinger'	B,C,DE,L,PK,S,SK,T
Tithonia rotundifolia 'Torch'	AP,B,C,DE,HU,JO,PI,PK, TE
Toddalia asiatica	B
Tofieldia calyculata	AP,B,C,DV,JE,KL,SG
Tofieldia glutinosa	B,C,JE,SG
Tofieldia pusilla	AP,C
Tolmiea menziesii	B,C,G,HP,JE,SA
Tolpis barbata	B,C,D,KS
Tonestus lyallii	HP,KL
Toona australis	B,EL,HA,NI,O
Toona serrata	FW
Toona sinensis	A,B,C,FW,HA,SA,WA
Tordylium aegyptiacum	B
Tordylium maximum	JD
Torenia flava 'Suzie Wong'	B,MO,PK,S
Torenia fournieri	B,DE
Torenia fournieri blue	PK
Torenia fournieri 'Clown' mix	B,C,CL,J,MO,SK,T,V
Torenia fournieri 'Nana Compacta Blue'	B
Torenia fournieri 'Pink Panda'	B,BS,MO,PK
Torilis arvensis	B,SG
Torilis japonica	B,LA
Torreya grandis	B,LN,SA
Torreya nucifera	B
Toumeya papyracantha	B
Townsendia alpigena	KL
Townsendia exscapa	AP,B,G,HP,KL,RM,SW
Townsendia florifera	SC
Townsendia formosa	AP,B,G,KL,SC,SW
Townsendia grandiflora	KL
Townsendia hirsuta	KL

TOWNSENDIA

Townsendia hookeri	KL
Townsendia incana	AP,B,RM,SC,SW
Townsendia montana	AP,CG,KL,RM,SC
Townsendia montana v minima	B,SW
Townsendia nuttallii	RM
Townsendia parryi	AP,B,CG,G,KL,SC
Townsendia rothrockii	AP,G,KL,SC,SG
Townsendia scapigera	KL
Townsendia speciosa	KL
Toxicodendron see Rhus	
Trachelium caeruleum	B,C,DE,G,SA
Trachelium caeruleum 'Album'	B,PK,SA
Trachelium caer. f1 'Passion in Violet'	B,F,T
Trachelium caer. f1 'Passion in Violet' p.s.	YA
Trachelium caeruleum 'Umbrella' mix	U
Trachelium caeruleum 'Umbrella Purple'	BS,CN,JE,MO,V
Trachelium caeruleum 'Umbrella White'	BS,CN,JE,MO
Trachelium caer. 'Violet Veil of Flowers'	C,HU,PK
Trachelium caer. 'White Veil of Flowers'	C
Trachelium rumelianum	B,HP,T
Trachelospermum asiaticum	B
Trachelospermum jasminoides	B
Trachyandra divaricata	B,SI
Trachyandra falcata	B,SI
Trachyandra hirsuta	B,SI
Trachyandra hirsutiflora	B,SI
Trachyandra revoluta	B,SI
Trachyandra tortilis	B,SI
Trachycarpus fortunei	A,B,C,CG,EL,FW,HA,O, SA,SH,T,VE
Trachycarpus martianus	B,C,O
Trachymene anisocarpa	O
Trachymene coerulea	AU,B,BS,C,DE,DI,EL,F, FR,HP,HU,KS,MO,NI,O, PI,PK,SA,V
Trachymene coerulea 'Alba'	B,KS
Trachymene coerulea 'Madonna'	BS,C,CO,JO,PL
Trachymene coerulea 'Rosea'	B,KS
Trachymene glaucifolia	B,NI
Trachymene oleracea	B,NI
Trachymene 'Sky Blue'	BS
Trachymene 'Wedding Party'	U
Trachys muricata	B
Trachyspermum ammi	HU
Tradescantia bracteata	B,PR
Tradescantia occidentalis	B,PR,SG
Tradescantia ohiensis	B,JE,PR
Tradescantia spathacea	B,C,PK,SA
Tradescantia subaspera montana	SG
Tradescantia virginiana	B,BD,BS,C,CN,MO,SA, TH
Tradescantia virginiana 'Alba'	B
Tradescantia virginiana 'Caerulea'	B
Tradescantia virginiana 'Rosea'	B
Tradescantia x andersoniana blue	JE
Tradescantia x andersoniana gr.	JE
Tradescantia x andersoniana hyb new	C
Tradescantia x andersoniana red	JE
Tradescantia x andersoniana white	JE
Tragia involucrata	B
Tragia plukenetii	B
Tragopogon balcanicus	B
Tragopogon dubius	B,HP,SG
Tragopogon floccosus	B
Tragopogon orientalis	B,SG
Tragopogon porrifolius	AP,B,CG,DD,G,HP,SC

Tragopogon pratensis	B,DD,G,HP,LA,SC,SG
Tragus roxburghii	B
Treculia africana	B
Trema orientalis	B,SI
Tremastelma palaestinum	CG
Tretrocarya cf pratensis	VO
Trevesia palmata	B,CA
Trianthema pilosa	B,NI
Trianthema portulacastrum	B
Trianthema turgidifolia	B,NI
Triaspis hypericoides ssp nelsonii	B,SI
Triaspis nelsonii	DD
Tribonanthes australis	C,NI
Tribulus cistoides	B
Tribulus hirsuta	B,NI
Tribulus platyptera aff	B,NI
Tribulus terrestris	B
Trichilia colimana	B
Trichilia dregeana	B,WA
Trichilia emetica	B,WA
Trichilia glabra	B
Trichocaulon piliferum	B,DV
Trichocaulon puntatus	CH
Trichocereus andalgensis	DV
Trichocereus atacamensis	B,Y
Trichocereus bridgesii	DV,HU
Trichocereus bridgesii see Echinopsis lageniformis	
Trichocereus bruchii	B
Trichocereus camarguensis	Y
Trichocereus candicans see Echinopsis	
Trichocereus catamarcensis	B
Trichocereus cephalomacrostibas	Y
Trichocereus chilensis v borealis	BC,DV
Trichocereus chilensis v panhoplites	BC,DV
Trichocereus culpinensis	DV,Y
Trichocereus culpinensis v monstrosus	B
Trichocereus escayensis	B
Trichocereus formosus	B
Trichocereus grandiflorus see Echinopsis huascha	
Trichocereus herzogianus	B
Trichocereus huascha	B,DV
Trichocereus lobivioides 'Grandiflorus'	B
Trichocereus lobivioides 'Purpureominiata'	B
Trichocereus longispinus	DV
Trichocereus macrogonus	B,DV,HU,Y
Trichocereus mix	Y
Trichocereus montanus	DV
Trichocereus narvaezensis	DV
Trichocereus orurensis	B
Trichocereus pachanoi	DV,HU,Y
Trichocereus pasacana	DV
Trichocereus peruvianus	DV,HU
Trichocereus peruvianus blue	HU
Trichocereus peruvianus f Ancash	HU
Trichocereus peruvianus f cuzcoensis	HU
Trichocereus poco	B,DV
Trichocereus puquiensis	Y
Trichocereus purpureopilosus	BC
Trichocereus randallii	B
Trichocereus santiaguensis	DV
Trichocereus schickendantzii	DV,Y
Trichocereus schickendantzii 'Paramount'	B
Trichocereus scopulicopus	Y
Trichocereus see Echinopsis	
Trichocereus shaferi	B,Y
Trichocereus smrzianus	B,DV

TRICHOCEREUS

Trichocereus sp	DV	Trifolium fragiferum 'Palestine'	B
Trichocereus strigosus	B	Trifolium fucatum	SZ
Trichocereus tacaquirensis	B,DV,Y	Trifolium hirtum	B
Trichocereus tarijensis v orurensis	B	Trifolium hirtum 'Hykon'	B
Trichocereus terschecki	B,DV,Y	Trifolium hirtum 'Kondinin'	B
Trichocereus thelegonoides	Y	Trifolium hybridum	B
Trichocereus thelegonus	B,DV,Y	Trifolium incarnatum	B,SU
Trichocereus totorensis	B,BC	Trifolium lupinaster	SG
Trichocereus trichosus	Y	Trifolium macrocephalum	B,DD
Trichocereus tunarensis	B,Y	Trifolium medium	SG
Trichocereus validus	B,DV,Y	Trifolium montanum	B,SG
Trichocereus werdermannianus	B,DV,Y	Trifolium nanum	RM
Trichocereus werdermann. v lecoriensis	B,Y	Trifolium ochroleucon	B,SG
Trichodesma zeylanicum	B,C,NI	Trifolium pannonicum	HP
Trichodiadema barbatum	B,DV	Trifolium parryi	RM
Trichodiadema densum	B,DV	Trifolium polyphyllum	VO
Trichodiadema intonsum	B	Trifolium pratense	AB,B,C,DD,DE,SC,SG
Trichodiadema mirabile	B,KB,Y	Trifolium pratense 'Redquin'	B
Trichodiadema stellatum	B,BC,DV,SI	Trifolium purpureum	B
Tricholaena rosea	C	Trifolium repens	A,B,C,FR,SG,SU
Trichopetalum plumosum B.C.W4116	MN	Trifolium repens f minus	B,CA
Trichosanthes cucumerina	B,C,NI	Trifolium rubens	A,AP,B,C,HP,JE,SA,T
Trichosanthes cucumerina v tricuspidata	B	Trifolium semipilosum	B
Trichostema arizonicum	B,SW	Trifolium semipilosum 'Safari'	B
Trichostema lanatum	AP,B,SW	Trifolium stellatum	AP,B,SC
Trichostema lanatum v parishii	B,SW	Trifolium striatum	CG
Tricoryne elatior	B,NI	Trifolium subterraneum cvs	B
Tricyrtis affinis	B,SG	Trifolium tomentosum	B
Tricyrtis bakeri see T.latifolia		Trifolium trichocephalum	SC,SG
Tricyrtis flava	B,KL	Trifolium vulgare	SG
Tricyrtis formosana	SG	Triglochin maritima	B,G,SG
Tricyrtis formosana amethystina	PK	Trigonella caerulea	B
Tricyrtis hirta	B,CG,JE,KL,SA,T,V	Trigonella foenum-graecum	B,CN,HU,KS,SG
Tricyrtis hirta 'Miyazaki'	AP,C,JE,PK	Trigonella sp	KL
Tricyrtis hirta 'Variegata'	B	Trigonidium egertonianum	B
Tricyrtis hyb Japanese	JE	Trillidium govanianum	AR
Tricyrtis hyb mix	T	Trillium chloropetalum	AP,AR,B,G,P,SC
Tricyrtis latifolia	AP,CG,G,JE,KL,SC,SG	Trillium cuneatum	G,PM
Tricyrtis macrantha	AP,I	Trillium erectum	AP,B,G,KL,P,PM,SC
Tricyrtis macrantha ssp macranthopsis	B	Trillium grandiflorum	AP,CG,G,KL,SC
Tricyrtis macropoda	AP,C,G,JE,KL,SC,SG	Trillium hibbersonii	AR
Tricyrtis maculata	JE	Trillium kamtschaticum	SG
Tricyrtis nana	B	Trillium ovatum	AP,B,P,SC,SG
Tricyrtis ohsumiensis	B	Trillium rivale	AR
Tricyrtis puberula	SC,SG	Trillium sessile	AP,B,G,P
Tricyrtis sp	LG	Trimeria trinervis	B,SI
Tridax procumbens	B	Trinia grandiflora	HP
Tridax trilobata	B,SG	Triodanis perfoliata	B,PR
Tridentea aperta	B	Triodia angusta	B,NI
Tridentea umdausensis	B	Triodia irritans v laxispicata	B,NI
Trifolium africanum	B,SI	Triodia mitchellii	B,NI
Trifolium alexandrinum	B	Triodia pungens	B,NI
Trifolium alpestris	B	Triodia wiseana	B,NI
Trifolium alpinum	B,C,JE,SA,VO	Triosteum perfoliatum	B
Trifolium ambiguum	SG	Tripetaleia bracteata	SG
Trifolium argutum	B	Triphasia trifolia	B
Trifolium arvense	B,SG	Triplaris surinamensis	B,HU
Trifolium atrorubens	KL	Triplaris weigeltiana	B
Trifolium aureum	B	Tripleurospermum inodorum	B,LA
Trifolium badium	B	Tripleurospermum inodorum 'Bridal Robe'	B,KS
Trifolium billardieri	B	Tripleurospermum maritima	HP
Trifolium campestre	B	Tripleurospermum maritima ssp inodorum	B,G
Trifolium clusii	B	Triplochiton zambesiacus	B,SI
Trifolium dubium	B	Tripsacum dactyloides	B,PR
Trifolium fragiferum	B	Tripteris clandestina	SI
Trifolium fragiferum 'O'connors'	B	Tripterococcus brunonis	B,NI

263

TRIPTERYGIUM

Tripterygium regelii	B,SA
Trisetum altaicum	SG
Trisetum flavescens	B,JE
Tristagma nivale	AR
Tristania conferta see Lophostemon confertus	
Tristania laurina see Tristaniopsis	
Tristania neriifolia	B
Tristaniopsis laurina	C,EL,HA,NI,O,SA
Triteleia hyacinthina	AP,B,G,MN,RH,SC,SG
Triteleia laxa	AP,B,C,G,RH,SC,SZ
Triteleia lemmoni	B,SW
Triteleia peduncularis	B,MN
Triteleia x tubergenii	AP,PM,SC
Trithrinax acanthocoma	B,C,CA,EL
Triticale 'Silver Tip'	JO
Triticum aestivum	B,DD,JO
Triticum aestivum 'Baart'	B
Triticum aestivum 'Pima Club'	B
Triticum aestivum v spelta	B
Triticum aestivum 'White Sonora'	B
Triticum durum black	B,HU,PI,SK
Triticum durum Black Tip	HU,JO,PK,SK
Triticum monococcum	SG
Triticum spelta	SG,T
Triticum turgidum v durum	C
Triticum turgidum v durum 'Bidi'	B
Tritoma see Knophofia	
Tritonia bakeri	B,RU
Tritonia crispa	B,SI
Tritonia crocata	AP,B,KB,MN,O,RU,SI
Tritonia deusta	B,KB,O,RU,SI
Tritonia deusta ssp miniata	B
Tritonia disticha ssp rubrolucens	B,C,P,SI
Tritonia dubia	AP,B,RU
Tritonia flabellifolia	B
Tritonia pallida	B,RU
Tritonia paniculata	B,SC,SI
Tritonia securigera	MN,RU,SC
Tritonia sp	SI
Tritonia squalida	B,KB
Tritoniopsis caffra	B,SI
Tritoniopsis dodii	B,SI
Tritoniopsis parviflora	B,SI
Tritoniopsis sp	SI
Triumfetta appendiculata	B,NI,SA
Triumfetta chaetocarpa	B,NI
Triumfetta rhomboidea	B
Trochetiopsis melanoxylon	SG
Trochocarpa thymifolia	B,C
Trochodendron aralioides	SA,SG
Trollius acaulis	AP,B,HP,KL,SC
Trollius altaicus	SG
Trollius altissimus	DV
Trollius asiaticus	AP,B,JE,SG
Trollius chinensis	AP,B,CG,CN,G,HP,KL,P, SA,SC,SG
Trollius chinensis 'Golden Queen'	AP,B,BD,BS,C,CL,CO, HP,JE,KI,MO,SC,V
Trollius Choice mix	U
Trollius dzhungaricus	VO
Trollius europaeus	AP,B,BS,C,CG,CN,F,G, HP,JE,KL,MO,PK,RS, SA,SC,SG,T,TH,VO
Trollius europaeus 'Superbus'	B,JE,SA
Trollius europaeus transilvanicus	SG
Trollius hondoensis	AP,B,HP,P

Trollius hybridus	T
Trollius laxus	B,JE,SW
Trollius laxus ssp albiflorus	RM
Trollius ledebourii h see T.chinensis	
Trollius patulus	VO
Trollius pumilus	AP,B,G,JE,KL,SC,SG
Trollius ranunculinus	AP,B,SC,SG
Trollius riederanus	VO
Trollius x cultorum hyb early	B,JE
Trollius x cultorum hyb new	B,BY,C,JE
Trollius x cultorum mix	PK
Trollius x cultorum 'Orange Globe'	B,JE
Trollius yunnanensis	G,SC,SG
Tropaeoleum 'Clotted Cream'	PL
Tropaeoleum 'Fruit Bowl' mix	PL
Tropaeoleum 'Mulberry' Fool	PL
Tropaeolum 'Alaska' (V)	w.a.
Tropaeolum azureum	AP,B,J,P,PL,SC,SE,T
Tropaeolum 'Black Prince'	C
Tropaeolum ciliatum	AP,B,C,P,MN,N,PL,SC
Tropaeolum majus	CA,SG,SU
Tropaeolum majus 'Apricot Trifle'	PL,SE
Tropaeolum majus 'Cherry Rose'	DN,PI,V
Tropaeolum majus 'Collection'	U
Tropaeolum majus Dark Leaved mix	BS,DT,SK
Tropaeolum majus 'Empress Of India'	BD,BS,C,CN,DI,DT,F,J, KS,MO,PK,S,SK,SU,T, TH,V,YA
Tropaeolum majus fragrant giants	PK
Tropaeolum majus 'Gleam Golden'	B,BS,BY,J,KI
Tropaeolum m. 'Gleam Hybrids' semi-dbl	BD,BU,C,CA,CN,D,DN, DT,F,J,KI,L,MO,PI,ST, TU,YA
Tropaeolum majus 'Gleam Scarlet'	B,BS,BY,D,J,KI
Tropaeolum majus 'Glorious Gleam' dbl	BS,C,T,V
Tropaeolum majus 'Golden Emperor'	B,DT
Tropaeolum majus hyb dbl choice	BY
Tropaeolum majus 'Jewel Cherry Rose'	B,C,T
Tropaeolum majus 'Jewel Golden'	B
Tropaeolum majus 'Jewel Mahogany'	B
Tropaeolum majus 'Jewel' mix	AB,BS,BU,CA,CL,CN,D, DN,DT,F,J,JO,KI,M,MO, PI,S,SK,ST,TE,VY,YA
Tropaeolum majus 'Jewel of Africa'	B,BS,MO,SE,T
Tropaeolum majus 'Jewel Primrose'	B,D,DT
Tropaeolum majus 'Jewel Scarlet'	B
Tropaeolum majus mix dw semi-dbl	U
Tropaeolum majus mix tall	AB,BY,C,CO,D,HU,J,KI, M,MO,PI,ST,SU,T,U,VY
Tropaeolum majus mix trailing	BS,DT,F,FR,JO,T,TE,VH
Tropaeolum majus 'Moonlight'	B,F,SE
Tropaeolum m. 'Pineapples/Strawberries'	F
Tropaeolum majus 'Queen Of The Dwarfs'	B
Tropaeolum majus 'Raspberry Sorbet'	PL,SE
Tropaeolum majus 'Salmon Baby'	BS,DT,F,KS,U,V
Tropaeolum majus 'Strawberries/Cream'	PL,SE,T,V
Tropaeolum majus 'Strawberry Ice'	SE,T,VH
Tropaeolum majus 'Tip Top Apricot'	B,BD,BS,D,DT,F,MO,T
Tropaeolum majus 'Tip Top Gold'	B,F
Tropaeolum majus 'Tip Top Mahogany'	B,T,TE
Tropaeolum majus 'Tip Top' mix	D,DT,J,T
Tropaeolum majus 'Tip Top Scarlet'	B
Tropaeolum majus 'Tom Thumb'	BD,BS,BY,C,CN,CO,F, J,KI,R,S,ST,T,TH,TU,VH
Tropaeolum majus 'Top Fl Series'	KS
Tropaeolum majus 'Vesuvius'	B,C,PI

TROPAEOLUM

Tropaeolum majus 'Whirlybird Cherry'	B,BS,C,SE,SK,T,TE
Tropaeolum majus 'Whirlybird Cream'	B,BS,T,V
Tropaeolum majus 'Whirlybird Gold'	B,BS,C,SK,V
Tropaeolum majus 'Whirlybird Mahogany'	B,BS,C,SK
Tropaeolum majus 'Whirlybird' mix	B,BD,BS,CL,CO,D,DT,F, GO,J,KI,KS,L,MO,PI,PK, S,SE,SK,ST,TU,U,VH, VY,YA
Tropaeolum majus 'Whirlybird Orange'	B,BS,C,SK
Tropaeolum m. 'Whirlybird Peach Melba'	B,BD,BS,CL,DI,DT,F, KS,MO,SK,T,TE,U
Tropaeolum majus 'Whirlybird Scarlet'	B,B,BS,SK
Tropaeolum majus 'Whirlybird Tangerine'	B,BS,SK,V
Tropaeolum peltophorum	RS
Tropaeolum peltophorum 'Spitfire'	C
Tropaeolum peregrinum	w.a.
Tropaeolum polyphyllum	B,F,P,PL,PM,SC,SG,T
Tropaeolum 'Roulette'	C
Tropaeolum sessilifolium	AR
Tropaeolum speciosum	AP,B,C,N,P,PL,SE,SG,T
Tropaeolum tricolor	AR
Tropaeolum tricolorum	AP,AR,B,F,MN,P,PL,T
Tropaeolum 'Wina'	BS,CO
Trymalium ledifolium	B,NI,SA
Trymalium myrtillus	B,NI
Trymalium spathulatum	B,NI
Tsuga canadensis	C,CA,CG,FW,G,LN,NO, SA,VE
Tsuga canadensis 'Pendula'	B
Tsuga canadensis prov.south/north	B
Tsuga caroliniana	B,FW,LN,SA
Tsuga chinensis	B,EL,LN,SA
Tsuga diversifolia	B,CG,FW
Tsuga heterophylla	AB,B,C,CA,DD,FW,G,LN, NO,SA,VE
Tsuga mertensiana	AB,B,FW,LN,NO,SA
Tsuga sieboldii	B,FW
Tuberaria lignosa	AP,HP,RS,SC
Tulbaghia acutiloba	B,SI
Tulbaghia cepacea	MN
Tulbaghia dregeana	B,SI
Tulbaghia fragrans see T. simmleri	
Tulbaghia galpinii	AP,HP,KL,MN,SC
Tulbaghia 'John Rider'	B,BS,C,MO,T
Tulbaghia leucantha	B,SI
Tulbaghia ludwigiana	B,SI
Tulbaghia maritima	B,MN
Tulbaghia natalensis	AP,B,C,I,KL,SC
Tulbaghia simmleri	AP,HP,KL,MN,SC
Tulbaghia sp	KL,SI
Tulbaghia violacea	AP,B,G,HP,KL,RU,SA,SI
Tulbaghia violacea pallida	I,MN,NG
Tulbaghia violacea v alba	AP,B,MN
Tulipa acuminata	SG
Tulipa agenensis ssp boisseri	B
Tulipa altaica	KL
Tulipa armena v lycica	AR
Tulipa australis	MN
Tulipa batalinii see T.linifolia Batalinii Gr	
Tulipa biflora	AP,CG,PM,SG
Tulipa bifloriformis	AR,G,PM,RS
Tulipa butkovii	MN
Tulipa calleri	SG
Tulipa clusiana	AP,AR,B
Tulipa clusiana 'Cynthia'	AP,HP,PM
Tulipa clusiana v chrysantha	AP,B,RS,SC

Tulipa didieri	CG
Tulipa hageri	SG
Tulipa heterophylla	VO
Tulipa hissarica	KL
Tulipa humilis	AP,B,PM
Tulipa h. v pulch. Albocaerulea Oculata Gr	JE,KL,SC
Tulipa humilis Violacea Gr	B,KL
Tulipa iliensis	AP,AR,CG
Tulipa julia	AR,KL
Tulipa kaufmanniana	AP,G,JE,KL,SC
Tulipa kaufmanniana 'Aurea'	KL
Tulipa kaufmanniana 'Brilliant'	KL
Tulipa kaufmanniana 'Jeantine'	KL
Tulipa kaufmanniana 'Scarlet Elegance'	PM
Tulipa kolpakowskiana	AP,CG,G,SC
Tulipa linifolia Batalinii Gr	AP,CG,MN,SC,SG
Tulipa 'Madame Lefeber'	HP
Tulipa montana	AP,SC,SG
Tulipa ostrowskiana	SG
Tulipa platystigma	SG
Tulipa polychroma	AR,KL
Tulipa pulchella humilis see T.humilis	
Tulipa pulchella see T.humilis v pulchella Albocaerulea Oculata Gr	
Tulipa regelii	AR
Tulipa sarracenica	CG
Tulipa saxatilis	AP,B,SC
Tulipa schrenkii	SG
Tulipa scithica	SG
Tulipa sprengeri	AP,AR,B,C,G,JD,JE,KL,L, G,MN,NG,PA,PM,RH, SA,SC
Tulipa sprengeri Trotter's form	NG
Tulipa sylvestris	AP,AR,B,CG,G,I,JE,KL, SC,SG
Tulipa sylvestris ssp australis	CG
Tulipa tarda	AP,B,CG,G,JE,KL,LG, RS,PM,SC,SG
Tulipa tetraphylla	KL
Tulipa tschimganica	AR
Tulipa turkestanica	AP,CG,G,JE,KL,LG,PM, SC,SG
Tulipa undulatifolia	CG
Tulipa urumiensis	AP,CG,G,JE,KL,SC,SG
Tulipa violacea see T. humilis Violacea Gr.	
Tulipa vvedenskyi	AP,KL,LG,PM,SC,SG
Tulipa vvedenskyi 'Tangerine Beauty'	KL
Tupidanthus calyptrata	CA,EL,HA,SA
Turbina corymbosa	B
Turbinicarpus dickisoniae	DV
Turbinicarpus flaviflorus	B,DV,GC,Y
Turbinicarpus gracilis	B,DV,Y
Turbinicarpus gracilis v dickisonii	B
Turbinicarpus hoferi	BC,DV
Turbinicarpus jauernigi	DV
Turbinicarpus klinkerianus	B,DV,Y
Turbinicarpus krainzianus	B,DV,Y
Turbinicarpus krainzianus v minimus	DV
Turbinicarpus laui	B,CH,DV,Y
Turbinicarpus lophophoroides	B,DV,Y
Turbinicarpus macrochele	B,DV,Y
Turbinicarpus macrochele v El Fraile	DV
Turbinicarpus polaskii	B,DV,Y
Turbinicarpus pseudomacrochele	B,DV,Y
Turbinicarpus pseudopectinatus	B,Y
Turbinicarpus roseiflorus	Y
Turbinicarpus roseiflorus v albiflorus	Y

TURBINICARPUS

Turbinicarpus schmiedickianus see Neolloydia	
Turbinicarpus schwarzii	B,DV,Y
Turbinicarpus swobodae	B,DV,Y
Turbinicarpus valdezianus	B,Y
Turbinicarpus valdezianus v albiflorus	B
Turnera ulmifolia v angustifolia	B
Turpinia nepalensis	B
Turraea obtusifolia	B,C,KB,O,SI
Turricula parryi	B
Turritis glabra	B
Tussilago farfara	CG
Tweedia caerulea	AP,B,C,CG,EL,G,HP,PM, SA,SC,SG,T,U
Tylecodon buchholtziana	BC
Tylecodon cacaloides	B,KB
Tylecodon hallii	B,SI
Tylecodon paniculatus	B,CH,DV,KB,SI
Tylecodon papillaris ssp wallichii	B,CH,DV,KB,SI,Y
Tylecodon pearsonii	B,SI,Y
Tylecodon racemosus	B,KB
Tylecodon reticulatus	B,DV,SI,Y
Tylecodon ventricosus	B
Tylecodon wallichii ssp ecklonianus	B,SI
Tylophora indica	B
Tylosema esculentum	B,DD,SI
Typha angustifolia	C,DE,JE,SA
Typha capensis	B,SI
Typha latifolia	AB,C,JE,SA,SG
Typha laxmannii	B,JE,SG
Typha minima	G,JE,KL
Typha muelleri	B
Typha shuttleworthii	B,JE
Typhonium diversifolium	B
Uapaca kirkiana	B,SA
Uebelmannia crebispina HU642	DV
Uebelmannia flavispina HU361	B,DV
Uebelmannia gummifera	CH,DV
Uebelmannia meninensis HU108	B,DV
Uebelmannia meninensis HU281	DV
Uebelmannia meninensis v rubra HU406	B,DV
Uebelmannia pectinifera	B,DV
Uebelmannia pectinifera v multicostata	B,DV
Ugni molinae	B,SA,SG
Ulex europaeus	A,AP,B,C,FW,LN,SA,VE
Ulex europaeus nanus see U.minor	
Ulex minor	B,SA
Ulmus americana	B,C,CA,FW,LN,SA
Ulmus campestris	VE
Ulmus davidiana	B,SA
Ulmus glabra	B
Ulmus japonica	CA,LN,SA,SG
Ulmus parvifolia	B,C,CA,EL,FW,LN,N,SA, WA
Ulmus pumila	A,B,CA,FW,LN,N,SA, SG,VE
Umbellularia californica	B,CA,LN,SA
Umbilicus erectus	AP,B,DV
Umbilicus horizontalis	B,DV
Umbilicus rupestris	B,C,DV,PM,SC,SG
Uncinia divaricata	B,SS
Uncinia macrantha 'Robusta'	HP
Uncinia rubra	AP,B,HP,SC
Uncinia uncinata	B,SA,SG
Ungnadia speciosa	B,SW
Urena lobata ssp lobata	B
Urena lobata ssp sinuata	B

Urginea capitata	B,SI
Urginea fugax	B
Urginea fugax S.F62 Morocco	MN
Urginea macrocentra	B,SI
Urginea maritima	AP,B,HP,HU,SA
Urginea multisetosa	B,SI
Urginea olivieri	B
Urginea olivieri S.L250 Tunisia	MN
Urginea sanguinea	B,SI
Urginea sp	SI
Urginea undulata MS529 Spain	MN
Urginea undulata S.F279 Morocco	MN
Urginea undulata S.F321 Morocco	MN
Urginea undulata S.L323/251 Morocco	MN
Urginea undulata S.L340 Morocco	MN
Urochloa mosambicensis	B
Urodon dasyphyllus	B,NI
Urospermum delachampii	AP,HP,LG,SC
Ursinia abrotanifolia	B,SI
Ursinia anthemoides	B,J,KB,PI,SG,SK,T,V
Ursinia cakilefolia	B,KB,SI
Ursinia calenduliflora	B,C,KB,SI
Ursinia chrysanthemoides	B,SI
Ursinia nana	B,SI
Ursinia paleacea	B,SI
Ursinia pulcherrima 'Solar Fire'	S
Ursinia sericea	B,SI
Ursinia sp	C,SI
Ursinia speciosa	B,C,KB,SI
Ursinia tenuiloba	B,SI
Ursinia tenuiloba v montana	C
Urtica cannabina	SG
Urtica dioica	B,CN,HU,SG,SU
Urtica galeopsifolia	B
Urtica incisa	DD
Urtica kioviensis	B
Urtica urens	B,HU
Utricularia alpina	B,DV
Utricularia arenaria	B
Utricularia benthamii	B
Utricularia bifida	B
Utricularia biloba	B
Utricularia bisquamata	B,DV
Utricularia caerulea	B
Utricularia calycifida	B
Utricularia capilliflora	B
Utricularia chrysantha	B,DV
Utricularia delicatula	B
Utricularia dichotoma	B
Utricularia endressii	B
Utricularia fistulosa	B
Utricularia hamiltonii	B
Utricularia helix	B
Utricularia hispida	B
Utricularia inaequalis	B,DV
Utricularia kamienskii	B
Utricularia kimberleyensis	B,DV
Utricularia lasiocaulis	B,DV
Utricularia lateriflora	B
Utricularia laxa	B
Utricularia leptoplectra	B,DV
Utricularia limosa	B,DV
Utricularia livida	B
Utricularia longifolia	B,DV
Utricularia menziesii	B
Utricularia monanthos	B

UTRICULARIA

Utricularia nigrescens	B
Utricularia novae-zelandiae	B
Utricularia odorata	B
Utricularia parthenopipes	B
Utricularia pusilla	B
Utricularia quinquedentata	B
Utricularia reniformis	B
Utricularia simplex	B
Utricularia simulans	B
Utricularia subulata	B,DV
Utricularia subulata f cleistogama	B
Utricularia tridactyla	B
Utricularia tridentata	B
Utricularia triflora	B,DV
Utricularia uliginosa	B
Utricularia violacea	B,DV
Utricularia volubilis	B
Uvularia grandiflora	AP,B,HP,SC
Vaccaria hispanica	B,SG
Vaccaria hispanica 'Florist Rose'	B
Vaccaria hispanica 'Florist Snow'	B
Vaccaria hispanica 'Pink Beauty'	B,V
Vaccaria hispanica 'White Beauty'	B
Vaccinium angustifolium	SG
Vaccinium corymbosum	B,FW,SA
Vaccinium macrocarpon	B,FW
Vaccinium membranaceum	AB,B,C,LN,NO
Vaccinium myrtillus	B,C,FW,JE,LN,PO,SA, SG
Vaccinium ovatum	AB,B,C,NO
Vaccinium padifolium	B
Vaccinium parvifolium	AB,B,C,LN,NO,SG
Vaccinium scoparium	NO
Vaccinium uliginosum	C,KL,SG
Vaccinium vitis-idaea	B,C,FW,JE,PO,SA,SG
Valeriana coccinea	BS,CO,KI,ST
Valeriana montana	B,CG,G
Valeriana officinalis	B,BH,BY,C,CN,DD,G,HP, HU,JE,KS,SA,SG,TH
Valeriana officinalis 'Anthos'	B
Valeriana officinalis 'Select'	B
Valeriana saliunca	B
Valeriana 'St.George'	U
Valeriana tripteris	B
Vancouveria hexandra	B,SC,SG
Vanda tricolor	B
Vanguieria edulis	EL,SA
Vangueria esculenta	BH,KB
Vangueria infausta	B,KB,SI
Vangueria madagascariensis	B
Vanheerdia angusta	B,DV
Vanheerdia divergens	B,DV,SI,Y
Vanheerdia primosii	B,DV,SI,Y
Vanheerdia roodiae	B,DV,SI,Y
Vanilla planifolia	B
Vatricania guentheri	B,DV,Y
Veitchia joannis	B,CA
Veitchia macdanielsii	B,CA
Veitchia merrillii	B,CA,EL,O,SA
Veitchia montgomeryana	B,CA,O
Veitchia winin	B
Vella spinosa	SC
Velleia discophora	B,CB,NI,SI
Velleia rosea	B,C,NI,O,SA
Velleia trinervis	B,NI,O
Veltheimia bracteata	AP,B,CF,DV,KB,LG,O,RU
	,SC,SI
Veltheimia capensis (viridiflora h.)	NG
Venegasia carpesoides	B
Venidium see Arctotis	
Ventilago maderaspatana	B
Ventilago viminalis	B,HA,NI,O,SA
Vepris lanceolata	B,KB,SI,WA
Veratrum album	B,BS,C,CG,HP,JE,SA,SG
Veratrum album ssp lobelianum	CG,G
Veratrum californicum	B,G,JE,SC
Veratrum lobelianum	SG
Veratrum maackii	SG
Veratrum nigrum	AP,B,C,G,HP,HU,JE,KL, LG,SA,SC,SG
Veratrum ussuriensis MW56R	X
Veratrum viride	AP,B,C,HP,JE,SA,SG
Verbascum adzurmericum	AP,SC,SE,T
Verbascum agrimanifolia ssp agriman.	T
Verbascum arcturus	G,HP,KL,SC,SG
Verbascum austriacum	CG
Verbascum bakerianum	C,SG
Verbascum blattaria	AP,B,BH,C,CP,DD,E,G, HP,HU,KL,SC,SG,T,V
Verbascum blattaria f albiflorum	B,C,E,HP,V
Verbascum blattaria f purpureum	KL
Verbascum blattaria Pink form	HP,T
Verbascum blattaria yellow	HP
Verbascum bombyciferum	AP,C,HP
Verbascum bombyciferum 'Polarsommer'	B,C,CL,CN,JE,JO,MO, SA,SK,T,V
Verbascum bombyciferum 'Silver Lining'	T
Verbascum chaixii	AP,B,BH,F,G,HP,JE,SC
Verbascum chaixii 'Cotswold King'	HP
Verbascum chaixii 'Cotswold Queen'	HP
Verbascum chaixii f album	AP,B,C,G,HP,I,JE,KS,PL, PM,RM,SC,SP,T,V
Verbascum chaixii 'Gainsborough'	HP,P
Verbascum chaixii 'Pink Domino'	AP,B,HP,P
Verbascum Cotswold Gr	KL
Verbascum creticum	E,SC
Verbascum densiflorum	B,C,G,HU,JE,SA,SG
Verbascum dumulosum	B,HP,SC,SG
Verbascum eremobium	B
Verbascum f1 'Southern Charm'	T
Verbascum Harkness Hybrids mix	BY
Verbascum hybridum 'Silberkandelaber'	JE
Verbascum hybridum 'Spica'	B,JE
Verbascum hybridum 'Wega'	JE
Verbascum longifolium	B,C,JE
Verbascum lychnitis	AP,B,C,G,HP
Verbascum nigrum	AP,B,BH,C,G,HP,LA,JE, RS,SA,SC,SG,SU
Verbascum nigrum 'Album'	B,C,JE,SA
Verbascum olympicum	AP,B,C,CP,E,G,HP,HU,J E,L,SA,SC,T
Verbascum phlomoides	B,BH,C,HP,RS
Verbascum phoeniceum	AP,B,C,CP,DD,DE,E,F,HP, J,JE,KI,KL,KS,MA,RM, SA,SC,SG,ST,SU,V
Verbascum phoeniceum 'Album'	HP,KL
Verbascum phoeniceum o-p hyb	HU
Verbascum phoeniceum 'Roseum'	KL
Verbascum phoenicium 'Flush of White'	BS,C,F,JE,KI,PL
Verbascum phoenicium hyb mix	BD,BS,C,CL,DT,L,MO,T
Verbascum phoenicium 'White Bride'	B
Verbascum pulverulentum	B,SG

VERBASCUM

Verbascum pyramidatum	B,G,JE,SA,SC
Verbascum roripifolia	B,C,HP,JE,SA
Verbascum 'Silver Candelabrum'	B
Verbascum 'Sunset Shades'	D,U
Verbascum thapsus	AP,B,C,CN,CO,CP,DD,E, HP,HU,LA,PM,SA,SG, TH
Verbascum undulatum	B
Verbascum virgatum	B,G,HU,SG
Verbascum 'Wega'	B
Verbascum wiedemannianum	AP,B,HP,KL,KS,RM,T
Verbena 'Adonis' s-c	BS,PL,S
Verbena 'Appleblossom'	S
Verbena atenuisecta	HW
Verbena aublieta perfecta	MO
Verbena bipinnatifida	B
Verbena bonariensis	AB,B,BS,C,CN,DI,F,G, HP,HU,JE,JO,MO,PI,PK, SA,SC,SZ,T,TH,V
Verbena canadensis	B,G
Verbena canadensis 'Compacta'	DT,F,V
Verbena canadensis 'Toronto'	B,BS
Verbena 'Celebration Mix'	U
Verbena 'Crown Jewels'	U
Verbena 'Derby' mix	BD,BS,CL,CN,J,MO,S, TU,YA
Verbena 'Derby' s-c	BS
Verbena encelioides	T
Verbena 'Garden Party' mix	CL
Verbena giant mix	S
Verbena gooddingii	B
Verbena hastata	AP,B,BH,C,CN,CP,G,HP, HU,JE,KL,PR,SA,SC,T
Verbena hastata 'Alba'	B,HP
Verbena 'Highlight' mix	S
Verbena Ideal Florist mix	BD,BS,PI,SE
Verbena 'Imagination'	B,BD,BS,CL,CO,DT,F,G, J,KI,L,M,MO,O,PK,S,SE, SK,ST,U,V,YA
Verbena lilacina	B
Verbena 'Misty'	U
Verbena nivalis nivea	HP
Verbena 'Novalis' mix	BD,BS,CL,DT,J,KI,L,MO, R,S,SK,YA
Verbena 'Novalis' primed seed	SK
Verbena 'Novalis' s-c	B,BS,CL,MO,SK
Verbena officinalis	C,CN,CP,G,KS,SA,SG, TH
Verbena 'Peaches & Cream'	B,BD,BS,C,CL,CN,D,F, T,J,KI,L,MO,O,PK,R,S, SE,SK,V,VH,VY,YA
Verbena 'Perfecta'	C,CL
Verbena peruviana	HP
Verbena polaris	B,DI,HU,PK
Verbena 'Quartz'	BS,CL,D
Verbena rigida	AP,B,BS,C,CL,G,HP,MO, PK,T
Verbena rigida 'Lilacina'	B
Verbena rigida 'Venosa'	DE,J,KS,V
Verbena 'Romance Lavender'	BS,SE,SK,V
Verbena 'Romance' mix	BS,CA,F,MO,PK,S,SK, VY
Verbena 'Romance Pastel' mix	BS,MO
Verbena 'Romance' s-c	BS,PL,SK
Verbena 'Sandy' mix	BS,KI,YA
Verbena 'Sandy' s-c	BS,CL,D,MO

Verbena scabra	B
Verbena 'Showtime'	BS,T
Verbena 'Sparkle' mix	CO,KI,M,TU
Verbena 'Sparkle' s-c	B
Verbena 'Sterling Star' mix	BD,BS,MO,PK
Verbena stricta	B,JE,PR
Verbena tenuisecta	B,C,JE,SA,V
Verbena tridens	AU
Verbena urticifolia	B,CP,KL
Verbena venosa see V.rigida	
Verbena 'Violet Profusion'	C
Verbena x hybrida 'Amour Light Pink'	T
Verbena x hybrida 'Amour' mix	PK
Verbena x hybrida 'Blaze'	T
Verbena x hybrida 'Blue Lagoon'	B,BS,CL,D,MO,T,U
Verbena x hybrida 'Dw Jewels'	T
Verbena x hybrida 'Mammoth'	BS,C,KI,MC,SG,ST,VH
Verbena x hybrida mix	BY,FR,TH
Verbena x hybrida 'Olympia'	BD,BS,C,J,MO
Verbena x hybrida pendula 'Elegance'	BS,F
Verbena x hybrida 'Raspberry Crush'	T
Verbena x hybrida 'Sweet Dreams'	F
Verbesina alternifolia	B
Verbesina alternifolia 'Goldstrahl'	JE
Verbesina encelioides	B,DD,G,SG
Verbesina occidentalis	B
Vernonia altissima	B,NT
Vernonia amygdalina	B,SI
Vernonia anthelmintica	B
Vernonia arkansana	NT
Vernonia baldwinii	B
Vernonia crinita	HP,JE
Vernonia fasciculata	B,JE,PR
Vernonia hirsuta	B,SI
Vernonia mespilifolia	B,BH,KB
Vernonia missurica	B,PR
Vernonia natalensis	B,KB
Vernonia neocorymbosa	B,SI
Vernonia noveboracensis	B,C,CP,G,JE,PR
Vernonia noveboracensis 'Albiflora'	JE
Vernonia oligocephala	B,SI
Veronica agrestis	B
Veronica allionii	KL
Veronica alpina	B,G,KL,SC
Veronica anagalis-aquatica	SG
Veronica aphylla	KL
Veronica arvensis	B
Veronica arvensis 'Chedglow' (V)	B,NS
Veronica austriaca	B,SG
Veronica austriaca ssp teucrium	AP,BS,HP,KI,SG
Veronica austriaca ssp teuc. 'Royal Blue'	B,C,DE,JE,L,PK,SA
Veronica au. ssp teucr. 'Crater Lake Blue'	T
Veronica bachofenii	T
Veronica beccabunga	B,SA
Veronica bellidioides	B,JE
Veronica bombycina ssp bolkardaghensis	KL
Veronica caespitosa	B,JE
Veronica cf macrostachya	RM
Veronica chamaedrys	B,C,CN,SU,TH
Veronica cuneifolia v cuneifolia	RM
Veronica cymbalaria	B
Veronica dentata	SG
Veronica dillenii	SG
Veronica fruticans	AP,B,C,CG,G,JE,KL,P, RM,SC
Veronica fruticulosa	AP,B,C,G,HP,JE,SG

268

VERONICA

Veronica gentianoides	AP,C,F,G,HP,JE,KL,PK, SA,SC,SE,SG,T,VO
Veronica gutheriana	AP,B,JE
Veronica hederifolia	B
Veronica incana see V. spicata ssp i.	
Veronica japonica	KL
Veronica latifolia royal blue	HU
Veronica longifolia	AP,B,C,G,HP,JE,RH,SA, SC,SG
Veronica longifolia 'Alba'	B,C,JE,SA
Veronica longifolia 'Oxford Blue'	DT,F
Veronica longifolia pink shades	B,BS,C,F,JE,KI,PK
Veronica minuta v glabrata	VO
Veronica minuta v minuta	VO
Veronica mix	T
Veronica officinalis	B,C,JE,SG
Veronica ornata	CG
Veronica peregrina	B
Veronica perfoliata see Parahebe	
Veronica persica	B
Veronica polita	B
Veronica prostrata	AP,B,JE,KL,SC
Veronica reptans	B,BS,C,J,JE,SA
Veronica satureioides	AP,B,C,KL,SC
Veronica schmidtiana	AP,G,KL,SG
Veronica scutellata	B,SG
Veronica serpyllifolia	B,SG
Veronica 'Shirley Blue'	B,BS,C,HP
Veronica sp	kL
Veronica spicata	AB,AP,B,BD,BS,C,CN,F, G,HP,JE,KS,MO,PI,RH, RM,SA,SC,SG,SK,SU,V
Veronica spicata 'Alba'	B,JE,SA
Veronica spicata Best Blue	JE
Veronica spicata 'Blue Bouquet'	CL,D,JE,MO,U
Veronica spicata blue spikes	HU
Veronica spicata 'Erika' (rosea)	B,C,DE,SA
Veronica spicata hybrida	NS
Veronica spicata red variations	JE
Veronica spicata 'Rosenrot'	JE,KL
Veronica spicata 'Sightseeing'	B,BD,BS,C,CL,CN,D,DE, DT,F,J,JE,JO,L,MO,PK, SK,U,V
Veronica spicata ssp incana	AP,B,BS,C,CL,F,JE,KL,L, MO,SA,SG,T
Veronica spicata ssp incana 'Silbersee'	B,JE
Veronica spicata ssp minor	B,JE,SA,T
Veronica spicata v nana 'Blue Carpet'	BS,C,JE,KI,PK
Veronica subsessilis	G
Veronica subsessilis 'Blue Pyramid'	JE
Veronica surculosa	VO
Veronica teucrium see V.austriaca ssp t.	
Veronica urticifolia	B,JE
Veronica virginica see Veronicastrum virginicum	
Veronicastrum sibiricum v japonicum	AP,B,SG
Veronicastrum sibiricum v jap. 'Album'	B
Veronicastrum virginicum	AP,B,C,DD,G,HP,HU, JE,P,PR,RH,SA,SG
Veronicastrum virginicum 'Alboroseum'	B,JE,SA
Veronicastrum virginicum album	AP,B,G,JE
Veronicastrum virginicum roseum see V. v. v incarnatum	
Veronicastrum virginicum v incarnatum	AP,B,JE
Verticordia acerosa	B,NI
Verticordia brachypoda	B,NI
Verticordia chrysantha	B
Verticordia chrysantha v preissii	AU,B,NI

Verticordia densiflora	B,NI,O,SA
Verticordia eriocephala	B,O
Verticordia fimbrilepis	B,NI
Verticordia forrestii	B,NI,O
Verticordia grandiflora	B,NI,O
Verticordia grandis	B
Verticordia huegelii	SA
Verticordia huegelii v decumbens	B,NI
Verticordia huegelii v huegelii	B,NI
Verticordia insignis	B,NI
Verticordia lindleyi	B,O
Verticordia monodelpha	B,NI
Verticordia muellerana	B,NI,O
Verticordia nitens	B,C,EL,NI,O,SA
Verticordia ovalifolia aff	B,NI
Verticordia pennigera	B,NI
Verticordia pennigera v prostrata	B
Verticordia picta	B,NI,O
Verticordia plumosa	B,NI,O
Verticordia preissii	O
Verticordia roei	B,NI,O
Verticordia serrata	B,NI,O
Vestia foetida	AP,B,C,HP,LG,P,SG
Viburnum acerifolium	B,FW,LN,SA
Viburnum betulifolium	B,RH,SA
Viburnum carlesii	B,HP,SC,SA
Viburnum cassinoides	B,G
Viburnum cotinifolium	A,SA
Viburnum dentatum	B,FW,LN,SA
Viburnum dilatatum	B,FW,G,LN,SA
Viburnum edule	A,NO
Viburnum erubescens	B
Viburnum furcatum	DD,SA
Viburnum henryi	B,SA
Viburnum ichangense	B,C,FW,SA
Viburnum lantana	B,C,FW,KL,LN,SA,SU, VE,VO
Viburnum lentago	A,B,FW,LN,SA
Viburnum macrocephalum	LN,SA
Viburnum odoratissimum	SA
Viburnum opulus	A,B,C,CA,FW,HU,LN,P, O,RH,RS,SA,SC,SU,VE
Viburnum opulus 'Compactum'	HP
Viburnum opulus 'Xanthocarpum'	B,HP
Viburnum orientale	B
Viburnum plicatum f tomentosum	B
Viburnum prunifolium	A,B,FW,LN,SA
Viburnum rhytidophyllum	B,C,FW,LN,SA,VE
Viburnum rufidulum	A,B,LN
Viburnum sargentii	B,FW,LN,SA
Viburnum setigerum	B,FW,LN,SA
Viburnum setigerum 'Aurantiacum'	B,FW,SA
Viburnum sieboldii	B,FW,LN,SA
Viburnum tinus	B,C,FW,HP,LN,SA,VE
Viburnum trilobum	A,B,FW,G,LN,SA
Viburnum trilobum 'Wentworth'	B,LN,SA
Viburnum wrightii	B,G,SA
Vicia alpestris	VO
Vicia americana	B
Vicia angustifolia see V.sativa ssp nigra	
Vicia benghalensis	B
Vicia cracca	B,C,HU,LA,SU
Vicia dasycarpa	B
Vicia ervilia	B
Vicia gigantea	B,C
Vicia hirsuta	B,DE,LA

VICIA

Vicia narbonensis	B
Vicia orobus	AP,HP,KL
Vicia palaestina	B
Vicia peregrina	B
Vicia sativa	B,C,LA
Vicia sativa ssp nigra	B,HA
Vicia sepium	B,LA
Vicia sylvatica	AP,B,SU
Vicia tenuifolia	CG
Vicia tetrasperma	B
Vicia unijuga	KL
Vigna aconitifolia	B,HU
Vigna angularis	DD
Vigna caracalla	B,HA
Vigna marina	DD
Vigna mungo	DD
Vigna umbellata	B
Vigna unguiculata	B
Vigna unguiculata cvs	B,DD
Vigna unguiculata ssp unguiculata	SI
Vigna vexillata	B
Viguiera deltoidea v parishii	B
Viguiera laciniata	B
Viguiera lanata	B
Viguiera multiflora	B,JE,NO
Vila aetolica	JE
Villarsia calthifolia	B,NI
Villarsia capensis	B,SI
Villarsia parnassifolia	B,NI
Viminaria denudata see V.juncea	
Viminaria juncea	B,C,DD,EL,HA,HU,NI, O,SA
Vinca minor	B
Vinca minor 'Argentovariegata'	B
Vincetoxicum hirundinaria	B,CG,G,JE,PO
Vincetoxicum nigrum	B,CG,G,HP,SC
Vincetoxicum officinale see V.hirundinaria	
Vincetoxicum pannonicum	B,SG
Vincetoxicum scandens	B
Viola adunca	AP,HP,SZ
Viola adunca 'Alba'	HP
Viola aetolica	AP,B,C,KL
Viola alba	B,C,G,HP,JE,SA
Viola alpina	KL
Viola arborescens	KL
Viola 'Arkwright's Ruby'	B,BS,BY,C,CL,L,MO,SA, SK,T
Viola arvensis	B,C,CG,LA
Viola 'Azurella'	B,BS,JE,MO
Viola 'Baby Franjo'	B,BS,BY,C,J,JE,MO,SA, U,V
Viola 'Baby Heather'	U
Viola 'Baby Lucia'	B,BD,BS,BY,C,J,JE,MO, SA,V
Viola 'Bambini'	BD,BS,BY,C,CN,F,J,JE, KS,L,MO,U,V
Viola bedding mix	S
Viola bertolinii	AP,HP,KL
Viola betonicifolia	AP,B,C,HP,NI,O
Viola betonicifolia albescens	P
Viola biflora	AP,B,CG,SC
Viola 'Bijou'	BS,KI
Viola 'Black Star'	J
Viola 'Black Velvet'	BS
Viola 'Blackjack'	BS,BY,F,L,MO,SK,VY
Viola 'Blaue Schonheit'	JE

Viola 'Blaue von Paris'	JE
Viola 'Blue Gem'	B,SA
Viola 'Blue Moon'	S
Viola 'Blue Perfection'	B,BS,BY,CL,JE,L,MO, PI,SA,SK
Viola 'Bluebird'	T
Viola Bolton's Superb Giant Strain	BO
Viola 'Bowles Black'	AP,B,BS,CL,JE,P,PK,PL, SC,SE,SU,T,V
Viola bubanii	KL
Viola calcarata	AP,B,JE,KL,SC,SA,VO
Viola canadensis	B,CG,SC,SW
Viola canina	CG
Viola 'Carpathian Spring'	B,C,JE
Viola celaminiera	CG
Viola cenisia	B,SC
Viola chaerophylloides see V.dissecta v c.	
Viola 'Chantreyland'	B,BS,BY,C,CL,JE,L,MO, SA,SK,T
Viola 'Charlotte'	B,P
Viola 'Columbine'	P
Viola comollia	B
Viola conspersa	PR
Viola 'Cornetto'	B,BD,BY,C,CN,F,JE,MO, SA
Viola cornuta	AP,B,CG,DN,G,HP,HW, KL,PM,SA
Viola cornuta 'Admiration'	B,BS,BY,C,JE,SK
Viola cornuta Alba Gr	AP,HP,SC
Viola cornuta 'Alba Minor'	AP,KL,P
Viola cornuta Collection	U
Viola cornuta hyb mix	FR
Viola cornuta hyb violet	FR
Viola cornuta lg fl mix	DE,F,MO
Viola cornuta Lilacina Group	AP,HP
Viola cornuta 'Lutea Splendens'	B,BS,CL,JE,PI
Viola cornuta maroon picotee	BS,BY,MO
Viola cornuta 'Minor'	AP,B,G,P,SC
Viola cornuta mix	SK
Viola cornuta 'Monarch Mix'	BS,DT,J
Viola cornuta 'Painted Black'	B,BD,BS,MO,SA
Viola cornuta 'Prince Henry'	B,BD,BS,BY,C,CL,CN, DT,MO,SU,W,U,YA
Viola cornuta purple picotee	BS,BY,MO
Viola cornuta 'Splendens'	SK
Viola 'Coronation Gold'	J
Viola corsica	AP,B,C,G,HP,JE,P,SC,SZ
Viola cotyledon	P
Viola cucullata striata 'Alba'	SE,T,V
Viola cunninghamii	B,SS
Viola 'Cuty'	B,BS,BY,CL,MO,PK,T,U
Viola declinata	CG,P
Viola declinata 'Melton Sapphire'	T
Viola dissecta v chaerophylloides	AP,CG,SC
Viola diversifolia	VO
Viola dubyana	AP,B,KL,SC
Viola elatior (erecta)	AP,B,C,CG,G,HP,I,KL, NG,P,PA,SC
Viola elegantula	KL
Viola eriocarpa	PR
Viola 'Evening Glow'	C
Viola ex 'Bowles Black'	RM
Viola f1 'Alpine Sky'	BS
Viola f1 'Alpine Spring'	BS,MO
Viola f1 'Alpine Summer'	BS,J,L,MO,V
Viola f1 'Alpine Sun'	BS

VIOLA

Viola f1 'Alpine Wing'	BS,MO
Viola f1 'Azure Blue'	S
Viola f1 'Bravissimo'	C
Viola f1 'Eclipse'	S
Viola f1 'Fanfare Mix'	BS,EL,L,MO,U
Viola f1 'Giant Fancy mix'	S
Viola f1 'Penny Series' s-c	CL,SE
Viola f1 'Skyline' s-c,mix	BS
Viola f1 'Sorbet Series' mix	BS,CA,CL,DT,KS,L,MO, PK,SE,SK,T,YA
Viola f1 'Sorbet Series' s-c	BS,DT,F,KS,MO,PK,PL, SK,T,VH
Viola f1 'Splendid' s-c	BS,YA
Viola f1 'Velour Blue'	BS,BY,CL,F,MO,O,SK, T,U,YA
Viola f1 'Velour' blue/blotch	BS,SK
Viola f1 'Velour Mix'	BS,F,MO,SK,U
Viola f1 'Velour Purple'	BS,BY,CL,MO,SK,U,YA
Viola f1 'Velour' white	BS,SK
Viola f1 'Velour' yellow	BS,SK
Viola f2 'Saint Tropez' mix	SK
Viola f2 'Toyland'	BS,BY,C,CL,MO
Viola 'Fancy Shades' mix	S
Viola 'Felix'	BS,D,DT,MO,SK
Viola 'Flame'	BY,C
Viola 'Funny Face'	D
Viola 'Glacier Ice'	BS,CO
Viola gracilis (velutina)	B,C,JE
Viola 'Green Jade'	P
Viola grisebachiana	KL,VO
Viola grypoceras v exilis	AP,B,P,SC
Viola hederacea	B
Viola hirta	AP,B,C,JE
Viola hybrida 'Blue Shades'	T
Viola issonensis	P
Viola jaubertiana	AP,CG
Viola 'Jersey Gem'	BY
Viola 'Johnny-jump-up'	B,BD,BS,BU,BY,C,CL, CN,DE,DN,F,GO,HU,JE, KI,KS,L,MO,PI,PK,SA, SE,VY
Viola jooi	AP,C,CG,G,I,JE,KL,SA
Viola jordanii	CG
Viola 'Juliette' mix	BS,D
Viola keiskei	AP,P
Viola 'King Henry'	B,JE,KS,SA,SK
Viola kitaibeliana	CG
Viola koreana see V.grypoceras v exilis	
Viola labradorica	AP,B,BH,C,JE,PL,SA, SC,T,TH
Viola labradorica v purpurea see V.riviniana Purpure Gr	
Viola lanceolata	AP,G,RS,SC
Viola lutea	AP,G,SC,W
Viola macedonica see V.tricolor ssp m.	
Viola macloskeyi v pallens	P
Viola maculata	CG
Viola mandshurica	AP,SA,SC
Viola mandshurica 'Grandiflora'	JE
Viola mirabilis	C,JE,SC
Viola nephrophylla	B,SW
Viola nigra	C,G,SA
Viola nipponica	KL
Viola obliqua see V.cucullata	
Viola ocucullata	B,JE
Viola odorata	AB,AP,B,BH,BS,C,CG, CN,CO,G,GO,HU,JE,KI, SA,ST,SU,TH,V
Viola odorata 'Alba'	B,CN
Viola odorata 'Czar'	B,BY,C,PK,SA,T
Viola odorata 'Empress Augusta'	B
Viola odorata 'Princesse de Galles'	T
Viola odorata 'Queen Charlotte'	B,BS,C,CN,DT,F,HU,JE, MO,PK,S,SA
Viola odorata 'Sulphurea'	AP,B,HU,JE,PL,T
Viola odorata 'Vilmoriniana'	B,C
Viola palmata	B,CG,G,JE,SA
Viola palmata x loveliana	P
Viola palustris	B
Viola 'Pariser' s-c	JE
Viola pedata	AP,B,G,JE,KL,PR,SC
Viola pedatifida	B,C,JE,KL
Viola 'Peppered Palms'	P
Viola pinnata	AP,CG,G,JE,SC
Viola 'Pretty'	BS,BY,C,JE,MO,U
Viola 'Prince John'	B,BS,BY,C,CL,CN,DE,L, MO,SU,SA,YA
Viola 'Prince William'	YA
Viola 'Princess' mix	BS,CL,D,DI,DT,KI,KS, MO,PL,SK
Viola 'Princess' s-c	BS,BY,CL,D,JE,L,MO, SK,U,Y
Viola pubescens	AP,B,P
Viola 'Purple Blaze'	B,SA
Viola pyrenaica	KL
Viola 'Raspberry Rose'	CG,JE,V
Viola reichenbachiana	B,C,JE
Viola reichi RB94126-94131	P
Viola riviniana	AP,B,C,CN,TH
Viola riviniana pink	B
Viola riviniana 'Purpurea'	AP,B,C,G,HP,I,P,SC,SU
Viola 'Roccoco' frilled	C,J,V
Viola 'Rodney Davey' (V)	AP,B,G,P,T
Viola rupestris	CG,G
Viola rupestris 'Rosea'	AP,B,JE,KL,P,T
Viola 'Sawyer's Black'	BS,C,CN,SU
Viola 'Scottish Hybrids'	BS,PK,SE,VY
Viola selkirkii	AP,B,P
Viola small fl	BS,L
Viola sororia	B,C,JE,SC,T
Viola sororia 'Albiflora'	B,G,JE,PL,SA
Viola sororia 'Freckles'	AP,B,BD,BS,BY,C,CO,JE, KI,L,MO,PK,PL,SA,SE,T, V
Viola sororia 'Rubra'	B,C,JE,T
Viola sp	AB,AP,BH
Viola stojanovii	AP,HP,KL
Viola Striped	SE
Viola suavis	CG
Viola 'Sunbeam'	BS,CL,MO,S,SE,SK,V
Viola 'Sunbeam & Blackjack'	SE
Viola 'Sunbeam, pale blue wing'	BS
Viola 'Sylettas'	T
Viola 'Symphonia'	KI,ST
Viola tricolor	AB,AP,B,BH,C,CN,CO, DE,DI,F,G,LA,SC,SU,T, TH,V
Viola tricolor 'Black'	B,CG,TH
Viola tricolor 'Blue Elf'	JO
Viola tricolor ssp curtisii	TH
Viola tricolor ssp macedonica	C,CG
Viola tridentata	AU
Viola 'Trimardeau' mix	C

VIOLA

Name	Code
Viola 'Ulla'	JE
Viola 'Velour Purple/White'	BS
Viola verecunda v yakusimana	AP,RM
Viola viarum	HP
Viola 'White Perfection'	B,BS,BY,C,CL,JE,L,MO,SA,SK,T
Viola x witt 'Aalsmeer Giant' mix	B,C,DE
Viola x witt 'Adonis'	PI
Viola x witt 'Amsterdam Giants'	BS
Viola x witt 'Aquarelle'	F
Viola x witt 'Atlas Series'	BS,VY
Viola x witt 'Beaconsfield'	BY,CA,PI
Viola x witt 'Black'	C,DE,DI
Viola x witt 'Black Devil'	SE
Viola x witt 'Black Pansy'	C,T,V
Viola x witt 'Blue Bird'	BS
Viola x witt 'Bravissimo' mix	FR
Viola x witt bronze tones	PI
Viola x witt 'Brown's Prizewinner'	BS
Viola x witt 'Brunig'	T
Viola x witt 'Burgundy laced Picotee'	PL
Viola x witt 'Butterfly' mix	PL
Viola x witt 'Celestial Queen'	BS,BY
Viola x witt 'Challenge Improved' s-c	R
Viola x witt 'Citrus Ice'	U
Viola x witt 'Clarion' s-c o-p	YA
Viola x witt 'Clear Sky Primrose'	T
Viola x witt 'Crown Exhibition'	BS
Viola x witt 'Delft'	CA
Viola x witt 'Dobies Emperor Strain'	D
Viola x witt 'Dream' mix	BS,BY,L,MO
Viola x witt 'Dream' s-c	BS,BY,MO
Viola x witt 'Early Flowering'	D,DT,F
Viola x witt 'Eclipse'	F
Viola x witt 'Engelmann's Mix'	BS,DT
Viola x witt f1 'Allegro' mix	DT,F,S
Viola x witt f1 'Banner Series'	CL
Viola x witt f1 'Berries and Buttermilk'	SE
Viola x witt f1 'Bingo' mix	SK,T
Viola x witt f1 'Bingo' s-c, mix	SK
Viola x witt f1 'Black Beauty'	D,S
Viola x witt f1 'Black Star'	BS
Viola x witt f1 'Challenge' s-c, mix	BS
Viola x witt f1 'Clear Crystal' black	B,KS,SK
Viola x witt f1 'Clear Crystals mix'	B,BS,BY,F,J,KI,S,SK,ST,SU,T,TU,U,V
Viola x witt f1 'Clear Crystals' s-c	HU,SK
Viola x witt f1 'Crown' mix	B,BS,MO
Viola x witt f1 'Crown' s-c	B,BS,MO
Viola x witt f1 'Crystal Bowl' mix	C,CA,JO,L,PK,SK
Viola x witt f1 'Crystal Bowl' s-c	SK
Viola x witt f1 'Delia Mix'	U
Viola x witt f1 'Delta' s-c, mix	BS,SK
Viola x witt f1 'Early Giants mix'	BD,BS,MO
Viola x witt f1 'Easter Parade'	U
Viola x witt f1 'Happy Face' mix	BS,MO,S
Viola x witt f1 'Happy Face' s-c	BS,MO
Viola x witt f1 'Imperial Antique Shades'	BS,CL,D,L,MO,PK,SK,T
Viola x witt f1 'Imperial Princess Gold'	BS,CL,L,MO,O,S,V
Viola x witt f1 'Imperial Series' mix	BS,CA,MO
Viola x witt f1 'Imperial Series' s-c	BS,BY,CL,L,MO,PK,PL,SK,T,U,V
Viola x witt f1 'Iona'	PL
Viola x witt f1 'Loyal Colours' s-c,mix	BS
Viola x witt f1 'Loyal King & Queen' mix	BS,R
Viola x witt f1 'Loyal King & Queen' s-c	BS
Viola x witt f1 'Majestic Giants'	BS,BY,C,CA,CL,CN,D,DT,J,KI,L,M,MO,PK,SE,SK,U,VH
Viola x witt f1 'Mammoth Giants'	BS,CL
Viola x witt f1 'Maxim'	BS,C,CA,DE,PK,SK
Viola x witt f1 'Maxim Marina'	DE,PK,SE,SK,T
Viola x witt f1 'Maxim' s-c, mix	SK
Viola x witt f1 'Miss Liberty'	BS,MO
Viola x witt f1 'Psychedelia'	U
Viola x witt f1 'Regal' s-c, mix	BS,MO
Viola x witt f1 'Reveille Series' mix	F
Viola x witt f1 'Reveille Series' s-c	F,YA
Viola x witt f1 'Rippling Waters'	AP,D,S,SE,T,V
Viola x witt f1 'Rock' s-c,mix	BS
Viola x witt f1 'Rococco'	BS,CA,PL
Viola x witt f1 'Scala Series' s-c	YA
Viola x witt f1 'Scimitar White'	BS
Viola x witt f1 'Springtime Black'	BD,BS,CL,MO
Viola x witt f1 'Springtime Lemon Splash'	BS,CL,MO,T
Viola x witt f1 'Sprite' s-c/mix	PK
Viola x witt f1 'Super Majestic Colossal'	BS
Viola x witt f1 'Turbo Series'	CL
Viola x witt f1 'Tutti Frutti'	BS,F,KI,U,YA
Viola x witt f1 'Ultima Impression Series'	T,YA
Viola x witt f1 'Ultima Lavender Shades'	BS,T
Viola x witt f1 'Ultima' mix	BD,BS,BY,C,CL,CN,D,DT,J,KI,MO,TU
Viola x witt f1 'Ultima Pastel' mix	D
Viola x witt f1 'Ultima pink'	CL,C,MO
Viola x witt f1 'Ultima Series' s-c	BS,CL,L,MO,YA
Viola x witt f1 'Ultima Silhouette' mix	BS,BY,CL,DT,JO,PK,PL,U
Viola x witt f1 'Universal mix'	BU,BY,D,F,J,SK,T,U
Viola x witt f1 'Universal Plus mix'	CA,CL,DT,PK,S,SE
Viola x witt f1 'Universal Plus' s-c	BY,CL,S,SE,SK
Viola x witt f1 'Watercolours'	BS,BY,DT,F,KI,L,MO,SE,SK,T,V
Viola x witt f1 'Winter Garden' mix	BS,PL
Viola x witt f1 'Winter Garden' s-c	BS,BY
Viola x witt f2 'Black Princess'	BS
Viola x witt f2 'Colour Festival'	BS,CL,CN,MO,S
Viola x witt f2 'Giants Goldsmith Colour Festival'	CA
Viola x witt f2 'Happy Flower Mix'	BS,SK,YA
Viola x witt f2 'Joker Light Blue'	BS,CL,DT,F,KS,S,SK
Viola x witt f2 'Joker' mix	BS,BY,CA,CL,DT,J,L,MO,SE,V
Viola x witt f2 'Joker Series' s-c	BS,CL,D,MO,SK,U,YA
Viola x witt f2 'Jolly Joker'	BD,BS,BY,C,CA,CL,CN,D,DE,DT,F,J,KI,KS,L,MO,PK,SE,ST,T,U,V,VH
Viola x witt f2 'New Faces'	BS
Viola x witt f2 'Northern Lights'	BS,SE
Viola x witt f2 'Padparadja'	BD,BS,BY,C,CL,CN,CO,D,DE,DT,F,J,KI,KS,MO,O,PK,S,SE,ST,T,U,V,YA
Viola x witt f2 'Pastiche'	BS
Viola x witt f2 'Premiere' mix	BD,BS,C,CL,D,L,MO
Viola x witt f2 'Premiere' s-c	CL,S
Viola x witt 'Fama' Series s-c/mix	MO
Viola x witt 'Floral Dance' mix	S,T
Viola x witt 'Floral Dance' s-c	T
Viola x witt 'Forerunner' mix	BS,CO,DT,J,L,MO,ST
Viola x witt 'Forerunner' s-c	BS,L,MO
Viola x witt 'Gay Jesters'	D
Viola x witt 'Harlequin Mix'	DT
Viola x witt 'Homefires'	U

VIOLA

Viola x witt 'Ice Queen'	BS	Viola 'Yellow Perfection'	B,BY,JE,L,SA
Viola x witt 'Impressions' mix	PL	Viola 'Yellow Prince'	C,JE
Viola x witt 'Jupiter'	B,BS,BY	Virgilia capensis	DD
Viola x witt 'Lace Series' s-c	SE	Virgilia divaricata	KB,O,SI
Viola x witt Large Fl mix	CL,CO,T,VH	Virgilia oroboides	B,O,SA,VE,WA
Viola x witt 'Lemon Ice'	BS	Viscaria see Lychnis	
Viola x witt 'Love Duet'	BS,D,J,MO,SE,U,V	Vitaliana primuliflora	AP,B,C,JE,SC,VO
Viola x witt 'Madame Steele'	PI	Vitaliana primuliflora ssp praetutiana	B,JE
Viola x witt 'Magic Fire'	BS	Vitex agnus-castus	A,AP,B,BH,C,CA,CP,EL,
Viola x witt 'March Beauty'	B,BS,BY		W,HU,JE,LN,SA,SC,VE
Viola x witt 'Marshall's Nene Giant Strain'	M	Vitex incisa	B
Viola x witt 'Mello 21'	T	Vitex keniensis	B
Viola x witt mix selection	F	Vitex lucens	B
Viola x witt mix special	DT,U	Vitex mombassae	B,SA
Viola x witt 'Moon Moth'	PI	Vitex negundo	C,CP,FW,HU,LN,SA
Viola x witt 'Moonlight'	T,U	Vitex payos	B,SI
Viola x witt 'North Pole'	B,BS,BY	Vitis amurensis	LN,SA
Viola x witt 'Oliver Twist'	PL,SE	Vitis amurensis MW140R	X
Viola x witt 'Paper White'	VH	Vitis californica	B
Viola x witt 'Pastel Butterflies'	T	Vitis coignetiae	B,C,FW,SA
Viola x witt 'Pay Dirt'	PI	Vitis davidii	B,HU
Viola x witt 'Pink Panther'	F	Vitis riparia	B,C,LN,NO,PR,SA
Viola x witt 'Poker Face'	D,PL	Vitis rotundifolia	B,HU
Viola x witt 'Prizewinner'	DT	Vitis thunbergii	B
Viola x witt Purple /Orange Bedder	MO	Vitis vinifera	B,SA
Viola x witt 'Querelle'	F	Vitis vinifera 'Brandt'	B
Viola x witt 'Rally' s-c	BS	Vitis vinifera 'Buckland Sweetwater'	B
Viola x witt 'Raspberry Rose'	BY,PI	Vitis vinifera 'Leon Millot'	B
Viola x witt 'Rhine Gold'	C,CG	Vitis vinifera 'Schiava Grossa'/Black Ham	B
Viola x witt 'Roggli Giants'	BS,CL,D	Vitis vulpina	B
Viola x witt 'Romeo and Juliet'	BS,F,J,KS,M,SE,T,V	Vittadinia australis	B,SS
Viola x witt S1 'Allegro'	BS	Voacanga africana	B
Viola x witt S1 'Armado'	F	Voandzeia subterranea white	B
Viola x witt 'Senator Series'	CL	Vriesea altodaserra	B
Viola x witt 'Silver Wings'	SE,T	Vriesea atra	B
Viola x witt 'Spanish Sun'	T	Vriesea barclayana	B
Viola x witt 'Sterling Silver'	T	Vriesea barilletii	B
Viola x witt 'Super Chalon Giants mix'	BD,BS,BY,CL,F,L,M,	Vriesea biguassuensis	B
	MO,S,SE,T,U,VH	Vriesea bituminosa	B
Viola x witt 'Superb Giant Strain'	MO,SK,U	Vriesea bleheri	B
Viola x witt Surprise mix	BY	Vriesea botafogensis	B
Viola x witt 'Swiss Giant Alpenglow'	B,BS,J,KI,MO,V	Vriesea brassicoides	B
Viola x witt 'Sw. G. Benary's Exhib. Strain'	L	Vriesea 'Brentwood'	B
Viola x witt 'Swiss Giant Coronation Gold'	B,BS,KI	Vriesea carinata	B
Viola x witt 'Swiss Giant Elite'	C	Vriesea chrysostachia	B
Viola x witt 'Swiss Giant' mix	BD,BS,BU,CA,CL,CO,	Vriesea corcovadensis	B
	DE,DN,DT,EL,F,J,KI,MC,	Vriesea declinata	B
	MO,R,PI,SK,ST,SU,TU,	Vriesea delicatula	B
	V,VY	Vriesea drepanocarpa	B
Viola x witt 'Swiss Giant Orange Sun'	B,BS,BY,KI	Vriesea duvaliana	B
Viola x witt 'Swiss Giant' s-c	B,BS,BY,EL,MO,SE	Vriesea 'Eico'	B
Viola x witt Swiss Giant 'Ullswater'	BY,C,J,KI,MO,T,V	Vriesea ensiformis	B
Viola x witt Swiss Giants 'Southbank Mix'	CL	Vriesea ensiformis v ensiformis	B
Viola x witt 'Swiss Master Mix'	CL	Vriesea ensiformis v striata	B
Viola x witt 'Swiss Velvet' mix	J	Vriesea erythrodactylon	B
Viola x witt 'Tequila' mix	BS	Vriesea erythrodactylon v striata	B
Viola x witt 'Tiara' mix	KI,ST	Vriesea 'Fascination'	B
Viola x witt 'True Blue'	T	Vriesea fenestralis	B
Viola x witt 'Wessel Ice'	L	Vriesea flammea	B
Viola x witt 'Wine Red'	BS,BY	Vriesea 'Flammenschwert'	B
Viola x witt 'Wink'	BS,KI	Vriesea fluminensis	B
Viola x witt 'Wink' s-c	MO	Vriesea fosteriana	B
Viola x witt 'Winter Flowering' mix	BS,BY,DT,F,KI,MC,S,ST,	Vriesea fosteriana v seideliana	B
	SU,TU,U,VH	Vriesea fosteriana v seideliana rubra	B
Viola x witt 'Winter Sun'	B,BS,BY	Vriesea fosteriana v seideliana-pallida	B
Viola x wittrochiana	CG	Vriesea friburgensii	B

VRIESEA

Vriesea friburgensis v paludosa	B
Vriesea 'Gemma'	B
Vriesea gigantea	B
Vriesea gigantea v seideliana	B
Vriesea gladioliflora	B
Vriesea glutinosa	B
Vriesea 'Goldfisch'	B
Vriesea graciliscapa	B
Vriesea gradata	B
Vriesea grande	B
Vriesea guttata	B
Vriesea guttata v striata	B
Vriesea heliconioides	B
Vriesea heterostachys	B
Vriesea hieroglyphica	B
Vriesea hieroglyphica v zebrina	B
Vriesea hoehneana	B
Vriesea hyb	B
Vriesea hyb 'Illustris'	B
Vriesea hyb 'Morreniana'	B
Vriesea hyb 'Rex'	B
Vriesea imperialis	B
Vriesea incurvata	B
Vriesea incurvata v longiflora	B
Vriesea inflata	B
Vriesea inflata v seideliana	B
Vriesea itatiaia	B
Vriesea jonghe	B
Vriesea 'Komet'	B
Vriesea longicaulis	B
Vriesea longiscapa	B
Vriesea lubbersii	B
Vriesea modesta	B
Vriesea neoglutinosa	B
Vriesea oligantha	B
Vriesea ourensis	B
Vriesea paratiensis	B
Vriesea pardalina	B
Vriesea pauperrima	B
Vriesea 'Perfecta'	B
Vriesea petropolitana	B
Vriesea petropolitana v virosa	B
Vriesea philippocoburgii	B
Vriesea philippocoburgii v philippocoburgii	B
Vriesea platynema	B
Vriesea platynema v albo - lineata	B
Vriesea platynema v flava	B
Vriesea platynema v rosea	B
Vriesea platynema v striata	B
Vriesea platynema v variegata	B
Vriesea platystachys	B
Vriesea platzmannii	B
Vriesea 'Poelmannii Selecta'	B
Vriesea poenulata	B
Vriesea procera	B
Vriesea procera v debilis	B
Vriesea procera v procera	B
Vriesea procera v rubra	B
Vriesea psittacina	B
Vriesea psittacina v psittacina	B
Vriesea psittacina v rubro-bracteata	B
Vriesea rastrensis	B
Vriesea regina	B
Vriesea regnelli	B
Vriesea retroflexa	B
Vriesea roberto-seidelii	B
Vriesea rodigasiana	B
Vriesea rodigasiana v maculata	B
Vriesea rodigasiana v purpurea	B
Vriesea 'Rubin'	B
Vriesea 'Sanderiana'	B
Vriesea sanguinea	B
Vriesea saundersii	B
Vriesea scalarii	B
Vriesea 'Sceptre D'or'	B
Vriesea sceptrum v flavobracteata	B
Vriesea seideliana	B
Vriesea simplex	B
Vriesea simplex v gigantea	B
Vriesea sparsiflora	B
Vriesea splendens	B,SG
Vriesea splendens v major	B
Vriesea splendens v mortefontanensis	B
Vriesea 'Splendide'	B
Vriesea sucrei	B
Vriesea taritubensis	B
Vriesea triangularis	B
Vriesea unilateralis	B
Vriesea vagans	B
Vriesea 'Vigeri'	B
Vriesea weberi	B
Vriesea x mariae	B
Wachendorfia brachyandra	B,RU
Wachendorfia paniculata	B,RU,SI
Wachendorfia parviflora	B,SI
Wachendorfia sp	AP,SI
Wachendorfia thyrsiflora	B,BH,C,KB,HP,RU,SI
Wahlenbergia albomarginata	AP,B,HP,JE,SS
Wahlenbergia albomarginata v saxicola	B
Wahlenbergia annularis	B,SI
Wahlenbergia capensis	B,HU,SI
Wahlenbergia congesta	AP,C,G,I,PM,SC
Wahlenbergia gloriosa	AP,AU,HP,SC
Wahlenbergia gracilis	CG
Wahlenbergia hederacea	CG
Wahlenbergia krebsii ssp krebsii	B,SI
Wahlenbergia lobelioides	CG
Wahlenbergia mathewsii	CG
Wahlenbergia 'Melton Bluebird'	BD,BS,MO,PK,SE,V
Wahlenbergia pendula	CG
Wahlenbergia procumbens	BH
Wahlenbergia prostrata	B,SI
Wahlenbergia pygmaea	B,SS
Wahlenbergia saxicola	AP,CG,G,SC
Wahlenbergia sp	AP,SI
Wahlenbergia thyrsiflora	HP
Wahlenbergia undulata	B,BH,HP,KB,SI
Waitzia acuminata v acuminata	B,NI,O
Waitzia acuminata v albicans	B,NI,O
Waitzia nitida	C,O
Waitzia suaveolens v flava	B,NI,O
Waitzia suaveolens v suaveolens	B,O
Waldheimia tridactylites see Allardia	
Waldsteinia fragarioides	KL
Wallichia densiflora	O,SA
Wallichia disticha	B
Walsura trifoliata	B
Waltheria indica	B
Washingtonia filifera	B,C,CA,CG,DV,EL,FW, HA,HU,O,SA,VE
Washingtonia robusta	B,C,CA,EL,FW,HA,O, SA,VE

WASHINGTONIA

Washingtonia sonorae	CG
Waterhousea floribunda	B,SA
Watsonia aletroides	B,C,RU,SI
Watsonia angusta	B,RU,SI
Watsonia angustifolia	B
Watsonia beatricis see W.pillansii	
Watsonia borbonica	CG,KB,RU,SI
Watsonia borbonica ssp ardernei	B,C,CG,KB,RU
Watsonia borbonica ssp borbonica	B,RU
Watsonia brevifolia see W.laccata	
Watsonia 'Candy Stripes'	B
Watsonia 'Cardinal'	B
Watsonia coccinea	B,SI
Watsonia 'Dawn'	B
Watsonia densiflora	B,SA,SI
Watsonia distans	B,SA,SI
Watsonia fourcadei	B,CG,RU,SI
Watsonia fulgens	B,SI
Watsonia humilis	B,RU
Watsonia hybrids	B,CG
Watsonia 'Jewel'	B
Watsonia laccata	B,RU,SI
Watsonia 'Lady Rose'	B
Watsonia latifolia	B,SI
Watsonia lepida	B,SI
Watsonia marginata	B,C,KB,RU,SI
Watsonia marginata v alba	B
Watsonia marginata v minor	B
Watsonia meriana	B,CG,RU,SI
Watsonia meriana v bulbifera	B,RU
Watsonia pillansii	AP,B,DV,LG,RU,SI,SZ
Watsonia 'Pink Lady'	B
Watsonia 'Purity'	B
Watsonia roseoalba see W.humilis	
Watsonia 'Shady Lady'	B
Watsonia sp	BH,SI
Watsonia sp/hyb mix	C,KB
Watsonia stenosiphon	B,SI
Watsonia tabularis	B,CG,KB,SA,SI
Watsonia vanderspuyae	B,SI
Watsonia versfeldii	B,SI
Watsonia watsonioides	B,SI
Watsonia wordsworthiana	B,KB
Wattakaka see Dregea	
Weberbauerocereus albus	DV
Weberbauerocereus churinensis	DV,Y
Weberbauerocereus horridispinus	DV
Weberbauerocereus johnsonii	B,DV,Y
Weberbauerocereus longicomus	DV
Weberbauerocereus rauhii	B,DV
Weberbauerocereus seiboldianus	DV
Weberbauerocereus weberbaueri	DV
Weberbauerocereus wint. v australis	DV
Weberbauerocereus winterienus	DV,Y
Wedelia trilobata	B
Wehlia thryptomenoides	B,NI
Weigela florida	B,FW,LN,SA
Weingartia see Rebutia	
Weinmannia racemosa	B,C,SA
Weinmannia trichosperma	B,SA
Welfia georgii	B,SA
Welwitschia mirabilis	B,SI
Westringia fruticosa	HP,O,SA
Wheat, organic 'Maris Widgeon'	CO
Whiteheadia bifolia	B,SI
Wiborgia monoptera	B,SI

Wicoxia schmollii	CH
Widdringtonia cedarbergensis	B,BH,C,KB,LN,SA,SI,WA
Widdringtonia cupressoides see W.nodiflora	
Widdringtonia nodiflora	B,BH,C,KB,SA,SG,SI,WA
Widdringtonia schwarzii	B,BH,KB,SI,WA
Widdringtonia whytei see W.nodiflora	
Wigandia caracasana	SG
Wigginsia see Parodia	
Wikstroemeria indica	B
Wilcoxia australis	DV,Y
Wilcoxia tamaulipensis deherdtii	BC
Wild bulb selection	PA
Wildeknowia incurvata	B,SI
Wildflower, Beneficial Insects	DI
Wildflower mix, Annual	DI,YS
Wildflower mix, Architectural/Bird/Bee mix	Z
Wildflower mix, Bats in the garden	CO
Wildflower mix, Bee	SU
Wildflower mix, Bird	NA,SU
Wildflower mix, Birds & Butterflies	PK
Wildflower mix, Bumblebee	CO,NA
Wildflower mix, Butterfly	CO,LA,NA,TU,SU,VY
Wildflower mix, Calcareous Meadow	LA
Wildflower mix, California	AV,CA
Wildflower mix, Continuous Colour	HW
Wildflower mix, Cornfield	CO,LA,NA,TU,SU,Z
Wildflower mix, Cottage Garden	LA,NA,PK,TU,YS,Z
Wildflower mix, Cut Flower	CA
Wildflower mix, Damp Meadow	LA,YS
Wildflower mix, Derelict Land	LA
Wildflower mix, Field and Hedgrow	CO
Wildflower mix, Flower Arrangers	CO
Wildflower mix, Flowering Lawn	CO,DI
Wildflower mix, Designated Areas	AB
Wildflower mix, Dry, Sun or Shade	BU
Wildflower mix, General	KI,Z
Wildflower mix, Golden Days ann	D
Wildflower mix, Haymeadow	SU
Wildflower mix, Hedgerow	NA,SU
Wildflower mix, Hedgerow/Shady Glade	LA
Wildflower mix, Herbaceous	NA
Wildflower mix, Leaves, and Shoots Salad	CO
Wildflower mix, Leaves/Stems /Roots Ed.	CO
Wildflower mix, Little Bit Shady	GO,HW
Wildflower mix, Long Season Meadow	NA
Wildflower mix, Meadow	DI,DN,PK,ST,VY,YS,Z
Wildflower mix, Mountain	AV,CA,SK
Wildflower mix, Northern Lights	JO
Wildflower mix, Old Flower Meadow	LA
Wildflower mix, 'Ozark'	HW
Wildflower mix, Patio	NA
Wildflower mix, Perennial	CA
Wildflower mix, Pond Edge	CO,LA,SU
Wildflower mix, Pond/Bog mix	Z
Wildflower mix, Queen Anne's Lace	LA
Wildflower mix, Rainbow Riot	
Wildflower mix, Riverside mix	Z
Wildflower mix, Scented	NA
Wildflower mix, Seed Head	LA
Wildflower mix, Shady	CA,VY
Wildflower mix, Short Meadow	GO,LA
Wildflower mix, Southwestern	AV,CA
Wildflower mix, Spring Meadow	LA,YS
Wildflower mix, Spring/Woodland mix	Z

WILDFLOWER

Wildflower mix, Summer Meadow	DI,LA,YS
Wildflower mix, Sun & Shade	AV
Wildflower mix, 'Texas'	AV,CA
Wildflower mix, Tropical	CA
Wildflower mix, Watermeadow	SU
Wildflower mix, Waterside	NA
Wildflower mix, Wayside	YS
Wildflower mix, Wet Land	YS
Wildflower mix, Wilderness	YS
Wildflower mix, Wildlife Garden (RSPB)	CO
Wildflower mix, Windowbox	CO
Wildflower mix, Woodland	CO,LA,NA,SU,YS
Wildflower mix, Woodland Edge	YS
Willdenowia incurvata	B,SI
Wisteria brachybotrys ' Murasaki Kapitan'	B
Wisteria brachybotrys 'Shiro Kapitan'	B
Wisteria floribunda	AB,B,EL,FW,HU,KL, LN,N,SA,VE
Wisteria floribunda 'Alba'	B,SA
Wisteria floribunda 'Macrobotrys'	B,C
Wisteria floribunda 'Multijuga'	HP
Wisteria floribunda 'Rosea' (Honbeni)	B
Wisteria frutescens	B,C,EL,FW,LN,N,SA
Wisteria sinensis	B,C,CA,CG,DE,DV,EL, FW,HA,HU,LN,N,PK, SA,T,U,VE
Wisteria sinensis 'Alba'	B,C,CA,EL,FW,HA,LN, PK,SA,VE
Wisteria x formosa	B,C,FW,N
Withania somnifera	BH,C,CP,DD,HU
Witheringia solanacea	B
Wittrockia amazonica	B
Wittrockia bahiana	B
Wittrockia campos - portos	B
Wittrockia smithii	B
Wittrockia superba	B
Wodyetia bifurcata	B,CA,EL,O
Woodwardia orientalis	B
Wrightia tinctoria	B,SA
Wrightia tomentosa	B
Wrixonia prostantheroides	B
Wulfenia amherstiana	KL
Wulfenia baldacii	JE
Wulfenia carinthiaca	AP,B,C,G,JE,KL,SA,SC
Wulfenia carinthiaca 'Alba'	AP,JE
Wurmbea diocia ssp alba	B
Wurmbea sp	SI
Wurmbea spicata	B,SI
Wyethia amplexicaulis	NO
Wyethia angustifolia	B,DD,KL
Wyethia glabra	B
Wyethia helenioides	B,C
Wyethia helianthoides	JE,NO
X Citrofortunella microcarpa	B,SA
X Homoglad hyb	SZ
X Pardancanda norrisii	B,C,DE,JE,PK,SA
Xanthisma texana	B,G,PK,SZ,T,U
Xanthisma texana 'Flower Power'	J
Xanthium spinosum	CG,G
Xanthium strumarium	CG,SG
Xanthocercis zambesiaca	B,SI,WA
Xanthocerus sorbifolium	AP,B,FW,G,HP,HU,LN, N,SA
Xanthorrhiza simplicissima	B,DD
Xanthorrhoea australis	B,C,CA,DD,EL,HA,HU, NI,O,SA,SH

Xanthorrhoea fulva	B,NI,O
Xanthorrhoea gracilis	B,NI,O,SA
Xanthorrhoea johnstonii	B,NI,O
Xanthorrhoea macronema	B,EL,HA,NI,O,SH
Xanthorrhoea media	B,EL,NI,O,SH
Xanthorrhoea minor	AU,HA
Xanthorrhoea preissii	AU,B,NI,O,SA
Xanthorrhoea quadrangulata	AU,B,O
Xanthorrhoea resinosa	C,HA,O
Xanthorrhoea semiplana	B,NI,O
Xanthorrhoea thorntonii	B,NI,O
Xanthosia atkinsoniana	B,NI
Xanthosia candida	B,NI,SA
Xanthosia rotundifolia	B,NI,SA
Xanthostemon chrysanthus	B,EL,NI,SA
Xeranthemum annuum	AB,BD,BS,BY,C,CO,D,D E,DT,F,HU,JO,KI,KS,L, PI,PK,S,SG,SK,ST,SU,T, TU,VY
Xeranthemum annuum 'Cherry Ripe' mix	BY,C
Xeranthemum annuum 'Lumina' mix	J,MO,KS,U,V
Xeranthemum annuum 'Snowlady'	BY,T
Xeranthemum ann. 'Superbissimum' s-c	B
Xeranthemum annuum 'Violet-purple'	B,BY
Xeranthemum cylindrica	T
Xeranthoxylum alatum	SA
Xeranthoxylum americanum	SA
Xeranthoxylum bungeanum	SA
Xeranthoxylum piperitum	SA
Xeroderris stuhlmannii	B,SI
Xeronema callistemon	AP,AR,B,C
Xerophyllum tenax	AB,B,C,DD,DV,JE,KS, LN,NO,SA
Xerophyta dasylirioides	SI
Xerophyta viscosa	B,SI
Xylococcus bicolor	B
Xylomelum angustifolium	B,NI,O,SA
Xylomelum occidentale	B,NI,O,SA
Xylomelum pyriformis	B,O
Xyris lanata	B,C,HU,NI,SA
Xyris operculata	B,NI
Xyris torta	B
Xysmalobium stockenstromense	B,C,SI
Xysmalobium undulatum	B,SI
Yakirra australiensis	B,HU,NI
Yateorhiza macrantha	B
Yucca aloifolia	B,C,CA,EL,FW,HA,SA,VE
Yucca aloifolia 'Marginata'	B,EL,SA
Yucca angustifolia see Y.glauca	
Yucca angustissima	B,SW
Yucca arizonica	B,SW
Yucca arkansana	DV
Yucca australis	B,DV
Yucca baccata	B,C,CA,DV,EL,FW,JE, LN,NO,SA,SW
Yucca baccata v thornberi	B
Yucca brevifolia	B,C,CA,DV,EL,HU,LN, SA,SW
Yucca brevifolia v jaegeriana	B
Yucca campestris	B,SW
Yucca carnerosana	B
Yucca elata	B,C,CA,DV,LN,SW
Yucca elephantipes	B,CA,SA,VE
Yucca fauxiana	DV
Yucca faxoniana	B
Yucca filamentosa	AP,B,BS,C,CA,CL,DE,

YUCCA

	DV,EL,FW,G,HU,JE,L, LN,MO,N,NO,SA,V,VE
Yucca filamentosa 'Bright Edge'	B
Yucca glauca	B,C,CA,DV,EL,FW,HU, JE,LN,NO,PR,SA,SW
Yucca glauca v baileyi	B
Yucca glauca v gurneyi	B,DV
Yucca glauca v intermedia	B,DV
Yucca glauca v kanabensis	B
Yucca glauca v radiosa	B,DV
Yucca gloriosa	B
Yucca harrimaniae	B,BC,SW
Yucca intermedia	DV
Yucca kanabensis	B,SW
Yucca mix outdoor vars	T
Yucca navajoa	B,SW
Yucca neomexicana	B
Yucca rigida	B,DV
Yucca rostrata	B,CA,DV,SA
Yucca rupicola	DV
Yucca schidigera	B,CA,SW
Yucca schottii	B,SW
Yucca sp mix	C
Yucca thompsoniana	B,DV
Yucca torreyi	B,C,CA,DV,SA,SW
Yucca whipplei	B,C,CA,EL,SA,SW
Yucca whipplei ssp caespitosa	B
Yucca whipplei ssp whipplei	B
Yucca whipplei v intermedia	B
Yucca whipplei v parishii	B
Yushania anceps	B
Zaleya decandra	B
Zaluzianskya capensis	B,DI,SG,SI,V,W
Zaluzianskya capensis 'Midnight Candy'	B,C,F,KS,SE
Zaluzianskya katherinae	B,SI
Zaluzianskya microsiphon	B,SI
Zaluzianskya ovata	B,SI
Zaluzianskya pulvinata	B,SI
Zaluzianskya sp	I,SI
Zaluzianskya spathacea	SI
Zaluzianskya villosa	B,SI
Zamia dominiquensis	B
Zamia fischeri	B,C,CA,O,SA
Zamia furfuracea	B,C,CA,EL,HA,O,SA
Zamia integrifolia	O
Zamia loddigesii	B,O
Zamia pumila	B,CA,O
Zamia skinneri	O
Zantedeschia aethiopica	B,C,CA,DV,EL,G,SA,SI
Zantedeschia aethiopica 'Crowborough'	B,LG,SC
Zantedeschia aethiopica 'Giant Vanetti'	B
Zantedeschia aethiopica 'Green Goddess'	B,EL,HA,MN
Zantedeschia albomaculata	B,G,MN,PK,SI
Zantedeschia elliottiana	B,C,G
Zantedeschia hybs	B
Zantedeschia mix	CA
Zantedeschia odorata	B
Zantedeschia 'Rainbow' mix	HA
Zantedeschia rehmannii	AP,B,DD,MN,SI
Zanthoxylum alatum	A,C,LN,SG
Zanthoxylum americanum	A,B,G
Zanthoxylum capense	B,SI
Zanthoxylum molle	B
Zanthoxylum piperitum	A,SG
Zanthoxylum simulans	B,G,LN,SG
Zanthoxylum sp AC1851	X

Zauschneria arizonica see Z.californica ssp latifolia	
Zauschneria californica	AP,C,G,HP,JD
Zauschneria californica 'Dublin'	PM
Zauschneria californica 'Etteri'	RM
Zauschneria californica 'Solidarity Pink'	RM
Zauschneria californica ssp cana	B,SS
Zauschneria californica ssp latifolium	B,RM,VO
Zauschneria latifolia	SW
Zea diploperennis	B
Zea gracillima	KS
Zea japonica	JO,KS
Zea japonica 'Red Berry'	L
Zea mays 'Arlecchino'	FR
Zea mays v gracillima	B,DD
Zea mays v gracillima 'Gelbe Beere'	CG
Zea mays v mexicana	B,DD,FR
Zea Strawberry Corn	FR,MO
Zelkova carpinifolia	B,C,FW,LN,N,SA
Zelkova hyrcania	SA
Zelkova schneiderana	B,LN,SA
Zelkova serrata	B,C,CA,EL,FW,HA,LN, N,SA,T,V,VE
Zelkova sinica	B,CA,FW,LN,N,SA
Zenobia pulverulenta	AP,B,CG,FW,KL,N,SC
Zephyranthes atamasco	AP,B
Zephyranthes aurea	KL
Zephyranthes candida	SG
Zephyranthes citrina	AP,B,C
Zephyranthes drummondii	AP,B
Zephyranthes grandiflora	AP,B,DD,EL,SC
Zephyranthes lindleyana	SG
Zephyranthes longifolia	B,G,SC,SW
Zephyranthes minima	LG
Zephyranthes pedunculata	RM
Zephyranthes rosea	AP,B,SC
Zephyranthes x lancasterae	AP,LG
Ziera smithii	HA
Zigadenus elegans	AP,B,HP,JE,KL,SA,SG
Zigadenus fremontii	B
Zigadenus glaucus	B,JE
Zigadenus nutallii	AP,B,HP,JE,SC
Zigadenus venosus	B,DD,JE,NO,RM
Zilla spinosa	B
Zingiber mioga	DD
Zingiber spectabile	B
Zingiber zerumbet	B
Zingiber zerumbet 'Darceyi'	B
Zinnia acerosa	B,DD
Zinnia angustifola see Z.haageana	
Zinnia 'Belvedere'	U
Zinnia 'Blue Point'	JO
Zinnia Burpee's Hybrids	BS,BY
Zinnia 'Button Box' mix	BU,SK
Zinnia Cactus Fl giant mix	C,L,PI,T,VY
Zinnia 'California Giants' mix	B,CA,DE,HU
Zinnia 'California Giants' s-c	BU
Zinnia 'Candy Cane'	C
Zinnia 'Chippendale'	B,DE,T,TE
Zinnia Chrysanthemum Fl mix	FR
Zinnia 'Classic'	PI
Zinnia 'Cupid' mix	SK
Zinnia Dahlia Fl mix	B,BS,BU,BY,C,CA,D,DD, DE,DT,FR,KI,L,MO,PI, PK,SE,ST,TU,VH,YA
Zinnia Dahlia Fl s-c	B,FR
Zinnia darwiniana	AP,B

ZINNIA

Zinnia 'Dasher' s-c, mix	BS,CA,PK,SK
Zinnia dwarf dbl mix	S,T
Zinnia 'Early Wonder'	C,F
Zinnia elegans	B,DD,G,SG
Zinnia elegans 'Beautiful' mix	AB,SD
Zinnia elegans, pink	SD
Zinnia elegans 'Scarlet Flame'	DE
Zinnia elegans 'Swirls' mix	DE,PL
Zinnia elegans 'Tufted Exemption'	F
Zinnia elegans 'Whirligig'	C,PK,S
Zinnia elegans 'Whirligig Imp'	T
Zinnia 'Envy' green	BS,C,DI,F,HU,JO,KS, MO,T
Zinnia f1 'Dreamland Series'	B,BS,MO,SE
Zinnia f1 'Fairyland'	D
Zinnia f1 'Parasol'	T
Zinnia f1 'Peter Pan' mix	CA,DI,MO,SK
Zinnia f1 'Peter Pan' s-c	BS,CL,DE,PK,SK,YA
Zinnia f1 'Ruffles'	CA,JO,PK,SK
Zinnia f1 'Short Stuff Series'	CA,CL
Zinnia f1 'Small World Cherry'	B,BS,CA,MO,PK,VY
Zinnia f1 'Small World Pink'	B,BS,MO,PK
Zinnia f1 'Sun'	PK
Zinnia 'Giant Fantasy'	BU
Zinnia grandiflora	AP,B,KL
Zinnia haageana	B,DD,FR,HU,PK,SG
Zinnia haageana 'Mandarin Orange'	J,PK
Zinnia haageana 'Orange'	B,V
Zinnia haageana 'Persian Carpet Mix'	B,BS,D,DE,DT,F,G,HU,J, KI,PI,S,SD,SK,T
Zinnia haageana 'Star Series'	BS,CL,PK,SK
Zinnia haageana 'Starbright'	BS,CL,F,KI,MO,S
Zinnia haageana 'White'	B,PK,SK
Zinnia haagena 'Star White'	DI
Zinnia 'Hobgoblin'	BS,MO
Zinnia 'Lilliput' mix	BS,BU,BY,FR,MO,PI,PK, SK,VY
Zinnia 'Lilliput' s-c	B,SK
Zinnia linearis	G,KS
Zinnia linearis 'White Star'	KS,M
Zinnia 'Mammoth'	BS
Zinnia mix giant dbl	J,S,T,V
Zinnia 'Oklahoma'	BS
Zinnia 'Old Mexico'	C,DE,TE
Zinnia 'Peppermint Stick'	BU
Zinnia peruviana	B
Zinnia peruviana 'Bonita Red'	B
Zinnia peruviana 'Bonita Yellow'	B
Zinnia 'Pinwheel' s-c	PK,V
Zinnia 'Pompon' mix see Lilliput	
Zinnia 'Pulcino' mix	PK,SK,VY
Zinnia 'Pulcino' s-c	SK
Zinnia 'Pumila' mix	BS,BY,DE,YA
Zinnia pumila salmon-rose	DE
Zinnia red mix	SD
Zinnia scabious fl mix	B,FR,T
Zinnia 'Sprite' mix	BD,J
Zinnia 'State Fair'	AB,B,BD,BS,C,JO,MO, VY
Zinnia 'Sunbow'	JO,PL,T
Zinnia 'Thumbelina'	B,BS,BU,C,CA,CO,D,FR, KI,L,MO,SE,SK,TE,TU,V
Zinnia 'Tropical Snow'	BS,T,TE
Zinnia 'Yoga'	BS,DE
Zinnia 'Youth and Old Age'	TH
Zinnia 'Zebra'	DT

Zinnia 'Zig Zag'	VY
Zizania aquatica	B
Zizia aptera	B,PR,SG
Zizia aurea	B,DD,G,HU,PR,SG
Ziziphus jujuba	A,C,CA,FW,HA,LN,SA, SI,VE
Ziziphus lotus	B
Ziziphus mauritanica	B
Ziziphus mucronata	B,C,LN,SA,SI,WA
Ziziphus mucronata ssp rhodesica	B,SI
Ziziphus oenoplia	B
Ziziphus rivularis	B,WA
Ziziphus spina-christi	B,HA,LN
Zoysia japonica	B,HA,PK,SA
Zygochloa paradoxa	B,NI
Zygophyllum aurantiacum	B,NI
Zygophyllum eremaeum	B,HU,NI,SA
Zygophyllum meyeri	B,SI
Zygophyllum morgsana	B,SA,SI
Zygophyllum sessilifolium	B,SI

VEGETABLES

Amaranth	CO,DD,RC,RI,SU
Amaranth, 'Bolivia'	AB
Amaranth, 'Bronze'	SP
Amaranth, 'Burgundy'	AB,DD,SD
Amaranth, 'Golden'	AB,DD,SD
Amaranth, 'Groenbladig type'	HU,SU,V
Amaranth, 'Hijau'	DD
Amaranth, 'Hopi Red Dye'	AB
Amaranth, 'K432'	SP
Amaranth, 'Kahulu'	AB
Amaranth, 'Kiwicha'	HU
Amaranth, 'Manna'	SD
Amaranth, 'Mayo Red'	HU
Amaranth, 'Merah'	DD,RC,SD
Amaranth, 'Mercado'	AB,SD
Amaranth, mix	SP
Amaranth, 'MT-3'	SP
Amaranth, 'Multicolor'	AB
Amaranth, 'Popping'	AB
Amaranth, 'Red Stripe Leaf'	HU
Amaranth, 'Roodbladig type'	SN,SP,V
Amaranth, 'Warihio'	SD
Amaranth, 'White leaf'	SU
Artichoke, 'Green Globe'	AB,B,BD,BH,BS,BY,C, CO,DE,DT,FJ,KI,L,M, MC,MO,RI,S,ST,SU,TE, TH,TU,U,V
Artichoke, 'Green Globe Imp'	KS,PI,T,VH
Artichoke, 'Green Star'	PK
Artichoke, 'Imperial Star'	GO
Artichoke, 'Purple Globe'	B,BS,BY,CO,KI,TH
Artichoke, 'Purple Romanesco'	FR,KS
Artichoke, 'Romagna'	V
Artichoke, 'Selma-Cynara' F1	V
Artichoke, 'Violetto di Chioggia'	B,BS,FR,HU,PI,TE
Artichoke, 'Violetto di Jesi'	KS
Asparagus	DI
Asparagus, 'Argenteuil Early'	FR,GO
Asparagus, 'Argenteuil Purple Imp'	BS
Asparagus, 'Conover's Colossal'	B,BD,BS,BY,C,CO,KI,L, MO,ST,SU,TH,TU,U,YA
Asparagus, 'Franklim' F1	B,KI,M,SU,TU,V
Asparagus, 'Geynlim' F1	DT
Asparagus, 'Jersey Knight Improved'	T
Asparagus, 'Larac' F1	DE
Asparagus, 'Limbras Franklim' F1	J
Asparagus, 'Mary Washington'	BS,BF,BU,DE,PI,SR,V, VH,VY
Asparagus, 'UC 157' F1	DE,VY
Asparagus, 'Viking KB3'	SK
Aubergine, African	BH,SN
Aubergine, 'Agora' hyb	SR
Aubergine, 'Antar' F1	BS,SN,TU
Aubergine, 'Avan' F1	BS
Aubergine, 'Bambino' F1	DE,PK,SK
Aubergine, 'Bandera' F1	T
Aubergine, black	SD
Aubergine, 'Black Beauty'	AB,B,BD,BF,BS,BU,DE, F,FR,MO,PI,RC,SD,SK, SN,SR
Aubergine, 'Black Bell' F1	J,JO,SK,SN,V,YA
Aubergine, 'Black Emperor'	U
Aubergine, 'Black Enorma' F1	VH
Aubergine, 'Black Magic' hyb	SN
Aubergine, 'Blacknite' hyb	SK

Aubergine, 'Blanca de Menorca' o-p	SN
Aubergine, 'Bonica' F1	BS,D,TU
Aubergine, 'Bride' F1	PI,SK,TE,V
Aubergine, 'Casper'	SK,SN,V
Aubergine, 'Chinese'	HD
Aubergine, 'Classic' F1	SK,SN
Aubergine, 'Classy Chassis' hyb	SK
Aubergine, 'Dusky' F1	PI,PK,SK,SR,TE
Aubergine, 'Dusky' o-p	SN,VY
Aubergine, 'Early Bird' F1	PK
Aubergine, 'Early Long Purple'	B,HU
Aubergine, 'Easter Egg'	FR,KS
Aubergine, 'Epic'	BS,KI,SR
Aubergine, 'Extra Long'	BH
Aubergine, 'Florence Round Purple'	KS
Aubergine, 'Florida Market'	HU
Aubergine, 'Foo Chow Round'	RC
Aubergine, 'Galine'	BS
Aubergine, 'Giullietta' hyb	SN
Aubergine, Heirlooms mix	DI
Aubergine, 'Highbush Select'	SK
Aubergine, 'Honey Pear'	BH
Aubergine, 'Ichiban' F1	DE,PI,PK,SR
Aubergine, 'Italian Pink Bicolor'	AB,SD,SK
Aubergine, 'Italian White'	AB,SD
Aubergine, 'Japanese Early Purple'	AB,SD
Aubergine, 'Jaxatus Soxna'	SN
Aubergine, 'Jersey King' F1	FR
Aubergine, 'Kurume Long Purple'	B,RI
Aubergine, 'Long Dk Red'	RC
Aubergine, 'Long Purple'	BS,BY,C,CO,DI,FR,GO,J, SN,SR,ST,TH,TU
Aubergine, 'Long Tom' F1	BS,CO,KS
Aubergine, 'Long White Streaked'	DI
Aubergine, 'Machiaw' F1	JO,SN
Aubergine, 'Megal' hyb	SR
Aubergine, 'Mini Bambino'	T
Aubergine, 'Mini Finger' hyb	SK
Aubergine, 'Mission Bell' F1	FR
Aubergine, 'Moneymaker' F1	B,BD,BS,DT,F,KI,L,MO, R,S,TU,VH
Aubergine, 'N'drowa Issia'	SN
Aubergine, 'Neon' F1	JO,SN
Aubergine, 'New York Round Purple'	BS,TH
Aubergine, 'No.226' F1	JO
Aubergine, 'Onita'	BS,SU
Aubergine, 'Orient Express' F1	JO,SN
Aubergine, Oriental 'Millionaire' F1	SK
Aubergine, 'Ova' F1	BS,C,CO,S,TU
Aubergine, 'Ping Tung Long' F1	AB,B,PI,PK,RC,V
Aubergine, 'Prelane' F1	SN
Aubergine 'Purple Balls'	SN
Aubergine, 'Purpura' F1	FR
Aubergine, 'Rosita' hyb	SK
Aubergine, 'Rotunda Bianca di Rosa' o-p	SN
Aubergine, 'Santana' hyb	SR
Aubergine, 'Short Tom' F1	BS,SU,TE
Aubergine, 'Sicilia' F1	FR
Aubergine, 'Silver Dollar'	DE
Aubergine, 'Slice Rite No.23'	M,U
Aubergine, 'Slim Jim'	FR,SN
Aubergine, 'Thai White'	DE
Aubergine, 'Turkish Gem'	DE,SD
Aubergine, 'Vernal' F1	BS,GO,SK
Aubergine, 'Violetti di Firenze'	FR,PI,SN
Aubergine, 'Vista' F1	BS,DT

AUBERGINE

Aubergine, 'Vittoria'	PK,SK
Aubergine, 'White Egg' F1	B,V
Balsam Pear, 'Moonshine'	BH
Barley, Hulless, 'Arabian Blue'	SP
Barley, Hulless, 'Arabian Purple'	SP
Barley, Hulless, easy thresh	SP
Barley, Hulless, 'Ethiopian'	SP
Barley, Hulless, 'Excelsior'	SP
Barley, Hulless, 'Faust'	SP
Barley, Hulless, 'Himalayan'	SP
Barley, Hulless, 'Lompoc'	SP
Barley, Hulless, mix	SP
Barley, Hulless, popping	SP
Barley, Hulless, 'Sangatsuga'	SP
Barley, Hulless, 'Sheba'	SP
Barley, Hulless, 'Thual'	SP
Beans, Adzuki	B,DD,HU,SP,T
Beans, Adzuki, 'Adzuki Express'	JO
Beans, Asparagus, black seeded	RC
Beans, Asparagus, 'Extra Early Ben'	F
Beans, Asparagus, 'Green Pod Kaohsiung'	V
Beans, Asparagus, 'Liana'	J
Beans, Asparagus, 'Long White Snake'	RC
Beans, Asparagus (Pea)	BS,BY,C,CO,D,F,KS,KI, MC,ST,SU,T,TH,TU,V
Beans, Asparagus, 'Purple Mart'	V
Beans, Asparagus, 'Sabah Snake'	RC
Beans, 'Azores'	SP
Beans, 'Boston Beauty'	SP
Beans, Broad, 'Acme' see Masterpiece Longpod	
Beans, Broad, 'Aquadulce'	AB,B,BD,BS,D,DE,DI, DT,F,FR,J,KI,MC,MO,S, SE,SK,SR,TH,VH
Beans, Broad, 'Aprovecho Large'	DD,SD
Beans, Broad, 'Aquadulce Claudia'	B,BS,BY,CO,D,KI,L,M, SE,SN,SU,T,TU,U,VR,YA
Beans, Broad, 'Banner'	DD
Beans, Broad, 'Bell'	SP
Beans, Broad, 'Bunyards Exhibition'	AB,B,BD,BS,CO,DT,F, J,KI,L,MC,MO,TH,TU, U,VH,VR
Beans, Broad, 'Chak'rusga'	SD
Beans, Broad, 'Con Amore'	VY
Beans, Broad, 'Cordiero'	SP
Beans, Broad, 'Crimson Flowered'	HD
Beans, Broad, 'Dreadnought'	BS,D,KI,VR,YA
Beans, Broad, 'Driemaal wit'	V
Beans, Broad, 'Excel'	DD
Beans, Broad, 'Express'	B,BS,CO,J,KI,M,MC, SU,T,TU,VR
Beans, Broad, extra early purple seed	FR
Beans, Broad, extra early white seed	FR
Beans, Broad, 'Fordhook 242 '	BU,JO,PK,SK,SR,TE,VY
Beans, Broad, 'Futura'	B,BD,BS,CO,MO
Beans, Broad, 'Giant Exhibition Longpod'	B,C,K,KI,MC,S,SB,SN, VR
Beans, Broad, 'Gloster Bounty'	HD
Beans, Broad, 'Guatemalan Purple'	SD
Beans, Broad, 'Hopi White Lima'	AB
Beans, Broad, 'Hylon'	BY,S,SN,TU
Beans, Broad, 'Iant's Yellow'	DD
Beans, Broad, 'Imperial Green Longpod'	AB,D,DT,FR,SK,T,VR
Beans, Broad, 'Imperial Green Windsor'	BS,J,TU,U
Beans, Broad, 'Jade'	BU,M,SE
Beans, Broad, 'Jubilee Hysor'	D,M
Beans, Broad, 'King of the Garden'	DE,PK,RC,SK

Beans, Broad, 'Martock'	HD
Beans, Broad, 'Masterpiece Gr. Longpod'	B,BD,BS,BY,C,CO,DT, F J,KI,L,MO,S,SU,TH,TU, VH,VR,YA
Beans, Broad, 'Meteor * Vroma'	M
Beans, Broad, 'Metissa'	CO
Beans, Broad, mix	DD,T
Beans, Broad, 'Mr. Barton's'	SP
Beans, Broad, 'Optica'	V
Beans, Broad, 'Perovka'	HD
Beans, Broad, purple	DD
Beans, Broad, 'Purple Fava'	SP
Beans, Broad, 'Red Epicure'	U,V
Beans, Broad, 'Reina Blanca'	M
Beans, Broad, 'Reina Mora'	FR
Beans, Broad, 'Relon'	D,S
Beans, Broad, 'Rognon de Coq'	D,S,SN
Beans, Broad, 'Sieva'	PI
Beans, Broad, 'Simmons Red Streak'	SD
Beans, Broad, 'Statissa'	T
Beans, Broad, 'Stereo'	D,DT,YA
Beans, Broad, 'Superaguadulce' giant	FR
Beans, Broad, 'Sweet Lorane'	DD,SD
Beans, Broad, 'Talia'	C
Beans, Broad, 'The Sutton'	B,BD,BS,BY,CO,D,DT,F, J,KI,L,M,MC,MO,S,SN, SU,T,TU,U,V,VH
Beans, Broad, 'Threefold White'	BY,J
Beans, Broad, 'Topic'	S
Beans, Broad, 'Verdy'	D,T,U,VH
Beans, Broad, 'Windsor Green'	AB,B,BU,CO,KI,PI,SR, SU,TE,TH,VR
Beans, Broad, 'Windsor White'	B,BS,BY,CO,DI,KI,S,TH, VR
Beans, Broad, 'Witkeim'	MO
Beans, Broad, 'Witkeim Manita'	B,BD,CO,DT,J,KI,SN,TU, VR
Beans, Broad, 'Witkeim Vroma'	D,F,V
Beans, Broad, 'Witkeim Major'	B,U,VH
Beans, Butter, 'Chico'	SP
Beans, Butter, 'Hopi Tan'	DD
Beans, Butter, 'Manitoba Brown'	B,SP
Beans, Butter, 'Natto'	SP
Beans, 'Candy'	SP
Beans, Cannellini	FR,JO,PI,PK
Beans, Climbing, 'Anellino Giallo'	FR
Beans, Climbing, 'Anellino Verde'	FR
Beans, Climbing, 'Aunt Jean's'	SP
Beans, Climbing, 'Barbarossa'	FR
Beans, Climbing, 'Bingo'	FR
Beans, Climbing, black seeded	FR
Beans, Climbing, 'Borlotto Lingua di Fuoco'	AB,B,D,FR,JO,KI,SP,ST, SU,V
Beans, Climbing, 'Brejo'	AB,DD
Beans, Climbing, 'Cherokee Cornfield'	AB,DD
Beans, Climbing, 'Dow Purple Pod'	AB,SD
Beans, Climbing, 'Emerite'	GO,PI,SK
Beans, Climbing, 'Fortex'	JO
Beans, Climbing French, 'Algarve'	D,YA
Beans, Climbing French, 'Blue and White'	HD
Beans, Clim. Fr., 'Blue Lake' White Seeded	AB,B,BS,BU,BY,C,CO,D, DI,DT,F,J,KI,L,M,MC, MO,PK,S,SK,SN,SU,TE, TU,VR,VY
Beans, Climbing French, 'Borlotto di Vigevano'	FR
Beans, Climbing French, 'Borlotto' white	FR

BEANS

Beans, Climbing Fr., 'Burro d'Ingegnoli' FR,SN,SU
Beans, Climb. Fr., 'Cherokee Trail of Tears' AB,HD
Beans, Climbing French, 'Coco Bicolour' HD
Beans, Climbing French, 'Corona D'Oro' J,KI,L,TU,VR
Beans, Climbing French, 'Cosse Violette' TU
Beans, Climbing French, 'Crystal' K,YA
Beans, Climbing French, 'Festival' MO
Beans, Climbing French, 'Florint' MO
Beans, Climbing French, 'Goldmarie' JO,S
Beans, Climbing French, 'Hunter' B,CO,DT,F,J,KI,L,M,S, SU,TU,VR
Beans, Climbing French, 'Jack Edward's' HD
Beans, Climbing French, 'Kentucky Blue' CO,K,KI,PK,T,TE,S,VY
Beans, Climbing French, 'Kingston Gold' RO
Beans, Climbing French, 'Kronos' MO
Beans, Climbing French, 'Kwintus' MO
Beans, Climbing French, 'Largo' M
Beans, Climbing French, 'Marvel of Venice' B,CO,FR,SU
Beans, Climbing French, Mix T
Beans, Climbing French, 'Musica' MO,VH
Beans, Climbing French, 'Neckargold' D,FR
Beans, Climbing French, 'Oregon Giant' HD
Beans, Climbing French, 'Pea Bean' BS,CO,MC,SU,TH
Beans, Climbing French, 'Purple Giant' HD
Beans, Climbing French, 'Purple King' DI,J,KI,V
Beans, Climbing French, 'Purple Podded' DI,HD,S
Beans, Climbing French, 'Red Robin' HD
Beans, Climbing French, 'Rob Roy' RO
Beans, Climbing French, 'Rob Splash' RO
Beans, Climbing French, 'Romano' DD,DE,DI,PI,RC,SD,SP, T
Beans, Climbing French, 'Selma Zebra' HD
Beans, Climbing French, 'Viola Cornetti' CO,SU
Beans, Climbing Fr., 'Violet Pod Stringless' F,TE
Beans, Climbing French, 'Yugoslavia No.1' HD
Beans, Climbing, 'Garafal Oro' PI
Beans, Climbing, 'Genuine Cornfield' RC
Beans, Climbing, 'Goja' J
Beans, Climbing, 'Gramma Walters' AB,SP
Beans, Climbing, 'Hickman's' SD
Beans, Climbing, 'Inge Hanle' SP
Beans, Climbing, 'Kapral' DD
Beans, Climbing, 'Lamon' FR
Beans, Climbing, long green FR
Beans, Climbing, 'Northeaster' JO
Beans, Climbing, 'Oregon Giant' AB,SD
Beans, Climbing, 'Purple Peacock' PI
Beans, Climbing, 'Rattlesnake Snap' DD,PI
Beans, Climbing, 'Robison Purple Pod' AB
Beans, Climbing, 'Scotch' AB
Beans, Climbing, 'Spagna' white FR
Beans, Climbing, 'Stregonta' FR
Beans, Cl., 'Superbo d'Ingegnoli Migliorato' FR
Beans, Climbing, 'Trionfo Violetto' FR,JO,SP
Beans, Climbing, 'True Cranberry' AB
Beans, Climbing, white seeded FR
Beans, Coloured Collection DT
Beans, 'Daytona' SK
Beans, Dwarf, 'Adventist' DD,SP
Beans, Dwarf, 'Agassiz Pinto' JO
Beans, Dwarf, 'Agate Pinto' AB
Beans, Dwarf, 'Algarrobo' AB
Beans, Dwarf, 'Anasazi' AB,DE,SP
Beans, Dwarf, 'Appaloosa' AB,PK,SP
Beans, Dwarf, 'Arikara Yellow' AB,SP
Beans, Dwarf, 'Arranesco' HD

Beans, Dwarf, 'Aztec Red Kidney' AB,BF
Beans, Dwarf, 'Baccicia' SD
Beans, Dwarf, 'Beautiful' SP
Beans, Dwarf, 'Beka Brown' SP
Beans, Dwarf, 'Benton' BU
Beans, Dwarf, 'Bert Goodwin's' SP
Beans, Dwarf, 'Black Canterbury' HD
Beans, Dwarf, 'Black Coco' JO,SD,SP,TE
Beans, Dwarf, 'Black Mexican' AB,HU,RC
Beans, Dwarf, 'Black Turtle' DE,PI,PK,SP
Beans, Dwarf, 'Black Turtle Soup,Midnight' JO,SP
Beans, Dwarf, 'Black Valentine' AB,HU,SP
Beans, Dwarf, 'Blower' DD
Beans, Dwarf, 'Bobis Bianco' FR
Beans, Dwarf, 'Boleta' SP
Beans, Dwarf, 'Bountiful' PI,SD
Beans, Dwarf, 'Boy' AB
Beans, Dwarf, 'Brittle Wax' HU
Beans, Dwarf, 'Buckskin' AB
Beans, Dwarf, 'Buckskin Girl' AB
Beans, Dwarf, 'Burpee's Imp Bush' BU
Beans, Dwarf, 'Butter Crisp' PK
Beans, Dwarf, 'Calypso' AB
Beans, Dwarf, 'Canada Wild Goose' DD
Beans, Dwarf, 'Canary' SP
Beans, Dwarf, 'Canberra' V
Beans, Dwarf, 'Castel' SR
Beans, Dwarf, 'Child's Delight' SP
Beans, Dwarf, 'Clem & Sarah's Big Bean' AB
Beans, Dwarf, 'Coco' AB,SD
Beans, Dwarf, 'Coco Nain Blanc Precoce' GO
Beans, Dwarf, 'Coquette' CO
Beans, Dwarf, 'Couch's' DD
Beans, Dwarf, 'Cranberry Horticultural' AB
Beans, Dwarf, 'Dandy' DE
Beans, Dwarf, 'Decibel' GO
Beans, Dwarf, 'Derby' PK,SK,SR,VY
Beans, Dwarf, 'Dog Bean' AB
Beans, Dw., 'Duane Baptiste's Potato Bean' SP
Beans, Dwarf, 'Earliserve' BU
Beans, Dwarf, 'Early Warwick' HD
Beans, Dwarf, 'English Long Green' SP
Beans, Dwarf, 'Ernie's Big Eye' HD
Beans, Dwarf, 'Etna' VY
Beans, Dwarf, 'Fisher' SP
Beans, Dwarf, 'Florence' PI,SP
Beans, Dwarf, 'Frazier's Choice' DD
Beans, Dwarf French, 'Admires z dr.' J,V
Beans, Dwarf French, 'Allure' FR
Beans, Dwarf French, 'Andrew Kent' JO
Beans, Dwarf French, 'Annabel' CO,D,KI,M,VR
Beans, Dwarf French, 'Aramis' T,TU,U
Beans, Dwarf French, 'Atlanta' K,T,VH
Beans, Dwarf French, 'Baffin' CO
Beans, Dwarf French, 'Brown Dutch' BS,CO,SP,SU
Beans, Dwarf French, 'Bush Blue Lake' B,BD,BS,BU,DE,K,PI, PK,SK,SN,SR
Beans, Dwarf French, 'Canadian Wonder' BS,BY,CO,J,KI,SU,TH, VR
Beans, Dwarf French, 'Capitole' DT,T
Beans, Dwarf French, 'Cascade' BD,MO
Beans, Dwarf French, Collection D
Beans, Dwarf French, 'Contender' BS,BU,CO,DE,DN,RC, SK,SR,SU
Beans, Dwarf French, 'Cropper Teepee' CO,F,J,KI,SU,TU
Beans, Dwarf French, 'Daisy' M,T

BEANS

Variety	Code
Beans, Dwarf French, 'Decibel'	SK
Beans, Dwarf French, 'Delinel'	M,RC,VY
Beans, Dwarf French, 'Deuil Fin Precoce'	CO,SU
Beans, Dwarf French, 'Dorabel'	SN
Beans, Dwarf French, 'Dutch Princess'	VH
Beans, Dwarf French, 'Fin de Bagnols'	B,GO,KS,SU
Beans, Dwarf French, 'Golddukat'	M,V
Beans, Dwarf French, 'Golden Butter'	CO,SU
Beans, Dwarf French, 'Golden Sands'	CO,SU
Beans, Dwarf French, 'Harvester'	BU
Beans, Dwarf French, 'Horsehead'	CO,U
Beans, Dwarf, 'French Horticultural'	HD,PI,SK,SR
Beans, Dwarf French, 'Irago'	TU
Beans, Dwarf French, 'Lasso'	F
Beans, Dwarf French, 'Laura'	YA
Beans, Dwarf French, 'Limelight'	SP
Beans, Dwarf French, 'Maradonna'	R
Beans, Dwarf French, 'Masai'	SN,T
Beans, Dwarf French, 'Masterpiece'	BS,BY,D,F,J,KI,MO,S,SU,VR
Beans, Dwarf Fr., 'Masterpiece Stringless'	D,M,RU
Beans, Dwarf French, 'Milagrow'	YA
Beans, Dwarf French Mix	GO,T
Beans, Dwarf French, 'Mondeo'	D
Beans, Dwarf French, 'Mont d'Or'	BS,BY,C,F,M,MO,S,T,TH,U,VR
Beans, Dwarf French, 'Montano'	DT,J,L,MO,V,YA
Beans, Dwarf French, 'Narbonne'	JO
Beans, Dwarf French, 'Nassau'	CO,DT,L,S
Beans, Dwarf, French Navy	SU
Beans, Dwarf French, 'Nerina'	FR,SP
Beans, Dwarf French, 'Odessa'	J
Beans, Dwarf French, 'Primel'	M,SE
Beans, Dwarf French, 'Processor'	MO
Beans, Dwarf French, 'Pros'	D
Beans, Dwarf French, 'Pros Gitana'	SE,U
Beans, Dwarf French, 'Provider'	AB,DN,JO,PI,SD,SK,SP,SU,VY
Beans, Dwarf French, 'Purple Queen'	F,L,S,SP,U
Beans, Dwarf French, 'Purple Teepee'	D,F,PK,SN,SU,T
Beans, Dwarf French, 'Radar'	T
Beans, Dwarf French, 'Rido'(Kenyan)	C
Beans, Dwarf French, 'Roma II'	PK,SK,SR,VY
Beans, Dwarf French, 'Roquencourt'	DT,GO,R,SN,SU
Beans, Dwarf French, 'Royalty Purple Pod'	AB,BF,BY,C,CO,DT,HU,JO,KI,M,SD,SP,SU,TU
Beans, Dwarf French, 'Safari'	K,M,S
Beans, Dwarf French, 'Safran'	F
Beans, Dwarf French, 'Slenderette'	FR,PK,SP
Beans, Dwarf French, 'Sprite'	BS,KI
Beans, Dwarf French, 'Sungold'	TU
Beans, Dwarf French, 'Sunray'	DT,L
Beans, Dwarf French, 'Tavera'	JO
Beans, Dwarf French, 'Tendercrop'	PK
Beans, Dwarf French, 'Tendergreen'	AB,B,BD,BF,BS,BY,CO,DT,F,J,KI,MC,MO,S,SK,TU,VR
Beans, Dwarf French, 'Tendergreen Imp'	BU,PI,SK
Beans, Dwarf French, 'The Prince'	BD,BS,BY,C,CO,DD,DT,F,K,KI,M,MO,S,T,TU,U,VR
Beans, Dwarf French, 'Top Crop'	SU
Beans, Dwarf French, 'Triomphe de Farcy'	B,GO,SU
Beans, Dwarf French, 'Vilbel'	T
Beans, Dwarf French, 'Wachs GoldPerle'	B
Beans, Dwarf, 'Frijol en Seco'	SP
Beans, Dwarf, 'Frijol Rojo'	RC
Beans, Dwarf, 'Garbanzo Black Kabouli'	AB,SD
Beans, Dwarf, 'Garbanzo Myles'	AB
Beans, Dwarf, 'Gatorgreen 15'	SR
Beans, Dwarf, 'Gaucho'	AB,SP
Beans, Dwarf, 'Geneva Bush'	SP
Beans, Dwarf, 'Gnuttle Amish'	DD,SP
Beans, Dwarf, 'Golden Rocky'	PI
Beans, Dwarf, 'Great Northern'	SP
Beans, Dwarf, 'Green Crop'	SR
Beans, Dwarf, 'Henderson Red'	SP
Beans, Dwarf, 'Henderson's Bush'	PI,PK,RC
Beans, Dwarf, 'Hialeah'	SK,SR
Beans, Dwarf, 'Hidatsa Red Indian'	AB,SP
Beans, Dwarf, 'Hignells Italian'	SP
Beans, Dwarf, 'Hopi Black'	AB,DD,SP
Beans, Dwarf, 'Humason's Best Bush'	AB
Beans, Dwarf, 'Hutterite Soup'	AB,HD,SD,SP
Beans, Dwarf, 'Ice/Crystal Wax'	HD
Beans, Dwarf, 'Immigrant'	AB,SP
Beans, Dwarf, 'Ireland Creek Annie's'	AB,SP
Beans, Dwarf, 'Jacob's Cattle'	AB,JO,PI,RC,SD,SP,VY
Beans, Dwarf, 'Jade'	JO,PK,SR,TE
Beans, Dwarf, 'Jumbo'	JO,PI,PK
Beans, Dwarf, 'Kebarika'	DD
Beans, Dwarf, 'Kenearly Baking Bean'	DD,VY
Beans, Dwarf, 'Kidney Dark Red'	SP
Beans, Dwarf, 'Kilham Goose'	AB
Beans, Dwarf, 'Kiva'	RC
Beans, Dwarf, 'Krol'	SP
Beans, Dwarf, 'Label'	SN
Beans, Dwarf, 'Landmark'	BU
Beans, Dwarf, 'Larry Locke's'	SP
Beans, Dwarf, 'Loreta'	JO
Beans, Dwarf, 'Low's Champion'	AB,JO,SP
Beans, Dwarf, 'Lucas Navy'	AB
Beans, Dwarf, 'Magpie'	AB,SD,SP
Beans, Dwarf, 'Maine Yellow Eye'	AB,JO,SP
Beans, Dwarf, 'Mansell Magic'	SP
Beans, Dwarf, 'Marbel'	SN
Beans, Dwarf, 'Marfax'	AB,SP
Beans, Dwarf, 'Mennonite'	SP
Beans, Dwarf, 'Minidor'	FR
Beans, Dwarf, 'Mirada'	SK,SR
Beans, Dwarf, 'Missouri Bill's'	DD
Beans, Dwarf, 'Mojave's'	SP
Beans, Dwarf, 'Molasses Face'	SP
Beans, Dwarf, 'Money'	AB,SP
Beans, Dwarf, 'Montcalm'	JO
Beans, Dwarf, 'Montezuma Red'	AB,SD,SP
Beans, Dwarf, 'Mountaineer'	PK
Beans, Dwarf Navy, 'Centralia'	SP
Beans, Dwarf, 'Negro Taxumal'	SP
Beans, Dwarf, 'Nez Perce'	AB,SP
Beans, Dwarf, 'Norwegian'	SP
Beans, Dwarf, 'Odawa Indian'	AB,DD
Beans, Dwarf, 'Orca'	SP
Beans, Dwarf, 'Oregon Trail'	SP
Beans, Dwarf, 'Paint' (Yellow Eye)	AB,DD
Beans, Dwarf, 'Painted Pony'	SP
Beans, Dwarf, 'Pawnee'	DD,SP
Beans, Dwarf, 'Pepa de Zapallo'	AB
Beans, Dwarf, 'Peregion'	AB
Beans, Dwarf, 'Pink'	SP
Beans, Dwarf, Pinto	PI
Beans, Dwarf, 'Plata'	AB

BEANS

Beans, Dwarf, 'Poroto Grenada'	SP	Beans, French Climbing, 'Epicure'	DI
Beans, Dwarf, 'Prelude'	GO,FR,J,V	Beans, French CL., 'Lazy Housewife's Bean'	DI
Beans, Dwarf, 'Prestige Salad'	DD	Beans, French, 'Cordoba'	V
Beans, Dwarf, 'Primo'	SK	Beans, French, 'Diamant'	DT
Beans, Dwarf, 'Prosperity'	VY	Beans, Dwarf French, 'Chopin'	DT
Beans, Dwarf, 'Rapids'	SR	Beans, Dwarf French, 'Pioneer'	DI
Beans, Dwarf, Red Kidney	BF,SK	Beans, Dwarf French,'Rasada'	D
Beans, Dwarf, 'Red Peanut'	SP	Beans, French, 'Nickel'	VY
Beans, Dwarf, 'Regal Salad'	PI	Beans, French, 'Vernel'	DE
Beans, Dwarf, 'Regalfin'	DD	Beans, 'Frenchie Green Bush'	SP
Beans, Dwarf, 'Remus'	PK,SP	Beans, Garbanzo	V
Beans, Dwarf, 'Robin's Egg Horticultural'	AB	Beans, Garbanzo, 'Black Kabouli'	DD
Beans, Dwarf, 'Rockwell'	AB	Beans, Garbanzo, 'Chestnut'	SP
Beans, Dwarf, 'Roma Gold'	PK	Beans, Garbanzo, Gene Pool mix	DD
Beans, Dwarf, 'Romanette'	DE	Beans, Garbanzo 'Hannan'	SP
Beans, Dwarf, 'Royal Burgundy'	DD,DE,PI,SK,SR,TE,VY	Beans, Garbanzo, 'Kala Channa'	HU
Beans, Dwarf, 'Ruckle'	SP	Beans, Garbanzo, 'Sarah'	DD
Beans, Dwarf, 'Rushmore'	SK,VY	Beans, 'Geril's'	SP
Beans, Dwarf, 'Sangre de Toro'	SP	Beans, 'Goodwin's Bush'	PI,SP
Beans, Dwarf, 'Santa Maria Pinquito'	RC,SP	Beans, 'Goodwin's Bush Butterbean'	SP
Beans, Dwarf, 'Sarah Ross' Black Bean'	SP	Beans, 'Goodwin's Green Bush'	SP
Beans, Dwarf, 'Scarlet Beauty'	SP	Beans, 'Goodwin's Tasmanian'	SP
Beans, Dwarf, 'Scuba'	FR	Beans, 'Gotlands Speckled'	SP
Beans, Dwarf, 'Seminole'	DD	Beans, 'Greencrop' see Bush Kentucky Wonder	
Beans, Dwarf, 'Sequoia'	JO,PI,PK,SD,SP	Beans , Guar (Cluster)	B,DD
Beans, Dwarf, 'Serene Bean'	SP	Beans, Haricot, 'Maxibel'	JO,PI
Beans, Dwarf, 'Seville'	PI,SK,SR	Beans, 'Hopi Purple'	SP
Beans, Dwarf, 'Shirokostruczkovnia'	HD	Beans, Lablab Climbing	PK,V
Beans, Dwarf, 'Six Nations'	AB,DD,SP	Beans, Lablab Climbing, 'Ruby Moon'	M
Beans, Dwarf, 'Snake Bean'	HD,DI	Beans, 'Landfrauen'	PK,SP
Beans, Dwarf, 'Soldier'	AB,HD,JO,RC,SP,VY	Beans, 'Large Speckled Christmas'	PK
Beans, Dwarf, 'Sonore'	FR	Beans, Lentil	HU
Beans, Dwarf, 'Spanish Tolosana'	SP	Beans, Lima, 'Dixie Butterpea'	PK
Beans, Dwarf, 'Spaulding'	DD	Beans, Lima, 'Dixie Butterpea Speckled'	PK
Beans, Dwarf, 'Speckled Bays' (Bale)	AB	Beans, Lima, 'Eastland'	PK,SK
Beans, Dwarf, 'Speculator'	SK	Beans, Lima, 'Jackson Wonder Bush'	DD,JO,PK,SP,SR,TE
Beans, Dwarf, 'Squaw Yellow'	AB,SD	Beans, Lima, 'Packer DM'	JO,PK
Beans, Dwarf, 'Steuben'	SP	Beans, Lima, 'Thorogreen Bush'	SR
Beans, Dwarf, 'Stregonta' dwarf	FR	Beans, Mini green	PK
Beans, Dwarf, 'Strike'	SK	Beans, Mini 'Mon Petit Cheri'	PK
Beans, Dwarf, 'Supermetis'	FR	Beans, Mini yellow	PK
Beans, Dwarf, 'Superpresto'	FR	Beans, mix, Heirloom Sampler	PK
Beans, Dwarf, 'Swedish Brown'	AB,SD,SP	Beans, Moth	HU
Beans, Dw., 'Taylor Horticultural Cranberry'	DD,SP	Beans, 'Mrs. Kramer's'	SP
Beans, Dwarf, 'Taylor's Dwarf Horticultural'	AB,SR,TE	Beans, 'Ojo de Cabra'	SP
Beans, Dwarf, 'Telstar'	FR	Beans, 'Old Romanian Romano'	SP
Beans, Dwarf, 'Tema'	SK	Beans, 'Old Rumanian'	SP
Beans, Dwarf, 'Texas Pink'	AB	Beans, 'Pa-Pa'	BH
Beans, Dwarf, 'Thousand to One'	SP	Beans, 'Parisian String'	SP
Beans, Dwarf, 'Topcrop'	BU	Beans, 'Rapier'	SP
Beans, Dwarf, 'Triumph de Farcy'	AB,JO	Beans, 'Rattlesnake'	SP
Beans, Dwarf, 'Trout Black/White'	AB	Beans, Red Kid., 'Bruine Noordhollandse'	V
Beans, Dwarf, 'Uncle Willie's'	AB,SP	Beans, 'Rhodonizer'	SP
Beans, Dwarf, 'Venture'	JO,PK,SP	Beans, 'Rice Bean'	SP
Beans, Dwarf, 'Vermont Cranberrry'	JO,PI,RC	Beans, Rice, 'Rojo de Seda'	SP
Beans, Dwarf, 'Wade'	FR	Beans, Runner, 'Achievement'	BD,J,M,MO,S,SB,SN, TU,VR
Beans, Dwarf, 'White Aztec'	PK		
Beans, Dwarf, White Marrow	SK	Beans, Runner, 'Aztec' (Half Runner)	SD
Beans, Dwarf, 'Yugoslavian No.4'	HD	Beans, Runner, 'Barnett'	AB
Beans, Dwarf, 'Zuni Shalako'	AB	Beans, Runner, 'Best of All'	S
Beans, Flageolet	B,DD,SP,V	Beans, Runner, 'Bird's Egg'	DD,SP
Beans, Flageolet, 'Chevrier Vert'	B,GO,SU,TH	Beans, Runner, 'Black'	PK
Beans, Flageolet, 'Flambeau'	JO,SP	Beans, Runner, 'Black Knight'	AB
Beans, 'Forks'	SP	Beans, Runner, 'Black Seeded Blue Lake'	SD
Beans, 'Fradinho'	SP	Beans, Runner, 'Blackcoat'	DD
Beans, French, 'Astrel'	DE	Beans, Runner, 'Bok'	HD

283

BEANS

Beans, Runner, 'Cave Bean' — DD
Beans, Runner, 'Chapman's Horticultural' — AB,DD
Beans, Runner, 'Crusader' — BD,BY,F,KI,L,MC,SB,SN
Beans, Runner, 'Czar' — CO,J,SN,SU,TH,TU
Beans, Runner, 'Don Collis' — SP
Beans, Runner, 'Droitwich Champion' — HD
Beans, Runner Dwarf, 'Hestia' — J
Beans, Runner, 'Enorma' — B,BD,BS,DD,DT,F,KI,J, L,M,MC,MO,R,S,SE, SN,TU,VH,VR,YA
Beans, Runner, 'Enorma Elite' — K
Beans, Runner, 'Erecta' — V
Beans, Runner, 'Fat White Boys' — SP
Beans, Runner, 'Galaxy' — U
Beans, Runner, 'Garden of Eden' — JO
Beans, Runner, 'Grammy Tilley' — PI
Beans, Runner, 'Hammonds Dwarf Scarlet' — B,BY,CO,KI,SN,SU,T,U, VH,VR
Beans, Runner, 'Japanese' — DD
Beans, Runner, 'Jembo Polish' — AB
Beans, Runner, 'Jerusalem' — DD
Beans, Runner, 'Kelvedon Marvel' — B,BD,BS,BY,CO,KI,M, MO,SN,SU,TU,U,VR, YA
Beans, Runner, 'Kentucky Wonder' — AB,BF,BU,DE,PI,PK,SD, SK,SR,TE
Beans, R., 'Kentucky Wonder, Mr Waters' — AB
Beans, R., 'Kentucky Wonder White Seed' — DE
Beans, Runner, 'Liberty' — BY,RO
Beans, Runner, 'Louisiana Purple Pod' — AB
Beans, Runner, 'Mortgage Lifter' — SP
Beans, Runner, 'Mrs. Cannell's Black' — HD
Beans, R, 'New Hampshire Horticultural' — AB
Beans, Runner, 'New Mexico Cave Bean' — AB
Beans, Runner, 'Nugget' — SR
Beans, Runner, 'Painted Lady' — B,BS,BY,CO,D,DI,DT,F, KI,M,MC,SN,SU,TE, TH,TU,VR
Beans, Runner, 'Prizetaker' — BS,KI
Beans, Runner, 'Prizewinner' — BS,BY,C,F,KI,S,SN,TH, TU,U,V
Beans, Runner, 'Red Rum' — T
Beans, Runner, 'Scarlet Emperor' — w.a.
Beans, Runner, 'Scarlet' see Scarlet Emperor
Beans, Runner, 'Streamline' — B,BD,BS,BY,C,CO,D,DT, F,J,KI,M,MO,T,TU,U, VH,VR,YA
Beans, Runner, 'Sunrae' — SR
Beans, Runner, 'Sunset' — HD
Beans, Runner, 'Trail of Tears' — DD
Beans, Runner, 'White Achievement' — S
Beans, Runner, 'White Emergo' — B,BD,BS,DT,F,KI,L,MO, U,YA
Beans, Runner, 'White Frost' — AB
Beans, Runner, 'White Half Runner' — SR
Beans, Runner, 'Zebra Horticultural' — AB,DD
Beans, Runner, 'Zembylas' — DD
Beans, 'Scarlet Bees' — SP
Beans, Soy, 'Agate' — SD,SP
Beans, Soy, 'Black Jet' — AB,B,JO,PI,SP
Beans, Soy, 'Butterbean' — B,JO
Beans, Soy, 'Butterpea' — SP
Beans, Soy, 'Early Hakucho' — B,PK
Beans, Soy, 'Envy' — B,JO
Beans, Soy, 'Gieso' — V
Beans, Soy, 'Grand Forks' — B,SP

Beans, Soy, green — CO
Beans, Soy, 'Hokkaido Black Soybean' — SP
Beans, Soy, 'Kura Kake Daizu' — SP
Beans, Soy, 'Lammer's Black' — SD
Beans, Soy, 'Prize Vegetable' — DE
Beans, Soy, 'Tohya' — SD
Beans, Soy, 'Verde' — AB
Beans, Soy, 'Vinton' — PI
Beans, Soy, yellow — BF
Beans, 'Stevenson Blue Eye' — SP
Beans, 'Stinger' — SP
Beans, Stringless Runner, 'Butler' — CO,KI,SR
Beans, Stringless Runner, 'Desiree' — BY,CO,DT,F,KI,M,MC,R, SN,T,V,VH,VR
Beans, Stringless Runner, 'Fergie' — DT,F
Beans, Stringless Runner, 'Gulliver' — D
Beans, Stringless Runner, 'Ivanhoe' — T
Beans, Stringless Runner, 'Kelvedon' — D
Beans, Stringless Runner, 'Lady Di' — DT,F,J,K,KI,L,SE,SN,T, TU,VH,VR
Beans, Stringless Runner, 'Mergoles' — D,DT,F,S
Beans, Stringless Runner, 'Pickwick' — BD,DT,F,J,M,MC,MO,S, TU,U
Beans, Stringless Runner, 'Polestar' — B,BD,CO,DT,F,J,M,MC, MO,S,U
Beans, Stringless Runner, 'Red Knight' — B,BY,CO,DD,F,KI,M,MC, SU,VH,VR
Beans, Stringless Runner, 'Royal Standard' — D,T
Beans, Tepary, 'Durango' — DD
Beans, Tepary, 'Light Brown' — RC
Beans, Tepary, 'Mitla Black' — AB,DD,SD,SP
Beans, Tepary, 'Sonoran Gold' — AB,SD,SP
Beans, Tepary, 'Warihio' — DD
Beans, Tepary, 'White' — AB
Beans, 'Ukranian' — SP
Beans, 'Urd' — SP
Beans, Wax, 'B.B.Wax' — PI
Beans, Wax Bush 'Buerre d'Rocquencourt' — AB,GO,SD
Beans, Wax Bush 'Cherokee' — AB,BU,DE
Beans, Wax Bush 'Dragon's Tongue' — AB,DD,DI,PI,SP,TE
Beans, Wax Bush 'Pencil Pod Wax' — AB,DE,PI,SP
Beans, Wax, 'Dorabel' — PI,SK
Beans, Wax, 'Fortin Wax' — SP
Beans, Wax, 'Galagold' — SP
Beans, Wax, 'Gold Crop' — SK
Beans, Wax, 'Gold Mine' — SK,VY
Beans, Wax, 'Gold Rush' — SK,VY
Beans, Wax, 'Golden Rod' — SK
Beans, Wax, 'Golden Wax' — DD
Beans, Wax, 'Goldkist' — JO,SK,SR,VY
Beans, Wax, 'Kentucky Wonder' — SK
Beans, Wax, 'Rapier Wax' — SP
Beans, Wax, 'Rocdor' — JO,RC,SD,SK,SN,SP
Beans, Wax, 'Romano/Italian' — AB,JO,PI,SK
Beans, Wax, 'Sally Sunshine' — SP
Beans, Wax, 'Slenderwax' — J
Beans, Wax, 'Valdor' — SK
Beans, Wax, yellow — BF
Beans, 'White Kahl' — SP
Beans, 'World War' — SP
Beans, Yard Long — AB,CO,FR,KS,PK,RI,SU
Beans, 'Yellow Green Kahl' — SP
Beans, 'Zert' — SP
Beet, Fodder — BY
Beetroot, 'Action' — JO,M,PI
Beetroot, 'Albina Vereduna' — DI,GO,KS,T,TE

BEETROOT

Beetroot, 'Always Tender' — VY
Beetroot, 'Avon Early' — BS,HD
Beetroot, 'Bikores' — B,BS,DT,J,KI,MO,VH
Beetroot, 'Boldet' — BS
Beetroot, 'Boltardy' — B,BD,BS,BY,C,CO,D,F,J,
KI,L,M,MC,MO,R,S,
SE,SN,ST,SU,T,TU,U,
V,VH,YA
Beetroot, 'Bonel' — BS,F
Beetroot, 'Boston' — BS
Beetroot, 'Bull's Blood' — AB,B,TH
Beetroot, 'Burpee's Golden' — BS,BY,C,D,DT,GO,J,L,
PI,S,SK,T,TH,TU,V,VY
Beetroot, 'Cheltenham Green Top' — B,BS,BY,KI,SU,TH
Beetroot, 'Cheltenham Green Top Select' — BD,BS,CO,MO
Beetroot, 'Cheltenham Mono' — BS,M
Beetroot, 'Chioggia' — AB,C,DD,DI,JO,PI,SD,
SN,T,TE,TH,V
Beetroot, 'Crimson King' — BS,KI,ST
Beetroot, 'Crosby's Egyptian' — AB,B,BF,DD,DE,DT,GO,
JO,PI,SD,TE
Beetroot, 'Cylindra' — AB,B,BS,BU,BY,DN,DT,
J,JO,KI,L,M,PI,PK,SK,
SU,T,TH,TU,U,VH
Beetroot, 'Cyndor' — VY
Beetroot, 'Detroit' — AB,BS,BU,DE,KI,PI,PK,
SB,SD,SK,SU,VH
Beetroot, 'Detroit 2' — J,M
Beetroot, 'Detroit 2 Little Ball' — BS,D,KS,M,S,TU
Beetroot, 'Detroit 2 Nero' — F
Beetroot, 'Detroit 2 New Globe' — BS,CO,D,S,YA
Beetroot, 'Detroit 2 Spinel' mini — VH
Beetroot, 'Detroit 2 Tardel' — BS,CO,SN,T
Beetroot, 'Detroit 6 Rubidus' — T
Beetroot, 'Detroit Crimson Globe' — BD,BS,BY,F,T
Beetroot, 'Detroit Globe' — BS,C,DI,MC,MO,ST,TU
Beetroot, 'Detroit Supreme' — SK,TE
Beetroot, 'Devoy' — HD
Beetroot, 'Dwergina' — B,BS,BY,C,KI,SN,ST
Beetroot, 'Early Wonder' see Crosby's Egyptian
Beetroot, 'Egyptian Turnip Rooted' — BS,TH
Beetroot, 'First Crop' — VY
Beetroot, 'Formanova' see Cylindra
Beetroot, 'Forono' — BS,CO,D,F,KI,S,ST,TE,
V,YA
Beetroot, 'Golden' — AB,B,BU,CO,DI,JO,KI,
KS,MC,PK,SU,TE
Beetroot, 'Golden Ball' — BS,SN,ST
Beetroot, 'Green Top Bunching' — SK
Beetroot, 'Kestrel' hyb — SR,TE
Beetroot, 'Libero' — BS,CO,KI,SN
Beetroot, Long K's selected — K
Beetroot, long season — HU
Beetroot, 'Lutz Green Leaf' — AB,DD,PI,PK,SD
Beetroot, 'Mammoth Long' — RO
Beetroot, Mini Gourmet — DI
Beetroot, Mix — AB,GO,T
Beetroot, 'Modena' — DT
Beetroot, 'Monaco' Mini — D
Beetroot, 'Mondella' — BS,BY,F
Beetroot, 'Moneta' — BS,KI,S,T,U
Beetroot, 'Monodet' Monogerm — BS,M
Beetroot, 'Monogram' — BS,J,PI,T,U,V
Beetroot, 'Monopoly' Monogerm — BS,CO
Beetroot, 'Motown' Monogerm — D,M
Beetroot, 'Nobolt' (Boltardy Selected) — BS

Beetroot, 'Pablo' F1 — BS,DT,K,L,PI,S,SB,TU,
VH,VY
Beetroot, 'Pacemaker III' F1 — SK,SR,TE
Beetroot, 'Paonazza d'Egitto' — FR
Beetroot, 'Perfect 2' — J
Beetroot, 'Perfect 3' — F
Beetroot, 'Pronto' — B,BD,BS,DT,K,MO,S
Beetroot, 'Red Ace' F1 — F,JO,K,PI,PK,RO,S,SE,
SK,T,TE,U,VY
Beetroot, 'Red Crapaudine' — GO
Beetroot, 'Regala' — BS,FR,SU,U
Beetroot, 'Rubigala' — BS
Beetroot, 'Ruby Queen' — BU,DE,DN,PI,RC,SK
Beetroot, 'Sangria' — BU
Beetroot, 'Sanguigna d'Ingegnoli' — FR
Beetroot, 'Scarlet Supreme' — DE,VY
Beetroot, 'Solo' F1 — SK,SR
Beetroot, special early — SK
Beetroot, 'Tonda di Chioggia' — B,BS,CO,FR,SU,TH
Beetroot, 'Warrior' hyb — SK
Beetroot, 'Winter Keeper' — AB,SK,TE
Beetroot, 'Wodan' F1 — K
Bitter Gourd, 'Halflange Groene' — V
Bitter Gourd, 'High Moon' F1 — V
Bitter Gourd, 'Long Green' — V
Broccoli, 'Albenga' — FR
Broccoli, 'Alverda' hyb — SR
Broccoli, 'Autumn Calabrese' — BH,TH,U
Broccoli, 'Boram 92' — PI
Broccoli, 'Captain' F1 — SK,SR
Broccoli, 'Caravel' F1 — T
Broccoli, Chinese — RC
Broccoli, 'Christmas Marvel' — M
Broccoli, 'Claret' F1 — DT,K,M,T
Broccoli, 'De Cicco' — AB,BS,DE,JO,SD,SU,TH
Broccoli, 'Dia Green' F1 — PI
Broccoli, 'Early Dividend' F1 — PI,VY
Broccoli, early green — SD
Broccoli, 'Early Purple Sprouting' — B,BS,BY,D,DT,F,KI,KS,L,
R,ST,TU,YA
Broccoli, 'Early Purple Sprouting Blend' — M
Broccoli, 'Early Purple Sprout. Red Arrow' — D, J, T
Broccoli, 'Early White Sprouting' — B,BS,BY,F,K,KI,M,SU,T,
TU,U,VH,YA
Broccoli, 'El Centro' — M
Broccoli, 'Emerald' F1 — PK,SK
Broccoli, 'Eureka' hyb — SK
Broccoli, 'Everest' F1 — SK,SR
Broccoli, 'Futura' F1 — V
Broccoli, 'Goliath' hyb — SK
Broccoli, 'Green King' — BH
Broccoli, 'Green Spring' — DD
Broccoli, 'Green Valiant' F1 — JO,SK,SR,TE,VY
Broccoli, 'Greenbelt' F1 — SR
Broccoli, 'Italian Sprouting' — DT,F,HU,PI,SK
Broccoli, 'Late Purple Sprouting' — B,BS,BY,DT,KI,L,M,ST,
SU,T
Broccoli, 'Late White Sprouting' — B,BS,BY,D,DT,KI,L,M
Broccoli, 'Late White Sprouting White Star' — K,T
Broccoli, 'Late Wh. Sp. White Star - Tozer' — BS
Broccoli, 'Legend' F1 — SK,SR
Broccoli, 'Mariner' F1 — SK,SR
Broccoli, 'Marshalls Long Season' — M
Broccoli, 'Minaret' — JO
Broccoli, 'Mix' — AB,BH,PK,SE,T,TE
Broccoli, 'Nine Star Perennial' — BS,C,KI,M,SD,TH

285

BROCCOLI

Broccoli, 'Paragon' hyb	GO,SK
Broccoli, 'Patriot' F1	SK,SR
Broccoli, 'Purple Sprouting'	AB,BD,BH,C,CO,J,MC, MO,S,SD,SU,TH,U,V,VH
Broccoli, 'Purple Sprouting Red Arrow'	BS,BY,CO,K,TU
Broccoli, 'Purple Sprouting Redhead'	BS
Broccoli, 'Queen' F1	V
Broccoli Raab	DD,DE,HU,JO,KS,PK, SR,TE
Broccoli Raab, 'De Brocoletto'	BS,SU
Broccoli Raab, 'Novantina'	PI
Broccoli Raab, 'Salad Rappone'	SK
Broccoli Raab, 'Sessantina Grossa'	JO
Broccoli Raab, 'Spring Rapini'	RI,SK
Broccoli, 'Red Spear' F1	BS,L
Broccoli, 'Regal' hyb	SR
Broccoli, 'Romanesco'	AB,BS,BY,C,CO,D,DI, DT,FR,HU,KI,KS,M, PI,SD,SU,TU,VH
Broccoli, 'Royal Banquet'	U
Broccoli, 'Rudolph'	BS,DT,TU
Broccoli, 'Saga' F1	JO
Broccoli, 'Signal' hyb	SR
Broccoli, 'Small Miracle'	PI,PK
Broccoli, 'Snow Star'	M
Broccoli, 'Super Dome' F1	BU,PI
Broccoli, 'Temple'	T
Broccoli, 'Titleist' hyb	SR
Broccoli, 'Tribute' F1	VH
Broccoli, 'Trixie' F1	BS,CO,DT,KI,T,TU,M, ST,SU,U,YA
Broccoli, 'Umpqua'	AB,TE
Broccoli, 'Violet Queen'	GO
Broccoli, 'Waltham 29'	AB,BF,BU,DN,SD
Broccoli, 'White Eye'	T
Broccoli, 'White Sprouting'	BD,C,CO,J,MC,MO,ST, TH,V
Broccoli, 'White Sprouting Imp'	S
Broccoli, 'Windsor' hyb	SR
Broccoli, 'Zeus' hyb	SR
Broccoli/Cauliflower, 'Floccoli' F1	V
Brussels Sprouts, '2Pk Peer Gynt/ Welland'	M
Brussels Sprouts, 'Acropolis' F1	BS
Brussels Sprouts, 'Adonis' F1	T
Brussels Sprouts, 'Ajax' F1	BS
Brussels Sprouts, 'Aries' F1	BS
Brussels Sprouts, 'Bedford'	D,DT,VH
Brussels Sprouts, 'Bedford Darkmar 21'	BS,BY,F,J,R,TU
Brussels Sprouts, 'Bedford Fillbasket'	B,BS,BY,C,KI,S,SD,ST, SU,T,VH
Brussels Sprouts, 'Bedford Winter Harvest'	S
Brussels Sprouts, 'Boxer' F1	B,BS,FR,MO,VH
Brussels Sprouts, 'Braveheart' F1	TU
Brussels Sprouts, 'Bubbles'	DE,PI,SK
Brussels Sprouts, 'Cambridge No 5'	BS
Brussels Sprouts, 'Cascade' F1	BS,D,DT,K,KI
Brussels Sprouts, 'Catskill'	AB,BU,DN
Brussels Sprouts, 'Cavalier' F1	B,BS,MO,T,TU,VH
Brussels Sprouts, 'Citadel' F1	BS,KI,ST,T,VH
Brussels Sprouts, 'Claudette' F1	BS,KI,M,SE,YA
Brussels Sprouts, 'Collette' F1	BS,KI,M,ST
Brussels Sprouts, 'Content' F1	BS,M,SK,TU
Brussels Sprouts, 'Cor' F1 (Valiant)	BS,BD,SK,VY
Brussels Sprouts, 'Darkmar 21'	B,BD,CO,KI,MO
Brussels Sprouts, 'Diablo' F1	BS,K,L,MO,TU,VH
Brussels Sprouts, 'Dolmic' F1	T

Brussels Sprouts, 'Early Half Tall'	B,BD,BS,CO,FR,MO
Brussels Sprouts, 'Edmund'	BS
Brussels Sprouts, 'Energy'	BS
Brussels Sprouts, 'Evesham Special'	B,BD,BS,BY,DT,F,J,KI,L, MC,MO,SU,V
Brussels Sprouts, 'Evident'	BS
Brussels Sprouts, 'Explorer'	BS
Brussels Sprouts, 'Falstaff'	D,S
Brussels Sprouts, 'Fortress' F1	J,ST,V
Brussels Sprouts, 'Golfer'	B,BS,KI,MO
Brussels Sprouts, 'Hamlet'	D,S
Brussels Sprouts, 'Hunter'	BS
Brussels Sprouts, 'Icarus' F1	T,VH
Brussels Sprouts, 'Jade Cross E'	PI,PK,SK,SR,VY
Brussels Sprouts, 'JBS' F1	JO
Brussels Sprouts, 'Long Island'	SD
Brussels Sprouts, 'Long Island Imp'	BF,HU,RC
Brussels Sprouts, 'Lunet' F1	BS,M,MO,TU
Brussels Sprouts, 'Mallard'	U
Brussels Sprouts, 'Masterline' F1	DT,PI
Brussels Sprouts, 'Mezzo'	FR
Brussels Sprouts, 'Montgomery' F1	BS,D,L,M
Brussels Sprouts, 'Noisette'	B,BS,CO,SU
Brussels Sprouts, 'Odette' F1	BS,SU,T,YA
Brussels Sprouts, 'Oliver' F1	BS,BY,CO,DT,JO,KI,L, SK,ST,T
Brussels Sprouts, 'Peer Gynt' F1	B,BD,BS,BY,CO,D,DT,F, J,KI,L,M,MC,MO,S,SE, ST,SU,T,U,VH
Brussels Sprouts, 'Perfect Line' F1	BS
Brussels Sprouts, 'Predora' F1	BS,M,MO
Brussels Sprouts, 'Prelent' F1	BS,MO,TU
Brussels Sprouts, 'Prince Marvel' F1	BS,DE,GO,KI,PK,ST,TE
Brussels Sprouts, 'Profline' F1	DT
Brussels Sprouts, 'Rampart' F1	BD,CO,D,DT,J,KI,L,MO, ST,SU,TU,U
Brussels Sprouts, 'Revenge' F1	K
Brussels Sprouts, 'Roger'	BS,BY
Brussels Sprouts, 'Rous Lench'	BS
Brussels Sprouts, 'Rubine'	B,BS,BY,C,CO,F,GO,MC, SU,TE,V
Brussels Sprouts, 'Ruby'	DI
Brussels Sprouts, 'Saxon' F1	S
Brussels Sprouts, 'Seven Hills'	B,BS,BY,CO,KI,ST,SU
Brussels Sprouts, 'Sheriff' F1	BS,CO,K,M,SE,T,VH
Brussels Sprouts, 'Solent' F1	BS
Brussels Sprouts, 'Stan' F1	RO
Brussels Sprouts, 'Stephen'	BY
Brussels Sprouts, 'Stockade' F1	BS,TU
Brussels Sprouts, 'Talent' F1	BS,TU
Brussels Sprouts, 'Tavernos' F1	T
Brussels Sprouts, 'The Wroxton'	BS,TH
Brussels Sprouts, 'Topline'	BS,BY,DT,U
Brussels Sprouts, 'Trafalgar' F1	T
Brussels Sprouts, 'Trimmer' F1	BS
Brussels Sprouts, 'Troika' F1	BS,D,F,J
Brussels Sprouts, TZ18977 red	BS
Brussels Sprouts, TZ9011	T
Brussels Sprouts, 'Uniline'	DT
Brussels Sprouts, 'United'	BS
Brussels Sprouts, 'Victor' F1	BS
Brussels Sprouts, 'Vittoria'	BS,MO
Brussels Sprouts, 'Warrior' F1	K
Brussels Sprouts, 'Welland'	M
Brussels Sprouts, 'Wellington' F1	BS,F,KI,U
Buckwheat, 'Mancan'	AB

BUCKWHEAT

Buckwheat, 'Medawask'	AB
Cabbage, 'Admiral'	BS
Cabbage, 'Advantage' F1	DT,S,TU
Cabbage, 'Albion' hyb	SK
Cabbage, 'Algro'	FR
Cabbage, 'All Year Selection'	DD,M,VY
Cabbage, 'Amager Green Storage'	BS
Cabbage, 'Apex' F1	BS
Cabbage, 'Applause' hyb	SK
Cabbage, 'Aquarius'	BY
Cabbage, 'Aquila' F1	BS
Cabbage, 'Arena' F1	BS,YA
Cabbage, 'Atria' hyb	SK
Cabbage, 'Augusta'	SR
Cabbage, 'Avalon' hyb	SK
Cabbage, 'Avonquest'	BS
Cabbage, 'B.G. 283'	BS
Cabbage, 'Balbro' F1	BS,SK
Cabbage, 'Bartolo' F1	BS,MO,VY
Cabbage, 'Baseball'	BS
Cabbage, 'Bently' hyb	VY
Cabbage, 'Bergkabis'	VY
Cabbage, 'Bewama'	BS
Cabbage, 'Big Ben' F1	BS
Cabbage, 'Bingo' F1	BS,T
Cabbage, 'Bison' F1	BS
Cabbage, 'Black Tuscany'	D,DT,S
Cabbage, 'Blue Pak'	SR
Cabbage, 'Blue Vantage'	SK,SR
Cabbage, 'Brunswick'	BS,FR,HU,K,KI,MC,VH
Cabbage, 'Calorsa' F1	D
Cabbage, 'Cape Horn' F1	BS,BY,F,KI,YA
Cabbage, 'Cardinal' hyb	SK
Cabbage, 'Carlton' F1	K
Cabbage, 'Carnival' F1	BS
Cabbage, 'Castello' F1 Mini	BS,BY,F,M,T
Cabbage, 'Cavalier'	SK,SR
Cabbage, 'Celtic' F1	BD,BS,BY,CO,D,DT,F,
	KI,M,MC,MO,S,TU,U,YA
Cabbage, 'Charmant' F1	SK,TE,VY,YA
Cabbage, 'Cheers' F1	SK,SR
Cabbage, 'Chieftain Savoy'	AB,SD
Cabbage, Chinese, 'Blues' F1	BD,BS,JO,MO,SK,SR
Cabbage, Chinese, 'China Express' F1	BS,KI,TE,SU
Cabbage, Chinese, 'China Flash'	PK
Cabbage, Chinese, 'China King No 14' F1	C
Cabbage, Chinese, 'Chine Pride' F1	C,FR,SK,SR
Cabbage, Chinese Flowering see Choy	
Cabbage, Chinese, 'Green Rocket' F1	BS,FR,KI,SU
Cabbage, Chinese, 'Hy Sawi Manis'	RC
Cabbage, Chinese, 'Jade Pagoda' F1	BH,BS,KI,SK,SR,SU,YA
Cabbage, Chinese, 'Kasumi' F1	BS,DT,L,M,SK,TU,VY
Cabbage, Chinese, 'Kyoto No. 3'	FR
Cabbage, Chinese, lettucy type	B,JO
Cabbage, Chinese, 'Mariko' F1	BS
Cabbage, Chinese, 'Market Pride'	SD
Cabbage, Chinese, 'Michihli'	AB,B,BF,BU,PI,PK,RI,SK
Cabbage, Chinese, mix	BH
Cabbage, Chinese, 'Monument' F1	J,SK,SR
Cabbage, Chinese, 'Nagaoka 60 Day' F1	BS,F
Cabbage, Chinese, 'Nekita' F1	S
Cabbage, Chinese, 'Nozaki Early'	AB
Cabbage, Chinese, 'Okido' F1	BS
Cabbage, Chinese, 'One Kilo SB' F1	YA
Cabbage, Chinese, 'Optiko' F1	PI
Cabbage, Chinese, 'Orange Queen' F1	BS,KI,SK,SU,T

Cabbage, Chinese, 'Pride No.2'	DE
Cabbage, Chinese, 'Ruffles' F1	D,S
Cabbage, Chinese, 'Santo'	B,BS,KS,SU
Cabbage, Chinese, 'Serifon'	V
Cabbage, Chinese, 'Shaho Tsai'	BS
Cabbage, Chinese, 'Shantung' o-p	C
Cabbage, Chinese, 'Sixtyres'	BH
Cabbage, Chinese, spring F1	PI
Cabbage, Chinese, 'Summer Bright'	BH
Cabbage, Chinese, 'Summer Sun'	BH
Cabbage, Chinese, 'Summer Top' F1	JO
Cabbage, Chinese, 'T-652' hyb	SK
Cabbage, Chinese, 'Tango'	BS
Cabbage, Chinese, 'Tiptop' F1	BS,BY,C,CO,J,TU,V
Cabbage, Chinese, 'Yuki' hyb	SR
Cabbage, 'Christmas Drumhead'	BS,BY,CO,D,J,KI,L,M,
	MC,MO,S,ST,SU,TH,
	TU,U,VH
Cabbage, 'CLX 514' F1	YA
Cab., 'Coeur de Boeuf Moyen de la Halle'	GO
Cabbage, 'Colt' F1	D,K
Cabbage, 'Columbia' F1	JO
Cabbage, 'Copenhagen Market'	BS,BU,SK
Cabbage, 'Cortina' F1	K
Cabbage, 'Cotswold Queen'	BS,DT
Cabbage, 'Custodian' F1	BS,MO
Cabbage, 'D'Aubervilliers'	GO
Cabbage, 'Danish Ballhead'	BU,PI
Cabbage, 'Decema'	BD,DT
Cabbage, 'Decema Extra'	BS
Cabbage, 'Delicatesse'	BS
Cabbage, 'Delphi' F1	BS,MO
Cabbage, 'Derby Day'	BS,BY,DT,F,L,M,MO,TE,
	TU
Cabbage, 'Destiny' F1	K
Cabbage, 'Discovery'	DE,PI
Cabbage, 'Dorado'	BS
Cabbage, 'Duchy' F1	BS,DT,K,T
Cabbage, 'Duncan' F1	BS,BY,M,MO,TU,U,YA
Cabbage, 'Durham Elf'	K
Cabbage, 'Dynamo' F1	JO,PK,SE,SK,VY
Cabbage, 'Earliana Green'	SD
Cabbage, 'Early 711' hyb	SK
Cabbage, 'Early Marvel'	SK
Cabbage, 'Elisa' F1	BS,PK,YA
Cabbage, 'Ellam's Early Dwarf'	BS,TH
Cabbage, 'Emerald Acre'	DI,SK
Cabbage, 'Enkhuizen Glory'	BS,FR,ST
Cabbage, 'Estron' F1	BS
Cabbage, 'Eureka' F1	YA
Cabbage, 'Excel' F1	K
Cabbage, 'Felix' F1	F
Cabbage, 'Fidelio' F1	K
Cabbage, 'First Early Market No.218'	BD,BS,MO,ST,TU,U
Cabbage, 'First of June'	BS
Cabbage, 'Flagship' F1	BS,CO,J,K,SU,TU
Cabbage, 'Fortuna' hyb	BU
Cabbage, 'Freshma' F1	BS,F,KI,YA
Cabbage, 'Galaxy' hyb	SK
Cabbage, 'Gideon' hyb	VY
Cabbage, 'Golden Acre'	AB,B,BS,BU,BY,C,CO,D,
	DN,F,FR,KI,L,MC,PI,R,
	SK,ST,U,VH,YA
Cabbage, 'Golden Acre - Earliana'	D,J,MO
Cabbage, 'Golden Acre May Express'	S
Cabbage, 'Golden Acre Primo 11'	DT,J,M,MO,S,TU

287

CABBAGE

Cabbage, 'Golden Acre Special'	BS
Cabbage, 'Golden Cross'	B,BS,BY,KI,MO
Cabbage, 'Gourmet' F1	DT,SK,SR
Cabbage, 'Grand Slam'	SR
Cabbage, 'Green Coronet'	BS
Cabbage, 'Green Cup'	SR
Cabbage, 'Green Express' F1	FR,KI,YA
Cabbage, 'Green Jewel' F1	PK
Cabbage, 'Green Wonder'	BS
Cabbage, 'Greensleeves'	BS
Cabbage, 'Greenstart' hyb	SK
Cabbage, 'Grenedier'	SR
Cabbage, 'Greyhound'	BD,BS,BY,C,CO,D,DT,F, J,KI,L,M,MC,MO,R,S, ST,SU,TU,U,VH,YA
Cabbage, 'Harbinger'	BS,J
Cabbage, 'Hardora' F1	BS,CO
Cabbage, 'Hawke' F1	BY,D,S
Cabbage, 'Heads Up' hyb	SK
Cabbage, 'Hercules'	V
Cabbage, 'Hidena' F1	BS,BY,FR,U
Cabbage, 'Hilton' hyb	SK
Cabbage, 'Hispi' F1	BD,BS,BY,D,DT,F,J,KI,L, MC,MO,S,SE,ST,SU, T,TU,U,V
Cabbage, 'Histona'	U
Cabbage, 'Holland Late Winter'	BS,CO,KI,ST,SU,TU
Cabbage, 'Holland Winter White Extra Late'	BS,M,S,TU,U
Cabbage, 'Houston Evergreen'	SK,VY
Cabbage, 'Hyjula' F1	BS,MO,U
Cabbage, 'Impala' F1	K,MO
Cabbage, 'Izalco'	SR
Cabbage, 'Jason' F1	K
Cabbage, 'Jersey Wakefield'	AB,BF,BS,BU,DE,HU, JO,TH
Cabbage, 'K K Cross' F1	FR
Cabbage, 'Kalorama'	DT
Cabbage, 'Kingdom 65'	BS
Cabbage, 'Kingspi'	M
Cabbage, 'Krautman'	PI,VH
Cabbage, 'Langedijk 4 (Holl. Winter E50)'	BY,F,J,KI,V
Cabbage, 'Lasso Red'	DD,PI
Cabbage, late flat Dutch	BF,DE
Cabbage, 'Lennox' hyb	VY
Cabbage, 'Lincoln Improved'	BS
Cabbage, 'Little Rock'	SR
Cabbage, 'Loose Leaf Golden'	BH
Cabbage, 'Loughton' hyb	SK
Cabbage, 'Marabel' F1	K,SE,T,VH
Cabbage, 'Marathon' F1	K
Cabbage, 'Marnah Allfruh'	BS,KI
Cabbage, 'Marvellon' F1	BS
Cabbage, 'Mastergreen'	M
Cabbage, 'Mayfield'	DT
Cabbage, 'Meggaton' F1	K
Cabbage, 'Minicole' F1	BS,BY,CO,D,DT,F,J,KI,L, MO,S,SE,SU,T,TU,U,VH, VY
Cabbage, mix	GO,PI,T
Cabbage, 'Multikeeper' hyb	SK
Cabbage, 'Multiton' F1	TU
Cabbage, 'Nobilis'	BS,YA
Cabbage, 'O-S Cross' F1	DN
Cabbage, 'Offenham'	BS
Cabbage, 'Offenham 1 Little Kempsey'	BS
Cabbage, 'Offenham 2 First and Best'	BS

Cabbage, 'Offenham 3'	BS,R
Cabbage, 'Offenham 3 Kempsey'	BD,BS
Cabbage, 'Offenham - Flower of Spring 2'	BD,BS,C,D,F,J,S,ST,TH, TU
Cabbage, 'Olympic'	SR
Cabbage, 'Ontario' hyb	SK
Cabbage, 'Pacifica'	SR
Cabbage, Palm Tree, 'Di Toscana'	KS
Cabbage, 'Parel' hyb	VY
Cabbage, 'Patron' F1	BS
Cabbage, 'Pedrillo' F1	BS,FR,V
Cabbage, 'Pennant'	SR
Cabbage, 'Perfect Ball' F1	T
Cabbage, 'Pixie'	BS,BY,D,DT,L,M,S,T,U
Cabbage, 'Pointer' F1	YA
Cabbage, 'Polar Green' hyb	SK
Cabbage, 'Polestar' F1	BS
Cabbage, 'Polinius' F1	BS
Cabbage, 'Primax'	BS,JO
Cabbage, 'Primissimo d'Ingegnoli'	FR
Cabbage, 'Primo' see Golden Acre	
Cabbage, 'Princess' F1	BS
Cabbage, 'Progress'	BS
Cabbage, 'Pruktor'	SR
Cabbage, 'Puma' F1	YA
Cabbage, 'Pyramid'	BS
Cabbage, 'Quick Green Storage'	SK
Cabbage, 'Quick Start'	SR
Cabbage, 'Quickstep' F1	M,T
Cabbage, 'Quisto'	SK,SR
Cabbage, 'Rapid' F1	BS
Cabbage, 'Rapidity'	BS
Cabbage, 'Rapier'	BS
Cabbage, 'Red Acre Early'	AB,BU
Cabbage, Red, 'Autura' F1	BD,BS,MO,TU,VH
Cabbage, Red, 'Cicero' F1	K
Cabbage, 'Red Debut'	VY
Cabbage, Red, 'Drumhead'	BD,BY,C,CO,DD,DI,J,KI, MC,MO,S,ST,SU,TH,TU
Cabbage, 'Red Express'	JO
Cabbage, Red, 'Fire Dance' hyb	SK
Cabbage, Red, 'Hardoro' F1	BS,BY,J,KI,TU
Cabbage, Red, 'Huzaro' F1	K
Cabbage, 'Red Jewel'	SR
Cabbage, Red, 'Jewel' hyb	SK
Cabbage, Red, 'Kissendrup'	BS
Cabbage, Red, 'Langedijk Red Late'	BS
Cabbage, Red, 'Langedijk Red Medium'	D
Cabbage, Red, 'Meteor'	SK
Cabbage, Red, 'Metro' F1	M
Cabbage, Red, 'Niggerhead'	BS,FR
Cabbage, Red, 'Normiro'	BS,KI
Cabbage, Red, 'Primero' F1	D,K
Cabbage, Red, 'Raven' hyb	SK
Cabbage, 'Red Regal'	SK,SR
Cabbage, Red, 'Rio Grande' hyb	SK
Cabbage, Red, 'Rodeo' F1	BS,TU
Cabbage, Red, 'Rodima' F1	BS,T,YA
Cabbage, Red, 'Rodon' F1	BS
Cabbage, Red, 'Roma' F1	VY
Cabbage, Red, 'Rondy' F1	BS
Cabbage, Red, 'Rookie' F1	BS,F,KS
Cabbage, 'Red Royale'	PK
Cabbage, Red, 'Ruby Ball' F1	DE,F,L,M,PI,U
Cabbage, Red, 'Sombrero'	PI
Cabbage, 'Red Success'	SR

CABBAGE

Variety	Code
Cabbage, 'Red Super 80'	JO,SK,SR
Cabbage, Red, 'Winner' F1	BS,DT,F,L,M,U,YA
Cabbage, 'Regalia' hyb	SK
Cabbage, 'Regina'	SR
Cabbage, 'Rio Verde'	SK,SR
Cabbage, 'Robinson's Champion Giant'	RO
Cabbage, 'Roulette'	M
Cabbage, 'Ruby Perfection' F1	JO
Cabbage, 'Safekeeper II' hyb	SK
Cabbage, 'Salarite' F1	F
Cabbage, 'Savana' F1	BS
Cabbage, Savoy	BF
Cabbage, Savoy, 'Ace'	PI,SR
Cabbage, Savoy, 'Alexander's No 1'	BS,M
Cabbage, Savoy, 'Alex.'s No 1 Lincoln Late'	BS
Cabbage, Savoy, 'Avon Coronet'	BS
Cabbage, Savoy, 'Best of All'	BS,BY,CO,D,KI,MC,MO, ST,SU,TU
Cabbage, Savoy, 'Cantasa' F1	BD,K,MO
Cabbage, Savoy, 'Capriccio'	M
Cabbage, Savoy, 'Chirimen' F1	BS,YA
Cabbage, Savoy, 'Colorsa' F1 (red)	T
Cabbage, Savoy, 'Concerto' F1	YA
Cabbage, Savoy, 'Daphne'	YA
Cabbage, Savoy, 'Dwarf Green Curled'	BS,TH
Cabbage, Savoy, 'Famosa' F1	K
Cabbage, Savoy, 'Genuine'	SR
Cabbage, Savoy, 'Harnasa' F1	BS,KI
Cabbage, Savoy, 'January King'	AB,BS,BY,C,CO,DD,DI, KI,J,M,MC,R,ST,SU,TE, TH,U,VH
Cabbage, Savoy, 'January King 3'	BD,BS,D,DT,J,L,S
Cabbage, Savoy, 'J. K. 3 Hardy Late 3'	M,MO,TU,YA
Cabbage, Savoy, 'J.King Imp Extra Late'	BS
Cabbage, Savoy, 'January King Special'	BS
Cabbage, Savoy, 'Julius' F1	JO,SK,T,TE
Cabbage, Savoy, 'King' F1	BS,DT,F,FR,KI,SE,T,U,VY
Cabbage, Savoy, 'Lisboa'	RC
Cabbage, Savoy, 'Midvoy' F1	BS,DT,R
Cabbage, Savoy, 'Novum'	BS
Cabbage, Savoy, 'Novusa'	BS,M,TU
Cabbage, Savoy, 'Ormskirk 1'(Early)	BD,BS,KI,MO,SU,TH
Cabbage, Savoy, 'Ormskirk 1(Extra Late)'	BS,BY,TU
Cabbage, Savoy, 'Ormskirk 1(Late)'	BS,C,CO,D,DT,J,L,M,ST, TU,U,VH
Cabbage, Savoy, 'Ormskirk 1(Med)'	BS
Cabbage, Savoy, 'Ormskirk 1 Rearguard'	C,D,J,L,M,U
Cabbage, Savoy, 'Ovasa' F1	VH
Cabbage, Savoy, 'Paravoy' F1	BS
Cabbage, Savoy, 'Paresa' F1	YA
Cabbage, Savoy, 'Perfection Drumhead'	BS,HU,TH
Cabbage, Savoy, 'Polasa' F1	K
Cabbage, Savoy, 'Primavoy' F1	BS,SK
Cabbage, Savoy, 'Protovoy' F1	BS,D,S,VH
Cabbage, Savoy, 'Rhapsody' F1	YA
Cabbage, Savoy, 'Rigoletto' F1	DT,YA
Cabbage, Savoy, 'Salarite'	FR,PK
Cabbage, Savoy, 'Solid'	SR
Cabbage, Savoy, 'Speedy'	SK
Cabbage, Savoy, 'Taler' F1	M,SK
Cabbage, Savoy, 'Tarvoy' F1	KI,T,TU
Cabbage, Savoy, 'Tombola' F1	BS
Cabbage, Savoy, 'Traviata'	YA
Cabbage, Savoy, 'Tundra' F1	BS,BY,CO,D,DT,F,J,L, M,MO,SE,T,TU,U,YA
Cabbage, Savoy, 'Winter King 2'	M
Cabbage, Savoy, 'Winter King Harda' o-p	BS
Cabbage, Savoy, 'Winter King Shortie'	BS
Cabbage, Savoy, 'Winter Star' F1	BS
Cabbage, Savoy, 'Winterkoning' o-p	BS,V
Cabbage, Savoy, 'Winterton'	J
Cabbage, Savoy, 'Wintessa' F1	BS,KI,SU
Cabbage, Savoy, 'Wirosa' F1	BS,BY,DT,FR,MO,TU,VY, YA
Cabbage, Savoy, 'Wivoy' F1	BS,D,M,TU
Cabbage, Savoy, Yellow	V
Cabbage, 'Scanbo' F1	YA
Cabbage, 'Scanita' hyb	YA
Cabbage, 'Scanner' F1	YA
Cabbage, 'Scanvi' F1	YA
Cabbage, 'Scarisbrick'	BS
Cabbage, 'Scout' F1	BS
Cabbage, 'Sparkle' F1	K
Cabbage, 'Spartan' F1	BS
Cabbage, 'Speedon' F1	BS
Cabbage, 'Spirant' F1	BS
Cabbage, 'Spirit' F1	BS
Cabbage, 'Spitfire' F1	BS,CO,KI,MO
Cabbage, Spring, 'April'	BS,BY,KI,MO,S,ST,SU, TH,TU,VH,YA
Cabbage, Spring, 'Cotswold Queen'	CO,YA
Cabbage, Spring, 'Durham Early'	BD,BS,BY,DT,KI,M,MO, ST,TU,U,VH
Cabbage, Spring, 'Durham Elf'	BS,J,K,TU,YA
Cabbage, Spring, 'Durham Elf Elite Strain'	K
Cabbage, Spring, 'Earliest of All'	BD,BS,KI,SU
Cabbage, Spring, 'Early Queen'	BS,KI,SU
Cabbage, Spring, 'Express'	V
Cabbage, Spring, 'Fem 218'	YA
Cabbage, Spring, 'Flower of Spring'	BY,CO,KI,MO
Cabbage, Spring, 'Hero' F1	BS,CO,D,F,J,KI,M,MO, SE,ST,SU,TU,U,YA
Cabbage, Spring, 'Off. 3 Winter Green'	BS,YA
Cabbage, Spring, 'Off. Myatts Compacta' 1	BS,BY,CO,DT,KI,L,M, MO,TU,YA
Cabbage, Spring, 'Pewa'	YA
Cabbage, Spring, 'Prospera' F1	BS,MO,V
Cabbage, Spring, 'Sparkel' F1	D,F,K
Cabbage, Spring, 'Vanguard' F1	SE
Cabbage, Spring, 'Wheeler's Imperial'	BD,BS,BY,C,D,J,KI,MO, S,ST,TH,TU,YA
Cabbage, Spring, 'Wintergreen'	BY,CO,KI,SU
Cabbage, 'Springtime'	BS
Cabbage, 'Standby'	BS
Cabbage, 'Starski'	KI
Cabbage, 'Starski' o-p	BS,YA
Cabbage, 'Steppe' F1	BS
Cabbage, 'Stonehead' F1	BD,BS,BY,CO,D,DT,F,K I,L,MO,SK,ST,TU,VY,YA
Cabbage, 'Storage No.4' F1	JO
Cabbage, 'Super Action' F1	BS
Cabbage, 'Supergreen' F1	CO
Cabbage, 'Sure Vantage'	SR
Cabbage, 'Survivor' hyb	SK
Cabbage, Taiwanese, Bai tsa	BH
Cabbage, 'Tasty' F1	PK
Cabbage, 'Tenacity' hyb	SK
Cabbage, 'Tropic Giant'	PK
Cabbage, 'Tucana' hyb	SK
Cabbage, 'Vantage Point' F1	BS,KI,SB,SR
Cabbage, Walking Stick	B,C,F,T,V
Cabbage, 'Wiam'	BS,FR

CABBAGE

Cabbage, 'Winchester' F1	K
Cabbage, 'Winnigstadt'	BS,BY,C,CO,D,J,KI,M, MO,ST,SU,TH,VH
Calabrese	AB
Calabrese, All Season Blend	VY
Calabrese, 'Arcadia' F1	BS,JO,KI,SK,SN,SR,TU, YA
Calabrese, 'Autumn Spear'	S
Calabrese, 'Cape Queen' F1	BS
Calabrese, 'Citation' F1	D
Calabrese, 'Colonel'	BS
Calabrese, 'Comet Imp'	VY
Calabrese, 'Corvet' F1	B,BS,BY,CO,D,DT,F,KI, M,MO,SE,SN,ST,SU,TU, U
Calabrese, 'Cruiser' F1	BS,MO
Calabrese, 'Dandy' F1	BS,FR
Calabrese, 'Dundee' F1	YA
Calabrese, 'Emerald City' F1	BS,BY,YA
Calabrese, 'Emperor' F1	BS,CO,JO,KI,SK,U.VY
Calabrese, 'Eusebio' F1	J
Calabrese, 'Express Corona' F1	S
Calabrese, 'Ginga' F1	BS,BY,YA
Calabrese, 'Green Comet'	B,BD,BS,DN,F,MO,PI, ST,T
Calabrese, 'Green Duke'	BS,BY
Calabrese, 'Green Sprouting'	B,BD,BS,BY,C,CO,D,DI, FR,J,MC,MO,RC,ST,SU, VH
Calabrese, 'Greenbelt' F1	BS,L,SR,YA
Calabrese, 'Jewel' F1 Mini	BS,F
Calabrese, 'Landmark' F1	HD,SR
Calabrese, 'Lord' F1	DT
Calabrese, 'Marathon' F1	BS,DT,K,KI,L,R,SN,SR, TU,YA
Calabrese, 'Mercedes' F1	BS,CO,M
Calabrese, 'Morses 4638'	BS
Calabrese, 'Pacifica'	BS
Calabrese, 'Packman' F1	BS,DE,JO,PI,PK,SK,SR
Calabrese, 'Pinnacle' F1	BS,FR
Calabrese, 'Pirate'	BS
Calabrese, 'Premium Crop' F1	BS,DI,PI,SK,SN,VY
Calabrese, 'Regilio'	MO
Calabrese, 'Romanesco Natalino'	F,FR
Calabrese, 'Roxette'	YA
Calabrese, 'S.G.1'	SN
Calabrese, 'S.G. 1 S.C. ' F1	BS
Calabrese, 'Samurai' F1	BS,L,TU,YA
Calabrese, 'Shogun' F1	BD,BS,CO,DT,F,J,KI,L, MO,SN,SU,TE,TU,YA
Calabrese, 'Small Miracle' F1	SN
Calabrese, 'Southern Comet' F1	BS,MO,TE
Calabrese, 'Stolto' F1	BS
Calabrese, 'Tiara'	BS
Calabrese, 'Viking' F1	K
Canola	BH
Cape Gooseberry, Physalis Edulis	AB,C,CO,DD,DE,DT,F, FR,J,JO,KS,S,SK,SN, SU,V,VS
Caper	C
Cardoon	BH,BY,C,DD,DE,KS,MC, RC,RI,S,TE,TH,TU,V
Cardoon, 'Gigante di Romagna'	CO,FR,SU
Cardoon, 'Plein Blanc'	GO
Cardoon, Spanish	BS
Cardoon, 'White Ivory'	KS

Carrot, 'All Season Topweight'	DI
Carrot, 'Almaro'	FR
Carrot, 'Amini'	DT,S,SK,YA
Carrot, 'Amsterdam Forcing 3 - Minicor'	AB,B,BD,BS,BY,CO,D, DD,F,GO,KI,KS,L,M,MO, S,SK,SN,SU,TU,V,VY
Carrot, 'Amsterdam Forcing' see A.M.3	
Carrot, 'Amsterdam Sweetheart'	BS,DT,FR,U
Carrot, 'Apache' F1	SK,SR
Carrot, 'Artist' F1	JO
Carrot, 'Astra'	BS
Carrot, 'Autumn King'	B,BD,BS,BY,C,CO,KI, MC,MO,SN,T,U,VH
Carrot, 'Autumn King 2'	D,F,J,S,T
Carrot, 'Autumn King 2 Vita Longa'	BS,KI,L,M,TU,U
Carrot, 'Autumn King - Giganta'	BS
Carrot, 'Autumn King Imp'	TU
Carrot, 'Autumn King Red Winter'	BS
Carrot, 'Autumn King Viking'	BS
Carrot, 'Avenger' hyb	SR
Carrot, 'Babette' o-p	PK,SR
Carrot, 'Baby'	DI
Carrot, 'Balin' F1	C
Carrot, 'Bangor' F1	S
Carrot, 'Banta'	BS
Carrot, 'Barbados' F1	K
Carrot, 'Berlanda' F1	BS,FR,VH
Carrot, 'Berlicum'	BS,KI
Carrot, 'Berlicum 2 * Berjo'	B,BD,BS,M,MO,SE,SU, TU,V,VH
Carrot, 'Berlicum 2 Oranza'	BS,DT,FR
Carrot, 'Berlicum Special'	BS
Carrot, 'Berltop'	VH
Carrot, 'Bertan' F1	BS, T
Carrot, 'Beta Champ' F1	PK
Carrot, 'Blaze' F1	JO,SR
Carrot, 'Bolero' F1	BS,DE,JO,SK,SR
Carrot, 'Boston' F1	J
Carrot, 'Calgary'	K
Carrot, 'Campestra'	BS
Carrot, 'Canada Gold' F1	PI
Carrot, 'Caro Choice' hyb	VY
Carrot, 'Carpa'	J
Carrot, 'Cartoga' F1	F
Carrot, 'Chanson'	K
Carrot, 'Chantenay 3 Comet'	BS
Carrot, 'Chantenay Babycan'	BS,SU
Carrot, 'Chantenay Canners' Favourite'	BS,YA
Carrot, 'Chantenay Long'	BS
Carrot, 'Chantenay Red Cored'	AB,B,BD,BS,BY,C,CO,KI, MC,PI,SD,SN,SR,ST,TH, VH,VY
Carrot, 'Chantenay Red Cored 2'	F,J,L,M,MO,TH,U
Carrot, 'Chantenay Red Cored 3 Supreme'	BS
Carrot, 'Chantenay Red Cored Fenman'	BS
Carrot, 'Chantenay Red Cored Gold King'	BS
Carrot, 'Chantenay Red Cored Royal 2'	BS,D,KI,SU
Carrot, 'Chantenay Royal'	BS,BU,DN,DT,FR,PK, SD,SK,T,TU
Carrot, 'Chayenne' F1	SK,SR
Carrot, 'Choctaw' F1	SK,SR
Carrot, 'Cobba' F1	YA
Carrot, 'Colora'	FR
Carrot, 'Comanche' hyb	SR
Carrot, 'Condor' hyb	SK
Carrot, 'Cordia'	BS

CARROT

Carrot, 'Corrie'	BS	Carrot, 'Mokum' F1	PI,T,TE
Carrot, 'Danro'	DD	Carrot, 'Monique' F1	PI
Carrot, 'Danvers'	AB,BS,BU,SK,SR,TE,TH	Carrot, 'Nabora' F1	YA
Carrot, 'Danvers 126'	TH	Carrot, 'Nairobi' F1	BS,KI,SU,TU
Carrot, 'Danvers Scarlet Half Long'	BF,DE,DT,PI	Carrot, 'Nanco' F1	BS,J,M,SK
Carrot, 'Danvers Scarlet Intermediate'	BS	Carrot, 'Nandor' F1	DT,PK,RO
Carrot, 'Decora'	BS	Carrot, 'Nantaise 2 -Michel'	BS
Carrot, 'Discovery'	K,SK,SR	Carrot, 'Nantaise Amelioree' half-long	GO
Carrot, 'Douceur', Baby Carrot	C,SK	Carrot, 'Nantes'	AB,BU,PI,PK,R,RC,SD,
Carrot, 'Eagle' hyb	SK		SR,TH,V
Carrot, 'Early French Frame'	BS,BY,DT,TH	Carrot, 'Nantes 2 Early'	F,J,L,M,U
Carrot, 'Early French Frame 4 * Lisa'	M	Carrot, 'Nantes 2 Romosa'	BS,DT
Carrot, 'Early Horn' (Scarlet)	AB,BY,DT,F,J,TH,U	Carrot, 'Nantes 3 TipTop'	BS,CO,FR
Carrot, 'Early Market'	J,KI,ST	Carrot, 'Nantes 5 Champion Scarlet Horn'	S
Carrot, 'Early Market Horn'	BY,TU	Carrot, 'Nantes 5 Early'	DT,S,TU
Carrot, 'Eurosweet' F1	PK	Carrot, 'Nantes 5- Tam Tam'	YA
Carrot, 'Fakkel Mix'	BS,TE	Carrot, 'Nantes Coreless'	SD
Carrot, 'Falcon II'	SK	Carrot, 'Nantes Duke'	BS
Carrot, 'Fancy'	BS,VY	Carrot, 'Nantes Early'	B,BD,BS,BY,KI,MC,MO,
Carrot, 'Favourite'	K,S		SK,ST,SU,T,TH,TU,VH
Carrot, 'Fedora'	U	Carrot, 'Nantes Express'	SE
Carrot, 'Feria' RZ F1	CO	Carrot, 'Nantes -Gringo'	YA
Carrot, 'Flak'	VH	Carrot, 'Nantes Scarlet'	BS,DE,DN,HU,JO,SD
Carrot, 'Flakee'	B,BS,BY,FR,KI,MC,SU,	Carrot, 'Nantes Special'	SK
	TU	Carrot, 'Nantucket' F1	TU
Carrot, 'Flame' hyb	SR	Carrot, 'Napoli' F1	PI,VH,VY
Carrot, 'Fly Away' F1	BD,BS,BY,CO,K,KI,MO,	Carrot, 'Narman' F1	B,BD,BS,MO
	ST,SU,T,TE,TU,V	Carrot, 'Narova' F1	BS
Carrot, 'Gold King' o-p	DN,SR	Carrot, 'Navajo' F1	JO,SR,VY
Carrot, 'Goliath' F1	SK,SR	Carrot, 'Navarre' F1	F
Carrot, 'Guerande'	BS	Carrot, 'Nelson' F1	S
Carrot, 'Healthmaster' hyb	VY	Carrot, 'Nelson' F1 pr.s	D
Carrot, Heirloom mix	DI	Carrot, 'Nevis' F1	JO
Carrot, 'Ideal' Mini	D	Carrot, 'New Radiance'	BS
Carrot, 'Ideal Red'	BS,SU	Carrot, 'New Red Intermediate'	K,S
Carrot, 'Imperator'	BS,BU	Carrot, 'Newmarket' F1	BS,CO,F,KI,SE
Carrot, 'Ingot' F1	BS,DT,F,KI,L,SE,T,U,V	Carrot, 'Obtuse de Doubs'	BS
Carrot, 'Invictor' F1	K	Carrot, 'Orangette' hyb	SK
Carrot, 'James Scarlet Intermediate'	BS,BY,C,CO,F,J,KI,ST,	Carrot, 'Oxheart'	AB,B,SD,SU,TH
	SU,T,TH,TU,U,VH	Carrot, 'Panther'	U
Carrot, 'Japanese Imperial Long'	SD	Carrot, 'Parabell'	BS,CO,KI,SN
Carrot, 'Jasper'	D	Carrot, 'Parano' F1	D
Carrot, 'Jumbo'	V	Carrot, 'Parmex'	BS,D,J,S,SU,U,V
Carrot, 'Junior' F1	DT	Carrot, 'Presto' hyb	SK
Carrot, 'Juwarot'	BS,J,SD,T	Carrot, 'Primo' F1	BU,DE,GO,K,M,U
Carrot, 'Kanzan'	K	Carrot, 'Processor II' hyb	SK
Carrot, 'Karotan'	BS,CO	Carrot, 'PS 70092' hyb	SR
Carrot, 'Kingston' F1	DT	Carrot, 'Rapier' F1	BS
Carrot, 'Kinko 4'	JO	Carrot, 'Red Intermediate Stump Rooted'	BY
Carrot, 'Kundulus' mini	VH	Carrot, 'Redca'	BS,CO,KI
Carrot, 'Kuroda'	PK	Carrot, 'Regulus'	BS
Carrot, 'Lagor' F1	M	Carrot, 'Rocket'	D,DT
Carrot, 'Lange Rote Stumpfe 2 Zino'	T	Carrot, 'Rubin'	BS,V
Carrot, 'Lange Stumpfe Winter - Laros'	BS	Carrot, 'Rubrovitimina'	FR
Carrot, 'Liberno' F1	T	Carrot, 'Rumba'	JO
Carrot, 'Lindoro'	PK	Carrot, 'Scarlet Keeper'	AB
Carrot, 'Little Finger'	DE,HU,PI	Carrot, 'Senior'	DT,U
Carrot, 'London Market'	HD	Carrot, 'Sheila' F1	YA
Carrot, Long Exhibition	SB	Carrot, Short Exhibition	SB
Carrot, 'Long Red Surrey'	CO,KI	Carrot, 'Spalding'	K
Carrot, Long (reselected)	K	Carrot, 'Spartan Premium 80' hyb	SK
Carrot, Long (St. Valery selected)	RO	Carrot, 'St. Valery'	BS,C,CO,D,DT,F,J,KI,M,
Carrot, 'Major' F1	BS,DT,K,TU		RC,S,SN,ST,SU,TH,TU,
Carrot, 'Marche de Paris'	GO		U
Carrot, 'Mini Round'	DI	Carrot, 'Stelio' F1	YA
Carrot, mix	AB,DE,GO	Carrot, 'Suko'	J,M,T

CARROT

Carrot, 'Sunrise' hyb	SK		L,M,MO,SU,ST,TU
Carrot, 'Supreme'	K	Cauliflower, 'Batsman'	F,TU
Carrot, 'Sweetness II' Hyb	VY	Cauliflower, 'Beauty' F1	D,K,M
Carrot, 'Sytan'	M	Cauliflower, 'Belot'	KI
Carrot, 'Tamino' F1	TE	Cauliflower, 'Boston Prize Early'	BS
Carrot, 'Thumbelina'	BS,DE,JO,PI,PK,SK,TE,	Cauliflower, 'Briac'	BS,YA
	VY	Cauliflower, 'Brocoverde'	BU
Carrot, 'Tokita's Scarlet' F1	PI	Cauliflower, 'Burgundy Queen' hyb	SK
Carrot, 'Topscore'	BS	Cauliflower, 'Cabrera' F1	D
Carrot, 'Topweight'	AB	Cauliflower, 'Calan'	BS
Carrot, 'Touchon'	AB,DE,GO,SK,VY	Cauliflower, 'Cambridge Early Giant'	BS
Carrot, 'Turbo' F1	YA	Cauliflower, 'Cambridge Mid Giant'	BS
Carrot, 'Waltham Hicolour'	BS	Cauliflower, 'Candid Charm' F1	BS,CO,KI,SR,ST,SU,TU
Carrot, 'Western Red'	DI	Cauliflower, 'Capella'	BS
Carrot, 'White Belgium'	HD	Cauliflower, 'Cappacio'	T
Carrot, 'Zino'	V	Cauliflower, 'Cargill'	T,VH
Cauli-Broc, F1	PK	Cauliflower, 'Carlos'	BS
Cauli/Broc, 'Chartreuse'	SK	Cauliflower, 'Carron' F1	YA
Cauliflower, 'A.G. 63'	BS	Cauliflower, 'Cashmere'	GO
Cauliflower, 'Ace Early'	B,BS,D,MO	Cauliflower, 'Castlegrant'	DT,M,U,YA
Cauliflower, 'Adam's Early White'	TH	Cauliflower, 'Celebrity'	BS
Cauliflower, 'Alban'	YA	Cauliflower, 'Centaurus'	BS,BY
Cauliflower, 'Albon No. 10'	BS	Cauliflower, 'Coleman'	K
Cauliflower, 'Alice Springs'	BS	Cauliflower, 'Colombo'	DT
Cauliflower, All Season Blend	VY	Cauliflower, 'Corvilia'	YA
Cauliflower, 'All The Year Round'	B,BD,BY,C,CO,D,DT,F,	Cauliflower, 'Cumberland' F1	JO,SK,SR
	FR,J,KI,L,M,MC,MO,R,	Cauliflower, 'Danish Perfection'	DT
	S,ST,SU,T,TU,U,V,VH,YA	Cauliflower, 'Dinnet' F1	YA
Cauliflower, 'Alpha 5'	FR,M	Cauliflower, 'Dok Elgon'	D,J,K,L,M,RO,S,SE,T,U,
Cauliflower, 'Alpha Ajubro' F1	BS		VH
Cauliflower, 'Alverda'	B,CO,KI,KS,SR,SU,TE,	Cauliflower, 'Dominant'	B,CO,KI,MO,SU
	TU,V,VY	Cauliflower, 'Dova' F1	BS, L
Cauliflower, 'Amazing'	JO	Cauliflower, 'Dunkeld' F1	YA
Cauliflower, 'Amelo'	BS	Cauliflower, 'Early Dawn' F1	PI,VY
Cauliflower, 'Andes' o-p	SK,SR,VY	Cauliflower, 'Early Feltham 2'	M,U
Cauliflower, 'Angers No 1'	BS	Cauliflower, 'Early Purple Sicilian'	AB
Cauliflower, 'Angers No 4 '	BS	Cauliflower, 'Elby' F1	BS,D,T
Cauliflower, 'Angers No 5'	BS	Cauliflower, 'Erfu'	BS
Cauliflower, 'Apex' hyb	SK	Cauliflower, 'Esmeraldo' F1	S,YA
Cauliflower, 'April Queen'	BS	Cauliflower, 'Fargo' F1	K,T
Cauliflower, 'Aprilex'	BS	Cauliflower, 'Firstman'	K,TU
Cauliflower, 'Arbon'	BS,TE	Cauliflower, 'Fleurly'	B,BS,D,MO
Cauliflower, 'Arcade'	M	Cauliflower, 'Flora Blanca'	S,SK
Cauliflower, 'Arctic' F1	VY	Cauliflower, 'Florian'	YA
Cauliflower, 'Armado April'	B,BS,BD,BY,CO,D,F,	Cauliflower, 'Florissant'	BS
	KI,L,M,MO,SE,ST,T,	Cauliflower, 'Fortuna'	BS
	TU,U,VH	Cauliflower, 'Fremont' F1	JO,K,MO,SK,SR,TE,VY
Cauliflower, 'Armado Mayo'	B,BS,KI,MO	Cauliflower, 'Galleon'	BS
Cauliflower, 'Armado Quick'	J,V	Cauliflower, 'Garant'	B,CO
Cauliflower, 'Armado Tardo'	B,BD,BS,FR,MO	Cauliflower, 'Giant Napoli Napolino'	FR
Cauliflower, 'Arminda'	BS	Cauliflower, 'Goodman'	VH
Cauliflower, 'Asmer Snowcap March'	M	Cauliflower, 'Grodan'	B,BS,FR,MO
Cauliflower, 'Asterix' F1	BD,MO	Cauliflower, 'Hawkesbury' F1	YA
Cauliflower, 'Aston Purple' F1	YA	Cauliflower, 'Icon' hyb	SK
Cauliflower, 'Astral' F1	YA	Cauliflower, 'Idol' Mini	B,BS,D,M,TU,V
Cauliflower, 'Atares'	BS	Cauliflower, 'Igloo'	DT
Cauliflower, 'Aubade'	F	Cauliflower, 'Inca'	B,BS,CO,K,KI,SU
Cauliflower, 'Autumn Giant'	B,BD,BS,BY,C,FR,J,KI,	Cauliflower, 'Incline' F1	PI
	M,MC,MO,ST,TH,VH	Cauliflower, 'Incomparable'	FR
Cauliflower, 'Autumn Giant 3'	BS,T	Cauliflower, 'Izoard' F1	FR
Cauliflower, 'A. G. 4 Veitch's Self Protecting'	BS,D,TH,S	Cauliflower, 'Janus'	BS,BY
Cauliflower, 'Autumn Glory'	BS,U	Cauliflower, 'Jaudy'	YA
Cauliflower, 'Baco'	BS	Cauliflower, 'Jerome'	M
Cauliflower, 'Balmoral' F1	DT,YA	Cauliflower, 'Jesi'	FR
Cauliflower, 'Bambi'	T	Cauliflower, 'Juno'	M
Cauliflower, 'Barrier Reef'	B,BD,BS,BY,C,DT,J,KI,	Cauliflower, 'Kestel'	TU

CAULIFLOWER

Cauliflower, 'Kibo'	V
Cauliflower, 'King'	B,BS,KI,MO,SB,U,YA
Cauliflower, 'Late June(EWK)'	BS,BY,KI
Cauliflower, 'Lateman'	DT,F,K,S,TU,VH
Cauliflower, 'Lawyna'	BS
Cauliflower, 'Leamington'	BS,TH
Cauliflower, 'Lecerf'	V
Cauliflower, 'Lenton Monarch'	BS
Cauliflower, 'Limelight'	J,M
Cauliflower, 'Lincoln Early'	BS
Cauliflower, 'Macerata Green'	FR
Cauliflower, 'Majestic' see Autumn Giant 3	
Cauliflower, 'Mariposa' hyb	SR
Cauliflower, ' Markanta'	F,M
Cauliflower, 'Marmalade' F1	BS,D,L,YA
Cauliflower, 'Mayflower'	BS,M
Cauliflower, 'Maystar'	BS,BY,CO,KI,SU,TU
Cauliflower, 'Mechelse-Carillon'	BS
Cauliflower, 'Medallion'	KI
Cauliflower, 'Metropole'	FR
Cauliflower, 'Milkyway' F1	PK
Cauliflower, 'Minaret' F1	BS,MO,TU
Cauliflower, mini	DI
Cauliflower, 'Minuteman' F1	SK,VY
Cauliflower, 'Montano'	M
Cauliflower, 'Napoletano Gennarese'	FR
Cauliflower, 'Nautilus' F1	DT,K
Cauliflower, 'Nevada'	BS
Cauliflower, 'November Heading'	B,BS
Cauliflower, 'Orange Bouquet'	JO,KS
Cauliflower, 'Oze White Top'	BS
Cauliflower, 'Pacific Charm'	BS
Cauliflower, 'Panda'	BS
Cauliflower, 'Penduick'	BS
Cauliflower, 'Perfection'	B,BS,KI,MO,SU,YA
Cauliflower, 'Pilgrim'	T
Cauliflower, 'Plana' F1	M,SE,T,TU,U
Cauliflower, 'Predial'	BS
Cauliflower, 'Predominant'	BS
Cauliflower, 'Prestige'	BS,DT
Cauliflower, 'Profil'	B,BS,MO
Cauliflower, 'Purple Cape'	B,BD,BS,BY,C,CO,D,DD,
	J,M,MO,SU,TH,TU,V
Cauliflower, 'Ravella' F1	PK,SR,TE
Cauliflower, 'Red Lion'	B,MO,TU
Cauliflower, 'Revito'	YA
Cauliflower, 'Romanesco'	B,BS,V
Cauliflower, 'Rosalind'	M
Cauliflower, 'Rushmore' F1	SK,SR
Cauliflower, 'Saint George'	BS,C,J
Cauliflower, 'Serrano' hyb	SK
Cauliflower, 'Shannon'	J
Cauliflower, 'Sierra Nevada' o-p	SK,SR
Cauliflower, 'Silver Cup 40' F1	PI
Cauliflower, 'Silver Cup 45' F1	PI
Cauliflower, 'Siria' F1	SK,VY
Cauliflower, 'Snow Cap'	B,BD,BS,BY,CO,FR,KI,
	MO,TU
Cauliflower, 'Snow Crown' F1	BY,FR,JO,KI,M,PI,SK,
	SR,TE,U
Cauliflower, 'Snow February'	BS
Cauliflower, 'Snow Grace' hyb	SR
Cauliflower, 'Snow King'	BS,FR
Cauliflower, 'Snow March'	BS
Cauliflower, 'Snow Prince'	BS,FR,KI,ST
Cauliflower, 'Snow's Winter White'	SD,TH

Cauliflower, 'Snowball'	AB,B,BD,BF,BS,BU,BY,
	D,DE,DN,F,HU,J,KI,MC,
	MO,PI,S,SK,ST,SU,TH,U
Cauliflower, 'Snowball Imp' o-p	SR
Cauliflower, 'Snowbred' F1	BS,BY,C,CO,KI,TU
Cauliflower, 'Snowflake' F1	BS
Cauliflower, 'Snowy River'	BS
Cauliflower, 'Solide'	B,BS,MO,SK
Cauliflower, 'Spalding'	K
Cauliflower, 'St. Mark'	BS
Cauliflower, 'Stella' F1	CO,KI
Cauliflower, 'Suprimax' o-p	SR
Cauliflower, 'Taroke'	BS
Cauliflower, 'Taymount' F1	DT,YA
Cauliflower, 'Thanet'(Walcheren Winter 3)	S
Cauliflower, 'Tico' F1	K
Cauliflower, 'Tosca'	BS
Cauliflower, 'Triskel'	YA
Cauliflower, 'Trisket No. 22'	BS
Cauliflower, 'Tulchan' F1	S,YA
Cauliflower, 'Uranus'	BS
Cauliflower, 'Valentine'	D
Cauliflower, 'Veitch's Self-Protecting'	TH
Cauliflower, 'Vidoke'	BS
Cauliflower, 'Vilna'	BS,DT,L
Cauliflower, 'Violet Queen'	BS,CO,FR,JO,KI,S,SK,
	SR,SU,T,TU,V
Cauliflower, 'Violet Sicilian'	FR,KS
Cauliflower, 'Vision'	BS,L,M
Cauliflower, 'Wainfleet'	K
Cauliflower, 'Wallaby'	B,BS,BY,CO,F,MO,T,VH,
	YA
Cauliflower, 'White Ball'	F
Cauliflower, 'White Corona' F1	PK
Cauliflower, 'White Dove'	YA
Cauliflower, 'White Fox'	BS
Cauliflower, 'White Queen' hyb	SK
Cauliflower, 'White Rock'	B,BS,BY,CO,DT,KI,MO,
	SB,SK,SR,TE
Cauliflower, 'White Sails' hyb	SK
Cauliflower, 'White Summer' o-p	SR
Cauliflower, 'Winter Selection'	M
Cauliflower, 'Woomera'	YA
Cauliflower, 'Yann'	BS,YA
Cauliflower, 'Yukon' hyb	SK
Cauliflower, 'Yuletide'	S
Cauliflower, 'YX D377' F1	YA
Cauliflower, 'Zara'	BS
Cauliflower, 'Zero'	BS
Celeriac, 'Alabaster'	BS,F,J,RI,V
Celeriac, 'Alba'	DD
Celeriac, 'Balder'	BS,C,CO,KI
Celeriac, 'Brilliant'	AB,D,JO,TE
Celeriac, 'Cesar' F1	L
Celeriac, 'Diament'	K
Celeriac, 'Giant Prague'	BD,BS,BY,DD,DE,DT,FR,
	GO,KI,KS,MC,MO,PI,
	SK,ST,SU,TH,TU,VY
Celeriac, 'Iram'	U
Celeriac, 'Marble Ball'	BS
Celeriac, 'Mentor'	T
Celeriac, 'Monarch'	BS,DD
Celeriac, 'Snehvide'	M
Celeriac, 'Tellus'	S
Celery, 'American Green'	BS
Celery, 'Avon Pearl'	BS

CELERY

Celery, 'Brydon's Prize Red' see Giant Red
Celery, 'Brydon's Prize White' TH
Celery, 'Celebrity' B,BS,D,DT,L,M,MO,SE,
   TU,YA
Celery, 'Celery Leaf' CO,GO
Celery, Chinese B,CO,DN,KS
Celery, 'Claudius' F1 BS
Celery, 'Clayworth Pink' see Giant Pink
Celery, 'Crystal' F1 BS
Celery, Cutting D,S,SU,V
Celery, 'Florida 683K' SK,SR
Celery, 'French Dinant' AB
Celery, 'Giant Green' BS,DE,FR
Celery, 'Giant Pink' B,SU,TH
Celery, 'Giant Red' B,BD,BS,BY,C,KI,M,MO,
   PI,TE,TH,TU,YA
Celery, 'Giant White' B,BD,BS,C,D,F,KI,ST
Celery, 'Giant White Pascal' FR,GO,MO,SD
Celery, 'Golden Boy' FR
Celery, 'Golden Plume' SK
Celery, 'Golden Self Blanching' B,BD,BF,BU,BY,C,CO,KI,
   MO,PI,RC,ST,TH
Celery, 'Golden Self Blanching 2' FR,TU
Celery, 'Golden Self Blanching 3' BS,F,J,S
Celery, 'Golden Spartan' BS
Celery, 'Green Utah' BS,BY,CO,KI
Celery, 'Greensleeves' BS
Celery, 'Greensnap' BS
Celery, 'Hopkins Fenlander' BS,L,M,T,VH
Celery, 'Ideal' K
Celery, 'Ivory Towers' BS,F,S
Celery, 'Lathom Blanching-Galaxy' T,VH
Celery, 'Lathom Self-Blanching' B,BS,MO,R,SU,U
Celery, 'Lathom Self-Blanching - Jason' BS
Celery, 'Mammoth White and Pink' RO
Celery, 'Martha Warde's' SP
Celery, 'Martine' RO
Celery, 'Matador' SK
Celery, 'Multipak' BS
Celery, 'New Dwarf White' BS
Celery, 'Pearly Queen' BS
Celery, 'Peto 285' SK
Celery, 'Picador' SK,SR
Celery, 'Pink Champagne' DT
Celery, 'Ponderosa' SR
Celery, 'Ponderosa' c.s SR
Celery, 'PS 285' SR
Celery, 'PS 285' c.s SR
Celery, 'Red Stalk' AB,SD
Celery, 'Selfire' BS
Celery, 'Solid Pink' CO,S
Celery, 'Solid White' BY,CO,S,TH,TU
Celery, Stringless DI
Celery, 'Tendercrisp' BS
Celery, 'Utah 52-70' AB,B,BS,BU,DN,PI,PK,
   SD,SK,VY
Celery, 'Utah Tall 52-70 R Imp' SR
Celery, 'Utah Tall Triumph' J,S,V
Celery, 'Ventura' JO,SK,SR,TE
Celery, 'Ventura' c.s. SR
Celery, 'Victoria' F1 BS,D,DT,M,MO,T
Celery, white K's selection K
Celery, 'White Pascal' BS,J,KI,SU
Celery, 'XP-85' SR
Celery, 'Zwolsche Krul' PI
Celery/Celeriac mix GO

Celtuce (Lettuce Stem) B,BH,BS,BY,CO,KS,MC,
   SK,SN,SU,T,TH,TU,VS
Celtuce, 'Majesty' V
Chard, mix VY
Chard, Perpetual Spinach B,BD,BH,BS,BY,C,CO,D,
   DT,F,J,KI,KS,L,M,MC,
   MO,S,SN,T,TH,TU,U,V,
   VS,VY,YA
Chard, Rhubarb AB,BD,BS,CO,D,J,JO,K,
   KI,L,MC,PI,RC,S,SD,SK,
   SR,ST,SU,T,TH,TE,TU,V
Chard, Rhubarb, Burpee's VY
Chard, Rhubarb, 'Charlotte' BS,DT,MO,PI
Chard, Rhubarb, 'Feurio' C,M
Chard, Rhubarb, 'Vulcan' F,PK
Chard, Swiss B,BD,BS,C,D,CO,F,KI,L,
   M,MC,MO,S,SG,ST,TH,
   TU
Chard, Swiss, 'Bright Lights' CO
Chard, Swiss, 'Broadstem Green' AB,DD,SD
Chard, Swiss, 'Dorat' GO
Chard, Swiss, 'Erbette' B,BS,FR,SU
Chard, Swiss, Five Colour Mix DI
Chard, Swiss, 'Fordbrook Giant' AB,DI,DN,JO,M,PI,RC,
   SK,TE,TH,U,VY
Chard, Swiss, 'French Green' AB
Chard, Swiss, Italian FR,SU
Chard, Swiss, 'Lucullus' AB,BS,PK,T,V,VY
Chard, Swiss, 'Lutz' DD,SP
Chard, Swiss, 'Mostruosa d'Ingegnoli' V
Chard, Swiss, of Geneva PK
Chard, Swiss, 'Palak Durga' RC
Chard, Swiss, San Francisco wild RC
Chard, Swiss, 'Silverado' SK,SR,VY
Chard, Swiss, 'Special Lg White Ribbed' BU,FR,PI,SK,SR
Chard, Swiss, 'Walliser' V
Chard, Swiss, 'White King' SK
Chard, Swiss, 'White Silver' BY,DE,DT
Chicory, 'All Seasons San Pasquale' B,SR
Chicory, 'Apollo' DT,M
Chicory, 'Bianca di Milano' BS,SU
Chicory, 'Biondissima di Trieste' SU
Chicory, 'Catalogna' FR,SK,SR
Chicory, 'Catalogna Special' FR,JO
Chicory, 'Cilantro' S
Chicory, 'Clio' F1 FR
Chicory, 'Del Veneto' KS
Chicory, 'Du Pere Vendi' SN,VS
Chicory, 'Extra Fine de Louvier' SN,VS
Chicory, 'Flash' F1 JO
Chicory, 'Gradina' BS
Chicory, 'Grumolo Bionda' KS
Chicory, 'Grumolo Verde' CO,FR,KI,KS,SU,V
Chicory, Italian Dandelion FR,HU
Chicory, 'Kristalkopf' T,V,VH
Chicory, Ige rooted coffee HU
Chicory, 'Magdeburg' (Ige root) BS,SK,SU,TH
Chicory, mix BH,DE
Chicory, 'Montmagny' SR
Chicory, 'Poncho' FR
Chicory, 'Puntarella' KS
Chicory, 'Soncino' FR
Chicory, 'Spadona' FR,KS
Chicory, 'Sugar Loaf' BS,BY,CO,DT,F,FR,HU,
   KI,M,S,ST,SU,TU
Chicory, 'Trieste' FR,KS

CHICORY

Chicory, 'Turbo' F1	GO,SK
Chicory, wild	FR,SD,TH
Chicory, Witloof (Brussels)	B,BD,BS,BY,C,CO,F,FR, J,KI,MO,PI,RC,RI,SK, SN,ST,SU,TH,TU
Chicory, 'Witloof- Rouge Carla' F1	V
Chicory, 'Witloof -Terosa'	V
Chicory, 'Witloof Zoom' F1	D,SU,V
Chicory, 'Zuckerhut'	KS
Chinese Broccoli	AB,BH,BS,KI,MC,RI,SN, SR,SU,YA
Chinese Broccoli, 'Kintsai'	AB,B,KI,MC,SR,SU
Chinese Melon, bitter	KS,SN
Chinese Melon, winter	KS,SN
Chives, 'Grolau'	BH
Choy Sum, 'Bouquet' F1	BS,KI,MC,SN,TU
Choy Sum, 'Flowering' F1	C,KS,PI,SU
Choy Sum, 'Flowering Purple'	AB,C,KS,MC,SN,TU
Choy Sum 'Purple'	SU
Cilantro, Slo-Bolt	DN,SP
Corn, Decorative Multicoloured	SN,VS
Corn, Dent, 'Alabama'	CS
Corn, Dent, 'Alamo-Navajo Blue'	JO
Corn, Dent, 'Apache Plume'	DD
Corn, Dent, 'Assiniboine'	AB
Corn, Dent, 'Bloody Butcher'	CS,PI,SR
Corn, Dent, 'Blue and White' (Cherokee)	CS
Corn, Dent, 'Chickasaw'	CS
Corn, Dent, 'Gaspe'	AB
Corn, Dent, 'Hickory King'	CS
Corn, Dent, 'Lancaster Surecrop'	CS
Corn, Dent, 'MN 13'	CS
Corn, Dent, 'Morado'	HU
Corn, Dent, 'Morado Peruvian'	HU
Corn, Dent, 'Mortgage Lifter'	CS
Corn, Dent, 'Mosbys'	CS
Corn, Dent, 'Murdock'	CS
Corn, Dent, 'Nothstine'	AB,JO
Corn, Dent, 'Oaxacan Green'	AB,SD
Corn, Dent, 'Old Hickory King'	CS
Corn, Dent, 'Silver Mine'	CS
Corn, Dent, 'Thompsons Prolific'	CS
Corn, Flint	CS
Corn, Flint, 'Blue'	CS
Corn, Flint, 'Rainbow Indian'	DD
Corn, Flour, 'Acoma Blue'	AB
Corn, Flour, 'Anasazi'	SD
Corn, Flour, 'Cherokee White'	AB
Corn, Flour, 'Cheyenne Red'	RC
Corn, Flour, 'Guadalajara All Purpose'	AB
Corn, Flour, 'Hopi Blue Flour'	AB,DD,PI
Corn, Flour, 'Hopi Blue Sawa-pu'	RC
Corn, Flour, 'Hopi Pink'	AB,SD
Corn, Flour, 'Hopi Purple'	SD
Corn, Flour, 'Hopi Purple 'Koko-ma'	RC
Corn, Flour, 'Hopi Red Pala-qa'	RC
Corn, Flour, 'Hopi Turquoise Flour'	AB
Corn, Flour, 'Hopi White'	AB,DD
Corn, Flour, 'Hopi White Qert-ca qa-er'	RC
Corn, Flour, 'Hopi Yellow Flour'	AB,DD
Corn, Flour, 'Hopi Yellow Taku-ri'	RC
Corn, Flour, 'Mandan Bride'	AB,JO
Corn, Flour, 'Mandan Red'	AB,DD
Corn, Flour, 'Pawnee Blue'	CS
Corn, Flour, 'Ponca Blue'	CS
Corn, Flour, 'Red Midget'	AB
Corn, Flour, 'Seibel's Red'	DD
Corn, Flour, 'Taos Blue'	RC
Corn, Flour, 'Taos Blue Flour'	AB
Corn Milling, White	BU
Corn, Ornamental, 'Black Amber'	SR
Corn, Ornamental, 'Blue Boy'	SR
Corn, Ornamental, 'Carousel'	SR,VY
Corn, Ornamental, 'Earth Shades'	SK
Corn, Ornamental, 'Fiesta' F1	JO,SK,SR,VY
Corn, Ornamental, Indian	BU,DI,SK
Corn, Ornamental, 'Laser Pretty Pop'	SK,SR
Corn, Ornamental, 'Little Boy Blue'	SR
Corn, Ornamental, 'Little Jewels'	JO
Corn, Ornamental, 'Little Miss Muffet'	SR
Corn, Ornamental, 'Purple Husk Rainbow'	SR
Corn, Ornamental, 'Red Stalker'	SR
Corn, Ornamental, 'Seneca'	PI
Corn Ornamental, Seneca Mini Indian	BU
Corn, Ornamental, 'Spectrum Pretty Pop'	SR
Corn, Ornamental, 'Strawberry Popcorn'	AB,BF,CO,HU,JO,SK,SR, U
Corn, Ornamental, 'Wampum'	JO
Corn, Parching, 'Aztec Red'	RC
Corn, 'Parching Lavender Corn'	AB
Corn, 'Parching Magenta'	SD
Corn, 'Parching Supai Red'	SD
Corn, Pod	CS,SR
Corn, Pop	SN,VS
Corn, Pop 'Bearpaw'	AB
Corn, Pop 'Black'	AB,DD
Corn, Pop, 'Early Pink'	PI
Corn, Pop 'Japanese Hulless'	AB,RC,SD
Corn, Pop, 'Lady Finger'	HU
Corn, Pop, Little Indian Popping	BU,SR
Corn, Pop, 'M-212' F1	JO
Corn, Pop, 'Miniature Blue'	AB,DI
Corn, Pop, Miniature coloured	CS,PK,SK
Corn, Pop, 'New England White'	DD
Corn, Pop, 'Peppy' F1	V
Corn, Pop, 'Purdue'	DE,SR
Corn, Pop, 'Rainbow'	AB
Corn, Pop, 'Robust 10-84'	SK
Corn, Pop, 'Robust 21-82' hyb	BU,SK
Corn, Pop, 'Robust 90135' hyb	BU,SR
Corn, Pop 'Robust 904677' F1	PK
Corn, Pop, 'Tom Thumb'	JO
Corn, Pop, 'White Cloud' hyb	SR
Corn, Pop, White Hulless see Japanese	
Corn, Pop, yellow	BF
Corn, Teosinte	RC
Cornsalad, 'Cavallo'	T,YA
Cornsalad, 'Coquille de Louviers'	GO
Cornsalad, 'Elan'	T,U
Cornsalad, 'Grote N-Hollandse'	BH,FR,RI,V
Cornsalad, 'Jade'	F,M
Cornsalad, Lamb's Lettuce	AB,B,BY,DD,HU,J,KS,M C,MO,SG,SK,ST,TH,VY
Cornsalad, 'Large Leaved'	BS,C,CO,D,FR,GO,KI,PI, PK,S,SU,TU
Cornsalad, mix	BH,GO
Cornsalad, 'Valgros'	FR,RC,TE
Cornsalad, 'Verte de Cambrai'	B,BF,BH,BS,CO,GO,K,PI, SK,SU,TH
Cornsalad, 'Vit'	B,JO,KI,SN,SU
Courgette, 'Acceste' F1	K
Courgette, 'All Green Bush'	BD,BS,BY,C,CO,DT,F,J,

COURGETTE

Courgette, 'Altea'	KI,MC,MO,SE,ST,T,VH SN
Courgette, 'Ambassador' F1	B,BD,BS,CO,D,DT,F,FR, L,M,MO,PI,R,SE,SN,TU, YA
Courgette, 'Aristocrat' F1	BS,DE,DN,FR
Courgette, 'Bambino'	BS,DT
Courgette, 'Belor' F1	BS,PI
Courgette, 'Black Jack'	BS,DN,FR,SK
Courgette, 'Botna' F1	C
Courgette, 'Brimmer'	BS
Courgette, 'Burpee Golden Zucchini'	BS,S,SN,ST
Courgette, 'Butterblossom' edible fl	GO,VY
Courgette, 'Caserta'	DN,SD
Courgette, 'Clarella'	BS,CO
Courgette, 'Clarion' F1	B,BS,KI,SN,SU
Courgette, 'Clarita'	BS,FR,U
Courgette, 'Cocozelle'	AB,B,BS,GO,SD
Courgette, 'Cocozelle v Tripolis' o-p org	SN
Courgette, 'Condor' F1	DE,GO,JO
Courgette, 'Cora' F1	K,YA
Courgette, 'Costata Romanesca'	RC,JO
Courgette, 'Dark Green'	AB
Courgette, 'Defender' F1	BS,CO,KI,S,SU,T,TU
Courgette, 'Di Faenza'	B,FR
Courgette, 'Diamant' F1	B,BS,FR,V
Courgette, 'Early Gem'	B,BD,BY,J,KI,MO,U
Courgette, 'Early Yellow Crookneck'	BF,BS,DI,PI,SU
Courgette, 'Elite' F1	BS,DT,FR,KI
Courgette, 'Embassy' F1	PK,SK
Courgette, 'Excalibur' F1	BS,YA
Courgette, 'French Early White' o-p org	SN
Courgette, 'Giada Blanca' hyb org	SN
Courgette, 'Giada' hyb org	SN
Courgette, 'Gold Rush' F1	w.a.
Courgette, 'Gold Slice'	VY
Courgette, 'Goldbar' F1	PI
Courgette, 'Golden Bush'	RC,SD
Courgette, 'Goldfinger'	SK
Courgette, 'Gourmet Globe' F1	PK
Courgette, 'Green Magic II' F1	PK
Courgette, 'Greyzini' F1	BS,FR,PI,T
Courgette, 'Grisette de Provence' hyb	SN
Courgette, 'Hercules'	V
Courgette, 'Ingot'	PI
Courgette, 'Jemmy' F1	BS,CO,KI
Courgette, 'Kojak'	BS,TU
Courgette, 'Kriti' F1	FR
Courgette, 'Leprechaun'	BS,TU
Courgette, 'Lynx' F1	DT
Courgette, 'Market King' F1	BS
Courgette, 'Milano Green'	FR
Courgette, 'Minipak'	SN
Courgette, mix	GO
Courgette, 'Moreno' F1	BS,F,YA
Courgette, 'Nice Long'	SN,VS
Courgette, 'Onyx' F1	VY
Courgette, 'Opal' F1	DT
Courgette, 'Patriot' F1	B,BD,M,MO,TU
Courgette, 'President' F1	B,BS,FR,MO,YA
Courgette, 'Raven' F1	F
Courgette, 'Richgreen' hyb	VY
Courgette, 'Rondo de Nice'	B,BS,CO,DE,F,FR,GO,KI, SD,SN,ST,SU,T,TH,VS
Courgette, Salad Collection	T
Courgette, 'Sardane' F1	T

Courgette, Selection	M
Courgette, 'Seneca Milano' F1	PK
Courgette, 'Seneca Zucchini' F1	BS,BU,SK,SR,YA
Courgette, 'Sofia'	FR
Courgette, 'Spacemiser'	DE,VY
Courgette, 'Spineless Beauty'	BS,SK,SR
Courgette, 'Storr's Green' hyb	FR,SN,YA
Courgette, 'Striato d'Italia'	FR
Courgette, 'Super Select'	BS,SK
Courgette, 'Supremo' F1	D,SE,T
Courgette, 'Tarmino'	U
Courgette, 'Taxi'	F,SN
Courgette, 'Tondo di Chiaro di Nizza'	BS,SN
Courgette, 'Triple 5'	DT,SN
Courgette, 'Tromboncino'	B,BS,CO,DI,FR,PI,SU, TH
Courgette, 'Zucchini Black'	BU,PI,SR,TE
Courgette, 'Zucchini Dark Green'	BS,DE,HU,SN
Courgette, 'Zucchini' F1	B,BF,BS,CO,D,DT,F,KI,M, MC,S,ST,SU,TU,U,VH
Courgette, 'Zucchini Select'	BS,SK
Cowpea, 'Arkansas Crowder'	DD
Cowpea, 'Banquet'	PK
Cowpea, 'Calhoun Purple Hull'	PK
Cowpea, 'California Blackeye'	BU,PK
Cowpea, 'Magnolia Blackeye'	SR
Cowpea, 'Minnesota Cow Pea'	AB
Cowpea, 'Mississippi Pinkeye Purplehull'	SR
Cowpea, 'Mississippi Purple'	SR
Cowpea, 'Mississippi Shipper'	SR
Cowpea, 'Mississippi Silver'	PK
Cowpea, 'Papago'	DD
Cowpea, 'Sunapee'	DD
Cress, 'Armada'	M
Cress, 'Cressonette Marocain'	SN
Cress, 'Curled'	AB,BH,C,J,M,PK,S,SK, TE
Cress, 'Double Curled'	ST
Cress, 'Extra Double Curled'	D
Cress, 'Fine Curled'	B,BS,DT,F,KI,SU,TU,U
Cress, Garden, 'Extra Curled'	T
Cress, 'Greek'	B,BS,CO,SU
Cress, 'Land' (American)	BS,BY,C,CO,D,J,JO,KI, M,MC,S,ST,SU,T,TH,TU, V,VH
Cress, 'Mega'	T
Cress, 'Moss Curled'	KS
Cress, Persian Broadleaf	AB,JO,SD
Cress, Plain	BD,BS,BY,FR,GO,JO,KI, L,MO,SD,ST,VH,VY,GO
Cress, Super Salad	D
Cress, 'Victoria'	M,PI
Cress, Water	AB,BD,BS,BY,C,CO,D, GO,HU,JO,KI,KS,MO, PK,ST,SU,TE,TU,VH
Cress, Water Imp Lge Leaved	BS,SK
Cress, Winter	AB,HU
Cucumber, 'Adora' F1	BS
Cucumber, African	RI
Cucumber, 'Aidas' F1	BS,K,T
Cucumber, 'Amira'	DE,GO,PI
Cucumber, 'Aramon' F1	B,BS,MO
Cucumber, 'Aria' F1	JO
Cucumber, 'Aricia' F1	SK
Cucumber, 'Armenian Yard Long'	AB,BU,DE,DI,GO,HU, KS,RC,SD,SN,TE

CUCUMBER

Cucumber, 'Athene' F1	M
Cucumber, 'Avanti' F1	BS,KI
Cucumber, 'Bedfordshire Prize Ridge'	BS,C,KI,MC,ST,YA
Cucumber, 'Bella' F1	S
Cucumber, 'Bestseller'	DT
Cucumber, 'Beta Alphee' F1	SU
Cucumber, 'Bianco Lungo di Parigi'	C,PI
Cucumber, 'Bimbostar' F1	V
Cucumber, 'Birgit' F1	B,BD,BS,D,DT,F,KI,L,MO,SE
Cucumber, 'Boothby's Blonde'	PI
Cucumber, 'Britania' F1	SK
Cucumber, 'Brocade'	V
Cucumber, 'Bronco' F1	YA
Cucumber, 'Brunex' F1	B,BS,MO,R,S,YA
Cucumber, 'Burpless Tasty Green' F1	B,BD,BS,BY,CO,DE,DT,F,KI,L,M,MO,PI,S,SE,SR,ST,SU,T,TU,U,V,VH
Cucumber, 'Bush Champion' F1	B,BS,CO,D,DT,F,KI,S,SD,SU,T
Cucumber, 'Bush Crop' F1	B,M,PI
Cucumber, 'Calypso' F1	PI
Cucumber, 'Carmen' F1	B,BS,SK,T,MO,VH,VY
Cucumber, 'Carosello Barese'	FR
Cucumber, 'Centurion' hyb	SR
Cucumber, 'Chinese Sweet and Striped'	DI
Cucumber, Chinese 'Tseng Gwa'	V
Cucumber, 'Cina'	FR
Cucumber, 'Comet II' hyb	SK
Cucumber, 'Conqueror'	CO,TH
Cucumber, 'Corona' F1	SK,V
Cucumber, 'Crystal Apple'	AB,B,BD,BS,BY,C,CO,DE,DT,KI,MO,S,SN,ST,SU,TH
Cucumber, 'Crystal Lemon' see Crystal Apple	
Cucumber, 'Cumlaud'	K
Cucumber, 'Dancer' F1	SR
Cucumber, 'Danimas' F1 Mini	D,T,YA
Cucumber, 'Dasher II' F1	SK,SR
Cucumber, 'Daytona' F1	SR
Cucumber, 'Diana' F1	BS,KI,SN,TU,U
Cucumber, 'Early Russian'	AB,SD
Cucumber, 'El Toro' F1	BS
Cucumber, 'Euphya' F1	B,BS,J,MO
Cucumber, 'Experimental TM/MO8'	T
Cucumber, 'Fanfare' F1	KS,PK,SK,VY
Cucumber, 'Farbiola' F1	BS
Cucumber, 'Fatum'	U
Cucumber, 'Femdan' F1	BS,DT
Cucumber, 'Femspot' F1	B,BS,F,MO,S,TU
Cucumber, 'Femunex' F1	B,BS,CO,KI,MC,ST,SU
Cucumber, 'Fitness' F1	YA
Cucumber, 'Flamingo' F1	BS,SK
Cucumber, 'Futura' F1	DT,SK
Cucumber, 'General Lee' F1	SK,SR
Cucumber, 'Gracius'	M
Cucumber, 'Green Fall' F1	FR
Cucumber, 'Hana' F1	BS
Cucumber, 'Harvestmore' F1	SR
Cucumber, 'Heiwa Gr. Prolific'	SD
Cucumber, 'II57' F1	YA
Cucumber, 'Indy' hyb	SR
Cucumber, 'Jamaican' o-p org	SN
Cucumber, 'Janeen' F1 Mini	YA
Cucumber, 'Japanese Yamoto'	BS,CO,KI,MC,SN,SU
Cucumber, 'Jaune Dickfleischige'	SN

Cucumber, 'Jazzer' F1	JO,PI,SK,SN,T,VH,VY
Cucumber, 'Jessica' F1	K
Cucumber, 'Jordan' F1	DN
Cucumber, 'Kalimero'	BS
Cucumber, 'King George'	RO
Cucumber, 'Kyoto'	BS,HU
Cucumber, 'Lebanese Mini Muncher'	DI
Cucumber, 'Lemon'	AB,DE,DI,GO,HU,JO,KS,SD,SK,TE
Cucumber, 'Long Green'	FR,V
Cucumber, 'Long Green Ridge'	BD,J,MO,S,TH,V
Cucumber, 'Marketer'	BS
Cucumber, 'Marketmore'	B,BS,BU,DT,FR,JO,M,SD,SK,SR,VY
Cucumber, 'Masterpiece'	BS,CO,KI,SN
Cucumber & Melon, Chitted Seed	M
Cucumber, 'Mervita'	V
Cucumber, 'Mideast Prolific'	SD
Cucumber, 'Mildama' F1	BS
Cucumber, 'Miniverde'	BS
Cucumber, 'Mistral' F1	D
Cucumber, mix	FR,GO
Cucumber, 'Muncher' o-p	BU
Cucumber, 'Mustang' F1	YA
Cucumber, 'New Pioneer' F1	FR
Cucumber, 'Niagara' F1	SK
Cucumber, 'Orient Express' F1	BU,SK,TE
Cucumber, Oriental	RI
Cucumber, Oriental 'Soo Yoh'	JO,KS,RC
Cucumber, 'Panther' F1	SK,SR,VY
Cucumber, 'Paska' F1	C,J
Cucumber, 'Passandra' F1	D
Cucumber, 'Pepinex 69' F1	BS,BY,D,DT,J,K,M
Cucumber, 'Perfection'	B,BS,BY,L,TH
Cucumber, 'Petita' F1	B,BD,BS,CO,D,DT,F,J,KI,L,MO,S,SN,SU,TU,U
Cucumber, Pickling see Gherkin	
Cucumber, 'Poinsett 76' o-p	BU
Cucumber, 'Prancer' hyb	SR
Cucumber, 'Precoce Grosso Bianco Crema'	RC
Cucumber, 'Pyralis'	BS,MO
Cucumber, 'Raider'	VY
Cucumber, 'Revenue' hyb	SK
Cucumber, 'Richmond Green Apple'	V
Cucumber, Russian	SN
Cucumber, 'Salad Bush' F1	BF,DE,PI,PK,VY
Cucumber, 'Sandra' F1	BS
Cucumber, 'Seneca Longbow' f1	BU,SK,TE
Cucumber, 'Seneca Trailblazer'	PI,VY
Cucumber, 'Simpson's Sweet Success' F1	SN
Cucumber, 'Slice King' F1	BS,CO,KI,SK,SN,SU
Cucumber, 'Slicemaster' F1	BU,PI,TE,VY
Cucumber, 'Sombrero' F1	BS
Cucumber, 'Southern Delight'	DE
Cucumber, 'Spacemaster'	DI,DN,PI,PK
Cucumber, 'Speedway' F1	SK,SR
Cucumber, 'Straight 8'	AB,SR
Cucumber, 'Straight 9'	PI
Cucumber, 'Superator'	B,BS,L,MO
Cucumber, 'Supersett' F1	JO
Cucumber, 'Support' F1	YA
Cucumber, 'Suprami' F1	BS,TU
Cucumber, 'Suyo Long'	B,PI,SD
Cucumber, 'Sweet Alphee' F1	BS,JO
Cucumber, 'Sweet Crunch' F1	FR
Cucumber, 'Sweet Delight' F1	BU

CUCUMBER

Cucumber, 'Sweet Slice' F1	GO,PK,SK,VY
Cucumber, 'Sweet Success' F1	DE,PI,PK
Cucumber, 'Tasty Green' F1	PK,VY
Cucumber, 'Tasty King' F1	PK
Cucumber, 'Telegraph'	BS,BY,CO,D,DI,J,R,S, SK,SN
Cucumber, 'Telegraph Imp'	B,BD,DT,F,KI,L,M,MO, S,ST,SU,TH,TU,U,VH
Cucumber, 'Thunder' F1	SK
Cucumber, 'Timun Hijan'	RC
Cucumber, 'Tokyo Slicer'	BS,FR,U
Cucumber, 'Topsy'	U
Cucumber, 'Toret'	BS
Cucumber, 'Toro'	BS
Cucumber, 'Triumph' F1	FR,PI
Cucumber, 'Turbo' F1	sk,SR
Cucumber, Turkish	SN
Cucumber, 'Tyria' ch.s	M
Cucumber, 'Tyria' F1	B,BS,M,MO
Cucumber, 'Ultraslice Early' F1	SK
Cucumber, 'Uniflora' F1	VH
Cucumber, 'Uzbekski'	AB
Cucumber, 'Vert Petit de Paris'	GO
Cucumber, 'White'	AB,DD,FR
Cucumber, 'White Wonder'	AB,B,DT,SN,V
Curled Mallow	AB
Dandelion, 'Pissenlit Imp'	GO
Dandelion, 'Thick Leaved'	BY,C,DD,DE,FR,RI,SN, SU,VS
Dandelion, 'Volhart'	V
Earth Chestnut	AB
Edible Flower Petal Salad	T
Edible Flowers Mixed	GO,T,V
Endive	AB
Endive, 'Atria'	YA
Endive, 'Batavian Broad Leaved' (Gr.)	B,BY,RI,TH,TU
Endive, 'Bossa'	B,V
Endive, 'Brevo'	V
Endive, 'Casca d'Oro'	FR
Endive, 'Coral'	B,JO
Endive, 'Dolly'	BS
Endive, 'Dorana'	YA
Endive, 'Elysee'	YA
Endive, 'Frisan'	DT,SK
Endive, 'Frisan' p.s	SK
Endive, 'Full Heart 65'	B,FR,PI,SK,SR
Endive, 'Full Heart' p.s.	SK
Endive, 'Galia'	DE
Endive, giant	FR
Endive, 'Glory'	BH,YA
Endive, 'Golda'	U
Endive, 'Green Curled'	B,BF,BY,DD,FR,KI,KS, SK,TH,VY
Endive, 'Green Curled' (Moss)	C,CO,J,MC,S,ST,TU,V
Endive, 'Grosse Bouclee'	GO,PI
Endive, 'Ione'	D
Endive, 'Italian Fine Curled'	KS
Endive, 'Jeti'	B,BS,KI,SN
Endive, 'Malan'	V
Endive, 'Markant'	SR
Endive, 'Minerva'	YA
Endive, 'Neos'	JO
Endive, 'No 52'	BS
Endive, 'Oxalie'	B,BD,MO
Endive, 'Pl. Leaf Winter En Cornet de Bord.'	B,SN,ST
Endive, 'President'	AB,TE

Endive, 'Red C'	B,DE
Endive, 'Rhodos'	JO
Endive, 'Riccia d'inverno'	FR
Endive, 'Riccia Pancalieri'	BS,CO,FR,KI,SN,SU
Endive, 'Ruffec'	BS,F,KS,TH
Endive, 'Saint Laurent'	KS
Endive, 'Salad King'	B,BU,SK,SR
Endive, 'Sally'	BS,M,YA
Endive, 'Scarola Verde'	B,SN
Endive, 'Stratego' RZ	CO
Endive, 'Tosca'	SK
Endive, 'Tres Fine Maraichere'	AB,B,GO,KS,SD,SU,T, VH
Endive, 'Twinkle'	SR
Endive, 'Wallonne'	SU
Endive, 'White Curled'	B,FR,KS
Escarole see Endive	
Fennel, 'Cantino'	CO,KI,M,MC,SU,TU
Fennel, 'Carmo'	FR
Fennel, 'Colossale d'Ignegnoli'	FR
Fennel, 'Cristal'	FR
Fennel, 'Di Firenzi'	B,C,F,RC,RI,SN,VS
Fennel, 'di Napoli'	FR
Fennel, 'Fino' (Zefa)	B,BD,BS,D,DT,F,JO,KS, L,MO,U,V
Fennel, Florence see Di Firenzi	
Fennel, 'Herald'	T
Fennel, 'Perfection'	SU
Fennel, 'Romanesco'	FR
Fennel, 'Rudy' F1	DT,JO
Fennel, 'Sirio'	S
Fennel, 'Sweet'	CO,DD,KI
Fennel, 'Tardo' (Zefa)	KS
Fenugreek, 'T&M Spicy'	T
Flax, Golden	SP
Garden Huckleberry o-p	SN
Garlic, Ramson's (Bear's)	BH
Garlic, wild	BH
Garlic, wild sweet scented	BH
Gherkin	BF,KI,SU
Gherkin, 'Accordia'	B,BD,L,MO
Gherkin, 'Alvin' F1	M,TU
Gherkin, 'Arena' F1	J
Gherkin, 'Bestal' F1	M
Gherkin, 'Bimbostar'	M
Gherkin, 'Boston Green'	AB,BS,TH
Gherkin, 'Bush Baby' hyb	SK
Gherkin, 'Bush Pickle'	PK,SK
Gherkin, 'Calypso' hyb	SK,VY
Gherkin, 'Carolina' hyb	BU
Gherkin, 'Chicago Pickling'	DE
Gherkin, 'Conda' F1	DT,U
Gherkin, 'County Fair'	TE
Gherkin, 'Cross Country' hyb	SK,VY
Gherkin, 'Eureka' F1	SK,SR
Gherkin, 'Experimental TM/MO7'	T
Gherkin, 'Fancipak' F1	PK
Gherkin, 'Fanfare' F1	F
Gherkin, 'Green Spear' hyb	SK
Gherkin, 'Hokus'	B,BS
Gherkin, 'Homemade Pickles'	PI,PK
Gherkin, 'Jackson Classic' F1	SR
Gherkin, 'Japanese Long Pickling'	SK
Gherkin, 'Lafayette' hyb	SK
Gherkin, 'Liberty' F1	T
Gherkin, 'Little Leaf'	JO,PK

GHERKIN

Gherkin, 'Lucky Strike'	DE	Kale, 'Cavalo Nero'	CO,M,SN
Gherkin, 'Lucky Strike' F1	DE,PI,SR	Kale, 'Champion' o-p	JO,SK,SR,TE
Gherkin, 'Napoleon Classic' F1	SK,SR	Kale, 'Cottagers'	BS,TH
Gherkin, 'National Pickling'	B,BS,C,CO,DE,PI,ST	Kale, 'Darkibor' F1	D,DT,L,TU
Gherkin, 'Northern Pickling'	JO,SD	Kale, 'Dw Blue Curled'	BF,BU,PI,SK,VY
Gherkin, 'Parigi'	FR	Kale, 'Dw Curled Scotch' see Dw Gr Curled	
Gherkin, 'Parisian Pickling'	BS,D,S,TH	Kale, 'Dw Green Curled'	AB,B,BD,BS,BY,CO,D,D
Gherkin, 'Pik-Rite' hyb	SK		N,DT,FJ,KI,L,M,MO,S,S
Gherkin, 'Pioneer'	BU,SK		K,SP,ST,SU,T,TH,TU,U,V
Gherkin, 'Pointsett'	BS	Kale, 'Dw Green Curled - Afro'	BS
Gherkin, 'Regal'	VY	Kale, 'Flash' F1	SK,SR
Gherkin, 'Salty' hyb	SK	Kale, 'Fribor' F1	BD,BS,BY,CO,KI,MO,
Gherkin, 'Smart Pickle'	SD		TU,VH
Gherkin, 'Spear-It' hyb	SK	Kale, 'Georgia'	DE,PK,RC
Gherkin, 'Sunre 3533 Classic' hyb	SR	Kale, 'Hevi-Crop' hyb	SR
Gherkin, 'Transamerica' hyb	SR	Kale, 'Hungry Gap'	M,TU
Gherkin, 'Venlo Pickling'	B,BS,BY,D,S	Kale, 'Konserva'	JO,PI
Gherkin, 'West India'	PI,RC	Kale, 'Lacinato'	AB,DI
Gherkin, 'Wisconsin SMR 58'	BU,SK,TE	Kale, 'Long Seasons'	AB
Golden Berry	T	Kale, 'Morton's Swarm'	DD
Good King Henry	BY,C,MC,SU,U, V	Kale, 'Nagoya Garnish Red'	JO,SR
Gourd, African	SN,VS	Kale, 'Nagoya Garnish White'	SR
Gourd, Antilles	SN,VS	Kale, 'Negro di Toscana'	TU
Gourd, Armenian	SN,VS	Kale, Palm Tree	RC
Gourd, Bitter, long	SR	Kale, 'Peacock' garnish red & white	JO
Gourd, Bitter, spindle	SR	Kale, 'Pentland Brig'	BS,BY,CO,DT,KI,M,MC,
Gourd, 'Blue Hill' F1	V		SU,TU,U
Gourd, Calabash	BH,DE,SN,VS	Kale, 'Ragged Jack'	HD
Gourd, Calabash Mini	SN,VS	Kale, 'Red Russian'	AB,HU,JO,KS,PI,SD,SP,
Gourd, 'Cheerer'	BH		TE,TU
Gourd, 'Cou Tors'	SN,VS	Kale, 'Redbor' F1	DT,K,TE
Gourd, Decorative	PI,SK,SN,TE,VS,VY	Kale, 'Savoy Salad'	KS
Gourd, Decorative 'Amphore'	SN,VS	Kale, 'Showbor' F1	D,K,S,SR
Gourd, Decorative 'Plate de Course'	SN,VS	Kale, 'Siberian'	AB,DE,HD,SD,TE
Gourd, Decorative 'Trombolino d'Albinga'	SN,VS	Kale, 'Smooth'	RC
Gourd, Devil's	SN,VS	Kale, Southern blue-gr	BF
Gourd, Edible	KS,RI	Kale, 'Spurt'	T
Gourd, 'Giant Bottle'	DE,FR,JO,SD,SK,V	Kale, 'Squire' o-p	SK,SR
Gourd, green & gold	BH	Kale, 'Starbor' F1	PI
Gourd, Jointed	V	Kale, 'Tall Green Curled'	B,BD,BH,BS,M,MO,TH,
Gourd, large	DD,FR,SK,SR		TU
Gourd, 'Long Green'	SN,VS	Kale, 'Thousand Head'	AB,B,BY,S,SU,TH,TU,U
Gourd, 'Marenka'	SN,VS	Kale, 'Top Bunch' hyb	PK,SK,SR
Gourd, 'Miniature Bottle'	KS,SK,V	Kale, 'Vates'	AB,BU,DN,PI,SD,SK,SR
Gourd, New Guinea Bean	DI	Kale, 'Vates Blue Curled'	AB,PK,SR
Gourd, 'Paris Long White'	SN,VS	Kale, 'Westfalian'	HD
Gourd, 'Paris Small Green'	SNVS	Kale, 'Westland Autumn'	D
Gourd, Russian	SN,VS	Kale, 'Winterbor' F1	BD,BS,F,JO,KI,MO,PK,
Gourd, 'Seven Star'	BH		SK,SR,TE,TU,YA
Gourd, small	DD,JO,SR,TE,VY	Kiwano	C
Gourd, 'Yard Long'	BH	Kohl Rabi, 'Danube Purple'	KI,PK,SR
Greens, Cooking mix	AB,JO	Kohl Rabi, 'Danube White'	CO,KI,SK,SR
Greens, Cooking 'Vitamin'	JO	Kohl Rabi, 'Express Forcer' F1	PK
Greens, Natural Garden mix	AB	Kohl Rabi, 'Gigante'	KS
Greens, Salad mix	AB	Kohl Rabi, 'Grand Duke' F1	SK,SR
Greens, Tyfon-Holland	PI	Kohl Rabi, 'Kolibri' F1	JO,PI
Huizontle	RC,RI	Kohl Rabi, 'Kolpak' F1	PI
Ice Plant	TH	Kohl Rabi, 'Lanro'	D,V
Jicama	C,DE,HU,KS,RC,RI	Kohl Rabi, 'Logo'	S
Kale, 'Asparagus'	HD	Kohl rabi, mix	BH
Kale, 'B.J. 1628' F1	K	Kohl rabi, 'Oestgota'	BH
Kale, 'Blue Ridge' hyb	SR	Kohl Rabi, 'Peking'	HU
Kale, 'Bornic' F1	BS	Kohl rabi, pink/blue	BH
Kale, Broccoli, 'Green Lance' F1	BS,C,CO,KI,MC,SN,SU,	Kohl Rabi, 'Quickstar' F1	DT
	V	Kohl Rabi, 'Rolano'	L
Kale, 'Buffalo' F1	BS	Kohl Rabi, 'Rolano' Mini	D

KOHL RABI

Kohl Rabi, 'Rowel'	M,U
Kohl Rabi, 'Super Schmelz'	TE,V
Kohl Rabi, 'Trero' F1	T
Kohl Rabi, 'Triumph' F1	SK
Kohl Rabi, 'Vienna Purple'	AB,B,BD,BF,BS,BY,C, CO,D,DE,DT,HU,J,KI,KS, L,MC,MO,S,SK,ST,SU, TH,TU,V,VY
Kohl Rabi, 'Vienna White' (green)	AB,B,BD,BS,BU,BY,C, C O,DE,DN,DT,F,J,KI,MC, MO,PI,S,SK,ST,SU,TH, TU
Kohl rabi, white	BH
Kohl Rabi, 'Winner' F1	JO,PI
Komatsuna	B,BS,CO,MC,PI,SU,TU, YA
Komatsuna, 'Green Boy'	MC,V
Komatsuna, 'Rondbladige (Roundleaf)'	V
Komatsuna, 'Summer Feast' F1	JO,V
Komatsuna, 'Tendergreen'	AB,BH,C
Kombucha bacterium live starter culture	RI
Lamb's Quarters see Corn Salad	
Leek, 'Alaska'	BS
Leek, 'Albinstar'	BS,BY,KI,S
Leek, 'Alcazar' RZ	CO
Leek, 'Alma'	BS
Leek, 'Alora' RZ	CO
Leek, 'American Flag'	RI
Leek, 'Ardea'	BS
Leek, 'Arial'	DT
Leek, 'Arkansas'	PK,SK,SR
Leek, 'Armor'	YA
Leek, 'Autumn Cortina'	SN
Leek, 'Autumn Giant 2-Argenta'	D,T,V
Leek, 'Autumn Giant 3 - Rami'	DT,S,YA
Leek, 'Autumn Mammoth 2'	DT,M,TU
Leek, 'Autumn Mammoth 2 - Governor'	BS
Leek, 'Autumn Mammoth Snowstar 2'	D,F,J
Leek, 'Autumn Mammoth Startrack'	BS,J
Leek, 'Autumn Mammoth Verina'	U
Leek, 'Autumn Mammoth Wintra RZ'	BD,MO
Leek, 'Autumn Profina'	SN
Leek, 'Bandit'	DT
Leek, 'Bastion'	B,BS
Leek, 'Blauwgroene Herfst Ardea'	MO
Leek, 'Blauwgroene Herfst Bastion'	MO
Leek, 'Blauwgroene Herfst Tadorna'	MO
Leek, 'Blauwgroene Wintra Laura'	MO
Leek, 'Bleu Solaize'	GO
Leek, 'Blizzard'	B,BS,MO,VH
Leek, 'Blue-Green Autumn Cortina'	J,TU,V
Leek, 'Bluestar' see Giant Winter 3	
Leek, 'Bulgaria'	BS
Leek, 'Bulgarian Giant'	U
Leek, 'Carina'	SR
Leek, 'Carlton' F1	D,S
Leek, 'Catalina'	BS
Leek, Chinese, Broad Leaf (Chinese Chives)	BF,BH,C,KS
Leek, 'Coloma'	HD
Leek, 'Colossal'	HD
Leek, 'Conora'	BS,CO,DT,KI,TU,YA
Leek, 'Derrick'	BS,KI,L
Leek, 'Elbeuf Elephant'	SN
Leek, 'Elephant'	BS,DI
Leek, 'Elina'	BS
Leek, 'Emperor'	BS

Leek, 'Falltime'	SD
Leek, 'Farinto'	C
Leek, 'Firena'	D,S
Leek, 'Gavia'	BS
Leek, 'Genita'	V
Leek, 'Gennevilliers Splendid'	BS,SK,SU,U
Leek, 'Giant Carentan'	AB,B,BS,CO,FR,JO,SU, TH
Leek, 'Giant Winter'	CO,FR,KI,MC,ST
Leek, 'Giant Winter 3'	BS,F
Leek, 'Giant Winter * Carina'	M
Leek, 'Giant Winter * Wila'	M
Leek, 'Goliath'	BS,BY,MC
Leek, 'Goliath'	TU
Leek, 'Hanniabal'	BS
Leek, 'Hivor'	PI
Leek, 'Jolant'	B,BD,BS,L,M,MO,ST, TU,VH
Leek, 'Kajak'	BS,BY,DD,KI,SU
Leek, 'Kelvedon King'	BS
Leek, 'Kilima'	SD,SR
Leek, 'King Richard'	BS,CO,D,DT,GO,JO,KI, M,PI,R,S,SE,SU,T,TE, TU,U,VH,YA
Leek, 'Lancelot'	K
Leek, 'Laura'	B,BS,JO,KI
Leek, 'Lavi'	BS,YA
Leek, 'Leefall'	SR
Leek, 'Lg American Flag'	BU,PI
Leek, 'Long Blanch'	K
Leek, 'Long Bow'	BS,DT
Leek, 'Longina'	BS,PK
Leek, 'Lungo d'Inverno'	RC
Leek, 'Lyon'	B,BS,BY,CO,DD,DT,J, KI,MC,ST,T,TH
Leek, 'Lyon 2 - Prizetaker'	BS,F,KI,S
Leek, 'Malabar'	BS
Leek, 'Mammoth Blanch'	BY,RO
Leek, 'Mammoth Pot'	RO
Leek, 'Maxim'	FR
Leek, 'Monstruoso di Carentan' see Giant Carentan	
Leek, 'Musselburgh'	B,BD,BS,BY,C,CO,D,DE, DT,F,J,KI,L,M,MC,MO,S, ST,SU,TH,TU,U,VH,VY
Leek, 'Musselburgh Improved'	T
Leek, 'Odin Longstanton'	BS
Leek, 'Otina'	SR
Leek, 'Pancho'	BS,D,SD,TU
Leek, 'Poribleu'	D
Leek, 'Poristo'	BS,F,TU
Leek, 'Pot Exhibition'	BY,SB
Leek, 'Pot K's strain'	K
Leek, 'Prenora'	BS,KI
Leek, 'Prizetaker' see Lyon	
Leek, 'Romil'	YA
Leek, 'Scotland'	SD
Leek, 'Senora'	YA
Leek, 'Sherwood'	SD
Leek, 'Siegfried Frost'	YA
Leek, 'Snowstar B'	BS
Leek, 'St. Victor'	AB,CO,DD,SN,SU
Leek, 'Sterna'	DT
Leek, 'Swiss Giant Coloma'	BS
Leek, 'Swiss Giant Marina'	SN
Leek, 'Tadorna'	B,BS,SK,SR
Leek, 'Thor'	BS

LEEK

Leek, 'Titan'	BS,SK
Leek, 'Toledo'	BS,T,TU
Leek, 'Tropita'	BS,KI
Leek, 'Unique'	SK
Leek, 'Upton'	T
Leek, 'Varna'	AB,JO,TE
Leek, 'Verina'	BS
Leek, 'Winora'	T,YA
Leek, 'Winter'	B,RO,SD
Leek, 'Winter Crop'	S
Leek, 'Winter Latina'	SN
Leek, 'Winterreuzen' see 'Giant Winter 3'	
Leek, 'Wintra'	B,BS,KI,L,SU
Leek, 'Yates Empire'	BS,U
Lentil, 'Ethiopian'	DD,SP
Lettuce, 'Abba'	K
Lettuce, 'Action'	F,SE
Lettuce, 'All The Year Round'	AB,BS,BY,C,CO,D,DT,F, J,KI,M,MC,S,ST,T,TH, TU,U,VH
Lettuce, 'Ambassador'	BS
Lettuce, 'American Brown'	BH
Lettuce, 'Anuenue'	JO
Lettuce, 'Arctic King'	BS,BY,KI,S,ST,TH,TU, VH
Lettuce, 'Attraction' see 'Unrivalled'	
Lettuce, 'Australian Yellow Leaf'	BH,DI
Lettuce, 'Avoncrisp'	BS,BY,CO,KI,M,ST
Lettuce, 'Avondefiance'	B,BD,BS,BY,CO,D,KI, L,M,MO,S,SU,YA
Lettuce, 'Baby Green'	SK
Lettuce, 'Babylon'	T
Lettuce, 'Balloon'	BS,BY,FR,KI,SN,SU,TH
Lettuce, 'Baltic'	M
Lettuce, 'Barbarossa'	BH
Lettuce, 'Barcarole'	HU,SD
Lettuce, 'Bastion'	J
Lettuce, Batavia 'Goutte de Sang'	SN,VS
Lettuce, Batavia 'La Brillante'	SN,VS
Lettuce, Batavia 'Laura'	AB,SD
Lettuce, Batavia 'Reine des Glaces'	SN,VS
Lettuce, 'Bath Cos'	HD
Lettuce, 'Beatrice'	B,BS,KI,SU,T,VH
Lettuce, 'Bella Green'	SK
Lettuce, 'Bikini'	YA
Lettuce, 'Bionda d'Ignegnoli'	FR
Lettuce, 'Bionda Ricciolina'	FR
Lettuce, 'Biondo Degli Ortolani'	FR
Lettuce, 'Biscia Rossa'	SU
Lettuce, 'Black Beauty'	DI
Lettuce, 'Black Seeded Simpson'	AB,BF,BU,DE,JO,KS, PI,SD,SK,SN,VY
Lettuce, 'Blonde Groene'	V
Lettuce, 'Blush'	D,T,YA
Lettuce, 'Borough Wonder'	TH
Lettuce, 'Bronze Arrow'	SD
Lettuce, 'Bronze Mignenette'	SD
Lettuce, 'Brown Edge Butterhead'	SP
Lettuce, 'Brown Goldring'	B,DD,HD
Lettuce, 'Bruna di Germania'	SU
Lettuce, 'Brune d'Hiver'	AB,GO,PI,SD
Lettuce, 'Brunia'	GO,PK,SK,SR,TE
Lettuce, 'Bubbles'	B,D,K,L,MO,T
Lettuce, 'Burgundy Boston'	BS,HU,KI,MC,SN
Lettuce, 'Burnia'	DE
Lettuce, 'Buttercrunch'	AB,B,BF,BS,BU,BY,CO, D,DE,DN,J,JO,KI,PI,PK, SD,SK,ST,SU,TE,U,VH
Lettuce, 'Butterking'	SD
Lettuce, 'Butterscotch'	T
Lettuce, 'Calmar'	VY
Lettuce, 'Capitaine'	SD
Lettuce, 'Capital'	L
Lettuce, 'Capuccio'	SN,VS
Lettuce, 'Carmona'	AB
Lettuce, 'Cartan'	BS
Lettuce, 'Catalogna'	BS,CO,SU,TU
Lettuce, 'Cavolo di Napoli'	FR
Lettuce, 'Celtic'	CO,MO
Lettuce, 'Centennial'	JO
Lettuce, 'Ceremony'	SP
Lettuce, 'Cerize'	S
Lettuce, 'Chadwick's Rodan'	SP
Lettuce, 'Challenge'	S
Lettuce, 'Cimmaron'	PI
Lettuce, 'Cindy'	MO
Lettuce, 'Clarion'	B,BS,DT,K,KI,L,MO
Lettuce, 'Cobham Green'	B,BS,BY,MO,SB
Lettuce, 'Cocarde' red	BS,CO,FR,JO,SN,SU
Lettuce, collection	KI,M
Lettuce, 'Columbus'	BS,D
Lettuce, 'Conny'	M,TU
Lettuce, 'Continuity' see 'Merveille des 4 saisons'	
Lettuce 'Cordoba'	MO
Lettuce, 'Corsair'	BS,D,DT,SE,T
Lettuce, 'Cortina'	BS,SU
Lettuce, 'Cosmic'	BS,D,DD,SE,T
Lettuce, 'Cosmo Savoy Leaf'	SD
Lettuce, 'Craquante D'Avignon'	DD
Lettuce, 'Cressonnette Marocaine'	SP
Lettuce, 'Crestana'	T
Lettuce, crisp	BF
Lettuce, 'Crispino'	F,JO
Lettuce, 'Curly Yellow'	BH
Lettuce, 'Cynthia'	BS,U
Lettuce, 'Daphne'	B,BS,MO
Lettuce, 'Dark Green Boston'	SR
Lettuce, 'Dark Green Cos'	BS
Lettuce, 'De Pologne'	SN,VS
Lettuce, 'Deep Red'	SK
Lettuce, 'Deer Tongue'	AB,JO
Lettuce, 'Deer Tongue Red'	AB,SD,SP
Lettuce, 'Delta'	AB,BS
Lettuce, 'Di Kagran 3'	FR
Lettuce, 'Diamant'	S
Lettuce, 'Diamond Gem'	KS
Lettuce, 'Diana'	BS
Lettuce, 'Divina'	DE,GO,PI
Lettuce, 'Dolly'	FR,U,VY
Lettuce, 'Drunken Woman'	RC,SP
Lettuce, 'Du Pere Vendee'	SN
Lettuce, 'Dynasty'	KI,SU
Lettuce, 'El Toro'	T
Lettuce, 'Ermosa'	JO
Lettuce, 'Escort'	SK,SR
Lettuce, 'Esmeralda'	SK,SR
Lettuce, 'Evola'	K
Lettuce, 'Express'	SN,VS
Lettuce, 'Favourite'	BS
Lettuce, 'Feuille de Chene'	HD
Lettuce, 'Flandria' RZ	CO
Lettuce, 'Fortune' see 'Hilde II'	

LETTUCE

Lettuce, Fresh Salad Mix	T
Lettuce, 'Frisby'	B,D,DT,J,M,MO,SE,T, TU,U
Lettuce, 'Gemini'	SK,VY
Lettuce, 'Goose'	DD
Lettuce, 'Grand Rapids'	BS,DN,PI,SK
Lettuce, 'Grasse Madrilene'	SN,VS
Lettuce, 'Great Lakes'	B,BS,BU,BY,DD,DI,DN, DT,FR,KI,M,MC,MO, ST,U
Lettuce, 'Great Lakes 659 Mesa'	BS
Lettuce, 'Green Ice'	KS,PI,PK
Lettuce, 'Green Towers'	SK,VY
Lettuce, 'Greenway'	YA
Lettuce, 'Guzmaine Tall'	SR
Lettuce, 'Hilde II'	BS,DT,M,S,VH
Lettuce, 'Hudson'	BS
Lettuce, 'Ibis'	K,PK
Lettuce, 'Iceberg'	B,BD,BS,BY,CO,J,KI, MC,MO,ST,SU,T,TH,VH
Lettuce, 'Iceberg 2'	TU
Lettuce, 'Ideal Cos'	SK
Lettuce, 'Imperial Winter'	B,BS,CO,DD
Lettuce, 'Impulse'	B,JO,K
Lettuce, 'Ithaca'	B,BS,MO,SK,SR,VY
Lettuce, 'Jackpot'	BS
Lettuce, 'Jaguar'	DT
Lettuce, 'Jericho'	SD
Lettuce, 'Jewel'	BS,DT,S
Lettuce, 'Kagraner Sommer'	PI,RI
Lettuce, 'Kalura'	JO
Lettuce, 'Karola'	V
Lettuce, 'Kathy'	MO
Lettuce, 'Kelly's'	B,BS,BY,DT,KI,L,M,MO, ST,SU,TU,U,V
Lettuce, 'Kelvin'	MO
Lettuce, 'Kendo'	F
Lettuce, 'King Crown'	BS,SN
Lettuce, 'Kloek'	BS
Lettuce, 'Kristine' RZ	CO
Lettuce, 'Kwiek'	AB,BS,CO,S
Lettuce, 'La Premiere'	SN,VS
Lettuce, 'Lactuca Angustana'	HD
Lettuce, 'Lake Nyah'	BS
Lettuce, 'Lakeland'	BS,D,DT,F,L,M,SE,U,VH
Lettuce, 'Leopard'	DT
Lettuce, 'Lianne'	S
Lettuce, 'Libusa' RZ	CO
Lettuce, 'Lilian'	BS,D
Lettuce, 'Little Gem'	w.a.
Lettuce, 'Little Gem Ferro'	K
Lettuce, 'Little Leprechaun'	BH,BS,CO,KI,SN,SU,V
Lettuce, 'Lobjoits Green Cos'	B,BS,BY,CO,F,J,KI,M, MO,R,S,SU,TH,TU,YA
Lettuce, 'Lollo Bionda'	B,BD,BS,CO,D,F,KI,KS, SU,M,MO,YA
Lettuce, 'Lollo Biondo - Lobi'	BH,J,V
Lettuce, 'Lollo' Mix	DI
Lettuce, 'Lollo Rosso'	w.a.
Lettuce, 'Lollo Rosso- Atsina'	J,V
Lettuce, 'Loma'	JO
Lettuce, 'Long Standing Batavian'	SD
Lettuce, 'Loos Tennis Ball'	HD
Lettuce, 'Lovina'	KS,YA
Lettuce, 'Luxor'	K
Lettuce, 'Malika'	BS

Lettuce, 'Marbello'	D
Lettuce, 'Marion'	MO
Lettuce, 'Martha'	FR
Lettuce, 'Mascara'	HU
Lettuce, 'Massa'	BS
Lettuce, 'May King'	BS,BY,CO,D,KI,ST,SU, TH
Lettuce, 'MDQS Chaperon'	DT,J,V
Lettuce, 'Merveille des Quatres Saisons'	B,BD,BS,BY,CO,DE,FR, GO,KI,KS,MC,MO,PI,RC ,SD,SN,ST,SU,TE,TH,TU
Lettuce, 'Mescher'	AB,HD
Lettuce, 'Milva'	BS,KI
Lettuce, 'Minetto'	BS
Lettuce, 'Mini Green'	BS,C,CO,DE,DT,KI,M, SK,SN,SU,TU,VH,VY
Lettuce, 'Miura'	T
Lettuce, Mixed	BH,DE,GO,PI,S,SD,SP
Lettuce, Mixed Leaf Salad	F,TE
Lettuce, Mixed Salad Leaves	D,F,KI,M, U
Lettuce, 'Monet'	VY
Lettuce, 'Montello'	SR
Lettuce, 'Musette'	B,BS,KI,S,SN,TU
Lettuce, 'Nancy'	B,BS,JO,MO,SR
Lettuce, 'Nevada'	GO,JO,M,PI,PK,SR,VY
Lettuce, 'New Red Fire'	AB,JO,PI,SK,T,TE
Lettuce, 'New York' see 'Webb's'	
Lettuce, 'North Pole'	SD
Lettuce, 'Novita'	BS,CO,KI,M,SE,SU,TU
Lettuce, 'Oak Leaf'	AB,B,BF,DD,DE,GO,HU, KS,PI,RC,SR
Lettuce, 'Oak Leaf Purple'	AB,DD,SD
Lettuce, 'Olga'	DE,PI,PK,VY
Lettuce, 'Optima'	JO,SR,TE
Lettuce, 'Oreilles du Diable'	SN
Lettuce, 'Pablo'	J
Lettuce, 'Pablo' Red	V
Lettuce, 'Parella, Green'	B,SU
Lettuce, 'Parella, Red'	SU
Lettuce, 'Paris White'	BS,BY,C,KI,KS,TH
Lettuce, 'Parris Island'	B,BS,DD,DE,DN,SB,SK, SN,SR,VY
Lettuce, 'Pasquier'	SN,VS
Lettuce, 'Patty'	FR
Lettuce, 'Pedro'	YA
Lettuce, 'Pennlake'	BS
Lettuce, 'Perlane'	BS
Lettuce, 'Pierre Benite'	U
Lettuce, 'Pinokkio'	D
Lettuce, 'Pirat Red'	BH,HU
Lettuce, 'Pirat Red & Green Butter'	SD
Lettuce, 'Piroga'	VY
Lettuce, 'Plato II'	PI
Lettuce, 'Plevanos'	BS
Lettuce, 'Polana'	YA
Lettuce, 'Poulton Market' see 'Hilde II'	
Lettuce, 'Prado'	V
Lettuce, 'Premier Great Lakes'	BS
Lettuce, 'Prestine'	BS
Lettuce, 'Prize Head'	AB,BU,K,RC,SD
Lettuce, ps	JO
Lettuce, 'PS 21192'	SR
Lettuce, 'PS 64289'	SR
Lettuce, 'Queen'	FR,VY
Lettuce, 'Rachel'	B,J,L,MO,YA
Lettuce, 'Raisa'	M

LETTUCE

Lettuce, 'Ravel'	B,BS,KI,MO,SU,TU
Lettuce, 'Red Butter'	SR
Lettuce, Red, 'Cerise'	JO
Lettuce, 'Red Fire'	BS,KI,KS,SN,SR,TU
Lettuce, 'Red Iceberg Sioux'	BS,BH,D,SD
Lettuce, Red, 'Jacqueline'	SK
Lettuce, 'Red Lettuce' Mix	T
Lettuce, 'Red Ridinghood'	SD
Lettuce, 'Red Sails'	BU,DE,DT,JO,KS,PI,SK, PK,TE
Lettuce, 'Red Splash'	HU
Lettuce, 'Red Velvet'	DI
Lettuce, 'Red Vogue'	PI,SK
Lettuce, 'Redcross'	FR
Lettuce, 'Redina'	JO,M,PI
Lettuce, 'Regina dei Ghiacci'	FR,SU
Lettuce, 'Regina di Maggio'	FR
Lettuce, 'Reine des Glaces'	SD,SN
Lettuce, 'Remus'	CO,K
Lettuce, 'Resisto'	FR
Lettuce, 'Reskia'	B,BS,BY,KI,MO
Lettuce, 'Ricardo'	BS,KI,TU
Lettuce, 'Ricciolina Bionda'	SU
Lettuce, 'Rigoletto'	AB,V
Lettuce, 'Robinson'	TU
Lettuce, 'Rolina'	SR
Lettuce, 'Romaine Dark Green'	AB,BF,BU
Lettuce, Romaine true	RC
Lettuce, Roman 'Chicon des Charentes'	SN,VS
Lettuce, Roman 'Pomme en Terre'	SN,VS
Lettuce, 'Romance'	J
Lettuce, 'Romulus'	JO
Lettuce, 'Rosalita'	JO,KS,SU
Lettuce, 'Rossa d'Amerique'	FR,SP
Lettuce, 'Rossa di Trento'	FR
Lettuce, 'Rossa Fruilana'	SU
Lettuce, 'Rossimo'	KS
Lettuce, 'Rouge d'Hiver'	AB,DI,GO,SD
Lettuce, 'Rouge de Grenoblaise'	BH,GO,PI,SD
Lettuce, 'Rougette du Midi'	BS,SU
Lettuce, 'Roxette' RZ	CO
Lettuce, 'Royal Frillice'	DT,J,V
Lettuce, 'Royal Green'	SK,SR
Lettuce, 'Royal Oak Leaf'	DI,KS,PK,SP
Lettuce, 'Royal Red'	SR
Lettuce, 'Ruben's Red'	AB,SD,SP
Lettuce, 'Ruby'	DN,HU,PI,SK
Lettuce, 'Rusty'	TU
Lettuce, 'Sabrina'	F
Lettuce, 'Salad Bowl'	AB,BF,BS,BU,BY,CO,D, DE,DN,DT,J,JO,KI,KS, M,S,ST,SU,TE,TU,VH
Lettuce, 'Salad Bowl, Red'	B,BF,BH,BS,BY,CO,D,DT, FR,JO,KI,KS,L,MO,PI, S,SK,SR,ST,SU,TU,VY
Lettuce, 'Salad Bowl,Red - Everest'	J, V
Lettuce, 'Salad Bowl', Red & Green Mix	DT,F
Lettuce, 'Salad Bowl Yellow'	BH
Lettuce, 'Salad Mix'	DT,TE
Lettuce, 'Saladin'	B,BD,BS,BY,C,CO,D,DT, F,J,K,KI,L,MO,SN,ST,TU, U,YA
Lettuce, 'Saladin Supreme'	BS
Lettuce, 'Saladin Zodiac'	MO
Lettuce, 'Saladini'	CO,TE
Lettuce, 'Salvo'	YA

Lettuce, 'Sandrina'	SD
Lettuce, 'Sangria'	JO,KS,S,SE,SK,SP
Lettuce, 'Santiago'	F
Lettuce, 'Sherwood'	T
Lettuce, 'Sierra'	JO,PI,TE,VY
Lettuce, 'Simpson Elite'	B,BU,DE,JO,KS,PI,PK, SK,SP,TE,VY
Lettuce, 'Slobolt'	FR,SK,SR,TE
Lettuce, 'Smooth Leaved Butter'	BH
Lettuce, 'Soprane'	YA
Lettuce, 'St. Anne's'	RC
Lettuce, 'St. Antoine'	SN,VS
Lettuce, 'St. Vincent'	SN
Lettuce, 'Stoke'	HD
Lettuce, 'Strada'	K
Lettuce, 'Sucrine' see 'Little Gem'	
Lettuce, 'Sudia'	DE
Lettuce, 'Summer Bibb'	SR
Lettuce, 'Summertime'	AB,PI,PK,TE,VY
Lettuce, 'Sunny'	DT
Lettuce, 'Super Prize'	SK
Lettuce, 'Suzan'	B,BS,BY,DT,KI,MO,S, ST,TU
Lettuce, 'Sweet Valentine'	SD,SR
Lettuce, 'Tango'	KS
Lettuce, 'Tania'	AB
Lettuce, 'Target'	MO
Lettuce, 'Thai Green'	B,SD
Lettuce, 'Tiger'	M
Lettuce, 'Till'	BH
Lettuce, 'Timo'	V
Lettuce, 'Titania'	MO,SK
Lettuce, 'Toledo'	M,VH
Lettuce, 'Tom Thumb'	B,BD,BS,BY,C,CO,D,DT, F,J,KI,L,M,MO,PI,S,SD, SN,ST,SU,TH,TU
Lettuce, 'Triumphator'	V
Lettuce, 'Trocadero Improved'	BD,FR,J,KI,MO,SU
Lettuce, 'Troubadour' RZ	CO
Lettuce, 'Two Star'	JO,SK
Lettuce, 'Unrivalled'	BS,BY,C,CO,KI,S
Lettuce, 'Val d'Orge'	SD
Lettuce, 'Valdai' RZ	CO
Lettuce, 'Valdor'	B,BS,BY,CO,D,KI,MO,S, SU,TU
Lettuce, 'Valeria'	D
Lettuce, 'Valeria (Red)'	F,HU,SN
Lettuce, 'Valmaine'	B,BD,BS,BY,CO,KI,MO, SN,SR,SU,TE,VH
Lettuce, 'Vanity'	JO
Lettuce, 'Vaux Self-Folding'	CO
Lettuce, 'Verpia'	B,SB
Lettuce, 'Verte Mar'	PI
Lettuce, 'Vulcan'	PI
Lettuce, 'Waldmann's'	AB,SK,SR
Lettuce, 'Warpath'	S
Lettuce, 'Webb's Wonderful'	B,BD,BS,BY,C,CO,D,DD, F,J,KI,M,MC,MO,S,SE, SN,ST,SU,T,TH,TU,U,VH
Lettuce, 'Windermere'	S
Lettuce, 'Winter Crop' see 'Imperial Winter'	
Lettuce, 'Winter Density'	AB,B,BD,BS,BY,C,CO,D, DT,F,J,JO,KI,M,MO,S, SD,SN,ST,TE,TU,U,V
Lettuce, 'Winter Green'	FR
Lettuce, 'Winter Imperial'	AB,J,KI,ST,V

LETTUCE

Lettuce, 'Winter Marvel' see 'Imperial Winter'	
Lettuce, 'Yellow Round Leaf'	BH
Lettuce 'Yvonne'	MO
Lettuce, 'Zodiac'	B,BS
Loofah	F,SN,SU,V,VS
Loofah, 'Large Fruit' Smooth	V
Loofah, 'San-C' F1	V
Loofah, 'Seven Star' F1	V
Malabar Spinach	KS,SU
Mallow, Curled	KS
Mangel	HU
Mangel, 'Feldherr'	BY
Mangel, 'Mammoth Long Red'	HU
Mangel, 'Prizewinner'	B,CO,KI,SU
Mangel, 'Wintergold'	BS,BY
Mangel, Yellow intermediate	SD
Marrow, 'Badger Cross' F1	BS,K,M,SE
Marrow, 'Bianco Friulano'	BS
Marrow, 'Cobra' F1	BS
Marrow, 'Cousa'	BS,SK
Marrow, 'Custard Yellow'	BS
Marrow, 'Emerald Cross' F1	B,BD,BS,KI,MO
Marrow, Ghada	SK
Marrow, 'Green Bush' F1	B,BD,C,CO,J,MO,R,S, ST,T,TH,VH,YA
Marrow, 'Green Bush Special'	BS
Marrow, 'Green Gem'	BS
Marrow, 'Long Green Bush'	BY,KI,MC,S,SK
Marrow, 'Long Green Bush 2'	BS,D,F,L,TU,U
Marrow, 'Long Green Bush 2' - Imp	BS,S
Marrow, 'Long Green Bush 3- Cobham'	BS
Marrow, 'Long Green Bush 3' - Smallpack	S
Marrow, 'Long Green Bush 4'	DT,M
Marrow, 'Long Green Striped' see Trailing	
Marrow, 'Long Green Trailing'	B,BD,BS,BY,CO,D,J,KI, M,MO,S,ST,TH,TU,U,VH
Marrow, 'Long White Trailing'	K
Marrow, 'Minipak'	BS,C,CO,KI
Marrow, Neapolitan	SN,VS
Marrow, 'Onyx' F1	BS
Marrow, 'Prepak'	BS
Marrow, 'Saracen'	BS
Marrow, 'Sundance'	BS
Marrow, 'Table Dainty'	BS,K,S
Marrow, 'Tender and True'	S
Marrow, 'Tiger Cross' F1	B,BS,CO,F,KI,L,MO,S, T,TU
Marrow, 'Zebra Cross'	B,BS,DT,M,MO,YA
Melon, 'Acor' F1	PI
Melon, 'Alaska' F1	PI,VY
Melon, 'Alienor' hyb	SK
Melon, 'Allsweet' o-p	B,SR
Melon, 'Amber Nectar'	B,PK,T
Melon, 'Ambrosia' F1	PI,PK
Melon, 'Ananas'	B,RC,SN,VS
Melon, 'Athena' hyb	JO,SR
Melon, 'Banana'	DE
Melon, 'Berlia'	BS
Melon, 'Blenheim Orange'	BS,BY,CO,KI,M,S,SD, ST,TH
Melon, 'Bolero' hyb	SR
Melon, 'Branco'	RC
Melon, 'Burpee' hyb	SK
Melon, 'Burrell's Jumbo'	BU
Melon, 'Canada Gem' hyb	SK
Melon, 'Casaba Golden Beauty'	BU

Melon, 'Casablanca' F1	PK
Melon, 'Charantais'	B,BS,DI,F,FR,GO,VH
Melon, 'Charmel II'	DE
Melon, 'Charmont' F1	FR
Melon, Chinese winter	RI
Melon, Chitted Seed	M
Melon, 'Classic' hyb	BU,SR
Melon, 'Clipper' F1	J
Melon, 'Cosenza Giallo'	FR
Melon, 'Creme de Menthe' hyb	SR
Melon, 'Crenshaw'	DE
Melon, 'Crete' hyb	SK
Melon, 'Crimson Sweet' o-p	B,SR
Melon, 'Delicious 51'	BU,PI
Melon, 'Dorado' hyb	SR
Melon, 'Earligold' hyb	JO,SR,TE,VY
Melon, 'Earliqueen' F1	JO,SK
Melon, 'Early Black Rock'	B,HU
Melon, 'Early Chaca' F1	PI
Melon, 'Early Dawn' F1	B,BS
Melon, 'Early Dew'	BS,JO,PI,SK,SR,TE
Melon, 'Early Hanover'	AB,DD
Melon, 'Early Large Prescott'	B,HU
Melon, 'Early Sweet'	BU,FR,S,SK,VY
Melon, 'Eclipse' hyb	SK
Melon, 'Eden Gem'	BU
Melon, 'Edisto'	BU,DE
Melon, 'Emerald Gem'	S
Melon, 'Experimental'	T
Melon, 'Extra Early Nutmeg'	AB
Melon, 'Fast Break' F1	BU,PI,SK,VY
Melon, 'Four-Fifty'	BU
Melon, 'Fuzzy'	KS
Melon, 'Galia' F1	B,BS,SR,T,YA
Melon, 'Gallicum' hyb	DE,FR,PK,SR
Melon, 'Geabel' F1	C
Melon, 'Gold King' hyb	SR
Melon, 'Golden Beauty' F1	JO
Melon, 'Golden Crispy'	DE
Melon, 'Golden Crown' F1	PK,T
Melon, 'Golden Honeymoon'	AB
Melon, 'Golden Light'	BH
Melon, 'Goldstar' F1	V
Melon, 'Grande Gold' hyb	BU
Melon, green climbing	HU
Melon, 'Green Flash'	FR
Melon, 'Green Meated' honeydew	BU
Melon, 'Green Nutmeg'	HD
Melon, 'Hale's Best Jumbo'	BF,FR
Melon, 'Haogen'	DI,SD
Melon, 'Harvest Queen'	DE,SD
Melon, 'Hearts of Gold'	BU,DE
Melon, Heirloom Melons of the World	DI
Melon, 'Honey Ice' F1	JO
Melon, 'Honey Orange' F1	JO
Melon, 'Honey World'	BH
Melon, 'Honeylope'	DD
Melon, 'Imperial 45-S12'	BU,DD
Melon, 'Iriquois' o-p	B,DD,DE,SR,TE
Melon, 'Jade Beauty'	BH
Melon, 'Jaune Canari'	BU,SD,SR
Melon, 'Jenny Lind'	AB,B,PI
Melon, 'Kazakh'	AB
Melon, 'Large White Prescott'	HU
Melon, 'Lunabel'	D
Melon, 'Luscious Plus' F1	PK

MELON

Melon, 'Market Pride'	BS
Melon, 'Market Star' F1	FR
Melon, 'Marygold' hyb	SK
Melon, 'Minnesota Midget'	AB,PI
Melon, mix	FR,GO
Melon, 'Napoletana Giallo' early green	B,FR
Melon, 'New Market' F1	FR
Melon, 'No Name'	V
Melon, 'Oasis' F1	PK
Melon, 'Ogen'	AB,B,BD,BS,BY,D,DT,J, KI,L,M,MC,MO,S,SE, ST,SU,T,TU,V
Melon, 'Orange Blossom'	DE,PI
Melon, 'Oranje Ananas'	BU,V
Melon, 'Oregon Delicious'	AB,DD
Melon, 'Passport' F1	GO,JO,PI,SK,SR,TE,VY
Melon, 'Pasteque a Confiture'	SN,VS
Melon, 'Peach Vine'	DE
Melon, 'Pear'	AB
Melon, Pickling, 'Katsura Giant'	SR
Melon, 'Pinonet Piel de Sapo' o-p	B,FR,SR
Melon, 'Planters Jumbo'	BU
Melon, 'Powdery Mildew Resistant No. 45'	BU
Melon, 'Pride of Wisconsin'	SD
Melon, 'Primo' F1	BU,SK,SR
Melon, 'Pulsar' F1	BU,SK,SR,TE
Melon, 'Queen Anne's Scented Pocket'	BH
Melon, 'Rapid'	BS
Melon, 'Rising Star'	SK
Melon, 'Rock Sunrise'	KS
Melon, 'Rock Sweet n' Early'	KS
Melon, 'Rocky Sweet' hyb	SR
Melon, 'Romeo' F1	M
Melon, 'Rugoso di Cosenza Giallo' F1	B,FR
Melon, 'Santa Clause'	BU
Melon, 'Saticoy' hyb	SR
Melon, 'Savor' F1	JO
Melon, 'Schoon's Hard-Shell'	BU,DE
Melon, 'Scoop II' F1	PK
Melon, 'Sharlyn'	AB,SD
Melon, 'Small Persian'	BU
Melon, 'Sparkle' hyb	BU
Melon, 'Spartan Rock' o-p	SR
Melon, 'Spear'	AB
Melon, 'Sprite' F1	PI
Melon, 'Starship'	SK
Melon, 'Summet' hyb	SK
Melon, 'Sungold'	SD
Melon, 'Super Market' F1	BU,FR
Melon, 'Swan Lake'	AB,B,SD
Melon, 'Sweet Delight' F1	PK
Melon, 'Sweet Granite'	AB,DI,JO
Melon, 'Sweetheart' F1	B,BD,BS,BY,CO,D,DT, F,J,KI,L,M,MO,PK,S, SE,ST,SU,T,TU,YA
Melon, 'Sweetie No.6' F1	JO
Melon, 'Tam Mayan Sweet'	DE
Melon, 'Topmark'	BU
Melon, 'Touchdown' F1	PI
Melon, 'Treasure' hyb	BU
Melon, 'Tropical'	KS
Melon, Turkish Leopard Melon	DI
Melon, 'Uncle E'	AB
Melon, 'Vector' F1	FR
Melon, 'Vieille France'	SN,VS
Melon, Water, 'Allsweet'	BU,SR

Melon, Water 'Arikara'	AB
Melon, Water, 'Arriba!' hyb	BU,SR
Melon, Water, 'Au Golden Producer'	B,SK
Melon, Water, 'Au Sweet Scarlet'	SK
Melon, Water, 'Baron' hyb	SR
Melon, Water, 'Big Crimson' F1	FR
Melon, Water, 'Black Boy' hyb	SR
Melon, Water, 'Black Diamond'	BU,DE,FR
Melon, Water, 'Black Diamond Yellow Belly'	BU
Melon, Water, 'Bush Baby II' F1	PK
Melon, Water, 'Bush Snakeskin'	SD
Melon, Water, 'Canada Supersweet' hyb	B,SK
Melon, Water, 'Carnival' hyb	SR
Melon, Water, 'Charleston Gray'	B,BD,BS,BU,BY,CO,DD, FR,KI,MC,MO
Melon, Water, 'Chilton'	SN,VS
Melon, Water, 'Christmas'	DD
Melon, Water, 'Cream of Saskatchevan'	DI
Melon, Water, 'Crimson Sweet'	AB,BS,BU,C,FR,J,SD, SK,SR,TE
Melon, Water, 'Crimson Trio' F1	SR
Melon, Water, 'Desert King'	SD
Melon, Water, 'Desert Storm' F1	BU,SR
Melon, Water, 'Early Moonbeam'	SD
Melon, Water, 'Fairfax'	HU
Melon, Water, 'Fiesta' hyb	BU,SR
Melon, Water, 'Fourth of July'	HU
Melon, Water, 'Garden Baby' F1	JO,PI
Melon, Water, 'Glory Sugar' F1	PI
Melon, Water, 'Golden Honey'	DE,SD
Melon, Water, 'Honey Queen'	HU
Melon, Water, 'Honey Red Seedless' F1	PK
Melon, Water, 'Hopi'	B,DD
Melon, Water, 'Hopi Red'	B,DD,HU
Melon, W., 'Hopi Yellow Jumbo Sikyatko'	HU
Melon, Water, 'Ice Cream'	B,DD
Melon, Water, 'Imperial Seedless' F1	BU,FR
Melon, Water, 'Jack of Hearts' hyb	SK
Melon, Water, 'Jade Star' F1	DE,SR,TE
Melon, Water, 'Jubilee'	BU
Melon, Water, 'Jubilee Registered'	BU
Melon, Water, 'Kenya'	B,DD
Melon, Water, 'King & Queen'	AB,RC
Melon, W., 'Klondike Striped Blue Ribbon'	FR
Melon, Water, 'Laurel' hyb	SR
Melon, Water, 'Louisiana Queen'	HU
Melon, Water, 'Malali'	SD
Melon, Water, 'Mardi Gras' hyb	SR
Melon, Water, 'Mickylee'	SK
Melon, Water, 'Mini Jubilee' F1	PK
Melon, Water, 'Moon and Stars'	AB,DI
Melon, Water, 'Navajo Sweet'	B,BU,DD,RC
Melon, Water, 'New Orchid' F1	BH,GO,JO
Melon, Water, 'Northern Sweet'	AB,B,DD,SD
Melon, Water, 'Nova' hyb	SR
Melon, Water, 'Orange Flesh TenderSweet'	BU,HU
Melon, Water, 'Paladin' F1	PK
Melon, Water, 'Patriot' hyb	SR
Melon, Water, 'Pony Yellow' F1	PI
Melon, Water, 'Premier Seedless' hyb	BU
Melon, Water, 'Regency' hyb	SR
Melon, Water, 'Royal Flush' hyb	SR
Melon, Water, 'Royal Jubilee' hyb	SR
Melon, Water, 'Royal Majesty' hyb	SR
Melon, Water, 'Royal Star' hyb	SR
Melon, Water, 'Royal Sweet' hyb	SR

MELON

Melon, Water, 'Sangria' hyb	BU,SR
Melon, Water, 'Seedless Supreme' F1	FR
Melon, Water, 'Sin' F1	D
Melon, Water, 'Sugar Baby'	AB,B,BF,BS,BU,C,DE,
	FR,GO,JO,PI,PK,RC,SK,
	SR,SU,TE,V,VY
Melon, Water, 'Sugar Bush'	DE
Melon, Water, 'Sugar' hyb	B,SK
Melon, Water, 'Sunshine' F1	JO
Melon, Water, 'Super Sweet'	BU
Melon, Water, 'Sweet Favourite' F1	JO,SK
Melon, Water, 'Sweet Heart' F1	PK
Melon, Water, 'Sweet Siberia'	DI
Melon, Water, 'Sweetmeat II WR' F1	FR
Melon, Water, 'Tiger Baby'	DE,SK
Melon, Water, 'Tiny Orchid'	V
Melon, Water, 'Tri-X 313' F1	SR
Melon, Water, 'Tri-X Chiffon' F1	SR
Melon, Water, 'Tri-X Triple Sweet' F1	SR
Melon, Water, 'Verona'	SD
Melon, Water, 'Wanli'	B,V
Melon, Water, 'Warpaint'	HU
Melon, Water, 'Yellow Baby' F1	BH,PK,SK
Melon, Water, 'Yellow Cutie' F1	FR
Melon, Water, 'Yellow Doll' F1	B,DE,SR,TE,VY
Melon, Water, 'Yellow Shipper'	BU
Melon, 'Yellow Canary Smooth'	B,HU
Melon, 'Zuccherino d'Ingegnoli'	B,FR
Mesclun	DI,DT,GO,KS,SU
Mesclun, Mild mix	JO,PK,SK
Mesclun, Oriental	KS
Mesclun, Provencal	DI
Mesclun, Tangy mix	DI,JO,PK
Mibuna Greens	CO,JO,KS,SU,TU
Millet	SN,VS
Millet, Japanese	AB
Millet, 'White Wonder'	AB
Miner's Lettuce, erect large leaf	SD
Miner's lettuce, 'Goldberg'	JO,PI
Miner's Lettuce, Golden	B,DD,GO,HU,SN,TH
Miner's Lettuce, 'Minutina'	JO
Miner's Lettuce(Winter Purslane)	AB,B,C,DD,HU,JO,M,
	RC,RI,S,SN,SU,TH,TU,V
Miscluglio	SU
Mitsuba	AB,BS,KI,KS,MC,SN,TU
Mizuna Greens	AB,B,BS,C,CO,JO,K,KI,
	KS,MC,PI,RC,RI,SD,SN,
	SR,SU,TU,V,YA
Mizuna Greens, 'Tokyo Belle'	KS,SK
Mizuna Greens, 'Youzen'	D
Mushroom 'Grey Oyster'	CO
Mushroom Spawn, 'Button'	CO,PI,PK,TU
Mushroom Spawn, 'Cultivated'	DT,FR,M
Mushroom Sp., 'Darlington's Grain Spawn'	S
Mushroom Sp., 'Darlington's Pellet Spawn'	S
Mushroom Spawn, 'Dobies Grain Spawn'	D
Mushroom Spawn, 'Dobies Pellet Spawn'	D
Mushroom Spawn, 'Oyster'	M,TE
Mushroom Spawn, Reishi	RI
Mushroom Spawn, Shiitake	PK,RI
Mustard	BH,BS,DI,K,SU
Mustard, black	BH,GO,RC
Mustard, 'Fine White'	B,BY,C,D,DT,F,J,M,S,
	SE,ST,SU,TU
Mustard 'Green Wave'	AB,B,JO,PI,SD,SK
Mustard Greens	CO,SU,SY

Mustard Greens, 'Florida Broad Leaf'	BU,SK,SR
Mustard Greens, lg curled	BF,BH
Mustard Greens, 'Mustard Lettuce'	KS,SP
Mustard Greens, 'Osaka Purple'	JO,RC,SD
Mustard Greens -red	BS
Mustard Greens, 'Red Giant'	AB,B,C,DI,DT,GO,JO,
	KS,PI,PK,SN,SR,SU,TE,
	TU,YA
Mustard Greens, small	AB
Mustard Greens, Swatow	BH,KS
Mustard, 'Hsueh-Si-Hung' (Serifon)	BH
Mustard old-fashioned	AB
Mustard, Salad 'Kingston'	B,KI,ST,SU,VH
Mustard, Southern Giant Curled	BU,PK,RI,SR
Mustard, Tilney	YA
Mustard, white	RC
Mustard-Horned see Swollen Stem	
Mustard-Salad	KS
New Zealand Spinach	AB,BF,BS,BY,C,CO,FR,
	GO,HU,J,JO,KI,KS,M,PI,
	RI,SK,SU,TH,V,VY
	SP
Oats, Hulless, 'James'	B,CG,L,KS
Okra	B,CG,L,KS
Okra, 'Annie Oakley' F1	BU,DE,GO,PI,SK,SR,TE
Okra, 'Artist'	V
Okra, 'Burgundy'	GO,KS,PK
Okra, 'Cajun Delight' F1	JO,PI,PK,SK,VY
Okra, 'Clemson Spineless'	B,BD,BS,BU,BY,C,DE,
	DT,F,HU,J,KI,MC,MO,PI,
	PK,RC,SK,SR,T,TE,TU,V
Okra, 'Dwarf Green Long Pod'	BS
Okra, 'Green Best' F1	PI,PK,SR
Okra, 'Green Velvet'	B,HU,U
Okra, 'Lee'	PK
Okra, 'Long Green'	D
Okra, 'Mammoth Spineless Long Pod'	SD
Okra, 'Pentagreen'	BS
Okra, 'Perkins Dw'	BF,BU,DE
Okra, 'Pure Luck' F1	B,BH,BS,KI,ST,SU,TU
Okra, Red	AB,DD,DE
Okra, 'Red Velvet'	SD
Okra, 'Star of David'	SD
Okra, 'White Velvet'	DE
Onion, '8838'	BS
Onion, 'A-1 ' (Sutton's)	BS
Onion, 'Ailsa Craig'	B,BD,BS,BY,C,CO,TH,J,
	JO,KI,L,M,MC,MO,ST,
	SU,TU,U,V,VH
Onion, 'Ailsa Craig' Crosslings Seedlings	BS
Onion, 'Ailsa Craig Prizewinner'	DT,F,PI,S
Onion, 'Ailsa Craig' Selected	BS,S
Onion, 'Ailsae'	K
Onion, 'Albion' F1	DT,F,J,M,SE,T,TU
Onion, 'Amigo'	F
Onion, 'Apriliatica'	FR
Onion, 'Augusta'	BS
Onion, 'Beacon' F1	DT,SE,T,V
Onion, 'Bedfordshire Champion'	B,BD,BS,BY,C,CO,D,
	DT,F,J,KI,L,M,MC,MO,
	S,ST,SU,TH,U
Onion, 'Best of Whites'	FR
Onion, 'Bingo' hyb	SK
Onion, 'Blanco Duro PVP'	BU,PI,TE
Onion, 'Brunswick'	BS,F,S
Onion, 'Buffalo' F1	B,BS,BY,D,JO,MO,T,
	TE,TU,VH

ONION

Onion, Bulbing, exhibition type	R	Onion, 'Ebeneezer'	BS
Onion, Bunching, 'Asagi'	DE	Onion, 'Eglisau Red'	DD
Onion, Bunching, 'Beltsville'	SK	Onion, 'Endurance' F1	SR
Onion, Bunching, common	DE	Onion, 'Eskimo' hyb	SK
Onion, Bunching, 'Deep Purple'	JO	Onion, Exhibition	U
Onion, Bunching, 'Emerald Isle'	DT,SK	Onion, 'Extra Early Kaizuka'	BS
Onion, Bunching, 'Evergreen White'	AB,B,DE,DN,FR,HU,JO, PI,PK	Onion, 'Frontier' hyb	SK
		Onion, 'Gazette' hyb	SK
Onion, Bunching, 'Guardsman'	BS,D,DT,M,TE,TU	Onion, giant white	FR
Onion, Bunching, 'Hardy White'	SK	Onion, 'Giant Zittau'	BS,CO,KI,M,TH
Onion, Bunching, 'Hikari'	B,BD,BS,BY,CO,MO,SU, TU,YA	Onion, 'Gold Coin'	JO
		Onion, 'Golden Bear'	BS,CO,KI,SU
Onion, Bunching, 'Ishiko' see Ishikura		Onion, 'Golden Cascade' F1	SR
Onion, Bunching, 'Ishikura'	B,BS,CO,DN,F,J,KI,MC, S,SD,SK,SR,SU,T,TU,V, VH,YA	Onion, 'Golden Summer' F1	FR
		Onion, 'Granex' F1	PK
		Onion, 'Headliner' F1	SK,SR
Onion, Bunching, 'Kaigaro'	BH	Onion, 'Hi Keeper' F1	K
Onion, Bunching, 'Kincho'	SK,SR,TE	Onion, 'Hygro' F1	B,BD,BS,BY,CO,DT,J,KI, L,M,MO,ST,TU,U
Onion, Bunching, 'Kyoto Market'	BS,D		
Onion, Bunching, 'Laser'	YA	Onion, 'Hyper' F1	BS
Onion, Bunching, 'Long White Summer'	SK	Onion, 'Hyrate' F1	BS
Onion, Bunching, 'Long White Tokyo'	C,SK,SR,VY	Onion, 'Hysam' F1	B,BS,K,MO
Onion, Bunching, 'Multi-Stalk Kujo Green'	B,C	Onion, 'Hyton' F1	BS,VH
Onion, Bunch., 'N. Holland Blood- Redmate'	DT,F,S,YA	Onion, 'James Longkeeper'	DD
Onion, Bunching, 'Parade'	VH,VY	Onion, Japanese, 'Express Yellow' F1	B,BS,CO,KI,MO,ST,SU
Onion, Bunching, Perennial	BH	Onion, Japanese, 'Imai Early Yellow'	B,BD,BS,M,MO,YA
Onion, Bunching, 'Perfecta'	BH	Onion, Japanese, 'Indared'	YA
Onion, Bunching, 'Red'	KS	Onion, Japanese 'Keepwell' F1	BS,KI
Onion, Bunching, 'Redbeard'	B,BS,CO,GO,HU,SK, SU,VY	Onion, Japanese, 'Senshyu Semi-Globe'	B,BD,BS,BY,CO,DT,J,KI, L,M,MO,S,ST,TU,U,V,YA
Onion, Bunching, 'Santa Clause'	T	Onion, 'Joint Venture' hyb	SK
Onion, Bunching, 'Savel'	M	Onion, K's selection	K
Onion, Bunching, 'Scallion'	B,SU	Onion, 'Lancastrian'	D,F,J,T
Onion, Bunching, 'Southport White'	SK	Onion, 'Legacy' F1	SK,SR
Onion, Bunching, 'SY 678'	BS	Onion, 'Long Red Florence'	B,BH,BS,SU,TH
Onion, Bunching, Welsh	B,F,KS,M,MC,ST,V	Onion, 'Lotus'	K
Onion, Bunching, Welsh Red	SU	Onion, 'Maggio' white	FR
Onion, Bunching, 'White Lisbon'	BD,BS,BY,C,CO,D,DE, DT,F,J,KI,L,M,MC,MO, R,S,SK,ST,SE,SU,T,TH, TU,U,V,VH,YA	Onion, 'Mambo' F1	BU
		Onion, 'Mammoth Improved'	BY,RO
		Onion, 'Mammoth Red'	BY,RO
		Onion, 'Maraton' F1 p.s	D
Onion, Bunching, 'White Lisbon Winter Hardy' see 'Winter-Over'		Onion, 'Marvel' F1	SR
Onion, Bunching, 'White Spear'	AB,BS,SR,YA	Onion, 'Marzatica' white	FR
Onion, Bunching, 'White Sweet Spanish'	BU,BY,PI,SK	Onion, 'Mercury' F1	SK,SR
Onion, Bunching, 'Winter White'	BS,M,T	Onion, mild red odourless	DI
Onion, Bunching, 'Yakko Summer'	RC	Onion, mix	BH,GO
Onion, 'Burgos' F1	SK,SR	Onion,'Monkston'	BS,BY,KI,ST
Onion, 'Burrell's Yellow Valencia'	BU	Onion, 'New York Early' o-p	JO,SK,SR
Onion, 'Candy' F1	SR	Onion, 'Norstar' F1	SK,SR,VY
Onion, 'Cannon'	VY	Onion, 'Oakey' see 'Reliance'	
Onion, 'Capable' F1	SK,SR	Onion, 'Oporto'	BS
Onion, 'Caribo' F1	T,VH	Onion, 'Owa'	F
Onion, 'Condor' hyb	SK	Onion, 'Own World Record Strain'	K
Onion, 'Contessa'	VH	Onion, 'Paragon' hyb	SR
Onion, 'Copper King' hyb	SK	Onion, Pickling, 'Barletta'	B,BH,BS,DI,FR,SK,SU, TH
Onion, 'Copra' F1	JO,SK,VH		
Onion, 'Creamgold'	DI	Onion, Pickling, 'Brown SY300'	D,DT,S,YA
Onion, 'Criterion' F1	SR	Onion, Pickling, 'Crystal Wax'	PK,VY
Onion, 'Crystal Wax White' o-p	SR	Onion, Pickling, 'Giant Rocca Brown'	BS,TH
Onion, 'Daytona'	VH	Onion, Pickling, 'North Holland Flat Yellow'	BS
Onion, 'Dessex' F1	SR	Onion, Pickling, 'Paris Silverskin'	B,BD,BH,BS,BY,C,CO, DT,F,J,KI,L,M,MO,S,ST, TH,TU,U,V,VH
Onion, 'Dorata di Parma'	FR		
Onion, 'Downing Yellow Globe'	BS		
Onion, 'Duraldo'	BS,KI	Onion, Pickling, 'Pompei'	BS,SK
Onion, 'Duration' F1	SK,SR	Onion, Pickling, 'Purplette'	AB
Onion, 'Early Yellow Globe'	AB,BS,PI	Onion, Pickling, 'Shakespeare Mini'	D,S,YA

ONION

Onion, Pickling, 'The Queen'	D	Onion, 'Super Bear'	BS,KI,ST
Onion, 'Prestige' hyb	SR	Onion, 'Sweet Georgia Brown'	PK
Onion, 'Prince' F1	JO	Onion, 'Sweet Sandwich' F1	CO,KI,ST,T,V,VH
Onion, 'Purplette'	B,CO,KS,SU	Onion, 'Sweet Spanish Colorado No.6'	BU
Onion, 'Radar' F1	B,BS,K,MO	Onion, 'Sweet Success' F1	SR
Onion, 'Ramata di Milano'	FR	Onion, 'Tarmagon' hyb	SK
Onion, 'Red Baron'	B,BD,BS,BY,D,DT,J,K,	Onion, 'Tarzan'	BS
	MO,SE,T,TU,V,VH	Onion, 'Texas Yellow Grano'	AB,BU,FR,TE
Onion, Red 'Burgermaster' F1	PI,PK,VY	Onion, 'Torpedo'	C
Onion, 'Red Eyes'	BU	Onion, 'Torque' F1	PI
Onion, 'Red Italian'	BS,TH	Onion, 'Toughball' F1	BS,K,YA
Onion, Red, 'Jon 190'	JO	Onion, 'TZ 8825' F1	BS
Onion, Red, 'Lucifer'	SK	Onion, 'Valencia'	FR,SD
Onion, Red, 'Mars' F1	JO,SK,SR	Onion, 'Walla Walla Sweet'	AB,GO,JO,PI,SD,TE
Onion, 'Red Moon'	L	Onion, 'White Keeper' F1	PI
Onion, 'Red Piroska'	BH	Onion, 'White Knight'	M
Onion, Red, 'Rossa di Milano'	FR,SD	Onion, 'White Portugal'	BS,TH
Onion, 'Red Ruby Globe'	DD	Onion, 'White Spanish'	BS,DE,SK
Onion, 'Red Simiane'	GO	Onion, 'Winter-Over'	BD,BS,CO,D,DT,F,J,KI,
Onion, Red, 'Stockton'	SD		MC,MO,R,S,ST,TU,U,
Onion, 'Red Torpedo'	PI		V,YA
Onion, Red 'Tropea Tonda Rossa'	PK,SD	Onion, 'X-201' hyb	BU
Onion, 'Red Wethersfield'	DD	Onion, 'X-202' hyb	BU
Onion, 'Redman'	AB	Onion, 'X-400' hyb	BU
Onion, 'Reliance'	BS,BY,CO,SU,TH	Onion, 'X-412' hyb	BU
Onion, 'Rijnsburger'	KI,SE,VH	Onion, 'X-636' hyb	BU
Onion, 'Rijnsburger 2 Sito'	F	Onion, 'Yellow Globe Danvers'	BS,TH
Onion, 'Rijnsburger 4'	F	Onion, 'Yellow Granex Imp' hyb	SR
Onion, 'Rijnsburger 5 Balstora'	B,BD,BS,DT,J,M,MO,V	Orach, Blonde	HU,SN,VS
Onion, 'Rijnsburger 5 Jumbo'	BS,D	Orach, Green	AB,HU,PI,RI,SN,TH,V,
Onion, 'Rijnsburger 5 -Toro'	BS		VS
Onion, 'Rijnsburger Reinaldo'	BS	Orach, Red	AB,HU,JO,PI,SN,SP,TH,
Onion, 'Rijnsburger Rocky'	YA		V,VS
Onion, 'Rijnsburger Tamrock'	YA	Orach, 'Ruby'	SD
Onion, 'Ringer Grano Imp' o-p	SR	Oriental Greens, 'Autumn Poem' F1	JO
Onion, 'Ringmaster' o-p	SR	Oriental Greens, 'Bau Sin'	B,BH,V
Onion, 'Robusta'	BS,BY,CO,KI	Oriental Greens, Burdock	BH
Onion, 'Romeo'	F	Oriental Greens, Chin-Chiang	AB,B
Onion, 'Rossa di Bassano'	B,C,FR	Oriental Greens, 'Chinese Green Giant'	KS
Onion, 'Rossa la Resistante'	FR	Oriental Greens, Chrysanthemum	AB,BS,C,CO,DT,F,GO,
Onion, 'Royal Oak' F1	BS,F		JO,KI,L,MC,PI,RI,SK,
Onion, Salad, 'Long White Tokyo'	KI		SR,SU,TU
Onion, Salad, 'Toga'	J	Oriental Greens, Express Vegetable Coll.	M
Onion, 'Sassy Brassy' F1	PK	Oriental Greens, 'Giant Purple'	KS
Onion, 'Savannah Sweet' hyb	SR	Oriental Greens, 'Green in Snow'	BS,CO,MC,KI,SN,SU,TU
Onion, 'Sentry'	BS	Oriental Greens, Headed Chinese Cabbage	B,BS,C,CO,DD,KI,SD,
Onion, Shallot, 'Ambition' F1	DT,F,K,ST,TE		SK,SN,SU,ST
Onion, Shallot, 'Atlas' F1	B	Oriental Greens, Joi Choi F1	CO,DT,GO,J,JO,KI,KS,
Onion, Shallot, 'Creation' F1	D,JO,PI,S,T,V,VH		M,MC,PK,SK,SN,SR,
Onion, Shallot, 'Ed's Red'	JO		SU,TU,U,V,YA,VY
Onion, Shallot, 'Golden Gourmet' F1	D,S,T,V	Oriental Greens, 'Kaisoi'	SU
Onion, Shallot, 'Matador' F1	S	Oriental Greens, 'Miike Giant Mustard'	B,SD,SR,SU
Onion, Shallot, 'Red Globe'	BH	Oriental Greens, Misome hyb	B,KS
Onion, Shallot Salad	DI	Oriental Greens, Mitoya Shirohada	AB,C,CO,SU,V
Onion, 'Sherpa' F1	DT,L	Oriental Greens, 'Pe Tsai San-Feng'	BH
Onion, 'Snow Baby' F1	JO	Oriental Greens, 'Savannah' F1	KS,PK,RI,SK,SR
Onion, 'Southport Red'	AB,BS,CO,DE,DT,KI,MC,	Oriental Greens, 'Shirona'	B,RC
	PI,SD,ST,SU,TH,U	Oriental Greens, 'Swollen Stem' F1	AB,B,KS,V
Onion, 'Southport White'	BS,DE,SK,SR,TH	Oriental Greens, Tah sai, Tai Sai, Tatsoi, Pe Tsai see Tah Tsai	
Onion, Spanish,'Celebrity' hyb	SK	Oriental Greens, 'Tah Tsai'	AB,BH,BS,CO,JO,KI,KS,
Onion, Spanish, 'Gringo' hyb	SK		MC,RC,SD,SK,SN,SR,
Onion, Spanish, 'Kelsae Sweet Giant'	BY,SK		SU,TU
Onion, Spanish, 'Riverside Sweet'	SK	Oriental Greens, 'Takinogawa'	KS
Onion, Spanish, Sweet yellow	BF	Oriental Greens, 'Takinogawa Long'	B,DD,JO,RI,SD,SR
Onion, 'Stunova'	V	Oriental Greens, Tsai-Shim	BS,CO,MC,SR,SU,TU,
Onion, 'Suntan' F1	BS		YA

ORIENTAL GREENS

Oriental Greens Veg Pack	T
Oriental Greens, 'Watanabe Early'	SR
Oriental Greens, 'Yu Choy'	AB,B
Pak Choi	AB,B,BH,BS,C,CO,DT,KI,
	JO,L,MC,RI,S,SK,SU,U
Pak Choi, 'Canton Dwarf'	DE,V
Pak Choi, Hon Sai Tai	B,BH,JO,SN
Pak Choi, 'Kaneko Cross' hyb	D
Pak Choi, 'Mei Qing Choi' F1	DT,JO,KS,PI,SK,SN,SR,
	V,YA
Pak Choi, 'Pueblo'	D,J
Pak Choi, 'Shanghai'	DE,V
Papaya	SU
Papaya, Chinese	BH
Papaya, Chinese, 'Red Lady'	BH
Papaya, 'K.Y. No.1' F1	V
Par-Cel, Plain Leaved	KS,T,V
Parsley, 'Bravour'	B,BS,MO,SK,TU,YA
Parsley, 'Calito'	YA
Parsley, 'Champion Moss Curled '	B,BS,BY,CO,K,MO,R,SK,
	TH
Parsley, 'Champion Moss Curled 2'	J,SE
Parsley, 'Champion Moss Curled 3'	TU
Parsley, 'Clivi'	BS,L
Parsley, 'Consort'	BS
Parsley, 'Curlina'	B,BS,D,M,SK
Parsley, 'Darki'	B,BS,SK,ST,TE,YA
Parsley, 'Dk Green Curled'	RC
Parsley, 'Envy'	D
Parsley, 'Evergreen'	BU
Parsley, 'Extra Triple Curled'	B,BS,KI,MC,V
Parsley, 'Fakir'	PI,VH
Parsley, 'Favorit'	S
Parsley, 'Forest Green'	JO,SK,SR,TE
Parsley, 'Garland'	SK,SR
Parsley, Hamburg	CO,DE,KI,SU,TH,V
Parsley, Hamburg, 'Bartowich Long'	JO,SK
Parsley, Hamburg, 'Berliner'	SK,U
Parsley, Hamburg, 'Early Sugar'	SK
Parsley, Hamburg 'Omega'	D
Parsley, Hamburg 'Triple Turnip Rooted'	BS,TU
Parsley, Hamburg 'Turnip Rooted'	B,BH,BY,HU,J,M,S,SR,
	ST,TU
Parsley, Italian	AB,BF,FR,JO,RC,SK,SR,
	TE
Parsley, 'Italian Giant'	RC,TU
Parsley, 'Japanese Giant'	SN
Parsley, mix	AB
Parsley, 'Moss Curled 2'	AB,BU,D,KI,L,M,S,ST
Parsley, 'M.C. * Krausa', Parsnip 'Arrow'	
Carrot 'Primo' Sp.s	J, M
Parsley, 'Moss Curled 2 * Krausa', Sp.s	M
Parsley, 'Pagoda'	VH
Parsley, 'Plain Leaved'	AB,B,BS,BU,CO,HU,J,
	KI,M,MO,SK,SR,ST,
	TU,YA
Parsley, 'Plain Leaved 2'	F,FR,J,M,S
Parsley, 'Regent'	BS
Parsley, 'Rich Green 2'	FR
Parsley, 'Robust'	K
Parsley, 'Sparticus'	BS
Parsley, 'Unicurl'	BF,SK
Parsley, 'Verdi'	BS
Parsnip, 'Alba'	BS
Parsnip, 'All American'	DE
Parsnip, 'Andover'	SK,VY

Parsnip, 'Archer'	K
Parsnip, 'Arrow'	F,K
Parsnip, 'Arrow', Sp.s	M
Parsnip, 'Avonresister'	B,BD,BS,CO,DT,F,J,KI,
	L,T,M,MO,ST,SU,TU,U,
	V,VH
Parsnip, 'Bayonet'	U
Parsnip, 'Bedford Monarch'	BS
Parsnip, 'Cambridge Imp Marrow'	BS
Parsnip, 'Cobham Imp Marrow'	BS,D,M
Parsnip, 'Eversham'	BS
Parsnip, 'Exhibition' (Dobies)	D
Parsnip, 'Exhibition Long'	BY,RO
Parsnip, 'Gladiator' F1	BS,CO,DT,F,K,L,S,SB,
	SE,SU,TE,U,V,VH
Parsnip, 'Guernsey'	GO
Parsnip, 'Harris Model'	BS,BU,PI,SK,VY
Parsnip, 'Hollow Crown'	AB,B,BD,BF,BS,BY,C,C
	O,DD,DN,DT,F,J,KI,L,
	MO,PK,ST,TH,TU,VH
Parsnip, 'Hollow Crown Imp'	D,DI,SK,U
Parsnip, 'Imperial Crown'	BS,KI
Parsnip, 'Improved Marrow'	BS,R,YA
Parsnip, Japanese	C
Parsnip, 'Javelin' F1	BS,DT,K,TU
Parsnip, 'Kingship'	DT,KI
Parsnip, 'Lancer'	BS,D,JO,M,S
Parsnip, 'Lisbonnais'	B,BD,BS,BY,F,MO
Parsnip, 'New White Skin'	BS,K,S
Parsnip, 'New White Skin' - pr.s	D
Parsnip, 'Offenham'	BS,BY,KI
Parsnip, 'Tender and True'	B,BS,CO,D,DT,F,J,KI,M,
	MC,S,SB,ST,SU,T,TH,TU
Parsnip, 'The Student'	AB,BS,CO,DT,KI,MC,S
	T,TH
Parsnip, 'Viceroy'	BS
Parsnip, 'White Diamond'	BS
Parsnip, 'White Gem'	BS,BY,DD,DT,F,J,KI,M,
	S,SU,TU,U,VH,YA
Parsnip, 'White King'	BS,CO,ST
Parsnip, 'White Spear'	TU
Parsnip, 'Yatesnip'	YA
Passion Fruit	SU,V
Peanut	FR
Peanut, 'Pronto'	DE
Peanut, 'Tennessee Red'	DE,RC
Peanut, 'Virginia Jumbo'	DI,PK
Peas, 'Alaska Early'	AB,BF,BU,DE,PI,RC
Peas, 'Alderman'	AB,B,BS,BY,CO,D,DT,J,
	KI,M,SB,SN,SU,TH,TU,
	U,VH,VR
Peas, 'Ambassador'	CO
Peas, 'Amplisimo Victoria'	SP
Peas, 'Australian'	SP
Peas, 'Banff'	CO
Peas, 'Bill Jump's Soup Pea'	AB,SP
Peas, 'Bolero'	SK
Peas, 'Bounty'	JO,SR
Peas, 'Buonissimo'	FR
Peas, 'Capucijner'	DD,SP
Peas, 'Capucijner Tall'	SP
Peas, 'Carlin'	HD,SP
Peas, 'Cavalier'	CO,DT,F,L,M,S
Peas, 'Century'	SP
Peas, 'Champion of England'	HD
Peas, 'Cockpit'	SN

PEAS

Peas, 'Corvalette'	DD
Peas, 'Cukor Borsi'	SP
Peas, 'Daybreak'	F,PI,SE,SN,T
Peas, 'Douce Provence'	B,BS,BY,F,M,MO,TU,VR
Peas, 'Early Frosty'	BF,BU,VY
Peas, 'Early Onward'	B,BS,BY,C,CO,D,DT,J, KI,M,MO,R,S,TU,U, VR,YA
Peas, Edible Pod, 'Ambrosia'	M
Peas, Edible Pod, 'Bayard'	F
Peas, Edible Pod, 'Carouby de Maussane'	BS,CO,DT,FR,GO,KI, SN,SU,TH,TU,VR
Peas, Edible Pod, 'Cascadia'	DD,JO,SD,SK
Peas, Edible Pod, 'Corgi'	BD,CO,JO,KI,SN,SU,TU
Peas, Edible Pod, 'Dw Gray Sugar'	AB,DN,HU
Peas, Edible Pod, 'Dwarf Sugar Sweet Gr.'	B,BD,BS,C,CO,D,DT, KI,L,MO,SN,SU,T,TU,VR
Peas, Edible Pod, 'Edula'	U
Peas, Edible Pod, 'Giant Dw Sugar'	SP
Peas, Edible Pod, 'Golden'	SP
Peas, Edible Pod, 'Golden Sweet'	DD
Peas, Edible Pod, 'Ho Lohn Dow'	SK,SP
Peas, Ed. Pod, 'Lage Grijze Roodbloeiende'	V
Peas, Edible Pod, 'Little Sweetie'	SK
Peas, Ed. Pod 'Mammouth Melting Sugar'	AB,RC
Peas, Edible Pod, mix	BH
Peas, Edible Pod, 'Nofila'	D
Peas, Edible Pod, 'Norli' see Sugar Dw. Sweet Gr.	
Peas, Edible Pod, 'Oregon Giant'	B,JO,PI,SD,SK,U,VY
Peas, Edible Pod, 'Oregon Sugar Pod'	AB,B,BD,BS,BY,DE, DN,DT,KI,M,RI,S,SN, SR,U,VH,VR,YA
Peas, Edible Pod, 'Oregon Sugar Pod II'	AB,B,PI,SD,SN,T,TE,VY
Peas, Ed. Pod, 'Rampicante Mangiatutto'	RC
Peas, Edible Pod, 'Record'	J
Peas, Edible Pod, 'Reuzensuiker'	J
Peas, Edible Pod, 'Sapporo Express'	RC
Peas, Edible Pod, 'Short n' Sweet'	PK
Peas, Edible Pod, Snow	AB,B,DI,KS,SP
Peas, Edible Pod, 'Snow Wind'	SN
Peas, Edible Pod, 'Snowhite'	DD
Peas, Edible Pod, 'Stam de Grace'	BD,MO,TH,V
Peas, Edible Pod, 'Sugar Ann'	AB,DN,GO,J,JO,PI,SE, SK,SR,T,VY
Peas, Edible Pod, 'Sugar Bon'	M,PK,S,TU,V
Peas, Edible Pod, 'Sugar Daddy'	AB,PK,SK,TE
Peas, Edible Pod, 'Sugar Gem'	S,SN,T,TU
Peas, Edible Pod, 'Sugar Pod'	SK
Peas, Edible Pod, 'Sugar Pop'	PK
Peas, Edible Pod, 'Sugar Rae'	BS,CO,D,KI,SN,SU,VR
Peas, Edible Pod, 'Sugar Snap'	w.a.
Peas, Edible Pod, 'Super Sugar Mel'	BU,PI,PK,SR
Peas, Edible Pod, 'Sweet Snap'	DE
Peas, 'Eminent'	V
Peas, 'Epicure'	HD
Peas, 'Espresso Generoso'	FR
Peas, 'Excellenz'	YA
Peas, 'Feltham Advance'	BS
Peas, 'Feltham First'	B,BD,BS,BY,CO,D,DT, F,J,KI,L,M,MC,MO,S, SU,TU,U,VR,VH,YA
Peas, 'Fortune'	BS,DT,KI,TU
Peas, 'Freezonian'	BU,DN
Peas, 'Fruher Heinrich'	HD
Peas, Garden Peas Mix	T
Peas, 'Goya'	FR

Peas, 'Gradus'	BS,BY,CO,J,KI,TH,TU, VR
Peas, 'Green Arrow'	AB,BU,DD,DN,PI,PK, SK,SR,VY
Peas, 'Greenfeast'	DI
Peas, 'Hatif de Annonay'	GO
Peas, 'Holiday'	S
Peas, 'Holland Brown'	SP
Peas, 'Hurst Beagle'	BD,BS,BY,DT,KI,M, MO,SP,U,VR
Peas, 'Hurst Green Shaft'	B,BD,BS,BY,C,CO,D,DT, F,J,KI,L,M,MC,MO,S, SE,SU,T,TU,U,VH,VR,YA
Peas, Johnsons Freezer	J
Peas, 'Kazankij'	SP
Peas, 'Kelvedon Monarch' see 'Victory Freezer'	
Peas, 'Kelvedon Wonder'	B,BD,BY,C,CO,D,DT,F,J, KI,L,M,MC,MO,R,S,SU, T,TU,U,V,VR,VH
Peas, 'Kickam'	SP
Peas, 'Kimberley'	SP
Peas, 'King Tut'	SP
Peas, 'Knight'	JO,PI,SR,TE,VY
Peas, 'Laxton's Progress Imp'	SK
Peas, 'Laxton's Progress' see 'Progress No.9'	
Peas, Leafless Pea Twiggy	T
Peas, 'Lincoln'	BD,BS,BU,BY,CO,FR,KI, PI,SK,SN,SU,TU,VR
Peas, 'Little Marvel'	AB,BS,BU,BY,CO,D,F,J, KI,M,S,T,TH,VR
Peas, 'Lord Chancellor'	BS,VR
Peas, 'Maestro'	AB,JO,PK,SK,SR,TE,VY
Peas, 'Magnum Bonum'	HD
Peas, 'Manitoba'	SP
Peas, 'Markana'	BS,CO,KI,M,TU,VR,YA
Peas, Marrowfat, 'Blauwschok Desiree'	SP,V
Peas, Marrowfat, 'Blauwschokkers'	V
Peas, 'Meraviglia d'Italia'	FR
Peas, 'Meteor'	B,BD,BS,BY,CO,F,KI, MO,SU,TU,U,VR
Peas, 'Minnow'	D
Peas, 'Miracle'	B,BS,BY,KI,SB,SN,VR
Peas, mix	GO
Peas, 'Mrs. Van's'	SP
Peas, 'Ne Plus Ultra'	HD
Peas, 'Northern Sweet'	AB
Peas, 'Novella II'	PI
Peas, 'Olympia'	SK
Peas, 'Onward'	B,BD,BS,BY,C,CO,D,DT, F,J,KI,L,M,MC,MO,S, TU,U,VH,VR,YA
Peas, 'Oregon Trail Green'	SD
Peas, 'Parsley'	DD
Peas, 'Patriot'	PK,SK
Peas, Petit Pois, 'Darfon'	J
Peas, Petit Pois 'Giroy'	PK
Peas, Petit Pois, 'Lynx'	F,SE,TU
Peas, Petit Pois, 'Prim d'Or'	PI
Peas, Petit Pois, 'Provencal'	GO
Peas, Petit Pois, 'Waverex'	BS,BY,C,CO,KI,L,M, MC,S,SU,TU,VR
Peas, 'Pioneer'	SD
Peas, 'Poppet'	HD
Peas, 'Premium'	TU
Peas, 'Progress No.9'	B,BS,BU,BY,D,FR,KI, MO,SR,VR

PEAS

PEPPERS

Pepper, Hot, 'NuMex Eclipse'	B,JO
Pepper, Hot, 'NuMex Joe E. Parker'	BU
Pepper, Hot, 'NuMex Sunrise'	B,JO
Pepper, Hot, 'NuMex Sunset'	B,JO
Pepper, Hot, 'NuMex Sweet'	KS
Pepper, Hot, 'Ortega'	B,JO
Pepper, Hot, 'Paper Dragon' F1	JO
Pepper, Hot, 'Papri Ace' hyb	SR
Pepper, Hot, Paprika	AB,B,BH,DD,DE,JO,PI, RC
Pepper, Hot, 'Pasilla'	KS,RI,SD,SN
Pepper, Hot, 'Pequin'	HU,RC
Pepper, Hot, 'Peruvian Purple'	SD
Pepper, Hot, 'Peter Pepper'	KS
Pepper, Hot, 'Piri Piri' (Pili?)	BH
Pepper, Hot, 'Portuguese Piri Piri'	BH
Pepper, Hot, 'Pretty in Purple'	B,JO
Pepper, Hot, 'Punjab Small Hot'	B,RC
Pepper, Hot, 'Purira'	B,SD
Pepper, Hot, 'Puya Chiltepin'	DD
Pepper, Hot, 'Rawit'	V
Pepper, Hot, 'Red Chili'	B,RC
Pepper, Hot, 'Relleno'	SD
Pepper, Hot, 'Ring of Fire'	SD,SK
Pepper, Hot, 'Rio Grande Hot'	SD
Pepper, Hot, 'Sandia'	RC
Pepper, Hot, 'Santa Fe Grande'	B,BU,RC,SN
Pepper, Hot, 'Santo Domingo'	B,RC
Pepper, Hot, 'Senorita' F1	PI,SN
Pepper, Hot, 'Serrano'	B,DE,KS,JO,PI,PK,RC, RI,SD,SN,SU,T
Pepper, Hot, 'Serrano Tampiqueno'	KS
Pepper, Hot, small red	DE,SN
Pepper, Hot, 'Spaanse' Red	V
Pepper, Hot, 'Spur'	HU
Pepper, Hot, 'Sugarchile' F1	JO
Pepper, Hot, 'Super Cayenne' F1	PK,SN,SR,T
Pepper, Hot, 'Super Chili' hyb	DE,JO,PK,SR
Pepper, Hot, 'Surefire'	VY
Pepper, Hot, 'Tabasco-Habernero'	B,KS,RC,SN,T
Pepper, Hot, 'Tabiche'	B,HU
Pepper, Hot, 'Tam Vera Cruz'	SN
Pepper, Hot, 'Taurus' o-p	SR
Pepper, Hot, 'Thai Dragon' F1	JO,SN
Pepper, Hot, 'Thai Nippon Taka'	PI
Pepper, Hot, 'Tri-Fetti'	PI
Pepper, Hot, 'Tula' F1	SR
Pepper, Hot, 'Tuste Blanco'	HU
Pepper, Hot, 'Volcano' F1	SR
Pepper, Hot, 'Yatsafusa'	BB,DD,RC
Pepper, Hot, 'Yellow Wax'	BH
Pepper, 'Italia'	JO
Pepper, 'Japones'	B,RC
Pepper, 'Jwala'	B,RC
Pepper, 'Manzano'	B,RC
Pepper, 'Merah'	B,RC
Pepper, Purple	SN,VS
Pepper, 'Pusa Jwala'	B,RC
Pepper, 'Scotch Bonnet'	B,RC
Pepper, 'Scotch Bonnet Early'	SN,SK
Pepper, 'Sunset Striped'	BH
Pepper, 'Suryamukhi'	RC
Pepper, Sweet, '860' F1	SR
Pepper, Sweet, 'Acapulco' F1	SR
Pepper, Sweet, 'Ace'	JO,M,SK,U
Pepper, Sweet, 'Aconcagua'	SD

Pepper, Sweet, 'Admiral' F1	SR
Pepper, Sweet, 'Albino'	SN
Pepper, Sweet, 'Andean'	DD
Pepper, Sweet, 'Antohi Romanian'	B,JO
Pepper, Sweet, 'Apple'	GO,JO
Pepper, Sweet, 'Ariane' F1	B,BS,CO,FR,J,KI,MO, TU,V
Pepper, Sweet, 'Aruba' F1	SR
Pepper, Sweet, 'Astra' F1	YA
Pepper, Sweet, 'Astrion' F1	SR
Pepper, Sweet, 'Baby Belle'	DT,SN
Pepper, Sweet, 'Banana'	BH
Pepper, Sweet, 'Banana Supreme' F1	SN,SR,TE
Pepper, Sweet, 'Banana Yellow'	KS,SK
Pepper, Sweet, 'Baron' hyb	SR
Pepper, Sweet, 'Beauty Bell' F1	B,BS,KI,ST,SU
Pepper, Sweet, 'Bell Boy' F1	BY,PI,SK,SN
Pepper, Sweet, 'Bell Captain' F1	SN,SR
Pepper, Sweet, 'Bellboy' F1	B,BS,CO,D,DE,DT,L, MO,SN,TU,YA
Pepper, Sweet, 'Bendigo'	BS,MO
Pepper, Sweet, 'Bianca' F1	B,BS,FR,MO,TU
Pepper, Sweet, 'Big Bertha' F1	SK,SN,T
Pepper, Sweet, 'Biscayne' F1	JO,SK,SR
Pepper, Sweet, 'Blockbuster' hyb	SK
Pepper, Sweet, 'Bonanza' F1	JO
Pepper, Sweet, 'Boyntan Bell' hyb	SK
Pepper, Sweet, 'Bull Nose'	AB,BS,TH
Pepper, Sweet, 'California Wonder'	B,BD,BS,BU,C,DE,F, FR,HU,J,KS,M,MO,PI, RC,SK,SN,TE,U
Pepper, Sweet, 'California Wonder Golden'	DE,FR,HU,KS,SN
Pepper, Sweet, 'Camelot' F1	SK,SR
Pepper, Sweet, 'Camelot X3R' hyb	SK
Pepper, Sweet, 'Canada Cheese'	SK
Pepper, Sweet, 'Canape' F1	D,SE,SN,T,U,VH
Pepper, Sweet, 'Carliston'	B,RC
Pepper, Sweet, 'Cayman'	SN
Pepper, Sweet, 'Centinel'	B,RC
Pepper, Sweet, 'Cherry'	DD,DE
Pepper, Sweet, 'Cherrytime'	B,JO
Pepper, Sweet, 'Chilancho' hyb	SK
Pepper, Sweet, 'Chinese Giant' o-p	DI,SN
Pepper, Sweet, 'Chocolate Beauty' F1	PI,SK,SN,VY
Pepper, Sweet, 'Clovis' hyb	SR
Pepper, Sweet, 'Commandant V.I.P.' F1	SK,SR
Pepper, Sweet, 'Corbaci'	RC
Pepper, Sweet, 'Corne de Bouc Jaune'	SN,VS
Pepper, Sweet, 'Corne de Bouc Rouge'	SN,VS
Pepper, Sweet, 'Corno di Toro'	B,FR,PI,SD,SN,TU
Pepper, Sweet, 'Corona' hyb	GO
Pepper, Sweet, 'Cubanelle' o-p	AB,BH,BU,DE,HU,PI, RC,SK,SN
Pepper, Sweet, 'Delphin' F1	B,BS,DT,MO,VH
Pepper, Sweet, 'Diablo Grande' hyb	SK
Pepper, 'Sweet Dwarf'	U
Pepper, Sweet, 'Eagle'	DT
Pepper, Sweet, 'Earlibird Series' hyb, s-c	SK
Pepper, Sweet, 'Earliest Red Sweet'	SD
Pepper, Sweet, 'Early Niagara Giant'	SK
Pepper, Sweet, 'Early Prolific' F1	M
Pepper, Sweet, 'Early Thickset' F1	PK
Pepper, Sweet, 'Ecuadorian Sweet Relleno'	SD
Pepper, Sweet, 'Elephant Trunk'	B,RC
Pepper, Sweet, 'Elisa' F1	SK,SR
Pepper, Sweet, 'Emerald Giant'	BU,SK

PEPPERS

Pepper, Sweet, 'Enza 31501' F1	SR
Pepper, Sweet, 'Ercole'	FR
Pepper, Sweet, 'Fat 'n Sassy'	SN
Pepper, Sweet, 'Feher'	V
Pepper, Sweet, 'Figaro' hyb	SR
Pepper, Sweet, 'Four Corners'	SN
Pepper, Sweet, 'Galaxy' hyb	SK,SR
Pepper, Sweet, 'Gambo'	SN,TU
Pepper, Sweet, 'Gator Belle'	SN
Pepper, Sweet, 'Giant Aconcagua'	SN
Pepper, Sweet, 'Giant Long Kashmir'	B,RC
Pepper, Sweet, 'Giant Sweet Green'	B,RC
Pepper, Sweet, 'Golden Arrow' F1	SK
Pepper, Sweet, 'Golden Bell' F1	BS,DT,PI,SN,TE,V
Pepper, Sweet, 'Golden Summer' F1	PK
Pepper, Sweet, 'Golden Treasure'	SN
Pepper, Sweet, 'Granny Smith'	SE,U
Pepper, Sweet, green	BF
Pepper, Sweet, 'Guantanamo' F1	SK
Pepper, Sweet, 'Guardian' hyb	SR
Pepper, Sweet, 'Gypsy' F1	F,PI,PK,T,S,SN,TE,VY
Pepper, Sweet, 'Hercules' hyb	SK
Pepper, Sweet, 'Hitower' F1	FR
Pepper, Sweet, Hybrid Mix F1	J
Pepper, Sweet, 'Islander' F1	JO
Pepper, Sweet, 'Islander Lavender'	GO
Pepper, Sweet, 'Italian Gourmet' F1	DE,SD,PK
Pepper, Sweet, 'Italian Red Marconi' o-p	AB,BS,DE,FR,KI,SN,SU,TH
Pepper, Sweet, 'Ivory' F1	PK,SK,SN,SR,TE
Pepper, Sweet, 'Jimmy Nardello's'	AB,DI,SD
Pepper, Sweet, 'Jingle Bells' F1 mini	DE,PI,SN,T,TE,VH,VY
Pepper, Sweet, 'Jumbo Sweet' F1	T
Pepper, Sweet, 'Jupiter' o-p	SK,SN,SR
Pepper, Sweet, 'Kandil'	B,RC
Pepper, Sweet, 'Keystone Resistant Giant'	BU,DE,SN
Pepper, Sweet, 'King Arthur' F1	JO,SK,SR
Pepper, Sweet, 'King Series' hyb, s-c	SK
Pepper, Sweet, 'Klondike Bell' hyb	SK
Pepper, Sweet, 'Lamuyo' F1	FR
Pepper, Sweet, 'Lantern' hyb	SR
Pepper, Sweet, 'Laparie' F1	SK
Pepper, Sweet, 'Lilac' hyb	PK,SN,SR,TE
Pepper, Sweet, 'Lipstick'	JO,SN
Pepper, Sweet, 'Little Dipper'	GO
Pepper, Sweet, 'Long French'	BH
Pepper, Sweet, 'Long Green Buddha'	PI
Pepper, Sweet, Long Red Marconi see Italian R.M.	
Pepper, Sweet, 'Long Red Rubens' F1	B,BS,SU
Pepper, Sweet, 'Long Yellow Ringo' F1	B,BS,SU
Pepper, Sweet, 'Luteus' F1	B,BS,KI,L,MO,S,ST,SU
Pepper, Sweet, 'Maite' F1	SR
Pepper, Sweet, 'Marquis' F1	SR
Pepper, Sweet, 'Martindale II' hyb	SK
Pepper, Sweet, 'Martindale III' hyb	SK
Pepper, Sweet, 'Mavras' F1	BS,CO,KI,MO,SR,V
Pepper, Sweet, 'Mayata' hyb	SK
Pepper, Sweet, 'Mazurka'	BS,MO
Pepper, Sweet, 'Memphis' F1	SR
Pepper, Sweet, 'Merit' F1	V
Pepper, Sweet, 'Merlin' F1	SK,SR
Pepper, Sweet, 'Midway' o-p	FR,SK,SN
Pepper, Sweet, mini	DI
Pepper, Sweet, 'Minibel'	M
Pepper, Sweet, mix	DI,FR,GO
Pepper, Sweet, 'Mogador' F1	FR,V
Pepper, Sweet, 'Mole'	DD
Pepper, Sweet, 'Nardello' see Jimmy	
Pepper, Sweet, 'Navarone' F1	SK
Pepper, Sweet, 'Neptune' hyb	SR
Pepper, Sweet, 'New Ace' F1	B,BD,BS,CO,DN,F,J,KI,MO,PI,R,SN,SU,VY
Pepper, Sweet, 'New Carnival Mix' F1	M
Pepper, Sweet, 'North Star' F1	SK,SN,SR,TE
Pepper, Sweet, 'Orange Sun'	SN
Pepper, Sweet, 'Ori' hyb	GO
Pepper, Sweet, 'Orobelle' F1	JO,KS
Pepper, Sweet, 'Pacific' F1	FR
Pepper, Sweet, 'Peperoncino' o-p	AB,SN,TE
Pepper, Sweet, 'Peto Wonder' F1	DE,PK,SN
Pepper, Sweet, 'Pimento Elite' o-p	DE,HU,SN
Pepper, Sweet, 'Pimento L' o-p	AB,DE,PI,SN
Pepper, Sweet, 'Pimento Red Heart'	AB,SD
Pepper, Sweet, 'Pimento Super Red'	SK
Pepper, Sweet, 'Pirati' hyb	SR
Pepper, Sweet 'Pot' F1	PK
Pepper, Sweet, 'Purple Beauty'	AB,DE,PI,PK,SN,T,TE
Pepper, Sweet, 'Queen' hyb	SR,TE
Pepper, Sweet, 'Rainbow' F1	F
Pepper, Sweet, 'Rampage' F1	DE,PI,SN,VY
Pepper, Sweet, 'Red Beauty' F1	DE,PI
Pepper, Sweet, 'Red Cherry L. Sweet' o-p	SN
Pepper, Sweet, 'Red Dawn' hyb	SK
Pepper, Sweet, 'Red Devil' F1	FR
Pepper, Sweet, 'Red Ruffled'	AB,SD
Pepper, Sweet, 'Redskin' F1	B,BD,BS,CO,DT,KI,L,MO,S
Pepper, Sweet, 'Redstart' hyb	SK
Pepper, Sweet, 'Roumanian Sweet' o-p	SN
Pepper, Sweet, 'Ruby King/Golden Queen'	DT
Pepper, Sweet, 'Salad Festival'	U
Pepper, Sweet, 'Salad Mix'	SE
Pepper, Sweet, 'Secret' F1	JO
Pepper, Sweet, 'Sentinel' hyb	SR
Pepper, Sweet, 'Sentry V.I.P.' hyb	SR
Pepper, Sweet, 'Slim Pin'	B,SU,TU
Pepper, Sweet, 'Sofia' F1	SK
Pepper, Sweet, 'Spanish Red and Green'	BS,KI,ST
Pepper, Sweet, 'Spanish Spice'	DE,SN
Pepper, Sweet, 'Spanish Topito Cheese'	SN
Pepper, Sweet, 'Staddon's Select'	VY
Pepper, Sweet, 'Sugar Banana' F1	SK
Pepper, Sweet, 'Summer Salad Mix' F1	SN,T,VH
Pepper, Sweet, 'Sunbright'	SN
Pepper, Sweet, 'Sunnybrook' o-p	SN
Pepper, Sweet, 'Sunrise Orange'	SD
Pepper, Sweet, 'Super Greygo' hyb	SK
Pepper, Sweet, 'Super Hungarian Hot' hyb	SK
Pepper, Sweet, 'Super set' hyb	SK
Pepper, Sweet, 'Super Shepherd'	AB,SK
Pepper, Sweet, 'Super Stuff'	SK
Pepper, Sweet, 'Super Sweet Banana' F1	BH,DE,SK,V
Pepper, Sweet, 'Super Sweet Cherry'	SK
Pepper, Sweet, 'Sweet Banana' o-p	AB,PI,SN
Pepper, Sweet, 'Sweet Cherry'	AB,BU,SK
Pepper, Sweet, 'Sweet Chocolate'	B,DI,JO,PK,T
Pepper, Sweet, 'Sweet Delight Mix'	DT,F,V
Pepper, Sweet, 'Sweet Green'	BS
Pepper, Sweet 'Sweet Pickle' F1	PK
Pepper, Sweet, 'Szegedi' o-p	SD,SK,SN
Pepper, Sweet, 'Szentesi Semi Hot'	SK
Pepper, Sweet, 'Tangerine'	SD

PEPPERS

Pepper, Sweet, 'Taurus'	SK	Potato, 'Duke of York' Red	HE,F,JM,SN,ST,TU,VR
Pepper, Sweet, 'Tequila' hyb	FR,SR	Potato, 'Dunbar Rover'	F
Pepper, Sweet, 'Top Banana' hyb	SN	Potato, 'Dunbar Standard'	F,SN,TU
Pepper, Sweet, 'Topepo Giallo' o-p	SN	Potato, 'Dunluce'	M,SN,TU,VR
Pepper, Sweet, 'Unicorn' F1	FR	Potato, 'Early Red Norland'	PI
Pepper, Sweet, 'Valencia' hyb	JO,PK,SR	Potato, 'Edzell Blue'	F,SN,TU,VR
Pepper, Sweet, 'Valiant' hyb	SR	Potato, 'Epicure'	HE,JM,SN,ST,TU,VR
Pepper, Sweet, 'Vidi' F1	DE,GO,PI,SR	Potato, 'Estima'	HE,JM,SN,ST,TU,VR
Pepper, Sweet, 'Viejo Arruga Dulce'	B,RC	Potato, 'Fiana'	SN,TU
Pepper, Sweet, 'Westlandse'	V	Potato, 'Florette'	SN,TU
Pepper, Sweet, 'White Fire' hyb	SK	Potato, 'Fontenot'	PI
Pepper, Sweet, 'Whopper Imp' hyb	SR,VY	Potato, 'Foremost'	HE,JM,M,S,SN,ST,TU,
Pepper, Sweet, 'World Beater'	DE,S,SN		VR
Pepper, Sweet, 'X3R Aladdin' hyb	SK,SR	Potato, 'Frontier Russet'	JO
Pepper, Sweet, 'X3R Camelot' hyb	SR	Potato, 'German Butterball'	SD
Pepper, Sweet, 'X3R Wizard' hyb	SR	Potato, 'Gladstone'	SD
Pepper, Sweet, 'Yankee Bell'	JO	Potato, 'Glamis'	VR
Pepper, Sweet, yellow	BF	Potato, 'Gold Rush Russet'	PI,PK
Pepper, Sweet, 'Yellow Cheese Pimento'	SK	Potato, 'Golden Wonder'	HE,SN,ST,TU,VR
Pepper, Sweet, 'Yolo Wonder'	BU,CO,SN	Potato, 'Green Mountain'	PI
Pepper, 'Tabasco'	RC	Potato, 'Heather'	M,SN
Pepper, 'Tepin'	B,RC,SN	Potato, 'Home Guard'	HE,JM,SN,ST,TU,VR
Pepper, 'Thai Hot'	B,DE,KS,PK,RC,RI,SN,	Potato, 'Irish Cobbler'	PI
	TU	Potato, 'Island Sunshine'	JO,VY
Pepper, 'Trupti'	B,RC	Potato, 'Jemseg'	VY
Pepper, 'Yellow Bumpy'	PI	Potato, 'Katahdin'	PI
Pepper, 'Yellow Squash'	PI	Potato, 'Kennebec'	FR,JO,PI
Pepper/Tomato Cross	SN,VS	Potato, 'Kerrs Pink'	CO,F,HE,SN,ST,TU,VR
Pepper/Tomato Cross 'Liebsapfel'	V	Potato, 'Kestrel'	D,DT,HE,JM,M,SN,ST,
Pepper/Tomato Cross 'Top Boy'	B,BD,BS,M,O,V		TU,VR
Pepper/Tomato Cross 'Top Girl'	B,BS,MO	Potato, 'King Edward'	HE,JM,SN,ST,TU,VR
Perilla Green and Purple	AB,BH,CO,HU,KS,TU	Potato, 'King Edward' Red	F,TU
Potato, 'Accent'	JM,M,SN,ST,TU	Potato, 'Kirsty'	SN
Potato, 'Ailsa'	SN,VR	Potato, 'Kondor'	M,SN,ST,TU
Potato, 'Alaskan Sweetheart'	SD	Potato, 'Lady Christl'	M
Potato, 'All-Blue'	SD	Potato, 'Linzer Delikatess'	M,S,SN,TU
Potato, 'Almaria'	SN	Potato, 'Mainestay'	JO
Potato, 'Aminica' org	CO,SN,TU	Potato, 'Majestic'	HE,JM,SN,ST,TU,VR
Potato, 'Arran Banner'	F,TU	Potato, 'Manna'	SN,TU
Potato, 'Arran Comet'	HE,SN,SU,TU	Potato, 'Marfona'	JM,M,SN,ST,TU,VR
Potato, 'Arran Consul'	F,TU	Potato, 'Maris Bard'	D,DT,HE,JM,M,SN,ST,
Potato, 'Arran Pilot'	DT,HE,JM,SN,ST,TU,VR		TU,VR
Potato, 'Arran Victory'	CO,SU,TU	Potato, 'Maris Peer'	D,HE,JM,SN,ST,TU,VR
Potato, 'Avalanche' org	CO,TU	Potato, 'Maris Piper'	D,DT,HE,JM,SN,ST,TU,
Potato, 'Ballydoon'	F		VR
Potato, 'Balmoral'	SN,TU,VR	Potato, 'Maxine'	JM,M,SN,TU,VR
Potato, 'Belle de Fontenay'	M,SN,TU	Potato, 'Mistral'	TU
Potato, 'BF15'	TU	Potato, 'Mona Lisa'	SN,TU,VR
Potato, 'Bintje'	M,SN,TU	Potato, 'Nadine'	D,HE,JM,M,SN,ST,TU,
Potato, 'British Queen'	F,TU		VR
Potato, 'Butte'	VY	Potato, 'Navan'	VR
Potato, 'Caesar'	SN,TU	Potato, 'Newleaf'	VY
Potato, 'Cara'	D,DT,HE,JM,M,SN,ST,	Potato, 'Nicola'	D,M,TU
	SU,TU,VR	Potato, 'Noisette'	TU
Potato, 'Carlingford'	SN,TU	Potato, 'Norland'	VY
Potato, 'Carole'	PI	Potato, 'Obelix'	SN
Potato, 'Catriona'	F,HE,JM,SN,ST,TU,VR	Potato, 'Pentland Crown'	HE,JM,SN,ST,TU,VR
Potato, 'Charlotte'	DT,JM,M,SN,TU,VR	Potato, 'Pentland Dell'	HE,SN,ST,TU,VR
Potato, 'Chipeta'	SD	Potato, 'Pentland Hawk'	HE,TU,VR
Potato, 'Concorde'	JM,M,SN,ST,TU	Potato, 'Pentland Ivory'	TU
Potato, 'Cultra'	VR	Potato, 'Pentland Javelin'	DT,HE,JM,SN,ST,TU,VR
Potato, 'Dark Red Norland'	JO,SD	Potato, 'Pentland Marble'	TU
Potato, 'Desiree'	CO,D,DT,HE,FR,JM,PK,	Potato, 'Pentland Squire'	HE,ST,TU,VR
	SD,SN,ST,SU,TU,VR	Potato, 'Picasso'	M,SN,TU,VR
Potato, 'Diana'	SN,TU,VR	Potato, 'Pink Fir Apple'	CO,D,DT,HE,JM,M,SN,
Potato, 'Duke of York'	CO,HE,JM,SN,ST,TU,VR		ST,SU,TU,VR

POTATO

Potato, 'Pomfine'	SN,TU
Potato, 'Pompadour'	SN,TU
Potato, 'Premiere'	SN,TU,VR
Potato, 'Purple Viking'	SD
Potato, 'Ratte'	DT,F,JM,M,SN,ST,TU,VR
Potato, 'Record'	DT,HE,SN,ST,VR
Potato, 'Red Sangre'	SD
Potato, 'Redsen'	PK
Potato, 'Remarka' org	CO,TU
Potato, 'Rocket'	DT,HE,JM,M,SN,ST,TU, VR
Potato, 'Romano'	HE,JM,SN,ST,TU,VR
Potato, 'Rooster'	HE,JM,SN,ST,TUD
Potato, 'Rosabelle'	TU
Potato, 'Rose Fin Apple'	JO
Potato, 'Rose Gold'	JO
Potato, 'Roseval'	M,SN,TU
Potato, 'Russet Burbank'	VY
Potato, 'Russet Nugget'	SD
Potato, 'Russian Banana'	JO
Potato, 'Samba'	SN,TU
Potato, 'Sante'	CO,M,SN,TU,VR
Potato, 'Saturna' org	CO,TU
Potato, 'Saxon'	DT,JM,SN,TU,VR
Potato Seed,pre-chitted	M
Potato, 'Sharpes Express'	CO,HE,JM,SN,ST,TU,VR
Potato, 'Shepody'	PI
Potato, 'Shula'	SN,TU,VR
Potato, 'Spunta'	FR
Potato, 'Stemster'	HE,JM,SN,ST,TU,VR
Potato, 'Stroma'	HE,JM,S,SN,ST,TU,VR
Potato, 'Superior'	VY
Potato, 'Swedish Peanut'	JO
Potato, 'Swift'	D,DT,HE,JM,M,SN,ST, TU,VR
Potato, 'Symphonia'	SN,TU,VR
Potato, 'Ulster Chieftain'	HE,JM,SN,ST,TU,VR
Potato, 'Ulster Prince'	SN,TU,VR
Potato, 'Ulster Sceptre'	HE,SN,TU,VR
Potato, 'Valor'	DT,JM,M,SN,ST,TU,VR
Potato, 'Vanessa'	D,HE,JM,S,SN,ST,TU, VR
Potato, 'Wilja'	D,DT,HE,JM,SN,ST, TU,VR
Potato, 'Winston'	D,HE,JM,M,SN,ST,TU
Potato, 'Yellow Finn'	PK,SD
Potato, 'Yukon Gold'	JO,PI,SD,VY
Pumpkin	SN,VS
Pumpkin, 'Apollo' F1	BS
Pumpkin, 'Appalachian' F1	BS,SK,SR
Pumpkin, 'Aspen'	BS,SK,SR,VY
Pumpkin, 'Australian Butter'	DI
Pumpkin, 'Autumn Gold'	BS,BU,M,PK,S,SR,VY
Pumpkin, 'Baby Bear'	BS,D,F,JO,PI,SN,SR, TU,VY
Pumpkin, 'Baby Boo'	BS,PK,SK,V
Pumpkin, 'Baby Pam' o-p	SR
Pumpkin, 'Big Autumn'	BS,BU
Pumpkin, 'Big Max'	BS,BU
Pumpkin, 'Big Moon'	BS,PK,TE
Pumpkin, 'Bohemian'	DI
Pumpkin, 'Buckskin' F1	BS,DE
Pumpkin, 'Casper'	SK
Pumpkin, 'Chinese Mini'	DD
Pumpkin, 'Cinderella' see Rouge Vif D'Etamps	
Pumpkin, 'Connecticut Field'	B,BF,BS,BU,PI,SK,SR,

	SU,TH,VY
Pumpkin, 'Crown Prince' F1	BS,M
Pumpkin, 'Dill's Atlantic Giant'	B,BS,DE,DT,F,JO,KS,M, PI,S,SE,SK,SN,SR,T,V, VH,VY
Pumpkin, 'Early Price'	CO
Pumpkin, 'Fall Star'	BS
Pumpkin, 'Frosty'	BS,DN,SK,SN,SR,VY
Pumpkin, 'Full Glory'	BH
Pumpkin, 'Funny Face'	BS,VY
Pumpkin, 'Ghost Rider'	BS,BU,SK,TU
Pumpkin, 'Half Moon'	BS
Pumpkin, 'Happy Jack'	BS
Pumpkin, 'Harvest Moon'	PI,SR,YA
Pumpkin, Heirloom Table Decorative	DI
Pumpkin, Heirloom Best Tasting mix	DI
Pumpkin, 'Howden'	BS,BU,JO,SK,SR,TE,VY
Pumpkin, 'Hundredweight'	KI,S,SN,ST,TU
Pumpkin, 'Jack Be Little'	AB,B,BS,BU,CO,DE,JO, KI,KS,PI,PK,SK,SN,SR, SU,TE,VS,VY
Pumpkin, 'Jack O Lantern'	AB,BS,BU,DE,KI,SN,ST, TU,VS
Pumpkin, 'Jack of All Trades' F1	BS,SK,SR
Pumpkin, 'Jack-o-Lite'	SD
Pumpkin, 'Jackpot'	BS,K,U
Pumpkin, 'Janne Gros de Paris'	BS
Pumpkin, 'Jarrahdale'	JO
Pumpkin, 'Kumi-Kumi'	KS
Pumpkin, 'Lady Godiva'	AB
Pumpkin, 'Large'	K
Pumpkin, 'Little Lantern' F1	BS,SK
Pumpkin, 'Long Island Cheese'	JO
Pumpkin, 'Lumina PVP'	BU,PI,PK,SK,SR,VY
Pumpkin, 'Mammoth'	BS,C,CO,D,J,L,MO,R,TH
Pumpkin, 'Mammoth Gold'	BS,F
Pumpkin, 'Mammoth Orange'	M
Pumpkin, miniature	BF
Pumpkin, mix	AB,GO
Pumpkin, 'Munchkin'	B,BD,BS,MO
Pumpkin, 'Musquee de Provence'	V
Pumpkin, 'New England Pie'	GO,JO
Pumpkin Nuts	C
Pumpkin, 'Pankow's Field'	VY
Pumpkin, 'Peek-A-Boo' F1	SR
Pumpkin, 'Phoenix'	BH
Pumpkin, 'Potimarron'	GO
Pumpkin, 'Prizewinner'	BS,KS,SK,SN,SR,TE
Pumpkin, 'Rebecca'	BS
Pumpkin, 'Rocket' F1	CO,JO
Pumpkin, 'Rouge Vif d'Etamps'	AB,B,BS,DE,GO,HU,JO, PI,SD,SN,SR,TE,TH,TU
Pumpkin, 'Show King'	SN,VS
Pumpkin, 'Small Sugar'	AB,B,BS,BU,CO,DE,L, PI,PK,RC,SD,SK,SN,SR, TE,TH,TU,YA,VY
Pumpkin, 'Spellbound'	BS,M
Pumpkin, 'Spirit' F1	B,BD,BS,DE,MO,PI,TE
Pumpkin, 'Spookie'	BS
Pumpkin, 'Spooktacular' F1	BS,DE,SK,SR
Pumpkin, 'Styrian Hulless'	HU
Pumpkin, 'Sumo'	BS,CO
Pumpkin, 'Sunny' F1	BS,DT
Pumpkin, 'Sweetie Pie'	BS,SK,V
Pumpkin, 'Tallman'	BS,SK
Pumpkin, 'Tom Fox'	BS,CO,JO

PUMPKIN

Pumpkin, 'Trick or Treat' F1	PI
Pumpkin, 'Trickster' F1	BS,SR,YA
Pumpkin, 'Triple Treat'	BS,DT,KI,SU
Pumpkin, 'Uchiki Kuri'	BS,CO,KI,TU,V
Pumpkin, White Large	SN,VS
Pumpkin, World's Largest	DI
Pumpkin, 'Young's Variety'	BS
Quinoa, 'Dave'	AB,SD
Quinoa, 'Faro'	AB,SD
Quinoa, 'Isluga Yellow'	AB,SD
Quinoa, 'Multi-hued'	HU,SP
Quinoa, 'Temuco'	SD
Radicchio	RI
Radicchio, 'Alouette'	F,T
Radicchio, 'Augusto'	F
Radicchio, 'Carmen' F1	GO,SK
Radicchio, 'Castelfranco'	KS
Radicchio, 'Castelfranco Variegata'	B,BS,C,FR,KI,SU,TH,V
Radicchio, 'Cesare'	DT,J,SU,V
Radicchio, 'Chioggia'	SU
Radicchio, 'Chioggia a Palla Blanca'	B,FR
Radicchio, 'Chioggia Giant'	KS
Radicchio, 'Chioggia Red Preco No.1'	JO
Radicchio, 'Fidelio' F1	YA
Radicchio, 'Fireball'	TU
Radicchio, 'Guilio'	KS,PK,SU
Radicchio, 'Medusa' F1	FR,JO
Radicchio, 'Milan'	DE,VY
Radicchio, 'Palla di Fuoco'	SU
Radicchio, 'Palla Rossa'	AB,B,BS,BY,KI,M,MC, SN,ST,TU,U
Radicchio, 'Palla Rossa Bella'	S
Radicchio, 'Palla Rossa Red Devil'	D,FR
Radicchio, 'Red Verona' see Rossa	
Radicchio, 'Rialto' F1	YA
Radicchio, 'Rossa di Chioggia' early	FR
Radicchio, 'Rossa di Chioggia' late	B,C,FR
Radicchio, 'Rossa di Chioggia' mid-season	FR
Radicchio, 'Rossa di Treviso'	B,BS,CO,DI,FR,GO,HU, JO,M,SN,SU,TH,VS
Radicchio, 'Rossa di Verona'	AB,BS,CO,FR,KS,PI,SU
Radicchio, 'Selvatica da Campo'	V
Radicchio, 'Silla'	PI
Radicchio, 'Variegata di Luisa'	B,FR
Radicchio, 'Varieg. di Sottomarina Precoce'	SU
Radish, '18 Day'	BS,GO,SU
Radish, 'Aomaru-Koshin'	KS
Radish, 'April Cross' F1	DT,M,PK,SE,SN,SR,U, V,YA
Radish, 'Attila' F1	YA
Radish, 'Beacon'	BS
Radish, 'Belrosa' RZ	CO
Radish, 'Black Spanish Long'	B,BD,BS,C,CO,KI,KS, PI,SN,SU,TH,V
Radish, 'Black Spanish Round'	AB,B,BS,BY,CO,DE,DT, HU,KI,M,S,SK,SN,SR, ST,SU,TH,TU,V
Radish, 'Buonissimo d'Ignegnoli'	FR
Radish, 'Cabernet' F1	SR
Radish, 'Candela di Fuoca'	SN
Radish, 'Caravella'	BS
Radish, 'Cavalier'	VY
Radish, 'Cello'	BS
Radish, 'Champion' o-p	DN,SK,SN,SR
Radish, 'Cherokee' F1	D,J,T,V
Radish, 'Cherriette' F1	PK,SR

Radish, 'Cherry Belle'	AB,B,BD,BS,BU,BY,D, DN,DT,KI,KS,L,M,MO,R, PI,SK,SN,SR,SU,T,TU, VH,VY,YA
Radish, 'China Rose'	B,BD,BS,BY,CO,DT,HU, J,KI,MO,PI,S,SK,SN,SR, ST,SU,TH,TU
Radish, Chinese Globe mix	M
Radish, 'Chinese White'	RC,SK
Radish, 'Comet'	SK,VY
Radish, 'Crimson Giant'	BS
Radish, 'Crunchy Red'	VY
Radish, 'Crystal Ball'	BS,S
Radish, 'Cyros' F1	BS,KI
Radish, 'D'Avignon'	BS,JO,KS,SU,TH
Radish, Daikon type	AB,BF,BH,RI,SK
Radish, 'Easter Egg'	BS,DI,JO,KS,PI,PK,SU, TE,VY
Radish, 'Edible Longpod'	DD
Radish, 'Eterna'	V
Radish, 'Fireball' F1	SR
Radish, 'Flair'	BS,MO
Radish, 'Fluo' F1	F,PI,SE,SN
Radish, 'Flyer' F1	BS,U
Radish, 'Fota'	BS
Radish, 'French Breakfast'	AB,B,BD,BS,BY,CO,DE, DN,KI,MC,MO,PI,SK, SN,ST,TE,TH,VH,VY
Radish, 'French Breakfast 2'	TU
Radish, 'French Breakfast 3'	C,D,DT,F,FR,J,L,S,SE, T,U,V
Radish, 'French Breakfast 3- Tozer'	BS
Radish, 'French Breakfast Forcing'	B,BS,MO
Radish, 'French Breakfast- Fusilier'	BS
Radish, 'Fr. Breakfast Large White Tipped'	BS
Radish, 'French Breakfast' o-p	SN
Radish, 'French Breakfast-Rafale'	BS
Radish, 'French Golden'	HD
Radish, 'Fuego' o-p	SR
Radish, 'Galahad'	SK
Radish, Globe Vars Mix	U,V
Radish, 'Hailstone'	BU
Radish, 'Helro' (Forcing)	BS,J
Radish, 'Icicle'	BU,TE
Radish, 'Icicle Long White'	B,BD,BS,BY,CO,F,HU, J,L,M,MO,S,SK,SN,ST, SU,TH,TU,V
Radish, Japanese	BH
Radish, 'Jolly'	DT,K
Radish, 'Juliette' F1	T
Radish, 'Jumbo'	BS
Radish, 'Korea Green'	HU
Radish, Lo Bok see Mino Early	
Radish, 'Long Scarlet'	HU
Radish, 'Mantanghong' F1	J,S,T,V,VH
Radish, 'Marabelle'	BS,JO
Radish, 'Mexican Bartender'	DE
Radish, 'Mino Early'	D,J,S,SK,TU,YA
Radish, 'Minowase' F1	AB,DN,SN
Radish, 'Minowase Summer Cross' F1	BY,FR,KI,PI,SR
Radish, 'Minowase Summer No 2' F1	BS,TE
Radish, 'Misato Green'	CO,DD,HU
Radish, 'Misato Rose Flesh'	BS,PK,SN
Radish, Mix	AB,BS,D,DT,GO,KI,M,PI, S
Radish, mix winter	SK

316

RADISH

Radish, 'Miyashige'	DD,JO,SD	Rhubarb, 'Holstein Bloodred'	BS
Radish, 'Mooli'	KI,KS,ST,SU	Rhubarb, 'Prince Albert'	BS,TH
Radish, 'Munchen Bier'	B,BS,CO,KI,KS,SU,TH,	Rhubarb, 'Redstick'	V
	VH	Rhubarb, 'Strawberry'	BS
Radish, 'Novired'	GO	Rhubarb, 'Victoria'	BD,BS,BY,DE,DT,GO,L,
Radish, 'Ohkura'	DD		MO,PI,S,TE,TH
Radish, 'Omny' F1	KS	Rice, wild	RI
Radish, 'Parat'	F,PI,SD,SN	Rocket	AB,B,BF,BH,C,CO,DD,
Radish, 'Pegaso'	BS,MO		DE,DI,FR,GO,KS,PI,PK,
Radish, 'Pernot'	DT		RC,RI,S,SK,SN,SP,SU,
Radish, 'Pink Beauty'	BS,CO,D,J,JO,KI,S		TH,TU,V,VY
Radish, 'Plum Purple'	PK	Rocket, 'Italian Wild Rustic'	BH,KS,SN
Radish, 'Poker' F1	BS	Rocket, 'Sylvetta'	FR,GO,JO,PI
Radish, 'Primella'	BS	Rocket, Turkish	C
Radish, 'Prinz Rotin'	BS,DE,DT,F,KI,M,SE,T,U	Rutabaga see Swede	
Radish, Rainbow Salad Mix	T	Salad, American	U
Radish, 'Rat's Tail'	HD,PI	Salad, 'El Toro'	SN,VS
Radish, 'Red Beret'	JO	Salad, 'Misticanza'	C,PI
Radish, 'Red Boy'	SK	Salad, Mixed Collection	TE,V
Radish, 'Red Flame'	PK	Salad, Purple Goosefoot	AB
Radish, 'Red Meat'	JO,SN	Salad, Rape	B,BS,BY,C,CO,FR,KI,
Radish, 'Red Silk'	SK		MO,ST,SU,V,YA
Radish, 'Revosa'	PI,VH	Salad, Roman Green 'Grass'	SN,VS
Radish, 'Ribella'	BS,M	Salad, Roman Red 'Les Oreilles du Diable'	SN,VS
Radish, 'Robino'	BS, M	Salad, Roman 'St. Martha'	SN,VS
Radish, 'Rond Rose a Bout Blanc National'	GO	Salad, Roman 'St. Vincent'	SN,VS
Radish, 'Rondeel' RZ	CO	Salad, Thai	CO,SU
Radish, 'Rota'	BD,BS	Saladisi	FR,T
Radish, 'Round Red Forcing Real'	BS,DI,FR	Salsify	DD,J
Radish, 'Rudi'	YA	Salsify, Giant see Mammoth	
Radish, 'Sabina'	BS,M,YA	Salsify, 'Mammoth'	B,M,S
Radish, 'Sakurajima Mammoth'	AB,KS	Salsify, 'Mammoth Sandwich Island'	AB,B,BS,BU,BY,C,CO,D
Radish, 'Saxa'	BS,BY,MO		E,DT,F,JO,KI,KS,MC,PI,
Radish, 'Scarlet Globe'	B,BF,BS,BU,C,CO,DN,		SK,SR,ST,SU,T,TH,TU
	F,FR,J,KI,MC,MO,S,	Salsify, 'Sandwich Island' See M.S.I.	
	SK,ST,TE,TH	Scorzonera	KS,L,RI,T,TH
Radish, 'Scharo'	BS,MO	Scorzonera, 'Duplex'	BH
Radish, 'Short Top Forcing'	BS,S	Scorzonera, 'Geante Noire de Russie'	FR,GO,S
Radish, 'Shunkyoh Semi-long'	JO,SN	Scorzonera, Giant Rooted	BS,FR
Radish, 'Sirri' RZ	CO	Scorzonera, 'Habil'	M
Radish, 'Snow Belle'	SK,VY	Scorzonera, 'Lange Jan'	BS,JO,V
Radish, 'Solar' F1	BS	Scorzonera, 'Long Black'	BY,C,KI,ST,SU
Radish, 'Sora'	JO,KS	Scorzonera, 'Maxima'	BS,CO,J,MC,TU
Radish, 'Sparkler'	BS,BU,BY,CO,DE,KI,SK,	Seedling Radish, 'Jaba'	B,BS,SU
	ST	Sesame, Afghani	SD
Radish, 'Sparkler 3'	D,F,J,S	Skirret	B,C,CN,DD,SU,TH
Radish, 'Spring Song' F1	JO	Sorghum, Broom, 'Black Amber'	PI
Radish, 'Summer Crunch'	BS,KI,SU	Sorghum, Broom, Hungarian	AB
Radish, Summer Mix	F	Sorghum, Broom, mix	SR
Radish, 'Tama' hyb	SN	Sorghum, Broom, red	B,SR
Radish, 'Tinto' hyb	SR	Sorghum, Broomcorn	AB,B,SK
Radish, 'Tokinashi'	KS,PI,RC	Sorghum, 'White Popping'	PI
Radish, 'Valentine'	SK	Spinach	BS
Radish, 'Vintage'	SK	Spinach, 'America'	BS,FR,SD,YA
Radish, 'Violet de Gournay'	SN	Spinach, 'Atlanta'	BS,KI,MC
Radish, 'Volcano'	F	Spinach, 'Avanti' F1 RZ	CO
Radish, 'White Giant Globe'	DE	Spinach, 'Avon' hyb	SR
Radish, 'White Hailstone'	BS	Spinach, 'Bakan'	L
Radish, 'White Icicle'	DE,DN,KI,PI,SD,SR,VY	Spinach, 'Bazaroet'	V
Radish, 'White Turnip'	BS,HU,TH	Spinach, 'Bergola'	BS,CO
Radish, 'Wood's Frame'	HD	Spinach, 'Bloomsdale'	AB,B,BS,BU,C,FR,HU,
Rampion	C,TH,V		KI,M,SN,ST,TE
Rhubarb	BH,DD	Spinach, 'Bloomsdale Winter'	AB,BF,DE,PI,RC,SK,SR
Rhubarb, 'Champagne Early'	M	Spinach, 'Bolero' F1	SK,SR
Rhubarb, 'Glaskins Perpetual'	BS,BY,C,KI,MO,ST,SU,	Spinach, 'Broad Leaf Prickly Standwell'	BS,CO
	T,TE,TU	Spinach, 'Broad Leaved Prickly'	BS,BY,C,K,MO

SPINACH

Spinach, 'Ceylon'	V	Spinach, 'Triathlon' F1	M,TU
Spinach, 'Coho' F1	SR	Spinach, 'Triathlon' &'Trinidad' F1, 2-pack	M
Spinach, cold resistant savoy	SK	Spinach, 'Tribute' F1	BS
Spinach, 'Correnta' F1	DE,PI,SR	Spinach, 'Trinidad' F1	M
Spinach, 'Dash' F1	BS	Spinach, 'Triptiek' F1	TU
Spinach, 'Dividend' o-p	SR	Spinach, 'Triton' F1	S,SE
Spinach, 'Dominant'	BS,BY,J	Spinach, 'Tyee'	BS,JO,PI,SK,SR,VY
Spinach, 'Estivato' o-p	SR	Spinach, 'Unipak 151' F1	SK,SR
Spinach, 'Fabris'	BS	Spinach, 'Viceroy' o-p	SR
Spinach, 'Fall Green' o-p	SR	Spinach, 'Vienna'	BS,PK,SK,SR,VY
Spinach, 'Five Star' F1	DI	Spinach, 'Viking'	BS,F
Spinach, 'Fordane'	DT	Spinach, 'Virkade'	BS
Spinach, 'Fortune'	FR	Spinach, 'Viroflay'	BS,FR,GO,SD,TH
Spinach, 'Giant New Prickly'	B,BS	Spinach, water	RI
Spinach, 'Giant Thick Leaved' see 'Broad Prickly'		Spinach, 'Winterriesen'	V
Spinach, 'Giant Winter'	AB	Spring Greens, 'Vanguard'	M
Spinach, 'Gigante d'Inverno'	AB	Sprouting, Mung Beans	BS,BY,CO,DE,FR,JO,KI,
Spinach, 'Grodane'	BS,KI,TU,YA		L,PI,PK,RC,S,SK,SU,TE,
Spinach, 'Hector'	JO		TU
Spinach, 'Hollandia'	BS	Sprouting , Quinoa	SU
Spinach, 'Indian Summer' hyb	BU,JO	Sprouting , Radish	CO,JO,PI,RC,SU,TE
Spinach, Japanese 'Summer Green'	KS	Sprouting Salad, T&M	T
Spinach, 'Kent' F1	FR	Sprouting Seeds, Alfalfa	BS,BY,CO,D,FR,J,JO,KI,
Spinach, 'King of Denmark'	BS,TH		L,M,PI,PK,RC,SU,T,TE,
Spinach, 'Long Standing'	T,VH		TU,V
Spinach, low acid	DD	Sprouting Seeds, Buckwheat	RC
Spinach, Malabar	PI	Sprouting Seeds, Chick Peas	CO,TE
Spinach, 'Matador'	FR	Sprouting Seeds, Chinese Cabbage	PI
Spinach, 'Mazurka' F1	BS,F,SR,TE	Sprouting Seeds, Fenugreek	BS,BY,CO,KI,SU,TU,V
Spinach, 'Medania'	B,BS,CO,DT,KI,L,ST,	Sprouting Seeds, Lentils	PI
	TU,U,YA	Sprouting Seeds, Mustard	TU
Spinach, 'Melody' F1	BS,DN,GO,PI,PK,SK,	Sprouting Seeds, Onion	FR,JO,PI
	SR,VY	Sprouting Seeds, Radish	RC
Spinach, 'Merlo Nero'	FR	Sprouting Seeds, Rocket	JO
Spinach, mix	GO	Sprouting Seeds, Spicy Fenugreek	J,L
Spinach, 'Monarch Long Standing'	U	Sprouting , Soya Beans	CO
Spinach, 'Monnopa'	BS,CO,KI,KS,T	Sprouting , Wheat	CO,JO,RC
Spinach, 'No.7-R' hyb	BU,SR	Squash, 'Alexandria'	S
Spinach, 'Nobel'	BS,BU,DE,HU,PI	Squash, 'All Seasons' F1	PK
Spinach, 'Nordic'	PK	Squash, 'Ambercup' F1	SK,SR,TE,VY
Spinach, 'Norfolk'	AB	Squash, 'Amerindian'	DD
Spinach, 'Novadane' F1	YA	Squash, 'Argentine'	DD
Spinach, 'Old Dominion'	DD	Squash, 'Arikara Round'	DD
Spinach, 'Olympia'	BS,DN,SK,TE	Squash, 'Autumn Cup' F1	PI,SR,TE
Spinach, 'Oscar' F1	BS	Squash, 'Autumn Queen'	SK,SN,U
Spinach, 'Patience'	GO	Squash, 'Aztec' hyb	BU
Spinach, 'Polka' F1	BS	Squash, 'Baby Delica'	BS
Spinach, 'Predane' F1	YA	Squash, 'Banana Blue'	SN,VS
Spinach, 'Resistoflay Securo'	V	Squash, 'Banana Pink Jumbo'	BS,DE,SN,VS
Spinach, 'Revenue' o-p	SR	Squash, 'Bennings Green Tint'	AB,JO,TE
Spinach, 'Rico' F1	J	Squash, 'Black Forest'	JO,SN
Spinach, 'Samish' F1	SR	Squash, 'Blue Ballet'	BS,JO,SD,SN
Spinach, 'Samson'	KS	Squash, 'Blue de Hongrie'	SN
Spinach, 'Sigmaleaf' F1	S	Squash, 'Boston Marrow' o-p	DD,SR
Spinach, 'Skookum' F1	SR	Squash, 'Brazilian Sugar'	SN,VS
Spinach, 'Space' F1	B,BD,BS,F,JO,KS,MO,PI	Squash, 'Brodee Galeuse'	SN,VS
Spinach, 'Spartacus'	BS	Squash, 'Bubble & Squeak'	U
Spinach, 'Spinoza'	BS	Squash, 'Burpee Butterbush'	PI
Spinach, 'Splendour' F1	B,BD,BS,DT,MO,VH	Squash, 'Bush Table Queen' o-p	BU
Spinach, 'Spokane' F1	D	Squash, 'Bushfire' F1	BS,YA
Spinach, 'Sprint' F1	BS	Squash, 'Butter Scallop' F1	PK
Spinach, 'Sputnik'	BS	Squash, 'Buttercup'	AB,B,BS,BU,D,PI,SD,
Spinach, 'Steadfast'	AB,TE		SK,SN,SR,SU,TU,VS
Spinach, Strawberry	CO,F,SN,U,V,VS	Squash, 'Buttercup Burgess' o-p	JO,SR,VY
Spinach, 'Teton' Summer Round	TE	Squash, 'Buttercup Emerald Bush'	VY
Spinach, 'Triade' F1	F	Squash, 'Butternut'	BF,DT,FR,KI,SN,SP,YA

SQUASII

Squash, 'Butternut Supreme' F1 — SK,SN,SR
Squash, 'Cee Gwa' — HU,SK
Squash, 'Chefini' F1 — DE
Squash, 'Chestnut' — DD,JO,TU
Squash, 'Chilacayote' — HU
Squash, 'Chioggia' — SN,VS
Squash, 'Chompa' — HU
Squash, 'Churimen, Abobora' — DE
Squash, 'Cobnut' — CO
Squash, 'Courge de Siam' — SN
Squash, 'Courge Marine de Ch' — SN
Squash, 'Courge Muscade' — SN
Squash, 'Courge Olive' — SN
Squash, 'Cream of the Crop' — BS,BU,CO,PK,SN,SR, VY

Squash, 'Creamy' F1 — PK
Squash, 'Crookneck PMR' F1 — PK
Squash, 'Crown Prince' F1 — S,TU,YA
Squash, 'Cucuzzi — PI
Squash, 'Cucuzzi Caravazzi' — HU
Squash, 'Cushaw Striped' — DD,PI,SN,VS
Squash, 'Custard White' — B,BS,BY,C,CO,KI,MO, SN,ST,TU,V

Squash, 'Dawn' — BS
Squash, 'Delicata' — AB,B,BS,DE,DI,F,JO,KS, MO,PI,SD,SK,SN,SR, TE,V,VY

Squash, 'Dividend' hyb — SK
Squash, 'Dixie' F1 — PK
Squash, 'Doe' — AB
Squash, 'Dw. Summer Crookneck' — BU
Squash, 'Early Acorn' — BS,CO,KI,SN
Squash, 'Early Butternut' F1 — BD,FR,MO,PI,PK,SK, SN,SR,VY

Squash, 'Early Pak' — SN
Squash, 'Early Prolific Straightneck' o-p — DN,SR
Squash, 'Early Yellow Crookneck' — AB,DE,JO,SD,SN
Squash, 'Ebony Acorn' — AB,BF,DD,JO
Squash, 'Etampes' — DD
Squash, 'Flat White Boer' — AB
Squash, 'Foo Gwa' — HU,RI
Squash, 'Furusato' — CO
Squash, 'Futsu' — AB,RC,SN,VS
Squash, 'Gemstore' F1 — BS,D
Squash, 'Gill's Golden Pippin' — AB,DD
Squash, 'Gold Nugget' — BS,CO,D,KI,ST,TE,TU, VY

Squash, 'Goldbar' F1 — SK,SR
Squash, 'Golden Delicious' — BS,SK,SN,TU
Squash, 'Golden Hubbard' — CO,PI,S,SK,SN,SR,SU, TH,VS

Squash, 'Golden Scallopini Bush' — SD
Squash, 'Goldfinger' F1 — DE
Squash, 'Goldkeeper' — BS
Squash, 'Green Delicious' — SK,SN
Squash, 'Greengold' — AB
Squash, 'Grey Zucchni' — BU
Squash, 'Heart of Gold' hyb — PK,SR
Squash, 'Hokkaido' — DD,SD
Squash, 'Hokkori' F1 — JO
Squash, 'Honey Delight' — JO,PI,SK,SN
Squash, 'Hopi Orange' — SD
Squash, 'Hopi Pale Grey' — AB,DD
Squash, 'Horn of Plenty' hyb — SR,VY
Squash, 'Hubbard' — FR
Squash, 'Hubbard Blue' — AB,BU,DE,HU,JO,PI,PK,

Squash, 'Hubbard Improved Green' — SN,SR,TE,VS / SD,SK,SN
Squash, 'Hubbard Mini Orange' — SK
Squash, 'Huicha' — HU
Squash, Italian Edible Gourd — DE
Squash, 'Jarrahdale' — JO
Squash, 'Jaspee de Vendee' — SN
Squash, 'Jersey Golden Acorn' — BS,DD,TU
Squash, 'Kuri Blue' — AB
Squash, 'Kuta' F1 — PK
Squash, 'Lady Godiva' — HD,SD
Squash, 'Lebanese' — KS
Squash, 'Libra' — SD
Squash, 'Little Gem' — AB,BS,DD,M,SU,VY
Squash, 'Long Island Cheese' F1 — JO
Squash, 'Lower Salmon River' — AB
Squash, 'Lumina' — BS,V
Squash, 'Mandan' — HD
Squash, 'Mao Gwa' — HU
Squash, 'Marblehead' — DD
Squash, 'Mayo Blusher' — AB
Squash, 'Medallion' F1 — BS
Squash, 'Melonette' — SN
Squash, 'Mesa Queen' hyb — SR
Squash, 'Mini Green Hubbard' — SK,SN,V
Squash, 'Minipop' F1 — SN
Squash, 'Monet' hyb — SR
Squash, 'Moschata' — SN
Squash, 'Neck Pumpkin' o-p — SR
Squash, 'New England Blue' — SK,SN
Squash, 'Nicklow's Delight' F1 — JO
Squash, 'NK 530' hyb — SR
Squash, 'North Georgia' — SN,VS
Squash, 'Nutty Delica' F1 — V
Squash, 'Olive' — HD,SN,VS
Squash, 'Olive' org — SN
Squash, 'Onion' — BS
Squash, 'Pacifica' F1 — BS,YA
Squash, 'Patisson Bunter' — SN,VS
Squash, 'Patisson Orange' — SN,VS
Squash, 'Patisson Patty Pan' — DT,KS,SN,VS
Squash, 'Patisson White' — SN,VS
Squash, 'Patty Pan' hyb — BU
Squash, 'Pepita' — SN,VS
Squash, 'Peruvian' — SN,VS
Squash, 'Peter Pan' hyb — BS,PK,SN,S,SR,V
Squash, 'Pink Banana' o-p — SR
Squash, 'Pink Jumbo' — BU,SN
Squash, 'Pompeon' — CO,SU
Squash, 'Ponca' — BS,DD,SR
Squash, 'Pontimarron' — SN,VS
Squash, 'Pontiron Chinese' — SN,VS
Squash, 'Pontiron Hungarian Blue' — SN,VS
Squash, 'Pontiron Rouge Vif d'Etamps' — SN,VS
Squash, 'Prince Regent' F1 — BS,YA
Squash, 'Queensland Blue' — BS
Squash, 'Red Kuri' — AB,BS,DI,JO,SD,SN
Squash, 'Revenue' hyb — SK
Squash, 'Rolet' — BS,CO
Squash, 'Round Zucchni' — BU
Squash, 'Scallop Scallopini' — BS,DE,SKSN,
Squash, Scallop, 'White Bush' — BS,BU,HU,SD,TH,VY
Squash, 'Scallop Yellow Bird' — BS
Squash, Scallop, 'Yellow Bush' — TH
Squash, 'Seneca Butterbar' F1 — PK
Squash, 'Seneca Prolific' hyb — BU,JO,SR

SQUASH

Variety	Code
Squash, 'Seneca Supreme' hyb	BU
Squash, 'Siamese'	SN,VS
Squash, 'Silver Bell'	AB
Squash, 'Stripetti' F1	BS,SK,SN
Squash, 'Sucriere du Bresil'	SN
Squash, 'Sugar Loaf' o-p	BS,BU,DD,JO
Squash, 'Sugarberry'	SN,VS
Squash, 'Sun Drops' hyb	PK,SN,SR
Squash, 'Sunbar' F1	SK,SR
Squash, 'Sunburst' F1	BS,C,CO,D,DT,JO,KI, PI,PK,SK,SN,SR,ST, TE,TU,V,VY
Squash, 'Supreme Delite' F1	D
Squash, 'Swan White Acorn'	BS,SK,SN
Squash, 'Sweet Dumpling'	AB,B,BS,C,D,DT,JO,KI, PI,SD,SK,SN,SR,SU,TU, V,VY
Squash, 'Sweet Keeper'	SD
Squash, 'Sweet Mama' F1	BS,CO,KI,MC,PK,SK, SN,SR,ST,TU,VY
Squash, 'Sweet Meat'	AB,BS,PI,TE
Squash, 'Sweet Nugget'	SN
Squash, 'Sweet Sensation' F1	S
Squash, 'Table Ace' F1	B,BD,BS,BU,L,MO,PI, PK,SK,SN,SR,TU
Squash, 'Table Gold'	SK,SN,SR,VS,VY
Squash, 'Table King'	SK,SN,SR,TE,VY
Squash, 'Table Queen'	AB,BS,BU,DE,SN,SR,TH
Squash, Tahini	BF
Squash, 'Tahitian'	AB,SD
Squash, 'Tamala de Carne'	HU
Squash, 'Tamala de Hueso'	HU
Squash, 'Tancheese'	SN,VS
Squash, 'Tasty Delite' hyb	FR,SR
Squash, 'Tay Belle'	SK,SN
Squash, 'Tetsukabuto'	PI
Squash, 'Tigress' hyb	SK
Squash, 'Tivoli' F1	BD,BS,D,DE,L,M,MO, PI,S,T,U,YA
Squash, 'Triamble'	B,SN,VS
Squash, 'True Hubbard'	AB
Squash, 'Tuffy'	JO
Squash, 'Turk's Hat Small'	SN,VS
Squash, 'Turk's Turban'	B,BS,BU,CO,DT,FR,JO, KI,SR,SU,TH,TU
Squash, 'Uchiki Kuru'	DE
Squash, 'Ultra Butternut' F1	BS,SK,SN,SR,VY
Squash, Vegetable Spaghetti	AB,BF,BS,BU,BY,C,CO, D,DI,F,FR,GO,J,JO,KI, MC,PI,RC,RI,SD,SK, SN,SR,TE,TU,V,VS,VY
Squash, Vegetable Spaghetti 'Orangetti'	BS
Squash,Vegetable Spaghetti, 'Pasta' F1	PK,SR
Squash, Vegetable Spaghetti 'Pyjamas'	BS
Squash, 'Waltham Butternut'	AB,B,BS,BU,GO,JO,PI, PK,SK,SN,SR
Squash, 'Warted Chicago Hubbard' o-p	BU
Squash, 'Warted Hubbard'	SK,SR,V,VY
Squash, 'Whangaparoa'	DD
Squash, 'White Zucchini' o-p	SR
Squash, 'Winterhorn'	SN,VS
Squash, 'Zahra' hyb	JO,SR
Squash, 'Zapallito di Tronco Redondo'	HD
Squash, 'Zapallo Macre'	DD
Squash, 'Zenith' F1	SK,SN,SR,TE
Squash, 'Zipinki Campana'	DD
Squash, 'Zucca Siciliano' o-p	SR
Strawberry, 'Alpine Alexandria'	B,BD,BY,CO,DE,GO,JE, JO,KI,MO,RI,SU,VH
Strawberry, 'Baron Solemacher'	B,J,L,V
Strawberry, 'D'ogni mese'	FR
Strawberry, 'Mignonette'	b,D,T
Strawberry, 'Sweet Sensation' F1	D
Strawberry Sweetcorn	SN,VS
Strawberry, 'Sweetheart' F1	CA,CO,GO,J,JE,MO,RI, SU,V
Strawberry, 'Temptation'	B,BD,DI,DT,J,KI,MO,S, SE,SK,T,U,V,VH,VY
Strawberry, 'Verbesserte Rugen'	B,JE,PI,RI
Strawberry, 'Yellow Wonder'	B,J,V
Sunflower, 'Mammoth Russian'	AB,FR
Sunflower, 'Rostov'	AB
Sunflower, 'Tarahumara White'	AB
Swede, 'American Purple Top'	BU,DE,DN,PK
Swede, 'Angela'	B,BS
Swede, 'Best of All'	B,BD,BS,D,DT,F,J,KI,M, MC,MO,T,U,VH
Swede, 'Champion'	VH
Swede, 'Champion Purple Top'	BS,TH
Swede, 'Devon Champion'	TU
Swede, 'Garden Purple Top Acme'	B,BD,BS,C,CO,KI,MC, MO,ST
Swede, 'Gilfeather'	JO
Swede, 'Joan'	JO,K,YA
Swede, 'Laurentian'	AB,BS,DD,PI,SK,SR,VY
Swede, 'Lizzy'	BS,D,DT,F,J,L,SE,V,VH
Swede, 'Magres'	BS,YA
Swede, 'Marian'	B,BD,BS,BY,CO,DT,F,KI, M,MO,ST,SU,TE,TU,U, VH,YA
Swede, 'Pike'	JO
Swede, 'Ruby'	BS,M,S,TU
Swede, 'Ruta Otofte'	B,BS
Swede, 'Yellow Fall Turnip'	BF
Swede, 'York'	VY
Sweetcorn, 'Aladdin' hyb	SK
Sweetcorn, 'Alpine' F1	PI,SK
Sweetcorn, 'Amarillo' Ancient Yellow	SN,VS
Sweetcorn, 'Ambrosia'	PK,SK
Sweetcorn, 'Anasazi'	CS
Sweetcorn, 'Argent' F1	JO,PK,SK,SR
Sweetcorn, 'Ashworth'	AB
Sweetcorn, 'Astarac' Ancient White	SN,VS
Sweetcorn, 'Athos' F1	JO,SK
Sweetcorn, 'Avalanche' hyb	SR
Sweetcorn, 'Baby' mini	B,VH
Sweetcorn, 'Balai'	SN,VS
Sweetcorn, 'Banker' F1	YA
Sweetcorn, 'Bi-Time' hyb	SR
Sweetcorn, 'Black Aztec'	AB,RC,SD
Sweetcorn, 'Blizzard Supersweet' hyb	SK
Sweetcorn, 'Bodacious' hyb	BU,PK,SR,TE
Sweetcorn, 'Breakthrough' F1	DI
Sw.c., 'Breakthrough Honey n' Cream' F1	DI
Sweetcorn, 'Bronze-Orange'	DD
Sweetcorn, 'BSS 1605 V.I.P.' hyb	SR
Sweetcorn, 'Bullion' F1	YA
Sweetcorn, 'Burgundy Delight' F1	PI
Sweetcorn, 'Butterscotch' F1	T
Sweetcorn, 'Candy Corner' hyb	SK
Sweetcorn, 'Challenger' F1	BS,F
Sweetcorn, 'Champ' F1	DT,F,M,T,VH

SWEETCORN

Sweetcorn, 'Citation' F1	BS	Sweetcorn, 'Jumpstart'	JO
Sweetcorn, 'Classic' F1	BS,VY	Sweetcorn, 'Kandy King' hyb	SR
Sweetcorn, 'Clockwork' F1	JO	Sweetcorn, 'Kandy Korn' hyb	BU,TE
Sweetcorn, 'Cobham Sweet' F1	BS	Sweetcorn, 'Kandy Treat' hyb	BU
Sweetcorn, 'Cochise' hyb	SK	Sweetcorn, 'Kelvedon Glory' F1	BD,BS,CO,F,KI,MO,ST
Sweetcorn, 'Colossal Bicolour' hyb	SK	Sweetcorn, 'King Arthur' hyb	SK
Sweetcorn, 'Colossal Yellow' hyb	SK	Sweetcorn, 'Kodiak' F1	BS
Sweetcorn, 'Conquest' F1	BD,BS,D,DT,MO,T	Sweetcorn, 'Lancelot' F1	PI,PK,SK,SR
Sweetcorn, 'Country Gentleman'	AB,RC	Sweetcorn, 'Lariat' F1	BS
Sweetcorn, 'Crisp- n- Sweet' F1	BS,BU,PI,SR,TU	Sweetcorn, 'Luther Hill'	DD
Sweetcorn, 'Custer' hyb	SK	Sweetcorn, 'Mainstay'	BS,MO
Sweetcorn, 'Dancer' F1	JO	Sweetcorn, 'Merit'	FR,PK
Sweetcorn, 'Dawn' F1	BS	Sweetcorn, 'Merlin'	PK,SK
Sweetcorn, 'Delectable' F1	JO,SK,SR	Sweetcorn, 'Midnight Snack'	AB
Sweetcorn, 'Dickson' F1	S,T,VH	Sweetcorn, 'Milk n' Honey' hyb	SK
Sweetcorn, 'Divinity' hyb	SK	Sweetcorn, 'Minipop' F1 Mini	BS,C,D,KI,S,TU
Sweetcorn, 'Double Gem' F1	JO,SR,TE	Sweetcorn, 'Minisweet' F1	CO
Sweetcorn, 'Double Treat' hyb	SK	Sweetcorn, 'Minor' F1	F,J,T,V
Sweetcorn, dwarf F1	DI	Sweetcorn, 'Miracle' F1	BS,BU,GO,ST,TE,VY
Sweetcorn, 'Eagle'	JO	Sweetcorn mix	GO
Sweetcorn, 'Earlibelle' F1	BS,TU	Sweetcorn, 'Monte Carlo' F1	SK,SR,VY
Sweetcorn, 'Earliking' F1	BS,BY,C,L,MO	Sweetcorn, 'Morning Sun'	BS
Sweetcorn, 'Earlivee' F1	BS,CO,JO,SK,VY	Sweetcorn, 'Native Gem' F1	SK,SR
Sweetcorn, 'Early Cup' F1	BS	Sweetcorn, 'North Star' F1	BS
Sweetcorn, 'Early Pak' F1	BS,KI,SU,YA	Sweetcorn, 'Northern Belle' F1	BS,MO
Sweetcorn, 'Early Sunglow' hyb	BU,PK	Sweetcorn, 'Northern Extra Sweet' F1	BS,CO,JO,SK,U
Sweetcorn, 'Extra Early Sweet' F1	BS,GO,KI,SK	Sweetcorn, 'Nova' F1	SK,SR
Sweetcorn, 'Fantasy'	B,JO	Sweetcorn, 'October Gold' F1	BS
Sweetcorn, 'Festival' F1	DT	Sweetcorn, 'Ovation' F1	BS
Sweetcorn, 'Fiesta' F1	BD,BS,F,L,MO,R	Sweetcorn, 'Peaches & Cream'	DE
Sweetcorn, 'First of All' F1	S	Sweetcorn, 'Pegasus' hyb	SR
Sweetcorn, 'Florida Stay Sweet' F1	BS	Sweetcorn, 'Phenomenal' F1	BU,PI,SK,SR
Sweetcorn, 'Fortune' F1	BS,SK,SR	Sweetcorn, 'Pilot' F1	JO
Sweetcorn, 'Genie' hyb	SK	Sweetcorn, 'Pinnacle' F1	BS
Sweetcorn, 'Geronimo' hyb	SK	Sweetcorn, 'Platinum Lady' F1	BU,PI
Sweetcorn, 'Golden Bantam' o-p	AB,BD,BF,BS,BU,DI,HU,	Sweetcorn, 'Polar Vee' hyb	DN,VY
	MO,SD,TH	Sweetcorn, 'Precious Gem' F1	SK,SR
Sweetcorn, 'Golden Beauty' hyb	BU	Sweetcorn, 'Pride and Joy'	VY
Sweetcorn, 'Golden Midget'	AB,SD	Sweetcorn, 'Prime Pak' F1	BS,KI,MC
Sweetcorn, 'Golden Queen'	PK	Sweetcorn, 'Prime Plus V.I.P.' F1	SR
Sweetcorn, 'Golden Sweet' F1	BS,CO,KI	Sweetcorn, 'Primetime' F1	SR
Sweetcorn, 'Gourmet' F1	BS,M	Sweetcorn, 'Pristine'	JO,PK
Sweetcorn, 'Grant' hyb	SK	Sweetcorn, 'Quest' F1	SR
Sweetcorn, 'Guinevere' hyb	SK	Sweetcorn, 'Quickie' F1	JO,VY
Sweetcorn, 'Herald' F1	BS,MO	Sweetcorn, 'Rainbow Inca'	AB,DD,SD
Sweetcorn, 'Honey and Cream' F1	M,PI	Sweetcorn, 'Reliance' F1	BS
Sweetcorn, 'Honey Bantam Bicolor (30)' F1	BS,T	Sweetcorn, 'Reward' F1	BS,J,TE
Sweetcorn, 'Honey n' Pearl'	PK	Sweetcorn, 'Rise N Shine' hyb	VY
Sweetcorn, 'Honeycomb' F1	BS,BY,KI,ST,SU	Sweetcorn, 'Rival' F1	FR
Sweetcorn, 'Honeydew' F1	BS,BY	Sweetcorn, 'Rosella 425' F1	BS
Sweetcorn, 'Hooker's Sweet Indian'	AB,SD,TE	Sweetcorn, 'RXW 6801' hyb	SR
Sweetcorn, 'Hopi White'	DD	Sweetcorn, 'Seneca Appaloosa' F1	SK,SR,TE,VY
Sweetcorn, 'How Sweet it is'	PK	Sweetcorn, 'Seneca Brave' hyb	SR
Sweetcorn, 'Hudson' hyb	SR	Sweetcorn, 'Seneca Chief'	PK
Sweetcorn, 'Illini Gold'	PK	Sweetcorn, 'Seneca Dawn' hyb	BU,VY
Sweetcorn, 'Imaculata' F1	SK,SR	Sweetcorn, 'Seneca Daybreak' F1	PI,SR,VY
Sweetcorn, 'Imp Golden Bantam'	AB	Sweetcorn, 'Seneca Horizon' F1	BS,BU,SK,TE,VY
Sweetcorn, 'Impulse' hyb	SR	Sweetcorn, 'Seneca RXB 6401' hyb	BU
Sweetcorn, 'Incredible' F1	BU,DT,F,PI,SR	Sweetcorn, 'Sensor' hyb	SK
Sweetcorn, 'Indian Dawn' F1	BS	Sweetcorn, 'Silver King' F1	SK,SR
Sweetcorn, 'Ivanhoe' hyb	SK	Sweetcorn, 'Silver Queen' F1	BU,DE,GO,JO,PK,SR
Sweetcorn, 'Jester II' hyb	SK	Sweetcorn, 'Sir Galahad' hyb	SK
Sweetcorn, 'J. Innes (Canada Cross)' F1	BS	Sweetcorn, 'Skyline'	JO
Sweetcorn, 'Joro' Ancient Red	SN,VS	Sweetcorn, 'Snowbird' F1	SK,SR
Sweetcorn, 'Jubilee' F1	BS,J,KI,L,MO,SK,SU,TU	Sweetcorn, 'Snowmass' F1	SK,SR
Sweetcorn, 'July Gem' hyb	SK	Sweetcorn, 'Sparkle' hyb	SK

SWEETCORN

Sweetcorn, 'Speedy Sweet' hyb — SK
Sweetcorn, 'Spring Snow' hyb — SR
Sweetcorn, 'Stardust' — PK
Sweetcorn, 'Starlite' F1 — BS,C,V
Sweetcorn, 'Stowell's Evergreen' — AB,RC,SD
Sweetcorn, 'Sugar Boy' F1 — BS
Sweetcorn, 'Sugar Buns' hyb — B,JO,SR,TE
Sweetcorn, 'Sugar Loaf' F1 — BS
Sweetcorn, 'Sugar Snow' F1 — SK,SR,TE
Sweetcorn, 'Sugar Snow II' hyb — SR
Sweetcorn, 'Summer Flavour ® 64Y' — T
Sweetcorn, 'Sun Up' F1 — BS
Sweetcorn, 'Sundance' F1 — BS,D,DT,S,SE,U
Sweetcorn, 'Sunrise' F1 — BS,M
Sweetcorn, 'Sweet 77' F1 — BS,MO
Sweetcorn, 'Sweet Mexi' F1 — BS
Sweetcorn, 'Sweet Nugget' F1 — BS,KI,TU
Sweetcorn, 'Sweet Rhythm' hyb — SK,VY
Sweetcorn, 'Sweet Season' F1 — BS
Sweetcorn, 'Sweet September' F1 — BS
Sweetcorn, 'Sweet Symphony' hyb — SK
Sweetcorn, 'Sweetheart' hyb — SK
Sweetcorn, 'Tasty Gold' F1 — BS,KI
Sweetcorn, 'Tasty Sweet' F1 — BS,KI,SU
Sweetcorn, 'Tasty Treat' F1 — BS,CO,ST
Sweetcorn, 'Tecumseh II' hyb — SK
Sweetcorn, 'Temptation' hyb — SK
Sweetcorn, 'Terrific' — BS
Sweetcorn, 'Triple Play' — SD
Sweetcorn, 'Trophy' F1 — V
Sweetcorn, 'True Gold' — AB,SD
Sweetcorn, 'True Platinum' — SD
Sweetcorn, 'Tuxedo' F1 — JO,SK,SR
Sweetcorn, 'Two's Sweeter' F1 — SE
Sweetcorn, 'Vail V.I.P.' hyb — SR
Sweetcorn, 'WSS 3680' hyb — SR
Sweetcorn, 'Xtra Sweet Early' — BS, U
Sweetcorn, 'Xtra Sweet Improved' — M
Sweetcorn, 'Yukon' F1 — BS,KI
Swiss Chard, 'Lily White' — B,C,DT,KI,MC,ST,SU,T
Swiss Chard, 'Ruby Red' — BY,DE,GO
Teff, Tan-Seeded — AB
Teff, White-Seeded — AB
Texel Greens — BS,CO,M,MC,SU,TU
Tomatillo — AB,C,DE,KS,PI,SN,SP, VS
Tomatillo 'Chilean Orange' org — SN
Tomatillo, 'De Milpa' — B,JO,SD
Tomatillo, Ige fruited — HU,RC
Tomatillo 'Mexican Green Husk' o-p org — SN
Tomatillo 'Peruvian Violet' org — SN
Tomatillo, 'Purple' — JO
Tomatillo, 'Rendidora' — RI
Tomatillo, 'Toma Verde' o-p — BU,JO,PK,SD,SK,VY
Tomatillo, Violet — SN
Tomato, 'Ace 55' o-p — DD,KI,SN,SR
Tomato, 'Ailsa Craig' — B,BS,BY,C,CO,D,DT,F, J,KI,L,M,MC,MO,R,S, SN,ST,SU,TH,U,VH,YA
Tomato, 'Alfresco' F1 — BS
Tomato, 'Alicante' — B,BD,BS,BY,CO,D,DT,F, J,KI,L,M,MO,R,S,SE, SN,ST,T,TU,U,VH,YA
Tomato, All Purpose — BF
Tomato, 'Allure' — SK
Tomato, 'Almetia' — AB

Tomato, 'Altaisky' — AB,SN,VS
Tomato, 'Amish Paste' o-p — DI,KS,SN
Tomato, 'Ananas' o-p EEC reg — SN,VS
Tomato, 'Andine Cornue' — SN,VS
Tomato, 'Angela' F1 — BS,MO
Tomato, 'Angora' — DD
Tomato, 'Arasta' F1 — B,BS,DT,KI,MO,SB,SN, ST
Tomato, 'Arkansas Traveller' — SD
Tomato, 'Aunt Ruby's German Green' — JO
Tomato, 'Auriga' — B,KI,SU
Tomato, 'Auriga' o-p — SN
Tomato, 'Azoychka' o-p — SN
Tomato, 'Aztec' hyb — SK
Tomato, 'Azure' — AB
Tomato, 'Balconstar' o-p — SN
Tomato, 'Banana Legs' — AB,DI,DD
Tomato, 'Basketvee' — AB,SK,VY
Tomato, 'Beaute Blanche' o-p — SN,VS
Tomato, 'Beef King' hyb — BU
Tomato, 'Beefmaster' F1 — BS,DE,FR,PI,PK,SK,SN, SR,V,VS
Tomato, 'Beefsteak Improved' — BS,SN,V,VS,VH
Tomato, 'Beefsteak' o-p — BU,DI,SK,SN,SR
Tomato, 'Bellstar' — AB,BS,JO,SK,TU
Tomato, 'Bernado' — BS
Tomato, 'Better Boy' F1 — BU,DE,PI,PK,SK,SN,SR
Tomato, 'Better Bush Cherry Imp' F1 — PK
Tomato, 'Bielo Russian' — AB
Tomato, 'Big Beef' F1 — DE,JO,SK,VY
Tomato, 'Big Beefie 6737' hyb — PK,SN
Tomato, 'Big Boy' F1 — BD,BS,BY,C,CO,DE,DT,F, KI,L,M,MO,PK,R,SN, SR,ST,SU,TU,U,YA
Tomato, 'Big Boy Giant Hybrid 6802' — SN
Tomato, 'Big Early 1200' hyb — SN
Tomato, 'Big Pack 6837' o-p — SN
Tomato, 'Big Rainbow' — DI,KS
Tomato, 'Big Rio' F1 — FR
Tomato, 'Big Star 1201' o-p — SN
Tomato, 'Black Krim' o-p — DI,SN,SP
Tomato, 'Black Plum' — SD
Tomato, 'Black Prince' o-p — AB,SN
Tomato, 'Black Russian' — DI,TU
Tomato, 'Blazer' hyb — VY
Tomato, 'Blizzard' F1 — BS,BY,F,KI,L,MO,SN,TU
Tomato, 'Boa' — SK
Tomato, 'Bonner Beste 6839' o-p — SN
Tomato, 'Bonny Best' — AB,PI,SP,SR
Tomato, 'Bonset' F1 — V
Tomato, 'Brandywine' o-p — AB,CO,JO,KS,PI,PK,RC, SD,SN,SP,TE,TU,VS
Tomato, 'Brandywine Yellow' — JO
Tomato, 'Brasero' Mini — BS, F
Tomato, 'Brin de Muguet' — SN
Tomato, 'Britain's Breakfast' — RO
Tomato, 'Broad Ripple' — AB
Tomato, 'Broadside Red' hyb — SK
Tomato, 'Bruinima Produckt' — AB
Tomato, 'Budai Torpe' o-p — SN,VS
Tomato, 'Buffalo' — BS,D,S
Tomato, 'Buissonante' — SN,VS
Tomato, 'Bullsheart' — AB
Tomato, 'Burbank Red Slicing' — SD
Tomato, 'Burpee Early Pick' — DE
Tomato, 'Burpee Supersteak' hyb — GO,SN

TOMATO

Tomato, 'Burpee's Delicious'	SN,VS
Tomato, 'Burpee's Long Keeper'	PI
Tomato, 'Cabot'	VY
Tomato, 'Cal-Ace' o-p	BU,FR,SR
Tomato, 'Cal-J'	FR
Tomato, 'Calabash Purple'	AB,DD,DI,HU,SN,VS
Tomato, 'Calabash Red'	SD
Tomato, 'Calypso'	BS
Tomato, 'Camello'	BS
Tomato, 'Campbells 1327' o-p	BU,SN,SR
Tomato, 'Campbells 28' o-p	SN
Tomato, 'Camporosso' o-p	SN
Tomato, 'Capri' hyb	SK
Tomato, 'Carmando' F1	FR
Tomato, 'Carnival' hyb	VY
Tomato, 'Caro' o-p	SD,SN,SP
Tomato, 'Caruso'	SK
Tomato, 'Celebrity' F1	BU,DE,FR,JO,PI,PK,SN, SK,SR,TE
Tomato, 'Cencara'	SK
Tomato, 'Cerisette'	SN,VS
Tomato, 'Cerisette Brin de Muguet' o-p	SN
Tomato, 'Chadwick's Cherry'	AB,SP
Tomato, 'Chello'	AB
Tomato, 'Cherokee Purple'	JO,KS,SP
Tomato, 'Cherry Belle' F1	D,YA
Tomato, 'Cherry Express II'	SK
Tomato, 'Cherry Grande' F1	SK,SR,VY
Tomato, 'Cherry Pink'	SK
Tomato, 'Cherry Wonder' F1	YA
Tomato, 'Chico 3'	DD
Tomato, 'Chinese'	AB
Tomato, 'Choice' F1	K
Tomato, 'Chonto Mejorado' o-p	SN
Tomato, 'Clear Pink'	AB
Tomato, 'Clementine' o-p	SN
Tomato, 'Cobra' F1	SK,VY
Tomato, 'Cocktail Clementine'	SN,VS
Tomato, 'Cocktail' mix	KS
Tomato, 'Cocktail Party'	BS
Tomato, 'Coldset'	AB
Tomato, 'Colorado' o-p	SN
Tomato, 'Cossack'	BS
Tomato, 'Costaloto Fiorentino'	B,F,RC,SD
Tomato, 'Count 11' hyb	SN
Tomato, 'Craigella'	DT,KI,SN
Tomato, 'Crimson Fancy'	SN
Tomato, 'Cristal' F1	BS,DT
Tomato, 'Currant Red'	AB,KS,SD
Tomato, 'Cyclon'	BS,MO,U
Tomato, 'Czech Select'	AB
Tomato, 'Dario'	M
Tomato, 'Daybreak' hyb	JO,SR
Tomato, 'Debarao'	JO
Tomato, 'Delicate' o-p	SN,VS
Tomato, 'Deweese Streaked'	AB
Tomato, 'Dombello' F1	BS,D,J,SN,TU
Tomato, 'Dombito' F1	BS,BY,M,SE,SN,T,YA
Tomato, 'Dona' hyb	DE,SN
Tomato, 'Double Rich'	SD
Tomato, 'Duke' hyb	FR,SN
Tomato, 'Dunkins Delight'	AB
Tomato, dwarf early and tasty	DI
Tomato, 'Earliana' o-p	AB,BS,SN
Tomato, 'Early Cascade' F1	JO,PK,VY
Tomato, 'Early Fuego' o-p	SN

Tomato, 'Early Girl' F1	DE,PI,PK
Tomato, 'Early Rouge'	DD
Tomato, 'Early Tanana'	DN
Tomato, 'Early Temptation' hyb	VY
Tomato, 'Earlypak No.7' o-p	BU
Tomato, 'Elios'	U
Tomato, 'Emperador' hyb	SR
Tomato, 'Empire' hyb	FR,SR
Tomato, 'Enchantment' F1	PI,PK,SN
Tomato, 'Eros'	AB
Tomato, 'Estrella' F1	BS,D,DT
Tomato, 'Eureka'	AB
Tomato, 'Eurocross BB' F1	BS,BY,J,KI,MO,YA
Tomato, 'Evergreen' o-p	CO,KS,SN,TU,VS
Tomato, 'Exclusive Collection'	T
Tomato, 'Experimental TM/MO5'	T
Tomato, 'Extase' F1	KI
Tomato, 'Fandango' F1	V
Tomato, 'Fantastic' F1	BU,SK,TE
Tomato, 'Firefly' F1	YA
Tomato, 'Fireworks'	AB
Tomato, 'First in the Field' o-p	B,BD,BS,BY,J,KI,MO,SU
Tomato, 'First Lady' F1	DE,JO,PI
Tomato, 'Flavormore 180' hyb	SR
Tomato, 'Floradade' o-p	BU,SN
Tomato, 'Floramerica'	DE
Tomato, 'Fond Red Mini Plum'	SE
Tomato, four colour sweet cherry	DI
Tomato, 'Fox Cherry'	SD
Tomato, 'Full Flavour Pack'	T
Tomato, 'Furon'	SK
Tomato, 'Galina'	SP
Tomato, 'Garden Pearl'	BS,DT
Tomato, 'Gardener's Delight' o-p	w.a.
Tomato, 'Gemini' F1	D
Tomato, 'German'	JO
Tomato, 'German Gold'	AB
Tomato, 'German Striped'	JO
Tomato, 'Giant, Experimental Variety SEY2'	SE
Tomato, 'Gioia della Mensa'	B,FR
Tomato, 'Glacier'	DN,SN,SP
Tomato, 'Glamour' o-p	SK,SR
Tomato, 'Gold Dust'	JO
Tomato, 'Gold Nugget'	AB,DD,JO,KS,PI,SP,TE
Tomato, 'Golden Boy' F1	BS,PI,PK,S,SN
Tomato, 'Golden Cherry' F1	SK,SN
Tomato, 'Golden Delight'	AB
Tomato, 'Golden Jubilee' F1	V
Tomato, 'Golden Queen'	PI,SP
Tomato, 'Golden Sunrise' o-p	BD,BS,BY,C,CO,D,DT,F, J,KI,L,MO,RO,S,SK,ST, SU,T,TH,TU,VH
Tomato, 'Golden Tomboy' F1	CO
Tomato, 'Goldie'	JO
Tomato, 'Goldstar' F1	K,KI,MO
Tomato, 'Gourmet'	U
Tomato, 'Gourmet Marmande' o-p	SN
Tomato, 'Graham's Good Keeper'	SP
Tomato, 'Grande Rose' hyb	SK
Tomato, 'Great White Beefsteak' o-p	KS,SN
Tomato, 'Green Bell Pepper'	AB,DI
Tomato, 'Green en Grappes'	AB,SN,VS
Tomato, 'Green Grape' o-p	DD,SN,TU
Tomato, 'Green Zebra' o-p	AB,DD,DI,SN,SP,VS
Tomato, Greenhouse Assortment	M
Tomato, 'Greenwich'	AB

TOMATO

Tomato, 'Grenadier' F1	BS, S
Tomato, 'GS 12' hyb	BU
Tomato, 'Guindilla'	BS
Tomato, 'Halley 3155' hyb	SR
Tomato, 'Harbinger' F1	BY,CO,D,KI,S,SU
Tomato, 'Harbinger' o-p	BS,SN,TH
Tomato, 'Harvestvee'	SK
Tomato, 'Harzfeuer' F1	V
Tomato, 'Hayslip' o-p	DD,SN
Tomato, 'Heart of the Bull'	AB,FR
Tomato, 'Heinz 1350'	BS
Tomato, 'Heinz 1439' o-p	BU,DD,SK
Tomato, 'Heinz 1765'	SK
Tomato, 'Herald'	M
Tomato, 'Hillbilly' o-p	SN
Tomato, 'Histon Early'	U
Tomato, 'Homestead' o-p	SN
Tomato, 'Husky Gold'	SK
Tomato, 'Husky Red'	SK
Tomato, 'Hy-Beef 9904' hyb	SK
Tomato, 'Immune'	AB
Tomato, 'Imur Prior Beta'	AB
Tomato, 'Incas' F1	D,S,SR
Tomato, 'Ingegnoli Giant'	FR,SN
Tomato, IPB	BF
Tomato, 'Ipsolon' F1	BS,D,S
Tomato, 'Italian Gold' F1	SK
Tomato, Italian Paste	BF
Tomato, 'Italian Stallion'	SP
Tomato, 'Ivory Egg' o-p	SN
Tomato, 'Jackpot' hyb	SN,SR
Tomato, 'Jaune St. Vincent' o-p	SN
Tomato, 'Jersey Devil'	AB
Tomato, 'Jetstar'	DE,SN
Tomato, 'Johnny's 361' F1	JO
Tomato, 'Joie de la Table' o-p	SN,VS
Tomato, 'Joker' hyb	SR
Tomato, 'JR-6' o-p	BS
Tomato, 'Jubilee'	BU,RO
Tomato, 'Jumbo'	AB,SK
Tomato, 'Kalimba' F1	FR
Tomato, 'Kentucky Beefsteak' o-p	SN
Tomato, 'Kootenai'	AB,TE
Tomato, 'Kotlas'	JO
Tomato, 'La Carotina' o-p	SN,VS
Tomato, 'La Rossa' F1	JO,PI,PK,SR
Tomato, 'Landry's Russian'	DE
Tomato, 'Large Red Cherry' o-p	AB,BF,BU
Tomato, 'Large Vida'	BS
Tomato, 'Lemon Boy' F1	DE,PK,SK,VY
Tomato, 'Lemon Plum' o-p	SN
Tomato, 'Libra' F1	BS,CO,DT,KI,SU
Tomato, 'Long Keeper'	AB,TE
Tomato, 'Long Red' o-p	SN
Tomato, 'Lunch Bucket'	SK,SP
Tomato, 'Lylia Cerisette'	SN,VS
Tomato, 'Lylia' o-p	SN
Tomato, 'Macero II' hyb	SK
Tomato, 'Madagascar' o-p	SN,VS
Tomato, 'Maja' o-p	B,SN,SU
Tomato, 'Mandarin'	AB
Tomato, 'Manhattan' F1	BS
Tomato, 'Manitoba'	SK
Tomato, 'Marglobe' o-p	BS,DE,RO,SN
Tomato, 'Marglobe Supreme Imp' o-p	SR
Tomato, 'Marion'	BS

Tomato, 'Marizol Purple'	DD
Tomato, 'Marmande Ancienne'o-p	SN
Tomato, 'Marmande' o-p	BD,BS,BY,C,D,DT,F,FR, GO,J,KI,S,SN,ST,SU,TH, U,V
Tomato, 'Marmande Super' o-p	BS,CO
Tomato, 'Marmande VF' super early	FR
Tomato, 'Mars'	SD
Tomato, 'Marvel Striped'	AB,SD
Tomato, 'Matador' F1	BS,FR,T
Tomato, 'Matt's Wild Cherry'	JO,SP
Tomato, 'Max' F1	FR
Tomato, 'Megatom'	TU,V
Tomato, 'Merced' F1	SK,SR
Tomato, 'Mexican'	SN,VS
Tomato, 'Mexican Honey' o-p	SN,VS
Tomato, 'MH 603'	SK
Tomato, 'Micado Violettor'	DD
Tomato, 'Micro-Tom'	PI
Tomato, 'Milano' hyb	SR
Tomato, 'Mini-Orange'	SN
Tomato, 'Minibel'	B,C,F
Tomato, 'Mirabel'	M
Tomato, 'Mirabelle Blanche' o-p	SN,VS
Tomato, 'Miracle Sweet'	DE,VY
Tomato, 'Mirror' F1	YA
Tomato, mix	GO
Tomato, mix sm fruited	PK,SK
Tomato, 'Money Cross'	B,BS,MO
Tomato, 'Moneymaker - Dutch Victory'	BS
Tomato, 'Moneymaker' o-p	B,BD,BS,BY,C,D,DT,F, J,KI,L,MC,MO,R,S,SN, ST,T,TU,U,V,VH,YA
Tomato, 'Monte's Gold'	DE
Tomato, 'Montecarlo VFN' F1	FR
Tomato, 'Montfavet'	GO
Tomato, 'Mortgage Lifter'	DI,KS,SP
Tomato, 'Moskvich'	JO
Tomato, 'Mountain Belle' hyb	SR
Tomato, 'Mountain Delight' F1	PK
Tomato, 'Mountain Fresh' F1	SK,SR
Tomato, 'Mountain Gold PVP' o-p	BU,SK,SR
Tomato, 'Mountain Pride' F1	BS,BU,DT,SK,SN,SR
Tomato, 'Mountain Spring' F1	SK,SR
Tomato, 'Mr.Stripey'	KS,SN
Tomato, 'MS-10 FT-R' F1	V
Tomato, 'Mt. Athos'	AB
Tomato, 'Napoli VF' o-p	B,DE,FR,SN
Tomato, 'Nebraska Wedding' o-p	AB,KS,SN
Tomato, 'Nemapeel' F1	FR
Tomato, 'Nemastar' hyb	SN
Tomato, 'Nepal'	AB,DD
Tomato, 'Neverwill'	AB
Tomato, 'New Yorker' o-p	SK,SN
Tomato, 'New Zealand Pear'	AB
Tomato, 'Niagara Belle'	SK
Tomato, 'Nigeria'	SP
Tomato, 'Nimbus'	S
Tomato, 'Noire Charbonneuse' o-p	SN,VS
Tomato, 'Nova'	AB
Tomato, 'Oaxacan Pink'	AB,DD
Tomato, 'Odessa'	AB
Tomato, 'Old German' o-p	SN
Tomato, 'Olomovic'	AB,DD
Tomato, 'Olympic' hyb	FR,SR
Tomato, 'Opal's Homestead'	AB

TOMATO

Tomato, 'Orange Jubilee'	DD
Tomato, 'Orange Queen'	SD,SK
Tomato, 'Oregon Oxheart' o-p	SN
Tomato, 'Oregon Spring'	AB,JO,PI,SD,TE
Tomato, 'Oroma'	DD
Tomato Ortigia	J
Tomato, 'Ostona'	BS
Tomato, 'Outdoor Girl'	B,BS,BY,CO,DT,J,KI, M,MO
Tomato, 'Oxheart Giant'	AB,SU
Tomato, 'Oxheart' o-p	BS,DE,HU,SN,TH
Tomato, 'Ozark Pink'	DD
Tomato, 'Palestinian'	AB,DD
Tomato, 'Palla di Fuoco'	B,FR
Tomato, 'Pannovoy'	K
Tomato, 'Patio' F1	DE,PK,SK,SR
Tomato, 'Payette'	DD
Tomato, 'Peacevine'	SD,SP
Tomato, 'Pearly Pink Cherry'	AB
Tomato, 'Pearson'	AB,BU
Tomato, 'Pepe' F1	FR
Tomato, Pepper	BF
Tomato, 'Perla Rossa'	BS
Tomato, 'Persimmon'	AB,DD,SN,TE
Tomato, 'Peruvian Horn'	SN
Tomato, 'Petit Coeur de Boeuf'	SN,
Tomato, 'Peto 76' o-p	SR
Tomato, 'Phyra' o-p	B,BS,C,CO,KI,MC,SU,V
Tomato, 'Pik Rite' hyb	SK
Tomato, 'Pilgrim' hyb	PK,SR,VY
Tomato, 'Pineapple'	CO,KS,SN,TU
Tomato, 'Pink KR-381' hyb	SK
Tomato, 'Pink Pear'	SN
Tomato, 'Pink Ping Pong'	AB
Tomato, 'Pioneer 2'	AB
Tomato, 'Piranto' F1	M
Tomato, 'Pixie' F1	BS,CO,M,ST,SU
Tomato, 'Plaisir d'Ete' o-p	SN
Tomato, 'Plumito'	RO
Tomato, 'Polar Baby'	AB,DN
Tomato, 'Polish Giant'	SD
Tomato, 'Pomme d'Amore'	AB,DD
Tomato, 'Pomme Rouge'	SN,VS
Tomato, 'Ponderosa' o-p	AB,HU,KS,SN
Tomato, 'Porter'	AB,DD
Tomato, Potato leaf	BF
Tomato, 'Potato Leaf White'	SP
Tomato, 'Potato Red Skins'	AB
Tomato, 'Potiron Ecarlate' o-p	SN,VS
Tomato, 'Prairie Fire'	SP,TE
Tomato, 'President' F1	DE
Tomato, 'Primato' F1	D
Tomato, 'Principe Borghese'	AB,B,DI,FR,JO,KS,PI, RC,SN,SP
Tomato, 'Prisca' F1	M
Tomato, 'Pritchard' o-p	SN
Tomato, 'Prize of The Trials'	SD
Tomato, 'Prometeo'	AB
Tomato, 'Pruden's Purple'	AB,DD,JO,PI
Tomato, 'PSX 537291' hyb	SR
Tomato, 'Puebla' hyb	SR
Tomato, 'Pusa Ruby'	AB,RC
Tomato, 'Quick Pick' F1	PK
Tomato, 'Red Alert'	B,BD,BY,CO,DT,F,J,KI, M,MO,SE,SN,ST,SU, U,VY

Tomato, 'Red Cherry'	AB,BH,RC,RO,SE,SR
Tomato, 'Red Currant'	DD,DE,HU,JO
Tomato, 'Red House'	SD
Tomato, 'Red Peach' o-p	DI,SN,TU
Tomato, 'Red Pear' o-p	AB,DE,JO,KS,SN
Tomato, 'Red Plum'	SN,VS
Tomato, 'Red Robin' F1	PK
Tomato, 'Red Rose'	SN
Tomato, 'Red Star' hyb	SN
Tomato, 'Red Sun' F1	JO
Tomato, 'Red Supreme'	AB
Tomato, 'Redheart'	AB
Tomato, 'Redrider' hyb	SK
Tomato, 'Redskin'	SN,VS
Tomato, 'Redstone' hyb	SK
Tomato, 'Reif Red Heart'	JO
Tomato, 'Reine de Claude Rouge' o-p	SN,VS
Tomato, 'Reine de Sainte Marthe' o-p	SN,VS
Tomato, 'Rio Fuego'	B,FR
Tomato, 'Rio Grande'	B,FR
Tomato, 'Rocamar'	BS
Tomato, 'Rocky' F1	FR
Tomato, 'Roma Puree'	AB,SD
Tomato, 'Roma VF'	AB,BD,BS,BU,DE,DT,F, KI,M,PI,PK,SK,SN,SP, SR,ST,TU,U,VY
Tomato, 'Roncardo'	BS
Tomato Rootstock, 'He Man' F1	DT
Tomato, 'Ropreco'	AB,SD
Tomato, 'Rose de Berne' o-p	SN,VS
Tomato, 'Rossol'	DD
Tomato, 'Royal Flush' hyb	SR
Tomato, 'Royale des Guineaux' o-p	SN,VS
Tomato, 'Ruby Cluster' F1	JO
Tomato, 'Ruby Rakes Yellow'	AB
Tomato, 'Ruffled'	DD,SN
Tomato, 'Russe' o-p	SN,VS
Tomato, Russian mix	DI
Tomato, 'Rutgers' o-p	BS,DE,HU,PK,SN,SR
Tomato, 'Saint Pierre' o-p	B,DD,GO,M,RC,PI,SN, SU,TH
Tomato, 'Sainte Lucie' o-p	SN,VS
Tomato, 'Saladette 3019' hyb	SR
Tomato, 'Saladmaster'	AB
Tomato, 'Saltspring Sunrise'	AB
Tomato, 'San Fran Frog'	DD,SP
Tomato, 'San Marzano'	AB,B,BF,BS,BY,C,CO, FR,KI,KS,MC,SK,SN, ST,SU,TH,V
Tomato, 'San Marzano - Lampadina'	B,FR,PI
Tomato, 'Sanibel' hyb	SR
Tomato, 'Santa'	B,BS,SN,T
Tomato, 'Santiam'	AB,DD
Tomato, 'Saucy'	DD
Tomato, 'Sausalito' hyb	VY
Tomato, 'Scarlet Empress' hyb	SK
Tomato, 'Schimmeig Creg'	AB
Tomato, 'Scotia'	SK,VY
Tomato, 'Seville Cross'	S
Tomato, 'Sheriff' F1	JO
Tomato, 'Sherry's Sweet Italian'	DI
Tomato, 'Shimmeig Creg'	DI
Tomato, 'Shirley' F1	BD,BO,BS,BY,CO,DT,F, J,KI,L,M,MO,R,S,SB, SE,SN,ST,T,TU, U,VH,YA
Tomato, 'Showell's Red'	SD

TOMATO

Name	Code
Tomato, 'Siberian'	AB,DD,DN
Tomato, 'Sigmabush'	S
Tomato, 'Siletz'	AB,DD,JO,TE
Tomato, 'Silvery Fir'	AB
Tomato, 'Sioux'	U
Tomato, 'Slava'	AB
Tomato, 'Sleaford Abundance'	M,SN
Tomato, 'Small Fry VFN' F1	FR,SK
Tomato, 'Snowball' o-p	SN
Tomato, 'Sonatine'	BY,S
Tomato, 'Spectra'	BS,MO
Tomato, 'Spectrum 882' F1	SK,SR
Tomato, 'Spitfire' F1	SK,SR
Tomato, 'Spoon' F1	PK
Tomato, 'Square Paste'	SK
Tomato, 'Stakeless' o-p	BU
Tomato, 'Starfire'	AB,SK
Tomato, 'Stone'	PI
Tomato, 'Stonor Exhibition'	BY,RO
Tomato, 'Stresa' F1	BS,MO,YA
Tomato, 'Stupice'	AB,SD,TE
Tomato, 'Sub-arctic Plenty'	AB,DN,HU,SK
Tomato, 'Sugar Bunch' F1	PK
Tomato, 'Sugar Lump'	DD
Tomato, 'Summerpink' hyb	SK
Tomato, 'Summerset' hyb	SK
Tomato, 'Sun Baby'	B,BD,DT,F,K,MO,TU
Tomato, 'Sun Belle'	B,F,L,MO
Tomato, 'Sun Cherry' F1	JO,KS
Tomato, 'Sunbeam' hyb	SK
Tomato, 'Sundrop'	AB,HU
Tomato, 'Sungold' F1	BD,BS,JO,L,MO,PI,T,TE,U
Tomato, 'Sunmaster' hyb	BU,PK,
Tomato, 'Super Bush' F1	PI
Tomato, 'Super Marmande'	AB,B,M,MO,SN,VH,VS
Tomato, 'Super Roma VF'	B,FR,T,VH
Tomato, 'Super Sarno' F1	FR
Tomato, 'Super Sioux' o-p	BU,SD
Tomato, 'Supersonic' hyb	SN
Tomato, 'Supersteak' F1	T,VH
Tomato, 'Supersweet' F1	M,MO,PK,SN,SU
Tomato, 'Supra' hyb	SR
Tomato, 'Sweet 100' F1 mini	BS,C,CO,DT,F,J,KI,S,SK,SN,T,U,V,VH
Tomato, 'Sweet Chelsea'	DE,PI,SK
Tomato, 'Sweet Cherry' F1	B,BS,F
Tomato, 'Sweet Cherry' o-p	SN
Tomato, 'Sweet Gold'	SK
Tomato, 'Sweet Million'	BS,GO,KS,PI,PK,SK,SN,TE,U,VY
Tomato, 'Sweet Orange'	SK
Tomato, 'Sweet Peel'	SN
Tomato, 'Sweetie'	DE
Tomato, 'Swifty Belle'	SK
Tomato, 'Tangerine' o-p	SN,VS
Tomato, 'Taxi'	AB,DD,JO,SP,TE,U
Tomato, 'Teardrop' F1	PK
Tomato, 'Thai Pink'	SP
Tomato, 'The Amateur'	BD,BS,BY,C,KI,MO,S,SN,U
Tomato, 'The Chef's Brigade'	T
Tomato, 'The Helen Hawkins' org	SN
Tomato, 'The John Hawkins' org	SN
Tomato, 'Thessaloniki' o-p	AB,SD,SN
Tomato, 'Tiger Stripe'	BF,SP
Tomato, 'Tigerella' o-p	AB,B,BS,CO,DE,DT,F,HU,KI,M,S,SK,SN,SP,SU,T,U,V,VH,VS
Tomato, 'Tiny Tim' o-p	B,BS,DT,KI,PI,SK,SN,SU,TU,VY
Tomato, 'Tip Top'	PI,SP
Tomato, 'Tomboy'	BS
Tomato, 'Tornado' F1	BS,BY,CO,D,F,KI,M,MO,S,TU
Tomato, 'Totem' F1	BS,BY,D,J,KI,MC,MO,SN,ST,U,VH
Tomato, trio	PL
Tomato, 'Trio' F1	BS,YA
Tomato, 'Tropic'	DN
Tomato, 'Tumbler' F1	BD,BS,D,DT,J,M,MO,R,S,SE,SN,T,U,VH,YA
Tomato, 'Turbo' F1	BS
Tomato, 'Typhoon' F1	BD,BS,D,DT,J,K,L,MO
Tomato, 'Ultra Boy' hyb	SK
Tomato, 'Ultra Girl' hyb	SK
Tomato, 'Ultra Magnum' hyb	SK
Tomato, 'Ultra Pink' hyb	SK
Tomato, 'Ultrasonic' hyb	SK
Tomato, 'Ultrasweet' hyb	SK
Tomato, 'Urbikany'	DD
Tomato, 'Valente VF'	FR
Tomato, 'Valerie' hyb	SN
Tomato, 'Vanessa'	K,BS
Tomato, 'Veeroma'	SK
Tomato, 'Ventura'	B,FR
Tomato, 'Vermillion'	AB
Tomato, 'Verna orange'	DI
Tomato, 'VF 6203' o-p	SR
Tomato, 'Victory'	B,SB
Tomato, 'Virginia'	K,BS
Tomato, 'Visitation Valley'	AB
Tomato, 'Vitador' F1	YA
Tomato, 'Viva Italia' F1	DE,GO,PK
Tomato, 'Walter' o-p	SN
Tomato, 'Washington'	DD
Tomato, 'Wayahead'	AB
Tomato, 'Weird and Wonderful'	DI
Tomato, 'West Virginia Hillbilly'	AB
Tomato, 'Whippersnapper'	JO
Tomato, 'White'	DD
Tomato, 'White Wonder' o-p	CO,SN,SP,TU
Tomato, 'Willamette'	DD
Tomato, 'Wonder Light'	JO
Tomato, 'World's Largest'	DI
Tomato, 'World's Smallest'	DI
Tomato, 'Yellow Belgium'	DD
Tomato, 'Yellow Bell'	PI
Tomato, 'Yellow Canary'	B,BS,MO
Tomato, 'Yellow Cherry' o-p	BH,SN,SP
Tomato, 'Yellow Cocktail' o-p	B,BS,C,KI,SU
Tomato, 'Yellow Currant'	DE,DI,JO,KS,RO,SD
Tomato, 'Yellow Debut' F1	BS,D,YA
Tomato, 'Yellow Delicious'	DI
Tomato, 'Yellow Peach' o-p	DI,SN,TU
Tomato, 'Yellow Pear' o-p	AB,DE,GO,JO,KS,PI,RC,SD,SN,SP,TE,TH,V
Tomato, 'Yellow Perfection'	AB,M,SD,U
Tomato, 'Yellow Plum'	DE,SN,VS
Tomato, 'Yellow River' F1	FR
Tomato, 'Yellow Ruffle'	AB,SD
Tomato, 'Yellow St. Vincent'	SN,VS

TOMATO

Tomato, 'Yellow Stuffer'	AB,DE,HU,SK,SN,VS
Tomato, 'Yellow Tangerine'	SP
Tomato, 'Zapotec'	AB,SD
Tronchuda	B,C,RC
Turnip, 'All Top' F1	PK
Turnip, 'Arcoat'	BS,S,YA
Turnip, 'Champion Green Top Yellow'	TU
Turnip, 'Gilfeather'	DI,EH,PI
Turnip, 'Golden Ball'	AB,B,BD,BS,BY,CO,D, DT,J,KI,M,MO,S,ST,SU, TH,TU,U
Turnip, 'Green Globe'	S
Turnip, 'Green Top Stone'	B,BS,BY,J,KI,L,M,MO, ST,TH,YA
Turnip, 'Hakurei' F1	JO
Turnip, 'Hakutaka' F1	D
Turnip, 'Ivory'	M
Turnip, 'Manchester Market' see Gr. Top	
Turnip, 'Market Express' F1	C,DT,KI,YA
Turnip,'Milan Purple Forcing'	BS
Turnip, 'Milan Purple Top'	AB,B,BD,BS,BU,D,DT, F,J,KI,MC,MO,S,ST,SU, TH,TU,U,VH
Turnip, 'Milan Red'	BS,GO,TH
Turnip, 'Milan White'	BS,BY,L,KS
Turnip, 'Milan White Forcing'	BS
Turnip, 'Model White'	BS,D
Turnip, 'Orange Jelly' see Golden Ball	
Turnip, 'Petrowski'	DD,DN
Turnip, 'Presto' (Tokyo Market Sagami)	C
Turnip, 'Purple Top White Globe' o-p	B,BF,DE,DN,JO,PI,PK, SK,SN,SR,TE,VY
Turnip, 'Red Round'	KS
Turnip, 'Royal Crest' hyb	SR
Turnip, 'Royal Crown' F1	BS,PI,PK,SK,SR,SU
Turnip, 'Scarlet Ball'	DD
Turnip, 'Seven Top' o-p	HU,SK,SR
Turnip, 'Shogoin'	B,DE
Turnip, 'Snowball'*Early White Stone	B,BD,BS,BY,C,CO,D, DT,F,J,KI,M,MC,MO,S, ST,SU,T,TH,TU,VH
Turnip, 'Sprinter' see 'Milan Purple Forcing'	
Turnip, 'Stanis'	BS
Turnip, 'Tokyo Cross' F1	BS,CO,D,F,KS,PI,S,SE, SU,T,TU
Turnip, 'Tokyo Market' Second Early	C,DE,DD
Turnip, 'Tokyo Top' F1'	BS
Turnip, 'Topper' hyb	SR
Turnip, 'Typhon'	BY
Turnip, 'Veitch's Red Globe'	BS,CO,KI,TH,TU
Turnip, 'Vertus'	GO
Turnip, 'White Egg'	DN,HU
Turnip, 'White Lady' F1	PK,SK
Turnip, 'Yellow Globe'	HU
Turnip, 'Yorii Spring'	AB
Vegetable Chinese/Oriental Collection	F
Vegetable Collection 1	F
Vegetable Collection 2	F
Vegetable Collections	BD
Vegetable Mini Collection	D,M
Vegetable Seed Collection, 13 Varieties	D
Vegetable Seed Collection , 26 Varieties	D
Vegetable Seed Collection , 'Mediterranean'	U
Vegetable 'Stir-Fry Collection'	D
Water Pepper	KS
Water Spinach	KS,SU

Wheat Grains, 'Alaska Spelt'	SP
Wheat Grains, 'Black Einkorn'	SP
Wheat Grains, 'Dw. Indian'	SP
Wheat Grains, 'Emmer'	SP
Wheat Grains, 'Ethiopian Mix'	SP
Wheat Grains, 'Hard Red Calcutta'	SP
Wheat Grains, 'Kamut'	SP
Wheat Grains, 'Khapli Spelt'	SP
Wheat Grains, 'Ladoga'	SP
Wheat Grains, 'Lavras Barzilian'	SP
Wheat Grains, 'Marquis'	SP
Wheat Grains, 'Red Fife'	SP
Wheat Grains, 'Spelta'	SP
Wheat Grains, 'Stanley'	SP
Wheat Grains, 'Thatcher'	SP
Wheat Grains, 'Triticum'	DD,RC,SP
Wheat Grains, 'Turkish Mix'	SP
Wheat Grains, 'Utrecht Blue'	SP
Wheat Grains, 'Vavilov'	SP
Wheat Grains, 'White Sonoran'	SP

HERBS

Agrimony	AB,BH,CE,H,JO,JV,PO, RI,SU		SU,TE,V,VY
Ajwain	B,C,RC,RI,SU	Basil, Lemon 'Mrs Burns'	B,C,RI
Ajwain, Bengal bold	RC	Basil, Lettuce Leaved	AB,B,BF,BH,C,CO,CP,
Ajwain, Bengal thin	RC		DD,DE,FR,GO,H,HU,JV,
Alexanders	AB,BH,CE,SU,TH		KS,PI,RI,SD,SK,SN
Alkanet	H,RI,SU,TH	Basil, Lime	JO
Ambrosia	AB,RI	Basil, Liquorice	AB,B,C,CA,CP,HU,PI,PK
Angelica	AB,BD,BH,BS,BY,C,CE,	Basil, 'Mammoth'	BH,FR,RI
	CO,J,JE,JO,KI,Mc,MO,	Basil, Mexican	C,DD,PI
	R,RI,SD,ST,SU,TE,TH,	Basil, 'Minette'	B,PK,RI
	U,V	Basil, mix	BH,PL
Anise	AB,BD,BS,BY,C,CA,CE,	Basil 'Napoletano'	B,BS,C,CP,HU,KS,RC,
	CO,DE,DI,FR,H,JE,JO,		SU
	JV,KI,Mc,MO,PI,PK,R,	Basil 'New Guinea'	B,C,CP
	RI,SK,ST,SU,TH,V,VY	Basil, 'Opal'	AB,BH,H,JV,PI
Anise Hyssop	AB,BH,GO,JO,PI,PO,RI,	Basil, 'Opal' purple variegated	SD
	SD,SP,SU,TE	Basil, 'Osmin Purple'	B,JO,PI
Annual Herb Mixture	M	Basil, 'Piccolo'	AB,B,RC
Arnica Chamissonis	BH,CE,JO,JV,RI,SU	Basil, 'Purple'	B,CE,CP,TH
Arnica Cordifolia	AB	Basil, 'Purple' dw	B
Arnica Montana	AB,PO,RI,SU	Basil, 'Red Rubin'	B,CE,D,JO,KS,RI,SK,S
Aromatic Seasonings	SE,T		R,SU,TE,V,VY
Artichoke, Globe	H	Basil, 'Ruffles Green'	B,BD,BH,BS,CE,JV,KS,
Arugula Special Select	SR		MO,RI,SK,SU,VY
Asafoetida	AB	Basil, 'Ruffles' Mixed	U
Ashwaganda	AB,PO,RI,SD,SP	Basil, 'Ruffles Purple'	B,BH,BS,CA,CE,DE,GO,
Balm	AB,BS,BY,C,J,L,JE,MC		H,JO,JV,K,KS,MO,PI,
	,MO,PO,R,RI,S,SK,V		PK,RI,S,SK,SU,TE,VY
Balm, Lemon	AB,BD,BH,CE,CO,CP,	Basil, 'Siam Queen'	B,F,JO,PK,RI,SK,TE,U,
	DD,DE,F,FR,JO,JV,KI,		VY
	KS,M,PI,PK,PO,RC,RI,	Basil, Special Select FT	RI
	SD,SK,ST,SU,T,TE,TH,	Basil, 'Spice'	B,CE,JO,RI,SU
	VH,VY	Basil, 'Spicy Globe'	B,C,GO,KS,RI,SK,SU,
Basil, African blue	RI		TE,VY
Basil, Anise	B,BH,BS,CE,DD,DE,JV	Basil, Sweet	w.a.
	KS,RC,RI,SD,SU	Basil, 'Sweet Green Bouquet'	B,BH,D,RI,SU
Basil, Bubikopf	BH	Basil, Thai	AB,B,BH,C,CE,CP,D,DD,
Basil, Bush (Greek)	w.a.		DT,JO,KS,PO,RC,RI,SD,
Basil, Camphor	BH,RI		SE,SN
Basil, 'Cinnamon'	AB,B,BD,BH,BS,C,CA,	Basil Thyme	RI
	CE,CP,D,DE,GO,HU,JO,	Basil, 'Valentino'	PK
	JV,KI,KS,MO,RI,SK,PI,	Basil, Wild	BH,RI
	PK,SD,SU,T,TE,VY	Bay Laurel	GO,RI
Basil, Clove	BH	Bergamot, Lemon	BS,BH,CE,DD,JV,MC,
Basil, Compatto FT	RI		PK,RI,S,SU
Basil, Culinary mix	PI	Bergamot, Mint	V
Basil, 'Dark Opal'	BD,BS,C,CO,DE,FR,HU,	Bergamot, Oswego tea	BD,BH,JE,SD
	KS,Mc,MO,PK,RI,ST,SU	Bergamot, Wild	AB,BH,DI,JO,JV,KI,RI,
Basil, East Indian	RI		SD,SU,TH
Basil, 'Fino Verde'	B,CP,DE,FR,HU,KS,PI,RI	Betony	AB,BH,CE,JV,PO,RI,SU
Basil, 'Genovese'	AB,B,BH,C,DD,JO,KS,	Borage	w.a.
	L,MO,RI,SD,SK,SN,SR,	Borage, White	CE,SU
	SU	Bugle	CE,RI
Basil, 'Genovese Giant'	KS	Burdock	AB,CE,JO,PO,RI
Basil, 'Greek Mini'	KS,SN,SU	Calamint	C,CE,JV,RI,SU,V
Basil, 'Green Globe'	RI,SU	Campion, Bladder	CE,SU
Basil, Holy	AB,C,CA,CE,DE,HU,JO,	Campion, Red	CE,SU
	KS,PI,PO,RI,S,SD,SU,V	Caper	DD,DI,PK,RI
Basil, Holy red & green	JO	Caraway	w.a.
Basil, 'Horapha'	CE,SU,V	Cardoon	AB,DD,H,KI,SR,ST
Basil, Italian	CA,CE,DE,FR,JO,PI,PK,	Catmint	AB,BH,CE,H,PK
	RC,SR,V	Catmint, 'Faassenii'	BH,JV,RI
Basil, Lemon	AB,BH,BS,CA,CE,CO,CP,	Catmint, Lemon	JV,PO
	DE,GO,H,HU,JO,JV,KS,	Catnip	AB,BH,BU,CA,CE,DD,
	PI,PK,RI,SD,SK,SN,SR,		DE,DN,GO,JO,JV,PI,PK,
			PO,RC,RI,SD,SK,SU,TE,

328

CATNIP

	VY
Catnip, Lemon	BH,CE,DD,PK,RI,SD,SU
Celandine, Greater	AB,BH,CE,PO,RI,SU,V
Celandine, Lesser	CE
Celery, Cutting	BH,DD,JO,M,TH
Celery, Par-cel	BH,H,M,PK,PO,RI,TH,U
Celery Parcel, 'Zwolsche Krul'	C,T
Centaury	CE,PO,RI,SU
Chamomile, Dyers	AB,CE,JV,PO,RI,SU
Chamomile, German	AB,BD,BH,C,CA,CE,CO,
	D,DE,FR,GO,H,JE,JO,
	MO,PK,PI,PO,RC,RI,
	SD,SK,SU,TE,TH,V,VY
Chamomile, Matricaria see German	
Chamomile, Roman	AB,C,BD,BH,BS,CE,CO,
	DE,F,H,JO,JV,KI,L,MC,
	MO,PI,PK,PO,R,RC,
	RI,ST,SUT,U,V
Chervil	w.a.
Chervil, Curled	BH,C,CA,DE,H,KI,MC,
	MO,PK,RI,S,SU,TH,VY
Chicory	AB,BH,CE,H,JV,RI,SU,V
Chives	w.a.
Chives, Fine Leaved	BH,H,JO,SU
Chives, Forcing	SU
Chives, Garlic	w.a.
Chopsuey Green	JV
Choy Sum	JV
Cicely, Sweet	AB,BD,BS,BY,C,CE,CO,
	DE,H,JV,Mc,MO,PK,PO,
	RI,TH
Cilantro, 'Festival'	PK
Comfrey	AB,C,PK,RI,ST,SU,V
Coriander	w.a.
Coriander, Cilantro Broad-leaf	PI,SD,SR
Coriander, Cilantro,Chinese Parsley	AB,B,BF,BU,C,CO,D,
	DE,GO,HU,JO,M,RC,
	RI,SE,SK,SR,T,TE,U,VY
Coriander, Dhani-ya	RC
Coriander, Leisure	PO
Coriander, Moroccan	KI,SU
Coriander, Roman	C,D,SU
Coriander, 'Santo'	H
Coriander, Tian Ching	RC
Coriander, Yen Sai	RC
Corn Salad	H,PO,TH
Cowslip	H,JV,PO,RI
Cress	BH,CA,DE,JO,PO,RI,SR
Cumin	AB,B,BD,BH,BS,BY,C,
	CA,CO,DE,GO,HU,KI,
	MC,MO,PI,PK,R,RC,
	RI,ST,SU,TE,TH,V,VY
Cumin, Black	BH,BS,DE,RI,SU
Dandelion	AB,B,BH,BS,CO,JO,
	RI,SK,SU
Dill	w.a.
Dill, Bouquet	AB,B,BS,BU,CA,DE,
	DN,G,JO,KI,KS,PK,RI,
	SD,SK,SR,SU,U,VY
Dill, Dukat	B,BS,GO,JO,K,PI,PO,
	RI,SD,SK,SR,SU,TE
Dill, 'Fernleaf'	BH,DD,DE,GO,JO,PI,
	PK,PO,SK,TE,VY
Dill 'Hercules'	B,C,RI
Dill, Indian	RC,RI,SU
Dill, Mammoth	AB,BF,BS,CA,DE,SD,

Dill, 'Sari'	SU,TE
Dill Tetra leaf	T,V
Dill, Tetraploid	RI
Dill, Vierling	BH
Dock	B,C,RI,SU
Dog Rose	AB,RI
Dong Quai	CO
Dropwort	RI
Dyers Greenwood	CE,RI
Dyers Weld	CE,SU
Echinacea see main section	CE
Elecampane	AB,BH,CE,H,JE,JO,JV,
	PO,RI,SU
Endive, 'Tres Fine'	SE
Epazote	DE,JO,PI,PK,RC,RI,SD,
	TE
Eucalyptus, Lemon	H,RISU
Eucalyptus, Peppermint	RI,SU
Evening Primrose	BH,CE,DI,JO,JV,KS,
	PO,RI,SP,SU,TE
Fennel, 'Cantino'	BS
Fennel, Sweet	w.a.
Fennel, Sweet Bronze	AB,BD,BH,C,CE,CO,DD,
	DI,F,JV,K,KI,MO,PI,PO,
	RC,RI,S,SD,SU,TE,TH,
	V,VY
Fennel, 'Zefa Fino'	BH,GO,SD,SR
Fenugreek	AB,C,DE,GO,PI,RC,RI,
	SP,SR,SU
Fenugreek, Durga	RC
Feverfew	AB,BD,BH,BS,BY,C,CE,
	CO,DE,J,JO,JV,KI,L,MC,
	MO,PO,RI,S,SD,ST,
	SU,TH,V
Feverfew, Golden	BS,CE,JV,PO,RI
Figwort	CE,RI
Flax	AB,CE,RI,SU
Flax, Red	CE
Fleabane	CE,SU
Foxglove, ambigua	H,JV
Foxglove, lanata	H,RI
Foxglove, lutea	H,RI
Foxglove, purpurea	SU,PO,RI
Garlic	AB,PO,SU
Garlic Mustard	BS,CO,SU,T
Garlic, society (Thulbaghia)	CA
Gayfeather	BH,CE,RI,SU
Germander	BH,PK,RI
Ginger, wild	RI
Gingko biloba	RI
Ginseng, Asiatic	DD,PK,PO,RI,SU
Ginseng, Panax	JE,JO,PO,RI
Ginseng, Siberian	PO,RI
Goats Rue	BH,CE,RI,SU
Goldenseal	DD,JO,RI
Good King Henry(Mercury)	BS,BY,CE,CO,DD,JV,
	KI,PO,R,RI,TH
Greater Knapweed	CE
Greater Knapweed, Golden	CE
Greater Stitchwort	CE
Gypsywort	AB,CE,PO,RI
Heartsease	CE,JV,PO,RI,SU
Henbane	AB,CE,PO,RI
Herb Bennet	CE,PO,SU
Herb Collection, Culinary	C,DN,JV,PI,PK,SD,VY

EDIBLE FLOWERS

Herb Collection, Edible Flower	JV	Marigold, Pot	BF,BH,BS,C,H,JE,JO,
Herb Collection, Herbal Tea	JV		JV,MO,PO,RI,SP,ST,
Herb Collection, Herbal Wild Flower	JV		SU,T,TH
Herb Collection, Salad Herb	JV	Marjoram, annual	SK
Herb Collections	BD,GO	Marjoram, Pot	BD,BS,BY,C,CE,CO,JE,
Herb Robert	CE,RI		JV,KI,MC,MO,PO,R,RI,
Herbs, Companion Plants	T		ST,SU,T,TH,V
Herbs, Medicinal	SD	Marjoram, Sweet	w.a.
Hollyhock	H,KI,RI,SU,V	Meadowsweet	BH,CE,JV,PO,RI,SU,T
Hop	RI,ST,SU	Mexican Tea	C
Hops, Japanese	RI	Mint	BH,J,JO,M,MO,PI,S,
Horehound	AB,BD,BH,BS,BY,C,CE,		T,VH,VY
	CO,DD,DE,GO,JE,JO,	Mint, Apple	RI,SU
	JV,KI,MC,MO,PK,PO,RI,	Mint, Emperor's	BH,C,JV,RI,SU
	SU,TE,TH,V	Mint, Korean	BH,JV,PO,RI,SD,SU
Horehound, Black	SU	Mint, Lemon	C,DD,DE,DI,PK,TE
Horseradish Tree	DD,RI,SU	Mint, Menthol	RI
Hungarian Blue Breadseed Poppy	B,C,DD	Mint, Mountain	BH,C,DD,PK,RI,SU
Hyssop	AB,BD,BS,BY,C,CE,CO,	Mint, Namibian	BH
	DD,DE,GO,J,JE,JO,L,	Mint, Peppermint	AB,BH,BS,BY,C,CA,
	MC,MO,PI,PK,RI,S,SD,		CO,DE,GO,L,JE,JO,MC,
	SP,ST,SU,TE,TH,V,VY		MO,PK,R,SE,SU,V
Hyssop, Blue Flowered	BH,CE,H,JV,KI,PO,SU,	Mint, Spearmint	AB,BS,C,CA,CO,DE,F,
	TE		JE,JO,KI,MO,PK,R,SK,
Hyssop, Pink Flowered	BS,C,CE,JV,PO,RI,SU		ST,SU,TE,TH,V
Hyssop, White Flowered	BS,C,CE,JV,PO,SU,TE	Mint, Water	RI,SU
Incense Plant	JV	Monkshood	CE,RI
Jacob's Ladder	BH,CE,DD,JV,PO,RI,SU	Motherwort	AB,BH,CE,DD,DE,JO,
Jacob's Ladder, White	CE		PO,RI,SD,SU
Japanese Green, Mizuna	JV	Motherwort, Siberian	RI
Japanese Parsley, Mitsuba	CE,JV	Mountain tobacco	JE
Jicama	CA,HU,PI	Mugwort	AB,C,CE,JE,JO,RC,RI,
Kidney Vetch	CE		SD,SU,V
Ladies Mantle	AB,BH,CE,DE,JO,KS,	Mullein, Greater	AB,CE,DD,DE,H,JO,
	RI,SU		PO,RI,SU,V
Lady's Bedstraw	BH,CE,RI,SU	Myrrh	JE,SU,T
Lavender, angustifolia	AB,BD,BH,CA,CO,DE,	Nasturtium	BF,CE,GO,JV,RI,SU,VH
	DI,DN,GO,JV,KI,MO,PK,	Nettle	AB,BH,DD,DE,JO,RI,SD
	RI,SP,ST,SU,V,VH,VY	Onion, Welsh	BD,BH,BY,CO,H,JV,KI,
Lavender, French	CE,RI,SU		MO,PO,RI,ST,SU,TH
Lavender, 'Hidcote'	BH,CE,DE,H,JV,PK,	Onion, Welsh red	SU
	PO,RI,SU,TE	Orach, Gold	BS,CE,SU,
Lavender, 'Lady'	BH,PK,RI,SK,TE,VY	Orach, Green	SU
Lavender, latifolia	BH,CO,FR,JE,MC,	Orach, Red	BS,CE,DD,JV,SU
	MO,PK,RI,SU	Oregano	w.a.
Lavender, 'Munstead'	BH,CE,DD,DE,GO,JO,	Oregano, Greek	AB,BH,BS,C,DE,DI,GO,
	JV,PI,PK,RI,SD,SK,SU,		JO,JV,KI,KS,PI,PK,PO,
	TE		RI,SD,SU,TE
Lavender, officinalis	JE,PI	Oregano, Showy	C
Lavender, rosea	PK,RI	Oregano, white	JV
Lavender, spica see latifolia		Ox-Eye Daisy	CE,SU
Lavender, viridis, Canary Island	RI,SD	Papalo	RC
Lavender, Woolly	BH,CE,RI,SU	Para Cress, Spilanthes	SD
Lemongrass, East Indian	BH,RI,TE	Parsley, Bravour	BD,DT,U
Lovage	w.a.	Parsley, 'Champion Moss Curled'	C,DE,DT,VH
Madder	BH,RI,SU	Parsley, 'Curlina'	DI,F,KS
Mallow, Common	CE,JV,RI,SU	Parsley, Curly	CE,DD,JV,MO,PO,SD,
Mallow, 'Crispa'	CE		SU
Mallow, Field	BH,CE	Parsley, 'Envy'	S
Mallow, Marsh	AB,BH,BS,CE,DE,H,JE,	Parsley, Forest Green	GO,VY
	JO,JV,PO,RI,SU,TH	Parsley, French	BY,CE,JV,K,PO,R,SU
Mallow, Musk	BH,CE,DD,JV,RI,SU	Parsley, Genovese	KS
Mallow, Musk White	BH,CE,PO	Parsley, Hamburg	BD,C,F,KS,RI
Mamang	C,RC	Parsley, Italian	BH,CA,CE,DE,GO,KS,
Mandrake, European	PO,RI		PK,RI,SD,SU,VY
Marigold, 'Fiesta'	JV	Parsley, Moss Curled	BD,F,H,RI,SD

PARSLEY

Parsley, Neapolitan — C
Parsley, 'Pagoda' — PK
Parsley, Plain Leaved — BD,BH,CA,H,JE,MO,PI, RI,TH,U
Parsley, 'Triple Curled' — C,CA,DN,KS,PI,VH
Parsley, Turnip rooted — BH
Parsley, 'Unicurl' — KS
Parsley, Wild — BH,T
Pennyroyal — AB,BD,BH,BS,CE,CO, DD,DE,F,H,JO,JV,KI,MC, PI,PK,PO,RC,RI,SD,SU, TE,TH
Perilla Frutescens — C,CE,DD,H,JO,JV,KS,RI, SD,SR,TH
Perilla frutescens, purple — BH,GO,JO,JV,RI,SD,TH
Pimpernel — DD,RI,V
Plantain — AB,DD,DE,FR,JE,JO,RI
Pleurisy Root — CE,DE,JO,RI,SU
Pokeroot — AB,CE,PO,RI,SU
Poppy — AB,DD,H,JO,PO,RI,SU, V
Purple Loosestrife — CE,RI,SU
Purslane — BD,BS,BY,C,CE,H,JV,Mc
Purslane, Golden — BS,C,CE,CO,DD,JV,MO
Purslane, Green — BY,C,CO,JV
Pyrethrum — BH,DD,DI,JV,PK,PO,RI, SU
Pyrethrum, Kenyan cert — RI
Quillquina — SD
Quinine, wild — RI
Rampion — JE,RI,SU
Rauwolfia — RI
Rhubarb — DD,JE,JO,RI
Rocket — BD,BH,BS,BY,CE,DD, J,JV,K,KI,M,Mc,MO,PO, RI,SE,SK,ST,SU,T,TH,U, VH
Rocket, Wild — BH,JV,SU,TH
Rosemary — w.a
Rue — AB,BD,BH,BS,BY,CE, CO,DE,FR,JE,JV,KI,MC, MO,PI,PK,PO,RI,S,SD, SK,SU,V
Rue, 'Harlequin' (V) — RI
Rue, Syrian — RI
Safflower — AB,BH,CE,DE,RI,SU
Sage — w.a
Sage, Clary — AB,BS,CE,CO,JO,JV,PO, RI,RC,SD,SU
Sage, 'Extrakta' — RI
Sage, Painted — BS,CE,SU
Sage, Red — BH,RI
Salad Burnet — AB,BD,BH,BY,C,CA,CE, CO,DD,DE,GO,H,JE,JO, JV,KI,T,Mc,MO,PI,PO, RC,RI,S,SU,TH,V,VY
Sassafras — RI
Savory, Broad Leaved — CE
Savory, Creeping — BH,CE,RI
Savory, Lemon — RI
Savory, Summer — w.a.
Savory, Summer 'Aromata' — RI
Savory, Winter — w.a.
Scabious, Devils Bit — CE,SU
Scabious, Field — CE,SU
Scabious, Sheeps — CE

Scabious, Small — CE,SU
Scurvy Grass — RI,SU,V
Self Heal — AB,BH,CE,DD,DE,JO, PO,RI,SU
Senna, Bladder — BH,RI
Senna, Chinese — RI
Sesame — BS,CA,DD,DE,GO,PI,PK, RI,SU,TH
Shiso see Perilla
Skullcap — AB,CE,DD,DE,JO,JV,PO, RI,SU
Skullcap, 'Baikal' — RI
Soapwort — AB,CE,CO,JV,RI,SU
Sorrell — AB,BH,BY,C,CA,CE,CO, DD,DE,J,JE,JO,JV,M, MC,PK,RI,SK,ST,V
Sorrell, Buckler Leaved — CE,CO,H,JV,PO,SU,TH
Sorrell, French (lge leaf) — AB,BD,BH,GO,H,HU,K, KI,MO,PK,PO,RI,S,SN, SR,SU,VY
St.John's Wort — BH,CE,DD,DE,JE,JO,PO, RI,SD,SP,SU
St.Johnswort, 'Elixir' — RI
St.Johnswort, 'Topas' — RI
St.Mary's Thistle — SP,V
Stone Orpine — JE,RI
Strawberry, Alpine — CE,RI
Strawberry, Sticks — KI,SU
Strawberry, Wild — JV,PO,RI,SU
Sweet Rocket — CE,JV,KS,RI
Tansy, Common — AB,BD,BH,BS,C,CE,CO, DD,DE,DI,JV,KI,KS,MC, MO,PI,PK,RI,S,SU,TH, V,VY
Tarragon — BD,BS,BY,C,CA,CO,DD, DE,J,JE,JO,KI,KS,L,MC, PI,PK,R,RC,RI,S,SU,T, TH,V
Tea Tree — RI
Teasel — CE,RI,SU
Thistle, Milk — DE,JO,PO,RI
Thyme — w.a.
Thyme, Broad Leaved — BH,U
Thyme, Creeping — BH,CA,CE,H,HU,JV,KS, PK,R,RC,SK,SU,TE,VY
Thyme,Fragrant/Orange — PO
Thyme, Old English — B,DE,DT,GO,K,MO,PK, RI,SE,T,TE,TH,VY
Toadflax — CE,JV,KS,SU
Toadflax, Purple — CE
Toothache Plant — AB,DD,RI,SD
Tormentil — AB,CE,PO,RI,SU
Valerian — AB,BH,CE,DD,DE,H,JE JO,JV,PK,PO,RI,SD,SU, V
Valerian, 'Anthos' — RI
Valerian, Red — DD,JV,PO,RI,SU
Valerian, select — RI
Vervain — AB,BH,CE,H,JO,JV,PO, RI,SU
Vervain, Blue — AB,CE,RI,SU
Viper's Bugloss — CE,DD,H,JV,SU
Vitex — CE,RI,SU
Watercress — DD,JE,RI,TH,V
Weld — AB,BH,H,PO,RI,SU
Woad — BH,CE,H,JV,KS,PO,RI,

WOAD/GREEN MANURES

Woad, Chinese	SU
Woodruff, Dyer's	RI
Woodruff, Sweet	RI
	BD,BH,BS,DE,JE,KS,
	PK,PO,RI,SU,V
Woodsage	CE,JV,PO,RI,SU
Wormwood	AB,BD,BH,BS,BY,CE,
	CO,DE,DI,JE,JO,JV,KS,
	MO,PI,PO,RC,RI,SU,V
Wormwood, Chinese	RI
Yarrow	AB,BH,DD,H,JE,JO,JV,
	KS,PO,RI,SU
Yellow Melilot	CE,RI

GREEN MANURES

Alfalfa	CD,CO,DI,JO,KI,PI,SU, TE,TU,V
Austrian Field Peas	TE
Bean, Fava	SD
Buckwheat	BY,CO,JO,KI,PI,SD,ST, SU,TE,TU,V
Clover Alsike	CA,CD,CO,JO,PI,TE
Clover, Crimson	CA,JO,KI,M,SD,ST,SU, TE,TU
Clover, Dutch white	PI
Clover, O' Connor's Strawberry	CA
Clover Red	CA,CO,JO,PI,ST,SU,TU, V
Common Vetch	CA,TE
Corn Salad	TE
Cowpea	SD
Crown Vetch	CA
Fenugreek	CO,KI,SU,TU
Field Beans	CO,D,JO,M,ST,SU,TU
Forage Pea Magnus	DT
Hairy Vetch	CA,JO,PI,SD,TE
Lupins	CO,KI,SU,TU,V
Medic(ago)	TE
Mustard	BY,CO,D,KI,M,ST,SU, TU,V
Oats	JO,PI,SD,TE
Pea, Austrian Winter	SD
Pea, Field	SD,ST
Phacelia	CO,D,DI,KI,M,ST,SU,TU, V
Radish	CO,TU
Rapeseed Ac Excel	JO,VY
Rye	CO,DT,JO,KI,PI,SD,ST, SU,TU
Sorghum, Black African	SD
Soybean	TE
Spring Green Manure mix	JO
Sunflowers	JO
Tares	CO,D,DT,KI,M,ST,SU
Trefoil	CA,CO,KI,SU,TE,TU
Tyfon	TE
Winter Wheat	TE

CODE-SUPPLIER INDEX

A Agroforestry Research Trust, 46 Hunters Moon, Dartington, Totnes, Devon. TQ9 6JT   CONTACT: Mr.M.Crawford CAT.COST:3x 1st class stamps   CAT OUT:Jan POSTAGE ON ORDERS:£1 for orders under £10 RETAIL/WHOLESALE:Retail mail order CULTURAL NOTES:Yes   SEED COUNT:Yes EXPORT:Yes SPECIALITIES:Trees, shrubs, perennials OTHER INFO:Profits go to research projects

AB Abundant Life Seed Foundation. P.O.Box 772. Port Townsend. WA 98368. USA. TEL: 360 385 5660   FAX: 360 385 7455 CAT COST: $2 Donation   CAT OUT: Jan POSTAGE: Charged   RETAIL/WHOLESALE: Retail mail order. SPECIALITIES: Open-pollinated, rare and endangered seeds. CREDUT CARDS: D,MC,V   CULTURAL NOTES: In cat. OTHER INFO: Overseas are asked to use credit cards and accept responsibility for conforming to regulations imposed by customs. Shipping costs plus $3 charged.

AL Allwood Bros. Mill Nursery. Hassocks. W.Sussex. BN6 9NB. TEL: 01273 844229   FAX:01273 846022 CAT COST: 2x 1st class stamps   CAT OUT:Dec WHOLESALE/RETAIL: Retail   CULTURAL NOTES: Yes EXPORT: Yes   CREDIT CARDS: Yes

AP Alpine Garden Society, AGS Centre, Avon Bank, Pershore. Worcs. WR10 3JP   CONTACT: Mr. W.J.Simpson TEL: 01386 554790   FAX: 01386 554801 CAT COST:Membership fee   CAT OUT:Dec POSTAGE ON ORDERS: £3   CULTURAL NOTES: Yes EXPORT: Seed exchange with overseas members OTHER INFO: Seed available to members only

AR Jim & Jenny Archibald. 'Bryn Collen'. Ffostrasol. Llandysul. Dyfed. SA44 5SB. Wales. FREE CAT OUT: Summer & Winter   EXPORT: Yes SEED COUNT: Yes SPECIALITIES: Many unusual seeds.

AS Ashwood Nurseries Ltd, Greensforge, Kingswinford. W.Midlands. DY6 0AE   CONTACT: Mr. T.D. Baulk TEL: 01384 401996   FAX: 01384 401108 OPENING TIMES: Everyday, except Xmas & Boxing Day. CAT COST: 4x 1st class stamps   CAT OUT:Autumn 1997 POSTAGE FOR ORDERS: Yes   WHOLESALE/RETAIL: Both CULTURAL NOTES: Yes   SEED COUNT:Yes EXPORT: Yes   CREDIT CARDS:A,V,AE SPECIALITIES: Auricula, Cyclamen, Hellebores, Lewisias.

AU Australasian Plant Society. Stonecourt. 74 Brimstage Rd, Heswall, Wirral. L60 1XQ   CONTACT: J.Irons CAT COST:Membership   CAT OUT:May CULTURAL NOTES: Yes SPECIALITIES: Australian & New Zealand sp. OTHER INFO: List may change from year to year. Seed available to members only.

AV Agua Viva Seed Ranch, R&I, Box 8, Taos, New Mexico 87571. U.S.A. TEL: (505) 758-4520   FAX: 505 758 1745 OPENING TIMES: M-F 9-5, Sat 10-4   CAT COST: $3 CAT OUT: Jan '97   WHOLESALE/RETAIL : Retail CULTURAL NOTES:Yes SPECIALITIES: Wildflower & Native Perennials EXPORT:Yes   CREDIT CARDS:Amex,Mc,V OTHER INFO: Pack by weight E-MAIL: aguaviva@taos.newmex.com

B B&T World Seeds. Rue des Marchandes. Paguignan, 34210 Olonzac. France   CONTACT: Mr.R.Wheatley TEL:00 33 468 912 963 FAX: 00 33 468 913 03 E-Mail:ralph@b-and-t-world-seeds.com OPENING TIMES: Dawn-Dusk 365 days   MIN ORDER: £5 CAT COST:EU £10, Elsewhere £14. Sublists 50p +.Disc £5. CAT OUT: Feb. Published quarterly. Sub-lists/discs ad hoc. POSTAGE ON ORDERS: Upto £20 -£1, £20-£50 -£2, £50+ qu. DISCOUNTS: Trade terms available, occasional special offers. WHOLESALE/RETAIL: Both. Limited stock held. Callers welcome   CULTURAL NOTES: (Yes) SEED COUNT:Rarely given   EXPORT: Yes CREDIT CARDS: Á,Eu,Ma,V SPECIALITIES: The exotic, obscure and/or hard to get. OTHER INFO:Over 30,000 seeds listed, divided into 187 sub-lists.

BA J & J Ainsworth. Bank Farm. Bank Head Ln, Bamber Bridge, Preston. PR5 6YR   CONTACT: J. Ainsworth TEL: 01772 321557 OPENING TIMES:By appt. One open day No cat. POSTAGE ON ORDERS: 26p.CULTURAL NOTES: Yes SEED COUNT:Min.   SPECIALITIES: Sarracenia seed. OTHER INFO: Limited quantities, sp & hyb, harvested Oct.

BC British Cactis & Succulent Society. Mr.P.Lewis, The Membership Secretary. 'Firgrove', 1 Springwoods, Courtmoor, Fleet, Hants. GU13 9SU   CONTACT: Mr. P.Lewis CAT COST:Free to members   CAT OUT:Nov EXPORT: Overseas members   SPECIALITIES:Cactus OTHER INFO: Seeds available to members only

BD Basically Seeds. Risby Business Park. Newmarket Rd. Risby. Bury St. Edmunds. IP11 8AS   CONTACT: V.Dahl TEL: 01284 811001   FAX:01284 811021 CAT COST: Free   CAT OUT:Sept   POSTAGE: Free OPENING TIMES:By arrangement. DISCOUNTS; Special offers in Mar.   WHOLESALE/RETAIL:Both SEED COUNT: Yes   EXPORT:Yes

BF Butterbrooke Farm. 78 Barry Rd. Oxford. CT 06478. USA. TEL: 203 888 2000   CONTACT: Tom WHOLESALE/ RETAIL: Both CAT COST: Sae or 1$US.   EXPORT: Yes POSTAGE: Charge basic postage plus handling charge. SPECIALITIES: Old time, pure-line varieties.

BH Blackwoods Herbs. P.O. Box 86. Hoekwil 6538. South Africa. Tel/Fax: 27 441 8501135.   E-Mail: yvwijk@pixie.co.za CONTACT: Y. Van Wijk CAT COST: £1   CAT OUT: Jan/Feb SPECIALITIES: Herbs, Unusual vegetables, S. African seed. EXPORT: Yes, but no phyto certificate. CULTURAL NOTES: On request.

BL Blackmore & Langdon. Pensford. Nr Bristol. BS18 4JL TEL:01275 332300   CONTACT:R.A.Langdon OPENING TIMES: M-Sa 9-5, Su 10-4   CAT OUT :Mar DISCOUNTS:Occasionally WHOLESALE/RETAIL:Retail CULTURAL NOTES: Yes   SEED COUNT: On request EXPORT:Yes   SPECIALITIES: Begonias,Delphiniums

BO Robert Bolton & Son. Birdbrook. Halstead. Essex. CO9 4BQ TEL: 01440 785246   FAX:01440 788000 FREE CAT OUT:Aug POSTAGE: Free over £10, Overseas £1.75 WHOLESALE/RETAIL: Retail   CULTURAL NOTES: Yes SEED COUNT:Yes   SEED COLLECTIONS:Yes EXPORT:Yes   CREDIT CARDS: Mc,V SPECIALITIES: Lathyrus odoratus (Sweet Peas).

CODE-SUPPLIER INDEX

BP Barnhaven Primroses. Langerhouad 22420. Plouzelambre. France CONTACT: A.Bradford E-MAIL:Bradford@wanadoo.fr TEL: (+33) 02 96 35 31 54   FAX:(+33) 96 35 31 55 CAT COST: £7 col cat., £1 seed list   CAT OUT: Oct POSTAGE ON ORDERS:£1   WHOLESALE /RETAIL: Retail CULTURAL NOTES: Yes   SEED COUNT: Yes EXPORT: Worldwide   CREDIT CARDS: MA,V SPECIALITIES: Primulas, Barnhaven Polyanthus.

BR British Clematis Society. 4 Springfield. Lightwater. Surrey. GU18 5XP   CONTACT: R.J.Stothard. (Sec) TEL: 01276 476387   CAT COST:Membership fee. CAT OUT: Spring POSTAGE:Free EXPORT: Overseas members OTHER INFO: Annual seed exchange available to members only.

BS Seeds-By-Size, 45 Crouchfield, Boxmoor, Hemel Hempstead, Herts. HP1 1PA   CONTACT: John Size TEL: 01442 251458   TEL. ANS. TIMES: 9-9 M-F, 9-12 Sa CAT COST: Free   CAT OUT:July   POSTAGE:77p for under £5 DISCOUNTS:£1 introductory voucher with first order WHOLESALE/ RETAIL: Both, wholesale on quotation CULTURAL NOTES:Some SEED COUNT:Some EXPORT:Yes SPECIALITIES: Cabbage, Marrow, Pumpkin, Squash, Lettuce, Cauliflower, Onions.   OTHER INFO:To sell seed in whatever quantity is required. 1350 veg, 3700 flowers listed

BU D.V.Burrell Seed Growers. P.O. Box 150. Rocky Ford. CO 81067. USA.   CONTACT: R.Burrell TEL : 719 254 3318   FAX: 719 254 3319 CAT COST: Free to USA, Overseas $5 each catalogue CAT OUT: Dec POSTAGE: Some items postage paid USA. WHOLESALE/RETAIL: Both   CULTURAL NOTES: Yes SEED COUNT: Certain items sold by seed count. EXPORT: Yes   CREDIT CARDS: MA, V SPECIALITIES: Cantaloupe, Melon, Squash, Tomato, Watermelon and Zinnia. OTHER INFO: Seed sold in bulk or packets.

BY J.W.Boyce. 237 Lower Carter St. Fordham. Ely. Cambs. CB7 5JU.   CONTACT: E. Morley TEL/FAX: 01638 721158 OPENING HOURS: M-F 9-1p.m. Sa 9-12 midday. FREE CAT OUT: Oct.   POSTAGE: 75p if under £10 Specialities: Viola x wittrochiana (Pansy) and vegetables. CREDIT CARDS: Yes   CULTURAL NOTES: Yes SEED COUNT: In most cases. OTHER INFO: Seed sold by count, weight and packet.

C Chiltern Seeds. Bortree Stile, Ulverston,Cumbria. LA12 7PB TEL: 01229 581137   FAX: 01229 584549 CAT COST:50p in stamps   CAT OUT: Dec POSTAGE:60p under £10, Europe £1 under £20, RoW £2 under £25 DISCOUNT: Trade discount WHOLESALE/RETAIL: Retail CULTURAL NOTES:Yes   SEED COUNT:If small no. of seeds EXPORT: Yes CREDIT CARDS: A,AE,EU,MA,SW,V OTHER INFO: Wide range E-mail: 101344.1340@compuserve.com

CA Carter Seeds. 475 Mar Vista Drive. Vista. CA 92083. USA. TEL: 760 724 5931   FAX: 760 724 8832 FREE CAT OUT: Oct POSTAGE: Shipping charged per invoice. MIN ORDER: US $6 on orders under US $20. WHOLESALE/RETAIL: Both. CULTURAL NOTES: Yes   SEED COUNT: Yes EXPORT: Yes CREDIT CARDS: MA, V. SPECIALITIES: Trees, shrubs, palms, tropicals, herbs, grasses.

CD Cotswold Grass Seeds Direct. The Barn Business Centre. Great Rissington. Cheltenham. Glos. GL54 2LH TEL: 01451 822055   FAX: 01451 810300 OPENING TIMES: M-F, 9-5   MIN. ORDER:£50 CAT COST: Free CAT OUT: Mar & July   POSTAGE:Free DISCOUNTS: On large orders WHOLESALE/RETAIL: Wholesale SPECIALITIES:All grass seed EXPORT: Yes   CREDIT CARDS: Yes OTHER INFO:Grass seed in bulk E-MAIL:caroline@cotseeds.demon.co.uk

CE Chesire Herbs, Fourfields. Forest Rd. Nr. Tarporley. Chesire. CW6 9ES   CONTACT:L & T Riddell TEL: 01829 760578   FAX:01829 760354 OPENING TIMES: 10-5 daily   CAT COST: 2nd class stamp CAT OUT: Jan POSTAGE:50p WHOLESALE/RETAIL:Retail CULTURAL NOTES:Yes   SPECIALITIES:Herbs OTHER INFO: Order unusual varieties in advance.

CF Cape Flora. P.O. Box 10556. Linton Grange. Port Elizabeth. 6015. RSA.   CONTACT: W. Cowley E-mail: capeflor@iafrica.com TEL: (041) 73 2096   FAX: (041) 73 3188 FREE CAT: Only changes with price change. POSTAGE: £2   MIN ORDER: £50   CREDIT CARDS: Yes EXPORT: Yes   CULTURAL NOTES: No SEED COUNT: Sold by quantity SPECIALITIES: Amaryllids, Pelargoniums, Clivias, Cycads. OTHER INFO: Additional costs for postage of heavy seeds.

CG Coombland Gardens Nursery. Coneyhurst. Billingshurst. W.Sussex. RH14 9DY TEL: 01403 741727   FAX: 01403 741079 OPENING TIMES: 2-4 pm week days   MIN. ORDER: £10 CAT. COST:£1   CAT OUT: Jan   POSTAGE:Free WHOLESALE/RETAIL: Retail   EXPORT:Yes

CH Craig House Cacti. 42 Brentwood Court. Southport. Lancs. PR9 9JW   CONTACT: G. MCLEOD TEL:01704 545077   POSTAGE FOR ORDERS: 35p CULTURAL NOTES: Yes   SPECIALITIES:Cactus

CL Colegrave Seeds Ltd. West Adderbury. Banbury. Oxon. OX17 3EY TEL:01295 810632 FAX:01295 812135 OPENING TIMES: Collection by appt   CAT OUT:Oct DISCOUNTS: Early orders WHOLESALE/RETAIL: Wholesale CULTURAL NOTES: Yes SEED COUNT: Unit weights EXPORT:Yes   CREDIT CARDS: Credit account

CN CN Seeds. Denmark House. Pymoor. Ely. Cambs. CB6 2EG. TEL: 01353 699413.   FAX: 01353 698806 FREE CAT OUT: Nov   WHOLESALE/RETAIL: Wh/s only. POSTAGE: Paid to UK address.   CREDIT CARDS: Yes EXPORT: Yes   CULTURAL NOTES: Supplied verbally SEED COUNT: Yes   SPECIALITIES: Herbs

CO The Organic Gardening Catalogue. River Dene Estate. Molesey Rd. Hersham. Surrey. KT12 4RG. TEL:01932 253666 FAX: 01932 252707 CONTACT:M.Hedges OPENING TIMES: 9-5 M-F   CAT COST: Free   CAT OUT:Oct POSTAGE: 75p orders under £14   DISCOUNT:10% HDRA members, RHS members. Group purchasing scheme WHOLESALE/RETAIL: Retail, mainly mail order, callers welcome CULTURAL NOTES: Yes   SEED COUNT:Yes   EXPORT:Yes SEED COLLECTIONS:As gift packs   CREDIT CARDS:Ma, V SPECIALITIES:Vegetables, herbs.Seed is untreated after harvest

CODE-SUPPLIER INDEX

CP Companion Plants. 7247 North Coolville Ridge, Athens, Ohio 45701. U.S.A CONTACT:Peter Borchard TEL: 614 592 4643 FAX: 614 593 3092 OPENING TIMES: 10-5 every day but Wed, no weekend hours in Dec, Jan, Feb CAT COST:$3 CAT OUT: Annually POSTAGE ON ORDERS: Yes WHOLESALE/RETAIL: Both CULTURAL NOTES:Yes DISCOUNTS:For W/sale bulk EXPORT: Yes CREDIT CARDS: MA,V SPECIALITIES:Culinary, Medicinal, Herbs E-MAIL: http://www.frognet.net/companion plants

CR Cravens Nursery. 1 Foulds Terrace. Bingley. W.Yorks. TEL: 01274 561412 CONTACT: S.R.Craven OPENING TIMES: Th-Su, please ring first MIN ORDER:£5 CAT COST: £1 POSTAGE:Yes DISCOUNTS:Yes WHOLESALE/RETAIL:Retail CULTURAL NOTES: Yes EXPORT: Yes SPECIALITIES: Show Auriculas, Primulas,Alpines

CS CORNS. Route 1. Box 32. Turpin. OK 73950. USA. TEL: (405) 778 3615 OTHER INFO: Infon letter with price list. CAT COST: US $2. MIN ORDER: US $15, postage included. EXPORT: No WHOLESALE/RETAIL: Retail mail order SPECIALITIES: Heirloom, open-pollinated corns.

CT CTDA. 174 Cambridge St. London. SW1V 4QE TEL:0171 9765115 CAT COST:Free CAT OUT: May POSTAGE:£1.50 WHOLESALE/RETAIL:Retail SEED COUNT: Yes EXPORT:Yes SPECIALITIES: Aquilegia, Cyclamen, Hellebores

D Samuel Dobie & Son Ltd, Broomhill Way, Torquay. Devon. TQ2 7QW TEL:01803 616281 FAX:01803 615150 CATCOST:Free CAT OUT:Oct POSTAGE:75p under £5 DISCOUNTS:For Horticultural Societies WHOLESALE/RETAIL:Retail CULTURAL NOTES:Yes SEED COUNT: Yes CREDIT CARDS:Yes

DD Deep Diversity.P.O. Box 15700. Santa Fe. NM 87506-5700. USA. CREDIT CARDS: MA,V. EXPORT: Yes POSTAGE: US $2.50, International charged. OTHER INFO: Gene pool resource. Sister co. of Seeds of Change.

DE De Giorgi Seed Company. 6011 "N" Street. Omaha. NE68117. USA. CONTACT: Rose Kleine TEL: 402 731 3901 FAX: 402 731 8475 WHOLESALE/RETAIL: Both, wh/s on request. FREE CAT OUT: Dec. MIN ORDER: US $10 POSTAGE: Yes EXPORT: Yes CREDIT CARDS: AE,D,MA,V CULTURAL NOTES: General SEED COUNT: Mostly

DG The Botanic Nursery. Bath Rd. Atworth. Melksham. Wiltshire. SN12 8HU. CONTACT: V.Baker TEL: Mobile 0850 328756 FAX:01225 700953 CAT COST: 1 x 1st class stamp(list) CAT OUT: Oct WHOLESALE/RETAIL: Retail mail order. MIN ORDER: £4.50 CULTURAL NOTES: Yes OTHER INFO: Descriptive leaflet SEED COUNT: Approx 50/100 seeds per pack. EXPORT: Yes SPECIALITIES: Digitalis

DI Digger's Club.105 La Trobe Parade. Dromana 3936.Vic. Australia. E-mail: orders@diggers.com.au TEL: 03 5987 1877 FAX: 03 5981 4298 DISCOUNTS: For members and for quantity. CAT COST: £1, US $2, 2 IRC's. CAT OUT: July POSTAGE: Yes. Overseas AU $5. WHOLESALE/RETAIL: Both

CULTURAL NOTES: Yes EXPORT: Yes CREDIT CARDS: MA, V (AU $10) SPECIALITIES: Heirloom vegetables

DN Denali Seed Company. P.O. Box 111425. Anchorage. AK 99511-1425.USA. CONTACT: Reg Yaple TEL: 907 344 0347 E-mail: seedforu@aonline.com CAT COST: US $2/ merchandise certificate US $2. CAT OUT: Dec MIN ORDER: US $5 POSTAGE: US $2.50 WHOLESALE/RETAIL: Retail Cultural Notes: Yes EXPORT: Yes CREDIT CARDS: Yes SPECIALITIES: Artic and sub-arctic varieties

DS Diane Sewell. Overdene. 81 Willingham Rd. Over. Cambridge. CB4 5PF. CONTACT: D. Sewell TEL: 01954 260614 FAX: 01954 260614 WHOLESALE/RETAIL: Mail order and retail at shows. FREE LIST OUT: July POSTAGE: Under £5 add 50p. CULTURAL NOTES: Yes SEED COUNT: Yes EXPORT: Yes SPECIALITIES: Lathyrus odoratus (Sweet peas) and species.

DT D.T.Brown & Co. Ltd. Station Rd. Poulton Le Fylde. Lancs. FY6 7HX TEL:01253 882371 FAX:01253 890923 OPENING HOURS:M-Th 8.30-5.30, F 8.30-4.30 CAT COST:Free CAT OUT:Sept POSTAGE:60p DISCOUNT:For Horticultural Clubs WHOLESALE/RETAIL:Both CULTURAL NOTES:Basic SEED COUNT:Yes EXPORT:Yes CREDIT CARDS:A,Sw,V SPECIALITIES: Flower & Veg

DV Doug and Vivi Rowland. 200 Spring Rd. Kempston. Bedford. MK42 8ND. FAX: 01234 358970 WHOLESALE/RETAIL: Retail mail order FREE CAT OUT: Dec EXPORT: Yes CULTURAL NOTES: Yes SEED COUNT: Yes SPECIALITIES: Cacti, Succulents, Desert Plants, Carnivorous.

E Elisabeth Goodwin Nurseries. Elm Tree Farm. 1 Beeches Rd. West Row. Bury St. Edmunds. Suffolk. IP28 8NP. TEL:01638 713050 OPENING TIMES: By appointment CAT COST:3 x 1st class stamps CAT OUT:Autumn POSTAGE ON ORDERS:Yes WHOLESALE/RETAIL:Retail CULTURAL NOTES:Yes SEED COUNT:For large/scarce seed SPECIALITIES: Plants for dry gardens

EH Elysian Hills Tree Farm. RR5 Box 452. Brattleboro. Vermont 05301. USA. CONTACT: M. L. Schmidt TEL: 802 257 0233 FAX: 802 257 1386 SPECIALITIES: Turnip Seed Only. WHOLESALE/RETAIL: Both MIN ORDER: Wh/s: 1 lb seed OR 100 packets. Retail: 1 pk. POSTAGE: Wh/S UPS;Retail, sae. EXPORT: Yes CULTURAL NOTES: On retail packet.

EL Ellison Horticultural Pty Ltd. P.O.Box 365. Nowra. NSW. Australia 2541. TEL: 044 214255 FAX: 044 230859 CAT COST: AU $5 or equivalent. WHOLESALE/RETAIL: Wh/s. MIN ORDER: AU $40. EXPORT: Yes CULTURAL NOTES: Yes SEED COUNT: Yes CREDIT CARDS: Yes. DISCOUNTS: Yes SPECIALITIES: Tree, Shrub and Palm seed. OTHER INFO: 2,000 varieties listed, 400 photographs.

F Mr.Fothergills Seeds. Kentford. Newmarket. Suffolk. CB8 7QB. TEL:01638 751161 FAX: 01638 751624 OPENING•TIMES: 9-5 FREECAT OUT: Oct CREDIT CARDS: Yes POSTAGE: 50p under £5 WHOLESALE/RETAIL:Retail outlets CULTURAL NOTES:Yes SEED COUNT:Yes EXPORT:Yes

CODE-SUPPLIER INDEX

FH Field House Alpines. Leake Rd. Gotham. Nottingham. NG11 0JN CONTACT:D.Lockhead TEL: 0115 9830278 OPENING TIMES: Every day exc. Th, 9-5 CAT COST: 4x 1st class stamps or 4x IRC (overseas) CAT OUT: Jan POSTAGE: EU 70p, £2 otherwiseWHOLESALE/ RETAIL: Retail CULTURAL NOTES: BriefSEED COUNT:Min 20 SEED COLLECTIONS:Yes EXPORT:Yes CREDIT CARDS:MA,V SPECIALITIES:Primula & Alpines

FR Fratelli Ignegnoli. Corso Buenos Aires. 54 20124 Milano. Italy. TEL: +39 2 29513167 FAX: +39 2 29529759 OPENING TIMES: 8.30-12.30, 14.30-16.30 Mon-Sat FREE CAT OUT: Jan MIN ORDER: Lire 50,000 WHOLESALE/RETAIL: Both CREDIT CARDS: Yes CULTURAL NOTES: Yes EXPORT: Yes SPECIALITIES: Unusual Vegetables

FW F.W.Schumacher Co., 36 Spring Hill Rd. Sandwich. MA 02563-1023. USA. TEL: 508 888 0659 FAX:508 833 0322 FREE CAT OUT: Nov POSTAGE: Yes CULTURAL NOTES/SEED COUNT: On request E-mail: treeseed@capecod.net

G Gesellschaft der Staudenfreunde e.V. Geshaftsstelle. Melensweg 1. D- 65795 Hattersheim. Germany. TEL: 0 61 90 36 42 FAX:0 61 90 71865 OPENING TIMES: Every day CAT COST:Membership fee CAT OUT:Dec POSTAGE ON ORDERS:Yes EXPORT:Overseas members OTHER INFO:Seeds for members only. Seeds may change from year to year.

GC Glenhirst Cactus Nursery. Station Rd. Swineshead. Boston. Lincs. PE20 3NX CONTACT: S.A.Bell TEL:01205 820314 OPENING TIMES:Th,F,Su 10-5 from 01/04 to 30/09 CAT COST: 2x stamps CAT OUT: Early '97 POSTAGE: Yes DISCOUNTS: On all seeds WHOLESALE/RETAIL:Retail CULTURAL NOTES:Yes SEED COUNT:Yes SEED COLLECTIONS:Yes EXPORT:Yes SPECIALITIES: Cactus & Succulents

GI Pinks & Carnations. 22 Chetwyn Ave. Bromley Cross. Bolton. BL7 9BN CONTACT: Tom Gillies TEL:01204 306273 FAX:01204 306273 OPENING TIMES: By appt only CAT COST: Stamp CAT OUT: Aug POSTAGE:Free in U.K, stamps for overseas WHOLESALE/RETAIL: Both SEED COUNT:Yes EXPORT:Yes CREDIT CARDS:A, V SPECIALITIES:Carnations, Pinks

GO Gourmet Gardener. 8650 College Boulevard. Suite Z. Overland Park. Kansas. 66210. USA. TEL: 913 345 0490 FAX: 913 451 2443 CAT COST: US $2. CAT OUT: Dec POSTAGE: Yes WHOLESALE/RETAIL: Retail CREDIT CARDS:Yes EXPORT: Yes, Fed X applied to credit card CULTURAL NOTES: Yes SEED COUNT: Yes SPECIALITIES: Gourmet herbs, Heirloom vegetables.

H The Cottage Herbery. Mill House. Boraston. Tenbury Wells. Worcs. WR15 8LZ TEL:01584 781575 FAX: 01584 781483 OPENING TIMES: 11-5 Su only May-July & by appt. CAT COST: £1 CAT OUT: Spring POSTAGE ON ORDERS:Yes WHOLESALE/RETAIL:Retail EXPORT:Yes SPECIALITIES: Herbs

HA Harvest Seeds. 325 McCarrs Creek Rd. Terrey Hills. NSW 2084. Australia. 1995 catalogue entered CONTACT: B.Harrold TEL: (02) 9450 2699 FAX:(02) 9450 2750 OPENING TIMES: M-F 8.30-4.30 MIN ORDER:$10.00 CAT COST:Free POSTAGE:Yes DISCOUNTS:Yes WHOLESALE/RETAIL: Wholesale CULTURAL NOTES:Yes SEED COLLECTIONS: Gift packs EXPORT:Yes SPECIALITIES:Native grasses OTHER INFO: Living cards

HD HDRA. Heritage Seed Library. Ryton Organic Gardens. Ryton-on-Dunsmore. Coventry. CV8 3LG TEL: 01203 303517 FAX:01203 639229 MIN ORDER: Max 6 pkts CAT COST: Free to members CAT OUT: Nov CULTURAL NOTES:Yes CREDIT CARDS: For membership fees SPECILIATIES:Unregistered vegetable seeds OTHER INFO: Seed exchange scheme for members only. E-MAIL: hsl@hdra.org.uk NOTE: List may vary year to year.

HE James Henderson & Sons. Kingholm Quay. Dumfries. DG1 4SU TEL: 01387 252234 FAX:01387 262302 CONTACT: Mr. Henderson OPENING TIMES:M-F 7.30-4.30 MIN ORDER: 3kg CAT COST: S.A.E. CAT OUT:Oct POSTAGE:Yes WHOLESALE/RETAIL:Both CULTURAL NOTES:Yes SPECIALITIES:Seed Potatoes only

HL Henllys Lodge Plants. Beaumaris. Anglesey. Gwynedd. TEL: 01248 810106 CONTACT:E.Lane CAT COST: 2x 1st class stamps CAT COST:Nov POSTAGE:40p WHOLESALE/RETAIL: Retail CULTURAL NOTES: On request SEED COUNT:For very small quantities SPECIALITIES: Hardy Geraniums

HP Hardy Plant Society. Little Orchard. Great Comberton.Pershore. Worcs. WR10 3DP. CONTACT: Mrs. P.Adams. TEL: 01386 710317 CAT COST: Membership fee. EXPORT: Overseas members. OTHER INFO: Seed available to members only.

HU J.L.Hudson, Seedsman. Star Route 2. Box 337. La Honda. CA 94020. USA. CAT COST: US $1 USA and Canada, Elsewhere US $4. CAT OUT: Jan WHOLESALE/RETAIL: Mainly retail, some wh/s POSTAGE CHARGED: Yes EXPORT: Yes CULTURAL NOTES: Yes SEED COUNT: For 10 seeds or less SPECIALITES: Unusual seeds, open-pollinated.

HW Holland Wildflower Farm. P.O.Box 328. Elkins. Arkansas 72727 TEL: 501 643 2622 FAX:501 643 2622 CONTACT:Julie Holland OPENING TIMES: By appt. MIN ORDER:$15 for credit card orders, otherwise no min. CAT COST:Free DISCOUNTS: On quantity WHOLESALE/RETAIL:Both CULTURAL NOTES:Extensive EXPORT: Yes CREDIT CARDS:Discover,MA,V SPECIALITIES:Eastern US natives, prairie, wetlands & forest OTHER INFO: Seed less than 1 ounce is sold by no. of sq.ft. coverage. E.g. 1 pkt covers 30 sq.ft. E-MAIL: info@hwildfower.com

I W.E.TH.Ingwersen Ltd. Birch Farm Nursery. Gravetye. East Grinstead. W.Sussex. RH19 4LE CONTACT: M.Green TEL: 01342 810236 OPENING TIMES:Every day 9-4, Mar-Sept. Rest of yr, 9-4, M-F. CAT COST: Free POSTAGE: S.a.e with order, 4 IRC (overseas) CAT OUT: Early 1997 WHOLESALE/RETAIL:Retail CULTURAL NOTES:Yes EXPORT:Yes SPECIALITIES:Alpines & Rock Garden Plants

CODE-SUPPLIER INDEX

IC International Clematis Society. 115. Belmont Rd. Harrow. Middlesex. HA3 7PL. CONTACT: F. Woolfenden (Secretary) TEL: +44 181 427 5340 E-MAIL: clematis@dial.pipex.com CAT COST: Free to members CAT OUT:Feb/Mar POSTAGE: Nominal CULTURAL NOTES:Relevant articles in journal EXPORT: Overseas members SPECIALITIES: Clematis only OTHER INFO: Seeds for members only.

J Johnsons Seeds. London Rd. Boston. Lincs. PE21 8AD TEL: 01205 365051 FAX:01205 310148 OPENING TIMES: M-F 8.30-5.30 FREE CAT OUT: Oct POSTAGE:Free DISCOUNTS: Yes WHOLESALE/RETAIL: Both CULTURAL NOTES: Yes SEED COUNT: Yes SEED COLLECTIONS: Yes EXPORT: Yes CREDIT CARDS:Yes SPECIALITIES: Grass seed

JD John Drake Aquilegias. Hardwicke Housen. Fen Ditton. Cambridge. CB5 8TF. TEL: 01223 292246 WHOLESALE/RETAIL: Mail order only CAT COST: 70p CAT OUT: August MIN ORDER: £12 CULTURAL NOTES: Yes EXPORT: Yes SPECIALITIES: Aquilegia and rare plants. Open-pollinated seed.

JE Jelitto Perennial Seeds. P.o. Box 1264. D-29685 Schwarmstedt. Germany. CONTACT: Georg Uebelhart TEL: 0049 5071 4085 FAX:0049 5071 4088 OPENING TIMES: M-F 8-4.45 CET MIN ORDER:£32 CAT COST: Free CAT OUT: Jan POSTAGE:Yes WHOLESALE/RETAIL:Wholesale. Happy to supply clubs/ individuals provided the £32 min is met. CULTURAL NOTES: Yes SEED COUNT:Gm needed to produce 1000 plants EXPORT:Yes CREDIT CARDS:Eu, Ma, V SPECIALITIES: Perennials, Grasses, Herbs, Patio-plants. Pre-treated seed for fast germination. OTHER INFO:Short plant description, over 50 colour pictures.

JM J.E.Martin. 4 Church St. Mkt Harborough. Leics. LE16 7AA TEL: 01858 462751 FAX:01858 434544 CONTACT:J.Martin-Proctor WHOLESALE/RETAIL:Both OPENING TIMES:M,Tu,Th,F 8.30-5.30, Sa 8.30-5, Wed 8.30-1 CAT COST:Free CAT OUT:Oct POSTAGE:Yes EXPORT:Yes SPECIALITIES: Potatoes

JO Johnny's Selected Seeds. RR1. Box 2580. Albion. Maine 04910-9731. USA E-mail: homegarden@johnnyseeds.com TEL: 207 437 9294 FAX: 207 437 2165 FREE CAT OUT: Dec POSTAGE: Yes EXPORT: Yes WHOLESALE/RETAIL: Both CREDIT CARDS: Yes CULTURAL NOTES: Yes SEED COUNT: Yes SPECIALITIES: Organic vegetable seed

JV Jekka's Herb Farm. Rose Cottage. Shellards Lane. Alveston. Bristol. BS12 2SY CONTACT: Jekka McVicar TEL: 01454 418878 FAX: 01454 411988 CAT COST:4x 1st class stamps CAT OUT:Jan POSTAGE:Free WHOLESALE/RETAIL: Yes, will stock retail outlets & retail at shows only. SEED COLLECTIONS: 6 new collections EXPORT:Yes SPECIALITIES: Herbs OTHER INFO:Full planting details on packets.

JW Jill White. 6 Edward Avenue. Brightlingsea. Essex. CO7 0LZ. TEL: 01206 303547 OPENING HOURS: By appointment. WHOLESALE/RETAIL: Both CAT COST: Sae CAT OUT: July to Oct POSTAGE: Yes EXPORT: Yes SPECIALITIES: Cyclamen

K Mr.K.Foster. Garden Cottage. Mulgrave Est. Lythe. Whitby. N.Yorks. TEL:01947 893315 FAX:01947 893315 CAT COST: S.a.e CAT OUT: Sept POSTAGE: Yes DISCOUNTS: Yes WHOLESALE/RETAIL: Retail CULTURAL NOTES: Yes SEED COUNT: Yes EXPORT:Yes SPECIALITIES: Leeks, onions, top grade veg seed OTHER INFO: Specialist seeds for show and kitchen use.

KB Kirstenbosch National Botanical Garden. National Botanical Institute. Private Bag X7. Claremont 7735. South Africa. TEL: 27 21 762 9120 FAX: 27 21 797 6570 CONTACT: A. Notton. Supervisor. Seed Section. WHOLESALE/RETAIL: Both CAT COST: R25 to cover air-mail CAT OUT: Mid-year. POSTAGE: Charged, plus R30 handling fee on overseas orders. CREDIT CARDS: Yes EXPORT: Yes SPECIALITIES: South African idigenous species CULTURAL NOTES: Not specifically SEED COUNT: Yes, seed priced per 100 or per 1000. OTHER INFO: Each item has a brief description. Conditions of sale are given in the price list. Seed sold on first-come-first-served basis. Explanatory notes in the catalogue give guidance on ordering.

KI E.W.King & Co. Monks Farm. Coggleshall Rd. Kelvedon. Essex. CO5 9PG TEL: 01376 570000 FAX: 01376 571189 CAT COST: Free CAT OUT: Sept POSTAGE: Free over £10, over £35 trade WHOLESALE/RETAIL: Both CULTURAL NOTES:Yes SEED COUNT: Yes SEED COLLECTIONS: Yes EXPORT:Yes CREDIT CARDS: Ma, V SPECIALITIES:Veg/flower, sweet pea

KL Klub Skalnickaru Praha (The Rock Garden Club Prague). Pod Zvonarkou 10, 12000 Praha 2. Czech Republic. CONTACT: V. Holubec E-MAil: holubec@genbank.vurv.cz CAT COST: Membership only. CAT OUT: Dec/Jan EXPORT: For members SPECIALITIES: Garden and wild collected seeds.

KS Kings Herbs Ltd. 1660 Gt North Rd, Avondale, Auckland. NZ TEL: +64-9-828 7588 FAX: +64-9-828 7588 OPENING TIMES: 9-5, daily except weekends RETAIL CAT: NZ $6 POSTAGE: Yes CULTURAL NOTES:Yes

L Milton Seeds. 3 Milton Ave. Blackpool. Lancs. FY3 8LY TEL:01253 394377 FAX:01253 305110CONTACT:B.J.Robertson MIN ORDER:£5 POSTAGE: 50p for under £10; £1 for orders containing peas and/or beans WHOLESALE/RETAIL: Retail SEED COUNT:Yes CREDIT CARDS:A,B,D,Ma,Sw,V

LA Landlife Wildflowers. The Old Police Station. Lark Lane. Liverpool. L17 8UU CONTACT: Ms.Watson TEL: 0151 728 7011 FAX:0151 728 8413 OPENING TIMES: 9-5 E-MAIL: info@landlife.u-net.com FREE CAT OUT: Jan POSTAGE:Yes DISCOUNTS:Yes WHOLESALE/RETAIL: Both CULTURAL NOTES: Yes SEED COUNT: Yes, seeds per gm SEED COLLECTIONS: Yes CREDIT CARDS:Yes SPECIALITIES: Native wildflowers

LG The RHS Lily Group. Rosemary Cottage. Lowbands. Redmarley. Gloucester. GL19 3NG CAT COST: Free to members CAT OUT: Jan SEED COUNT: Average 10-15 seeds per pk OTHER INFO: Seed distribution for members only

CODE-SUPPLIER INDEX

LN Lawyer Nursery, Inc. 950 Highway 200 West Plains, MT 59859.
USA. E-mail: lawyrnsy@montana.com CONTACT: J.M. Lawyer
TEL: 406 826 3881   FAX: 406 826 5700
FREE CAT OUT: July   WHOLESALE/RETAIL: Wholesale
MIN ORDER: US $50   POSTGAE: Charged at cost
EXPORT: Yes   CREDIT CARDS: MA, V
CULTURAL NOTES: Limited SPECIALITIES: Tree/shrub seed.

M Marshalls. Wisbech. Cambs. PE13 2RF
TEL:01 945 466 711 FAX: 01 945 588 235
Phone lines: Jan-Apr 8.30-5.30 M-F, 9-4 Sa; May-Dec 9-4 M-F
FREE CAT OUT:Oct, June POSTAGE:95p under £15
DISCOUNTS: Allotments, societiesWHOLESALE/RETAIL:Retail
CULTURAL NOTES:Yes SEED COUNT:No. of seeds/min no. of
plants you can expect   CREDIT CARDS:Yes
EXPORT:Details on request
SPECIALITIES:Potatoes, veg OTHER INFO:Pre-chitted potato

MA The Marches Nursery. Presteigne. Powys. LD8 2HG
TEL: 01544 260474 FAX:01544 260474 CONTACT:J.Cooke
CAT COST: S.a.e   CAT OUT: Spring   POSTAGE:Free
WHOLESALE/RETAIL: Retail   CULTURAL NOTES:Yes
SEED COUNT: Yes   EXPORT: Yes
SPECIALITIES:Hardy Perennials

MC S.M.McArd. 39 West Rd. Pointon. Sleaford. Lincs. NG34 0NA
TEL: 01529 240765 FAX: 01529 240765 CONTACT: S.M.McArd
CAT COST: 2x 2nd class stampsCAT OUT: Nov, Supplement
each month   POSTAGE: 40p WHOLESALE/RETAIL: Retail
CULTURAL NOTES:Some   SEED COUNT:Not on plain pks
EXPORT: EU only SPECIALITIES: Unusual veg
OTHER INFO: Flower seeds free from all chemical treatment

MN Monocot Seeds. Jacklands. Jacklands Bridge. Tickenham.
Clevedon. BS21 6SG   TEL: 01275 810394
CAT COST: S.a.e. 50p stamps   CAT OUT: Oct
WHOLESALE/RETAIL: Retail   EXPORT: Yes
SPECIALITIES: Bulbous & tuberous rooted

MO Moles Seeds. Turkey Cock Lane, Stanway. Colchester. Essex.
CO3 5PD.
TEL: 01206 213213   FAX: 01206 212876
FREE CAT OUT: Sept   WHOLESALE/RETAIL: Wholesale only.
OPENING DAYS: Commercial gowers only, August.
POSTAGE: Free on flowers, small charge on peas/beans.
DISCOUNT: Cash with order.   EXPORT: Yes
CULTURAL NOTES: Yes   SEED COUNT: Yes

MS Matthewman's Sweetpeas. 14 Chariot Way. Thorpe Audlin.
Pontefract. W.Yorks. WF8 3EZ   CONTACT: P. Matthewman
TEL: 01977 621381
CAT OUT: Autumn   POSTAGE: 50p under £10
WHOLESALE/RETAIL: Retail SEED COUNT: Yes EXPORT:Yes
SPECIALITIES: Lathyrus odoratus (Sweet peas)
OTHER INFO: Offer lecture/talk on sweet pea culture

N Andrew Norfield Seeds. Lower Meend. St. Briavels. Glos. GL15
6RW
TEL: 01594 530134 FAX: 01594 530113
MIN ORDER: No min for retail, £20 wholesale
CAT COST: 1st class stamp   CAT OUT: Dec
DISCOUNT:Free pkt for 8 pkts ordered
WHOLESALE/RETAIL: Both   CULTURAL NOTES: Yes
SEED COUNT: Yes   EXPORT:Yes
SPECIALITIES: Pre-germinated seed of hardy trees, shrubs,
palms & cycads.

NA Naturescape. Lapwing Meadows. Coach Gap Lane. Langar.
Notts. NG13 9HP CONTACT: E.A.Scarborough
TEL: 01949 851045/860592 FAX: 01949 850431
OPENING TIMES: See cat.   CAT COST: 4x 1st class stamps
POSTAGE: Free over £5   WHOLESALE/RETAIL: Both
CULTURAL NOTES: Yes   SEED COUNT: Yes
SPECIALITIES: Wild Flowers

NG North Green Seeds. 16 Witton La. Little Plumstead. Norwich.
Norfolk NR13 5DL
MIN ORDER: £5   CAT COST: £1.25, 4x IRC (overseas)
CAT OUT: Late Autumn   POSTAGE:26p
WHOLESAE/RETAIL: Both   CULTURAL NOTES: General
EXPORT: Yes
SPECIALITIES:Helleborus, Fritillaria, Galanthus.

NI Nindethana Seed Service Pyt Ltd. P.O. Box 2121. ALBANY WA
6330. Western Australia.
TEL: 098 44 3533   FAX: 098 44 3573
BUSINESS HOURS: 8.30-4.30 Mon-Fri(West Australia time).
Callers by appointment only.
POSTAGE: Yes, Regular or Express.
EXPORT: Yes. Please determine if you need Phytosanitary
certificates and request with order.

NO Northplan/Mountain Seed. P.O. Box 9107 Moscow. ID 83843-
1607. USA.   CONTACT: L.M. Jones
TEL: 208 882 8040   FAX: 208 882 7446
WHOLESALE/RETAIL: US $1 or Sae US postage
POSATGE: Yes   EXPORT: Yes
CULTURAL NOTES: On request if known.
SPECIALITIES: Native, wildland species seed.

NP National Collection of Passiflora. Lampley Rd. Kingston
Seymour. Clevedon. N.Somerset. BS21 6XS
TEL: 01934 833350 FAX:01934 877255
CONTACT: J. Vanderplank OPENING TIMES:9-1, 2-5 M-Sa
MIN ORDER: No min. U.K., £5 EU   CAT COST: £1
CAT OUT: Oct   CULTURAL NOTES: Yes
WHOLESALE/RETAIL: Both SEED COUNT: Yes EXPORT:Yes
SPECIALITIES: Passiflora only   CREDIT CARDS:Yes

NS Natural Selection. 1 Station Cottages. Hullavington.
Chippenham. Wilts. SN14 6ET   CONTACT: M.J.Cragg Barber
TEL: 01666 837369   CAT COST: S.a.e
CAT OUT: Aut   POSTAGE: 26p WHOLESALE/RETAIL: Retail
SPECIALITIES:Obscure British natives

NT Native Gardens. 5737 Fisher Lane. Greenback. TN 37742. USA.
TEL: 423 856 0220 FAX: 423 856 0220 CONTACT:M.Bradforth
OPENING TIMES: By appt.   CAT COST: £2
CAT OUT: Spring, autumn update WHOLESALE/RETAIL: Both
CULTURAL NOTES: Yes   SEED COUNT:Min 25 , usually 100
EXPORT:Yes SPECIALITIES: Native seed of mid & eastern US
E-MAIL:R.copallina@aol.com

O D.Orriell - Seed Exporter. 45 Frape Ave. Mt Yokine 6060. Perth.
W.Australia   CONTACT: P.Orriell
TEL:+619 344 2290 FAX: +619 344 8982
OPENING TIMES: M-F, 9-5. Phone & fax 24hr service
MIN ORDER: Aus$25 CAT COST: US$6   CAT OUT: July
POSTAGE:Yes DISCOUNT: Lge orders WH/SALE/RETAIL: Both
CULTURAL NOTES:Some   SEED COUNT: Some
EXPORT:Yes SPECIALITIES: Native Australian seeds, palms,
cycads OTHER INFO: Vice President, member of Fleuroselect
group. Distributor of Kirstenbosch seed primer.

CODE-SUPPLIER INDEX

P Plant World. St. Marychurch Rd. Newton Abbot. Devon. TQ12 4SE
TEL/FAX: 01803 872939   CONTACT:Ray Brown
OPENING TIMES:Gardens open 9.30-5 , Easter- Sept
MIN ORDER: £8 UK, £20 overseas
CAT COST: 3x 1st class stamps or 2IRC (overseas)
CAT OUT: Oct   POSTAGE: 50p for under 10 pk, £1 overseas
DISCOUNT:Free pk for friend's name, or 10pks ordered. Trade
WHOLESALE/RETAIL: Retail   CULTURAL NOTES: Brief
SEED COUNT: Some   EXPORT:Yes
CREDIT CARDS:A,Eu,Ma,V   SPECIALITIES:
Primula, Hardy Geraniums, Aquilegias, Euphorbias, Mecanopsis

PA The Paradise Centre. Twinstead Rd. Lamarsh. Nr Bures. Suffolk. CO8 5EX
TEL: 01787 269449 FAX: 01787 269449
OPENING TIMES: Sa,Su & Bank Hols   MIN ORDER:£7.50
CAT COST: £1 or 4x 1st class stamps   CAT OUT: Jan
DISCOUNT: Several   WHOLESALE/RETAIL: Retail
CULTURAL NOTES: On request   EXPORT: Yes
CREDIT CARDS: Yes   SPECIALITIES: Unusual sp
OTHER INFO: Seeds suitable for growing abroad

PG Graysons Seeds. 34 Glenthorne Cl. Brampton. Chesterfield. Derbyshire. S40 3AR   CONTACT: P.Grayson
TEL: 01246 278503 FAX: 01246 566918
OPENING TIMES: By appt only CAT COST: Free CAT OUT: Oct
POSTAGE: 50p DISCOUNT: Trade WHOLESALE/RETAIL: Both
CULTURAL NOTES: Yes   SEED COUNT: Yes
SPECIALITIES: Alcea & Lathyrus   EXPORT:Yes
OTHER INFO: Produces own cultivars

PH Phedar Nursery. Bunkershill. Romiley. Stockport. SK6 3DS
TEL: 0161 430 3772 FAX:0161 430 3772
CONTACT:Will McLewin
CAT COST: S.a.e   CAT OUT:Hellebores Jul, Paeonia Oct
POSTAGE: Nominal   WHOLESALE/RETAIL:Both
CULTURAL NOTES: Basic   EXPORT: Yes
SPECIALITIES: Hellebore & paeonia
OTHER INFO: Accurate, authentic seed, provenance not hybrid
cultivated seed. Mainly wild-collected. Advance orders advised.

PI Pinetree Garden Seeds. Box 300. New Gloucester. ME 04260.USA.
TEL: 207 926 3400   FAX: 888 527 3337
FREE CAT OUT: Dec   POSTAGE: Yes, as per shipping costs.
WHOLESALE/RETAIL: Retail mail order only
CREDIT CARDS: Yes   CULTURAL NOTES: Yes
SEED COUNT: Yes   E-mail:superseeds@worldnet.ATT.NET

PK Park Seed Company. 1 Parkton Ave.Greenwood.SC 29647. USA
TEL:864 223 7333   FAX:864 941 4206
FREE CAT OUT: Retail in Dec, Wh/S in June
WHOLESALE/RETAIL: Both, export for wh/s only.
POSTAGE: Yes   E-mail: info@parkseed.com
CULTURAL NOTES: Yes   SEED COUNT: Yes
CREDIT CARDS:Yes   SPECIALITIES: Untreated heirlooms.

PL Plants of Distinction. Abacus House. Station Yard. Needham Market. Suffolk. IP6 8AS.   CONTACT: S. Missing
TEL: 01449 721720   FAX:01449 721722
FREE CAT OUT: OCT MIN ORDER: £10
WHOLESALE/RETAIL: Both   DISCOUNTS: By negotiation
CULTURAL NOTES: Yes   SEED COUNT: Yes
CREDIT CARDS: Yes   EXPORT: Yes
SPECIALITIES: Meconopsis, Cyclamen

PM Potterton & Martin. The Cottage Nursery. Moortown Rd. Nettleton. Nr Caistor. Lincs. LN7 6HX CONTACT: R.Potterton
TEL: 01472 851792   FAX:01472 851792
OPENING TIMES: 9-5 CAT COST:1st class stamp CAT OUT:Nov
POSTAGE: Free WHOLESALE/RETAIL: Both EXPORT: Yes
CREDIT CARDS:Yes   SPECIALITIES:Rare Alpines

PO Poyntzfield Herb Nursery. Black Isle. By Dingwall. Ross & Cromarty. Scotland.   CONTACT: D W Ross
TEL/FAX: 01381 610352 OPENING HOURS: 1-5 Mon-Sat.
Cat Cost: 4 x 1st class stamps. WHOLESALE/RETAIL: Retail
MIN ORDER: U.K. £5, Overseas £10.   EXPORT: Yes
POSTAGE: U.K. 50p, Overseas £1.50.
CULTURAL NOTES: Yes   SEED COUNT: On request
SPECIALITIES: Herbs and seeds of Scottish natives.

PR Prairie Moon Nursery. RR3 Box 163. Winona. MN55987. USA.
TEL: 507 452 1362   FAX:507 454 5238
OPENING TIMES:8-5 M-F Mail order only
CAT COST : $2.00 , $4 outside of USA   CAT OUT: Jan
POSTAGE: Yes   WHOLESALE/RETAIL: Retail
CULTURAL NOTES:Yes   SEED COUNT: Yes
SEED COLLECTIONS: Custom mixes   EXPORT: Yes
SPECIALITIES: 350 sp of native seeds
OTHER INFO: International customers expected to know their
countries' customs regulations. Pay in US funds in advance.

PT Philip Tivey & Sons. 28 Wanlip Rd. Syston. Nr Leicester. LE7 1PA   CONTACT:S.P.Tivey
TEL: 0116 269 2968   SPECIALITIES: Dahlia Exhibition Seed

PV Pleasant View Nursery. Pleasant View. Two Mile Oak. Newton Abbot. Devon. TQ12 6DG.   CONTACT: C.Yeo
TEL: 01803 813388   FAX: 01803 813388
OPENING HOURS: 10-5, Wed- Sat, Mid March to mid Oct.
WHOLESALE/RETAIL: Retail mail order.
CAT COST: 2x 2nd class stamps or 2 IRC's.   CAT OUT: Oct
MIN ORDER: £10 + p&p.   EXPORT: Yes
POSTAGE: U.K. 50p, EU £1, elsewhere £1.50
SPECIALITIES: Salvia seed only

R Range Nurseries. The Range. Clement St. Hextable. Swanley. Kent. BR8 7PQ
TEL: 01 322 661049   Phone, best bet 2-5   MIN ORDER: £3
FREE CAT OUT: Sept POSTAGE: Free   EXPORT: Possible
WHOLESALE/RETAIL:Both, wh/s on quotation
CULTURAL NOTES: Some SEED COUNT: Yes

RC Redwood City Seed Co. P.O. Box 361. Redwood City. California 94064. USA.
TEL: 415 325 7333
Internet: http://www.batnet.com.rwc-seed/
FREE CAT OUT: Dec   POSTAGE: See Catalogue
WHOLESALE/RETAIL: Both, separate lists.
CULTURAL NOTES: Yes   SEED COUNT: Yes, usually 100
EXPORT: Yes   SPECIALITIES: Endangered cultivated plant
seeds, heirloom vegetables, unusual culinary and medicinal
herbs. Hot capsicum varieties.
OTHER INFO: Gives historical, anecdotal, ethnobotanical uses.

RE Rainforest Seed Co. Box 241, San Jose 1017, Costa Rica.
TEL: 506 231 0980   FAX: 506 232 9260
CAT COST: US $2   SPECIALITIES: Exotic rainforest sp
OTHER INFO: Seed mostly from our own 1,500 acre virgin
rainforest. Portion of profits go to rainforest conservation
organisations.

CODE-SUPPLIER INDEX

RH Royal Horticultural Society. RHS Garden. Wisley. Woking. Surrey. GU23 6QB
TEL: 01483 224234 FAX:01483 212343
CAT COST: S.a.e, members only
CAT OUT: Nov, details provided on membership uptake
POSTAGE: £4 UK members, free to overseas members
EXPORT: RHS members only   CULTURAL NOTES: Yes
OTHER INFO: List changes annually, seeds available to members only.

RI Richters Herbs. 357 Hwy 47. Goodwood. ON LOC 1A0. Canada.
TEL: 1-905-640-6677   FAX: 1-905-640-6641
FREE CAT OUT: Jan
POSTAGE: $4 on orders under $40, otherwise none.
WHOLESALE/RETAIL: Both   e-mail: catalog@richters.com
CULTURAL NOTES: Yes   CREDIT CARDS: Yes
EXPORT: Yes
SPECIALITIES: Herbs

RM Rocky Mountain Rare Plants. 1706 Deerpath Rd. Franktown.
CO 80116-9462. USA.
TEL: 303 660 6498   FAX: 303 660 6498
FREE CAT OUT: Oct   WHOLESALE/RETAIL: Retail
POSTAGE: US $4 N.America, US $5 elsewhere.
CULTURAL NOTES: Yes   SEED COUNT:Yes
CREDIT CARDS: Yes   EXPORT: Yes
SPECIALITIES: Alpines e-mail: bskowron@harvest.com

RO W.Robinson & Sons Ltd. Sunnybank, Forton. Nr. Preston. PR3
0BN   CONTACT: I/E.Robinson
TEL: 01524 791210 FAX: 01524 791933
OPENING TIMES: Mar-Dec times vary   CAT COST:Free
CAT OUT: Sept   POSTAGE:Free WHOLESALE/RETAIL: Both
CULTURAL NOTES: Yes SEED COUNT: Yes   EXPORT: Yes
CREDIT CARDS: Yes
SPECIALITIES: Mammoth Strain veg

RS Richard Stockwell. Rare Plants. 64, Weardale Rd, Sherwood,
Nottingham. NG5 1DD   CONTACT:R. Stockwell
TEL: 0115 969 1063 FAX: 0115 969 1063
OPENING TIMES: Mail order only
CAT COST: 4x 2nd class stamps or 2 IRC (overseas)
CAT OUT: Dec, updated July for Southern hemisphere
POSTAGE: Free UK, overseas £1
WHOLESALE/RETAIL: Both
CULTURAL NOTES: Detailed germination guide on all genera
SEED COUNT: If less than 10   EXPORT:Yes
SPECIALITIES: Rare climbers, dwarf sp

RU Rust-en-Vrede Nursery. P.O. Box 753. Brackenfell 7560. RSA.
TEL: 27-21-9814515   FAX: 27-21-9810050
CONTACT: Alan Horstmann
CAT COST: $2   CAT OUT: Jan   MIN ORDER: $30
WHOLESALE/RETAIL: Retail mail order.
CULTURAL NOTES: Yes SEED COUNT: Yes EXPORT: Yes
SPECIALITIES: Indigenous seed, Cape flora.

S Suttons Seeds. Hele Rd. Torquay. Devon. TQ2 7QJ
TEL: 01803 612011 FAX: 01803 615747
OPENING TIMES: 8.30-5, M-F   CAT COST: Free
CAT OUT: Mid-Oct   POSTAGE:Free over £5
DISCOUNT: Trade/Associations WHOLESALE/RETAIL: Retail
CULTURAL NOTES: Yes
SEED COUNT: pks of under200 seeds
SEED COLLECTIONS: Yes EXPORT: Yes
CREDIT CARDS:Yes   OTHER INFO: Est. 1806

SA Sandeman Seeds. The Croft. Sutton. Pulborough. W.Sussex.
RH20 1PL   CONTACT: JCP Sandeman
TEL: 01798 869315 FAX`: 01798 869400
OPENING TIMES: 8.30-5.30   MIN ORDER: £40
CAT COST: Free to trade only CAT OUT: Sept   EXPORT:Yes
POSTAGE: Yes DISCOUNTS:Over £1000 CULTURAL NOTES:
Yes WHOLESALE/RETAIL: Wh/s   SEED COUNT: On request
E-MAil: Sandemanseeds@btinternet.com
SPECIALITIES: Woody plant seeds and perennials
OTHER INFO: Info such as provenance etc. on request

SB S&N Brackley. 117 Winslow Rd. Wingrave. Aylesbury. Bucks.
HP22 4QB.
TEL: 01296 681384   OPENING HOURS: By Appointment.
FREE CAT OUT: August   WHOLESALE/RETAIL: Both
POSTAGE: Yes   DISCOUNTS: Yes   EXPORT: Yes
CULTURAL NOTES: Yes   SEED COUNT: Yes
SPECIALITIES: Lathyrus odoratus, Exhibition vegetables.
OTHER INFO: Specialist hybridisers and raisers of Lathyrus
and Exhibition vegetables.

SC Scottish Rock Garden Club. PO Box 14063. Edinburgh. EH10
4YE
TEL: 01786 824064
MIN ORDER: £2.50   CAT COST: Free to members
CAT OUT: Dec/Jan   POSTAGE: Free
CULTURAL NOTES: Yes   EXPORT: Overseas members
SPECIALITIES:Hardy plants & bulbs
OTHER INFO:List may be subject to slight changes from year
to year. Seed exchange available to members only. Wild &
garden sources from around the world

SD Seeds of Change. P.O. Box 15700. Santa Fe NM 87506. USA.
TEL: 1-888 762 7333   FAX: 505 438 7052
CAT COST: Free POSTAGE: Yes WHOLESALE/RETAIL: Both
CREDIT CARDS: Yes EXPORT: Yes
CULTURAL NOTES: Yes   SEED COUNT: Yes
e-mail: gardener@seedsofchange.com
internet: http://www.seedsofchange.com

SE Seymour Selected Seeds. Admail 962 Farm Lane. Spalding.
Lincs. PE11 1TD
TEL: 01481 65270 FAX:01481 64552 Answer machine 24hr
CAT COST: Free   CAT OUT: Early Oct   POSTAGE:Yes
DISCOUNT:Yes   WHOLESALE/RETAIL: Mail order
CULTURAL NOTES: Yes   SEED COUNT: Yes
CREDIT CARDS:Yes   SPECIALITIES: Flower & veg

SG The Seed Guild. The Coach House. Carnwath. Lanark. ML11
8LF.   CONTACT: D. McDougall
TEL: 01555 841450 FAX: 01555 841480
CAT COST: 3x 2nd class stamps   CAT OUT: Autumn
POSTAGE: Free over £10   WHOLESALE/RETAIL: Both
EXPORT: Yes   CREDIT CARDS:Yes
SPECIALITIES: Seeds from botanical gardens around the world
Internet: http://www. Gardenweb.com/seedgd
E-MAIL: 100104.346@compuserve.com

SH The Seed House. 9a Widley Rd. Cosham. Portsmouth. PO6
2DS
TEL: 01705 325639
MIN ORDER: £5   CAT COST: 4x 1st class stamps or 4IRC's
CAT OUT: On request with updated lists   DISCOUNTS:Trade
WHOLESALE/RETAIL: Both   CULTURAL NOTES: Yes
EXPORT: Yes SEED COUNT: Depends on cost, pks at unit price.
SPECIALITIES: Australian & N.Z seeds for European climate

340

CODE-SUPPLIER INDEX

SI Silverhill Seeds. P.O.Box 53108. Kenilworth. 7745 South Africa
TEL: +27 21 762 4245 FAX: +27 21 797 6609
CONTACT: R.Saunders e-mail: silseeds@iafrica.com
CAT COST: £1 CAT OUT: Jan POSTAGE: Min £2
DISCOUNTS: Bulk discounts WHOLESALE/RETAIL: Both
CULTURAL NOTES: Yes EXPORT: Yes
SEED COUNT: Seeds normally sold by no., not by weight
SPECIALITIES: South African seeds

SK Stokes Seeds Inc. Box 548 Buffalo NY 14240-0548. USA.
TEL: 716 695 6980 FAX: 716 695 9649
OPENING HOURS: 8-6 FREE CAT OUT: Nov
WHOLESALE/RETAIL: Both CREDIT CARDS: Yes
EXPORT: Yes CULTURAL NOTES:Yes SEED COUNT:Yes
SPECIALITIES: Vegetables, Herbs, Flowers.
OTHER INFO: Also at: Box 10. St. Catharines. Ontario. L2R
6R6. Canada. TEL: 905 688 4300. FAX: 905 684 9649

SN Simpson's Seeds. 27 Meadowbrook. Old Oxted. Surrey.
TEL: 01883 715242 FAX: 01883 715242
OPENING TIMES: By appt, late Aug/early Sept
CAT COST: Free CAT OUT: Late Oct DISCOUNTS: Several
WHOLESALE/RETAIL: Both CULTURAL NOTES: Yes
SEED COUNT: Yes EXPORT: Yes CREDIT CARDS: Yes
SPECIALITIES: Tomatoes, unusual veg, gourmet potatoes &
peppers.
OTHER INFO: M.A.F.F. registered growers & distributors
No:2620. Newsletter & helpline for tomatoes. Organic seed

SO Southfield Nurseries. Boune Rd. Morton. Bourne. Lincs. PE10
ORH
TEL: 01778 570168 CONTACT: B.Goodey
POSTAGE: 60p WHOLESALE/RETAIL: Retail
CULTURAL NOTES: Yes SEED COLLECTIONS: Yes
SPECIALITIES: Cactus

SP Salt Spring Seeds. P.O. Box 444 Ganges. Salt Spring Island.
B.C. Canada. V8K 2W1. CONTACT: D.Jason
TEL: 250 537 5269 WHOLESALE/RETAIL: Retail
CAT COST: $2 CAT OUT: Dec EXPORT: Yes
CULTURAL NOTES: Yes SEED COUNT: Yes
SPECIALITIES: Beans, Grains, Lettuce, Tomato.
OTHER INFO: All seeds ceritified organic.

SR Siegers Seed Co. 8265 Felch St. Zeeland. MI 49464. USA.
TEL: 1 800 962 4999 FAX: 616 772 0333
FREE CAT OUT: Nov CONTACT: D. Siegers
POSTAGE: Orders over $200 free. EXPORT: Limited
SEED COUNT: Mostly WHOLESALE/RETAIL: Both
CREDIT CARDS: Yes
SPECIALITIES: Vegetables, Herbs.

SS Southern Seeds. The Vicarage. Sheffield. Canterbury. New
Zealand 8173
TEL: 03 31 83 814 FAX: 03 31 83 814
OPENING TIMES: Mail order MIN ORDER: NZ $25
CAT COST: NZ $5 or £2 sterling CAT OUT: Mid year
POSTAGE: NZ $10 WHOLESALE/RETAIL: Retail
CULTURAL NOTES: Yes EXPORT: Yes
SPECIALTIES: N.Z alpines/ South Island
OTHER INFO: Seed mainly collected from the wild

ST Stewarts (Nottm) Ltd. The Garden Shop. 3 George St. Nottm.
NG1 3BH
TEL: 0115 9476338 FAX:0115 9410720

OPENING TIMES: 9-5.30, 6 days MIN ORDER: 1 pk
CAT COST: 2x 1st class stamps CAT OUT: Dec
POSTAGE: Yes DISCOUNT: Early orders
WHOLESALE/RETAIL: Retail CULTURAL NOTES: Some
SEED COUNT:Some EXPORT: If necessary
CREDIT CARDS: Yes SPECIALITIES: Potatoes, grass , veg

SU Suffolk Herbs, Monks Farm. Kelvedon. Essex. CO5 9PG
TEL: 01376 572456 FAX: 01376 571189
CAT COST: Free CAT OUT: Sept WHOLESALE/RETAIL: Both
POSTAGE: Mail order free, trade free over £35
CULTURAL NOTES: Yes SEED COUNT: Yes EXPORT: Yes
SEED COLLECTIONS: Yes CREDIT CARDS: Yes
SPECIALITIES: Herbs, oriental veg, wild flowers and vegetable

SW Southwestern Native Seeds. Box 50503. Tuscon. Arizona
85703.USA. CONTACT: J. Walker .
OPENING TIMES: Mail order only MIN ORDER: $13
CAT COST: $2 CAT OUT: Oct
POSTAGE; $1 US, $2 overseas WHOLESALE/RETAIL: Retail
CULTURAL NOTES: Yes EXPORT: Yes
SPECIALITIES: Wild collected native ornamentals

SZ Seedhunt. P.O. Box 96. Freedom. CA 95019-0096. USA.
TEL: 408 763 1523 e-mail: seedhunt@aol.com
CAT COST: US $1 in USA, US $2 overseas or 3IRC's.
CAT OUT: Dec POSTAGE: US $2
WHOLESALE/RETAIL: Retail EXPORT: Yes
CULTURAL NOTES: On request only SEED COUNT: Yes
SPECIALITIES: Salvias, uncommon annuals, Mediterranean
plant seeds. OTHER INFO: List varies a little from year to year.

T Thompson & Morgan, Poplar Lane, Ipswich. Suffolk. IP8 3BU
TEL: 01473 688588 FAX: 01473 680199
OPENING TIMES: 9-5, M-F CAT COST: Free
CAT OUT: Oct POSTAGE: 70p
DISCOUNTS: Various. For horticultural socieies & clubs.
WHOLESALE/RETAIL: Both CULTURAL NOTES: Yes
SEED COUNT: Yes SEED COLLECTIONS: Yes
EXPORT: Yes SPECIALITIES: Wide range
OTHER INFO: Biggest illustrated seed catalogue in the world

TE Territorial Seed Co. P.O. Box 157. 20 Palmer Ave. Cottage Grove.
OR 97424. USA. CONTACT: Tom John
TEL: 541 942 9547 FAX: 541 942 9881
FREE CAT OUT: Dec WHOLESALE/RETAIL: Retail
CREDIT CARDS: Yes EXPORT: Yes
SPECIALITIES: Many Northwest heirlooms.

TH Thomas Etty Esq.. 45 Forde Ave.Bromley. Kent. BR1 3EU.
TEL/FAX: 0181 466 6785 CONTACT: R. Warner
E-Mail: rwarner@cix.co.uk WEBSITE:Yes
CAT COST: 4 x 1st class stamps MIN ORDER: £5
POSTAGE: On orders under £10
WHOLESALE/RETAIL: Retail EXPORT: Yes
SPECIALITIES: Vegetables, Flowers from 15-19 century.

TT Three Trees Trading Co. Ltd. Suite 699. 2 Old Brompton Rd.
London. SW7 3DQ. CONTACT: E.Baum
TEL: 0171 413 9921 FAX: 0171 581 4445
FREE CAT OUT: Feb MIN ORDER: £5 EXPORT: Yes
CULTURAL NOTES: Yes SEED COUNT: Yes
WHOLESALE/RETAIL: Both e-mail: ebaum@patril.i-way.co.uk
SPECIALITIES: Sustainably harvested tropical rainforest seeds,
species germination tested in th UK.
OTHER INFO: European distributors for Rainforest Seed Co.

CODE-SUPPLIER INDEX

TU Edwin Tucker & Sons Ltd. Brewery Meadow. Stonepark.
Ashburton. Newton Abbot, Devon. TQ13 7DG
TEL: 01364 652403   FAX: 01364 654300
CONTACT: Geoff Penton OPENING TIMES: M-F 8-5, Sa 8-12
CAT COST: Free   CAT OUT: Oct
POSTAGE: For small orders   DISCOUNTS: Various
WHOLESALE/RETAIL: Retail   CULTURAL NOTES: Yes
SEED COUNT: Yes   EXPORT: Yes (some restrictions)
CREDIT CARDS: Yes   SPECIALITIES: Potatoes

U Unwins Seeds Ltd. Cambridge CB4 4ZZ
TEL: 01945 588 522   FAX: 01945 475 255
FREE CAT OUT: Summer, mid-autumnPOSTAGE: Free over £15
DISCOUNTS: See catalogue WHOLESALE/RETAIL: Mail order,
Retail stockists CULTURAL NOTES: Yes SEED COUNT: Yes
SEED COLLECTIONS: Yes   EXPORT: By agreement
CREDIT CARDS: Yes   SPECIALITIES: Sweet peas

V Vreeken's Zaden. Voorstraat 448, 3311 ex Dordrecht. Holland
TEL: 00-31-78-6135467   FAX: 00-31-78-312198
OPENING TIMES:Vary   MIN ORDER: £6
CAT COST: £3   CAT OUT: Nov   POSTAGE: Free over £14
WHOLESALE/RETAIL: Both   CULTURAL NOTES: Yes
SEED COUNT: Most EXPORT: EU CREDIT CARDS: Eu, Ma, V
SPECIALITIES: Rare varieties veg & flowers

VE Versepuy. 1 Chemin Sainte catherine. B.P.9- 43001 Le Puy-
en-Velay. Cedex. France.   CONTACT: J. Schmitt (Export)
TEL: (33) 4 71 05 60 80 FAX: (33) 4 71 05 91 01
OPENING HOURS: 8-7.   EXPORT: Yes
CAT COST: Free to trade, 15ff for individuals.   CAT OUT: Dec
CULTURAL NOTES: Yes   SEED COUNT: Yes

VH The Van Hage Garden Co. Great Amwell. Ware. Herts. SG12
9RP
TEL: 01920 870811 FAX: 01920 871861
OPENING TIMES: M-F 9-6, Sa 9-6, Su 10.30-4.30
CAT COST: Free   CAT OUT: Oct   POSTAGE: 50p
DISCOUNTS:Yes   WHOLESALE/RETAIL: Retail
EXPORT: Yes   SPECIALITIES: Dutch seed, giant carrot Flak

VO Wild Collected Seeds. Voltech Holubec. Sidlistni 210. 16500
Praha 6. Czech Republic.   e-mail: holubec@genbank.vurv.cz
TEL: 420-2/360851   FAX: 365228
CAT COST: US$ 2.   CAT OUT: Nov   POSTAGE: US$ 3
CULTURAL NOTES: General   OTHER INFO: Descriptive cat.
SPECIALITIES: Rare alpines from Turkey, Caucasus, Russia.

VR R.V.Roger Ltd, The Nurseries. Pickering.N.Yorks. YO18 7HG.
TEL: 01751 472226 FAX: 01751 476749
CAT COST: Sae   CREDIT CARDS: Yes
SPECIALITIES: Seed Potatoes

VS Samen Catalogue c/o Vreeken's Zaden. Voorstraat-West 448.
Postbus 182. 3300 AD Dordrecht. The Netherlands.
TEL: 00 31 78 6135467   FAX: 00 31 78 6312198
CAT OUT: Mar   WHOLESALE/RETAIL: Retail
EXPORT: Yes   SPECIALITIES: Rare veg seeds
OTHER INFO: Distributed through Vreekens.

VY Vesey's Seeds Ltd. York. Prince Edward Island. Canada. C0A
1P0.   CONTACT: Allen Perry
TEL: 902 368 7333   FAX: 902 566 1620
FREE CAT OUT: Dec   POSTAGE: $2.50 handling charge
CREDIT CARDS: Yes   EXPORT: Small quantities
WHOLESALE/RETAIL: Retail e-mail: catalog@veseys.com

CULTURAL NOTES: Yes   SEED COUNT: Some
SPECIALITIES: Seeds for shorter seasons

W c/o National Auricula, & Primula Society (Southern), 67
Warnham Court Rd, Carshalton Beeches, Surrey. SM5 3ND
CONTACT: L.E.Wigley
CAT COST: S.a.e. CAT OUT: Jan POSTAGE: S.a.e. with order
CULTURAL NOTES: Yes   EXPORT: Yes
SPECIALITIES: Auricula, Primula , Campanula.
OTHER INFO: List contains hand-fertilised items.

WA Seed Center: Dept Water Affairs & Forestry. P.O. Box 727
Pretoria 0001. RSA.   CONTACT: Officer in Charge
TEL: 012 3274168/9   FAX: 012 3274175
CAT: Free   MIN ORDER: 10g and multiples thereof.
POSTAGE: Yes   WHOLESALE/RETAIL: Wh/s EXPORT: Yes
CULTURAL NOTES: Yes   SEED COUNT: Yes
SPECIALITIES: Trees, Shrubs

WO F.A. Woodcock. Lawn Rd Nurseries. Lawn Rd. Walmer. Deal.
Kent. CT14 7ND.
TEL: 01304 374238   Contact: F.A.Woodcock
CAT COST: S.a.e.   POSTAGE: 80p
WHOLESALE/RETAIL: Retail   EXPORT: Yes
SPECIALITIES: Lathyrus odoratus (Sweet peas)

X Rhododendron, Camellia & Magnolia Group (RHS), Whitehills,
Newton Stewart. DG8 6SL
TEL: 01671 402049 FAX: 01671 403106
CAT COST: £1, £2 overseas   CAT OUT: Jan
WHOLESALE/RETAIL: Members only
EXPORT: For members SPECIALITIES: Rhododendron
OTHER INFO: List includes wild-collected, hand and open-
pollinated sp. Seed available to members only.

Y Roy Young Seeds. 23 Westland Chase. West Winch. King's
Lynn. Norfolk. PE33 0QH
TEL: 01553 840867 FAX: 01553 840867
CAT COST: Stamp UK, 2x IRC (overseas) each list
CAT OUT: Oct   POSTAGE: 65p UK, £1 EU, £1.50 elsewhere
WHOLESALE/RETAIL: Both   SEED COUNT:Yes
EXPORT: Yes   SPECIALITIES: Cactus & succulents
OTHER INFO: Over 1,500 varieties in retail catalogue.

YA Samuel Yates Ltd. Withyfold Drive. Macclesfield. Chesire. SK10
2BE   CONTACT: Charles Seddon
TEL: +44 (0)1625 427823 FAX: +44 (0)1625 422843
WH/S/RETAIL: Wh/s   MIN ORDER: £50   POSTAGE : Free
CULTURAL NOTES:Yes   SEED COUNT:On request
CREDIT CARDS: CWO or credit accounts only
SPECIALITIES: Sakata bred veg & flower seed
OTHER INFO: Subsidiary of Sakata Seed Corporation, Japan.

YS YSJ Seeds. Kingsfield Conservation Nursery. Broadenham
Lane. Winsham. Chard. Somerset. TA20 4JF.
TEL/FAX : 01460 30070   CONTACT: M.A. White
Catalogue Cost: 31p stamp   CAT OUT: Oct POSTAGE: Yes
WHOLESALE/REATIL: Both   EXPORT: Yes
SPECIALITIES: British natives

Z Wild Seeds. Branas. Llandderfel, Gwynedd. LL23 7RF
CONTACT: Mike Thorne
OPENING TIMES: Mail order only
CAT COST: Free   POSTAGE: Free over £40
DISCOUNT: 10% over £100   CULTURAL NOTES: Yes
EXPORT: Yes   SPECIALITIES: Wildflowers

342

SUPPLIER- CODE INDEX

343

SUPPLIER-CODE INDEX

Please note new companies in this edition are in bold.

COMMON NAMES- BOTANICAL

Botanical	Common	Botanical	Common
Yucca filamentosa	Adam's Needle	Hyacinthoides	Bluebell
Arctotis	African Daisy	Vaccinum	Blueberry
Agapanthus	African Lily	Andromeda	Bog Rosemary
Saintpaulia	African Violet	Borago	Borage
Tillandsia	Air Plant	Callistemon	Bottlebrush
Alnus	Alder	Brachychiton	Bottletree
Anchusa	Alkanet	Pandorea jasminoides	Bower Plant
Calycanthus	Allspice	Gillenia trifoliata	Bowman's Root
Dierama	Angel's Fishing Rod	Buxus	Box
Datura	Angel's Trumpet	Cotula coronopifolia	Brass Buttons
Brugsmansia	Angel's Trumpets	Francoa	Bridal Wreath
Fraxinus	Ash	Cytisus	Broom
Callistephus	Aster, Chinese	Genista	Broom
Banksia	Australian Honeysuckle	Eriogonum	Buckwheat
Grevillea	Australian Silky Oak	Ajuga	Bugle
Colchicum	Autumn Crocus	Typha	Bullrush
Geum	Avens	Sanguisorba	Burnet
Nemophila menziesii	Baby Blue Eyes	Bassia	Burning Bush
Gypsophila	Baby's Breath	Dictamnus	Burning Bush
Platycodon	Balloon Flower	Browallia	Bush Violet
Melissa	Balm	Impatiens	Busy Lizzie
Impatiens balsamina	Balsam	Ranunculus	Buttercup
Bambusa	Bamboo	Buddleja	Butterfly Bush
Musa/Ensete	Banana	Schizanthus	Butterfly Flower
Actaea	Baneberry	Cordyline	Cabbage Palm
Adansonia digitata	Baobab Tree	Acinos	Calamint
Acanthophoenix	Barbel Palm	Kalmia latifolia	Calico Bush
Berberis	Barberry	Phacelia	Californian Bluebell
Hordeum	Barley	Ceanothus	Californian Lilac
Epimedium	Barrenwort	Eschscholzia	Californian Poppy
Ocimum basilicum	Basil	Cinnamonum camphora	Camphor Tree
Tacca chantrierei	Bat Flower	Lychnis	Campion
Campanula trachelium	Bats-in-the-Belfry	Tropaeolum peregrinum	Canary Creeper
Laurus nobilis	Bay Laurel	Iberis	Candytuft
Aciphylla	Bayonet Plant	Campanula medium	Canterbury Bells
Melia azedarach	Bead-tree	Streptocarpus	Cape Primrose
Acanthus	Bear's Breeches	Cynara	Cardoon
Penstemon	Beard Tongue	Dianthus caryophyllus	Carnation
Kolkwitzia	Beauty Bush	Ricinus	Castor Oil Plant
Pelargonium	Bedding Geranium	Avena	Cat Grass
Galium	Bedstraw	Silene	Catchfly
Fagus	Beech	Cobaea scandens	Cathedral Bell
Campanula	Bell Flower	Calamintha	Catmint
Moluccella	Bells of Ireland	Nepeta	Catmint
Monarda	Bergamot	Chelidonium majus	Celandine, Greater
Acaena	Bibi-bidi	Ranunculus ficaria	Celandine, Lesser
Craspedia	Billy Buttons	Agave	Century Plant
Betula	Birch	Chamaemelum	Chamomile
Strelitzia	Bird of Paradise	Vitex agnus-castus	Chaste Tree
Gilia	Birds' Eyes	Heliotropium arborescens	Cherry Pie
Persicaria	Bistort	Castanea	Chestnut (Sweet)
Cardamine	Bittercress	Eccremocarpus	Chilean Glory Vine
Celastrus	Bittersweet	Ornithogalum thyrsoides	Chincherinchee
Cimicifuga	Black Snake Root	Cynoglossum	Chinese Forget-me-Not
Rudbeckia fulgida/hirta	Black-Eyed Susan	Rehmannia	Chinese Foxglove
Thunbergia	Black-Eyed Susie	Physalis	Chinese Lantern
Colutea	Bladder Senna	Akebia	Chocolate Vine
Utricularia	Bladderwort	Aronia	Chokeberry
Gaillardia	Blanket Flower	Blandfordia	Christmas Bells
Liatris	Blazing Star	Schlumbergera	Christmas Cactus
Mentzelia	Blazing Star	Dendranthema	Chrysanthemum
Dicentra	Bleeding Heart	Leucanthemum	Chrysanthemum
Sanguinaria	Blood Root	Cuphea	Cigar Plant
Scilla	Blue Bells	Potentilla	Cinquefoil
Trachymene	Blue Lace Flower	Trifolium	Clover
Sisyrinchium	Blue-Eyed Grass	Celosia	Cockscomb
		Cocos	Coconut

COMMON NAMES-BOTANICAL

Botanical	Common	Botanical	Common
Aquilegia	Columbine	Crepis	Hawksbeard
Rudbeckia	Cone Flower	Calluna	Heather
Heuchera	Coral Bells	Carya	Hickory
Erythrina	Coral Tree	Alcea	Hollyhock
Antigonon	Coral Vine	Lunaria	Honesty
Agrostemma	Corn Cockle	Cerinthe	Honeywort
Centaurea	Cornflower	Ptelea	Hop Tree
Bidens	Cosmos	Carpinus	Hornbeam
Onopordum	Cotton Thistle	Glaucium	Horned Poppy
Geranium	Crane's Bill	Aesculus	Horse Chestnut
Codiaeum	Croton	Achimenes	Hot Water Plant
Araujia	Cruel Plant	Sempervivum	House Leek
Nierembergia	Cup Flower	Lablab	Hyacinth Bean
Catanache	Cupid's Dart	Agastache	Hyssop
Chamaecyparis	Cypress	Canna	Indian Shot
Bellis Perennis	Daisy	Polemonium	Jacob's Ladder
Commelina	Day Flower	Fatsia Japonica	Japanese Aralia
Hemerocallis	Day Lily	Cryptomeria	Japanese Cedar
Adenium	Desert Rose	Sophora	Japanese Pagoda Tree
Anethum	Dill	Coix lacryma jobi	Job's Tears
Dracaena	Dragon Tree	Cercis	Judas Tree
Ratibida pinnata	Drooping Coneflower	Anigozanthos	Kangaroo Paw
Aristolochia	Dutchman's Pipe	Agathis	Kauri Pine
Chamaerops	Dwarf Fan Palm	Archontophoenix	King Palm
Convolvulus	Dwarf Morning Glory	Actidinia deliciosa	Kiwi Fruit
Bergenia	Elephant's Ears	Alchemilla	Lady's Mantle
Calendula	English Marigold (Pot)	Adenophora	Ladybell
Oenethera	Evening Primrose	Stachys	Lamb's Ears
Rhodanthe	Everlasting	Consolida	Larkspur
Lathyrus	Everlasting Pea	Lavendula	Lavender
Schefflera elegantissima	False Aralia	Santolina	Lavender Cotton
Baptisia	False Indigo	Ligularia	Leopard Plant
Foeniculum	Fennel	Lilium	Lily
Delonix	Flamboyant Tree	Lithops	Living Stones
Anthurium	Flamingo Flower	Lysimachia	Loosestrife
Linum	Flax	Arum	Lords and Ladies
Dianella	Flax Lily	Amaranthus caudatus	Love Lies Bleeding
Erigeron	Fleabane	Nigella	Love-in-a-Mist
Ageratum	Floss Flower	Adiantum	Maidenhair Fern
Malus	Flowering Crab	Ginkgo	Maidenhair Tree
Abutilon	Flowering Maple	Lavatera	Mallow
Chaenomeles	Flowering Quince	Malva	Mallow
(Japanese)		Archtostaphylos	Manzanita
Myosotis	Forget-me-Not	Acer	Maple
Digitalis	Foxglove	Tagetes	Marigold
Alopecurus	Foxtail Grass	Caltha	Marsh Marigold
Eremurus	Foxtail Lily	Althaea	Marshmallow
Hedysarum	French Honeysuckle	Mirabilis	Marvel of Peru
Limnanthes	Fried Eggs	Alonsoa	Mask Flower
Acca	Fruit Salad Bush	Astrantia	Masterwort
Corydalis	Fumitory	Panacratium	Mediterranean Lily
Cardiocrinum	Giant Lily	Choisya	Mex. Orange Blossom
Alpinia	Ginger Lily	Tithonia	Mexican Sunflower
Gomphrena globosa	Globe Amaranth	Hunnemannia	Mexican Tulip Poppy
Globularia	Globe Daisy	Reseda	Mignonette
Trollius	Globe Flower	Asclepias	Milkweed
Echinops	Globe Thistle	Mentha	Mint
Gloriosa	Glory Lily	Mimulus	Monkey Flower
Chionodoxa	Glory of the Snow	Aconitum	Monkshood
Aruncus	Goat's Beard	Ipomoea	Morning Glory
Galega	Goat's Rue	Leonurus	Motherwort
Anthemis	Golden Chamomile	Sorbus	Mountain Ash
Ulex	Gorse	Linanthus	Mountain Phlox
Aegopodium	Ground Elder	Arnica	Mountain Tobacco
Eucalyptus	Gum Tree	Anacyclus	Mt. Atlas Daisy
Celtis	Hackberry	Verbascum	Mullein

346

COMMON NAMES- BOTANICAL

Botanical	Common	Botanical	Common
Myrtus	Myrtle	Leucojum	Snowflake
Tropaeoleum	Nasturtium	Amelanchier	Snowy Mespilus
Celmisia	New Zealand Daisy	Polygonatum	Solomon's Seal
Phormium	New Zealand Flax	Bolusanthos	South African Wisteria
Arrhenantherum	Oat Grass	Veronica	Speedwell
Physostegia	Obedient Plant	Cleome	Spider Flower
Olea	Olive Tree	Picea	Spruce
Allium	Onion	Euphorbia	Spurge
Origanum	Oregano	Paradisea	St.Bruno's Lily
Brassica oleracea	Ornamental Cabbage	Hypericum	St.John's Wort
Carex	Ornamental Sedge	Xanthisma	Star of Texas
Cortaderia	Pampas Grass	Osteospermum	Star of the Veldt
Viola x wittrochiana	Pansy	Matthiola	Stocks
Aloe variegata	Partridge Breasted Aloe	Stokesia	Stokes Aster
Pulsatilla	Pasque Flower	Sedum	Stonecrop
Passiflora	Passion Flower	Arbutus	Strawberry Tree
Anaphalis	Pearl Everlasting	Bracteantha bracteata	Strawflower
Catharanthus	Periwinkle	Portulaca	Sun Plant
Alstroemeria	Peruvian Lily	Helianthus	Sunflower
Adonis	Pheasant's Eye	Brachyscome	Swan River Daisy
Anagallis	Pimpernel	Lobularia	Sweet Alyssum
Pinus	Pine	Artemisia annua	Sweet Annie
Ananas	Pineapple	Liquidamber	Sweet Gum
Dianthus	Pinks	Lathyrus odoratus	Sweet Pea
Plantago	Plantain	Hesperis	Sweet Rocket
Macleaya	Plume Poppy	Amberboa	Sweet Sultan
Hypoestes	Polka Dot	Dianthus barbatus	Sweet William
Papaver	Poppy	Athrotaxis	Tasmanian Cedar
Eustoma	Prairie Gentian	Emilia	Tassel Flower
Acanthostachys	Prickle Ear	Dipsacus	Teasel
Argemone	Prickly Poppy	Armeria	Thrift
Amaranthus cruentus	Purple Amaranth (Red)	Thymus	Thyme
Rhodochiton	Purple Bell Vine	Linaria	Toad Flax
Lythrum	Purple Loosestrife	Nicotiana	Tobacco Plant
Antennaria	Pussy Toes	Gerbera	Transvaal Daisy
Ramonda	Pyrenean Primrose	Clematis vitalba	Traveller's Joy
Briza	Quaking Grass	Gazania	Treasure Flower
Camassia	Quamash	Dicksonia	Tree Fern
Aporocactus	Rat's tail Cactus	Campsis	Trumpet Flower
Echinacea	Red Cone Flower	Chelone	Turtlehead
Kniphofia	Red Hot Poker	Peltiphyllum	Umbrella Plant
Sequoia	Redwood	Centranthus	Valerian
Arabis	Rock Cress	Dionaea	Venus Fly Trap
Androsace	Rock Jasmine	Specularia	Venus' Looking Glass
Cistus	Rock Rose	Ionopsidium	Violet Cress
Helianthemum	Rock Rose	Malcomia	Virginian Stock
Rosa	Rose	Erysimum	Wallflower
Aiphanes	Ruffle Palm	Sparaxis	Wand Flower
Perovskia	Russian Sage	Alisma	Water Plantain
Carthamus	Safflower	Acacia	Wattle
Acoelorraphe	Saw Palm	Abeliophyllum	White Forsythia
Scabiosa	Scabious	Morina	Whorl Flower
Arenaria	Scotch Moss	Asarum	Wild Ginger
Coccoloba	Sea Grape	Epilobium	Willow Herb
Eryngium	Sea Holly	Anemone	Wind Flower
Mimosa	Sensitive Plant	Stylomecon	Wind Poppy
Nicandra	Shoo Fly Plant	Ammobium	Winged Everlasting
Bombax	Silk Cotton Tree	Eranthis	Winter Aconite
Albizia	Silk Tree	Solanum	Winter Cherry
Periploca	Silk Vine	Chimonanthus	Wintersweet
Abies	Silver Fir	Hamamelis	Witch Hazel
Calceolaria	Slipper Flower	Asperula	Woodruff
Phaseolus	Snail Flower	Artemisia	Wormwood
Antirrhinum	Snapdragon	Helleborus	Xmas Rose
Helenium	Sneezeweed	Achillea	Yarrow
Galanthus	Snowdrop	Bupthalmum	Yellow Ox Eye Daisy

SYNONYMS

Acca	Feijoa	Epilobium	Chamaenerion
Aeonium	Megalonium	Epipremnum	Scindapsus
Aethionema	Eunomia	Episcia	Alsobia
Agastache	Brittonastrum	Episcia	Alsobia
Agathis	Dammara	Erysimum	Cheiranthus
Albizia	Paraserianthes	Eustoma	Lisianthus
Allamanda	Allemanda	Fallopia	Bilderdyckia
Amsonia	Rhazya	Fatsia	Aralia
Amygdalus	Prunus	Felicia	Agathaea
Androsace	Douglasia	Fremontodendron	Fremontia
Anredera	Boussingaultia	Gaultheria	Pernettya
Arctostaphylos	Comarostaphylos	Gaultheria	X Gaulnettya
Arctotis	Venidium	Genista	Chamaespartium
Arctotis	x Venidioarctotis	Genista	Echinospartium
Arecastrum	Syagrus	Gladiolus	Aciderantha
Asarum	Heterotropa	Gladiolus	Homoglossum
Asarum	Hexastylis	Hacquetia	Dondia
Asplenium	Ceterach	Hatiora	Rhipsalidopsis
Asplenium	Phyllitis	Hedychium	Brachychilum
Aster	Crinitaria	Helipterum	Rhodanthe
Aurinia	Alyssum	Hepatica	Anemone
Bassia	Kochia	Herbertia lahue	Alophia lahue
Bergenia	Megasea	Hibbertia	Candollea
Bignonia	Doxantha	Howea	Kentia
Bixa orellana	Annatto	Humea	Calomeria
Brachyglottis	Senecio	Hyacinthoides	Endymion
Brachyscome	Brachycome	Hymenocallis	Ismene
Bracteantha	Helichrysum	Incarvillea	Amphicome
Brevoortia	Dichelostemma	Ipomea	Mina
Browningia	Azurocereus	Ipomea	Pharbitis
Buddleja	Buddleia	Jeffersonia	Plagiorhegma
Calomeria	Humea	Juniperus	Sabina
Caralluma	Frerea	Justicia	Beloperone
Cardamine	Dentaria	Justicia	Drejerella
Centaurium	Erythraea	Justicia	Duvernoia
Chamaedaphne	Cassandra	Justicia	Libonia
Clarkia	Eucharidium	Kalanchoe	Bryophyllum
Clarkia	Godetia	Kennedia	Kennedya
Clematis	Atragene	Kitaibela	Kitaibelia
Consolida	Delphinium	Lablab	Dolichos
Cornus	Chamaepericlymenum	Lamium	Galeobdolon
Cornus	Dendrobenthamia	Lamium	Lamiastrum
Cornus	Thelycrania	Leschenaultia	Lechenaultia
Corryocactus	Erdisia	Leucanthemopsis	Chrysanthemum
Corydalis	Fumaria	Leucanthemum	Chrysanthemum
Corydalis	Pseudofumaria	Leucophyta	Calocephalus
Corydalis	Pseudofumaria	Lobularia	Alyssum
Crocosmia	Antholyza	Lotus	Dorycnium
Cyathea	Alsophila	Lychnis	Silene
Cyathia	Alsophila	Lychnis	Viscaria
Cyrtomium	Phanaeophlebia	Macfadyena	Doxantha
Cyrtomium	Phanerophlebia	Mackaya	Asystasia
Cytisus	Argyrocytisus	Macleaya	Bocconia
Darmera	Peltiphyllum	Maclura	Cudrania
Dendranthema	Chrysanthemum	Mammillaria	Mammilopsis
Dichelostemma	Brevoortia	Mandevilla	Dipladenia
Disporum	Prosartes	Mauranya	Asarina
Dorotheanthus	Mesembryanthemum	Melicytus	Hymenanthera
Dregea	Wattakaka	Melinis	Rhynchelytrum
Drimys	Tasmannia	Mimulus	Diplacus
Drimys	Tasmannia	Morina	Acanthocalyx
Eleutherococcus	Acanthopanax	Muscari	Muscarimia
Elymus	Leymus	Neoregelia	Aregelia
Emilia	Cacalia	Oemleria	Nuttallia
Ensete	Musa	Onopordum	Onopordon
Epilobium	Chamaenerion	Oreocereus	Borzicactus

SYNONYMS

Osmanthus	X Osmarea	Thuja	Platycladus
Pachycereus	Lophocereus	Trachelium	Diosphaera
Parahebe	Derwentia	Trachymene	Didiscus
Paris	Daiswa	Tradescantia	Zebrina
Parodia	Eriocactus	Tripetaleia	Elliottia
Parodia	Notocactus	Tulipa	Amana
Parodia	Wigginsia	Tweedia	Oxypetalum
Passiflora	Granadilla	Verbascum	Celsia
Paxistema	Pachistema	Verbena	Glandularia
Pericallis	Cineraria Flowering	Veronicastrum	Veronica
Persicaria	Aconogonon	Viola	Erpetion
Persicaria	Bistorta	Vitaliana	Douglasia
Persicaria	Polygonum	x Amarcrinum	x Crinodonna
Persicaria	Tovara	Yucca	Hesperoyucca
Petrophytum	Petrophyton	Yushania	Arundinaria
Photinia	Heteromeles	Zauschneria	Epilobium
Photinia	Stranvaesia	Zephyranthes	Cooperia
Phuopsis	Crucianella		
Pisonia	Heimerliodendron		
Poncirus	Aegle		
Potentilla	Comarum		
Potentilla	Comarum		
Probiscidea	Martynia		
Prunus	Amygdalus		
Pulsatilla	Anemone		
Rebutia	Sulcorebutia		
Rebutia	Weigartia		
Retama	Lygos		
Rhodanthe	Acroclinium		
Rhodanthe	Helipterum		
Rhodanthemum	Chrysanthemopsis		
Rhodanthemum	Pyrethropsis		
Rhododendron	Azalea		
Rhus	Toxicodendron		
Ruellia	Dipterocanthus		
Saccharum	Erianthus		
Schefflera	Brassaia		
Schlumbergera	Zygocactus		
Sclerocactus	Ancistrocactus		
Sedum	Hylotelephium		
Senecio	Cineraria		
Senecio	Kleinia		
Senna	Cassia		
Shortia	Schizocodon		
Solanum	Lycianthes		
Soleirolia	Helxine		
Solenopsis	Isotoma		
Solenopsis	Laurentia		
Solenostemon	Coleus		
Sparrmannia	Sparmannia		
Sphaeralcea	Iliamna		
Stachys	Betonica		
Stenocactus	Echinofossulocactus		
Stenomesson	Urceolina		
Stenotus	Happlopappus		
Stewartia	Stuartia		
Stipa	Achinatherum		
Swainsona	Swainsonia		
Syagrus	Arecastrum		
Tanacetum	Balsamita		
Tanacetum	Pyrethrum		
Tecoma	Tecomaria		
Tetradium	Euodia		
Tetradium	Evodia		
Tetrapanax	Fatsia		

HAZARDOUS PLANTS

Aconitum
Actaea
Aquilegia
Caltha
Chelidonium
Colchicum
Daphne
Datura
Delphinium
Digitalis
Euphorbia
Gaultheria
Helleborus
Ipomoea
Iris
Kalmia
Laburnum
Lobelia
Lupinus
Narcissus
Ornithogalum
Polygonatum
Ruta
Zigadenus
Achillea
Acokanthera
Adenium
Aesculus
Agrostemma
Allamanda
Alocasia
Alstroemeria
Amsonia
Anemone
Anthurium
Arnica
Asclepias
Berberis
Brugmansia
Caladium
Calla
Colocasia
Cichorium
Cionura
Clivia
Codiaeum
Colutea
Consolida
Convallaria
Coriaria
Cornus
Cotoneaster
Crataegus
Crinum
x Cupressocyparis
Cyclamen
Cymbidium
Cytisus
Dendranthema
Dicentra
Dictamnus
Dieffenbachia
Dorstenia
Echium
Epipremnum
Eranthis

Euonymus
Ficus
Fremontodendron
Galanthus
Glaucium
Gloriosa
Gomphocarpus
Grevillea
Haemanthus
Hedera
Helenium
Helianthus
Hippeastrum
Hyacinthoides
Hyacinthus
Hydrangea
Hyoscyamus
Jatropha
Juniperus
Lagunaria
Lantana
Lathyrus
Lonicera
Mandevilla
Mandragora
Menispermum
Monstera
Nerine
Nerium
Nicotiana
Paeonia
Paphiopedilum
Parthenocissus
Pedilanthus
Periploca
Persicaria
Petteria
Phacelia
Philodendron
Physalis
Phytolacca
Pieris
Platanus
Podophyllum
Pulsatilla
Pyracantha
Ranunculus
Rhamnus
Rheum
Rhus
Ricinus
Robinia
Rumex
Ruscus
Scopolia
Sedum
Senecio
Skimmia
Solanum
Solenopsis
Sorbus
Spathiphyllum
Symphoricarpos
Symphytum
Synadenium
Syngonium

Tagetes
Tanacetumn
Taxus
Thevetia
Thuja
Tradescantia
Ulex
Veratrum
Viburnum
Vinca
Zantedeschia

The above is a list of hazardous plants, and I feel all growers should be aware of these. The majority of garden plants are safe. Children are at risk, as they can be tempted by seeds which may look like sweets and could cause stomach upset if ingested. Please keep all seeds out of reach of children.

Adverse reactions to plant substances can occur on contact or through ingestion. Many plants have yet to be scientifically screened. Foliage or sap may irritate, aggravate existing allergies, or cause photodermatitis (severe sensitivity to sunlight). Reaction can be delayed and may include itching, redness or blistering.

Seek medical attention immediately if you think you have an adverse reaction to a plant substance, take a sample of the plant with you if you can. Do not force the sufferer to vomit.

ORDER FORM

To order further copies of this edition direct, please fill in the form below with your details (you may photocopy this page only, or write on a piece of paper) and send together with a cheque/P.O. for the full amount made payable to Karen Platt to:
35 Longfield Rd. Crookes. Sheffield. S10 1QW.
Orders are normally sent out within one week, but please allow 28 days for delivery.

Name _____

Address _____

_____

_____

Postcode _____

Telephone No. _____

Price: £10.99 less discount, £1, plus postage; £1.75 U.K. £2.75 EU, £3.50 Non-EU, £5 USA, £6 rest of world

To order copies of The Seed Search, third edition, please see details above.
The third edition is expected to be published in December 1998. Please check price and postage before ordering .
Tel: 0114 268 1700 for details.

BIBLIOGRAPHY

The following is a list of useful books related to growing from seed and gardening in general.

GENERAL

Barton, Barbara J. 1997. Gardening By Mail. Fifth Ed. Houghton Mifflin Co. 215 Park Avenue South. New York. New York 10003.
Brickell, C.D. (ed) 1992. The RHS Encylopaedia of Plants and Flowers. Dorling Kindersley, London.
Brickell, C.D. (ed) 1992. The RHS Encyclopaedia of Gardening. Dorling Kindersley, London.
Brickell,C.D. (ed) 1996. The RHS A-Z Encyclopaedia of Garden Plants. Dorling Kindersley, London.
Davis, B & Knapp, B. 1992. Know Your Common Plant Names. MDA Publications, Newbury, Berks.
The RHS Plant Finder. 1997/8. Dorling Kindersley Ltd. 9 Henrietta St. London. WC2E 8PS.
Philip, C. The Plant Finder CDRom.1996/7. Lakeside. Whitbourne. Worcs. WR6 5RD.

JOURNALS
Van Der Werff, D. Plants, New, Rare & Elusive. A journal for New Plant Hunters. Aquilegia Publishing. 2 Grange Close. Hartlepool. Cleveland. TS26 0DU. (Available on subscription).

SEED REFERENCE BOOKS

There are many general reference books with section on propagating from seed. The following a more specific.
Ashworth, S. 1991. Seed To Seed.Seed Saver Publications. Iowa.
Bubel, N. 1988. The New Seed Starter's Handbook. Rodale Press. Emaus. Pennsylvania.
Cherfas, J & Fanton, M & J. 1996. The Seed Savers' Handbook. Grover Books.
Deno, N.C. Seed Germination Theory and Practice. 2nd Supplement out late 1997. 139 Lenor Drive. State College. PA 16801. USA.
Deppe, C. 1993. Breed Your Own Vegetable Varieties. Little Brown.
F.A.O. 1961. Agricultural and Horticultural Seeds. Rome.
French, J. 1991. New Plants From Old. Aird, Melbourne.
Harkness, M.G. The Bernard Harkness Seedlist Handbook. 2nd. Edition. 1993. Timber Press. (Available from Batsford Books).
Nabhan, G. 1989. Enduring Seeds. North Point Press, Berkley, California.
Whealy, K.1995. Garden Seed Inventory. Fourth Edition. Seed Saver Publications. 3076 North Winn Rd. Decorah. Iowa 52101.

JOURNALS/NEWSLETTERS
Harvest Edition. 1987. The Seed Saver's Exchange, Rural Route 3, Decorah. Iowa. USA.
HDRA News. Ryton Organic Gardens. Ryton-on-Dunsmore. Coventry. CV8 3LG.
Seed News. Newsletter for seed savers. Heritage Seed Library. HDRA. Ryton Organic Gardens. Ryton-on-Dunsmore. Coventry. CV8 3LG.
Seedling. Quarterly Newsletter of Genetic Resources Action International (GRAIN), Girona 25 pral, E-8010 Barcelona. Spain.
The Seed Savers' Network Newsletter. Box 975. Byron Bay. NSW 2481.